KT-210-225

AA

ROAD BOOK OF BRITAIN

AA Publishing

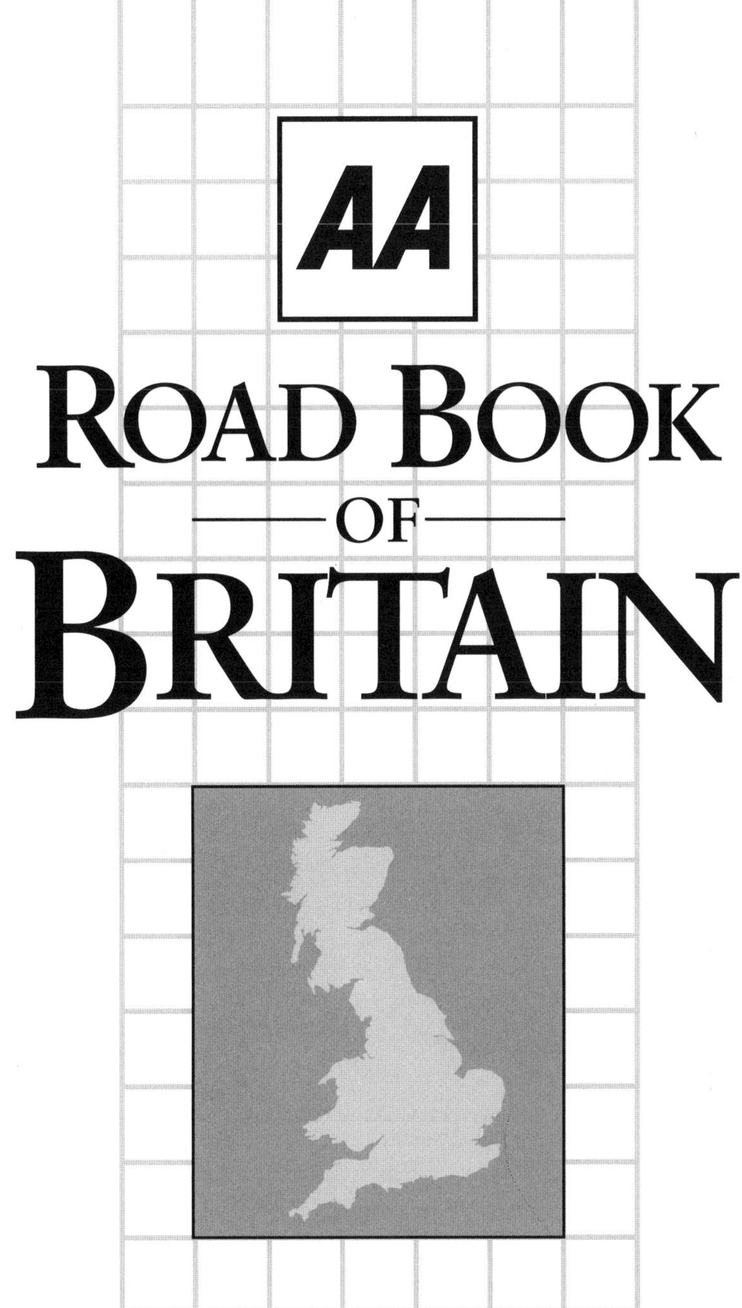

A-Z GAZETTEER

The reference guide to places in Britain

General Editor: Richard Cavendish

General Editor: Richard Cavendish
Southwest and southern England: Jo Draper
Channel Islands, Isles of Scilly: Gail Dixon-Smith
Southeast England: Helen Livingston
London and the northern home counties: Richard Cavendish
East Anglia: Liz Cruwys, Beau Riffenburg
Central eastern England: Margaret Fotheringham
Central western England: Lawrence Garner
Wales: Roger Thomas
Northern England: Alice Ferguson
Scotland: Sally Roy

Consultant Editors: Virginia Langer, Jane Franklin

Copy Editor: Rebecca Snelling

Published by AA Publishing, a trading name of Automobile Association Developments Limited, whose registered office is Norfolk House, Priestley Road, Basingstoke, Hampshire RG24 9NY. Registered number 1878835.

A catalogue record for this book is available from the British Library.

ISBN 0 7495 1140 0

Page make-up, origination, reproduction: Anton Graphics Ltd, Andover, Hampshire
Printed and bound by: Mladinska Knija Tiskarna, Slovenia

CONTENTS

FACTFILE

Preface

In the 1950s and 60s the AA published the *Road Book of England and Wales*, the *Road Book of Scotland* and the *Road Book of Ireland*. All these titles went into several different editions and remain, even to this day, perhaps the best known reference works on Britain that the AA ever produced.

The new *Road Book of Britain* (which includes gazetteer entries for England, Scotland and Wales) is a completely new book, researched and written all over again and reflecting the face of Britain today. Many of the best-loved features of the old *Road Books* remain – the county profiles, the line drawings, the extensive gazetteer. National grid references are provided for all the places described in the gazetteer and the book is designed to be used with any of the widely available AA road atlases which are updated annually.

'Where to find ...' (page 652) lists places of interest which, although described in the gazetteer, appear as part of the text under a settlement heading. For example Blenheim Palace, which appears under the heading 'Woodstock' in the gazetteer, is indexed alphabetically in 'Where to find ...' with a cross-reference to Woodstock.

Finally we would like to acknowledge the help of all the people who provided information for the book and checked the copy. We are particularly grateful to the Tourist Information Centres and to those individuals whose detailed knowledge of their own locality has proved so useful.

FOREWORD

People have always turned to the AA for reliable information about Great Britain, whether through our members' information services, the *AA Handbook* or our huge list of guides and atlases. That is why I welcome this new edition of one of our great publishing classics. I still have a copy of the original *Road Book of England and Wales*, purchased more than 20 years ago. It has been well used and I have no doubt that this new edition, which has been completely rewritten and brought up to date, will prove equally invaluable to a new generation of readers for years to come.

Simon Dyer, Director General

COUNTIES OF BRITAIN

England

1 Avon
2 Bedfordshire
3 Berkshire
5 Buckinghamshire
6 Cambridgeshire
8 Cheshire
9 Cleveland
11 Cornwall
12 Cumbria
13 Derbyshire
14 Devon
15 Dorset
17 Durham
19 East Sussex
20 Essex
22 Gloucestershire
24 Greater London
25 Greater Manchester
28 Hampshire
29 Hereford and Worcester
30 Hertfordshire
32 Humberside
33 Isle of Man
34 Isle of Wight
35 Isles of Scilly
36 Kent
37 Lancashire
38 Leicestershire
39 Lincolnshire
41 Merseyside
43 Norfolk
44 Northamptonshire
45 Northumberland
46 North Yorkshire
47 Nottinghamshire
49 Oxfordshire
52 Shropshire
53 Somerset
55 South Yorkshire
56 Staffordshire
58 Suffolk
59 Surrey
61 Tyne and Wear
62 Warwickshire
65 West Midlands
66 West Sussex
67 West Yorkshire
68 Wiltshire

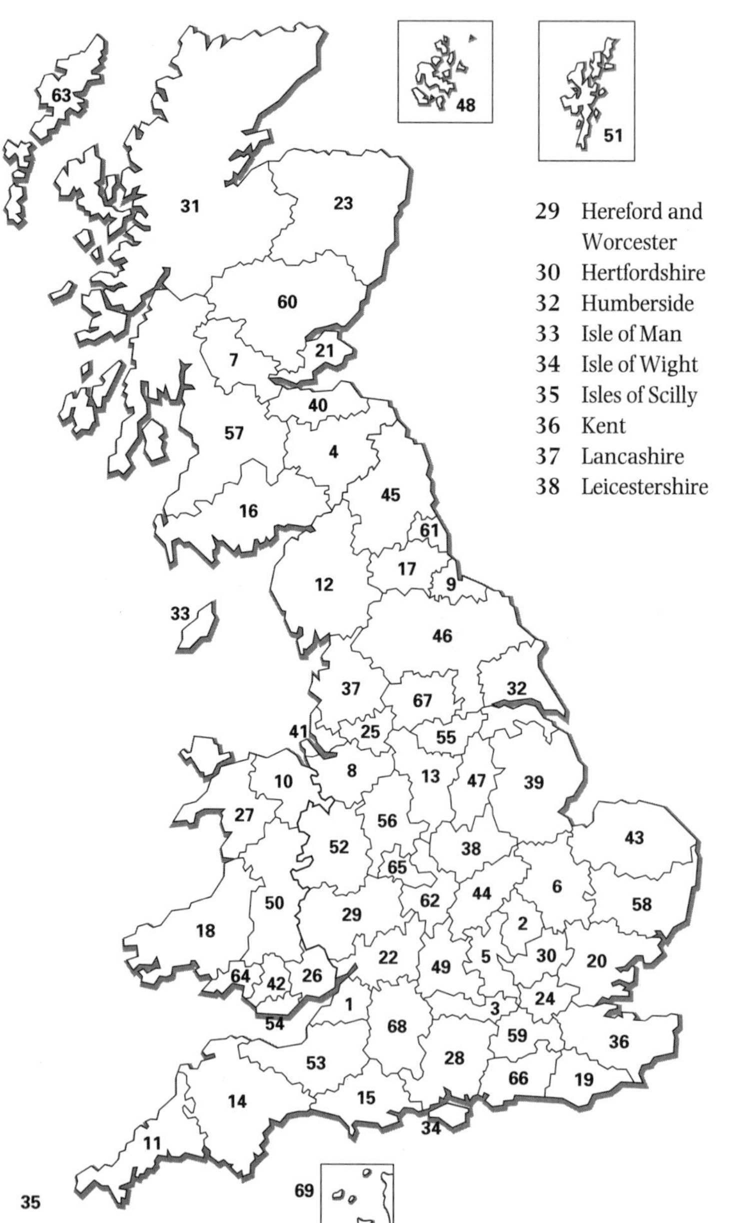

Scotland

4 Borders
7 Central
16 Dumfries and Galloway
21 Fife
23 Grampian
31 Highland
40 Lothian
48 Orkney
51 Shetland
57 Strathclyde
60 Tayside
63 Western Isles

Wales

10 Clwyd
18 Dyfed
26 Gwent
27 Gwynedd
42 Mid Glamorgan
50 Powys
54 South Glamorgan
64 West Glamorgan

69 Channel Islands

POPULATION

Populations based on 1991 census figures

England – population 46,382,051

Greater London: 6,393,568
Inner London boroughs: 2,343,133
Outer London boroughs: 4,050,435

Metropolitan counties/districts
Greater Manchester: 2,455,093
Merseyside: 1,380,465
Administrative centre: Liverpool
South Yorkshire: 1,253,959
Administrative centre: Barnsley
Tyne and Wear: 1,089,808
Administrative centre: Newcastle
West Midlands: 2,511,007
Administrative centre: Birmingham
West Yorkshire: 1,991,540
Administrative centre: Wakefield

Non-metropolitan counties/districts
Avon: 924,459
Administrative centre: Bristol
Bedfordshire: 514,399
Administrative centre: Bedford
Berkshire: 724,661
Administrative centre: Reading
Buckinghamshire: 620,188
Administrative centre: Aylesbury
Cambridgeshire: 643,439
Administrative centre: Cambridge
Cheshire: 940,887
Administrative centre: Chester
Cleveland: 544,440
Administrative centre: Middlesbrough
Cornwall and Isles of Scilly: 470,912
Administrative centre: Truro
Cumbria: 489,354
Administrative centre: Carlisle
Derbyshire: 918,648
Administrative centre: Matlock
Devon: 1,015,969
Administrative centre: Exeter
Dorset: 647,245
Administrative centre: Dorchester
Durham: 593,195
Administrative centre: Durham
East Sussex: 683,404
Administrative centre: Lewes
Essex: 1,500,210
Administrative centre: Chelmsford
Gloucestershire: 523,610
Administrative centre: Gloucester
Hampshire: 1,523,742
Administrative centre: Winchester
Hereford and Worcester: 671,971
Administrative centre: Worcester
Hertfordshire: 960,564
Administrative centre: Hertford
Humberside: 847,987
Administrative centre: Hull
Isle of Wight: 127,232
Administrative centre: Newport
Kent: 1,493,891
Administrative centre: Maidstone
Lancashire: 1,370,331
Administrative centre: Preston
Leicestershire: 865,133
Administrative centre: Leicester
Lincolnshire: 580,114
Administrative centre: Lincoln
Norfolk: 742,080
Administrative centre: Norwich
Northamptonshire: 570,598
Administrative centre: Northampton
Northumberland: 301,882
Administrative centre:
Newcastle upon Tyne
North Yorkshire: 703,076
Administrative centre: Northallerton
Nottinghamshire: 984,990
Administrative centre: Nottingham
Oxfordshire: 556,390
Administrative centre: Oxford
Shropshire: 403,478
Administrative centre: Shrewsbury
Somerset: 461,647
Administrative centre: Taunton
Staffordshire: 1,022,901
Administrative centre: Stafford
Suffolk: 633,098
Administrative centre: Ipswich
Surrey: 1,000,885
Administrative centre:
Kingston upon Thames
Warwickshire: 479,208
Administrative centre: Warwick
West Sussex: 694,550
Administrative centre: Chichester
Wiltshire: 555,843
Administrative centre: Trowbridge

Wales – population 2,811,865

Clwyd: 402,927
Administrative centre: Mold
Dyfed: 342,952
Administrative centre: Carmarthen
Gwent: 434,244
Administrative centre: Cwmbrân
Gwynedd: 240,170
Administrative centre: Caernarfon
Mid Glamorgan: 527,595
Administrative centre: Cardiff
Powys: 116,801
Administrative centre:
Llandrindod Wells
South Glamorgan: 388,576
Administrative centre: Cardiff
West Glamorgan: 358,600
Administrative centre: Swansea

Scotland – population 4,962,152

Borders Region: 103,311
Administrative centre:
Newton St Boswells
Central Region: 268,251
Administrative centre: Stirling
Dumfries and Galloway Region:
147,732
Administrative centre: Dumfries
Fife Region: 340,138
Administrative centre: Glenrothes
Grampian Region: 493,760
Administrative centre: Aberdeen
Highland Region: 209,746
Administrative centre: Inverness
Lothian Region: 724,107
Administrative centre: Edinburgh
Strathclyde Region: 2,219,110
Administrative centre: Glasgow
Tayside Region: 385,136
Administrative centre: Dundee
Orkney Islands Area: 19,328
Administrative centre: Kirkwall
Shetland Islands Area: 22,163
Administrative centre: Lerwick
Western Isles Islands Area: 29,370
Administrative centre: Stornoway

Channel Islands

Alderney – population 2,297

Guernsey – population 58,867
Castel Parish: 9,068
Forest Parish: 1,386
St Andrew Parish: 2,357

St Martin Parish: 6,082
St Peter Port Parish: 16,648
St Peter's in the Wood Parish: 2,248
St Sampson Parish: 8,048
Toteval Parish: 976
Vale Parish: 9,530

Jersey – population 84,082

Grouville Parish: 4,297
St Brelade Parish: 9,331
St Clement Parish: 7,393
St Helier Parish: 28,123
St John Parish: 2,440
St Lawrence Parish: 4,561
St Martin Parish: 3,258
St Mary Parish: 1,449
St Ouen Parish: 3,612
St Peter Parish: 4,231
St Saviour Parish: 12,747
Trinity Parish: 2,640

Sark – population (est) 550

Isle of Man – population 69,788

Areas of residence:
Designated towns
Castletown: 3,152
Douglas: 22,214
Peel: 3,829
Ramsey: 6,496
Village districts
Laxey: 1,367
Michael: 1,244
Onchan: 8,483
Port Erin: 3,024
Port St Mary: 1,762
Parish districts
Andreas: 1,156
Arbory: 1,661
Ballaugh: 802
Braddan: 2,046
Bride: 418
German: 1,025
Jurby: 682
Lezayre: 1,503
Lonan: 1,232
Malew: 2,216
Marown: 1,553
Maughold: 828
Patrick: 1,192
Rushen: 1,446
Santon: 457

CHANGING BOUNDARIES

Following government reviews of local authority organisation, many county boundaries in England and Wales and region boundaries in Scotland are set to change.

Background Local government was reorganised in the 1970s, so that local services were provided by both county councils and district councils. Some traditional county identities were abolished – Rutland, for instance – and amalgamations of old counties were created, such as Avon and Humberside, causing considerable controversy. In an attempt to reduce the numbers of local authorities, central government initiated the reviews of the 1990s, re-establishing some of the pre-1974 boundaries. Changes in Wales and Scotland were directed by the government, introducing the new authorities listed below. In England an extensive public consultation process was underway in 1995 to determine future changes.

These changes have been in progress during the preparation of this book, so to ensure a consistent approach in the gazetteer, we have used the counties as they appear on the page 8, prior to the changes listed below.

New Welsh authorities
(Welsh names in brackets)

Counties
Anglesey *(Sir Fôn)*
Caernarfonshire and Merionethshire *(Sir Gaernarfon a Meirionnydd)*
Cardiff *(Caerdydd)*
Cardiganshire *(Sir Aberteifi)*
Carmarthenshire *(Sir Gaerfyr/ddin)*
Denbighshire *(Sir Ddinbych)*
Flintshire *(Sir y Fflint)*
Monmouthshire *(Sir Fynwy)*
Pembrokeshire *(Sir Benfro)*
Powys
Swansea *(Abertawe)*

County boroughs
Aberconwy and Colwyn *(Aberconwy a Cholwyn)*
Blaenau Gwent
Bridgend *(Pen-y-bont ar Ogwr)*
Caerphilly *(Caerffili)*
Merthyr Tydfil *(Merthyr Tudful)*
Neath and Port Talbot *(Castell-nedd a Phort Talbot)*
Newport *(Casnewydd)*
Rhondda, Cynon, Taf
Torfaen
The Vale of Glamorgan *(Bro Morgannwg)*
Wrexham *(Wrecsam)*

New Scottish authorities
Aberdeenshire
Angus
Argyll and Bute
Borders
City of Dundee
City of Edinburgh
City of Glasgow
Clackmannan
Dumfries and Galloway
Dumbarton and Clydebank
East Ayrshire
East Dunbartonshire
East Lothian
East Renfrewshire
Falkirk
Fife
Highland
Inverclyde
Midlothian
Moray
North Ayrshire
North Lanarkshire
Orkney
Perthshire and Kinross
Shetland
Stirling
South Ayrshire
South Lanarkshire
Western Isles
West Lothian

Profiles of the Counties and Regions of Britain

PROFILES

Profiles of the counties and regions of Britain

The county or 'shire' (the older, Anglo-Saxon word) was for centuries the basic administrative division of England for local government purposes, and from England the system was extended to Scotland and Wales. The counties built up strong individual identities and traditions, and became the focus of deeply-felt affections and loyalties. Their boundaries have been changed from time to time and in 1974 some traditional English counties were abolished, amalgamated or altered and new ones were created. In Scotland and Wales the traditional counties were scrapped altogether in favour of new regions. Now fresh changes are underway, but the situation at the moment is far from clear. The following notes are based on the position at the time of writing.

England

England is the largest and most heavily populated area in Britain, occupying more than half the land surface of England, Scotland and Wales combined, with over 85 per cent of the population. The highland zone of England lies in the north and west, with the centre and south predominantly a lowland zone. In the north, the Pennines run up like a backbone from Derbyshire to the whale-backed Cheviot Hills along the Scots border. The North York Moors are set off to the east, with the Lake District mountains to the west and high ground barricading the Welsh Marches further south. In the rest of the country the prevailing lowlands are broken by higher ground here and there, by the North and South Downs, the Chilterns, the Cotswolds and Salisbury Plain, the Mendips and the granite humps of Dartmoor and Bodmin Moor in the far southwest. East Anglia is famously flat and the lowest country of all is in the Cambridgeshire Fens, parts of which are below sea level.

Avon

The county of Avon was formed in 1974 out of southern Gloucestershire and northern Somerset, but has never established a clear identity. Its name came from the River Avon, one of several Avon rivers in England (it was simply the ancient Celtic word for 'river', surviving in Welsh as *Afon*). This one enters the county at the eastern border and runs westwards through Bath and Bristol, beneath Isambard Kingdom Brunel's suspension bridge at Clifton – a magnet for suicides ever since it was built – and through a narrow, scenic gorge to the Bristol Channel at the busy port of Avonmouth.

Bristol is the biggest town in the southwest of England, a hive of commercial and industrial activity, a cathedral and university town, and a major communications and entertainments centre. Bath meanwhile, set on hills rising steeply from the Avon, is one of England's most satisfyingly beautiful cities, possessed of the finest 18th-century townscape in Britain with its crescents, squares and terraces built of the mellow local stone. Bath's long history as a spa goes back far beyond its 18th-century days when anyone who was anyone went there, back to and beyond its Roman incarnation as *Aquae Sulis*; the remains of the Roman bath complex, down below the 18th-century Pump Room, are a leading visitor attraction. The only other town of any size in the county is Weston-Super-Mare, a popular resort and retirement town on the Bristol Channel. Also on the Bristol Channel, but somewhat quieter, the town of Clevedon has a notable Victorian pier. Inland from Clevedon lie the Mendip Hills and the reservoirs in the Chew Valley.

Bedfordshire

One of the smaller counties, Bedfordshire is largely prosperous arable farming and London-commuter territory, with market gardening in the Brussels sprouts belt around Biggleswade and Sandy. The land is generally flat, with the highest ground rising to about 700ft (210m) on the Chilterns outliers in the southwest of the county, where gliders soar from the steep sides of the Dunstable Downs and exotic animals roam the Whipsnade Wild Animal Park. There are sandy, pine-clad heaths north of Woburn, where another collection of exotic animals is at home to visitors in Europe's largest drive-through safari park, and the Duke of Bedford's palatial mansion is the doyen of Bedfordshire's stately homes. The Great Ouse winds and loops its way across the northern half of the county past attractive villages and beneath many an ancient bridge. It was in the Ouse Valley that the Bedfordshire lace industry developed in the 16th century.

The county town, Bedford, is set pleasantly on the Ouse. It prides itself on its links with John Bunyan and many sites in the county are supposed to have inspired the scenery of *Pilgrim's Progress*. Leighton Buzzard and Ampthill are attractive towns, but much the biggest town in Bedfordshire is Luton, a thriving industrial centre with an international airport in the south of the county, with Dunstable on its western edge. There is a psychological gulf between northern and southern Bedfordshire, which tend to behave as if they were completely separate areas. Both Luton and Dunstable were important centres for the manufacture of straw hats from the 17th century to the 20th – straw hats only went out of fashion in the 1930s. The two towns were surrounded by their tributary straw-plaiting villages. Bedfordshire also has an old tradition of brick-making, carried on today on a diminished scale at Stewartby, while Totternhoe stone was used in the construction of many important buildings, including Westminster Abbey.

Berkshire

The changes of 1974 cut off a substantial chunk of northern Berkshire and handed it to Oxfordshire on a plate, and the acquisition of Slough at the eastern end of the county was not universally regarded as adequate compensation. The Thames previously formed the northern border of Berkshire, but now the line runs across the Berkshire Downs north of Lambourn, to strike the river at the Goring Gap. Then the county boundary follows the river eastwards past Reading and along the delectable reaches by Sonning, Bisham and Cookham. At Reading the other principal Berkshire river, the Kennet, comes in from the west to join the Thames, closely accompanied by the Kennet and Avon Canal, with its narrow-boat cruises and towpath walks.

The Berkshire Downs to the north are rolling chalk grassland, known for the breeding and training of fabulously expensive racehorses. In the south, beyond the Kennet, high ground along the Hampshire border rises to Inkpen Beacon. The valleys of the Kennet and the Thames have provided one of the main routes into London from the west since time immemorial and today the M4 motorway, the A4 road and the main railway line from Exeter all go this way.

The county proudly calls itself Royal Berkshire because of Windsor, where the massive castle is the royal family's principal residence outside London and a magnet to visitors. Reading, the county town and much the biggest town in Berkshire, best known at one time for Sutton's seeds and Huntley and Palmer's biscuits, is now busy with electronics and engineering.

East of Reading, Berkshire is largely urban. Slough, the county's next biggest centre, is an industrial town close to London Airport. Bracknell has swelled since the 1950s as a New Town and Maidenhead is gracelessly post-war residential. In the more rural western half of the county, however, Newbury has kept its character more successfully and Hungerford with its fine old coaching inns is full of charm and antiques shops.

Buckinghamshire

Close enough to London to attract the rich and powerful, Buckinghamshire sports a procession of grand houses and estates headed by the superb Rothschild château of Waddesdon Manor and the stately grounds of Stowe, and including Claydon House with its memories of Florence Nightingale and Hughenden Manor, where Benjamin Disraeli lived. The Thames runs sweetly along the county's southern border past Marlow and through the idyllic Cliveden Reach to Taplow. The Chiltern Hills sweep splendidly across the south of the county, with their deep, enticing beech woods, and Buckinghamshire's name may come from the Old English word for beech, 'bece'.

The steep northern scarp commands broad prospects over the rich farming country of the Vale of Aylesbury, where cattle and ducks have been fattened for centuries for the London market, and towards the flatter landscape of northern Buckinghamshire with its peaceful thatched villages. Closeness to London is a key factor in the south, where dairy, pig and poultry farming supply the capital, while Wendover, Chesham, Amersham, the Chalfonts, Gerrards Cross and Beaconsfield are expensive London dormitories along the main road and rail routes through the gaps in the Chilterns.

High Wycombe is the principal market and shopping town here, though it is not high at all, but set in a deep Chilterns valley, and Burnham Beeches is the most famous beauty spot. The county town of Aylesbury was badly damaged by post-war development, but further north Buckingham is pleasingly unspoiled and a fascinating experiment has been going on at Milton Keynes, where a new city has been brought into being since the 1960s, a development from the garden city movement of earlier in the century, cocooned at the heart of a network of fast roads and studded with attractive towns, villages, parks and lakes.

Cambridgeshire

This is quite a sizeable county, which forms the western march of East Anglia and includes the old county of Huntingdon and two other areas which once enjoyed their own separate identities – the Isle of Ely and the Soke of Peterborough, the districts immediately round the two cathedral cities. Cambridgeshire contains much of the Fens, which have been so efficiently drained over the centuries by the Romans, the medieval monasteries, Dutch engineers in the 17th century and renewed efforts in the 19th that only the nature reserve of Wicken Fen, owned by the National Trust, still survives in its earlier state. Elsewhere the flat, open landscape, with the least woodland of any county in England, is threaded by rivers and criss-crossed by ruler-straight cuts and canals, with the banks of the principal drains rising high above the prevailing level. The soil of the county is extremely fertile and grows fruit and vegetables in great abundance, while Ely Cathedral with its spectacular towers and lantern floats above the surrounding landscape like a great liner in harbour.

The principal Cambridgeshire rivers are the Great Ouse, which is like a loose belt across the county's midriff, and the Nene which runs across further north. The county town is Cambridge itself, in the chalk downland of southern Cambridgeshire, famed for its beauty and its university, for the soaring spider's web of fan vaulting in King's College Chapel and the satisfying parade of colleges along the Backs beside the Cam. In the north, Peterborough, with a less dramatically striking cathedral than Ely, has expanded considerably since the 1970s with new factories and housing estates in an area formerly known for bricks and sugar beets. March was once a railway town and the county town of the Isle of Ely, and Wisbech is a busy inland port on the Nene. Over to the west is Huntingdon,

Oliver Cromwell's birthplace, formerly the capital of its own small county and a coaching town on the line of the Roman Ermine Street. St Neots is a pleasant old market town on the River Great Ouse, and St Ives is another, with a bridge chapel, a rarity in England.

Cheshire

At the northern end of the Welsh Marches, Cheshire was once both a bastion of defence against Welsh incursions and a base for inroads into Wales. Chester, the prosperous county town and one of the most rewarding cities in England to visit, began life as a major Roman army base on the River Dee and the circuit of its old walls is one of its most engaging attractions. The M6 motorway negotiates the rich green pastures of the gently undulating central area of the county, a placid dairy-farming region noted for Cheshire cheese, which preserves much of the black and white, half-timbered architecture for which the county is celebrated. Some of the finest examples are glittering Victorian creations in Chester itself, but perhaps the most spectacular of all is Little Moreton Hall, which is leaning about at the craziest angles and looking as if it is bound to fall down at any moment.

Most of the Wirral peninsula in the northwest, Cheshire's most densely inhabited area, was handed over to Merseyside in 1974. On the north bank of the River Mersey, however, Cheshire gained the vast modern chemical industry concentration around Widnes with its strange, futuristic landscape of huge tanks and pipes, and the thriving New Town of Warrington. Motorways zoom to and fro on the Mersey's southern bank. In more rustic mood, there is boating and walking along the canals in Cheshire, notably the Shropshire Union Canal, which runs up to Ellesmere Port on the Mersey. Further east, Northwich and Middlewich were centres of the historic Cheshire salt industry, going back to before Roman times. Picturesque Nantwich was once a salt town, too, while at the National Trust's Quarry Bank Mill at Styal you can rediscover the days of the Industrial Revolution in textiles in the 1830s. Here in the northeast of the county, the scenery becomes much more dramatic, first where the high ridge of Alderley Edge rises abruptly from the plain, and then in the rugged country immediately east of the town of Macclesfield, set in the western reaches of the Peak District National Park.

A fountain in Great Court, Trinity, Cambridge.

Cleveland

The handkerchief-sized new county of Cleveland was created by joining segments of Durham and the North Riding of Yorkshire, drawn together by the zip-fastener of the River Tees as it makes its final drive towards the North Sea. At this point the river negotiates one of Britain's most important industrial regions, with Middlesbrough, the county town, on the southern bank and Stockton-on-Tees on the northern.

Cleveland was an old name for the area and the Cleveland Hills run along the county's southern boundary in the North Yorkshire Moors National Park. The high point of Roseberry Topping is right on the county boundary and on the North Sea shore the towering rampart of Boulby Head is the highest cliff on the eastern English coast at 660ft (210m). Further northwest the shore is weighed down by heavy industry, power stations, chemical plants, oil installations and the debris of coal mines, but even so there are beaches of gleaming golden sand at the resorts of Marske-by-the-Sea, Redcar and Seaton Carew. Inland, Guisborough is a pleasant market town and the old capital of the Cleveland district.

Cornwall

Protruding into the Atlantic in the southwest, separated from the rest of England by the River Tamar and preserving an isolated Celtic heritage, Cornwall has its own unmistakable character, and place-names beginning with Cornish 'Tre', 'Pol' and 'Pen'. Granite houses crouch low against the sea winds, diminutive villages cluster in green valleys and rocky coves and little granite churches preside peacefully over weathered graveyards. There are numerous ancient crosses and holy wells, and prehistoric sites include the impressive 'quoits' with their giant stone slabs, eerie stone circles and standing stones, and the remains of Iron Age settlements. Nowhere in Cornwall is more than 20 miles (32km) from the sea. Down the sea-beaten northern coast strides cliff after titanic cliff, headland after adamantine headland, strung with a necklace of gleaming golden beaches. Tintagel was the birthplace of the legendary King Arthur, and the legendary St Ia brought the Christian faith to St Ives in the Dark Ages, floating miraculously across the Irish Sea on a millstone. The town was later known for its artists' colony. There are tales of mermaids, and here and there the engine houses of abandoned tin mines cling to the cliffs, their seams and tunnels running far out beneath the sea.

Land's End is the most westerly point on the English mainland. About 28 miles (45km) further out lie the Isles of Scilly with their twin harvest of wrecks and spring flowers.

The southern Cornish coast, the Cornish Riviera, is generally kinder and milder, with fishing harbours and their salt-streaked boats and tangled nets lying in quiet coves. They have strange evocative names – Mevagissey and Mousehole, Mullion and Marazion. The tales here are of wrecking and smuggling, and offshore from Marazion a causeway leads to legend-haunted St Michael's Mount. Inland the granite hump of lonely Bodmin Moor rises to about 1,400ft (425m).

Truro, the county town, has a stunning 19th-century cathedral, Falmouth is a port on the huge natural harbour of Carrick Roads, Penzance is close to the Land's End peninsula and nearby Newlyn, Cornwall's principal fishing port, attracted a well-known school of artists at the turn of the century. Tin mining is at its last gasp, but near St Austell blazing white hills of spoil stud the weird, unearthly moonscape of the china-clay country.

Cumbria

Combining the former Cumberland and Westmorland with parts of Lancashire and Yorkshire in the angle of the Irish Sea and the Solway Firth, Cumbria is the second largest of the English counties (after North Yorkshire). The name is Celtic and reflects the fact that the British Celts preserved their independence against the invading Saxons in these northwestern fastnesses. Later came strong Norse influence, as Viking longships prowled down the coast. The county town is Carlisle with its cathedral and castle, close to the Scottish border and the western end of Hadrian's Wall, for centuries an English bastion against marauding Scots and a base for English armies invading Scotland.

To the south lies the Lake District, where the shining waters of Windermere, Derwentwater, Coniston Water, Grasmere, Ullswater and the rest reflect the highest peaks in England – Scafell Pike, Scafell, Skiddaw, Helvellyn, the Langdale Pikes and many more – in a magical clarity and quality of light. Stone circles recall the rituals of long-vanished generations and far back in prehistoric times there were stone axe factories among the peaks. This is wonderful walking, climbing and touring country, crowded in the season, and enriched by associations with Wordsworth and Ruskin, Arthur Ransome and Hugh Walpole.

The valley of the Eden separates the Lake District fells from the western edge of the Pennines, where Cross Fell rises to 2,930ft

(893m) and Alston claims to be England's highest market town. South of Penrith the M6 motorway, the A6 road and the railway line clamber over high Shap Fell. Kendal has a reputation for its strengthening mint cake and Keswick for lead pencils, while diminutive Appleby was once Westmorland's county town.

Running down the west coast, a succession of ports on the Irish Sea – Maryport, Workington, Whitehaven – is followed by the landmark of St Bee's Head, with the nuclear industry established further south at Sellafield. In the extreme southwest the Furness peninsula stands between the Irish Sea and the sandflats of Morecambe Bay. Barrow-in-Furness is an oil town and former ship-building centre.

Derbyshire

Geologically speaking, Derbyshire is where the North begins, at the southern end of the Pennine Chain, near Wirksworth and Cromford in the scenic valley of the Derwent. Sir Richard Arkwright's mill and company town at Cromford are early landmarks of the Industrial Revolution. Further south lies a notable inheritor of this legacy, Derby itself, a busy industrial centre with a heritage of fine china and Rolls Royce cars, whose noble 18th-century church is now a cathedral.

The River Trent glides across the southern part of the county, where stately mansions include Robert Adam's elegant Kedleston Hall and the wonderfully eccentric 'time capsule' of unmodernised Calke Abbey.

The more dramatic scenery, however, is in the northern half of Derbyshire, where the Pennines head up towards Yorkshire through the Peak District National Park, past rattling, dust-hung quarries and sheer stone cliffs, sheep and cattle grazing in small fields penned in by drystone walls, the deep, intriguing caves in the limestone at Castleton, the shivering landslip-prone mountain of Mam Tor and the broad, lonely windswept moors of Kinder Scout (the Peak District does not run to many peaks). In the west the scenic beauties of Dovedale embellish the border with Staffordshire. The River Wye runs through Miller's Dale and Monsal Dale. Villages 'dress' their wells delightfully with flower-pictures in spring and summer, and there are giant reservoirs on the Derwent. Great houses include Chatsworth, with its fountains and waterworks, medieval Haddon Hall and 16th-century Hardwick Hall, 'more glass than wall'.

The county town is not Derby, but Matlock, a former spa set deep in the gorge of the Derwent. The twisted spire of Chesterfield's church can be seen for miles. Buxton is a former spa of character, with a delightful Edwardian opera house and a well-known mineral spring. Ashbourne, too, is known for spring water, and Bakewell for tart, while Glossop is a former cotton town and Eyam holds vivid and tragic memories of the plague.

Devon

The third largest English county (after North Yorkshire and Cumbria) is known for its enchanting scenery and its long tradition of seafaring – the heroic tradition of Sir Francis Drake and Sir John Hawkins, who sallied out in little ships to beat the overbearing galleons of the Spanish Armada. Along the southern coast, Plymouth Sound is a spacious and beautiful natural harbour and the Pilgrim Fathers sailed for the New World from Plymouth, now a cross-Channel ferry port and naval base. There are impressive cliffscapes in the South Hams district to the east and the National Trust protects a particularly splendid stretch towards Bolt Head. Dartmouth and Brixham, where the hymn 'Abide With Me' was written, are old ports and fishing towns, and sunny, sheltered Torbay is a tourist honeypot. From here the characteristic red cliffs of South Devon line the coast to the charming little Regency resort of Sidmouth, where the poor, baffled River Sid runs into a large shingle bank a few yards from the sea.

Inland is the county town and cathedral city of Exeter, a Roman base in its time, badly bombed in World War II and the possessor of a network of underground passages originally constructed to bring water into the town and now an idiosyncratic visitor attraction.

North Devon has a spectacular coastline of its own, with high cliffs along the Bristol Channel coast past Lynton and Combe Martin, a Victorian seaside resort at Ilfracombe and jutting headlands protecting broad expanses of sandy beaches against the Atlantic tides at Woolacombe and Saunton. Barnstaple and Bideford are venerable ports and market towns. Further west Clovelly tumbles down its cliff in a cataract of white cottages and an iron coastline of massive cliffs extends on past the savage rocks of Hartland Point. To the south are green hills, thatched cottages built of cob, cream teas, the valleys of the Torridge and the Taw and enjoyable walking in the *Tarka the Otter* country. South again, the wild moorland of Dartmoor rises abruptly to above 2,000ft (600m) in weathered, weirdly shaped rocky tors. There are wild ponies here, as well as the country's best-known prison and an abundance of prehistoric sites, and Devon also includes the western reaches of Exmoor in the northeast.

Dorset

Loved for its poetic, melodious or sometimes comical place-names, its Ryme Intrinsecas and Fifehead Magdalens and Melbury Bubbs, Dorset is a peaceful, profoundly rural county of chalk downland and open heath, the setting for many of the novels of Thomas Hardy. He was born at Higher Bockhampton, outside Dorchester, and his heart was buried with his ancestors in the quiet country churchyard of nearby Stinsford. Dorchester, which was Hardy's 'Casterbridge', is the soothingly dignified county town. To the south is the great hump of Maiden Castle, one of the most impressive Iron Age strongholds in Britain, successfully stormed by the Roman legionaries in AD43. There are other evocative prehistoric fortresses high on Hod Hill and Hambledon Hill, and the notorious Cerne Abbas Giant is impressively endowed.

Dorset has a spectacular and geologically rewarding coastline along the English Channel, running from Lyme Regis with its fossil finds eastwards past the long pebble ridge of Chesil Bank to Portland Bill, source of Portland building stone, and the Georgian seaside resort of Weymouth. Further east lie the great chalk arch of Durdle Door, the beauty spot of Lulworth Cove and the Isle of Purbeck, of Purbeck marble fame. Swanage is another pleasant seaside resort and Poole has a big natural harbour, which laps the fringes of Dorset's largest town, the sedate resort of Bournemouth. Inland, Shaftesbury commands sweeping views from its 700ft (210m) hill, with attractive Cranborne Chase to the south; Wimborne Minster, Blandford Forum and Sherborne are towns of character and charm.

Durham

One of the most breathtaking views in England is the prospect of Durham's massive Norman cathedral, set on its towering rock above a horseshoe bend of the River Wear. The great church stands above the spot where the bones of St Cuthbert, most revered saint of the North, were buried at the end of the 10th century after long wanderings. With the duty of defending England against attack from Scotland, the Prince-Bishops of Durham ruled as potentates for centuries from their castle high on the rock, now part of Durham University. The eastern half of the county developed into a major coal-mining region in the 19th century, but the industry is in sharp decline. Working life at the turn of the century is vividly re-created at Beamish, at the excellent North of England Open Air Museum.

Darlington in the far south of the county is a historic railway town, where George Stephenson's Stockton to Darlington Railway opened to passengers in 1825. The county's finest scenery is to be found in the west, inland along the valleys of the Wear and especially the Tees. At Barnard Castle the grey battlements of the ruined castle rear up high above the river and the Bowes Museum holds the riches of 18th-century French decorative art. Further west beyond Middleton-in-Teesdale the Tees hurls itself over the waterfalls of High Force and Cauldron Snout. To the north, in the hills above Weardale, a 19th-century lead-mining site is preserved at Killhope Wheel.

Essex

Much of the southwest of the county has been swallowed by London's gaping maw and virtually the whole of Essex – originally the territory of the East Saxons, and not strictly speaking part of East Anglia – betrays the influence of the capital. The north bank of the Thames from Purfleet to Grays and Tilbury sports a formidable array of oil and gas installations and container ports, and a swathe of suburbs, New Towns and post-war housing estates stretch across the county from Harlow and Brentwood through Billericay, Basildon and Wickford to the sprawling Southend-on-Sea conurbation and the post-modernist preserve of South Woodham Ferrers.

Chelmsford is the county town, but Colchester, which has outstanding Roman and Norman remains and proudly proclaims itself England's earliest recorded town, has greater character. So has the old town of Harwich, now an adjunct to a major passenger and container port for Northern Europe, and demure Saffron Walden in the north, which owes its name to its crocus beds. Essex is flat and open, mainly, but there are isolated hilly areas near Danbury and Basildon, Epping Forest is an oasis of woodland and the county has its share of the Constable Country in the Stour Valley. The watery fingers of the Crouch, the Blackwater and the Colne probe far inland among marshes and creeks, full of waterfowl, nature reserves and small-boat sailors. Burnham-on-Crouch is one of England's leading yachting centres and Maldon a historic harbour town, while beyond the sands, donkey rides and cheerful amusements of Clacton-on-Sea are the cliffs and creeks of the Naze.

Gloucestershire

The county divides into three main areas: the Cotswold Hills, the Vales of Severn and Berkeley, and the Forest of Dean. The Cotswolds run up the eastern side of Gloucestershire, and the steep escarpment on their western edge affords compelling views towards Wales. The native Cotswold limestone in subtle shades of brown and grey is used for towns and villages, churches and manor houses, barns and field walls, which consequently seem to have grown naturally out of the land. Chipping Campden, Stow-on-the-Wold, Bourton-on-the-Water and Painswick are among the most attractive small towns in England and there are many entrancing villages. Below the Cotswold scarp the Vales of Severn and Berkeley are flat and green, rich farming land, traversed in huge sweeping loops by the Severn – the longest river in Britain and one of the most capricious and dangerous, known for its strange reverse tidal wave, the 'bore'. West of the river lie the rides and thickets of the Forest of Dean, nothing like as impenetrable a region as it once was, but still with a remoteness and singularity about it.

Gloucester, the county town, held a strategic position as the first place upstream at which the Severn was bridged – until the modern suspension bridge was opened in 1966 – and its noble cathedral saw the first flowering of the Perpendicular style of architecture. The county's second town, Cheltenham, is a smart and stylish Regency creation and former spa. Cirencester is a flourishing market town with a notable Roman museum and Stroud was once the centre of a thriving textile industry.

Greater London

The Thames runs across the centre of the area on course for its estuary and the North Sea. On either side are hills, along the Northern Heights through Hampstead and Highgate, and in the south along the line of the North Downs, rising to above 700ft (210m) in the Biggin Hill area in the southeast. The M25 motorway approximately circles the perimeter. All through its history London has drawn in immigrants from the rest of the country – and some from abroad – and bulged out over the surrounding countryside to house them. The process gained tremendous momentum in the 19th century when the railways made it possible for ordinary people to work in London while living much further afield.

Substantial areas of Surrey, Kent, Essex, Hertfordshire and Middlesex were overwhelmed by a tidal wave of suburban bricks and mortar. Between the censuses of 1801 and 1901 the population of what is now the Greater London area increased by a factor of six, from about 1 million to some 6.5 million, and by 1938 the figure was 8.5 million, though it has shrunk back again since. An inevitable consequence of the expansion was that newly conquered territories passed out of control of the counties. The old county of Middlesex, north and west of the capital, was done away with altogether by the Government of London Act of 1963, to survive only as a postal address. The Act replaced 87 former local authorities with 32 London Boroughs plus the City of London. The Greater London Council, which had certain overall functions and responsibilities, was abolished altogether in 1986.

Today's Greater London occupies about 610 square miles (1,525sq km) of remarkable contrasts between town and country, city and suburb, teeming streets and leafy rusticity.

Greater Manchester

Created by the reorganisation of 1974, Greater Manchester bit off most of southern Lancashire with extra mouthfuls of Cheshire and the old West Riding of Yorkshire, but the metropolitan council was abolished in 1986. In the county are Wigan, Bolton, Bury, Rochdale, Oldham and Stockport, which all played leading parts in the booming Lancashire cotton industry of the 19th century, spawned by the Industrial Revolution. Wigan Pier, which began as a music-hall joke, is now a remarkable museum of the area's past, Bury has a special reputation for black puddings, and the building where the Co-operative Movement began has been preserved in Rochdale. Manchester itself, or 'Cottonopolis', prospered and grew as the manufacturing, trading and financial hub of the textile belt. Like the rest of the area, it has come through hard times with the decline of heavy industry, but is still busy with engineering, chemicals and textiles, and has an important airport. It is also a leading financial and cultural centre and a cathedral and university city.

Hampshire and the Isle of Wight

Hampshire is close enough to London to provide comfortable homes for well-to-do commuters and far enough away to preserve genuine countryside. In the southwest the woods and heaths of the New Forest are inhabited by deer and wild ponies and the occasional adder. Lyndhurst is its principal town and its port is Lymington, now a magnet to small-boat sailors. East along the English Channel coast, in contrast, are two of England's busiest harbour towns. Southampton, handling passenger and container ships, is a major port for Europe and the cross-Atlantic traffic. Portsmouth is an important naval base which mounts the country's most powerful broadside of naval heritage attractions, including Nelson's *Victory* and Henry VIII's cherished *Mary Rose*.

Inland, the county town and cathedral city of Winchester, once the capital of the kingdom of Wessex, is one of the most prosperous towns in England and full of interest. Romsey has a Norman abbey church and Petersfield is a charming Georgian town close to Butser Hill and the Queen Elizabeth Country Park in the South Downs, which sweep across the south of Hampshire. More chalk downland rises in the northern part of the county. Here the influence of London is more evident. Andover swelled with London overspill housing estates in the 1960s and so did Basingstoke, which has burgeoned as a business centre. Aldershot in the heathland of the northeast is at the heart of a military area and nearby Farnborough is linked with aviation.

Across the water from Southampton and Portsmouth, the enjoyable miniature touring ground of the Isle of Wight has drawn holiday-makers since Queen Victoria and Prince Albert built themselves Osborne House as a summer retreat near the yachting centre of Cowes. Newport is the county town.

Chalk downs run across the centre of the island, and there is an impressive southern coastline from the dramatic Needles and Tennyson Down at the western end, past wooded chines and round St Catherine's Point to the resorts of Ventnor, Shanklin and Sandown.

Hereford and Worcester

The 1974 grouping joined the two old counties of Herefordshire and Worcestershire together, lying respectively southwest and northeast of each other, and sharing the shapely, evocative Malvern Hills, with their prehistoric hillforts and dramatic views over the surrounding countryside.

Herefordshire is quiet, rural and surprisingly unspoiled, famed for its red cattle, its cider orchards and its gleaming black and white, half-timbered, spick-and-span villages, such as Weobley and Eardisland. In the west is remote, wooded, hilly country along the Welsh border, where the Black Mountains encroach into England and the gentle Golden Valley stretches from Dorstone to Abbey Dore.

Another invader from Wales is the River Wye, which runs east and south across southern Herefordshire, rolling past the quiet cathedral city of Hereford and the town of Ross-on-Wye, perched high above the water, and gliding on in great scenic loops and bends to curve beneath the high viewpoint of Symonds Yat.

The Severn and the M5 motorway run roughly north–south through the central plain of Worcestershire, and through or close to Worcester itself, the county town, a handsome cathedral city which has survived the authorities' earnest post-war efforts to spoil it. It is best known for its Royal Worcester china factory and museum, for Worcester Sauce, made to a secret recipe, and for its musical tradition. Sir Edward Elgar's birthplace at Lower Broadheath is a shrine to him and Worcester shares the Three Choirs Festival with Hereford and Gloucester.

In the southeast, Broadway is an expensively smart village beneath the rim of the Cotswolds and the smiling Vale of Evesham is famous for fruit and vegetables. Bredon Hill is a commanding viewpoint. In the northeast lie attractive hill country and the outer fringes of the Birmingham conurbation. Kidderminster is one of England's least engaging towns, but it does have the Severn Valley Railway to console it, and Bewdley is a delight, while the River Teme brings lovely river scenery to the northwest.

Hertfordshire

Hertfordshire is London commuterland and the county has long been heavily influenced by the capital. Much praised for the pure quality of its air, it has lived for centuries by supplying Londoners with food and country residences, and it lies athwart London's communications to the north. The Great North Road through Hatfield has been replaced by the M1 and A1, Watling Street runs to the northwest through St Albans, the old Cambridge road through Ware is now the A10, while the A41 and the Grand Union Canal from London to the Midlands run by the towns of Watford, Hemel Hempstead and Tring through a narrow gap in the Chiltern Hills.

At the turn of the century, when anxiety about London's remorseless expansion became acute, Hertfordshire was the site of the 'garden cities' of Letchworth and Welwyn Garden City, and after World War II three New Towns for London overspill were located in the county – at Stevenage, Hemel Hempstead and Hatfield. Suburbs crowd the southern border from Rickmansworth to Watford and Potter's Bar, and the whole area down the River Lee from Hoddesdon south through Broxbourne, Cheshunt and Waltham Cross is built-up sprawl.

Even so, much quiet countryside has survived off the main routes, around George Bernard Shaw's beloved Ayot St Lawrence, for example, or Much Hadham or Furneux Pelham. The New River, constructed to supply water to London in the 17th century, starts in a delectable spot at Great Amwell, and the Ashridge estate among the hills and beech woods of the Chilterns is rewardingly lovely.

Harpenden, Sawbridgeworth and Ware are engaging towns and Hatfield enjoys the Jacobean splendours of Hatfield House. There are associations with the sculptor Henry Moore at Perry Green and the author George Orwell at Wallington. Hertford is the county town, but St Albans tends to draw the visitors, to its Roman sites and its cathedral, largely a 19th-century creation that dominates the surrounding area from its hilltop vantage.

Humberside

The subject of heated dispute between its detractors and its defenders, the artificial county of Humberside was created in 1974 by marrying most of the old East Riding of Yorkshire to the northern part of Lincolnshire, across the broad estuary of the rolling Humber. Beverley, with its beautiful medieval minster, was chosen as the county administrative centre, but much the biggest town is Hull, a major industrial city, university town, container and passenger port for Northern Europe, and a far more rewarding and enjoyable place to visit than is generally realised.

East of Hull, the flat, farming country of the Holderness peninsula terminates in a long spit of sea-eroded land leading down to solitary Spurn Head. Further north, the quiet seaside resort of Bridlington is sheltered by the towering ramparts of Flamborough Head and inland from here lies the mild, undulating landscape of the Yorkshire Wolds. The Humber is formed by the Yorkshire Ouse and the Trent, and the two sides of the estuary are connected by the beautiful Humber Bridge, the longest single-span suspension bridge in the world when it opened in 1981.

Commercial harbours on the southern bank are the wonderfully named Goole, Immingham and Grimsby, which is Britain's largest fishing port. On the edge of Grimsby, the resort of Cleethorpes was developed in the 1860s originally by the Great Northern Railway Company, whose trains unloaded Yorkshire holiday-makers from the Sheffield area straight onto the bracing sea front, while Scunthorpe, inland, made its name as an iron and steel town. John Wesley grew up at the Old Rectory in nearby Epworth, now a place of pilgrimage for Methodists from all over the world.

Kent

Kent's reputation as 'the Garden of England' grew from its fertile green fields and orchards feeding London, and its closeness to the capital encouraged wealthy Londoners to build themselves country retreats in Kent, from moated and idyllic Ightham Mote to the princely splendours of Knole.

Armies of middle-class London commuters have their homes in the county today and Greater London has swallowed a sizeable helping of western Kent. The county is the nearest part of England to the mainland of Europe and the flow of incoming people and ideas, and stands astride the main routes between London and the Continent. Julius Caesar landed in Kent in 55BC. The invading Roman army in the 1st century AD established its main base in Kent, at Richborough, where Herculean Roman walls stand to this day, and the Romans built the main road from Dover to London.

Hengist and Horsa, leaders of the Saxons, landed in Kent in the 5th century in Pegwell Bay, according to tradition, and so did St Augustine and his party of missionaries from Rome in 597.

Fourteenth-century bridge across the Medway at Aylesford, Kent.

They made for Canterbury, which is still a magnet for visitors with its magnificent cathedral, the mother church of Anglican Christianity.

The Pilgrim's Way footpath to Canterbury follows the long ridge of the North Downs, which cross the county in the north above the M2 motorway. To the south in the shelter of the downs lies the countryside of the Weald with its neat little towns and villages, its hop-gardens and oasthouses, its time-honoured amicable pubs. In the far southwest the wet, flat, cattle-grazed country of Romney Marsh is agog with romantic tales of smugglers. Along the coast, Dover Castle, high above the ferry port and the famous white cliffs, stares watchfully across the heaving sea to France, and Kent's other main passenger and commercial ports for the Continent are Folkestone, where the new Channel Tunnel comes ashore, Ramsgate and Sheerness. Maidstone is the county town. Margate made its reputation as a brash and breezy resort for Londoners on the spree, Tunbridge Wells, in upper-crust contrast, as a smart spa. Chatham's historic dockyard is enthralling and Rochester, with England's second cathedral, exudes dignified charm.

Lancashire

The county of Lancashire suffered severely in the reorganisation of 1974. Its industrial belt in the south was taken away and turned into Merseyside and Greater Manchester, while its contrastingly scenic northern enclave of Furness in the Lake District was confiscated for Cumbria. Lancashire was left with the central part of its ancestral domain, as a predominantly rural, farming county, traversed north–south by the M6 motorway, with a varied and interesting coastline and some significant reminders of the Industrial Revolution in towns like Burnley, Blackburn and Preston, which is the county town, the largest town and the centre of extensive development since the 1970s. Preston is on the Ribble, which runs clear across the county. On the coast, Blackpool, the North of England's answer to Brighton, continues to prosper with its pleasure beach and its famous tower and ballroom, its breathless roller-coaster rides, giant ferris wheel and nostalgic little trams.

Lytham St Anne's to the south is more restrained. Further north the vast, treacherous sandflats of Morecambe Bay glisten as the tide retreats far out into the Irish Sea, before it floods swiftly in again. Lancaster, on the Lune, is a historic and attractive university town, while inland from Morecambe Bay are the farms of the flat Fylde district, giving way further east to the Forest of Bowland. Bowland is forest no longer, but an area of high, peaty moorland on the edge of the Pennines, fine walking country, crossed by a road which goes down through the valley of the Trough of Bowland. The district round Pendle Hill holds memories of witches. Further south, the high moors of the West Pennines loom up on the border with West Yorkshire.

Leicestershire and Rutland

Geographically at the centre of England, known for fox-hunting, Red Leicester and Stilton cheese and Melton Mowbray pork pies, Leicestershire is divided in two by the M1 motorway and the River Soar, which runs roughly south to north to join the Trent. On the Soar lies Leicester, the county town and by a considerable margin the biggest town. Stockings and hose have a long history in Leicester, which today is a centre of engineering and the hosiery, knitwear and footwear industries, with a cathedral and a university, and a substantial immigrant population.

Further north in the Soar Valley, the town of Loughborough makes church bells, in one of England's only two remaining bell-foundries, with a unique museum. West of the Soar the county's highest land rises in the remnants of Charnwood Forest, with the bracken-covered heathland, woods and rocks of Bradgate Park. The battlefield of Bosworth, where the Tudor dynasty won the throne in 1485, appeals to visitors further south, and further south again is another historic hosiery town, Hinckley. In the other half of Leicestershire, lying east of the Soar, the handsome old town of Market Harborough close to the Northamptonshire border boasts a notable church and several coaching inns. Melton Mowbray is another veteran market town, which in the 19th century acquired toothsome repute for the making of pork pies, as the ideal snack for fox-hunters to carry in their pockets. In the northeast the Duke of Rutland's palace of Belvoir Castle looks out over the surrounding lands from its eyrie over the fertile Vale of Belvoir.

The reorganisation of 1974 made Rutland part of Leicestershire, to considerable local indignation. England's smallest county, with an area of 152 square miles (380sq km), has a history as a shire going back to at least the 12th century and its county town, Oakham, has a Norman castle. Much of the county now lies drowned under Rutland Water, one of the biggest man-made lakes in Europe, created in the 1970s as a reservoir for the East Midlands, attractively landscaped and today a popular sailing and watersports centre with paths and picnic spots along its shores.

Lincolnshire

One of England's larger counties, Lincolnshire is rich agricultural and horticultural land, well stocked with windmills, generally flat, but with the Lincolnshire Wolds going up to above 550ft (168m) on the county's eastern side. The Holland area in the southeast is a continuation of the Cambridgeshire fen country, lying inland from the Wash and drained in the 17th century. The bulb-fields round Spalding and Holbeach are a blaze of colour in the spring, and Spalding stages a tremendous Tulip Parade in May, while Boston Stump, the stately tower of St Botolph's Church in the old market town and port of Boston – which gave its name to Boston, Massachusetts – is a landmark for miles around across the flat fields and the winding creeks close to the shore. Stamford, tucked away in the extreme southwestern corner of Lincolnshire on the River Welland, is one of England's most sympathetic and satisfying towns in its creamy stone and, like Grantham, is a former coaching town on the route of the Great North road.

Lincoln, the county town and once an important Roman base, is set on two levels. The castle and the magnificent cathedral are poised dramatically on a ridge of rock above the lower town, and one of the narrow medieval streets is simply and justifiably called Steep Hill. Outside the cathedral is a statue of Lord Tennyson, greatly admired in his home county. He grew up at Somersby, where his father was rector, and went to school in Louth, a market town of character below the Wolds. Gainsborough, Horncastle and Spilsby are pleasant country towns. The quiet of Lincolnshire's low-lying, solitary North Sea coastline is broken by Skegness, a brash, bracing seaside resort where the first Butlin's holiday camp opened in the 1930s.

Merseyside

The county of Merseyside was cut out of Lancashire and Cheshire in 1974 to cover Liverpool and its environs on both sides of the River Mersey, but the metropolitan council was abolished in 1986. Three miles (5km) inland from the Irish Sea, Liverpool is Britain's leading trans-Atlantic port. With 2,000 acres (810ha) of docks handling close to 28 million tons of cargo a year, it is one of the liveliest and most fascinating cities in the country. It has Church of England and Roman Catholic cathedrals of note, as well as two top football teams, its impressive 19th-century docks are being refurbished, its Beatles memories and its sardonic humour are both intact and it owns some of the most rewarding art galleries in the kingdom. One of them is across the Mersey in the Wirral peninsula, in the intriguing soap-company town of Port Sunlight. There are notable golf courses here, too. Up the coast lie sandy beaches and miles of dunes, nature reserves, natterjack toads and the resort of Southport.

Norfolk

Flatness, enormous panoramic skies and cloudscapes, windmills and turkeys are all associated with Norfolk, a county whose distinctive identity has been supported by its relative isolation from the rest of the country and the fact that it is as close to Amsterdam as it is to its own capital, London.

Cold-shouldered by the Industrial Revolution, it is mainly prosperous and efficient arable farming country, with few towns of any size. In the northwest the fens spill over from Cambridgeshire, and the delightful old town of King's Lynn is an inland port on the Great Ouse, close to the Wash. Northeast from here are the royal estate of Sandringham and the scented lavender fields at Heacham. A chain of nature reserves stretches along the low-lying North Norfolk coast with its small harbours, saltmarshes and mudflats carpeted in sea lavender, where diminutive rivers wriggle their way to the North Sea through channels and creeks, attracting walkers, small-boat sailors, cockles and whelks, and multitudes of birds. Norfolk's great naval hero, Lord Nelson, came from Burnham Thorpe, where his father was rector.

The shrine to the Virgin Mary at Walsingham draws many pilgrims, while Cromer is a pleasant seaside resort with a famous lifeboat. Further on down the coast are sand and shingle beaches and a constant battle against the encroaching sea. People digging for peat inland in medieval times unintentionally created the Broads, northeast of Norwich, which provide some 200 miles (320km) of inland waterways for cruising and sailing.

Norwich itself, the county town, is a lively and enjoyable market, financial, cultural and university centre, with a beautiful cathedral of Caen stone, brought from Normandy by water, and one of the best museums in the country in an odd-looking Norman castle. Great Yarmouth, a popular resort on the coast, was a redoubtable herring port until overfishing put paid to the industry after World War II.

Thetford has an abundance of Georgian and medieval houses in its pretty centre. The town is the capital of the Breckland of southwestern Norfolk, stretching across the border into Suffolk, an area of sandy heaths, marshes and diminutive lakes, which was covered with conifers by the Forestry Commission in the period between the two world wars.

Northamptonshire

A smallish county in the quiet, unspectacular but endearing landscape of the English Midlands, Northamptonshire is primarily farming country, though Northampton itself, the county town, has a long history in the boot and shoe trade which prompted the witty 17th-century Northamptonshire antiquarian Thomas Fuller to remark that the town could be said 'to stand chiefly on other men's legs'. Northampton is still an active manufacturing centre, and it also has one of England's few round churches.

The shoe trade also industrialised the towns of Kettering, Higham Ferrers and Rushden to the northeast. Irthlingborough was once an iron town and Corby was a thriving iron and steel town until its giant steelworks closed suddenly in 1979. Since the disaster it has recovered admirably, pulled itself up by its own bootstraps and attracted new businesses.

An undulating line of limestone hills, with fine views to the west, runs up the western side of the county, not rising much above 700 ft (210m). The highest point is Arbury Hill, near Badby. Below to the east, the M1 motorway, Watling Street, the Grand Union Canal and the main London–Birmingham railway go hand-in-hand towards the Watford Gap.

Up on high ground near the Civil War battlefield of Naseby is one of England's major watersheds, where the Avon, the Nene and the Welland all rise: the Avon to head for Shakespeare's Stratford-upon-Avon, the Nene to flow through most of its native county by Northampton and Wellingborough towards the Fens, and the Welland to run along the Leicestershire border to Stamford. The mellow stone townscape of Stamford dates mostly from the 17th and 18th centuries.

An engagingly eccentric note is struck by the symbolic creations of pious Sir Thomas Tresham in the 17th century: the triangular lodge at Rushton and Lyveden New Bield. Little is left of what was once the great Forest of Rockingham, but much of 'the county of spires and squires' is still agreeably rural.

Northumberland

England's most northerly county is also one of the most unspoiled and remote. Its peacefulness belies an ancient history of war, raiding, rustling and rapine across the Scots border. Ruined castles and the remains of peles and bastles stand as mute witnesses to a turbulent past.

The original Northumbria was a powerful Anglo-Saxon kingdom, whose rulers presided over the introduction of Christianity to the North and a 'golden age' of art exemplified by the Lindisfarne Gospels. By the 12th century it had been reduced to a county of roughly today's proportions, except that it lost Newcastle upon Tyne in the 1974 reorganisation. The western marches are formed by the high moors, solitary hill farms and drystone walls of the Pennines, with the huge artificial lake of Kielder Water at the heart of a heavily forested area. Further north, the lonely Cheviot Hills patrol the border with Scotland. The tragic battlefield of Flodden lies here and the walled fortress-town of Berwick-upon-Tweed changed hands between English and Scots many times in the past. Down the coast, Lindisfarne or Holy Island is a magical place, and the bird-haunted Farne Islands lie offshore.

Across the farming country of central Northumberland the rivers Aln, Coquet, Wansbeck and Blyth thread their way eastwards to a beautiful North Sea coastline of long sandy beaches, dunes and cliffs, old fishing harbours, and around Craster the salutary reek of kippers. Morpeth, the county town, has a unique museum of bagpipes. Wild white cattle graze the park at Chillingham, Alnwick was the headquarters of the formidable Percy dynasty, which held the North against the Scots, and there are notable castles at Bamburgh, Dunstanburgh and Warkworth. Further south a much older fortification climbs and swoops its way across country, worn by time and human depredations, but still powerfully impressive – Hadrian's Wall, which the Romans built to hold back the tribesmen to the north. Further south, beyond the market town of Hexham, the Derwent forms the border with Durham.

Nottinghamshire

Lying mainly in low ground in the basin of the River Trent in the northern Midlands, the county blends coal-mining and industry with arable and livestock farming. Traditions of Robin Hood and Little John cling to the remnants of Sherwood Forest, which once covered much of the area north of Nottingham. Clumber Park was one of the grand aristocratic estates of the Dukeries, while caves once inhabited by Neanderthal families can be seen at Cresswell Crags. The industrial towns are in the western part of the county towards the Derbyshire border, where the M1 carves its way north – Beeston, Hucknall, Mansfield and Eastwood, where D H Lawrence's birthplace is a museum to him. Not far away, and in marked contrast, is romantic Newstead Abbey in its delectable grounds, the ancestral home of another famous writer – Lord Byron.

Nottingham, on the Trent, the county town and by a long chalk the largest town, is a lively industrial, engineering, university and sporting centre, celebrated for lace and for Boot's the Chemist, which Jesse Boot started here. It still holds its famous Goose Fair in October. Southwell is a delightful little miniature city, home to one of England's smallest cathedrals, and Newark is a historic town on the Great North road with a handsome market square and a ruined castle frowning beside the Trent. Further north, Worksop is a market town with a notable priory church and the village of Laxton has kept its medieval strip-farmed fields.

Oxfordshire

Oxfordshire swelled in size by more than a third after the changes of 1974 presented the county with a substantial area south of the Thames previously belonging to Berkshire. This included the Vale of the White Horse, with the spectacular Iron Age hill figure called the White Horse of Uffington, the oldest of its breed, connected in legend with the story of St George and the Dragon; as well as the market town of Wantage, where King Alfred was born, the railway town of Didcot and the handsome Thames-side town of Abingdon. From here the Thames loops its way southeastwards past the noble abbey church at Dorchester to Goring and on down to Henley-on-Thames and its prestigious regatta.

The Chiltern Hills carry their beechwoods in a scenic curve across the southeastern section of Oxfordshire, cut through by the M40 motorway on its way towards Oxford and Birmingham. Oxford itself, the county town, is the only town of any size in Oxfordshire and the centre of most attention, which it commands for its venerable university, its college buildings of mellow stone, its charming riverside and its cultural attractions. However, Oxford has another contrasting side to it which tourists seldom see, as an industrial town, making cars in Cowley.

On the western side of the county the Cotswold Hills encroach attractively from Gloucestershire, with many delightful villages in mellow stone. Burford is a particularly smart and pleasing small town, Witney has a reputation for carpets, and Woodstock bows before the titanic splendours of Blenheim Palace, where Sir Winston Churchill was born. Thame and Bicester in the east are minor market towns, and the busy Banbury in the north of the county boasts a big livestock market, the Banbury Cross of the nursery rhyme and a special type of cake.

Shropshire

Rural, agricultural and still comparatively unspoiled, Shropshire is paradoxically the place where the Industrial Revolution began, in the picturesque Ironbridge Gorge of the Severn in the 18th century. The famous Iron Bridge itself, built in 1779, is now at the heart of a fascinating complex of industrial museums. Not far away there is a parallel contrast between the isolated wooded hump of the Wrekin and the new town of Telford, developed since the 1960s among exhausted coal mines.

The Severn flows right across Shropshire from the Welsh border in the west to Shrewsbury, past the Roman site of Wroxeter and beneath the Iron Bridge, and on down by Bridgnorth, perched on its high cliff above the river, in the southeast. Shrewsbury, the county town, keeps its half-timbered buildings and its considerable attractions inside a horseshoe loop of the river so extreme that it almost joins up in a circle.

North of Shrewsbury and the river lies mainly flat country, a rich dairy and arable farming region, dotted with small lakes or 'meres' around Ellesmere and rising to hills in the northwest around the market town of Oswestry. South of the river is where the more dramatic scenery is to be found, among the 'blue remembered hills' of A E Housman's oft-quoted lines, marching southwards in fine style towards Herefordshire. Among the Stretton Hills is the pointed peak of Caer Caradoc, in legend the place where the British chieftain made his last stand against the conquering Romans. Church Stretton is a neat former spa town sheltering below the burly hump of the Long Mynd. In high, solitary country further south the strange rock outcrops of the Stiperstones break the surface. To the east runs the long, narrow ridge of Wenlock Edge and in the southeast of the county the high Clee Hills are rich in folklore and tales of witchcraft. Ludlow in the far south is a showplace old market town and Much Wenlock, set at the northern end of Wenlock Edge is another delight.

Somerset

Along the county's northern edge, the Mendip Hills are as full of holes as a colander, as caves and potholes and hidden streams wind their mysterious way beneath the ground. The caves at Wookey Hole are well known, as are those in the spectacular Cheddar Gorge, which carves its path through the hills. Cheddar, of course, gave its name to the cheese.

Below the Mendips, Wells is a charming old town with a strikingly beautiful medieval cathedral, and further south lies the county's central plain and the flat, peaty marshland of the Somerset Levels, drained for dairy farming. At Cadbury Castle and Glastonbury, the last hippy capital of the West, where the Tor rises enigmatically above the Isle of Avalon, Somerset has the strongest associations with the Arthurian legends of any area in Britain. In the Levels, among the straight irrigation ditches called 'rhines', are Athelney, where King Alfred hid from the Danes and burned the cakes, and the 17th-century battlefield of Sedgemoor.

Burnham-on-Sea and Minehead are popular resorts with holiday camps and caravan parks on the Bristol Channel, and Bridgwater is a bustling market town astride the River Parrett. The county town, Taunton, is set in an area rich in cider orchards, but Somerset's fastest expanding town is Yeovil, a business and industrial centre in the southeast. In the western part of the county the roller-coaster Quantock Hills with their superb views run inland from the Bristol Channel coast and the Blackdown Hills line the border with Devon. The Brendon Hills act as curtain-raiser to the high plateau of Exmoor, with its deer and wild ponies, rising to 1,707ft (520m) at Dunkery Beacon, the highest point in Somerset. The National Trust owns the bewitching Holnicote estate and further west lurk the haunts of the legendary Doones.

Staffordshire

The county lost a stretch of heavily industrialised territory in the Black Country to the West Midlands under the changes of 1974, but retained the Potteries, the famed 'five towns' (actually six towns) of the industrial city of Stoke-on-Trent, celebrated for the production of fabulously beautiful objects under such names as Wedgwood, Minton and Spode. With its satellite of Newcastle-under-Lyme, close to the M6 motorway, Stoke is the world's largest producer of china, earthenware and other clayware, and is also busily engaged with steel, chemicals and engineering, while Burton upon Trent is the capital of England's brewing industry.

Staffordshire has many miles of canal, and has bred its own brand of bull terrier. Most of the county is farming country and it is richly endowed with attractive scenery. In the north are the high Staffordshire Moorlands and the Peak District valleys of the Hamps, the Manifold and the Dove, with their caves and waterfalls and rock formations. Leek is the principal town here, the pleasure park at Alton Towers is one of the most successful visitor attractions in Britain and the Rudyard Lake reservoir gave a visiting couple named Kipling a first name for their infant son.

Further south there is peace and seclusion to be found among the woods and heaths of Cannock Chase, with its touching war cemeteries, and the Vale of Trent in the east of the county is delightful. Staffordshire's cathedral city, Lichfield, preserves a Georgian dignity and memories of Dr Johnson, while Tamworth, Uttoxeter and the lively county town of Stafford, are all pleasant market centres for the county.

Suffolk

Much of previously remote and idiosyncratic Suffolk has fallen to the London commuter, but the county still enjoys beautiful farming countryside, associated with the Suffolk Punch breed of heavy horse, and a coastline which intriguingly blends nature and commerce. Felixstowe, at the southern end, is both a seaside resort and a busy modern container and ferry port for Holland. To the north lies a low, bleak, shingly shore studded by Martello towers, marshes and teeming bird sanctuaries. The Ore and the Alde wriggle their way behind the long silt spit of Orford Ness. The little fishing town of Aldeburgh has an international reputation for its music festival and its links with Benjamin Britten, and the avocet and the nightingale flourish among reed-fringed lagoons, heaths and woods at Minsmere.

This part of the coast is under constant attack from the eroding sea. Most of Dunwich disappeared under the waves long ago, which did not prevent it continuing to send its accustomed two members to Parliament, but Walberswick and Southwold are resorts of charm and character, and the fishing port of Lowestoft is the most easterly town in England.

Inland, Suffolk is best known for Flatford Mill and the idyllic scenery which John Constable loved to paint in the valley of the Stour. The other great Suffolk painter, Gainsborough, came from Sudbury, where his house is open to visitors. Lavenham and Long Melford are exceptionally attractive former wool towns with thrilling churches, while Ipswich, the county town and largest town, is very much part of today's world as a business and industrial centre. In the north lies the open heath country of the Breckland. Bury St Edmunds makes a prosperous and attractive setting for its ruined abbey and its lovely gardens, and strings of expensive thoroughbreds and the Jockey Club's headquarters make red-brick Georgian Newmarket the leading horse-racing town in England.

Surrey

The county's writ once ran all the way up to the south bank of the Thames, but London has eaten into its territory to such an extent that Surrey's administrative centre itself is in Greater London, at Kingston upon Thames. The area which is still Surrey is inevitably commuterland. The smart, well-to-do, neatly trimmed and packaged small towns and villages are dependent on and heavily dominated by the capital, but less regimented countryside has survived. The North Downs run across northern Surrey from Guildford eastwards and Box Hill, above the valley of the Mole north of Dorking, is a notable beauty spot. In the south another ridge of hills, greenly garlanded with woods, rises to Surrey's highest point at Leith Hill and skirts the deep chasm of the Devil's Punchbowl near Hindhead.

The M3 motorway cuts through the open heathland between Bagshot and Chertsey, while the narrow ridge of the Hog's Back commands huge panoramas west of Guildford. At Guildford the red-brick tower of the 1930s cathedral is a commanding sight, but Farnham, with its handsome Georgian streets, probably takes the prize as Surrey's most engaging town, perhaps with Godalming as runner-up. Redhill, Reigate, Leatherhead, Woking and Staines are primarily residential centres and London satellites. The attractive town of Epsom, where Epsom Salts came from, is famed for horse-racing and especially the Derby. Outside Egham the Thames ripples through the historic meadows of Runnymede, where King John reluctantly put his signature to Magna Carta.

Sussex, East and West

The kingdom of the South Saxons originally, Sussex is known for the Weald, the South Downs and the English Channel coast. All of it is well in commuting range of London, but there are some quiet and little explored corners. Rudyard Kipling, who lived in Sussex, loved its 'blunt, bow-headed, whale-backed Downs', which enter the county from Hampshire in the west and run for 50 miles (80km) or so southeast to meet the sea at the towering chalk cliff of Beachy Head outside Eastbourne. Their green slopes support eye-catching clumps of trees like Chanctonbury Ring, which suffered in the 1987 hurricane. North of the downs is the rich farming country of the Weald, an almost impenetrable forest when the Romans came, subsequently a major iron-working area – the industry left its hammerponds behind it – and gradually cleared. Ashdown Forest is more heath than woodland now, but there are remnants of St Leonard's Forest near Horsham. The highest ground in Sussex is not in the South Downs, but at Blackdown, 919ft (280m) up in the sandy heaths and pines of the north western corner.

Along the coast, the 'Sussex by the sea' of the sprightly song features a succession of resorts with shingle beaches, iron piers and high sunshine counts, tending to run into each other all the way from Bognor Regis and Littlehampton to Bexhill and Hastings. The queen of them is certainly Brighton, smart and lively, unabashedly devoted to pleasure and elegantly adorned with Regency terraces and the brilliantly eccentric oriental pleasure-dome of the Pavilion. Eastbourne is thoroughly attractive, too, if quieter, and right along at the eastern end of the Sussex coast, the picturesque old town of Rye is a delight. Another charmer is Lewes, East Sussex's county town. The county town of West Sussex is Chichester, known for its fine cathedral and

Georgian streets, modern art and fish paste. Among the inlets of Chichester Harbour, Bosham is an old-fashioned treat, and further inland are Arundel, Steyning, Midhurst and Petworth, all stylish country towns. Crawley, by contrast, has been developed since 1945 as a New Town, close to Gatwick Airport.

Tyne and Wear

The county was created in 1974 to cover Newcastle, Gateshead, Sunderland and their hinterland. It was named after the two principal rivers, but its metropolitan council was abolished in 1986. In the 19th century this was Britain's leading coal-exporting region, with a major ship-building industry and important armaments and chemical plants, but it fell into decline from the 1930s onwards. Newcastle upon Tyne started life soon after the Norman Conquest as a bastion against the Scots and developed into an important provincial centre, a coal-mining town (hence the expression about not carrying coals to Newcastle) and later the heart of industrial Tyneside. It is an impressive and enjoyable city, a commercial, sporting and cultural base, and a ferry port for Northern Europe, with a cathedral and university, a splendid sheaf of seven bridges crossing the river and a handsome 18th-century Promenade in Grey Street. At Tynemouth, to the east, the river is guarded by a ruined castle and priory, and to the north is the seaside resort of Whitley Bay. On the Tyne's southern bank, Gateshead boasts the biggest drive-in shopping centre in Europe. Down river at Jarrow, the simple little Church of St Paul, which the Venerable Bede knew in the 8th century, stands marooned in the midst of a grim industrial landscape. Sunderland, on the Wear, was another coal port.

Warwickshire

One of the smaller counties, Warwickshire lost Birmingham and Coventry to the West Midlands in 1974 and ended up shaped like a banana. The Avon runs across the south of the county, where Stratford upon Avon, the capital of the Shakespeare Country, welcomes droves of pilgrims to the Bard's birthplace, the other sites associated with him and the Memorial Theatre. Many of the surrounding villages with their thatched, half-timbered cottages have traditional associations with Shakespeare as well. Not much is left of the Forest of Arden, but Henley-in-Arden is a little town of enduring charm.

The Cotswolds touch the county's southern borders, but Warwickshire's highest point is the Edge Hill ridge near Kineton, known for the Civil War battle and providing fine views. Close by is the M40 motorway, which runs diagonally across the county on its way between London and the Birmingham conurbation. Leamington Spa has a dignified collection of Regency and Victorian buildings, nicely set off by gardens, and the county town, Warwick, is a thoroughly rewarding place, with a massively formidable castle and a particularly beautiful church. Another historic fortress of exceptional grandeur looms up at nearby Kenilworth. Rugby is enduringly famous for its school and its brand of football, and in the far north of the county, at the thinner end of the banana, the town of Nuneaton prides itself on its connections with another famous author, George Eliot.

West Midlands

The county was carved out of Warwickshire and Staffordshire in 1974 for the Birmingham and Coventry conurbation, but its metropolitan council was abolished in 1986. The area is the central hub of the motorway system, as it was earlier of the canal network. The Industrial Revolution turned Birmingham and its surrounding towns into one of Britain's most important manufacturing regions and the view as you drive in from the east on the M6 motorway is still grimly impressive. The coal and iron towns of the Black Country – Dudley, West Bromwich, Wednesbury, Walsall, Wolverhampton – merged into each other in the 19th century in a polluted landscape of chimneys, furnaces, flames and smoke which Charles Dickens described as an industrialised realisation of hell.

Despite the decline in heavy industry, the West Midlands is a major business centre and Birmingham has an international airport and the National Exhibition Centre, as well as a university, and is an important cultural and sports centre. Coventry, whose new cathedral rose from the bombed-out ruins of the old one in 1962, is busy with motor vehicles, machine tools and the telecommunications industry. There are pleasant, leafy suburbs with their own character in places like Solihull and Sutton Coldfield.

Wiltshire

Wiltshire cherishes Britain's leading concentration of major prehistoric sites – led by the giant, evocative and mysterious stone circles of Stonehenge and Avebury and the enigmatic man-made mound of Silbury Hill, but extending to many other sites, barrows, hillforts and ancient trackways. The county is dominated by the central high chalk plateau of Salisbury Plain, parts of which are reserved for the military.

The pleasant, fertile Vale of Pewsey lies immediately to the north, and the old Bath road, the A4, runs through the woods of Savernake Forest and through Britain's widest main street in the town of Marlborough. North from here is the rolling chalk downland of the Marlborough Downs, studded with Iron Age hillforts, with the M4 motorway on the northern side. Swindon, a 19th-century railway town, has been developing rapidly as an electronics and pharmaceuticals centre and is Wiltshire's largest town.

Further west and south, Devizes and Chippenham are solid, pleasant country towns; Malmesbury has an imposing abbey church, Corsham and Bradford-on-Avon are particularly attractive in their locally quarried Bath stone and Lacock is a National Trust showplace. Trowbridge is the county town of Wiltshire, Westbury boasts a notable white horse, outside Warminster the Longleat lions roam their safari park in the grounds of the Marquess of Bath's palatial mansion, and near the charming town of Mere is the delectable landscape garden at Stourhead. Carving through Salisbury Plain and running south, the valleys of the Wylye and the Wiltshire Avon converge at the city of Salisbury, Wiltshire's most attractive town, with its beautiful, tall-spired cathedral, cattle-grazed watermeadows and charming close. Nearby Wilton is famous for carpets and for another palatial mansion, Wilton House, which contains some of the most beautiful rooms in England, while among the most intriguing of Wiltshire's many hill figures are the series of regimental badges carved into a chalk hillside near Fovant.

An old lock-up at Shrewton, Wiltshire.

The Yorkshires

Far and away Britain's largest county, Yorkshire was traditionally divided into three ridings (literally 'thirdings'): east, north and west. The 1974 reorganisation created three new divisions of Yorkshire – north, south and west – while hiving off most of the east riding to the new county of Humberside and passing other slices of traditional Yorkshire politely to Lancashire, Cumbria, Durham and Cleveland.

North Yorkshire is still the biggest English county. The Pennines run up the western marches through some of the most breathtaking scenery in England, in the Yorkshire Dales National Park, starting with the remarkable caves and limestone landscape of Malham Cove, Gordale Scar and the Three Peaks in the southwest. The scenic Settle–Carlisle railway line crosses this territory by way of the Ribblehead Viaduct. The principal North Yorkshire dales, from the south, are: Wharfedale, with a particularly enticing stretch around Bolton Abbey; Wensleydale, known for cheese and spectacular scenery around Hawes; and lonely Swaledale, with its waterfalls and its sheep. The Swale rushes deep below the battlements of Richmond Castle and further south are ruined Fountains Abbey and the diminutive cathedral city of Ripon. Harrogate, 18th-century spa and now smart conference centre, is further south again. In the centre of the county lie the prosperous farms of the Vale of York.

Northallerton is North Yorkshire's county town, but the area is dominated by the historic city of York, with its ancient walls and mighty church. Further east, the high North York Moors make their solitary way over to the North Sea coast, the seaside resort of Scarborough and the picturesque old port of Whitby.

South Yorkshire is primarily an industrial region dominated by Sheffield, with Rotherham, Barnsley and Doncaster as outliers. This was a principal coal-mining area, but the industry has been steadily running down. Famed for its cutlery, Sheffield boomed as a steel town in the 19th century, still manufactures special steels, and is also a financial, university and cultural centre.

Where North Yorkshire is predominantly rural and South Yorkshire industrial, West Yorkshire is a mixture of the two. The industrial revolution turned it into a great wool manufacturing district. Bradford, once a leading wool town, has broadened out into engineering, micro-electronics and financial services, and has attracted a substantial immigrant population, while its neighbour and rival, Leeds, is a commercial, service industry and communications centre. Wakefield and Huddersfield are other industrial towns adjusting to today's climate, as is Halifax, an attractive town set beautifully among hills. Meanwhile there's entrancing Pennine scenery in the west of the county, where Holmfirth attracts 'Last of the Summer Wine' devotees and Haworth draws pilgrims to the Brontë Country and the romantic moors of *Wuthering Heights*.

Scotland

There are three natural divisions of Scotland. North of the English border rise the southern uplands. North of them lie the central lowlands, the valleys of the Clyde, Forth and Tay, with the bulk of the population. North again is the mountain mass of the Highlands. Scotland is far less densely inhabited than England. In an area equal to about 60 per cent of the size of England, Scotland has a population of only some 11 per cent of England's figure. Under the reorganisation of the 1970s, the existing Scots counties were abolished, with their accumulated baggage of history and tradition, and replaced by 12 new 'regions'.

Borders

Covering the former counties of Berwick, Roxburgh, Selkirk and Peebles, with a bit of Midlothian thrown in, this was for centuries the war-torn land north of the border with England, fought over from Roman times to the 17th century, trodden and devastated by armies, and restless with raiding and rustling even in times of peace or truce. Hermitage Castle's grim and solitary hold and the ruined abbeys of Melrose, Jedburgh, Kelso and Dryburgh bear gaunt witness to a violent past in what is today pleasant farming, forest and hill country, known for peaceable tweeds and knitted goods. Towns like Kelso, Hawick and Selkirk keep up their historic 'common riding' customs and Peebles and Galashiels are textile centres. The Tweed and the Teviot are famous fishing rivers. Sir Walter Scott's home at Abbotsford can be visited below the magical Eildon Hills. To the west are the remains of the great Forest of Ettrick and John Buchan's favourite Tweedsmuir Hills, while Traquair, near Innerleithen, is one of the most romantic houses in all Britain. To the north lies the lonely moorland of the Lammermuirs.

Central

Clackmannanshire, the smallest county in Scotland, was included in the Central region with most of Stirlingshire and the southwestern part of Perthshire to create an area which straddles Lowlands and Highlands. The River Forth runs across the middle of the region, which embraces the lochs and glens of one of the most famously scenic districts in Scotland – the Trossachs – and extends westwards to Loch Lomond, with Ben Lomond towering above, and north to the 'Rob Roy' country and the deer forests of Breadalbane. Historic Stirling Castle crouches menacingly on its high, bare rock above the Forth and the battlefield of Bannockburn, where Robert the Bruce resoundingly defeated the English. Falkirk and Alloa are in the industrial area in the southeast.

Dumfries and Galloway

The old shires of Wigtown, Kirkcudbright and Dumfries made up the new Dumfries and Galloway region. The Galloway area in Scotland's extreme southwest was an independent lordship until the 11th century and preserved a measure of independence until the 15th. The area lies off the beaten track today, occupied with raising cattle and sheep, arable farming, forestry and tourism, but for centuries before the coming of the railways and modern roads the harbours here offered the swiftest routes to the northwest of England, the north of Wales and Ireland. Portpatrick was the equivalent of Gretna Green to eloping Irish couples and Stranraer in the shelter of Loch Ryan is still a major port for Northern Ireland. The first Christian missionary to Scotland, St Ninian, worked at Whithorn. Further east, Kirkcudbright is a dignified old harbour town on the Dee and the region's capital, Dumfries, is linked with Robert Burns, who spent the last years of his life there. Threave Castle is a grim stronghold of the Black Douglases, while the rose-red ruins of Caerlaverock Castle gaze out over the flats and bird sanctuaries of the Solway Firth, fed by the rivers Annan, Nith and Esk. In the north deer and wild goats roam the huge Galloway Forest Park.

Fife

This was the one old Scottish county to survive intact as a region. Lying between the Firth of Tay and the Firth of Forth, the Fife peninsula has a long record as an identifiable entity, packed full of historic sites, old fishing ports and industrial towns. Robert the Bruce and many of his successors lie buried at Dunfermline, the old royal capital, later a textile town and the birthplace of the business tycoon and philanthropist Andrew Carnegie. Falkland, with Britain's oldest tennis court, was a favourite hunting and relaxation retreat of James IV, James V and Mary, Queen of Scots. Cowdenbeath was a centre of the old Fife coalfield. The Scottish Fisheries Museum in the veteran herring port of Anstruther records one of Scotland's major industries until recent decline – sea fishing and whaling. Out on the shore of the grey North Sea, the dignified town of St Andrews guards with proper pride Scotland's oldest university, as well as the Holy Grail of the golfing world, the famed Old Course of the Royal and Ancient Golf Club.

Grampian

Uniting most of Morayshire with the old counties of Banff, Aberdeen and Kincardine, the Grampian region in the northeast is a delectable blend of mountains, forests, sea coast and the famous river valleys of the Spey and the Dee.

Speyside is known for its fishing and its whisky distilleries. Deeside for the royal family's summer home at Balmoral and the Highland Games at Braemar. Beetling cliffs, sandy beaches and picturesque fishing towns and villages are ranged along the long Grampian coast. The spectacular ruins of Dunnottar Castle lie close to the harbour town and resort of Stonehaven. The region's capital and largest town, the granite cathedral and university city of Aberdeen, is a major North Sea oil port and a thriving business and financial centre, and the next largest town, Peterhead, is Scotland's principal fishing port. More old fishing harbours line the northern coast, where Banff and Elgin are historic towns of character.

Highland

The huge Highland region is the biggest administrative district in Britain, far larger than any English or Welsh county, covering some 10,000 square miles (25,000sq km) and some of the most breathtakingly spectacular scenery in the entire country. These are the realms of the eagle, the stag, the wild cat, the otter and the seal, among soaring peaks, sparkling lakes and salmon rivers, grouse moors and deer forests, craggy shores and sea-lochs shimmering under spectacular sunsets.

The region joins the former counties of Caithness, Sutherland, Ross and Cromarty, Inverness, Nairn and parts of Argyll and Morayshire in about one-third of the entire land area of Scotland. It extends from haunting and dramatic Glen Coe of massacre fame in the south up past Ben Nevis, Britain's highest peak, with Fort William at its foot, to beautiful Loch Torridon and the snow-capped summits of Wester Ross, and on across the trackless wastes of Sutherland to Cape Wrath, the wild waters of the Pentland Firth and finally John o' Groats and Dunnet Head in the far north. Slashing diagonally is the Great Glen with the Caledonian Canal and Loch Ness concealing its legendary monster.

Straddling the border betweeen Grampian and Highland, between the Spey and Dee, rise the snow-crowned peaks of the Cairngorms – nine of them topping 4,000ft (1,200m) – with their ski resorts and mountain walking and the winter sports centre of Aviemore. Just north of Aviemore are the ospreys at Loch Garten. The region is run from the principal town, Inverness, a centre of road, rail and air communications, east of which lies the tragic battlefield of Culloden. The other main towns – Nairn, Dingwall, Wick and Thurso – are all on the eastern and northeastern coast. Across at the other side, the jewel in the glittering western sea is the island of Skye with the far Cuillins dominating the horizon. It is intensely romantic country, shot through with memories of the clans and of Prince Charles Edward and the last, doomed attempt to regain the throne for the Stuarts, in 1745.

Lothian

Edinburgh inevitably dominates the Lothian region, as it did the old counties of West Lothian, Midlothian and East Lothian. The name Lothian itself originally belonged to an ancient kingdom which was often under the sway of the English kings of Northumbria, until King Malcolm II of Scots defeated the Northumbrians in a decisive battle in the 11th century. Edinburgh eventually became the capital of Scotland and today, below its impregnable castle rock, is one of Britain's most attractive, civilised and enjoyable cities, dominated by its ancient castle and the home of the country's most prestigious arts festival.

To the south are the Pentland Hills and the Lammermuirs. To the west lie the new town of Livingston, with the microchip industries of 'Silicon Glen', and the twin rail and road bridges which swoop triumphantly over the Forth at South Queensferry. Further west, Linlithgow holds memories of James IV and Mary, Queen of Scots, who was born and christened there. Going the other way from Edinburgh, eastwards, there is attractive country and coastline with some notable golf courses in what used to be East Lothian. Haddington is a particularly handsome old town and on the coast below North Berwick, the ruins of Tantallon Castle, titanic stronghold of the Red Douglases, command a thrilling view of the offshore hump of the Bass Rock and its screaming and wheeling gulls.

Orkney

Some 90 small islands and islets, of which 20 or so are inhabited, make up the Orkney group, lying off the north coast of mainland Scotland, across the Pentland Firth. Flat and generally low-lying, the islands enjoy a gentler climate than might be expected. They live by cattle-farming, by tourism and by North Sea oil, with a major terminal on the island of Flotta. They have a strong Norse tradition, were governed by their own Norse jarls or earls until the 13th century and were not annexed to Scotland until the 15th. The capital is the cathedral town of Kirkwall on Mainland, the biggest of the islands, which is also the site of the giant prehistoric monument of Maes Howe and the remarkable Stone Age village of Skara Brae. The huge natural harbour of Scapa Flow has memories of the two world wars.

Shetland

Some 50 miles (80km) out beyond the Orkneys, there are about 100 islands in the Shetland group, of which 15 or so are inhabited. Muckle Flugga with its lighthouse is the most northerly point in the British Isles. Sheep-farming and fishing are the main pursuits, with North Sea oil again an important factor in the economy. Sullom Voe on the biggest island, Mainland, is Europe's biggest oil terminal. The Shetlands share the Norse tradition of the Orkneys and Shetland-Norse sentiment has strengthened in recent years. The wildly spectacular winter fire festival of Up Helly Aa at Lerwick, the capital on Mainland, is an expression of it. There are fine cliffs and beaches, and multitudes of seabirds. Striking prehistoric sites include the Bronze Age village of Jarlshof and the Iron Age fortress of Mousa Broch. The small but tough Shetland ponies were bred here, and distinctive Fair Isle sweaters and Shetland knitwear enjoy a high reputation.

Ruins of 15th-century Loch Leven Castle, Tayside

Strathclyde

The second biggest of the Scottish regions, Strathclyde was put together from the former counties of Argyll, Dunbarton, Renfrew, Lanark and Ayr, with their outlying islands. Strathclyde was the name of a British Celtic kingdom of the Dark Ages in southwestern Scotland, before the original Scots came from Ireland and settled in Argyll in the 6th century. The most famous of the new arrivals was St Columba. Today's Strathclyde includes the largest city in Scotland, Glasgow with its rewarding architecture, townscape and cultural attractions. It also includes the old Clydeside docks and ship-building area, and Scotland's principal industrial region with towns like Airdrie, Motherwell, Hamilton, Kilmarnock and Paisley clustered round Glasgow in the most heavily populated part of the country.

To the south, the old county of Ayrshire is known for its Robert Burns connections and its golf courses and seaside resorts along the Firth of Clyde coast. West of Glasgow are the islands of Bute and Arran, and north is Loch Lomond, Britain's biggest expanse of inland water. Northwest lies the beautiful coastline of Argyll and the sea-lochs whose long fingers reach far inland. This is Campbell country and the chief of that formidable clan, the Duke of Argyll, has his palatial seat at Inverary on Loch Fyne. Further north, Oban is the port for ferries and cruises to the magical islands in the gleaming western sea – Mull, Colonsay, Jura, Islay and the rest with their romantic past and their delectable whiskies. The queen of them is tiny Iona, St Columba's base and the burial place of Scotland's ancient kings.

Tayside

The 'silvery Tay' of the poet McGonagall's lugubrious verse is Scotland's longest river and the Tayside region united most of Perthshire with Angus and Kinross in an area centred on the river. The region runs from the Forest of Atholl in the north and the giant hydro-electric schemes at Loch Rannoch and Loch Tummel, with Schiehallion looming above them, down by way of Loch Tay itself to Strath Earn and through the Ochil Hills south to Loch Leven, with its island-prison from which Mary, Queen of Scots romantically escaped.

This is primarily farming country, though Dundee on the Firth of Tay, the region's capital and by far its biggest town, is an industrial centre, once famous for the jute industry and for marmalade. Perth, on the Tay inland, has a long history and John Knox preached with formidable effect from the pulpit of St John's. Arbroath on the Angus coast is known for 'smokies', Forfar is a town of some style and at Crieff cattle-drovers from the Highlands used to bring thousands of beasts to market to sell to buyers from the south. Pitlochry is an attractive inland resort and at Blair Atholl the Dukes of Atholl command Britain's only surviving private army.

Western Isles

The Western Isles region is formed by the Outer Hebrides – the sparsely populated islands of Lewis and Harris, North Uist, Benbecula, South Uist and Barra with their subordinate islets – lying out in the Atlantic west of the Scottish mainland and stretched out over a distance of some 130 miles. Prehistoric sites culminate in the remarkable stone circles at Callanish on Lewis. The Norse ruled here until the 13th century, succeeded by the Macdonalds, Lords of the Isles, who held sway with a fleet of war galleys for another 200 years. The small port of Stornoway on Lewis is the capital, the best-known product is Harris tweed, wildflowers and midges are abundant and the sunsets over the western ocean here are wonderfully spectacular.

Wales

Wales is a country of mountains and high moorland cut by deep river valleys, with low ground around the coast. Like Scotland, Wales is more sparsely inhabited than England, with a population numbering only about 6 per cent of England's in an area which amounts to about 16 per cent of England's size. The changes in 1974 threw the 13 traditional counties of Wales into the waste-basket of history – or were meant to – and replaced them with eight new counties, based largely on early Welsh realms and princedoms.

Clywd

Clwyd in northeastern Wales amalgamated the old county of Flint with the bulk of Denbighshire. It included the curious old anomaly of the Part of Flint, or English Maelor, a little separated-off patch of land east of Wrexham, English in character but which belonged to Flint for reasons lost in the mists of time. The new county's name came from the River Clwyd, flowing through its lush green vale with its farmsteads and churches below the Clwydian Hills, which range away southeast from the coast with the highest point at Moel Fammau, 1,820ft (555m). Much the biggest town is industrial Wrexham, dominated by its 16th century St Giles Cathedral. Mold is the county town and a sandy parade of cheap and cheerful resorts struts along the coast from Prestatyn and Rhyl to Colwyn Bay.

Inland are the more dignified towns of Rhuddlan and Denbigh with their castles, and St Asaph with its diminutive cathedral. Further south, beyond the scenic Horseshoe Pass, is Llangollen. Famed for its International Musical Eisteddfod, the town is set in the bewitching valley of the River Dee, where the high arches of the noble Pontcysyllyte Aqueduct stride impressively across the river.

Dyfed

The biggest of the new 1974 Welsh counties, Dyfed combined Pembrokeshire with Carmarthenshire and Cardiganshire in the southwestern corner of Wales. It is noted for the magnificent cliff and shore scenery of the Pembrokeshire Coast National Park and the haunting moors and prehistoric sites of the Preseli Hills inland. Dyfed was one of the four 'ancient kingdoms' of Wales in early times, with much Irish and later Norman and English immigration. This is largely farming country, with a major fishing and oil port at Milford Haven.

The county town is Carmarthen. Aberystwyth on Cardigan Bay is the principal commercial centre of central Wales, with the Rheidol Valley and the Devil's Bridge lying enticingly inland. The River Teifi, famed for its coracles, flows out to the sea through Cardigan and the Taf and the Tywi run south to the Bristol Channel. St David, the patron saint of Wales, was born and worked in Pembrokeshire and St David's today is Britain's smallest city. Fishguard is known for the Irish ferries, Pembroke for its towering castle and Laugharne for its Dylan Thomas connections, while Llanelli is a vigorous industrial and rugby-playing town.

The Glamorgans

West, Mid and South Glamorgan replaced the former county of Glamorgan, which was originally another of the 'ancient kingdoms' of Wales, Morgannwg, in the south. It became one of the great Norman power bases in Wales, as Caerphilly Castle dramatically demonstrates. Cardiff, with its Roman and Norman remains and its amazing Victorian castle, is the delightful capital city and chief cultural centre of Wales, and by a wide margin the principality's largest town, while Swansea is the second biggest town in Wales. Both are former major industrial ports which have had to adjust themselves to a changed world. So has the Valleys area, from which black rivers of coal poured down into the docks of Cardiff and Barry for export to the wider world. Hardly a nugget of coal is mined there today and the area has been extensively 'greened'.

West of Cardiff lies the peaceful agricultural Vale of Glamorgan with its small farming villages, and south of Swansea are the cliffs and beaches of the beautiful Gower Peninsula, but the busy, bristling steel town of Port Talbot is still an important industrial centre.

Gwent

The smallest of the new Welsh counties, Gwent was the former Monmouthshire, which had been an English county from the time of Henry VIII until 1974. In character this is the least Welsh area in Wales. The name Gwent came originally from *Venta Silurum*, the Roman town of Caerwent. There is another major Roman site at Caerleon and ruined Marcher castles, including Chepstow and Raglan, show how Norman warlords fastened their grip on this region. The rich agricultural land of the coastal plain along the Bristol Channel is protected by a high sea wall.

Cwmbran, Wales's only New Town, is the county town, but far the biggest urban centre is industrial Newport on the River Usk. Ebbw Vale is a former iron and steel town in an area which is being 'greened'. Abergavenny is a centre for the Black Mountains and Monmouth is in the entrancing valley of the Wye, which winds its rippling way down the border with England past the hallowed ruins of Tintern Abbey.

Gwynedd

Gwynedd in the northwest, by contrast, is the most Welsh area in Wales and prides itself on the purity of its spoken Welsh. Combining Anglesey, Caernarfonshire and most of Merioneth with a bit of Denbighshire, it is dominated by Snowdon and the other mighty peaks of the Snowdonia National Park, which once rose as high as the Himalayas. They are superbly seen from across the water in Anglesey, the Druids' island where the Tudor dynasty originated. To the south of the main massif is legend-haunted Cader Idris. Bala Lake is the largest natural lake in Wales.

In the 6th century AD, the ruler of Gwynedd, the 'island dragon', was the most powerful figure in Britain. His successors were the ancestors of the Welsh princes of Wales and today the castles of Caernarfon, Conwy, Harlech and Beaumaris bear witness to Edward I of England's determination to reduce Wales to subjection. Sheep and cattle are raised in Gwynedd, the source of some of the tastiest of the celebrated Welsh lamb. It is a land of mountain and sea, and there are no large towns.

Caernarfon is the county town of Gwynedd, Bangor commands the Menai Strait and Thomas Telford's majestic suspension bridge, and Llandudno, brimming with Victorian charm, is the popular queen of the North Wales seaside resorts. The remote Lleyn peninsula with its fine cliff and beach scenery was once pilgrim country and there are dramatic remains of slate quarrying in Snowdonia.

Powys

Covering a quarter of the whole country, this is the only entirely inland Welsh county, lying along the border with England and uniting the former shires of Montgomery, Radnor and Brecknock. The Welsh kingdom of Powys was successor to an earlier British Celtic realm that stretched into Shropshire and the West Midlands. It is engagingly remote hilly country of oak and ash woods, and green fertile river valleys, living by farming and forestry, plus tourism, fairly sparsely populated and with no large towns.

Llandrindod Wells, the county town, is a former spa, as are Builth Wells and Llanwrtyd Wells. Welshpool is a market town, Hay-on-Wye has Britain's longest mileage of second-hand bookshop shelves and Brecon, with its castle and cathedral, is a base for the mountain country of the Brecon Beacons National Park, a magnet for walkers, cavers and pony trekkers, with the Black Mountains lying to the east. Both the Severn and the Wye rise on the high, bleak moors of Plynlimon in the west of Powys. The Elan Valley with its reservoirs supplying water to Birmingham is a notable beauty spot, and another is man-made Lake Vyrnwy, which supplies Liverpool.

Isle of Man

Set in the Irish Sea, the Isle of Man is British but not part of the United Kingdom, which allows it to add being a tax haven to its other attractions. It has its own laws and its own distinctive heritage, and its Court of Tynwald is the world's oldest parliament with an uninterrupted tradition, but the island's Celtic language, Manx, is scarcely used now except on ceremonial occasions. There are no large towns. The capital, Douglas, is about the size of Bishop Aukland or Chippenham. Douglas and the other principal towns – Ramsey, Peel, Castletown – are all on the coast and developed as seaside resorts in the 19th century. Sea-beaten cliffs and wooded valleys make Man scenically attractive and its mountains rise to 2,036ft (621m) at Snaefell. Tourism is a major industry and the island is also known for its curious three-legged badge, tail-less Manx cats and the spectacular TT motorcycle races.

Channel Islands

Lying in the English Channel close to the coast of Normandy, the Channel Islands are part of the British Isles but not part of the United Kingdom – making them a tax haven – and they have their own traditions. During World War II they were occupied by the Germans and there are many intriguing reminders of that time. The four main islands are Jersey, Guernsey, Alderney and Sark, and there are numerous smaller islets, but all told the Channel Islands add up to only about 75 square miles (187sq km) of land. They have a gentle, pleasant climate and are known for their flowers, fruit and vegetables, as well as their own traditional sweaters and breeds of cattle. Tourism is a major source of income.

A

AB KETTLEBY
Leicestershire SK7223

Village on A606, 3 miles (5km) NW of Melton Mowbray

High on Leicestershire Wolds, ironstone village with 13th-century church on its southern edge and 17th-century ironstone manor house with barn and dovecote.

ABBAS COMBE
Somerset ST7022

Village on A357, 4 miles (6km) S of Wincanton

Really part of Templecombe (see), Abbas Combe is the older part, with a medieval church. Medieval painting found locally which resembled the head of Christ on the Turin shroud.

ABBERLEY/ABBERLEY COMMON
Hereford and Worcester SO7567

Village off A443, 5 miles (8km) SW of Stourport-on-Severn

A campanile in the grounds of Abberley Hall (school) is the landmark for this village where there are two churches of very different ages and interesting buildings. Abberley Common, wooded hillside, near by.

ABBERTON
Essex TM0019

Village off B1025, 4 miles (6km) S of Colchester

The big Abberton Reservoir, crossed by B1026, is a magnet to wildfowl. Nature reserve with birdwatching hide and picnic area.

ABBESS RODING
Essex TL5711

Village off B184, 5 miles (8km) N of Chipping Ongar

Once owned by the nunnery at Barking, hence the name. Good late 15th-century church with monuments.

ABBEY DORE
Hereford and Worcester SO3830

Village on B4347, 2 miles (3km) N of Pontrilas

The centrepiece of this village at the foot of the Golden Valley is St Mary's, adapted in the 17th century from the 13th-century chancel and transepts of a Cistercian abbey church. Famous Herefordshire craftsman John Abel carved the magnificent chancel screen, stalls, pulpit and west gallery. Abbey Dore Court gardens (open in summer), opposite the church, incorporate the River Dore and feature woodland, pond, rockery, nursery and walled garden.

ABBEY ST BATHANS
Borders NT7661

Village off B6355, 5 miles (8km) N of Duns

Tiny and remote village in the Lammermuir Hills on the Whiteadder Water. Edinshall Broch, a prehistoric stone tower near by, is rare example outside Highlands.

ABBEY TOWN
Cumbria NY1750

Village on B5302, 4 miles (6km) SE of Silloth

St Mary's, the parish church, was built in the 12th century as the Cistercian monastery, Holm Cultram Abbey.

ABBEYCWMHIR
Powys SO0571

Hamlet off A483, 6 miles (10km) N of Llandrindod Wells

Traditional burial place of Llywelyn the Last, last native Prince of Wales, after death in skirmish.

ABBEYDALE
South Yorkshire SK3281

District of Sheffield

A reconstructed 18th-century industrial village with a forge and counting house, as well as terraced workmen's cottages.

St Mary's, Abbey Dore.

ABBOTS BROMLEY Staffordshire SK0724
Village on B5234, 6 miles (10km) S of Uttoxeter
This attractive village in the Vale of Trent has some pleasant old buildings but is best known for the annual Horn Dance on the first Monday following the first Sunday in September. 'Deermen' and other traditional characters make an early morning start and tour local farms before the climax of the dance in the main street, where deermen act out mock combat with deer heads and reindeer antlers.

ABBOTS LANGLEY Hertfordshire TL0901
Village off A405, 3 miles (5km) N of Watford
Now part of Watford. Close to River Gade and Grand Union Canal. Church of St Lawrence the Martyr. The Boy's Home pub has a sentimental sign.

ABBOTS MORTON Hereford and Worcester SP0255
Village off A422, 7 miles (11km) N of Evesham
Once the Abbot of Evesham's summer residence (signs of his fishponds remain), the village is highly picturesque, with an array of timber-framed cottages.

ABBOTSBURY Dorset SY5785
Village on B3157, 8 miles (13km) NW of Weymouth
Picture-postcard stone and thatch village, once the site of a monastery – little remains except the huge barn (with rural display inside) and St Catherine's Chapel on top of a hill. Large sub-tropical garden. On the shore of the lagoon enclosed by Chesil Bank (see) is the Swannery where 800 mute swans breed.

ABBOTSFORD Borders NT5034
see Melrose

ABBOTSHAM Devon SS4226
Village off A39, 2 miles (3km) W of Bideford
On a slope a little back from rocky cliffs and shore. Medieval church with interesting 16th-century bench-ends. The Big Sheep is an amusement park with sheep racing.

ABBOTSINCH Strathclyde NS4766
Location of Glasgow Airport, off M8, 8 miles (13km) W of city centre
Home of Glasgow Airport, Scotland's biggest and busiest; handles scheduled and charter international flights and regular flights to other British airports.

ABBOTTS ANN Hampshire SU3243
Village off A343, 3 miles (5km) SW of Andover
Dense and pretty village, lots of thatched cottages and interesting church of 1718 with maidens' garlands to those who died single.

ABDON Shropshire SO5786
Village off B4368, 8 miles (13km) N of Ludlow
High on the slopes of Brown Clee, Shropshire's highest hill, where open moorland rises to 1,770ft (540m). Small, primitive 14th-century church.

ABER Gwynedd SH6572
Village off A55, 2 miles (3km) SW of Llanfairfechan
Base for exploring 100ft (30m) Aber Falls (Rhaeadr

Abbotsford House, Sir Walter Scott's 19th-century home.

Fawr) and accompanying nature reserve. Paths lead alongside valley through pine forest and scree. Of historical interest is the site of Llywelyn the Great's motte and bailey and the place where Llywelyn the Last refused Edward I's demand for sovereignty.

ABERAERON Dyfed SN4562
Small town on A487, 14 miles (23km) SW of Aberystwyth
Brightly painted Cardigan Bay sea town, well laid out, mainly Georgian in character. Quay is focal point, where sailing has replaced ship-building. Novel aerial ferry across quay, bee exhibition, honey products at Hive on the Quay. Sea Aquarium. Crafts at attractively converted range of old buildings known as Clìs Pencarreg. Chiefly pebble beach. The late Sir Geraint Evans lived here.

ABERCARN Gwent ST2195
Town on A467, 7 miles (11km) NW of Newport
Typical linear valleys town in steep-sided setting. Conifers clothe the hillsides. Noted Church of St Luke, built in 1920s.

ABERCORN Lothian NT1378
see South Queensferry

ABERDARE (ABERDAR) Mid Glamorgan SO0002
Town on A4059, 11 miles (18km) NW of Pontypridd
Old coal and iron town at the head of the Cynon Valley. St John's Church survives from 12th century with iron gate made by local ironworks. Dare Valley Country Park's acres have transformed colliery waste tip into a place for natural history, industrial heritage, walks, fishing and other recreational activities. Attractive town park.

ABERDARON Gwynedd SH1726
Village on B4413, 12 miles (19km) SW of Nefyn
On western tip of Llyn peninsula. Long sandy beach. Popular with today's holiday-makers and 14th-century pilgrims *en route* to Bardsey Island (see).

ABERDEEN Grampian NJ9306
City on A92/A93, 10 miles (16km) NE of Stonehaven
Scotland's third largest city, granite-built and flower-bedecked, lies on the estuaries of the rivers Dee and Don. For years dependant on ship-building and fishing, the city's prosperity since the 1970s has been linked with oil and gas from the North Sea. Affluence fluctuates, but the solid, prosperous appearance of this industrial, business and administrative centre tells no lies.

City charters date back to 1179 when it was already becoming a major trading centre. Today, outlying Old Aberdeen, united with Aberdeen in 1891, still shows the medieval street layout. At its heart lies the Cathedral of St Machar, an early granite building, with a twin-towered west front and wooden nave ceiling. Near by is King's College Chapel (1495), an admirable early university edifice.

Mile-long Union Street is the heart of modern Aberdeen, lined with imposing stone buildings and shops and surrounded by the city's main attractions. Provost Skene's House belonged to a prosperous 17th-century merchant, and there are several interesting churches. Pinnacled and exuberant Marischal College, part of the University, is the world's second largest granite building and houses the fascinating Anthropological Museum. The art gallery, which contains the important MacDonald bequest, lies to the north. South of Union Street is the harbour area, containing Aberdeen's oldest building, the many-windowed Old Provost Ross's House, now the Maritime Museum. The harbour and fish market, bustling and crammed with supply ships, are a reminder of both sources of Aberdeen's affluence.

Known as the Granite City, Aberdeen softens this image with vast floral displays all over the city, as well as lovely parks; Duthie Park has wonderful roses and Europe's largest indoor garden, the Winter Garden. Civic pride manifests itself in festivls throughout the year; some specifically Scots and some arts or family-oriented.

ABERDOUR Fife NT1985
Small town on A92, 3 miles (5km) W of Burntisland
Small town on Firth of Forth with good beach. Fourteenth-century towered castle has St Fillan's Church, complete with leper window, in its grounds; also beehive-shaped 16th-century dovecote. Offshore Inchcolm Island has some of Scotland's most complete monastic remains: St Colomba's Abbey, founded in 1123. The island also offers opportunities for seal-spotting.

ABERDOVEY Gwynedd SN6196
Small town on A493, 4 miles (6km) S of Tywyn
Spectacularly sandwiched between mountains and the sandy Dovey estuary. Sailing and watersports, 18-hole golf. Birthplace of the Outward Bound movement.

ABERDULAIS West Glamorgan SS7799
Village on B4434, 2 miles (3km) NE of Neath
The photogenic waterfalls have powered industry since the 16th century. Europe's largest electricity-generating waterwheel is here. Visitor centre (National Trust). Canal basin close by.

ABEREDW Powys SO0747
Village off B4567, 3 miles (5km) SE of Builth Wells
By tributary of River Wye, shielded by giant outcrop of Aberedw Rocks. Interesting church with 14th-century rood screen and hammerbeam roof.

ABERFAN Mid Glamorgan SO0700
Village off A470, 4 miles (6km) S of Merthyr Tydfil
In 1966 a coal tip engulfed the local primary school killing almost 150 children and adults. Intensive programme of land reclamation followed in industrial valleys.

ABERFELDY Tayside NN8549
Small town on A827, 8 miles (13km) SW of Pitlochry
On the River Tay, here spanned by General Wade's fine bridge of 1733, which is flanked by a monument to the Black Watch, raised locally in 1740. Restored early 19th-century watermill, powered by water from the picturesque Urlar Burn, the inspiration for Burns' *The Birks of Aberfeldy*. Distillery tours.

ABERFFRAW Gwynedd SH3569
Village on A4080, 12 miles (19km) W of Menai Bridge
Ancient seat of powerful Princes of Gwynedd, commemorated at Llys Llywelyn Coastal Heritage Centre. Barclodiad-y-Gawres is a superb neolithic tomb with decorated stones.

ABERFORD West Yorkshire SE4337
Village off A1, 8 miles (13km) S of Wetherby
Lotherton Hall was built in the mid-18th century. An extension to the east was completed in 1896 and the west in 1903. The hall houses the Gascoigne collection of pictures, furniture, silver and porcelain of 17th and 18th centuries. There is also a bird park. St Ricarius' Church has an early Norman tower, the rest was built by Salvin in 1861.

ABERFOYLE Central NN5200
Village on A81, 8 miles (13km) SW of Callander
Known as Gateway to the Trossachs, a resort town to the east of Loch Ard, and an excellent centre for exploring the Trossachs, with good tourist facilities. Visitor centre to north of town through Duke's Pass, reached on winding road (A821) through forested hills.

ABERGAVENNY (Y-FENNI) Gwent SO2914
Town on A40, 9 miles (14km) N of Pontypool
Abergavenny is a busy, prosperous market and shopping centre where the River Usk emerges from the Brecon Beacons National Park's mountainscapes into an ever-widening vale. Markets are an integral part of life here. The Tuesday livestock and general markets draw in the crowds, and there are regular craft and antiques fairs in addition to a yearly medieval market.

The much-ruined castle was the stage for a deed unsurpassed in its infamy when, in 1175, the Norman baron William de Braose invited local chieftains to a Christmas feast and promptly did them to death. Part of the castle precinct has been turned into a local museum with a replica farmhouse kitchen. Nostalgia holds sway over the Museum of Childhood and the Home's array of playthings in matching period room settings in an old chapel. St Mary's Church is notable for an outstanding series of monuments covering 13th to 17th centuries.

Abergavenny's environs make for good walking – the Monmouthshire and Brecon Canal's level towpath for easy going, the surrounding hills for the more energetic. Nearby Skirrid-fawr is cleft by a chasm which opened, it is said, when Christ died.

ABERGELE Clwyd SH9477
Town off A55, 4 miles (6km) SW of Rhyl
Market centre's seaside face has shingle/sand beach and family fun. Quiet uplands rise behind busy coast. Battlemented Gwrych Castle completed 1815.

ABERGLASLYN, PASS OF Gwynedd
see Beddgelert

ABERGWESYN Powys SN8552
Hamlet off A483, 4 miles (6km) NW of Llanwrtyd Wells
Isolated spot in Irfon Valley. Old cattle drovers' route twists and climbs through the Abergwesyn Pass, up Devil's Staircase, to Tregaron. Abergwesyn Common is National Trust land.

ABERGWILI Dyfed
see Carmarthen

ABERLADY Lothian NT4679
Village on A198, 6 miles (10km) SW of North Berwick
Once the trading port for Haddington until the river silted up, this long and scattered village has a medieval church with fine stained-glass windows. Near by are good beaches and dunes; Aberlady Bay Nature Reserve lies east, good bird-watching on the saltmarshes. Nearby Gosford House (limited opening) is an impressive Robert Adam mansion.

ABERLEMNO Tayside NO5255
Village on B9134, 5 miles (8km) NE of Forfar
Four remarkable Pictish stones, the 8th-century finest, 7ft (2m) tall and intricately carved. Two ruined castles and an Iron Age fort near by.

ABERNETHY Tayside NO1816
Village on A913, 3 miles (5km) SW of Newburgh
Conservation village with substantial Iron Age and Roman remains near by. Important Pictish settlement. Abernethy Round Tower, probably 11th century, is 74ft (23m) high.

ABERPORTH Dyfed SN2651
Village on B4333, 6 miles (10km) NE of Cardigan
Green hillsides, sheltered sands, watersports. Clifftop walks along Ceredigion Heritage Coast. Exotic butterfly centre near by. Military testing station around headland.

ABERSOCH Gwynedd SH3128
Village on A499, 6 miles (10km) SW of Pwllheli
Developed from fishing village to resort favoured by yachting fraternity. Two sandy bays, harbour. Boat trips, regattas, golf. Peaceful Llanengan's church worth visiting.

ABERTILLERY Gwent SO2104
Town on A467, 5 miles (8km) S of Brynmawr
Ex-coal town. Six Bells colliery disaster killed 45 men in 1961. Small museum in library promotes a trail around streets.

ABERYSTWYTH Dyfed SN5881
Town on A44/A487, 40 miles (65km) N of Carmarthen
Aberystwyth, the 'capital' of Mid Wales, combines the roles of university seat and Victorian-flavoured resort on Cardigan Bay. On rising ground at Penglais sit two major institutions: the University of Wales College with its attendant Arts Centre, and the National Library of Wales, storehouse of a priceless collection of Celtic literature which includes the oldest Welsh-language manuscript, the *Black Book of Carmarthen*.

Down on the seashore the promenade curves around a shingle-and-sand beach bounded to the south by Pen Dinas's Iron Age fort and neighbouring harbour, to the north by Constitution Hill. From this summit, climbed by a 19th-century cliff railway, vast vistas can be seen from another Victorian-style device, the Camera Obscura. Dividing the bay is a promontory occupied by traces of a 13th-century castle.

By the foreshortened pier stands the original university building, a Victorian neo-Gothic pile, while back from the seafront are the Ceredigion Museum's interesting folk collections in a restored Edwardian theatre known as the Coliseum. At Llanbadarn Fawr, now a suburb of Aberystwyth, stands one of Wales's largest cruciform churches. From the station, the scenic narrow-gauge Vale of Rheidol Railway climbs to Devil's Bridge.

ABINGDON Oxfordshire SU4997
Town off A34, 6 miles (10km) S of Oxford
Abingdon has a long history as a commercial, ecclesiastical and administrative centre, and its ancient heart offers a wealth of interesting buildings. The surviving portions of the Norman and medieval abbey include a 16th-century long gallery, a medieval gateway (later a prison) and the Checker Hall, now a theatre.

An attractive mixture of timber-framed and Georgian buildings make up East St Helen's Street, leading to the impressive Parish Church of St Helen, which is chiefly famous for the 14th-century Tree of Jesse painted on the roof of the Lady Chapel. In its shadow stand the unusual Long Alley almshouses, founded in 1446 and incorporating a full-length timber cloister. Two sets of 18th-century almshouses stand near by. Abingdon's commercial centre is the market place, dominated by the free-standing 17th-century County Hall, an impressive symbol of prosperity built by one of Wren's masons. Its upper floor houses a local history museum.

Abingdon's tradition of adapting old buildings is illustrated at the Old Gaol, built in about 1810 and now a leisure centre. It stands close to the bridge, which retains two of its medieval arches.

ABINGER HAMMER Surrey TQ0947
Village on A25, 5 miles (8km) W of Dorking
In the Tillingbourne Valley, where hammerponds from the vanished forge are used as watercress beds. The working smith continues the iron-working tradition and the bell on the jaunty clock tower is struck hourly by the model of a blacksmith. Medieval church and manor house at Abinger Common, the mother village, high on hill to southeast.

ABLINGTON Gloucestershire SP1007
Village off B4425, 1 mile (2km) NW of Bibury
The manor house of this Coln Valley village was the home of Arthur Gibbs, author of best-selling classic *A Cotswold Village* (1898).

ABOYNE Grampian NO5298
Village on B968, 10 miles (16km) E of Ballater
Deeside resort, well known for its September Highland Gathering, and for rest and rehabilitation centre run by the International League for the Protection of Horses.

ABRIDGE Essex TQ4696
Village on A113, 3 miles (5km) S of Epping
Known as 'Little Sodom' by 19th-century puritans, now home of the BBC Essex Garden and a good pub, the White Hart.

ACASTER MALBIS North Yorkshire SE5845
Village off A19, 4 miles (6km) S of York
Romans constructed a fort here to protect the river route, along the River Ouse, to York. Acaster is Latin for water fort.

ACCRINGTON Lancashire SD7628
Town on A679, 5 miles (8km) E of Blackburn
Principal town of Hyndburn with a fine Victorian market hall. Town developed rapidly during the Industrial Revolution making textile machinery and producing and finishing cotton. Haworth Art Gallery houses Europe's largest collection of Tiffany glass, presented to the town in 1933 by Joseph Briggs, a native of Accrington who worked for Louis Tiffany in New York.

ACHILTIBUIE Highland NC0208
Village off A835, 10 miles (16km) NW of Ullapool
Scattered crofting township overlooking and providing access to Summer Isles. Popular holiday base for walkers and climbers. Hydroponicum is unique soil-less indoor growing environment.

ACHNACARRY Highland NN1787
see Spean Bridge

ACKLAM Cleveland NZ4817
Village off A19 in S outskirts of Middlesbrough
An ancient village on the outskirts of Middlesbrough. Acklam Hall, built in 1678 by the Hustler family, is now a school.

The peak of Ben More Coigach near Achiltibuie.

The round tower of St Edmund's Church, Acle.

ACLE Norfolk TG4010
Small town on A47, 8 miles (13km) W of Great Yarmouth
The pleasant village of Acle stands in some of Norfolk's most beautiful and important wetland countryside. Acle was granted a market charter in the 13th century, and market day is still an important event in the area. The Church of St Edmund King and Martyr is more than 900 years old, and has an interesting round tower.

ACOMB Northumberland NY9366
Village off A6079, 1 mile (2km) NE of Hexham
Name means 'the place where the oaks are'. The village has a mining past and is now favoured by Tyneside commuters.

ACORN BANK GARDEN Cumbria NY6228
see Temple Sowerby

ACTON Cheshire SJ6352
Village on A534, 1 mile (2km) W of Nantwich
Village was used as a garrison by Royalists in the Civil War. Dorfold Hall is open to the public.

ACTON Greater London TQ2080
District in borough of Ealing
A spa briefly in the 18th century and a smart London suburb until canals facilitated 19th-century industrial growth and workers' housing. Goldsmiths' almshouses, 1811, on north side of Acton Park. Parish Church of St Mary rebuilt 1860s/1870s. Art by Graham Sutherland and Carel Weight in 1960s Roman Catholic Church of St Aidan.

ACTON Suffolk TL8945
Village off B1071, 3 miles (5km) N of Sudbury
All Saints' Church contains one of the most famous military brasses in England and dates from 1302. The 'Acton Miser' inspired Dickens' *Bleak House*.

ACTON BRIDGE Cheshire SJ6075
Village on A49, 4 miles (6km) NW of Northwich
A village on the River Weaver and near the Trent and Mersey Canal. It was once called Acton-in-Delamere.

ACTON BURNELL Shropshire SJ5302
Village off A458, 7 miles (11km) S of Shrewsbury
Richard Burnell, Chancellor to Edward I, paid for the finely crafted church of about 1270 with elaborate groups of lancets and rich detailing. Next to the church are substantial ruins of Burnell's fortified manor house – tall, square and with angle towers (English Heritage). Surviving gable ends in adjacent field are reputed to be those of the building where Parliament met during a visit by Edward I.

ACTON ROUND Shropshire SO6395
Village off A458, 3 miles (5km) S of Much Wenlock
Isolated in hilly country are a fine Queen Anne mansion and a Norman and medieval church with Acton family chapel of 1750s.

ACTON SCOTT Shropshire SO4589
Village off A49, 3 miles (5km) S of Church Stretton
A popular attraction here is the re-creation of a Victorian working farm, with rare breeds, seasonal demonstrations, restored buildings and craftspeople at work.

ADCOTE Shropshire SJ4219
see Little Ness

ADDERBURY Oxfordshire SP4735
Village on A4260, 3 miles (5km) S of Banbury
Divided by the Sor Brook, the original village centre is rich in old houses and dominated by an impressive medieval church.

ADDINGHAM West Yorkshire SE0749
Village on A65, 3 miles (5km) NW of Ilkley
An industrial village once devoted to domestic, as opposed to factory, weaving. Was once a crossroads on the old turnpike system.

ADDINGTON Greater London TQ3664
District in borough of Croydon
Awash with golf courses. Addington Palace, former Surrey residence of 19th-century Archbishops of Canterbury, now Royal School of Church Music.

ADDISCOMBE Greater London TQ3366
District in borough of Croydon
Basically a 19th-century Croydon suburb. Eccentric 1860s Church of St Mary Magdalene, Canning Road, has interior described as 'nightmarish'.

ADDLESTONE Surrey TQ0464
Town on B3132, 2 miles (3km) W of Weybridge
Famed for the ancient Crouch Oak, meeting place for centuries, this suburbanised town grew with the coming of the railway; it is now close to M25.

ADDLETHORPE Lincolnshire TF5468
Hamlet off A52, 4 miles (6km) N of Skegness
Just inland from busy Skegness and Ingoldmells resorts. Fine marshland church with superb south porch; 18th-century almshouses and Bede Cottages.

ADEL West Yorkshire SE2740
Area in N Leeds
Old village with a magnificent church dating mainly from the 12th century. The church is noted as one of the most complete Norman churches in Britain.

ADISHAM Kent TR2253
Village off B2046, 3 miles (5km) SW of Wingham
Scattered village in wooded undulating country, with cruciform church containing 13th-century painted woodwork salvaged from Canterbury Cathedral.

ADLESTROP Gloucestershire SP2426
Village off A436, 4 miles (6km) E of Stow-on-the-Wold
Jane Austen visited her relatives at the manor house and her uncle at the rectory long before Edward Thomas immortalised Adlestrop in a poem of that name.

ADLINGTON Cheshire SJ9180
see Prestbury

The medieval church at Adderbury.

ADLINGTON Lancashire SD6013
Town on A6, 7 miles (11km) NW of Bolton
First British muslins woven here in 1764; the town is now better known for Leonard Fairclough civil engneering business.

ADUR, RIVER West Sussex
River
Wealden headstreams meet near Henfield and flow south through gap in South Downs to reach sea at Shoreham.

ADWICK LE STREET South Yorkshire SE5308
Town on A638, 4 miles (6km) NW of Doncaster
Adwick Hall was once home to the Washington family. The stars and stripes on the family coat of arms suggest ancestors of George Washington.

AE VILLAGE Dumfries and Galloway NX9889
Village off A701, 8 miles (13km) N of Dumfries
The Forestry Commission founded this community in 1947 to house their workers engaged in planting Ae Forest on the hills between Annandale and Nithsdale.

AFFPUDDLE Dorset SY8093
Village on B3390, 2 miles (3km) W of Bere Regis
In the watermeadows of the River Piddle. Magnificent 15th-century church tower. Very fine 16th-century woodwork inside, especially the pulpit. Affpuddle Heath.

AFTON Isle of Wight SZ3486
Beauty spot off A3055, 1 mile (2km) S of Freshwater
Part of the smooth chalk down which succumbs to the sea at the Needles. The Tennyson Trail (see Tennyson Down) runs along Afton Down.

AILSA CRAIG Strathclyde NX0199
Island off Ayrshire coast
Island is volcanic lump, 1,114ft (339m) high, 2 miles (3km) in circumference, with lighthouse. Noted bird sanctuary. Former quarry produced special granite for curling stones.

AINDERBY STEEPLE North Yorkshire SE3392
Village on A684, 2 miles (3km) SW of Northallerton
Church of St Helen has a 15th-century tower and a 14th-century chancel restored in 1870.

AINSDALE Merseyside SD3112
District of Southport
Old fishing village near beach to the south of Southport. Surrounding dunes are a nature conservation area and home to the rare Natterjack toad.

AINSTABLE Cumbria NY5246
Village off B6413, 10 miles (16km) N of Penrith
A quiet village. The Church of St Michael was built in 1872, and a church has been on this site for 900 years.

AINTREE Merseyside SJ3898
District in N Liverpool
Famous as the home of the Grand National Steeplechase. The racecourse first opened in 1829 on land leased from the Earl of Sefton.

AIRA FORCE Cumbria NY4020
Waterfall in Aira Beck, near Dockray
The waterfall and nearby beauty spot give rise to several legends, a poem by Wordsworth and a story by De Quincey.

AIRDRIE Strathclyde NS7565
Town on A89, 11 miles (18km) E of Glasgow
Huge growth in 19th century disfigured surrounding landscape as town changed from cotton town to major coal-mining centre. Part of Glasgow's industrial sprawl.

AIRE, RIVER North Yorkshire
River
River's source is in Malhamdale; it joins River Ouse near Airmyn. In 1826 the Aire and Calder Navigation Company cut a canal to link the River Ouse to the West Riding industrial towns. Along with the Leeds and Liverpool Canal, it provides a waterway link between Irish Sea and North Sea.

AIRMYN Humberside SE7224
Village off A614, 2 miles (3km) NW of Goole
On bank of River Aire near confluence with River Ouse. Elegant stone clock-tower commemorates George Percy becoming Duke of Northumberland in 1865. Formerly in Yorkshire West Riding.

AIRTH Central NS9087
Village on A905, 8 miles (13km) SE of Stirling
Port until 1740s, now lying inland. In Dunmore Park lies The Pineapple, unusual structure built in 1761 as summerhouse, in shape of fruit.

AKELD Northumberland NT9529
Hamlet on A697, 2 miles (3km) W of Wooler
A tiny hamlet on the edge of the Northumberland National Park overlooked by Humbleton Hill. Near by is a battlefield marked by the Bendor Stone.

AKEMAN STREET Hertfordshire
Roman road
Name later given to Roman road which ran from St Albans to Berkhamsted and Aylesbury, and on to Cirencester.

ALBERBURY Shropshire SJ3614
Village off B4393, 8 miles (13km) W of Shrewsbury
Reminders of its medieval importance are the crumbling castle (not open), scanty remains of a priory and a large church with notable 14th-century chapel.

ALBOURNE West Sussex TQ2516
Village on B2116, 1 mile (2km) W of Hurstpierpoint
Tucked away from main roads with church at end of winding lane. Plaque to James Starley, inventor of the modern bicycle, born here 1831.

ALBRIGHTON Shropshire SJ8004
Town off A41, 7 miles (11km) NW of Wolverhampton
This pleasant small town, with attractive old buildings at its centre, has now become a popular commuter base for Wolverhampton.

ALBURY Surrey TQ0447
Village on A248, 4 miles (6km) E of Guildford
Picturesque village in gentle landscape of Tillingbourne Valley. Tudor Albury Park, remodelled in the 19th century, is famous for its 63 ornate chimneys.

ALCESTER Warwickshire SP0857
Town on A435, 7 miles (11km) W of Stratford-upon-Avon
A church of the 1730s stands at the head of a High Street lined with good vernacular architecture. Other interesting buildings stand in Henley Street, Church Street, Butter Street. Ancient timber-framed houses in Malt Mill Lane. To the southwest is 17th-century Ragley Hall, with fine plasterwork, furniture and paintings. The 14th-century Kinwarton Dovecote (National Trust), to the east, has been fully restored.

ALCISTON East Sussex TQ5005
Village off A27, 6 miles (10km) E of Lewes
Its cottages snuggle under the South Downs. Court House Farm was a grange of Battle Abbey. Magnificent tithe barn. Skipping races at inn every Good Friday.

ALCONBURY Cambridgeshire TL1875
Village off A1, 4 miles (6km) NW of Huntingdon
Near the pleasant village of Alconbury is Monks Wood Nature Reserve (Nature Conservancy Council, limited opening), an ancient tract of woodland noted for its variety of butterflies and moths.

ALDBOROUGH North Yorkshire SE4066
Village off B6265, 1 mile (2km) SE of Boroughbridge
Stands on the foundations of a thriving Roman city. Maypole on village green still used for traditional May Day dances.

ALDBOURNE Wiltshire SU2676
Village on B4192, 6 miles (10km) NE of Marlborough
A large village on the chalk, with a central green, some good cottages facing it and an interesting medieval church.

ALDBROUGH Humberside TA2438
Village on B1242, 6 miles (10km) SE of Hornsea
A coastal village; the Church of St Bartholomew dates from the 13th century and contains a Saxon sundial and a Norman arch.

ALDBURY Hertfordshire SP9612
Village off A41, 3 miles (5km) E of Tring
Delightfully pretty with green, duck pond, stocks, Valiant Trooper and Greyhound pubs. Chilterns walks. Below Bridgewater Monument, National Trust viewpoint.

ALDEBURGH Suffolk TM4656
Town on A1094, 3 miles (5km) S of Leiston
Aldeburgh is a lively fishing town with fine medieval buildings, a handsome church, and some splendid inns. It was once an important port, but has waged a long battle with the sea, and the early 16th-century Moot Hall that once formed the centre of the town is now right at the water's edge. The Romans settled in Aldeburgh, but the ruins of their village have long since been devoured by the encroaching sea.

Aldeburgh is perhaps best known for its music. In 1967, the composer Benjamin Britten and the singer Peter Pears opened a magnificent new concert hall to accommodate the world-famous Aldeburgh Festival. Sadly, an electrical fault destroyed the interior two years later, but it was restored within a year, and the Queen returned to open it a second time. The Aldeburgh Festival, a joyous celebration of music, is every June, and all year round there are classes in the School for Advanced Musical Studies that are open to the general public.

George Crabbe, an Aldeburgh resident, wrote poetry that inspired Britten to write his opera *Peter Grimes*.

ALDENHAM Hertfordshire TQ1498
Village off B462, 2 miles (3km) NE of Watford
Near M1 in the Colne Valley. Letchmore Heath manor house owned by Hindu religious movement. For Aldenham Country Park, see Elstree.

ALDERLEY EDGE Cheshire SJ8478
Town on A34, 2 miles (3km) S of Wilmslow
With the expansion of the railways system, Alderley Edge grew to accommodate Victorian houses of wealthy Manchester businessmen drawn here by the incentive of free first-class travel. The Edge, a National Trust countryside property, overlooks the Cheshire Plain, and was once mined for copper. The area is steeped in tales of witchcraft and legend, featuring in the books of Alan Garner.

ALDERMASTON Berkshire SU5965
Village on A340, 8 miles (13km) E of Newbury
Pleasant brick and timber-framed cottages, but known mainly for the Aldermaston marches of the late 1950s and 60s. The 'Ban the Bomb' protesters walked annually from here to London. The Atomic Weapons Research Establishment is in Aldermaston Court, rebuilt in 1850 after a fire. Aldermaston Wharf has a canal basin and lock, with visitor centre.

ALDERMINSTER Warwickshire SP2348
Village on A3400, 4 miles (6km) SE of Stratford-upon-Avon
Large and popular main-road village, which retains its attraction in pleasant rural surroundings beside the River Stour.

ALDERNEY Channel Islands
Island in English Channel
The northernmost of the Channel Islands, 4 miles (6km) long, 2 miles (3km) wide. Plateau to the west, the rest low-lying. Few roads, fortified coastline.

ALDERSHOT Hampshire SU8650
Town on A323, 8 miles (13km) W of Guildford
Home of the British Army from 1854, when 6,000 acres (2,400ha) of barren heathland were purchased. Permanent barracks were built, and Aldershot grew from a tiny village to a sizeable town by the end of the 19th century, housing not only those who supplied the camp, but also the thousands employed building the barracks.

The town still has many small-scale Victorian buildings. However, the army camp is mostly 1960s and 70s buildings, with lots of trees and playing fields. A few red-brick barracks survive from the 1890s. The army term 'glasshouse' for prison came from the glass-roofed detention barracks here.

Soldiers everywhere, and a number of military museums, some of which are actually inside the barracks. The Aldershot Military Museum gives the history and development of the area, and the Airborne Forces Museum is large and good. Royal Corps of Transport and even Royal Army Dental Corps museums.

ALDFIELD North Yorkshire SE2669
Village off B6265, 3 miles (5km) W of Ripon
St Lawrence's Church has a pleasant, unassuming exterior with a delightful interior including a ribbed plaster vault, box pews, three-decker pulpit, and Gothic Decalogue.

ALDFORD Cheshire SJ4159
Village on B5130, 5 miles (8km) S of Chester
Roman ford 1/2 mile (1km) from village crosses River Dee. Part of Eaton estate, rebuilt in mid-Victorian period by John Douglas.

ALDINGHAM Cumbria SD2870
Hamlet on A5087, 5 miles (8km) S of Ulverston
Coastal village with fabulous views across the bay. Church of St Cuthbert features a crooked chancel arch, which represents the body of Christ with his head leaning on one side.

ALDINGTON Kent TR0736
Village off B2067, 6 miles (10km) W of Hythe
Set on higher land west of Romney Marsh, this dispersed village, where Erasmus was briefly rector, has a splendid Tudor church tower.

ALDRIDGE West Midlands SK0500
Town on A454, 3 miles (5km) NE of Walsall
Conservation area protects the old centre of this former mining community on the fringe of Birmingham's northern green belt.

ALDSWORTH Gloucestershire SP1509
Village off B4425, 6 miles (10km) W of Burford
Of equal fame in tranquil Aldsworth are the church's Norman carvings and Kilkenny Farm, where Robert Garne ensured survival of the famous Cotswold sheep.

ALDWINCLE Northamptonshire TL0081
Village off A605, 4 miles (6km) SW of Oundle
Nene Valley village where stone houses line long main street. Unusually, there are two churches, opposite one of which the poet Dryden was born.

ALDWORTH Berkshire SU5579
Village on B4009, 3 miles (5km) W of Streatley
Downland village, well known for the 14th-century stone effigies in the church – the Aldworth Giants. Eight of them, all members of the de la Beche family, dominate the church. They are not really giants, but normal-size effigies, rather bashed about over the years.

ALEXANDRIA Strathclyde NS3979
Town off A82, 3 miles (5km) N of Dumbarton
Former manufacturing town in Vale of Leven once noted for production of Argyll motors. Birthplace of author Tobias Smollett in 1721.

ALFOLD Surrey TQ0333
Village on B2133, 4 miles (6km) SW of Cranleigh
Tiny village on Sussex border with pretty centre of tile-hung cottages beneath church on little triangular green.

ALFORD Grampian NJ5715
Small town on A944, 23 miles (37km) W of Aberdeen
Founded as terminus for Great North Scotland Railway and now home to Grampian Transport Museum. Birthplace of poet Charles Murray.

ALFORD Lincolnshire TF4575
Small town on A1104, 11 miles (18km) SE of Louth
Lively market town between seaside and Lincolnshire Wolds. Fine 16th- and 17th-century thatched Manor House, now local museum with chemist's shop, cobbler's, Victorian room. Town noted for craft markets on summer Fridays, craft fair at Spring Bank Holiday and popular August Bank Holiday festival. Five-sailed working windmill of 1813. Georgian and Victorian shops and cottages.

ALFORD Somerset ST6032
Village on B3153, 2 miles (3km) W of Castle Cary
Small stone-built village in flat countryside; isolated 15th-century church, good roof, wooden screen and bench-ends.

ALFRED'S CASTLE Oxfordshire SU2885
see Ashbury

ALFRETON Derbyshire SK4155
Town on A61, 10 miles (16km) S of Chesterfield
Market town close to Nottinghamshire border, whose main street broadens uphill to red-brick shopping centre. Town Council offices are in stone 17th-century Alfreton House. Alfreton Hall, late 19th century, is an Adult Education Centre, with leisure centre with swimming pool close by. St Martin's Church has some 13th-century work and later features, with Victorian additions.

ALFRISTON East Sussex TQ5103
Village off A27, 6 miles (10km) W of Eastbourne
Popular village of tile-hung and timber-framed houses and cottages in Cuckmere Valley; once a notorious haunt of smugglers. Several inns; the Star is one of the oldest in England. The Clergy House (National Trust), a 14th-century thatched priest's house; reconstructed stump of Saxon market cross; cruciform church, 'the cathedral of the Downs', built 1360.

ALGARKIRK Lincolnshire TF2935
Village off A16, 6 miles (10km) SW of Boston
Small fenland village with large cruciform church, medieval with 19th-century restoration; impressive range of clerestory windows, and aisles on transepts.

ALKBOROUGH Humberside SE8821
Village off B1430, 7 miles (11km) N of Scunthorpe
Close to the River Trent, the village has an ancient turf maze, Julian's Bower. The maze was cut by monks in the Middle Ages.

The Star inn at Alfriston.

ALKHAM Kent TR2542
Village off A20, 4 miles (6km) W of Dover
Secluded and pretty village in wooded Dour Valley. On hilltop to south are ruins of St Radegund's Abbey.

ALLEN, RIVER (EAST AND WEST) Northumberland
River
Allen Banks is a lovely woodland site near the meeting point of the River Allen and River South Tyne, owned by the National Trust.

ALLENDALE TOWN Northumberland NY8355
Small town on B6303, 5 miles (8km) S of Haydon Bridge
Market town, on banks of River West Allen, which claims to be the geographical centre of Britain.

ALLENHEADS Northumberland NY8645
Village on B6295, 4 miles (6km) N of Wear Head
Pretty moorland village with visitor centre open all year. Attractions include a hydraulic engine house and riverside walks.

ALLER Somerset ST4029
Village on A372, 2 miles (3km) NW of Langport
On the edge of Somerset Levels, medieval church.

ALLERFORD Somerset SS9046
Village on A39, 1 mile (2km) E of Porlock
Well known for its picturesque packhorse bridge and stone cottages; little museum of west Somerset.

ALLERTON Merseyside SJ3987
District on A562 in SE outskirts of Liverpool
A district of Liverpool once home to the richer merchants of the city. Notable buildings include Allerton Hall, Springwood House and Allerton Tower.

ALLERTON MAULEVERER North Yorkshire SE4158
Hamlet off A1, 6 miles (10km) S of Boroughbridge
Allerton Park (limited opening) was used as the setting for the Sherlock Holmes film *The Sign of Four*.

ALLHALLOWS Kent TQ8377
Village off A228, 8 miles (13km) NE of Rochester
Seaside spot on wide open land on northeast tip of Hoo peninsula near mouth of River Thames.

ALLINGTON Kent TQ7557
Village off A20, 2 miles (3km) NW of Maidstone
Set on a great bend of the River Medway with a romantic-looking medieval castle built to guard the strategic point.

ALLINGTON Lincolnshire SK8540
Village off A52, 5 miles (8km) NW of Grantham
Poet George Crabbe was rector at mainly medieval church. Allington Hall, 17th century and later. Ironstone Old Manor House (17th century).

ALLITHWAITE Cumbria SD3876
Village on B5278, 1 mile (2km) SW of Grange-over-Sands
A coastal village with a well that was thought by local miners to cure illnesses caused by their employment.

ALLOA Central NS8892
Town on A907, 6 miles (10km) E of Stirling
Important coal port in 18th century known for glass-making. This is still a major industry and Alloa has the largest bottle-production in Britain. Spinning is an old-established industry, still thriving, as is the brewery, famed for traditional ales. Connected with Mary Stuart.

ALLONBY Cumbria NY0842
Village on B5300, 5 miles (8km) NE of Maryport
An 18th-century sea-bathing resort which retains much of its original charm. Was an important centre of herring fishing.

ALLOWAY Strathclyde NS3318
Village on B7024, 2 miles (3km) S of Ayr
Now suberb of Ayr and famous as the birthplace of Robert Burns in 1759. Family cottage has adjoining museum with memorabilia. Land o' Burns fills in the history of 18th-century Ayrshire. Burns Monument, neo-classical temple, contains relics of poet; 15th-century Brig o' Doon and the roofless church used as setting for *Tam o' Shanter*. Burns' father is buried in churchyard.

ALMELEY Hereford and Worcester SO3351
Village off A480, 4 miles (6km) SE of Kington
Characteristic Welsh border village. Church has Elizabethan painted roof. Almeley House (not open) is a 15th-century timber-framed house.

ALMONDBURY West Yorkshire SE1614
Area in SE Huddersfield
Mainly residential area with mixture of small terraced cottages and large detached homes. Superb views from Castle Hill, historic site.

ALMONDSBURY Avon ST6084
Village off A38, 7 miles (11km) N of Bristol
The parish is dominated by motorways, which join here in Britain's first four-level motorway crossing, 1966. Medieval church with prominent broach spire.

ALNE North Yorkshire SE4965
Village off A19, 3 miles (5km) SW of Easingwold
A pretty village with long curving main street, houses and cottages set well back. St Mary's Church dates from 12th century.

ALNHAM Northumberland NT9810
Hamlet off A697, 5 miles (8km) W of Whittingham
An isolated hamlet with the hillfort, High Knowes, believed to date back to the Iron Age, and a ruined castle demolished in 1532.

ALNMOUTH Northumberland NU2410
Village off A1068, 4 miles (6km) SE of Alnwick
A charming seaside village popular with Victorians and once used as a port by smugglers. *Aln* is the Celtic word for 'bright water'.

ALNWICK Northumberland NU1813

Town off A1, 17 miles (27km) N of Morpeth

The town grew up around Alnwick Castle, an 11th-century border stronghold. In 1309 the castle came into possession of the Percy family and the 1st Earl of Northumberland's famous son, Harry Hotspur, was born here. The estates were temporarily confiscated after the planned revolt against Henry IV and the Battle of Shrewsbury where Hotspur was killed, but they were later restored to his son and the Duke of Northumberland, of the same family, lives there still.

In the 15th century the town was given the protection of stout gatehouses which served until peace was finally made between England and Scotland in the 17th century. From then on Alnwick thrived, as county town and staging post on the Great North Road. The castle was renovated in the 18th and 19th centuries and landscaped by Capability Brown. The town's walls are almost gone but the sturdy, stone buildings, coaching inns and cobbled streets remain, the 800-year-old market place is still a focal point and much of Alnwick is a conservation area.

Alnwick's Medieval Fair is an annual summer event, costumed and based on a 13th-century market fair.

Malcolm's cross in Alnwick.

ALPERTON Greater London TQ1883

District in borough of Brent

Middlesex village where Grand Union Canal spurred 19th-century industrial development; 1930s Piccadilly Line tube station by Charles Holden.

ALPHINGTON Devon SX9190

Suburb of Exeter

An old village now being engulfed by Exeter. Some early 19th-century parts remain.

ALPORT Derbyshire SK2264

Village off B5056, 3 miles (5km) S of Bakewell

Attractive village in the White Peak limestone area, where rivers Lathkill and Bradford meet. The 18th-century cornmill with its wheel is still intact.

ALRESFORD Essex TM0621

Village on B1027, 2 miles (3km) E of Wivenhoe

Pronounced 'Arlsf'd'. There were Roman villas here and local legend has the stammering Emperor Claudius sailing down the River Colne from Colchester to Alresford Creek on a visit. Sailing, birdwatching and picnicking on creek today, with riverside path to Wivenhoe (see). Village church burned down 1971, new one dedicated 1976.

ALRESFORD, NEW AND OLD Hampshire SU5832

Town off A31, 7 miles (11km) E of Winchester

New Alresford was founded in 1199 by a Bishop of Winchester, with a huge pond dammed to power a mill. It is now a handsome small town with a very wide street filled with 17th- and 18th-century houses and cottages. The Watercress Line (steam) runs from here to Alton. Old Alresford is the original village, with a handsome mid-18th-century brick church and plain classical Old Alresford House, 1750s, built by Admiral Lord Rodney.

ALREWAS Staffordshire SK1614

Village on A513, 5 miles (8km) NE of Lichfield

Village beside the River Trent with a wealth of picturesque timber-framed cottages and Wychnor deserted village near by.

ALSAGER Cheshire SJ7955

Town on B5077, 6 miles (10km) E of Crewe

A small Cheshire town near the Staffordshire border, with a heath and a mere, which took its name from the Alsager family, who built Christ Church, in Oxford, in 1789. Until the coming of the railway in 1848, Alsager was an agricultural village. Since then it has developed a pottery industry and during World War I there was an ammunitions factory near by.

ALSOP EN LE DALE Derbyshire SK1554

Hamlet off A515, 6 miles (10km) N of Ashbourne

Hamlet with largely Norman church, close to the Ashbourne – Buxton road, in good walking country (Tissington Trail close by). Bronze Age burial mounds near by.

ALSTON Cumbria NY7146

Small town on A686, 16 miles (26km) NE of Penrith

The highest market settlement in England. Sits just

below the Pennine watershed, high in the valley of the River South Tyne. At the heart of the newly-designated North Pennines Area of Outstanding Natural Beauty. Now a busy service centre but has retained cobbled streets and traditional shop fronts. Popular as a base for touring North Pennines.

ALSTONEFIELD Staffordshire SK1355
Village off A515, 6 miles (10km) N of Ashbourne
Izaak Walton fished from a riverside house in this village where the River Dove winds through a dramatic ravine.

ALTARNUN Cornwall SX2281
Village off A30, 7 miles (11km) W of Launceston
Picturesque stone village on the edge of Bodmin Moor (see), with a packhorse bridge over the little river and lots of trees. Famous church for woodwork, especially the 79 early 16th-century carved bench-ends with musicians, angels and so on. At Trewint is Wesley Cottage, where John Wesley preached, preserved as in his time.

The lock-up in Alton, Staffordshire.

ALTCAR Lancashire SD3206
Village on B5195, 2 miles (3km) E of Formby
An old farming village, on the River Alt, not far from the coast. Also known as Great Altcar.

ALTHORNE Essex TQ9198
Village on B1010, 3 miles (5km) NW of Burnham-on-Crouch
Church on ridge, attractive houses, impressive views.

ALTNAHARRA Highland NC5635
Village on A836, 17 miles (27km) S of Tongue
Township at west end of Loch Naver at road junction in midst of wild and desolate landscape, mainly noted as angling centre. Prehistoric remains near by.

ALTOFTS West Yorkshire SE3823
Village off A642, 3 miles (5km) NE of Wakefield
This old colliery village on the banks of the River Calder was the birthplace of the seafarer, Martin Frobisher.

ALTON Hampshire SU7139
Town on A339, 10 miles (16km) SE of Basingstoke
Set in a gap in the low chalk hills, Alton developed as a proper market town on the road from London. Happy mixture of buildings, with good Georgian brick and some Victorian flint. The prominent church was the scene of a battle in the Civil War – 500 soldiers made their final stand actually inside the church in 1643. Local museum and the Allen Gallery with pottery and paintings.

ALTON Staffordshire SK0741
Village off B5032, 4 miles (6km) E of Cheadle
Pugin's huge Gothic Alton Towers, built between 1809 and 1813, is now ruined, but its superb gardens with Pagoda Fountain, Chinese Temple and other elaborate follies are open to the public. The earlier 800 acre (324ha) park by 'Capability' Brown now accommodates one of Britain best-known leisure parks, with many entertainments including spectacular rides.

ALTON BARNES/ALTON PRIORS Wiltshire SU1062
Villages adjoining, off A345, 4 miles (6km) NW of Pewsey
Two small villages nestled next to one another in the Vale of Pewsey, with the chalk downs to the north. The two small and ancient churches stand only a stone's throw apart. On the downs is carved the White Horse of 1812, and many archaeological remains including Knap Hill, an enclosure, and Adam's Grave, a long barrow. Both are neolithic.

ALTRINCHAM Greater Manchester SJ7687
Town on A560, 8 miles (13km) SW of Manchester
An historic market town which developed as a residential area in the 19th century. The Booth family estate, Dunham Massey Hall and Park, now owned by the National Trust, is open to the public. The hall exhibits the impressive family collection of Huguenot silver; watermill, originally used for grinding corn; gardens; large deer park.

ALUM BAY Isle of Wight SZ3085
Beach on B3322, 1 mile (2km) SW of Totland
The technicolour sands of the cliffs at Alum Bay are well known, but still startle. Chair-lift down to the beach. Nestling next to the Needles (see). The Needles Pleasure Park is at Alum Bay.

ALVA Central NS8897
Town on A91, 7 miles (11km) S of Stirling
Small weaving town since 16th century beneath Ochil Hills. Nearby Alva Glen had silver mine; two communion cups in church made from local silver.

ALVECHURCH Hereford and Worcester SP0272
Village on A441, 3 miles (5km) N of Redditch
Birmingham dormitory on the slopes of the Lickey Hills with school, rectory and restored church by celebrated Victorian architect William Butterfield.

ALVECOTE Warwickshire SK2404
Hamlet off B5493, 3 miles (5km) E of Tamworth
The ruins of a medieval Benedictine priory are now the centre of a nature reserve and walks that take in nearby Alvecote Pools.

ALVELEY Shropshire SO7584
Village off A422, 6 miles (10km) SE of Bridgnorth
Old village centre with pleasant traditional cottages survives among much modern building, the result of a former colliery on the opposite bank of the River Severn.

ALVESTON Warwickshire SP2356
Village off B4086, 2 miles (3km) E of Stratford-upon-Avon
The village, in a loop of the River Avon, has expanded in recent years, but its attractive old centre remains.

ALVINGHAM Lincolnshire TF3691
Village off A16, 3 miles (5km) NE of Louth
Two 12th-century churches in one churchyard, approached through a farmyard. Fine 17th-century working watermill on River Lud.

ALWALTON Cambridgeshire TL1396
Village on A605, 4 miles (6km) SW of Peterborough
Pretty village on the River Nene. Birthplace of Henry Royce, of Rolls-Royce cars.

ALWINTON Northumberland NT9106
Village off B6341, 9 miles (14km) NW of Rothbury
The last English village in the Cheviot Hills, in the valley of the River Coquet, situated in prime walking country.

ALYTH Tayside NO2448
Small town on B958, 6 miles (10km) NE of Blairgowrie
A market and milling town in fertile Strathmore, once a cloth-manufacturing centre, with a mercat cross and the 16th-century Auld Brig.

The 17th-century market hall in Amersham.

AMBERLEY West Sussex TQ0213
Village off B2139, 5 miles (8km) N of Arundel
Picturesque friendly village on meander of River Arun, backed by watermeadows (nature reserve) and smooth green downs. Norman castle, strengthened 1380, now hotel, rises straight from river. Thatched cottages grouped by church, old houses with wisteria, village shop and two pubs. Chalk Pits Museum, a working industrial museum. Amberley villagers used to wassail their bees.

AMBLE Northumberland NU2604
Small town on A1068, 7 miles (11km) SE of Alnwick
A busy harbour town on the Coquet estuary, once important for the export of coal and now popular for sailing and fishing. Coquet Island lies 1 mile (2km) offshore and is now an RSPB reserve noted for its colonies of puffins, terns and eider ducks. The island once had a monastic foundation known as Cocwadae, and a Benedictine settlement.

AMBLESIDE Cumbria NY3704
Small town on A591, 4 miles (6km) NW of Windermere
Popular tourist centre that gets very crowded in summer. On the shore of Windermere; lake cruises go from here to Newby Bridge and Bowness. The tiny Old Bridge House, perched on old packhorse bridge, once housed a family with six children; now a National Trust shop.

AMERSHAM Buckinghamshire SU9597
Town on A416, 3 miles (5km) S of Chesham
Old Chilterns market town in Misbourne Valley, broad High Street, many houses of 16th, 17th and 18th centuries, coaching inns, 17th-century market hall raised on brick pillars. Church of St Mary with monuments of Drake family of Shardeloes House. Amersham on the Hill is newer settlement, developed since 1892 arrival of the Metropolitan railway.

AMESBURY Wiltshire SU1541
Town on A345, 7 miles (11km) N of Salisbury
On the edge of Salisbury Plain, mostly small-scale modern but with a large medieval church, partly 13th century. Big army camps either side.

AMLWCH Gwynedd SH4492
Small town on A5025, 15 miles (24km) NW of Menai Bridge
The old metal workings that scar Parys Mountain, once the world's largest source of copper, transformed 18th-century Amlwch into a populous and prosperous port. Now it is a fishing and holiday centre with a Friday general market. A modern Roman Catholic church, a representation of an upturned boat, contrasts with St Eilian's 15th-century contents.

AMMANFORD Dyfed SN6212
Town on A483, 12 miles (19km) N of Swansea
Former coal-mining town at crossroads in western valleys. Terraced houses back on to unspoilt wildernesses of Black Mountain.

AMPFIELD Hampshire SU4023
Village on A31, 3 miles (5km) E of Romsey
Wooded village, with the Hillier Gardens and Arboretum, 160 acres (65ha), boasting the largest collection of hardy plants in the country.

AMPLEFORTH North Yorkshire SE5878
Village off A170, 10 miles (16km) E of Thirsk
College, founded by Benedictine Father Bolton in 1802, now one of the country's largest Roman Catholic schools. Abbey church designed by Sir Giles Gilbert Scott.

AMPNEY CRUCIS Gloucestershire SP0601
Village off A417, 3 miles (5km) E of Cirencester
The main attraction of the largest of the Ampney villages is the Saxon and medieval church, with its rare 15th-century churchyard cross.

AMPORT Hampshire SU3044
Village off A303, 4 miles (6km) W of Andover
Big green, lots of old cottages including almshouses called Charity Square. Early 14th-century church with good Victorian stained glass.

AMPTHILL Bedfordshire TL0337
Town on B530, 8 miles (13km) S of Bedford
Attractive old coaching town with Georgian houses and picturesque cottages. Sand-loving insects lurk in Cooper's Hill Nature Reserve, while Ampthill Park, landscaped in 18th century by Capability Brown, commands fine views. To the north is the romantic shell of Houghton House, traditionally the model for the 'House Beautiful' in Bunyan's *Pilgrim's Progress.*

AMPTON Suffolk TL8671
Village off A134, 4 miles (6km) N of Bury St Edmunds
A pretty village near a mere. Ampton Hall (not open) was the home of Robert Fitzroy, captain of the *Beagle*, on which Charles Darwin was naturalist.

AMROTH Dyfed SN1607
Village off A477, 2 miles (3km) NE of Saundersfoot
At southernmost end of Pembrokeshire Coast National Park and Coast Path. Long, south-facing sands, shallow waters, submerged forest. Delightful Colby Woodland Garden (National Trust).

ANCASTER Lincolnshire SK9843
Village on A153, 5 miles (8km) W of Sleaford
Roman station on Ermine Street, linking London, Lincoln, York. Source of durable Ancaster limestone, strikingly seen in houses lining long main street.

ANCRUM Borders NT6224
Village on B6400, 3 miles (5km) NW of Jedburgh
Stands round green on River Ale near junction with River Teviot. Iron Age and Roman hillforts in neighbourhood.

ANDERTON BOAT LIFT Cheshire SJ6475
Industrial archaeology site 1 mile (2km) NW of Northwich
Amazing and enormous boat lift, built in 1875 by Leader Williams, engineer of the Manchester Ship Canal. Connects Trent and Mersey Canal with Weaver Navigation.

ANDOVER Hampshire SU3645
Town on A3057, 8 miles (13km) N of Stockbridge
A medieval town, but small until the 1960s when it was selected to take London overspill. The centre is partly modern, partly older. The Andover Museum and the

Museum of the Iron Age are good. Finkley Down Farm Park (2 miles/3km east) has a great variety of farm animals and rural bygones.

ANDREAS Isle of Man SC4199

Village on A19, 4 miles (6km) NW of Ramsey

Carved stones and crosses in the church reflect village's Viking connections. Spire of separate church tower removed in 1940 in case of danger to wartime aircraft.

ANERLEY Greater London TQ3369

District in borough of Bromley

Developed after railway arrived 1840s, previously notorious for highwaymen. Swedenborgian church in Waldegrave Road, curious 1880s Gothic in pink concrete.

ANFIELD Merseyside SJ3793

District of Liverpool

A district of Liverpool famous as the home of Liverpool Football Club. There is also a football museum at the ground.

ANGLE Dyfed SM8602

Village on B4320, 8 miles (13km) W of Pembroke

Outlying village at mouth of Milford Haven Waterway. Tiny Fishermen's Chapel, characterful pubs. Extensive sea views take in Thorn Island's unusual 19th-century fort-cum-hotel.

ANGLESEY Gwynedd

Island off NW coast of Wales

Anglesey is known in Welsh as Ynys Môn, often with the title 'Mam Cymru', or 'Mother of Wales'. This description derives from Anglesey's once-abundant cornfields which fed Snowdonia's barren heartlands. Those days are recalled by Llynon Mill at Llanddeusant, the only windmill on Anglesey where the milling process survives.

Flattish, with small fields, stone walls and white houses, the island is pastoral now in nature, more English than Welsh in appearance. The 125 mile (201km) coastline, an Area of Outstanding Natural Beauty, is varied and, where access allows, very popular. First settled by mesolithic hunters, Anglesey possesses the greatest concentration of prehistoric sites in Wales. A stronghold of the Druids, spiritual leaders of the Celts, it was the last corner of Wales to fall to the Romans. The island became, in turn, a seat of the mighty Princes of Gwynedd who were eventually conquered by Edward I.

Separated from the mainland by the Menai Strait, the island is bridged by Telford's suspension bridge of 1826, a true engineering feat. Another such was Robert Stephenson's Britannia tubular rail bridge of 1850. Burned down in 1970, its piers carry the modern road and railway on their way to Holyhead and the Irish ferries.

ANGMERING West Sussex TQ0604

Town on A280, 3 miles (5km) NE of Littlehampton

Old village centre set around a green lies inland from the 19th- and 20th-century coastal development of Angmering-on-Sea.

The five-arched packhorse bridge at Anstey.

ANGUS Tayside
Historic region of Scotland
Until 1975 a Scottish county, formerly known as Forfarshire, after the county town of Forfar. The main industries are agriculture and fishing, with Dundee, once famed for its jute industry, being the main industrial and population centre. The countryside ranges from the deep northern glens to the cultivated Vale of Strathmore and the fine coastline to the east.

ANNAN Dumfries and Galloway NY1966
Town on A75, 15 miles (24km) E of Dumfries
Market town near Solway Firth, with bridge designed by Robert Stevenson. Connections with historian Thomas Carlyle who was educated, and later taught, at Annan Academy.

ANNANDALE Dumfries and Galloway NY1966
Valley of River Annan
Valley of River Annan, long stretch of upland heath between Border and Moffat. Traversed by busy A74, quickest way to cross southern Scotland.

ANNESLEY Nottinghamshire SK5053
Village on A611, 2 miles (3km) S of Kirkby-in-Ashfield
Poet Byron's love Mary Chaworth lived in Annesley Hall (private), beside ruined church replaced by 19th-century hilltop church. Kodak works are near by.

ANNFIELD PLAIN Durham NZ1651
Town on A693, 2 miles (3km) SW of Stanley
Originally a sheep-farming area, after the first pits were sunk in the 19th century this became a typical mining community.

ANSFORD Somerset ST6433
Village on A371, 1 mile (2km) N of Castle Cary
Now almost part of Castle Cary, with lots of modern building. James Woodforde, the famous diarist, was born here in 1740.

ANSTEY Hertfordshire TL4033
Village off B1368, 4 miles (6km) NE of Buntingford
Handsome old church that escaped Victorian restorers, with Norman font carved with mermen, misericords, medieval graffiti. Earthworks of vanished Norman castle.

ANSTON, NORTH AND SOUTH South Yorkshire SK5284
Town off A57, 5 miles (8km) NW of Worksop
Area in two distinct parts, separated by A57. South Anston, still a pleasant village, with a pretty church.

ANSTRUTHER Fife NO5703
Town on A917, 9 miles (14km) SE of St Andrews
Rivalled Pittenweem (see) as Fife's major fishing port; two now almost joined. Since 1929 town has incorporated Cellardyke and Kilrenny; fishing fleet known as 'Dykers', main catch cod and herring. Many typical Fife crow-stepped 17th- and 18th-century houses and Scotland's oldest inhabited manse. Interesting Scottish Fisheries Museum. Craggy Isle of May offshore, well-known nature reserve and bird sanctuary.

ANSTY West Sussex TQ2923
Village on A272, 1 mile (2km) SW of Cuckfield
Small hilltop village on the old Brighton road with pleasant timber-framed and brick houses. Legh Manor gardens to southwest.

ANTHORN Cumbria NY1958
Village off B5307, 15 miles (21km) W of Carlisle
Situated on the shores of Moricambe Bay with a NATO radio station whose masts dominate the skyline.

ANTINGHAM Norfolk TG2533
Village off A149, 3 miles (5km) NW of North Walsham
Small, attractive village standing on the banks of the River Ant. It is on the main railway line to Cromer from Norwich.

ANTONINE WALL Strathclyde/Central
Roman fortification
Built AD140 to push back northern barbarians. It stretched from River Clyde to River Forth with 17 forts, abandoned after 25 years.

ANTONY Cornwall SX4054
Village on A374, 2 miles (3km) W of Torpoint
Small stone village on the edge of St Germans estuary, with good river views. Antony House (2 miles/3km east, National Trust) has huge woodland gardens, with even better views. Early 18th-century house with good paintings. Fort Tregantle prominent on the coast dates from the 1860s, and is still used as a firing range.

ANTROBUS Cheshire SJ6480
Hamlet on A559, 2 miles (3km) NW of Great Budworth
A 19th-century village known for its much older 'souling' custom. The Soul Caking play was revived by naturalist Major Arnold Boyd, and is once again performed on or around All Soul's Day. A pleasant area that has attracted new residential development.

ANWICK Lincolnshire TF1150
Village on A153, 4 miles (6km) NE of Sleaford
Fenland village where land was drained in the 18th century. Fourteenth-century sculpture of Virgin and Child was found during 19th-century church restoration.

APETHORPE Northamptonshire TL0295
Village off A43, 4 miles (6km) SW of Wansford
Dominated by splendours of its hall, now a school, which is late 15th century, Jacobean and later. Church with fine monuments. Stocks and whipping post.

APPIN Highland/Strathclyde
Historic region of Scotland
Traditional name for country lying between Loch Creran and Ballachulish. Best known for Appin Murder of 1752, used by Robert Louis Stevenson in *Kidnapped*.

Wren's 17th-century grammar school at Appleby Parva.

APPLEBY, MAGNA AND PARVA Leicestershire SK3109/SK3008
Villages off M42, 5 miles (8km) SW of Ashby-de-la-Zouch
Staffordshire/Derbyshire/Warwickshire meet near by. Gatehouse of moated medieval manor adjoins 16th-century timber-framed house. Old Grammar School (1690s) built to Wren's designs.

APPLEBY-IN-WESTMORLAND Cumbria NY6820
Small town off A66, 12 miles (19km) SE of Penrith
Former county town of Westmorland dominated by Appleby Castle, dating from Norman times. Rare Breeds Survival Trust Centre. Famous for Appleby Horse Fair, the largest gypsy gathering in Britain; the fair is 300 years old and takes place in June. Church of St Lawrence houses one of the oldest organs in Britain, moved here from Carlisle Cathedral. Lady Anne Clifford, who restored several buildings in the town, is buried here.

APPLECROSS Highland NG7144
Village off A896, 20 miles (32km) SW of Shieldaig
Remote and lovely crofting settlement on sheltered bay founded 673 by St Maelrubha. Difficult access over 2,000ft (608m) Bealach na Ba Pass, or along coast.

APPLEDORE Devon SS4630
Small town on A386, 3 miles (5km) N of Bideford
On the junction of the big estuaries of the Taw and Torridge, narrow streets packed with plain whitewashed cottages run up a gentle hill and along the estuary. Shipyards further up the Torridge River. Good views, with Braunton Burrows sand dunes (see) up the coast and the hills inland. North Devon Maritime Museum.

APPLEDORE Kent TQ9529
Village on B2080, 5 miles (8km) SE of Tenterden
Pleasing village with wide street of contrasting old houses set above the Royal Military Canal on the edge of Romney Marsh.

APPLETON Oxfordshire SP4401
Village off A420, 4 miles (6km) NW of Abingdon
Lanes lead down to the Thames from this straggling village set within an arc of woodland.

APPLETON THORN Cheshire SJ6484
Village off A49, 3 miles (5km) SE of Warrington
Heavy traffic passes through here to the M56 and M6 motorways, and large industrial estate. Older centre, with much new residential development.

APPLETON-LE-MOORS North Yorkshire SE7387
Village off A170, 5 miles (8km) NW of Pickering
Good example of single-street village of traditional houses with parallel back lanes, tofts and crofts and a common.

APPLETON-LE-STREET North Yorkshire SE7373
Village on B1257, 4 miles (6km) W of Malton
All Saints' Church is mainly 13th century, although the lower part of the tower is Saxon.

APPLETREEWICK North Yorkshire SE0560
Village off B6160, 2 miles (3km) SE of Burnsall
Onion Lane recalls days when village was famous for its onions. Mock Beggar Hall has an eccentric projecting wing.

APULDRAM West Sussex SU8403
Village off A286, 1 mile (2km) SW of Chichester
A tiny place at head of creek of Chichester Harbour, with 13th-century church originally chapel of Bosham Abbey.

AQUALATE MERE Staffordshire SJ7621
see Newport, Shropshire

ARBIGLAND Dumfries and Galloway NX9857
see Kirkbean

ARBOR LOW Derbyshire SK1663

Prehistoric site off A515, 3 miles (5km) W of Youlgreave

This important Bronze Age henge monument, in the Peak District National Park, near the Ashbourne – Buxton road, is approached through a farmyard. A 250ft (76m) diameter outer bank and ditch surround a circle of 47 stones, with three central stones, all lying down. Early Bronze Age barrow in the bank.

ARBORFIELD Berkshire SU7567

Village on A327, 5 miles (8km) SE of Reading

In three parts – Arborfield itself with the church, Arborfield Cross on the crossroads and Arborfield Garrison with the Royal Electrical Mechanical Engineers complex and museum.

ARBROATH Tayside NO6441

Town on A92, 15 miles (24km) NE of Dundee

This ancient seaside town, which James VI made a royal burgh in 1599, had become a major trading and manufacturing centre by the 18th century and is today an important fishing port and visitor resort.

The sandstone ruins of Arbroath Abbey, founded in 1178, dominate the town and include the west doorway and the south transept window, known as the 'Round O' and once lit with a beacon to guide coastal shipping. In 1320 the Declaration of Arbroath was signed here by Robert I, establishing Scottish independence from England: 'so long as a hundred of us remain alive, we will yield in no least way to English dominion.' The Abbot's House has a small museum, which includes a collection of Scottish medieval art. The Signal Tower, built in 1813 as a signalling station for the offshore Bell Rock Lighthouse (1808), nowadays houses a local museum.

The cliff path along Whiting Ness gives good views to sea and leads to the ancient and picturesque village of Auchmithie.

Smokies, delicately oak-smoked haddock, are Arbroath's main culinary claim to fame.

ARBURY HALL Warwickshire SP3189

see Astley

ARDELEY Hertfordshire TL3027

Village off B1037, 5 miles (8km) NE of Stevenage

Green with well, village hall, thatched cottages – charming scene created from 1917 on. Restored 17th-century windmill on outskirts.

ARDEN, FOREST OF Warwickshire

Historic region of England

The Forest of Arden, immortalised by Shakespeare in *As You Like It*, once covered most of Warwickshire north-west of the River Avon and the area is still noticeably well wooded in places such as Tanworth-in-Arden. Elms predominated and became known as 'the Warwickshire weed'. The memory of the forest is preserved in placenames like Henley-in-Arden.

ARDINGLY West Sussex TQ3429

Village on B2028, 4 miles (6km) N of Haywards Heath

Compact village street grouped around a crossroads with church lying to south. Famous school, Ardingly College (St Saviour's), established under Woodard Foundation, 1858. South of England Showground hosts major agricultural shows. Wakehurst Place is leased by National Trust from Kew Gardens; dramatic parkland and gardens with superb collection of exotic plants and mature trees in geographical settings.

ARDINGTON Oxfordshire SU4388

Village off A417, 2 miles (3km) E of Wantage

Victorian village built for workers on Lockinge estate. The craft centre at Ardington Home Farm is open to visitors.

ARDLEIGH Essex TM0529

Village on A137, 5 miles (8km) NE of Colchester

Victorian church by William Butterfield with earlier Tudor tower and porch vividly decorated in flint and brick. Ardleigh Reservoir to southwest.

Cottages facing Applecross Bay at Applecross.

ARDNAMURCHAN Highland
Historic region of Scotland
Remote peninsula stretching to Ardnamurchan Point, the most westerly point on the British mainland. Varied upland landscape of great beauty, crofting townships, Kilchoan the principal.

ARDRISHAIG Strathclyde NR8585
Town on A83, 2 miles (3km) S of Lochgilphead
Lies at southern end of Crinan Canal on Loch Gilp; once a herring port. Birthplace of John Smith, leader of Labour Party in 1990s.

ARDROSSAN Strathclyde NS2342
see Saltcoats

ARELEY KINGS Hereford and Worcester SO7970
Village off A451, 1 mile (2km) SW of Stourport-on-Severn
Severnside village with an interesting church and associated buildings. Redstone Rock, an outcrop overlooking the river, contains caves inhabited until the 19th century.

ARENIG FAWR Gwynedd SH8236
Mountain off A4212, 6 miles (10km) E of Trawsfynydd
Summit (2,800ft/854m) is surmounted by memorial to the eight crew of a United States Flying Fortress which crashed here in 1943. Splendid views.

ARGYLL Strathclyde
Historic region of Scotland
Before government reorganisation in 1975 a large county, more than 100 miles (160km) from north to south, including 90 islands, among them Mull, Islay and Jura. Mainland is largely formed of peninsulas with many sea-lochs and beautiful coastline, over 2,000 miles (3,200km) in length. Economy based on fishing, agriculture, whisky and tourism. Lochgilphead was old county town.

ARISAIG Highland NM6586
Village on A830, 7 miles (11km) S of Mallaig
Crofting and tourist centre around rock-strewn sandy bay, excellent beaches in vicinity. Associations with Prince Charles Edward and Jacobites. *Local Hero* filmed near by.

ARKENGARTHDALE North Yorkshire SE0498
Valley of the Arkle Beck
Most northerly of Yorkshire dales. Arkle Beck runs down the valley into the River Swale. Hamlets in the dale are early Norse settlements.

ARKESDEN Essex TL4834
Village off B1039, 5 miles (8km) SE of Saffron Walden
Attractive place near Audley End (see), on diminutive stream, the Wicken Water. Village green, thatched cottages, church with monuments.

ARKSEY South Yorkshire SE5806
N suburb of Doncaster
Charming rural village with 17th-century almshouses and school house, once owned by Sir John Falstaff, who was immortalised by Shakespeare.

ARLEY Hereford and Worcester SO7680
see Upper Arley

ARLINGHAM Gloucestershire SO7010
Village off A38, 9 miles (14km) NW of Stroud
Prehistoric travellers and Welsh cattle-drovers used this River Severn fording point, where St Mary's Church has some of Gloucestershire's oldest stained glass.

ARLINGTON Devon SS6140
Hamlet off A9, 6 miles (10km) NE of Barnstaple
Really only the big house and a church. Arlington Court (National Trust) is Regency with mid-Victorian additions and interior. Large collection of carriages.

ARLINGTON MILL Gloucestershire SP1106
see Bibury

ARMADALE Highland NG6303
Village on A851, 17 miles (27km) S of Broadford
Situated on southern slopes of fertile Sleat peninsula overlooking Sound of Sleat. Car ferry connections to Mallaig on mainland.

ARMATHWAITE Cumbria NY5046
Village off A6, 9 miles (14km) SE of Carlisle
Armathwaite Castle was home to John Skelton, Poet Laureate to Henry VIII. Church contains stained-glass windows made by William Morris workshops in 1926.

ARMITAGE Staffordshire SK0715
Village on A513, 3 miles (5km) SE of Rugeley
A name famous throughout Britain, thanks to the sanitary ware produced here. Less well known is the splendid Norman font in the church.

ARNCLIFFE North Yorkshire SD9371
Village off B6160, 7 miles (11km) NW of Grassington
Charles Kingsley wrote part of *The Water Babies* while staying here. The hero, Tom, fell into the River Skirfare before becoming a water baby.

ARNE Dorset SY9788
Hamlet off A351, 3 miles (5km) E of Wareham
Huge wild parish stretching from the shore of Poole Harbour, much of it a heathland nature reserve.

ARNOLD Nottinghamshire SK5845
Town in N outskirts of Nottingham
Once a separate Urban District, the town adjoins Nottingham's northern boundary. Nearby Burntstump Country Park has woodland walks and picnic sites.

ARNSIDE Cumbria SD4578
Town on B5282, 6 miles (10km) N of Carnforth
In 19th century was a busy holiday resort and port, with pleasure boats coming in from Morecambe and Fleetwood and barges bringing coal and taking limestone to Blackpool. The estuary of the River Kent, on which village stands, is a haven for birds and wildlife. A viaduct carries the railway from Arnside, over estuary, to Grange-over-Sands. Arnside Knott (521ft/158m) belongs to the National Trust.

ARRAN, ISLE OF Strathclyde
Island in Firth of Clyde
Most southerly of the Scottish islands, Arran claims to be a Scotland in miniature, with scenically a little bit of everything, making it a favourite holiday area for outdoor enthusiasts. Measuring 20 miles (32km) by 10 miles (16km) and divided by the Highland fault, the north is mountainous and bleak while the south provides a more rounded and fertile contrast. The highest point is Goat Fell (2,868ft/872m). The east coast has sheltered bays and beaches with sailing and watersports centres.

Chambered cairns, stone circles, standing stones, duns and forts testify to Arran's ancient history; there are good examples around Lamlash Bay and Machrie Moor. Sacked by the Vikings in the 8th century, it became part of Scotland in 1266 and was granted by royal charter in 1503 to the Hamilton Earls of Arran, who played an important role in Scottish politics over the centuries. They cleared many people off the land in the 19th century to establish large sheep farms and deer forests.

Tourism is the main industry, and its growth has resulted in a living community without the depopulation problems of other west coast islands. See Brodick.

ARRETON Isle of Wight SZ5386
Village on A3056, 3 miles (5km) SE of Newport
Small, with medieval church, big tithe barn, and a handsome 17th-century stone manor house. Arreton Manor also has the National Wireless Museum. Haseley Heritage, at Haseley Manor to the south, has a Victorian kitchen.

ARRINGTON Cambridgeshire TL3250
Village off A1198, 6 miles (10km) N of Royston
Arrington boasts the splendid 18th-century Wimpole Hall (National Trust, limited opening), the 19th-century thatched Home Farm, and beautiful St Nicholas' Church.

ARROCHAR Strathclyde NN2904
Village on A83, 1 mile (2km) W of Tarbet
At the end of Loch Long, with so-called Arrochar Alps behind; good base for exploring northern Argyll National Park.

ARROW, RIVER Hereford and Worcester
River
Rising in the Radnor Hills, it flows eastward from Kington and passes through Staunton, Pembridge and Eardisland before joining the River Lugg south of Leominster.

ARTHOG Gwynedd SH6414
Village on A493, 2 miles (3km) NE of Fairbourne
Originally built for quarry workers. A panoramic road winds up from houses on Mawddach estuary to beautiful Cregennen Lakes on the flank of Cader Idris.

ARUN, RIVER West Sussex
River
River rises in Weald, flows through gap in South Downs past Amberley and Arundel to the sea at Littlehampton.

ARUNDEL West Sussex TQ0106
Town on A27, 5 miles (8km) N of Littlehampton
In a glorious location on the edge of the downs above the River Arun, the town piles up the hillside dominated by its great bulky castle. Seen from the watermeadows Arundel still closely resembles an engraving of it made by Holler in the 16th century. The High Street descends to the river lined by some attractive houses. There are many antique shops and a museum and heritage centre.

The first castle on the site, an earthen motte and bailey, was constructed in 1067 by the cousin of William the Conqueror, Roger Montgomery. The stone castle keep was built in the 12th century and the barbican a century later. Ruined in the Civil War, the castle remained ruinous until the 1790s when it was rebuilt only to be substantially reconstructed in the Gothic style in 1890.

Arundel Park contains a famous cricket ground, while the Wildfowl and Wetlands Trust runs a reserve by the river. Since the 13th century the town and surrounding lands have been in the hands of one family, the Fitzalans and their descendants, the Howards, Dukes of Norfolk. The Duke is England's premier Roman Catholic layman. The Roman Catholic cathedral was completed in 1873.

ASCOT Berkshire SU9268
Town on A329, 6 miles (10km) SW of Windsor
A very small town, dominated by its famous racecourse. The first horse-racing on Ascot Heath, conveniently close to Windsor, was under the patronage of Queen Anne in 1711. Royalty have continued to attend the June meeting, with a procession in carriages marking the opening.

ASCOTT-UNDER-WYCHWOOD Oxfordshire SP3018
Village off B4437, 4 miles (6km) W of Charlbury
Stone cottages and a Norman church lie in the Evenlode Valley beneath the ancient Wychwood Forest.

ASFORDBY Leicestershire SK7019
Village off A6006, 3 miles (5km) W of Melton Mowbray
Wreake Valley village, older buildings around 13th-century church. Iron worked extensively to 1960s, now producing small castings. Showpiece coal mine opened 1980s.

ASH Kent TR2858
Village on A257, 3 miles (5km) W of Sandwich
Pleasant old village of brick, tile and timber with some modern housing. Tall copper church spire has long been a navigational mark for seamen.

ASHAMPSTEAD Berkshire SU5676
Village off B4009, 3 miles (5km) SW of Streatley
High woody downland village, with a large green and a medieval church with 13th-century wall-paintings.

ASHBOURNE Derbyshire SK1746
Town on A52, 13 miles (21km) NW of Derby
This attractive market town lies just south of the Peak District National Park, a good centre from which to explore Dovedale and the Manifold Valley. The cobbled

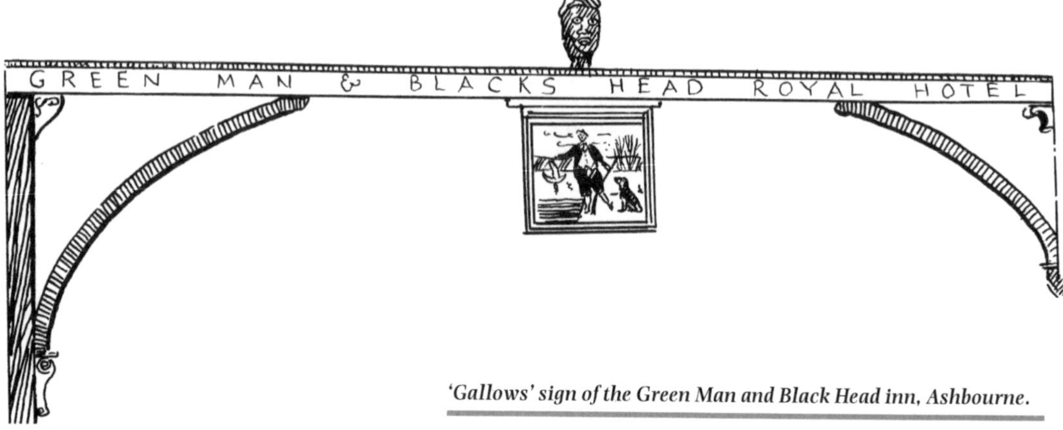

'Gallows' sign of the Green Man and Black Head inn, Ashbourne.

market place is triangular, stretching up the hill along the road leading north to Buxton. The many outstanding Georgian buildings include almshouses, town houses and inns such as the Green Man and Blacks Head. The latter is no longer an inn, but it still retains its rare 'gallows' inn sign across the main street. The church, at the west end of the town, was described by novelist George Eliot as 'the finest mere Parish Church in England'. It has the tallest spire in the Peak District, 212ft (65m), and a touching marble monument to Penelope Boothby, aged five when she died.

Dr Johnson was a frequent visitor to his friend Dr Taylor's house. Today's visitors can enjoy traditional Ashbourne gingerbread, washed down with Ashbourne water drunk from a glass made from the local Derwent Crystal. On Shrove Tuesday or Ash Wednesday, all the streets are taken over by the traditional 'football' game, with hundreds of players on each side.

ASHBURNHAM PLACE East Sussex TQ6814
Village off B2204, 6 miles (10km) W of Battle
Estate village hidden in a steep valley centred on Ashburnham Place (1680s). The iron furnace (closed 1813) was the last to operate in the Weald.

ASHBURTON Devon SX7570
Town off A38, 7 miles (11km) W of Newton Abbot
A quiet market town, large and important in the medieval period as one of the stannary towns (where tin from Dartmoor was taken to be weighed and taxed) and for cloth manufacture. Pleasant buildings, many slate-hung and an interesting granite church. Local museum. River Dart Country Park and Holme Park.

ASHBURY Oxfordshire SU2685
Village on B4000, 7 miles (11km) E of Swindon
Chalk and brown stone were the building materials for the medieval church, manor house and other old dwellings in this village lying beneath the Ridgeway. On the downs above is the elegant Ashdown Park of 1660, the 3,500-year-old chambered tomb called Wayland's Smithy, and Alfred's Castle, an Iron Age hill-fort.

ASHBY CUM FENBY Humberside TA2500
Village off B1203 5m (8km) S of Grimsby
Village adjacent to the Roman 'Barton Street'. The Wray almshouses were built in 1641 by Lady Wray.

ASHBY DE LA LAUNDE Lincolnshire TF0555
Village off B1191, 6 miles (10km) N of Sleaford
The hall, mainly 19th-century but with Elizabethan origins, in parkland, is now a country club. Mid-19th-century Gothick cottages.

ASHBY FOLVILLE Leicestershire SK7012
Village on B674, 5 miles (8km) SW of Melton Mowbray
Elizabethan Manor of 1520, restored 1890s after fire and 16th-century tithe barn, with Swithland slate roof replacing thatch. Church founded 1220.

ASHBY ST LEDGERS Northamptonshire SP5768
Village off A361, 4 miles (6km) N of Daventry
Mansion dates from 16th-century and later and is home of the Catesbys, where Gunpowder Plot conspirators met in Elizabethan gatehouse. Thatched cottages by Lutyens.

ASHBY-DE-LA-ZOUCH Leicestershire SK3516
Town on A50, 16 miles (26km) NW of Leicester
Historic market town and former spa, with Georgian buildings, old coaching inns, impressive 15th-century church. Substantial castle ruins (English Heritage) were 15th-century manor of Lord Hastings. Walter Scott used nearby fields as setting for novel *Ivanhoe*, title used for spa baths. Popularity as a spa was short-lived, but some buildings remain to enhance town.

ASHCOMBE Devon SX9179
Village off B3192, 3 miles (5km) E of Chudleigh
Tiny village – church, vicarage and a couple of cottages in the bottom of a little combe.

ASHDON Essex TL5842
Village off B1053, 4 miles (6km) NE of Saffron Walden
Near Suffolk border. Bartlow Hills north of village are Romano-British burial mounds still standing 20ft to 40ft (6m to 12m) high.

ASHDOWN FOREST East Sussex TQ4530
Ancient forest
Sandstone ridge on watershed of the Weald. Highest point, Crowborough Beacon, 792ft (240m); best views from Camp Hill. Former royal hunting forest. Board of Conservators set up 1870s. Commoners have rights over 6,000 acres (2,400ha). Excellent walking and bird- watching. Heath and bracken, dark woods and rocky outcrops give it a Scottish rather than south country feel.

ASHDOWN HOUSE Gloucestershire SU2782
see Ashbury

ASHFORD Kent TR0142
Town on A20, 19 miles (31km) SE of Maidstone
Bustling modern town of offices and industry with historic core of old buildings centred on large medieval church.

ASHFORD CARBONEL Shropshire SO5270
Village off A49, 3 miles (5km) S of Ludlow
Small, attractive village beside the River Teme. Its interesting Norman and medieval church has a fine timber roof.

ASHFORD IN THE WATER Derbyshire SK1969
Village off A6, 2 miles (3km) NW of Bakewell
Picturesque Peak District village on the River Wye, close to Monsal Dale, bypassed by the busy A6. One of the three bridges, once used by packhorses, has a stone enclosure beside it in which sheep were washed. Once the centre of the ornamental black marble industry, creative talent is now expressed in the traditional well-dressings.

ASHINGDON Essex TQ8693
Village off B1013, immediately N of Rochford
Great battle fought here in 1016 when Danes under Canute defeated English. Model Viking ship in church, huge Thames estuary views.

ASHINGTON Northumberland NZ2687
Town on A196, 5 miles (8km) E of Morpeth
Childhood home of footballing heroes Jack and Bobby Charlton. Woodhorn Church Museum is housed in a restored Saxon church and contains a collection of medieval carved stones. In the Queen Elizabeth II Silver Jubilee Park the Woodhorn Colliery Museum recalls the mining and social history of the area. Sits on banks of River Wansbeck.

ASHLEWORTH Gloucestershire SO8125
Village off A417, 5 miles (8km) N of Gloucester
Set beside the River Severn is a picturesque group made up of a 15th-century manor house, a church with fine medieval screen and a huge tithe barn of 1500 (National Trust).

ASHLEY Northamptonshire SP7990
Village off B664, 5 miles (8km) NE of Market Harborough
In Welland Valley, close to Leicestershire border, with Gothic school and medieval church remodelled by Sir George Gilbert Scott.

Tithe barn, Ashleworth.

ASHLEY Staffordshire SJ7636
Village off A53, 6 miles (10km) NE of Market Drayton
Pleasant old village hidden among high-hedge lanes and close to fine woodland.

ASHMANSWORTH Hampshire SU4157
Village off A343, 9 miles (14km) NE of Andover
The highest chalkland village in England at 800ft (235m). Flint and brick cottages and an interesting church, never Victorianised.

ASHMORE Dorset ST9117
Village off B3081, 9 miles (14km) N of Blandford Forum
Hilltop downland village in Cranborne Chase (see), centred around its famous, supposedly Roman, pond.

ASHOVER Derbyshire SK3463
Village off B6036, 3 miles (5km) W of Clay Cross
Steep hills surround the village, beside the Amber Valley, at the heart of this large northeast Derbyshire parish. The buildings are of limestone and gritstone, quarried locally. The Crispin inn claims to date from the Agincourt period, but is more likely 17th century. Next to it, surrounded by ancient trees, the imposing church contains fine tombs and wall monuments.

ASHOW Warwickshire SP3170
Village off B4115, 2 miles (3km) SE of Kenilworth
Charmingly situated beside the River Avon, the village has some well-preserved thatched cottages and a church of great interest.

ASHPRINGTON Devon SX8157
Village off A381, 2 miles (3km) SE of Totnes
Beautiful scenery on the Dart River and Bow Creek. Many pretty 19th-century estate cottages. Avenue Cottage Gardens have woodland walks as well.

ASHRIDGE Hertfordshire SP9912
see Little Gaddesden

ASHTEAD Surrey TQ1857
Suburb, NE Leatherhead
Originally a main-road village on chalk springline, has retained friendly character with church and Ashtead Park set slightly above on North Downs.

ASHTON Northamptonshire TL0588
Village off A605, 1 mile (2km) E of Oundle
Model village of picturesque thatched Tudor-style cottages around village green, built in 1900 for Charles Rothschild. Huge crowds gather on second Sunday each October for World Conker Championships, held outside Chequered Skipper pub. Fish Museum and rural life exhibits in former mill, with late 19th-century machinery for water and electricity supply.

ASHTON, HIGHER AND LOWER Devon SX8484
Villages off B3193, 3 miles (5km) N of Chudleigh
Higher Ashton church is on a rocky knoll. Good interior – wooden screens with paintings. Lower Ashton on the River Teign; wonderful scenery.

ASHTON KEYNES Wiltshire SU0494
Village off B4696, 4 miles (6km) W of Cricklade
On the upper Thames, surrounded by lakes formed by gravel extraction, now the Cotswold Water Park with nature trails, angling, sailing. Good Georgian houses in the village.

ASHTON UNDER HILL Hereford and Worcester SO9937
Village off A435, 4 miles (6km) SW of Evesham
Small village below Bredon Hill. Church has interesting 17th- and 19th-century features. Bredon Springs (organic garden) open in summer.

ASHTON UPON MERSEY Greater Manchester SJ7892
see Sale

ASHTON-IN-MAKERFIELD Greater Manchester SJ5798
Town on A49, 4 miles (6km) S of Wigan
Three Sisters Recreation Area includes an international karting circuit. In the church, the Holy Hand of St Edmund Arrowsmith is said to have miraculous powers.

ASHTON-UNDER-LYNE Greater Manchester SJ9399
Town on A627, 6 miles (10km) E of Manchester
An industrial mill town in the foothills of the Pennines with its own canal. The Grade I Listed Church of St Michael and All Angels has a spectacular stained-glass window. Portland Basin Heritage Centre tells the social and industrial history of the Tameside area, while the Museum of Manchester tells the story of the Manchester Regiment.

ASHURST West Sussex TQ1715
Village on B2135, 3 miles (5 km) N of Steyning
Secluded village above River Adur with church hidden among trees containing rare 'vamping horn'. Village celebrated in Hilaire Belloc's *The Four Men.*

ASHWELL Hertfordshire TL2639
Village off A505, 4 miles (6km) NE of Baldock
Highly attractive, chic commuter village at source of River Rhee. Old houses from 14th century on. Spacious church with tall tower, medieval graffiti and drawings, including one of Old St Paul's. Brewing centre until 1950s, retains good pubs – Three Tuns, Rose and Crown, Bushel and Strike. Arbury Banks near by is Iron Age fort.

ASKAM IN FURNESS Cumbria SD2177
Village on A595, 3 miles (5km) N of Dalton-in-Furness
Old ironworks town with spectacular views of the Duddon estuary. K Shoes factory has been developed as a visitor attraction.

ASKHAM Cumbria NY5123
Village off A6, 4 miles (6km) S of Penrith
Askham Hall home to Earls of Lonsdale. Fifth Earl instituted Lonsdale belt award for boxing and was first president of Automobile Association.

ASKHAM BRYAN North Yorkshire SE5548
Village off A64, 4 miles (6km) SW of York
A small village with a Norman church with a fish window, a delightful village pond and an Institute of Agriculture.

ASKRIGG North Yorkshire SD9491
Village off A684, 4 miles (6km) NW of Aysgarth
Small market town once famous for hand-knitting and clock-making; now best known as location for the television series *All Creatures Great and Small.*

ASLACKBY Lincolnshire TF0830
Village off A15, 7 miles (11km) N of Bourne
Pronounced 'aiz-el-by'. Pretty village in valley off main road, Georgian Old Rectory and other houses around 14th-century and later church.

ASLOCKTON Nottinghamshire SK7440
Village off A52, 2 miles (3km) E of Bingham
Peaceful village, birthplace of Thomas Cranmer who became supportive Archbishop to Henry VIII and wrote the Book of Common Prayer.

ASPATRIA Cumbria NY1441
Small town on A596, 8 miles (13km) NE of Maryport
Elaborate memorial fountain to 'Watery Wilfred', Sir Wilfred Lawson MP, crusader of Temperance Movement. Church contains ancient relics including Viking hogback tombstone.

ASPLEY GUISE Bedfordshire SP9335
Village off A5130, 2 miles (3km) N of Woburn
The village is known particularly for its towering holly hedges. Set among pinewoods and sandy hills, it was renowned for its gentle climate and salubrious air in Victorian times. Plenty of convalescent homes in the area, good walking on Wavendon Heath and a notable Victorian church at Aspley Heath, to the south.

ASTBURY Cheshire SJ8461
Village on A34, 1 mile (2km) S of Congleton
The churchyard boasts a 1,000-year-old yew tree and the church has an unusual detached tower and steeple. Little Moreton Hall, just outside the village, is a National Trust property and a fine example of a black and white Tudor hall. May Day is still observed, with dancing round a maypole in the grounds of the Queen Anne rectory.

ASTHALL Oxfordshire SP2811
Village off A40, 2 miles (3km) E of Burford
A medieval church of great interest is among the attractions of this idyllic crossing-point on the River Windrush.

ASTLEY Hereford and Worcester SO7867
Village off B4196, 3 miles (5km) SW of Stourport-on-Severn
Prime Minister Stanley Baldwin resided in this hillside village, which has an outstanding Norman and medieval church. Astley Vineyard is open to visitors.

ASTLEY Warwickshire SP3189
Village off B4102, 4 miles (6km) SW of Nuneaton
The church, rebuilt in the 1600s, is noted for its chancel stalls of about 1400. Arbury Hall (limited opening), the childhood home of Lady Jane Grey, is a Tudor house, Gothicised in the 18th century, with a fine interior and extensive grounds. The novelist George Eliot was born at South Farm on the Arbury estate in 1819 (see Chilvers Coton).

ASTLEY ABBOTS Shropshire SO7096
Village off B4373, 2 miles (3km) N of Bridgnorth
Dunval Hall (not open) is a superb example of an Elizabethan timber-framed manor house. The church, Norman and later, has a good 17th-century hammerbeam roof.

ASTON West Midlands SP0888
Area in Birmingham
An imposing church and Aston Hall, a splendid Jacobean mansion open to the public since 1858, distinguish this inner Birmingham suburb. Birmingham's second university 1½ miles (2km) to the south.

ASTON BLANK Gloucestershire SP1219
Village off A429, 3 miles (5km) NE of Northleach
Visitors to this exposed village, once known as Cold Aston, come to inspect the ancient church and to drink at the 17th-century pub, the Plough.

ASTON CANTLOW Warwickshire SP1460
Village off B4089, 4 miles (6km) NE of Alcester
The 17th-century King's Head stands near picturesque Guild House. Shakespeare's father John is reputed to have married Mary Arden in the church in 1557.

ASTON CLINTON Buckinghamshire SP8812
Village on A41, 4 miles (6km) E of Aylesbury
On busy Aylesbury–Tring road, soon to be bypassed. Evelyn Waugh wrote part of his first novel, *Decline and Fall*, while teaching at a school here, 1925. Bell inn is smart former coaching hostelry. Signs of Rothschild influence, but Sir Anthony de Rothschild's grand Victorian mansion in Green Park was knocked down in 1950s.

ASTON MUNSLOW Shropshire SO5186
Village on B4368, 7 miles (11km) NE of Craven Arms
Pretty Corvedale village where the pub is one of several attractive timber-framed buildings.

ASTON ON CLUN Shropshire SO3981
Village on B4368, 3 miles (5km) W of Craven Arms
A highly individual village with mock-Gothic pub, a round house and a tree ceremonially decked with flags on 29 May each year.

ASTON ROWANT Oxfordshire SU7299
Village off B4009, 4 miles (6km) NE of Watlington
Beneath the wooded edge of the Chilterns, the Norman and medieval church stands among a mixture of old cottages and modern houses.

ASTON SUBEDGE Gloucestershire SP1441
Village on B4035, 2 miles (3km) N of Chipping Campden
With its back to the Cotswold Edge and facing the Vale of Evesham, the village boasts a notable Georgian church and attractive manor house.

ASTON TIRROLD Oxfordshire SU5586
Village off A417, 3 miles (5km) SE of Didcot
The ancient church with its Saxon doorway stands near the 18th-century Chequers inn in this pleasant village below the downs.

ASTON-UPON-TRENT Derbyshire SK4129
Village off A6, 6 miles (10km) SE of Derby
Attractive dormitory village for Derby, set in farmland beside Trent and Mersey Canal. Prehistoric monuments revealed by 1960s aerial survey.

ASWARBY Lincolnshire TF0639
Hamlet off A15, 4 miles (6km) S of Sleaford
Road curves around park of demolished hall. Tudor-style estate cottages. Birthplace of George Bass, who sailed round Tasmania 1798, and named Bass Strait.

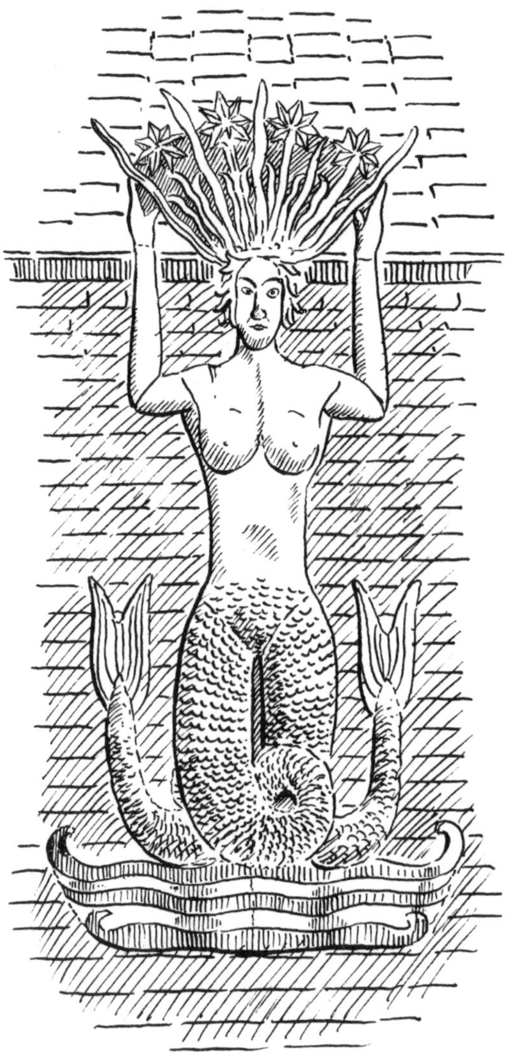

Sign in the courtyard of the Mytton and Mermaid inn at Atcham.

ATCHAM Shropshire SJ5409
Village on B4380, 4 miles (6km) SE of Shrewsbury
The estate village for nearby Attingham Park (National Trust), a sophisticated house of 1783 with fine furniture and silver and a notable picture gallery by Nash. St Eata's Church has Roman stones in the tower, Saxon window, good Norman doorway and medieval and Elizabethan glass. A modern bridge over the River Severn stands side-by-side with a redundant bridge of 1770.

ATHELHAMPTON Dorset SY7694
Hamlet on A35, 1 mile (2km) E of Puddletown
Handsome house with a Hall of 1500, surrounded by formal gardens designed in the 1890s.

ATHELNEY Somerset ST3428
Hamlet off A361, 5 miles (8km) W of Langport
Supposedly where King Alfred burnt the cakes, and the site of an abbey founded by him, now gone.

ATHERINGTON Devon SS5922
Village on B3217, 7 miles (11km) S of Barnstaple
High up, with wide views. Fifteenth-century church with the only medieval rood loft surviving in Devon and medieval monuments .

ATHERSTONE Warwickshire SP3097
Town on A5, 5 miles (8km) NW of Nuneaton
Handsome buildings dating from the 16th to 19th centuries abound in the streets of this old market town, with the timber-framed Old Swan a major attraction. St Mary's is an interesting former friary church. The nearby ruins of Merevale Abbey, founded in 1148, are worth visiting for the Church of Our Lady, which has a wealth of fascinating medieval features.

ATHERTON Greater Manchester SD6703
Town on A577, 4 miles (6km) SW of Bolton
Once had a thriving cotton industry, now diversified. Dorma factory and Barrs soft drinks are two main employers today.

ATHOLL Tayside
Historic region of Scotland
Mountainous region including most of north Perthshire and bounded by Badenoch, Rannoch Moor, Loch Tummel and Glenshee; it contains the vast Forest of Atholl .

ATTENBOROUGH Nottinghamshire SK5034
Hamlet on A6005, 1 mile (2km) S of Beeston
Hamlet with beautiful 13th- to 14th-century and later church. Former Trent Valley gravel pits flooded to create 360 acre (145ha) nature reserve.

ATTINGHAM PARK Shropshire SJ5409
see Atcham

ATTLEBOROUGH Norfolk TM0495
Small town off A11, 5 miles (8km) SW of Wymondham
This busy market town dating from Saxon times has a Norman church. Some townspeople sailed with the Pilgrim Fathers to America.

ATWORTH Wiltshire ST8565
Village on A365, 3 miles (5km) NW of Melksham
Large village, with the older part up towards the church, on a by-road. Oddly detached 15th-century church tower. Local museum.

AUBOURN Lincolnshire SK9262
Village off A46, 6 miles (10km) SW of Lincoln
Hall dating from the 16th century and later, with old church beside; redundant Victorian church at other end of village, which has two parallel streets.

AUCHTERARDER Tayside NN9412
Small town on A824, 8 miles (13km) SE of Crieff
Royal burgh with one long street which was once a linen-weaving and woollen-manufacturing centre. The famous Gleneagles Hotel and golf courses are near by.

AUCHTERMUCHTY Fife NO2311
Small town on A91, 9 miles (14km) W of Cupar
A royal burgh since 1517, Auchtermuchty was once royal hunting base on the edge of the fertile Howe of Fife before becoming a handloom weaving centre. It retains many 18th-century houses including the Town House. Myres Castle dates from 1549 and was a Z-plan castle belonging to the Scrymgeour family.

AUDENSHAW Greater Manchester SJ9197
Town off M67, 5 miles (8km) E of Manchester
The council offices are housed in Ryecroft Hall, originaly the home of Abel Buckley, owner of the Ryecroft mills at Ashton-under-Lyne.

AUDLEM Cheshire SJ6543
Village on A529, 6 miles (10km) N of Market Drayton
Most southerly town in Cheshire, served by the Shropshire Union Canal. The canal was once used to carry locally-produced cheese to Liverpool and Birmingham. The wharf now serves the leisure craft which frequent the canal, the warehouse having been turned into a pub and the mill into a gift shop.

AUDLEY Staffordshire SJ7950
Village on B5500, 4 miles (6km) NW of Newcastle-under-Lyme
Hilltop village overlooking Cheshire Plain, with history of coal-mining and nail-making.

AUDLEY END Essex TL5337
Hamlet off B1383, 1 mile (2km) W of Saffron Walden
Dominated by the colossal Jacobean mansion completed in 1616, originally far bigger than today – 'too large for a king', as James I commented – now English Heritage. Beautiful 17th-century screen in great hall, Robert Adam interiors. Park landscaped by 'Capability' Brown with Adam bridge and temple. Victorian garden has been restored.

AUGHTON Humberside SE7038
Village off B1228, 11 miles (18km) W of Market Weighton
Earthworks of a motte and bailey castle are visible. The 'tump' near the church is the site of Aske family's fortified dwelling.

AUGHTON Lancashire SD3905
Village off A59, 2 miles (3km) SW of Ormskirk
Old village with two historically interesting churches, now one of the more attractive residential areas in the heart of rich farmland.

AULDEARN Highland NH9255
Village off A96, 2 miles (3km) E of Nairn
Village site of battle in 1645 when Montrose defeated Covenanters. Late 17th-century Boath Doocot (dovecote), circular building (National Trust for Scotland).

The 17th-century Boath dovecote at Auldearn.

AULT HUCKNALL Derbyshire SK4665
Hamlet off A617, 5 miles (8km) NW of Mansfield
Hamlet on the ridge close to Nottinghamshire border, neighbouring Hardwick Park and Hall. Philosopher Hobbes is buried in Norman and later church.

AUST Avon ST5788
Village off A403, 4 miles (6km) W of Thornbury
The little village on the Severn estuary where the huge Severn Bridge takes off for Wales (once the ferry base). The suspension bridge is enormous – the towers 400ft (133m) and the main span 3,240ft (1,000m). Wide views from the bridge and from Aust. The bridge was opened in 1966 and increasing traffic has made a second bridge necessary.

AUSTERFIELD South Yorkshire SK6694
Village on A614, 1 mile (2km) NE of Bawtry
Austerfield Manor was the birthplace of Nonconformist William Bradford, a pilgrim on the *Mayflower*.

AVEBURY Wiltshire SU1069
Village on A4361, 6 miles (10km) W of Marlborough
The village is partly tucked inside a 4,500-year-old circular bank and ditch enclosing 28 acres (11ha), along with the famous big stone circle. Stone avenues lead to the enclosure. Just outside is the partly Saxon church and Avebury Manor (National Trust), early 16th century with topiary and flower gardens. The Alexander Keiller Museum (English Heritage) explains the prehistory of this important area, and the Great Barn Museum in the 17th-century thatched barn has bygone Wiltshire life. See Silbury and West Kennett.

AVELEY Essex TQ5680
Town off A13, 3 miles (5km) NW of Grays
Once a village, now mostly post-war housing estates. Belhus Woods Country Park to north, old woodland with gravel pits, walking, fishing, riding.

AVENING Gloucestershire ST8898
Village on B4104, 2 miles (3km) SE of Nailsworth
A large village, formerly a cloth-making centre, perched on a steep hillside. The church, with Saxon and Norman work, has a monument to reformed pirate Henry Brydges.

AVERHAM Nottinghamshire SK7654
Village off A617, 2 miles (3km) W of Newark
Pronounced 'Air-am'. Overlooked by Staythorpe Power Station, but still an attractive village whose Norman and later church stands beside the River Trent, with fine monuments to the Suttons. Donald Wolfit made his first stage appearance at the Robin Hood Theatre, built by an early 20th-century rector in the rectory grounds, and still a theatre today.

AVETON GIFFORD Devon SX6947
Village off A379, 3 miles (5km) NW of Kingsbridge
Pronounced Orton Jifford.The church was ruined by a bomb in 1943, and rebuilt afterwards. On the road from Modbury to Kingsbridge, a medieval causeway nearly 3/4 mile (1km) long across watermeadows.

AVIEMORE Highland NH8913
Village off A9, 11 miles (18km) NE of Kingussie
Lying in wooded stretch of Spey Valley and developed in 1960s as year-round resort. Wide range of facilities, accommodation and easy access to other areas make it popular holiday centre. Cairngorm Ski Area 8 miles (13km) distant, watersports on Loch Morlich, hill-walking and climbing in Cairngorms and varied low-level walking, all in surroundings of great natural beauty.

AVINGTON Berkshire SU3767
Hamlet off A4, 2 miles (3km) E of Hungerford
Tiny and pretty, with a small and interesting Norman church – elaborate and sagging chancel arch and font carved with strange compressed figures.

AVINGTON Hampshire SU5332
Hamlet off B3047, 4 miles (6km) NE of Winchester
Small village close to Avington Park, a large brick mansion mostly of 1710 with good later 18th-century interiors. Best Georgian church in the county – austere brick, complete inside with original fittings of 1770. Mahogany pews, and hat pegs along the side walls.

AVON, RIVER Avon
River
The river gives its name to the new county, fittingly, as it runs right through the middle. The Kennet and Avon Canal (1790s) is beside it to the edge of Bath, and to Bristol the river itself was used as a canal from 1727. From Clifton (see) the river runs through a deep picturesque gorge, then widens and joins the Severn estuary at the modern port of Avonmouth (see).

AVON, RIVER Warwickshire
River
The Avon enters Warwickshire near Rugby (see) in the northeast and flows southwest through the county. Access from the River Severn at Tewkesbury (see) made it an important trading route, contributing to the growth of major towns like Warwick and Stratford (see). These towns, and the many riverside villages, still benefit from its attractions. Navigable up to Stratford, it remains popular for cruising.

AVON, RIVER Wiltshire/Dorset
River
Starting as small streams in the Vale of Pewsey, the young Avon River turns south, still through chalk, and is lined with villages all the way down to Salisbury. There tributaries increase as the river wanders through the wider valley below Salisbury, with the Avon Forest Park at Ringwood, finally meeting the sea at Christchurch Harbour.

AVONCROFT MUSEUM OF BUILDINGS Hereford and Worcester SO9668
see Bromsgrove

AVONMOUTH Avon ST5178
Town on A403, 6 miles (10km) NW of Bristol
Developed at the mouth of the Avon in the later 19th century because ships were becoming larger and could not get up the narrow river to Bristol. From 1868 docks were constructed, and a big smelting plant followed. The docks still flourish, recently on the south bank as well, and there is much industry.

AWLISCOMBE Devon ST1301
Village on A373, 2 miles (3km) NW of Honiton
Prominent medieval church and the village down in the little valley. St Cyres Hill above gives long views.

AXBRIDGE Somerset ST4354
Small town off A371, 2 miles (3km) W of Cheddar
Once a town, with a market place and town hall of 1833. King John's Hunting Lodge (National Trust) is a 15th-century jettied timber-framed house, much too late for King John. The church is 15th century, very fine, with a fan vault and unusual plaster ceiling of 1636.

AXE EDGE Derbyshire SK0271

Beauty spot on A53, 2 miles (3km) SW of Buxton

Dramatic views from Buxton – Leek road, A53, along this gritstone escarpment, source of the rivers Manifold, Dove, Wye, Goyt and Dane.

AXHOLME, ISLE OF Humberside SE7080

Historic region

Until 17th century was actually an inland island. Charles I engaged Dutch engineer Vermuyden to drain the Chace and Isle of Axholme in 1626. The Dutch influence is as strong as ever with flat fertile fields, deep dykes, straightened watercourses and windmill towers dotting the landscape. Even the buildings of the Isle feature bright clay pantiles which originated in Holland.

AXMINSTER Devon SY2998

Small town on A35, 5 miles (8km) NW of Lyme Regis

A proper small market town with many pleasant 18th- and 19th-century houses. Prominent medieval church, and the main street curves through a little market place. The famous Axminster carpet factory started here in 1755, and made large and fine carpets for great houses such as Saltram and Powderham (where they still survive).

AXMOUTH Devon SY2591

Village on B3172, 1 mile (2km) NE of Seaton

On the wide Axe estuary, set just back from the sea. A neat village running down the hill, with thatched cottages and a medieval church down by the river. All the way to Lyme Regis in Dorset is a wide belt of wooded coastal landslips, impenetrable apart from one footpath.

AYCLIFFE Durham NZ2822

Village on A167, 5 miles (8km) N of Darlington

Older village near Newton Aycliffe (see). St Andrew's Church of Saxon origin with 12th- and 13th-century expansions.

AYDON Northumberland NZ0066

Hamlet on B6321, 2 miles (3km) NE of Corbridge

Aydon Castle, built at the end of the 13th century and converted to a farmhouse in the 17th century.

AYLESBURY Buckinghamshire SP8213

Town on A41, 36 miles (58km) NW of London

The county town of Buckinghamshire since the 18th century, Aylesbury has suffered badly from post-war planning and development. At the heart of the old town is the cobbled market square with the 18th-century County Hall (where the Great Train Robbers were tried), the mock-Jacobean corn exchange of 1865, the 1870s Gothic clock tower and statues including local notable John Hampden.

The parish church, St Mary's, was so dilapidated it had to be almost rebuilt by Sir George Gilbert Scott from 1849 onwards. Prebendal House close by was once the home of the 18th-century reformer John Wilkes. The National Trust cherishes the 15th-century King's Head inn, with its fine contemporary heraldic window, and the county museum of local history in Church Street preserves the 18th-century grammar school, with a pair of 15th-century houses opposite it in the town's best street. Temple Square is rewarding, too.

The town has always been the principal market centre for the Vale of Aylesbury, stretching out below the Chiltern Hills. For centuries the Vale has fattened cattle for London tables on its lush grass and reared the celebrated Aylesbury ducks.

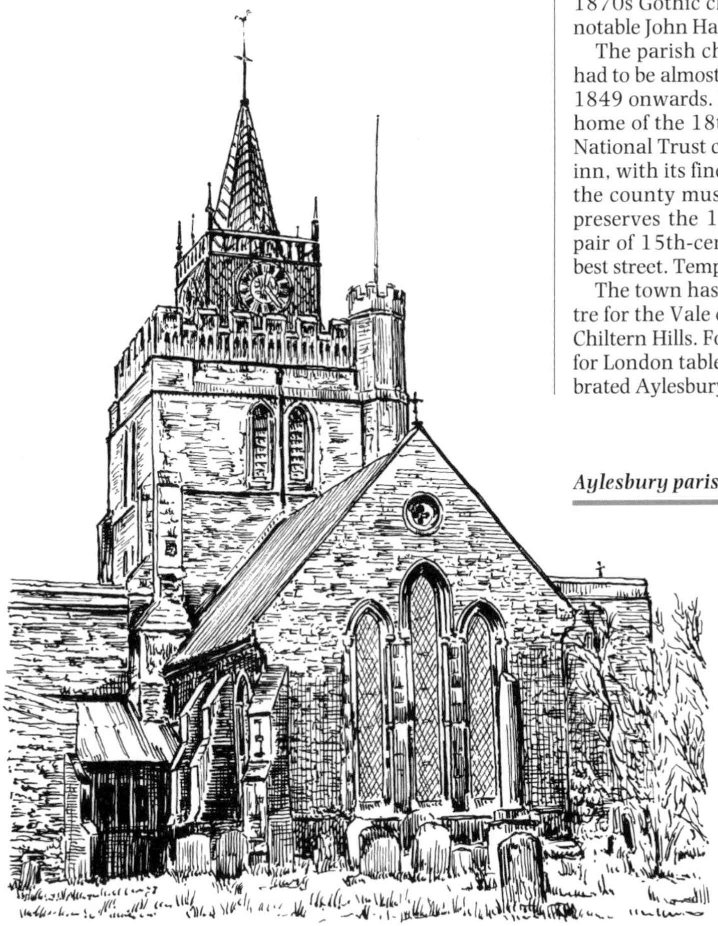

Aylesbury parish church.

AYLESFORD Kent TQ7358

Village off A20, 3 miles (5km) NW of Maidstone

Charming historical village on River Medway with busy industrial suburb. A place of many battles; Hengist beat the British here, AD455, and Alfred the Great and Edmund Ironside beat the Danes, AD893 and AD1016. Medieval bridge on site of ancient ford for long only Medway crossing between Maidstone and Rochester. Carmelite friary, founded 1240, rededicated 1949, now place of pilgrimage.

AYLESTONE Leicestershire SK5700

District of Leicester

Now absorbed into Leicester. Long medieval packhorse bridge and causeway. Aylestone Hall, 19th-century appearance concealing Elizabethan parts, belonged to Vernon family.

AYLSHAM Norfolk TG1926

Small town on B1354, 12 miles (19km) N of Norwich

A flourishing market town that grew to prosperity under the ownership of John of Gaunt, son of Edward III. Steam trains run on the Bure Valley Railway to Wroxham, a pleasant journey through the Broadlands. The flint-faced Church of St Michael has the grave of the landscape gardener Humphry Repton.

AYMESTREY Hereford and Worcester SO4265

Village on A4110, 6 miles (10km) NW of Leominster

An 18th-century bridge crosses the River Lugg, which runs through a steep-sided gorge here. Church worth visiting for 16th-century chancel screen.

AYNHO Northamptonshire SP5133

Village on B4100, 6 miles (10km) SE of Banbury

Neat ironstone village overlooking River Cherwell and M40, close to Oxfordshire border. Aynhoe Park, Jacobean, Carolean and early 18th-century mansion, with early 19th-century work by Soane (now apartments but limited opening), stands in park landscaped by Capability Brown in 1760s. Seventeenth-century grammar school, 19th-century almshouses. Village stocks. Medieval church rebuilt in 18th century.

AYOT ST LAWRENCE Hertfordshire TL1916

Village off B656, 2 miles (3km) W of Welwyn

Attractive village, secluded in woodland. Shaw's Corner (National Trust) was home of George Bernard Shaw 1906–50. *Pygmalion* and *Saint Joan* both written here. Shaw plays acted on lawn in summer. Striking 18th-century church with Greek-style portico and colonnades, picturesque ruins of medieval church. Brocket Arms inn is said to go back to the 14th century and is haunted.

AYOT ST PETER Hertfordshire TL2115

Hamlet off B656, 1 mile (2km) SW of Welwyn

Church (1870) by JP Seddon, notable Arts and Crafts interior. Ayot Greenway is an attractive footpath along former railway line.

AYR Strathclyde NS3321

Town on A79, 12 miles (19km) SW of Kilmarnock

Ayrshire's commercial and administrative centre is the biggest town on the Firth of Clyde coast, with remnants of the close-packed alleys of the medieval town near the River Ayr and wide Victorian streets to the southwest behind the long sandy beach. It was chartered as a royal burgh in 1202 and rivalled Glasgow as a trading centre and port up until the early 1800s. Cromwell chose to make it his administrative centre and built a fortress here, now destroyed, although the Auld Kirk, with its mort safe to protect graves, was funded by him and still stands.

Robert Burns was christened here and born in nearby Alloway (see). Ayr is the capital of Burns Country, and the cobbled 13th-century Auld Brig features in the poem *Twa Brigs*, which saved it from destruction in the 1900s.

The arrival of the railway in 1840 opened up the area to tourism, which helped fund the building of the prosperous and spacious new town area. There are good shops and entertainment facilities, three golf courses, and Scotland's main racecourse, venue for the Scottish Grand National.

AYSGARTH North Yorkshire SE0088

Village on A684, 7miles (11km) W of Leyburn

On hill above River Ure, crossed by attractive stone arch bridge, and has an impressive set of waterfalls. Carriage Museum at Yore Mill houses a collection of horse-drawn vehicles. St Andrew's Church above mill has a splendid rood screen and abbot's stall from Jervaulx Abbey. Yorkshire Dales National Park information centre is near by.

AYSTON Leicestershire SK8600

Hamlet off A47, 1 mile (2km) N of Uppingham

Ironstone Rutland village with old cottages and estate houses; 1807 Ayston Hall; 13th-century and later church with 15th-century stained glass.

B

BABBACOMBE Devon SX9265

Suburb of Torquay

Originally a little fishing hamlet, but from the middle of the 19th century it grew villas as part of Torquay. Rich and splendid 1860s church, All Saints', by William Butterfield, and a few old cottages surviving on the cliff top. Cliff railway running down to the sea. Babbacombe Model Village.

BABCARY Somerset ST5628

Village off A37, 3 miles (5km) NW of Sparkford

Small stone-built village, where James Woodforde, the diarist, was curate in the 1760s.

BABWORTH Nottinghamshire SK6880

Hamlet on A620, 2 miles (3km) W of Retford

William Bradford and William Brewster were worshippers at this 13th-century church before sailing in the *Mayflower* with the Pilgrims to the New World.

BACONSTHORPE Norfolk TG1236
Village off A148, 3 miles (5km) SE of Holt
The small village is dominated by the romantic ruins of Baconsthorpe Castle (English Heritage), a fortified manor house built in the 15th century.

BACTON Hereford and Worcester SO3732
Village off B4347, 4 miles (6km) NW of Pontrilas
Lonely settlement tucked away on slopes of Golden Valley. Small church has famous memorial to Blanche Parry, lady-in-waiting to Elizabeth I.

BACTON Norfolk TG3433
Village on B1159, 5 miles (8km) NE of North Walsham
The glittering lights of the vast Bacton Gas terminal contrast vividly with the lonely ruins of Broomholm Priory.

BACTON Suffolk TM0567
Village off B1113, 5 miles (8km) N of Stowmarket
An agricultural village, once the scene of a brutal murder, with handsome church dating from 14th and 15th centuries.

BACUP Lancashire SD8622
Town on A671, 6 miles (10km) S of Burnley
One of Rossendale's main towns, it is the best remaining example of a small Lancashire cotton town, although many of the terraced houses and mills have disappeared. Market hall, the Maden Baths and the Conservative Club are fine examples of Victorian architecture. The old sandstone setted roads still remain in places.

BADBURY RINGS Dorset ST9603
see Shapwick

BADBY Northamptonshire SP5658
Village off A361, 3 miles (5km) SW of Daventry
Attractive thatched ironstone cottages. Knightley Way footpath skirts ancient beeches of Badby Wood. Iron Age hillfort on Arbury Hill, county's highest point.

BADDESLEY CLINTON Warwickshire SP2070
Village off A4141, 7 miles (11km) NW of Warwick
Baddesley Clinton House (National Trust) is an intriguing 14th-century moated manor house altered in 1634. There is a 16th-century window in the church.

BADGEWORTH Gloucestershire SO9101
Village off A46, 3 miles (5km) SW of Cheltenham
In an unromantic setting, the church has a 14th-century gem of a chapel. The rare 'Badgeworth Buttercup' is carefully conserved near by.

BADINGHAM Suffolk TM3068
Village off A1120, 3 miles (5km) NE of Framlingham
Badingham House is the home of the Academy of Transcendental Meditation. The grounds are open in the summer for walks through the woods.

BADMINTON (GREAT BADMINTON) Avon ST8082
Village off B4040, 5 miles (8km) E of Chipping Sodbury
Home of the famous annual Horse Trials, held in the park of Badminton House. The house is huge, 17th and 18th century. The game of badminton was invented here. The village has colour-washed cottages, and some elaborate thatched ones. Almshouses of 1714.

BADSEY Hereford and Worcester SP0743
Village off B4035, 2 miles (3km) E of Evesham
In the heart of market garden country, Badsey is famous for asparagus. Fine stone and timber manor house, once the property of Evesham Abbey.

BADSWORTH West Yorkshire SE4614
Village off A638, 5 miles (8km) S of Pontefract
An estate village until 1926 when the Badsworth Hall estate was broken up. Only one working farm remains.

BAG ENDERBY Lincolnshire TF3472
Hamlet off A16, 5 miles (8km) NW of Spilsby
Pleasant Wolds hamlet where Tennyson's father was rector, as well as neighbouring Somersby. Annual commemorative services alternate between the two.

BAGENDON Gloucestershire SP0106
Village off A435, 3 miles (5km) N of Cirencester
Deep in the wooded Churn Valley are an intriguing Norman church and the surviving earthworks of the Celtic capital of the Dubonni tribe.

BAGGY POINT Devon SS4140
see Croyde

BAGINTON Warwickshire SP3474
Village off A46, 3 miles (5km) S of Coventry
On the edge of Coventry Airport is the Midland Air Museum. The village also has an interesting 13th-century church and earthworks of a 14th-century castle.

BAGSHOT Surrey SU9063
Town on A30, 4 miles (6km) NE of Camberley
Formerly wild and dangerous heath, haunt of highwaymen along the Portsmouth road. Since early 19th century heath has been enclosed for housing and tamed so that it is genteel and discreet. Town centre consists of a few 19th-century buildings, the rest a land of villas, shrubs and evergreen hedges. Bagshot Heath is a country park.

BAILDON West Yorkshire SE1539
Town off A6038, 4 miles (6km) N of Bradford
The Parish Church of St John was built in 1848 and Baildon Hall has been altered many times over the years.

BAINBRIDGE North Yorkshire SD9390
Village on A684, 4 miles (6km) E of Hawes
Village green still displays stocks. The tradition of horn-blowing to guide travellers from the forest is still practised on winter evenings.

BAINTON Humberside SE9652
Village on A163, 5 miles (8km) SW of Great Driffield
Fine church built in 16th century believed to be fourth on this site since the 7th century. Norman font preserved from a former church.

BAKEWELL Derbyshire SK2168
Town on A6, 7 miles (11km) NW of Matlock
Attractive market town in heart of Peak District National Park, on River Wye. Noted particularly for Bakewell pudding, delicious result of mistake by cook at inn now the Rutland Arms. Haddon Hall, home of Dukes of Rutland, is unspoilt medieval manor house 1 mile (2km) south. Major agricultural show in August and weekly cattle market on Mondays.

BALA (Y BALA) Gwynedd SH9236
Town on A494, 12 miles (19km) SW of Corwen
Major watersports centre by Bala Lake (Llyn Tegid), Wales's largest natural sheet of water, alongside which runs a narrow-gauge railway. The town, encircled by mountain ranges, developed around a wooded mound, Tomen-y-Bala, of Norman or earlier origin. Thriving woollen industry here in 18th century. Town's many memorials testify to its important place in the Nonconformist movement.

BALCOMBE West Sussex TQ3130
Village on B2036, 5 miles (8km) N of Haywards Heath
Friendly little village, retaining its identity with pub and school, lying in beautiful wooded landscape of hills and streams.

BALDOCK Hertfordshire TL2434
Town on A505, 6 miles (10km) N of Stevenage
Romantically named after old Baghdad by the medieval Knights Templar, who founded it. Developed as market town on Great North Road.

BALERNO Lothian NT1666
Village off A70, 4 miles (6km) SW of Edinburgh
Now a dormitory suburb of Edinburgh but once known for its corn and papermills, powered by Water of Leith. Malleny House incorporates old royal hunting lodge.

BALLACHULISH Highland NN0858
Village on A82, 15 miles (24km) S of Fort William
Roof-slate quarrying village from 17th century until 1950s, attractively situated beside Loch Leven to east of new road bridge.

BALLANTRAE Strathclyde NX0882
Village on A77, 12 miles (19km) SW of Girvan
Once a fishing village, now holiday and retirement centre. Not the inspiration for Robert Louis Stevenson's *Master of Ballantrae*; he just used the name.

BALLATER Grampian NO3695
Small town on A944, 14 miles (23km) NW of Aberdeen
Resort on Deeside in wooded hills, former rail-stop for Balmoral, and overlooked by Lochnagar. Near by lies Pannanich Wells, historic healing spa.

BALLINDALLOCH Grampian NJ1636
Hamlet on A95, 7 miles (11km) SW of Charlestown of Aberlour
Turreted 16th-century castle in lovely grounds with fine interior. Nearby Glenfarclas Distillery run by Grant family for 150 years with visitor centre.

BALLOCH Strathclyde NS3982
Village off A82, 5 miles (8km) N of Dumbarton
Resort on River Leven at southern end of Loch Lomond. Base for first steamer on loch in 1816, still centre for boating and pleasure trips.

BALLOCHMYLE Strathclyde NS5126
Hospital, off B705, 1 mile E of Mauchline
Near by are 200 prehistoric cup-and-ring markings dating from neolithic to early Bronze Age, one of top ten sites in Britain.

BALMACARA Highland NG8028
Village on A87, 3 miles (5km) E of Kyle of Lochalsh
Fine views across Loch Alsh and down the coast. National Trust for Scotland's Balmacara estate has walks in wooded lochside garden, in process of restoration.

BALMAHA Central NS4290
Village on B837, 3 miles (5km) W of Drymen
Watersports centre opposite group of wooded islands on east shore of Loch Lomond on route of West Highland Way.

BALMERINO Fife NO3524
Village off A914, 5 miles (8km) SW of Newport on Tay
Ruined Cistercian abbey in serene wooded position on south of Firth of Tay. Founded 1229 from Melrose (see) with lovely 15th-century chapter house.

BALMORAL CASTLE Grampian NO2595
Royal mansion off A93, 7 miles (11km) E of Braemar
Originally a Deeside 16th-century tower house, castle was rebuilt in present Scottish baronial style after its purchase by Queen Victoria in 1852. The Queen's summer home, not visible from road and only open when the royal Family are not in residence. Extensive gardens, laid out by Prince Albert.

BALQUHIDDER Central NN5320
Village off A84, 4 miles (6km) SW of Lochhearnhead
Burial place at foot of Braes of Balquidder of Rob Roy MacGregor, famous 18th-century Scottish cattle-lifter, outlaw and Jacobite supporter, pardoned in 1725.

BALSALL West Midlands SP2476
Small town on A452, 5 miles (8km) NW of Coventry
Extensive residential area of Balsall Common dwarfs older village of Balsall Street, where Magpie Farm survives as notable timber-framed house.

BAMBURGH Northumberland NU1734
Village on B1340, 5 miles (8km) E of Belford
The castle dates from 12th century when Bamburgh was the capital of the region ruled by the Saxon kings. Restored in the 18th and 19th centuries, the castle often features in films. St Aiden's Church is named after the founder of Lindisfarne Priory. The Grace Darling Museum tells the story of her life and heroism; her tomb is in the churchyard.

BAMFORD Derbyshire SK2083
Village on A6013, 2 miles (3km) NW of Hathersage
Pleasantly situated between the Hope Valley and

Ladybower Reservoir, on the hillside above the River Derwent.

BAMPTON Devon SS9522

Town on B3190, 6 miles (10km) N of Tiverton

In rich farmland just south of Exmoor, really only a large village on the River Batherm. Many Georgian buildings of stone from the local quarries. The village was important in the wool cloth trade in the 18th century. Big medieval church. Local museum.

BAMPTON Oxfordshire SP3103

Small town on A4095, 5 miles (8km) SW of Witney

Famous for its Morris dancers, Bampton is a quiet, stone-built town with a wealth of old buildings and a richly rewarding church.

BANBURY Oxfordshire SP4540

Town on A361, 6 miles (10km) N of Deddington

The famous Banbury Cross, several old inns, a wide range of shops and the attractive People's Park are features of this busy market town. A museum tells the story of Banbury's cloth-making (and its cakes), and a visit to Europe's largest cattle market demonstrates the importance of the town today.

BANBURY LANE Northamptonshire/Oxfordshire

Ancient track between Northampton and Banbury

Ancient trackway, part of Jurassic Way from Cotswolds to the Humber, used as drove road for trading purposes.

BANCHORY Grampian NO6995

Small town on A93, 17 miles (27km) SW of Aberdeen

Known as Gateway to Deeside and beautifully situated between hills and river. Excellent chance of spotting a salmon leaping at the Bridge of Feugh. Birthplace of fiddler James Scott Skinner. Good local walks.

BANFF Grampian NJ6863

Small town on A98, 3 miles (5km) W of Macduff

Architecturally rich ancient seaport, royal burgh and resort on wide Banff Bay with a 16th century market cross and 17th-century town houses. Duff House near by is William Adam's 1735 classical masterpiece, a huge and elaborate mansion, whose grounds are now a park. Local history in museum.

BANGOR Gwynedd SH5771

Town off A5, 14 miles (23km) NW of Capel Curig

The largest town in northwest Wales stands at the foot of a valley beside the Menai Strait. The cathedral has probably been in continuous use longer than any other in Britain. On a site established by St Deiniol, the present restored building goes back to the 13th century. A notable feature is the life-sized carving of Christ of 1518, and in the former cathedral close plants associated with the Bible and medieval church are grown. Across from the cathedral and mirroring its architecture is the University College of North Wales. There is more greenery here, in Treborth Botanical Gardens.

The town's museum exhibits period costume and furniture, the most complete Roman sword in Wales, and mementoes of Thomas Telford. Telford's bridge to Anglesey is one of the sights from Bangor's renovated Victorian pier.

At nearby Tal-y-bont is 15th-century Cochwillan Old Hall and working mill with old weaving machinery. Also close by, 19th-century Penrhyn Castle's neo-Norman bulk (National Trust) conceals an elaborate interior. The solid slate bed reflects the past owners' slate interests and the Industrial Railway Museum contains rolling stock used between their Bethesda quarries and Port Penrhyn.

The gabled vicarage at Banbury.

BANGOR-ON-DEE Clwyd SJ3845
Village on B5069, 5 miles (8km) SE of Wrexham
Also known as Bangor-is-y-coed. Great Celtic monastic site destroyed by Saxons in the early 7th century. Picturesque medieval bridge. Racecourse.

BANHAM Norfolk TM0687
Village on B1113, 6 miles (10km) NW of Diss
This lovely old village, with attractive buildings clustered around a rectangular green, has been a cider-making centre for hundreds of years.

BANKFOOT Tayside NO0635
Village on B867, 5 miles (8km) SE of Dunkeld
Village at the western end of Strathmore at the foot of the Highland line. The Perthshire visitor centre explores the fact and fiction surrounding Macbeth.

BANNOCKBURN Central NS8190
Village on A29, 2 miles (3km) SE of Stirling
Coal-mining village near battlefield where Robert Bruce defeated English in 1314, achieving Scots independence. National Trust for Scotland Heritage Centre with equestrian statue marks site.

BANSTEAD Surrey TQ2559
Town off A2022, 3 miles (5km) S of Sutton
Suburbia has spread over the downs trapping the ancient village once famous for wool and mutton from downland sheep.

BANTHAM Devon SX6643
Hamlet off A379, 4 miles (6km) W of Kingsbridge
At the mouth of the wide Avon estuary, sheltered from the storms by rocky headlands. Sand dunes. Foot ferry across the river.

BANWELL Avon ST3959
Village off A371, 5 miles (8km) E of Weston-super-Mare
Big village, on the junction of three roads. Banwell Castle is a 19th-century folly. Huge 15th-century church tower. Inside, a roof with angels and a rood screen of 1522.

BARBON Cumbria SD6282
Village off A683, 3 miles (5km) N of Kirby Lonsdale
Church of St Bartholomew, built 1892, believed to replace church from 12th century. Interior decoration carved by local craftsmen.

BARBURY CASTLE Wiltshire SU1576
Prehistoric site off B4005, 5 miles (8km) S of Swindon
Big Iron Age hillfort on the Marlborough Downs, with country park.

BARCALDINE Strathclyde NM9641
Village on A828, 5 miles (8km) N of Connel
Village north of Oban and site of Oban Sea Life Centre, with underwater and shoreline displays, seal pools and a seal pup nursery.

BARCHESTON Warwickshire SP2639
Village off B4035, 1 mile (2km) SE of Shipston on Stour
The church of this village beside the River Stour has a leaning tower and two fine doorways. Manor House Farm (not open) has traces of the home of William Sheldon, who imported Flemish weavers in about 1560 to create the first English tapestries. His best-known products were county maps, some of which are preserved in the Victoria and Albert Museum.

BARCOMBE East Sussex TQ4114
Village off A275, 3 miles (5km) N of Lewes
Main village at Barcombe Cross. Barcombe Mills by the River Ouse once had three watermills. Roman road crossed the Ouse here.

BARDEN TOWER North Yorkshire SE0557
Site on B6160, 3 miles (5km) NW of Bolton Abbey
Barden Tower is a hunting lodge dating from 1485. Barden Bridge is 17th century.

BARDNEY Lincolnshire TF1269
Village on B1190, 9 miles (14km) W of Horncastle
Some relics of former Benedictine abbey in St Lawrence's Church, with 15th-century brick chancel. Massive sugarbeet-processing plant on village edge.

BARDON MILL Northumberland NY7764
Village on A69, 4 miles (6km) W of Haydon Bridge
Near the confluence of River Allen and River South Tyne in the heart of Roman Northumberland. Bardon Mill Pottery.

BARDSEA Cumbria SD3074
Village off A5087, 3 miles (5km) S of Ulverston
Village on northern shore of Morecambe Bay, with a country park along the coast. Chapel Island, just off coast, was inhabited in past times by monks who provided refuge for travellers negotiating the quicksands. Conishead Priory, in Gothic Revival style, built on site of former priory, is an Institute of Buddhist Studies.

BARDSEY West Yorkshire SE3643
Village off A58, 7 miles (11km) NE of Leeds
A village with picturesque stone cottages interspersed by large modern detached houses. The church is near the remains of a castle motte.

BARDSEY ISLAND Gwynedd SH1221
Island off SW tip of Lleyn Peninsula
In Welsh 'Ynys Enlli', the 'Island of Currents'. Also called the 'Island of 20,000 Saints'. Three pilgrimages here equalled one to Rome. Although nothing is left of the earliest monastic site, remnants of 13th-century Augustinian abbey, tower and churchyard containing some of the 20,000 reputedly buried here remain. Now a Site of Special Scientific Interest noted for its birdlife.

BARDWELL Suffolk TL9473
Village off A143, 2 miles (3km) N of Ixworth
A 16th-century inn and a 19th-century mill characterise this attractive village.

BARFORD Warwickshire SP2760
Village off A429, 3 miles (5km) S of Warwick
Joseph Arch, agricultural labourer and later an MP

who inspired the first farmworkers' union, was born and died here. His small cottage stands near the church.

BARFORD, ST MICHAEL AND ST JOHN Oxfordshire SP4332
Villages off B4031, 2 miles (3km) W of Deddington
The attractive Barfords, St Michael and St John, face each other across the River Swere, each with a notable Norman church.

BARFRESTON Kent TR2650
Hamlet off A256, 6 miles (10km) NW of Dover
Remote, pretty village with remarkable Norman church of 1080, arguably the best in England. Magnificent, sometimes bizarre carvings, especially over south doorway, reminiscent of Rochester Cathedral. Said to have been built by Adam de Port.

BARGOED Mid Glamorgan ST1599
Town on A469, 8 miles (13km) N of Caerphilly
Rows of terraced houses line this Rhymney Valley town. There is a chance to view glass production at Stuart Crystal's Pengam Glassworks in neighbouring Aberbargoed.

BARHAM Kent TR2050
Village off A2, 6 miles (10km) SE of Canterbury
Little village nestled in beautiful Elham Valley, with pleasant brick and timber-framed houses, restored windmill and nearby vineyard and winery.

BARHAM Suffolk TM1451
Village off A14, 5 miles (8km) N of Ipswich
The fine 13th-century church has a Henry Moore sculpture of the Madonna and Child. Near by is Shrubland Hall, an exclusive health clinic.

BARKBY Leicestershire SK6309
Village off A607, 5 miles (8km) NE of Leicester
Farming village, with stream flowing through it. Thirteenth-century church with interesting Victorian furnishings, and Rysbrack monument to Charlotte Pochin of Barkby Hall.

BARKING Greater London TQ4484
District in borough of Barking and Dagenham
Developed from Saxon times, fishing town at head of Barking Creek. Some remains of Barking Abbey, major medieval nunnery. Eastbury House, Eastbury Square, 16th-century manor house (National Trust), used as arts centre. Elizabeth Fry, 18th-century prison reformer, buried in Quaker cemetery, commemorated in St Margaret's Church. Much industrial development in the 19th and 20th centuries.

BARKING Suffolk TM0753
Village on B1078, 4 miles (6km) S of Stowmarket
Ancient woodland surrounds this farming village. It also has the Tye, 50 acres (20ha) of common land on which cattle graze.

BARKSTON Lincolnshire SK9341
Village off A607, 4 miles (6km) NE of Grantham
Old Manor House on site of monastic grange. Medieval church with ironstone tower and Ancaster stone spire, on edge of Syston Park.

BARKWAY Hertfordshire TL3835
Village on B1368, 4 miles (6km) SE of Royston
Delightful High Street houses on what was once main coaching road from London to Cambridge, with ornate 18th-century milestone.

BARLASTON Staffordshire SJ8938
Village off A34, 3 miles (5km) N of Stone
Village now home to the Wedgwood factory, moved here from Etruria, Stoke-on-Trent, in the early 1940s. The factory is set in estate surroundings near Barlaston Hall (undergoing restoration). An adjacent visitor centre displays Wedgwood ware from 1750 onwards, and other attractions include an art gallery, craftsmen at work and a reconstruction of an original 18th-century workshop at Etruria.

BARLBOROUGH Derbyshire SK4777
Village on A619, 7 miles (11km) W of Worksop
Grey stone, red-roofed village close to the Nottinghamshire/Yorkshire border, with 16th-century hall now used as a school.

BARLEY Hertfordshire TL4038
Village on B1039, 3 miles (5km) SE of Royston
Hunt chases fox across road on gallows sign of the Fox and Hounds. Old houses. Tudor village hall smartly restored in 1970s.

BARLING Essex TQ9389
Village off B1017, 3 miles (5km) N of Shoeburyness
The church tower and spire make a landmark in flat and desolate country of marshes and creeks north of Southend (see).

BARMBY MOOR Humberside SE7748
Village on B1246, 2 miles (3km) W of Pocklington
Allerthorpe Common, a remnant of a once-mighty York forest. Now owned by Forestry Commission.

BARMBY ON THE MARSH Humberside SE6928
Village off A63, 4 miles (6km) W of Howden
Isolated position created by junction of rivers Derwent and Ouse, with a tidal barrage on the River Derwent.

BARMOUTH (ABERMAW) Gwynedd SH6115
Town on A496, 8 miles (13km) W of Dolgellau
Steep-banked holiday centre at mouth of Mawddach estuary. Sands, amusements, passenger ferry to Fairbourne. Around the quayside are the small Lifeboat Museum, Ty Crwn's shipwreck exhibits and Ty Gwyn's Tudor displays. Amongst choice of walks: Dinas Oleu's viewpoint (the National Trust's first-ever property) and path over the Cambrian Coast Railway's bridge. Noteworthy church at Llanbedr.

BARMSTON Humberside TA1659
Village off A165, 5 miles (8km) S of Bridlington
On the coast with fine stretches of firm sands and cliff nooks. Barmston was once the military capital of East Yorkshire.

BARNACK Cambridgeshire TF0705
Village on B1433, 3 miles (5km) SE of Stamford
With a tower windmill, Barnack is a pretty village with stone-built houses and inns. South of the village are the grassy knolls of a quarry (the Hills and Holes Nature Reserve) which provided stone for the village, Ely and Peterborough cathedrals and some Cambridge colleges. Charles Kingsley was born in the Old Rectory (not open).

BARNARD CASTLE Durham NZ0516
Town on A67, 15 miles (24km) W of Darlington
Small market town on the banks on the River Tees. The castle, built in 12th century by Bernard Balliol, an ancestor of John Balliol who founded Balliol College, Oxford, is now a ruin. The Bowes Museum contains a fine collection of furniture, paintings and ceramics, best known is the Silver Swan by John Cox, first mentioned in 1774.

BARNBY DUN West Yorkshire SE6109
Village off A18, 5 miles (8km) NE of Doncaster
Situated by a canal, this village has a medieval centre. The church has an exceptionally fine 14th-century aisle displaying some bold gargoyles.

BARNBY IN THE WILLOWS Nottinghamshire SK8552
Village off A17, 4 miles (6km) E of Newark
Secluded beside the River Witham which forms the boundary with Lincolnshire. Round dovecote. Medieval church with intriguing tracery and box pews.

BARNBY MOOR Nottinghamshire SK6684
Village on A638, 4 miles (6km) NE of East Retford
Bypassed by the A1 but formerly on Great North road, once an important coaching centre whose main inn remains a hotel.

BARNES Greater London TQ2276
District in borough of Richmond
Smart suburb. Central green and pond, 18th-century Sun pub. Jazz at Bull's Head. Church restored after 1978 fire.

BARNINGHAM Durham NZ0810
Village off A66, 4 miles (6km) SE of Barnard Castle
An attractive Teesdale village. Barningham Park was home of the Milbanke family and near by is Stang Forest.

BARNINGHAM Suffolk TL9676
Village on B1111, 5 miles (8km) NE of Ixworth
James Fison built a steam mill in Barningham in the 18th century and began the agro-chemical company that still bears his name. The church is 500 years old.

BARNOLDSWICK Lancashire SD8746
Town on B6251, 4 miles (6km) N of Colne
Set in the heart of Pendle farmland, the main industry is engineering: home to the Rolls-Royce aero-engine plant. The Bancroft Mill Engine Museum houses a preserved steam engine, one of the few remaining which used to power the mills of Lancashire and Yorkshire. The Anglican Church of St Mary Le Gill has an unusual three-decker pulpit.

Tablet on the Horwood's almshouses in Barnstaple.

BARNSLEY Gloucestershire SP0704
Village on B4425, 4 miles (6km) NE of Cirencester
A very picturesque single-street village, where garden-lovers flock to visit Rosemary Verey's Barnsley House Garden.

BARNSLEY South Yorkshire SE3406
Town on A628, 12 miles (19km) N of Sheffield
Industrial town north of Sheffield founded in Saxon times. The town hall was built of Portland limestone in 1933. St Mary's Church dates back to 1300. The Cooper Gallery collection includes several English watercolours. Much of Barnsley's shopping centre is pedestrianised and the markets are busy and popular.

BARNSTAPLE Devon SS5633
Town on A39, 9 miles (14km) NE of Bideford
On the lowest fordable point of the Taw estuary, Barnstaple has been a town since the 10th century (big medieval castle mound), and was the biggest port on the north Devon coast until the river started silting up in the 18th century. The massive bridge is 15th century, much mended. Many Georgian houses and cottages all through the town survive from prosperous times when the town imported Irish wool and traded to America. An elegant merchant's exchange of 1708 (now Queen Anne's Walk) preserves the Tome Stone where merchants sealed their bargains.

The old centre is around the Church of St Peter and St Paul, with the 14th-century St Anne's Chapel (now a museum) and Horwood's Almshouses and school (now a shop), both mid-17th century. Several other almshouses around the town attest to 17th-century riches and piety. The guildhall of 1826 is smooth Greek in style, and the town's market is in a remarkable 320ft (97m) long market house of 1856 with an even longer Butchers' Row. The Museum of North Devon shows the history of the area.

Barnstaple was known for its pottery from the 17th century (some went to America) and Brannam's pottery still survives, a handsome 1886 terracotta showroom with bottle kiln behind. The town is now a bustling regional shopping centre.

BARNSTON Merseyside SJ2783
Village on A551, 2 miles (3km) S of Birkenhead
A quiet village whose 18th- and 19th-century buildings enclose the village green. Now a commuter suburb.

BARNWELL, ST ANDREW AND ALL SAINTS
Northamptonshire TL0584
Villages off A605, 2 miles (3km) S of Oundle
Attractive villages with stone cottages beside stream. French/Italian-type castle of about 1266, first in Britain of type with square plan, round corner towers. Manor House replaces Elizabethan mansion in castle courtyard, country estate of Duke of Gloucester (closed). Chancel remains of All Saints' Church; 13th- and 14th-century St Andrew's. Waterbirds, fishing, picnics at Barnwell Country Park.

BARRA Western Isles NF6801
Island in Outer Hebrides, S of South Uist
Eight miles (13km) long by 4 miles (6km) wide and mainly noted for its tranquillity and scenic beauty, a combination of hills, fertile croftland, rocky bays and sandy beaches. Economy based on crofting, fishing and tourism. Prehistoric cairns and brochs. Catholic community with strong Gaelic culture and musical tradition. Good coastal and inland walks.

BARRHEAD Strathclyde NS4958
Town on A736, 4 miles (6km) S of Paisley
Small industrial town once noted for textile industry. Shanks, famous firm of sanitary engineers, founded here in 1856.

BARRINGTON Cambridgeshire TL3849
Village off A10, 6 miles (10km) NE of Royston
A small village around a spacious green. Handsome thatched and tiled houses line the green. The timber-framed Royal Oak is a popular pub.

BARRINGTON Somerset ST3818
Village off B3168, 3 miles (5km) NE of Ilminster
Stone and thatch cottages, picturesque church, and the handsome, large, 16th-century Barrington Court (National Trust) with good gardens.

BARRINGTON, GREAT AND LITTLE Gloucestershire SP2013
Villages off A40, 3 miles (5km) W of Burford
Old quarrying villages connected by a medieval bridge over the River Windrush, with pleasant churches and attractive cottages of many ages.

BARROW Shropshire SJ6500
Village off B4376, 2 miles (3km) E of Much Wenlock
Isolated cluster of hall, school, 1816 almshouses and small, primitive church with Saxon chancel and Norman nave.

BARROW BRIDGE Greater Manchester SD6811
Village off A58, 2 miles (3km) NW of Bolton
A model industrial settlement of the 19th century where the village's social, educational and economic life was completely integrated to form a close-knit community.

BARROW HILL Derbyshire SK4275
Village off A619, 4 miles (6km) NE of Chesterfield
Mid-19th-century housing for the Staveley Coal and Iron Company.

BARROW UPON SOAR Leicestershire SK5717
Village on B675, 3 miles (5km) SE of Loughborough
Large residential village, growing from defensive River Soar position. Hosiery and knitwear industries. Many prehistoric finds from limeworks now in Leicester Museum.

BARROW UPON TRENT Derbyshire SK3528
Village on A5132, 5 miles (8km) S of Derby
Pleasant residential village between the Trent and Mersey Canal and the River Trent, with several fine 17th- to 19th-century houses.

BARROW-IN-FURNESS Cumbria SD2068
Town on A590, 18 miles (29km) NW of Lancaster
Barrow, on the Furness peninsula, is a 19th-century industrial town with long, narrow streets of terraced houses around a busy centre. Like many such towns it grew up around a railway, built to transport locally produced iron ore, slate and limestone to a new deep-water port. Prosperity came to the town in the 19th century with the steel production and ship-building industries.

Furness Abbey is one of the most important monastic sites in the country and is now managed by English Heritage. Built in the 12th century of the local red sandstone and absorbed into the Cistercian order, Furness Abbey became the second wealthiest monastery in Britain after Fountains Abbey in Yorkshire, despite its remote location. The monks established themselves as guides across the treacherous sands of Morecambe Bay. After dissolution in 1537 it became part of Thomas Cromwell's estate and fell into disrepair. Now an elegant ruin with tall arches, it still stands to its full height in some parts.

A bridge at Barrow Docks joins nearby Walney Island to the peninsula, where there are two important nature reserves.

BARROW-UPON-HUMBER Humberside TA0620
Village off A1077, 3 miles (5km) E of Barton-upon-Humber
Was once a port. To the north is a mound where a castle once stood, some remains are clearly visible. Mudflats noted for snipe.

BARROWBY Lincolnshire SK8736
Village off A52, 2 miles (3km) W of Grantham
Seventeenth-century halls and cottages, ironstone hill-top church overlooking Vale of Belvoir, with monument to Charles I's chaplain. Almost joined to Grantham.

BARROWDEN Leicestershire SK9400
Village off A47, 5 miles (8m) E of Uppingham
Pretty Rutland village, greens, duck pond. In 1830, local farmer's daughter married village missionary who later found worldwide fame as Thomas Cook, travel pioneer.

BARROWFORD Lancashire SD8539
Town on A682, 1 mile (2km) N of Nelson
Large village alongside Pendle Water. The deer park in the grounds of Carr Hall is inhabited by Australian wallabies. The Pendle Heritage Centre, housed in a Lancashire yeoman's house, was once home to the Bannister family of Dr Roger Bannister, the first man to run a mile in under four minutes. Its collection includes an audio-visual display on the Pendle Witches.

BARRY South Glamorgan ST1168
Town on A4055, 7 miles (11km) SW of Cardiff
Town's resort, Barry Island, is actually a peninsula possessing all the traditional seaside trappings. Main sandy beach is Whitmore Bay, backed by a pleasure park with over 50 rides. The Knap is pebbled and quieter, with Roman remains. Remnants of Barry's 13th-century castle lie en route to Porthkerry Country Park. Birds of prey fly at the Welsh Hawking Centre.

BARSHAM Suffolk TM3989
Village on B1062, 2 miles (3km) W of Beccles
Barsham church has seen misfortune since 1806. Lightning damaged the altar, and later the thatched roof caught fire, damaging the interior.

BARSTON West Midlands SP2078
Village off A452, 4 miles (6km) E of Solihull
In pleasant countryside, this traditional village with several old houses is contained within a meander of the River Blythe.

BARTHOMLEY Cheshire SJ7652
Village off A500, 4 miles (6km) SE of Crewe
The last wolf in England was reputed to have been shot in a wood at Barthomley. Village also has Civil War connections.

BARTON BROAD Norfolk TG3621
Lake on the River Ant, 5 miles (8km) NE of Wroxham
A beautiful reed-fringed broad on the River Ant. Near by is Barton Turf, a tiny village with a church that has a fine rood screen.

BARTON IN FABIS Nottinghamshire SK5132
Village off A453, 6 miles (10km) SW of Nottingham
Octagonal dovecote built by the Sacheverell family whose monuments lie in the medieval church, near the Trent.

BARTON IN THE BEANS Leicestershire SK3906
Village off A447, 7 miles (11km) SE of Ashby-de-la-Zouch
As implied by name, an agricultural settlement, now become residential. Samuel Deacon's fine clockmaker's workshop moved in 1951 to Newarke Houses Museum, Leicester.

BARTON MILLS Suffolk TL7173
Village on A11, 8 miles (13km) NW of Newmarket
In the 13th century, the rector of Barton Mills, Jacobus de Scabelli, became Pope Honorius IV (1285–7). The village has a pretty bridge.

BARTON ON SEA Hampshire SZ2393
Suburb in E area of Christchurch
Developed from the 1920s as a seaside settlement set back from the low cliffs. Wonderful views of the Solent and Isle of Wight.

BARTON SEAGRAVE Northamptonshire SP8877
Area of SE Kettering
Separated from the rest of Kettering by the River Ise. Impressive Norman parish church with beautifully carved tympanum.

BARTON UPON IRWELL Greater Manchester SJ7697
District in Eccles
Site of the famous aqueduct, built in 1761 by James Brindley, which carries the Bridgewater Canal over the River Irwell.

BARTON-LE-CLAY Bedfordshire TL0830
Village off A6, 6 miles (10km) N of Luton
Much sprawling post-1960s development here. The

Barton Hills to the south are supposed to have inspired Bunyan's *Delectable Mountains*.

BARTON-ON-THE-HEATH Warwickshire SP2532
Village off A44, 3 miles (5km) E of Moreton-in-Marsh
Village of Cotswold character, site of the 'Four Shires Stone', where Warwickshire, Worcestershire, Oxfordshire and Gloucestershire used to meet. Interesting Norman church.

BARTON-UNDER-NEEDWOOD Staffordshire SK1818
Village on B5016, 5 miles (8km) SW of Burton upon Trent
Large and lively village with six pubs and an interesting church.

BARTON-UPON-HUMBER Humberside TA0221
Town on B1218, 6 miles (10km) SW of Hull
Once a Roman signal station, later a flourishing medieval port, eventually eclipsed by Hull. Baysgarth Museum, housed in an 18th-century mansion house, has collections relating to geology, archaeology and later history of the district. Clay Pits Country Park includes marshland and lakes formed from clay pits, and has five nature reserves.

BARWICK Somerset ST5513
Village off A37, 2 miles (3km) S of Yeovil
On the edge of Yeovil, famous for the follies erected in the late 18th century on the boundaries of the park – a pillar, a cone standing on an arch, a tower and a tower on an arch.

BARWICK IN ELMET West Yorkshire SE4037
Village off A64, 7 miles (11km) NE of Leeds
The area was once the tiny Saxon kingdom of Elmet and the village retains extensive remains of earthworks.

BASCHURCH Shropshire SJ4221
Village on B4397, 7 miles (11km) NW of Shrewsbury
Village centre has interesting 16th-century yeomen's cottages. In a nearby field, The Berth is thought to be the headquarters of Cynddylan, a 6th-century Welsh chieftain.

BASILDON Essex TQ7189
New town off A127, 11 miles (18km) E of Romford
Once an obscure Essex village not far inland from the Thames estuary, Basildon developed rapidly in a higgledy-piggledy way earlier this century and has been transformed since the 1950s into a New Town, which covers several previously independent villages. Sir Basil Spence was consultant architect to the New Town, consisting of ten 'neighbourhoods' with a centre. In the centre is a pedestrian precinct with shops, tall modern blocks, trees, pools, fountains and modern statues. Close by is the 1960s Church of St Martin with stained-glass windows by Joseph Nuttgens. The old church of Holy Cross, Basildon, goes back to the 14th century, with the chancel rebuilt in brick in the 1590s.

Other former villages have churches of note, including St Nicholas, Laindon, with its broach spire, stout wooden belfry and 17th-century priest's house, and the 11th-century church of All Saints' in Vange. In Vange, too, are the big cats, birds of prey and endangered species of Basildon Zoo.

Pitsea Hall Country Park is in Pitsea (see), while the Langdon Hills Country Park with its woods and nature trails provides sweeping views across southern Essex.

St Nicholas, Laindon, now in Basildon.

BASILDON, UPPER AND LOWER Berkshire SU6078
Villages on A329, 2 miles (3km) NW of Pangbourne
Upper Basildon is a sizeable downland village; Lower Basildon has the old church and big house. The church with its brick tower of 1734 is down by the Thames. Basildon Park (National Trust) is the best Georgian mansion in the county, severe classical stone of 1776, splendid inside, with an octagonal room and much fine plasterwork. Beale Bird Park in gardens by the Thames.

BASING, OLD Hampshire SU6652
Village off A30, 2 miles (3km) E of Basingstoke
Basing House was the scene of the most famous siege of the Civil War, and was levelled to the ground afterwards. Picturesque brick village, interesting church restored after damage in the Civil War. Many cottages are of small Tudor bricks looted from the ruins of the big house.

BASINGSTOKE Hampshire SU6352
Town on A30, 17 miles (27km) SW of Camberley
A pleasant market town until the 1960s, when it was expanded to take London overspill. The population quadrupled, most of the town centre was demolished to make way for a new elevated pedestrian shopping area, and big business arrived. Gigantic office buildings ring the town, like bits of the City of London but with more space and trees. Local museum.

BASLOW Derbyshire SK2572
Village on A623, 3 miles (5km) NE of Bakewell
On northern border of Chatsworth estate, beside River Derwent, below gritstone edge of moors. Unusual church clock commemorates Queen Victoria's 1897 Jubilee.

BASS ROCK Lothian NT6087
Island in Firth of Forth
Basalt outcrop, 350ft (106m) high, in Firth of Forth; landmark visible for miles. Lighthouse. Provides nesting for huge colonies of seabirds.

BASSENTHWAITE Cumbria NY2332
Village off A591, 6 miles (10km) N of Keswick
Village located near lake of same name, with remains left behind by ancient Britons and the Romans.

BATCOMBE Somerset ST6939
Village off A359, 3 miles (5km) N of Bruton
Pretty village with a handsome church with a big 16th-century tower. Wonderful views from churchyard.

BATECOMBE Dorset ST6103
Village off A37, 4 miles (6km) NW of Cerne Abbas
Scattered village set in a wide combe, with high chalk downs behind and a huge view of the Blackmore Vale.

BATH Avon ST7464
City on A4, 11 miles (18km) SE of Bristol
Bath is the most elegant town in the country, with acres of handsome Georgian buildings in the creamy orange local stone and surrounded by small green hills. The town has always been based on its natural hot springs, the largest producing a million litres a day of red-stained hot water.

The Romans built their baths around the spring, with a temple dedicated to Minerva and the Iron Age god Sulis, providing a mixture of physical healing and spiritual refreshment, doubtless, as later, relieved with more social amusements.

The Roman baths were rediscovered in the later 19th century, and can be seen along with the little medieval King's Bath, and displays of finds which include Roman sculpture and Roman curses inscribed on little rolls of lead which were thrown into the spring.

Medieval Bath was small, with a big monastery, whose large and handsome early 16th-century church survives as Bath Abbey, fan-vaulted and with a famous west front.

The 17th-century town was promoted as a spa, and really took off from 1725, becoming the most fashionable resort in the country. Present-day Bath is the stylish town created for those who came to bathe and to drink the water in the Georgian period.

Two people heavily influenced the town: 'Beau' Nash, the official Master of Ceremonies for 50 years who made the resort genteel, and the architect John Wood who designed many areas of Bath including the Circus (1754), the large circular terrace. His son designed the Royal Crescent (no 1 is open to the public) and the Assembly Rooms in the 1760s, while Robert Adam produced Pulteney Bridge at the same time. Other notable buildings include the guildhall (1776) and the Pump Room (1789), but fine as these individual buildings are, it is Bath as a whole which impresses, miles of Georgian houses, mostly in terraces, looking much as they did when Jane Austen or Gainsborough visited. Royal Victoria Park (laid out from 1830) and the Botanic Gardens in the northwest part are fine Victorian additions to the town, although by then it had ceased to be fashionable. The best view of the city is from the wooded ridge to the south.

Two of Jane Austen's novels, *Northanger Abbey* and *Persuasion*, are partly set in Regency Bath and give a good picture of the social life then, as do the Assembly Rooms and the Museum of Costume.

Today Bath attracts visitors from all over the world, and has masses of smart shops. The annual summer music festival holds concerts in many of the Georgian buildings, and the Holbourne of Menstrie Museum (in a hotel of 1796) and the Victoria Art Gallery have temporary exhibitions as well as their permanent displays. The Building of Bath Museum has details of the construction of the Georgian town. Bath is always bustling and always beautiful.

BATHAMPTON Avon ST7766
Village off A36, 2 miles (3km) NE of Bath
Tucked into a curve of the River Avon, with the Kennet and Avon Canal right by the church. The modern campus of Bath University (founded 1966) is on the side of Bathampton Down.

BATHEASTON Avon ST7767
Suburb in NE area of Bath
Virtually part of Bath, although originally a separate village. Many elegant 17th- and 18th-century stone houses. Bathford just to the south is similar, with the woods of the down making a good backdrop.

BATHGATE Lothian NS9768
Town on A89, 5 miles (8km) S of Linlithgow
Industrial town in central belt known at various times for weaving, coal-mining, paraffin refinery and car and truck manufacture.

BATLEY West Yorkshire SE2224
Town on A652, 7 miles (11km) SW of Leeds
North Kirklees town near Dewsbury in the Pennine moorland. Bagshaw Museum houses local displays, the Hilditch collection of Oriental art and an Egyptology section. The Butterfly Conservation Centre is next door. The Batley Art Gallery is above the library in the market place.

BATSFORD Gloucestershire SP1833
Village off A429, 1 mile (2km) NW of Moreton-in-Marsh
The celebrated arboretum and charming gardens of Batsford Park, childhood home of the Mitford sisters, are a prime tourist attraction.

BATTERSEA Greater London TQ2776
District in borough of Wandsworth
Market gardening area until 19th-century railway and industry developments. Battersea Old Church, 18th century, on Thames bank. Battersea Park opened 1853, has 1985 Buddhist peace pagoda. Covent Garden Market moved to former Nine Elms railway yard 1974. Striking 1980s Marco Polo Building, Queenstown Road. Future of 1930s power station by Sir Giles Gilbert Scott in doubt.

BATTLE East Sussex TQ7515
Town on A2100, 6 miles (10km) NW of Hastings
Attractive town with pleasing variety of architecture. Grew up on site of Battle of Hastings around Battle Abbey (completed 1095). Magnificent abbey gatehouse (1338) overlooks triangular market place. Abbey dissolved 1537, and abbey church, with high altar where Harold fell, destroyed. Ruins open to public. Abbot's house now a school.

BATTLEFIELD Shropshire SJ5117
Site of battle off A49, 3 miles (5km) N of Shrewsbury
After defeating the rebel army at Shrewsbury (1403), Henry IV founded a church on the edge of the battlefield. It still stands, although it is now redundant.

BATTLESBRIDGE Essex TQ7894
Village off A130, 2 miles (3km) E of Wickford
Known for its antiques centre, with more than 80 dealers. Supported by furniture workshops, pub, coffee shop and weekend motorcycle museum.

BATTLESDEN Bedfordshire SP9628
Hamlet off A4012, 3 miles (5km) SE of Woburn
Tiny little place built by Duke of Bedford in 1880s. Church in surviving Paxton-designed grounds of Battlesden Park.

BAULKING Oxfordshire SU3191
Village off A417, 4 miles (6km) SE of Faringdon
This small settlement marooned in the Vale of the White Horse is worth visiting for its sturdy little 13th-century church.

BAUNTON Gloucestershire SP0204
Village off A435, 2 miles (3km) N of Cirencester
Now caught up in Cirencester's residential fringe, the village has a Norman church with a huge wall-painting of St Christopher.

BAWBURGH Norfolk TG1508
Village off A47, 5 miles (8km) W of Norwich
A mill still stands astride the River Yare in this pretty village. St Walstan is buried here, and pilgrimages were made to St Walstan's Well.

BAWDSEY Suffolk TM3440
Village on B1083, 7 miles (11km) SE of Woodbridge
Bawdsey Manor (not open) was where radar was developed in World War II. Bawdsey is associated with war heroine Edith Cavell.

BAWTRY South Yorkshire SK6593
Small town on A638, 6 miles (10km) SE of Doncaster
Once an inland port on the River Idle and a major stage-coach stop on the Great North road.

BAYFORD Hertfordshire TL3108
Village off B158, 3 miles (5km) S of Hertford
Expensive commuter village in wooded countryside. Victorian church. Grand Baker family mansion of Bayfordbury, now a college, has beautiful grounds.

BAYSWATER Greater London TQ2580
District in City of Westminster
North of Hyde Park, grew up round rustic springs supplying water to London. Built up from east end of Bayswater Road (Roman road originally) from early 19th century to 1850s. Impressive squares and terraces include Orme Square and Lancaster Gate. Victorian churches and numerous hotels. Former Whiteley's department store, Queensway, in glamorous Edwardian building, reopened as shopping complex.

BEACHAMWELL Norfolk TF7505
Village off A1122, 5 miles (8km) SW of Swaffham
Standing near a Saxon earthwork called Devil's Dyke, Beachamwell is a sleepy, peaceful village that boasts four churches. The oldest is Saxon and has a thatched roof; on a pillar is the 'Beachamwell Demon' poking its tongue out at the congregation. Semi-detached cottages line the village green, with the church at one end, and the pub at the other.

BEACHY HEAD East Sussex TV5895
Headland off B2103, 3 miles (5km) SW of Eastbourne
Highest cliff on south coast (536ft/163m), formed where South Downs plunge into the sea. Notorious place with superb views. The name is Norman French *beau-chef*. Borough of Eastbourne owns whole headland (Beachy Head Countryside Centre). Old Belle Tout lighthouse on cliff top (1831) superseded by one at cliff foot (1902), now unmanned.

BEACONSFIELD Buckinghamshire SU9490
Town on A40, 5 miles (8km) SE of High Wycombe
Pronounced 'Beckonsfield' and once a coaching town on the London–Oxford route. Writers GK Chesterton,

Robert Frost and Enid Blyton are among famous residents. Broad streets, handsome Georgian houses and inns. Church with notable monuments and glass. Bekonscot Model Village has more than 70 miniature buildings and a miniature railway; 20th-century development in Beaconsfield New Town to north.

BEADNELL Northumberland NU2229
Village on B1340, 2 miles (3km) S of Seahouses
Former fishing village, it is the only east coast port with a west-facing harbour. Was once a smugglers' haunt.

BEAFORD Devon SS5515
Village on B3220, 5 miles (8km) SE of Great Torrington
Just up the wooded Torridge Valley, which has wonderful river scenery.

BEAL Northumberland NU0642
Hamlet off A1, 6 miles (10km) NW of Belford
Small village marking the crossing point to Lindisfarne. The causeway is impassable for two hours before and three-and-a-half hours after each high tide.

BEAMINSTER Dorset ST4701
Small town on A3066, 5 miles (8km) N of Bridport
Pronounced 'Bemminster'. Small, handsome rural town, surrounded by green hills. Many Georgian houses and cottages, and a good medieval church with a splendid tower all in local creamy-orange limestone. Parnham House (3/4 mile/1km south) is a really romantic (and large) stone manor house. Now John Makepeace Furniture Workshops. Early 1900s formal gardens and woodland walks.

BEAMISH Durham NZ2253
Village off A693, 2 miles (3km) E of Stanley
Best known for the award-winning open-air museum which tells the social history of the North of England.

BEARPARK Durham NZ2343
Village off A167, 2 miles (3km) W of Durham
Former colliery village near Durham. Excavations have revealed remains of Beau Repaire Priory, which was started in 1195.

BEARSDEN Strathclyde NS5372
Town off A82, 5 miles (8km) NW of Glasgow
Select and prosperous Glasgow suburb, which became burgh in 1958. Known as Kirktoune until 19th century. Remains of Antonine Wall, including bathhouse.

BEARSTED Kent TQ8055
Village off A20, 2 miles (3km) E of Maidstone
Attractive village grouped round its historic green, famed for its village cricket. The church tower has curious sculptures of lions on the battlements.

BEATTOCK Dumfries and Galloway NT0802
Village on A74, 2 miles (3km) S of Moffat
Tiny settlement on the desolate hills of Upper Annandale, familiar to those driving north on the A74.

BEAUCHAMP RODING Essex TL5809
Hamlet off B184, 2 miles (3km) S of Leaden Roding
One of the eight Rodings. Isolated Church of St Botolph in fields with landmark 15th-century tower.

BEAULIEU Hampshire SU3802
Village on B3054, 6 miles (10km) NE of Lymington
The name means beautiful place, which it is: on a tidal estuary and the edge of the New Forest. Palace House was part of an abbey, and still has medieval vaulting. Ruins of more of the abbey in the grounds, and an interesting parish church made from the refectory of the abbey. The National Motor Museum has more than 200 cars and many displays on the history of motoring. Beaulieu village is small and pretty.

BEAULY Highland NH5246
Town on A862, 10 miles (16km) W of Inverness
Stone-built town, noted for salmon-fishing and tweed, with spacious square and ruins of 13th-century Beauly Priory.

BEAUMARIS Gwynedd (Anglesey) SH6076
Town on A545, 4 miles (6km) NE of Menai Bridge
The predominantly English feel of Beaumaris, a resort and sailing centre on the eastern approach to the Menai Strait, stems from medieval times when Edward I evicted the area's native inhabitants and created a garrison town. Of its wealth of historic buildings, none is finer than Edward's castle (Cadw), last of the 'iron ring' of fortresses thrown around North Wales to subdue the Welsh. Created on a flat, virgin site – the *beau marais* ('fair marsh') of the Norman French – it was uncompleted through lack of funds. Once across the moat, the sophisticated concentric defences become apparent, the epitome of medieval military architecture even without the planned towers. It is now a World Heritage Site.

Opposite, the courthouse dated 1614 still functions. The nearby Victorian gaol, forbidding in its punishment cell and treadmill, was ahead of its time in amenities like running water and toilets. The exhibits in the Museum of Childhood and Marine World strike a happier note.

Noteworthy among the town's many gracious buildings are Ye Olde Bull's Head (a characterful old inn), the Tudor Rose (one of Wales's oldest houses), and the 14th-century church containing the coffin of Llywelyn the Great's wife.

BEAUMONT Cumbria NY3459
Village off B5307, 4 miles (6km) NW of Carlisle
Hadrian's Wall runs through the village. Disused railway line, closed 1964, was laid along the bed of the Carlisle Canal.

BEAUWORTH Hampshire SU5726
Hamlet off A272, 4 miles (6km) S of Alresford
Very remote, with old plain brick and thatch cottages and an austere little church of 1838 enlivened by 1989 stained glass.

BEBINGTON Merseyside SJ3383
Town off A41, 3 miles (5km) S of Birkenhead
Stone for building the ancient church was mysteriously transported here from Tranmere. The church was mentioned before AD735 by the Venerable Bede.

BECCLES Suffolk TM4289
Town on A145, 8 miles (13km) W of Lowestoft
A series of fires in the 16th and 17th centuries did much damage to medieval Beccles, but out of the ashes rose a splendid town of elegant Georgian buildings of red brick. Nelson's parents were married in the imposing 14th-century Church of St Michael in 1749, and Beccles offers two informative and interesting museums.

BECK HOLE North Yorkshire NZ8202
Village off A169, 7 miles (11km) SW of Whitby
A village in the North York Moors National Park, well known for the steep incline on the railway line between Beck Hole and Goathland.

BECKENHAM Greater London TQ3769
Town in borough of Bromley
Prosperous suburb. St George's Church, 19th-century Gothic, claims Britain's oldest lych-gate, 13th century. Beckenham Park, Kelsey Park.

BECKFORD Hereford and Worcester SO9736
Village off A435, 6 miles (10km) E of Tewkesbury
Bredon Hill village, where Norman/medieval church has notable sculpted doorways. Former rectory is now Beckford Silk (visitor centre open all year).

BECKINGTON Somerset ST8051
Village off A36, 3 miles (5km) NE of Frome
Lots of stone buildings, 16th century onwards. Unusual big Norman church tower.

BECKLEY East Sussex TQ8523
Village on B2165, 5 miles (8km) NW of Rye
Strung along a ridge, a street of tile-hung, weather-boarded and timber-framed buildings. Beckley Furnace made great guns for Parliament in the Civil War.

BECKLEY Oxfordshire SP5611
Village off B4027, 5m (8km) NE of Oxford
The scattered village, with a fine medieval church in its old centre, sprawls across a hillside overlooking the expanse of Otmoor (see).

BECKWITHSHAW North Yorkshire SE2653
Village on B6161, 3 miles (5km) SW of Harrogate
A residential area with converted older buildings and new residential developments. Nineteenth-century church has beautiful stained glass.

BEDALE North Yorkshire SE2688
Small town on A684, 7 miles (11km) SW of Northallerton
An old settlement with a 14th-century market cross. Bedale Hall, a Georgian mansion with ornate plaster ceiling, now houses district council offices and a small museum. With a fortified tower, the Church of St Gregory incorporates architectural styles from 1000 to 1500. Restored buildings and machinery of Crakehall Watermill now produce wholemeal flour. Thorpe Perrow Arboretum contains over 1,000 species of tree and shrub.

BEDDGELERT Gwynedd SH5948
Village on A4085, 13 miles (21km) S of Caernarfon
Houses, bridge and monument, all of stone, where Colwyn and Glaslyn's rivers meet in shadow of Snowdon's peaks. Story goes that monument is burial place of Prince Llywelyn's heroic dog, Gelert, mistakenly slain after saving his son. River Glaslyn flows down from rocky Aberglaslyn Pass. Sygun Copper Mine depicts Victorian mining conditions, and Cae Du Farm shows rural life.

BEDFORD Bedfordshire TL0449
Town on A6, 19 miles (31km) N of Luton
Bedfordshire's amiable county town is famed particularly for its links with John Bunyan, the 17th-century author born at nearby Elstow (see), who wrote *Pilgrim's Progress* while imprisoned for his opinions in Bedford town gaol. The Bunyan Meeting Museum has a riveting collection of his belongings, including his walking stick and his iron violin, and copies of *Pilgrim's Progress* in practically every language on earth. Scenes from the book are carved on the doors of the Bunyan Meeting church itself and a fine Victorian statue of the author surveys the scene outside St Peter's Church.

The town's setting on the Great Ouse has given it outstandingly pretty riverside gardens and walks, and there are rewarding tree trails and an 1880s pedestrian suspension bridge. The Cecil Higgins Art Gallery, in the Higgins family's Victorian home, shows Bedfordshire lace and fabulous glass and ceramics, with watercolours and prints from Turner to Picasso. Bedford's main church, St Paul's, at the heart of the town, has enjoyable misericords in the choir and outside is a statue by Sir Alfred Gilbert of John Howard, the 18th-century prison reformer.

BEDFORD PARK Greater London TQ2179
District in W London
Delightful red-brick garden suburb of 1870s/1880s, mainly designed by Richard Norman Shaw. St Michael's Church. Near Turnham Green station.

BEDGEBURY FOREST Kent TQ7134
Woodland off B2079, S of Goudhurst
Large (2,500 acres/1,012ha) area of forest run by the Forestry Commission, popular with walkers and picnickers. Includes Bedebury Pinetum, the national collection of specimen conifers and the largest in the world, established in 1925 by the Forestry Commission and the Royal Botanical Gardens, Kew. Nature trails, picnic area and visitor facilities. Programme of organised outings.

BEDLINGTON Northumberland NZ2681
Town on A1068, 4 miles (6km) SE of Morpeth
The main street of this small market town is a conservation area. Famous as the home of the Bedlington Terrier, and Sir Daniel Gooch, founder of the Great Western Railway, was born here. St Cuthbert's Church was founded in 12th century. Plessey Woods Park lies on the north bank of River Blyth.

BEDMOND Hertfordshire TL0903
Village off A41, 4 miles (6km) SE of Hemel Hempstead
Birthplace of Pope Adrian IV in the 12th century. Little corrugated iron church with toy spire. Copy of Marie Antoinette's Versailles dairy farm.

BEDRUTHAN STEPS Cornwall SW8469
Beach off B3276, 6 miles (10km) NE of Newquay
On the dark rocky north Cornwall coast; a name applied to either small islets in the sandy beach (called giants' stepping stones) or the steep steps leading down the cliff.

BEDSTONE Shropshire SO3676
Village on B4367, 6 miles (10km) NE of Knighton
On the southeast fringe of Clun Forest, with a small Norman church, fine Elizabethan yeoman's house and spectacular Victorian mansion in mock timber-framing.

BEDWORTH Warwickshire SP3687
Town on B4113, 5 miles (8km) N of Coventry
Old market centre, later a mining and silk-weaving town, has former weavers' cottages in Mill Street and pleasant almshouses of 1840 in the market place.

BEELEY Derbyshire SK2667
Village on B6012, 5 miles (8km) N of Matlock
Estate village largely laid out by Paxton at southern end of Chatsworth Park, below Beeley Moor.

BEER Devon SY2289
Village on B3174, 1 mile (2km) W of Seaton
A pretty seaside village, with a little stream running down the main street. Good cottages of brick, flint and the local Beer stone. Beer Head to the south has chalk cliffs, with the Pinnacles, remains of old landslips. Beer Quarry caves are open. Pecorama Pleasure Gardens and Exhibition.

BEESTON Cheshire SJ5458
Hamlet off A49, 3 miles (5km) S of Tarporley
Beeston Castle (English Heritage) was originally occupied by the Romans and in the 13th century became a key point in the border strongholds. The Image House, according to legend, was built in one night. John and Robert Naylor who lived at Beeston Towers in the 18th century were probably the first to complete the Land's End to John O' Groats walk.

BEESTON Nottinghamshire SK5236
Town on A6005, in SW outskirts of Nottingham
Home of Boots pharmaceutical factory, whose founder Jesse Boot was also a benefactor of Nottingham University near by in its parkland campus.

BEESTON REGIS Norfolk TG1642
Area of E Sheringham
Standing proud and lonely on Beeston Regis Common in the eastern outskirts of Sheringham are the ruins of a priory.

BEESTON ST LAWRENCE Norfolk TG3222
Village on A1151, 4 miles (6km) NE of Wroxham
Beeston Hall is at Beeston St Lawrence – an elegant Georgian mansion in Gothic Revival style containing memorabilia from before the Russian Revolution. Extensive grounds.

BEETHAM Cumbria SD4979
Village on A6, 6 miles (10km) N of Carnforth
One hundred Norman coins found during restoration work to church. German prisoners were held at nearby Bela Camp during World War II.

BEGUILDY Powys SO1979
Village on B4355, 7 miles (11km) NW of Knighton
In tranquil Teme Valley amongst rolling green hills of Welsh/English border. Church has old woodwork, including a finely preserved painted screen.

BEINN EIGHE Highland NG9561
Mountain group off A832, W of Kinlochewe
Nine-peaked massif of Torridonian sandstone with Caledonian pine, alpine flora and abundant wildlife. National Nature Reserve run by Scottish Natural Heritage; climbing, walking and countryside centre.

BEITH Strathclyde NS3553
Town on A737, 6 miles (10km) NE of Dalry
Manufacturing town with Auld Kirk dating from 1556 with inscribed stone and bell dating from 1614.

BEKESBOURNE Kent TR1955
Village off A2, 3 miles (5km) SE of Canterbury
Lovely group of old buildings around church. Nearby Howletts Zoo Park with rare and endangered wild animals in natural settings.

BELAS KNAP Gloucestershire SP0225
Prehistoric site off B4632, 2 miles (3km) S of Winchcombe
This neolithic long barrow (English Heritage) on its hilltop site has four burial chambers with a false entrance lined with fine drystone walls.

BELAUGH Norfolk TG2818
Village off B1354, 1 mile (2km) W of Wroxham
A pleasant village hugging the banks of the River Bure. In the summer, it is busy with tourists enjoying boating on Norfolk's beautiful Broads.

BELBROUGHTON Hereford and Worcester SO9277
Village on B4188, 5 miles (8km) S of Stourbridge
Large village on fringe of Black Country, where handsome Georgian houses stand round the green with Norman/medieval church near by.

BELCHAMP ST PAUL Essex TL7942
Village off B1064, 5 miles (8km) W of Sudbury
Attractive village belonged to St Paul's Cathedral, London. Misericords in 15th-century church, an Essex rarity.

BELCHAMP WALTER Essex TL8240
Village off A131, 3 miles (5km) W of Sudbury
Belchamp Hall (open by appointment), Queen Anne-style historic seat of Raymond family, stables, gardens. Church with 15th-century tower near by.

BELFORD Northumberland NU1034
Village off A1, 14 miles (23km) SE of Berwick-upon-Tweed
Small agricultural and market town. Blue Bell hotel is a historic coaching inn. Belford Hall recently reconstructed by Northern Heritage Trust.

BELGRAVIA Greater London TQ2879
District in City of Westminster
Expensively grand area of stuccoed squares, terraces centred on Belgrave Square. Laid out by Thomas Cubitt for Grosvenor family from 1820s.

BELLE ISLE Cumbria SD3996
Island in Lake Windermere
Largest island on Lake Windermere. Belle Isle house, built in 1774, home of the Curwen family and first round house built in England, burnt down in early 1990s.

BELLEAU Lincolnshire TF4078
Village off A16, 4 miles (6km) NW of Alford
Named from streams bubbling from Wolds. Tudor brick barn and other traces of Willoughby's medieval manor; 13th-century knight's effigy in church.

BELLINGHAM Northumberland NY8383
Small town on B6320, 14 miles (23km) NW of Hexham
Small market town which claims to be the capital of North Tynedale, the heart of raiding country, and a good centre for exploring the Kielder Forest and Northumberland National Park. St Cuthbert's Church has an unusual stone roof built as protection against fire after the church was burnt several times by border raiders. Pronounced 'Bellinjum'.

BELLSHILL Strathclyde NS7360
Town off M74, 2 miles (3km) NW of Motherwell
A former mining town in the northeast of the Clyde Valley.

BELMONT Lancashire SD6715
Village on A675, 5 miles (8km) NW of Bolton
Set on the edge of Anglezarke Moor, the village grew up round Belmont Dye Works as part of the thriving textile industry.

BELPER Derbyshire SK3447
Town on A6, 7 miles (11km) N of Derby
Developed from 1770s with coming of the Strutt textile mills on River Derwent, with fine examples of industrial housing.

BELSAY Northumberland NZ0978
Village on A696, 5 miles (8km) NW of Ponteland
The English Heritage-owned estate of hall, castle and gardens encapsulates 600 years of the region's often turbulent past. Sir Charles Monck, the 19th-century owner of Belsay, based the design of the hall on the classical buildings he studied in Greece. The castle, built in the 14th century, is a fine example of a border tower house.

BELSTONE Devon SX6293
Village off A30, 2 miles (3km) SE of Okehampton
Right on the edge of Dartmoor, the moors rising high to the south. The Belstone Cleave is a little gorge with the River Tor at the bottom.

BELTINGHAM Northumberland NY7863
Hamlet off A69, 3 miles (5km) W of Haydon Bridge
Very pretty village with small 15th-century Church of St Cuthbert. Ridley Hall, 17th century, was country seat of Bowes Lyon family.

BELTON Lincolnshire SK9339
Village off A607, 3 miles (5km) NE of Grantham
Nineteenth-century estate village of Belton House, splendid Restoration country house (National Trust); tapestries, furniture, portraits, porcelain, formal gardens, landscaped park.

BELTON Norfolk TG4802
Village off A143, 4 miles (6km) SW of Great Yarmouth
An old market-garden town that has changed considerably during the last 40 years. The Barn Restaurant was once a blacksmith's forge.

BELTON IN RUTLAND Leicestershire SK8101
Village off A47, 3 miles (5km) W of Uppingham
Pleasing Rutland village on hill above Eye Brook. Medieval church, ironstone cottages, 17th-century Old Hall. Leicestershire Round footpath passes through.

BELTRING Kent TQ6747
Hamlet on B2015, 2 miles (3km) N of Paddock Wood
Tiny place dominated by Whitbread Hop Farm, home to the largest group of Victorian oasthouses in the world.

BELVIDE RESERVOIR Staffordshire SJ8309
see Bishop's Wood

BELVOIR Leicestershire SK8133
Hamlet off A52, 6 miles (10km) W of Grantham
Battlements, towers, golden-toned stone, commanding hilltop site overlooking beautiful Vale of Belvoir: what more could anyone want of a fairytale castle? Seat of Dukes of Rutland since Henry VIII's time, present Belvoir Castle was built by Wyatt in 1816. Pictures and fine furniture in staterooms, interesting kitchen and cellars, lovely gardens, jousting and special events.

BEMBRIDGE Isle of Wight SZ6488
Village off B3330, 4 miles (6km) SE of Ryde
The easternmost part of the island. Complicated coastline – rocky on the Foreland with a long pier over the rocks for the lifeboat, sandy beach and then the harbour, partly closed by a huge sandbar. Houseboats on the harbour edge, and lots of yachts. Shipwreck Centre and Maritime Museum, and on the hill Bembridge Windmill (National Trust), complete and 18th century.

BEMERTON Wiltshire SU1230
District in W area of Salisbury
Once a separate village, but now joined to Salisbury. The 17th-century poet George Herbert was rector here in the 1630s.

BEMPTON Humberside TA1972
Village on B1229, 3 miles (5km) N of Bridlington
An attractive village near the North Sea coast, with nearly perpendicular cliff precipices upwards of 400ft (122m). An RSPB bird sanctuary near the cliffs provides a home to many species. St Michael's Church has some interesting early 13th-century features, including a screen incorporating the Royal Arms. The old mansion of Buckton Hall was home to the Robinson family.

BEN LAWERS Tayside NN6341
Mountain off A827, NE of Killin
Highest peak in Breadalbane Range (3,984ft/1,214 m). National Nature Reserve noted for its Arctic-alpine flora. Visitor centre provides interpretation and ranger services.

BEN LOMOND Central NN3602
Mountain near N end of Loch Lomond, 3 miles (5km) N of Rowardennan
Rising above the eponymous loch and the most southerly Munro (3,192ft, 973m), Ben Lomond is familiar from countless photographs. Best climbed from Rowardennan.

BEN NEVIS Highland NN1671
Mountain off A82, SE of Fort William
Highest mountain in Great Britain, 4,406ft (1,343m). Provides testing climbing year-round as well as an easy walk to the summit plateau, where there are remains of the meteorological station, manned 1883–1904. Superb views, occasionally as far as Irish coast, and attractive walking in Glen Nevis.

BEN RHYDDING West Yorkshire SE1347
District of Ilkley
The Cow and Calf Rocks are a prominent local feature, popular with climbers.

BENBECULA Western Isles NF8251
Island in Outer Hebrides between N and S Uist
Low-lying island with army presence manning missile range and radar station. Flora MacDonald sailed from here to Skye with Prince Charles Edward in 1746.

BENEFIELD, UPPER AND LOWER Northamptonshire SP9988
Villages on A427, 3 miles (5km) W of Oundle
Twin villages on Oundle–Corby road. Lower Benefield has a fine 19th-century church with work by Comper, and a castle site (1208).

BENENDEN Kent TQ8033
Village on B2086, 3 miles (5km) SE of Cranbrook
Attractive village strung along ridge with spacious green, famous for cricket. The girls' public school lies on the west of the village.

BENGEO Hertfordshire TL3213
District in N Hertford
Swallowed up in Hertford now, but village nucleus survives with surprisingly unspoiled Norman and medieval church, wall-paintings and tiles.

BENINGBROUGH North Yorkshire SE5257
Hamlet off A19, 6 miles (10km) NW of York
Beautifully restored Beningbrough Hall (National Trust), was built in 1716 and is set in parkland.

BENINGTON Hertfordshire TL2923
Village off A602, 4 miles (6km) E of Stevenage
Picturesque green and cottages. Benington Lordship Gardens on Norman castle site, sloping down hill to ponds; snowdrops, roses, nursery garden,

BENLLECH Gwynedd (Anglesey) SH5182
Village on A5025, 8 miles (13km) SE of Amlwch
Two miles (3km) of sands and cliffs make this a favourite family resort. Headland hillfort possibly occupied by Romans. Rhuddlan Fawr Farm has museum and trails.

BENSON Oxfordshire SU6291
Village on B4009, 2 miles (3km) N of Wallingford
Thames-side village, once an important stage-coach stop and still boasting fine coaching inns, at the edge of a well-known RAF station.

BENTHALL Shropshire SJ6602
Village on B4375, 1 mile (2km) SW of Ironbridge
The Benthall family still occupy thelate 16th-century hall (National Trust), an intriguing house. Interesting church of 1667 with motley additions.

BENTLEY Hampshire SU7844
Village on A31, 4 miles (6km) SW of Farnham
Large village, mostly brick. Jenkyn Place has perhaps the best garden in the county, in many different styles and with unusual plants.

BENTLEY South Yorkshire SE5605
Town on A19, immediately NW of Doncaster
A suburb of Doncaster and the home of Doncaster Rugby League Club. The Church of St Peter is impressive both inside and out.

BENTLEY Suffolk TM1138
Village off A137, 5 miles (8km) SW of Ipswich
Legend has it that buried treasure lies beneath the great stone that is all that remains of Dodnash Priory.

BENWELL Tyne and Wear NZ2164
District in Newcastle upon Tyne
This settlement dates back to Roman times when there was a temple dedicated to the god Antenociticus. There was also a *Vallum* (ditch) crossing.

BENWICK Cambridgeshire TL3490
Village on B1093, 4 miles (6km) NW of Chatteris
On the banks of the Old Nene, Benwick stands exposed on the great flat expanses of the Fens. The pub is called The Five Alls.

BEOLEY Hereford and Worcester SP0669
Village on B4101, 2 miles (3km) NE of Redditch
Norman and medieval church contains monument to William Sheldon (died in around 1570), who introduced tapestry-weaving to England (see Barcheston).

BERDEN Essex TL4629
Village off B1038, 5 miles (8km) NW of Bishop's Stortford
Medieval church with Roman tiles in its walls. 'Boy Bishop' custom occasionally revived here. Elizabethan manor house and former priory.

BERE ALSTON Devon SX4466
Village off B3257, 5 miles (8km) SW of Tavistock
A large village, the centre of a market gardening area, with daffodil growing. Had silver mines in medieval times.

BERE FERRERS Devon SX4563
Village off A386, 7 miles (11km) S of Tavistock
On a spit of land cut off on two sides by the wide estuaries of the Tamar and Tavey. The village runs down to the Tavey, with the church right by the water an interesting building, with good fittings.

BERE REGIS Dorset SY8494
Village off A35, 7 miles (11km) NW of Wareham church
Old-fashioned main street with lots of brick buildings erected after a bad fire in 1788. One of the most interesting churches in Dorset, with a very pretty tower and an elaborate timber roof of 1475. Tombs and a stained-glass window are memorials to the Turbervilles, used by Thomas Hardy in his novel *Tess of the D'Urbervilles.*

BERKELEY Gloucestershire ST6899
Village on B4509, 5 miles (8km) W of Dursley
The 'capital' of the Severnside region of scattered farms known as the Vale of Berkeley, this pleasant town is dominated by the extensive and well-preserved castle, with its keep, great hall, state apartments and cell where Edward II was murdered in 1327. An interesting church is set within the castle bounds. The Jenner Museum (Church Lane) commemorates the pioneer of smallpox vaccines.

BERKHAMSTED Hertfordshire SP9907
Town on A41, 6 miles (10km) SE of Tring
Busy shopping town in narrow Chilterns Gap guarded by ruined Norman castle (English Heritage) and traversed by River Bulbourne, Grand Union Canal, road and railway. Attractive canalside with Boat pub. Old houses in Castle Street and High Street. Original 16th-century premises of Berkhamsted School, whose old boys include Graham Greene. Outside town to north is Berkhamsted Common (National Trust).

BERKSWELL West Midlands SP2479
Village off A452, 6 miles (10km) W of Coventry
The old heart of this popular village is carefully conserved, with its outstanding Norman church, former 17th-century rectory and Elizabethan Bear inn. The stocks and whipping post stand on the village green, and a 19th-century four-storey windmill with most of its machinery intact has been restored to the south of the village (limited opening).

BERMONDSEY Greater London TQ3479
District in borough of Southwark
Former docks and slum area southeast of London Bridge. Bermondsey Abbey here in Middle Ages. St Mary Magdalene, mainly 17th century. Riverside wharves and warehouses attractively redeveloped. London Dungeon, if you dare (children lap it up), Design Museum, HMS *Belfast* moored near Tower Bridge. Thames views from Angel pub, known to Pepys and Laurel and Hardy.

BERRIEW Powys SJ1801
Hamlet on B4385, 5 miles (8km) SW of Welshpool
Church and half-timbered old buildings cluster around river. Museum presents work of modern sculptor Andrew Logan. Black and white Lion inn is a well-known hostelry.

BERRINGTON HALL Hereford and Worcester SO5164
see Eye

BERRY POMEROY Devon SX8261
Village off A385, 2 miles (3km) E of Totnes
Small village with good views and a nice medieval church, best known for its castle (1 mile/ $^1/_2$km) northeast – English Heritage)which is romantically sited in woodland and looking over a small ravine. It is mostly ruins apart from the strong gatehouse.

BERRYNARBOR Devon SS5646
Village off A399, 3 miles (5km) SE of Ilfracombe
In a steep valley just back from the sea, with tightly packed white-painted cottages; picturesque setting. Watermouth Castle, down by the sea, is a large mock castle of 1825 and 1845, now an amusement centre.

BERSHAM Clwyd SJ3049
Village on A483, 2 miles (3km) W of Wrexham
Ironworks and heritage centre re-create area's pioneering industrial past, heavily influenced by John 'Iron Mad' Wilkinson. Part of Clywedog Valley Heritage Trail.

BERWICK East Sussex TQ5105
Village on A27, 7 miles (11km) SE of Lewes
Beneath South Downs. Church (murals by Clive Grant, Vanessa and Quentin Bell), pub and cottages. Nearby Drusilla's, with zoo, country gardens and craft centre.

BERWICK BASSETT Wiltshire SU0973
Village off A4361, 2 miles (3km) N of Avebury
Below the Marlborough Downs, with two old manor houses and a church built from Sarsen stone.

BERWICK-UPON-TWEED Northumberland NT9953
Town on A1, 58 miles (93km) NW of Newcastle upon Tyne
England's most northerly town, on the Tweed estuary, changed hands no less than 14 times during that turbulent period of history when the English and Scots fought to control the Border lands. Berwick-upon-Tweed was first fortified in the 13th century and subsequent modifications by Henry VIII form the basis of the Elizabethan walls which now encircle the town centre.

Berwick Castle ruins date from the 13th century but where the great hall once stood is now the site of the railway station platform, although the west curtain wall is still visible. Holy Trinity Parish Church is one of only two built during the reign of Oliver Cromwell, and is notable for the renaissance pulpit panels of Swiss or German glass, and an impressive west doorway.

The town has three distinctive bridges spanning the River Tweed, the oldest being the 17th-century, 15-arch Berwick bridge. The Royal Border bridge was designed by Robert Stevenson and opened by Queen Victoria in 1850 to carry mainline trains between Edinburgh and London. Berwick's traditional industries of salmon netting and sea fishing are still very much in evidence today.

BERWYN MOUNTAINS Clwyd
Mountain range
Few roads cross these silent, heather-topped heights pierced by steep, tree-clad valleys. Moel Sych highest point at 2,713ft (827m).

BESSACARR South Yorkshire SE6100
District on A638, on SE edge of Doncaster
A popular residential district of Doncaster which expanded rapidly after World War II.

BESTWOOD Nottinghamshire SK5746
District in N Nottingham
Former royal deer park and reclaimed colliery tip make up Bestwood Country Park. The colliery's steam winding engine and headstocks are architecturally listed. Bestwood Pumping Station, 1871–4, Gothic with tall chimney, stands in landscaped park. Bestwood Lodge, now a hotel, is a flamboyant Victorian building by Teulon. Model Aviation Museum near by.

BETCHWORTH Surrey TQ2150
Village off A25, 3 miles (5km) E of Dorking
Satisfying long street between River Mole and the North Downs. Church surrounded by mellow cottages beside grounds of Betchworth House.

BETHERSDEN Kent TQ9240
Village off A28, 6 miles (10km) SW of Ashford
Cosy, unassuming village with some medieval and some modern houses, separated by bright gardens. Known for its marble, quarried in the Middle Ages.

BETHESDA Gwynedd SH6266
Town on A5, 5 miles (8km) SE of Bangor
At foot of Nant Ffrancon Pass and below huge hillside amphitheatre sculpted by world's largest open-cast slate mine, Penrhyn Slate Quarry, developed in the 18th and 19th centuries.

BETHNAL GREEN Greater London TQ3482
District in borough of Tower Hamlets
Appalling East End Victorian slum, cleared after 1945. Museum of Childhood with Victoria and Albert Museum's collection.

BETLEY Staffordshire SJ7548
Village on A531, 6 miles (10km) W of Newcastle-under-Lyme
Very pretty mereside village. Unusual church with wooden columns and timber-framed clerestory.

BETTWS-NEWYDD Gwent SO3605
Hamlet off B4598, 3 miles (5km) W of Raglan
Pleasantly situated in rolling, rural surroundings of Vale of Usk. Church has remarkable late 15th-century rood screen.

BETTWS-Y-CRWYN Shropshire SO2081
Hamlet off B4368, 6 miles (10km) W of Clun
In a lonely situation high above the Clun Valley, St Mary's, the 'farmers' church', has fine roof timbers and a delicate chancel screen.

BETTYHILL Highland NC7061
Village on A836, 9 miles (14km) SW of Strathy
Major crofting township on estuary of River Naver, noted salmon river. Extensive Bronze Age and Pictish remains in Strathnaver, part of which forms Invernaver Nature Reserve, noted for birds and alpine plants. Museum in old Farr church with emphasis on appalling local Clearances by Duke of Sutherland and exceptional 9th-century Pictish cross in churchyard.

BETWS-Y-COED Gwynedd SH7956
Village on A5, 18 miles (29km) NW of Corwen
This mountain-ringed village has been a very popular inland resort since Victorian times and the coming of the railways. Trains still operate, north to Llandudno Junction, southwest to Blaenau Ffestiniog to link up with the narrow-gauge Ffestiniog Railway.

In a setting of afforested mountain, glen and river, the village attracts many outdoor enthusiasts. Footpaths, often used by the old lead-miners, fan out to much-visited spots. Favourites are the Miners' Bridge, spectacular Conwy Falls (separated by a stretch of white water from the Fairy Glen), the foaming Swallow Falls, and Ty Hyll, the Ugly House, an odd edifice of boulder-like stones. In the valley is the confluence of the Conwy, Lledr and Llugwy rivers, spanned by some fine bridges. Stone-arched Pont-y-Pair, the 'Bridge of the Cauldron', is aptly named. Thomas Telford designed the graceful iron Waterloo Bridge of 1815.

Along with many craft and outdoor equipment shops and Victorian hotels are a railway museum, motor museum and, in the Royal Oak hotel's stables, a visitor centre spotlighting the natural history of the Snowdonia National Park and Gwydyr Forest. The 'Old Church' houses an unusual effigy of Dafydd Goch, Llywelyn the Last's great-nephew.

BEVERLEY Humberside TA0339
Town on A164, 8 miles (13km) N of Hull
Beverley is a very pretty market town with elegant Georgian terraces and promenades, described by Sir John Betjeman as 'a place for walking in and living in', and which the National Council of Archaeology has declared 'so splendid and precious that the ultimate responsibility for it should be a national concern'.

A retreat for John, Bishop of York 1300 years ago, the town became a place of pilgrimage for believers in his miracles. When he was canonised St John of Beverley, the first Minster was granted lands and privileges by King Athelstan. Through Viking and Norman conquests the buildings were changed and destroyed until 1220, when the Minster standing today was begun, a splendid example of Gothic architecture. St John's tomb is marked by a giant slab in the centre of the Minster.

Beverley's other great church, St Mary's, was built 700 years ago with money raised by the ancient guilds which represented the town's cloth-weaving, tanning and dyeing trades. Between the two churches is the town's market centre which also separates the Saturday and Wednesday market places.

BEVERSTONE Gloucestershire ST8694
Village on A4135, 2 miles (3km) W of Tetbury
A prim Victorian estate village, with evidence of greater antiquity in Saxon sculpture on church tower and remains of medieval castle.

BEWCASTLE Cumbria NY5674
Hamlet off B5318, 9 miles (14km) N of Brampton
Close to England–Scotland border. Well known to drovers taking sheep to market in the south; an inn still called the Drove between Bewcastle and Roadhead.

BEWDLEY Hereford and Worcester SO7875
Town off A456, 3 miles (5km) W of Kidderminster
Until the 18th century Bewdley was a major river port for the Midlands with its own prosperous trade in brass, horn and leather goods. Its decline began when neighbouring Stourport acquired a canal link with the Midlands, but much remains of a gracious little town, especially the harmonious buildings on the long waterfront and in Load Street, which resembles a market square closed off by the classical St Anne's Church. Prominent here are the George hotel, a coaching inn, and the guildhall of 1808, next to which is the Shambles, a former butchers' market now housing a lively local history museum, a reconstructed brass foundry and craft displays. Behind the church, Park Lane leads to Tickenhill Manor, an 18th-century mansion on the site of a medieval royal palace.

Other attractive buildings abound in High Street and Lower Park, especially the Bailiff's House of 1610, the Manor House, the Sayers Almshouses and Lower Park House, birthplace of Stanley Baldwin, whose constituency this was.

Across Thomas Telford's elegant bridge of 1798 is the headquarters of the Severn Valley Railway, Britain's longest restored standard-gauge line, which carries steam train services between Kidderminster and Bridgnorth.

West Midlands Safari and Leisure Park near by (open in summer).

BEWHOLME Humberside TA1649
Village off B1242, 3 miles (5km) NW of Hornsea
A small village with a church dedicated to St John the Baptist, built in 1905, and a 17th-century manor house.

BEWL BRIDGE RESERVOIR/BEWL WATER East Sussex TQ6833
Reservoir off B2100, 2 miles (3km) S of Lamberhurst
One of England's largest reservoirs. Bewl Water activity centre: water sports and adventure centre (open all year).

BEXHILL East Sussex TQ7407
Town on A259, 5 miles (8km) W of Hastings
Genteel seaside resort developed from the 1880s and still overwhelmingly Victorian. Some newer tower blocks. The 1930s De la Warr Pavilion crouches on the front overlooking the wide sandy beach. Submerged forest off Galley Hill. Old Bexhill, swamped by the resort, stands on the hill inland with some pretty houses and cottages near the church.

BEXLEY Greater London TQ4973
District in borough of Bexley, SE London
Old Bexley village on River Cray and grand estates islanded in 20th-century suburbia. Bexley Museum in Hall Place, 16th century, with gardens, topiary, park. In neighbouring Bexleyheath are Red House (open by appointment) built 1860 by Philip Webb for William Morris, and Danson Place in Capability Brown grounds.

BIBURY Gloucestershire SP1106
Village on B4425, 7 miles (11km) NE of Cirencester
William Morris's 'most beautiful Cotswold village' has an ancient church of great interest, but its famous attractions are Arlington Row (National Trust – not open), a line of 17th-century weavers' cottages, and Arlington Mill, a 17th-century watermill (housing a museum) restored to working order. Bibury Trout Farm is open for fishing, exhibitions and sales.

BICESTER Oxfordshire SP5823
Town on A421, 11 miles (18km) NE of Oxford
An ancient town of Roman origin, Bicester serves the needs of an extensive rural community and also prospers from the big army and RAF installations near by. Its old market town character survives in the venerable buildings at its centre, especially in Market End and Sheep Street. The Church of St Edburgh is also worth a visit.

BICKENHILL West Midlands SP1882
Village off A45, 3 miles (5km) NE of Solihull
The giant National Exhibition Centre, opened here in 1976, stages large-scale exhibitions and performance events. The National Motorcycle Museum near by displays 650 machines.

BICKER Lincolnshire TF2237
Village on A52, 2 miles (3km) NE of Donington
Former port on Bicker Haven, now several miles inland thanks to Fen drainage. Impressive cruciform church with outstanding Norman nave.

BICKLEIGH Devon SS9407
Village on A396, 4 miles (6km) S of Tiverton
Lies across the Exe Valley, with thatched cottages and a 16th-century bridge making a pretty picture. The castle (really a fortified manor house) has an idyllic setting by the river. The mill has crafts, rural displays and animals.

BICKNACRE Essex TL7802
Village on B1418, 5 miles (8km) SW of Maldon
A single, solitary arch is all that is left of a medieval priory. Long a hamlet, but much new post-war housing.

BICKNOLLER Somerset ST1139
Village off A358, 4 miles (6km) SE of Watchet
Picturesque thatched cottages; 15th-century church with good wooden screen and bench-ends.

BICTON Devon SY0686
Site on A376, 3 miles (5km) N of Budleigh Salterton
Bicton Park Gardens have 60 acres (24ha) of formal gardens and parklands, a big palm house of 1840, a bird garden and a woodland miniature railway.

BIDBOROUGH Kent TQ5643
Village on B2176, 3 miles (5km) SW of Tonbridge
Delightful village with bungalows and newer houses set among the older cottages with pretty gardens. Superb views across High Weald.

BIDDENDEN Kent TQ8538
Village on A262, 6 miles (10km) NW of Tenterden
Main street with attractive houses and village green. Dole still handed out at Easter in terms of bequest of 'Biddenden Maids', 12th-century Siamese twins.

BIDDENHAM Bedfordshire TL0250
Village off A428, 2 miles (3km) W of Bedford
Attractive village in a bend of the Great Ouse, outside Bedford. Thatched cottages, village pond, church near the river.

BIDDESTONE Wiltshire ST8673
Village off A420, 4 miles (6km) W of Chippenham
Stone houses and cottages around a green, with a village pond. Church Norman onwards, still with Georgian box pews and gallery.

BIDDULPH Staffordshire SJ8858
Town on A527, 7 miles (11km) N of Stoke-on-Trent
Isolated moorland town with famous Biddulph Grange Garden (National Trust). Exotic themed areas, rock and water features, unusual buildings.

BIDEFORD Devon SS4526
Town off A39, 9 miles (14km) SW of Barnstaple
A successful port from the late 17th century, on the big estuary of the River Torridge. There are fine 17th- and 18th-century merchants' houses in Bridgeland Street, but the town is now mostly rather neglected-looking. Large 1883 covered market, narrow twisting streets up the hill. The long bridge is basically 13th century, much repaired. Burton Gallery, local museum.

BIDFORD-ON-AVON Warwickshire SP1052
Village on B439, 7 miles (11km) W of Stratford-upon-Avon
The riverside park close to a medieval bridge over the River Avon is popular in summer. Shakespeare is reputed to have drunk at the former Falcon inn.

BIDSTON Merseyside SJ2890
District in Birkenhead
An attractive village dominated by Bidston Hill with an observatory and windmill at the summit.

BIERTON Buckinghamshire SP8415
Village on A418, 2 miles (3km) NE of Aylesbury
Human settlement here since Iron Age and in Roman and Saxon times. Attractive 14th-century church.

BIGBURY-ON-SEA Devon SX6544
Village on B3392, 3 miles (5km) S of Modbury
The seaside off-shoot from an inland village, mostly modern with good sea views. Wide sandy beaches and rocky cliffs. See Burgh Island.

BIGGAR Strathclyde NT0437
Small town on A702, 13 miles (21km) W of Peebles
Lowland market town in sweeping Vale of Biggar with plethora of museums devoted to local history; including Victorian everyday life and a gasworks.

BIGGIN Derbyshire SK1559
Village off A515, 8 miles (13km) N of Ashbourne
In Peak District National Park, close to beautiful Dovedale. Cyclists and walkers can approach along Tissington Trail, a former railway route.

BIGGIN HILL Greater London TQ4159
Village in borough of Bromley
Celebrated Battle of Britain airfield, with model Spitfire and Hurricane planes at gate, north of post-war housing sprawl.

BIGGLESWADE Bedfordshire TL1944
Town off A1, 9 miles (14km) SE of Bedford
Not Bedfordshire's most prepossessing town. On River Ivel and now bypassed by the Great North road. White Hart survives from days when it was a flourishing coaching stop.

BIGHTON Hampshire SU6134
Village off B3046, 2 miles (3km) NE of Alresford
Agreeable village – brick, flint and timber-framing all mixed up, some thatch. Tiny and charming church, partly Norman.

BIGNOR West Sussex SU9814
Village off A29, 5 miles (8km) S of Petworth
Old-fashioned little place of half-timbered houses built around quadrangle of narrow lanes. Famed for its Roman villa with superb mosaics.

BILDESTON Suffolk TL9949
Village on B1115, 5 miles (8km) N of Hadleigh
Terraces of weavers' cottages lead off from the long winding High Street flanked by timber-framed houses dating from the 16th century.

BILLERICAY Essex TQ6794
Town on A129, 5 miles (8km) E of Brentwood
Post-war residential and industrial estates have changed this old town, now an outlier of Basildon (see). The 16th-century Chantry House was a meeting place for the Pilgrim Fathers. Cater museum of local history opened 1960, Barleylands Farm Museum has agricultural displays and vintage farm machinery. Norsey Wood, where 1381 Peasants' Revolt was crushed, is a nature reserve.

BILLESDON Leicestershire SK7202
Village on A47, 8 miles (13km) E of Leicester
Grew from agricultural settlement to 19th-century coaching stop. Many attractive ironstone buildings. Surrounding land developed as hunting country for Quorn Hunt.

BILLINGBOROUGH Lincolnshire TF1133
Village on B1177, 9 miles (14km) N of Bourne
Large village on edge of Fens, centred around church with tall tower and spire. Several 17th-century buildings, some altered later.

BILLINGFORD Norfolk TM1678
Village on A143, 2 miles (3km) E of Diss
There is a fine five-storey windmill open at weekends, splendid with its bright white sails. The Church of St Leonard has early 14th-century wall-paintings.

BILLINGHAM Cleveland NZ4624
Town off A19, 2 miles (3km) NE of Stockton-on-Tees
An ancient village transformed when a factory opened during World War I to produce nitrogen. Town now dominated by chemical industry.

BILLINGSHURST West Sussex TQ0825
Small town on A29, 6 miles (10km) SW of Horsham
Attractive small town with High Street on line of Roman Stane Street. Fine old timbered houses and tasteful modern development.

BILSTHORPE Nottinghamshire SK6460
Village off A617, 4 miles (6km) S of Ollerton
Close to Sherwood Forest, the old village and church remain secluded from the inter-war housing which grew up around the colliery.

BILSTON West Midlands SO9596
District in SE area of Wolverhampton
Poet Henry Newbolt was born in this former steel-making town where the museum has a fine collection of painted enamels, once a Black Country speciality.

The stocks on the village green at Bilton.

BILTON Warwickshire SP4873
District in SW area of Rugby
The old village survives in the Rugby suburbs with a good 14th-century church and Bilton Hall (not open), home of essayist Joseph Addison.

BINBROOK Lincolnshire TF2093
Village on B1203, 7 miles (11km) NE of Market Rasen
Former Wolds market town, clustered around hillside market place and grand Victorian church. Base for World War II No 1 Bomber Squadron.

BINCHESTER BLOCKS Durham NZ2232
Roman Site off A689, 1 mile (2km) N of Bishop Auckland
The site of a Roman fort called Vinovia built around AD80 as one of a chain guarding the road between York and Hadrian's Wall.

BINEGAR Somerset ST6149
Village off A37, 4 miles (6km) N of Shepton Mallet
Mostly modern, in the Mendips.

BINFIELD Berkshire SU8471
Village on B3034, 2 miles (3km) NW of Bracknell
Now partly suburban, but the further parts still rural. The 15th-century church tower is of the odd local building stone – dark brown conglomerate.

BINGHAM Nottinghamshire SK7039
Village on A52, 8 miles (13km) E of Nottingham
Busy village bypassed by the Nottingham – Grantham road and the Fosse Way, with butter cross, 1861, in the market place. The steepled Church of All Saints' has interesting medieval features, including monument to an early 14th-century knight, possibly Richard de Bingham. Henry IV's supporter Thomas de Rempstone and his son who fought at Agincourt are buried here.

BINGLEY West Yorkshire SE1039
Town on A650, 5 miles (8km) NW of Bradford
A market town in the Aire Valley, headquarters of the Bradford and Bingley Building Society and known nationally as a centre for thermal underwear. The Three and Five Rise Locks on the Leeds and Liverpool Canal raise the canal by over 59ft (18m) and were a major engineering feat of the 18th century.

BINHAM Norfolk TF9839
Village on B1388, 5 miles (8km) SE of Wells-next-the-Sea
A compact little flint-built village with the remains of a once-splendid Benedictine monastery. The fine Norman abbey church is still used.

BINSEY Oxfordshire SP4907
Hamlet off A420, 2 miles (3km) NW of Oxford
This rural oasis, with its tiny church and holy well, is a popular destination for gentle walks out from north Oxford.

BINSTEAD Isle of Wight SZ5892
Site off A3054, 2 miles (3km) W of Ryde
Almost part of Ryde now. Brickfields Horsecountry; shire horses, farm museum and carriage rides.

BINSTED Hampshire SU7741
Village off A31, 4 miles (6km) NE of Alton
Large, very rural village, with oasthouses and malthouses. Once a hop-growing area. The fine medieval church is the burial place of Viscount Montgomery of Alamein.

BINTON Warwickshire SP1454
Village off B439, 4 miles (6km) W of Stratford-upon-Avon
In this hillside village overlooking the River Avon the church has a pictorial window commemorating Captain Scott's fatal Antarctic expedition.

BIRCHAM NEWTON Norfolk TF7733
Village on B1153, 3 miles (5km) S of Docking
On the fringe of the Sandringham estate, beautiful Bircham Newton is a conservation area. All Saints' Church is one of the smallest in England.

BIRCHINGTON Kent TR3069
Village off A28, 4 miles (6km) W of Margate
Relatively quiet Thanet resort with cliffs and bays on north coast. Burial place of the pre-Raphaelite artist and poet, Dante Gabriel Rossetti. Quex House, with its remarkable museum, stands in its park near by dominated by the extraordinary bell tower, with a peal of 12 bells, and an openwork spire of cast iron.

BIRCHOVER Derbyshire SK2362
Village off B5056, 4 miles (6km) W of Matlock
On Stanton Moor hillside, in Peak District National Park. Houses of warm local stone. Eighteenth-century clergyman carved Rowtor Rocks into seats.

BIRDLIP Gloucestershire SO9214
Village on A417, 5 miles (8km) SW of Cheltenham
Sitting 1,000ft (300m) up on a Cotswold escarpment, the village commands panoramic views across the Severn Valley to the Malvern Hills and Welsh mountains.

BIRDOSWALD Cumbria NY6166
Roman site off B6318, 1 mile (2km) W of Gilsland
One of the best-preserved sections of Hadrian's Wall, where a Roman fort was built guarding the bridge over the River Irthing.

BIRGHAM Borders NT7939
Village on A698, 3 miles (5km) W of Coldstream
The Treaty of Birgham (1290) established details of Scotland's independence. 'Go to Birgham!' old local pejorative exclamation, Birgham being furthest south possible without crossing border.

BIRKENHEAD Merseyside SJ3288
Town on A41, across the River Mersey from Liverpool
The ship-building industry has now declined but Birkenhead has made great efforts to regenerate the town. Birkenhead Waterfront is developing as a visitor attraction with a heritage trail. The Woodside Ferry Terminal still provides a transport link with Liverpool, and displays the history of Mersey Ferries and the tourist information centre is also here. On East Float Dock Road a pair of historic warships are now museums; Frigate HMS *Plymouth* and submarine HMS *Onyx* served during the Falklands War. Both are open to the public.

Birkenhead Park, designed by Sir Joseph Paxton and opened in 1847, was the first public park in the country and provided the model for New York's Central Park. Sandstone lodges at the various entrances were built to reflect different periods of architecture.

At the Williamson Art Gallery and Museum the main attractions are a collection of English watercolours, Liverpool porcelain, Della Robia pottery and a display of ferry models.

Birkenhead Priory is Merseyside's oldest building, established in 1150 by Benedictine monks who also operated the first-ever ferry service across the Mersey.

BIRKIN North Yorkshire SE5326
Village off A645, 3 miles (5km) NE of Knottingley
Village situated on what is known as the Old Eye, once the course of the River Aire.

BIRLING Kent TQ6860
Village off A20, 6 miles (10km) NW of Maidstone
Unpretentious little village compactly grouped beneath the North Downs with its church on a hill rising steeply to the north.

BIRMINGHAM West Midlands SP0786
City off M5/M6/M42, 100 miles (161km) NW of London
From the 14th century the village of Birmingham was noted for its ironwork, and centuries of expertise in the metal trades gave Birmingham a head start during the Industrial Revolution of the 18th century, when its plentiful supplies of coal and iron made it a major industrial centre. A population of 35,000 in 1760 grew to 233,000 by 1851, when Birmingham was gaining its reputation as 'the workshop of the world'.

Demand for its multifarious products kept the city buoyant throughout the 19th century and well into the 20th, but the decline of large-scale metal industries after World War II brought a change of direction. Its position at the centre of England and the developing motorway network made it an ideal base for the new service industries. The 1960s saw massive redevelopment as Birmingham set out to provide hotels, office complexes and shopping facilities worthy of England's 'second city'.

It has been especially successful in exploiting London's congestion to promote rival venues for exhibitions, conventions and cultural events. The National Exhibition Centre at Bickenhill, with Birmingham International Airport next door, is complemented by the International Convention Centre in Broad Street.

The city's new international status has wrought a transformation in shopping and entertainment. Sophisticated shopping centres like the Bull Ring, the City Plaza, The Pallasades and Pavilions co-exist with traditional street shops. The nightlife, too, has become distinctly metropolitan, with a wide choice of cinemas, night clubs and theatres (notably the Hippodrome, the Alexandra and the famous Birmingham 'Rep'). Significantly, the former Sadler's Wells company has relocated to the city as the Birmingham Royal Ballet, and the Convention Centre houses the much-acclaimed Symphony Hall, home of the world-class City of Birmingham Symphony Orchestra. The Museum and Art Gallery in Chamberlain Square is famous for its Pre-Raphaelite collection, while a rich industrial history is vividly portrayed at the Museum of Science and Industry in Newhall Street.

The transformation of central Birmingham has not banished more traditional attractions, and the city makes much of its Victorian heritage. The focal points are Victoria Square and Chamberlain Square, which feature some fine 19th-century buildings, notably the town hall in Victoria Square, a multi-columned temple by Joseph Hansom, and the neighbouring Council House, the equally impressive municipal headquarters erected in the 1870s. Opposite the town hall is the château-like General Post Office of 1890, and the mid-1970s Central Library (the largest public library in Europe) stands near by. In Bath Street is Pugin's twin-spired Roman Catholic Cathedral of St Chad, while its Anglican counterpart, a splendid baroque building, stands in Colmore Row.

One of the few surviving traditional industries continues to thrive in the jewellery quarter near St Paul's Square, which attracts thousands of visitors to its many workshops and retail outlets (a visit to St Paul's Church is also recommended). Another industrial survival is the complex canal network, and the lively Gas Street Basin, next to the International Convention Centre, is a major attraction.

BIRMINGHAM INTERNATIONAL AIRPORT West Midlands SK1984
see Elmdon

BIRNAM Tayside NO0341
Village on A9, 1 mile (2km) S of Dunkeld
On River Tay and famous through Shakespeare's *Macbeth*, when Birnam Wood advanced to Dunsinane. The original home of Beatrix Potter's Peter Rabbit.

BIRNIE Grampian NJ2058
Village off A941, 3 miles (5km) S of Elgin
Parish church claims to be oldest in continuous use in Scotland. Churchyard contains the Celtic 'Ronnel Bell'.

BIRSAY Orkney HY2527
Hamlet on A966, 1 mile (2km) E of Brough Head
Centre of Norse power before construction of Kirkwall Cathedral. Remains of Earl's Palace, built in 1570s, originally grandiose structure surrounded by gardens.

Church of St Martin, Birmingham.

BIRSTALL Leicestershire SK5909
Northern area of Leicester
Large residential area adjoining north Leicester. Timber-framed cottages near church by River Soar. Restored steam Great Central Railway's southern terminus.

The 'Swan' tomb in the Thames-side church at Bisham.

BIRSTALL West Yorkshire SE2225
Town on A62, 2 miles (3km) NW of Batley
Tudor Oakwell Hall appears in Charlotte Brontë's novel *Shirley* as Fieldhead, home of the heroine Shirley Keeldar.

BIRSTWITH North Yorkshire SE2359
Village off B6165, 5 miles (8km) NW of Harrogate
A pleasant village just outside Harrogate with an attractive footbridge built in 1822 over the River Nidd.

BIRTLEY Tyne and Wear NZ2756
Town on A167, 5 miles (8km) S of Gateshead
Developed with its industries of iron-making and coal-mining, which have now ceased. Light industry and chemicals have replaced them.

BIRTSMORTON Hereford and Worcester SO8035
Hamlet off A438, 6 miles (10km) west of Tewkesbury
Picturesque Birtsmorton Court (not open), where the future Cardinal Wolsey was family chaplain, stands next to church with much medieval glass.

BISHAM Berkshire SU8485
Village off A404, 5 miles (8km) NW of Maidenhead
Right on the River Thames, with woody hills behind. Pretty village, with a suspension bridge of 1836 over to Marlow. Norman church tower, and a remarkable collection of monuments inside; churchyard bordering the river, good views.

BISHOP AUCKLAND Durham NZ2028
Town on A688, 9 miles (14km) SW of Durham
Ancient market town with town hall, a Grade 1 Listed Building, in the market place which now houses a library, art and exhibition galleries and the tourist information centre. Auckland Castle, built 12th century by Bishop Puiset, principal residence of Prince Bishops since Norman times, and more recently the Bishops of Durham.

BISHOP BURTON Humberside SE9839
Village on A1079, 3 miles (5km) W of Beverley
Picturesque village with duck pond. Bishop Burton College of Agriculture has parkland, woodland walks, a Victorian conservatory and farmland.

BISHOP MIDDLEHAM Durham NZ3231
Village off A177, 2 miles (3km) NW of Sedgefield
Named after its long-gone medieval bishop's castle. Mainsford Hall was home of Robert Surtees, famous County Durham historian.

BISHOP MONKTON North Yorkshire SE3266
Village off A61, 3 miles (5km) S of Ripon
A pretty village near Ripon which earned itself a reputation as a 'hot-bed of gambling' when whist drives were illegal.

BISHOP WILTON Humberside SE7955
Village off A166, 5 miles (8km) E of Stamford Bridge
On a Roman road with little bridges connecting the narrow streets. Tiny Norman Church of St Edith has a rare black and white mosaic floor.

BISHOP'S CASTLE Shropshire SO3288

Small town off A488, 8 miles (13km) NW of Craven Arms

The long main street of this miniature market town, lined with houses spanning several centuries, rises from the church, with its squat Norman tower, to the remains of the castle behind the Castle hotel of 1719. The 18th-century town hall has a lock-up in the basement. Real-ale enthusiasts relish famous home-brewed beers at the Three Tuns.

Half-timbered 'House on Crutches' in Bishop's Castle.

BISHOP'S CLEEVE Gloucestershire SO9627

Village on A435, 4 miles (6km) N of Cheltenham

Now a Cheltenham dormitory, this old village has a fascinating Norman and medieval church and a community centre fashioned from a 15th-century barn.

BISHOP'S FROME Hereford and Worcester SO6648

Village on B4214, 4 miles (6km) S of Bromyard

Two interesting monuments in the village church, of a medieval knight drawing a sword and an Elizabethan lady kneeling above her skeleton.

BISHOP'S ITCHINGTON Warwickshire SP3857

Village on B4451, 3 miles (5km) SW of Southam

A 17th-century stone manor house is one of the attractions of a village centre surrounded by much modern development.

BISHOP'S NYMPTON Devon SS7523

Village off B3227, 3 miles (5km) SE of South Molton

Sloping village with thatched cottages and a prominent church tower.

BISHOP'S STORTFORD Hertfordshire TL4821

Town on A120, 8 miles (13km) N of Harlow

Old market and coaching town on River Stort. Owned by Bishops of London, who used Waytemore Castle as prison; the castle mound survives. Shopping and commuter centre today with much post-war development. Impressive Greek Revival former Corn Exchange, St Michael's Church on hill. House where diamond magnate and empire-builder Cecil Rhodes was born in 1853 is now museum to him.

BISHOP'S SUTTON Hampshire SU6032

Village on A31, 1 mile (2km) SE of Alresford

Watercress-growing area. An austere church of the 12th and 13th centuries, with super Norman doorway decorated with stylised birds' heads.

BISHOP'S TACHBROOK Warwickshire SP3161

Village off A452, 3 miles (5km) S of Leamington

This commuter village on the Leamington fringe was the early home of poet Walter Savage Landor, who is commemorated in St Chad's Church.

BISHOP'S TAWTON Devon SS5729

Village on A377, 2 miles (3km) S of Barnstaple

Small and picturesque church, large village with some thatched cottages. Codden Hill to the southeast gives good views.

BISHOP'S WALTHAM Hampshire SU5517

Small town off B2177, 7 miles (11km) N of Fareham

Densely packed with small Georgian houses and cottages, mostly brick. Several humble Victorian shop fronts survive, and the whole little town has a happy old-fashioned air. Unusual church tower of 1589, 17th-century aisles. The Bishop's Palace (English Heritage) is an impressive ruin, 12th to 15th century. Local museum.

BISHOP'S WOOD Staffordshire SJ8309

Village off A5, 8 miles (13km) NW of Wolverhampton

From its high position near the Shropshire border fine views extend to Cannock Chase and Wrekin. Nearby Belvide Reservoir attracts bird-watchers.

BISHOPBRIGGS Strathclyde NS6070

District on A803, in N Glasgow

District on the northern outskirts of Glasgow with good civic amenities. Near by is the Forth–Clyde Canal and the line of the Roman wall.

BISHOPS CANNINGS Wiltshire SU0364

Village off A361, 3 miles (5km) NE of Devizes

Small village with a huge church, built here because the estate belonged to the Bishop of Salisbury. Mostly 13th-century, in style like Salisbury Cathedral, with a tower and spire. Inside, a curiosity – a 17th-century penitential seat for the repentant sinner, with a huge hand painted on it. Timber-framed thatched cottages.

BISHOPS LYDEARD Somerset ST1729
Village off A358, 5 miles (8km) NW of Taunton
Large, mostly modern. The start of the West Somerset Railway (steam) which runs to Minehead. One of the best Somerset church towers – 15th century, red sandstone.

BISHOPSBOURNE Kent TR1852
Village off A2, 4 miles (6km) SE of Canterbury
Quiet village in peaceful and green valley of infant River Stour, lying between parkland grounds of two great houses.

BISHOPSTEIGNTON Devon SX9073
Village off A381, 2 miles (3km) W of Teignmouth
Close to the River Teign's short wide estuary, with good views and several 19th-century villas. The roads at Little Haldon, to the north, give wider views of the whole coast.

BISHOPSTOKE Hampshire SU4619
Village on B3354, 2 miles (3km) E of Eastleigh
On the wide River Itchen, which runs alongside the road. A large medieval village, grown even bigger since the 1960s.

BISHOPSTON West Glamorgan SS5789
Village off B4436, 5 miles (8km) SW of Swansea
Narrow and wooded Bishopston Valley leads down from village to secluded Pwlldu Bay, 2 miles (3km) away.

BISHOPSTONE East Sussex TQ4701
Village off A259, 1 mile (2km) N of Seaford
In a fold of the South Downs overlooking the sea; a cluster of houses and a remarkable church with Saxon nave and south porch.

BISHOPSTONE Wiltshire SU2483
Village on B4192, 6 miles (10km) E of Swindon
On the edge of the chalk downs, with thatched cottages, a pond and predominantly 15th-century church.

BISHOPSTONE Wiltshire SU0625
Village off A354, 4 miles (6km) SW of Wilton
In the valley of the River Ebble, chalk downs rising either side. Big, mostly 14th-century church.

BISHOPTHORPE North Yorkshire SE5947
Village off A64, 3 miles (5km) S of York
Contains the Archbishop of York's Palace. Chapel dates from 1241 but main palace was built in 15th century.

BISHOPTON Durham NZ3621
Village off A66, 5 miles (8km) W of Stockton-on-Tees
St Peter's Church contains fragments of medieval stones. The village is now a conservation area, and a popular residence for commuters.

BISHOPTON Strathclyde NS4371
Small town on A8, 6 miles (10km) NW of Paisley
Centre of dairy cattle industry until the 1930s when Royal Ordnance Factory constructed on previous farm land. Acquired by British Aerospace in 1987.

BISLEY Gloucestershire SO9005
Village off A419, 4 miles (6km) E of Stroud
At the head of the Toadsmoor Valley, windswept Bisley has a 16th-century pub and seven wells that are decorated on Ascension Day.

BISLEY Surrey SU9559
Village on A322, 4 miles (6km) W of Woking
Tiny place best known for its National Rifle Association shooting ranges on heath to west, moved here from Wimbledon Common in 1890.

BIX Oxfordshire SU7284
Village on A4130, 3 miles (5km) NW of Henley-on-Thames
This pleasant, scattered village on the edge of the Chiltern Hills has lonely ruins of a Norman church.

BLACK BOURTON Oxfordshire SP2804
Village on B4020, 6 miles (10km) SW of Witney
Overshadowed by the huge Brize Norton air base, but the church with its rare 13th-century wall-paintings deserves a visit.

BLACK COUNTRY West Midlands
Region NW of Birmingham
Formerly independent towns, with distinct regional character, have now become a conurbation centred on Dudley. Strong tradition of mining and specialist metal manufacturing.

BLACK DOWN Dorset SY6187
Hill off B3157, 5 miles (8km) SW of Dorchester
On top of the chalk downs, a stone tower to the memory of Admiral Sir Thomas Masterman Hardy, hero of Battle of Trafalgar. Splendid viewpoint.

BLACK DOWN West Sussex SU9129
Beauty spot off B2131, 3 miles (5km) SE of Haslemere
Highest hill in Sussex, 918ft (280m). Superb viewpoint looking to Mount Harry, 30 miles (48km) away, and through Arun Gap to sea.

BLACK ISLE Highland NH6557
Region in Scotland
Fertile peninsula lying between Cromarty Firth and the Firths of Beauly and Moray, with prosperous farming and woodlands. Ancient remains. Named possibly for lack of frost due to mild climate.

BLACK MOUNTAIN Dyfed/Powys SN7182
Mountain range in Wales
Wild ridge in west of Brecon Beacons National Park, rising to 2,630ft (802m) at Fan Brycheiniog. One of the twin glacial lakes, Llyn-y-fan Fach, figures in famous folk tale.

BLACK MOUNTAINS Powys
Mountain range crossing Wales/England border
Borderland chain of mountains which stretches southwards from Hay-on-Wye in far east of Brecon Beacons National Park. Offa's Dyke Path runs across summits.

BLACK NOTLEY Essex TL7620
Village off B1018, 2 miles (3km) S of Braintree
Celebrated tuberculosis sanatorium is now a general hospital. Pioneer 17th-century botanist John Ray, born and lived here, buried in churchyard.

BLACK TORRINGTON Devon SS4605
Village off A3072, 5 miles (8km) W of Hatherleigh
Last home of the Reverend John (Jack) Russell, who bred the terriers which bear his name, in the 19th century.

BLACKBURN Lancashire SD6827
City on A666, 21 miles (34km) NW of Manchester
The cotton industry was responsible for the good fortunes of Blackburn during the 19th century, and like other towns in this region the architecture reflects Victorian prosperity. Brewing was also important to the town and Daniel Thwaites, founder of Thwaites Brewery, is buried in the churchyard of St John's Church.

The town hall was built in the early 1850s after Blackburn was granted a royal charter and bears an unmistakable resemblance to the Mansion House in London. Opposite is the Exchange building, built in the 1860s as the town's main trading centre for cotton. Blackburn has one of the country's most interesting modern cathedrals. In 1926 a new diocese was carved out of the Diocese of Manchester and the Bishop's throne was placed in Blackburn Parish Church, thus turning it into the new cathedral. As well as works of art there are fragments of a 16th-century window.

Lewis Textile Museum is dedicated to the history of the cotton industry, and the Museum and Art Gallery in Museum Street includes paintings by Turner, the Hart collection of medieval manuscripts and an important collection of Eastern European icons.

BLACKBURN Lothian NS9865
Town on B792, 2 miles (3km) S of Bathgate
Former industrial and coal-mining town in the central belt which recently experienced economic difficulties; lies close to the M8.

BLACKDOWN HILLS Somerset/Devon
Hill range in SW England
Long and woody ridge in south Somerset, forming the border to Devon. Huge Wellington monument, 170ft (52m) obelisk commemorating the Duke of Wellington, the victor of Waterloo.

BLACKFORDBY Leicestershire SK3217
Village off A50, 2 miles (3km) NW of Ashby-de-la-Zouch
Residential village close to south Derbyshire border, with 1850s parish church.

BLACKGANG Isle of Wight SZ4876
Village on A3055, 6 miles (10km) W of Ventnor
At the western end of the landslip, where slips still happen. Big and popular theme park. Viewpoint just to the west looks all along one side of the island to the Needles. St Catherine's Hill, a high downland ridge, has the Oratory, a unique 14th-century stone lighthouse looking like a rocket, or pepper-pot.

BLACKHALL Durham NZ4539
Village off A19, 5 miles (8km) NW of Hartlepool
A village inland from the coast and supportive to Blackhall Colliery, one of the big undersea coal mines in the North East.

BLACKHEATH Greater London TQ3876
District in borough of Lewisham
Attractive suburb with England's oldest golf and rugby clubs. Heath for kite-flying, fairs. Ranger's House, 18th century, has a portrait collection.

BLACKMOOR VALE Somerset/Dorset
Region in SW England
Rich dairying country of north Dorset and south Somerset. Flattish, with small hillocks, winding high-hedged lanes and lots of cows. Sometimes spelt Blackmore Vale.

BLACKMORE Essex TL6001
Village off A414, 7 miles (11km) SW of Chelmsford
Attractive village near River Can. St Laurence's Church has one of England's finest wooden towers, an ingenious masterpiece of carpentry added in 15th century to Norman priory church and topped by broach spire. Strong Henry VIII connection, too, as he visited mistress Elizabeth Blount here at house called Jericho (hence, supposedly, the saying 'Go to Jericho').

BLACKNESS Central NT0580
Village off A904, 4 miles (6km) E of Bo'ness
Old port of Linlithgow with views down Firth of Forth to Bridges from 15th-century Blackness Castle. The House of the Binns lies to south, three-storey tower house in courtyard with encircling crenellated wall, dating from about 1440, where Royal Scots Greys Regiment was raised in 1681.

BLACKPOOL Lancashire SD3036
Town off M55, 15 miles (24km) W of Preston
It was the combination of the Irish Sea and the railway that first made Blackpool such a popular seaside resort. Visitors began to come here in the 18th century to take advantage of the healthy attributes of the sea. It soon became a fashionable resort and the rich, when they were not bathing or even indulging in the national craze of drinking the sea-water, rode in carriages along the promenade, then only a 200yd (182m) stretch of grass.

In 1846 the railway came to Blackpool, offering cheap excursion trains from industrial Lancashire and Yorkshire. The resort was hardly prepared for the thousands of visitors who started to pour in from the densely populated areas of Manchester and Leeds, but it quickly set about making adequate provisions. The Promenade was opened in 1856 and in 1863 the cast-iron North Pier was opened, an exclusive promenade for 'quality' visitors, now a listed building. In 1867 the Prince of Wales Arcade opened, now the site of Blackpool Tower. Open-air dancing for the working classes was introduced on the Central Pier and in 1872 the outdoor Pleasure Gardens were opened at Raikes Hall.

Visitors continued to flock to Blackpool and in 1885 the world's first electric street tramway opened to transport people along the sea front. Today Blackpool is still principally a seaside resort, its main attraction being the Pleasure Beach, a huge fun park with the world's highest and fastest rollercoaster ride and the famous annual Blackpool Illuminations. Live shows and casinos animate the town at night, and amusement arcades line the pavements of the Golden Mile next to stalls selling sticks of rock and candy floss.

BLACKROD Greater Manchester SD6110

Village on A6, 4 miles (6km) NW of Wigan

Arley Hall is a picturesque moated manor house situated on the site of an old abbey, near the Leeds–Liverpool Canal.

BLACKSTONE EDGE West Yorkshire SD9717

Roman site off A58, 8 miles (13km) SW of Halifax

A remarkable stretch of Roman road set on a moorland ridge on the borders of Greater Manchester and West Yorkshire.

BLACKWATER, RIVER Essex

River, flows from near Braintree to Maldon

Flows through Coggeshall and Witham to scenic estuary at Maldon which gave marauding Saxons and Danes a convenient entry into England.

BLACKWOOD Gwent ST1797

Town off A4049, 7 miles (11km) N of Caerphilly

Busy town and shopping centre on hill beside River Sirhowy in eastern valleys of South Wales. Stuart Crystal Glassworks at nearby Aberbargoed has factory tours.

BLADON Oxfordshire SP4514

Village on A4095, 1 mile (2km) S of Woodstock

The estate village on the edge of Blenheim Park draws thousands of visitors to the grave of Sir Winston Churchill.

BLAENAFON Gwent SO2508

Town on A4043, 5 miles (8km) N of Pontypool

Coal and iron were all-pervading here. Big Pit, closed in 1980, is a museum with a difference. Authentic underground tours complete with hats and lamps, conducted by ex-miners plus surface mining paraphernalia. Iron is represented at Europe's best-preserved 18th-century ironworks (Cadw). Blast furnaces, water-balance lift, workers' cottages. St Peter's Church has iron door, font and gravestones.

BLAENAU FFESTINIOG Gwynedd SH7045

Town on A470, 17 miles (27km) SE of Caernarfon

Slate still dominates the landscape and economy of former slate 'capital' of Wales. The industry lives on in two slate mines: Gloddfa Ganol has self-guided tour and reproduction quarrymen's cottages, Llechwedd's tours offer choice of underground transportation. Narrow-gauge Ffestiniog Railway now carries passengers, not slate, to Porthmadog. Ffestiniog Pumped Storage Power Station operates guided tours.

BLAGDON Avon ST5059

Village on A368, 7 miles (11km) NE of Axbridge

Big village set on the lower slope of Blagdon Hill, edge of the Mendips, with Blagdon Lake (a reservoir of 1900) below. Big 15th-century church tower.

BLAIR ATHOLL Tayside NN8665

Village on B8079, 6 miles (10km) NW of Pitlochry

Village around baronial Blair Castle dating from 1269 with 18th- and 19th-century alterations and additions. Duke of Atholl's Atholl Highlanders form only private army in Britain. Viscount Claverhouse, victor of nearby Battle of Killiecrankie, buried in St Bride's churchyard. Three miles (5km) west lies scenic walk around Falls of Bruar and Robertson Clan Museum.

The footbridge at Blair Atholl.

BLAIR DRUMMOND Central NS7399
Safari park on A84, 5 miles (8km) NW of Stirling
Scotland's only African wildlife safari park in grounds of Blair Drummond Castle. Wide variety of animals, children's rides and cinema. Good family outing.

BLAIRGOWRIE Tayside NO1745
Town on A93, 17 miles (27km) NW of Dundee
Popular tourist and golfing centre in Perthshire's raspberry-growing district. Old jute and flax mill is visitors' centre with the largest working waterwheel in Scotland.

BLAIRLOGIE Central NS8396
Village on A91, 3 miles (5km) NE of Stirling
Miniscule conservation village surrounded by gardens on lower slopes of Ochil Hills, once a goat-milk spa.

BLAISDON Gloucestershire SO7017
Village off A4136, 4 miles (6km) NE of Cinderford
Pretty village on the fringe of the Forest of Dean, much visited in spring, when the plum trees blossom.

BLAISE HAMLET Avon ST5678
Site off B4055 in N suburbs of Bristol
The most picturesque hamlet in England, and designed to be so. Built for the owners of Blaise Castle by John Nash from 1811, as homes for old retainers. All the cottages are different, all complicated and set around an undulating green, with curving paths. Blaise Castle is much more sober, 1796, now a museum. Behind on the wooded hill is an Iron Age hillfort.

BLAKEMERE Hereford and Worcester SO3641
Village on B4352, 9 miles (14km) W of Hereford
Small settlement with timber-framed cottages against a backdrop of hills.

BLAKENEY Gloucestershire SO6707
Village on A48, 4 miles (6km) NE of Lydney
An unglamorous former industrial village on the upper Severn estuary, where 19th-century Forest of Dean colliers built cottages and created smallholdings.

BLAKENEY Norfolk TG0243
Village on A149, 5 miles (8km) NW of Holt
A charming village set in lonely marshland, Blakeney was once a port. A combination of silt accumulation and larger ships heralded the end of Blakeney's port days, but it has acquired new life as a centre for small boats. Picturesque fishermens' cottages huddle along the narrow cobbled streets. Blakeney Point is a nature reserve for birds and seals.

BLAKESLEY Northamptonshire SP6250
Village off A5, 4 miles (6km) NW of Towcester
Attractive ironstone village, a conservation area, with fine 17th- and 18th-century houses, and ironstone church with grey stone tower.

BLANCHLAND Northumberland NY9650
Village on B6306, 9 miles (14km) S of Hexham
Historic and completely unspoilt hamlet which grew around the abbey. The abbey was founded by monks of the Premonstratensian order in 1165, who wore white habits and hence the name of the village. The Lord Crewe Arms hotel, which originally housed the abbey kitchens as well as the abbot's lodge and guest house, is said to be haunted.

BLANDFORD FORUM Dorset ST8806
Town on A354, 16 miles (26km) NW of Bournemouth
The most perfect small Georgian town in the country, rebuilt after a bad fire in 1731 destroyed the whole of the town centre and made 480 families homeless. The rebuilding was dominated by a local building firm – John and William Bastard. They designed many of the new buildings, including the church and town hall. The town centre remains much as they left it, with the town hall and church of stone, and most of the houses fine red brick. The church is plain and classical, the town hall a little more elaborate with open arches in the ground floor for market stalls. The Forum in the name means market, not Romans. Local museum.

At Blandford Camp, 2 miles (3km) north, is the Royal Signals Museum.

BLANTYRE Strathclyde NS6957
Town on A724, 2 miles (3km) N of Hamilton
Originally a 18th-century cotton town, now a suburb of Hamilton. Birthplace of David Livingstone, explorer and missionary; museum on his life and work.

BLAYDON Tyne and Wear NZ1863
Town off A695, 5 miles (8km) W of Gateshead
The town developed around its coal-mining, engineering and chemical industries. The name means 'black hill'. Blaydon Burn is to the west.

BLEAN Kent TR1260
Village on A290, 3 miles (5km) NW of Canterbury
A scatter of houses on the hills north of Canterbury amid the dwindled remains of ancient forest of Blean, the former domain of royal huntsmen and later a haunt of smugglers. Blean Woods, the surviving part of the forest, is a nature reserve managed as coppice with a wide variety of woodland plants and animals.

BLEASBY Nottinghamshire SK7149
Village off A612, 3 miles (5km) S of Southwell
Quiet village in the valley of the River Trent, served by the Nottingham – Newark railway. Eighteenth-century Hall; 13th- and 19th-century church.

BLEDINGTON Gloucestershire SP2422
Village on B4450, 4 miles (6km) SE of Stow-on-the-Wold
Village in the Evenlode Valley with a large green and a 15th-century church, famous for its splendid medieval glass.

BLEDLOW Buckinghamshire SP7702
Village off B4009, 2 miles (3km) NE of Chinnor
Conservation and commuter village, landscaped ravine called the Lyde, Tudor cottages, delightful medieval church, cross cut in chalk hillside.

BLENHEIM PALACE Oxfordshire SP4616
see Woodstock

BLETCHINGLEY Surrey TQ3250
Village on A25, 3 miles (5km) E of Redhill
Attractive former market town on the sandstone ridge; wide High Street with tile-hung and gabled buildings. Whyte Hart, an inn since 1388. Middle Row, which forks from High Street, built in centre of old market square. Until Reform Act, 1832, a borough returning two members to Parliament. One of the last was Lord Palmerston.

BLETCHLEY Buckinghamshire SP8633
Town off A5, S part of Milton Keynes
Bletchley Park was key wartime intelligence centre. Much 1970s development in town which became part of Milton Keynes (see) in previous decade.

BLETSOE Bedfordshire TL0258
Village off A6, 6 miles (10km) N of Bedford
Henry VII's mother born in castle of which only one later bit survives. Nice old houses, cottages and Falcon pub.

BLEWBURY Oxfordshire SU5385
Village on A417, 3 miles (5km) S of Didcot
A fine medieval church and picturesque cottages lie close to the large Iron Age hillfort on Blewburton Hill.

BLICKLING Norfolk TG1728
Village off B1354, 1 mile (2km) NW of Aylsham
The village grew up around the manor house, now destroyed, but first built in 1390. Blickling Hall (National Trust) is a splendid 17th-century mansion in red brick.

BLIDWORTH Nottinghamshire SK5956
Village on B6020, 5 miles (8km) SE of Mansfield
Twentieth-century coal-mining expanded this village in Sherwood Forest. Woodland walks and picnic sites at Blidworth Bottoms and Haywood Oaks. Reputed burial place of outlaw Will Scarlet, hilltop church vies with Edwinstowe as the place where Maid Marion married. Ancient rocking ceremony in February, baby boy being rocked in 18th-century cradle, representing taking boy Jesus to the temple.

BLISLAND Cornwall SX1073
Village off A30, 4 miles (6km) NE of Bodmin
On the edge of Bodmin Moor, all stone houses and cottages, many of them around the big village green. The Church of St Protus and St Hyacinth (oddest dedication in the county) has leaning granite columns and colourful woodwork. The moor to the north is full of archaeological remains, with a stone circle, hut circles and barrows.

BLISWORTH Northamptonshire SP7253
Village off A43, 4 miles (6km) NE of Towcester
Beside the Grand Union Canal, at the end of the longest navigable tunnel on British Waterways system, 3,075yd (2,812m) long, completed 1805.

BLITHFIELD Staffordshire SK0424
Hamlet on B5013, 4 miles (6km) N of Rugeley
Medieval church of great interest. The reservoir on Blithfield estate is a haven for waterfowl and accessible to the public.

BLO' NORTON Norfolk TM0179
Village off A1066, 7 miles (11km) W of Diss
Hugging the banks of the Little Ouse River, Blo' Norton's dominant feature is its windmill, one of many in the area.

BLOCKLEY Gloucestershire SP1634
Village on B4479, 3 miles (5km) NW of Moreton-in-Marsh
Old silk-weaving mills, millworkers' cottages and church with fine array of monuments are attractive features of this terraced hillside village.

BLOOMSBURY Greater London TQ2982
District in borough of Camden
District near British Museum, developed by Dukes of Bedford in 18th and 19th centuries. Famed for intellectuals, writers and artists of inter-war Bloomsbury Group (Virginia Woolf, Lytton Strachey, John Maynard Keynes, among others). London University buildings include 1930s Senate House by Charles Holden. Dickens House Museum. Numerous scholarly institutions, hospitals, hotels.

BLOXHAM Oxfordshire SP4336
Village on A361, 4 miles (6km) SW of Banbury
A village museum tells the story of this hillside village with its rich, imposing church and wealth of ancient buildings.

BLOXWICH West Midlands SJ9902
District in NW area of Walsall
Modern housing estates on the fringe of Walsall's northern green belt dominate the old town, once famous for its harness ironmongery.

BLUE ANCHOR Somerset ST0243
Hamlet on B3191, 2 miles (3km) W of Watchet
Tiny modern resort, named after a pub. Sandy beach, and a stop on the West Somerset Steam Railway.

BLUE POOL Dorset SY9383
Beauty spot off A351, 3 miles (5km) NW of Corfe Castle
A lake created by old clay digging, surrounded by pines and heathland. It really is blue.

BLUNDELLSANDS Merseyside SJ3099
District in NW Liverpool
Blundellsands Park was laid out in the 19th century as a high-class residential area by Nicholas Blundell of nearby Crosby Hall.

BLUNDESTON Suffolk TM5297
Village off A12, 4 miles (6km) NW of Lowestoft
Charles Dickens thought the sign to Blundeston read 'Blunderstone', a name which was later immortalised in *David Copperfield*.

BLUNHAM Bedfordshire TL1551
Village off A1, 2 miles (3km) NW of Sandy
Village of limestone, brick and thatch; double-humped bridge over River Ivel. Seventeenth-century poet John Donne was non-resident rector.

BLYTH Northumberland NZ3181
Town on A193, 8 miles (13km) N of Tynemouth
Blyth, the largest town in the county, is a busy seaport. The Royal Northumberland Yacht Club has its headquarters in a converted lightship in the town. Seaton Delaval Hall, a Vanbrugh house, comprises a centre block between two arcaded and pedimented wings. The east wing contains fine stables and there are gardens with statues.

BLYTH Nottinghamshire SK6287
Village off A1, 6 miles (10km) NW of East Retford
On old Great North road, a Georgian coaching stop, but now bypassed by A1. Elegant wide main street and magnificent priory church which survived destruction of monastic Benedictine priory at Reformation. Sturdy Norman pillars, round arches and later work. Huge medieval wall-painting of Last Judgement revealed in 1980s. Late 14th-century tower 100ft (30m) high.

BLYTHBURGH Suffolk TM4475
Village on A12, 4 miles (6km) W of Southwold
In 1577, the Devil is said to have toppled the spire from Blythburgh church, killing two people. Near by, an ancient king was killed in battle.

BO' NESS Central NS0081
Town on A904, 3 miles (5km) N of Linlithgow
Industrial town and port, the name a contraction of Borrowstouness, on Forth estuary. James Watt experimented with steam on nearby Kinneil estate, making Bo'ness an apt site for Scotland's biggest vintage train centre. The eastern end of the Antonine Wall (AD140) was here.

BOARHUNT Hampshire SU6008
Hamlet off A32, 2 miles (3km) NE of Fareham
Isolated church, on the side of the chalk hump of Portsdown Hill. Late Saxon, small and simple.

BOARSTALL Buckinghamshire SP6214
Hamlet off B4011, 6 miles (10km) SE of Bicester
Known for its rare 18th-century duck decoy, owned by the National Trust, now used for ringing migrant duck, which are then released. Previously provided winter meat for Aubrey family of Boarstall Tower (open by written appointment), gatehouse of vanished medieval fortified manor house, damaged in Civil War by Parliamentarian troops who also destroyed village.

BOAT OF GARTEN Highland NH9319
Village off A95, 5 miles (8km) NE of Aviemore
Resort in Spey Valley, named for ferry which provided crossing until bridge was built in 1898. Eastern terminus of Strathspey Steam Railway from Aviemore. Near by is Loch Garten, a Royal Society for the Protection of Birds reserve with hide facilities and the first nesting site of ospreys on their return to Britain in 1954 after absence of 50 years.

BOBBINGTON Staffordshire SO8090
Village off A458, 6 miles (10km) E of Bridgnorth
Commuter village in pleasant agricultural surroundings with Halfpenny Green airfield near by.

BOCKHAMPTON Dorset SY7292
Hamlet off A35, 2 miles (3km) NE of Dorchester
Famous as the birthplace of Thomas Hardy, the novelist and poet whose books reveal so much about 19th-century Dorset. He was born in a thatched cottage at the end of a narrow woody lane in the small hamlet of Higher Bockhampton and lived there until he was 22, later returning to write several novels.

BOCKING Essex TL7623
District in NW area of Braintree
Restored windmill in attractive village swallowed by Braintree (see). Church is mainly 15th century. Courtauld factory, once specialising in mourning crêpe, now itself departed.

BODDAM Shetland HU3915
Village off A970, 5 miles (8km) S of Sandwick
Village on south mainland. The Croft House Museum re-creates stone-built Shetland croft and interior fittings.

The lighthouse at Boddam.

BODELWYDDAN Clwyd SJ0075
Village off A55, 2 miles (3km) W of St Asaph
Local limestone forms the landmark white spire of 19th-century 'Marble Church'. Inside, marble appears in arcade and font. Castle's beautifully restored Victorian interior a backdrop to finest portrait collection of that era outside London, thanks to its status as a country arm of National Portrait Gallery. Victorian-style family diversions (including toys), woodland walks. Adults-only hotel attached.

BODENHAM Hereford and Worcester SO5350
Village off A417, 7 miles (11km) N of Hereford
A 13th-century church, a village green and an array of timber-framed and Georgian houses. Bodenham Vineyard open to visitors.

BODIAM East Sussex TQ7825
Village off A268, 2 miles (3km) SW of Sandhurst
Pronounced 'Bod-jem'. In the Rother Valley. Attractive village is adjunct to romantic moated castle ruins (National Trust). Built 1386; 'slighted' by Cromwell.

BODINNICK Cornwall SX1352
Village off B3269, opposite Fowey
On the wide River Fowey, with the car ferry across to the town of Fowey. A pretty hamlet running up the hill. Novelist Daphne du Maurier lived here before her marriage.

BODMIN Cornwall SX0667
Town off A30, 18 miles (29km) E of Newquay
Established in the 6th century when St Petroc settled here, and although only feeling like a market town, the capital of Cornwall from 1835 until 1989. On the edge of Bodmin Moor (see) and the Camel (see), trail for cycling and walking.

St Petroc's Church reflects Bodmin's importance in medieval times, being large (the largest church in the county) and impressive. It mostly dates from the late 15th century. Holy well tucked in beside it.

Bodmin's streets are narrow and hilly. At the centre are the Victorian buildings for the courts. The market of 1839 has bulls and rams in the decorative frieze. The big memorial obelisk of 1856 on the hill above the town is a prominent feature.

Bodmin Museum has displays on the area, and the prison of 1855 is also a museum. The Duke of Cornwall's Light Infantry Museum is in the Victorian barracks. Bodmin and Wenford Railway runs steam trains to Bodmin Parkway, with stations for Cardinham Woods (see) and Lanhydrock House (National Trust, $2^1/_2$ miles/4km southeast), the grandest house in Cornwall, 17th century and 1880s with lovely grounds. Pencarrow House (4 miles/6km northwest) is Georgian and handsome, with woodland gardens.

BODMIN MOOR Cornwall
Region in SW England
About 100 square miles (258 sq km) of moorland, cut across the middle by the A30. The highest and wildest parts are in the north – Rough (pronounced Row) Tor, and Brown Willy which is Cornwall's highest point at 1,377ft (418m). Lots of prehistoric remains are preserved on the moor – standing stones, cairns, stone circles and hut circles. See Dozmary and Bolventor.

BOGNOR REGIS West Sussex SZ9399
Town on A29, 6 miles (10km) SE of Chichester
Seaside town with safe sandy beaches and seaside entertainment at Butlin's Southcoast World. Fishing hamlet in Middle Ages and coast was empty expanse until attempt to develop it as select resort 200 years ago. Centred on Steyne, in imitation of Brighton. The town has grown piecemeal, filling out properly since Victorian times. Acquired royal suffix in 1929.

BOLAM Northumberland NZ1082
Village off A696, 3 miles (5km) N of Belsay
St Andrew's Church has a late Saxon tower and a Norman chancel arch. Bolam Lake Country Park is noted for its birdlife.

BOLDON Tyne and Wear NZ3561
Town on A184, SW of South Shields
This is a conservation area made up of East and West Boldon and Boldon Colliery. The latter is portrayed as 'Fellburn' in Catherine Cookson novels.

BOLDRE Hampshire SZ3198
Village off A337, 2 miles (3km) N of Lymington
On the edge of the New Forest, very scattered hamlet. Mostly 13th-century church. Spinners, in the south, is a fine woodland garden.

BOLHAM Devon SS9515
Hamlet on A396, 2 miles (3km) N of Tiverton
Knightshayes Court (National Trust) is a quirky 1870s house designed by William Burges. Good gardens and grounds.

BOLLINGTON Cheshire SJ9377
Town on B5090, 3 miles (5km) NE of Macclesfield
Stone-built former cotton village. On nearby Kerridge Ridge is White Nancy, a folly, built to commemorate the Battle of Waterloo.

BOLNEY West Sussex TQ2622
Village just off A23, 4 miles (6km) W of Haywards Heath
Bypassed by huge new A23 in deep Wealden country. Attractive single street. Norman church has peal of eight bells.

BOLSOVER Derbyshire SK4770
Town on A632, 6 miles (10km) E of Chesterfield
Splendid remains of 17th-century castle dominate hilltop, guarding town from hostile approaches from valley below. Norman castle occupied site earlier. Present building by Bess of Hardwick's son, Charles Cavendish, is romantic mansion, for show rather than defence. Magnificent 17th-century Riding School. Town market is 700 years old. Georgian houses. Church has fine Cavendish family monuments.

BOLSTERSTONE South Yorkshire SK2796
Village off A616, 1 mile (2km) S of Stocksbridge
Situated in the beautiful Ewden Valley, near to the reservoir where, during World War II, the Dambusters practised their low-level flying over water.

BOLT HEAD Devon SX7235

Beauty spot off A381, 2 miles (3km) S of Salcombe

Rocky headland which protects Salcombe and the Kingsbridge estuary from the sea. Good views and rocky shore all the way to Bolt Tail, another headland 4 miles (6km) west.

BOLTON Cumbria NY6323

Village off A66, 8 miles (13km) SE of Penrith

The village is situated on rising ground above the flood plain of the River Eden and has a 12th-century church.

BOLTON Greater Manchester SD7109

Town on A666, 10 miles (16km) NW of Manchester

Like many other Lancashire towns, Bolton owes its growth and prosperity to the Industrial Revolution, and its majestic town hall, opened in 1873, reflects the town's civic pride. Bolton is a most handsome Victorian town but it has a much earlier history too. On Churchgate is Bolton's oldest hostelry, The Man and Scythe, dating from 1251. Richard Arkwright lived and worked on Churchgate before moving to Nottingham where he built his famous spinning machine. Across Bradshawgate is Nelson Square, presided over by the statue of Bolton's most famous son, Samuel Crompton, who invented the spinning mule and helped to make this region a world leader in the textile industry. Samuel Crompton is buried in the churchyard of Bolton Parish Church, a magnificent Victorian Gothic church built on a grand scale.

William Lever, later Lord and ultimately Viscount Leverhulme, one of Bolton's most important benefactors, was born on Wood Street, close to the church. He bought and restored Samuel Crompton's home, medieval Hall i'th'Wood, for the town and gave Leverhulme Park.

Today Bolton is a popular shopping centre with thriving markets, the renowned Octagon Theatre and good facilities for residents.

BOLTON ABBEY North Yorkshire SE0753

Village on B6160, 5 miles (8km) NW of Ilkely

Historic estate village with the famous Bolton Priory. This Augustinian priory was founded in the 1120s by Cicely de Romille. It was sold after the Dissolution of the Monasteries to Henry Clifford and passed on to the Cavendish family. The nave was retained at the dissolution and is a well cared for and well-attended parish church. Bolton Hall, now a shooting lodge, was built on to the 14th-century gatehouse of the priory.

BOLTON BY BOWLAND Lancashire SD7849

Village off A59, 3 miles (5km) W of Gisburn

Greens on either side of the church have war memorial, market cross, stocks and Old Courthouse, where Forest Law used to be proclaimed.

BOLTON LE SANDS Lancashire SD4867

Town on A6, 4 miles (6km) N of Lancaster

Mother parish for Slyne-with-Hert and originally a fishing village. Features an assortment of stone cottages. The Lancaster Canal runs around village.

BOLTON PERCY North Yorkshire SE5341

Village off B1223, 3 miles (5km) SE of Tadcaster

Remote village near the River Wharfe with the strikingly handsome limestone All Saints' Church, consecrated in 1424.

BOLTON-ON-SWALE North Yorkshire SE2599

Village on B6271, 5 miles (8km) SE of Richmond

An attractive village in Swaledale. The church contains a monument to Henry Jenkins, recording that he lived to be 169.

BOLVENTOR Cornwall SX1876

Village off A30, 9 miles (14km) NE of Bodmin

This was the only village on the bleak road running across Bodmin Moor (see), but now bypassed. The Jamaica Inn, an important coaching stop in the 18th century, inspired Daphne du Maurier's novel of the same name after she visited in 1930. Mr Potter's Museum of Curiosity is a fanciful Victorian display of stuffed animals.

BONAR BRIDGE Highland NH6191

Village on A949, 14 miles (23km) W of Dornoch

Named for bridge spanning channel between Inner Dornoch Firth and Kyle of Sutherland, now bypassed. Salmon netting station. Prehistoric remains near by.

BONCHURCH Isle of Wight SZ5778

Village off A3055, 1 mile (2km) NE of Ventnor

Entirely picturesque, a romantic village largely built in the 1840s along the steep slopes of the Underhill. Well wooded, big pond; old St Boniface Church is medieval and charming.

BONNINGTON Kent TR0535

Village off B2067, 5 miles (8km) SE of Ashford

Scattered in woodland above Romney Marsh, with a history of smuggling and a little grey church beside the Royal Military Canal.

BONNYRIGG Lothian NT3065

Town on A6094, 2 miles (3km) SW of Dalkeith

Joined to Lasswade since 1929 and noted as manufacturing town in 18th and 19th centuries, particularly for mills and carpet factories. Stands on River North Esk.

BONSALL Derbyshire SK2758

Village off A5012, 2 miles (3km) SW of Matlock

Peak District village, former lead-mining and textile centre, with medieval stone cross on 13 circular steps, surrounded by 17th-century limestone cottages.

BOOSBECK Cleveland NZ6617

Village off A173, 3 miles (5km) S of Saltburn-by-the-Sea

A tiny village with workmen's terraced cottages and the Margrove Heritage Centre which explains the geological formation of the surrounding countryside.

BOOT Cumbria NY1700

Hamlet off A595, 6 miles (10km) NE of Ravenglass

At the Eskdale end of the Ravensglass and Eskdale Railway, a tiny village which also marks the beginning of the climb up Hardknott Pass.

BOOTHBY GRAFFOE Lincolnshire SK9859
Village on A607, 8 miles (13km) S of Lincoln
On Lincoln Cliff. Views from Viking Way footpath across Brant, Witham and Trent valleys. Remains of 13th-century Somerton Castle, now a farm.

BOOTHBY PAGNELL Lincolnshire SK9730
Village on B1176, 5 miles (8km) SE of Grantham
'The most important small Norman manor house in England' (Pevsner), limited opening, in garden of 1825 hall. Norman church, restored 1890s.

BOOTLE Merseyside SJ3495
Town on A565, immediately N of Liverpool
The first settlers in 7th century were attracted by the supply of soft spring water. At the beginning of the 19th century it was a fashionable resort with villas and mansions. Later these were demolished when the docks were built on Bootle's Mersey waterfront. Much of the town was destroyed in World War II.

BORDON Hampshire SU7935
Small town on A325, 7 miles (11km) SW of Farnham
Only sandy heathland with a few farms until the army arrived in 1903. Now a huge village, with vast army camp.

BOREHAM Essex TL7609
Village on B1137, 4 miles (6km) NE of Chelmsford
Unusual church monument of three Earls of Sussex side by side. They lived at historic New Hall (not open), now a convent and girls' school.

BOREHAMWOOD Hertfordshire TQ1996
Town off A1, 3 miles (5km) N of Edgware
Has far outgrown its companion Elstree (see). Mostly London overspill housing estates. Home of Elstree film and television studios.

BORERAIG Highland (Skye) NG1853
Hamlet off B884, 7 miles (11km) N of Dunvegan
North-coast site of famous MacCrimmon piping school from 1500–1800. There is a modern Piping Heritage Centre, telling story of school and bagpipes.

BORGUE Dumfries and Galloway NX6248
Village on B727, 4 miles (6km) SW of Kirkcudbright
Overlooking Kirkcudbright Bay, this tranquil village was used by RL Stevenson as a setting for part of *The Master of Ballantrae.*

BORLEY Essex TL8443
Hamlet off B1064, 2 miles (3km) NW of Sudbury
Notorious for strange and frightening occurrences at its former rectory, 'the most haunted house in England'. It was demolished in the 1940s.

BOROUGH GREEN Kent TQ6157
Village off A25, 5 miles (8km) E of Sevenoaks
Pleasant, large modern village developed around the railway station between the North Downs and the Kentish orchards.

BOROUGHBRIDGE North Yorkshire SE3966
Small town on B6265, 6 miles (10km) SE of Ripon
This was once an important coaching stop on the Great North road; now bypassed by A1. It has a mixture of Regency, Georgian and Victorian architecture with an elaborate fountain dominating St James' Square. The nearby legendary Devils' Arrows are three stone monoliths dating from 2000BC, the largest is 30ft (9m) high. Market day Thursday.

BORROWASH Derbyshire SK4234
Village off A52, 4 miles (6km) E of Derby
Commuter village between Derby and Nottingham, close to an old Roman road and the winding River Derwent.

BORROWDALE Cumbria NY2514
Valley of River Derwent S of Derwent Water
Often considered the prettiest valley in the Lake District. Valley of the River Derwent, mostly belonging to the National Trust.

BORSTAL Kent TQ7366
Village off B2097, 1 mile (2km) S of Rochester
Now a suburb of Chatham, Borstal looks over the River Medway to Rochester and is best known for its reformatory prison.

BORTH Dyfed SN6089
Village on B4353, 5 miles (8km) N of Aberystwyth
Shingle bank separates low-lying village from miles of sands. Small-scale resort, with watersports and golf. Animalarium a family attraction.

BORTH-Y-GEST Gwynedd SH5637
Village off A487, 1 mile (2km) S of Porthmadog
Pretty little seaside spot on southern outskirts of Porthmadog. Attractive sand-and-pebble beach close to mouth of Traeth Bach estuary.

BOSBURY Hereford and Worcester SO6943
Village on B4220, 4 miles (6km) N of Ledbury
Fine church with beautiful 15th-century embellishments and good Tudor monuments. Interesting buildings include the ancient Crown inn with its Elizabethan parlour.

BOSCASTLE Cornwall SX0990
Village on B3263, 5 miles (8km) N of Camelford
The most dramatic of all the Cornish harbours: a dog-leg through the black cliffs, with small jetties in the inner part. The dramatic coastal scenery contrasts with the popular walk up the sheltered wooded Valency Valley to St Juliot: The whole area is closely associated with Thomas Hardy, and features in his novels and poetry.

BOSCOBEL HOUSE Shropshire SO7907
see Tong

BOSCOMBE Wiltshire SU2038
Village on A338, 7 miles (11km) NE of Salisbury
Best known for Boscombe Down, the huge airfield. The village is in the valley, downs rising either side. Near by is Figsbury Ring (National Trust), an Iron Age hillfort with magnificent views.

BOSHAM West Sussex SU8003
Village off A27, 4 miles (6km) W of Chichester
Picturesque village on creek in Chichester Harbour. Once had abbey with royal connections. High Street is a narrow lane of flint, tile-hung and brick cottages with little green called Quay Meadow. Sailing craft all over the place, with road beside harbour flooded at high tide. Traditionally place where Canute unsuccessfully bid the tide retreat.

BOSHERSTON Dyfed SR9694
Village off B4319, 5 miles (8km) S of Pembroke
Lily pools lead to beautiful Broad Haven beach. Ancient, legend-steeped St Govan's Chapel remarkable in cliff cleft. Ministry of Defence range near by.

BOSLEY Cheshire SJ9165
Village on A52, 5 miles (8km) S of Macclesfield
Scattered village dominated by The Cloud, the penultimate peak of the Pennine chain. Also famous for the set of 12 locks on the Macclesfield Canal.

BOSSINGTON Somerset SS8947
Village off A39, 1 mile (2km) NE of Porlock
On the shore below high wooded hill, picturesque with thatched whitewashed cottages. Lynch, just to the north, has a small, early 16th-century chapel.

BOSTON Lincolnshire TF3343
Town on A16, 28 miles (45km) SE of Lincoln
The sight of the magnificent octagonal lantern tower of St Botolph's Church greets visitors approaching this historic market town from miles across the Fens. Inappropriately but affectionately known as Boston Stump, this is the largest parish church in England, whose architectural treasures include its misericords. Tudor composer John Taverner is buried here, and John Foxe, author of the *Book of Martyrs*, is a native.

In 1607, a group of pilgrims from Nottinghamshire and Lincolnshire, seeking religious freedom in Holland, were betrayed by their ship's captain as they left nearby Scotia Creek. They were tried in the town's guildhall, where their cells now form part of a fascinating museum illustrating Boston's history. Eventually many found a fresh start in the New World, travelling on the *Mayflower*. In 1633, rector John Cotton and his companions followed them to America, founding Boston's namesake in Massachusetts.

No longer Britain's second most important port, the original Boston still draws the crowds, to events at its Arts Centre in 13th-century Blackfriars, to Sam Newsom Music Centre in a converted warehouse, to visit the Maud Foster windmill, and especially to Boston's lively market, popular since 1308.

BOSTON SPA West Yorkshire SE4245
Village on A659, 4 miles (6km) NW of Tadcaster
A pretty place on the River Wharfe, with many Georgian houses surviving from the time when the spa was a popular resort. The growth of the town began in 1774 when the discovery of a spring was made by a local labourer called John Shires. From then until well into the 19th century the town was known as Thorp Spa.

The octagonal tower of St Botolph's Church in Boston.

BOSWORTH BATTLEFIELD Leicestershire SK4100
see Sutton Cheney

BOTHAL Northumberland NZ2386
Village off A197, 3 miles (5km) E of Morpeth
Bothal Castle, a fortified manor house dating from 1343, was a place of refuge from border raiders.

BOTHAMSALL Nottinghamshire SK6773
Village off B6387, 4 miles (6km) NE of Ollerton
Attractive village with pantiled farm buildings. Castle Hill, ancient site topped by oaks and sycamores, overlooks Meden and Maun valleys.

BOTHWELL Strathclyde NS7058
Town on A74, 2 miles (3km) NW of Hamilton
Bothwell Castle is massive and impressive sandstone pile in dramatic position, parts date from 1200s. Built for defence against English and changed hands frequently.

BOTLEY Hampshire SU5113
Small town on A334, 6 miles (10km) E of Southampton
One of the handsomest small towns in the county, really a village. Everything around the main square is Georgian brick except the little stone market hall of 1848.

BOTTESFORD Leicestershire SK8038
Village on A52, 7 miles (11km) W of Grantham
Peacefully set in loop of River Devon, tall-spired church has astonishingly fine collection of monuments of Earls of Rutland, two by Grinling Gibbons.

BOTUSFLEMING Cornwall SX4061
Village off A338, 2 miles (3km) NW of Saltash
In a steep combe leading down to the Tamar estuary, once with extensive cherry orchards, now mostly gone. Holy well by the church.

BOUGHTON Northamptonshire SP7565
Village off A508, 4 miles (6km) N of Northampton
Residential village of fine houses and cottages. Obelisk 1764. Castellated follies and lodges by 2nd Earl of Strafford, 1750s–1770s.

BOUGHTON ALUPH Kent TR0348
Village off A28, 4 miles (6km) NE of Ashford
A classic group of manor house and church hidden up a no-through road and home to the Stour Music Festival.

BOUGHTON MALHERBE Kent TQ8849
Hamlet off A20, 2 miles (3km) SW of Lenham
Little hillside hamlet among the orchards above the headwaters of the River Stour and River Beult, with pleasant views.

BOUGHTON MONCHELSEA Kent TQ7749
Village off A229, 4 miles (6km) S of Maidstone
Church and lovely 16th-century Boughton Monchelsea Place perch halfway down steep Quarry Hills with views right over the Weald. Modern village on hilltop.

BOUGHTON STREET Kent TR0559
Village off A2, 5 miles (8km) W of Canterbury
Attractive village of Tudor and 18th-century houses on Watling Street, route of Canterbury pilgrims whose first glimpsed cathedral from hill beyond.

BOULBY Cleveland NZ7618
Hamlet off A174, 1 mile (2km) W of Staithes
On the edge of the North York Moors, the Boulby Mine produces potash used in the Middlesbrough chemical industry.

BOULGE Suffolk TM2552
Hamlet off A12, 2 miles (3km) N of Woodbridge
The grave of the Suffolk sailor and eccentric Edward Fitzgerald lies in the peaceful churchyard.

BOULMER Northumberland NU2614
Village off B1339, 5 miles (8km) E of Alnwick
A small coastal village, once the haunt of smugglers. It has sandy beaches that alternate with rocky foreshores which are habitually the home of seabirds.

BOURN Cambridgeshire TL3256
Village off B1046, 8 miles (13km) W of Cambridge
Seventeenth-century Bourn Hall is now an internationally known fertility clinic. Bourn Mill, built in 1636, is one of the oldest in England.

BOURNE Lincolnshire TF0920
Town on A15, 10 miles (16km) W of Spalding
Crossroads market town on western edge of Fens, supposed birthplace of Hereward the Wake, rebellious Saxon chieftain. Birthplace of William Cecil who became Lord Burghley, chief minister to Elizabeth I. Remains of Roman Car Dyke, earthworks of Norman castle, parish church survival of 12th-century Augustinian Abbey. Seventeenth-century Red Hall; 18th- and 19th-century shops and houses.

BOURNE END Buckinghamshire SU8987
Small town on A4155, 3 miles (5km) E of Marlow
Prosperous London commuter town, set pleasantly on the Thames. Started to grow in later Victorian days with popularity of Thames boating.

BOURNE END Hertfordshire TL0206
Village on A41, on W edge of Hemel Hempstead
Quiet backwater on River Bulbourne and Grand Union Canal, once known for its watercress beds.

BOURNEMOUTH Dorset SZ0890
Town on A35, 24 miles (39km) SW of Southampton
Difficult to believe that there was nothing on the site of this massive conurbation until 1810, when a single house was built in heathy wasteland. Up to the 1880s growth was slow, and mostly as a select seaside resort. Pine trees were planted to improve the surroundings, and they are still a feature of the town.

After the railway arrived growth speeded up, and engulfed several inland villages. The long sandy beach backed by short cliffs and large public gardens still attract many visitors, but the town is now also an important business centre and shoppers come from a wide area.

Few Victorian buildings survive, but there are two very fine Victorian churches (St Stephen's and St Peter's, both close to the centre) and the Russell-Cotes Art Gallery and Museum is in a rich late 19th-century house (good collections too).

The huge central gardens run back from the sea into the centre of the town, and then continue, less formally, inland.

Boscombe, to the east, was a separate but similar development which started in the 1850s. Small museum to the poet Shelley in the Art School (once the manor house).

BOURNVILLE West Midlands SP0481
Suburb in Birmingham on A38
Cadbury's chocolate factory moved to a rural site here in the 1880s, and soon afterwards the 'model' village

for workers was started. The estate has grown independently of the factory, but original buildings still stand in the centre. Cadbury World, Linden Road, tells the story of chocolate and Cadbury's contribution. Also worth visiting are two medieval houses making up Selly Manor Museum in Maple Road.

BOURTON ON DUNSMORE Warwickshire SP4370
Village off B4453, 5 miles (8km) SW of Rugby
The village pays its annual dues to the Duke of Buccleuch, lord of the manor, at the 800-year-old Wroth Silver ceremony in November.

BOURTON-ON-THE-HILL Gloucestershire SP1732
Village on A44, 2 miles (3km) W of Moreton-in-Marsh
A steep hillside village with ornate church and 18th-century pub. Nearby Sezincote is an exotic Indian-style mansion with oriental water gardens.

BOURTON-ON-THE-WATER Gloucestershire SP1620
Small town off A429, 4 miles (6km) SW of Stow-on-the-Wold
Footbridges span the River Windrush as it runs beside the main street between impeccable old houses and manicured lawns. Among many attractions in this Cotswold showpiece are Birdland, Folly Farm Waterfowl, a miniature village, a model railway layout and a perfumery. A motor museum and toy collection are housed in a restored watermill. There is a fine painted ceiling in the church.

BOUTH Cumbria SD3285
Village off A590, 5 miles (8km) NE of Ulverston
Pretty village on a hill, with a village green next to old coaching inn, the White Hart.

BOVEY TRACEY Devon SX8178
Small town on A382, 5 miles (8km) NW of Newton Abbot
In the wooded Bovey Valley on the edge of Dartmoor, with the river running through the middle. Pleasant small town. The medieval Church of St Thomas is on the east side, mostly 15th century with good fittings of that date. The headquarters of the National Park are at Parke just to the north, with 200 acres (81ha) of parkland and woods (National Trust) and a rare breeds centre.

BOVINGDON Hertfordshire TL0103
Village on B4505, 3 miles (5km) SW of Hemel Hempstead
Attractive village which has grown considerably this century. Youth prison. Disused airfield was World War II bomber base.

BOVINGTON CAMP Dorset SY8389
Army site off A352, 6 miles (10km) W of Wareham
The army has used this area since World War I, and it is now a large army camp for the Royal Armoured Corps, surrounded by heathland. Tanks are a common sight. The Tank Museum has old and new ones. About $1^1/_2$ miles (2km) west is Clouds Hill (National Trust) which belonged to TE Lawrence (of Arabia). A tiny, fascinating cottage.

BOW Devon SS7201
Village on A3072, 7 miles (11km) W of Crediton
Central Devon with red soils. On the main road, with some cob and thatch; high pavement with steps.

BOW Greater London TQ3783
District in borough of Tower Hamlets
Deep in East End. Bryant and May match factory, now housing. Ragged School Museum, Copperfield Road. St Paul's, Burdett Road, 1950s.

BOWERS GIFFORD Essex TQ7588
Village off A13, 3 miles (5km) E of Basildon
Little isolated marshland church with 14th-century brass of Sir John Gifford, who fought at Battle of Crécy.

BOWES Durham NY9913
Small town off A66, 4 miles (6km) SW of Barnard Castle
Historic village with coaching inn, the Unicorn, visited by Dickens while researching *Nicholas Nickleby*; the sadistic Wackford Squeers was based on local headmaster W Shaw and the house at the end of the village was the model for 'Dotheboy's Hall'. Bowes Castle has a massive stone keep dating from 1170 and is set within the earthworks of a Roman fort.

BOWLAND, FOREST OF Lancashire
Scenic region in NW England
An Area of Outstanding Natural Beauty, the Forest of Bowland is popular for walking and drives in lovely countryside. Many of the stone-built villages have Saxon names, and there is also a Norse influence. During the 13th century Cistercian monks did much to cultivate the land for farming sheep and other livestock, and crop-growing.

BOWLING Strathclyde NS4373
Village on A82, 2 miles (3km) SE of Dumbarton
At west end of Forth and Clyde Canal and thus industrially important in 18th century. Experiments with first steamship by Henry Bell here in 1802.

BOWMORE Strathclyde (Islay) NR3159
Village on A846, 4 miles (6km) S of Bridgend
Eighteenth-century planned village built on grid plan, now the administrative capital of Islay. Round parish church.

BOWNESS-ON-SOLWAY Cumbria NY2262
Village off B5307, 4 miles (6km) N of Kirkbride
A compact village of narrow streets lined with sandstone cottages, Bowness was founded by Romans as Maia, the last fort on Hadrian's Wall.

BOWNESS-ON-WINDERMERE Cumbria SD4097
Suburb on A592, immediately S of Windermere
Busy tourist town on the edge of Windermere, which developed when the railway line opened, being the nearest accessible point on the lake. Most of the lake cruisers operate from here on the 10 mile (16km) stretch of Windermere. 'World of Beatrix Potter' at The Old Laundry is a popular attraction.

BOX Wiltshire ST8268
Village on A4, 5 miles (8km) NE of Bath
Large stone-built village, with the Box Tunnel, an early railway wonder, 2 miles (3km) long with castellated entrances designed by Brunel in 1837. The church was extended to accommodate the railway workers.

BOX HILL Surrey TQ1951
Beauty spot off A24, 1 mile (2km) NE of Dorking
National Trust owns 800 acres (324ha) of this wooded chalk hill, the southeast bluff of Mole Gap through North Downs. Famous beauty spot for over 200 years, visited by Jane Austen, John Keats and RL Stevenson, it rises 400ft (121m) from River Mole, with magnificent views. During French Revolution Juniper Hall was home of French *émigrés*.

BOXFORD Berkshire SU4271
Village off B4000, 4 miles (6km) NW of Newbury
Picture-postcard village of thatched cottages on the Lambourn River. The church tower of brick and flint (1692) adds to the charm.

BOXFORD Suffolk TL9640
Village off A1071, 4 miles (6km) W of Hadleigh
An old weaving town with colourful houses and a 14th-century wooden porch in the church – said to be the oldest in the country.

BOXGROVE West Sussex SU9007
Village off A27, 3 miles (5km) NE of Chichester
On the coastal plain just beneath the downs. Attractive cottages in quiet lane leading to parish church, the former church of Boxgrove Priory, dissolved 1538. Finest monastic church in Sussex, with superb painted roof. Extensive palaeolithic finds in nearby sand and gravel pit, including early hominid thigh bone, discovered 1993, dubbed 'Boxgrove Man'.

BOXLEY Kent TQ7758
Village off A249, 2 miles (3km) N of Maidstone
Pleasant village at foot of steep wooded North Downs. Church, associated with notorious Boxley Abbey, retains chamber for viewing relics.

BOXTED Essex TL9933
Hamlet off A134, 5 miles (8km) N of Colchester
A Salvation Army colony here once, more recently known for Methodist Silver Band. Famous American fighter base in World War II.

BOYNTON Humberside TA1367
Village on B1253, 3 miles (5km) W of Bridlington
Boynton Hall's Strickland family introduced the turkey, commemorated by the carving on the 18th-century church's lectern.

BOYTON Cornwall SX3292
Village off B3254, 5 miles (8km) N of Launceston
So close to the Tamar boundary that the village mill is in Devon. Small, properly rural village with the medieval church in the middle.

BOYTON Wiltshire ST9539
Village off A36, 3 miles (5km) SE of Heytesbury
Small, well-wooded village in the Wylye Valley.

BOZEAT Northamptonshire SP9058
Village off A509, 6 miles (10km) S of Wellingborough
Lively village bypassed by Wellingborough–Bedford road, formerly a centre of the shoe trade.

BRABOURNE Kent TR1041
Village off A20, 6 miles (10km) E of Ashford
Cluster of cottages with pub and sturdy church tucked beneath the steep-faced North Downs in gently rolling country.

BRACEBOROUGH Lincolnshire TF0713
Village off A6121, 5 miles (8km) NE of Stamford
Small village beside River Glen, between Stamford and Market Deeping, with unfulfilled 19th-century ambitions to become a famous spa.

BRACKLEY Northamptonshire SP5837
Town on A43, 8 miles (13km) E of Banbury
Attractive town close to Oxfordshire and Buckinghamshire border, with trees and warm-toned stone buildings lining broad main street and market place, with 1706 town hall. Magdalen College, Oxford, sought refuge here from 16th-century plague and moved into 12th-century Hospital of St John and St James. Magdalen College School still occupies many of the town's fine buildings.

BRACKNELL Berkshire SU8769
New Town on A329, 4 miles (6km) E of Wokingham
A small town in poor sandy heathland until 1948, when it was made a New Town. Now vast, with one of the first purpose-built pedestrian shopping centres of the 1960s (open-air). Huge office blocks around the middle, many for computer firms. Lots of green spaces. Vast area of coniferous woods to the south, with Caesar's Camp (actually an Iron Age hillfort pre-dating Caesar) and the Look-out Countryside and Heritage Centre.

BRACO Tayside NN8309
Village on B8033, 6 miles (10km) NE of Dunblane
Huge earthworks, one of largest in Britain, at Ardoch Roman Camp, dating from the time of Hadrian (AD76–138), serving 40,000 soldiers.

BRADENHAM Buckinghamshire SU8297
Village off A4010, 4 miles (6km) NW of High Wycombe
Almost entire village belongs to National Trust. Lovely beech woods. Manor house (not open) was home of Benjamin Disraeli's father, Isaac.

BRADENHAM, WEST AND EAST Norfolk TF9108
Villages off A1075, 5 miles (8km) SW of East Dereham
These two East Anglian villages each have a splendid church – St Mary's in East Bradenham is 14th and 15th century and has a lovely medieval altar stone; St Andrew's in West Bradenham has some handsome 13th-century arches. Nelson's sister lived in West Bradenham Hall, and aired out the uniforms returned to her after his death near the front gates.

BRADFIELD Berkshire SU6072
Village off A340, 3 miles (5km) SW of Pangbourne
Wooded, and with Victorian brick buildings of Bradfield College, a school founded in 1850. Sir George Gilbert Scott rebuilt the church (apart from the 16th-century tower) picturesquely in 1848. Many Georgian brick houses.

The church and manor house at Bradenham, Buckinghamshire.

BRADFIELD Essex TM1430
Village on B1352, 3 miles (5km) E of Manningtree
Splendid views from south side of Stour estuary. Good pubs with unusual names – Stranger's Home, Ram and Hogget.

BRADFIELD South Yorkshire SK2692
Village off A616, 6 miles (10km) NW of Sheffield
In a fine Pennine setting. Now part of the city of Sheffield. Beautiful 12th-century Church of St Nicholas in High Bradfield.

BRADFIELD COMBUST Suffolk TL8957
Village on A134, 5 miles (8km) SE of Bury St Edmunds
According to local legend, the curious name of this attractive village derives from the fact that the hall was burned down during 14th-century riots.

BRADFORD West Yorkshire SE1632
City off M62, 8 miles (13km) W of Leeds
In 1801 Bradford was a country market town with 6,000 inhabitants. Only 30 years later the population had grown to 97,000 as the textile industry transformed the town, and by the end of the century Bradford handled 90 per cent of the world's wool trade and was known as the wool capital of the world. The prosperous Victorians backed a massive building programme using local Pennine stone, creating splendid public buildings, German merchants built ornate warehousing in the area of the town known as Little Germany, mills were modelled on Italian palaces and impressive private homes sprang up. Today over 4,000 buildings in the Bradford district are listed for their architectural or historical significance.

Bradford also led the way in social reform, introducing public education, school meals, public baths and medical examinations. Campaigners battled to reform working conditions and this was the birthplace of the Independent Labour Party.

Heavy engineering, print and packaging firms, financial and export businesses thrived upon Bradford's success in the textile industry for many years, until in the 1960s and 1970s this core trade declined sharply, putting 50,000 people out of work. Bradford responded to this economic disaster by establishing the country's first Economic Development Unit to attract new investment and to launch the town and its district as a tourist destination, which it has done with remarkable success. Its large Asian population has provided one of Bradford's most popular features, and the town makes much of its reputation for having the finest curry houses in the country.

Although Bradford is less dependent on textile production these days, it still plays a vital role in the local economy. The mills are highly mechanised and specialise in top-quality fabrics and yarns, many of which are exported to Japan and Europe. The mill shops are also a great attraction, selling their produce to the public often at wholesale prices.

The National Museum of Film, Photography and Television, in the centre of the town, houses Britain's only IMAX screen which stands five storeys high. Bradford's Colour Museum reflects the town's industrial past, showing how colour is used in textiles and printing, and the Industrial Museum chronicles the history of the town's textile and manufacturing industry. Treadwell's Art Mill in the historic quarter of Little Germany contains the world's biggest collection of Super Humanism art and sculpture. The Alhambra Theatre, a provincial Edwardian theatre, is a major venue for touring productions by English National Ballet, Scottish Opera, Opera North and the Royal Shakespeare Company.

BRADFORD ABBAS Dorset ST5813
Village off A30, 4 miles (6km) SE of Yeovil
Large north Dorset village with a beautiful medieval church. Handsome tower.

Bradford-on-Avon: the old bridge with its rare bridge chapel converted to a lock-up in the 17th century.

BRADFORD-ON-AVON Wiltshire ST8261

Town on A363, 3 miles (5km) NW of Trowbridge

One of England's prettiest stone small towns, with steep streets and the River Avon completing the picture. Seventeenth-century stone bridge and big Victorian mill – a reminder that the town was founded on woollen cloth manufacture. Many 17th- and 18th-century stone houses and cottages line the streets. There are three churches, the smallest of which (St Lawrence) is the most interesting – a tiny but complete Saxon church of 8th–10th centuries, a rare survival.

The 14th-century tithe barn (English Heritage) is large, built of stone, 168ft (51m) long with big original roof. The Kennet and Avon Canal loops around the town, making an interesting walk. Local museum. Barton Farm Country Park is set in meadows.

BRADFORD-ON-TONE Somerset ST1722

Village off A38, 3 miles (5km) NE of Wellington

The ford was superseded by a 15th-century bridge. Thatched cottages. Near by, Sheppy's Cider and Rural Life Museum.

BRADGATE PARK Leicestershire SK4914

see Charnwood Forest

BRADING Isle of Wight SZ6087

Village on A3055, 2 miles (3km) N of Sandown

A port in medieval times, but now miles inland because the estuary has filled in. Isle of Wight Wax Museum in one of the oldest houses, and Lilliput Museum of toys and dolls. Nunwell House, 17th century and Georgian, has gardens, park and the Home Guard Museum, and Morton Manor (1670 and Georgian) has gardens and a vineyard. Brading Roman Villa is famous for its fine mosaics.

BRADNINCH Devon SS9904

Small town off B3181, 8 miles (13km) NE of Exeter

A very small town, once important through the wool and lace industries, but now only paper-making survives at Hele to the south.

BRADSHAW Greater Manchester SD7312

Village on A676, 2 miles (3km) N of Bolton

Home of the only church in England dedicated to St Maxentius, a 6th-century French abbot.

BRADWELL Derbyshire SK1781

Village on B6049, 4 miles (6km) W of Hathersage

Peak District village ready for all weathers: home of delicious ice cream, birthplace of umbrella frame inventor. Massive Bagshawe Cavern.

BRADWELL-ON-SEA Essex TM0006

Village off B1021, 7 miles (11km) NE of Burnham-on-Crouch

Solitary by the sea wall among desolate North Sea flats, an astonishing survival – the simple little 7th-century church built here for missionary St Cedd, now used for services in summer. Attractive village with largely 18th-century church. Tom Driberg, Labour MP, lived at Bradwell Lodge. Sailing at Bradwell Waterside on Blackwater estuary.

BRADWORTHY Devon SS3214

Village off A338, 7 miles (11km) N of Holsworthy

Large village set around a square. The Gnome Reserve at West Putford has about 1,000 gnomes and some pixies.

BRAELOINE VISITOR CENTRE Grampian

see Glen Tanar

BRAEMAR Grampian NO1591

Village on A93, 7 miles (10km) SW of Balmoral

Best-known of the Deeside resorts lying on Clunie Water. September Braemar Gathering is most famous Highland games, attended by royal family, and first held in 11th century. Braemar Castle (1628) destroyed after 1715 Rebellion and rebuilt 1746. Birchwood Nature Reserve has good examples of native upland birches.

BRAINTREE Essex TL7523

Town off A120, 11 miles (18km) NE of Chelmsford

Old cloth-weaving town, long owned by the Bishops of London, later owed much to Courtauld family of local silk mills, now closed (see Bocking). Local history, textile heritage in Working Silk Museum and District Museum, art gallery in 1920s town hall. Statue of John Ray (see Black Notley) and public gardens contain knot garden in his memory.

BRAITHWAITE Cumbria NY2323

Village on B5292, 2 miles (3km) W of Keswick

Village at foot of Whinlatter Pass surrounded by mountains, formerly the seat of the woollen industry.

BRAMBER West Sussex TQ1810

Village off A283, 4 miles (6km) NW of Shoreham-by-Sea

Compact little place on River Adur, centre of conservation area, including Grade I St Mary's House. Through traffic follows bypass on old railway line. Was important river port and administrative centre of wide district from Norman times, but declined as river silted. Norman castle on mound by river; one gaunt bleak tooth remains since its destruction in Civil War.

BRAMCOTE Nottinghamshire SK5037

District on A52 in S outskirts of Nottingham

Residential area adjoining the city of Nottingham. Medieval tower of old church is all that remains. Replaced by Victorian church.

BRAMDEAN Hampshire SU6128

Village on A272, 3 miles (5km) SE of Alresford

Georgian brick houses and cottages. Bramdean Common is still open grazing and has a little corrugated iron church of 1883, built for the gypsies who used the common. Bramdean House gardens are good.

BRAMFIELD Hertfordshire TL2915

Village off A602, 3 miles (5km) NW of Hertford

Quiet country place with village green, cottages and Victorianised church, the kneelers worked by the locals. Thomas Becket's first benefice.

BRAMFORD Suffolk TM1246

Village on B1067, 3 miles (5km) NW of Ipswich

A meadow opposite the pretty church leads down to the River Gipping. Near by, Suffolk Water Park offers canoeing and windsurfing.

BRAMHALL Greater Manchester SJ8984

Town on A5102, 4 miles (6km) S of Stockport

A well-to-do suburb of Stockport with Bramall Hall. Dating from 1375, it retains its classic black and white Tudor appearance.

The Old Bridge of Dee at Braemar.

BRAMHAM West Yorkshire SE4242
Village off A1, 4 miles (6km) S of Wetherby
Bramham Park is a rare example of a fine Queen Anne mansion with grand views. The privately owned house was created during the first half of the 18th century and contains fine furniture, pictures and porcelain. Set in magnificent grounds with ornamental ponds and cascades, it is known as a miniature Versailles.

BRAMHOPE West Yorkshire SE2543
Village on A660, 7 miles (11km) NW of Leeds
The interesting Chapel of St Giles was built by the Lord of the Manor in 1649. It has unusually complete Puritan furnishings.

BRAMLEY Surrey TQ0044
Village on A281, 3 miles (5km) S of Guildford
Long winding street in wooded valley on Guildford to Horsham road. Wide green space of Gosden Common at north end of village is nice foil to Victorian and older cottages further south. Both canal (Wey and Arun) and railway have come and gone, but grassy trackway, aqueduct and combined rail and canal bridge survive.

BRAMPFORD SPEKE Devon SX9298
Village off A377, 4 miles (6km) N of Exeter
Lots of cob and thatch cottages down by the River Exe.

BRAMPTON Cambridgeshire TL2170
Village off A141, 2 miles (3km) SW of Huntingdon
A pleasant jumble of architectural styles around an attractive village green. Samuel Pepys lived here during the plague of 1665.

BRAMPTON Cumbria NY5361
Small town on A69, 9 miles (14km) NE of Carlisle
Founded by Augustinian monks of Lanercost Priory in 1166. Most of the church dates from 13th century with tall lancet windows. Naworth Castle, home of the Earl of Carlisle, is an ancient border fortress. The Moot Hall, in the market place, was built in 1817. Village destroyed by Robert the Bruce and later suffered from Scottish raids.

BRAMPTON ABBOTS Hereford and Worcester SO6026
Village off A40, 2 miles (3km) N of Ross-on-Wye
St Michael's Church has a Norman nave and chancel, 14th-century timbered south porch and timber bell turret.

BRAMPTON BRYAN Hereford and Worcester SO3772
Village on A4113, 5 miles (8km) E of Knighton
Reconstruction by Parliamentarian landowners after a Civil War battle gave this Temeside village a severe church of rare 1656 date with a triple hammerbeam roof, together with several new thatched and timber-framed cottages. Some church timbers were recycled from the demolished castle, of which the 14th-century gatehouse survives in the grounds of the manor house.

BRAMSHOTT Hampshire SU8432
Village off A3, 1 mile (2km) N of Liphook
More like Surrey than Hampshire, short steep heathy ridges. Lots of trees in the village, and deep roads. Waggoner's Wells to the east is a series of large ponds, well wooded around.

BRANCASTER Norfolk TF7743
Village on A149, 4 miles (6km) W of Burnham Market
A straggling village now a centre for golfing, sailing and holidays. West of Brancaster is Titchwell Marsh, a nature reserve under the care of the Royal Society for the Protection of Birds. This expanse of reedbeds, lagoons, saltmarsh and sandy beaches offers a refuge to many birds, including nesting avocets, marsh harriers and bitterns.

BRANCASTER STAITHE Norfolk TF7944
Village on A149, 3 miles (5km) W of Burnham Market
The village surrounds the large harbour with its colourful flotilla of small boats. Boats can be hired from Brancaster Staithe to Scolt Head Island, a finger of sand and shingle about 3 miles (5km) long that has a large breeding colony of terns. The island is managed by English Nature.

BRANCEPETH Durham NZ2237
Village on A690, 4 miles (6km) SW of Durham
Attractive stone cottages built as 19th-century estate village. The grand castle, now in private use, was once home to the famous Nevill family and was substantially rebuilt in the 19th century. The Parish Church of St Brandon has very fine woodwork.

BRANDESBURTON Humberside TA1147
Village on A165, 6 miles (10km) W of Hornsea
St Mary's Church was originally built in 12th century. Golf course; Cottage Crafts Exhibition.

BRANDON Durham NZ2340
Town on A690, 3 miles (5km) SW of Durham
A small colliery town with the largest parish church in the county. The church's greatest feature is its Saxon cross.

BRANDON Suffolk TL7886
Town on A1065, 15 miles (24km) S of Swaffham
This town was once a thriving port, but is perhaps better known for flint. Many of its houses are built from flint, and generations of Brandon families specialised in the art of flint-knapping. Flints were used in flintlock guns, and 2,000-odd gun clubs in the United States keep knappers employed in Brandon. Near by is Brandon Country Park.

BRANDS HATCH Kent TQ5764
Car racing track off A20, 3 miles (5km) SE of Farningham
World-famous Motor-racing circuit, hosting British Grand Prix, other major Formula One races and variety of other motoring events.

BRANDSBY North Yorkshire SE5872
Village on B1363, 4 miles (6km) NE of Easingwold
Set on the slopes of Howardian Hills overlooking the Vale of York. Sandstone cottages; All Saints' Church built by T Atkinson.

BRANKSOME Dorset SZ0492
District off A35, between Poole and Bournemouth
A smart suburb of Poole; well wooded. The little ravine of Branksome Chine runs through the middle to the sea.

BRANSCOMBE Devon SY1988
Village off A3052, 5 miles (8km) E of Sidmouth
Long pebbly beach (National Trust). Steep wooded valleys just inland, with hamlets and cottages scattered around picturesquely. Lots of thatch. Interesting church, partly Norman. The Old Bakery (National Trust) now a baking museum.

BRANSGORE Hampshire SZ1897
Village off A35, 4 miles (6km) NE of Christchurch
On the edge of the New Forest, with lots of pine trees. Unusual little classical church of 1906 at Thorney Hill, and superb acid gardens at MacPennys.

BRANSTON Lincolnshire TF0166
Village on B1188, 4 miles (6km) SE of Lincoln
Residential village, older buildings just off Lincoln road around part-Saxon and Norman church, restored in 19th century and after 1960s fire.

BRANSTON Staffordshire SK2221
Village off A38, 2 miles (3km) SW of Burton upon Trent
The famous pickle factory has gone, but Water Park is popular for fishing and watersports. Good walking through bankside woods and meadowland.

BRANT BROUGHTON Lincolnshire SK9154
Village off A17, 7 miles (11km) E of Newark-on-Trent
Attractive village with broad main street lined with 17th- and 18th-century houses. Outstanding medieval and 19th-century church with tall elegant spire.

BRANTINGHAM Humberside SE9429
Village off A63, 2 miles (3km) N of Brough
An estate village in the scenic Elloughton Dales near the River Humber. Was the site of a Roman villa.

BRANXTON Northumberland NT8937
Village off A697, 9 miles (14km) NW of Wooler
The site of the Battle of Flodden Field in 1513, the last and most bloody battle to be fought in Northumberland. The monument to the battle contains information about the fight between the English army and the Scots. A cement menagerie, a most unusual attraction, displays figures and animals set in a local garden.

BRASSINGTON Derbyshire SK2254
Village off B5056, 4 miles (6km) W of Wirksworth
Former lead-mining village of grey stone, above Carsington Reservoir (known as Carsington Water), which changed local landscape attractively from 1990s.

BRASTED Kent TQ4755
Village on A25, 2 miles (3km) E of Westerham
Delightfully rural village of tile-hung cottages on land which rises southwards to the renowned Emmetts Garden (National Trust) on Ide Hill.

BRATTON Wiltshire ST9152
Village on B3098, 3 miles (5km) E of Westbury
Big village, tucked up under the edge of Salisbury Plain downs. Several Georgian brick houses and older timber-framing. Brick Baptist chapel of 1734; 15th-century church. To the southwest is Bratton Camp, an Iron Age hillfort with massive banks. Close by, cut into the chalk, is the Westbury White Horse of the early 18th century.

BRATTON CLOVELLY Devon SX4691
Village off B3218, 8 miles (13km) W of Okehampton
Good views of Dartmoor away to the southwest. To the west, beyond wonderfully named Broadwoodwidger, is Roadford Reservoir, a large artificial lake.

BRATTON FLEMING Devon SS6437
Village off A39, 6 miles (10km) NE of Barnstaple
In the Exmoor foothills, with the main street climbing the hill. Exmoor Animal and Bird Gardens at South Stowford 2 miles (3km) north.

BRAUGHING Hertfordshire TL3925
Village off B1368, 1 mile (2km) N of Puckeridge
Picturesque, pronounced 'Braffing', often used as film set. Ford over River Quin, pargetted cottages, old houses, notable 15th-century church.

BRAUNSTON Leicestershire SK8306
Village off A606, 2 miles (3km) SW of Oakham
Quietly situated Rutland village, Norman and later church, Elizabethan Chapter Farm and, on the green, Quaintree Hall, retaining 1295–1305 hall roof.

BRAUNSTON Northamptonshire SP5466
Village off A45, 3 miles (5km) NW of Daventry
Alongside Grand Union Canal at its junction with Oxford Canal, with a marina and several pubs serving village and visitors.

BRAUNTON Devon SS4836
Village on A361, 5 miles (8km) NW of Barnstaple
A huge village which claims to be the largest in the country. The old part is up the valley, around the church, which is large and has an interesting roof with bosses, lots of bench-ends and other good fittings. Village Life and Farming Museum. Braunton Marsh was reclaimed from the sea about 1810 and still has banks and sluices of that date. Braunton Burrows, on the coast, is the largest area of sand dunes in the country, up to 100ft (30m) high, now a nature reserve. Braunton Great Field still farmed in medieval strips.

BRAY Berkshire SU9079
Village off A308, 1 mile (2km) SE of Maidenhead
Down by the Thames and still rural. Big church, where the famous Vicar of Bray survived all the religious changes of the 16th century, becoming a byword for adaptability and lack of religious scruples.

BRAYBROOKE Northamptonshire SP7684
Village off A6, 3 miles (5km) SE of Market Harborough
Close to Leicestershire border, with triple-arched medieval bridge, site of 14th-century castle, and a remarkable Norman font in church.

BRAYFORD Devon SS6834
Village off A399, 6 miles (10km) NW of South Molton
Just off Exmoor, with wooded valleys and small steep hills. The church is at High Bray, isolated on a spur above the river.

BRAYTON North Yorkshire SE6030
Village on A19, 1 mile (2km) SW of Selby
St Wilfrid's Church has a superb Norman tower, and an octagonal spire and lantern which dominates the surrounding countryside.

BREADALBANE Tayside
Historic region of Scotland
Splendid landscape of Breadalbane (Gaelic Braid-Alban means upper Alba) originally comprised the Upper Tay river system, greatly enlarged under the Campbell Earls of Breadalbane.

BREADSALL Derbyshire SK3639
Village off A38, 2 miles (3km) NE of Derby
Close to Derby but still rural, with fine steepled church. Remains of 13th-century Augustinian priory incorporated into Jacobean mansion, now a hotel.

BREAGE Cornwall SW6128
Village off A394, 3 miles (5km) W of Helston
Pronounced to rhyme with 'vague'. The 15th-century church is famous for its medieval wall-paintings. Godolphin House (limited opening, 2 miles/3km north) is 16th and 17th century.

BREAMORE Hampshire SU1517
Village on A338, 3 miles (5km) N of Fordingbridge
Very pretty village, with a big boggy green, thatched cottages and an interesting, mostly Saxon church. Breamore House is Elizabethan, restored after a Victorian fire. Countryside and carriage museums as well.

BREAN Somerset ST2956
Village off A370, 4 miles (6km) N of Burnham-on-Sea
A long, thin and mostly modern resort village, with a thin rocky headland (Brean Down) protruding into the Bristol Channel. Brean Down (National Trust) is good walking, with the remains of a fort of 1867 at the sea end. Tropical Bird Garden.

BRECHFA Dyfed SN5230
Village on B4310, 10 miles (16km) NE of Carmarthen
Away from it all on southern fringe of Brechfa Forest's large tract of conifers. Fishing in River Cothi.

BRECHIN Tayside NO6060
Town on A935, 7 miles (11km) W of Montrose
Town on the River South Esk with a cathedral founded in 1150. The adjacent Round Tower dates from the 10th century and was built for defence against the Vikings by Irish clergy, it is 87ft (26m) high and one of only two in Scotland (see Abernethy). Eighteenth-century Brechin Castle is the seat of the Earls of Dalhousie.

BRECKLAND Norfolk
Area of SW Norfolk
Once called the 'great East Anglian desert', the Breckland is chalk covered by wind-blown sand. The Forestry Commission planted huge tracts of pine trees, such as Thetford Forest. Between the pine plantations are heathlands, dry, uncultivated areas of wilderness with outcrops of heather here and there. Open skies, scrubby heath and silent forests make it a place of undeniable beauty.

BRECON (ABERHONDDU) Powys SO0428
Town on A470, 14 miles (23km) N of Merthyr Tydfil
This characterful market town, terminus of the Monmouthshire and Brecon Canal, is a year-round base for exploring the Brecon Beacons National Park as well as being a famous music venue in summer when its acclaimed international jazz festival takes to the streets. The central square houses the Brecknock Museum with its 19th-century assize court and collection of love spoons, the equivalent of the engagement ring. The nearby South Wales Borderers' Museum gives a fascinating insight into the regiment's heroic stand at Rorke's Drift, immortalised in the film *Zulu*. Further out is Wales's only distillery and the Welsh Whisky Experience.

On a hill above the River Honddu looms the cathedral, the Priory Church of St John, with some original Norman work. Down towards the River Usk, the remains of the medieval castle make up part of the Castle hotel, while across the river Christ College public school surrounds a ruined 13th-century Dominican friary church.

Outside the town the Mountain Centre near Libanus is an excellent focal point for the national park with inspiring views across to the flat-topped summits of its highest peaks.

BRECON BEACONS Powys
Mountain range S and SW of Brecon; national park
The distinctively shaped sandstone summits of the Brecon Beacons lend their name to a national park occupying 519 square miles (1,344 sq km) and consisting of four mountain ranges with the Beacons at the heart. Pen y fan is highest point at 2,901ft (886m). Contains Monmouthshire and Brecon Canal, Llangorse Lake (largest natural lake in South Wales), waterfalls, caves, forests and reservoirs.

BREDE East Sussex TQ8218
Village on A28, 6 miles (10km) N of Hastings
Pleasant hillside village. Small green; tiled and timbered cottages. Church originally built 1140. Brede Furnace made guns, later converted to a gunpowder mill.

BREDFIELD Suffolk TM2653
Village off A12, 3 miles (5km) N of Woodbridge
A plaque in a Bredfield inn states, 'On this spot 1742 absolutely nothing happened.' Sixty-seven years later, poet Edward Fitzgerald was born here.

BREDON Hereford and Worcester SO9236
Village on B4079, 3 miles (5km) NE of Tewkesbury
The spire of St Giles's Church soars above this Avonside village, with a huge medieval tithe barn (National Trust),

a 16th-century rectory and Georgian stone manor house at its centre. Old houses line the main street. Impressive church has much Norman work with fine medieval additions, including floor tiles and glass. Sumptuous monument (1611) to Sir Giles and Lady Reed.

BREDON HILL Hereford and Worcester SO9540
Hill off B4080, 5 miles (8km) NE of Tewkesbury
Various paths lead up this low circular outlier of the Cotswolds with Iron Age hillfort and remains of 18th-century folly on summit.

BREDWARDINE Hereford and Worcester SO3344
Village on B4352, 11 miles (18km) W of Hereford
Victorian diarist Francis Kilvert (vicar 1877–9) lies in the graveyard of St Andrew's Church, isolated beside the River Wye and close to the motte of a Norman castle. Church has Norman masonry and carving and a chancel of about 1300 at an angle to the nave. An 18th-century bridge stands to the north. The village, with its 17th-century Red Lion inn, stands well to the west.

BREEDON ON THE HILL Leicestershire SK4022
Village on A453, 5 miles (8km) NE of Ashby-de-la-Zouch
Fascinating church, perched precariously on top of hill being quarried away to east, on site of Iron Age hillfort and Saxon monastic foundation. Twelfth-century tower, 13th-century chancel, important early 9th-century Saxon sculptural fragments placed in interior walls. Elaborate Shirley Pew of 1627, almost a chapel within a chapel. Village lock-up beside main road at foot of hill.

BREMHILL Wiltshire ST9773
Village off A4, 2 miles (3km) NW of Calne
Set high, as the name suggests, with thatched cottages in the middle. At Wick Hill to the northwest is a monument of 1838 to the memory of Maud Heath, who left money in 1474 for a causeway from Wick Hill to Chippenham.

BRENCHLEY Kent TQ6741
Village off B2162, 7 miles (11km) NE of Tunbridge Wells
Pleasing, sizeable Wealden village of timbered and tile-hung cottages set round tiny triangular green, with Marle Place gardens near by.

BRENDON Devon SS7748
Village off A39, 3 miles (5km) SE of Lynton
Little village on the East Lyn River; wooded in the valley, the upper parts Exmoor moorland.

BRENDON HILLS Somerset
Hill range in SW England
On the eastern side of Exmoor, and inside the national park, the Brendon Hills are more wooded than most of the Moor, and have more farming, but still with areas of moorland.

BRENT ELEIGH Suffolk TL9448
Village on A1141, 2 miles (3km) SE of Lavenham
The pretty Church of St Mary has wall-paintings that have been dated to 1290. They depict the crucifixion, with kneeling Mary and Doubting Thomas.

BRENT KNOLL Somerset ST3350
Village off B3140, 2 miles (3km) NE of Burnham-on-Sea
Village at the bottom of the prominent hill of the same name. Interesting church. Wide views of the Somerset Levels and Bristol Channel from the top. Iron Age hillfort.

BRENT PELHAM Hertfordshire TL4330
Village on B1038, 5 miles (8km) E of Buntingford
Church has a curious tomb linked with legend of local dragon-slayer. Village stocks and whipping post, thatched cottages.

BRENT RESERVOIR Greater London TQ1984
Reservoir in boroughs of Barnet and Brent
Also known as the Welsh Harp, large reservoir in course of River Brent. Watersports, nature reserve, great crested grebe nesting.

BRENT TOR Devon SX4881
Hill off A386, 5 miles (8km) N of Tavistock
On the edge of Dartmoor – the most dramatically placed church in Devon – perched, all alone, on the summit of a high rocky knoll, 1,100ft (335m) high. A landmark from miles around, and with enormous views from the top. Church small and medieval. North Brentor village is away to the northeast, with its own, newer church.

BRENTFORD Greater London TQ1777
District in borough of Hounslow
On Thames opposite Kew (see), on main road to London from west and at ford over River Brent. Largely rebuilt post-war. Elevated stretch of M4 runs through. Kew Bridge Steam Museum preserves vast working engines of West London Pumping Station. Musical Museum of automatic instruments in former St George's Church. Waterman's Arts Centre, Waterman's Park.

BRENTINGBY Leicestershire SK7818
Hamlet off B676, 2 miles (3km) E of Melton Mowbray
Near River Eye. Fourteenth-century church tower cared for by Redundant Churches Fund; 14th-century nave and chancel, remodelled 1660, converted to house in 1970s.

BRENTWOOD Essex TQ5993
Town off A12, 11 miles (18km) SW of Chelmsford
Pleasant shopping, entertainment and London commuter town on old pilgrim and coaching routes. Now mainly post-war in style and atmosphere, graced by a Roman Catholic cathedral designed by Quinlan Terry, dedicated in 1991. Ford Motors headquarters here. Local history museum in disused cemetery. Thorndon Country Park and Weald Country Park outside town, both former stately deer parks, now provide enjoyable walking, riding, fishing.

BRENZETT Kent TR0027
Village on A259, 5 miles (8km) NW of New Romney
Minute settlement on Rhee Wall, an ancient, probably Roman, sea embankment on wide Romney Marsh. The Peasants' Revolt mustered here.

BRERETON GREEN Cheshire SJ7764
Village on A50, 5 miles (8km) NW of Congleton
Pretty 15th-century Church of St Oswald is reached through the castellated Lodge Gates to Brereton Hall. The Bear's Head, focal point of the village, is a typical black and white Tudor building.

BRESSAY Shetland HU5441
Island off E coast of mainland
Fertile island with cliffs to the south with good walking, once had famous stud for Shetland ponies. Ferry gives access to Noss National Nature Reserve on uninhabited Noss Island; vast nesting colonies of seabirds around 500ft (152m) seacliff called Noup of Noss, particularly skuas, guillemots and puffins. Good day outing from Lerwick.

BRESSINGHAM Norfolk TM0780
Village on A1066, 3 miles (5km) W of Diss
Home to the Bressingham Steam Museum, with its parkland of perennial and alpine plants. Engines can be seen in full steam puffing around the village.

BRETFORTON Hereford and Worcester SP0944
Village on B4035, 4 miles (6km) E of Evesham
The medieval/Tudor Fleece inn (National Trust) stands out among a wealth of interesting buildings around the village green.

BREWOOD Staffordshire SJ8808
Small town off A5, 7 miles (11km) N of Wolverhampton
Attractive canalside town with interesting churches (one by Pugin) and a wealth of homely Georgian architecture. Near by is Chillington Hall (limited opening), a fine Georgian mansion.

BREYDON WATER Norfolk TG4907
Lake off A47, W of Great Yarmouth
Expanse of tidal salt water that disintegrates into shiny stretches of mud at low tide. Norfolk wherries (black-sailed boats) raced here in bygone days.

BRIANTSPUDDLE Dorset SY8193
Village off B3390, 2 miles (3km) SW of Bere Regis
Many of the cottages are 'model' ones built in traditional styles (some thatched) early this century by the local landowner.

BRICKET WOOD Hertfordshire TL1202
Area of NE Watford
In jaws of M1 and M25. Woods known for pre-war nudist colonies. Building Research Establishment, Garston, studies methods, materials.

BRIDESTONES, THE North Yorkshire SE8791
Rocks off A169, 12 miles (19km) S of Whitby
Curiously shaped rock masses formed by erosion, the largest of which is known as 'The Pepper Pot'. A National Trust site.

BRIDESTONES, THE Staffordshire SJ9062
Prehistoric site off A527, 5 miles (8km) SE of Congleton
Neolithic burial chamber. Original barrow, apparently removed in 18th century, estimated to have been 100yds (90m) long.

BRIDFORD Devon SX8186
Village off B3212, 4 miles (6km) E of Moretonhampstead
Once a lead-mining and granite-quarrying area, now agricultural, with wooded valleys. The church has a fine wooden screen of about 1530.

BRIDGE OF ALLAN Central NS7997
Town on A9, 3 miles (5km) N of Stirling
Agreeable Victorian spa town at foot of Ochil Hills on Allan Water. The Wallace Monument looms on a hill above the town affording magnificent views; built in 1869 to commemorate William Wallace's victory over the English at the Battle of Stirling Bridge in 1297. Stirling University campus to east; purpose-built in late 1960s round Airthrey Castle with beautifully landscaped grounds.

The bridge at Bridge of Orchy, on the West Highland Way.

BRIDGE OF ORCHY Strathclyde NN2939
Village on A82, 6 miles (10km) N of Tyndrum
Minuscule village to south of Rannoch Moor; lies on West Highland Way, excellent local and long-distance walking.

BRIDGE OF WEIR Strathclyde NS3965
Small town on A761, 6 miles (10km) W of Paisley
Residential town on the Gryfe Water with good local facilities, dormitory town for Paisley and Glasgow in pleasant country.

BRIDGEND Mid Glamorgan SS9079
Town off A48, 18 miles (29km) W of Cardiff
Industrial centre known for its concentration of Japanese manufacturers. Coity Castle better preserved than Newcastle's remains. Bryngarw Country Park near by, with Japanese garden.

BRIDGNORTH Shropshire SO7193
Town on A458, 13 miles (21km) NW of Kidderminster
Once a thriving river port, Bridgnorth has a unique character. The town centre (High Town) stands on a dramatic sandstone bluff; the later suburb (Low Town) spreads along the opposite bank of the River Severn and pedestrians between the two take a vertiginous cable railway. At the southern end of the bluff St Mary's Church, a classical design by Thomas Telford, rubs shoulders with the crazily leaning keep of the castle. From here a once-fashionable 18th-century thoroughfare leads to the long High Street, where the 17th-century town hall stands in the middle of the bustling road pleasantly lined with timber-framed Georgian and Victorian buildings.

At the northern end St Leonard's Church is the centrepiece of a close of interesting buildings, and steps from here descend to the old quayside, passing Bishop Percy's House, a fine timber-framed mansion. From the riverside road it is possible to see caves, inhabited well into the 19th century.

The former GWR station is now the northern terminus of the Severn Valley Railway, Britain's longest restored standard-gauge line, running from here to Kidderminster.

BRIDGWATER Somerset ST2937
Town on A39, 9 miles (14km) NE of Taunton
Port at the head of the Parrett estuary, quite a way inland. A town from 1200. Big market place, with classical 1834 market hall and big medieval church. Good Georgian houses, especially in Castle Street and West Quay. Bridgwater Carnival in November is said to have the largest procession in Europe. Admiral Blake Museum has the history of the town and the admiral.

BRIDLINGTON Humberside TA1866
Town on A165, 10 miles (16km) SE of Filey
Traditional family seaside resort with harbour, cliff walks around Flamborough Head, coastal wildlife and sandy beaches. Usual resort attractions on the sea front and many watersports activities and events. Sewerby Hall, an early 18th-century house, contains a room dedicated to Amy Johnson, the aviation pioneer. The Harbour Museum and Aquarium tells the history of Bridlington Harbour.

BRIDPORT Dorset SY4692
Town on A35, 14 miles (23km) W of Dorchester
The main town of west Dorset, surrounded by small but prominent green hills. Still a proper old-fashioned market town with two main streets, almost all of stone but with a classical Georgian town hall of brick right in the middle. Rope and net have been made here since the 13th century. Local museum.

BRIERFIELD Lancashire SD8436
Town off M65, immediately SW of Nelson
An industrial town, Brierfield looks up to the Pennines. There is a large war memorial in the main street.

BRIERLEY HILL West Midlands SO9186
District in SW Dudley, on A461
Straggling town once famous for Marsh and Baxter pies and steel production at Round Oak works. The steelworks site is now occupied by the huge Merry Hill shopping centre, where a monorail service takes customers round 260 shops in environmentally controlled conditions. The Royal Brierley Crystal factory in North Street still operates and offers factory tours and shop.

BRIGG Humberside TA0007
Small town on A18, 7 miles (11km) E of Scunthorpe
On the River Ancholme, the medieval town grew around a bridging point of the river and is the subject of a 1907 tone poem *Brigg Fair* by Delius. Brigg is the Old English for bridge. Henry III granted a charter in 1235 to hold a market each Thursday and a horse fair each summer. Town is now a conservation area.

BRIGHOUSE West Yorkshire SE1422
Town on A644, 4 miles (6km) N of Huddersfield
Dates back to Roman times but grew rapidly as a textile town. Famous for the Brighouse and Rastrick Brass Band.

BRIGHSTONE Isle of Wight SZ4282
Village on B3399, 2 miles (3km) W of Shorwell
Lots of thatched cottages, some of the local hard chalk, some a jumble of all sorts of stone. Medieval church.

BRIGHTLING East Sussex TQ6820
Village off B2096, 5 miles (8km) NW of Battle
Tiny village on wooded hillside. Thirteenth-century church dwarfed by pyramidal mausoleum of Jack Fuller (died 1833). Gypsum mine; aerial ropeway to Mountfield.

BRIGHTLINGSEA Essex TM0817
Town on B1029, 8 miles (13km) SE of Colchester
Former Colne estuary port, known for oysters, now a sailing centre and retirement town. Impressive church with tall 15th-century tower.

BRIGHTON East Sussex TQ3104
Town on A23, 48 miles (77km) S of London
Now the largest town in Sussex, 'Brighthelmstone' was mentioned in Domesday Book as a prosperous fishing village. It remained a fishing village until the mid-18th century when a Lewes doctor, Richard Russell, published a treatise on the beneficial effects of sea water and

Brighton's fortunes rose dramatically. Well placed to receive visitors from London, the town was already a fashionable spa when in 1782 the Prince of Wales (later George IV) arrived and Brighton became the most elegant – and rakish – of bathing resorts. Up went handsome squares, gracious terraces and fine crescents, the distinguished architecture which gives present-day Brighton so much of its appeal. The Prince's seaside home, the 'Marine Pavilion', was built in 1786 and then entirely remodelled in the Hindu style. It is unique, one of the most extraordinary buildings in Britain. It is open to the public – an experience not to be missed. The railway reached Brighton in 1841 and soon the *Brighton Belle* was bringing Londoners to enjoy themselves at the seaside.

The original fishing village lay in the area known as 'the Lanes' which, although the houses date only from the 18th and 19th centuries, preserves the feel of a medieval town – a mass of alleyways and passages, filled today with antique shops and restaurants. The restored Palace Pier provides seaside amusements; Volk's electric railway was one of the earliest in the world; Brighton museum and art gallery are impressive; there is an aquarium, a race course, several golf courses, and numerous parks, while the 1980s marina has allowed Brighton to develop as a sailing centre.

Brighton festival takes place every May and the London – Brighton Veteran Car Run every November. Brighton is an exciting place – fully deserving of its title of 'London by the Sea'.

BRIGHTWALTON Berkshire SU4279
Village off B4494, 8 miles (13km) N of Newbury
Downland village, with some thatched cottages, and a set of church, school and rectory, all designed by GE Street in the 1860s and 70s.

BRIGHTWELL BALDWIN Oxfordshire SU6595
Village off B480, 2 miles (3km) W of Watlington
A fascinating church and the 17th-century Lord Nelson inn stand at the heart of this small village in a parkland setting.

BRIGHTWELL-CUM-SOTWELL Oxfordshire SU5790
Village off A4130, 2 miles (3km) NW of Wallingford
Despite proximity of Wallingford, the twin villages retain their old centres, together with the ancient Church of St Agatha.

BRIGSTOCK Northamptonshire SP9485
Village off A6116, 7 miles (11km) SE of Corby
Ancient centre of Rockingham Forest administration. Fine Saxon church tower, market cross, 16th-century manor house, 19th-century factory. Country park and herb garden.

BRILL Buckinghamshire SP6513
Village off B4011, 6 miles (10km) NW of Thame
Weatherboarded 17th-century windmill perches high up on the common, with sweeping views to the Cotswolds. Attractive old houses.

BRILLEY Hereford and Worcester SO2648
Village off A438, 5 miles (8km) NE of Hay-on-Wye
Northeast of this hill village is Cwmmau Farmhouse (National Trust), a preserved example of a 17th-century stone and timber house with traditional hall.

BRIMHAM ROCKS North Yorkshire SE2064
Rocks off B6265, 3 miles (5km) E of Pateley Bridge
Fantastic stacks of millstone grit, carved out over many years by the effects of the weather.

BRIMPSFIELD Gloucestershire SO9312
Village off A417, 6 miles (10km) S of Cheltenham
A small hill village close to Cotswold Edge. The Norman/medieval church stands alone in a field near earthworks of the castle, demolished in 1322.

BRIMPTON Berkshire SU5564
Village off A340, 2 miles (3km) W of Aldermaston
On the side of the Kennet Valley, with some Georgian brick. Flint church of the 1870s.

BRINGSTY Hereford and Worcester SO6655
see Brockhampton

BRINKLOW Warwickshire SP4379
Village on B4027, 6 miles (10km) E of Coventry
The substantial motte and double bailey of an early medieval castle lies close to the church, which is also worth a visit.

BRINSLEY Nottinghamshire SK4548
Village on A608, 9 miles (14km) NW of Nottingham
DH Lawrence's father worked at the colliery here. Pit headstocks re-erected as starting point of Lawrence trails.

BRINSOP Hereford and Worcester SO4444
Village off A480, 5 miles (8km) NW of Hereford
Church interior is rich in beautiful craft work from 12th to 19th centuries. Wordsworth was a visitor to medieval Brinsop Manor.

BRISCO Cumbria NY4252
Hamlet off A6, 3 miles (5km) SE of Carlisle
A ribbon of dwellings once part of the Woodside estate. St Ninian's Well dates back to AD400.

BRISTOL Avon ST5972
City off M4/M5, 106 miles (171km) W of London
A huge city on the River Avon and a port from medieval times, when it was almost as large as London. The medieval town was based around a bridge across the river, and traded with France, Spain, Portugal and Holland, importing many luxury goods such as wine and exporting woollen cloth. Bombing in World War II removed many medieval buildings, but many medieval churches remain. The cathedral was the abbey church and still has the Norman chapter house and three gateways besides the church itself, which is later medieval with a very fine Lady Chapel. St Mary Redcliffe is considered the best medieval parish church in the country; 13th and 14th century, large, rich and intricate with a soaring spire.

The harbour was improved in the 13th century, and reached its present form with the floating harbour (a harbour always full of water) and basins in the early 19th century. It is no longer a commercial port (the docks are at the mouth of the Avon), but the docks still dominate the middle of the city and have become an attraction, with the Maritime Heritage Centre, Bristol Industrial Museum, ferries, occasional steam trains and most famously the SS *Great Britain*, Brunel's vast steam ship of 1843, now being fully restored. Harvey's Wine Cellars Museum is a reminder of one famous part of Bristol's trade. Some big 17th-century timber-framed houses and inns survive, and the Tudor Red Lodge has early furniture as well.

After a decline, Bristol again became the city with the second largest population in the country in the first half of the 18th century, and there are many Georgian houses still surviving, including squares and even a crescent. Queen Square is the most impressive, and Georgian House has been furnished as a museum of 18th-century life. John Wesley's chapel dates from 1739, and is the earliest Methodist building in the world.

The Exchange (classical, 1740s) has earlier bronze pillars outside called Nails, where the merchants paid out – the origin of 'to pay on the nail'.

Bristol was on the early Great Western Railway, and part of Temple Meads Station is one of the earliest stations in the country, castellated stone of 1839. Nineteenth-century Bristol processed tobacco and made chocolate, both industries being based on local imports. Soap and glass were also produced, blue glass being a Bristol speciality.

The town centre is very diverse, with many Victorian commercial buildings including a covered market, the big Victorian City Museum, and a mixture from Georgian to modern. The huge Gothic tower of the Wills Memorial Building (1925, part of the University) is a particular landmark. There are two theatres (one 18th century) and a concert hall. Christmas Steps is lined with old buildings.

The best view of the city is from Cabot Tower, Brandon Hill. The little Gothic tower (1897) is a memorial to the great sailor who left from Bristol in 1496 to discover Newfoundland (he thought it was China).

Bristol today spreads across several hills, and in contrast to its genteel neighbour, Bath, is a functional city, lively and cosmopolitan, but still very human despite its great size.

BRITFORD Wiltshire SU1627
Village off A338, 1 mile (2km) SE of Salisbury
Small and pretty village right down in the Avon Valley, with good views of Salisbury and its cathedral spire. The Georgian big house (not open) has fancy Gothic windows and an older moat. Saxon arches in the church.

BRITON FERRY West Glamorgan SS7494
Town on A474, 2 miles (3km) S of Neath
Bridges have long since replaced ferry across mouth of River Neath. Old docks date from industrial times.

BRITWELL SALOME Oxfordshire SU6792
Village on B4009, 1 mile (2km) SW of Watlington
A small village on the edge of the Britwell estate beneath Swyncombe Downs and the Ridgeway.

BRIXHAM Devon SX9255
Town on A3022, 5 miles (8km) S of Paignton
Still a fishing centre, with an attractive harbour and old cottages around it. Narrow old streets and steps. A replica of Drake's ship *Golden Hind* is kept in the inner harbour. Berry Head Country Park is the rocky headland to the east, high and wild with good sea views and cliffs. Remains of 1790s fort. Local museum.

BRIXTON Greater London TQ3175
District in borough of Lambeth
Lively Brixton market in Electric Avenue reflects substantial West Indian population. Restored windmill, Blenheim Gardens. Brixton Prison opened 1820.

BRIXWORTH Northamptonshire SP7470
Village on A508, 7 miles (11km) N of Northampton
Magnificent church on rise at northern edge of village, is 'perhaps the most imposing architectural memorial of the seventh century surviving north of the Alps' and, according to Pevsner, 'surpasses all other Anglo-Saxon churches in England'. Fine 18th- and 19th-century houses, dating from establishment of Pytchley Hunt here, 1766. Country park with views of Pitsford Water.

BRIZE NORTON Oxfordshire SP2907
Village off A40, 4 miles (6km) W of Witney
Home of the RAF's principal air transport centre; fine Norman and medieval Church of St Britius.

BROAD CHALKE Wiltshire SU0325
Village off A30, 5 miles (8km) SW of Wilton
In two parts across the River Ebble, with watercress beds and some thatch. Big medieval church.

BROAD HAVEN Dyfed SM8613
Village on B4341, 6 miles (10km) W of Haverfordwest
This popular little resort with wide sandy beach on St Bride's Bay contrasts with quieter havens along cliff-backed coast. Traditional Welsh entertainment at Celtic Corner.

BROAD HINTON Wiltshire SU1075
Village off A4361, 4 miles (6km) N of Avebury
Largish, mostly modern village. Restored medieval church with fine monuments including a colonel killed fighting for the king in 1645. Figure in armour with his real armour above.

BROADBRIDGE HEATH West Sussex TQ1431
Village off A264, 2 miles (3km) W of Horsham
Retains its village identity despite proximity to Horsham and its own growth of suburban housing. The poet Shelley was born in Field Place.

BROADCLYST Devon SX9897
Village on B3181, 5 miles (8km) NE of Exeter
A large, unspoilt, well-preserved village with its own suburb called Dog Village. Killerton House (National Trust) to the north has superb shrub and tree gardens, laid out from the late 18th century onwards. Good woodlands too, especially Killerton Clump. The house is also open; smallish but interesting with costume displays in period rooms. Marker's Cottage (National Trust) is a medieval cob house.

BROADFORD Highland (Skye) NG6423
Village on A850, 7 miles (11km) SW of Kyleakin
Main 'town' in southern Skye, stretching round Broadford Bay with easy access to Cuillins. Tourist centre with good facilities.

BROADHEMBURY Devon ST1004
Village off A373, 5 miles (8km) NW of Honiton
Lots of pretty thatched cottages, some of them terraced along the main street. Hembury hillfort 1 1/2 miles (2km) southeast is the best prehistoric earthwork in the county – neolithic and Iron Age.

BROADS, THE Norfolk/Suffolk
Region
Rippling lakes, mysterious reed-choked channels leading away from streams, and rivers which look down on the surrounding countryside. All these features can be found in the Broads, a triangular area that runs from Stalham in the north, to Norwich in the west, and Lowestoft in the southeast. In the summer, the six great rivers (Yare, Waveney, Bure, Thurne, Chet and Ant) that link the Broads seethe with pleasure crafts, as hundreds of people explore the waterways.

The Broads are strings of lakes, teeming with fish and wildfowl. Small islands rising out of the shallow waters offer refuge to a wide variety of plants, animals and birds, many of them now rare as human development has whittled away their habitats. Dotted sparsely around the Broads are isolated villages which are invariably pretty.

The only real way to explore the Broads is by boat: roads simply do not go to some of the meres and channels. Despite the massive growth of tourism recently, it is possible to escape the crowds down some of the smaller waterways. Here the Broads work their magic, offering stillness and peace along silent tree-lined avenues of water.

BROADSTAIRS Kent TR3967
Town on A255, 2 miles (3km) N of Ramsgate
Family seaside resort on Isle of Thanet between Ramsgate and Margate. Grew by amalgamation of St Peter's, a mile inland, and Broadstairs and Reading Street on the coast. Retains village atmosphere. Annual Dickens Festival celebrates the novelist's attachment to the place. Annual Folk Festival Week in August is leading folk festival in southern England.

BROADWAS Hereford and Worcester SO7555
Village on A44, 6 miles (10km) W of Worcester
The church stands beside the River Teme, away from the modern village. Timber tower containing bell of 1346, 13th-century nave, 14th-century chantry chapel.

BROADWATER West Sussex TQ1404
Suburb in N area of Worthing
Inland from coast, old centre of Worthing with pleasant cottages and modern shopping centre. Suburban now right on to South Downs.

BROADWAY Hereford and Worcester SP0937
Small town on A44, 5 miles (8km) SE of Evesham
One of England's showpieces, lying beneath a Cotswold escarpment. Impeccably preserved buildings include the 17th-century Lygon Arms, the medieval Abbot's Grange and a rich array of old farmhouses and cottages. Ancient Church of St Eadburga stands well to the south. At the top of Fish Hill is Broadway Tower, a neo-Norman folly of 1793, spectacular viewpoint and centrepiece of country park.

BROADWELL Oxfordshire SP2504
Village off A361, 4 miles (6km) NE of Lechlade
An unexpectedly grand church presides over a village with attractive stone houses and a characterful pub.

BROADWINDSOR Dorset ST4302
Village on B3162, 3 miles (5km) W of Beaminster
Large village whose centre seems little changed since the 19th century. Southwest (3 miles/5km) is Pilsden Pen, the highest point in Dorset (908ft/277m) crowned with an Iron Age hillfort. Wide and wonderful views from the top.

BROBURY Hereford and Worcester SO3444
Hamlet off A438, 11 miles (18km) W of Hereford
Brobury House, Garden and Gallery offers extensive semi-formal gardens beside the River Wye and a fine collection of watercolours.

BROCKENHURST Hampshire SU3002
Village on A337, 4 miles (6km) S of Lyndhurst
Right in the New Forest, and small until the railway arrived in 1849. All around the outskirts are Lawns, the New Forest name for open areas of grazing. Isolated medieval church, the tower smothered by an ancient yew.

BROCKHALL Northamptonshire SP6362
Village off A5, 4 miles (6km) E of Daventry
Small village in centre of estate of Brockhall Hall, Elizabethan and later (closed), now flanked by M1.

BROCKHAM Surrey TQ1949
Village off A25, 2 miles (3km) E of Dorking
Delightfully satisfying with Box Hill behind as a spectacular backdrop. Village grouped around green, one side cottages, the other Regency and trees.

BROCKHAMPTON (NEAR BROMYARD) Hereford and Worcester SO6855
Hamlet off A44, 2 miles (3km) E of Bromyard
Good walking on Bringsty Common. Lower Brockhampton Manor (National Trust) is a moated, timber-framed house dating from about 1400 with gatehouse and 12th-century chapel.

BROCKHAMPTON (NEAR ROSS-ON-WYE) Hereford and Worcester SO5931
Village off B4224, 5 miles (8km) N of Ross-on-Wye
Gem of the village is William Lethaby's homely thatched church of 1901–2, with Burne-Jones tapestries and floral carvings on chancel stalls.

BROCKHOLE Cumbria SD3901
Site on A591, 2 miles (3km) NW of Windermere
A large house on eastern shores of Lake Windermere, now the Lake District National Park information centre.

BROCKLESBY Humberside TA1311
Village on B1211, 9 miles (14km) W of Grimsby
Estate village at gates of Brocklesby Park, home of the Earls of Yarborough. At one time the largest estate in Lincolnshire.

BROCKWORTH Gloucestershire SO8916
Village off A417, 4 miles (6km) SE of Gloucester
This old village, engulfed in Gloucester's suburbs, has a 14th-century church and 16th-century manor house, but is best known for Cooper's Hill, to the south: a nature reserve and site of the annual cheese-rolling contest on Spring Bank Holiday, when competitors chase replicas of Double Gloucester cheeses down a dangerously steep slope. Winners receive real cheeses.

BROCTON Staffordshire SJ9619
Village off A34, 4 miles (6km) SE of Stafford
On the slopes of Cannock Chase. Good walks to nature reserve in flooded quarry and ancient oak woods at Brocton Coppice.

BRODICK Strathclyde (Arran) NS0135
Town on A841, 7 miles (11km) N of Lamlash
Set on sandy bay and backed by mountains, capital and main ferry terminal of Arran, with good tourist services. Nearby Brodick Castle was seat of Dukes of Hamilton, central tower is 15th century, although building had 19th-century additions; fine furniture, porcelain and pictures and beautiful gardens running down to sea.

BRODSWORTH South Yorkshire SE5007
Village on B6422, 5 miles (8km) NW of Doncaster
Brodsworth Hall designed by Cavaliere Casentini provides a unique experience of life in a Victorian country hall.

BROKERSWOOD Wiltshire ST8352
Hamlet off A350, 3 miles (5km) W of Westbury
The Woodland Park and Woodland Heritage Museum, in 80 acres (32ha) of ancient woodlands, nature trails, lake and waterfowl.

BROME Suffolk TM1376
Village off B1077, 2 miles (3km) N of Eye
This delightful village has links with the Cornwallis family (surrendered to George Washington). Works by Suffolk sculptor James Williams adorn the church.

BROMFIELD Shropshire SO4876
Village on A49, 3 miles (5km) NW of Ludlow
A 15th-century priory gatehouse stands close to the church, which has a naively painted chancel ceiling. Picturesque estate cottages beside main road.

BROMHAM Bedfordshire TL0051
Village off A428, 3 miles (5km) W of Bedford
Bedford dormitory village, noble 26-arched bridge over the Great Ouse, watermill restored to working order. Church with squires' monuments.

BROMHAM Wiltshire ST9665
Village off A342, 4 miles (6km) NW of Devizes
Straggling village, with timber-framed cottages in the centre, and a timber lock-up in the churchyard. Ornate side chapel of 1492 in church, with many 15th- and 16th-century memorials.

Brodick Castle on the Isle of Arran.

BROMLEY Greater London TQ4069
District in SE London borough
Old Kentish market town before railway arrived in 1850s, now London suburb and major shopping, entertainment and education centre. Bromley College almshouses, 17th century and later. Edwardian and 1930s red-brick town hall. St Peter and St Paul Church restored after 1941 bomb damage. Brutal 1970s theatre and public library. Bromley Museum is in Orpington (see).

BROMPTON BY SAWDON North Yorkshire SE9482
Village on A170, 7 miles (11km) SW of Scarborough
Castle once stood here when the area belonged to the Kingdom of Northumbria. Mary Hutchinson, wife of William Wordsworth, was born here and the two were married in the village.

BROMPTON-IN-ALLERTONSHIRE North Yorkshire SE3796
Village off A684, 1 mile (2km) N of Northallerton
Lovely village surrounding a large green intersected by Brompton Beck. The site of a battle is near by.

BROMSGROVE Hereford and Worcester SO9670
Town on A38, 12 miles (19km) SW of Birmingham
The town's industrial and social history is explained at the Bromsgrove Museum in Birmingham Road, which also features work of famous Bromsgrove guild of craftsmen and life of poet AE Housman, born here in 1859. Avoncroft Museum of Buildings at Stoke Heath specialises in rescuing interesting buildings, moving them to site and restoring them. Post mill, merchant's house, 1946 prefab among those on show.

BROMYARD Hereford and Worcester SO6554
Town on A44, 12 miles (19km) W of Worcester
Bustling market town in striking hill setting with pretty centre, including two old coaching inns and timber-framed and Georgian houses. St Peter's church is Norman (fine south doorway) and medieval, with notable Walker organ. Heritage centre, Rowberry Street, displays local history, especially hop-growing. Good walking and panoramic views on the Bromyard Downs.

BROOK Isle of Wight SZ3983
Village off A3055, 4 miles (6km) W of Shorwell
A long village with a long green, running down to crumbly yellow cliffs and the sea.

BROOK Kent TR0644
Village off A28, 4 miles (6km) E of Ashford
Scattered village with pleasant houses and cottages and a remarkable Norman church in wooded farmland beneath the North Downs.

BROOKE Leicestershire SK8405
Hamlet off A6003, 2 miles (3km) S of Oakham
Remote site of Augustinian priory. Tiny gem of church, 13th-century tower, Norman work, rebuilt about 1579 with contemporary box pews, pulpit and other woodwork.

BROOKE Norfolk TM2899
Village on B1332, 7 miles (11km) SE of Norwich
Delightful village blending old with new. The meres have a rare fungus, and the woods at Shrieking Woman Grove are said to be haunted.

BROOKLAND Kent TQ9926
Village on A259, 5 miles (8km) W of New Romney
Attractive village on little knoll that was once an island in Romney Marsh. Church has unusual, separate 13th-century bell tower.

BROOKMANS PARK Hertfordshire TL2404
Village off A1000, 2 miles (3km) N of Potters Bar
Little Miss Muffet lived at Moffats Farm, supposedly. Two great houses here have gone, leaving only 18th-century folly arch behind.

BROOKSBY Leicestershire SK6715
Hamlet off A607, 5 miles (8km) SW of Melton Mowbray
Brooksby Hall – birthplace 1592 of George Villiers who became Duke of Buckingham, royal favourite of Stuart kings – now Leicestershire's Agricultural College.

BROOKWOOD Surrey SU9557
Village on A324, 4 miles (6km) W of Woking
Village tucked between railway and Basingstoke Canal with huge cemetery, London's necropolis founded in 1854, at one time largest in world.

BROOMFIELD Essex TL7010
Village off A130, 2 miles (3km) N of Chelmsford
Northern suburb of Chelmsford. Church has Norman round tower and Roman bricks. Burial of pagan Saxon king discovered here.

BROOMFIELD Somerset ST2232
Hamlet off A38, 4 miles (6km) W of North Petherton
The highest settlement on the Quantock Hills, with a beautifully sited and interesting church. Many 16th-century bench-ends. Fyne Court, Somerset Wildlife Trust, displays, nature trails and interpretive centre.

BROOMFLEET Humberside SE8827
Village off B1230, 4 miles (6km) SW of South Cove
The Humber Wildfowl Refuge provides a sanctuary for the protection of wild birds which winter on the nearby Whitton sandbanks.

BRORA Highland NC9103
Village on A9, 10 miles (16km) SW of Helmsdale
Lies at mouth of River Brora with small harbour. Clynelish Distillery is Scotland's most northerly. Also high-quality tweed mill.

BROSELEY Shropshire SJ6701
Large village on B4373, 1 mile (2km) S of Ironbridge
The imposing church of 1845 stands at the edge of this former industrial village, a centre of coal-mining, iron-founding, brick-making and clay pipe manufacture. John Wilkinson, famous 18th-century ironmaster, lived at The Lawns opposite church. The main street is a living museum of early Victorian vernacular architecture.

BROTTON Cleveland NZ6819
Town on A174, 2 miles (3km) SE of Saltburn-by-the-Sea
Built during the ironstone mining boom of the 1880s, now an interesting mix of ironstone miners' cottages and modern housing.

BROUGH Cumbria NY7914
Village on A685, 4 miles (6km) N of Kirkby Stephen
Made up of Market Brough, Church Brough and Brough Sowerby, this natural trading point has been occupied since Roman times. The ruins of Brough Castle (English Heritage), built by Normans on the site of a Roman fort, are still visible. Brough Hill Fair, an annual gathering of gypsies, takes place in September and dates back 600 years.

BROUGH OF BIRSAY Orkney HY2328
Island off NW coast of mainland
Pictish and Viking remains of great historical interest on small tidal island which can be reached on foot for two hours each side of low water. Eleventh-century Earl Thor Finn established Orkney's first bishopric here and built cathedral, exact location unknown. Outline of walls of St Peter's Church, dating from 1200s, can still be seen on island.

BROUGHAM Cumbria NY4328
Site off A66, 2 miles (3km) SE of Penrith
Outlines of a Roman fort can still be seen at this site along with the ruined Brougham Castle (English Heritage) and a church. The great castle keep was built in 1170s and the curtain wall in the 13th century. St Ninian's Church dates from Norman times. Both the castle and church were restored by Lady Anne Clifford in 17th century.

BROUGHTON Borders NT1136
Village on A701, 4 miles (6km) E of Peebles
Tweed Valley village where writer John Buchan, Lord Tweedsmuir, spent many holidays. Scottish baronial Broughton Place designed by Sir Basil Spence.

BROUGHTON Buckinghamshire SP8939
Village on A5130, 3 miles (5km) SE of Newport Pagnell
Close to the M1, tiny place known for its church wall-paintings of the 14th and 15th centuries, including Last Judgement, St George and Dragon, unusual *pietà.*

BROUGHTON Humberside SE9608
Village on B1207, 3 miles (5km) NW of Brigg
Village on the Roman Ermine Road, one of Britain's straightest roads built on a ridge to avoid surrounding marshes.

BROUGHTON Northamptonshire SP8375
Village off A43, 3 miles (5km) SW of Kettering
Large residential village, with notable 17th-century listed buildings, and Norman and 14th-century church. The A43 bypass has made the village quieter, except on first Sunday after 12 December each year, when villagers bang kettles and cans in midnight Tin Can Band parade, shattering the peace, a continuing tradition despite unsuccessful efforts to stop it in 1929.

BROUGHTON Oxfordshire SP4138
Village on B4035, 3 miles (5km) SW of Banbury
The moated castle, home of the Fiennes family since 1451, was converted to a house in the 16th century but still stands on its romantic island site. As well as the fine ceilings, panelling, furniture and paintings there are memorabilia of the Civil War. Standing in the castle park, St Mary's Church has a splendid east window and rare medieval features.

BROUGHTON ASTLEY Leicestershire SP5292
Village on B581, 5 miles (8km) N of Lutterworth
Large residential village. Fourteenth-century granite church beside brook. Wide north aisle gives appearance of two naves. Baptist chapel of 1815.

BROUGHTON GIFFORD Wiltshire ST8763
Village off B3107, 2 miles (3km) W of Melksham
Long thin village, still with a large open common at one end.

BROUGHTON-IN-FURNESS Cumbria SD2187
Village on A593, 8 miles (13km) NW of Ulverston
Name derived from old English word meaning 'stronghold'. Was of strategic importance through centuries of invasion from Scotland and overseas.

BROUGHTY FERRY Tayside NO4630
Suburb in E Dundee
Developed as eastern residential suburb of Dundee during 19th-century jute heyday. Some original fisher cottages still exist, and castle houses fishing museum.

BROWN CLEE HILL Shropshire SO5987
see Abdon

BROWNHILLS West Midlands SK0405
Town on A5, 5 miles (8km) NE of Walsall
Housing and industrial estates now dominate this old mining settlement. Chasewater, a large recreational reservoir, and Chasewater Pleasure Park are major attractions.

BROWNSEA ISLAND Dorset SZ0288
Island in Poole Harbour
The largest of several islands in Poole Harbour (National Trust). Only accessible by boat, which gives good views of the fancy mock castle (not open) and other buildings. Most of the island is a nature reserve, and still has red squirrels. The first Boy Scout camp was held here in 1907. Inland is a well-fitted Victorian church.

BROXBOURNE Hertfordshire TL3606
Village on A1170, 2 miles (3km) S of Hoddesdon
Old settlement by River Lee, developed after railway arrived 1840, now continuous with Hoddesdon (see). Parish church with notable brasses, in attractive setting among meadows by New River. Pleasant walks here. Lee Valley boat centre for boating, cruising. Nazeing Glass Works with factory shop. To west are Bencroft Wood and Broxbourne Woods with Paradise Wildlife Park's wild animals.

BROXBURN Lothian NT0872
Town on A899, 11 miles (18km) W of Edinburgh
Town with food-processing and light industry. Near by is Niddry Castle, five-storey L-plan tower-house, built in 1500s by Setons.

BRUNDALL Norfolk TG3308
Village off A47, 6 miles (10km) E of Norwich
Elegant Edwardian residences lie on the north bank of the River Yare. To the south are Broadland marshes littered with reeds.

BRUNTINGTHORPE Leicestershire SP6089
Village off A50, 9 miles (14km) S of Leicester
Seventeenth-century timber-framed farm and 1870s church. Former airfield closed in early 1970s, now proving ground for vehicles, with occasional air displays.

BRUSHFORD Somerset SS9225
Village on B3222, 2 miles (3km) SE of Dulverton
Large and partly modern – older parts round the medieval church. Exebridge, hamlet down on the river, is picturesque.

BRUTON Somerset ST6835
Small town on A359, 7 miles (11km) SE of Shepton Mallet
Tiny old-fashioned town, good buildings including Hugh Sexey's superb almshouses of 1636 (with chapel). Bartons (alleyways) run under houses and down to the river; glimpses of the huge medieval dovecote on hill beyond. Two old stone bridges down by the impressive church: 102ft (31m) tower, splendid wooden roof and unusual Georgian chancel. Local museum.

BRYHER Isles of Scilly SV8714
Island
Rocky formations on the Atlantic coast, to the east and south sandy beaches and peaceful bays. Bronze Age cairns on Samson Hill.

BRYMBO Clwyd SJ2953
Town on B5433, 3 miles (5km) NW of Wrexham
Former steelworking town has links with pioneering industrialist John 'Iron Mad' Wilkinson. Large steelworks site now closed. Nearby Minera once important for its lead mines.

BRYNEGLWYS Clwyd SJ1447
Village on A5104, 5 miles (8km) NE of Corwen
Church contains chapel in memory of Yale University's founding family. Elihu Yale's ancestral home, Plas-yn-Yale (Ial), close by.

BRYNMAWR Gwent SO1911
Town on A467, 7 miles (11km) W of Abergavenny
On high ground above Clydach Gorge, surrounded by moors at head of industrial valleys. Iron-masters built Nantyglo's two round towers.

BRYNSIENCYN Gwynedd (Anglesey) SH4867
Village on A4080, 6 miles (10m) SW of Menai Bridge
By Menai Strait. Popular Anglesey Sea Zoo gives close-ups of marine creatures. Bodowyr Burial Chamber, Caer Làb earthworks, Foel Farm Park all near by.

BUBWITH Humberside SE7136
Village on A163, 5 miles (8km) NW of Howden
On the banks of the River Derwent, an important winter habitat for significant numbers of wildfowl. Interesting 12th-century church.

BUCHAN Grampian
Historic region of Scotland
Flat, north-eastern sector of Grampian mainly bounded by the sea, and including ports of Peterhead and Fraserburgh, with inland pasture and arable.

BUCKDEN Cambridgeshire TL1967
Village off A1, 4 miles (6km) SW of Huntingdon
Imposing Buckden Palace (English Heritage, not open) was built by Bishops of Lincoln in the 15th century. The gatehouse dates from Tudor times. Catherine of Aragon was imprisoned here, and two of Lady Jane Grey's uncles, fleeing to Buckden to escape the plague, died of the sickness within 30 minutes of each other. Writer Lawrence Sterne was ordained in Buckden church.

BUCKDEN North Yorkshire SD9477
Village on B6160, 4 miles (6km) N of Kettlewell
Once the headquarters of the officers of the hunting forest of Langstrothdale, and a popular starting point for climbing Buckden Pike.

BUCKFAST Devon SX7467
Village off A38, 1 mile (2km) N of Buckfastleigh
In the Dart Valley, and only just off Dartmoor. In medieval times there was a large monastery, abolished with all the others in the 1530s. In 1882 French Benedictines acquired the site and set out to rebuild it, finishing the buildings in 1938. Large church, and still a working monastery.

BUCKFASTLEIGH Devon SX7366
Town off A38, 5 miles (8km) NW of Totnes
An early industrial centre, particularly for the manufacture of woollen cloth, with several mills surviving. Buckfast Butterfly Farm and Dartmoor Otter Sanctuary, and the Primrose Line, the Dart Valley Light Railway (steam) which runs to Totnes.

BUCKHAVEN Fife NT3598
Town off A955, 7 miles (11km) NE of Kirkcaldy
Once a fishing port with ferry serving Leith and Edinburgh, now part of a continuous stretch of coal-mining towns.

BUCKIE Grampian NJ4265
Town off A98, 17 miles (27km) W of Banff
Small fishing town with satellite villages along adjacent cliffs which boomed during heyday of herring industry. Maritime Heritage Centre tells local fisheries story.

BUCKINGHAM Buckinghamshire SP6933
Town on A422, 11 miles (18km) W of Bletchley
Unspoiled pre-Victorian market town in the far north-west of the county, nowhere near a railway or a motorway, formerly the county town. Narrow streets, attractive 18th-century houses built after 1725 fire, big church on hill with tall spire and views. Old Gaol

has local history museum. Home of University of Buckingham since 1970s.

BUCKLAND Oxfordshire SU3498
Village off A420, 4 miles (6km) NE of Faringdon
Norman ironwork on the door is one of many good reasons for visiting the church in this village overlooking the Thames Valley.

BUCKLAND IN THE MOOR Devon SX7273
Hamlet off B3357, 3 miles (5km) NW of Ashburton
Lives up to its name – Dartmoor edge, with steep moorland and wooded valleys. Little medieval granite church, thatched stone cottages. Buckland Beacon to the east has the Ten Commandments carved in granite.

BUCKLAND MONACHORUM Devon SX4968
Village off A386, 4 miles (6km) S of Tavistock
Interesting church, mostly 16th century, with a hamerbeam roof with angels playing musical instruments. Buckland Abbey (1 mile/2km south) is an Elizabethan mansion, constructed actually in the abbey church, a rare conversion. Sir Francis Drake lived here from 1581, and the museum in the house has some relics.

BUCKLEBURY Berkshire SU5570
Village off B4009, 6 miles (10km) NE of Newbury
A hamlet down by the River Pang; interesting church with complex Norman doorway and 18th-century box pews. Woodlands and commons to the south, with more hamlets. Bucklebury Farm Park, with deer too.

BUCKLERS HARD Hampshire SU4000
Hamlet off B3054, 2 miles (3km) SE of Beaulieu
Two rows of brick cottages either side of an extraordinarily wide street (with the river beyond) are all that were built of a new town intended to import and refine sugar. From the 1740s it became a ship-building centre. The Maritime Museum illustrates the history of the area, and several cottages have displays.

BUCKS MILLS Devon SS3523
Hamlet off A39, 3 miles (5km) SE of Clovelly
Tiny picturesque fishing village in a steep valley; wooded shore. A miniature Clovelly.

BUDE Cornwall SS2105
Town off A39, 15 miles (24km) NW of Launceston
The only port on the harsh northern Cornwall coast. It developed faster after the Bude Canal to Launceston was built in the 1820s. The impressive sea lock survives (and a couple of miles of the canal), but the town now relies on its stretches of sandy beaches for most of its trade. The arrival of the railway in the 1880s (now closed) put the canal out of business and brought the holiday-makers.

BUDLEIGH SALTERTON Devon SY0682
Town on B3178, 4 miles (6km) E of Exmouth
A seaside town which started as a resort in the early 19th century. Some villas and cottages of that date survive, along with seaside architecture of later date. Occasional walls and even buildings of pebbles from the beach. Local museum.

BUDOCK WATER Cornwall SW7831
Village off A39, 2 miles (3km) W of Falmouth
The mother parish to Falmouth, just inland. Still rural, tucked in the valley.

BUGBROOKE Northamptonshire SP6757
Village on B4525, 5 miles (8km) SW of Northampton
Substantial village around historic centre of 17th- and 18th-century stone and brick buildings. Thirteenth-century and later parish church. Baptist church 1808.

BUGLE Cornwall SX0158
Village on A391, 4 miles (6km) N of St Austell
In the 'White Alps', Cornwall's china-clay-mining area. A new village of terraces built in the 19th century to house the miners. Conveyor belts across roads and a huge tip behind.

Georgian houses in the street leading to the sea in Buckler's Hard.

BUGTHORPE Humberside SE7757
Village off A166, 4 miles (6km) NE of Stamford Bridge
A particularly pleasant village with a sloping rectangular green, the church on one side and Victorian school on the other.

BUILDWAS Shropshire SJ6204
Village on B4380, 3 miles (5km) N of Much Wenlock
A giant power station is neighbour to a Norman Cistercian abbey (English Heritage), of which splendid nave arcades of church and vaulted chapter house survive.

BUILTH WELLS (LLANFAIR-YM-MUALLT) Powys SO0451
Town off A470, 14 miles (23km) N of Brecon
Farming centre and market town set on River Wye's banks is host to Royal Welsh Agricultural Show every July. Earthworks of a Norman castle indicate Builth's origins, later to develop into a spa town. The Victorian assembly room has become Wyeside Arts Centre. At nearby Cilmery a monument to Llywelyn the Last marks his killing by an English soldier in 1282.

BULBARROW HILL Dorset ST7706
Hill off A357, 5 miles (8km) S of Sturminster Newton
The second highest point in Dorset, on the edge of the chalk and giving the longest view in the county.

BULFORD Wiltshire SU1643
Village off A303, 2 miles (3km) NE of Amesbury
Small village on the Avon, with Bulford Army Camp, started in World War I and now much larger than the village. Bulford Kiwi is a chalk-cut figure on the hillside.

BULLO PILL Gloucestershire SO6909
Site off A48, 1 mile (2km) S of Newnham
This 19th-century dock on the tidal inlet of the River Severn once shipped Forest of Dean coal, transported here on a tramway.

BULMER North Yorkshire SE6967
Village off A64, 6 miles (10km) SW of Malton
The village was part of the Castle Howard estate (see Welburn) and the church is noted for its Saxon wheel cross.

BULPHAN Essex TQ6385
Village on A128, 5 miles (8km) SW of Basildon
Once known for sheep's cheese. London commuter and weekend settlement since railway came. Church noted for fine timberwork and tile-hung tower.

BULWICK Northamptonshire SP9694
Village on A43, 6 miles (10km) NW of Oundle
Attractive stone village, home of Fitzurse, knight to Henry II and one of Becket's murderers. Seventeenth-century hall, home of military Tryon family.

BUNBURY Cheshire SJ5657
Village off A49, 3 miles (5km) S of Tarporley
Original Tudor houses fell victim to World War II bombings of nearby Crewe. Free grammar school, founded 1594, still belongs to Haberdashers' Company.

BUNGAY Suffolk TM3389
Town off A143, 14 miles (23km) SE of Norwich
A raging fire in 1688 destroyed much of Bungay, and many buildings are 18th century. The butter cross in the market place was built in 1689. Bungay Castle dates from 1165, built by the powerful Bigods, but has been a ruin since the 14th century. The River Waveney sweeps around the town, protecting it on three sides.

Sign showing the castle in Bungay.

BUNNY Nottinghamshire SK5829
Village on A60, 7 miles (11km) S of Nottingham
Eccentric 'wrestling baronet' Sir Thomas Parkyns designed parts of Bunny Hall, school, cottages and almshouses. His striking monument dominates nave of 14th-century church.

BUNTINGFORD Hertfordshire TL3629
Small town off A10, 10 miles (16km) N of Ware
Grew up on Ermine Street at crossing of River Rib. Attractive High Street, unusual 17th-century church, handsome almshouses.

BURBAGE Derbyshire SK0472
Village on A53, on W outskirts of Buxton
Former quarrying centre, now virtually suburb of Buxton, below Grin Low Bronze Age barrow and Solomon's Temple look-out tower.

BURBAGE Leicestershire SP4492
Village on B578, on SE outskirts of Hinckley
Attractive residential village with two timber-framed buildings, Georgian houses, church heavily restored in Victorian times. Burbage Common and Woods, visitor centre.

BURBAGE Wiltshire SU2261
Village on A346, 4 miles (6km) E of Pewsey
Long narrow village, with a wharf on the Kennet and Avon Canal (see). Still has a wharf crane.

BURE, RIVER Norfolk
River, flows from near Melton Constable
Called the 'North River' by Broadsmen, the Bure meanders across the beautiful Norfolk Broads from Melton Constable to Great Yarmouth.

BURFORD Oxfordshire SP2512
Small town off A40, 7 miles (11km) W of Witney
A medieval bridge crosses the River Windrush at the foot of the mellow, harmonious main street of this showpiece town. Profits from the wool trade paid for some notable buildings, including the magnificent church, the Lamb inn, Bay Tree hotel, Falkland Hall and grammar school. The Tolsey old market hall is now a museum. Cotswold Wildlife Park off A361 to south.

BURFORD Shropshire SO5868
Village on A456, 1 mile (2km) W of Tenbury Wells
Small Temeside village noted for a church with an astonishing range of monuments and for plantsman John Treasure's nursery and garden (open) at Burford House.

BURGESS HILL West Sussex TQ3218
Town on B2113, 9 miles (14km) N of Brighton
Sprawling suburban growth, a new town of 19th and particularly 20th centuries. The best lies close to the spacious cricket green.

BURGH BY SANDS Cumbria NY3259
Village off B5307, 5 miles (8km) NW of Carlisle
Notable for its massive church tower. Burgh is pronounced 'Bruff'.

BURGH CASTLE Norfolk TG4805
Village off A143, 3 miles (5km) SW of Great Yarmouth
The main attraction of this village is the impressive ruins of a Roman fortress, Burgh Castle (English Heritage) lying to the south. Called *Gariannonum* by the Romans, it was built in the 3rd century as a defence against marauding Saxons. Originally on an estuary, it is now 3 miles (5km) from the sea on flat marshland.

BURGH ISLAND Devon SX6444
Island off Bigbury-on-Sea
A small rocky island just off the south Devon coast, linked to land by a tidal causeway. See Bigbury-on-Sea.

BURGH LE MARSH Lincolnshire TF5065
Village on A158, 5 miles (8km) W of Skegness
Old market town with large marshland church. Five-sailed windmill uses bracing winds for which Skegness area is noted to produce flour.

BURGH ST MARGARET Norfolk TG4413
Village on A1064, 4 miles (6km) NE of Acle
Home of the Bygone Heritage Village, a reconstruction of a 19th-century town with steam locomotives, fire appliances, houses, cars, sawmill, animals and crafts.

BURGH ST PETER Norfolk TM4693
Village off A143, 5 miles (8km) NE of Beccles
The tall square tower of the church, some distance from the village, is a landmark to sailors on the River Waveney.

BURGHCLERE Hampshire SU4761
Village off A34, 5 miles (8km) NW of Highclere
Gentle hills and many trees. The Sandham Memorial Chapel was built in the 1920s to house Stanley Spencer's paintings of World War I.

BURGHEAD Grampian NJ1168
Village on B9013, 8 miles (13km) NW of Elgin
Major Pictish centre in 4th–5th century. Fishing village with lighthouse, and sweeping sands in Burghead Bay.

BURGHFIELD Berkshire SU6668
Village off A4, 4 miles (6km) SW of Reading
Wooded but suburban (to Reading). Odd neo-Norman church of 1843. Burghfield Common is a much larger settlement.

BURGHWALLIS South Yorkshire SE5311
Village off A1, 6 miles (10km) N of Doncaster
Attractive village surrounded by fields and woodland. Burghwallis Hall (not open) was built in 1797.

BURITON Hampshire SU7419
Village off A3, 2 miles (3km) S of Petersfield
Narrow roads cut deeply into the soft greensand. Picturesque village, with a large pond in front of the largely Norman church. Queen Elizabeth Country Park to the south, including downland on Butser Hill and beech woods.

BURLEY Leicestershire SK8810
Village on B668, 2 miles (3km) NE of Oakham
'Rutland Dwarf' sprang out of pie to entertain Charles I. Present House completed 1700, converted into housing, overlooks Rutland Water.

BURLEY IN WHARFEDALE West Yorkshire SE1646
Village on A65, 3 miles (5km) E of Ilkley
A pleasant village beside the River Wharfe. Stone-built cottages were built by mill owners, now desirable homes for commuters.

BURNESTON North Yorkshire SE3084
Village on B6160, 2 miles (3km) W of Ripley
A small village with 17th-century almshouses, a stately 15th-century church. Part of village is a conservation area, with much new building surrounding.

BURNHAM Buckinghamshire SU9282
Village off A4, 3 miles (5km) NW of Slough
On Slough outskirts. Big private houses, medieval church with monuments and 18th-century anti-papist

graffiti. To north is famous Chilterns beauty spot of Burnham Beeches, whose pollarded trees in over 500 acres (202ha) go back to 16th century. Bought for the public by City of London 1879. Deer, birds, newts and dragonflies in the ponds. Spectacular autumn colours.

BURNHAM DEEPDALE Norfolk TF8044
Hamlet on A149, 2 miles (3km) NW of Burnham Market
Once joined to the other Burnhams, this hamlet is now separated from them. The church has a Saxon tower and a fascinating Norman font.

BURNHAM MARKET Norfolk TF8342
Village off A149, 5 miles (8km) W of Wells-next-the-Sea
The Burnhams form a group of seven villages spread along the Burn Valley. Burnham Market encompasses Burnhams Westgate, Sutton and Ulph. It has a spacious village green fringed with some elegant 18th-century houses. The main crop of the 19th century in nearby farms was barley, and several maltings have been converted into houses.

BURNHAM NORTON Norfolk TF8343
Hamlet on A149, 1 mile (2km) N of Burnham Market
Burnham Norton is an unspoiled hamlet standing at the edge of the reclaimed saltmarshes. A painted wine-glass pulpit is in the church.

BURNHAM OVERY Norfolk TF8442
Hamlet on B1155, 1 mile (2km) NE of Burnham Market
Burnham Overy was once a port, but as the sea began to recede, Overy Staithe was built. Burnham Overy is a charming village with a watermill and windmill standing side by side. Across lavender-covered saltmarshes stands Overy Staithe with a fine range of granaries and maltings owned by the National Trust.

BURNHAM THORPE Norfolk TF8541
Village off B1155, 2 miles (3km) SE of Burnham Market
The Lord Nelson inn reveals that Burnham Thorpe was the birthplace of Lord Admiral Horatio Nelson. The church bears tribute to him with a bust above his father's tomb and flags from battleships. Nelson's actual house no longer exists, but the village is a pleasant place to visit with a wide green surrounded by Georgian buildings.

BURNHAM-ON-CROUCH Essex TQ9496
Town on B1010, 9 miles (14km) SE of Maldon
Prestigious yachting centre on wide stretch of River Crouch, ranked second only to Cowes. Pleasant walk along river front, White Harte is old-style, nautical-flavour hostelry, plenty of good pubs. Notable 1930s building of Royal Corinthian Yacht Club, while the Long Row of 24 houses under single slate roof went up in 1890s for oystermen. Church at town's edge.

BURNHAM-ON-SEA Somerset ST3049
Town on B3140, 8 miles (13km) N of Bridgwater
A small village which became a resort from the 1830s, with long sandy beaches. Largely modern.

BURNHOPE Durham NZ1948
Village off A691, 2 miles (3km) E of Lanchester
A former colliery village on hilltop near Lanchester, with simple rows of miners' cottages built for the workers by the pit owners.

BURNLEY Lancashire SD8432
Town off M65, 22 miles (35km) N of Manchester
The town was first established around AD800, in a basin between the River Calder and the River Brun, from which it gets its name, and grew in status when it was granted a market charter in the 13th century. The first fulling mill built here signalled the beginning of the textile industry which was to dominate this region throughout succeeding centuries.

The Leeds and Liverpool Canal, constructed between 1770 and 1816 and one of the most prosperous canals in the country, runs through the town centre and brought great wealth to Burnley during the Industrial Revolution. This section was one of the most difficult to build, including the 'straight mile', a remarkable embankment which carries the canal above the town. By the end of the 19th century Burnley was the world's leading producer of cotton cloth. The former Mechanics Institute was re-opened in 1986 as Burnley Mechanics Arts and Entertainments Centre, and is now well known nationally as a jazz and blues venue. Towneley Hall, home of the Towneley family from the early 1400s until 1902, is now the town's art gallery and museum.

BURNMOUTH Borders NT9560
Village on A1, 2 miles (3km) S of Eyemouth
Fishing village tucked under steep sandstone cliffs where two treaties were signed between Scotland and England in late Middle Ages.

BURNOPFIELD Durham NZ1757
Village on B6310, 3 miles (5km) NW of Stanley
Popular residential village with excellent views of Derwent Valley, which grew with coal-mining industry. Employment now at industrial estates and in Newcastle.

BURNSALL North Yorkshire SE0361
Village on B6160, 3 miles (5km) SE of Grassington
Ancient gritstone village with attractive bridge across River Wharfe. Two Viking hogback tombstones and village stocks in grounds of St Wilfred's Church.

BURNTISLAND Fife NT2385
Town on A921, 4 miles (6km) SW of Kirkcaldy
On Firth of Forth with hill known as The Binn behind; great efforts are in progress to change Burntisland's industrial image as a ship-building, coal and aluminium town to that of holiday resort. Originally prosperous medieval royal burgh trading with Baltic and France, trade declined after Act of Union but prosperity returned with 19th-century industrialisation.

BURNTWOOD Staffordshire SK0509
Village on A5190, 5 miles (8km) W of Lichfield
This collection of hamlets with a history of coal-mining and nail-making makes up a large and expanding village on the edge of Cannock Chase.

BURPHAM West Sussex TQ0308
Village off A27, 5 miles (8km) N of Littlehampton
Downland village on no-through road above River Arun with lovely centre, pub and cottages. Church crowns little knoll. Saxon fort by river.

BURRATOR RESERVOIR Devon SX5568
Reservoir off B3212, 2 miles (3km) NE of Yelverton
The first reservoir to be made on Dartmoor, in 1898; extended 1928. Lots of archaeology on the moors around.

BURRINGTON Avon ST4859
Village off A368, 1 mile (2km) W of Blagdon
The village is situated below the wooded limestone scarp of the Mendips. Above is Burrington Combe, a steep limestone valley – a smaller Cheddar with many caves. The hymn 'Rock of Ages' was written here by Reverend Toplady.

BURRINGTON Devon SS6416
Village off A377, 4 miles (6km) NW of Chulmleigh
High up, with views all round and the Taw Valley below. Thatched cottages close together. Sixteenth-century church with good roof and screen.

BURRINGTON Hereford and Worcester SO4472
Village off A4110, 5 miles (8km) SW of Ludlow
Secluded among hills, village has church with unusual cast-iron grave slabs of Knight family, iron-founders at Bridgnorth.

BURROUGH ON THE HILL Leicestershire SK7510
Village off A606, 5 miles (8km) S of Melton Mowbray
Site of Iron Age hillfort. Splendid views from country park and Leicestershire Round footpath. Village has fine 18th-century houses.

BURRY HOLMS West Glamorgan SS4092
Island off the Gower Peninsula, N end of Rhossili Bay
High-tide islet at north end of Rhossili's vast bay. Iron Age earthworks, medieval monastic chapel ruins.

BURSLEDON Hampshire SU4809
Village off A27, 6 miles (10km) NW of Fareham
On the big Hamble estuary, a medieval ship-building centre, still producing yachts. Bursledon Windmill has been restored.

BURSLEM Staffordshire SJ8649
Town on A53, in Stoke-on-Trent
One of the six towns of Stoke-on-Trent immortalised by Arnold Bennett in his novel as Five Towns, at the heart of the conurbation. Its 18th-century origins show in good Georgian architecture in the town centre; otherwise it is characterised by small pottery works in terraced streets. The principal manufacturer is Royal Doulton, whose Nile Street factory, together with museum and showroom, is open for tours.

BURSTON Norfolk TM1383
Village off A140, 3 miles (5km) NE of Diss
Burston was the scene of the longest strike in British history – 25 years. The museum in the 'strike school' contains interesting photographs and memorabilia.

BURSTOW Surrey TQ3141
Village off B2037, 4 miles (6km) NE of Crawley
Set on the Wealden plain near the Sussex border, a scattered village with compact group by church sheltered by tall trees.

Gatehouse to Elizabethan Burton Agnes Hall.

BURSTWICK Humberside TA2227
Village off B1362, 3 miles (5km) E of Hedon
The Royal Arms of Charles I hang under an arch in All Saints' Church so the reverse side depicting his execution can be seen.

BURTON Cheshire SJ3174
Village off A540, 3 miles (5km) SE of Neston
Burton Mill Wood (National Trust), named after mill which once stood overlooking the village, is noted for wildlife and superb views of Dee estuary.

BURTON Wiltshire ST8179
Village on B4039, 8 miles (13km) NW of Chippenham
Small straggling stone village. Medieval church with fine 15th-century tower.

BURTON AGNES Humberside TA1062
Village on A166, 5 miles (8km) SW of Bridlington
A pretty village with cottages around a tree-shaded duck pond and Norman church. Burton Agnes Hall is a late Elizabethan house built around 1600 and containing a valuable collection of paintings, furniture and pine carvings. The courtyard between the imposing gatehouse and the hall is formally laid out as a topiary garden.

BURTON BRADSTOCK Dorset SY4889
Village on B3157, 3 miles (5km) SE of Bridport
A large and pretty village, set a little back from the sea. Lots of thatched cottages, mostly built from the local stone. Tiny green, and a pleasant late medieval church. The sea shore has impressive cliffs. The Bredy Farm Collection (2 miles/3km east) has farming and craft bygones.

BURTON CONSTABLE Humberside TA1836
Estate immediately N of Sproatley Hall and Country Park
Burton Constable Hall is one of the most important houses of Holderness, built in 1570 and redesigned in the 18th century by William Constable. The hall contains a collection of paintings and Chippendale furniture. The park was laid out by Capability Brown and has a model railway and boating lake.

BURTON DASSETT Warwickshire SP3951
Hamlet off B4100, 4 miles (6km) E of Kineton
Splendid Norman church with dramatically sloping floor. Nearby country park on Burton Hills provides superb views.

BURTON FLEMING Humberside TA0872
Village off A165, 7 miles (11km) NW of Bridlington
Queen Henrietta Maria is said to have stayed at the Manor House and an ancient British chieftain is buried at a site called Willy Howe.

BURTON JOYCE Nottinghamshire SK6443
Village off A612, 5 miles (8km) NE of Nottingham
Residential commuter village in the Trent Valley close to Nottingham. Thirteenth-century and later church.

BURTON LATIMER Northamptonshire SP9074
Town on A6, 3 miles (5km) SE of Kettering
Several notable ancient buildings, including thatched Old School House, 1622, and Manor House, 1704. Wall-paintings and brasses in church.

BURTON LAZARS Leicestershire SK7716
Village on A606, 2 miles (3km) SE of Melton Mowbray
Hillside village, site of important 13th-century leper (lazar) hospital, depending on perceived healing properties of local spring water.

BURTON ON THE WOLDS Leicestershire SK5821
Village on B676, 4 miles (6km) E of Loughborough
Farming village in Leicestershire Wolds. Burton Hall, begun about 1740, became hunting box 50 years later, now a nursing home.

BURTON UPON STATHER Humberside SE8717
Village on B1430, 5 miles (8km) N of Scunthorpe
Normanby Hall, a Regency mansion built for the former Dukes of Buckingham, was designed by Sir Robert Smirke, architect of the British Museum.

BURTON UPON TRENT Staffordshire SK2323
Town off A38, 11 miles (18km) SW of Derby
The 'capital' of East Staffordshire and also of the brewing industry is a no-nonsense town with a wealth of solid Victorian architecture typified by the magnificent Midland Railway Grain Warehouse, the bustling maket hall and the Gothic splendour of its town hall.A Benedictine abbey was founded here in 1100, and the monks were not the first to find that the Burton well water is specially suited to brewing. William Worthington and William Bass started major commercial production in the mid-18th century, and at one time over 40 breweries were operating in the town. Today Bass Charrington dominates, and their Bass Museum visitor centre in Horninglow Street is a major attraction. It tells the story of Bass brewing with a reconstructed brewhouse and machinery, a fleet of old vehicles and the famous Bass shire horses.

Rubber (Pirelli) and Marmite are other important industries. Church enthusiasts will enjoy the classical St Modwen's (1726), and St Chad's (1910), the last church built by the eminent Victorian architect GF Bodley.

The Brewhouse Arts Centre is noted for theatre, film and dance, and shoppers are provided for by a modern shopping centre.

BURTON-IN-LONSDALE North Yorkshire SD6572
Village on A687, 3 miles (5km) W of Ingleton
Situated on the River Greta, the main streets are arranged in a rectangle up the hillside. The village was once famed for its potteries.

BURTONWOOD Cheshire SJ5692
Village off A49, 4 miles (6km) NW of Warrington
A small community depending on agriculture and coal-mining. It is also famous for the Burtonwood Brewery.

BURWASH East Sussex TQ6724
Village on A265, 6 miles (10km) NE of Heathfield
Pronounced 'Burrish'. Handsome village on ridge top. Interesting old cottages and splendid 17th- and 18th-century houses, the variation giving a colourful effect. The church contains the earliest known cast-iron tomb slab (14th century). Village has its own volunteer fire brigade. Rudyard Kipling lived at Batemans (National Trust), southwest of the village, for 34 years from 1902.

BURWELL Cambridgeshire TL5866
Village on B1102, 4 miles (6km) NW of Newmarket
Castle ruins, a vast church and an old wharf can be seen in this attractive old village. In 1727 a barn fire killed 82 people.

BURWICK Orkney ND4384
Village on A961, 21 miles (34km) S of Kirkwall
On southern tip of South Ronaldsay with daily summer passenger ferry across the Pentland Firth to John O' Groats; service started in 16th century.

BURY Greater Manchester SD8010
Town off M66, 8 miles (13km) N of Manchester
The name comes from the Saxon and means 'a stronghold' but little now remains of the castle built by Thomas Pilkington in 1465. Bury came into its own during the Industrial Revolution, when a suitable water supply was needed to power the new machinery of the cotton mills. The River Irwell provided such a supply, creating a thriving industry for the town. Papermills drew upon the same source of power, and side by side the two industries flourished. In 1791 a canal was built to link Bury to Bolton and Manchester and in 1846 the East Lancashire Railway Company began to operate services linking the valley's mill towns with Manchester. When the textile industry fell into decline the railway closed for many years, but the local preservation society has reopened the station at Bury and restored steam trains carry passengers along the Irwell Valley.

Sir Robert Peel, founder of the Metropolitan Police and later Prime Minister, was born here. Bury Art Gallery has an important collection of Turner and Constable paintings, but the town is probably best known for its black pudding.

BURY West Sussex TQ0113
Village off A29, 4 miles (6km) N of Arundel
Secluded among its trees beside the River Arun, the village street descends steeply from the main road to reach the river opposite Amberley (see).

BURY ST EDMUNDS Suffolk TL8564
Town off A14, 23 miles (37km) NW of Ipswich
In 870 Edmund, King of England, was brutally murdered by Danes. He was buried in Hoxne (see) and miracles were associated with his tomb. He was made a saint, and his bones taken to Beodericsworth, which changed its name to St Edmundsbury. The town became an important pilgrimage site, and the fine abbey ruins dating from the 14th century and earlier can still be seen. It was in this important abbey that the barons drew up the conditions of Magna Carta in 1214.

Modern Bury St Edmunds is a bustling town boasting many fine buildings. Handsome Moyse's Hall may be the oldest domestic building in East Anglia, and is a museum (housing, among other things, the death mask of a local murderer and a book bound in his skin).

The town centre is based upon Angel Hill with its fine Norman tower, the 16th-century St James' Cathedral, and the elegant Athenaeum, where Dickens gave public speeches. The beautiful Abbey Gardens offer walks along the murmuring River Lark, and through scented groves of trees and flowers.

The town offers good shopping, an art gallery, and an ice rink.

BUSCOT Oxfordshire SU2298
Village on A417, 2 miles (3km) SE of Lechlade
Owned by the National Trust, this small Thames-side estate village offers two notable 18th-century houses: the Old Parsonage (limited opening) and Buscot Park, which houses the distinguished Faringdon Collection of paintings (notable Burne-Jones series), together with fine furniture and porcelain. Formal water gardens. Riverside church should not be missed.

BUSHBY Leicestershire SK6503
see Thurnby

BUSHEY Hertfordshire TQ1395
Town on A411, 3 miles (5km) SE of Watford
London satellite town that still has something of earlier atmosphere at centre, with small green and pond and a pleasant High Street. Georgian and Edwardian houses. Parish church, substantially restored and enlarged in 1870s, boasts flamboyant Jacobean pulpit. Public garden now on site of painter Sir Hubert Herkomer's studio and art school – artists used to love Bushey Heath and its views.

BUSHLEY Hereford and Worcester SO8734
Village off A438, 1 mile (2km) NW of Tewkesbury
The most impressive building in this far-flung outpost of Worcestershire is Pull Court (school), neo-Jacobean mansion of about 1840. Victorian church.

BUSHMEAD PRIORY Bedfordshire TL1160
Site off B660, 8 miles (13km) NE of Bedford
Duloe Brook runs past ruins of Augustinian priory founded at end of 12th century. Refectory has fine roof. Wall-paintings.

BUTE Strathclyde
Island in Firth of Clyde
Fifteen mile (24km) long island, popular holiday resort, renowned for mild climate, serving Clydeside since 1900s. Bulk of population live on east coast, leaving south and hillier north isolated, with good walking. Attractive bays on west coast. Archaeologically interesting. St Ninian's Point has 6th-century chapel ruins; remains of St Blane's Chapel date from 12th century.

BUTLEY Suffolk TM3650
Village on B1084, 4 miles (6km) W of Orford
Charming village with a reed-roofed church, the remains of an abbey, a dense wood of oak and holly and remnants of a neolithic village.

BUTTERMERE Cumbria NY1717
Hamlet on B5289, 8 miles (13km) SW of Keswick and lake
Surrounded by high fells, this popular beauty spot lies between Lake Buttermere and Crummock Water. The village is connected with a great 19th-century scandal, when Mary Robinson, the 'Beauty of Buttermere', thought she had married the Earl of Hopetoun's brother only to discover that her husband was a bankrupt impostor. He was later hanged.

BUTTERSTONE Tayside NO0645
Village on A923, 3 miles (5km) NE of Dunkeld
Tiny village in attractive countryside best known for neighbouring Loch of the Lowes Nature Reserve, noted for osprey nesting site.

BUTTERTON Staffordshire SK0756
Village off B5053, 6 miles (10km) E of Leek
High moorland village close to Manifold Valley and within Peak District National Park.

BUTTERTUBS PASS North Yorkshire SD8796
Site off B6270, 2 miles (3km) SW of Thwaite
A scenic road named for the strange series of little potholes near the summit of the pass.

BUXHALL Suffolk TM0057
Village off B1115, 3 miles (5km) W of Stowmarket
A quiet, sprawling village with some fine 18th-century buildings, a sail-less windmill and an ancient wood called Pye Thatch.

BUXTED East Sussex TQ4923
Village on A272, 2 miles (3km) NE of Uckfield
Old cottages, railway station and inn cluster at gate of Buxted Park (rebuilt 1941). Church set in picturesque parkland. Modern village sprawls along main road.

BUXTON Derbyshire SK0572
Town on A515, 18 miles (29km) NW of Ashbourne
The Romans valued *Aquae Arnemetiae* for its waters, a constant 82 degrees Fahrenheit (28 degrees Celsius). Later Buxton visitors included Mary Stuart, suffering rheumatism while held in Derbyshire under Elizabeth I's instructions.

Intended to rival Bath, the elegant 1780s Crescent, by John Carr of York for the 5th Duke of Devonshire, accommodated those coming to take the waters. After severe neglect, restoration of The Crescent began in the 1990s. In 1880, the largest unsupported dome in the world was built to enclose the courtyard of 18th-century stables, now the Devonshire Royal Hospital.

The River Wye runs through an attractive park overlooked by the 1870s iron and glass Pavilion Gardens conservatories, restaurants, and Octagon Hall for events. The elegant Edwardian Opera House, restored in 1979, inspired the Buxton International Festival, held each July/August. The former thermal baths are transformed into a pleasant shopping mall. St Ann's Well houses the intriguing Micrarium, displaying the natural world under the microscope. Poole's Cavern has dramatic stalagmites and stalactites.

Surrounded by glorious Peak District countryside, England's highest market town, at 1,000 ft (305m), continues its tradition of welcoming visitors.

BUXTON Norfolk TG2322
Village off B1354, 4 miles (6km) SE of Aylsham
The birthplace of Thomas Cubitt, the entrepreneur who built more of 19th-century London than anyone else.

BWLCH Powys SO1422
Village on A40, 5 miles (8km) NW of Crickhowell
Translates into English as 'pass'. Just north are vestiges of a Norman castle. Quaint, very narrow stone bridge over River Usk below hillside village on the way to Llangynidr.

BYFLEET Surrey TQ0661
Village off A245, 4 miles (6km) NE of Woking
Old village, a former royal manor, lies between River Wey and Navigation. Few old houses left swamped by intrusive post-war development. West Byfleet around railway station, widely spaced houses of pre-war stockbroker belt. To north, Brooklands Museum, classic cars and aircraft displayed at first purpose-built motor racing circuit (1907), later an important airfield.

BYGRAVE Hertfordshire TL2636
Village off A505, 2 miles (3km) NE of Baldock
Isolated little place. Church too humble to have a tower. Strip farming in open, unenclosed fields lasted to 1920s here.

BYRNESS Northumberland NT7602
Hamlet on A68, 6 miles (10km) SE of Carter Bar
A Forestry Commission village southeast of Catcleugh Reservoir. In the tiny church is a memorial to the construction workers who died while building the reservoir.

BYWELL Northumberland NZ0461
Hamlet on A695, 4 miles (6km) SE of Corbridge
A small hamlet with two Saxon churches, St Andrew's and St Peter's, although the latter displays mainly 13th-century features.

C

CABOURNE Lincolnshire TA1401
Village on A46, 2 miles (3km) E of Caistor
In hollow of Lincolnshire Wolds. Pelham's Pillar commemorates 1st Lord Yarborough's planting of over 12 million trees on his vast local estates.

CADBURY Devon SS9105
Village off A3072, 6 miles (10km) NE of Crediton
High up, with views of both Exmoor and Dartmoor. Cadbury Castle to the northeast is an Iron Age hillfort, but not the famous Arthurian one (see South Cadbury). Fursdon House (limited opening) looks Georgian but has earlier parts.

CADBURY CASTLE Somerset ST6325
see South Cadbury

CADDINGTON Bedfordshire TL0619
Village off A5, 2 miles (3km) SW of Luton
Caddington Grey bricks used to be quarried here in deep pits. Now a dormitory town for Dunstable and Luton.

CADE STREET East Sussex TQ6020
Hamlet on B2096, 1 mile (2km) E of Heathfield
Associated with rebel Jack Cade, allegedly killed here in 1450. Monument by roadside east of pub, but name is corruption of 'Cart Street'.

CADEBY Leicestershire SK4202
Village off A447, 1 mile (2km) SE of Market Bosworth
Several listed buildings including Tudor cruck cottage, stone church with bell tower. Narrow-gauge steam railway (limited opening) at Old Rectory.

CADELEIGH Devon SS9108
Village off A3072, 4 miles (6km) SW of Tiverton
A small village deep in Devon, high on a ridge with good views on both sides.

CADER IDRIS Gwynedd SH7113
Mountain 3 miles (5km) SW of Dolgellau
Massive and unmistakable with its 2,927ft (892m) domed ridge, the 'Chair of Idris', legendary giant. A National Nature Reserve. Glacial lakes, marvellous views.

CADGWITH Cornwall SW7214
Hamlet off A3083, 3 miles (5km) NE of Lizard Point
Charming small-scale village on steep slopes by the sea, lots of thatch and buildings of the Serpentine rock peculiar to the Lizard peninsula.

CADNAM Hampshire SU3013
Village on A336, 4 miles (6km) W of Totton
Once a hamlet on the edge of the New Forest, but now a suburb of Southampton.

CADNEY Humberside TA0103
Village off B1434, 3 miles (5km) SE of Brigg
The village has an early 13th-century church, with a Norman font, and there are opportunities for watersports on the reservoir.

CAEO Dyfed SN6739
Village off A482, 1 mile (2km) SE of Pumsaint
Sleepy village in countryside where the Romans mined for gold. Church dates from 13th century, Methodist chapel from 18th.

CAERGWRLE Clwyd SJ3057
Village on A541, 5 miles (8km) N of Wrexham
Good views from hilltop remnants of native border fort built by Llywelyn the Last's brother, Dafydd. Burned down in 1282.

CAERHUN Gwynedd SH7770
Site on B5106, 4 miles (6km) S of Conwy
Church is situated on the site of a Roman fort on the River Conwy. Nearby Pen-y-Gaer hillfort has quite extensive remains and views.

CAERLAVEROCK Dumfries and Galloway NY0265
Site off B725, 6 miles (10km) SE of Dumfries
Caerlaverock Castle, a 13th-century Maxwell stronghold, was attacked by Edward I in 1300 and finally destroyed after siege of 1640. Thought to be the inspiration for 'Ellangowan' in Scott's *Guy Mannering*. Caerlaverock Wildlife and Wetlands Centre is well provided with hides to observe the barnacle geese overwintering on the saltmarsh.

CAERLEON Gwent ST3390
Small town on B4236, 3 miles (5km) NE of Newport
Caerleon is a place of history and legend. Called *sca* by the Romans after the River Usk on which it stands, it is one of Europe's most significant Roman military sites. Over 5,000 soldiers from the elite Second Augustan Legion were based here from AD75 to 290, initially to subjugate the native tribe known as the Silures. The town's centrepiece is the extraordinary Fortress Baths complex (Cadw), hub of the soldiers' off-duty hours. Modern interpretative techniques describe the intricate bathing process in sight of pools, a cold hall and changing room.

Many of the objects unearthed during almost continual excavations this century are on show at the Legionary Museum. From here, Fosse Lane leads to the vast, grassed arena of the amphitheatre, scene of bloody entertainment and combat. This was once known as 'King Arthur's Round Table' and Arthurian legend drew Tennyson here to stay at the Hanbury Arms for inspiration for his poem *Idylls of the King*. Prysg Field accommodates the only legionary barrack blocks still visible in Europe, across the road from the surviving fortress wall. Tucked away in a courtyard are Ffwrrwm's antiques, crafts and curiosities.

CAERNARFON Gwynedd SH4762
Town on A487, 8 miles (13km) SW of Bangor
The military settlement called *Segontium* was founded here around AD78 by the Romans. The excavated remains are on the town's hilly outskirts, together with a museum explaining the fort's layout and displaying the finds. The much later occupation of Caernarfon has left a more conspicuous legacy in the shape of its mighty medieval castle (Cadw), a World Heritage Site. A link in the chain of colossal fortresses constructed by Edward I along the North Wales coast to defeat the Welsh, it is now Wales's most famous castle. Prince Charles was invested Prince of Wales here in 1969, thus reviving a tradition supposedly begun when the reigning monarch, Edward I, presented his eldest son to the townspeople as their prince.

The town walls that accompanied the building of the castle are now mostly hemmed in by shops, but one section is easily accessible where a 14th-century church, the Chantry of St Mary, is incorporated into the actual structure. Just the other side of the wall, in Victoria Dock, a maritime museum features an old dredger and the last ferry to work the Menai Strait. Castle Square (Y Maes) is the scene of a Saturday market.

CAERPHILLY Mid Glamorgan ST1586
Town on A469, 6 miles (10km) N of Cardiff
Europe's second largest castle, with its massive water defences and mighty walls (Cadw), dominates this town at southern gateway to industrial valleys. Castle dates from 13th century with concentric fortifications. Alarmingly askew tower resulted from Oliver Cromwell blowing it up. Caerphilly cheese still made here at nearby Courthouse. Comedian Tommy Cooper, and Evan James, composer of Welsh National Anthem, are two famous local sons.

CAERSWS Powys SO0391
Village on A470, 5 miles (8km) W of Newtown
Romans garrisoned strategic spot at meeting of three rivers. Local stationmaster poet John Ceiriog Hughes is buried at Llanwnog church, which possesses a fine rood loft.

CAERWENT Gwent ST4690
Village on A48, 5 miles (8km) SW of Chepstow
This was *Venta Silurum*, market town of the Silures, a native tribe forcibly relocated from their hillfort at Llanmelin by the conquering Romans. Unique in Wales as a Romano-Celtic civilian, rather than military, settlement; massive stone ramparts survive to be explored. Excavated dwellings and temple are visible across from the church, which has unusual inscribed stones

CAERWYS Clwyd SJ1272
Village on B5122, 4 miles (6km) SW of Holywell
In its heyday an important market town and medieval borough. Finest hour came in 1568 when a competitive cultural festival held here marked the revival of the eisteddfod.

CAIRNBULG Grampian NK0365
Village off B9033, 5 miles (8km) SE of Fraserburgh
Originally a fishing village, now more a dormitory for Fraserburg, with a good beach. Cairnbulg Castle was restored in 1890s.

CAIRNDOW Strathclyde NN1810
Village on A83, 3 miles (5km) NE of Inverarary
Pronounced Cairndoo, lies on Loch Fyne with salmon and oyster farming. Neighbouring woodland gardens at Ardkinglas have reputedly tallest tree in Britain (*Abies grandis*, 210ft/63m).

CAIRNGORM MOUNTAINS Highland/Grampian
Mountain range in Scotland
Largest British area of ground over 4,000ft (1,216m), flat-topped mountains with extensive corries. Composed of granite, yielding Cairngorm stone, used in traditional jewellery. Remains of Caledonian forest on lower slopes, plateau bare and rocky. Four major peaks, including Ben MacDhui overlooking Lairig Ghru pass leading to Dee from Speyside. Excellent climbing and hill-walking; some skiing.

CAIRNRYAN Dumfries and Galloway NX0668
Village on A77, 5 miles (8km) N of Stranraer
Car ferry terminal to Larne in Northern Ireland. Naval base in World War II which constructed components for Mulberry Harbour, used in Normandy landings.

CAISTER-ON-SEA Norfolk TG5112
Small town off A149, 3 miles (5km) N of Great Yarmouth
Caister has a long and fascinating history. It was settled by the Romans, and remains of their camp (English Heritage) can still be visited. In 1432, the powerful Fastolf family built Caister Castle, one of the first brick buildings in England. In 1904, a tragic lifeboat disaster robbed Caister women of husbands, sons and brothers.

CAISTOR Lincolnshire TA1101
Small town on A46, 8 miles (13km) N of Market Rasen
Perched on western edge of Lincolnshire Wolds, this attractive market town was, as name indicates, a Roman camp site: part of wall survives. Timber-framed buildings demolished by 1681 fire. Town rebuilt, with attractive red-brick 18th- and 19th-century buildings around market place, Cornhill, and near church, which has curious Gad Whip, traditionally cracked on Palm Sunday.

CAISTOR ST EDMUND Norfolk TG2303
Village off A47, 3 miles (5km) S of Norwich
The rugged outlines of sturdy Roman walls with the little Saxon church huddled against them are evocative of the history of this ancient village. It is thought that Queen Bodicea had her headquarters here, or near by, when she fought against the Romans. It is possible that a Roman capital was built here to quell further uprisings by the Iceni.

CAITHNESS Highland
Historic region of Scotland
Most northeasterly area of mainland Britain, came under Scottish crown in 1196. Low-lying interior and magnificent coastline; main industries agriculture and fishing.

CALBOURNE Isle of Wight SZ4286
Village off B3401, 5 miles (8km) SW of Newport
Picture-postcard village, with thatched cottages, most picturesquely at Winkle Street, with a stream alongside. Medieval church above the green. Calbourne watermill and Rural Museum has a working waterwheel.

CALDBECK Cumbria NY3240
Village on B5299, 7 miles (11km) SE of Wigton
Name means 'cold brook' and water used to be harnessed to drive a variety of mills for grinding corn and weaving. John Peel is buried in the churchyard where his tombstone bears a carved hunting horn. Mary Robinson, the 'Beauty of Buttermere', is also buried here. The old brewery, which once supplied 16 inns in the village, is still standing.

CALDECOTE Hertfordshire TL2338
Hamlet off A1, 3 miles (5km) N of Baldock
Deserted medieval village, abandoned in the 15th and 16th centuries. A few houses still, and sad redundant church.

CALDER BRIDGE Cumbria NY0306
Village on A595, 4 miles (6km) SE of Egremont
Originally this was an agricultural community but has now changed into a residential village for workers at the Sellafield Nuclear Power Station. The power

station's visitor centre explains the workings of the nuclear power industry. Calder Abbey, just outside the village, was founded as a Cistercian abbey; now a ruin.

CALDER, RIVER West Yorkshire
River, tributary of the Aire
The River Calder rises near Todmorden and flows east to join the River Aire at Castleford. The Calder and Hebble Navigation connects with the Wakefield branch of the Aire and Calder Navigation at Wakefield. It was built initially as a river navigation and opened in 1779 with a few canal cuts. The River Calder is liable to heavy flooding.

CALDICOT Gwent ST4888
Town off B4245, 5 miles (8km) SW of Chepstow
Restored castle dating from 12th century houses local history museum, costumes and art exhibitions, and hosts medieval banquets. Important Bronze Age finds in surrounding country park.

CALDRON SNOUT (OR CAULDRON SNOUT) Cumbria/Durham NY8128
Waterfall, 4 miles (6km) off B6277, at Langdon Beck
A spectacular mountain cascade where Langdon Beck runs into the River Tees. Highest waterfall in England.

CALDY ISLAND (OR CALDEY ISLAND) Dyfed SS1496
Island in Carmarthen Bay, off Tenby
Known for its religious communities dating from 5th century. Men only allowed in modern Cistercian abbey. Ogham stone, monks' perfume shop, birds, seals.

CALF OF MAN Isle of Man SC1565
Island off SW end of Isle of Man
This tiny island just off the Isle of Man is a bird sanctuary reached by a short boat trip from Port Erin.

CALGARY Strathclyde (Mull) NM3751
Village on B8073, 12 miles (19km) SW of Tobermory
Crofting township and holiday centre with marvellous sandy bay and exceptional views. Emigrants from here founded the eponymous Canadian city.

CALKE ABBEY Derbyshire SK3721
See Ticknall

CALLALY Northumberland NU0509
Site off A697, 2 miles (3km) SW of Whittingham
In Callaly Park there is a cave that was hewn out as a safe place for Catholic priests in the 17th century.

CALLANDER Central NN6207
Town on A84, 14 miles (23km) NW of Stirling
A good touring base on the edge of the Trossachs at the Highlands' southern boundary, Callander was the location for the original *Doctor Finlay's Casebook* television series. Designed by military architects after the 1745 Rebellion, it stands on the River Teith with good, undemanding local walking. Rob Roy and Trossachs visitor centre gives introduction to the history of the area.

CALLANISH Western Isles (Lewis) NB2133
Village on A858, 13 miles (21km) W of Stornoway
Village noted for around 20 neighbouring neolithic archaeological stone circle sites which date from 3000–500BC. Main group is impressive Callanish Standing Stones, nearly 50 Lewisian gneiss boulders up to 15ft (3m) high in cruciform layout. Much on-going scholarly argument over their purpose; popular theory holds they were astronomical observatory for predicting seasonal cycles.

CALLINGTON Cornwall SX3669
Town on A388, 8 miles (13km) NW of Saltash
A small town with good views, especially from Kit Hill to the north. A copper- and tin-mining area in the 19th century, of which relics remain, including a huge chimney on Kit Hill. At Dupath to the southwest is a holy well still covered by a little medieval building.

CALMSDEN Gloucestershire SP0508
Hamlet off A435, 4 miles (6km) N of Cirencester
An isolated group of estate cottages notable for a rare example of a 14th-century wayside cross.

CALNE Wiltshire ST9971
Town on A4, 5 miles (8km) SE of Chippenham
Once the centre of the Wiltshire bacon industry, with Harris's huge factory in the middle. Georgian houses around the green, and 17th-century ones (including almshouses of 1682) near the big 15th-century church which was built from profits of the woollen cloth trade. Bowood House is part of an 18th-century mansion (open, with museum). The grounds are some of the finest in the country, with exotic trees and a lake. Atwell-Wilson Motor Museum.

CALSTOCK Cornwall SX4368
Village off A390, 5 miles (8km) E of Callington
On the banks of the Tamar, with wonderful river scenery. Impressive railway viaduct of 1907 across the river at Cotehele, and a quay used by sailing barges until the railway came. Cotehele House (National Trust) is a virtually unaltered late medieval house, a rare survival, with a proper hall and courtyards. Romantic wooded setting and wonderful gardens.

CALVERHALL Shropshire SJ6037
Village off A41, 5 miles (8km) SE of Whitchurch
Tranquil village with 1870s church by Eden Nesfield (one window with glass by Edward Burne-Jones), attached to attractive almshouses of 1724.

CALVERTON Nottinghamshire SK6149
Village off B6386, 7 miles (11km) NE of Nottingham
Probable birthplace of William Lee, inventor of stocking-frame. Some framework knitters' cottages remain. Folk Museum (by appointment) and Patchings Farm Art Centre.

CAM, RIVER Cambridgeshire
River
Rising in Essex and Hertfordshire, the Cam winds north through medieval Cambridge. It was called the *Granta* by the Romans.

CAMBER East Sussex TQ9618

Village off A259, 3 miles (5km) E of Rye

Conglomeration of post-war bungalows on sand dunes east of Rother estuary. Wide sandy beach. Holiday camp.

CAMBERLEY Surrey SU8860

Town on A325, 6 miles (10km) S of Bracknell

Expanding modern town just beyond London's green belt. Streets on grid pattern in York Town, landscaping in Upper Camberley.

CAMBERWELL Greater London TQ3276

District in borough of Southwark

In 1830 still a village where the Camberwell Beauty butterfly roamed, soon to become a fashionable Victorian suburb. Georgian houses in Camberwell Grove. St Giles Church, 1840s by Sir George Gilbert Scott with east window designed by John Ruskin, other glass by Comper. South London Art Gallery, Peckham Road, next to Camberwell School of Arts and Crafts, both 1890s.

CAMBLESFORTH North Yorkshire SE6426

Village on A1041, 3 miles (5km) N of Snaith

A village with the only public house in Britain named after Comus, the son of Bacchus, Greek god of wine.

CAMBO Northumberland NZ0285

Village on B6342, 11 miles (18km) W of Morpeth

Wallington Hall (National Trust) was built in 1688 on the site of a medieval castle and is surrounded by 100 acres (40ha) of woodland and lakes. Remodelled in the 1740s by Daniel Garrett, the house is renowned for its Italian plasterwork and porcelain collection. It also contains an important dolls' house collection and a museum of curiosities.

CAMBORNE Cornwall SW6440

Town on A3047, 11 miles (18km) W of Truro

Formerly the capital of the principal Cornish tin- and copper-mining district, and now forming a single built-up area with Redruth (see), Camborne was a small village until the late 18th century, when mining expanded. Today, long low terraces of granite houses built for miners and their families, and numerous Nonconformist chapels are legacies of the past, as are the surrounding country's melancholy chimneys and ruined engine houses, needed for the pumps to extract water. The deepest mine was Dalcoath at 3,300ft (1,003m). Camborne Museum covers mining and minerals, with material on Richard Trevithick, the great mining engineer born in 1771 at nearby Illogan. His statue stands outside the building and his cottage at Penponds (National Trust, open by appointment) has survived.

At Pool, which is part of the Camborne-Redruth complex, the Geological Museum of Camborne School of Mines has impressive displays of rocks and minerals, while the National Trust's nearby Cornish Engines are two giant steam engines used for pumping water out of the mines, lowering men into the black depths to work, and bringing up the ore.

CAMBRIDGE Cambridgeshire TL4458

City off M11, 49 miles (79km) N of London

In the 13th century, scholars were hanged in Oxford, causing their colleagues to flee to Cambridge. A rival university was founded, which is now one of the best in the world. Today, visitors can wander through the ancient college buildings of Peterhouse (founded 1281), Clare (1326), Pembroke (1347), Trinity Hall (1350) and Corpus Christi (1352) to name but a few (limited opening). The university continues to grow: its newest college, Robinson, was founded in 1977.

The castle at Camber.

Dominating this beautiful city is the magnificent King's College Chapel, famous for its Christmas carol service, superb choir and fabulous fan vaulting. It also has Rubens' painting *The Adoration of the Magi*, now protected by alarms because a visitor once slashed it with a knife. For music lovers, the choir of St John's College is equally fine, and few experiences can match listening to the pure voices of the boys soaring through the college chapels.

Cambridge has many fine churches besides King's chapel. St Bene't's is the oldest, with a Saxon tower. The Round Church is one of a handful of such churches in England, the design of which was based upon the Holy Sepulchre in Jerusalem. It was restored, rather over-enthusiastically, by the Victorians. St Mary the Great stands over the market square, and has been the university church since the 1300s.

The first of the Trinity milestones at Cambridge.

Many famous people have studied or lived in Cambridge. Trinity, founded by Henry VIII, boasts a gallery of poets including Byron, Marvell, Dryden, and Tennyson. Newton, Bacon and Rutherford (of atom-splitting fame) were also at Trinity, as were composer Vaughan Williams and several prime ministers. Former Pembroke students include the poet Spenser and Pitt the Younger, and Erasmus was at the fine Tudor college of Queens'. John Harvard, who founded the American university that bears his name, was at Emmanuel. The gardens at Christ's College are particularly fine, and it is easy to imagine Milton or Darwin walking in some of the bowers.

The colleges have some outstanding architectural features. The Bridge of Sighs at St John's, which spans the murky green waters of the Cam, was built in 1831, modelled on the bridge in Venice. The Mathematical Bridge at Queens' is said to have been built on physical principles and needed no bolts (a Victorian scientist took it apart, and it is now held by thick black nuts and bars). Magdalene College houses Pepys' collection of books, while Pembroke's chapel was designed by Wren.

The city also has the excellent Fitzwilliam Museum, and the peaceful botanic gardens. But perhaps most famous of all is the Backs, an ancient strip of land that runs behind the colleges by the River Cam. In the early morning, a pale mist often hovers over the river and the beautiful old college buildings, giving them a peace that is absent later in the day when the tourists arrive. Sheep sometimes graze on the common land right in the city centre, giving this wonderful medieval city a rural air.

CAMBUSLANG Strathclyde NS6460

Town on A749, 5 miles (8km) SE of Glasgow

Former industrial iron- and steel-manufacturing town. There are wide views from Cathkin Braes.

CAMDEN TOWN Greater London TQ2883

District in borough of Camden

North of Euston and St Pancras railway stations, intersected by railway lines and 1820s Regent's Canal. Attractive Camden Lock area with weekend crafts and flea market and Camden Passage antiques shops, canal cruises, floating restaurants. Round House (1847), former engine shed and arts centre, future in doubt. Camden Town Art Group formed round painter Walter Sickert in Edwardian period. Jewish Museum.

CAMEL, RIVER Cornwall

River, reaches sea in Padstow Bay

Runs into the only big estuary on the north Cornwall coast. The track of the old railway is now converted into a cycle path and walk from Poley's Bridge below Bodmin Moor to Padstow (see).

CAMELEY Avon ST6157

Village off A37, 4 miles (6km) NW of Midsomer Norton

Now very small and rural, but in the 19th century a busy industrial centre with coal and iron-ore mines, a brickworks and a quarry.

CAMELFORD Cornwall SX1083

Small town on A39, 11 miles (18km) NE of Wadebridge

A small town, really one long street down the hill. Mostly slate, with a town hall of 1806. Lanteglos to the southwest was the original settlement, and has the medieval church. North Cornwall Museum.

CAMERTON Cumbria NY0330

Village off A596, 3 miles (5km) NE of Workington

Church of St Peter contains an effigy of a local character known as Black Tom.

CAMPBELTOWN Strathclyde NR7120

Town on A83, 30 miles (48km) S of Tarbert

Argyll's second most important town on Campbeltown Loch. Founded in 1607 with Lowland settlers to subdue area, thrived in 1800s on herring fishing and 34 whisky distilleries, both industries still existing but much reduced. Fine late medieval market cross with Celtic carving. Nearby tidal Davaar Island has 19th-century cave-painting of crucifixion. Birthplace of landscape painter William MacTaggart.

CAMPSALL South Yorkshire SE5413

Village off A1, 7 miles (11km) N of Doncaster

The Church of St Mary Magdalene has many impressive features including a Norman west tower, medieval screen, Flaxman sculpture and Pugin-designed altar. The Campsall Country Park is set in the grounds of a now demolished 18th-century hall, with lakes and picnic areas.

CAMPSEA ASH Suffolk TM3356

Village on B1078, 2 miles (3km) E of Wickham Market

Alternatively called Campsie Ash, Campsey Ashe or Campsey Ash. A priory of Austin nuns once stood here, founded about 1195. Parts of the priory still survive in a house.

CAMPSIE Strathclyde NS6079

Village off A891, 2 miles (3km) NW of Lennoxtown

Village at foot of low range known as Campsie Fells. Term used to mean area between River Clyde at Dumbarton and River Forth at Stirling.

CAMPTON Bedfordshire TL1238

Village off A507, 1 mile (2km) SW of Shefford

Quiet backwater near Shefford. Monuments of the Osborns of Chicksands Priory (see Shefford) in the church. Half-timbered 1590s manor house.

CANADA Hampshire SU2818

Village off A36, 3 miles (5km) N of Cadnam

A long thin settlement on the edge of the New Forest, once for squatters, now prosperous.

CANADA, UPPER AND LOWER Avon ST3658

Hamlets off A371, 3 miles (5km) SE of Weston-super-Mare

Two hamlets on Bleadon Hill, the westernmost hill of the Mendips.

CANEWDON Essex TQ9094

Village off B1013, 3 miles (5km) NE of Rochford

Isolated deep in the marshlands between the Crouch and Roach rivers, Canewdon was notorious as a centre of witchcraft into the 20th century. The last of the feared witch-masters and village wise men, George Pickingale, a farm labourer, died in 1909 aged 93. Village pond with ducks.

The most northerly church in Scoland, at Canisbay.

CANFORD CLIFFS Dorset SZ0589

Suburb on B3065 in SW Bournemouth

Borders both the sea and Poole Harbour. Overlooking the harbour is Compton Acres, a series of formal themed gardens – Roman, Italian, Japanese, heather and so on – mostly laid out between the wars.

CANFORD MAGNA Dorset SZ0398

Hamlet off A31, 2 miles (3km) SE of Wimborne Minster

A huge Victorian mock-Tudor house (now a school, not open) and an interesting church with Saxon features, in the wide Stour Valley.

CANISBAY Highland ND3472

Village off A836, 2 miles (3km) W of John O' Groats

Overlooks Gills Bay; church is most northerly on mainland and churchyard contains grave of Jan de Groot, who gave his name to John O' Groats.

CANNA Highland NG2405

Island in Inner Hebrides, NW of Rum

Tiny National Trust for Scotland island 1 mile (2km) by 5 miles (8km). Early Christian settlement, population evicted in 1820 after decline of kelp industry.

CANNINGTON Somerset ST2539

Village off A39, 3 miles (5km) NW of Bridgwater

Large village, now bypassed; lots of Georgian houses around the large medieval church. Cannington College Gardens are interesting.

CANNOCK Staffordshire SJ9810

Town on A34, 9 miles (14km) S of Stafford

An important market centre for centuries, Cannock still attracts people from a wide area to its attractive central market place, supplemented by a modern precinct. Nearby St Luke's Church is Norman in origin but has been modified from the Middle Ages until the 1950s. Other interesting buildings include the impressive former council house overlooking an old bowling green and 18th-century waterworks.

CANNOCK CHASE Staffordshire

Scenic region N of Cannock

Surprisingly wild for an area near densely populated conurbations, Cannock Chase offers 20,000 acres (8,100ha) of heath and woodland designated as an Area of Outstanding Natural Beauty. Of this, 3,000 acres (1,350ha) form a country park with appropriate facilities.

The Chase is the remnant of an oak forest that was the hunting preserve of Norman kings and later of the Bishops of Lichfield, and deer are still plentiful (Sherbrook Valley is a good sighting-point). Among modern conifers old oak woods can still be found, notably at Brocton Coppice, and rare plants survive in less-trodden areas like the marshy ground at Womere.

The Chase provides opportunities for outdoor recreation ranging from picnics and gentle walks from the car to more strenuous rambles. Popular objectives are viewpoints such as Coppice Hill, Brereton Spurs and Castle Ring, an impressive Iron Age hillfort, and many visitors are attracted to the unique military cemeteries near Broadhurst Green, where some 5,000 Germans lie. A published 'trail' explains these and the remnants of a World War I training area and prisoner-of-war camp. Full information about the Chase is available at the Marquis Drive visitor centre.

CANONS ASHBY Northamptonshire SP5750

Village off B4525, 10 miles (16km) NE of Banbury

Parts of the medieval priory church are virtually all that remain of once-larger village. Priory land was later incorporated into the grounds of 16th-century Canons Ashby House (National Trust), a fine manor with Elizabethan and Jacobean features, home of Dryden family, visited by the poet and now open to visitors.

CANTERBURY Kent TR1457

City off A2, 54 miles (87km) SE of London

Canterbury is a bustling modern city of venerable age, a place of pilgrimage for the historically-minded. It was capital of the Iron Age kingdom of the Cantii – the name survives in today's city and in the county of Kent – and then an important Roman town. In AD602 St Augustine re-dedicated a deserted Roman church within the city wall, creating Christchurch Cathedral, and Canterbury has been the spiritual capital of England ever since. By about 1100 it also had a Norman castle.

The cathedral was rebuilt in 1170 and 1175, creating the bulk of the present magnificent Gothic building. The nave was rebuilt again in 1380 and the great central tower went up in 1500. The shrine of Thomas Becket, murdered here in 1170, was particularly sumptuous. For 200 years it was, Rome apart, the most popular shrine in Europe, thronged by pilgrims, most of whom travelled from London, as did Chaucer's famous group of 1388. The shrine declined in the 15th century and in 1538 it was wrecked by Henry VIII's officers.

Industry flourished when 16th-century Flemish refugees set up a woollen cloth industry, while in the late 17th century Huguenot refugees developed silk weaving. The Weavers' Houses in High Street date from this time, as does St Dunstan's Street.

Devastating bombing in World War II destroyed much of the city's historic heart, but the cathedral survived, as do many timber-framed buildings of the 16th and 17th centuries. Particularly good are Mercery Lane with overhanging buildings and glimpses of the cathedral and the tiny butter market outside Christchurch Gate of 1517. Post-war clearance has opened up the area around the medieval city walls which run along the Roman lines. Canterbury became a university city in 1962.

CANTLEY South Yorkshire SE6202

Village off A638, 4 miles (6km) SE of Doncaster

An old village, known locally as Old Cantley. Cantley Hall was the home of wealthy landowning family, the Childers.

CANTLOP BRIDGE Shropshire SJ5305

see Condover

CANVEY ISLAND Essex TQ7983
Town on A130, 7 miles (11km) SE of Basildon
On land reclaimed and embanked in the 17th century by Dutch engineers. One of their tiny, two-roomed houses is now the Dutch Cottage Museum, but little else pre-dates rapid residential and industrial development from 1930s on. Thames estuary views from the sea walls. Bus museum. Lobster Smack inn appears in Dickens' *Great Expectations*.

CANWICK Lincolnshire SK9869
Village off B1188, 1 mile (2km) SE of Lincoln
On hillside across River Witham from Lincoln's hilltop cathedral. Hall was home of Sibthorpe family, including botanist founder of Linnaean Society.

CAPE WRATH Highland NC2574
Headland on NW point of Scotland
Dramatic and lonely headland at the extreme north-western point of mainland Britain; accessible by ferry and rough track.

CAPEL Surrey TQ1740
Village off A24, 6 miles (10km) S of Dorking
Strung out along old London – Worthing road, weather boarded and tile-hung cottages, 19th-century brick houses and Friends' Meeting House, 1725.

CAPEL CURIG Gwynedd SH7258
Hamlet on A5, 5 miles (8km) W of Betws-y-coed
Classical view of Snowdon's 'horseshoe' of peaks is gained from Llynau Mymbyr. By these twin lakes stands Plas-y-Brenin, the National Mountaineering Centre.

CAPEL LE FERNE Kent TR2539
Village off B2011, 3 miles (5km) NE of Folkestone
Large residential village perched above the English Channel. Name comes from the little church, originally outlying chapel of St Radegund's Abbey, Alkham (see).

CAPEL ST MARY Suffolk TM0838
Village off A12, 5 miles (8km) SE of Hadleigh
Capel St Mary has dramatically expanded with the addition of housing estates. Good shopping and facilities. Constable sketched here.

CAPEL-Y-FFIN Powys SO2531
Site off A465, 3 miles (5km) NW of Llanthony
Once an isolated religious, artistic retreat. Nineteenth-century monastic remains have chequered history. Gospel Pass climbs to Hay-on-Wye for far-reaching views.

CAPHEATON Northumberland NZ0380
Hamlet off A696, 5 miles (8km) NW of Belsay
A small village where novelist Algernon Swinburne spent his childhood holidays, at Capheaton Hall. The village appears in his novel *Lesbia Brandon*.

CAR COLSTON Nottinghamshire SK7142
Village off A46, 2 miles (3km) NE of Bingham
Attractive village with two greens and several fine houses. Home of Dr Robert Thoroton, author of *Antiquities of Nottinghamshire*.

CARBIS BAY Cornwall SW5238
Town off A3072, 1 mile (2km) SE of St Ives
A modern seaside settlement which developed from a small mining centre. Abuts St Ives, and has a wide sandy beach.

CARBROOKE Norfolk TF9402
Village off B1108, 2 miles (3km) NE of Watton
Fine St Peter and St Paul's Church dates from the 13th century. There are coffin lids with flowered crosses belonging to the Countess of Clare.

CARDIFF (CAERDYDD) South Glamorgan ST1876
City off M4, 130 miles (209km) W of London
Wales's principal city and one of Europe's youngest capitals, Cardiff mushroomed from a small fishing village in the 19th century into one of the world's busiest coal-exporting ports. But its history reaches much further back, to Roman times when a fort was built alongside the River Taff, the foundations of which are still visible as part of the city-centre castle. Two regimental museums and a Norman keep are contained within the perimeter walls, but essentially the castle is a flamboyant Victorian make-over of buildings from previous centuries'. The wealth of the Bute family, creators of Cardiff's docklands, was displayed loud and clear at their castle home. The third Marquess, reputedly the richest man in the world, commissioned 19th-century opium-smoking genius William Burges to transform his residence into a no-expense-spared medieval fantasy palace decorated with astonishing detail. Medieval banquets now take place here.

Across in Cathays Park, the splendid civic centre consists of elegant neo-classical edifices in white Portland stone. The Welsh Office, University of Wales College and Temple of Peace are grouped behind the Law Courts and City Hall with its dragon-crowned dome and Marble Hall of heroic Welsh figures. Also fronting the civic centre is the National Museum of Wales, which tells the story of Wales through the ages. Of particular note is the innovative natural history gallery. The museum also boasts an outstanding collection of French Impressionist paintings, with works by Cézanne, Monet, Renoir and Van Gogh.

Cardiff's green belt stretches from the castle past the National Sports Centre for Wales and Glamorgan's cricket ground all the way to Llandaff a mile or so northwest. Another oasis is Roath Park's lake where a monument commemorates Captain Scott; his ill-fated Antarctic expedition left from Cardiff.

The compact shopping centre just south of Cathays Park has several modern malls amidst distinguished Victorian and Edwardian buildings interspersed with canopied period arcades. The Victorian market hall, selling Welsh delicacies such as laverbread (a type of seaweed), stands between the slender 15th-century spire of St John's Church and the colonnaded façade of the Old Library (now a crafts centre). Another central landmark is Brain's Brewery, known for its local 'dark' beer.

Among the city's sporting venues are the world-famous rugby citadel, Cardiff Arms Park, and the Wales National Ice Rink, home of the phenomenally successful Cardiff Devils ice hockey team. On the entertainments front, the large, modern Cardiff International Arena and St David's Hall both stage major concerts and shows, while the Sherman Theatre, Chapter Arts Centre and St Stephen's Theatre Space offer repertory, touring and experimental productions. The Edwardian New Theatre remains the base for the prestigious Welsh National Opera until it moves to Cardiff Bay.

At the old docklands, the waterfront development – one of the world's largest – is transforming legendary Tiger Bay, singer Shirley Bassey's birthplace. A tube-like visitor centre, Techniquest's entertaining hands-on science demonstrations and the imaginative Welsh Industrial and Maritime Museum's exhibits epitomise the area's blend of old and new.

CARDIGAN (ABERTEIFI) Dyfed SN1846
Town on A487, 16 miles (26km) NE of Fishguard
Ancient borough on Teifi estuary. Pleasant hotch-potch of buildings. Good covered market. Castle shell reputedly site of first eisteddfod in 1176.

CARDINGTON Bedfordshire TL0847
Village off A603, 3 miles (5km) SE of Bedford
Dominated by its two gigantic sheds, used for 1920s airships; the ill-fated R101 left on her last voyage from here in 1930. Due to their enormous size they almost have their own mini-climate inside and the sheds are used for research. Monument to R101 victims in graveyard opposite church, rebuilt about 1900. Monuments of the Whitbread brewing dynasty, lords of the manor .

CARDINGTON Shropshire SO5095
Village off B4371, 4 miles (6km) NE of Church Stretton
Lying beneath the peak of Caer Caradoc, the isolated village has a notable church of the 12th and 13th centuries with a splendid timber roof.

CARDINHAM Cornwall SX1268
Village off A30, 4 miles (6km) NE of Bodmin
On the edge of Bodmin Moor (see), with steep wooded valleys to the south. Small village with prominent medieval church. Cardinham Woods can be reached via the Bodmin and Wenford Steam Railway.

CAREW Dyfed SN0403
Village off A477, 4 miles (6km) E of Pembroke
Tiny place with three notable attractions. A strikingly carved 11th-century Celtic cross, 14ft (4m) high, now the symbol of Cadw, stands at the roadside. Picturesquely situated by River Carew is an imposing castle which evolved from a medieval defensive site to Tudor manor. Restored French Mill is the only one in Wales to be powered by the tide.

CARHAMPTON Somerset ST0042
Village on A39, 1 mile (2km) SE of Dunster
On the main road; church with very fine wooden screen, repainted in the original colours. Caesar's Camp, an Iron Age hillfort, to the west.

CARISBROOKE Isle of Wight SZ4888
Village on B3401, 1 mile (2km) SW of Newport
Village with a large and prominent medieval church (high 15th-century tower). Castle Street is the picturesque part. Carisbrooke Castle (English Heritage) is famous as the place where King Charles I was imprisoned. Best medieval parts are the gatehouse and the high keep. Battlement walks. Sixteenth-century well-house has the donkey wheel still worked by donkeys. Isle of Wight Museum inside the castle, with Tennyson relics and much else.

CARK Cumbria SD3676
Village on B5278, 2 miles (3km) SW of Cartmel
This small village takes its name from the Celtic word '*carrec*', meaning 'rock'. Holker Hall, owned by the Cavendish family, is near by.

CARLBY Lincolnshire TF0413
Village off A6121, 5 miles (8km) N of Stamford
On Rutland border in attractive limestone country; church faces open fields at corner of village.

CARLETON North Yorkshire SD9749
Village off A629, 2 miles (3km) SW of Skipton
Also called Carleton-in-Craven, this sizeable village lies south of the River Aire near Skipton.

CARLISLE Cumbria NY3956
City off M6, 19 miles (31km) NW of Penrith
The strategic importance of Carlisle goes back over 2,000 years, the name being derived from the Celtic word '*caer*', meaning fort. The Romans established a military base here in the 1st century called *Luguvalium*, and there followed a period of prosperity and luxurious living until the 9th century, when it was devastated by invading Danes. The following 600 years were the most turbulent in the city's history as Scotland and England fought each other to take control of the border regions, or 'debatable lands' as they were known.

Airship sheds at Cardington in Bedfordshire.

Carlisle Castle (English Heritage), originally a Norman castle made of wood, was rebuilt using stone taken from Hadrian's Wall and today dominates the city, having been added to and repaired over the centuries. Carlisle Cathedral was founded in 1122 as a Norman Priory for Augustinian canons. The chancel roof is magnificently decorated and the cathedral features an exquisite east window. The Citadel was built in 1541 as an additional fortification and marks the gateway to the city. Carlisle's award-winning museum, Tullie House, vividly tells much of the history of the city and its surrounding border regions.

CARLOWAY Western Isles (Lewis) NB2042
Village on A858, 4 miles (6km) SW of Shawbost
Site of Dun Carloway, one of Scotland's best-preserved brochs, 30ft (9m) high, with double walls and inner yard, on imposing rocky outcrop above sea.

CARLTON Bedfordshire SP9555
Village off A428, 7 miles (11km) NW of Bedford
In a loop of the Great Ouse, with stone and thatched houses.

CARLTON Cleveland NZ3921
Village off A177, 4 miles (6km) NW of Stockton-on-Tees
A small, agricultural village, once home to freed Norse slaves, called 'karls'. Victorian Gothic church has a fine lych-gate.

CARLTON North Yorkshire NZ5004
Village off A172, 3 miles (5km) S of Stokesley
Sometimes known as Carlton-in-Cleveland. Once provided shelter for alum miners and this long-dead industry is recalled in the name of the stream, Alum Beck, which runs through village. St Botolph's Church was destroyed by fire in 1881. Present church was once run by Canon John Kyle, who bought and managed the village pub so that he could close it on Sundays.

CARLTON North Yorkshire SE6423
Village on A1041, 1 mile (2km) N of Snaith
Carlton Towers, a conventional Jacobean house, was turned into a mock-medieval fantasy by two young eccentrics in the 1870s.

CARLTON Nottinghamshire SK6041
Town on B686, in E Nottingham
Also known as Carlton-le-Willows, to distinguish from other Nottinghamshire Carltons. Now joined on to Nottingham suburbs. Early hosiery factories. Massive Victorian church.

CARLTON COLVILLE Suffolk TM5189
Village off A12, 3 miles (5km) S of Lowestoft
The superb East Anglia Transport Museum is based in this pleasant village. Constantly changing, the museum features all kinds of transport.

CARLTON HUSTHWAITE North Yorkshire SE4976
Village off A19, 5 miles (8km) N of Easingwold
A small village sheltering in the lee of a gorse-covered mound which is an ancient earthwork.

CARLTON IN LINDRICK Nottinghamshire SK5883
Village on A60, 3 miles (5km) N of Worksop
Pleasant village with 18th–19th-century buildings, including watermill, now a rural museum. Major golf course just in neighbouring South Yorkshire.

CARLTON SCROOP Lincolnshire SK9445
Village on A607, 6 miles (10km) NE of Grantham
Small village of stone houses and a part-Norman church, rebuilt in two years after the spire fell in 1630.

CARLTON-ON-TRENT Nottinghamshire SK7963
Village off A1, 6 miles (10km) N of Newark
Formerly on the Great North road, with pleasing 18th-century houses, and old forge marked by an outsize brick horseshoe.

CARLUKE Strathclyde NS8450
Town on A73, 5 miles (8km) NW of Lanark
In Clyde Valley at centre of fruit- and tomato-growing area. Birthplace of General William Roy (1726–90), the military cartographer who directed first British ordnance surveys.

CARLYON BAY Cornwall SX0552
Village off A3390, 2 miles (3km) E of St Austell
Modern seaside village, with big sandy beach.

CARMARTHEN (CAERFYRDDIN) Dyfed SN4120
Town on A40, 22 miles (35km) NW of Swansea
Administrative and trading centre of region, thronged on market days. Links with legendary wizard Merlin (Myrddin). Site of Romans' most westerly fort in Britain. Remnants of Roman amphitheatre and medieval castle. Oldest existing Welsh manuscript written here. Oriel Myrddin Gallery promotes arts and crafts. Excellent museum in former Bishop's Palace at Abergwili on outskirts. Masses of pubs, old buildings. Gwili Railway steams at nearby Bronwydd Arms.

CARNABY Humberside TA1465
Village on A166, 2 miles (3km) SW of Bridlington
Here you will find a well-known rock factory, John Bull's World of Rock. Tours show confectionery being made in the traditional way.

CARNFORTH Lancashire SD4970
Town on A6, 6 miles (10km) N of Lancaster
Opening of Lancaster Canal in 1797 stimulated local quarry industry, and by 1857 the railway line provided connection to the iron-mining district of Furness. Steamtown is one of the largest mainline steam locomotive depots in Britain; home to *Flying Scotsman*, open to the public, offering steam rides. Carnforth station was the setting for the film *Brief Encounter.*

CARNOUSTIE Tayside NO5534
Town on A930, 6 miles (10km) SW of Arbroath
Select commuter town for Dundee and holiday resort on North Sea coast with championship golf course and good sandy beach.

CARPERBY North Yorkshire SE0089
Village off A684, 1 mile (2km) N of Aysgarth
A pretty village with a market charter dating from 1305, and a large Quaker Meeting House built in 1864. James Herriot spent his honeymoon at The Wheatsheaf.

CARRAWBURGH Northumberland NY8671
Roman site on B6318, 4 miles (6km) W of Chollerford
Remains of a fort constructed astride the Vallum, the ditch that ran behind Hadrian's Wall, with 3rd-century temple to the sun god Mithras.

CARRBRIDGE Highland NH9022
Village off A9, 7 miles (11km) N of Aviemore
Stands on River Dulnain, spanned by old bridge of 1715. Landmark visitor centre is a Highland heritage centre and educational adventure park.

CARRICK Strathclyde
Historic region of Scotland
Scenic region south of River Doon extending to Galloway Hills with some exceptional coastline. Former capital Maybole. Earldom of Carrick held by heir to throne.

CARRICK ROADS Cornwall SW8334
Harbour on estuary of the Fal, running down to Pendennis Point
The huge deep estuary running north from Falmouth. Famous for yachts and large ships, it is one of the largest natural harbours in the world.

CARRONBRIDGE Dumfries and Galloway NX8698
Village off A76, 2 miles (3km) NW of Thornhill
In Nithsdale, with two ruined castles, Morton and Tibber's, and imposing 17th-century Drumlanrig Castle, seat of Dukes of Queensberry, containing splendid paintings and furniture.

CARSHALTON Greater London TQ2764
District in borough of Sutton
Attractive former Surrey village. Heritage centre for Sutton borough. Little Holland House (limited opening) is a remarkable Arts and Crafts building.

CARSPHAIRN Dumfries and Galloway NX5693
Village on A713, 9 miles (14km) SE of Dalmellington
Birthplace of John MacAdam (1756–1835), inventor of hard road-surfacing process. Surrounding hills yielded iron, lead, copper, silver and zinc; now heavily forested.

CARTER BAR Northumberland/Borders NT6906
Site on A68, 10 miles (16km) SE of Jedburgh
The border point between England and Scotland on A68. Located on the crest of the Cheviot ridge between England and Scotland, this was part of the lawless Middle March region.

CARTERTON Oxfordshire SP2706
New Town off A40, SW of Brize Norton
Small New Town created originally to serve residential needs of Brize Norton air base. Has now attracted its own new industry and commerce.

CARTHEW Cornwall SX0056
Village on A391, 3 miles (5km) N of St Austell
In the 'White Alps', Cornwall's china-clay-mining district. Tiny old village in a tight valley, surrounded by huge tips, some overgrown, some bare. Just to the south is the Wheal Martyn Museum, displaying the history, machinery and buildings of the industry, which started to grow from 1800, and is now enormous.

CARTMEL Cumbria SD3878
Village off A590, 4 miles (6km) S of Newby Bridge
Attractive village on the River Aye dominated by the remains of Cartmel Priory (National Trust), founded in 1188 by Augustine canons after St Cuthbert appeared in a vision to the monastic architect and ordered him to build the priory next to water. Cartmel steeplechase racecourse; legend has it that the monks started Cartmel Races as their Whitsun recreation.

CARVORAN Northumberland NY6665
Roman site off B6318, 5 miles (8km) NW of Haltwhistle
The site of a Roman farm. The Roman Army Museum provides reconstructions of Roman life along Hadrian's Wall.

CASCOB Powys SO2366
Hamlet off B4372, 5 miles (8km) SW of Knighton
In quiet farming country around Radnor Forest. Unusually proportioned half-timbered tower of church; inside, a restored 16th-century rood screen.

The church at Cascob with its half-timbered belfry.

CASTLE

CASSINGTON Oxfordshire SP4511
Village off A40, 5 miles (8km) NW of Oxford
Straggling away from the A40, the village boasts a church with outstanding Norman and medieval work.

CASTLE ACRE Norfolk TF8115
Village off A1065, 4 miles (6km) N of Swaffham
The village stands between the lonely ruins of the magnificent Cluniac priory, and the sturdy ruins of the 11th-century flint keep (both English Heritage). The priory boasts the beautiful Prior's House and a splendid west front. The castle's walls are crumbling, but the huge grassy ramparts are still formidable. Houses of flint and brick stand along the village High Street.

CASTLE ASHBY Northamptonshire SP8659
Village off A428, 6 miles (10km) SW of Wellingborough
Small village dominated by Marquess of Northampton's magnificent Elizabethan mansion, which has fine pictures and furnishings, 17th-century woodwork, and lettered stone parapet surrounding house, and in which conferences, product launches and prestige events take place. Capability Brown parkland, lakes, extensive gardens with Camellia House and Victorian terrace gardens open to visitors. Craft workshops in former farmyard.

CASTLE BOLTON North Yorkshire SE0391
Village off A684, 5 miles (8km) W of Leyburn
Village dominated by Bolton Castle. At the end of 14th century Richard le Scrope was given permission to fortify his manor against Scots raiders; he built the castle instead. Mary Stuart was imprisoned here after her arrival in England. The castle has a huge hall and chambers, a monk's cell, an ale house and an armourer's forge.

CASTLE BROMWICH West Midlands SP1489
Suburb in E area of Birmingham
Castle Bromwich was earmarked in the 1930s for an ambitious programme of new municipal housing, and the process has continued since. The Church of St Mary and St Margaret (1726–31) replaced an older church by simply encasing its timbers. A growing visitor attraction is the on-going restoration of Castle Bromwich Hall Garden, a fine early 18th-century English formal garden, in Chester Road.

CASTLE BYTHAM Lincolnshire SK9818
Village off B1176, 8 miles (13km) N of Stamford
Pretty stone village on the winding West Glen River, close to the Rutland border. Houses have Collyweston slate and red-tiled roofs. Of the Norman castle which gives its name, substantial earthworks remain. The hilltop cruciform church has a long 14th-century chancel and, under the tower, a ladder which used to be the 17th-century maypole.

CASTLE CARROCK Cumbria NY5455
Village on B6413, 4 miles (6km) S of Brampton
There is no castle here, but there was once a fortified manor house with moat. Evidence exists of early habitation during Stone and Bronze Ages.

CASTLE CARY Somerset ST6432
Small town on B3152, 3 miles (5km) SW of Bruton
A charming small town with narrow twisty streets and stone buildings. Rather pompous market hall, partly 1616, partly 1855, and a famous lock-up of 1779 – a tiny circular building with dome. Little remains of the castle. Local museum.

CASTLE COMBE Wiltshire ST8477
Village off B4039, 5 miles (8km) NW of Chippenham
Perfect picture-postcard stone village, in a wooded hollow with a stone bridge over the river. Market cross in the centre, many gabled cottages and a pretty church with a fine tower. Everything is in the local golden stone. Local museum. Remnants of a medieval castle overlook the village, and to the east is a motor-racing circuit.

CASTLE DONINGTON Leicestershire SK4427
Village on B6540, 7 miles (11km) NW of Loughborough
Almost a small town, with site of Norman castle on hillside, timber-framed and Georgian buildings. On edge of town, Donington Collection of single-seater racing cars, and adjoining motor-racing circuit which draws crowds to its special events. Busy East Midlands International Airport with aeropark, viewing mound and visitor centre illustrating history of flight.

CASTLE DOUGLAS Dumfries and Galloway NX7662
Town on A75, 9 miles (14km) NE of Kirkcudbright
Pleasant market town, whose name was changed from Carlingwalk by William Douglas in the 18th century. Threave Castle, 14th century, a Douglas stronghold, was wrecked by Covenanters in 1640. Nearby Threave estate is National Trust for Scotland's School of Horticulture, with stunning gardens and woodlands and a visitor centre.

CASTLE EATON Wiltshire SU1496
Village off A419, 3 miles (5km) E of Cricklade
Close to the Thames, with stone cottages. Church down beside the river.

CASTLE EDEN Durham NZ4238
Village off A1086, 2 miles (3km) S of Peterlee
Small scattered village adjacent to Castle Eden which gives the village its name. Part of the castle gardens is now a National Nature Reserve.

CASTLE FROME Hereford and Worcester SO6645
Village on B4214, 6 miles (10km) S of Bromyard
St Michael's Church has an exceptional Norman font and is rich in other Norman and medieval work.

CASTLE GATE Cornwall SW4934
Hamlet on B3311, 3 miles (5km) NE of Penzance
Superb view across Mount's Bay with the best prospect of St Michael's Mount. Smaller view of north Cornwall.

CASTLE HEDINGHAM Essex TL7835
Village on B1058, 4 miles (6km) NW of Halstead
Impressive 12th-century fortress with keep almost 100ft (30m) high, Hedingham Castle was owned by the De Veres, Earls of Oxford, for over 500 years.

Fencing made from local flagstones at Castletown in Scotland.

Exceptionally attractive village of medieval, Tudor and Georgian houses clustered round the old market square. Pottery open. The Colne Valley Railway's steam trains have their base here, too.

CASTLE KENNEDY Dumfries and Galloway NX1159
Village off A75, 3 miles (5km) E of Stranraer
Eighteenth-century gardens, some of Scotland's loveliest, laid out by Earl of Stair around ruined 17th-century castle, restored 1840s. Baronial Loch Inch Castle dates from 1867.

CASTLE RISING Norfolk TF6624
Village off A149, 4 miles (6km) NE of King's Lynn
The village is dominated by one of the most splendid Norman keeps in England (English Heritage). Built in the 12th century, this forbidding castle was for many years the home of Queen Isabella, mother of Edward III, after her part in the murder of Edward II. The village has a row of red-brick almshouses built in 1807, and a 15th-century cross.

CASTLEBAY Western Isles (Barra) NL6698
Small town on A888 in S of Island
Old herring-port with ferry connections to Oban and Lochboisdale. Kisimul Castle harbour stronghold of MacNeils of Barra since 1427.

CASTLEFORD West Yorkshire SE4225
Town on A656, 10 miles (16km) SE of Leeds
This former coal-mining town is on the River Aire at the confluence with the River Calder. The town stands on the site of the Roman fort *Lagentium*, the most important Roman site in West Yorkshire as it straddled the Great North road. There is an RSPB reserve at an old coal workings, Fairburn Ings.

CASTLETHORPE Buckinghamshire SP8044
Village off A508, 3 miles (5km) N of Stony Stratford
Close to the River Tove in the far north of the county; a Norman castle's earthworks loom up by the village church.

CASTLETON Derbyshire SK1582
Village on A625, 5 miles (8km) W of Hathersage
Beautifully situated at the head of the Hope Valley in the Peak District National Park, Castleton shelters beneath the Norman ruin of Peveril Castle (English Heritage) and is overlooked by Mam Tor, topped by a Bronze and Iron Age hillfort and known as the 'shivering mountain' because of its instability.

Light traffic can leave the valley by spectacular Winnats Pass, a narrow limestone gorge. These hills are the unique source of Blue John, a fluorspar whose attractive purplish veining is seen in huge vases and urns at many historic houses and at the village's Ollerenshaw Collection. Pendants, brooches and earrings are produced from the smaller quantities of Blue John mined today from Treak Cliff Cavern. Cave tours show off stalactites and stalagmites here and at Blue John Cavern higher up the hillside. Speedwell Cavern is visited by a 1 mile (2km) underground boat journey, and Peak Cavern has a 400-year-old ropewalk in its entrance.

Each May the traditional Garland Ceremony attracts crowds, with much music and merrymaking. Special interest holidays can be enjoyed at the Peak National Park's Study Centre at 19th-century Losehill Hall.

CASTLETON North Yorkshire NZ6808
Village off A171, 8 miles (13km) W of Egton
Typical small central Moors village. Beautifully preserved wayside station serving the branch line through Eskdale.

CASTLETOWN Highland ND1967
Village on A836, 5 miles (8km) E of Thurso
Nineteenth-century centre south of impressive Dunnet Bay with purpose-built harbour for production of Caithness flagstones, used locally for fencing.

CASTLETOWN Isle of Man SC2667
Small town on A5, 9 miles (14km) SW of Douglas
Capital of the Isle of Man until 1869, this harbour town is dominated by Castle Rushen. The well-preserved medieval castle has displays of medieval and 17th-century life. The last Viking King, Magnus, died here in 1265. Nautical Museum contains the *Peggy*, an 18th-century armed yacht, which lay undisturbed after her owner's death and was rediscovered in 1935.

CASTON Norfolk TL9597
Village off B1077, 3 miles (5km) SE of Watton
A well-kept village green around which stand a church, a school and the Old Rectory. The nearby windmill is also part of the village.

CASTOR Cambridgeshire TL1298
Village on A47, 4 miles (6km) W of Peterborough
Visitors to Castor should ensure they turn off the main road to see the village green, the narrow High Street and the church, all of which are to one side of the A47. Blue-grey Roman pottery has been found in and around Castor, and, in about AD650, Kyneburgha, daughter of a Mercian king, founded a convent here.

CAT AND FIDDLE INN Cheshire SK0071
Inn on A537, 4 miles (6km) W of Buxton
Second highest inn in England, 1,690ft (515m), perhaps named from picture given to landlord by Duke of Devonshire, 1857.

CATCLEUGH RESERVOIR Northumberland NT7403
Reservoir on A68, 3 miles (5km) SE of Carter Bar
Completed in 1906, the reservoir is fed by the River Rede and lies at the edge of Redesdale Forest.

CATCLIFFE South Yorkshire SK4288
Village off B6066, 3 miles (5km) E of Sheffield
The village, on the banks of the River Rother, is home to one of Europe's remaining glass-blowing kilns.

CATERHAM Surrey TQ3455
Town off A22, 6 miles (10km) S of Croydon
Old centre on downs, Norman church and old cottages, surrounded by 1930s housing, merged with Victorian centre by station in valley.

CATHERINGTON Hampshire SU6914
Village off A3, 1 mile (2km) NW of Horndean
Still rural, and very scattered. Good views of Langstone Harbour and the chalk downs.

CATMOSE, VALE OF Leicestershire SK8709
District around Oakham
Area of outcropped clay.

CATON Lancashire SD5364
Village on A683, 4 miles (6km) NE of Lancaster
Village founded by Norseman called Katti. Subjected to harsh treatment by Scottish border raiders, especially Black Douglas in 14th century.

CATRINE Strathclyde NS5225
Village on B705, 2 miles (3km) SE of Mauchline
Industrial Revolution cotton-milling town on River Ayr in Burns country, relatively thriving until mill burnt down in 1960s.

CATSFIELD East Sussex TQ7213
Village on B2204, 2 miles (3km) SW of Battle
Hilltop village, dominated by spire of Methodist church (1912). Parish church lies to the south by the manor house.

CATTERICK North Yorkshire SE2397
Village off A1, 5 miles (8km) SE of Richmond
A large military camp is based here. Site of a Roman settlement on the main London to Newcastle highway. Near by, Paulinus, Bishop of York and creator of first York Minster, baptised 10,000 Christians in River Swale. A Roman garrison was once situated 3 miles (5km) away at *Cataractonium*. Catterick Racecourse lies to the north of the village.

CATTISTOCK Dorset SY5999
Village off A356, 1 mile (2km) N of Maiden Newton
Thatched brick and stone cottages, and a fine Victorian church with a vast tower.

CAUNTON Nottinghamshire SK7460
Village off A616, 5 miles (8km) NW of Newark
Home of founder of National Rose Society. An attractive village with Norman and medieval church beside The Beck.

CAVENDISH Suffolk TL8046
Village on A1092, 4 miles (6km) W of Long Melford
An attractive group of pink-walled, thatched cottages huddle around the large 14th-century church. The cottages are about 400 years old, but have been rebuilt several times. Dating from Saxon times, Cavendish's name comes from *Cafa's Edisc*, meaning the Enclosure of Caffa's People. The Old Rectory is owned by Sue Ryder, benefactor of the Foundation for the Sick and Disabled.

CAVERSFIELD Oxfordshire SP5825
Village off A421, 2 miles (3km) N of Bicester
Caversfield House, its small village and the ancient church dating from Saxon times remain snugly secluded from the encroachments of Bicester.

CAVERSHAM Berkshire SU7274
District in N area of Reading, N of the Thames
Separated from Reading by the Thames, but really part of that town. Victorian urban buildings and some villas, but more 20th century.

CAVERSWALL Staffordshire SJ9542
Village off A521, 4 miles (6km) W of Cheadle
Despite its proximity to Stoke-on-Trent, Caverswall remains a quiet backwater with traditional pub, and stocks on display in the village square.

CAWDOR Highland NH8450
Village on B9090, 5 miles (8km) SW of Nairn
Pretty village clustered just outside the entrance to Cawdor Castle, a fairytale 14th-century building with later additions and pleasing gardens, inhabited for 600 years by the Cawdor family. Shakespeare's Macbeth was predicted to become Thane of Cawdor by the three witches, setting off his tragic desire to become king.

CAWFIELDS Northumberland NY7166
Roman site off B6318, 1 mile (2km) N of Haltwhistle
The remains of a milecastle on the crags of Whin Sill, one of the most rugged sections of Hadrian's Wall.

CAWOOD North Yorkshire SE5737
Village on B1223, 4 miles (6km) NW of Selby
Once known as the Windsor of the north because of its medieval castle which was made into a palace in the 14th century. Seven Archbishops of York lived at the castle and Henry VIII visited with Catherine Howard. Most tragic occupant was Cardinal Wolsey, who retired there only to be arrested for high treason by a guest.

CAWSAND Cornwall SX4350
see Kingsand

CAWSTON Norfolk TG1323
Village on B1145, 4 miles (6km) SW of Aylsham
Cawston boasts a splendid 15th-century church and the curious Duelling Stone. This great stone ball, mounted on a plinth and standing at the side of the road, commemorates a duel fought in 1698 between two men over heated words during an election campaign. One was killed, and the other fled to Holland and was later acquitted.

CAWTHORNE South Yorkshire SE2808
Village off A635, 4 miles (6km) W of Barnsley
Cannon Hall and the country park were built in the 18th century by John Carr; it is now run by Barnsley Council as a museum.

CAXTON Cambridgeshire TL3058
Village on A1198, 9 miles (14km) W of Cambridge
A grim reminder of crime and punishment in past times is Caxton Gibbet. Near by is a post mill with a pitched roof.

CAYNHAM Shropshire SO5573
Village off A49, 3 miles (5km) SE of Ludlow
Scattered settlement below prominent Iron Age hillfort. Church has curious Norman chancel arch with three openings.

CAYTHORPE Lincolnshire SK9348
Village off A607, 8 miles (13km) N of Grantham
Large village of golden-toned ironstone. One mile (2 km) east, Caythorpe Court agricultural college forms part of De Montfort University.

CEMAES Gwynedd (Anglesey) SH3793
Village off A5025, 5 miles (8km) W of Amlwch
Wales's northernmost village with most northerly pub, Stag inn. Sands, pretty harbour. Llanbadrig Church has surprising Islamic-style restoration. Windmill farm, tours of Wylfa Head Nuclear Power Station.

CENARTH Dyfed SN2641
Village on A484, 3 miles (5km) W of Newcastle Emlyn
Much-visited spot on River Teifi. Salmon falls, stone bridge. National Coracle Centre, restored 17th-century flour mill.

CERES Fife NO4011
Village on B939, 3 miles (5km) SE of Cupar
Pretty village – pronounced 'Series' – with village green and pleasant buildings. Fife Folk Museum, mainly farming and agricultural. June Games celebrate return from Bannockburn (see).

CERNE ABBAS Dorset ST6601
Village on A352, 7 miles (11km) N of Dorchester
A flourishing small market town until it was bypassed by the railways. Handsome 15th-century church, very pretty village centre, especially Abbey Street. Remains of the abbey include an elaborate late 15th-century hall, and tithe barn (not open). St Augustine's Well in the graveyard pre-dates everything except perhaps the Cerne Giant, a 180ft (54m) figure cut into the chalk above the village. He may be Roman.

CHACEWATER Cornwall SW7544
Village off A390, 5 miles (8km) W of Truro
Small village on the edge of a copper-mining area, with many chimneys still surviving.

CHACOMBE Northamptonshire SP4944
Village off A361, 3 miles (5km) NE of Banbury
Conservation area with remains of 12th-century priory incorporated into house, 14th-century church with rare stone porch, wall-paintings and locally-cast bells.

CHADDERTON Greater Manchester SD9005
Town on A669, 6 miles (10km) NE of Manchester
An industrial town whose manor house, Foxdenton Hall, was home to two Royalists who were killed at the battle of Edgehill in 1642.

CHADDESDEN Derbyshire SK3836
Village off A52, 2 miles (3km) E of Derby
Now a suburb of Derby. Mid-14th-century church an important example of one completed before the Perpendicular style took over.

CHADDESLEY CORBETT Hereford and Worcester SO8973
Village off A448, 4 miles (6km) SE of Kidderminster
The picture-postcard village street is famous for the variety and harmony of its buildings dating from the 16th to 19th centuries (timber-framed Talbot inn is outstanding). The uniquely dedicated St Cassian's Church has an extravagantly beautiful Norman font and outstanding features of the 14th and 15th centuries. The oaks of Chaddesley Wood are protected as a nature reserve.

CHAGFORD Devon SX7087
Small town off A382, 4 miles (6km) NW of Moretonhampstead
A proper tiny market town on the edge of Dartmoor, with steep deeply wooded river valleys and the moors above. A stannary town, where the tin was taken to be weighed and taxed. Lots of good cottages (some still thatched) and in the middle a little octagonal market house of 1862 and a fine 15th-century church.

CHAILEY East Sussex TQ3919
Village on A275, 6 miles (10km) N of Lewes
Village centre is tucked in valley: a small green and church. To north, the beautiful common and its windmill.

CHALBURY COMMON Dorset SU0206
Hamlet off B3078, 4 miles (6km) N of Wimborne Minster
High on the chalk, with deep, narrow roads. The white-painted church has good 18th-century fittings and wide views.

CHALDON Surrey TQ3155
Village off B2031, 2 miles (3km) NW of Caterham
High on the downs with housing straggling towards it from Caterham. Church stands alone, contains unique 'Doom' painting, about 1200.

CHALDON HERRING Dorset SY7983
Village off A352, 4 miles (6km) SW of Wool
Also known as East Chaldon. A sparse village, mostly thatched cottages. Well known as the home of the brothers TF and Llewellyn Powys, some of whose books use the area.

CHALE Isle of Wight SZ4877
Village on A3055, 5 miles (8km) W of Ventnor
Very open landscape, with long views to the Needles. Medieval church, estate cottages and, at Chale Green, a long thin green with some old cottages.

CHALFIELD, GREAT Wiltshire ST8663
Hamlet off B3107, 3 miles (5km) W of Melksham
A wonderful late medieval group of Manor House (National Trust), gatehouse and church, with a moat. Good fittings in both buildings.

CHALFONT ST GILES Buckinghamshire SU9893
Town off A413, 3 miles (5km) SE of Amersham
Best known for Milton's Cottage, where the blind poet retreated from the London plague of 1665 and completed *Paradise Lost*. Chiltern Open Air Museum preserves historic buildings from 15th century to Edwardian times. Medieval wall-paintings in Church of St Giles and grave of circus magnate Bertram Mills. Shire horses at Model Farm. (For Jordans, see Seer Green.)

CHALFONT ST PETER Buckinghamshire TQ0090
Town on A413, 5 miles (8km) SE of Amersham
Commuter town, a junior relative of Chalfont St Giles. Fine old Greyhound pub in High Street. Obelisk on common commemorates George III killing a stag.

CHALFORD Gloucestershire SO8903
Village off A419, 4 miles (6km) SE of Stroud
Rising by terraces on the steep side of the Frome Valley, this village was once a busy cloth-making centre, and has an array of 18th- and 19th-century houses and cottages built for mill owners and workers. Some mill buildings remain below the village beside the river. The Company's Arms inn is said to have been a 15th-century manor house.

CHALGRAVE Bedfordshire TL0127
Site on A5120, 4 miles (6km) N of Dunstable
Solitary church with medieval wall-paintings and possibly the tomb of Conan Doyle's 'Sir Nigel', who owned the manor.

CHALGROVE Oxfordshire SU6396
Village off B480, 4 miles (6km) NW of Watlington
Modern housing has not entirely erased the charm of thatched cottages, old pubs and a church with unique series of 14th-century wall-paintings.

CHALLACOMBE Devon SS6940
Village on B3358, 5 miles (8km) W of Simonsbath
On the edge of Exmoor; the name means 'cold valley'. The church is at Barton Town on a hill to the west, and Shoulsbarrow to the southeast on the moors is a large Iron Age hillfort.

CHALLOCK LEES Kent TR0050
Village on A252, 4 miles (6km) E of Charing
Village dispersed around wide spacious green with the church 1 mile (2km) away in Eastwell Park near the manor house.

CHALTON Hampshire SU7315
Village off A3, 3 miles (5km) NE of Horndean
On the slope of a chalk down, with a prominent timber-framed thatched pub on the little green.

CHANCTONBURY RING West Sussex TQ1412
see Wiston

CHANDLER'S FORD Hampshire SU4320
District off M3, in NW Eastleigh
Huge area of housing, mostly 1930s onwards, all well wooded. Chandler's Ford Lake is a big pond created by clay-digging for the 19th-century brick industry.

CHAPEL OF GARIOCH Grampian NJ7124
Village off A96, 4 miles (6km) NW of Inverurie
Garioch, pronounced 'Geerie', is known for nearby Maiden Stone, 10ft (3m) high Pictish symbol stone with relief carvings.

CHAPEL ST LEONARDS Lincolnshire TF5672
Village off A52, 6 miles (10km) N of Skegness
Popular seaside resort on bracing Lincolnshire coast, with a village atmosphere, caravan and chalet parks, and wide sandy beaches.

CHAPEL-EN-LE-FRITH Derbyshire SK0580
Town off A6, 5 miles (8km) N of Buxton
Market town on border of Peak District National Park, whose name means 'chapel in the forest'. Chapel, consecrated 1225, expanded early 14th century with some later alterations, is dedicated to St Thomas Becket. Seventeenth-century market cross in market place. Most notable buildings are Victorian. Otters and owls bred at Chestnut Centre Conservation Park on edge of town.

CHAPEL-LE-DALE North Yorkshire SD7477
Hamlet on B6255, 4 miles (6km) NE of Ingleton
Once made its money by manufacturing shoes. Dominated by the sheer bulk of Whernside and Ingleborough mountains.

CHAPPEL Essex TL8928
Village on A604, 5 miles (8km) E of Halstead
Pretty place in Colne Valley. Magnificent 30-arched railway viaduct, Knights Farm dried-flower centre. East Anglian Railway Museum. Merges with Wakes Colne (see).

CHARD Somerset ST3208
Town on A30, 9 miles (14km) W of Crewkerne
A proper small town, with classical town hall (1834, two storeys of pillars), 16th- to 19th-century houses, almshouse and chapels. The museum is in one of the 16th-century houses. Tiny thatched and verandahed circular turnpike cottage. To the north Hornsbury Mill, rural life displays. Forde Abbey to south – beautiful house, abbot's hall, cloisters and huge gardens.

CHARING Kent TQ9549
Small town off A20, 6 miles (10km) NW of Ashford
Compactly clustering between fork in two main roads on the steep slopes of the North Downs. The attractive High Street, with Tudor houses, climbs the steep hill. Possible site of Roman town *Durolenum*, and certainly one of Kent's oldest townships, with former palace of Archbishops of Canterbury where both Henry VII and Henry VIII stayed.

CHARLBURY Oxfordshire SP3519
Small town on B4026, 6 miles (10km) SE of Chipping Norton
A tall church tower guides you to this tranquil old weaving town beside the River Evenlode. Corner House Museum portrays its interesting history.

CHARLECOTE Warwickshire SP2656
Village off B4086, 4 miles (6km) E of Stratford-upon-Avon
Charlecote House (National Trust), home of Lucy family since the 13th century, has a fascinating interior and splendid deer park. Lucy monuments in church.

CHARLESTOWN Cornwall SX0351
Village off A390, 1 mile (2km) SE of St Austell
Small harbour built in the 1790s to ship copper ores, later used for china clay; often has tall ships in. Terraces of cottages and few larger houses are all of around 1800. Unspoilt. Shipwreck and Heritage Centre.

CHARLESTOWN OF ABERLOUR Grampian NJ2643
Small town on A95, 4 miles (6km) S of Rothes
Founded in the 19th century by Charles Grant, and named after him. Several famous distilleries in neighbourhood. Aberlour House is now a school.

CHARLTON Hertfordshire TL1728
Village off A602, 1 mile (2km) SW of Hitchin
Charlton House was the 1813 birthplace of Sir Henry Bessemer, inventor of Bessemer steel-making process, who grew up here.

CHARLTON West Sussex SU8812
Village off A286, 1 mile (2km) E of Singleton
Flint-built village without a church set high on the downs and famous in the annals of hunting.

CHARLTON Wiltshire ST9588
Village on B4040, 2 miles (3km) NE of Malmesbury
Cotswold-like stone village, with Charlton House and its big park to the north. The house dates from 1607 and 1770s (limited opening).

CHARLTON ABBOTS Gloucestershire SP0324
Hamlet off A436, 3 miles (5km) S of Winchcombe
A lofty hill village with fine views, an Elizabethan manor house and barn (not open). Norman tub font in church.

CHARLTON KINGS Gloucestershire SO9621
Town on A40, immediately E of Cheltenham
An early Cheltenham suburb, which gives its name to the Common, an extensive stretch of open grassland on the northern edge of Leckhampton Hill.

CHARLTON MACKRELL Somerset ST5328
Village off B3153, 3 miles (5km) E of Somerton
The last part the name of a person, not a fish. Lytes Cary (National Trust) to the south is a perfect ancient manor house, small and medieval.

CHARLTON MARSHALL Dorset ST9004
Village on A350, 2 miles (3km) SE of Blandford Forum
A spread-out village along a main road, with a fine church of 1713.

CHARLTON-ALL-SAINTS Wiltshire SU1723
Village off A338, 5 miles (8km) S of Salisbury
Right down by the River Avon, with mid-Victorian church, vicarage and school. Clearbury Ring is a small Iron Age hillfort on a knoll.

CHARLTON-ON-OTMOOR Oxfordshire SP5616
Village off B4027, 4 miles (6km) S of Bicester
At the centre of Otmoor stands the village whose church boasts the most magnificent rood screen in Oxfordshire.

CHARLWOOD Surrey TQ2441
Village off A23, 3 miles (5km) NW of Crawley
Picturesque village centre of timber-framed and tile-hung cottages, cricket ground and ancient church which preserves excellent medieval wooden screen.

CHARMINSTER Dorset SY6792
Village on A352, 1 mile (2km) N of Dorchester
Neat and prosperous, with some thatch. Sturdy and handsome church tower of 1525, built by the owner of Wolfeton House (to the south), a later 16th-century house with a gatehouse of 1500.

CHARMOUTH Dorset SY3693
Small town off A35, 2 miles (3km) NE of Lyme Regis
Tucked in behind the coast, with one long street running up a steep hill. Many early 19th-century houses, when the town started as a resort. Cliffs on the shore, good views. Charmouth Heritage Coast Centre near the beach.

CHARNEY BASSETT Oxfordshire SU3894
Village off B4508, 4 miles (6km) N of Wantage
Isolated in the Vale of the White Horse, the village has a good Norman church and paths to Cherbury Camp, an Iron Age settlement.

CHARNOCK RICHARD Lancashire SD5515
Village off A49, 2 miles (3km) SW of Chorley
A small Lancashire village near the River Yarrow, best known for its Camelot Theme Park.

CHARNWOOD FOREST Leicestershire SK4914
Scenic area SW of Loughborough
Attractive area of high undulating countryside with rocky granite outcrops, woodland, picturesque grey stone villages. Visitor centre at Bradgate Park, family home of Lady Jane Grey, tells story of England's 'nine days queen'. Tudor brick house ruins (limited opening) surrounded by extensive deer park. On hilltop, Old John Tower is a landmark for miles around.

CHARSFIELD Suffolk TM2556
Village off B1078, 3 miles (5km) W of Wickham Market
Ronald Blythe wrote *Akenfield*, a book based on Charsfield. A cottage garden, open to visitors, is named after the book and is full of flowers and vegetables.

CHARTERHOUSE Somerset ST4955
Hamlet off B3371, 3 miles (5km) NE of Cheddar
On top of the Mendips, where the Romans mined lead. A small Roman amphitheatre survives. Mining continued from medieval times until 1885.

CHARTHAM Kent TR1054
Village off A28, 3 miles (5km) SW of Canterbury
Large village in valley of Great Stour beneath wooded downs; clusters around green with stately church. Known for the manufacture of quality paper .

CHARWELTON Northamptonshire SP5356
Village on A361, 5 miles (8km) SW of Daventry
Originally two villages, church and manor house are 1 mile (2km) away. Packhorse bridge over River Cherwell which has its source near by.

CHASTLETON Oxfordshire SP2429
Village off A44, 4 miles (6km) NW of Chipping Norton
Small, attractive Cotswold village where church has interesting work of Norman period and later, including medieval floor tiles. Chastleton House (closed for restoration), with its multi-gabled front and splendid long gallery, was built in the early 1600s, probably by Robert Smythson, who created Derbyshire's famous Hardwick Hall. The 18th-century dovecote is an added attraction.

CHATHAM Kent TQ7567
Town on A2, 28 miles (45km) E of London
A busy town on the River Medway with a history of ship-building. It was first used as safer anchorage than Portsmouth by Henry VIII and developed by Elizabeth I against the Armada, when a large dockyard and arsenal were built. It prospered, but in 1667 the Dutch fleet sailed up the Medway and burnt the English fleet. In response forts were built along the river. The Napoleonic wars saw further dockyard expansion and Nelson's *Victory* was launched here.

As a child, Charles Dickens lived in Chatham where his father worked in the Navy Pay Office. Chatham remained England's prime naval dockyard throughout the 19th century and with the arrival of cement and engineering industries became the largest industrial centre in Kent.

Today, as in the last 400 years, this cheerful, crowded town lives for its dockyards, now an important tourist attraction run as a living museum with flags, sails and rope made in the time-honoured way. There are few old houses, but there is the tiny quadrangle with chapel and houses of the Sir John Hawkins Hospital, founded in 1592 by the famous navigator 'for poor decayed mariners and shipwrights'.

CHATHILL Northumberland NU1827
Hamlet off B1340, 4 miles (6km) SW of Seahouses
The 14th-century Preston pele tower which is still standing is one of the 78 such towers originally listed in 1475.

CHATTERIS Cambridgeshire TL3985
Small town off A141, 7 miles (11km) S of March
Surrounded by Tick, Horseley and Langwood Fens, Chatteris is an ancient town that, like Ely, was once an island in the marshes.

CHATTISHAM Suffolk TM0942
Village off A1071, 4 miles (6km) E of Hadleigh
In the 1640s, two Chattisham villagers were accused of witchcraft. Charity Farm dates from the 14th century.

Chastleton House in Oxfordshire.

CHATTON Northumberland NU0528
Village on B6348, 4 miles (6km) E of Wooler
The Church of the Holy Cross was built to provide tithes for Alnwick Abbey. The present church has an organ from Magdalen College, Oxford.

CHAWLEIGH Devon SS7112
Village on B3042, 2 miles (3km) SE of Chulmleigh
Remote and very rural village, just above the wooded valley of the Little Dart River.

CHAWTON Hampshire SU7037
Village off A31, 1 mile (2km) SW of Alton
Revered as the village where Jane Austen spent the last eight years of her life, and wrote three of her novels. A single street of brick houses and cottages, with the Austen house on the corner, only a fair-sized village house. Many relics and some rooms looking much as in her time. Chawton House (not open), where one of her brothers lived, is also little changed.

CHEADLE Greater Manchester SJ8688
Town on A34, 3 miles (5km) W of Stockport
A smart suburb of Stockport, parts of which lie in a conservation area. Abney Hall (now offices) was built by the Watt family who, along with many other leading Manchester industrialists, made their home here. The Church of St Mary dates from 1520 and contains a Saxon cross from the 11th century.

CHEADLE Staffordshire SK0043
Town on A522, 8 miles (13km) E of Stoke-on-Trent
Centuries of quiet market-town prosperity show in good timber-framed and Georgian houses around the 17th-century market cross near the Wheatsheaf inn. The outstanding building is Pugin's Roman Catholic church of 1846, with a 200ft (60m) spire and rich interior embellishment. Cheadle Mill (1790s), in Tape Street, is a striking example of an early iron-frame construction.

CHEAM Greater London TQ2463
District in borough of Sutton
Whitehall, a 16th-century house, restored in 1970s, is now a museum. Nonsuch Park, grounds of vanished Tudor palace. Victorian parish church with monuments.

CHEARSLEY Buckinghamshire SP7110
Village off B4011, 1 mile (2km) NE of Long Crendon
Attractive village among winding lanes with thatched cottages and a simple church; good place to see Buckinghamshire 'witchert' or earth walls, made of soil and straw.

CHEBSEY Staffordshire SJ8528
Village Off A5013, 5 miles (8km) NW of Stafford
Village on River Sow with good Norman church. Near by is Izaak Walton's Cottage (limited opening) where the author of *The Compleat Angler* spent much of his life.

CHECKENDON Oxfordshire SU6683
Village off A4074, 4 miles (6km) NE of Goring
High in the Chiltern Hills, timber-framed cottages stand round a green close to a Norman church with wall-paintings and brasses.

CHECKLEY Staffordshire SK0237
Village on A522, 5 miles (8km) NW of Uttoxeter
Rewarding church with Norman font, doorway and arcades, fine chancel of about 1300 with medieval glass, stalls of 1540s and remains of Saxon crosses.

CHEDDAR Somerset ST4553
Town on A371, 8 miles (13km) NW of Wells
Famous for its deep limestone gorge and the caves below. Cliffs of 400ft (120m) either side of the gorge, with the road in the bottom. The 274 steps of Jacob's Ladder lead to the upper level from the village. The caves are large, with stalagmites and so on, and had evidence of occupation in palaeolithic times. The Cheddar pink grows only here, and the cheese was named after the area.

CHEDDINGTON Buckinghamshire SP9217
Village off B488, 4 miles (6km) N of Tring
Once known for plum orchards, damsons and greengages, but now famed for the rich pickings of the Great Train Robbery, in 1962, at railway crossing here.

CHEDDLETON Staffordshire SJ9752
Village on A520, 3 miles (5km) S of Leek
Popular for its restored flint mill beside Caldon Canal and steam railway museum at station. The church's richly decorated chancel should not be missed.

CHEDGRAVE Norfolk TM3699
Village off A146, 7 miles (11km) NW of Beccles
The thatched tower of All Saints' Church dominates the village. The stained glass was once thought to have come from Rouen Cathedral.

CHEDISTON Suffolk TM3577
Village off B1123, 2 miles (3km) W of Halesworth
Chediston is noted for its fruit farms and old moated Chediston Grange. It is a lively village that has attracted talented craftsmen.

CHEDWORTH Gloucestershire SP0512
Village off A429, 4 miles (6km) SW of Northleach
Spread along wooded slopes, this village has notable 15th-century features in its church, but most visitors come to see the nearby Roman villa (National Trust), one of the best-preserved in Britain. It dates from the 2nd and 3rd centuries, with mosaic floors in the bath complex and dining room, garden colonnade and water tank showing Christian 'chi-ro' symbol. Visitor centre and museum.

CHEDZOY Somerset ST3437
Village off A39, 3 miles (5km) E of Bridgwater
Small village in the Somerset Levels; medieval church with crude 1550s bench-ends.

CHEESDEN Greater Manchester SD8216
Village on A680, 5 miles (8km) NW of Rochdale
The village flourished during the 18th and 19th centuries when the cotton industry provided employment for several hundred people.

CHELFORD Cheshire SJ8174
Village on A537, 6 miles (10km) W of Macclesfield
Typical rural village which grew up round church, farm and manor house. Famous for its thriving cattle market.

CHELLASTON Derbyshire SK3730
Village on A514, 4 miles (6km) SE of Derby
Site of medieval quarries of alabaster, intricately carved into figures by Nottingham artists. Small church with tower rebuilt 1842.

CHELMORTON Derbyshire SK1169
Village off A5270, 4 miles (6km) SE of Buxton
In Peak District, second highest village in country. Stone walls enclose narrow fields behind farms which line village street up to church.

CHELMSFORD Essex TL7007
City off A12, 30 miles (48km) NE of London
The first small settlement here, where the rivers Can and Chelmer join, grew up on the Roman road between Colchester and London. The road ran along today's Moulsham Street, with its pubs and small shops. Essex's county town today, however, is directly descended from a new town planned by the Bishop of London in 1199. In the centre are the principal inn, the Royal Saracen's Head, and the elegant Shire Hall of 1792, by a distinguished local architect, John Johnson, who also designed the bridge over the Can.

It was Johnson, again, who rebuilt the Parish Church of St Mary, with its 15th-century tower, when most of it fell down in 1800. The church became the cathedral of the new diocese of Chelmsford, created in 1913, was further enlarged in the 1920s by Sir Charles Nicholson, and reorganised inside in 1983. For plays and concerts, Chelmsford has its Civic Theatre and craft workshops now crowd Moulsham Mill, a converted 18th-century watermill. Local and natural history can be explored in the Chelmsford and Essex Museum, which also covers the fighting history of the Essex Regiment.

CHELSEA Greater London TQ2778
District in borough of Kensington and Chelsea
Pricey Bohemia, famous for artists and writers, smart shopping. Annual flower show in grounds of Royal Hospital, old soldiers' home by Sir Christopher Wren. National Army Museum near by, and Carlyle's House Museum. Cheyne Walk beside Thames Embankment. Albert Bridge, delightful 1870s iron cat's cradle. Chelsea Old Church. Royal Court Theatre, avant garde.

CHELSHAM Surrey TQ3758
Village off B269, 1 mile (2km) E of Warlingham
Scattered downland village of homespun cottages around large rough green surrounded by little woods and rolling fields with isolated church.

CHELSWORTH Suffolk TL9748
Village on B1115, 4 miles (6km) NW of Hadleigh
The shallow, rippling waters of the River Brett murmur softly through this lovely old village. Chelsworth has an aura that is quintessentially English.

CHELTENHAM Gloucestershire SO9422
Town on A40, 8 miles (13km) E of Gloucester
A visit by George III in 1788 transformed the small spa village of Cheltenham into the elegant town that attracts so many visitors today. They come to see the avenues, crescents and squares of one of England's finest Regency towns and to sample attractions that include splendid shopping centres in the Promenade and Montpellier Street and notable museums. The Art Gallery and Museum has an outstanding collection of furniture, silver and Arts and Crafts exhibits, while costume and local history are featured at the Pittville Pump Room museum. The birthplace of composer Gustav Holst in Clarence Road is a museum with an 'upstairs, downstairs' theme.

One of the few pre-Regency buildings is St Mary's, a 14th-century rebuilding of a Norman church, a striking contrast to the sumptuous Victorian Gothic of All Saints' in Pittville. Enjoyable open spaces like the Montpellier Gardens, the Imperial Gardens and Pittville Park add to a civilised environment that is an appropriate setting for prestigious annual festivals of literature and music.

But Cheltenham does not rely on the glories of the past. It is a thriving regional centre with a major share of modern commerce and industry.

CHENIES Buckinghamshire TQ0198
Village off A404, 4 miles (6km) E of Amersham
Above the River Chess. Chenies Manor is delightful lived-in Tudor house with ornamental chimneys, mysterious secret passages and limping ghostly presence of Henry VIII, who stayed here; charming garden. In church close by is fabulous mausoleum of Dukes of Bedford with huge monuments, private but glimpsed enticingly through window in church wall. Also 15th–16th-century brasses.

CHEPSTOW (CAS-GWENT) Gwent ST5393
Town on A48, 14 miles (23km) E of Newport
Hilly town near mouth of River Severn boasting Britain's first stone-constructed castle, a mighty border stronghold on River Wye's sheer cliffs (Cadw). Medieval town walls and gate, local history museum, glass-engraving centre, pottery. Racecourse hosts Welsh Grand National. Start of long-distance Offa's Dyke Path and Wye Valley Walk. Riverside plaque commemorates transportation of Chartist Movement's leaders.

CHERBURY CAMP Oxfordshire SU3896
see Charney Bassett

CHERHILL Wiltshire SU0370
Village on A4, 3 miles (5km) E of Calne
Large village below the chalk downs, with a white horse cut into the chalk slope in 1780, and on top an obelisk, a memorial of 1845.

CHERITON Hampshire SU5828
Village on B3046, 3 miles (5km) S of New Alresford
Neat and rural, with a river through the middle. The Battle of Cheriton (1644) was one of the most important in the Civil War – the Royalists lost for the first time.

CHERITON Kent TR2037
Village off M20, in N outskirts of Folkestone
Former hamlet in valley above coast with fine 13th-century church, now suburb of Folkestone and site of Channel Tunnel terminal.

CHERITON BISHOP Devon SX7793
Village off A30, 6 miles (10km) SW of Crediton
Church set in a hollow, in the hilly country northeast of Dartmoor. Toll house of 1838 from a Turnpike Trust.

CHERITON FITZPAINE Devon SS8606
Village off A3072, 4 miles (6km) NE of Crediton
Pretty village, with many thatched cottages and almshouses of 1594, with chimneys like buttresses to the street.

CHERRINGTON Shropshire SJ6619
Hamlet on B5062, 5 miles (8km) W of Newport
A handful of houses dominated by Cherrington Manor (1635), a superb example of a timber-framed manor house.

CHERRY BURTON Humberside SE9841
Village off A1079, 3 miles (5km) NW of Beverley
A row of ancient yew trees survives at Cherry Burton House. Once agricultural, now largely a dormitory village.

CHERRY HINTON Cambridgeshire TL4856
Area of SE Cambridge
A suburb of Cambridge, this village boasts Cherry Hinton Hall (limited opening), home to the annual Cambridge Folk Festival.

CHERRY WILLINGHAM Lincolnshire TF0372
Village off A158, 4 miles (6km) E of Lincoln
Residential village close to Lincoln. Attractive small Georgian church, built 1753, with cupola, colourful interior and original furnishings.

CHERTSEY Surrey TQ0466
Town on A320, 3 miles (5km) S of Staines
Pleasing town on River Thames with an 18th-century air, especially on Windsor Street and Guildford Street. River spanned by elegant seven-arch bridge built 1780s; marina to south, Abbey Barge Club to north. Scanty remains of splendid Benedictine abbey. Church maintains ancient custom of ringing curfew on abbey bell (29 September to 25 March).

CHESHAM Buckinghamshire SP9601
Town on A416, 3 miles (5km) NE of Amersham
London commuter town squeezed into valley of River Chess, on trade route through Chilterns used since prehistoric times. Source of Chess in Lowndes Park. The Moor public meadow has a riverside walk. Some old houses, largely Victorian church. Arrival of Metropolitan railway in 1889 opened area up to Londoners. Chesham Bois is leafy suburb among wooded hills to south.

CHESHUNT Hertfordshire TL3502
Town off A10, 14 miles (23km) N of London
Part of built-up stretch from London edge to Hoddesdon (see). Largely 20th century, but Churchgate, Church Lane area near 15th-century parish church, retains a little of earlier character. Dewhurst Charity School, 17th century. Victorian Gothic buildings of Bishop's College originally housed Countess of Huntingdon's Connection theology college, now council offices. See also Waltham Cross.

CHESIL BEACH Dorset SY5882
Scenic feature on S coast of England
A huge ridge of shingle which runs 8 miles (13km) on the shore from Portland to Abbotsbury, cutting off a long lagoon known as the Fleet.

CHESSINGTON Greater London TQ1863
District in borough of Kingston
Still a Surrey village in Edwardian days, rapidly suburbanised after World War I, now on edge of Greater London. Medieval flint church, St Mary the Virgin. Area is best known for Chessington World of Adventures, theme park with rides and zoo developed in 1980s by Madame Tussaud's organisation from former Chessington Zoo, opened 1931.

CHESTER Cheshire SJ4066
City off M53, 34 miles (55km) SW of Manchester
The history of this ancient walled city begins in AD79 with the Romans, who built the fortress *Deva* here, in a bend of the River Dee, as a base for military operations against the Welsh. Later it became a 'citizen fortress' and a trading centre until the Romans withdrew in AD383. They certainly left their mark; Chester now claims the largest Roman amphitheatre ever uncovered in Britain, superb city walls, and a remarkable collection of Roman artefacts now housed in the Grosvenor Museum. The Roodee, once the site of the Roman harbour, is now a racecourse, the only one in the country where horses race anti-clockwise!

Less is known about the following 600 years, although Saxons apparently settled in AD650. Saxon King Aethelred of Mercia is credited with founding the Church of St Peter and St Paul, later rededicated to St Werburgh, on the site of Chester's present cathedral. Chester was captured by William of Normandy in 1072, and was ruled by a succession of eight Norman earls until 1237. During this time the River Dee provided access to the sea and the city's port flourished, importing hides, Irish linen, French wines, Spanish fruits and spices, and exporting cheese, salt and candles. In 1092 a Benedictine abbey was founded at the Church of St Werburgh, which flourished until the Dissolution of the Monasteries in 1540. A year later it became the cathedral, now one of Chester's most significant landmarks.

During the Tudor period Chester continued to prosper, and the black and white buildings are still a hallmark of the city, as are the Rows, two-tier shopping galleries dating from the Middle Ages which contribute to Chester's popularity as a shopping centre.

CHESTER-LE-STREET Durham NZ2751
Town off A1(M), 6 miles (10km) N of Durham
As its name implies, the town stands astride what was once a Roman road and was originally a fort called *Conganium*. In AD883, the monks of Lindisfarne arrived with St Cuthbert's body and made Chester-le-Street the seat of the diocese of Lindisfarne. Only a few stones of the original church remain and these are incorporated into the fabric of the medieval Parish Church of St Mary and St Cuthbert. Inside the 14 Lumley Warriors lie in the Aisle of Tombs. Within the church is the Ankers House Museum, the anchorite where the Ankers order of monks lived their solitary lives of prayer in the 14th and 15th centuries. It houses a Roman stone with inscription, the shaft of a Saxon cross and the stone head of a Roman emperor.

Across the River Wear are the parklands of Lambton and Lumley Castle which provide an attractive backcloth. Lambton Castle is a mock castle built around the ancient Harraton Hall by the Lambton family between 1794 and 1932. Lumley Castle is genuinely 14th-century, now a luxury hotel.

CHESTERFIELD Derbyshire SK3871
Town on A61, 10 miles (16km) S of Sheffield
The crazily twisted 228ft (69m) lead-covered spire of St Mary and All Saints' Church is Chesterfield's best-known landmark, caused by the use of unseasoned timber. The large and fascinating church beneath has fine monuments to the Foljambe family from 1510.

The heart of the town is the popular open market, established for 800 years, and claimed to be England's largest. The market square narrowly escaped total change in the 1970s. Wiser counsel prevailed, however, traditional frontages were retained, and the Pavements Shopping Centre constructed behind to maintain the town's role as a major shopping centre.

The 16th-century timber-framed former Peacock inn, now the tourist information centre, and other jettied Tudor buildings confirm Chesterfield's long history, but the black and white timbering in Knifesmithgate is a 1930s whim, inspired by Chester. The impressive red-brick town hall opened in 1938.

Chesterfield's industrial development owed much to George Stephenson, who lived at Tapton House and is buried at Holy Trinity Church. Leisure facilities include Queen's Park Sports Centre, the Pomegranate Theatre, the Museum and Art Gallery telling the story of Chesterfield, the Winding Wheel entertainment centre, annual well-dressings, and numerous special events.

CHESTERFORD, LITTLE AND GREAT Essex TL5042
Villages on B184, 3 miles (5km) NW of Saffron Walden
Two smart villages on the River Cam. The Manor House (not open) at Little Chesterford is 12th century and may be Essex's oldest inhabited house.

CHESTERHOLM Northumberland NY7766
Roman site off B6318, 1 mile (2km) SE of Twice Brewed
The site of *Vindolanda*, an impressive Roman fort and civilian settlement excavation, with an excellent museum which illustrates all aspects of civilian and military life.

CHESTERTON Cambridgeshire TL4660
Area of NW Cambridge
Chesterton village has maintained a separate identity from Cambridge, although they adjoin. The village has a fine 14th-century tower house (not open).

CHESTERTON GREEN Warwickshire SP3558
Hamlet off B4100, 5 miles (8km) SE of Leamington Spa
Best known for its elegant stone windmill of 1632, reputedly by Inigo Jones. Exterior can be viewed.

CHESWARDINE Shropshire SJ7130
Village off A529, 4 miles (6km) SE of Market Drayton
St Swithin's Church has a highly embellished 15th-century tower and good 13th-century interior. Much glass by CE Kempe.

CHESWICK GREEN West Midlands SP1376
Village off B4102, 3 miles (5km) NW of Hockley Heath
The A34 separates this compact residential 'island' from Solihull to the north. Skirted by the River Blythe and the Stratford Canal.

CHETTLE Dorset ST9513
Village off A354, 3 miles (5km) S of Tollard Royal
On the edge of Cranborne Chase (see). Good brick cottages and Chettle House, also brick, of about 1710.

CHETWODE Buckinghamshire SP6429
Hamlet off A421, 5 miles (8km) SW of Buckingham
Remote place with church which belonged to small medieval priory. Fine 13th-century interior, with wall-paintings and notable stained glass.

CHEVENING Kent TQ4857
Hamlet off A25, 3 miles (5km) NW of Sevenoaks
Cluster of cottages and a church in wooded country at the gates of Chevening Park, official residence of Foreign Secretary.

CHEVIOT HILLS Northumberland
Hill range along English–Scottish border
A range of rounded, grass-covered hills which straddle the border of England and Scotland and carry the Northumberland National Park boundary from Carter Bar to Yetholm Mains, a distance of some 28 miles (45km). Excellent and challenging walking country. The highest peak, The Cheviot, is 2,684ft (816m). In the surrounding foothills, glacial features are apparent.

CHEW MAGNA Avon ST5763
Village on B3130, 6 miles (10km) S of Bristol
Almost a small town, with Georgian houses in the High Street and 15th-century church with a high tower, one of the famous Somerset church towers.

CHEW STOKE Avon ST5561
Village off B3114, 7 miles (11km) S of Bristol
Sizeable village, close to Chew Valley Lake, a reservoir created in 1956 to provide water for Bristol and now used for sailing and fishing as well.

CHEWTON MENDIP Somerset ST5953
Hamlet on A39, 6 miles (10km) NE of Wells
On the Mendips, with one of the famous Somerset church towers, one of the highest in the county – 126ft (38m) and beautiful. Chewton Cheese Dairy demonstrates cheese-making.

CHICHELEY Buckinghamshire SP9046
Village on A422, 2 miles (3km) NE of Newport Pagnell
Handsome 1720s house with naval collection relating to Admiral Beatty, World War I hero. Church with 18th-century chancel.

CHICHESTER West Sussex SU8604
City on A27, 9 miles (14km) E of Havant
Chichester preserves something of its origin as a Roman town: the walls follow the Roman lines and some of the streets mirror the Roman grid-iron pattern. The octagonal market cross of 1501 marks the crossing of the four main streets, today partly pedestrianised. The ring road to the southwest has cut across the former rough grazing land that used to press right up to the town walls.

Chichester was a port and owes much of its prosperous architecture to its coastal trade in the 18th and 19th centuries. Today, Georgian red-brick merchants' houses and flint and stone buildings give the city its character. The cathedral was begun in 1080 to replace Selsey which was rapidly being swallowed by the sea. It stands on Roman foundations and Roman mosaics found during restoration are displayed behind glass. It has a unique detached bell tower and unusual double aisles in the nave. The soaring spire is a replica of the one that collapsed in 1861. The intimate little cathedral close leads to the cloister.

There is plenty to see: among the most interesting areas are the Pallant which was fashionable in Georgian times; the little Georgian cameos of St John's Street and Little London; and St Martin's Square, Georgian again, but with the medieval St Mary's Hospital thrown in for good measure. There is busy modern shopping in North Street where the tiny church of St Olave is tucked among the shops which jostle the 1807 market house by John Nash. Further along the street is the large projecting council house of 1773, with a Roman inscription preserved under the porch.

Modern Chichester is bustling and alive. The Festival Theatre, opened in 1962, has established an enviable reputation.

CHICHESTER HARBOUR West Sussex SU7700
Scenic area 7 miles (11km) W of Chichester
An Area of Outstanding Natural Beauty, with fine open water and navigable creeks, developed as most important recreational harbour on south coast.

CHICKNEY Essex TL5728
Hamlet off B1051, 3 miles (5km) SW of Thaxted
Isolated, tree-sheltered Church of St Mary preserves its Saxon nave with original windows and finely carved 14th-century font.

CHIDDINGFOLD Surrey SU9635
Village on A283, 5 miles (8km) SE of Milford
Large village near Sussex border, centre of medieval glass-making industry of west Surrey. Large green with village pond, church and inn clustered at one end. Some good-looking 16th- and 17th-century houses. Further south along village street are 17th- and 19th-century terraces of tile-hung cottages.

CHIDDINGLY East Sussex TQ5414
Hamlet off A22, 4 miles (6km) NW of Hailsham
Tiny shrunken place, hidden from the modern world in a maze of lanes. Great house reduced to a fragment. Imposing monument to former owners in church (1612).

CHIDDINGSTONE Kent TQ5045
Village off B2027, 4 miles (6km) E of Edenbridge
Picturesque village owned by the National Trust, arguably prettiest place in Kent. Lovely street of weather-boarded and tile-hung 16th- and 17th-century houses. Chiddingstone Castle, a 17th-century house castellated in 19th century, houses a museum. The 'Chiding Stone', a block of sandstone, said to be where nagging wives were scolded.

CHIDEOCK Dorset SY4292
Village on A35, 3 miles (5km) W of Bridport
The village runs up and down steep hills, with some thatched stone cottages and later houses in the local orangey stone. To the south is Seatown, right on the shore. Golden Cap (National Trust) to the west is the highest sea cliff on the south coast (618ft/188m) and gives wonderful views along the coast and inland.

The brick church at Chignall Smealy.

CHIGNALL SMEALY Essex TL6611
Hamlet off A130, 4 miles (6km) NW of Chelmsford
Also called Brick Chignall. The brick Tudor church even has a brick font. Some of the old houses are of local brick, too.

CHIGWELL Essex TQ4494
Town on A113, 3 miles (5km) NE of Woodford
London commuter town in the Roding Valley close to the M11, known for its schools and not such an 'out of the way rural place' as it was when Dickens came here and used the venerable King's Head inn as the model for the 'Maypole' in *Barnaby Rudge*. Imposingly Victorianised church with some attractive Georgian houses.

CHILCOMB Hampshire SU5028
Hamlet off A31, 2 miles (3km) SE of Winchester
Rustic hamlet with the tiny Norman church away under the downs.

CHILCOMPTON Somerset ST6451
Village off B3355, 2 miles (3km) SW of Midsomer Norton
In the Mendips, the older part with several stone Georgian houses and a stream by the road.

CHILD OKEFORD Dorset ST8312
Village off A357, 3 miles (5km) SE of Sturminster Newton
A big village but properly rural. To the east the tall hill of Hambledon with the clear ramparts of its Iron Age hillfort on top.

CHILDREY Oxfordshire SU3687
Village on B4001, 2 miles (3km) W of Wantage
Lying beneath the steep Hackpen Hill, this traditional village has a church with fine medieval features.

CHILDSWICKHAM Hereford and Worcester SP0738
Village off A44, 2 miles (3km) NW of Broadway
On the Cotswold fringe, the old centre is a picturesque mixture of timber, brick and stone cottages, together with manor house and church.

CHILDWALL Merseyside SJ4189
Village on A5080, in W outskirts of Liverpool
A village dating from Norse times with Liverpool's only remaining medieval church, All Saints', dating from the 14th century.

CHILGROVE West Sussex SU8314
Hamlet off B2141, 3 miles (5km) NW of Singleton
Handful of cottages and inn in verdant wooded valley of scattered farms with a long history. Remains of two Roman villas.

CHILHAM Kent TR0653
Village off A28, 6 miles (10km) SW of Canterbury
Recognised beauty spot set high on the downs above the Stour Valley. Village of delightful, pretty houses with rambling flowers. Church and timbered cottages grouped around square by the castle gates where Pilgrims' Fayre is held annually in medieval costume. Castle of noble pedigree replaced in 1616 by mansion with gardens laid out by Tradescant.

CHILLENDEN Kent TR2653
Village off B2046, 3 miles (5km) SE of Wingham
Village with small Norman church in wooded country overlooked by great white post mill of 1868, restored in 1958.

CHILLINGHAM Northumberland NU0525
Village off B6348, 4 miles (6km) E of Wooler
A charming village with a medieval castle complete with dungeons. The castle dates from 12th century with Tudor and Georgian additions. Renovations are ongoing and it is open to the public for the first time in 800 years. The Wild White Cattle at Chillingham Castle are a unique herd which has roamed freely for hundreds of years. Ross Castle hillfort is near by.

CHILMARK Wiltshire ST9732
Village on B3089, 8 miles (13km) W of Wilton
Famous Chilmark stone, used for Salisbury Cathedral and many other buildings, was quarried here. Many 17th-century Chilmark stone cottages in the village.

CHILTERN HILLS Buckinghamshire/Hertfordshire/Oxfordshire
Scenic area in Central England
Largely an official Area of Outstanding Natural Beauty, the chalk Chilterns range crosses Oxfordshire, Buckinghamshire, Hertfordshire and Bedfordshire from Goring on the River Thames to the Luton area. The western end of the range is noted for beech woods, with deer and abundant birdlife – Burnham Beeches being the best-known example – and the beech trees supported the traditional Chilterns furniture industry. At the eastern end are rolling grass downs, such as Dunstable Downs. The steep scarp faces north and behind it the land slopes gently down towards London. The highest point is Coombe Hill, rising to 852ft (260m) above Wendover.

The main routes from London to the northwest run through gaps in the Chilterns. The chalk is mixed with flint, accounting for the area's flint churches. For centuries sparsely settled, for lack of springs and surface water, it remained wild, unruly country until the 19th-century railways opened the Chilterns up to settlement by Londoners. Today, commuter towns and villages fill the valleys and lower slopes. On the higher ground substantial unspoiled areas are preserved, with much land owned by the National Trust.

CHILTHORNE DOMER Somerset ST5219
Village off A37, 3 miles (5km) NW of Yeovil
Stone village. Interesting medieval church has an unusual square bell-cote over the west gable.

CHILTON Buckinghamshire SP6811
Village off B4011, 4 miles (6km) N of Thame
Attractive village on high ground with good views and cottage gardens. Church with stumpy tower, curious 13th-century figure of mailed knight high on exterior nave wall, massive Croke monument and Loos battlefield cross from World War I. Chilton House, 18th century, now a nursing home. Dorton House (limited opening), in next village to north, now school.

CHILTON FOLIAT Wiltshire SU3170
Village on B4192, 2 miles (3km) NW of Hungerford
Right on the River Kennet (very wide here), with older brick houses and cottages.

CHILTON POLDEN Somerset ST3740
Village off A39, 5 miles (8km) NE of Bridgwater
On the Polden ridge; Chilton Priory is a folly castle built in the 1830s.

CHILVERS COTON Warwickshire SP3690
District off A444, in S area of Nuneaton
The church where novelist George Eliot was baptised contains craft work by German prisoners who repaired it after wartime bomb damage.

CHILWORTH Surrey TQ0347
Village on A248, 2 miles (3km) SE of Guildford
Village once famous for gunpowder mills, below the steep wooded North Downs, with St Martha's Chapel, rebuilt following explosion, 1854, on Pilgrims' Way.

CHINGFORD Greater London TQ3894
Town in borough of Waltham Forest
Close to massive River Lea reservoirs. Queen Elizabeth Hunting Lodge, 16th century, is now small museum of Epping Forest (see).

CHINLEY Derbyshire SK0482
Village on B6062, 2 miles (3km) NW of Chapel-en-le-Frith
Two massive viaducts testify to skills of Victorian railway engineers in coping with Peak District gradients. Galleried 18th-century Independent Chapel.

CHINNOR Oxfordshire SP7501
Village on B4445, 4 miles (6km) SE of Thame
A village below the Chilterns whose attractions defy the giant cement works. Medieval church of exceptional interest, with astonishing collection of brasses.

CHIPPENHAM Cambridgeshire TL6669
Village on B1085, 4 miles (6km) N of Newmarket
'Model village' created by Lord Orford in 17th century. Has handsome school (1714), and present mansion (not open, built 1886). Chippenham Fen is a well-preserved peat fen.

CHIPPENHAM Wiltshire ST9173
Town on A4, 12 miles (19km) NE of Bath
A town since Saxon times, now large and bustling. The old centre is tucked into a loop of the River Avon, with the best parts around the church (with an unusual imitation medieval spire and tower of 1633). The Old Yelde Hall, formerly the town hall, is 16th century, timber-framed and now the museum. Maud Heath left money in 1474 for a causeway from Wick Hill. Statue to her of 1838. Other timber-framed buildings, and Georgian houses.

CHIPPERFIELD Hertfordshire TL0401
Village off A41, 4 miles (6km) S of Hemel Hempstead
Attractive tree-shaded common, cricket ground and veteran Two Brewers pub, with memories of great 19th-century prize fighters who trained here.

CHIPPING Lancashire SD6243
Village off B6243, 4 miles (6km) N of Longridge
Started life as a market place and later became an important wool centre. In 17th century, a variety of cottage industries grew up, including chair-making. Factory remains, and its original waterwheel can still be seen. Famous son, John Brabin, bequeathed the grammar school and almshouses, and once lived in the post office.

CHIPPING BARNET (OR HIGH BARNET) Greater London TQ2496
Town in borough of Barnet
Successively market town, 17th-century spa, coaching town on old Great North road, then developed as suburb in 19th century. Parish Church of St John the Baptist with monuments and 1875 tower by Butterfield. Barnet Museum of local history, Wood Street, has material on 1471 battle (see Monken Hadley). The annual September fair survives.

CHIPPING CAMPDEN Gloucestershire SP1539
Small town on B4081, 8 miles (13km) SE of Evesham
A market centre that grew rich on wool in the Middle Ages, Chipping Campden offers a harmonious main street lined with Cotswold stone buildings ranging over six centuries. Outstanding among them are the 14th-century house of wool merchant William Grevel, the Woolstaplers' Hall of 1487 (now a museum of local life), the 15th-century grammar school, the pillared market hall of 1627 and the elegant 18th-century Bedfont House. The large Church of St James has the rich embellishments of the late 15th century and contains some fine monuments to wool merchants, including Sir Baptist Hicks, who, in 1612, endowed the picturesque almshouses in Church Street. The ruins of his house, Campden Manor, stand near by.

The preservation of the town owes much to the Campden Trust, a group of craftsmen inspired by CR Ashbee, who moved his Guild of Handicrafts here from London in 1902, inaugurating a craft tradition that still survives. Dover's Hill (National trust), to the east, is the site each June of the 'Cotswold Olympicks'. These traditional games, established by Robert Dover in 1612 and revived in 1951, are followed by the Scuttlebrook Wake Fair on the following day.

CHIPPING NORTON Oxfordshire SP3127
Town on A44, 18 miles (29km) NW of Oxford
On a breezy hillside, this old wool town has handsome buildings and pleasant shops around its market square, including a 19th-century town hall. The fine 15th-century church stands between earthworks of Norman castle and almshouses of 1640, but even more striking is the huge Tweed Mill of 1872 (now flats) in valley to the west.

CHIPPING ONGAR Essex TL5503
Small town on A128, 6 miles (10km) NW of Brentwood
Shopping centre, as name (from 'cheaping', 'market') implies. Big Norman castle mound, Norman church. Writer of *Twinkle, twinkle, little star* lived here.

CHIPPING SODBURY Avon ST7282
Town on A432, 11 miles (18km) NE of Bristol
The wide main street is lined with stone buildings, ranging from the 16th century to the 20th, all in scale with each other. The 'Chipping' part of the name means 'market', which was held in the broad street. Big early 16th-century church tower.

CHIPPING WARDEN Northamptonshire SP4948
Village on A361, 6 miles (10km) NE of Banbury
Steps of market cross and 'Chipping' name indicate existence as medieval market site. Many old cottages and 16th-century manor house.

CHIPSTEAD Surrey TQ2757
Village off A23, 5 miles (8km) NW of Redhill
Old Chipstead high on downs with lovely church by green pleasant Victorian houses by Ellmore Pool and new housing in Chipstead Valley.

CHIRBURY Shropshire SO2698
Village on A490, 3 miles (5km) NE of Montgomery
Big medieval/18th-century church has the timber-framed village school behind it. Stunning views from Mitchell's Fold, Bronze Age stone circle, on hills above.

CHIRK Clwyd SJ2937
Small town off A5, 5 miles (8km) N of Oswestry
Stands at gateway to Vale of Ceiriog. Chirk Castle (National Trust) is exceptional for uninterrupted occupation since 13th-century founding. Home of Myddleton family for 400 years, it juxtaposes dungeon and stateroom. Offa's Dyke crosses castle's parkland, which is entered by elaborate iron gates, work of the Davies brothers of Bersham. Near by, Telford's aqueduct carries Shropshire Union Canal high over river valley.

CHIRNSIDE Borders NT8756
Village on B6355, 6 miles (10km) E of Duns
Philosopher David Hume retired here in 1749. Jim Clark, motor-racing world champion, lived here and is buried in churchyard; clock commemorates him.

CHIRTON Wiltshire SU0757
Village off A342, 5 miles (8km) SE of Devizes
In the Vale of Pewsey, with thatched cottages and Georgian houses.

CHISELDON Wiltshire SU1880
Village on B4005, 4 miles (6km) SE of Swindon
Growing fast because close to Swindon. Richard Jefferies, the famous countryside writer, was born at Coate farmhouse to the north in 1848, and the building is now a museum dedicated to his life and work (limited opening).

CHISLEHAMPTON Oxfordshire SU5999
Village on B480, 7 miles (11km) SE of Oxford
The gem of this small village beside the River Thame is its tiny church built in 1762, complete with elegant Georgian fittings.

CHISLEHURST Greater London TQ4470
District in borough of Bromley
Well-to-do suburb with pleasant common. Church of St Nicholas is 15th century with impressive monuments and glass; also fine Victorian Church of the Annunciation. Chislehurst Caves, extensive underground system left over from ancient chalk mines, date back to Roman period. They were used during World War II as air-raid shelter.

CHISLET Kent TR2264
Village off A28, 4 miles (6km) SE of Herne Bay
Scattered north Kent village on marshy land overlooking Chislet Marshes, once an arm of the sea which has silted up since Roman times.

CHISWELLGREEN (OR CHISWELL GREEN) Hertfordshire TL1304
Village off A405, 2 miles (3km) SW of St Albans
Home of 30,000 rose plants in the Gardens of the Rose, the Royal National Rose Society's scented showpiece collection.

CHISWICK Greater London TQ2078
District in borough of Hounslow
In loop of River Thames, developed after railways arrived. Strand-on-the-Green riverside houses, City Barge and Bull's Head pubs. St Nicholas, Church Street, largely rebuilt 1880s, at heart of original village, with old houses around. Chiswick House was Lord Burlington's grand 18th-century house to show off his pictures; grounds by William Kent. Hogarth's House was artist's summer place.

CHITTERNE Wiltshire ST9843
Village on B390, 8 miles (13km) E of Warminster
In a chalk valley, with a stream running through, little triangular green and prominent chequered flint and stone church tower (1863).

The handsome church tower at Chittlehampton.

CHITTLEHAMPTON Devon SS6325
Village off B3227, 5 miles (8km) W of South Molton
Thatched cottages and a village square, with the church prominent. It is dedicated to St Hieritha, a local martyr, who was cut to pieces by heathen locals with scythes in the 6th century. Large, mostly 15th-century, still with a shrine. Best tower in Devon.

CHITTOE Wiltshire ST9566
Village off A342, 5 miles (8km) SE of Chippenham
A few thatched cottages and a church of 1845.

CHIVELSTONE Devon SX7838
Hamlet off A379, 8 miles (13km) SE of Kingsbridge
At the centre of the remote windswept peninsula cut off by the Kingsbridge estuary.

CHOBHAM Surrey SU9762
Village on A319, 3 miles (5km) NW of Woking
Compact village centre with pleasant cottages, church and small green. To the north, birch trees, heath and gorse of expansive Chobham Common.

CHOLDERTON Wiltshire SU2242
Village on A338, 5 miles (8km) E of Amesbury
Tiny village, with flint and brick cottages. The church of 1840 has a medieval hammerbeam roof brought here from Ipswich.

CHOLESBURY Buckinghamshire SP9307
Village off A416, 4 miles (6km) NW of Chesham
Among the beech woods of the Chilterns' northern edge. Village church is set inside the earthworks of a prehistoric fort.

CHOLLERFORD Northumberland NY9170
Roman site on B6318, 4 miles (6km) N of Hexham
Chesters, a large 2nd-century Roman fort whose visible remains include defences and the commandant's house as well as the regimental bathhouse. In AD635 King Oswald of Northumbria defeated Caedwallon, King of North Wales at Heavenfield. This led to the re-establishment of Christianity in Northumbria. The battlefield is marked by a wooden roadside cross.

CHOLLERTON Northumberland NY9371
Village on A6079, 5 miles (8km) N of Hexham
In the Church of St Giles, Roman monolithic columns are incorporated into the 12th-century nave.

CHOLSEY Oxfordshire SU5886
Village off A329, 2 miles (3km) SW of Wallingford
Novelist Agatha Christie and her husband are buried beside the Norman church of this expanding village.

CHOPWELL Tyne and Wear NZ1158
Village off B6315, 3 miles (5km) SE of Prudhoe
Chopwell found fame during the General Strike of 1926 when, due to its miners' militancy, it acquired the name 'Little Moscow'.

CHORLEY Lancashire SD5817
Town on A6, 10 miles (16km) NW of Bolton
Compact and atmospheric, traditional market town with a unique weekly 'Flat Iron' market, named after the ancient practice of laying out wares on the ground. Astley Hall, now owned by the Tatton family, has been home to the Charnocks of Charnock Richard and the Brooke family. Duxbury Park contains an abundance of wildlife including red squirrels, foxes and herons.

CHORLEYWOOD Hertfordshire TQ0396
Town on A404, 2 miles (3km) NW of Rickmansworth
Once Charley Wood, now a select London commuter town in the Chilterns, popular with media people, entertainers and well-to-do businessmen. Views over Chess Valley. Grew relatively late, after the railway's arrival in 1880s. Extensive common with woods, abundant gorse and heather, golf course. St Andrew's Church gained reputation as charismatic centre in 1990s.

CHORLTON CUM HARDY Greater Manchester SJ8293
District in SW area of Manchester
Hough End Hall is the only major Elizabethan mansion in the Manchester area. The district is named after two former villages.

CHRISTCHURCH Dorset SZ1592
Town on A35, 5 miles (8km) E of Bournemouth
A large town which has grown from a little Saxon settlement on the junction of the rivers Stour and Avon. It gained a medieval castle, of which only ruins remain (the so-called Constable's House was the castle hall) and had an important priory. Most of the priory buildings have disappeared, but the church became the parish church and so survives. It is the best medieval church in Dorset, and the longest parish church in the country. The nave, crossing and north transept are all Norman – the transept decoration is particularly good outside. Lots of good tombs and chantries.

Many riverside walks and views, and a pretty high street. Place Mill is open, and there are three museums – Southern Electric Museum, The Tricycle Museum and Red House Museum with local history, geology and so on.

Hengistbury Head, to the south, is a heathy headland which forms one side of the large natural harbour. Two long sand spits make another side. The Head, a nature reserve, is the only really wild place on this built-up coastline. The prominent double bank cutting it off probably dates from the late Iron Age when Hengistbury was a port.

CHRISTIAN MALFORD Wiltshire ST9678
Village off B4069, 4 miles (6km) NE of Chippenham
On the River Avon, with a 13th- and 14th-century church.

CHRISTLETON Cheshire SJ4465
Village off A41, 3 miles (5km) E of Chester
Picturesque village on the Shropshire Union Canal was Parliamentarians' headquarters for the attack on Royalist Chester. Name means 'Christ's little town'.

CHRISTMAS COMMON Oxfordshire SU7193
Hamlet off B480, 2 miles (3km) SE of Watlington
A Victorian church and a scatter of cottages in beech woods on top of the Chilterns.

CHRISTOW Devon SX8385
Village off B3193, 4 miles (6km) NW of Chudleigh
In an old mining area. Fine 1630 granite church tower. Big reservoirs to the west supply Torquay with water. Two miles (3km) south is Canonteign Falls and Nature Reserve.

CHUDLEIGH Devon SX8679
Small town off A38, 5 miles (8km) N of Newton Abbot
A small market town, now bypassed; mostly burnt down in 1807, so has many early 19th-century buildings. One mile (2km) south is Ugbrooke House, of 1760 in Norman style with fine Adam decoration inside. Good parkland.

CHULMLEIGH Devon SS6814
Small town on B3096, 8miles (13km) S of South Molton
A small, quiet hilltop town which was left off the turnpike road in 1830 and later bypassed by the railways. Pleasant buildings and good views, especially over the Little Dart River.

CHURCH Lancashire SD7429
Town on A679, immediately W of Accrington
Settlement here since 1200. Calico-printing industry established here by an uncle of Sir Robert Peel.

CHURCH EATON Staffordshire SJ8417
Village off A518, 6 miles (10km) SW of Stafford
Scattered village in pleasant countryside near Shropshire border. Interesting church has fine east window.

CHURCH FENTON North Yorkshire SE5136
Village off A162, 2 miles (3km) NE of Sherburn in Elmet
Local magnesian limestone gives a distinctive colour to building stone. Handsome church with unusual carved effigy.

CHURCH HANBOROUGH Oxfordshire SP4213
Village off A4095, 5 miles (8km) NE of Witney
On a popular walking route, the hillside village overlooks the Evenlode Valley. Its rewarding church, with notable chancel screen, is much visited.

CHURCH KNOWLE Dorset SY9481
Village off A351, 1 mile (2km) W of Corfe Castle
A Purbeck village, with local stone farms and cottages. Interesting medieval church.

CHURCH LANGTON Leicestershire SP7293
Village off A6, 4 miles (6km) N of Market Harborough
One of attractive group of villages called The Langtons. Eighteenth-century rectory built for William Hanbury, who organised first parish church performance of Handel's *Messiah*, 1759.

CHURCH LAWFORD Warwickshire SP4576
Village on A428, 4 miles (6km) W of Rugby
Small village with interesting church, attractively situated on upper reaches of the River Avon.

CHURCH LEIGH Staffordshire SK0235
Village off A50, 5 miles (8km) NW of Uttoxeter
Beside the River Blythe and at the centre of 11 hamlets forming the village of Leigh. Notable church windows include some by Burne-Jones.

CHURCH MINSHULL Cheshire SJ6660
Village on B5074, 4 miles (6km) NW of Crewe
Typical 17th-century black and white Cheshire village by the River Weaver, home of Elizabeth Minshull before she became John Milton's wife in 1660.

CHURCH STOWE Northamptonshire SP6357
see Stowe IX Churches

CHURCH STRETTON Shropshire SO4593
Town on A49, 12 miles (19km) S of Shrewsbury
Tucked beneath the Long Mynd (see), much of the town's architecture and character derives from brief 19th-century popularity as a spa. Long Mynd hotel, high above town, was the hydro. Church, mainly Norman and 13th century, has rare *sheila-na-gig* (pagan fertility figure) over door. Nearby Cardingmill Valley (National Trust) is a dramatic ravine carved out of the hillside.

CHURCH WILNE Derbyshire SK4431
Hamlet off B6540, 3 miles (5km) SW of Long Eaton
Willoughby family monuments in church, now separated from village whose residents moved to escape frequent flooding of River Derwent.

CHURCHDOWN Gloucestershire SO8819
Village off A40, 4 miles (6km) E of Gloucester
Visitors come here to climb Chosen Hill, on which stands a church of Saxon origin with interesting Norman and medieval features.

CHURCHILL Avon ST4459
Village off A368, 3 miles (5km) S of Congresbury
At the foot of the Mendip Hills. Ancestors of the Churchills in the church, and on the high hill to the south, Dolebury Camp, one of the largest Iron Age hill-forts in the country.

CHURCHILL Oxfordshire SP2824
Village on B4450, 3 miles (5km) SW of Chipping Norton
Only the chancel remains of a church well known to Warren Hastings, Governor-General of India, and William Smith, pioneer geologist, both born here.

CHURCHTOWN Lancashire SD4843
Village on A586, 1 mile (2km) S of Garstang
Historic town which has changed little. St Helen's Church contains examples of almost every style of architecture since the Norman Conquest.

CHURSTON FERRERS Devon SX9056
Village on A3022, 1 mile (2km) W of Brixham
One of the few wild areas in Torbay; still rural, with rocky cliffs and coves.

CHURT Surrey SU8538
Village on A287, 3 miles (5km) NW of Hindhead
In hilly wooded country between sandy commons and clay vale. Attractive stone, brick and tile-hung cottages clustering around green at crossroads.

CHYSAUSTER ANCIENT VILLAGE Cornwall SW4735
Prehistoric site off B3311, 3 miles (5km) NW of Gulval
Famous group of courtyard houses (English Heritage), once thought to be Iron Age, now thought to be Roman. The remains are impressive – walls survive to virtually their original height (nearly 6ft/2m in some cases) and all that is missing are the roofs. Small houses cluster around open courtyards, with the groups enclosed by outer walls. One roof has been reconstructed.

CILCAIN Clwyd SJ1765
Village off A541, 4 miles (6km) W of Mold
In Clwydian Range. Medieval church with double nave, hammerbeam roof, stained glass. Path up to summit of Moel Famau.

CILGERRAN Dyfed SN1943
Village off A484, 2 miles (3km) SE of Cardigan
Dwarfed by crag-top castle, a celebrated River Teifi beauty spot. Annual coracle regatta. Welsh Wildlife Centre close by.

CINDERFORD Gloucestershire SO6514
Town on A4151, 11 miles (18km) W of Gloucester
A former mining town whose utilitarian character is a reminder of the industrial history and distinctive culture of the Forest of Dean.

CIRENCESTER Gloucestershire SP0201
Town off A419, 14 miles (23km) NW of Swindon
Britain's second largest Roman town, strategically placed at the crossing of the Fosse Way and Ermin Way, became the site of a large Saxon abbey, prospered as a centre of the medieval wool trade and went on to become an important market town. Some of this history is still visible in a Roman amphitheatre (English Heritage) and buildings that include the Norman abbey gatehouse, the remains of the 13th-century St John's Hospital, the Weavers' Hall of the 1430s and the old grammar school of 1464, as well as an array of houses of the 17th and 18th centuries.

St John's is one of the finest 'wool' churches of the Cotswolds, mainly 15th century, with a tall tower, a huge and highly embellished south porch (used for many years as a town hall), several 16th-century chapels and an exceptional array of medieval brasses and later monuments.

Cirencester's Roman story is told at the Corinium Museum in Park Street. The vast and magnificent Cirencester Park was established outside the town by Lord Bathurst at the turn of the 17th century.

CISSBURY RING West Sussex TQ1408
see Findon

CLACKMANNAN Central NS9191
Town off A907, 2 miles (3km) E of Alloa
Small erstwhile wool-manufacturing town with old tolbooth and stepped town cross. The virtually derelict 79ft (24m) Clackmannan Tower dates from 14th–15th centuries and has connections with Robert Bruce. Near by is the Gartmorn Dam Country Park with islanded bird-watching reservoir.

CLACTON-ON-SEA Essex TM1715
Town on A133, 13 miles (21km) SE of Colchester
A byword for brash, bright and breezy seaside atmosphere and entertainment, with a 7 mile (11km) stretch of sand, colourful public gardens and all the expected amusements, it started life unobtrusively as Great Clacton, a village 1 mile (2km) inland. The seaside resort was developed for profit from the 1860s on by a railway promoter backed by a steamship company, to attract London holiday-makers. A small pier, later greatly enlarged, and the first hotel, the Royal, opened early in the 1870s and the arrival of the railway in the next decade sealed the resort's success.

Lively attractions include the pier with rides and cafés, the Magic City indoor play centre for children, the Living Ocean aquarium with sharks, rays, sealions, touch pool, daily fish feeding. Princes Theatre for concerts, big-name stars and everything from wrestling to ballet. The town is a showcase of Victorian suburban architecture. Jaywick Sands is a bungalow development along the shore to the southwest.

CLAINES Hereford and Worcester SO8558
Hamlet off A38, 3 miles (5km) N of Worcester
The old village, now a satellite of Worcester, has a 15th-century church and a collection of gracious Georgian houses.

CLANFIELD Oxfordshire SP2801
Village on A4095, 4 miles (6km) N of Faringdon
The 17th-century Plough inn is one of the attractions of this straggling village with a strong Cotswold flavour.

CLAPHAM Bedfordshire TL0352
Village on A6, 2 miles (3km) NW of Bedford
On the Great Ouse, known for massive Saxon church tower, possibly built for defence against the Danes.

CLAPHAM Greater London TQ2975
District in borough of Lambeth
Rows of later 19th-century and 20th-century terraced houses. Fairs and circuses on Clapham Common.

CLAPHAM North Yorkshire SD7469
Village off A65, 6 miles (10km) NW of Settle
Popular centre for Three Peaks region, with Gaping Gill, the largest pothole in country. The cave chamber is large enough to house York Minster; it was first descended by a Frenchman in 1895. Reginald Farrer, from a local family, became a celebrated botanist specialising in alpine species. The local nature trails commemorate his work. Also Ingleborough Cave.

CLAPHAM West Sussex TQ0906
Village off A280, 4 miles (6km) NW of Worthing
Unpretentious village set on hillside on South Downs with 13th-century church with memorials to the Shelley family.

CLAPTON Somerset ST4106
Village on B3165, 3 miles (5km) SW of Crewkerne
Small village with Clapton Court (gardens only open).

CLAPTON-IN-GORDANO Avon ST4773
Village off B3128, 3 miles (5km) SE of Portishead
The name means 'Clappa's enclosure, wedge-shaped, in a vale'! Long thin village, with the church, separate, strikingly placed on a steep hill.

CLARBOROUGH Nottinghamshire SK7383
Village on A620, 2 miles (3km) NE of Retford
Canal-side village, not far from Sherwood Forest, with medieval church restored in the 19th century.

CLARE Suffolk TL7745
Town on A1092, 6 miles (10km) W of Long Melford
Clare commanded an important position on one of England's main medieval roads – the Icknield Way. A Norman castle was raised here in the 11th century by the de Clare family, and the jagged walls and towering mound can still be seen. There is a splendid pargetted 15th-century priests' house, and a pleasant park.

CLARENCEFIELD Dumfries and Galloway NY0968
Village on B724, 7 miles (11km) W of Annan
Cumlongon Castle, well-preserved 15th-century tower with massive walls, lies just to the west of the village.

CLATTERINGSHAWS LOCH Dumfries and Galloway NX5476
Reservoir on A712, 5 miles (8km) W of New Galloway
Hydro-electric reservoir. Nearby is Bruce's Stone, marking Robert the Bruce's victory over English in 1307and Galloway Deer Museum.

CLAUGHTON Lancashire SD5566
Village on A683, 6 miles (10km) NE of Lancaster
Pronounced 'Clafton'. St Chad's Church contains one of the oldest bells in the country, dated 1296.

CLAVERDON Warwickshire SP1965
Village on A4189, 3 miles (5km) E of Henley-in-Arden
The Stone Building and imposing tomb in the church are reminders that this was the domain of a branch of the Spencers of Althorp.

CLAVERING Essex TL4731
Village on B1038, 7 miles (11km) N of Bishop's Stortford
On the diminutive River Stort. Earthworks of vanished castle, 15th-century church with good stained glass, photogenic ancient guildhall.

CLAVERLEY Shropshire SO7993
Village off A454, 5 miles (8km) E of Bridgnorth
Picturesque place with much timber-framing. Among many interesting features in the church is a painted frieze of about 1200, reminiscent of the Bayeux tapestry.

CLAVERTON Avon ST7864
Village on A36, 3 miles (5km) E of Bath
Tiny village on the Avon and Kennet and Avon Canal, famous for Claverton Manor, the American Museum in Britain. Neo-classical mansion of 1820, with superb reconstructed and furnished rooms ranging from 17th-century New England to Greek Revival of the 1830s. Good gardens too, and a folk art gallery.

CLAY CROSS Derbyshire SK3963
Town on A61, 5 miles (8km) S of Chesterfield
Industrial town on high ridge, developed after George Stephenson found coal while building railway tunnel. Engineering, iron works, busy market.

CLAYBROOKE, MAGNA AND PARVA Leicestershire SP4988
Villages on B577, 4 miles (6km) NW of Lutterworth
Twin villages near High Cross junction of Roman Fosse Way and Watling Street. Formerly centres for frame-knitting industry. Working watermill (limited opening).

CLAYDON Oxfordshire SP4549
Village off A423, 6miles (10km) N of Banbury
Simple Norman church and Granary Museum showing countryside bygones are worth visiting. Oxford Canal narrowboats negotiate laborious series of locks near by.

CLAYDON Suffolk TM1349
Village off A14 (A45), 4 miles (6km) NW of Ipswich
The Church of St Peter was declared redundant in 1975, and stands forlorn on the hill overlooking the village. Chalk was quarried here.

CLAYPOLE Lincolnshire SK8449
Village off A1, 5 miles (8km) SE of Newark-on-Trent
Substantial village, beside River Witham and Nottinghamshire border, whose impressive cruciform church with tall spire is one of Lincolnshire's glories.

CLAYTON West Sussex TQ2914
Village on A273, 6 miles (10km) N of Brighton
Tucked under the South Downs, a village of ancient buildings famed for 12th-century wall-paintings in church and Jack and Jill windmills on hilltop.

CLEADON Tyne and Wear NZ3862
Village on A1018, 3 miles (5km) S of South Shields
The village lies north of Sunderland near the North Sea coast. It is home to the South Shields Golf Club and Cleadon Country Park.

CLEARWELL Gloucestershire SO5608
Village on B4228, 2 miles (3km) S of Coleford
This ancient iron-mining centre has a flamboyant Victorian church in red, white and blue stone and a 'castle' that is in fact a battlemented 'Gothick' mansion of 1727 (now a hotel). Its main attraction, however, is the extensive series of miners' tunnels known as Clearwell Caves, where the more accessible and spectacular areas are illuminated for visitors.

CLEATOR Cumbria NY0115
Village on A5086, 2 miles (3km) N of Egremont
Cleator Moor, former iron-mining district built on limestone between Whitehaven coal-measures and the Skiddaw slate of the fells. Village of Cleator to the south.

CLECKHEATON West Yorkshire SE1825
Town off M62, 4 miles (6km) NW of Dewsbury
The site of a Roman iron workings where heaps of clinker were identified in the 18th century.

The old village cross in Clearwell.

CLEE ST MARGARET Shropshire SO5684

Village off B4364, 7 miles (11km) NE of Ludlow

Attractive hillside settlement with one road submerged under a stream. Tiny church has early Norman chancel. Good views from Nordybank, hillfort to northeast.

CLEEHILL Shropshire SO5975

Village on A4117, 5 miles (8km) E of Ludlow

Village resulting from 19th-century quarrying operations. Car access to spectacular viewpoint just under summit of Titterstone Clee at 1,740ft (533m).

CLEETHORPES Humberside TA3008

Town on A1098, immediately S of Grimsby

One of England's finest seaside resorts with over 3 miles (5km) of golden beaches; they can be hazardous, as the tide comes in very fast. Old part of the town is called Old Clee and has a Norman church. There are parades and carnivals throughout the summer, an all-weather Leisure Centre, a totally refurbished pier and Jungle World.

CLEEVE HILL Gloucestershire SO9822

Village on B4632, 4 miles (6km) NE of Cheltenham

A scattered hillside settlement lying beneath the highest point in the Cotswolds, 1,083ft (330m) here. Views stretch to Wales and the Malverns.

CLEEVE PRIOR Hereford and Worcester SP0849

Village on B4085, 5 miles (8km) NE of Evesham

Overlooks River Avon from its position on Cleeve Hill. Elizabethan manor house and inn, church with notable 1902 window. Nature reserve near by.

CLEISH Tayside NT0998

Village off B9097, 3 miles (5km) SW of Kinross

Situated at foot of Cleish Hills, with 16th-century castle and rare burial boundary stone in churchyard wall.

CLENT Hereford and Worcester SO9279

Village off A491, 4 miles (6km) SE of Stourbridge

Attractively sited in a fold of the Clent Hills (National Trust), 5 mile (8km) range that rises to 1,000ft (300m) and forms a popular 'green lung' on the edge of the Birmingham conurbation. Clent Hills Country Park to northeast of village offers woodland and hillside walks.

CLEOBURY MORTIMER Shropshire SO6775

Large village on A4117, 10 miles (16km) E of Ludlow

The main street has a distinguished Queen Anne house and buildings of the 17th and 18th centuries. Elegant school building of 1740. The church, with its twisted spire, stands above the street and contains good Norman and 13th-century features. East window commemorates poet William Langland, believed to have been born here in about 1330.

CLERKENWELL Greater London TQ3182

District in Camden and Islington

Grew up round Clerks' Well, spring supplying medieval monasteries here. St John's Gate, 1504, survives from Knights Hospitallers' priory, with museum of Order of St John. Priory church restored after wartime bombing. Charterhouse almshouse (limited opening). Marx Memorial Library, Clerkenwell Green, honours Karl Marx. Sadler's Wells Theatre, Rosebery Avenue, famous for ballet, and opera by visiting companies.

CLEVEDON Avon ST4171

Town on B3124, 8 miles (13km) NE of Weston-super-Mare

A Regency and early Victorian resort, overtaken by Weston-Super-Mare later because Clevedon was not on the railway. Still with many villas, and a large church of 1839 and a long but simple iron pier of 1868. Clevedon Court (National Trust) is inland, an interesting medieval manor house with a 12th-century tower, 13th-century hall, and 18th-century terraced garden.

CLEVELAND HILLS North Yorkshire

Hill range in North York Moors National Park

The distinctive summits of the Cleveland Hills, like Roseberry Topping, escaped the effects of ice pressing round their slopes during various Ice Ages to give them the shape seen today. Beacons warned of the Armada from Roseberry Topping and celebrated the coronation of Queen Elizabeth II. The long-distance footpath, Cleveland Way, runs alongside the hills.

CLEVELEYS Lancashire SD3143

Town on A587, 5 miles (8km) N of Blackpool

A popular resort, situated on the Fylde coast just north of Blackpool, with all the usual seaside attractions.

CLEWER Somerset ST4351

Hamlet off B3151, 2 miles (3km) SW of Cheddar

Tiny hamlet on the edge of the Axe Valley.

CLEY HILL Wiltshire ST8344

Hill off A362, 2 miles (3km) W of Warminster

Isolated chalk knoll with an Iron Age hillfort on top. Famous for manifestations of Unidentified Flying Objects, apparently seen here frequently from 1965.

CLEY-NEXT-THE-SEA Norfolk TG0444

Village on A149, 4 miles (6km) NW of Holt

Traces of an old quay and an 18th-century windmill stand on the windblown expanses of the Norfolk marshes.

CLIDDESDEN Hampshire SU6349

Village on B3046, 2 miles (3km) S of Basingstoke

Rural despite proximity to Basingstoke. Pond, some thatch and a farm in the middle.

CLIFFE Kent TQ7376

Village on B2000, 5 miles (8km) N of Rochester

Large village important in Saxon times. Built on chalk hills at northwest corner of Hoo peninsula looking over Thames marshes and estuary.

Old windmill at Cley-next-the-Sea.

CLIFFORD Hereford and Worcester SO2445

Village on B4350, 2 miles (3km) NE of Hay-on-Wye

Welsh border village with ruined castle on bluff overlooking River Wye. The castle was the home of 'Fair Rosamund', mistress of Henry II (limited opening).

CLIFFORD West Yorkshire SE4344

Village off A1, 3 miles (5km) SE of Wetherby

The church was built in 1845-8 to a design by a Scotsman named Ramsay who had been influenced by his travels on the Continent.

CLIFFORD CHAMBERS Warwickshire SP1952

Village on B4632, 2 miles (3km) S of Stratford-upon-Avon

A pleasant cluster of buildings beside the River Stour includes an early 18th-century manor house and an interesting Norman church.

CLIFTON Avon ST5773

District in W of Bristol

Starting as an 18th-century spa based on a hot spring down in the valley, Clifton developed as an elegant suburb of Bristol with its own strong style. Mostly Grecian and therefore plainish, the best parts are 1820-40s, with terraces, squares and the largest crescent in England. The hilly site and the downs to the north add to the charm. Clifton Suspension Bridge (toll) was one of the wonders of Victorian England, and still amazes. Designed in 1829 by Brunel, but not finished until 1864, it crosses the deep rocky Avon Gorge, the muddy bed of the river way below. Near by is a little observatory with a Camera Obscura. A rare survival. Bristol Zoo on Clifton Down.

CLIFTON Cumbria NY5326

Village on A6, 3 miles (5km) S of Penrith

Site of the last battle of the Jacobite Rebellion on English soil. Nearby cliffs overlook the River Lowther.

CLIFTON Nottinghamshire SK5434

Village on A453, 3 miles (5km) SW of West Bridgford

Old village beside River Trent on southern edge of Nottingham, its hall and other buildings now used by Nottingham Trent University.

CLIFTON CAMPVILLE Staffordshire SK2510

Village off B5493, 5 miles (8km) NE of Tamworth

Staffordshire's best village church has a two-storey late Norman north transept: an upper room with latrine and a vaulted lower room. The 14th century provided the south aisle, chapel and tower, and spire supported by flying buttresses; in the 15th century the chancel arch was added, and the low-pitched roof at the east end is 16th century. Monuments include alabaster table tomb (1545) of Sir John Vernon. Other fine details abound.

CLIFTON HAMPDEN Oxfordshire SU5495

Village on A415, 3 miles (5km) E of Abingdon

This venerable Thames-side village is a popular day out for Oxonians. The Barley Mow, immortalised in *Three Men in a Boat*, is a special attraction, standing opposite the picturesque riverbank cottages and the church on its commanding site. Reward for climbing to church is some notably ornate Victorian craft work in chancel.

CLIFTON REYNES Buckinghamshire SP9051
Village off A509, 5 miles (8km) N of Newport Pagnell
Attractive stone village. Church with rare wooden effigies and unusual monument showing pet dog with his name, Bo, on his collar.

CLIFTON UPON DUNSMORE Warwickshire SP5376
Village on B5414, 2 miles (3km) NE of Rugby
Now almost a suburb of Rugby, the village has a good medieval church that was once the 'parent' parish church of the town.

CLIFTON UPON TEME Hereford and Worcester SO7161
Village on B4204, 6 miles (10km) NE of Bromyard
A pleasant mix of old houses in this hilltop settlement includes the medieval Lion hotel. Church contains monument by Grinling Gibbons.

CLIFTONVILLE Kent TR3771
Area of Margate, on B2051
The select eastern district of Margate, laid out in parallel streets on the clifftop above the beach. An impressive aquarium on the cliff.

CLIMPING West Sussex TQ9902
Village off A259, 2 miles (3km) W of Littlehampton
No real centre to this little coastal village with 13th-century church and unspoilt sandy beach backed by dunes.

CLIPSHAM Leicestershire SK9716
Village off A1, 7 miles (11km) NW of Stamford
Broad topiary avenue, with yews clipped into birds and animals, leading to east front of Clipsham Hall.

CLIPSTON Northamptonshire SP7181
Village on B4036, 4 miles (6km) SW of Market Harborough
Close to Leicestershire border, in undulating country. Medieval church contains monuments to the Buswell family of London merchants; 17th-century school.

CLIPSTONE Nottinghamshire SK6064
Village on B6030, 5 miles (8km) NE of Mansfield
Old Sherwood Forest settlement. New Clipstone colliery village near by. Ruins of King John's Palace, royal hunting lodge. Archway Lodge, now house, built as school in imitation of Worksop Priory Gatehouse, with figures of Robin Hood and friends. Rare breeds at Sherwood Forest Farm Park. Walks and cycle trails in Clipstone Forest. Center Parcs Holiday Village near by.

CLITHEROE Lancashire SD7441
Town on A671, 10 miles (16km) NE of Blackburn
Ancient market town. Only the Norman keep remains of Clitheroe Castle, one of the smallest in the country and one of the earliest stone buildings in Lancashire. Church of St Mary Magdalene, built in 1828 and incorporates a medieval tower. Local limestone quarrying industry reached its peak in 19th and early 20th century. Browsholme Hall, home of the Parker family, lies to northwest.

CLIVE Shropshire SJ5124
Village off B5476, 3 miles (5km) S of Wem
The village's presence on the slopes of Grinshill Hill is proclaimed by the prominent spire of the church, where Victorian restoration left north and south Norman doorways.

CLOFORD Somerset ST7244
Village off A359, 4 miles (6km) SW of Frome
Across the Nunney Brook; very rural with big stone manor house of 1633 (not open).

CLOPHILL Bedfordshire TL0838
Village on A6, 11 miles (18km) N of Luton
Attractive 17th- and 18th-century houses, old lock-up and pound on village green. Cainhoe Castle earthworks.

CLOPTON Suffolk TM2253
Hamlet on B1079, 4 miles (6km) NW of Woodbridge
A small huddle of houses around the attractive Church of St Mary. Nearby Clopton Hall (limited opening) dates from about 1500, but has an 18th-century façade.

CLOTTON Cheshire SJ5264
Hamlet on A51, 2 miles (3km) NW of Tarporley
Excellent examples of 'cops', hedges standing on top of a sandstone wall, found throughout the village. Now a conservation area.

CLOVA Tayside NO3273
Village on B955, 12 miles (19km) N of Kirriemuir
At northern end of Glen Clova, village makes good centre for exploring valley meadows and rocky uplands of this beautiful Angus glen.

CLOVELLY Devon SS3124
Village off A39, 9 miles (14km) W of Bideford
Whitewashed cottages tumble down the steep street to the wooded shore, with a little harbour. A tourist attraction for over a century, Clovelly is a quaint showplace, the one street cobbled and with steps. No cars, only sledges and donkeys. The Clovelly Centre at the top of the hill has a display on the village. The Milky Way and North Devon Bird of Prey Centre.

CLOVENFORDS Borders NT4536
Village on A72, 3 miles (5km) W of Galashiels
Local connection with Sir Walter Scott and memorial window at nearby Caddenfoots church. Vineyards here in 1860s heated by 5 miles (8km) of cast-iron pipes.

CLOWNE Derbyshire SK4875
Small town on B6417, 3 miles (5km) NE of Bolsover
Grew up around coal-mining industry. Away from centre, Norman and later St John Baptist Church has Salome pictured in a window.

CLUMBER PARK Nottinghamshire SK6274
Estate off A57, 4 miles (6km) SE of Worksop
Owned by National Trust, 3,800 acre (1,918ha) former estate of Dukes of Newcastle, open to visitors. Dukes Drive is double avenue of limes nearly 3 miles (5km) long, large lake, cricket pitch, woodlands, walled kitchen gardens, cycle trails, caravan park, shop and

restaurant. Fine 1880s Gothic Revival chapel, Duke's study, stables. Foundations of house, which was demolished 1938.

CLUN Shropshire SO3080
Small town on A488, 5 miles (8km) N of Knighton
A tiny market town in the Clun Forest. Original settlement centred on church, which retains massive Norman tower and interior arcades. Main part of town grew up around later castle across the river, still reached by medieval packhorse bridge. Huge earthworks and remains of tall keep survive. The architectural gem of the town is Trinity Hospital; almshouses of 1618.

CLUNGUNFORD Shropshire SO3978
Village on B4367, 4 miles (6km) SW of Craven Arms
Backed by hills, the village is a bridging point over the River Clun. The mainly 13th-century church stands alone beside the river.

CLWYDIAN RANGE Clwyd
Hill range in Wales
Smooth-browed slopes ascend from the broad and fertile Vale of Clwyd to command distant views. Traversed by Offa's Dyke. Area of Outstanding Natural Beauty.

CLYDACH Gwent SO2213
Village off A465, 2 miles (3km) E of Brynmawr
At bottom of tree-lined gorge containing traces of 18th-century ironworks. Trails encompass industrial relics and natural beauty. Cwm Clydach National Nature Reserve.

CLYDE, RIVER Strathclyde
River
Scotland's third largest river, of vital importance in development of Glasgow. Rises in Lowther Hills and flows predominantly north through open country to Lanark; valley below here extensively used for market-gardening. After Hamilton and Motherwell, runs through Glasgow, once base of world's largest ship-building industry. Opens north of Erskine into Firth of Clyde.

CLYDEBANK Strathclyde NS4970
Town on A814, 6 miles (10km) NW of Glasgow
On north bank of River Clyde and once important ship-building town whose dockyards produced the *QEII*. Native town of pop group Wet, Wet, Wet.

CLYFFE PYPARD Wiltshire SU0777
Village off A3102, 4 miles (6km) S of Wootton Bassett
Built into the hillside, picturesque view down the street. Woody, with scarp above. In the church a huge memorial to Thomas Sprackman, a local carpenter who made a fortune in London; he died in 1786.

CLYNNOG-FAWR Gwynedd SH4149
Village on A499, 9 miles (14km) SW of Caernarfon
Pilgrims to Bardsey Island (see) helped build huge 16th-century church beneath the mountains, overlooking the sea. Much of interest inside. Museum of Welsh country life near by.

CLYRO Powys SO2143
Village off A438, 1 mile (2km) NW of Hay-on-Wye
In rolling border country, made famous by Francis Kilvert, local curate and diarist of the 19th century, who lived opposite Baskervill Arms.

CLYST ST MARY Devon SX9791
Village off A3052, 4miles (6km) E of Exeter
Beside a medieval bridge over the River Clyst (the oldest bridge in Devon), the village is split by the main road. Crealy Country Park – animals and amusement park.

COALBROOKDALE Shropshire SJ6604
see Ironbridge

COALCLEUGH Northumberland NY8045
Hamlet off A689, 2 miles (3km) NE of Nenthead
The highest village in Northumberland; little remains of this one-time lead- and coal-mining settlement.

COALPORT Shropshire SJ6902
see Ironbridge

COALVILLE Leicestershire SK4214
Town on A50, 12 miles (19km) NW of Leicester
Snibston Discovery Park occupies former colliery site on edge of town, illustrating local industrial heritage; 'hands-on' science exhibits, events.

COATBRIDGE Strathclyde NS7365
Town off M8, 9 miles (14km) E of Glasgow
Former major industrial town which boomed in 1800s and declined after 1934 when steel-workers moved to Corby (see). Industrial museum and good leisure facilities.

COBBATON Devon SS6126
Hamlet off B3227, 6 miles (10km) SE of Barnstaple
Only a hamlet, but the northern part is called Traveller's Rest. Cobbaton Combat Collection to the south has military vehicles.

COBERLEY Gloucestershire SO9616
Village off A436, 4 miles (6km) S of Cheltenham
Lying near the source of the River Churn (also claimed locally as source of the River Thames), the village has a church containing the tomb of Dick Whittington's mother.

COBHAM Kent TQ6768
Village on B2009, 4 miles (6km) SE of Gravesend
Historic village south of the old Dover road. Tudor almshouses, called Cobham College, 1598, incorporate hall of chantry college of 1362; half-timbered inn, the Leathern Bottle, features in writing of Dickens; church contains most notable brasses in England. Inigo Jones and Robert Adam involved in design of magnificent Cobham Hall, now a girls' school.

COBHAM Surrey TQ1060
Small town on A245, 4 miles (6km) NW of Leatherhead
Lying in a great meander loop of the River Mole, two villages, Church Cobham on the Leatherhead road and Street Cobham on the London to Portsmouth road, have grown together and amalgamated during the

20th century. Painshill Park to west is superb historic landscape garden of lakes, follies and parkland, created 1738-73, renovated since 1981.

COCKAYNE HATLEY Bedfordshire TL2649
Village off B1040, 2 miles (3km) E of Potton
Splendid baroque woodwork in church, and brasses. Grave of WE Henley, allegedly the original Long John Silver.

COCKBURNSPATH Borders NT7770
Village on A1, 8 miles (13km) SE of Dunbar
Pronounced 'Coeburnspath'. At end of Southern Upland Way with unattractive Torness Power station near by. Just north is 14th-century cruciform Dunglass Collegiate Church.

COCKENZIE AND PORT SETON Lothian NT4075
Town on B1348, 4 miles (6km) NE of Musselburgh
Town on Firth of Forth dominated by bulky power station, with Seton Sands holiday beach close by.

COCKERHAM Lancashire SD4651
Village on A588, 6 miles (10km) SW of Lancaster
Cockerham Hall, dating from the 1470s, is a rare example of a medieval timber-framed hall. Fluke fishing is a local custom.

COCKERMOUTH Cumbria NY1230
Town off A66, 8 miles (13km) E of Workington
Birthplace of Lakeland's most famous poet William Wordsworth and of Fletcher Christian, the man who led the mutiny on the *Bounty*. Wordsworth House (National Trust) was built in 1745, where the poet was born. Wordsworth's father is buried in the churchyard.

COCKFIELD Durham NZ1224
Village off A688, 2 miles (3km) N of Staindrop
Peaceful hilltop village based around the coal industry. Main street runs to Holymoor, once famous for its geese.

COCKING West Sussex SU8717
Village on A286, 3 miles (5km) S of Midhurst
Roadside village in wooded gap in South Downs, owned by Cowdray estate, the cottages' woodwork painted the estate's regulation yellow.

COCKINGTON Devon SX8963
Village in W outskirts of Torquay
A really pretty and well-preserved thatch, cob and stone village, now on the outskirts of the Torbay development. Interesting church.

COCKLEY CLEY Norfolk TF7904
Village off A1065, 4 miles (6km) SW of Swaffham
Charming hamlet (pronounced 'Cly') with reconstructed Iron Age (Iceni tribe) village. A rectangular moat encloses the thatched huts and long houses.

COCKTHORPE Norfolk TF9842
Hamlet off A149, 4 miles (6km) E of Wells-next-the-Sea
Seven rooms in the 16th-century Cockthorpe Hall are a toy museum, filled with toys from the 1800s to the 1960s.

CODDENHAM Suffolk TM1354
Village on B1078, 6 miles (10km) N of Ipswich
A single street winds up the hill through Coddenham's attractive half-timbered houses, with their pargetting. Gryffon House, which served for many years as the Crown inn, is said to be the home of an archer who was knighted by Henry V for his courage at the Battle of Agincourt in 1415.

CODDINGTON Nottinghamshire SK8354
Village on A17, 3 miles (5km) E of Newark
Pleasant brick-built village, with Old Manor Farm 1714. Civil War earthworks. Church has 19th-century work by Morris and Burne-Jones.

CODFORD Wiltshire ST9739
Village off A36, 4 miles (6km) SE of Heytesbury
Codford St Mary and Codford St Peter have been united as one village, but still have their own churches. The Woolstore at St Peter is now a theatre.

CODICOTE Hertfordshire TL2118
Village on B656, 2 miles (3km) NW of Welwyn
Medieval pilgrims to St Albans used former George and Dragon inn. Attractive houses in old central market place, post-war housing estates.

CODNOR Derbyshire SK4149
Village on A610, 2 miles (3km) SE of Ripley
Codnor Castle, remains of 13th- and 14th-century crenellated manor house (closed), with adjoining 17th-century farmhouse. Pretty Victorian church.

CODSALL Staffordshire SJ8603
Village off A41, 4 miles (6km) NW of Wolverhampton
This Wolverhampton fringe village was once famous for its lupins. Exceptional views from church, which is the 'highest point between Codsall and Russia'.

COGGES Oxfordshire SP3609
Hamlet off B4022, immediately SE of Witney
Defended by the River Windrush from encroaching Witney suburbs, the village has a good farm museum and a church with lively medieval carving.

COGGESHALL Essex TL8522
Village off A120, 6 miles (10km) E of Braintree
Showpiece old cloth and lace town. Paycocke's House (National Trust), about 1500, is one of the finest half-timbered buildings in England. National Trust also owns 12th-century Grange Barn, spectacular with enormous roof, Europe's oldest timber-framed barn. Venerable inns, ancient brick bridge. Church with rare dedication to St Peter ad Vincula, restored after direct hit by 1940 bomb.

COLCHESTER Essex TL9925
Town off A12, 51 miles (82km) NE of London
Now a busy shopping and services centre, Colchester claims to be Britain's oldest recorded town, the pre-Roman settlement where the Romans established their first legionary base and capital in AD43. Part of the Roman town wall still stands. The unusual-looking castle of 1076, possessor of Europe's largest Norman keep,

is now a museum with top-flight archaeological collections. To the south stand the ruins of St Botolph's Priory Church, battered by Cromwellian besiegers in 1648.

Two other churches, All Saints' and Holy Trinity, have become museums of natural and social history respectively, while Colchester-made clocks and watches pass the time serenely in the Tymperleys Clock Museum and the Hollytrees Museum is packed with toys, curios and historic costumes. Notable buildings range from the 15th-century half-timbered Red Lion to grand Georgian town houses, the colossal Victorian water tower known as Jumbo and the grandiloquent 1902 town hall, with its 162ft (49m) tower. Rollerworld boasts Europe's biggest maple roller-skating floor while Colchester Zoo breeds endangered species in 40 acres (16ha) of gardens sheltering majestic Siberian tigers, snow leopards and elephants.

COLD ASHBY Northamptonshire SP6576
Village on B4036, 6 miles (10km) SW of Market Harborough
Small rural village, less isolated since construction of A14 road close by, linking A1 and M1.

COLD ASHTON Avon ST7572
Village off A46, 5 miles (8km) N of Bath
Small pretty village, with a church rebuilt 1508-40 by the rector.

COLD ASTON Gloucestershire SP1219
see Aston Blank

COLD NORTON Essex TL8500
Village off B1012, 4 miles (6km) S of Maldon
Tiny place until 1960s, when big water tower built. Junction of 'ley lines' (mysterious force patterns) sometimes claimed to explain oddly high birth rate.

COLDHARBOUR Surrey TQ1443
Village off A24, 4 miles (6km) S of Dorking
Remote little hamlet of stone cottages strewn along Leith Hill near Iron Age Anstiebury Camp, with superb views southwards across the Weald.

COLDINGHAM Borders NT9065
Village on A1107, 3 miles (5km) NW of Eyemouth
Mainly 18th-century village inland from sandy Coldingham Bay. Priory founded 7th century, repeatedly destroyed; remains now form part of church. Impressive red cliffs of St Abb's Head rise over 300ft (91m) to north, huge seabird nesting colony and nature reserve. Ruined and precipitous Fast Castle up coast featured in Scott's *Bride of Lammermuir*.

COLDRIDGE Devon SS6907
Village off B3220, 4 miles (6km) E of Winkleigh
Lives up to its name, being on top of a ridge. Good church with better fittings – wooden screen.

COLDSTREAM Borders NT8439
Small town on A697, 9 miles (14km) NE of Kelso
Border town on busy A697 with ford, used for numerous English invasions until present bridge built in 1776. Associated with Coldstream Guards; name originally nickname for Second Foot Guards raised near by, Regimental Museum. Rideouts in August to commemorate Flodden. The Hirsel (1640s) is family seat of Earls of Home – pronounced 'Hume' – with splendid grounds.

COLEBROOK Devon SS7700
Village off A377, 4 miles (6km) W of Crediton
Small village in the red soil area of Devon; isolated medieval church with good wooden fittings, especially the screen.

COLEBY Lincolnshire SK9760
Village off A607, 7 miles (11km) S of Lincoln
Attractively sited on the Lincoln Cliff, looking across the Brant, Witham and Trent valleys. Viking Way footpath passes through.

COLEFORD Gloucestershire SO5710
Town on B4228, 4 miles (6km) SE of Monmouth
The 'capital' of the Forest of Dean has a stranded church tower at its centre, many chapels and, near by, the Speech House, still used as the Forest Court.

COLEHILL Dorset SU0201
Village off B3078, immediately NE of Wimborne Minster
A large rural suburb of Wimborne, with a surprising 1890s brick and half-timbered church.

COLERNE Wiltshire ST8271
Village off A4, 6 miles (10km) W of Chippenham
Large village, set high on the edge of the Cotswolds, with a wide view. Fine 15th-century church tower, and inside part of a very fine 9th-century stone cross shaft with intricate interlaced dragons.

COLESHILL Buckinghamshire SU9495
Village of A355, 2 miles (3km) SW of Amersham
Pretty village with green, pond, old houses, impressive water tower and a Victorian church by GE Street. Birthplace of Edmund Waller, 17th-century poet.

COLESHILL Oxfordshire SU2393
Village on B4019, 4 miles (6km) W of Faringdon
Bordered by the River Coke and the extensive park of vanished Coleshill House, the pleasant village has a church full of character.

COLESHILL Warwickshire SP2089
Town on B4117, 9 miles (14km) E of Birmingham
Attractive hilltop town on Birmingham fringe with an impressively spired church of the 14th/15th centuries and many handsome Georgian buildings.

COLINSBURGH Fife NO4703
Village on B942, 2 miles (3km) NW of Elie
Founded by Earls of Balcarres; their mansion house, Balcarres House, dating from 1595, stands outside the village.

COLL Strathclyde
Island in Inner Hebrides, off Mull
Idyllic sparsely-populated crofting and holiday island, 3 miles (5km) by 13 miles (20km), with lovely beaches. Ferry to main settlement, with services, of Arinagour.

COLLATON ST MARY Devon SX8660
Village on A385, 2 miles (3km) W of Paignton
Small village, now on the edge of Paignton. Church, school and vicarage all built in the 1860s.

COLLIESTON Grampian NK0328
Village on B9003, 3 miles (5km) NE of Newburgh
Originally a fishing village, now a holiday resort with many second homes. Smugglers' caves in cliffs.

COLLINGBOURNE DUCIS Wiltshire SU2453
Village on A346, 2 miles (3km) NW of Ludgershall
Thatched cottages, timber-framed and brick, with a winterborne river – the Bourne – which only flows in winter.

COLLINGBOURNE KINGSTON Wiltshire SU2355
Village on A338, 4 miles (6km) NW of Ludgershall
Tiny, with farms in the middle.

COLLINGHAM Nottinghamshire SK8361
Village on A1133, 6 miles (10km) NE of Newark
Formerly separate North and South Collingham parishes now one long village, beside River Trent, with fine Georgian and earlier houses.

COLLINGTREE Northamptonshire SP7555
Village off A508, 3 miles (5km) S of Northampton
Sandwiched between Northampton town and the M1, yet retaining its individuality, with a 12th- and 13th-century church.

COLLYWESTON Northamptonshire SK9902
Village on A43, 3 miles (5km) SW of Stamford
Home of famous Collyweston slates seen on roofs not only in this village, but in many other buildings in fine towns and villages near and far. Handsome Saxon and medieval church, late 17th-century manor house, and the barn, dovecote and sundial of the demolished mansion which belonged to Thomas Cromwell, Treasurer to Henry VI.

COLMONELL Strathclyde NX1485
Village on B734, 5 miles (8km) NE of Ballantrae
Village in pretty Stinchar Glen with five ruined castles in vicinity, mainly Kennedy strongholds.

COLMWORTH Bedfordshire TL1058
Village off B660, 7 miles (11km) NE of Bedford
Set draughtily near the Cambridgeshire border, village with beautiful, tall-spired 15th-century church.

COLN ROGERS Gloucestershire SP0809
Village off A429, 4 miles (6km) SW of Northleach
Beautifully situated in the Coln Valley, this village boasts one of the best-preserved Saxon churches in the county.

COLN ST ALDWYNS Gloucestershire SP1405
Village off B4425, 2 miles (3km) SE of Bibury
Splendid Norman doorway in a church where the famous 19th-century divine John Keble was curate. Elizabethan manor house and attractive cottages.

COLN ST DENNIS Gloucestershire SP0810
Village off A429, 3 miles (5km) SW of Northleach
Idyllically situated beside the River Coln, St James's Church has a massive Norman tower and grotesque carvings on its walls.

COLNBROOK Greater London TQ0277
Village off A4, 4 miles (6km) SE of Slough
Partly in Buckinghamshire, near Heathrow Airport. There has been a pub on the site of the Ostrich since the 12th century.

COLNE Lancashire SD8939
Town on A56, 6 miles (10km) NE of Burnley
This 19th-century cotton town has much older roots and boasts Pendle's oldest building, St Bartholomew's Church, built in 1122. The Colne Heritage Centre, next to the church, was formerly the grammar school. The town's stocks can be seen here. The local government shares responsibility for governing Pendle district with nearby Nelson.

COLNE, RIVER Essex
River
Flows across the county of Essex from northwest by Halstead, Colchester and Brightlingsea to North Sea below Mersea Island.

COLNEY Norfolk TG1807
Village on B1108, 3 miles (5km) W of Norwich
Pleasant village centred around a church with a splendid Anglo-Saxon round tower. Colney Hall (not open) is a handsome neo-Georgian building.

COLNEY STREET Hertfordshire TL1502
Village on A5183, 3 miles (5km) S of St Albans
Named after River Colne, which runs through Colney Heath, once highwaymen's haunt. Numerous pubs along Watling Street, former coaching route.

COLONSAY AND ORONSAY Strathclyde
Islands in the Inner Hebrides, NW of Jura
Two small islands, joined at low tide, with superlative plant and birdlife and excellent beaches. Sub-tropical gardens at Colonsay House, and ruined priory on Oronsay.

COLSTERWORTH Lincolnshire SK9324
Village off A1, 7 miles (11km) S of Grantham
Pretty stone village, where Roman Ermine Street leaves Great North road. Close by at Woolsthorpe Manor (National Trust), Isaac Newton was born on Christmas Day 1642. Returning during 1660s plague years, he did much of his major work here. An apple tree in the orchard is descended from the one whose falling fruit inspired his theory on gravity.

COLSTON BASSETT Nottinghamshire SK7033
Village off A46, 4 miles (6km) S of Bingham
Picturesque village in Vale of Belvoir, with dairy making famous Stilton cheese. Lavish Victorian church commemorating squire's wife and son.

COLTISHALL Norfolk TG2719
Village on B1354, 8 miles (13km) NE of Norwich
Elegant Dutch-gabled houses and grassy watermeadows characterise this pretty village. Patrons of several pubs spill out on to the common on fine days.

COLTON Cumbria SD3185
Hamlet off A5092, 5 miles (8km) N of Ulverston
Tiny hamlet which comprises a handful of farms and cottages. Colton Old Hall was seat of the Sandy family in 17th century.

COLWALL Hereford and Worcester SO7542
Village off B4218, 3 miles (5km) NE of Ledbury
Original medieval village stands apart from sprawling modern development on slopes of Malverns. St James's Church has medieval tiles and fine timber roof.

COLWICH Staffordshire SK0121
Village off A51, 3 miles (5km) NW of Rugeley
Traversed by river, railway and canal, this Trent Valley village has an ornate Victorian church worth visiting.

COLWYN BAY Clwyd SH8479
Town off A55, 10 miles (16km) W of Rhyl
Wooded hills overlook resort popular since last century. Miles of sand are bordered by a promenade backed by Eirias Park's gardens, sport and leisure facilities, and Dinosaur World. The Welsh Mountain Zoo features free-flying birds of prey, Jungle Adventureland and Chimpanzee World, all in a panoramic setting. Green, unspoiled hinterland.

COLYFORD Devon SY2592
Village on A3052, 2 miles (3km) N of Seaton
Really the southern part of Colyton (see) with the ford and later the bridge over the River Coly.

COLYTON Devon SY2494
Village on B3161, 3 miles (5km) N of Seaton
A little market town set in the river valley with good views and many pleasant buildings.

COMBE Berkshire SU3760
Hamlet off A4, 6 miles (10km) SE of Hungerford
An isolated hamlet, close to Walbury Hill with its Iron Age hillfort – the highest hill in the county at 974ft (297m). Wonderful views from the ridge. Combe Gibbett just to the west of the hill is large and high, supposedly erected in 1676 to hang a local couple who had murdered their children.

COMBE FLOREY Somerset ST1531
Village off A358, 6 miles (10km) NW of Taunton
Red sandstone village, famous as home of the novelist Evelyn Waugh from 1956. Fine 1593 gatehouse. Stone cottages.

COMBE MARTIN Devon SS5846
Small town on A399, 4 miles (6km) E of Ilfracombe
One very long street running down a shallow valley, with a pretty bay at the end. Fine rocky coast, especially eastwards to Hangman Point. Red sandstone 15th-century church with good wooden screens. Holdstone Down to the east gives panoramic views. Combe Martin Wildlife and Dinosaur Park sounds Jurassic. Farm World at Berry Down. Combe Martin Motor Cycle Collection. Local museum.

COMBEINTEIGNHEAD (OR COMBE IN TEIGNHEAD) Devon SX9071
Village off A382, 3 miles (5km) E of Newton Abbot
Set in a combe running down to the Teign estuary, the position giving the complex name. Coombe Cellars (National Trust) is right on the shore.

COMBERBACH Cheshire SJ6477
Village off A559, 3 miles (5km) NW of Northwich
Originally only a small cluster of thatched cottages; the Spinner and Bergamot inn is named after two racehorses belonging to Smith-Barry of nearby Marbury Hall.

COMBERTON Cambridgeshire TL3856
Village on B1046, 4 miles (6km) W of Cambridge
The remains of a medieval hall are incorporated into the Old Vicarage near St Mary's Church. There is a good village college.

COMBERTON, GREAT AND LITTLE Hereford and Worcester SO9542/SP9643
Villages off B4080, 2 miles (3km) S of Pershore
Pretty Bredon Hill villages, with interesting churches and pleasant old houses. Fine manor house at Little Comberton, also Nash's Farm with big stone dovecote.

COMBS Suffolk TM0456
Village off B1115, 2 miles (3km) S of Stowmarket
Comb Wood Reserve is home to the rare hawfinch. Some fine medieval glass in the church was damaged in an explosion in a nearby factory.

COMBWICH Somerset ST2542
Village off A39, 4 miles (6km) NW of Bridgwater
Pronounced 'Cummitch'. Once a little port with a ferry on the Parrett estuary, very flat area around.

COME-TO-GOOD Cornwall SW8140
Hamlet off A39, 3 miles (5km) S of Truro
A very simple thatched Quaker meeting house, built in 1710. The name is ancient, and not derived from the meeting house. Very rural setting.

COMPSTALL Greater Manchester SJ9690
Village on B6104, 2 miles (3km) E of Romiley
Etherow Country Park is a nature reserve on the River Etherow with woodland walks, an old mill, sailing and a braille trail for the blind.

COMPTON Devon SX8664
Hamlet off A380, 3 miles (5km) W of Torquay
Compton Castle (National trust) is one of the best fortified medieval manor houses in the country. Great hall, solar and chapel.

COMPTON Surrey SU9546
Village on B3000, 3 miles (5km) SW of Guildford
Cosy 19th- and 20th-century cottages dispersed along

the village street in intricate hilly country just south of the Hog's Back. The 11th-century church crowns a little knoll and larger houses hide among trees. Art gallery devoted to paintings of GF Watts (1817–1904), and in cemetery, extraordinary 'art nouveau' Watts memorial chapel by his wife.

COMPTON ABBAS Dorset ST8618
Village off A350, 3 miles (5km) S of Shaftesbury
Running up a combe in the chalk, with steep downs on three sides. Fontmell Down, to the south, is well-preserved downland.

COMPTON ABDALE Gloucestershire SP0516
Village off A40, 4 miles (6km) NW of Northleach
The church, with strange carvings on its tower, stands aloof on a terrace above cottages set in a deep combe.

COMPTON BASSETT Wiltshire SU0372
Village off A4, 3 miles (5km) NE of Calne
A straggling but pretty village; 12th- and 15th-century church, with a very elaborate and rare stone screen of the 14th century.

COMPTON BEAUCHAMP Oxfordshire SU2786
Village on B4507, 5 miles (8km) S of Faringdon
A chalk-built church with medieval glass and Victorian wall-painting is the main attraction of this village, situated beneath wooded downland slopes.

COMPTON CHAMBERLAYNE Wiltshire SU0229
Village off A30, 5 miles (8km) W of Wilton
Pretty, well-wooded village, with timber-framed and thatched cottages.

COMPTON DANDO Avon ST6464
Village off A39, 7 miles (11km) W of Bath
Mostly Victorian church, but one corner of the tower has a large stone carved with two figures – part of Roman altar from Bath.

COMPTON DUNDON Somerset ST4932
Village off B3151, 5 miles (8km) S of Glastonbury
Tucked under Dundon Hill, a woody and secluded village. The 300ft (90m) hill has an Iron Age hillfort on the top.

COMPTON MARTIN Avon ST5457
Village on A368, 3 miles (5km) S of Chew Stoke
On the edge of the Mendips. Fine Norman church, with one unusual spiral-fluted column.

COMPTON VERNEY Warwickshire SP3152
Mansion on B4086, 7 miles (11km) E of Stratford-upon-Avon
Early 18th-century house (not open), home of the Verney family. Attributed to Vanbrugh and remodelled by Adam. Verney monuments in church.

COMPTON WYNYATES Warwickshire SP3341
Mansion off B4035, 5 miles (8km) E of Shipston on Stour
Early Tudor house (not open) in brick and timber-framed, built around courtyard. Restoration chapel preserved in near-original form.

COMRIE Tayside NN7722
Village on A85, 6 miles (10km) W of Crieff
Pretty village which straddles the Highland boundary fault on the upper River Earn; this results in more seismological activity here than anywhere else in Britain. The granite obelisk on Dunmore Hill commemorates Henry Dundas, 1st Viscount Melville, the powerful 18th-century Scottish politician, who spent his retirement at Comrie. Near by is the Drummond Fishery and the Auchingarrich Wildlife Centre.

CONDOVER Shropshire SJ4905
Village off A49, 4 miles (6km) S of Shrewsbury
A magnificent E-shaped sandstone mansion of about 1598 (now a school) adjoins the church, where rebuilding of the 17th and 19th centuries has left a striking hammerbeam roof and outstanding monuments in the chapel by artists including Louis Roubiliac and GF Watts. Near by, to the east, is Cantlop Bridge (English Heritage), a single span of cast iron by Thomas Telford.

CONEY WESTON Suffolk TL9578
Village off B1111, 5 miles (8km) N of Ixworth
The ancient footpath Peddars Way passes through this delightful village. Many of the 17th-century buildings are Listed.

CONGLETON Cheshire SJ8562
Town on A54, 11 miles (18km) N of Stoke-on-Trent
Mill town which rose to prominence in the Tudor period when it prospered in lace-making and leather-working, later in silk and cotton industry; Venetian Gothic town hall. The Cloud, penultimate peak of the Pennine chain, is visible for miles around. Bridestones, remains of a chambered tomb thought to have been built in the Stone Age.

CONGRESBURY Avon ST4363
Village on A370, 5 miles (8km) S of Clevedon
Big village across the Congresbury Yeo, a small port until 1900 and supposedly founded by St Congar, from whose walking stick the ancient yew in the churchyard is supposed to have grown. Interesting church, mostly 15th century outside and 13th century inside. To the north is an Iron Age hillfort usually known as Cadbury-Congresbury.

CONINGSBY Lincolnshire TF2257
Village on A153, immediately SW of Tattershall
Eye-catching feature of the massive church tower is its huge one-handed clock, possibly the world's largest. At Coningsby's Royal Air Force base, the Battle of Britain Memorial Flight has its home. Spitfires, a Hurricane and Lancaster are on display, except during their summer weekend programme, when they do demonstration flights at numerous air displays.

CONINGTON Cambridgeshire TL3266
Village off A14 (A604), 9 miles (14km) NW of Cambridge
Small village just off a Roman road in the heart of Fen country. St Mary's Church was largely rebuilt in the 18th and 19th centuries.

CONINGTON Cambridgeshire TL1885
Village off A1, 2 miles (3km) SE of Stilton
Conington is home to Peterborough airport. It is surrounded by beautiful fenland, including Holme Fen, the lowest place in Britain.

CONISBROUGH South Yorkshire SK5098
Town on A630, 5 miles (8km) SW of Doncaster
Strategically set in the Don valley and a significant administrative unit in Anglo-Scandinavian times. Conisbrough Castle, built in 1170s by Hameline Plantagenet, was the principal northern stronghold of the Earls of Surrey until 1347. It became a royal castle when Edward IV ascended the throne in 1461, and was Athelstane in Walter Scott's novel *Ivanhoe*.

CONISHOLME Lincolnshire TF4095
Village on A1031, 7 miles (11km) NE of Louth
Just off winding coast road, medieval church, once much larger, now an intriguing architectural puzzle, with Anglo-Saxon sculpture; 16th-century brass.

CONISTON Cumbria SD3097
Village on A593, 6 miles (10km) SW of Ambleside
Name derived from Anglo-Saxon for 'king's village'. In the churchyard a cross with one side depicting an artist at work marks the grave of John Ruskin. His home, Brantwood, overlooks the lake and now houses a museum commemorating his life and work. Donald Campbell died on Coniston Water in 1967 attempting to break the water speed record. The Old Man of Coniston is 2,635ft (803m) high.

CONISTONE North Yorkshire SD9867
Village off B6160, 2 miles (3km) NW of Grassington
Pretty limestone cottages and barns surround the village green. On the hill behind the village is a rocky outcrop called 'The Pie', on Dalesway long-distance footpath.

CONNAH'S QUAY Clwyd SJ2969
Town on A548, 4 miles (6km) SE of Flint
Conurbation at start of Dee estuary supposedly named after a publican. No longer a port of significance. Wooded valley of Wepre Park. Large Deeside Leisure Centre at neighbouring Queensferry.

CONNEL Strathclyde NM9134
Village on A85, 5 miles (8km) NE of Oban
At mouth of Loch Etive with its turbulent sea rapids, Falls Of Lora. Near by is 13th-century Ardchattan Priory.

CONSETT Durham NZ1051
Town on A694, 12 miles (19km) SW of Newcastle upon Tyne
Dramatically sited on the edge of the North Pennines with views over the hills and moors beyond. This was once a major iron and steel centre; the steelworks closed in 1980 and its site has now been restored. Consett is a local administrative centre with shopping and recreational facilities. Two disused railway lines provide walks to Sunderland and Swalwell.

CONSTABLE BURTON North Yorkshire SE1690
Village on A684, 3 miles (5km) E of Leyburn
Recorded in the Domesday Book as Bortone. Constable Burton Hall, originally built in 1328, has fine gardens.

CONSTABLE COUNTRY Suffolk
Scenic area
The journey through beautiful Dedham Vale (an Area of Outstanding Natural Beauty) from Dedham (where Constable went to school) to East Bergholt (where he was born) inspired many of his paintings.

CONSTANTINE Cornwall SW7329
Village off B3291, 5 miles (8km) SW of Falmouth
Large hilltop village just above the Helford estuary, mostly built of locally quarried granite.

CONTIN Highland NH4556
Village on A835, 2 miles (3km) SW of Strathpeffer
Stands on River Blackwater. To the north, the water cascades over rocks at picturesque Falls of Rogie, where there are riverside walks.

CONWY Gwynedd SH7877
Town off A55, 3 miles (5km) S of Llandudno
One of Europe's best-preserved medieval walled towns lies between a wooded estuary and the northern foothills of Snowdonia. Edward I's castle and the fortified town walls which even now shelter most of Conwy are a World Heritage Site (Cadw). Approaching from the west, Telford's suspension bridge of 1826, joined now by rail and road bridges, echoes the architecture of the stronghold that forms a link in the 'iron ring' devised to conquer the Welsh. The best vantage point from the partly walkable walls is the Upper Gate.

Within the town there are many historic buildings. The 14th-century stone and timber Aberconwy House (National Trust) was the home of a merchant. Much of the original decoration survives at Plas Mawr, home of an Elizabethan adventurer. On the site of a Cistercian abbey is the 14th-century Church of St Mary and All Saints. Along the busy quayside is the famous 'Smallest House', a minuscule dwelling. Another unusual attraction is the Teapot Museum, an amazing array of rare, beautiful and quirky teapots. Other places of interest include a visitor centre, art gallery, butterfly 'jungle' and aquarium.

CONWY, RIVER Gwynedd
River
Starts its journey at Llyn Conwy, high above tourist honeypot of Betws-y-coed. Flows through beautiful vale to sea at Conwy.

COODEN East Sussex TQ7107
Suburb on W edge of Bexhill
Suburb of Bexhill overlooking Hooe Level (nature reserve), a modern golfing resort with course for national championships. Submerged forest below beach.

COOKHAM Berkshire SU8985
Small town off A4094, 3 miles (5km) NE of Maidenhead
A tiny, pretty town on the Thames, surprisingly rural with many woods and meadows. Proper High Street,

with a good mixture of buildings. The medieval church is right down on the river. Cast-iron bridge over the Thames, 1867. Sir Stanley Spencer, the well-known painter, was born at Cookham and lived here most of his life. The Stanley Spencer Gallery has several of his large, strange paintings, many set in the town.

COOLHAM West Sussex TQ1122
Village on A272, 3 miles (5km) SE of Billingshurst
Small crossroads village near River Adur with famous Quaker Meeting House, the Blue Idol, attended by William Penn.

COOLING Kent TQ7575
Village off B2000, 5 miles (8km) NE of Rochester
Little marshland village on Hoo peninsula associated with Dickens' *Great Expectations*. Its massive ruinous castle, 1381, was once owned by Sir John Oldcastle, Shakespeare's Falstaff.

COOMBE BISSETT Wiltshire SU1026
Village on A354, 3 miles (5km) SW of Salisbury
On the River Ebble. Prominent stone and flint church with prettily chequered tower. Some cottages in the same style.

COOMBES West Sussex TQ1808
Village off A283, 2 miles (3km) SE of Steyning
Norman church in a farmyard in the Adur Valley with dramatic wall-paintings of about 1100.

COOPER'S HILL Gloucestershire SO8815
see Brockworth

COOPER'S HILL Surrey SU9972
Site off A328, 1 mile (2km) N of Englefield Green
Green hill overlooking Runnymede, above peaceful River Thames, crowned by Sir Edward Maufe's great memorial tower to 20,455 Commonwealth aircrew killed 1939–45.

COPDOCK Suffolk TM1242
Village off A12, 3 miles (5km) SW of Ipswich
Known locally as Copdock and Washbrook. Saved from the constant thunder of traffic by the opening of a new road.

COPFORD GREEN Essex TL9222
Village off A12, 5 miles (8km) W of Colchester
Attractive green, houses, barns. Copford church is Norman with Roman and early medieval brickwork, remarkable 12th-century wall-paintings.

COPINSAY Orkney HY6101
Island off mainland of Scotland
Royal Society for the Protection of Birds island reserve to southeast of mainland, noted for breeding colonies of seabirds.

COPLE Bedfordshire TL1048
Village off A603, 4 miles (6km) E of Bedford
Quiet Bedford dormitory village, with notable array of 15th- and 16th-century brasses in the 15th-century church.

COPPLESTONE Devon SS7702
Village on A377, 5 miles (8km) NW of Crediton
Surrounded by red hills, and named after a 10th-century boundary stone, which still survives 10ft (3m) high.

COPTHORNE West Sussex TQ3139
Small town on A264, 3 miles (5km) NE of Crawley
This town sprawls around its wide common close to Gatwick Airport and is known for immense Copthorne hotel, virtually a self-contained village.

COQUET, RIVER Northumberland
River
The river rises on the border of England and Scotland in the Cheviot Hills and flows into the North Sea at Amble.

CORBRIDGE Northumberland NY9964
Small town off A68, 3 miles (5km) E of Hexham
Attractive market town on the north bank of the River Tyne, a strategic point for the important Roman garrison of Corstopitum. The garrison was built in AD90 and extended over the following 250 years; objects of Roman life can be seen at the Corbridge Roman Museum. St Andrew's Church and the vicar's pele tower were built with stone from Corstopitum.

CORBY Northamptonshire SP8988
Town off A6003, 7 miles (11km) N of Kettering
Rural village burgeoned into modern town when 1930s steel-making brought huge influx of workers. Closure of steelworks in 1980 caused heavy job losses, but council successfully attracted modern industries to town, surrounded by pleasant Rockingham Forest area. East Carlton Countryside Park and magnificent historic houses, including Kirby Hall (English Heritage), home of Elizabeth I's Lord Chancellor, Christopher Hatton.

CORBY GLEN Lincolnshire SK9924
Village on A151, 7 miles (11km) NW of Bourne
Stone-built former market town on hillside. Fine medieval wall-paintings discovered in church, 1939. Apt epitaph in churchyard to local auctioneer.

CORFE CASTLE Dorset SY9681
Village on A351, 4 miles (6km) SE of Wareham
An attractive stone village nestling under the castle, impressively placed in the only gap in the chalk ridge which cuts Purbeck off. The castle (National Trust) is on a high mound, and was a large and important royal castle in medieval times. The outer wall and towers were mostly undermined after the Civil War, leaving them split or spilled down the bank. The inner buildings are impressive and the views fine. Local museum.

CORHAMPTON Hampshire SU6120
Village on B3035, next to Meonstoke
Deep in the Meon Valley, with a notable Saxon church, which has good later medieval wall-paintings. A huge ancient yew nearly fills the churchyard.

CORLEY Warwickshire SP3085
Village on B4098, 5 miles (8km) NW of Coventry
Hilltop village. Corley Hall thought to be original of Hall Farm in George Eliot's *Adam Bede*.

CORNFORTH Durham NZ3134
Village on B6291, 4 miles (6km) NW of Sedgefield
Former colliery village with green and Victorian church. Dominated by cement works and nearby motorway.

CORNHILL-ON-TWEED Northumberland NT8639
Village on A697, 1 mile (2km) E of Coldstream
Border town with elegant bridge over River Tweed, built between 1763 and 1766, linking Cornhill in England with Coldstream in Scotland.

CORNWELL Oxfordshire SP2727
Hamlet off A44, 3 miles (5km) W of Chipping Norton
Cornwell's appeal results from restoration by Clough Williams-Ellis, architect of Portmeirion (see), commissioned by an American couple, who bought the manor house and hamlet in the 1930s.

CORNWOOD Devon SX6059
Village off A38, 3 miles (5km) NW of Ivybridge
On the edge of Dartmoor, its land stretching far into the moor, with many archaeological remains.

CORNWORTHY Devon SX8255
Village off A381, 4 miles (6km) SE of Totnes
On a hill sloping down to the Dart estuary, beautiful countryside. Interesting church because it escaped Victorian restoration.

CORRIESHALLOCH GORGE Highland NH2077
Beauty spot on A835, 11 miles (18km) S of Ullapool
A 200ft (61m) deep canyon (National Trust for Scotland) providing special habitat for ferns and shrubs. The spectacular Falls of Measach drop 150ft (46m) through this gorge; there is a good bridge and viewing platform. Six miles (10km) north on Loch Broom are Lael Forest Gardens, with walks through species woodland laid out by Forest Enterprise.

CORRINGHAM Essex TQ7083
Town off A1014, 4 miles (6km) S of Basildon
Former village engulfed in housing estates. Attractive green, old cottages and church with impressive Norman tower.

CORRINGHAM Lincolnshire SK8791
Village on A631, 4 miles (6km) E of Gainsborough
Saxon church tower commands village from northern end of long main street. Fine Victorian restoration of church, with stencilled ceiling.

CORRIS Gwynedd SH7507
Village on A487, 4 miles (6km) N of Machynlleth
Hemmed in by forested mountains, Corris once echoed to sounds of slate-quarrying and locomotives. Railway museum, craft centre and underground boat ride to King Arthur's Labyrinth.

CORSHAM Wiltshire ST8770
Town off A4, 4 miles (6km) SW of Chippenham
The most picturesque town in Wiltshire, the centre full of stone houses, many of them 17th century and gabled. Stone Georgian houses too, a town hall of 1784, and Hungerford almshouses, 1668 with a very pretty porch. Corsham Court (in the town) is Elizabethan and Victorian imitation Elizabethan, with fine paintings and furniture and park and gardens, partly laid out by 'Capability' Brown and Repton. The Underground Quarry Centre is a Bath stone quarry.

CORSLEY Wiltshire ST8246
Village off A362, 3 miles (5km) NW of Warminster
Parish with several hamlets, churches in two of them. Stone cottages.

CORSTORPHINE Lothian NT1972
Area in W Edinburgh
Village swamped by spread of Edinburgh in 1920s. Corstorphine Hill has tower commemorating Sir Walter Scott and Edinburgh Zoo, run by Royal Scottish Zoological Society.

CORTON Suffolk TM5497
Village off A12, 3 miles (5km) N of Lowestoft
A long, pale yellow stretch of sand and shingle beach that is exceptionally clean. The southern area has been set aside for naturists.

CORWEN Clwyd SJ0743
Small town on A5, 8 miles (13km) W of Llangollen
By River Dee. Associated with Owain Glyndwr, whose estate was near by. Interesting church and Iron Age promontory fort with stone rampart. Livestock market.

CORYTON Essex TQ7382
Town on A1014, 5 miles (8km) S of Basildon
Giant Thames-bank industrial site named after Cory Brothers, creators of oil refinery/storage facility here, modernised by Mobil Oil in 1950s.

COSELEY West Midlands SO9494
Town off A4123, 3 miles (5km) SE of Wolverhampton
Houses and light industry have replaced the coal-pits and nail works of this former smoky town in the heart of the Black Country.

COSFORD Shropshire SJ8005
Village on A41, 2 miles (3km) NW of Albrighton
Next to the RAF station is Cosford Aerospace Museum, with a huge display of military and civil aircraft and a specialist collection of missiles and rockets.

COSGROVE Northamptonshire SP7942
Village off A508, 1 mile (2km) N of Stony Stratford
In curve of Great Ouse River on the Buckinghamshire boundary. Charming Gothick bridge over Grand Union Canal whose two halves met here, 1800.

COSHAM Hampshire SU6505
Suburb in N Portsmouth
Originally a village close to the bridge over to Portsmouth, but since the 1930s really a suburb of that city. Distinctive 1936 Church of St Philip, austere outside and superbly fitted inside. Miles of terraced and semi-detached houses, 1930s onwards.

COSSALL Nottinghamshire SK4842
Village off A6096, 6 miles (10km) W of Nottingham
Attractive village with fine brick almshouses, 1685, and old cottages in its conservation area.

COTHELSTONE Somerset ST1831
Hamlet off A358, 6miles (10km) NW of Taunton
Hamlet in the Quantocks – manor house, 15th-century church and a few cottages – set in a good walking area.

COTHERIDGE Hereford and Worcester SO7855
Hamlet off A44, 4 miles (6km) W of Worcester
Limewashed Norman church has timber-framed tower, with lower stage consisting of tongued and grooved oak planks, 17th-century pulpit and box pews.

COTHERSTONE Durham NZ0119
Village on B6277, 3 miles (5km) NW of Barnard Castle
Pretty village with a group of stone cottages. Famous for its cheese. Remains of a Norman castle are to the north of the village.

COTON Cambridgeshire TL4058
Village off A1303, 3 miles (5km) W of Cambridge
An attractive village with a Norman church. Near by, between Coton and Madingley (see), is the American Military Cemetery.

COTON Northamptonshire SP6771
Village off A50, 9 miles (14km) NW of Northampton
Coton Manor country gardens attract visitors to see wildfowl, flamingos and tropical birds, in mellow ironstone village close to Ravensthorpe Reservoir.

COTSWOLD HILLS Gloucestershire/Oxfordshire
Hill range
The Cotswolds are a formation of rounded hills that begin their rise at Meon Hill, south of Stratford-on-Avon, and stretch southwest to a point north of Bath. Their most striking feature is the 'Edge' – the steep western escarpment that reaches a high point of 1,083ft (330m) at Cleeve Hill above Cheltenham. To the south and east the land slopes away from the Edge, forming the characteristic wolds landscape of rolling hills divided by eight rivers that flow off the hills as tributaries of the Thames or Severn. In the Stroud area the distinctive landscape of deep valleys and fast-flowing streams encouraged a local textile industry, but the main source of Cotswold prosperity was sheep-farming, to which the high expanses of open grassland were particularly suited.

The underlying oolitic limestone has been heavily quarried for centuries to produce the mellow stone buildings and drystone walls that are the major attraction of the Cotswold landscape. Careful preservation of this hill landscape, now an Area of Outstanding Natural Beauty, has given the Cotswolds a new prosperity from tourism.

COTTAM Humberside SE9964
Hamlet off B1249, 5 miles (8km) N of Great Driffield
This deserted medieval village also has a ruined church and near by there is a disused airfield.

COTTENHAM Cambridgeshire TL4467
Village on B1049, 6 miles (10km) N of Cambridge
Once famous for its cheeses, Cottenham stands on land that is above flood level. The church has curious onion-shaped pinnacles.

COTTESBROOKE Northamptonshire SP7173
Village off A50, 9 miles (14km) N of Northampton
Magnificent Cottesbrooke Hall, built 1702-13, has fine pictures, furniture, porcelain. Lovely medieval church with box pews, a three-decker pulpit and a two-storey family pew.

COTTESMORE Leicestershire SK9013
Village on B668, 4 miles (6km) NE of Oakham
Rutland Railway Museum re-creates ironstone quarry activity, operating industrial steam and diesel locomotives and rolling stock on former mineral line.

COTTINGHAM Humberside TA0432
Town on NW edge of Hull
Claims to be the largest village in England, also known as the 'university village' as many students from Hull University live here.

COTTISFORD Oxfordshire SP5831
Hamlet off A43, 5 miles (8km) N of Bicester
Flora Thompson, born at nearby Juniper Hill, went to school at Cottisford which became 'Fordlow' in her autobiographical classic *Lark Rise to Candleford.*

COTTON Suffolk TM0666
Village off B1113, 5 miles (8km) N of Stowmarket
The village is home to the fascinating Mechanical Music Museum, displaying all manner of contrivances from organs to music boxes.

COUGHTON Warwickshire SP0860
Village on A435, 2 miles (3km) N of Alcester
Coughton Court (National Trust) is rich in history. Home of the Catholic Throckmorton family since 1409, the present house is of 16th-century origin (impressive battlemented gatehouse survives) with subsequent developments of the 18th and 19th centuries. Chapel, secret rooms, paintings, tapestries and intriguing historical exhibits (wives of Gunpowder Plotters sheltered here). St Peter's Church well worth visiting.

COULSDON Greater London TQ2959
District in borough of Croydon
Former Surrey village on London–Brighton road, now thoroughly suburbanised. Village green with medieval church, enlarged in 1950s.

COUND Shropshire SJ5505
Village on A458, 6 miles (10km) SE of Shrewsbury
Cound Hall is a notable 'provincial baroque' house of 1704, elaborately embellished. On the A458, near by, a former 17th-century manor house now serves as pub.

COUNDON West Midlands SP3181
District on NW outskirts of Coventry
This green-belt residential suburb of Coventry, with a Jaguar factory near by, still retains hints of its former village character.

COUPAR ANGUS Tayside NO2239
Small town on A94, 4 miles (6km) SE of Blairgowrie
Strathmore market town, centre for surrounding soft-fruit-growing area. Traces of nearby Roman camp and Cistercian abbey.

COVEHITHE Suffolk TM5282
Hamlet off A12, 4 miles (6km) N of Southwold
A new church was built inside an old one in 1672, and stands against the magnificent backdrop of the rugged Suffolk coast.

COVENTRY West Midlands SP3378
City off M6, 17 miles (27km) E of Birmingham
The ancient, huddled centre of Coventry, prosperous since the Middle Ages from wool-trading and later from precision engineering, was demolished by three nights of bombing in 1940. The present city is largely the result of post-war reconstruction, the symbol of which was Basil Spence's Cathedral of St Michael, opened in 1962 beside the ruins of the old building. Dominated by Graham Sutherland's huge tapestry *Christ in Majesty*, it contains outstanding work by other artists of the 1950s.

Among other innovations Coventry introduced pedestrian precincts and 'people-friendly' traffic management that placed major industrial sites close to out-of-town main roads. The result is a fairly tranquil centre in which some old buildings survive, for example the almshouses known as Ford's Hospital (Greyfriars Lane) and Bond's Hospital (Hill Street), and the medieval Guildhall of St Mary in Bayley Lane. Other old buildings have been moved and re-erected in Spon Street. The Herbert Art Gallery and Museum, near the cathedral, traces Coventry's history and displays furniture and silver, while the Museum of British Road Transport in Hales Street portrays one of Coventry's best-known industries.

COVERACK Cornwall SW7818
Village on B3294, 10 miles (16km) SE of Helston
A fishing village tucked in behind Dolor Point on the east side of the Lizard peninsula. The little harbour is of the local Serpentine stone and has a date stone of 1724. Very plain cottages, some thatched. Unspoilt, somehow empty, with wild coast to the south.

COVERHAM North Yorkshire SE1086
Hamlet off A6108, 2 miles (3km) SW of Middleham
Hamlet in Coverdale founded by Premonstratensian monks who built an abbey and the first bridge over River Cover.

COW GREEN RESERVOIR Durham NY8129
Reservoir off B6277, 9 miles (14km) NW of Middleton in Teesdale
Upland reservoir located in the heart of the North Pennines. Provides quality fishing for brown trout.

COWAN BRIDGE Lancashire SD6376
Village on A65, 2 miles (3km) SE of Kirkby Lonsdale
Charlotte Brontë attended School for Clergymen's Daughters here and used the unhappy experience in her novel *Jane Eyre*.

COWBIT Lincolnshire TF2617
Village on A1073, 3 miles (5km) S of Spalding
Pronounced 'Cubbit'. Beside River Welland and fen drains. Norman stone shaft 2 miles (3km) south may mark Croyland Abbey's boundary.

COWBRIDGE South Glamorgan SS9974
Town off A48, 12 miles (19km) W of Cardiff
Prosperous market town in lush Vale of Glamorgan known for quality shops, crafts. Beaupre Castle's Elizabethan ruins (Cadw) near by . Llanerch Vineyard tours.

COWDEN Kent TQ4640
Village off A264, 5 miles (8km) E of East Grinstead
Hidden among leafy lanes on the Sussex border, compact village of weatherboarded and half-timbered houses; iron grave slabs in churchyard.

COWDENBEATH Fife NT1691
Town on A909, 5 miles (8km) NE of Dunfermline
Once Fife's most important coal-mining town, whose population soared between 1860 and 1920, Cowdenbeath is now economically ruined by the decline in the industry.

COWES Isle of Wight SZ4996
Town on A3020, 4 miles (6km) N of Newport
West Cowes is the most famous yachting centre in the country, with Cowes Week in August the premier event. A large town running along the shore, where yachts, seaplanes, hovercraft and all sorts of ships have been built. The Royal Yacht Squadron clubhouse uses the base of a Henry VIII fort to fire the guns which start races. Two marine museums – Sir Max Aitken Museum and Cowes Maritime Museum. Norwood House of 1840 is the best building, high above the town with the oddest church tower in the country; close by – St Mary's of 1816 by John Nash, Greek in style.

Just over the river mouth, connected by a floating bridge, is the much smaller East Cowes, with large industrial buildings. Car ferries for Southampton leave from here. Cowes Roads are the deep and sheltered waters close to Cowes. Much traffic – yachts, ferries and large ships en route for Southampton or Portsmouth.

Queen Victoria and Prince Albert built Osborne House (English Heritage) in 1845 as an informal family home. Large and Italianate, it has intricately decorated and furnished rooms.

COWFOLD West Sussex TQ2122
Village on A272, 6 miles (10km) SE of Horsham
Attractive friendly village of brick, timber and tile-hung cottages with a wide green and lovely intimate grouping round church.

COWLEY Oxfordshire SP5304
District in SE Oxford
District famous for churches, monks and especially motor cars, following establishment of factory by William Morris (Lord Nuffield).

COWLINGE Suffolk TL7154
Village off A143, 6 miles (10km) NE of Haverhill
This small village is dominated by the splendid brick tower of St Margaret's Church. The body of the church is early 14th century.

COWPEN BEWLEY Cleveland NZ4824
Village off A1185, 2 miles (3km) NE of Billingham
Cowpen (pronounced 'Coo-pen') Nature Reserve, is a haven for wildlife, on marshland, with many waders and wildfowl.

COWSHILL Durham NY8540
Village on A689, 1 mile (2km) N of Wear Head
Located at head of Upper Weardale. Once centre of intense lead-mining region based around Killhope.

COWTHORPE North Yorkshire SE4252
Village off A1, 3 miles (5km) NE of Wetherby
Remote rural Church of St Michael was built in 1450s by Brian Roucliffe.

COXHOE Durham NZ3136
Village on A177, 5 miles (8km) SE of Durham
Nearby Coxhoe Hall, now demolished, was the birthplace of Elizabeth Barrett Browning.

COXWOLD North Yorkshire SE5377
Village off A19, 5 miles (8km) N of Easingwold
Oliver Cromwell's daughter, Mary, married Thomas, Earl of Fauconberg, after whom 17th-century inn is named. Cromwell's body is believed to have been secretly buried at Newburgh Priory after the restoration of Charles II. Eccentric literary figure Laurence Sterne was vicar here for last eight years of his life. He bought Shandy Hall, which appears in one of his best-known novels, *Tristram Shandy*.

CRACKINGTON HAVEN Cornwall SX1496
Village off A39, 5 miles (8km) NE of Boscastle
A small village on the rockiest part of the rocky north Cornish coast. Steep roads and woody valleys inland.

CRACKPOT North Yorkshire SD9796
Hamlet off B6270, 1 mile (2km) SW of Low Row
The name is said to be Norse, meaning 'cave frequented by crows'. Confusingly, ruined Crackpot Hall stands near Swinnergill, at the back of Kisdon Hill; it was abandoned in the 1950s due to mining subsidence.

CRADLEY Hereford and Worcester SO7347
Village off A4103, 3 miles (5km) W of Great Malvern
A 15th-century parish hall is among several timber-framed buildings in the village. Section of Saxon frieze in tower wall of church.

CRAGHEAD Durham NZ2150
Village on B6313, 2 miles (3km) SE of Stanley
A former mining village at the head of Upper Weardale. A woodland trail links displays of early mining.

CRAIG-Y-NOS Powys SN8315
Site on A4067, 10 miles (16km) SW of Sennybridge
The 19th-century castle was home to the celebrated operatic singer Madame Adelina Patti. Her bijou theatre is still used occasionally and the parkland is now an attractive country park. Dan-yr-Ogof Showcaves complex is reputedly largest in western Europe and includes main cave system, Cathedral Cave and Bone Cave; also a Dinosaur Park, museum, dry skiing, pony trekking.

CRAIGELLACHIE Grampian NJ2844
Village on A95, 3 miles (5km) S of Rothes
Village in heart of distillery country with cooperage for whisky barrels. Pleasant walks along Spey which is crossed by Telford's cast-iron bridge.

CRAIGIEVAR CASTLE Grampian NJ5609
Mansion off A980, 4 miles (6km) S of Alford
Quintessential example of turreted tower house in charming position, completed in 1620s and unchanged since. Notable interior ceilings and vaulted hall.

CRAIGMILLAR Lothian NT3071
Area in S Edinburgh
Lying near southern edge of Edinburgh and dominated by impressive ruins of Craigmillar Castle; L-shaped tower house dating from 1600s with intact great hall, enclosed by later wall with corner towers. One of best-preserved Scottish medieval fortresses and scene of plot to murder Lord Darnley, second husband of Mary Stuart.

CRAIGNURE Strathclyde (Mull) NM7236
Village on A849, 18 miles (29km) SE of Tobermory
Main ferry port on Mull. Nineteenth-century Torosay Castle is a baronial pile chiefly remarkable for gardens, linked to village by narrow-gauge railway.

CRAIL Fife NO6107
Small town on A917, 10 miles (16km) S of St Andrews
Granted a charter in 1178, making it the oldest of the five royal burghs in the East Neuk (see). Nowadays more a tourist centre than fishing village with attractive and typical crow-stepped red-tiled houses clustered round the harbour and some interesting old buildings. Crail 'capon', or smoked haddock, was an early export.

CRAMLINGTON Northumberland NZ2676
Town off A1, 8 miles (13km) N of Newcastle upon Tyne
A new town centred around the ancient village centre of Smithy Square with its typical village green still intact.

CRAMOND Lothian NT1976
Village off A90, 5 miles (8km) W of Edinburgh
Site of Roman settlement and port; church stands on site of fort. Eighteenth-century industrial village, restored in 1960s, with attractive step-gabled houses on Firth of Forth, with passenger ferry across river since 1550s and pretty local walks. Off-shore Cramond Island reachable on foot at low tide. Attractive old inn.

CRANBORNE Dorset SU0513
Village on B3081, 8 miles (13km) NW of Ringwood
Once an important settlement, the centre of Cranborne Chase (see), but it declined to a backwater when it was left off the railway lines. Mostly 18th century and brick. Interesting late medieval church, with Norman doorway. Cranborne Manor gardens are very fine (limited opening).

CRANBORNE CHASE Dorset
Scenic region on Dorset/Wiltshire border
An Area of Outstanding Natural Beauty. From medieval times until 1830 a hunting forest, where the deer were encouraged and protected. Originally bordered by Ringwood, Salisbury, Shaftesbury and Blandford, but the name really applies to the still wooded area around Cranborne village. Early medieval kings hunted here.

CRANBOURNE Berkshire SU9272
Village off A330, 3 miles (5km) N of Ascot
Small village, close to Windsor Forest. Church 1849 with William Morris stained glass.

CRANBROOK Kent TQ7736
Small town off A229, 7 miles (11km) W of Tenterden
Delightful little town, 'capital' of Kentish Weald, lying among gentle hills near headwaters of River Crane. Raised pavements, weatherboarded, brick and timber houses built in prosperous days as centre of cloth weaving, 14th–19th centuries. Church, known as 'cathedral of the Weald' has tall tower, but Cranbrook is dominated by Union Mill, the largest working windmill in England.

CRANFIELD Bedfordshire SP9542
Village off A422, 8 miles (13km) SW of Bedford
Parish pump on the green, Quaker almshouses, wartime airfield and former well-known college of aeronautics.

CRANFORD Greater London TQ1076
District in borough of Hounslow
Once Middlesex's prettiest village, suburbanised from 1930s. Village lock-up in High Street. Notable monuments, 1930s fittings in St Dunstan's Church.

CRANFORD, ST ANDREW AND ST JOHN
Northamptonshire SP9277/SP9276
Villages on A14, 4 miles (6km) E of Kettering
Twin villages, with 15th-century circular dovecote in beautiful parkland, and brass to Henry VI's nurse in St Andrew's Church.

CRANLEIGH Surrey TQ0539
Town on B2128, 8 miles (13km) SE of Guildford
Cheerful small town, once a centre for iron industry, with friendly tree-lined green that narrows to become the High Street.

CRANMORE Somerset ST6643
Villages off A361, 4 miles (6km) E of Shepton Mallet
Home of the East Somerset Steam Railway and with the largest Mendip quarry, producing limestone for road making, taken out by its own railway.

CRANTOCK Cornwall SW7960
Village off A3075, 2 miles (3km) SW of Newquay
A little village opposite Newquay which has gained some seaside development. Rocky headlands to the west.

CRANWELL Lincolnshire TF0349
Village on B1429, 4 miles (6km) NW of Sleaford
Small village whose name is best known in connection with Royal Air Force College, completed 1933. Nearby aviation heritage centre.

The 16th-century tower house at Crathes.

CRARAE Strathclyde NR9897
Village on A83, 9 miles (14km) SW of Inverary
In superb setting on Loch Fyne with Sir George Campbell's spectacular azalea and rhododendron gardens, planted mainly in 1920s, in ravine around Crarae Lodge.

CRASTER Northumberland NU2519
Village off B1339, 6 miles (10km) NE of Alnwick
Picturesque fishing village famous for its delicious smoked kippers. There is a pleasant coastal walk to Dunstanburgh Castle (see Embleton).

CRASWALL Hereford and Worcester SO2735
Hamlet off B4350, 5 miles (8km) SE of Hay-on-Wye
Remote Black Mountain hamlet with primitive church and, to the north, ruins of priory founded in 1222.

CRATFIELD Suffolk TM3175
Village off B1123, 5 miles (8km) W of Halesworth
About 150 houses dating from 1700s to 1900s make up Cratfield. Trees and hedgerows have been carefully tended, making the village a haven for wildflowers.

CRATHES Grampian NO7596
Village off A93, 3 miles (5km) E of Banchory
Lovely gardens surround fine 16th-century towerhouse with picturesque turrets and gables. Inside, splendid woodwork and painted ceilings.

CRATHIE Grampian NO2695
Village on A93, 1 mile (2km) E of Balmoral
Granite church built in 1895 to serve Balmoral Castle. John Brown, Queen Victoria's ghillie, buried in churchyard. The Princess Royal married Commander Tim Laurence here.

CRAVEN North Yorkshire
District in NW Yorkshire
An historic region, the Craven Lowlands stretch towards Morecambe Bay and to both north and south there is a marked step up on to the limestone plateau of the Craven Uplands. The Craven Faults, dominating this great step, constitute a major break in the bedrock geology and displacement of the limestone beneath the surface of the lowlands.

CRAVEN ARMS Shropshire SO4382
Small town on A49, 7 miles (11km) NW of Ludlow
Named after the Craven Arms hotel on the main road, this is a haphazard 19th-century town, built at a railway junction as a market and distribution depot for sheep, mainly from Wales. To the south is Stokesay Castle (English Heritage), an exceptionally well-preserved 13th-century fortified manor house with an impressive great hall and exuberant Elizabethan gatehouse.

CRAWFORD Strathclyde NS9520
Village off A702, 2 miles (3km) SE of Abington
River Clyde proper considered to start in the rolling hilly area around this village off the A74. Many local Iron Age hillforts.

CRAWLEY Hampshire SU4235
Village off A272, 5 miles (8km) NW of Winchester
A single dense street with an unusual combination of plain old cottages and fancy newer ones built by the estate 1900–20. The model village had a bathhouse and even a roller-skating rink.

CRAWLEY West Sussex TQ2836
New Town off M23, 9 miles (14km) S of Reigate
Vibrant modern town designated New Town in 1947. Has grown rapidly around old village, a wide and pleasing tree-lined street of old houses including the George hotel with 'gallows' sign overhanging road. Modern town centres on Queen Square, just behind High Street, linked to it through the churchyard. Beyond are large housing districts with their own amenities.

CRAWSHAWBOOTH Lancashire SD8125
Village on A682, 2 miles (3km) N of Rawtenstall
The village was an important settlement in the old hunting forest of Rossendale. It has a local animal sanctuary and graveyard.

CRAYFORD Greater London TQ5175
District in borough of Bexley
Where Watling Street crosses River Cray, former company town of Maxim's and Vickers' armaments works. Norman and later church with monuments.

CRAYKE North Yorkshire SE5670
Village off A19, 2 miles (3km) E of Easingwold
On a low hill in the Vale of York, Crayke was the birthplace of the celebrated and controversial churchman Dean Inge (1860–1954).

CREAKE, NORTH AND SOUTH Norfolk TF8538
Villages on B1355, 7 miles (11km) NW of Fakenham
North and South Creake are two villages linked by the River Burn. North Creake is noted especially for the ruins of Creake Abbey, once an important stopping-off place for pilgrims travelling to Walsingham. The peaceful ruins are well worth a visit. A three-storeyed corn mill in West Street is said to be the smallest in Norfolk. Situated on the gently flowing River Burn, South Creake's pretty flint cottages have little wooden footbridges for residents. Also has a derelict 1920s razorblade factory.

CREDENHILL Hereford and Worcester SO4543
Village on A480, 4 miles (6km) NW of Hereford
Poet Thomas Traherne was the vicar of St Mary's Church, which has an unusual chancel screen and other striking medieval details. National Snail Farming Centre.

CREDITON Devon SS8300
Small town on A377, 8 miles (13km) NW of Exeter
Birthplace of St Boniface in the 7th century; an old monastic settlement. A sleepy market town, with many 18th- and 19th-century buildings: the earlier ones were destroyed by fires. Big red sandstone church, mostly 15th century.

CREECH ST MICHAEL Somerset ST2725
Village off A358, 3 miles (5km) E of Taunton
On the Bridgwater and Taunton Canal as well as the River Tone, and growing because it is close to Taunton. Interesting medieval church.

CREED Cornwall SW9347
Hamlet off A390, 6 miles (10km) SW of St Austell
Tiny hamlet on the side of the Fal Valley with church for several larger settlements.

CREETOWN Dumfries and Galloway NX4759
Village on A75, 6 miles (10km) SE of Newton Stewart
Called Ferrytown until 1791. Nineteenth-century granite quarries which supplied stone for Thames Embankment. Area used by Scott in *Guy Mannering*.

CREMYLL Cornwall SX4553
Village on B3247, 3 miles (5km) NE of Millbrook
A few old houses with wide views of Plymouth, just across the Sound. A foot ferry runs between the two. See also Mount Edgcumbe.

CRESSAGE Shropshire SJ5904
Village on A458, 3 miles (5km) NW of Much Wenlock
Attractive Severnside village believed to have been a Celtic preaching place. Church of 1841 on site of Celtic Church of St Sampson.

CRESSING Essex TL7920
Village off B1018, 3 miles (5km) SE of Braintree
Two fine 13th-century barns on former estate of Knights Templar with farmhouse of about 1600, Elizabethan court hall.

CRESSINGHAM, LITTLE AND GREAT Norfolk TF8700
Villages off B1108, 3 miles (5km) W of Watton
Little and Great Cressingham are pleasant villages, with a ruined church and some Bronze Age barrows in which a skeleton was found.

CRESSWELL Northumberland NZ2993
Village off A1068, 4 miles (6km) N of Ashington
A coastal village on Druridge Bay known for its sand dunes. Cresswell Pond nature trail was developed in 1991.

CRESWELL Derbyshire SK5274
Village on A616, 4 miles (6km) NE of Bolsover
Limestone gorge of Creswell Crags, on Derbyshire/Nottinghamshire border, has 26 caves dating back 100,000 years, used as shelter by Neanderthal Man while hunting. Tours bookable through visitor centre where finds are displayed. Nearby Whalley Thorns heritage centre continues story of human activity in area from Stone Age to coal industry and agriculture.

CRETINGHAM Suffolk TM2260
Village off A1120, 4 miles (6km) SE of Debenham
A delightful village with a fine Tudor pub boasting oak-beamed ceilings and half-timbered walls. A vicar was once murdered in Cretingham by his curate.

CREWE Cheshire SJ7056
Town on A532, 12 miles (19km) NW of Stoke-on-Trent
Founded on the fortunes of the Grand Junction Railway Company, Crewe is also famous as the original home of the Rolls-Royce motor car. The history of the town and its important links with the railways is explored at The Railway Age in the town centre. The Crewe Lyceum Theatre is a fine Edwardian building.

CREWE GREEN Cheshire SJ7255
Hamlet on B5077, 2 miles (3km) E of Crewe
Village hall, formerly the local school, features a decorated outside south wall with unusual inscriptions.

CREWKERNE Somerset ST4409
Town on A30, 8 miles (13km) SW of Yeovil
A proper old-fashioned market town, with lots of stone buildings, a market square nearly filled by Victoria Hall (1900) and many second-hand bookshops. Large church, mostly of around 1500.

CRIANLARICH Central NN3825
Village on A82, 5 miles (8km) SE of Tyndrum
Important road junction with rail connections to Glasgow and Fort William. Position on West Highland Way and surrounding scenic splendour make it good walking base.

CRICCIETH Gwynedd SH5038
Town on A497, 15 miles (24km) S of Caernarfon
Two-beached resort of Victorian pedigree on southern side of Lleyn peninsula (see). Dividing headland dramatically topped by Welsh castle, captured by English, reoccupied by Welsh (Cadw). Its natural defensive position was enhanced by Edward I's fortifications, especially twin-towered gatehouse. Wonderful outlook. David Lloyd George lived near by. Annual festival (mainly music) has good reputation.

CRICH Derbyshire SK3454
Village on B5035, 4 miles (6km) N of Belper
Large village with hilltop church and market cross, gritstone cottages leading downhill to broadening of street beside solid chapel. National Tramway Museum developed in former quarry beneath Crich Stand, inland lighthouse monument to Sherwood Foresters Regiment. Vintage trams from Britain and around world, many operated for visitors to ride through Edwardian street, with exhibitions, special events.

CRICHTON Lothian NT3862
Village on B6367, 2 miles (3km) S W of Pathhead
Close by is ruined Crichton Castle, 14th-century basic keep transformed into Renaissance residence with arcaded courtyard by 5th Earl of Bothwell.

CRICK Northamptonshire SP5872
Village on A428, 6 miles (10km) E of Rugby
Between M1, which used to end here, and Grand Union Canal, a pleasant village dominated by its 14th-century ironstone church.

CRICKET MALHERBIE Somerset ST3611
Hamlet off A358, 3 miles (5km) NE of Chard
Hamlet on a hill slope, the name meaning 'little hill'. Owned by the Malherbie family.

CRICKET ST THOMAS Somerset ST3708
Hamlet off A30, 3 miles (5km) E of Chard
Below Windwhistle Ridge, with the large Cricket St Thomas Wildlife Park, gardens, exotic animals and birds, railway, and National Heavy Horse Centre. House, 1801 (not open), used for television programme *To the Manor Born.*

CRICKHOWELL Powys SO2118
Small town on A40, 6 miles (10km) NW of Abergavenny
Iron Age fort on Table Mountain overlooks this pretty little town with attractive shops. Stone-arched bridge across River Usk, Norman-castled mound. Bear hotel is an old coaching inn.

CRICKLADE Wiltshire SU0993
Village off A419, 7 miles (11km) NW of Swindon
Saxon town, still with the square earthen defences built in Alfred's time. Church with a very prominent 16th-century tower, and another little Norman one tucked into the High Street. Seventeenth-century and Georgian stone and stucco houses, mixed with modern. Robert Jenner's school of 1651 is pretty. Local museum. A meadow to the north has thousands of fritillaries in May.

CRICKLEWOOD Greater London TQ2385
District in borough of Brent
Countryside until late 19th century. Edwardian churches and Baptist chapel, brick waterworks. Mosque and Islamic Centre in former Congregational church.

CRIEFF Tayside NN8621
Town on A85, 6 miles (10km) E of Comrie
Ancient town on Highland Line where several drove roads converged, Crieff was important cattle trading centre until 18th century, and developed as spa town after arrival of railway in 1856. Tenth-century market cross. Outside town Scotland's oldest distillery, Glenturret, was established in 1775. Popular holiday centre with many attractions for visitors.

CRIMOND Grampian NK0556
Village on A952, 8 miles (13km) NW of Peterhead
Best known for Loch of Strathbeg Nature Reserve, good information on winter goose population and observation hides. Remains of Rattray Castle on lochside.

CRINAN Strathclyde NR7894
Village off B841, 6 miles (10km) NW of Lochgilphead
At west end of Crinan Canal, linking Loch Fyne with Sound of Jura. Small fishing port, but chiefly holiday and boating centre, with superb views.

CROCKHAM HILL Kent TQ4450
Village on B2026, 2 miles (3km) S of Westerham
Late Victorian mansions set on sandstone ridge with wonderful views south over the Weald and to the north over the common of bracken and gorse.

CROFT Hereford and Worcester SO4465
Site off B4362, 5 miles (8km) NW of Leominster
Extensive National Trust estate. On its northern edge Croft Ambrey, Iron Age hillfort, stands at 1,000ft (300m) on ridge. To the south the medieval exterior of Croft Castle hides an elegant 18th-century house with fine interior decoration. Church of 1660s. Good walking on Bircher Common to east of castle and in wooded gorge known as Fishpool Valley.

CROFT Lincolnshire TF5061
Hamlet off A52, 2 miles (3km) NE of Wainfleet
Hamlet behind Skegness. Late Georgian rectory grouped with fine marshland church, with 1615 pulpit, pews with doors, early brass of knight.

CROFT-ON-TEES North Yorkshire NZ2809
Village on A167, 3 miles (5km) S of Darlington
This village on the River Tees straddles the Yorkshire and Cleveland border. Built of colourful stone, the Church of St Peter contains good 14th- and 15th-century work, 15th- to 18th-century monuments and a sculpture reputed to be Romano-British. Lewis Carroll's father was rector here for a number of years, and Lord Byron was a visitor.

CROICK CHURCH Highland NH4591
Site off A836, 10 miles (16km) W of Bonar Bridge
Evicted Clearance tenants sheltered in graveyard of isolated church in Strath Carron; they scratched still-legible messages on church windows. 'Glencalvie people was here May 24 1845.'

CROMARTY Highland NH7867
Small town on A832, 18 miles (29km) NE of Inverness
Lies just inside Cromarty Firth and is perfect example of 18th-century burgh and port which escaped later development. Harbour, linen and ironworks, brewery, Fishertown area and two churches survive from 18th century. Courthouse (1773–83) is now award-winning museum. Hugh Miller, geologist, stonemason and writer, was born here; his cottage (1711) is now run by National Trust for Scotland.

CROMER Norfolk TG2242
Town on A140, 21 miles (34km) N of Norwich
Generous expanses of clean, amber sand and extravagant Victorian hotels teetering on the cliff tops are Cromer's hallmark. It first became a popular seaside resort in the late 18th century, although long before that it was an important centre for fishing. Crabbing has remained one of Cromer's mainstays, and Cromer crabs are famous all over the country.

Cromer's popularity as a holiday resort has persisted, and many of the fine, spacious hotels built for Victorians who expected luxury and elegance, still exist. Nearby Overstrand Hall is a classic example, built by Edwin Lutyens. No one expects a British holiday to be entirely rain-free, and Cromer has two museums to amuse visitors in inclement weather. The Lifeboat Museum at the pier has a large collection of photographs and models, along with the medals of the local lifeboat hero Henry Bloggs. The new lifeboat is called *Ruby and Arthur Read II* and can be viewed at the Lifeboat House.

The 160ft (49m) tower of the Church of St Peter and St Paul soars above the town, and is the tallest church tower in the county.

CROMFORD Derbyshire SK2956
Village on A5012, 2 miles (3km) N of Wirksworth
World-renowned site of Richard Arkwright's first successful cotton-spinning mill, 1771, harnessing the power of River Derwent. Mill open with explanatory displays, craft shops and restaurant. Willersley Castle, built as Arkwright's home, is now Methodist holiday centre. Canalside walks and picnics at Cromford Wharf. Market place and model housing for Arkwright's workers in Cromford village, across busy A6.

CROMWELL Nottinghamshire SK7961
Village off A1, 5 miles (8km) N of Newark
On the old Great North road. Seventeenth-century Old Rectory now setting for Vina Cooke Museum of Dolls and Bygone Childhood.

CRONDALL Hampshire SU7948
Village off A287, 3 miles (5km) NW of Farnham
Between the chalk of the North Downs and heathlands, large village with houses and cottages of brick, timber-framing and even some flint.

CRONTON Merseyside SJ4988
Village on A5080, 5 miles (8km) W of Warrington
An ancient settlement with one of the last surviving groups of pre-18th-century buildings in the Merseyside area.

CROOK Cumbria SD4695
Village on B5284, 4 miles (6km) NW of Kendal
A pleasant Lakeland village midway between Kendal and Bowness-on-Windermere. The church has a bell dating from the 14th century.

CROOK Durham NZ1635
Town on A689, 5 miles (8km) NW of Bishop Auckland
Small market town and administrative centre of Wear Valley. New industries have now taken over from coal-mining.

CROOME D'ABITOT Hereford and Worcester SO8844
Site off A38, 7 miles (11km) S of Worcester
Croome Court, a distinguished Palladian house, 1751, is not open, but church with Robert Adam interior and fine monuments can be visited.

CROPREDY Oxfordshire SP4646
Village off A423, 4 miles (6km) N of Banbury
Royalists and Parliamentarians fought in 1644 for possession of Cropredy's strategic bridge over River Cherwell. Today the Oxford Canal runs side by side with the river through the peaceful village. The spacious medieval church possesses a rare Spanish lectern of the 15th century.

CROPTHORNE Hereford and Worcester SO9945
Village off A44, 3 miles (5km) W of Evesham
Avonside village worth visiting for pleasing variety of dwellings and Norman church possessing fine monuments and rare Saxon stone cross of about 800.

CROPTON North Yorkshire SE7589
Village off A170, 4 miles (6km) NW of Pickering
Nearby Cawthorn Camps was a remarkable Roman military encampment. William Scoresby, navigator and Arctic explorer, was born here in 1760.

CROPWELL, BISHOP AND BUTLER Nottinghamshire SK6835/SK6837
Villages off A46, 8 miles (13km) SE of Nottingham
Formerly Crophill, after rounded hill now called Hoe Hill. Possessed respectively by Archbishop of York and Butler family.

CROSBY Merseyside SJ3198
Town off A565, 6 miles (10km) N of Liverpool
Coastal town which developed in 19th century when Liverpool businessmen came to live here. Crosby channel runs parallel to shore close to the beach.

CROSBY GARRETT Cumbria NY7209
Village off A685, 3 miles (5km) W of Kirkby Stephen
Dominated by the viaduct of the Settle–Carlisle railway. Traces of prehistoric settlements have been found on the surrounding fells.

CROSBY RAVENSWORTH Cumbria NY6214
Village off B6260, 5 miles (8km) SW of Appleby-in-Westmorland
Ancient village in the valley of the River Lyvennet. Ewe Close, a Celtic settlement of 2nd or 3rd century BC, takes the form of a complicated series of enclosure walls and hut circles. The Church of St Lawrence contains the tomb of Sir Lancelot Threlkeld, who saved the young Cliffords in the Wars of the Roses.

CROSCOMBE Somerset ST5944
Village on A371, 3 miles (5km) E of Wells
Steep little valley, lots of stone cottages. Medieval church, one of the finest sets of 17th-century fittings in the country – screen, pulpit, box pews.

CROSS IN HAND East Sussex TQ5521
Village on B2102, 1 mile (2km) W of Heathfield
Old cottages and pub surrounded by modern housing on breezy hilltop dominated by particularly fine smock mill.

CROSSCANONBY Cumbria NY0739
Hamlet off A596, 3 miles (5km) NE of Maryport
Originally just four farms and four cottages. Formerly part of the salt trade, at Salt Pans, deep-dug basins remain.

CROSSFORD Strathclyde NS8246
Village on A72, 3 miles (5km) SW of Carluke
On junction of River Clyde with River Nethan and downstream from ruined Craignethan Castle (1530s), last major castle to be built in Scotland.

CROSSKEYS Gwent ST2291

Village on A467, 6 miles (10km) NW of Newport

At junction of Ebbw and Sirhowy valleys, surrounded by forested hillsides regenerated after coal-mining past. Cwmcarn Forest Drive is 7 miles (11km) long with wide-ranging views, adventure play area and picnic places, leading to Twmbarlwm hillfort. Neighbouring Sirhowy Valley's large country park offers walks, Land Rover safaris and a working farm. Babell Chapel is local poet Islwyn's memorial.

CROSTHWAITE Cumbria SD4391

Hamlet off A5074, 5 miles (8km) W of Kendal

The name means 'cross in a clearing' and it is thought there has been a chapel or church here for centuries.

CROSTON Lancashire SD4818

Village on A581, 6 miles (10km) W of Chorley

Pretty village with 17th-century almshouses and weavers' cottages. Old packhorse bridge dated 1682, but was actually built in 1671.

CROUGHTON Northamptonshire SP5433

Village on B4031, 4 miles (6km) SW of Brackley

Close to Oxfordshire border, with thatched Victorian school, and 12th-century church with timber roof and 14th-century wall-paintings.

CROVIE Grampian NJ8065

Village off B9031, 7 miles (11km) E of Banff

Picturesque fishing village nestled against tall cliffs on Gamrie Bay and sheltered by Crovie Head. Impressive viewpoint on cliff top.

CROWBOROUGH East Sussex TQ5131

Town on A26, 7 miles (11km) SW of Tunbridge Wells

Populous modern town spreading around Ashdown Forest's highest hill – Crowborough Beacon – at 729ft (240m) although most is lower, and known for its bracing air. Golf course.

CROWCOMBE Somerset ST1436

Village off A358, 6 miles (10km) SE of Watchet

Tucked under the Quantocks, a large village with an interesting church whose spire was destroyed by lightning in 1725. Bench-ends of 1534, and 1729 rood screen and pulpit, replacing those destroyed by the lightning. The 16th-century Church House is a rare survival.

CROWELL Oxfordshire SU7499

Hamlet on B4009, 3 miles (5km) NW of Stokenchurch

Hamlet nestles beneath chalk pits at the edge of Chiltern Hills, overlooked by the ancient Ridgeway.

CROWFIELD Suffolk TM1457

Village off A1120, 4 miles (6km) SW of Debenham

Pleasing mixture of old and new houses line an old Roman road. The church is isolated from the rest of the village, but well worth visiting.

CROWHURST Surrey TQ3847

Hamlet off A22, 3 miles (5km) S of Oxted

Tiny rural place in rolling clay country near the Kent border, famed for the hollow yew in its churchyard.

The hollow yew in the churchyard at Crowhurst.

CROWLAND (OR CROYLAND) Lincolnshire TF2410
Small town on B1166, 8 miles (13km) NE of Peterborough
Fenland site of great 8th-century Benedictine abbey, founded by King Ethelbald in memory of St Guthlac, who sought refuge in this isolated spot. Spectacular Norman arch and 13th-century west front remain, with 15th-century bell tower and north aisle as parish church. Unique 14th-century triangular bridge provided crossing over confluence of three streams, but now on dry land.

CROWLE Hereford and Worcester SO9256
Village off A422, 5 miles (8km) E of Worcester
The handsome Chequers inn stands in long and appealing village street. Rare carved stone lectern of early 13th century in the church.

CROWLE Humberside SE7712
Village on A161, 10 miles (16km) SE of Goole
This former market town is now a conservation area with fine Georgian and Victorian buildings, particularly around the market square.

CROWMARSH GIFFORD Oxfordshire SU6189
Village on A4130, 1 mile (2km) E of Wallingford
The 19th-century Howbery Park now houses offices and laboratories, but the Norman church and medieval Queen's Head are reminders of village's long history.

CROWTHORNE Berkshire SU8464
Town on A3095, 4 miles (6km) SW of Bracknell
Mostly recent, but with two famous institutions – Broadmoor Hospital, with high walls, opened in 1863, and Wellington College, the public school founded in memory of the Duke of Wellington in 1853. Fancy French-style brick buildings, very impressive.

CROXALL Staffordshire SK1913
Hamlet off A513, 6 miles (10km) N of Tamworth
Little more than a church and hall (not open). The church has an unusual south wall comprising blocked arcade with medieval windows re-set.

CROXDALE Durham NZ2636
Village off A167, 2 miles (3km) N of Spennymoor
Rows of miners' cottages line main street, the old Great North road. There are dramatic bridges crossing the deep cleft made by the River Wear.

CROXDEN Staffordshire SK0639
Hamlet off B5032, 4 miles (6km) SE of Cheadle
Remnants of a Cistercian abbey (English Heritage) include the west front, south transept wall and east range of cloisters, all of the late 13th century.

CROXLEY GREEN Hertfordshire TQ0795
Village on A412, 1 mile (2km) NE of Rickmansworth
Green with some attractive houses and a partly Edwardian church. Rivers Gade, Chess, Colne near by and Grand Union Canal; towpath walks.

CROXTON Cambridgeshire TL2460
Hamlet on A428 (A45), 4 miles (6km) E of St Neots
This hamlet with its 17th- and 18th-century cottages and crumbling hall has an abandoned, but peaceful, atmosphere.

CROXTON KERRIAL Leicestershire SK8329
Village on A607, 7 miles (11km) SW of Grantham
Ironstone village high on Wolds, overlooking Belvoir Castle and, if clear, Lincoln Cathedral. Waterspout on main road fed by never-failing spring water.

CROYDE Devon SS4439
Village on B3231, 7 miles (11km) SW of Ilfracombe
Thatched cottages mixed with modern seaside development. Croyde Bay sandy and backed by dunes. Baggy Point gives wide views, including Lundy Island, and has a huge cave (Baggy Hole) under the Point.

CROYDON Cambridgeshire TL3149
Village off A1198, 6 miles (10km) NW of Royston
Set in pretty countryside among woods and a hill, Croydon was the home of George Downing, Cromwell's spy, who built Downing Street, in London.

CROYDON Greater London TQ3265
Borough in S London
Major Surrey town before merging into London. Centre full of giant post-war blocks. Fairfield Halls, 1960s concert hall, theatre complex. Shopping centres, street market. Parish church rebuilt by Sir George Gilbert Scott, 1860s, next to former palace of Archbishops of Canterbury, now a school. Sixteenth-century almshouses, 1890s town hall. Airfield was London's 1920s airport, closed 1959.

CRUACHAN RESERVOIR Strathclyde NN0828
Reservoir off A85, 6 miles (10km) W of Dalmally
Reservoir in a dammed glacial corrie on Ben Cruachan serving Cruachan Power Station, a hydro-electric plant in a cavern excavated within the mountain. Water is recycled for use in generating, being pumped back up to the reservoir during off-peak hours. Visitor centre and guided tours into the mountain.

CRUDEN BAY Grampian NK0836
Village on A975, 7 miles (11km) S of Peterhead
Seashore village with beach, renowned for its golf course. North lie Bullers of Buchan, 245ft (74m) deep chasm surrounded by rocks where sea 'bulls' or boils.

CRUDWELL Wiltshire ST9593
Village on A429, 4 miles (6km) NE of Malmesbury
Attractive stone-built village with an interesting medieval church.

CRUMMOCK WATER Cumbria NY1519
Lake off B5289, next to Buttermere
Lake fed by Scale Force, the highest waterfall in the Lake District. Ancient name was Cromack Water.

CRUWYS MORCHARD Devon SS8712
Hamlet off B3137, 5 miles (8km) W of Tiverton
Tiny – just the big house, 18th century with earlier part behind (not open), and the church with an interesting Georgian interior.

CRYNANT West Glamorgan SN7904
Village on A4109, 5 miles (8km) NE of Neath
In the Dulais Valley. Cefn Coed Colliery Museum on site of Blaenant Colliery, once world's deepest anthracite mine. Simulated mining gallery, working winding engine.

CRYSTAL PALACE Greater London TQ3371
District in S London
The giant prefabricated glasshouse that housed London's 1851 Great Exhibition was taken down and re-erected here, only to be destroyed by fire, 1936. Its plaster prehistoric animal figures survive engagingly along a stream and the extensive grounds now include the National Sports Stadium. Concert bowl. Museum in Anerley Hill.

CUBERT Cornwall SW7857
Village off A3075, 3 miles (5km) SW of Newquay
A large village inland from the huge sand dunes – up to 300ft/91m – of Penhale. Mostly modern but the church has a 14th-century tower and spire.

CUBLINGTON Buckinghamshire SP8422
Village off A418, 6 miles (10km) N of Aylesbury
In 1971 successfully resisted plan to site new London airport here. Traces of previous village to west, with Norman castle mound.

CUCKFIELD West Sussex TQ3025
Small town on B2036, 2 miles (3km) W of Haywards Heath
Delightful compact small town with attractive street of brick and stone houses, many with Horsham slate roofs.

CUCKMERE HAVEN East Sussex TV5197
Beauty spot off A259, 3 miles (5km) SE of Seaford
Unspoilt mouth of River Cuckmere, lying between Seaford Head and the Seven Sisters. Area of Outstanding Natural Beauty. Only undeveloped estuary in the southeast in England.

CUCKNEY Nottinghamshire SK5671
Village on A60, 7 miles (11km) N of Mansfield
Sherwood Forest village, meeting point of several roads on edge of the Dukeries, with 12th-century castle remains, and Greendale Oak inn.

CUDDESDON Oxfordshire SP5903
Village off A329, 6 miles (10km) SE of Oxford
Set on a hill overlooking the Thame Valley, this village has a church with fine Norman and Victorian features, but is best known for its theological college, started in 1854 and the first major work by ecclesiastical architect GE Street, who also designed some brick cottages. The 17th-century Denton House was built for bishops of Oxford.

CUDDINGTON Buckinghamshire SP7311
Village off A418, 4 miles (6km) NE of Thame
Prize-winning 'best kept' village, with houses originally built of 'witchert' (soil and straw). Work by GE Street in church.

CUFFLEY Hertfordshire TL3003
Village on B157, 2 miles (3km) W of Cheshunt
Sought-after, suburban, stockbrokery, mock-Tudor, in farming countryside. Obelisk marks shooting down of Zeppelin in 1916. Country park noted for fungi.

CUILLIN HILLS Highland (Skye) NG4422
Mountain range in S Skye
Steepest and most dramatic mountain range in Britain with over 20 Munros; precipitous slopes offer advanced rock-climbing and mountaineering and there is also excellent hill-walking. Glen Sligachan divides main ridge, 6 mile (10km) semi-circular jagged peaks of Black Cuillins, composed of gabbro and overlooking Loch Coruisk, from the granite and more symmetrical Red Cuillins.

CULBONE Somerset SS8448
Site off A39, 3 miles (5km) W of Porlock
The church claims to be the smallest in the country, but it is not. Perfectly set on a wooded hillside with little stream and sea views. Tiniest spirelet.

CULDROSE Cornwall SW6725
Site off A394, immediately SE of Helston
The largest helicopter station in Britain, with a small museum and viewing area.

CULFORD Suffolk TL8370
Village on B1106, 4 miles (6km) N of Bury St Edmunds
One of five villages which made up the Culford estate that thrived for nearly 400 years. It is a pretty village surrounded by woodland.

CULLEN Grampian NJ5167
Village on A98, 6 miles (10km) E of Buckie
Planned village of 1820s, with old fishing quarter. Three Kings of Cullen are large off-shore rocks. Interesting local garden with historical collection of old flower bulbs.

CULLERCOATS Tyne and Wear NZ3570
Village between Tynemouth and Whitley Bay
A fishing village which has a magnificent sandy bay. As well as fishing, the harbour was used for the export of salt and coal. St George's Church is a perfect example of Gothic Revival architecture by John Loughborough Pearson. It was built in 1884 by the 6th Duke of Northumberland, with fine stone vaulting and detail.

CULLODEN MOOR Highland NH7445
Battlefield off B9006, 4 miles (6km) E of Inverness
Last battle fought on British soil on 16 April 1745 here marked end of Jacobite rebellion and consequent end of clan system; turning point in Scottish history. Battlefield, including Graves of the Clans, owned by National Trust for Scotland, who operate the visitor information centre. Clava Cairns, impressive Bronze Age standing stones and burial cairns 1 mile (2km) southeast.

CULLOMPTON Devon ST0207
Small town on A396, 5 miles (8km) SE of Tiverton
A very important centre for the wool trade until the late 18th century, but now mostly 19th century because

fires destroyed all the earlier buildings. One long main street, very narrow in parts. St Andrew's Church is one of the best in Devon, with a richly coloured wooden screen and roof, and the famous fan-vaulted aisle, built from 1526 by John Lane, a rich local cloth merchant.

CULMSTOCK Devon ST1013
Village on B3391, 5 miles (8km) SW of Wellington
Once a small market town, with a considerable woollen industry. At Prescott (1 mile/2km west) is Spicelands, a Quaker Meeting House of 1815, complete with fittings of that date.

CULROSS Fife NS9886
Small town off A985, 7 miles (11km) W of Dunfermline
Archetypal 16th-century burgh – pronounced Cooross – restored by National Trust for Scotland, with fine examples of buildings, streets and open spaces. Fortunes founded by salt-panning and coal-mining, built up by Sir George Bruce, who built Culross Palace in walled courtyard by sea in the 1600s. The cobbled streets called Causeys (Causeways) are typical of contemporary town planning.

CULZEAN CASTLE Strathclyde NS2310
Mansion off A719, 4 miles (6km) W of Maybole
Considered one of Robert Adam's triumphs, Culzean – pronounced Cul-lane – was commissioned on an existing Kennedy stronghold site in 1777. Exterior is sham Gothic complete with castellations; within are harmonious classical elements typical of Adam, including magnificent oval staircase. President Eisenhower had lifetime flat here. Castle (National Trust for Scotland) is surrounded by large country park including gardens, beach and woodlands.

CUMBERNAULD Strathclyde NS7674
New Town on A8011, 12 miles (19km) NE of Glasgow
One of central Scotland's planned New Towns, developed in 1956 to house Glasgow's overspill population.

CUMBRAE (GREAT CUMBRAE) Strathclyde NS1656
Island in Firth of Clyde
Small and hilly island just off coast with capital Millport overlooking south bay. Extremely popular and busy in summer.

CUMNOCK Strathclyde NS5620
Town on A70, 14 miles (23km) E of Ayr
Once-important covenanting town with early market cross (1509). Centre of coal-mining area. James Keir Hardie, founder of Independent Labour Party, lived here.

CUMNOR Oxfordshire SP4504
Village on B4017, 4 miles (6km) W of Oxford
Worth negotiating the busy A420 to visit St Michael's Church and drink at the 16th-century Bear and Ragged Staff.

CUPAR Fife NO3714
Town on A91, 10 miles (16km) NE of Falkland
Royal burgh with charter from 1363, although always ecclesiastically over-shadowed by St Andrews (see). Nowadays market and service town with medieval layout and largely Georgian and Victorian architecture. Near by is Hill of Tarvit, admirable Edwardian mansion with fine furniture and picture collection, designed by Sir Robert Lorimer. Seventeenth-century Scotstarvit Tower near house.

The road to Carnwath at Currie.

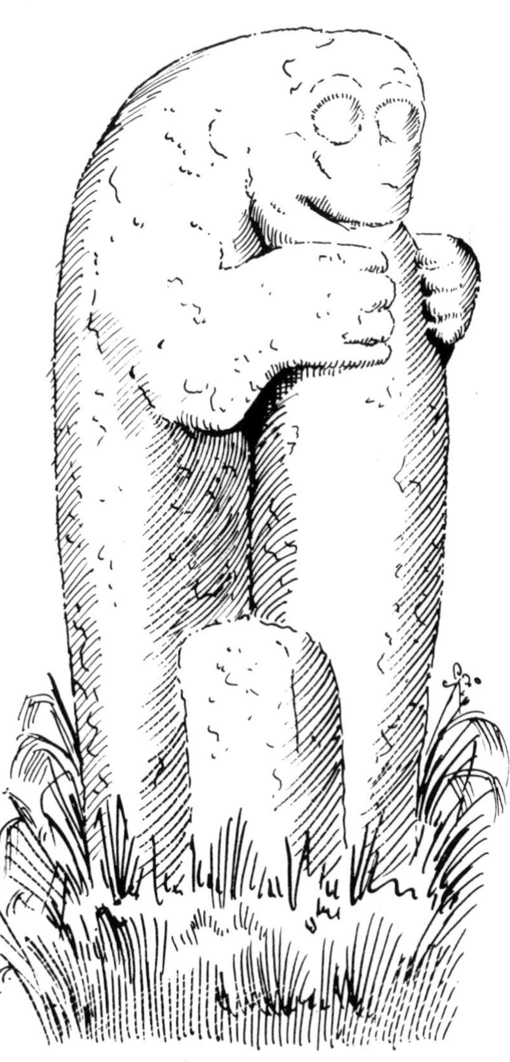

One of four stone bears in Dacre.

CURRIE Lothian NT1867
Village on A70, 5 miles (8km) SW of Edinburgh
Became Edinburgh suburb in 1975. Lies on Water of Leith, which provided power for number of mills.

CURRY MALLET Somerset ST3221
Village off A378, 7 miles (11km) E of Taunton
Scattered village, big partly 16th-century manor house in one part, the 14th-century church in another. Good 17th-century monuments.

CURRY RIVEL Somerset ST3925
Village on A378, 2 miles (3km) SW of Langport
Thatched cottages around a green, with handsome church. Prominent column at Burton Pynsent to the west, 1767.

CUTTHORPE Derbyshire SK3473
Village on B6050, 3 miles (5km) NW of Chesterfield
Two historic halls, 1625 and 16th–18th centuries, in pleasant Old Brampton parish. Lakeside walks at Linacre reservoirs near by.

CUXHAM Oxfordshire SU6695
Village on B480, 5 miles (8km) NE of Wallingford
Set on a long, stream-bordered village street, the old Half Moon inn and a sturdy Norman church help to make this an idyllic place.

CWMBRAN Gwent ST2894
Town on A4051, 4 miles (6km) N of Newport
New Town with pedestrianised shopping, leisure centre, athletics stadium and theatre. Greenmeadow Community Farm a hit with children. Llantarnam Grange Arts Centre.

CWMMAU FARMHOUSE Hereford and Worcester SO2648
see Brilley

CYMMER West Glamorgan SS8696
Village on A4107, 3 miles (5km) N of Maesteg
Old coal-mining community located amongst steep hills in forested Afan Valley, the 'Little Switzerland' of South Wales. Scars of mining removed or hidden away by conifers. Nearby Afan Argoed Country Park has a countryside centre and beautiful woodland walks. Park also contains a little museum which movingly tells the story of the life of a Welsh miner.

D

DACRE Cumbria NY4526
Village off A592, 4 miles (6km) SW of Penrith
Dalemain House has remained in the same family since 1679. The oldest part is a pele tower dating from the 15th century; now contains the museum of local yeomanry. Dacre Castle belonged to one of the four great northern families until the 16th century. The village was possibly the site of a monastery as early as AD698.

DAGENHAM Greater London TQ5084
District in borough of Barking and Dagenham
Urbanised this century. Industrial area with massive Ford car works, here since 1930s. Ancient Cross Keys inn is the area's oldest building.

DAGLINGWORTH Gloucestershire SO9905
Village off A417, 3 miles (5km) NW of Cirencester
Three precious carved panels are among the Saxon features of the church. The manor house (closed) has a rare medieval dovecote complete with revolving ladder.

DAILLY Strathclyde NS 2701
Village on B741, 7 miles (11km) NE of Girvan
Dailly stands in the valley of Water of Girvan. Old and new Dalquharran Castles are situated near by, Kennedy strongholds, both ruined.

DAIRSIE Fife NO4117
Village on A91, 3 miles (5km) NE of Cupar
Small village near River Eden, here spanned by 16th-century bridge, and overlooked by ruined Dairsie Castle.

DALBEATTIE Dumfries and Galloway NX8361
Small town on A711, 13 miles (21km) SW of Dumfries
Town has fine buildings of granite from quarries at nearby Craignair. Established 1800 with world-wide market in 19th century, today they produce road chippings.

DALE Derbyshire SK4338
Hamlet off A6096, 3 miles (5km) SW of Ilkeston
Twelfth-century hermit's sandstone cave; 13th-century chancel arch of Premonstratensian abbey. Tiny Norman church with 17th-century furnishings shares roof with house.

DALE Dyfed SM8005
Village on B4327, 12 miles (19km) SW of Haverfordwest
Sheltered sailing and watersports centre on western shores of Milford Haven Waterway, with shingle beach. Victorian Dale Fort, now a Field Study Centre, one of a series of old coastal defences still much in evidence. Mill Bay witnessed Henry Tudor's landing in 1485, prior to the long march to Bosworth to defeat Richard III and found the Tudor dynasty.

DALGETY BAY Fife NT1683
Town off A921, 3 miles (5km) E of Inverkeithing
Sprawling new residential development on shores of Dalgety Bay, dormitory for Dunfermline and Edinburgh. Twelfth-century ruined St Bridget's Kirk near by.

DALHAM Suffolk TL7261
Village on B1085, 5 miles (8km) E of Newmarket
The pretty village of Dalham lies neatly on both banks of the River Kennet, spanned by attractive white footbridges. There are thatched, white-walled cottages, and the entire village nestles in gently rolling wooded hills. The Duke of Wellington lived in nearby Dalham Hall (not open), and Cecil Rhodes bought it, although he never lived here.

DALKEITH Lothian NT3367
Town on A68, 6 miles (10km) SE of Edinburgh
Busy market town, once a centre for agriculture and Lothian coalfields. Dalkeith House is a superb early classical mansion around earlier castle (not open).

DALLAS Grampian NJ1252
Village off B9010, 9 miles (14km) SW of Elgin
Thought to have given its name to Dallas, Texas. Secluded village on River Lossie with circular Dallas Lodge, built in 1680.

DALLINGTON East Sussex TQ6519
Village off B2096, 5 miles (8km) SE of Heathfield
Homely hilltop village. Church has rare stone spire, duplicated in the folly at Wood's Corner.

DALLINGTON Northamptonshire SP7362
N area of Northampton
Now part of Northampton, with distinctive character in ironstone houses, 13th-century and later church, 17th-century almshouses; 18th-century hall now hospital.

DALMALLY Strathclyde NN1627
Village on A85, 12 miles (19km) W of Tyndrum
Tiny settlement at west end of Glen Lochy with interesting octagonal church built in 1811.

DALMELLINGTON Strathclyde NS4705
Small town on B741, 13 miles (21km) SE of Ayr
Once an iron-working town, now home to the Scottish Industrial Railway Centre with locomotives and rolling stock used for heavy industry, agriculture and whisky.

DALMENY Lothian NT1477
Village off A90, 1 mile (2km) E of South Queensferry
Dalmeny House, seat of Earls of Rosebery, overlooks Firth of Forth in landscaped grounds and replaced earlier Barnbougle Castle in 1820s. House is excellent and early example of Tudor Gothic Revival; superb collections of Spanish tapestries and French carpets and furniture. Dalmeny Kirk in estate village is one of best preserved Norman churches in Britain.

DALRY Strathclyde NS2949
Town off A737, 6 miles (10km) NE of Ardrossan
Originally 18th-century weaving centre, textiles important until 1930s. Near by is Blair House, a huge 17th-century mansion, and Duisk Glen, with stalactite-hung Cleave's Cove.

DALSTON Cumbria NY3650
Village on B5299, 4 miles (6km) SW of Carlisle
The prosperity brought to the village in the late 18th century by the cotton and flax industries is still evident today.

DALSWINTON Dumfries and Galloway NX9385
Village off A76, 6 miles (10km) N of Dumfries
Burns wrote *Tam o' Shanter* at local Ellisland Farm. He was also a passenger when Patrick Millar experimented with steam-driven vessel on Dalswinton Loch.

DALTON-IN-FURNESS Cumbria SD2274
Town off A590, 4 miles (6km) NE of Barrow-in-Furness
Dalton is historically the ancient capital of Furness where a castle (National Trust) was built to defend Furness Abbey at Barrow. The castle stands above the town and served mainly as a courthouse and prison. George Romney, the last of the great 18th-century painters, was born here in 1734. His grave can be seen in the parish churchyard.

DALTON-LE-DALE Durham NZ4048
Village off A19, 2 miles (3km) SW of Seaham
Twelfth-century church with remains of internal sundial. Near by is Dalden Tower, the ruined remains of a medieval hall.

DALWHINNIE Highland NN6384
Village on A889, 12 miles (19km) SW of Kingussie
Highest village in Highlands (1,200ft/365m) at north of Drumochter Pass on route of railway. Old-established distillery.

DALWOOD Devon ST2400
Village off A35, 3 miles (5km) NW of Axminster
Loughwood Meeting House (at Loughwood Farm, 1 mile/2km south, National Trust) is one of the earliest Baptist chapels in England, with records back to 1653. Simple Georgian fittings.

DANBURY Essex TL7805
Small town on A414, 5 miles (8km) E of Chelmsford
Essex's second highest spot. Country park. Medieval wooden knights' effigies in church and carved pew ends by World War I troops.

DANBY North Yorkshire NZ7008
Village off A171, 12 miles (19km) W of Whitby
Typical Moors village with a delightful wayside station on the Esk Valley railway, with unspoiled inns and pleasant cafés. The Moors Centre at Danby Lodge is the North York Moors National Park Authority's major visitors' centre. It has excellent and informative displays on natural and local history, conservation and programmes of organised events.

DARENTH Kent TQ5671
Village off A225, 2 miles (3km) SE of Dartford
Old village by River Darent keeps its integrity round little green, despite proximity of M25 and huge creeping development from Dartford.

DARESBURY Cheshire SJ5882
Village off A56, 4 miles (6km) SW of Warrington
Birthplace of Lewis Carroll; the church, where his father was rector, has a stained-glass window featuring *Alice in Wonderland* characters.

DARLASTON West Midlands SO9796
Town on A463, in W Walsall
Mrs Henry Wood wrote her famous novel *East Lynne* in King Street, when Darlaston was at the height of its Victorian fame as a producer of precision gun components and more mundane nuts and bolts. Today the town's older buildings are protected in a pleasant conservation area at the centre of extensive residential estates.

DARLEY DALE Derbyshire SK2663
Hamlet on A6, 3 miles (5km) NW of Matlock
Alongside River Derwent, linked to Matlock by restored Peak Railway. Ancient yew tree in churchyard. Stancliffe Quarry supplied Trafalgar Square flagstones.

DARLINGTON Durham NZ2814
Town off A1(M), 18 miles (29km) S of Durham
The town grew world famous with the opening of the world's first public passenger steam railway, which was sponsored by Darlington's far-sighted Quaker families. George Stephenson's *Locomotion* steam engine, which pulled the first train, can be seen at Darlington Railway Centre and Museum.

The architecture of the town dates from the 19th century, a wealthy period under the influence of Quakers, when industrial expansion was at its height, fuelled by the pioneering Stockton and Darlington Railway Company.

The Victorian market hall is still the focus for shopping, open every day except Sunday. Modern-day bank holiday markets in Darlington perpetuate the old fair days when agricultural workers came to offer their labour for the coming season. St Cuthbert's Church in the market place was built between 1183 and 1230 as a collegiate church for the Bishop of Durham. Its slender lancet windows and steep roofs lend an especially elegant air which has earned this church the name 'Lady of the North'.

Lewis Carroll spent his youth near Darlington and the local legend of the Sockburn Worm is thought to have inspired his poem *The Jabberwocky*.

DARRINGTON West Yorkshire SE4820
Village on A1, 2 miles (3km) SE of Pontefract
Has a Norman church, dedicated to St Luke and All Saints, built of Tadcaster limestone and with an unusual arcaded gallery.

DART, RIVER Devon
River; two branches – East and West Dart
The East and West Dart rivers start as tiny streams high on Dartmoor, joining at Dartmeet, one of the most picturesque spots on the whole moor. To Buckfast the valley is steep and wooded, and below the South Devon Railway runs to Totnes, through fine scenery. The huge estuary is a drowned river valley, with several side creeks.

DARTFORD Kent TQ5474
Town off M25, 12 miles (19km) NW of Rochester
Industrial town with long history, built where Roman Watling Street crossed River Darent south of the Thames. Church with Norman foundations and priory of 1359. Pioneer of Industrial Revolution, important for ship-building. Burial place of Richard Trevithick, Cornish engineer who worked at shipyards. Today known for Dartford Tunnel and Queen Elizabeth II bridge, both carrying traffic across Thames.

DARTINGTON Devon SX7862
Village on A384, 2 miles (3km) NW of Totnes
Dartington Hall (very limited opening) is famous for its medieval architecture, for music and for glass. The 14th-century hall makes one side of a fine court of buildings. Good gardens. Dartington Cider Press Centre is in 16th- and 17th-century stone buildings.

DARTMOOR Devon
Scenic area NE of Plymouth
High, bleak and wild, Dartmoor is the only true wilderness in southern England. It is only too easy to get lost walking in these rolling granite uplands, especially when the weather is bad. Its association with endurance tests, and a tough prison, suits the moor well.

Blanket bogs of peat cover most of the higher parts, with bare tors of granite at the very tops. These stark outcrops of the underlying rock are picturesque, if often windswept. The valleys have bogs too.

As the many archaeological remains indicate, Dartmoor was well populated until the end of the Bronze Age, when the climate deteriorated and the area became deserted moorland. Stone rows, cairns and hut circles all survive because they were built of the granite. The densest concentration is in the southern valleys.

From medieval times Dartmoor has been worked for tin, usually by sorting the gravels in rivers. Streams were diverted for this, and there are ruins of many small buildings used by the industry on the moor.

The margins of the moor are different: deeply cut and wooded small valleys, with big streams, often dyed brown from the peat on the moor. The 365 square miles (913 sq km) of Dartmoor became a national park in 1951.

DARTMOUTH Devon SX8751
Town on A379, 7 miles (11km) SE of Totnes
An ancient port, sheltering inside the mouth of the Dart estuary, and built up a steep hillside. Houses line the riverside, and the town generally has a charming mixture of buildings, with some timber-framing. The 17th-century Butterwalk (with the museum) is particularly fine. Two ferries (one for vehicles) across the river to Kingswear, and another (vehicles) a little north on the main road, by the huge late Victorian Royal Naval College. Dartmouth Castle (English Heritage) is on the rocks at the river entrance, dates from the 1480s, and has a large church of 1642 beside it.

DARVEL Strathclyde NS5637
Town on A71, 9 miles (14km) E of Kilmarnock
Upland town at edge of fells, once known for its lace-making. Birthplace of Sir Alexander Fleming, discoverer of penicillin.

DARWEN Lancashire SD6922
Town on A666, 4 miles (6km) S of Blackburn
Darwen Tower, erected to commemorate the Diamond Jubilee of Queen Victoria in 1897, is part of the Three Tower Walk.

DATCHET Berkshire SU9877
Town off M4, 2 miles (3km) NE of Windsor
Just over the Thames from Windsor Home Park, mostly modern but still with a green. Queen Mother Reservoir is huge.

DAVENTRY Northamptonshire SP5762
Town off A45, 12 miles (19km) W of Northampton
Stone Age hillfort and Roman site on Borough Hill superseded by radio masts bringing Daventry's name to wider audience. Once important coaching stop on London–Holyhead road, planned town expansion and motorway communications established Daventry as major industrial and distribution centre. Elegant 18th-century town church, busy market, museum in 17th-century Moot Hall, country park on edge of town.

DAVIOT Grampian NJ7428
Village off B9001, 5 miles (8km) NW of Inverurie
In upper River Nairn Valley surrounded by moorland. Near by is Loanhead stone circle, recumbent stones 4,000 years old.

DAWLEY Shropshire SJ6808
Town, part of Telford New Town
A former industrial settlement on a Shropshire coalfield, Dawley retains its Victorian character. Birthplace of Captain Matthew Webb, first man to swim the English Channel.

DAWLISH Devon SX9576
Town on A379, 12 miles (19km) S of Exeter
An early seaside resort, which started developing from the little inland village in the 1790s. Lots of early 19th-century villas, especially around the Lawn, the central garden. The railway of 1846 runs straight along the beach, cutting it off from the town. Local museum. To the north is Dawlish Warren, a wide sandspit which juts into the Exe estuary mouth.

DEAL Kent TR3752
Town on A258, 8 miles (13km) NE of Dover
Delightful, friendly seaside resort with noble history. Upper Deal was original village, later spreading towards beach. Member of Confederation of Cinque Ports under Sandwich. Castle built 1540, part of coastal fortifications. Attractive 18th- and 19th-century houses on lanes off High Street. Fascinating Time Ball tower on front, and famous Royal Cinque Ports Golf Club.

DEAN, FOREST OF Gloucestershire SO6310
Scenic area W of River Severn
From Roman times the Forest was exploited for timber, iron and coal. Signs of this history, strikingly revealed at the Dean Heritage Centre (Soudley), can be seen at Clearwell Caves and in industrial settlements like Coleford and Cinderford. Today a network of trails and footpaths crosses the expanse of heath and woodland, making it a mecca for walkers and riders.

DEAN FOREST RAILWAY Gloucestershire SO6303
see Lydney

DEAN PRIOR Devon SX7363
Hamlet on A38, 2 miles (3km) S of Buckfastleigh
A hamlet on the edge of Dartmoor, with a little medieval church.

DEANE Greater Manchester SD6907
District on A58, SW area of Bolton
On the southern outskirts of Bolton, the village has a 15th-century church built by the monks of Whalley Abbey.

DEANE Hampshire SU5450
Hamlet off B3400, 6 miles (10km) W of Basingstoke
Often visited by Jane Austen, with Deane House (not open) still as she would have known it. The church (1818) is unusual and many of its details are in artificial stone.

DEANSHANGER Northamptonshire SP7639
Village off A422, 2 miles (3km) W of Stony Stratford
Near the Buckinghamshire border, a large industrial village producing ferrous oxide. Nineteenth-century almshouses overlook the green.

DEBENHAM Suffolk TM1763
Small town on B1077, 11 miles (18km) N of Ipswich
Gurgling water winds its way down Debenham's streets until it joins the River Deben. Some of the picturesque timber-framed houses that line the streets date from the 14th century, while others are 17th century. One village resident founded a chain store that he named 'Debenhams'.

DEDDINGTON Oxfordshire SP4631
Village on A4260, 6 miles (10km) S of Banbury
The fine medieval church overlooks a spacious square, where a market hall of 1806 indicates the village's former importance. Other reminders are earthworks of a Norman castle (English Heritage), almshouses of 1818, the 17th-century King's Arms and the Georgian Crown and Tuns. Leadenporch House and Castle House are both of medieval origin.

DEDHAM Essex TM0533
Small town on B1029, 6 miles (10km) NE of Colchester
Near River Stour in beautiful surroundings, a lovely, tranquil old place with memories of painters Constable and Munnings and, ironically, famous forger Tom Keating is buried here. Church tower Constable loved to paint, fine High Street of Tudor and Georgian houses. Castle House, now museum to Munnings. Rare Breeds Centre. (For Dedham Vale, see Constable Country.)

DEE, RIVER Clwyd
River, runs through Clwyd to Irish Sea
Rises in Bala Lake, flows through Vale of Llangollen to estuary on the English border northwest of Chester.

DEE, RIVER Grampian
River
Important river, rising in Cairngorms and reaching North Sea at Aberdeen. Most famous stretch below Linn of Dee between Ballater and Braemar, known as Royal Deeside.

DEENE Northamptonshire SP9492
Village off A43, 4 miles (6km) NE of Corby
Deene Park, home of Brudenell family since 1514, has lake, gardens and memorabilia of Earl of Cardigan who led Charge of the Light Brigade.

DEEPING ST JAMES Lincolnshire TF1609
Village on B1166, immediately E of Market Deeping
Along north bank of River Welland, joining Market Deeping. Grand church of Benedictine priory, with rare Georgian tower, Norman arches inside.

DEERHURST Gloucestershire SO8730
Village off B4213, 7 miles (11km) NW of Cheltenham
This Severnside village has two important Saxon buildings. St Mary's Church contains rare features dating from the 8th and 9th centuries, with fascinating later additions that include a pet dog named Tirri, immortalised on a 14th-century tomb. To the west is Odda's Chapel, discovered within a timber-framed house and yielding an inscription dating it precisely to 12 April 1056.

DEFYNNOG Powys SN9227
Village on A4067, 1 mile (2km) S of Sennybridge
Mainly 15th-century church bears traces from 5th and 6th centuries. Font believed to have the only Runic inscription in Wales.

DEGANWY Gwynedd SH7779
see Llandudno

DELABOLE Cornwall SX0683
Village on B3314, 2 miles (3km) W of Camelford
Slate has been quarried here since the 14th century, and the huge quarry, 500ft (152m) deep and more than 1/2 mile (1km) across, is still in use (viewing platform). The sails of the new wind farm for generating electricity are prominent. The village expanded with the quarrying, and is mostly 19th century.

DELAMERE Cheshire SJ5668
Village on A556, 6 miles (10km) W of Winsford
Often regarded as a district, Delamere is best known for its forest which was once full of game and used as a royal hunting ground.

DELPH Greater Manchester SD9807
Village on A62, 4 miles (6km) NE of Oldham
A pretty village in Saddleworth. Castleshaw Roman Fort, above Delph, was one of a series built on the Roman road between Chester and York.

DENBIGH (DINBYCH) Clwyd SJ0566
Town on A525, 10 miles (16km) S of Rhyl
Possesses many historic buildings, chief amongst which is a castle (Cadw) conspicuous on its high outcrop. Ingenious defensive features remain, along with a stretch of town wall affording excellent views of Clwydian Range. Good local museum. Famous sons include HM Stanley, rescuer of Doctor Livingstone, and bard Twm o'r Nant (died 1810).

DENBURY Devon SX8268
Village off A381, 3 miles (5km) SW of Newton Abbot
A village which tried to become a town in medieval times. Little Conduit House of 1771 turned into a war memorial. To the southwest is a big Iron Age hillfort, Denbury Camp.

DENBY Derbyshire SK3946
Village off A609, 3 miles (5km) S of Ripley
Distinctive pottery produced here has made the village's name famous, attracting crowds to its factory tours and fascinating visitor centre and factory shop.

DENBY DALE West Yorkshire SE2208
Town on A636, 8 miles (13km) W of Barnsley
The Iron Age hillfort above the village shows traces of an impressive bank and ditch. Near by is the isolated Quaker settlement of High Flatts.

DENFORD Northamptonshire SP9976
Village on A45 (A605), 1 mile (2km) S of Thrapston
Small attractive stone village beside River Nene. Holy Trinity Church has fine 13th-century tower.

DENHAM Buckinghamshire TQ0487
Village off A412, 2 miles (3km) NW of Uxbridge
Concealed at the heart of 20th-century sprawl is a choice old village of mellow red brick in spanking condition with houses of 17th and 18th centuries and church with brasses and monuments. Famous residents galore, from Napoleon's brothers to Oswald Mosley and John Mills, while Alexander Korda founded Denham film studios in 1930s. Small aerodrome near by.

DENHOLM Borders NT5718
Village on A698, 5 miles (8km) NE of Hawick
Birthplace of John Leyden, 18th-century poet and friend of Sir Walter Scott. Stands on River Teviot.

DENMEAD Hampshire SU6512
Village on B2150, 2 miles (3km) SE of Hambledon
A scattered old village, now much developed. At World's End is a pillar box of 1859, believed to be the oldest still in use.

DENNINGTON Suffolk TM2867
Village on A1120, 2 miles (3km) N of Framlingham
An oak tree in the square marks the centre of this attractive village. The square lost its grass from the hooves of Suffolk heavy horses. The church was built in the 14th century, although there was probably a much earlier one. Carvings include Britain's only representation of a sciapod, a mythical creature with a huge boat-shaped foot.

DENNY (AND DUNIPACE) Central NS8182
Town on A883, 5 miles (8km) W of Falkirk
Small manufacturing town, lying to east of Kilsyth Hills, and virtually connected to neighbouring Dunipace. Both towns lie on River Carron.

DENSHAW Greater Manchester SD9710
Village on A672, 4 miles (6km) NE of Oldham
A village with weavers' cottages and early textile mills. It was part of the Friarmere division of Saddleworth and belonged to monks until the Dissolution.

DENSTON Suffolk TL7652
Village off A143, 5 miles (8km) N of Clare
Has of the finest medieval churches in Suffolk. It is 15th century, and has some especially attractive carvings of animals.

DENSTONE Staffordshire SK0940
Village on B5032, 5 miles (8km) N of Uttoxeter
Famous for damsons and their May blossom, this Churnet Valley village boasts some notable work by Victorian architect GE Street.

DENT Cumbria SD7086
Small town off A684, 4 miles (6km) SE of Sedbergh
Remote but very picturesque village in Dentdale. Main street is cobbled and only wide enough for single-file traffic. Near the church, a huge slab of granite with a drinking fountain commemorates Adam Sedgwick, a native of Dent and pioneer of geology. Marble from nearby quarries was used for the floor of the church's sanctuary.

DENTON Greater Manchester SJ9295
Town off M67, 4 miles (6km) NE of Stockport
A market town which thrived on the textile boom during the Industrial Revolution. Grade II Listed church.

DENTON Kent TR2147
Village on A260, 7 miles (11km) N of Folkestone
Cheerful handful of timbered cottages away from the main road in wonderfully verdant countryside, with church hidden among trees in Denton Park.

DENTON Lincolnshire SK8632
Village on A607, 4 miles (6km) SW of Grantham
Honey-toned ironstone village close to Leicestershire border and Belvoir Castle (see). Nineteenth- and 20th-century estate cottages wrapped around Georgian parkland of Welby estate. The present manor is 17th century, enlarged in 1950s. Of Arthur Blomfield's Victorian house, the gatehouse and stabling remain. In 1888 he restored medieval church with interesting monuments. Salvin designed 1840s Old Rectory.

DENTON North Yorkshire SE1448
Village off A65, 2 miles (3km) NE of Ilkley
Village in Wharfedale with Denton Hall, home to Thomas, Lord Fairfax, who was a general to Oliver Cromwell during the Civil War.

DENVER Norfolk TF6001
Village off A10, 1 mile (2km) S of Downham Market
West of Denver village is Denver Sluice, built to control tides up the River Great Ouse. Swans glide in the water at this peaceful spot.

DEOPHAM Norfolk TG0400
Village off B1108, 4 miles (6km) W of Wymondham
For a small village, Deopham's church is disproportionately large. It has a fine tower that looms impressively over the village.

DEPTFORD Greater London TQ3777
District in borough of Lewisham
Fishing village on Thames originally, important in naval history as dockyard from Tudor times, subsequently Royal Victoria Victualling Yard. Sir Francis Drake knighted by Elizabeth I on *Golden Hind* here. St Paul's, tremendous 18th-century baroque church by Thomas Archer. Christopher Marlowe buried in graveyard of St Nicholas. Town hall in Edwardian baroque, 1907. Street market.

DERBY Derbyshire SK3536
City on A6, 15 miles (24km) W of Nottingham
Commercial and industrial city whose famous products include exquisite Royal Crown Derby porcelain and powerful Rolls-Royce aero-engines. Fine porcelain and a superb collection of paintings by 18th-century Joseph Wright of Derby, characterised by unusual effects of light, are among the treasures in the City Museum and Art Gallery. Pickford's House Museum provides the setting for Georgian domestic items, while the Industrial Museum exhibits aero engines and other local products in the Old Silk Mill, the earliest factory building, beside the River Derwent.

Near by is Derby Cathedral, an airy 1720s building by James Gibbs, with an early 16th-century tower, and beautiful wrought-iron screen by Robert Bakewell. The splendid monuments include the tomb of Bess of Hardwick, whose progressively wealthy marriages financed her passion for building fine houses.

Derby was at the heart of national events in 1745, when Prince Charles Edward held his final War Council here and decided to turn his army back for Scotland. Today, Derby serves as a major shopping and entertainment centre, with a busy indoor market, theatre at Derby Playhouse and the Guildhall, and concerts at the Assembly Rooms.

DERBYSHIRE DALES Derbyshire

Scenic region

Dramatic limestone gorges, wooded dales, picturesque villages and market towns in the southern part of the Peak District National Park.

DERE STREET Northumberland

Roman road from Corbridge to the border

A Roman road crossing the River Tyne at Corbridge and running to the border with Scotland.

DEREHAM Norfolk TF9813

see East Dereham

DERSINGHAM Norfolk TF6830

Village off A149, 7 miles (11km) S of Hunstanton

Large village with fine houses of Carr stone, and pleasant views over the Wash and the Sandringham estate.

DERVAIG Strathclyde (Mull) NM4352

Village on B8073, 5 miles (8km)SW of Tobermory

Lies at head of sheltered sea loch in lovely scenery. Home of Mull Little Theatre, whose two resident actors make it one of world's smallest.

DERWEN Clwyd SJ0750

Village off A494, 5 miles (8km) N of Corwen

Unusually fine 15th-century rood screen and loft in St Mary's Church. Village also has one of Wales's best churchyard crosses.

DERWENT, RIVER Derbyshire

River, rises near Glossop and joins the Trent

From Peak District moors above Glossop, flows through valleys which were broadened to create Derwent Reservoir, through attractive villages beneath gritstone edges, past magnificent Chatsworth House, through Matlock Bath's limestone gorge to Cromford, where Arkwright harnessed its power for cotton-spinning, fuelling the Industrial Revolution, past Belper's mills, on through city of Derby, before flowing into River Trent at Sawley.

DERWENT, RIVER Durham/Northumberland

River, tributary of the Tyne

Flows down Forge Valley to join the River Ouse near Selby. Early 19th-century sea cut was created to improve agricultural potential of Vale of Pickering, directing part of the river straight to the sea.

DERWENT, RIVER North Yorkshire

River, tributary of the Ouse

During end of last Ice Age, the River Derwent overflowed south, carving Forge Valley to reach the Vale of Pickering.

DERWENT WATER Cumbria NY2521

Lake off B5289, SW of Keswick

A popular lake which can be explored by boat from Keswick. The lake has two islands, St Herbert's Island and Derwent Island, each steeped in history. On the east side of Derwent Water is Friar's Crag, from which there is a famous view of the lake, considered by John Ruskin to be one of the finest views in Europe.

DESBOROUGH Northamptonshire SP8083

Small town on A6, 5 miles (8km) NW of Kettering

Pleasantly sited above River Ise, site of archaeological finds including Desborough Mirror, now in British Museum. Thirteenth-century and later church.

DESFORD Leicestershire SK4703

Village on B582, 7 miles (11km) W of Leicester

Large Leicestershire village, with some older buildings, and newer residences for expanding population. Industrial concerns on edge. Community College.

Ornate 'gallows' town sign in Dereham.

DEVIL'S BRIDGE Dyfed SN7376
Hamlet on A4120, 10 miles (16km) E of Aberystwyth
Three bridges span scenic wooded gorge, the oldest the subject of a popular legend. Dramatic waterfalls. Terminus of narrow-gauge Vale of Rheidol Railway.

DEVIL'S CHIMNEY Gloucestershire SO9518
see Leckhampton Hill

DEVIL'S DYKE West Sussex TQ2611
Scenic feature off A23, 7 miles (11km) NW of Brighton
Steep dry valley on north face of South Downs. Beyond is hilltop viewpoint looking over Weald to Ashdown Forest, the Surrey Hills and North Downs.

DEVIL'S PUNCHBOWL Surrey SU8936
Scenic feature off A3, 3 miles (5km) N of Haslemere
Steep-sided valley (National Trust) in sandstone, deepest of many on slopes of Gibbet Hill. Superb views.

DEVIZES Wiltshire SU0061
Town on A342, 10 miles (16km) SE of Chippenham
Proper country town, with some early cottages and many handsome Georgian buildings. The market place is especially good, with a fancy market cross of 1814. The medieval castle has been replaced by a more elaborate Victorian one, with a big gatehouse. Classical town hall of 1806, and many inns, because Devizes was a coaching stop. The Kennet and Avon Canal has a famous flight of 29 locks in only 2 miles (3km) to the west of the town; canal museum too. Devizes Museum includes archaeology, art and natural history.

DEVONPORT Devon SX4554
Town on A374, across River Tamar from Plymouth
The huge naval dockyard was started in 1685, and expanded greatly through the 18th century. Until 1824 it was known as Dock, and a large column in the middle commemorates the renaming. Prominent wall to the dockyard, and many 19th-century terraces. Three huge covered docks of 1977. The Tamar Bridges loom. Car ferry to Torpoint.

DEVORAN Cornwall SW7939
Village off A39, 4 miles (6km) SW of Truro
On Restronguet Creek. Mostly built in the 1830s and 40s to house tin-workers.

DEWSBURY West Yorkshire SE2421
Town on A638, 8 miles (13km) SW of Leeds
The capital of the 'Heavy Woollen District' of North Kirklees, where methods for reprocessing cloth, to make blankets, work clothes and uniforms, were pioneered in the early 19th century. The Dewsbury Museum concentrates on children at work, play and school. Dewsbury market specialises in textiles. The town centre is a designated conservation area.

DIBDEN PURLIEU Hampshire SU4106
Village on A326, 6 miles (10km) S of Southampton
On the edge of the New Forest, with views of Southampton docks across the water. The church was bombed in 1940, and parts still show the effects.

DICKER, UPPER AND LOWER
East Sussex TQ5510
Hamlets off A22, 2 miles (3km) W of Hailsham
Two villages above River Cuckmere in area once known as 'Dyker Waste'. Lower, which had a well-known pottery working Weald clay, is strung along the Hailsham–Uckfield road. Upper, centred on a minor crossroads, is famed for nearby Michelham Priory, founded in 1229 for Augustinian canons, dissolved in 1537 and later turned into a farmhouse for the Sackville family.

Old lock-up or wellhead in Digby.

DICKLEBURGH Norfolk TM1682
Village on A140, 4 miles (6km) NE of Diss
This heathland village is the birthplace of George Cattermole, best known for his illustrations in Sir Walter Scott's novels.

DIDCOT Oxfordshire SU5290
Town off A34, 10 miles (16km) S of Oxford
Railway Centre is a mecca for Great Western Railway buffs. The 15th-century church and huge power station (limited opening) are also worth a visit.

DIDDLEBURY Shropshire SO5085
Village off B4368, 5 miles (8km) NE of Craven Arms
Corvedale village, its attractive old centre to the east of modern houses. Church of Saxon and Norman origins close to Delbury Hall (1750s).

DIDMARTON Gloucestershire ST8287
Village on A433, 6 miles (10km) SW of Tetbury
Pleasant village on the edge of Badminton Park. Old church, now redundant, has an interesting 18th-century interior.

DIDSBURY Greater Manchester SJ8490
District in S Manchester
A fashionable residential area also popular with students. Fletcher Moss Botanical Gardens contains many rare plants in rock garden settings.

DIGBY Lincolnshire TF0854
Village on B1188, 6 miles (10km) N of Sleaford
Lock-up or wellhead shaped like a pepperpot. Village cross. Church shows evidence of Saxon and Norman work, with Victorian chancel.

DIGSWELL Hertfordshire TL2415
Village off A1000, in N outskirts of Welwyn Garden City
Imposing 40-arched 1850 viaduct carries railway across River Mimram here. Medieval church enlarged 1960s. Digswell lake and park.

DILHORNE Staffordshire SJ9743
Village off A521, 2 miles (3km) W of Cheadle
In open, rising countryside, the village has a medieval church worth a visit. Foxfield Steam Railway runs near by.

DILTON MARSH Wiltshire ST8449
Village on B3099, 2 miles (3km) W of Westbury
Grew from the late 18th century as a hand-weaving centre; the many weavers' cottages now mixed with modern development.

DILWYN Hereford and Worcester SO4154
Village off A4112, 6 miles (10km) SW of Leominster
Pretty black and white village. Unusually grand and lofty church resulting from medieval association with Wormsley Priory. Intricate chancel screen and other fine details.

DINAS DINLLE Gwynedd SU4356
Beach/prehistoric site off A499, 1 mile (2km) W of Llandwrog
On western edge of north-facing finger of level land. Long sandy surfing beach. Prehistoric fort. Caernarfon Airport's Air World Museum has pleasure flights.

DINAS EMRYS Gwynedd SU6049
Hill off A498, 1 mile (2km) NE of Beddgelert
Iron Age site the subject of legends. One concerns Vortigen's attempts to build tower, thwarted, according to Merlin, by red and white dragons.

DINAS MAWDDWY Gwynedd SH8514
Hamlet on A470, 8 miles (13km) E of Dolgellau
Quiet spot in bowl of wild, wooded mountains. Old inn: Llew Coch/Red Lion. Meirion Mill for Welsh woollens. Highest road in Wales ascends over Bwlch y Groes to Bala.

DINDER Somerset ST5744
Village off A371, 2 miles (3km) SE of Wells
On the edge of the Mendips, a pretty village. Dinder House (not open), 1801, is close to the 15th-century church.

DINGWALL Highland NH5458
Town on A862, 11 miles (18km) NW of Inverness
Market town, once county town of Ross and Cromarty, on Cromarty Firth, royal burgh since 1226, and once a thriving port, with harbour (now choked) designed by Telford. Eighteenth-century town house and tolbooth and remains of mercat cross. Monument on cemetery hill to Sir Hector Archibald MacDonald, hero of Second Afghan War. Town is now bypassed.

DINMORE HILL/DINMORE MANOR Hereford and Worcester SO5052
see Hope under Dinmore

DINNET Grampian NO4598
Village on A93, 6 miles (10km) E of Ballater
Deeside village in pleasant hill-country with good walking and bird-watching at nearby Muir of Dinnet Nature Reserve.

DINNINGTON South Yorkshire SK5285
Small town on B6060, immediately N of North Anston
Former coal-mining village; the pit has been closed and buildings demolished. Area undergoing regeneration, now mainly residential.

DINTON Buckinghamshire SP7610
Village off A418, 4 miles (6km) SW of Aylesbury
Church distinguished for elaborate Norman carving of south door. Many 'witchert' (earth and straw) cottages. Dinton Castle is an 18th-century eyecatcher.

DINTON Wiltshire SU0131
Village on B3089, 5 miles (8km) W of Wilton
Woody, with a big green. Interesting medieval church. Philipps House (National Trust, limited opening) is Greek in style, of 1816.

DIRLETON Lothian NT5184
Village on B1435, 2 miles (3km) W of North Berwick
Charming picture-postcard village of pantiled cottages set about two greens with extensive remains of 13th-

century Dirleton Castle, destroyed by Cromwell, on rocky mound behind. Well-tended castle grounds have 17th-century dovecote and bowling green. Church dates from same century. Open Arms, famous inn, overlooks green and castle.

DISLEY Cheshire SJ9784

Town on A6, 2 miles (3km) W of New Mills

Pretty village on outskirts of Stockport. Lyme Park, set in hundreds of acres of park and moorland, is the largest house in Cheshire; parts of original Elizabethan house survive, with 18th- and 19th-century additions by Giacomo Leoni and Lewis Wyatt; contains Mortlake tapestries, Grinling Gibbons carvings and unique collection of English clocks.

DISS Norfolk TM1180

Town off A1066, 19 miles (31km) SW of Norwich

The name comes from an Anglo-Saxon word meaning 'standing water', so the pretty mere in the centre of this busy town is probably very ancient. A pleasing jumble of Tudor, Georgian and Victorian houses surrounds the mere, while narrow streets lead up the hill to the market square. Diss stands in the beautiful Waveney Valley.

DITCHEAT Somerset ST6236

Village off A371, 3 miles (5km) NW of Castle Cary

An attractive village; large medieval church, with wall-painting of St Christopher of around 1500.

DITCHINGHAM Norfolk TM3391

Village on B1332, 1 mile (2km) N of Bungay

The grounds of Ditchingham Hall (not open) were designed by Capability Brown. The Victorian writer Rider Haggard lived in the hall for many years.

DITCHLEY Oxfordshire SP3920

Village off B4022, 2 miles (3km) NE of Charlbury

Ditchley Park, a fine house of the 1720s by James Gibbs (now a conference centre) became famous as strategic planning headquarters during World War II.

DITCHLING East Sussex TQ3215

Village on B2112, 3 miles (5km) SE of Burgess Hill

Thriving timber and brick village set on crossroads beneath South Downs and famous Ditchling Beacon (813ft/247m). Oldest part to west of crossroads. Tudor Anne of Cleves House possibly on site of King Alfred's royal manor. Strong association with the arts: Eric Gill and Frank Brangwyn lived here, Dame Vera Lynn still does. Wide grassy common to north.

DITTISHAM Devon SX8655

Village off A3122, 3 miles (5km) N of Dartmouth

On the Dart estuary, with a passenger ferry across. Pretty village, stone and thatch, with plum orchards.

Tudor Anne of Cleves House in Ditchling.

DOBCROSS Greater Manchester SD9906
Village off A670, 4 miles (6km) E of Oldham
An attractive Pennine village which has changed little. It was used as the setting for the film *Yanks*.

DOBWALLS Cornwall SX2165
Village on A38, 3 miles (5km) W of Liskeard
Large modern village, with Dobwalls Family Adventure Park to the north.

DOCKING Norfolk TF7636
Village on B1454, 11 miles (18km) NW of Fakenham
The Seal Rescue Unit, run by the Royal Society for the Prevention of Cruelty to Animals, was founded in Docking during the epidemic that killed hundreds of British seals.

DODDINGTON Cambridgeshire TL4090
Village on B1093, 3 miles (5km) N of Chatteris
Christopher Tye, one of Doddington's rectors, wrote the music to 'While shepherds watched their flocks by night'. The church has a window by William Morris.

DODDINGTON Kent TQ9357
Village off A2, 4 miles (6km) SE of Sittingbourne
Church and vicarage group together in a steep lane, focal point of this village in wooded countryside. Spectacular Doddington Place has gardens covering 10 acres (4ha).

DODDINGTON Lincolnshire SK8970
Village on B1190, 5 miles (8km) W of Lincoln
Romantic red-brick Elizabethan mansion (open in summer), by Robert Smythson, with elegant Georgian rooms, fine contents, gatehouse and walled gardens.

DODDINGTON Northumberland NT9932
Village on B6525, 3 miles (5km) N of Wooler
A village of stone-built houses sited above the floodplains of the River Till. Iron Age hillfort called Dod Law and several of the moorland rocks here are marked with cup-and-ring carvings. The Dod Well, in the shape of a cross, used to supply the whole village with water.

DODDISCOMBSLEIGH Devon SX8586
Village off B3193, 6 miles (10km) SW of Exeter
Beautiful scenery. The church has five 15th-century windows still with their original stained glass, a very rare survival.

DODFORD Northamptonshire SP6160
Village off A45, 3 miles (5km) SE of Daventry
Attractively secluded from nearby A5, main Euston railway and Grand Union Canal, with Norman and later church rich in monuments.

DODLESTON Cheshire SJ3661
Village off A55, 4 miles (6km) SW of Chester
Originally built for workers on the Grosvenor family estate; each cottage had its own pump and pigsty.

DODMAN POINT Cornwall SX0039
Headland off B3273, 4 miles (6km) S of Mevagissey
Prominent headland with long views of the south Cornwall coast. Cut off by an Iron Age bank. Deep-cut wriggly roads inland.

DOGS, ISLE OF Greater London TQ3878
District in borough of Tower Hamlets
Peninsula containing old West India and Milwall docks, redeveloped since 1980s as heart of London Docklands. Docklands Light Railway runs through. Dominating 50-storey Canary Wharf Tower, 800ft (244m) high. London Arena, new Billingsgate Market. Pedestrian tunnel to Greenwich (see) and wonderful view of Greenwich across River Thames from Island Gardens.

DOLGELLAU Gwynedd SH7217
Town on A470, 10 miles (16km) E of Barmouth
Solid stone market town, base for exploring Cader Idris and Mawddach estuary. Scenic paths include Torrent and Precipice Walks, as well as up Cader. Welsh Gold Centre is starting point for unique tour of working gold mine. Area supplied gold for royal wedding rings. Visitor centre tells of persecution of 17th-century Quakers. St Mary's Church has fine stained glass.

DOLLAR Central NS9698
Small town on A91, 6 miles (10km) NE of Alloa
Prosperous-looking grey-stone town dominated by Playfair's Academy buildings. Evocative Castle Campbell in Dollar Glen dates mainly from late 15th century.

DOLTON Devon SS5712
Village on B3217, 7 miles (11km) SE of Torrington
Above the wooded Torridge Valley. The church has a remarkable font made from two pieces of Saxon cross.

DOLWYDDELAN Gwynedd SH7352
Village on A470, 5 miles (8km) SW of Betws-y-coed
Built by Princes of Gwynedd, taken and extended by Edward I, Dolwyddelan's stark and isolated castle tower (Cadw) broods over peaceful Lledr Valley.

DON, RIVER Grampian
River, rises S of Tomintoul
Rises south of Tomintoul in Highlands and enters North Sea at Aberdeen. Stately river, big enough in lower reaches to serve industrial needs.

DON, RIVER South Yorkshire
River, tributary of the Ouse
One of Britain's most polluted rivers, but now recovering. It rises close to Holmfirth and flows into the Humber estuary.

DONCASTER South Yorkshire SE5703
Town off A1(M), 17 miles (27km) NE of Sheffield
A busy market town on the River Don, Doncaster has seen many recent changes in its community as it witnessed the decline of South Yorkshire's mining industry. However, it commands an excellent position as a principal town on the Great North road, the Roman route from London, and this advantage has always served the town well. The Romans established a fort here called *Danum;* later Doncaster became an important trading centre in the Middle Ages and a major coaching town during the 18th century.

Doncaster also has a famous railway heritage; the steam locomotives *The Flying Scotsman* and *The Mallard* were built here. The racecourse is home of the St Leger, the oldest of English Classic horse races. The town's most notable building is the Mansion House, designed by James Paine and finished in 1748, and one of only three civic mansion houses in England.

Doncaster is still a major market town for the region, and as the surrounding collieries have closed the town has turned its attention to the leisure industry, investing in multi-million-pound sports and recreational facilities.

DONINGTON Lincolnshire TF2035
Town on A152, 9 miles (14km) N of Spalding
A small market town with several 17th- and 18th-century buildings. Birthplace in 1774 of Matthew Flinders, explorer of Tasmania and Australia.

The bow-windowed Georgian King's Arms in Dorchester.

DONINGTON LE HEATH Leicestershire SK4212
Village off B591, 1 mile (2km) S of Coalville
Medieval manor house of early 14th century with 16th- to 17th-century alterations, oak furniture of the period, herb garden (limited opening).

DONNINGTON Berkshire SU4668
Village in N area of Newbury
Still a village, despite Newbury's proximity. Imposing and prominent gatehouse from a castle of 1386 (English Heritage), with earthworks.

DONNINGTON Shropshire SJ7013
Town off A518, N of Oakengates
An early iron- and coal-mining centre, Donnington has now acquired housing and industrial estates as part of Telford. Military ordnance depot near by.

DONYATT Somerset ST3314
Village on A358, 1 mile (2km) W of Ilminster
Attractive village, almshouses of 1624 and 15th-century church. Pottery produced here in the 17th and 18th centuries – one area is called Crock Street.

DORCHESTER Dorset SY6990
Town on A35, 17 miles (27km) SW of Blandford Forum
The county town of Dorset, not large but with a long history. The present town is on the site of the Roman one, and until the late 19th century the town stayed inside the line of the Roman walls, laid out as tree-lined walks in the 18th century. Remains of a Roman town house and a mosaic are exposed in Colliton Park.

The handsome High Street runs down the hill, with Georgian town houses in great variety. In the centre is St Peter's, the only surviving medieval church. Thomas Hardy worked as an architect in South Street, and William Barnes, the Dorset poet, lived next door. Hardy's novel *The Mayor of Casterbridge* depicts the town in the mid-19th century. Shire Hall of 1797 contains the old county court – preserved as a memorial to the Tolpuddle Martyrs who were tried here in 1834.

Maumbury Rings, just to the south, is a neolithic henge remodelled in Roman times as an amphitheatre. Maiden Castle (see), further out, is the largest Iron Age hillfort in the county. To the southeast is Fordington, a proper village, unusual so close to a town. Max Gate just beyond is the house Thomas Hardy built for himself (limited opening).

The Dorset County Museum has Thomas Hardy's study, and extensive displays on Dorset history, archaeology, geology. The Keep is a military museum. Tutankhamun Exhibition and Dinosaur Museum.

On the western outskirts is Poundbury, the new development for the Prince of Wales, demonstrating his ideas on architecture.

DORCHESTER Oxfordshire SU5794
Village off A4074, 4 miles (6km) NW of Wallingford
Some traces remain of the Roman origins of this ancient settlement, site of a vanished Saxon cathedral of AD634. Imposing church incorporates Norman abbey and is noted for a chancel containing remarkable medieval glass. The White Hart and the George hotel, a coaching inn with galleried courtyard, are

among an array of fine old buildings. Abbey Museum explains village's history.

DORKING Surrey TQ1649
Town on A24, 5 miles (8km) S of Leatherhead
The only Surrey town to be dominated by its church spire which stands out in distant views. Dorking is a bustling town with modern amenities, but retains its charm, and Box Hill (see) is still visible from the High Street. In the Middle Ages Dorking was famous for its poultry market and breed of five-toed chickens.

DORMINGTON Hereford and Worcester SO5840
Village off A438, 5 miles (8km) E of Hereford
On the church door is a replica of a very rare piece of Norman ironwork: a closing ring featuring a cat with large eyes and teeth.

DORMSTON Hereford and Worcester SO9857
Hamlet off A422, 6 miles (10km) W of Alcester
Offers twin attractions of homely, rustic church and 700-nest dovecote (1660s) at Moat Farm, restored by Avoncroft Museum of Buildings.

DORNEY Buckinghamshire SU9378
Village on B3026, 3 miles (5km) W of Slough
The Pineapple pub recalls first English cultivation of pineapples at Dorney Court, Palmer family's delightfully atmospheric Tudor manor house.

DORNIE Highland NG8826
Village on A87, 8 miles (13km) E of Kyle of Lochalsh
Once an important fishing village. Access on foot to the dramatic Falls of Glomach (350ft/106m drop), on the National Trust for Scotland's Kintail estate.

DORNOCH Highland NH7989
Small town on A949, 12 miles (19km) E of Bonar Bridge
Royal burgh since 1628, with a tiny, heavily-restored cathedral (1224), fortified 16th-century Bishop's Palace (now a hotel) and Old Town Jail set, with other good examples of vernacular architecture, around spacious square. Witch's Stone commemorates the last witch-burning in 1722. Popular holiday resort with good beaches and championship golf course.

DORSTONE Hereford and Worcester SO3141
Village off B4348, 6 miles (10km) E of Hay-on-Wye
'Arthur's Stone', north of the village, is a late neolithic burial chamber, with hexagonal capstone on six verticals (English Heritage).

DOUGHTON Gloucestershire ST8791
Village on A433, 1 mile (2km) SW of Tetbury
Small village with attractive old cottages on the edge of the Highgrove estate, the 18th-century residence of HRH Prince of Wales.

DOUGLAS Isle of Man SC3875
Town on A5, 9 miles (14km) NE of Castletown
The capital and main harbour of this independent island country, where the River Glass joins the River Dhoo and runs into the sea, Douglas is a busy commercial and finance centre. Horse-drawn trams still run the length of the town's promenade on the sea front, the focus of the island's nightlife. The Douglas Bay Horse Tramway was designed by Thomas Lightfoot, a civil engineer who retired to the Isle of Man.

The Manx Museum relates the fascinating history of the Isle of Man, beginning around 10,000 years ago when the meltwater of the Ice Age raised the sea level. Among the first arrivals after this were the Vikings and many of their hidden treasures have been unearthed and are on display at the Manx Museum. The Vikings also established the Manx governmental system known as Tynwald, which has survived to this day as an independent government.

Sir William Hilary, founder of the Royal National Lifeboat Institution, lived in a mansion overlooking Douglas Bay, and he built the Tower of Refuge on Conister Rock in the bay, to provide shelter for shipwrecked mariners.

The 17th-century Moat Farm, Dormston.

DOUGLAS Strathclyde NS8330
Small town on A70, 8 miles (13km) S of Lanark
Granted in 13th century to powerful Douglas family, whose family stronghold, Douglas Castle, was demolished in 1938 because of coal-mining subsidence.

DOULTING Somerset ST6443
Village on A361, 2 miles (3km) E of Shepton Mallet
In the Mendips; many buildings in the locally quarried stone, which was also sent further afield. Large 15th-century tithe barn.

DOUNE Central NN7201
Village on A820, 4 miles (6km) W of Dunblane
Doune Bridge was built in 1535 to ruin the livelihood of the ferry man by a wealthy local tailor who had been refused passage. Doune Castle dates from 15th century when town was renowned for pistol manufacturing and, later, cotton milling. Today, it caters mainly for tourists.

DOUNREAY Highland NC9867
Site off A836, 8 miles (13km) W of Thurso
Scotland's first nuclear power station with distinctive silver sphere. Major local employer, but fast reactor soon to close.

DOVE, RIVER Derbyshire
River, tributary of the Trent
Forms much of Derbyshire/Staffordshire border, rising on Axe Edge (see), through dramatic Dovedale, past Tutbury Castle into River Trent at Newton Solney.

DOVER Kent TR3241
Town off A2, 15 miles (24km) SE of Canterbury
One of England's most important sea ports with exciting docks, owing its very existence to its proximity to France – the Eastern Docks are a busy cross-Channel port. The Romans developed Dover as their main naval base and it continued to be important becoming a founder member of the Confederation of Cinque Ports founded by Edward I. Slowly the old harbour silted up, it now lies under the town, and a new harbour was built out into the English channel in the 19th century.

Two World Wars have destroyed much of old Dover – this was 'Hell Fire Corner' – and the town itself is a jumble of modernity. Castle Street is the one good street remaining, while the best of the old buildings are Maison Dieu Hall, in the High Street, founded 1220, and Maison Dieu House (1665), now the library. Tourist attractions include The White Cliffs Experience and Dover Old Town gaol.

Dover Castle is one of Europe's most impressive medieval fortresses. The keep was finished in the 1180s, but the whole castle was remodelled substantially during the Napoleonic wars.

DOVER'S HILL Gloucestershire SP1639
see Chipping Campden

DOVERCOURT Essex TM2431
District off A120, S area of Harwich
Seaside resort and retirement town, originally developed by local MP from about 1850. Harwich has been called its 'poor relation'.

DOVERIDGE Derbyshire SK1133
Village off A50, 2 miles (3km) E of Uttoxeter
Commuter village with 16th- to 18th-century houses. Mainly 13th-century church with ancient yew, quietly situated beside River Dove, the Staffordshire border.

DOWLAIS Mid Glamorgan SO0707
NE area of Merthyr Tydfil
Eighteenth-century ironworks was first of those in and around Merthyr Tydfil which led to the town becoming Wales's largest. The narrow-gauge Brecon Mountain Railway leaves from Pant.

DOWLISH WAKE Somerset ST3712
Village off A358, 2 miles (3km) SE of Ilminster
Picture-postcard golden stone village, with stream. Perry's Cider Mill also has a small rural life museum.

DOWN AMPNEY Gloucestershire SU0996
Village off A419, 2 miles (3km) N of Cricklade
The village gives its name to a famous hymn tune by Ralph Vaughan Williams, born at the vicarage in 1872. All Saints' Church, mainly 13th and 14th century, has a fine Jacobean painted screen and impressive array of Arts and Crafts woodwork. The 15th-century Down Ampney House was partly remodelled by Sir John Soane in about 1800.

DOWN HATHERLEY Gloucestershire SO8622
Village off A38, 4 miles (6km) NE of Gloucester
On Gloucester's northern fringes, close to Staverton Airport, this village has a Victorian church with a rare lead font.

DOWN ST MARY Devon SS7404
Village off A377, 7 miles (11km) NW of Crediton
Remote, the church with interesting fittings including 16th-century bench-ends. Cob bus shelter of 1978.

DOWNE Greater London TQ4361
Village off A233, 2 miles (3km) NE of Biggin Hill
Still a country village. Charles Darwin wrote *The Origin of Species* at Down House, his home for 40 years, now a museum.

DOWNHAM Cambridgeshire TL5284
Village on B1411, 3 miles (5km) N of Ely
Downham was a favoured residence of the Bishops of Ely until 1642. The Norman church has 26 carved heads.

DOWNHAM Essex TQ7296
Village off A132, 2 miles (3km) NW of Wickford
Church with brick Tudor tower, gutted by fire in 1977 arson attack, restored by parishioners. Wildfowl at Hanningfield Reservoir.

DOWNHAM Lancashire SD7844
Village off A59, 3 miles (5km) NE of Clitheroe
Village is well preserved thanks to the Assheton family, now the Clitheroes. Often used in film and television.

DOWNHAM MARKET Norfolk TF6103
Town on A1122, 10 miles (16km) S of King's Lynn
Once a horse-market town, Downham Market still retains an air of bustle and activity. Handsome buildings of Carr (or iron) stone line the streets, some of them, such as Dial House in Railway Road, dating from the 1600s. An elegant cast-iron clock tower adorns the market place, and the parish church has a 1730 glass chandelier.

DOWNSIDE Surrey TQ1057
Hamlet off A245, 1 mile (2km) S of Cobham
Victorian model cottages surround the wide rough green of this little hamlet in the Mole meadows.

DOWNTON Wiltshire SU1821
Village on B3080, 6 miles (10km) S of Salisbury
A pretty village lying across the Avon Valley, the part to the west called The Borough, a New Town of the 13th century, now a very wide street with cottages either side (some thatched). Across the river is the big tannery, still producing leather. Paper was once made here too. The Moot is a large brick house of 1700 (not open) on the site of a medieval castle. Interesting Norman and later church with fine 18th-century monuments.

DOZMARY POOL Cornwall SX1974
Lake off A30, 9 miles (14km) NE of Bodmin
A lake high on Bodmin Moor; a mysterious place as no streams feed it. By legend this is where King Arthur's sword, Excalibur, was hidden.

DRAKE'S ISLAND Devon SX4652
Island in Plymouth Sound
Out in the sound, Plymouth's natural outer harbour, used as the site of a fort from the 1860s. Very much part of the stunning view from Plymouth Hoe (see).

DRAX North Yorkshire SE6726
Village off A1041, 5 miles (8km) SE of Selby
Skyline of Drax is dominated by the towers of the nearby power station and the ancient Saxon Church of St Peter and St Paul.

DRAYCOTT Somerset ST4751
Village on A371, 2 miles (3km) SE of Cheddar
Strawberry-growing area on the edge of the Mendips, with a golden local building stone known as Draycott marble.

DRAYCOTT IN THE MOORS Staffordshire SJ9840
Village off A50, 3 miles (5km) SW of Cheadle
Pleasantly situated on the River Blythe, the village has a church with several memorials to the Draycott family, lords of the manor from 1496.

DRAYTON Oxfordshire SU4894
Village on B4017, 2 miles (3km) SW of Abingdon
Popular residential village has attractive old houses in High Street and a medieval church of considerable interest.

DRAYTON Somerset ST4024
Village off A378, 2 miles (3km) SW of Langport
Small stone village, with Elizabethan Midelney Manor away to the south (limited opening).

DRAYTON BASSETT Staffordshire SK1900
Village off A4091, 3 miles (5km) SW of Tamworth
Well known for Drayton Manor Theme Park and Zoo on Sir Robert Peel's former estate. Hair-raising rides a speciality.

DRAYTON BEAUCHAMP Buckinghamshire SP9011
Village off A41, 1 mile (2km) W of Tring
At the foot of the Chilterns with a striking 15th-century church with brasses and monuments of the Cheyne lords of the manor.

DREFACH Dyfed SN3538
Village off A484, 3 miles (5km) E of Newcastle Emlyn
At the centre of one-time thriving Teifi Valley woollen trade. Bygone times remembered in the Museum of the Welsh Woollen Industry, which includes a working mill.

DREWSTEIGNTON Devon SX7391
Village off A382, 3 miles (5km) N of Moretonhampstead
Attractive granite village in striking scenery, with steep wooded river valleys, especially at Fingle Bridge. On a granite bluff to the southwest is Castle Drogo (National Trust), an extraordinary granite house like a castle, by Lutyens, 1911–30.

DRINKSTONE Suffolk TL9561
Village off A14, 6 miles (10km) NW of Stowmarket
On the old stagecoach road between Colchester and Bury St Edmunds, Drinkstone is an ancient village with fine houses and scattered farmsteads.

DROITWICH Hereford and Worcester SO8963
Town off A38, 6 miles (10km) NE of Worcester
The heritage centre explains the town's history as source of salt and later as a curative spa. Some town-centre buildings lean at crazy angles, the result of underground brine extraction. Notable buildings include Regency town hall, timber-framed Raven hotel, Norman/medieval Anglican church and Roman Catholic church with spectacular mosaics. Outside the town is an architectural extravaganza called Chateau Impney (now a hotel), built by salt tycoon John Corbett.

DRONFIELD Derbyshire SK3578
Town off A61, 5 miles (8km) N of Chesterfield
Important market town, later developed industrially. Fourteenth-century church and many fine 17th- and 18th-century buildings in its conservation area.

DROXFORD Hampshire SU6018
Village on A32, 5 miles (8km) N of Wickham
One of the largest and prettiest villages in the Meon Valley, many Georgian houses and beautiful water-meadows. The church tower is dated 1599 and the rest is basically Norman.

DROYLSDEN Greater Manchester SJ9197
Town in E area of Manchester
An industrial town with the Fairfield Moravian Settlement. The model village, centred on the church built in 1785, is a living community.

DRUMELZIER Borders NT1334
Village on B712, 8 miles (13km) SW of Peebles
Drumelzier – pronounced 'Drummelier' – said to be burial place of Merlin. Dawyck – pronounced 'Doick' – Botanic Gardens near by, branch of Edinburgh's Royal Botanic Gardens; numerous rare shrubs and trees, particularly conifers.

DRUMNADROCHIT Highland NH5030
Village on A82, 14 miles (23km) SW of Inverness
Straggling village at head of Glen Urquhart on fertile bay of Loch Ness and major tourist, boating and monster-watching centre, with two exhibitions devoted to Nessie. Strone Point is site of ruined Urquhart Castle, built during the 13th–15th centuries to guard Great Glen, which played an important part in the Wars of Independence. Destroyed in 1692.

DRYBURGH Borders NT5932
Village on B6404, 1 mile (2km) N of St Boswells
Incredibly romantic sandstone ruins of Dryburgh Abbey stand amidst stately trees and lawns beside River Tweed. Founded by David I in 1150, frequently damaged during Border Wars, and mouldered from 1600s. Ruins of church, monastic buildings and chapter house still extant. Burial place of Sir Walter Scott and Field Marshal Earl Haig.

DRYMEN Central NS4788
Village on A811, 7 miles (11km) NE of Balloch
At the west of the Campsie Fells and overlooking Endrick Water. Easy access to Loch Lomond and very popular in summer.

DRYSLWYN Dyfed SN5520
Hamlet on B4297, 5 miles (8km) W of Llandeilo
Ruins of early Welsh castle crown a prominent mound by crossing point of River Towy. Overlooked by 18th-century folly, Paxton's Tower.

DUART POINT Strathclyde (Mull) NM7435
Headland off A849, NE of Lochdonhead
Evocative 13th-century castle, seat of Macleans, in dramatic and defensive position on spit of land overlooking Firth of Lorne and Sound of Mull.

DUCKLINGTON Oxfordshire SP3507
Village off A415, 1 mile (2km) S of Witney
Village preserves its picturesque green and strong tradition of Morris dancing. St Bartholomew's Church is a treasurehouse of medieval artistry.

DUDDINGSTON Lothian NT2872
Area in E Edinburgh
Former village at foot of Arthur's Seat and beside Bowsinch Bird Reserve. Norman church, some pretty houses, 18th-century Sheep's Heid inn.

DUDDINGTON Northamptonshire SK9800
Village on A43, 5 miles (8km) SW of Stamford
Pretty Rockingham Forest conservation village of local stone, beside River Welland, the boundary with Rutland. At centre of village, Stocks Hill Farm dates in part from 1601. Fourteenth-century bridge relieved of heavy traffic since village was bypassed in 1973. Among other pleasant buildings are converted 17th-century watermill, manor house, dovecote, and 12th-century and later church.

The jougs or iron collar in Duddington.

DUDDO Northumberland NT9342
Hamlet on B6354, 7 miles (11km) SW of Berwick-upon-Tweed
Duddo Stones in the village centre is one of the best-preserved stone monuments in Northumberland. Duddo Tower is now a shapeless ruin.

DUDDON Cheshire SJ5164
Village on A51, 3 miles (5km) NW of Tarporley
Once a farming community where farm workers lived in tied cottages, now a cosy dormitory village, with an allegedly haunted pub.

DUDLEY West Midlands SO9490
Town off M5, 8 miles (13km) W of Birmingham
The old 'capital of the Black Country' boasts several attractions, including Dudley Zoo absorbed into the castle ruins, the Black Country Museum with outdoor reconstructions of regional life and industry, and the Museum and Art Gallery housing fine paintings, furniture and ceramics in addition to a specialist fossil collection. Town-centre nature reserve at Wren's Nest rock also worth visiting.

DUFFIELD Derbyshire SK3443
Village on A6, 5 miles (8km) N of Derby
Church isolated beside River Derwent, with cottages along banks of River Ecclesbourne and Georgian houses towards scanty remains of Norman castle.

DUFFTOWN Grampian NJ3240
Small town on A941, 7 miles (11km) SE of Rothes
Planned village founded 1817 by James Duff, Earl of Fife. Near by are two ruined castles: 15th-century Balvenie with its 'yett', or original iron gate, and Auchindoun, an 11th-century hill-top foundation. Several distilleries roundabout, notably Glenfiddich, founded by William Grant in 1886 and producing world-famous single malt whisky.

DUFFUS Grampian NJ1668
Village on B9012, 5 miles (8km) NW of Elgin
Duffus Castle is exceptional example of motte and bailey, originally surrounded by loch. Gordonstoun School, in 17th-century mansion, is near by.

DUFTON Cumbria NY6825
Village off A66, 3 miles (5km) N of Appleby-in-Westmorland
A centre of lead mining in the 18th and 19th centuries. The London Lead Company, a Quaker concern, built the village.

DUKERIES, THE Nottinghamshire
Historic area in N part of Sherwood Forest
Several Dukes had their homes here, Newcastle at Clumber (see), Portland at Welbeck (see), Kingston at Thoresby (see Ollerton).

DUKINFIELD Greater Manchester SJ9497
Town off A635, 6 miles (10km) E of Manchester
Industrial area in East Manchester which built up around the Peak Forest Canal, close to the junction of Ashton and Huddersfield canals.

DULL Tayside NN8049
Village off B846, 3 miles (5km) W of Aberfeldy
Centre of learning and worship since 8th century and burial place of St Adamnan, biographer of St Colomba, though insignificant today. Prehistoric remains.

DULOE Cornwall SX2358
Village on B3254, 4 miles (6km) S of Liskeard
A stone village with a medieval church, a holy well and a prehistoric stone circle – a good Cornish combination.

DULVERTON Somerset SS9127
Small town on B3222, 10 miles (16km) N of Tiverton
On the southern edge of Exmoor, in the wooded Barle Valley. Pretty little town, with the headquarters of the national park in the old workhouse (visitor centre) and an unusual town hall with a big arched external staircase of 1927. Fifteenth-century stone bridge over the Barle River, and local museum.

DULWICH Greater London TQ3373
District in borough of Southwark
Dulwich Picture Gallery, designed by Sir John Soane in early 19th century, notable collection. Rhododendrons in Dulwich Park. Fine Victorian buildings of Dulwich College.

DUMBARTON Strathclyde NS3975
Town off A82, 14 miles (23km) NW of Glasgow
Lying on the River Leven, Dumbarton became a royal burgh in 1222 and rivalled Glasgow as an important market town. By the 18th century the growth of ship-building and engineering was changing the town to an important industrial centre; by 1853 there were five shipyards. William Denny was the town's largest employer for more than a century, and the firm struggled on until 1963. In its heyday it built the famous tea-clipper *Cutty Sark* in 1869. Since the decline of ship-building,

Dumbarton Rock with its castle.

whisky distilling and light industry have taken over as the main employers in this sprawling industrial town.

Dumbarton Rock is on a commanding site overlooking the River Clyde with magnificent views; there has been a fortress here since Roman times, and it was briefly a royal castle in the Middle Ages. The present castle buildings date mainly from the 1600s and are approached from the solid 18th-century Governor's House up steps through a cleft between two rocks. Little else remains of the old town except one arch from St Mary's Collegiate Church.

DUMFRIES Dumfries and Galloway NX9776

Town on A75, 29 miles (47km) NW of Carlisle

A prosperous historic border town, Dumfries is known for its spinning and weaving industry and its strong links with Robert Burns. A royal burgh since 1186, it changed hands frequently during the Wars of Independence and the subsequent struggles. After the Act of Union the town benefited economically, it became an important North American port until the late 1900s.

The original castle was demolished; its site is now occupied by Greyfriars Church, near by is Midsteeple, a three-storeyed towered tolbooth built in 1707. The oldest bridge is the 15th-century Devorguilla Bridge, now pedestrianised.

Burns came to Dumfries in 1791 as excise man and lived in a house, now a museum, on the present-day Burns' Street until his death in 1796. The Globe inn, the Kings Arms and the Hole in the Wa' Tavern all have links with the poet and he was buried with his wife and five of his children in St Michael's churchyard. His original grave was replaced with a mausoleum containing his statue; another statue stands in the High Street. There are several tourist attractions, including a Burns Interpretative Centre in the Old Town Mill.

DUMMER Hampshire SU5846

Village off A30, 5 miles (8km) SW of Basingstoke

Famous as the home of the Duchess of York before her marriage. Small, with a proper village pond.

DUMPLING GREEN Norfolk TG0011

Village off A47, 1 mile (2km) SE of East Dereham

Birthplace (1803) of the writer George Borrow, whose love of travelling caused him to write several books on the gypsy way of life.

DUNADD Strathclyde NR8393

Prehistoric site on A816, 4 miles (6km) NW of Lochgilphead

Iron Age fort on high crag, important Celtic site. Associated with first dynasty of Scottish kings, Stone of Destiny may have been first used here.

DUNBAR Lothian NT6778

Town on A1087, 27 miles (43km) E of Edinburgh

On North Sea coast with intricate double harbour dating from fishing heyday and overlooked by castle ruins. Wide High Street has 17th-century six-sided town house, oldest civic building in constant use in Scotland. Birthplace of John Muir, conservationist and founder of North American National Park system; nearby John Muir Country Park commemorates him.

DUNBEATH Highland ND1629

Village on A9, 18 miles (29km) SW of Wick

Cliff-top crofting community with 15th-century castle and sheltered harbour, once important herring-fishing port. Birthplace of Neil M Gunn, author of *The Silver Darlings*.

DUNBEG Strathclyde NM8833

Village on A85, 2 miles (3km) NE of Oban

Nearby Dunstaffnage Castle had vital strategic importance from earliest times. Controlled by Campbells from 1409, its ruins date from 1200s. Outstanding Early Gothic chapel.

DUNBLANE Central NN7801

Small town off A9, 5 miles (8km) N of Stirling

Pleasant town on River Allan with historic core of buildings round cathedral which dates from 13th century, although a Celtic ecclesiastical centre dedicated to St Blane dates from 7th century. Cathedral restored since its virtual destruction during Reformation. Crow-stepped Leighton Library was purpose-built for bishop's books in 1680s and may be oldest in Scotland.

DUNCANSBY HEAD Highland ND3872

Headland off A9, 1 mile (2km) E of John O' Groats

Magnificent headland with lighthouse and superb views to Orkneys and along coast. Adjacent stacks and geos and abundant birds.

DUNCHIDEOCK Devon SX8787

Hamlet off A30, 4 miles (6km) SW of Exeter

A scattered village; little church with interesting fittings including bench-ends. On Haldon Hill, 1 mile (2km) south, is Lawrence Castle, a triangular monument with a statue, built in 1788. Prominent from miles around.

DUNCHURCH Warwickshire SP4871

Village on A426, 3 miles (5km) SW of Rugby

Gunpowder plotters and associates met at picturesque 'Guy Fawkes House'. Dun Cow hotel, famous coaching inn, among several other interesting buildings in village.

DUNCTON West Sussex SU9617

Village on A285, 3 miles (5km) S of Petworth

Scattered village straggling along road under Duncton Hill with splendid view to south. To north, wooded expanse of Duncton Common.

DUNDEE Tayside NO4030

City on A92, 18 miles (29km) NE of Perth

Overlooking the Tay estuary and backed by the volcanic hill called the Law, the site of a Roman hillfort, Dundee was granted a royal charter in 1190 and is today Scotland's fourth largest city. Many old buildings were destroyed in the 18th century, leaving only the Old Steeple of the City Churches as a 15th-century landmark.

The city boomed in the 19th century when it was the centre of the jute industry, employing as many as 7,000 as late as the 1950s. It claims to have invented marmalade but was also noted for jam-manufacturing and journalism, both of which are still major employers today, though modern industries are being introduced.

The restored ship *Discovery*, built in Dundee, which Captain Scott used for his Antarctic expedition in 1901, is now the centrepiece of a major tourist attraction on the waterfront.

The present rail bridge across the Firth of Tay replaced that destroyed in the Tay Bridge Disaster of 1879, which collapsed during a storm while a train was crossing, with heavy loss of life.

DUNDONALD Strathclyde NS3634

Village on B730, 4 miles (6km) NE of Troon

Ruined Dundonald Castle, mainly 14th-century; occupied till 1600s. Robert II and Robert III died here.

DUNDRENNAN Dumfries and Galloway NX7447

Village on A711, 5 miles (8km) SE of Kirkcudbright

Stone from ruined Dundrennan Abbey was used in construction of this secluded village near which Mary Stuart embarked for England after her last night in Scotland.

A 13th-century monument to a former Abbot of Dundrennan Abbey.

DUNDRY Avon ST5666

Village off A38, 4 miles (6km) SW of Bristol

High on a hill, with the church tower built in 1484 by the Merchant Venturers of Bristol as a beacon to guide sailors. Huge view of Bristol.

DUNFERMLINE Fife NT0987

Town off M90, 13 miles (21km) NW of Edinburgh

Scotland's capital until the Union of the Crowns in 1603, Dunfermline was founded by Malcolm III in the 1070s. His son, David I, built the first abbey in 1150s; this was destroyed by Edward I and rebuilt by Robert the Bruce, who is buried here, although his heart lies in Melrose Abbey (see). Only the Norman nave and parish church remain. Near by is the remaining façade of the palace, once the guesthouse of the monastery founded by Margaret, Malcolm III's wife. Charles I was born here in 1600.

Andrew Carnegie, the American industrialist and philanthropist, was born in the town and emigrated as a child. He purchased Pittencrieff Park in 1902 and donated this large flower-filled area and Pittencrieff House to the town, also founding the first of the Carnegie libraries here.

Dunfermline has prospered since the 18th century, first from coal-mining and weaving, today thanks to an electronics industry. The town centre, on the top of the hill round the abbey, is an attractive shopping area with cobbled streets, and there are good recreational Centre.

DUNGENESS Kent TR0916

Headland off B2075, 5 miles (8km) SE of Lydd

Glorious shingle foreland with expanse of marshland, wild, remote nature reserve with lighthouse, on Kent's southerly tip, brooded over by nuclear power stations.

DUNIPACE Central NS8083

see Denny

DUNKELD Tayside NO0242

Small town on A923, 10 miles (16km) W of Blairgowrie

The impressive medieval cathedral ruins of Scotland's 9th-century ecclesiastical capital beside the Tay overlook Telford's graceful bridge (1809). Many old Scottish vernacular townhouses have been restored by the National Trust for Scotland which also owns the nearby Hermitage, a charming waterside 18th-century folly in the woods near Inver, home of Neil Gow, the famous 18th-century fiddler.

DUNKERY BEACON Somerset SS8941

Hill off B3224, 6 miles (10km) SW of Minehead

Highest point on Exmoor, 1,705ft (519m); the only prominent peak on the moor, big cairn and panoramic views.

DUNKESWELL Devon ST1407

Village off A373, 5 miles (8km) N of Honiton

Two miles (3km) north are the ruined remains of an abbey, with parts of the gatehouse and a little church of 1842.

DUNLOP Strathclyde NS4049

Village on A735, 2 miles (3km) N of Stewarton

Renowned from 17th century for Dunlop cheese, a hard cheese made from unskimmed milk; the technique was introduced from Ireland.

DUNNET Highland ND2171

Village on A836, 7 miles (11km) E of Thurso

On sweeping Dunnet Bay, surfers' mecca and nearest habitation to Dunnet Head, most northerly point of British mainland. Neighbouring Castle of Mey belongs to Queen Mother (limited opening).

DUNNING Tayside NO0114

Village on B934, 5 miles (8km) E of Auchterarder

Lies at foot of Ochil Hills in Strathearn. Medieval church tower and memorial to west commemorating the burning of a witch in 1657.

DUNNOTTAR Grampian NO8783

Site off A92, 1 mile (2km) S of Stonehaven

Splendid ruins of great castle on 200ft (60m) high fortified promontory soaring above North Sea. Chapel and tower date from 1390s. In 1650s Scottish regalia was brought here and, when castle fell to Cromwell's troops, smuggled to safety at Kinneff church by minister's wife. Buildings deteriorated after 1715 Rebellion.

DUNOON Strathclyde NS1776

Town on A815, 2 miles (3km) S of Sandbank

Quintessential 'doon the watter' Clyde resort, reached by ferry from Gourock, with ruined Campbell castle. Grew fast in 19th century, many Victorian and Edwardian seaside buildings. Still popular today; sailing and local walking and climbing. Statue to Robert Burns' 'Highland Mary'. Cowal Highland Gathering is one of Scotland's largest.

DUNS Borders NT7853

Small town on A6105, 13 miles (21km) W of Berwick-upon-Tweed

Market town with castle and wildlife reserve lying in fertile farmland at foot of Duns Law, pleasant walk with fine views. Birthplace of racing driver Jim Clark, with small museum. Probable birthplace of 13th-century philosopher John Duns Scotus. Sumptuous Manderston House, huge Edwardian pile, is near by with stunning rhododendron and azalea gardens.

DUNS TEW Oxfordshire SP4528

Village off A4260, 2 miles (3km) S of Deddington

Pleasant and very traditional grouping of 18th-century manor house, impressive old rectory, pub, houses and church of Norman origin.

DUNSFOLD Surrey TQ0035

Village off B2130, 4 miles (6km) SW of Cranleigh

Brick and tile houses straggle alongside a shaggy common near airfield, while church, holy well and old cottages lie to the west.

DUNSFORD Devon SX8189

Village off B3193, 4 miles (6km) NE of Moretonhampstead

In the Teign Valley, a pretty village with cob and thatch. Wonderful scenery. The wooded river valley is a nature reserve with wild daffodils.

DUNSTABLE Bedfordshire TL0122

Town on A5, 5 miles (8km) W of Luton

Notable coaching town on Watling Street in its day and once a hat-making centre. Impressive priory church, old Saracen's Head and Old Sugar Loaf pubs; 1960s buildings include circular Church of Our Lady Immaculate. Much post-war development. Lovely country immediately outside on Dunstable Downs for walking, gliding, golf and Five Knolls prehistoric burial mounds.

DUNSTER Somerset SS9943

Village on A39, 2 miles (3km) SE of Minehead

This supremely picturesque and much-visited tiny town is actually better than its photographs. The view down the perfect main street with the Yarn Market (16th century, octagonal) towards the castle is balanced by the opposite view, with a tower folly on the wooded hillside. Dunster Castle (National Trust) is partly medieval (gatehouse) but the scenic upper parts are Victorian. Dunster watermill still grinds corn. Superb church with 16th-century wooden screen and roofs. Dunster Forest to the south has marked trails and England's highest tree, a Douglas Fir, 187ft (57m).

The saddleback tower of the church at Dunnet.

DUNSTON Lincolnshire TF0662

Village off B1188, 8 miles (13km) SE of Lincoln

Dunston Pillar, 1751, lighthouse to guide heath travellers. George III statue replaced lantern in 1810, but was removed as danger to aircraft during World War II.

DUNTISBOURNES, THE Gloucestershire SO9706/7

Villages and hamlets off A417, 5 miles (8km) NW of Cirencester

A quartet of attractive settlements (Abbots, Leer, Middle, Rouse) strung along Dunt Brook. Leer and Middle are quiet farm hamlets. Rouse has an unusual Saxon and Norman church on a steep hillside with an interior rich in history. The road at Abbots is partly submerged beneath the brook, and St Peter's Church has a notable Norman font and ancient ironmongery on its door.

DUNURE Strathclyde NS2515

Village off A719, 5 miles (8km) NW of Maybole

Fishing village with impressive ruins of Dunure Castle looming over it. Kennedy Castle, mainly 14th century, scene of roasting alive of Commendator of Crossraguel Abbey.

DUNVEGAN Highland (Skye) NG2547

Village on A850, 23 miles (37km) W of Portree

Dunvegan Castle stands north of village; seat of MacLeods since 13th century and Scottish castle longest occupied by same family. Fortress-like structure on rocky outcrop originally approachable only by sea, with various architectural additions to structure from 15th–19th centuries. Interior has clan relics, including Fairy Flag, silk Middle-Eastern banner from about 5th century, revered by all MacLeods.

DUNWICH Suffolk TM4770

Village off B1125, 4 miles (6km) SW of Southwold

Dunwich is one of many Suffolk villages that wage a constant battle against the advance of the sea. Medieval Dunwich was a powerful port, boasting a shipyard and a thriving fishing industry. Today, many old buildings have been claimed by the sea, and Dunwich's architecture is predominantly modern. It is, nevertheless, attractive, and is surrounded by forest and marshland.

DURGAN Cornwall SW7727

Hamlet off A39, 4 miles (6km) SW of Falmouth

Picturesque stone hamlet right down on the bank of the Helford River estuary. The school of 1876 is right on the shore.

DURHAM Durham NZ2742

City off A1(M), 14 miles (23km) S of Newcastle upon Tyne

Known as the cradle of Christianity in England, and the historic capital of the northeast, the centre of Durham, where the magnificent Norman cathedral and Durham Castle stand side by side, is acknowledged as a World Heritage Site. The first church was built in 995, where Durham Cathedral now stands, when monks from Lindisfarne arrived on Durham's rocky outcrop and chose this as a safe place for the shrine of St Cuthbert, whose remains they had been carrying with them since he died in 687. The cathedral also contains the shrine of the Venerable Bede. The castle was founded soon after the Norman Conquest, and from this time until 1836 Durham was known as a 'palatinate', because the bishops who ruled the territories enjoyed all the powers and influence normally vested only in royalty, and were known as 'Prince Bishops'. Durham Castle was their home and they gradually transformed it from a military fortress into a lavish residence. The castle was handed over to the newly established Durham University in the 1830s and the bishops moved out to the castle at Bishop Auckland. It is now used for student halls of residence and accommodation for visitors during the summer vacations.

The porch of the almshouses founded in 1666 in Durham.

The River Wear almost encircles the peninsula upon which Durham was built, and is crossed by three bridges of note: Framwellgate Bridge, dating from 1120, Elvet Bridge, from the same period and Prebends Bridge, built in 1777, which offers superb views of the cathedral. Durham Light Infantry Museum depicts the 200-year history of the county regiment and Durham Art Gallery is housed in the same building. The site is often used for outdoor performances through the summer, and the Oriental Museum contains important collections of Chinese ceramics and jades.

DURISDEER Dumfries and Galloway NS8903
Village off A702, 5 miles (8km) N of Thornhill
Remains of a Roman fort lie near this tiny place with its monument to the Duke of Queensberry in the church.

DURNESS Highland NC4068
Village on A838, 10 miles (16km) NW of Hope
Coastal crofting township with ruins of 12th-century church and good beach walks. One mile (2km) east lies the large limestone Smoo Cave.

DURRINGTON Wiltshire SU1544
Village off A345, 2 miles (3km) N of Amesbury
In a loop of the River Avon, and with army camps each side. Woodhenge is a ceremonial monument about 4,300 years old, like Stonehenge but six circles of wooden posts, now marked by concrete piles, inside a bank and ditch.

DURSLEY Gloucestershire ST7598
Town on A4135, 7 miles (11km) SW of Stroud
At the old centre of the sprawling modern town are the Old Bell hotel, the market house (1738), on pillars, and some pleasant 18th-century houses, reminders of Dursley's former cloth-making prosperity. St James's Church, mainly 15th century and built in local tufa, has an unusual large vaulted porch. Dursley is well known as the home of Lister engines.

DURWESTON Dorset ST8508
Village on A357, 2 miles (3km) NW of Blandford Forum
A mixture of thatched cottages and 19th-century estate cottages. Bryanston, the big house, is in woodlands to the south, a huge mansion of brick and stone of the 1890s (not open).

DUXFORD Cambridgeshire TL4846
Village off A505, 7 miles (11km) NE of Royston
Famous for its Imperial War Museum, Duxford has two churches with Norman towers, a chapel, a mill and two old pubs.

DYCE Grampian NJ8812
Village on A947, 5 miles (8km) NW of Aberdeen
Once-distinct community, but now swallowed up by Aberdeen. Home to Aberdeen Airport, whose heliport for North Sea rigs is one of the world's busiest.

DYFFRYN ARDUDWY Gwynedd SH5823
Village on A496, 5 miles (8km) N of Barmouth
Pre-eminent in coastal area full of prehistoric sites is prominent neolithic tomb whose long cairn covered two burial chambers of different dates.

DYKE Grampian NJ9858
Village off A96, 3 miles (5km) W of Forres
Brodie Castle (National Trust for Scotland) lies to west, site inhabited continuously by Brodies since the 12th century. Present castle is Z-shaped tower-house built in 1560s, with notable collections of paintings and furniture and spacious gardens. To the south is Darnaway Castle, mainly modern, with 15th-century banqueting hall.

DYLIFE Powys SN8694
Hamlet off B4518, 8 miles (13km) NW of Llanidloes
Former lead-mining community in wild, lonely mountain setting. Old Star inn. Memorial to broadcaster Wynford Vaughan Thomas at spectacular roadside viewpoint.

DYMCHURCH Kent TR1029
Small town on A259, 5 miles (8km) SW of Hythe
Seaside resort with chalets, holiday camps and funfairs, enjoying a sandy beach and the diminutive Romney, Hythe and Dymchurch Railway. This is the ancient 'capital of Romney Marsh', on edge of reclaimed levels $7^1/_2$ ft (2m) below high tides, protected from sea by Dymchurch Wall. The 'Lords of the Level' still meet at New Hall.

DYMOCK Gloucestershire SO7031
Village on B4215, 4 miles (6km) NW of Newent
A good early Norman church, but the village is remembered for its remarkable community of poets who lived and worked here immediately before World War I.

DYRHAM Avon ST7475
Hamlet off A46, 4 miles (6km) S of Chipping Sodbury
Dyrham Park (National Trust) is a handsome late 17th-century mansion, still with many interiors of that date, and the ancient deer park still has its herd of fallow deer.

DYSART Fife NT3093
NE area of Kirkcaldy, on A955
Once a prosperous little royal burgh with some picturesque 16th-century buildings, Dysart has been swallowed up to become a suburb of Kirkcaldy.

DYSERTH Clwyd SJ0579
Village on A5151, 3 miles (5km) S of Prestatyn
Located below Graig Fawr's slopes (a Site of Special Scientific Interest) rich in fossils deposited 300 million years ago. Waterfall plunges 60ft (18m). Parish church dates from 13th century. Bodrhyddan Hall near by. Dating from 17th century, its treasures include Egyptian mummy, Inigo Jones well-house, paintings, armour, period furniture and formal garden.

E

EAGLE Lincolnshire SK8766
Village off A46, 7 miles (11km) SW of Lincoln
Between Lincoln and River Trent. Nearby 1820 folly, The Jungle, sham castle where eccentric builder kept kangaroos and other animals.

EAGLESCLIFFE Cleveland NZ4215
Area in Stockton-on-Tees
Now a suburb of Stockton, surrounded by farmland. Stockton–Darlington Railway Line once ran through Eaglescliffe.

EAGLESFIELD Cumbria NY0928
Village off A5086, 2 miles (3km) SW of Cockermouth
Birthplace of John Dalton, originator of atomic theory and also of Robert Eaglesfield, confessor to Queen Philippa, wife of Edward III.

Tablet to John Dalton at Eaglesfield.

EAGLESHAM Strathclyde NS5751
Village on B764, 4 miles (6km) SW of East Kilbride
Attractive open-plan 1790s village, with green space between the rows of houses. It was built for a cotton factory which later burnt down, halting its growth.

EAKRING Nottinghamshire SK6762
Village off A616, 4 miles (6km) S of Ollerton
In 1669, William Mompesson came as rector, from the Derbyshire plague village of Eyam (see). In 1939, oil was struck.

EALING Greater London TQ1780
Borough in W London
Best known for films made in the 1950s at the studios on Ealing Green. Pitshanger Manor, now a museum with curious Martinware pottery collection, was home of architect Sir John Soane, who rebuilt it imposingly about 1800. Georgian houses from here to St Mary's Church, rebuilt about 1870 by SS Teulon with improbably huge battlemented tower.

EAMONT BRIDGE Cumbria NY5228
Village on A6, immediately S of Penrith
The remains of two ancient fortifications can still be seen here, Mayburgh Henge dating to about 2500BC, and King Arthur's Round Table, of about 1800BC.

EARBY Lancashire SD9046
Town off A56, 4 miles (6km) N of Colne
Museum of Mining, in old grammar school, tells story of lead-mining in the Pennines.

EARDISLAND Hereford and Worcester SO4158
Village off A44, 5 miles (8km) W of Leominster
Idyllic, manicured village where timber-framed houses are grouped beside the River Arrow and a millpond. Notable among them are the medieval Staick House and Knapp House, a 17th/18th-century manor house with brick dovecote and Millstream Cottage (former school of 1650s). On the fringe of the village, Burton Court has a 14th-century hall within an 18th-century exterior and houses a costume collection.

EARDISLEY Hereford and Worcester SO3149
Village on A4111, 5 miles (8km) S of Kington
Welsh border village where earthworks of Norman castle stand near church with outstanding Norman font. Tram inn commemorates early Kington–Hay industrial tramway.

EARITH Cambridgeshire TL3875
Village on A1123, 7 miles (11km) S of Chatteris
Starting point of the parallel canals that run for 21 miles (34km). Civil War barracks near by is called 'The Bulwark'.

EARL SHILTON Leicestershire SP4697
Small town on A47, 4 miles (6km) NE of Hinckley
Cottage workshops and 19th-century factories for footwear and hosiery industry. Richard III's officers slept in church before Battle of Bosworth, 1485.

EARL SOHAM Suffolk TM2363
Village on A1120, 3 miles (5km) W of Framlingham
This beautiful old village has a long winding High Street that was once part of a Roman road. The Romans were foiled in their penchant for straight roads by a large mere that was only drained in 1970. The village has a lovely church, and a large number of 16th- and 17th-century buildings.

EARL STERNDALE Derbyshire SK0966
Village off B5053, 4 miles (6km) SE of Buxton
Peak District quarrying village, whose Quiet Woman inn has headless woman on sign. Nineteenth-century church rebuilt in 1950s after war damage.

EARL STONHAM Suffolk TM1059
Village on A1120, 4 miles (6km) E of Stowmarket
Based around three village greens – Forward Green, Middlewood Green and Broad Green – this lovely old village boasts a pretty church, a thriving cricket club and a fruit packing business. It is sometimes confused with Earl Soham. One villager was a blacksmith for a record-breaking 80 years before his death in 1988.

EARL'S COURT Greater London TQ2578
District in borough of Kensington and Chelsea
Named after Earls of Warwick's courthouse. Post-war Australian outpost. Exhibition Hall, 1937, was then Europe's biggest reinforced concrete building.

EARL'S CROOME Hereford and Worcester SO8642
Village on A38, 6 miles (10km) N of Tewkesbury
Former manor of the Earls of Warwick has splendid Elizabethan manor house and well-preserved Norman church.

EARLEY Berkshire SU7472
District in E area of Reading
Huge suburban area of Reading, developed from the early 19th century. The Whiteknights estate has been the home of the University of Reading since 1947; modern campus buildings with the excellent Museum of English Rural Life.

EARLHAM Norfolk TG1908
Area of W Norwich
Earlham Hall forms the centre of the University of East Anglia (UEA). In its grounds is the Sainsbury Centre for Visual Arts.

EARLS BARTON Northamptonshire SP8563
Village off A45, 4 miles (6km) SW of Wellingborough
Substantial village famed for late Saxon tower of All Saints' Church, often featured in architectural texts as best preserved of its type in England. Church also has Norman and medieval work. Traditional boot and shoe making still flourishes. Prefix from Earls of Huntingdon and Northampton whose home is across River Nene at Castle Ashby.

EARLS COLNE Essex TL8528
Village on A604, 3 miles (5km) SE of Halstead
Named after the De Veres of Castle Hedingham (see), Earls of Oxford, who were buried in priory church on site where 18th-century Colne Priory house stands. Village church has handsome tower overlooking Colne Valley and showing the De Vere stars. World War II bomber airfield converted to golf course.

EARLSFERRY Fife NO4800
see Elie

EARSHAM Norfolk TM3289
Village on A143, 1 mile (2km) S of Bungay
Set in the rolling pastures of the Waveney Valley, Earsham is home to the Otter Trust, where these engaging animals thrive.

EARTHAM West Sussex SU9309
Village off A27, 5 miles (8km) W of Arundel
Pleasant flint and brick village on the southern slopes of the South Downs set in beautiful countryside near Roman Stane Street.

EAS COUL AULIN Highland NC2827
Waterfall off A894, near the head of Loch Glencoul
Britain's highest waterfall (658ft/200m) at the head of Loch Glencoul. Access via a tough two-hour walk, or by boat from Kylestrome.

EASBY North Yorkshire NZ1800
Hamlet off B6271, 1 mile (2km) SE of Richmond
The substantial remains of Easby Abbey stand in this beautiful setting by the River Swale near Richmond.

EASBY North Yorkshire NZ5708
Hamlet off A173, 2 miles (3km) SE of Great Ayton
The monument to Captain Cook, erected in 1827 by Robert Campion, a Whitby banker, overlooks Easby Moor.

EASDALE Strathclyde NM7417
Island off W coast of Seil
Tiny island famed for slate production until quarries flooded in 1880s. Workers' cottages now holiday homes.

EASEBOURNE West Sussex SU9023
Village on A272, 1 mile (2km) NE of Midhurst
A Cowdray estate village , with woodwork painted their regulation yellow, on the edge of Cowdray Park overlooking romantically ruined Cowdray House.

EASHING Surrey SU9443
Village off A3, 2 miles (3km) W of Godalming
Pretty National Trust village on River Wey with timber and stone houses, fine row of cottages and medieval bridge.

EASINGTON Durham NZ4143
Village on B1283, 2 miles (3km) NW of Peterlee
An important settlement since early times, the village retains its mainly rural and residential character, even though it lies in the heart of the East Durham Coalfield. The Church of St Mary has some fine 17th-century woodwork. Seaton Holme, in the centre of the village, was the home of Nicholas Breakspear, later Adrian IV, the only English pope.

EASINGWOLD North Yorkshire SE5269
Small town off A19, 12 miles (19km) NW of York
Once stood in the midst of the Forest of Galtres, a Norman hunting preserve. Impressive market cross and outline of bull-baiting ring can be seen.

EAST ALLINGTON Devon SX7748
Village off A381, 3 miles (5km) NE of Kingsbridge
Small, with a 15th-century church. Very rural.

EAST ANGLIA
Historic region of England
Much of East Anglia lies only a few feet above sea level, with Fens to the west and Broads to the east. Some of the earliest evidence of human settlement comes from Grimes Graves (English Heritage), a stone age flint mine. The Romans built fortresses here during Bodicea's revolt, and there are some splendid medieval castles at Castle Rising and Norwich.

EAST BARSHAM Norfolk TF9133
Village on B1105, 3 miles (5km) N of Fakenham
The glorious East Barsham Manor (not open) greets the traveller in a riot of moulded brickwork and ten carved chimneys. It was built around 1520.

EAST BERGHOLT Suffolk TM0734
Village off A12, 7 miles (11km) NE of Colchester
Birthplace of Constable. Both Flatford Mill and Willy Lot's Cottage (National Trust), painted by Constable,

still stand and are usually thronged with tourists. The village also offers a pretty church with an unfinished tower, and the bells still hang in their 16th-century housing, waiting to be installed.

EAST BRENT Somerset ST3451
Village off A370, 3 miles (5km) NE of Burnham-on-Sea
Tucked under Brent Knoll. Church has elegant spire, once whitewashed to act as a seamark, pretty ceiling of 1637 and rare 15th-century wooden lectern.

EAST BRIDGFORD Nottinghamshire SK6943
Village off A46, 8 miles (13km) E of Nottingham
Wooded village between the River Trent and the Fosse Way, where the Roman camp of *Margidunum* was sited.

EAST BUDLEIGH Devon SY0684
Village off B3197, 2 miles (3km) N of Budleigh Salterton
A port until the 16th century when the river silted up. Lots of cob and thatch in the centre, 15th-century church, with 63 bench-ends dating from 1537. Raleigh was born here at Hayes Barton, 1 mile (2km) west.

EAST CLANDON Surrey TQ0651
Village off A346, 4 miles (6km) E of Guildford
Genuine village on winding main street with timber and brick cottages, on estate of Hatchlands, the National Trust mansion east of village.

EAST COKER Somerset ST5412
Village off A30, 3 miles (5km) SW of Yeovil
A pretty, orange ham-stone village, lots of good cottages and houses including a row of almshouses of 1640. Mostly 15th-century church. The poet TS Eliot is buried here.

EAST COWES Isle of Wight SZ5095
see Cowes

EAST DEAN East Sussex TV5598
Village off A259, 4 miles (6km) W of Eastbourne
Flint-built village cupped in hollow of downs close to sea. Working farm (Seven Sisters Sheep Centre) at Birling Manor.

EAST DEREHAM Norfolk TF9913
Town on A47, 16 miles (26km) W of Norwich
In 984, monks from Ely came to East Dereham and stole the bones of St Withburga, who was buried here. Her grave immediately filled with water, and became a pilgrimage site. East Dereham was the home of the morose poet William Cowper, and has a pretty row of thatched cottages named after 'Bloody Bonner', a bishop who burned Protestants.

EAST DONYLAND Essex TM0221
see Rowhedge

EAST FARLEIGH Kent TQ7353
Village on B2010, 2 miles (3km) SE of Maidstone
Village on River Medway among hop gardens and orchards with superb medieval stone bridge, some old cottages, bungalows, caravan parks and boatyards.

EAST GARSTON Berkshire SU3576
Village off A338, 3 miles (5km) SE of Lambourn
Straddles the Lambourn River, with lots of little bridges. Some thatched and timber-framed cottages. Racehorses often about. Basically Norman church, a little apart.

EAST GRINSTEAD West Sussex TQ3938
Town on A22, 30 miles (48km) S of London
On Surrey border 400ft (122m) up on sandstone hills. A borough by 1235, then market town and centre of iron industry. Grew rapidly with coming of railway and now divided in two – around famous High Street with extraordinary range of medieval buildings, and 19th- to 20th-century centre by railway. Standen, to south, is a Philip Webb house with William Morris fittings.

EAST HAGBOURNE Oxfordshire SU5288
Village on B4016, 1 mile (2km) SE of Didcot
Satellite of Didcot, but well worth visiting for fine church interior and cottages around village cross.

EAST HAM Greater London TQ4283
District in borough of Newham
Quiet Essex country village until 1880s. Elizabeth Fry, 18th-century prison reformer, lived in Plashet area. Grand Edwardian town hall with clock tower. Parish Church of St Mary Magdalene is astonishing Norman survival with Tudor tower. Huge overgrown churchyard is now a flourishing nature reserve with foxes, lizards etc. Visitor centre in Norman Road.

EAST HARLING Norfolk TL9986
Village on B1111, 7 miles (11km) NE of Thetford
Deep in Breckland country, the attractive town of East Harling boasts a beautiful 15th-century church. Unusually for Norfolk, it has a spire. Inside is the marble tomb of Robert Harling, one of Henry V's knights who died at the siege of Paris in 1435. Harling's body was stewed so that it could be brought to East Harling for burial.

EAST HENDRED Oxfordshire SU4588
Village off A417, 4 miles (6km) E of Wantage
Late medieval Hendred House (home of Eyston family for 500 years) has its own 13th-century chapel and is an integral part of the village centre that also features the impressive King's Manor and other timber-framed buildings. Among them stands a church with notable 14th-century carving in its nave. Another 15th-century chapel near by has a timber-framed priest's house attached.

EAST HESLERTON (OR HESLERTON) North Yorkshire SE9276
Village on A64, 9 miles (14km) E of Malton
A village situated near the route of the Wolds Way footpath. The church contains figures designed for Bristol Cathedral.

EAST HORNDON Essex TQ6389
Hamlet on A128, 4 miles (6km) SE of Brentwood
Solitary brick church on hilltop above busy road junction with Tyrell monuments. According to legend, Sir James Tyrell slew a dragon here.

EAST HORSLEY Surrey TQ0952
Village on B2039, 7 miles (11km) E of Guildford
Suburbanised in the 20th century with no real centre. At southern end is extraordinary East Horsley Towers, manor house of 1820, embellished in range of 'Gothick' styles from 1847 by Earl Lovelace. Village near big house remodelled 1856–67 in self-assured red-brick and flint with heraldic devices over houses, cottages, school and pub.

EAST ILSLEY Berkshire SU4980
Village off A34, 9 miles (14km) N of Newbury
A big old village, until 1934 the site of a large annual sheep market, a centre for the downlands around. Large Georgian houses in the village indicate its importance in the 18th century. Now a racehorse training area.

EAST KILBRIDE Strathclyde NS6354
New Town off A726/A749, 7 miles (11km) SE of Glasgow
First, and quite successful, example of Scottish New Town, planned in 1940s and constructed in 1950s and 1960s to attract industry and solve Glasgow's housing shortage. Torrance House is headquarters for Development Corporation. First Scottish meeting of Society of Friends held in original town. Calderglen Country Park lies to south.

EAST KIRKBY Lincolnshire TF3362
Village on A155, 5 miles (8km) SW of Spilsby
Under slope of Lincolnshire Wolds; 14th-century church sympathetically restored 1900s, stands apart from main road village. Lincolnshire Aviation Heritage Centre.

EAST KNOYLE Wiltshire ST8830
Village on A350, 5 miles (8km) N of Shaftesbury
Scattered settlements and woody landscape. Sir Christopher Wren was born here in 1631, and the intricate plaster decoration in the chancel of the church was designed by his father, rector here.

EAST LAMBROOK Somerset ST4318
Village off B3165, 2 miles (3km) W of Martock
Small village, visited for the fine garden of East Lambrook Manor (15th-century house, not open) created in cottage style by Margery Fish, the gardening writer.

EAST LAVINGTON West Sussex SU9416
Hamlet off A285, 5 miles (8km) SW of Petworth
Small place at wooded downs' foot – the clump that crowns the down is Bishop's Ring, after Bishop Wilberforce who lived at Lavington Place, now Seaford College.

EAST LEXHAM Norfolk TF8517
Village off B1145, 6 miles (10km) NE of Swaffham
One of a group of four neighbouring villages with fine Anglo-Saxon churches that escaped Norman rebuilding for reasons that are unclear.

EAST LINTON Lothian NT5977
Small town off A1, 6 miles (10km) W of Dunbar
Small town on River Tyne, 16th-century bridge carried Edinburgh–London mail road. Downstream, river powers Preston Mill, restored 18th-century working corn mill. Phantassie Doocot lies to south with nesting for 500 birds. Two miles (3km) outside town on river is ruined Hailes Castle, complete with original water gates and dungeon. Demolished by Cromwell in 1650.

EAST LOOE Cornwall
see Looe

EAST LOTHIAN Lothian
Historic region of Scotland
Consisted of coastal strip and hinterland east of Edinburgh bordered to south by Lammermuir Hills. Industry mainly agriculture and fishing, some coal-mining.

EAST LULWORTH Dorset SY8682
Village on B3070, 3 miles (5km) S of Wool
Picturesque stone and thatch village. To the west is Lulworth Castle, built from 1608, a fanciful imitation castle, now a shell because of a fire in 1929. Close by is the Catholic Church of St Mary, built in the 1780s and deliberately looking like a house. George III is said to have given permission for the church, but only if it didn't look like one.

EAST MALLING Kent TQ7056
Village off A20, 4 miles (6km) W of Maidstone
Old buildings in village centre with pleasant Kentish cottages by church, modern development in old park of Clare House. Famed for horticultural research station.

EAST MARKHAM Nottinghamshire SK7373
Village off A57, 1 mile (2km) N of Tuxford
Large village with grand 15th-century church containing tomb-chest of Sir John Markham who drew up document deposing Richard II.

EAST MEON Hampshire SU6822
Village off A272, 5 miles (8km) W of Petersfield
The highest village in the Meon Valley, picturesque and much-visited. The young Meon River runs down one side of the main street, with handsome houses and cottages around. On the fringes are timber-framed cottages. The church, which stands apart, sidling up under a big chalk down, is largely Norman, with a black marble font (also Norman) vigorously carved with figures.

EAST MOLESEY Surrey TQ1467
Suburb of London on A3050/B369
At confluence of River Mole and River Thames opposite Hampton Court Palace. Some Victorian buildings, but modern houses have spread across the former Hurst Park racecourse.

EAST NEUK OF FIFE Fife
Historic region on E end of Fife peninsula
East Neuk ('corner' or 'promontory'), is extreme eastern corner of Fife peninsula. Includes several picturesque coastal towns. 'Golden fringe on the beggar's mantle' (James II).

EAST PECKHAM Kent TQ6648
Village off B2016, 4 miles (6km) NE of Tonbridge
Large village with several outlying hamlets which are set in beautiful countryside deep among the hop gardens.

EAST PENNARD Somerset ST5937
Village off A37, 4 miles (6km) SW of Shepton Mallet
A winding street with stone cottages. Well wooded.

EAST PORTLEMOUTH Devon SX7538
Village on E bank of Kingsbridge estuary
Passenger ferry across from Salcombe; good creeks to the north on the estuary and cliff walks to the south on the shore.

EAST PRESTON West Sussex TQ0602
Town off A259, 3 miles (5km) E of Littlehampton
Seaside village with some flint cottages, but village swamped by 20th-century sprawl. Church has very slim stone spire, rare in Sussex.

EAST QUANTOXHEAD Somerset ST1343
Village off A39, 4 miles (6km) E of Watchet
Small and rural, just back from the sea at the end of the Quantock Hills, with thatched cottages and a duck pond.

EAST RAYNHAM Norfolk TF8825
Village on A1065, 3 miles (5km) SW of Fakenham
East Raynham has one of Norfolk's most splendid 17th-century houses – Raynham Hall – built in 1622 for the Townshend family (not open).

EAST RETFORD Nottinghamshire SK7081
see Retford

EAST RIDDLESDEN West Yorkshire SE0742
see Riddlesden

EAST RIDING Humberside
Historic region in NE England
Old region which, after the boundary changes in 1974, became the county of Humberside.

EAST ROUNTON North Yorkshire NZ4203
Village off A19, 7 miles (11km) NE of Northallerton
Small village. The church was built in 1884 and contains Renaissance woodwork from Newcastle Cathedral.

EAST SHEEN Greater London TQ2075
District in borough of Richmond
Almost entirely 20th-century suburb on north side of Richmond Park. National Trust owns East Sheen Common.

EAST STOKE Nottinghamshire SK7549
Village on A46, 4 miles (6km) SW of Newark
On the Fosse Way. Site of battle, 1487, in which Lambert Simnel's supporters were defeated in his claim for the throne.

EAST STRATTON Hampshire SU5440
Village off A33, 2 miles (3km) NE of Micheldever
Lots of thatched cottages, including five brick pairs designed by London architect George Dance.

EAST TILBURY Essex TQ6877
Village off A1089, 3 miles (5km) E of Tilbury
In the marshes by the Thames with a Norman church, a 19th-century fort (limited opening) and a 1930s shoe factory estate.

EAST TISTED Hampshire SU7032
Village on A326, 4 miles (6km) S of Alton
Many decorative estate cottages. Rotherfield Park is a sham castle of 1820 with good views and gardens.

EAST WELLOW Hampshire SU3020
Hamlet off A27, 3 miles (5km) W of Romsey
Florence Nightingale spent much of her youth here (the house has been rebuilt) and she is buried in the churchyard. Medieval wall-paintings in the church.

EAST WEMYSS Fife NT3497
Village on A955, 5 miles (8km) NE of Kirkcaldy
Formerly a small coal port with nearby caves, or weems, in the cliffs. Ruined MacDuff's castle is near by.

EAST WITTON North Yorkshire SE1486
Village on A6108, 2 miles (3km) SE of Middleham
Quiet estate village, once an important market place being situated between the abbeys of Jervaulx and Middleham. The present village, with pairs of houses facing each other across a wide green, was built by the Earl of Ailesbury in 1809. On the green is a stone dated 1839 with a tap set in it – this was the village's water source.

EAST WRETHAM Norfolk TL9190
Village off A1075, 5 miles (8km) NE of Thetford
A small village standing in some of the finest grassland and woodland heath in England. Local industry revolves around the huge chicken factory.

EASTBOURNE East Sussex TV6199
Town on A22, 70 miles (113km) S of London
Lies under the lee of Beachy Head and is considered by some the most aristocratic of Sussex watering places, with its expansive seafront parades, Carpet Gardens and architecture that echoes Regency Brighton, although it is, in fact, Victorian. The earliest guide book to Eastbourne dates from 1799, but it was not until 1851 that the landlord, the Duke of Devonshire, began to develop the place in earnest. Up went the three-tiered parades overlooking the sea, the hotels, the churches (the best is St Saviour's, South Street), the railway station and the town hall, and old Eastbourne, set a mile inland, was swamped. The old town consists of St Mary's Church, a timber-framed inn and a parsonage (16th-century) set close together. The 18th-century manor house is now the Towner Art Gallery.

As for the new town, it does not try to compete with the gaudier amusements offered by other resorts, retaining a genteel atmosphere in keeping with its popularity as a place to retire. Amusements tend to cluster at the eastern end of town towards the shingle spread of the Crumbles. The Eastbourne Sovereign centre is a large indoor water leisure complex. There is international tennis at Devonshire Park, bowls, golf, cricket, sailing from the beach and fishing from the pier, itself a fantasy of Victorian ironwork and glass. There are several theatres. The Butterfly Centre on Royal Parade is a tropical house with exotic butterflies. The Wish Tower on King Edward's Parade, a Martello Tower built against the Napoleonic threat, in 1806, houses a permanent exhibition.

Nearby is the Lifeboat Museum. The famous bandstand on Devonshire Place seats 3,500 spectators. Eastbourne hosts an Air Festival and an International Folk Festival.

EASTBURY Berkshire SU3477
Village off B4001, 2 miles (3km) SE of Lambourn
In the Lambourn Valley, with many old buildings including a dovecote of 1620 with 999 nesting holes and weatherboarded thatched barns. Victorian church.

EASTCHURCH Kent TQ9871
Village on B2231, 2 miles (3km) SE of Minster
Agricultural village, developed but pleasing, built among trees on a little height in the middle of the Isle of Sheppey, on the island's only east–west road. Eastchurch Aerodrome was Britain's first airfield, 1909; both Lord Brabazon and Sir Winston Churchill learnt to fly here. Later it was important during the Battle of Britain.

EASTER ROSS Highland
Historic region of Scotland
Part of Ross and Cromarty before 1975, the name was given to the flat, relatively lush eastern area between the Dornoch and Cromarty Firths.

EASTGATE Durham NY9538
Village on A689, 10 miles (16km) SW of Consett
The village is the eastern 'gate' of the Bishop of Durham's 16th-century deer park in Weardale.

EASTHORPE Essex TL9121
Hamlet off A12, 6 miles (10km) SW of Colchester
On a Roman road. Old houses and a little Norman church with 13th-century wall-painting.

EASTINGTON Gloucestershire SO7705
Village off A419, 5 miles (8km) W of Stroud
This ill-defined dormitory village in the lower Frome Valley has an isolated riverside church with interesting medieval details.

EASTLEACH, MARTIN AND TURVILLE Gloucestershire SP1905
Villages off A361, 4 miles (6km) N of Lechlade
The two settlements, each with an interesting medieval church, confront each other across the River Leach, connected by an ancient clapper bridge.

EASTLEIGH Hampshire SU4519
Town on A335, 8 miles (13km) NE of Southampton
Until 1839 Eastleigh was just a farm. Then several railways crossed here, and it developed fast as a railway town, with big carriage works. Miles of terraced houses were built for the workers. Modern development now blurs the Victorian layout. To the south is Southampton Airport, by 1934 the third busiest airport in the country, but now only of regional importance. Local museums.

EASTNOR Hereford and Worcester SO7237
Village on A438, 2 miles (3km) E of Ledbury
Attractive estate village at gates of Eastnor Castle (open in summer), built 1812 with impressive interior and fine deer park. Interesting church.

EASTON Dorset SY6971
Village in Portland
Village in centre of Portland (see). The superb classical church (1750s) of St George Reforne to the east. Portland Museum in an old cottage at Wakeham, adjacent to the ruins of Rufus Castle and the medieval church. Portland Bill, the southern tip of the peninsula, has lighthouses to warn of the dangerous current just beyond.

EASTON Hampshire SU5132
Village off B3047, 2 miles (3km) NE of Winchester
Beautifully placed just above the River Itchen. Large village with a mostly Norman church.

EASTON Suffolk TM2858
Village off B1116, 2 miles (3km) NW of Wickham Market
In the spring and summer, Easton is an explosion of colours from well-tended gardens. It has an undulating brick (or 'crinkle-crankle') wall that belonged to the hall.

EASTON GREY Wiltshire ST8887
Village on B4040, 3 miles (5km) W of Malmesbury
A stone village on the River Avon, with picturesque views across the river and meadows. Westonbirt Arboretum, to the north, is enormous with a huge collection of trees and shrubs and a visitor centre.

EASTON MAUDIT Northamptonshire SP8858
Village off A509, 2 miles (3km) E of Castle Ashby
Johnson, Goldsmith and other literary figures visited 18th-century author Dr Percy, rector. Intriguing rustic thatched lodge on lane to Castle Ashby.

EASTON NESTON Northamptonshire SP7049
Mansion off A43, 1 mile (2km) NE of Towcester
Mansion designed in Wren's office by Hawksmoor, finished 1702, seat of Hesketh family (closed). Towcester racecourse is part of park.

EASTON ON THE HILL Northamptonshire TF0104
Village on A43, 2 miles (3km) SW of Stamford
Beautiful limestone hill village above River Welland, with church at highest point. Pre-Reformation Priest's House (National Trust) is open by appointment.

EASTON ROYAL Wiltshire SU2060
Village off B3087, 3 miles (5km) E of Pewsey
Neat village, with thatched cottages and Georgian houses in the main street, and the chalk downs above.

EASTON-IN-GORDANO Avon ST5175

Town off A369, 3 miles (5km) E of Portishead

Small old centre, with medieval church tower, but has spread since World War II to meet Pill (see).

EASTRINGTON Humberside SE7929

Village off B1230, 3 miles (5km) NE of Howden

Former stretch of embankment of the Hull to Barnsley railway line has been transformed into a wildlife park and amenity area.

EASTRY Kent TR3054

Village on A256, 3 miles (5km) SW of Sandwich

Interesting village with many historical connections, built along the straight Roman road from Richborough to Dover. Eastry Court stands on the site of a palace of Saxon Kentish kings, where Thomas Becket hid in 1164 on his flight to France. Nelson stayed at Heronden House, and one of his officers, Captain John Harvey, is buried here.

EASTWOOD Nottinghamshire SK4646

Town off A608, 8 miles (13km) NW of Nottingham

Displays in the miner's terraced house where DH Lawrence was born illustrate the background to his life in this 'country of my heart', the setting for his semi-autobiographical novel *Sons and Lovers* and other works. Oppressive conditions of the close-knit coal-mining community here meet the open spaces of Moor Green Reservoir and the surrounding countryside.

EATON BISHOP Hereford and Worcester SO4439

Village off B4352, 4 miles (6km) W of Hereford

Popular commuter village with 13th-century church worth visiting for remarkably beautiful glass of about 1320 in east window.

EATON BRAY Bedfordshire SP9720

Village off A4146, 3 miles (5km) W of Dunstable

Long, straggling village, church in local Totternhoe stone with magnificent 13th-century interior, stone carving, ironwork.

EATON SOCON Cambridgeshire TL1759

Village on A428, 1 mile (2km) SW of St Neots

The White Horse inn dates from the 13th century. Start of the 26 mile (42km) Ouse Valley Way to Earith (see). Was once a castle here.

EBBERSTON North Yorkshire SE8982

Village on A170, 6 miles (10km) E of Pickering

Ebberston Hall is a Palladian gem, the interior being a miniature version of Castle Howard.

EBBOR GORGE Somerset ST5248

Beauty spot off A371, 3 miles (5km) NW of Wells

Wooded limestone gorge with wide views of the Somerset Levels from the hills above.

EBBSFLEET Kent TR3464

Site on A256, immediately SW of Cliffs End

Dominated by its power station on a great meander loop near mouth of River Stour. Landing place of Hengist and Horsa, AD499 and St Augustine, AD597.

EBBW VALE Gwent SO1609

Town on A4046, 17 miles (27km) NW of Newport

One-time coal, iron and steel town *par excellence*. The giant steelworks closed in 1978, leaving a tinplate works and the future site of Britain's 1992 – and final – Garden Festival. Victoria Park an attractive leftover. Monument to Aneurin Bevan, the area's formidable Member of Parliament, stands on town's outskirts where the long, crowded valley meets the moors of the Brecon Beacons.

EBCHESTER Durham NZ1055

Village on A694, 3 miles (5km) N of Consett

Roman settlement on Roman Dere Street, with remains of Vindomora Fort. Derwent Walk Country Park accessed from the old station yard.

EBRINGTON Gloucestershire SP1840

Village off B4035, 2 miles (3km) NE of Chipping Campden

An appealing village lodged on a steep valley-side. St Eadburga's Church has good Norman and medieval features and some interesting monuments.

ECCLEFECHAN Dumfries and Galloway NY1974

Village off A74, 5 miles (8km) N of Annan

Several Roman forts in vicinity, including a ballistics practice range. Mainly noted as the birthplace of Thomas Carlyle (1795–1881), historian and essayist, who is commemorated by a statue. He was born in the Arched House, now a museum, and is buried in the churchyard. Name derived from 'eaglais', or church.

Statue of Thomas Carlyle at Ecclefechan.

ECCLES Greater Manchester SJ7798
Town on A57, 4 miles (6km) W of Manchester
The Church of St Mary dates back to Norman times but the name Eccles is derived from the Celtic word for church, so there was probably a place of worship here much earlier. Following the building of the Bridgewater Canal, the town developed with the cotton-spinning and weaving industry.

ECCLESFIELD South Yorkshire SK3593
District in N outskirts of Sheffield, on A6135
St Mary's Church is set in a fine churchyard with a central tower; it was rebuilt in the late 15th century.

ECCLESHALL Staffordshire SJ8329
Small town on A519, 7 miles (11km) NW of Stafford
Leisurely little town with wide, harmonious High Street. The medieval bishops of Lichfield lived in the former castle; the imposing church is their legacy.

ECCLESTON Cheshire SJ4162
Village off A55, 3 miles (5km) S of Chester
This estate village just outside Chester is dominated by Eaton Hall, the house of the Duke of Westminster and his ancestors since 1758, and Eaton Stud which has turned out many champion racehorses. The village was once occupied by the Romans and also became a Parliamentary garrison during the Civil War.

ECCLESTON Merseyside SJ4895
District on B5201, in W area St Helens
With a Tudor old hall, the village was the childhood home of Richard Seddon, who became Prime Minister of New Zealand.

ECHT Grampian NJ7405
Village on B977, 12 miles (19km) W of Aberdeen
Area very rich in prehistoric remains; most important is Barmekin of Echt, Pictish fort on isolated hill surrounded by five concentric defensive walls. Used as setting for end of Lewis Grassick Gibbons' *A Scots Quair*. Stone circles at Sunhoney, Cullerlie and Midmark Kirk.

ECKINGTON Derbyshire SK4379
Village on B6056, 7 miles (11km) NE of Chesterfield
Straggling village with imposing church, near Yorkshire border. Renishaw Hall with Jacobean core and later enlargements, home of literary Sitwells.

ECKINGTON Hereford and Worcester SO9241
Village on B4080, 3 miles (5km) SW of Pershore
Splendid 15th-century church roof, but village is best known for five-arched bridge of 1729 over Avon to north of village.

ECTON Northamptonshire SP8263
Village off A4500, 5 miles (8km) E of Northampton
American statesman Benjamin Franklin's blacksmith ancestors buried in churchyard. Mellow ironstone houses, Early Gothic Revival Hall, 17th-century Ecton House now a retreat.

EDALE Derbyshire SK1285
Village off A625, 5 miles (8km) NE of Chapel-en-le-Frith
Peak District village in valley of River Noe, last civilisation before wild peat moors from which Pennine Way stretches 250 miles (402km) to Scottish border. Walkers must be well equipped to cope with sudden weather changes, but spectacular Kinder Downfall waterfall is worth the effort. Peak National Park Information Centre, camping facilities, accommodation, youth hostel.

EDAY Orkney
Island between Stronsay and Westray
Sparsely inhabited island, with peat and quarrying industry. Rich in prehistoric remains; 15ft (4m) standing stone, chambered cairns. Carrick House (1633). Good walking.

EDBURTON West Sussex TQ2311
Hamlet off A2037, 3 miles (5km) S of Henfield
Tiny little place below the South Downs with the great hill behind named after it and crowned by small motte and bailey.

EDEN, RIVER Cumbria
River, runs through Carlisle to Solway Firth
At Rockcliffe, River Eden has cut small, red sandstone cliffs. The river estuary is a centre for birdlife.

EDEN, RIVER Gwynedd
River
A tributary of the River Mawddach running through the Ganllwyd Valley and ancient mixed woodlands of Coed y Brenin.

EDEN, RIVER Surrey/Kent
River
Small Wealden river which rises near Crowhurst and flows past Edenbridge to join the River Medway at Penshurst.

EDEN, RIVER Tayside/Fife
River
Rises in Lomond Hills to flow eastwards through Howe of Fife and Cupar, before entering North Sea at Guardbridge, northwest of St Andrews.

EDENBRIDGE Kent TQ4446
Small town on B2026, 6 miles (10km) S of Westerham
Characterful old town with some light industry on River Eden with straight High Street on Roman line upgraded in the 18th century. Some good timber houses in High Street between the Crown hotel and the river, including Taylor House with wall-paintings in an upper room and attractive Tanyard House. The surrounding countryside is delightful.

EDENHALL Cumbria NY5632
Hamlet off A686, 4 miles (6km) NE of Penrith
Once property of the Musgrave family who improved the village in the 19th century. Their mansion house has since been demolished.

EDENHAM Lincolnshire TF0621
Village on A151, 3 miles (5km) NW of Bourne
Attractive village in wooded countryside. Monuments of Willoughby de Eresby family, later Dukes of Ancaster, are important feature of church. Their Grimsthorpe Castle (limited opening), probably Lincolnshire's grandest house, lying in spacious parkland, shows four architectural periods: 13th-century castle; quadrangular Tudor house; Vanbrugh's 1720s north front probably completed by Hawksmoor; 19th-century west façade, with fine 18th-century furniture, gardens.

EDENSOR Derbyshire SK2469
Village off B6012, 2 miles (3km) E of Bakewell
Chatsworth estate village planned by Paxton for 6th Duke of Devonshire, as old village spoiled view. President Kennedy's sister, married into ducal family, buried in churchyard of George Gilbert Scott's church, as is Paxton. Chatsworth enjoys Peak District setting for splendid state rooms, fine contents, extensive gardens with fountains, cascades, farmyard, River Derwent flowing through park.

EDGBASTON West Midlands SP0684
District in SW Birmingham
Birmingham's once-fashionable Victorian suburb is dominated by the university, its original Edwardian buildings marked by a tall campanile. Among its associated buildings are the Barber Institute of Fine Arts (art gallery and concert hall). Long-established Botanical Gardens (tropical plants) are a major attraction, as are Cannon Hill Park (houses Midland Arts Centre) and Edgbaston Reservoir (watersports).

Figure on a roof in Ramsay Gardens, Edinburgh, originally a representation of 'Auld Nick' but now eroded to look more like a cat.

EDGCOTE Northamptonshire SP5047
Village off A361, 5 miles (8km) NE of Banbury
Peaceful parkland setting of early 13th-century church, 18th-century house and rectory near battle sites of 914 and 1469.

EDGEHILL Warwickshire SP3747
Hill off A422, 7 miles (11km) NW of Banbury
Edgehill Tower (1749) commemorates the site of the first battle of the Civil War in October 1642. Good walking with fine views.

EDGEWORTH Gloucestershire SO9406
Village off B4070, 5 miles (8km) NW of Cirencester
Isolated above the wooded Frome Valley, the village has a large Jacobean manor house and a church with notable Saxon, Norman and medieval work.

EDGMOND Shropshire SJ7119
Village on B5062, 2 miles (3km) W of Newport
Ornate 15th-century exterior conceals church's Norman origins. Old rectory incorporates 14th-century hall. Harper Adams Agricultural College on outskirts.

EDGWARE Greater London TQ1991
District in borough of Barnet
Middlesex village suburbanised mainly after 1920s arrival of underground railway. Edgware Road was originally Watling Street, Roman London–Chester road.

EDGWORTH Lancashire SD7416
Village off B6391, 5 miles (8km) N of Bolton
Originally a farming community, grew when mills were attracted to water power in nearby valley. Has a medieval footbridge.

EDINBURGH Lothian NT2573
City on A1, 413 miles (661km) N of London
This beautiful capital city, known as either 'Auld Reekie' or 'Athens of the north', is the administrative, legal and financial centre of Scotland, with three universities, fine buildings and abundant parks. The city stretches from the port of Leith to Queensferry and the Forth Bridges. It is essentially non-industrial, although there is a brewing and distilling tradition, and the 20th century has seen much urban expansion. With its renowned International Festival and excellent museums it is a cultured and fascinating place, which retains a strong sense of autonomy.

Founded on the defensive Castle Rock and well established by the 13th century, it became Scotland's capital in 1532. Reformation concepts found support in the 1550s with Presbyterianism dominating by the late 1600s. The Union of the Crowns (1603) and the Union of the Parliaments (1707) shifted prestige to London, although Edinburgh retained control of the church and Scotland's legal and educational systems, ensuring its status as a capital city.

The city has two distinct parts: the narrow streets of the unremittingly medieval Old Town and the spacious squares and terraces of the Georgian New Town. The Old Town sprawls down the hill from the ancient fortress of Edinburgh Castle, set high above the city, to the Palace of Holyroodhouse and the adjacent abbey, a stretch lined with tall stone tenement buildings with atmospheric wynds and closes leading off, known as the Royal Mile. Some of Edinburgh's best-known monuments are here, including sombre St Giles Cathedral, Parliament House, now housing the Law Courts, and John Knox's House. There are fine churches and secular buildings, some occupied by museums devoted to Edinburgh and its history. Near by, the open spaces of the Lawnmarket and the Grassmarket recall medieval times, while the neighbouring University of Edinburgh buildings and Scotland's National Library and Royal Museum represent intellectual life. North of the castle, across gardens formed by draining the old North Loch, lies the splendid New Town, built on a grid pattern between the 1770s and 1830s. Princes Street faces the castle, providing one of Europe's finest city views, although other New Town streets are architecturally better preserved. Along Princes Street lie fine Georgian civic buildings, among them Register House, the Royal Academy and the National Gallery of Scotland, while the Victorian Scott Monument gives a bird's-eye view of the city centre, also obtainable from Calton Hill near by. The New Town's elegant streets spread north down the hill towards the Firth of Forth, with the Royal Botanic Gardens below, one of Edinburgh's numerous parks and recreational areas.

Edinburgh, as a major tourist centre, is well provided with hotels, restaurants and other facilities, including some modern business and conference centres and a fine new Opera House. Shopping is more than adequate, with many specialist shops tucked off the beaten track. There is a full range of sports amenities and other entertainment, although clearly Edinburgh shows its best face to the visitor during the Festival.

Inscription at the entrance of World's End Close, Edinburgh.

EDINGTON Wiltshire ST9253
Village on B3098, 4 miles (6km) E of Westbury
Scattered villages supposedly the site of the Battle of Ethandune in 878, when King Alfred defeated the Danes. The church is beautiful, and dates from the late 14th century, elaborate inside and out. In the 1449 Peasants' Revolt the Bishop of Winchester was dragged from this church and stoned to death.

EDITH WESTON Leicestershire SK9205
Village off A6003, 5 miles (8km) SE of Oakham
Edward the Confessor gave his Queen Edith this part of Rutland, hence name of village. Now prettily sited on south shore of Rutland Water, where Rutland Sailing Club has its base, with views across to Hambleton peninsula. Graceful 14th-century church tower with spire. Monument by Rysbrack to a founder of Bank of England, Sir Geoffrey Heathcote.

EDLESBOROUGH Buckinghamshire SP9719
Village off A4146, 4 miles (6km) SW of Dunstable
On Bedfordshire border, isolated redundant church on mound has marvellous 15th-century interior. Brasses include one with unusual rose design.

EDLINGHAM Northumberland NU1109
Village off B6341, 5 miles (8km) SW of Alnwick
The village is situated in a remote and picturesque valley with a splendid viaduct and castle ruin. Edlingham Castle is a complex fortified house with a 13th-century hallhouse. The mainly 12th-century Church of St John the Baptist has a Saxon foundation and west wall, as well as a distinctive 14th-century tower.

EDMONDBYERS Durham NZ0150
Village on B6278, 1 mile (2km) W of Bishop Auckland
Small village set in heather moorland on the Durham and Northumberland border. The churchyard contains the remains a witch.

EDMONDSHAM Dorset SU0611
Village off B3078, 1 mile (2km) S of Cranborne
Once part of Cranborne Chase (see) and still wooded. Mostly brick, including Edmonsham House (1589 and 18th century) whose good gardens are sometimes open.

EDMONDTHORPE Leicestershire SK8517
Village off B676, 6 miles (10km) N of Oakham
Scattered village with ruins of Edmondthorpe Hall. Monument in church to Roger Smith and two wives, one thought to be a witch.

EDMONTON Greater London TQ3492
District in borough of Enfield
Once popular Londoners' day out resort. Charles and Mary Lamb lived at Lamb's Cottage, Church Street; they are buried in All Saints' churchyard.

EDNAM Borders NT7337
Village on B6461, 2 miles (3km) N of Kelso
Claim to fame as birthplace of Henry Lyte, who wrote words of '*Abide with me*', and James Thomson, writer of '*Rule Britannia*'.

EDSTASTON Shropshire SJ5132
Hamlet on B5476, 2 miles (3km) N of Wem
The church has some of Shropshire's best Norman work, including elaborate north and south doorways, another in the south chancel wall and a finely carved chancel window.

EDVIN LOACH Hereford and Worcester SO6658
see Edwyn Ralph

EDWARDSTONE Suffolk TL9442
Village off A1071, 4 miles (6km) E of Sudbury
Roman coins have been found at Edwardstone, and it was mentioned in Domesday Book. Its church once stood in the grounds of the hall (not open).

EDWINSTOWE Nottinghamshire SK6266
Village on A6075, 2 miles (3km) W of Ollerton
Church is reputed scene of Robin Hood's marriage to Maid Marion, beside oaks, beeches and silver birches of Sherwood Forest. Pleasant country park walks lead from visitor centre to huge ancient Major Oak, in whose hollow trunk the Merry Men are supposed to have hidden. Craft workshops and a summer amusement fair near by.

EDWYN RALPH Hereford and Worcester SO6457
Village on B4214, 2 miles (3km) N of Bromyard
St Michael's has two fine 14th-century monuments, and at nearby Edvin Loach are remains of a Saxon church (English Heritage).

EDZELL Tayside NO6068
Village on B966, 6 miles (10km) N of Brechin
Attractive village at south of Glen Esk on River North Esk with ruins of 16th-century Edzell Castle behind. Pleasant, formal walled garden of 1604.

EFFINGHAM Surrey TQ1153
Village on A246, 4 miles (6km) SW of Leatherhead
Small old cottages and modern houses make up this old springline village which runs downhill for 3 miles (5km) from the downs to the clay vale. Baron Howard of Effingham, Elizabeth I's Lord High Admiral, victor over the Spanish Armada of 1588, held the manor here – the modern village sign shows a 16th-century warship.

EGERTON Kent TQ9147
Village off A20, 3 miles (5km) SW of Charing
On a hill above the River Great Stour, the older parts of the village nestle into the valley with newer housing around the church.

EGGESFORD Devon SS6811
Hamlet on A377, 2 miles (3km) S of Chumleigh
In the wooded Taw Valley; no proper village, just a railway station and the church alone to the south. Eggesford Country Centre offers woodland and riverside trails. All trains stop here because the local landowner made that a condition when the line was built in 1854.

EGGINTON Derbyshire SK2628
Village off A38, 4 miles (6km) NE of Burton upon Trent
Rural village where 13th-century bridge crosses River Dove. Brindley's brick aqueduct carries Trent and Mersey Canal over river. Church about 1300.

EGGLESCLIFFE Cleveland NZ4113
Area in Stockton-on-Tees
Village is noted for its ancient Church of St John the Baptist. Fragments of Saxon stonework can be seen in the porch.

EGHAM Surrey TQ0071
Town off A30, 2 miles (3km) W of Staines
Town on River Thames with attractive winding main street and pretty riverside cottages at Egham Hythe. The church houses magnificent monument to Sir John Denham (1638), shown rising from the dead. Southwards the Victorian red-brick towers and turrets of Royal Holloway College dominate the skyline. Southeast stands 16th-century Great Fosters, now a hotel.

EGILSAY Orkney HY4730
Island E of Rousay
St Magnus murdered here 1115. Ruined 12th-century round-tower church, dedicated to saint, dominates low-lying landscape.

EGLETON Leicestershire SK8707
Village off A6003, 1 mile (2km) SE of Oakham
Site of Rutland Water's nature reserve, with visitor centre. Church, once much larger, has fine Norman doorway and other Norman work.

EGLOSHAYLE Cornwall SX0072
Village on A389, 1 mile (2km) NE of Wadebridge
Very close to Wadebridge, but a separate village with slate houses and cottages on the bank of the Camel estuary (see).

EGLOSKERRY Cornwall SX2786
Village off B3254, 4 miles (6km) NW of Launceston
Granite village, on an old road, so larger than its position suggests. Penheale Manor (1 mile/2km north) is 1620–40 and 1920s (not open).

EGLWYSFACH (FURNACE) Dyfed SN6895
Site on A487, 5 miles (8km) SW of Machynlleth
Silver-refining and iron-smelting took place here, the latter in the 18th-century Dyfi Furnace (Cadw) by the River Einion's tumbling waters. Secluded Cwm Einion or Artists' Valley continues to Plynlimon's foothills. Bordering the furnace is the Royal Society for the Protection of Birds' Ynyshir Nature Reserve with its wide range of habitats.

EGMANTON Nottinghamshire SK7368
Village off A6075, 1 mile (2km) S of Tuxford
Medieval centre of pilgrimage, revived 1896 when Duke of Newcastle had Comper restore medieval church. Motte and bailey castle.

EGREMONT Cumbria NY0110

Small town off A595, 5 miles (8km) SE of Whitehaven

Small market town with annual crab apple celebration dating from 13th century, which features the World Gurning Championship. Wordsworth's poem *The Horn of Egremont Castle* is based on a local medieval legend, whereby a great horn hanging in the castle can only be blown by the rightful lord. In this instance the impostor flees to a monastery.

EGTON/EGTON BRIDGE North Yorkshire NZ8006

Villages off A171, 6 miles (10km) SW of Whitby

Exposed and windswept villages on the North Yorkshire Moors. Egton Bridge claims to grow the finest gooseberries in the world and an annual Gooseberry Show, now over 200 years old, is held in August. The massive Catholic Church of St Edda, built 1866, overshadows the village of Egton. The name comes from 'Egetune', meaning 'town of oaks'.

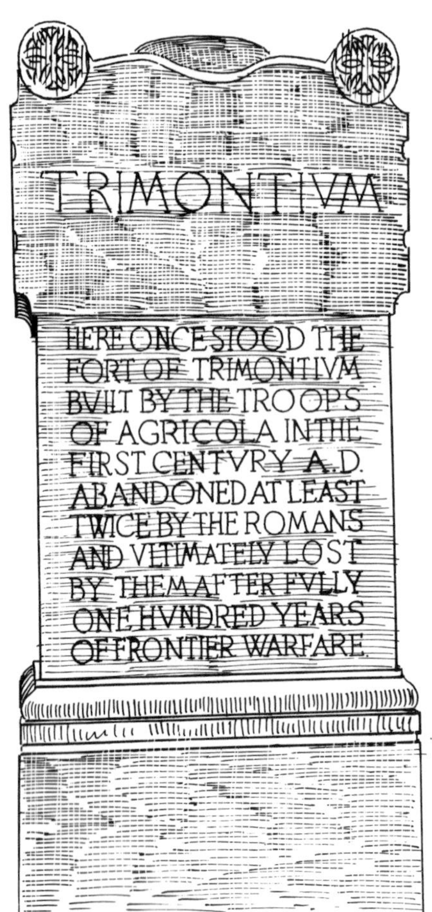

Monument on Leaderfoot Hill in the Eildon Hills.

EIGG Highland NM4687

Island in Inner Hebrides, SE of Rum

Five miles (8km) by 7 miles (11km) and distinguished by the Sgurr, a basalt ridge whose protection makes this beautiful island unusually fertile. Gaelic name means 'notch', which divides the island. Settled since prehistoric times, and Clanranald stronghold until 19th century. Since then owned by various incomers, and inhabited by fluctuating population of under 100 crofters, some involved in tourism.

EIGHT ASH GREEN Essex TL9425

Village on A604, 3 miles (5km) W of Colchester

Scattered greens among Colchester commuter housing estates. Fordham Heath is one of largest Essex greens. Iron Latch Meadow Nature Reserve.

EILDON HILLS Borders NT5432

Hills S of Melrose

Triple-peaked volcanic mounds, Roman Trimontium, (1,385ft/421m), are a 4 mile (6km) walk from Melrose. Legendary resting place of King Arthur and his knights, sleeping under a spell.

EILEAN BAN Highland NM6992

Island between Kyle of Lochalsh and Skye coast

One of two islands between Kyle of Lochalsh and Skye. Supports for Skye road bridge stand here and bridge soars overhead.

EILEAN DONAN CASTLE Highland NG8825

Castle off A87, 7 miles (11km) E of Kyle of Lochalsh

Much photographed and heavily restored 18th-century castle on 13th-century site reached across causeway and bridge on Loch Duich, overlooking Skye.

EILEAN MOR Western Isles NA7246

Island W of Lewis

Largest of Flannan Islands with lighthouse dated 1899 from which three keepers mysteriously disappeared in 1900, possibly washed away by freak wave.

ELAN VALLEY Powys SN9365

Scenic area on B4518, 3 miles (5km) SW of Rhayader

The four reservoirs constructed between 1892 and 1903 to supply Birmingham's water are the oldest, most natural looking of Mid Wales's many man-made lakes. A fifth was later added at nearby Claerwen. The poet Shelley's honeymoon retreat was among the buildings submerged. Area is the haunt of the rare red kite and other birdlife. A visitor centre provides a wide range of information.

ELDERSLIE Strathclyde NS4462

Small town on A737, W of Paisley

Small town chiefly renowned as being the traditional birthplace of William Wallace, with a monument to his memory.

ELFORD Staffordshire SK1810

Village off A513, 4 miles (6km) N of Tamworth

Good monuments in the church of this lonely village and good views over the Tame Valley towards Lichfield.

ELGIN Grampian NJ2162
City on A96, 36 miles (58km) E of Inverness
Royal burgh and market town, Elgin has been an important administrative and commercial centre since the 1300s. Recent building has failed to obliterate the outlines of the medieval street plan, and there are some fine buildings around the High Street, from which attractive wynds and pends lead off. Good examples of Scottish vernacular arcaded town houses exist, including Braco's Banking House. Near by is Elgin Museum, one of Britain's oldest collections, which includes some idiosyncratic anthropological exhibits.

The original castle was demolished in the 16th century and only the impressive remains of the cathedral still stand; first built in the 1220s, it was burnt by the Wolf of Badenoch in 1390, then rebuilt, only to crumble during the Post-Reformation period, when it was used as a quarry by local builders. It had replaced the cathedral at Spynie in 1224, although the bishops continued to live in Spynie Palace until after the Reformation. The gateway is the oldest part of these romantic 15th-century ruins.

Today, this bustling service town has good parks, hotels, and recreational amenities.

ELGOL Highland NG5213
Village on A881, 14 miles (23km) SW of Broadford
Dramatically sited village at foot of Cuillins on Loch Scavaig. Two famous caves: Suidhe Biorach sheltered Prince Charles Edward; Spar Cave renowned for stalactites.

ELHAM Kent TR1744
Village off A260, 6 miles (10km) NW of Folkestone
In the pastoral Elham Valley above course of River Little Stour – a 'nailbourne' or intermittent stream. Elham was once a market town, its charter granted by Edward I, and the delightful market square stands at the centre surrounded by timbered and brick houses and brick and tile cottages with new buildings that harmonise pleasingly.

ELIE Fife NO4900
Small town on A917, 5 miles (8km) W of Anstruther
Elie and Earlsferry amalgamated in 1929. Pretty harbour on lovely sandy bay, attractive village with green and good local walking and golf course.

ELING Hampshire SU3612
Village off A326, 1 mile (2km) SE of Totton
On a side estuary to Southampton Water, a pretty village with a toll road over the dam which impounds water for the tide mill, which still works.

ELISEG'S PILLAR Clwyd SJ2044
Site off A542, 1 mile (2km) NW of Llangollen
Remains of 9th-century cross honouring Eliseg of the princely house of Powys. Monument gives its name to nearby Valle Crucis Abbey (Cadw).

ELKSTONE Gloucestershire SO9612
Village off A417, 6 miles (10km) S of Cheltenham
Standing high above a steep drop into the Churn Valley, Elkstone has a splendid Norman church with a unique pigeon loft over the chancel.

ELLAND West Yorkshire SE1020
Village off A629, 4 miles (6km) NW of Huddersfield
Haunted village with a local industry based on textiles. The name is derived from 'Ealand', meaning 'land by water'.

ELLASTONE Staffordshire SK1143
Village on B5032, 4 miles (6km) SW of Ashbourne
Divided from Derbyshire by the River Dove, the village became 'Hayslope' in George Eliot's *Adam Bede*.

ELLESMERE Shropshire SJ3934
Small town on A495, 8 miles (13km) NE of Oswestry
Former canal town with wealth of timber-framed and Georgian buildings bordering The Mere, a haven for waterfowl and the largest of several local lakes.

ELLESMERE PORT Cheshire SJ4076
Town on A5032, 7 miles (11km) N of Chester
Prospered with the development of the Shropshire Union Canal and later the Manchester Ship Canal. Ellesmere Port Boat Museum depicts canal life, with boats and displays of narrowboat crafts.

ELLINGHAM Hampshire SU1408
Village off A338, 2 miles (3km) N of Ringwood
Tiny village on the edge of the New Forest, with an interesting, unaltered church.

ELLINGHAM Norfolk TM3592
Village off A143, 2 miles (3km) NE of Bungay
A mill and a granary have been converted into houses that stand on the banks of the River Waveney, each with picturesque, well-tended gardens.

ELLINGTON Cambridgeshire TL1671
Village off A14, 5 miles (8km) W of Huntingdon
Ellington and Ellington Thorpe are near the man-made reservoir, Grafham Water. There are nature trails, bird hides and watersports.

ELLON Grampian NJ9530
Small town off A92, 15 miles (24km) N of Aberdeen
Pleasant market town in agricultural country on the River Ythan, once the capital of Buchan and nowadays largely inhabited by Aberdeen commuters. Ellon Castle belonged to the Earls of Aberdeen; the 3rd Earl used it as a home for one of his three mistresses.

ELM Cambridgeshire TF4707
Village on B1101, 2 miles (3km) S of Wisbech
Dense trees and carved tombstones make All Saints' Church an atmospheric place. The Black Horse inn is just one of many fine buildings.

ELMDON Essex TL4639
Village off B1039, 5 miles (8km) W of Saffron Walden
Tucked away in a quiet corner of Essex, close to the Hertfordshire border among low hills and ancient earthworks.

ELMDON West Midlands SP1783
District off A45, in E Birmingham
Birmingham's new International Airport opened here in 1984. Its passenger terminals are linked to the nearby National Exhibition Centre by a magnetic levitation rail system.

ELMET West and North Yorkshire
Historic region between Leeds and Selby
An historic region containing many ancient settlements; it was once the Saxon kingdom of Elmet.

ELMLEY CASTLE Hereford and Worcester SO9841
Village off A44, 4 miles (6km) SW of Evesham
At the centre of this pretty Bredon Hill village are an Elizabethan inn and an ornate 15th-century church with unusual font and remarkable monuments.

ELMORE Gloucestershire SO7815
Village off B4008, 4 miles (6km) SW of Gloucester
Attractive Severnside village with an interesting medieval church. Close to Stonebench, a popular point for viewing the Severn Bore.

ELMSTEAD MARKET Essex TM0624
Village on A133, 4 miles (6km) E of Colchester
On old road to Harwich, named after medieval market on green. King's Arms, 17th century; Bowling Green pub with bowler sign.

ELMSTED Kent TR1144
Hamlet off B2068, 7 miles (11km) E of Ashford
Truly rural little place, with church, farm and cottages tucked in a fold of the downs above the Canterbury road.

ELMSTONE HARDWICKE Gloucestershire SO9125
Hamlet off A4019, 3 miles (5km) NW of Cheltenham
Isolated church in a tiny settlement, once the property of Deerhurst Priory. Norman and medieval, with fine east window and giant Victorian reredos.

ELMSWELL Suffolk TL9964
Village off A14 (A45), 5 miles (8km) NW of Stowmarket
The imposing flint tower of the church looms over the village. A housing estate in the 1960s heralded a sudden growth in Elmswell's population.

ELPHIN Highland NC2111
Village on A835, 7 miles (11km) S of Inchnadamph
Remote village in wild Assynt. Highland and Rare Breeds Farm has collection of traditional varieties of farm animals, including Hebridean and Soay sheep and Highland cattle.

ELRIG Dumfries and Galloway NX3248
Village off A747, 3 miles (5km) N of Port William
Author Gavin Maxwell described his childhood here in *The House of Elrig* (1965). Good walking country, prehistoric remains and later earthworks. Elrig Loch near by.

ELSDON Northumberland NY9393
Village on B6341, 3 miles (5km) E of Otterburn
Once a fortified village with a large green surrounded by houses, it has an inhabited pele tower and the remains of a Norman motte and bailey castle. The sinister Winter's Gibbet stands near by on Gallow's Hill. Some of the fallen of the Battle of Otterburn were brought to Elsdon church. Redesdale Sheep Dairy is open to the public.

ELSENHAM Essex TL5326
Village on B1051, 4 miles (6km) NE of Bishop's Stortford
Known for jam made at factory started by squire Sir Walter Gilbey, and for late Dorothy Paget's steeplechasers at Elsenham Hall.

ELSFIELD Oxfordshire SP5410
Village off A40, 3 miles (5km) NE of Oxford
Writers John Buchan and RD Blackmore are buried in the churchyard of this small hill village overlooking Oxford. Fine east window in church.

Moot Hall at Elstow.

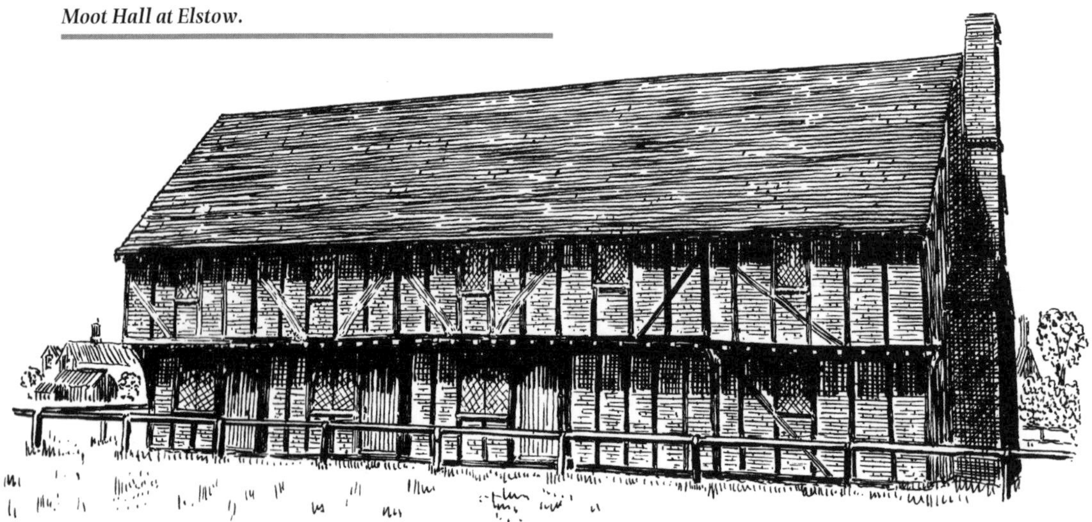

ELSHAM Humberside TA0312
Village off B1204, 4 miles (6km) NE of Brigg
Elsham Hall Country and Wildlife Park is set in the Old Hall's gardens. Beyond some disused quarries is an airfield used in both world wars.

ELSTEAD Surrey SU9043
Village on B3001, 4 miles (6km) SW of Godalming
In watermeadows of River Wey, with cosy cottages at village centre beside triangular green and graceful medieval bridge.

ELSTED West Sussex SU8119
Village off A272, 5 miles (8km) W of Midhurst
At the downs' foot, a compact little village with brick and chalk cottages and church rehabilitated in 1951 after a century of dereliction.

ELSTOW Bedfordshire TL0546
Village off A6, 2 miles (3km) S of Bedford
Birthplace of John Bunyan, 1628, and parts of the attractive village still look much as they did then. The Moot Hall museum on the green displays life in Bunyan's day, while in the massive Norman church is the font where he was baptised. The Whitbread brewing dynasty owned Elstow and helped to preserve it.

ELSTREE Hertfordshire TQ1795
Village on A5183, 5 miles (8km) E of Watford
On Watling Street, best known for film studios, but they are actually in Borehamwood (see). The Aldenham Country Park reservoir was dug in the 1790s by French prisoners-of-war to replenish the River Colne, depleted by canal building. Today there are watersports, rare breeds of farm animals and a nature trail.

ELSWORTH Cambridgeshire TL3163
Village off A14, 7 miles (11km) SE of Huntingdon
Originally a forest clearing, Elsworth has some handsome 16th-century buildings. A stream still trickles through Brook Street.

ELTERWATER Cumbria NY3204
Village on B5343, 3 miles (5km) W of Ambleside
An unspoilt village and smallest of the Lakes, surrounded by volcanic crags and waterfalls. The name means 'swan lake' in Norse.

ELTHAM Greater London TQ4274
District in borough of Greenwich
Eltham Palace (limited opening) was a favourite residence of English kings from 14th to 16th centuries. Great hall has third largest hammerbeam roof in England. Tudor Barn and Well Hall Pleasaunce survive from Tudor mansion where E Nesbit wrote *The Railway Children*. Other famous residents included Bob Hope and Frankie Howerd. Bob Hope Theatre.

ELTISLEY Cambridgeshire TL2759
Village off A428 (A45), 6 miles (10km) E of St Neots
A village in the Great Ouse Valley with an ancient history that includes two old English saints and a famine.

ELTON Cambridgeshire TL0893
Village off A605, 4 miles (6km) S of Wansford
Splendid Elton Hall (limited opening) and some fine 17th-century buildings mark Elton village. The River Nene to the west has a lock near the mill buildings.

ELTON Cleveland NZ4017
Village on A66, 3 miles (5km) W of Stockton-on-Tees
A suburban village centred around the church, a reconstruction of a former Norman church. Elton Hall looks Queen Anne but is actually 20th century.

ELTON Derbyshire SK2260
Village off B5056, 5 miles (8km) W of Matlock
Peak District village where limestone and gritstone meet, reflected in varied stone of 17th- and 18th-century houses. Former lead-mining centre.

ELTON Hereford and Worcester SO4570
Hamlet off A4110, 4 miles (6km) SW of Ludlow
Tiny settlement with church and hall attractively situated beneath wooded hills.

ELVASTON Derbyshire SK4032
Village off A6, 4 miles (6km) SE of Derby
South Derbyshire village gathered around edge of Elvaston Castle parkland. Nineteenth-century house (closed) designed by James Wyatt. Estate buildings and workshops operate as Working Estate Museum, illustrating crafts and tasks of 1910. Grounds designed 1830–50 for Earl of Harrington; formal, topiary and walled gardens, parkland, lake, woodland, nature trails open as country park.

ELVEDEN Suffolk TL8280
Village on A11, 4 miles (6km) SW of Thetford
Elveden Hall's most famous resident was Prince Duleep Singh, an exiled Indian maharajah who was persuaded to present the Koh-i-Noor diamond to Queen Victoria (hall not open). Much of the present village comprises red-brick houses dating from the 1890s, while the most recent innovation is Elveden Forest Village, built by Center Parcs.

ELVETHAM Hampshire SU7856
Village off A30, 1 mile (2km) SE of Hartley Wintney
Just a huge house of 1860 in hot red-brick striped with black, and a little neo-Norman church of 1840.

ELWICK Cleveland NZ4532
Village off A19, 3 miles (5km) W of Hartlepool
An ancient rural village established long before the Norman Conquest and originally part of the 'wapentake' of nearby Sadberge.

ELY Cambridgeshire TL5480
City off A10, 14 miles (23km) NE of Cambridge
Ely's name stems from a once major industry: eeling. It was originally on an island that stood above the surrounding marshes. The fen was a labyrinth of treacherous channels and tangled foliage, and those fighting against William the Conqueror made it their stronghold in the 11th century.

The octagon tower of the magnificent cathedral can

be seen from miles, towering above the low-lying land. It was founded by St Etheldreda in 673, although the present building is mostly 12th century.

Oliver Cromwell lived in Ely, and his house is open to visitors, a splendid black and white timbered building with a 17th-century kitchen.

Beyond the lovely medieval buildings associated with the cathedral – the old Bishops' Palace, the 15th-century Monks' Granary, and parts of what are now the King's School – lies the lazy River Great Ouse. Several pubs lend a holiday-like atmosphere to this attractive quayside, and the Maltings has been lovingly restored for public use.

Ely has some good shops, elegant Georgian buildings and a large park. To one side of the park, swathed in shrubs and almost forgotten, is the mound of a 12th-century castle.

EMBERTON Buckinghamshire SP8849
Village on A509, 1 mile (2km) S of Olney
Farming village set round 1846 clock tower, with enjoyable country park and lakes in former gravel workings by Great Ouse.

EMBLETON Northumberland NU2322
Village on B1339, 7 miles (11km) N of Alnwick
Dunstanburgh Castle (National Trust) was built in 1316 by Thomas Earl of Lancaster and enlarged later by John of Gaunt. The ruins of the castle are situated in a dramatic setting on rocky ledge overlooking the splendid beach. Holy Trinity Church existed in medieval times but unfortunately was rather badly restored in the 19th century.

EMBO Highland NH8192
Village off A949, 2 miles (3km) N of Dornoch
Popular holiday centre on coast with sandy beaches. Remains of two Stone Age burial sites.

EMLEY West Yorkshire SE2413
Village off A637, 1 mile (2km) S of Flockton
Dormitory village, with old and new dwellings. On nearby Emley Moor stands a television mast which is one of the tallest structures in Europe.

EMNETH Norfolk TF4807
Village off A1101, 2 miles (3km) SE of Wisbech
Typical village with a church and a pub. The village stands on marshland, rather than fenland, and is renowned for strawberries and folk songs.

EMPINGHAM Leicestershire SK9408
Village on A606, 5 miles (8km) W of Stamford
Substantial stone village at eastern end of Rutland Water. Large church with tall 14th-century tower reflects medieval importance.

EMPSHOTT Hampshire SU7531
Village off B3006, 2 miles (3km) SE of Selborne
Hilly wooded countryside, deep lanes, stone cottages. Early 13th-century church with pretty fittings.

EMSWORTH Hampshire SU7406
Small town on A259, 2 miles (3km) S of Havant
Picturesque and much visited, a yachting centre at the head of one of the muddy arms of Chichester Harbour. All lanes lead to the shore, and are lined with Georgian houses and cottages, brick, or brick and flint. Two huge mill ponds add to the picture. Local museum.

ENBORNE Berkshire SU4365
Village off A343, 3 miles (5km) SW of Newbury
Tiny village, with a small, partly Norman, church and a farm.

ENFIELD Greater London TQ3597
Town in borough of Enfield
On London's northern edge. Handsome old houses in Gentleman's Row and the Forty Hill area, where William-and-Mary-style Forty Hall is now a museum in an attractive park. Trent Country Park is in former Enfield Chase hunting forest, house now used by Middlesex University.

ENFORD Wiltshire SU1351
Village on A345, 2 miles (3km) S of Upavon
In the Avon Valley, small with older thatch and banded flint cottages, Georgian houses down by the river. More over the river at Longstreet. Interesting and pretty church, partly Norman.

ENGLEFIELD Berkshire SU6272
Village off A4, 6 miles (10km) W of Reading
Huge mansion, partly Elizabethan, partly Victorian, with elaborate church of 1857 designed by Sir George Gilbert Scott. The village was moved away from the house, and mostly neat estate cottages remain in the grounds.

ENGLISH BICKNOR Gloucestershire SO5815
Village on B4228, 3 miles (5km) N of Coleford
High above the meandering River Wye, the village has a Norman and medieval church on the site of a 12th-century castle.

ENGLISHCOMBE Avon ST7162
Village off A367, 3 miles (5km) SW of Bath
Now on the edge of Bath, but still rural. Partly Norman church.

ENHAM ALAMEIN Hampshire SU3649
Village on A343, 3 miles (5km) N of Andover
A hamlet which was developed after World War I to house disabled servicemen, second name added after World War II.

ENMORE Somerset ST2435
Village off A39, 4 miles (6km) W of Bridgwater
Remnants of a 1750s mock castle survive (not open) close to the church. To the northwest is Barford Park, a handsome house of 1710 with good gardens.

ENNERDALE WATER Cumbria NY1015
Lake off A5086, 1 mile (2km) E of Ennerdale Bridge
A remote corner of the Lake District. The lake and nearby village of Ennerdale Bridge take their name from the River Ehen.

ENSTONE Oxfordshire SP3724
Village on A44, 4 miles (6km) E of Chipping Norton
Two settlements divided by the Glyme Valley. Church Enstone has older buildings, including a good medieval church and tithe barn of 1382.

ENVILLE Staffordshire SO8286
Village on A458, 5 miles (8km) W of Stourbridge
Norman and medieval church worth visiting for fine monuments and entertaining misericords in chancel stalls.

EOLIGARRY Western Isles (Barra) NF7007
Village at N end of the island
Barra's beach landing strip near by, only airport in Britain 'subject to tides'. Sir Compton MacKenzie lived here, buried in churchyard. Ferry to South Uist.

EPNEY Gloucestershire SO7611
Hamlet off A38, 7 miles (11km) SW of Gloucester
Gastronomically famous as the depot for the annual catch of Severn elvers (small eels), netted during spring migration.

EPPERSTONE Nottinghamshire SK6548
Village off A6097, 7 miles (11km) NE of Nottingham
Attractive village with Georgian, Victorian and earlier houses, and several dovecotes.

EPPING Essex TL4502
Town on B1393, 17 miles (27km) NE of London
Market town of character outside Epping Forest (see). Camille Pissarro painted it. Eminent moth expert Henry Doubleday lived here.

EPPING FOREST Essex TL4196
Scenic area on A104, SW of Epping
Renowned for hornbeams and nightingales, almost 6,000 acres (2,400ha) survives of the old, once far more extensive forest. A forerunner of the green belt, maintained by the City of London. Besides woodland, there is heath, grassland and bog. Information centre, High Beach, Loughton (see), museums in Chingford (see), Waltham Abbey (see).

EPSOM Surrey TQ2160
Town on A24, 6 miles (10km) S of Kingston
This large town with a country feel, due in part to its rough common, possesses the widest High Street in Surrey. It was only a village when the medicinal spring on the common was discovered in 1619, heralding its development as a spa town. It obtained its charter as a market in 1685 and the assembly rooms arrived in 1690, as did the New Tavern on High Street which still stands. Wealthy city types patronised the spa at the well on the common, whose waters rich in 'Epsom Salts' were reputed a superb cure for indigestion.

Soon Epsom was a residential suburb of London and by the 1720s city men commuted to London by coach in the summer. Later a second well was opened in the town but by the 1740s those 'taking the waters' had declined in numbers.

There had been racing on the Epsom Downs since the early 17th century but once properly organised races were held, The Oaks in 1779 and The Derby in 1780, Epsom's popularity increased. These two races continue in importance and the big grandstand was rebuilt in the 1980s.

EPWELL Oxfordshire SP3540
Village off B4035, 7 miles (11km) W of Banbury
Isolated and deeply rural settlement on Oxfordshire's western border, with medieval Church of St Anne at its heart.

EPWORTH Humberside SE7803
Small town on A161, 9 miles (14km) N of Gainsborough
The home of World Methodism. John Wesley, founder of Methodism, was born here in 1703 at the Old Rectory. House later burnt down by a mob politically opposed to the views of his father, the rector. Now rebuilt and preserved. Charles Wesley, John's brother, writer of hymns, was also born here.

ERBISTOCK Clwyd SJ3541
Village off A539, 1 mile (2km) W of Overton
Border village attractive in its setting on banks of River Dee. Boat inn very popular, especially in summer.

ERDINGTON West Midlands SP1191
Suburb in NE Birmingham
Good Victorian and Edwardian architecture, plus a popular 15th-century pub in Bromford Lane, survive in an area of large housing estates near 'Spaghetti Junction'.

ERIDGE GREEN East Sussex TQ5535
Village on A26, 3 miles (5km) SW of Tunbridge Wells
Small village clusters around church and pub at gates to Eridge Park (costume museum). Station, and Bowles Outdoor Centre to south.

ERISKAY Western Isles NF7910
Island in the Outer Hebrides, between South Uist and Barra
Hilly island with strong musical tradition. Eriskay ponies are last survivors of Scottish native ponies; conservation breeding scheme. First landing place of Prince Charles Edward in 1745, islanders told him to go home. Fishing, crofting, knitting. SS *Politician* sank here in 1941 with 24,000 cases of whisky, inspiring Sir Compton MacKenzie's *Whisky Galore* and the subsequent film.

ERISWELL Suffolk TL7278
Village on B1112, 2 miles (3km) NE of Mildenhall
During the Napoleonic wars, the warrens at Eriswell provided thousands of rabbits for the army. The missionary New England Company was based here for 200 years.

ERITH Greater London TQ5177
District in borough of Bexley
High-rise blocks and factories grimly arrayed on south bank of River Thames. Erith Museum (limited opening), local history.

ERLESTOKE Wiltshire ST9653
Village on B3098, 6 miles (10km) E of Westbury
In a wooded valley, and remodelled in the late 18th century by the owner of the now-demolished big house. Ornamental thatched cottages, and bits of sculpture set in other cottages.

Sculpture set into a cottage in Erlestoke, a feature introduced by an 18th-century landlord.

ERMINE STREET Greater London
Roman road
Main Roman road from London to Lincoln and York, followed today by sections of A1 (M), A15 and B1207 north of Lincoln.

ERMINGTON Devon SX6353
Village on A3121, 2 miles (3km) S of Ivybridge
Famous for its twisted, 14th-century spire. Flete is a big house, Elizabethan and 1879 (limited opening).

ERPINGHAM Norfolk TG1931
Village off A140, 3 miles (5km) N of Aylsham
The mighty Church of St Mary the Virgin stands on Gallows Hill overlooking the village. Shakespeare wrote about Thomas Erpingham in *Henry V*.

ERROL Tayside NO2422
Village off A85, 8 miles (13km) E of Perth
Near the Firth of Tay in the fertile farmland of the Carse of Gowrie. Near by are the 16th-century castles of Megginch and Fingask.

ERWARTON Suffolk TM2234
Village off B1456, 2 miles (3km) W of Shotley Gate
A heart-shaped casket lends credence to the local story that Anne Boleyn's heart was buried at Erwarton church.

ERWOOD Powys SO0943
Village on A470, 6 miles (10km) SE of Builth Wells
Perched on River Wye's banks where cattle drovers of old used shallow crossing. Henry Mayhew conceived *Punch* magazine while staying here in 1841.

ESCOMB Durham NZ1830
Hamlet off B6282, 1 mile (2km) NW of Bishop Auckland
Small village on River Wear on outskirts of Bishop Auckland. Church is the oldest complete Saxon church in England.

ESCRICK North Yorkshire SE6242
Village off A19, 6 miles (10km) S of York
A well-planned village with a fine Victorian church. Escrick Hall was originally built in the 1680s by Henry Thompson, mayor and MP of York.

ESH Durham NZ1944
Village off A691, 5 miles (8km) W of Durham
The unusual name is from the Old English for 'ash tree'. The Hall, of which little remains, is incorporated in a farmhouse on that site.

ESHER Surrey TQ1364
Town on A307, 4 miles (6km) SW of Kingston
Pleasant little town with gently sloping green surrounded by cottages and pub. High Street mainly neo-Tudor and neo-Georgian, but 15th-century Waynflete Tower stands alone beside River Mole, the red-brick gatehouse of vanished bishops' palace. South of town is Claremont Landscape Garden (National Trust), created 1715–74, covering 50 acres (20ha) in the grounds of Claremont House.

ESHOLT West Yorkshire SE1840
Village off A65, 3 miles (5km) NE of Shipley
Better known as Beckindale from the television series *Emmerdale*; the Woolpack inn from the programme is a real functioning pub.

ESKDALE Dumfries and Galloway NH4540
River valley
Rather bleak upland area now largely forested. Roman remains near Eskdale church and meteorological observatory for cold and rainfall.

ESKDALE North Yorkshire NZ8205
Region off A171, 5 miles (8km) SW of Whitby
The valley of the River Esk. The Esk Valley Walk, a series of linking trails, explores the length of this historic and beautiful valley.

ESTON Cleveland NZ5418
Town off A174, 4 miles (6km) E of Middlesbrough
Suburb of Middlesbrough. Much mining around here in 1850s, contributing greatly to the Tees-side iron industry. Eston Nab is a prehistoric site.

ETAL Northumberland NT9339
Village on B6354, 8 miles (13km) NW of Wooler
A village of thatched cottages with ruined Etal Castle. Heatherslaw water-driven corn mill was built in 19th century; its products are much in demand.

ETCHILHAMPTON Wiltshire SU0460
Village off A342, 3 miles (5km) E of Devizes
Pronounced 'Ashelton'. Very rural, with some thatch and timber-framing. On the A342 a monument with a seated lion on top commemorates road improvements of 1768.

ETCHINGHAM East Sussex TQ7126
Village on A265, 7 miles (11km) N of Battle
Quiet village on railway beside confluence of rivers Dudwell and Rother. Splendid collegiate church (1360) containing renowned brasses.

ETON Berkshire SU9677
Town across the Thames from Windsor
A small town on the Thames with a handsome High Street and a good views of Windsor, but known principally for Eton College, the most famous public school in England, founded in 1440 and still using the original 15th-century buildings. The courtyards of brick buildings are similar to those of a Cambridge college, with proper gatehouse tower and lovely stone chapel. Very atmospheric.

ETRURIA Staffordshire SJ8647
District in Stoke-on-Trent
Settlement originally created in once rural valley by Josiah Wedgwood in 1769 as a factory for his pottery and a village for his workers. Etruria Hall, his house, remains on the site of the National Garden Festival but the factory has gone (see Barlaston). Etruria Industrial Museum displays steam-powered potters' mill and other exhibits. Caldon Canal starts here.

ETTINGTON Warwickshire SP2749
Village on A422, 6 miles (10km) SE of Stratford-upon-Avon
Tower of old church stands near new church of 1903. Ettington Park (hotel) is a remarkable Gothic house of 1862 with a spectacular interior.

ETTON Cambridgeshire TF1406
Village off B1443, 6 miles (10km) NW of Peterborough
Etton stands at the western edge of the Bedford Levels. Near by is part of Car Dyke, a Roman canal that was navigable to York.

ETTON Humberside SE9743
Village off B1248, 4 miles (6km) NW of Beverley
The village below the Church of St Mary is laid out with attractive red and white cottages.

ETTRICK Borders NT2714
Village off B709, 15 miles (24km) W of Hawick
Tiny hamlet in Ettrick Forest, once heavily wooded, now sheep country. Birthplace of James Hogg, 'The Ettrick Shepherd', important 19th-century poet and novelist.

ETWALL Derbyshire SK2631
Village off A516, 6 miles (10km) SW of Derby
Almshouses and family monuments in church illustrate influence of Sir John Port, founder of nearby Repton School; 17th- to 19th-century houses.

EUSTON Suffolk TL8979
Village on A1088, 3 miles (5km) SE of Thetford
Black and white cottages huddle along Euston's High Street. Near by is the splendid 17th-century palace, Euston Hall.

EVANTON Highland NH6066
Village off A9, 6 miles (10km) NE of Dingwall
Noted for Fyrish Monument on hill behind village; built by General Sir Hector Munro to commemorate his capture of Seringapatam in India in 1781.

EVENLODE Gloucestershire SP2229
Village off A429, 3 miles (5km) NE of Stow-on-the-Wold
Compact and solitary, at the head of Evenlode Valley, with an Elizabethan manor house and an interesting Norman and medieval church.

EVERCREECH Somerset ST6438
Village on B3081, 4 miles (6km) SE of Shepton Mallet
On the edge of the Mendips, with what has been claimed as the best church tower in the whole country, 15th century. Fine painted medieval roof. Around the church a large square of stone cottages and a school.

EVERDON Northamptonshire SP5957
Village off A361, 4 miles (6km) SE of Daventry
Secluded village, 14th-century church beside manor house. Old House (1690) at Little Everdon. Everdon Stubbs, ancient woodland; birdlife, wildflowers.

EVERINGHAM Humberside SE8042
Village off A1079, 5 miles (8km) W of Market Weighton
Magnificent Roman Catholic church dedicated to St Mary and St Everilda; design is neo-classical; altar is marble, inset with polished porphyry.

EVERSHOLT Bedfordshire SP9833
Village off A4012, 3 miles (5km) E of Woburn
Old houses, excellent cricket ground. In the church, paintings by local artist Edward Aveling Green (died 1930).

EVERSLEY Hampshire SU7762
Village on A327, 5 miles (8km) SW of Wokingham
Rural woody parish, with small scattered hamlèts. Charles Kingsley, the author of *The Water Babies*, was rector at Eversley 1844–75, and wrote most of his books here. The rectory (not open) looks as he left it, and there are big half-timbered labourers' cottages built as a memorial to him. Jacobean Bramshill House is now a police college.

EVERTON Bedfordshire TL2051
Village off B1042, 2 miles (3km) NW of Potton
Witch judge's monument in the church. Tower shortened in 1974 after lightning struck, the bells sold to America.

EVERTON Merseyside SJ3491
District in NE Liverpool
Home to the famous football club and the black and white striped mints, both of the same name.

EVESHAM Hereford and Worcester SP0344
Town off A44, 13 miles (21km) SE of Worcester
Pleasant riverside gardens are dominated by the impressive bell tower of 1539, sole reminder of powerful Evesham Abbey. The two churches, standing side by side, both contain rich 15th-century work inspired by Abbot Clement Lichfield. Among many attractive buildings are 15th-century Booth Hall and the Almonry, which houses an information centre and museum of local history.

EWELL Surrey TQ2062
Town off A24, 5 miles (8km) SE of Kingston
Twisting streets and streams and pools of Hogsmill River make this an enchanting little town between Nonsuch Park and expansive Horton Country Park.

EWELME Oxfordshire SU6491
Village off B4009, 3 miles (5km) SW of Watlington
The church, school (still used) and almshouses (still occupied) form the unique medieval heart of this Chiltern village, all founded in the 1430s by the benevolent Duke and Duchess of Suffolk. The Duchess, grand-daughter of poet Geoffrey Chaucer, has a sumptuous tomb in the splendid church. Writer Jerome K Jerome lies in the churchyard.

EWENNY Mid Glamorgan SS9077
Village on B4524, 2 miles (3km) S of Bridgend
Fortified Benedictine priory founded in 1141. Priory church has medieval rood screen and some good Norman work. Long-established working pottery.

EWERBY Lincolnshire TF1247
Village off A17, 4 miles (6km) E of Sleaford
Long village with tall spired church and market cross. Thomas Becket sheltered from Henry II at nearby Haverholme Priory in 1164.

EWHURST Surrey TQ0940
Village on B2127, 2 miles (3km) E of Cranleigh
Straggling Wealden village set around little square with long green to south, overshadowed to north by looming heights of wooded Hurtwood Common.

EWLOE Clwyd SJ2966
Village off A55, 1 mile (2km) NW of Hawarden
Castle ruins hidden in steeply wooded glen, a stronghold both of Llywelyn the Great and Llywelyn the Last. Recreational facilities of Wepre Park near by.

EWYAS HAROLD Hereford and Worcester SO3828
Village on B4347, 1 mile (2km) NW of Pontrilas
Earthworks of Norman castle survive to the east of church with impressive tower and reredos made up of 16th-century carved panels.

EXBOURNE Devon SS6002
Village on B3217, 4 miles (6km) NE of Okehampton
In the Okemont Valley, red Devon soil. The church has a fine early 14th-century east window. Rubble and cob cottages.

EXBURY Hampshire SU4200
Village off A326, 3 miles (5km) SW of Fawley
On the edge of the New Forest, with a famous garden. Exbury Gardens have every type of rhododendron, and many other trees and plants which enjoy acid soils. Huge, with woodlands and ponds; some more formal areas (limited, seasonal opening).

EXE, RIVER Devon
River
Starts only 5 miles (8km) from the north coast of Devon, but runs all the way from Exmoor to Exeter on the south coast, with a big estuary below to Exmouth.

EXETER Devon SX9292
City off M5, 64 miles (103km) SW of Bristol
Historically and psychologically the capital of the southwest, the cathedral city is the county town of Devon, a university town and a major focus of road and rail routes. Although severely damaged in World War II, it has retained much history and charm. The city stands on the site of a Roman fort on a hill above the River Exe. Stretches of the Roman wall have been kept in repair ever since.

The cathedral is distinguished by two massive Norman towers and 300ft (91m) of the longest unbroken stretch of tierceron vaulting in the world. Standing beneath it in the nave has been compared to being inside a whale. There is also an elaborate medieval clock, the first English attempt to depict an elephant and delightful carvings done when bomb damage was repaired after 1945 – among them the one-eyed cathedral cat. The cathedral library contains the fabled Exeter Book, the premier manuscript of Anglo-Saxon poetry.

Little city churches in the local crumbly red sandstone were fitted into bustling medieval Exeter at odd angles. The guildhall is one of Britain's oldest municipal buildings and the Ship inn was Sir Francis Drake's favourite hostelry. The Royal Albert Memorial Museum and Art Gallery is in a fine Victorian building, and part of the medieval St Nicholas Priory can be visited. There are elegant Georgian streets and the old canal docks house the world's biggest boat collection in the lively Maritime Museum. Guided tours through the medieval Underground Passages (originally for water) are irresistible except for the claustrophobic. Today a premier administrative, financial and business centre, Exeter prides itself on excellent shopping and attractive gardens.

EXFORD Somerset SS8538
Village on B3224, 9 miles (14km) SW of Dunster
The first, but by no means the last settlement on the River Exe. In the middle of Exmoor and sometimes called its capital. Small green and medieval stone bridge. The church of St Salvyn stands a little apart, with a rich wooden screen and 16th-century tower.

EXMINSTER Devon SX9487
Village off A379, 4 miles (6km) SE of Exeter
Along the Exe estuary, now partly a suburb to Exeter. The old village has a 14th-century church with exceptional plasterwork of 1633.

EXMOOR Devon/Somerset
Scenic area in SW England
Exmoor, sometimes seen as the poor relation to Dartmoor, has its own strong character and particular scenery. It is a high moorland plateau in northern Devon and Somerset (mainly Somerset) bordering the Bristol Channel. The national park of 265 square miles (685 sq km), designated in 1954, includes the Brendon Hills (see) in a landscape which blends moor and heath with farms and swift streams in deep, lushly wooded valleys, and England's highest sea cliffs on the Bristol Channel coast.

Once all wild hunting country, Exmoor was partly tamed in the 19th century by a rich ironmaster, John Knight, who turned 15,000 acres into farmland planting miles of beech hedges which still survive. Today there are miles of enjoyable walking routes, prehistoric sites, ancient packhorse bridges and whortleberry bushes, with red deer and wild ponies, although the pony population is declining (to below 200 in 1994).

The highest point is Dunkery Beacon at 1,705ft (502m), commanding huge views, in an extensive National Trust estate. The valleys of the Barle, the Exe and the twin Lyn rivers are especially lovely. Romantic associations with RD Blackmore's *Lorna Doone* draw visitors to Badgworthy Water and the Doone Valley, and the diminutive church at Oare (see), where Lorna Doone and John Rigg were married.

EXMOUTH Devon SY0081
Town on A376, 9 miles (14km) SE of Exeter
Sandy beach one side, estuary the other. A small fishing port until the early 18th century when it became the first sea-bathing resort in Devon. A la Ronde to the north is an extraordinary house (National Trust) – 16-sided and built in 1798 with a shell-lined gallery. Chapel and almshouses of 1811 close by. The World of Country Life amusement park.

EXNING Suffolk TL6265
Village on B1103, 2 miles (3km) NW of Newmarket
The origins of Exning are shrouded in mystery. St Felix came in AD636, and the village stands near Devil's Dyke, an Anglo-Saxon earthwork.

EXTON Leicestershire SK9211
Village off A606, 4 miles (6km) NE of Oakham
Very attractive Rutland village, with thatched 18th-century cottages around village green. Church contains outstanding range of monuments from 16th to 18th centuries, some by Gibbons and Nollekens. Exton Park is home of Earls of Gainsborough. Old Hall burnt out 1810, present hall dates from 1811 and 1850s (closed). Fort Henry, 1780s Gothick summerhouse on lake.

EYAM Derbyshire SK2176
Village off A623, 5 miles (8km) N of Bakewell
Pronounced 'Eem'. 'Plague village' where rector William Mompesson persuaded villagers into voluntary quarantine, 1666, to prevent spread of plague. Over 250 people, two-thirds of population, died. Open-air service at Cucklet Dell each August commemorates villagers' self-sacrifice, with well-dressing as thanksgiving for pure water. Summer concerts at the 17th-century Eyam Hall; family portraits, tapestries, old kitchen.

EYDON Northamptonshire SP5449
Village off A361, 8 miles (13km) NE of Banbury
Conservation area with many fine ironstone 17th-century and later buildings, restored 13th-century church, 18th-century hall, waterpump and stocks.

EYE Cambridgeshire TF2202
Village off A47, 4 miles (6km) NE of Peterborough
Eye (meaning 'island' in Anglo-Saxon) lies on the great expanse of low-lying farmland of the north Bedford Levels.

EYE Hereford and Worcester SO4964
Hamlet off A49, 3 miles (5km) N of Leominster
Church has fine medieval interior. Nearby Berrington Hall (National Trust) is 18th century, with splendid plasterwork, interesting bygones, park by Capability Brown.

EYE Suffolk TM1473
Small town on B1077, 4 miles (6km) SE of Diss
Eye's heyday was in the mid-1800s, when it was a thriving market town seething with tradesmen and craftsmen. It suffered when the mainline railway went to Diss. Modern Eye is an attractive little town that spans the banks of the River Dove, overlooked by the castle mound. Black and white houses and a 12th-century church complete the picture.

EYEMOUTH Borders NT9464
Town off A1107, 8 miles (13km) NW of Berwick-upon-Tweed
Picturesquely situated, an active herring fishing town focused round harbour, granted free port charter in 1597. Renowned as smuggling centre in 1700s with secret passages all over town; Robert Adam's Gunsgreen House was centre of this. Museum contains Eyemouth Tapestry, woven in memory of disastrous storm of 1881 when 129 fishermen were drowned. Thriving community, popular with holidaymakers.

EYEWORTH Bedfordshire TL2545
Village off B1042, 4 miles (6km) E of Biggleswade
Largely Victorian. Anderson family monuments in tree-cloaked church, whose steeple was destroyed in fierce 1967 storm.

EYKE Suffolk TM3151
Village on A1152, 3 miles (5km) NE of Woodbridge
A farming village with a church dating from 1150, and some 17th-century buildings. Near by is the former US Air Force base of Bentwaters.

EYNESBURY Cambridgeshire TL1859
District of St Neots on B1046
Once a separate village on a tributary of the River Great Ouse, Eynesbury has become part of a continuous development from St Neots.

EYNSFORD Kent TQ5465
Village on A225, 5 miles (8km) S of Dartford
Picturesque and popular village beside a narrow hump-backed bridge and ancient ford in the Darent Valley. Here the picture-postcard Plough Inn, old timbered cottages and slim-spired church group themselves beside the ruined 11th-century castle (English Heritage). The rest of the village is strung along the main road.

EYNSHAM Oxfordshire SP4309
Town off A40, 6 miles (10km) NW of Oxford
A tollbridge of 1769 over the River Thames still gives access to this ancient market town. Reminders of its past importance are traces of a 13th-century abbey, a fragile medieval market cross and 17th-century town hall. Streets of pleasant buildings in various materials radiate from a centre still busy with modern commerce. Morris dancing flourishes.

EYPE Dorset SY4491
Village off A35, 2 miles (3km) SW of Bridport
Close to the sea, with deep narrow lanes and plain cottages. Thorncombe Beacon to the west has impressive 500ft (155m) cliffs.

EYTHORNE, UPPER AND LOWER Kent TR2849
Village off A256, 5 miles (8km) N of Dover
Lower Eythorne is an attractive Kentish village of pretty cottages and church with rare lead font. Newer houses in Upper Eythorne, an old colliery village.

EYTON Hereford and Worcester SO4761
Village off B4361, 2 miles (3km) NW of Leominster
Timber-framed Eyton Court is reputed to be the birthplace of Richard Hakluyt, Elizabethan travel writer. Fine rood screen in the church.

F

FADMOOR North Yorkshire SE6789
Hamlet off A170, 2 miles (4km) NW of Kirkbymoorside
A farming hamlet on the edge of the Moors which only received electricity in 1948–9, and still has no street lighting.

FAILSWORTH Greater Manchester SD8901
Town on A62, 5 miles (8km) NE of Manchester
A mixed industrial and residential area which developed in the 19th century with Manchester's cotton boom. Now surrounded by light industry and warehousing.

FAIR ISLE Shetland HZ2172
Island about 25 miles (40km) SW of Sumburgh Head
Magnificently bleak island (National Trust for Scotland) with a famous bird observatory and a tiny population. Famous for unique knitting patterns, possibly introduced by shipwrecked Spanish Armada seamen.

FAIRBOURNE Gwynedd SH6112
Village off A493, 8 miles (13km) SW of Dolgellau
Holiday village at sandy mouth of Mawddach estuary backed by mountain heights of Cader Idris. Fairbourne and Barmouth Steam Railway is the smallest of Wales's narrow-gauge trains (just over 12in/31cm gauge) and trains run from Fairbourne to Porth Penrhyn, with ferry connections across estuary to Barmouth. Huge, west-facing beach.

FAIRBURN North Yorkshire SE4727
Village off A1, 2 miles (3km) N of Ferrybridge
A residential area of modern housing estates. Fairburn Ings RSPB Nature Reserve is set around a lake created from flooded coal workings.

FAIRFIELD Hereford and Worcester SO7275
Village off A491, 3 miles (5km) N of Bromsgrove
Haphazard village south of Clent Hills with the big Pepper Wood to the west and church by celebrated Victorian architect Benjamin Ferry.

FAIRFORD Gloucestershire SP1501
Small town on A417, 8 miles (13km) E of Cirencester
This attractive Coln Valley market town, birthplace of famous priest John Keble, has a High Street full of harmonious buildings and a square dominated by the picturesque Bull inn. The outstanding attraction is St Mary's Church (1497), containing rich furnishings and a wealth of 15th-century glass illustrating Bible stories – the finest collection in England.

FAIRLIE Strathclyde NS2055
Town on A78, 3 miles (5km) S of Largs
Former resort and Clyde steamer departure point, now largely a retirement and commuter town. Racing and cruising yachts were built here. Kelburn Castle and country centre near by.

FAIRLIGHT East Sussex TQ8612
Village off A259, 3 miles (5km) E of Hastings
Village church 500ft (152m) up on the clifftop, with old coastguard cottages. A modern settlement of seaside houses sits down by Fairlight Cove. Hastings Country Park on wooded cliffs.

FAIRSTEAD Essex TL7616
Hamlet off A12, 4 miles (6km) W of Witham
Norman church built using Roman bricks, with notable 13th-century wall-paintings of scenes from the life of Christ.

FAKENHAM Norfolk TF9229
Town off A148, 23 miles (37km) NW of Norwich
Straddling the River Wensum, Fakenham is an attractive country town with 18th-century brick houses clustered around its fine market place. The old corn mill, beside the mill race, is now the Old Mill hotel with rooms overlooking the pond. There is a large church with colourful Victorian stained glass. Near by is Thorpland Hall (not open), a Tudor wool merchant's mansion.

FAL, RIVER Cornwall
River, forms estuary of Carrick Roads
The River Fal rises near Roche in the clay-quarrying area of Cornwall. The lower part of the valley is wide, tidal and muddy, wooded right to the shore, becoming the vast Carrick Roads (see) before reaching the sea.

FALKENHAM Suffolk TM2939
Village off A14 (A45), 3 miles (5km) N of Felixstowe
Adjoining Kirton, Falkenham lies near the mouth of the River Deben. The 1987 hurricane deprived it of trees (now replanted).

FALKIRK Central NS8880
Town on A803, 7 miles (11km) W of Linlithgow
Sprawling, centrally-situated town with much ribbon development between Edinburgh and Stirling and the rivers Forth and Clyde, once Scotland's most important cattle market. Substantial remains of Antonine Wall near by, including the fort of Rough Castle. Ornate Callendar House was built around a 14th-century tower house. There were two Battles of Falkirk, in 1298 and 1746.

FALKLAND Fife NO2507
Small town on A912, 4 miles (6km) N of Glenrothes
Falkland is one of Scotland's prettiest royal burghs, with 18th-century weavers' cottages bordering its cobbled streets and a spacious square dominated by the superb Scottish Renaissance Falkland Palace (National Trust for Scotland).

The original stronghold belonged to the Earls of Fife but passed in the 15th century to the Stuarts, who made it their royal hunting lodge. The palace was built between 1501 and 1541 by James IV and James V, and Mary Stuart spent some of her girlhood here. It was deserted after the Jacobite rising of 1715 and fell into ruin, until being beautifully restored by the 3rd Marquess of Bute in the late 19th century. The most notable rooms of the interior are the king's bedchamber and the queen's room, while the tapestry gallery, hung with 17th-century Flemish tapestries, leads to the serene and lovely chapel royal, still used for Mass. The verdant expanse of lawn in the garden is surrounded by well-stocked herbaceous borders and mature trees and shrubs. The oldest royal tennis court in Britain stands here too; it was built in 1539 and is still in use.

FALMER East Sussex TQ3508
Village on B2133, 4 miles (6km) NE of Brighton
Pleasant flint and brick cottages and old dewpond in downland village, separated from Sussex University by the A27.

FALMOUTH Cornwall SW8032
Town on A39, 12 miles (19km) S of Truro
Now the largest town in Cornwall, Falmouth is also one of the most recent. It was only a tiny village until the 17th century, and the deep-water natural harbour of Carrick Roads (see) made it one of the largest trading ports in the country in the 18th century (see Pendennis Castle).

The main street, with large Georgian and Victorian buildings, runs parallel to the shore and then further along turns its back on it. The early 19th-century Greek-style custom house has a brick chimney called the Queen's Pipe. The town church dates from 1660–1, with classical pillars and a plaster ceiling but medieval-style windows. Modern docks are tucked up under the headland, and the whole area is a popular yachting centre. Small passenger ferries run to St Mawes and to Flushing. The railway of 1863 made the town, with beaches on its southern side, into a resort. An art gallery and the Cornwall Maritime Museum are based here.

FANGFOSS Humberside SE7653
Village off A166, 4 miles (6km) SE of Stamford Bridge
This agricultural village is near the Roman road to York and was mentioned in Domesday Book as 'Frangefosse'.

FAR FOREST Hereford and Worcester SO7275
Village off A4117, 4 miles (6km) W of Bewdley
Scattering of cottages on edge of Wyre Forest. Settlement created by squatters who carried on traditional forest trades. Forest visitor centre near by.

FAR SAWREY Cumbria SD3795
see Near Sawrey

FARCET Cambridgeshire TL2094
Village on B1091, 3 miles (5km) S of Peterborough
Near old course of the River Nene, a small village standing close to some attractive Fens.

FAREHAM Hampshire SU5706
Town off M27, 6 miles (10km) NW of Portsmouth
The High Street of this old market town and river port is the finest in the county, with superb Georgian brick houses of all sizes and styles. The commercial focus has moved to West Street. Quays survive on the river, mostly now pleasure boats. Fareham Museum has fine new displays.

FARINGDON Oxfordshire SU2895
Town off A420, 11 miles (18km) NE of Swindon
Rich medieval work and monuments in All Saints' Church reflect medieval prosperity of this quiet market town on hills overlooking the upper Thames Valley. It retains its 17th-century town hall on piers, but the character of its streets is mainly Georgian. Crown hotel, Faringdon House and Church Farm House stand out among a variety of handsome buildings.

FARINGTON Lancashire SD5325
Village off A59, 2 miles (3km) N of Leyland
Residential and commercial district of Leyland, with modern housing and business park. Leyland Trucks are the main employers.

FARLEIGH HUNGERFORD Somerset ST8057
Village on A366, 4 miles (6km) W of Trowbridge
A village with the ruins of a large 14th-century castle. The chapel inside is complete, with many memorials from the 14th century onwards, and 17th-century German stained glass. Museum.

FARLEIGH WALLOP Hampshire SU6246
Village off B3046, 3 miles (5km) S of Basingstoke
A village of 1930s estate cottages and a church, with the big house away to the south (not open).

FARLEY Wiltshire SU2229
Village off A36, 5 miles (8km) E of Salisbury
Wooded, scattered village with an unusual, rather plain, classical church. It was completed in 1690, possibly designed by Sir Christopher Wren. Almshouses of 1681.

FARLEY CHAMBERLAYNE Hampshire SU3927
Hamlet off A3090, 4 miles (6km) W of Hursley
Only farms and an isolated church, high on the chalk. Farley Mount Country Park to the northeast is 1,000 acres (405 hectares) of woods and downland. Farley Mount, a barrow with a little pyramid on the summit, is a 1733 memorial to a horse.

FARMERS Dyfed SN6444
Hamlet off A482, 5 miles (8km) SE of Lampeter
Hamlet on crossroads deep in the country. Located on the Sarn Helen Roman road – the approach from the south off the A482 is a characteristically straight one.

FARMINGTON Gloucestershire SP1315
Village off A40, 2 miles (3km) E of Northleach
A large green with a Victorian pumphouse is the centre of this pleasant village above the Leach Valley, with Norbury Camp, an Iron Age hillfort, near by.

FARNBOROUGH Berkshire SU4381
Village off B4494, 4 miles (6km) SE of Wantage
In the north Berkshire chalklands, with a window by John Piper in the church and a memorial to John Betjeman, who lived here for a time.

FARNBOROUGH Hampshire SU8755
Town off M3, 4 miles (6km) S of Camberley
This large modern town grew because His Majesty's Balloon Factory (now the Royal Aircraft Establishment) moved here in 1906. The huge Farnborough Air Show is in September every even-numbered year. St Michael's Abbey, on the outskirts, was built in French medieval style in 1887 as a mausoleum for Napoleon III of France.

FARNBOROUGH Warwickshire SP4349
Village off A423, 6 miles (10km) N of Banbury
Among the stone and thatched cottages stands the 17th-century Butcher's Arms, close to the Norman and medieval church. Farnborough Hall (National Trust), with its terraced gardens and follies, dates from 1684 and contains Italian paintings and much fine plasterwork. In estate buildings are displays relating to the Civil War Battle of Edgehill (see).

FARNDON Cheshire SJ4154
Village on B5130, 6 miles (10km) NE of Wrexham
An old Cheshire village close to the Welsh border with many typical black and white houses. Stone bridge of 1345.

FARNE ISLANDS Northumberland
Islands in North Sea, off Bamburgh
The 28 islands of hard dolerite rock are famous as a bird sanctuary and breeding ground for the grey seal. The largest is Inner Farne, with a lighthouse and chapel, and landings are permitted here and on Staple. The lighthouse on Longstone (National Trust) was manned by Grace Darling and her father.

FARNHAM Dorset ST9515
Village off B3081, 2 miles (3km) SE of Tollard Royal
A pretty, wooded village, with many thatched cottages.

FARNHAM Surrey SU8446
Town off A31, 10 miles (16km) W of Guildford
Farnham Castle provides the backdrop for this attractive brick-built town on the River Wey. The first castle keep was raised in 1138 by Henry of Blois, Bishop of Winchester, and replaced about 100 years later. Most of the present fabric dates from the 15th to the 17th centuries, including Bishop Waynflete's Tower (1470–5), which dominates distant views of the castle.

Farnham is a planned town, its streets laid out on a grid in the 12th century; but the whole flavour of the town is Georgian, as it was virtually rebuilt on the wealth generated by its 18th-century corn market, the largest in England.

Castle Street and West Street are the show streets, broad and lined by handsome houses, including Willmer House, 1718, now housing the museum. Elsewhere the town displays its brick-built elegance in little lanes and squares, and in the 20th-century developments to which it has taken kindly, since most have succeeded in blending old and new. The Lion and Lamb Yard shopping centre (1980s) is one of many schemes that have preserved the shells of the old buildings and given them new life.

FARNINGHAM Kent TQ5466
Village off A225, 5 miles (8km) S of Dartford
Attractive village on the River Darent, close to the M20, with good 18th-century houses and a church in a grove of yew trees.

FARNLEY North Yorkshire SE2148
Hamlet on B6451, 2 miles (3km) NE of Otley
All Saints' Church, originally built in 1250, was restored in 1851 by Francis Fawkes. Turner the painter was a frequent visitor.

FARNLEY TYAS West Yorkshire SE1612
Village off A629, 3 miles (5km) SE of Huddersfield
Noted for its scenic beauty. Much larger in the 19th century when cloth-making was an important industry here.

FARNWORTH Greater Manchester SD7306
Town off M61, 2 miles (3km) SE of Bolton
Grew up around the cotton industry; there are many mill shops in the area.

FARRINGFORD Isle of Wight
see Freshwater

FARSLEY West Yorkshire SE2135
Village off A647, 1 mile (2km) N of Pudsey
A textile village, now with only one working worsted mill, which is home to the TV series *Emmerdale*.

FARTHINGHOE Northamptonshire SP5339
Village on A422, 4 miles (6km) NW of Brackley
Hilltop village on the Brackley–Banbury road, close to the Oxfordshire border. Fine church monument of man in slippers and nightcap, relaxing with book.

FARTHINGSTONE Northamptonshire SP6154
Village off A5, 5 miles (8km) SE of Daventry
Attractive village in undulating country, with stone and timber-framed buildings. Castle Dykes earthwork of motte and bailey close by.

FARWAY Devon SY1895
Village off A3752, 4 miles (6km) S of Honiton
Small and rural stone and cob village with a beautifully set church and, to the south, Farway Countryside Park, tropical garden with butterflies and animals.

FAULKBOURNE Essex TL7917
Hamlet off A12, 2 miles (3km) NW of Witham
The village pond is an old holy well visited by medieval pilgrims. Norman church in stately grounds of Faulkbourne Hall (not open).

FAVERSHAM Kent TR0161
Town off M2, 8 miles (13km) SE of Sittingbourne
A superb small town amid orchards at the head of a creek, Faversham was attached to the Cinque Port of Dover from 1225 and still possesses a commercial quay. Long associated with gunpowder mills, bricks and brewing, the town is now a centre for packaging and the distribution of fruit, and is still the brewing capital of Kent.

Faversham was granted its first charter in AD811, and the town centres on Market Square, where a market is still held. Abbey Street is the show street, restored since 1961 as part of a conservation scheme. It is named after the abbey founded by King Stephen in 1147 and destroyed at the Reformation. The houses in Abbey Street are mellowed brick and half-timber, leading to 17th-century warehouses on Standard Quay, built with reused stone and timbers from the abbey. Number 80 is part of the abbey gatehouse, rebuilt 1538–40 for Thomas Arden, mayor. He was murdered here in 1550 and his tale told in *Arden of Faversham*, a play of 1592.

West Street is another rewarding street of half-timbered buildings. The church has a graceful 'flying spire', a well-loved landmark.

FAWLEY Berkshire SU3981
Village off A338, 4 miles (6km) S of Wantage
Sometimes called Great Fawley. Fine austere church of 1866 by GE Street, and 17th-century manor house (not open).

FAWLEY Buckinghamshire SU7586
Village off B480, 3 miles (5km) N of Henley-on-Thames
Notable 18th-century fittings in church. Fawley Court (in Oxfordshire) has remarkable Polish military collection and beautiful Capability Brown grounds by the River Thames.

FAWLEY Hampshire SU4503
Village on A326, 10 miles (16km) SE of Southampton
This industrial area, bordered by Southampton Water and the New Forest, has the largest oil refinery in Britain and a huge power station. Calshot, the spit protruding into the mouth of Southampton Water, has a little 1530s castle (English Heritage).

FAWSLEY Northamptonshire SP5656
Site off B4037, 4 miles (6km) S of Daventry
Rebuilt by Salvin in 1868, 16th-century Fawsley Hall was home to the powerful Knightley family, whose monuments enhance the church.

FAXTON Northamptonshire SP7875
Deserted village off A508, 6 miles (10km) W of Kettering
This 12th-century village site was deserted after the 18th century and artefacts from its demolished church removed to Lamport and Kettering.

FAZELEY Staffordshire SK2001
Small town on A4091, 2 miles (3km) S of Tamworth
Unremarkable village in the Tame Valley with a notable industrial monument: the giant steam mill of 1883 beside the Birmingham and Fazeley Canal.

FEARBY North Yorkshire SE1981
Village off A6108, 2 miles (3km) W of Masham
An old farming community, at one time famous for its geese, with a Druidical folly built in the early 19th century.

FECKENHAM Hereford and Worcester SP0162
Village off B4090, 7 miles (11km) SE of Bromsgrove
Village with attractive green and array of timber-framed and Georgian houses, close to Roman road to Droitwich. Bird reserve in marshland near by.

FEERING Essex TL8720
Village off A12, 5 miles (8km) NE of Witham
Lively village with a green, cottages, church and inns. Feeringbury Manor garden is by the River Blackwater. Local history museum at Kelvedon (see).

FELBRIGG Norfolk TG2039
Village off A148, 2 miles (3km) S of Cromer
Pretty village with large medieval church, and the splendid Jacobean Felbrigg Hall (National Trust). Nearby Felbrigg Great Wood is a belt of ancient beech trees.

FELIXKIRK North Yorkshire SE4684

Village off A170, 3 miles (5km) NE of Thirsk

This pretty village once had a timber castle, the motte of which can still be seen. The gardens of Mount St John are open occasionally.

FELIXSTOWE Suffolk TM3034

Town off A14 (A45), 11 miles (18km) SE of Ipswich

Felixstowe presents two faces to the world. There is the bustle of the huge container port, one of the largest in Europe, and there is the genteel Edwardian seaside resort. It has a long sand and shingle beach, with the mouths of the rivers Deben and Orwell at either end, while in the middle is the fine pier, leading back to the neat lawns and colourful flower beds of the Promenade.

At the southernmost tip of the Felixstowe peninsula stands Landguard Point, a nature reserve that is home to coastal plants and migrating birds. The Point is still guarded by two martello towers, built in the 1800s, and Landguard Fort (English Heritage), built in 1718. The fort has an exhibition of its history and is open on some summer afternoons.

Felixstowe's history revolves around the sea, although it was a dangerous port in which to linger in the days of the pressgangs. The Dooley pub has many doors that allowed its patrons to escape. Smugglers also used the doors when avoiding Revenue officers. Felixstowe offers an annual folk festival, motor-racing, a drama festival, tennis championships and a lively carnival.

FELLING Tyne and Wear NZ2861

Town on A184, immediately E of Gateshead

An industrial area of Tyneside with terraced streets and tower blocks on a hillside above the River Tyne. Site of the Gateshead International Stadium.

FELMERSHAM Bedfordshire SP9957

Village off A6, 6 miles (10km) NW of Bedford

Eye-catching village with one of Bedfordshire's best churches, and a medieval tithe barn converted to housing.

FELMINGHAM Norfolk TG2529

Village on B1145, 2 miles (3km) W of North Walsham

Picturesque village surrounded by lovely Norfolk heath and moorland. Felmingham also has a church with a dominating 16th-century tower, and the Belaugh Pottery.

FELPHAM West Sussex SZ9599

Suburb off A259, on E outskirts of Bognor

Once a little flint-built fishing village, now tacked on to the resort of Bognor Regis, with a good sandy beach. Some old thatched cottages survive in Blakes Lane, where William Blake, artist, poet and philosopher, lived 1801–4 under the patronage of William Hayley. Blake wrote *Jerusalem* here but the cottage where he lived is not open to the public.

Thatched cottage of 1713 at Fen Drayton.

FELSHAM Suffolk TL9457
Village off A14 (A45), 7 miles (11km) SE of Bury St Edmunds
Two village greens and a church form the centre of Felsham. There are striking contrasts in architectural styles. Annual flower show and street fair.

FELSTED Essex TL6720
Village on B1417, 3 miles (5km) E of Great Dunmow
The massive church monument to Lord Rich, who founded Felsted School in 1564, shows him in his robes as Lord Chancellor, improbably accompanied by personifications of various virtues. The original school building is now a bookshop. Lord Rich lived at Leez Priory (limited opening) at Hartford End. Felsted Vineyard at Crix Green is open to visitors.

FELTHAM Greater London TQ1073
District in borough of Hounslow
One-time Middlesex village, now a modest residential and light industrial suburb in West London sprawl. Much 1960s and 1970s development.

FELTON Northumberland NU1800
Village off A1, 8 miles (13km) S of Alnwick
A straggling village with two bridges crossing the River Coquet, one modern and the other dating from the 15th century, now closed to traffic.

FELTWELL Norfolk TL7190
Village on B1386, 5 miles (8km) NW of Brandon
A sizeable village much under the influence of the nearby airbase at Lakenheath (see). It has two churches and several new housing estates.

FEN DRAYTON Cambridgeshire TL3368
Village off A14, 7 miles (11km) SE of Huntingdon
Connected to the River Ouse by a small stream. The High Street and Cootes Lane have several restored thatched, gabled, and timbered cottages.

FENCE Lancashire SD8237
Village on A6068, 2 miles (3km) W of Nelson
The area is known as 'Old Laund Booth', a straggling village which stretches to Wheatley Lane. Ye Olde Sparrow Hawk is an impressive Tudor-style building.

FENISCOWLES Lancashire SD6426
Village on A674, 3 miles (5km) SW of Blackburn
Residential district of Blackburn on the Leeds–Liverpool Canal, comprising mainly 1950s and 1960s housing.

FENITON Devon SY1099
Village off A30, 4 miles (6km) W of Honiton
Set in park-like countryside with a pretty 15th-century church with wooden screens of the same date.

FENNY BENTLEY Derbyshire SK1750
Village on A515, 2 miles (3km) N of Ashbourne
Southern Peak District village, with a medieval hall, now part of a farm. It lies near the Tissington Trail, a cycling and walking route on a former railway line.

FENNY COMPTON Warwickshire SP4152
Village off A423, 8 miles (13km) N of Banbury
This large village at the foot of the Dassett Hills has some venerable buildings and a wharf on the Oxford Canal.

FENNY DRAYTON Leicestershire SP3596
Village on A444, 3 miles (5km) N of Nuneaton
On low-lying land close to Roman Watling Street (modern A5) and the Warwickshire border. Monument commemorates birth in 1624 of Quaker George Fox.

FENNY STRATFORD Buckinghamshire SP8734
Village off A5, on E outskirts of Bletchley
On the River Ouzel and Grand Union Canal, and now part of the Milton Keynes (see) complex. Built in the 1720s by the antiquary Browne Willis, St Martin's Church has been enlarged several times. Inside are his tomb and his Fenny Poppers, miniature cannon still fired off every St Martin's Day to commemorate him and his family.

FENS, THE Cambridgeshire
Scenic and historic region of E England
This land of black soil and mysterious waterways extends over much of Cambridgeshire from the Wash. Flat and dotted with isolated farmsteads and 'islands' that rise above the surface, such as at Ely and Boston. These wild lands were a haven for the rebel Hereward the Wake in the 11th century, but were drained in the 17th century.

FENSTANTON Cambridgeshire TL3168
Village on A14 (A604), 5 miles (8km) SE of Huntingdon
The Church of St Peter and St Paul contains the tomb of 'Capability' Brown. A fine clock tower stands in the village centre.

FENTON Staffordshire SJ8944
Town on the edge of Stoke-on-Trent
Not a pretty town, but offering much to people who enjoy Victorian architecture. Restored traditional potbank in Chilton Street.

FEOCK Cornwall SW8238
Village off B3289, 5 miles (8km) S of Truro
Pretty village with thatched cottages in the middle, and views of Carrick Roads (see).

FERNDOWN Dorset SU0700
Small town off A31, 6 miles (10km) N of Bournemouth
Large and mostly modern, on the edge of the New Forest. Area was heathland, and some pines survive.

FERNHAM Oxfordshire SU2991
Village on B4508, 3 miles (5km) S of Faringdon
The pleasant village, with its manor house and park, looks across the Vale of White Horse to the Lambourn Downs.

FERNHURST West Sussex SU8928
Village on A286, 3 miles (5km) S of Haslemere
Under the wooded slopes of Black Down, a pleasant tile-hung and stone village, partly grouped round the green and partly fronting the main road.

FERRING West Sussex TQ0902
Village off A259, 3 miles (5km) W of Worthing
Popular resort with a centre of flint-built cottages by the church. To the east, a large, open green space faces the sea, a real rarity along the coast hereabouts. Highdown Chalk Garden contains plants from all over the world.

FERRYBRIDGE West Yorkshire SE4824
Town off A1, immediately W of Knottingley
Former coal-mining village on the River Aire with elegant eight-arched bridge designed by John Carr. Ferrybridge Pottery has a shop and exhibitions.

FERRYHILL Durham NZ2832
Town off A167, 6 miles (10km) S of Durham
A steep hill leads to a narrow market place with Victorian town hall. The 16th-century manor house on top of the hill is now a hotel.

FERRYSIDE Dyfed SN3610
Village off A484, 7 miles (11km) S of Carmarthen
Forgotten Ferryside stands on eastern bank of beautiful Towy estuary, hidden on a minor road. Cockle-picking past. Low-tide sandbanks, views across to castle-crowned Llanstephan.

FERSFIELD Norfolk TM0683
Village off A1066, 4 miles (6km) NW of Diss
St Andrew's Church, with its 15th-century arcades and 1311 wooden effigy, stands with the Old Rectory amid fine old trees.

FETCHAM Surrey TQ1455
District in W Leatherhead
Originally a Saxon village, now an urban area facing Leatherhead across the River Mole. Church with Saxon foundations and re-used Roman tiles.

FETLAR Shetland HU6391
Island E of Yell
Noted for its fertile soil and good grazing and once intensively farmed, the island has prehistoric sites. Rare bird visitors have included the snowy owl in 1967.

FETTERCAIRN Grampian NO6573
Village on B974, 11 miles (18km) NW of Montrose
Picturesque village with distinctive houses around the square, where the old 'ell' measure – 3ft 1½ ins – is marked on a mercat cross. The Gothic arch commemorates Queen Victoria's visit in 1861. Fettercairn Distillery is Scotland's second oldest. Ruined Kincardine Castle, near by, is associated with Macbeth. Fasque House, a rambling Victorian mansion, was the home of Prime Minister Gladstone.

FFESTINIOG Gwynedd SH7042
Village on A470, 3 miles (5km) S of Blaenau Ffestiniog
Village of terraced stone houses at the gateway to the upper part of the Vale of Ffestiniog where Snowdonia's natural beauty begins to meet evidence of Blaenau Ffestiniog's historic slate industry. On doorstep of inhospitable, uninhabited moorlands known as the Migneint. Cynfal Falls a local beauty spot.

FIDDLEFORD Dorset ST8013
Village off A357, 1 mile (2km) E of Sturminster Newton
A few cottages and an early 14th-century manor house, with the original roof and many 16th-century fittings (English Heritage).

Shaft of the old town cross at Fettercairn.

The tiny church at Fifield Bavant.

FIDDLER'S HAMLET Essex TL4701
Hamlet off B1393, 1 mile (2km) SE of Epping
In farming country close to noisy junction of M11 and M25. Named after 400-year-old Merry Fiddler's inn.

FIELD BROUGHTON Cumbria SD3795
Hamlet off A590, 2 miles (3km) N of Cartmel
Farming village with a lime kiln by the church which was used until 1922 for producing quicklime. Coppices were also grown for charcoal-burning.

FIELD DALLING Norfolk TG0039
Village off A148, 4 miles (6km) W of Holt
Handsome tombstones litter the leafy churchyard of St Andrew's Church. There are some especially picturesque cottages in the village.

FIFEHEAD MAGDALEN Dorset ST7821
Village off A30, 5 miles (8km) SW of Shaftesbury
Fifehead means 'five hides', a Saxon land measure. The stone village is mostly 19th century but has some older cottages.

FIFEHEAD NEVILLE Dorset ST7610
Village off A357, 2 miles (3km) SW of Sturminster Newton
A scattered, prettily wooded village, with a tall packhorse bridge to the west, medieval but restored.

FIFIELD Berkshire SU9076
Village on B3024, 4 miles (6km) W of Windsor
Mostly modern settlement just back from the Thames. Moneyrow Green to the west.

FIFIELD Oxfordshire SP2318
Village off A424, 4 miles (6km) N of Burford
On hills overlooking Evenlode Valley near border with Gloucestershire, the attractive village, once noted for hurdle-making, has a worthwhile medieval church.

FIFIELD BAVANT Wiltshire SU0125
Hamlet off A30, 7 miles (11km) SW of Wilton
A tiny hamlet of just a few cottages, a farm and one of the smallest churches in the country.

FILBY Norfolk TG4613
Village on A1064, 5 miles (8km) NW of Great Yarmouth
Pretty Broadland village with a traditional 17th-century Norfolk pub. Filby Broad is a beautiful stretch of water easily accessible by road.

FILEY North Yorkshire TA1180
Town off A165, 7m (11km) SE of Scarborough
This traditional seaside resort has a long sandy beach, and the fishing fleet still lands at Coble Landing. The rock formation of Filey Brigg offers excellent sea-fishing

and the Filey Dams Nature Reserve provides a freshwater habitat for wildlife. The older fishermen's cottages contrast with the elegant Edwardian architecture in the town centre.

FILKINS Oxfordshire SP2304
Village off A361, 4 miles (6km) NE of Lechlade
This enterprising village preserves its old stone cottages and has the additional attractions of a working woollen mill, a museum of bygones and an art gallery.

FILLEIGH Devon SS6628
Village off B3226, 3 miles (5km) NW of South Molton
Dominated by the big house, Castle Hill (not open), and by the church filled with memorials to the owners of the house.

FILLINGHAM Lincolnshire SK9485
Village off B1398, 9 miles (14km) N of Lincoln
Charming stone village with lake, and church rebuilt in 18th century. On ridge above is Gothic Fillingham Castle (not open), perhaps by Carr of York.

FILLONGLEY Warwickshire SP2887
Village on B4098, 6 miles (10km) NW of Coventry
In rural belt between Coventry and Birmingham with earthworks of a Norman castle and a church with medieval glass and good Victorian chancel.

FILTON Avon ST6079
Area of N Bristol
Centre of the Bristol aircraft industry, which started in 1910. Huge runway and hangars. The city has grown out to meet it.

FIMBER Humberside SE8960
Village on B1251, 2 miles (3km) NE of Fridaythorpe
A charming hillside village whose name is pronounced 'Fimmer' by the locals.

FINAVON Tayside NO4956
Hamlet on A90 (A94), 5 miles (8km) NE of Forfar
Tiny village on the River South Esk with ruined Finavon Castle and a vitrified fort on the Hill of Finavon behind it.

FINCHALE PRIORY Durham NZ2947
Site by River Wear, 3 miles (5km) NE of Durham
Ruins of a Benedictine priory (English Heritage) on the wooded banks of the River Wear.

FINCHAM Norfolk TF6806
Village on A1122, 5 miles (8km) E of Downham Market
This interesting village has several notable buildings, including Talbot Manor (not open) with its famous gardens set in rich farmland.

FINCHAMPSTEAD Berkshire SU7963
Village on B3348, 4 miles (6km) SW of Wokingham
Pretty village with several 17th-century brick houses, and the brick church tower of 1720. Finchampstead Ridges lie to the east, with fine views.

FINCHINGFIELD Essex TL6832
Village on B1053, 8 miles (13km) NW of Braintree
Showplace commuter and retirement village, one of England's most photogenic, depicted on innumerable postcards and calendars. Green and duck pond, humpbacked bridge, venerable church, the Fox pub and old houses in varied styles create a charming picture. To top it all off, just round the corner is an 18th-century windmill. Museum in former guildhall (limited opening).

FINCHLEY Greater London TQ2690
District in borough of Barnet
The name means 'wood with finches', but the area is now a prosperous North London suburb. The London Museum of Jewish Life is at 18th-century Finchley Manor House, now a synagogue. Rare trees stand in the grounds of Avenue House, once owned by 'Inky' Stephens of the ink dynasty, a predecessor of Lady Thatcher as Finchley's MP.

FINDERN Derbyshire SK3030
Village off A38, 5 miles (8km) SW of Derby
Cottages and a Victorian church around a small green, near the Trent and Mersey Canal. Willington power station near by.

FINDHORN Grampian NJ0364
Village on B9011, 4 miles (6km) N of Forres
Resort and fishing village on a sandy bay probably best known as the base of Findhorn Community, an international centre for 'spiritual and holistic education'.

FINDOCHTY Grampian NJ4667
Village on A942, 3 miles (5km) NE of Buckie
Pronounced 'Finechty', this pretty fishing village with brightly painted houses stands around a tidal harbour and is a popular sailing base.

FINDON West Sussex TQ1208
Village off A24, 4 miles (6km) N of Worthing
A neat little flint village on the South Downs, under the lee of Church Hill, almost joined to Worthing by a valley development known as Findon Valley. Near by is Cissbury Ring, an Iron Age hillfort, the interior ploughed by the Romans and then refortified against the Saxons. At the west end are the shafts and galleries of neolithic flint mines, 6,000 years old.

FINDON (FINNAN) Grampian NO9397
Village off A90, 5 miles (8km) S of Aberdeen
Tiny fishing village above the cliffs south of Aberdeen. Traditional home of the 'Finnan haddie', local haddock lightly cured over peat.

FINEDON Northamptonshire SP9172
Town on A510, 3 miles (5km) NE of Wellingborough
The honey tones of ironstone, formerly worked here, are seen in the splendid, gracefully spired 14th-century church, and other buildings, several Victorian mock-Gothic.

FINGEST Buckinghamshire SU7791
Village off B482, 5 miles (8km) N of Henley-on-Thames
Solitary little place among wooded valleys, where the Bishops of Lincoln once had a palace. Remarkable church with big Norman tower topped by eccentric double saddleback roof. It is plain and narrow inside, with walls leaning outwards. By custom every bridegroom must hoist his bride over the church gate after the wedding or the marriage is doomed.

FINGRINGHOE Essex TM0220
Village off B1028, 4 miles (6km) SE of Colchester
The village has a green, pond and smugglers' tales to add to vistas over the Roman river valley. Smugglers allegedly hid contraband on the roof of the Norman church. Herons and waterfowl, kingfishers and nightingales can be seen at Fingringhoe Wick Nature Reserve to the southeast, by the River Colne, with hides, an observation tower and an interpretation centre. Firing ranges to the south.

FINMERE Oxfordshire SP6332
Village on B4031, 4 miles (6km) W of Buckingham
Right on the Buckinghamshire border, this popular village has expanded out of its old centre. Church has good 15th-century windows.

FINNINGLEY South Yorkshire SK6799
Village on A614, 4 miles (6km) N of Bawtry
A small village on the borders of Nottinghamshire, Lincolnshire and South Yorkshire with five village greens.

FINSBURY Greater London TQ3182
District in borough of Islington
A northern extension of the City, originally fens outside the walls where people went skating in winter. John Bunyan, Daniel Defoe and William Blake are all buried in Bunhill Fields opposite John Wesley's chapel and house on the City Road. Close by are the headquarters of the Honourable Artillery Company (museum open by appointment).

FINSTHWAITE Cumbria SD3687
Hamlet off A590, 1 mile (2km) N of Newby Bridge
The village can trace its history back to Viking times. The extensive surrounding woodlands of oak, birch and hazel have been cut and used in the furniture and building trades. The Stott Park Bobbin Mill was opened in 1835 to make bobbins for the growing textile industry.

FINSTOCK Oxfordshire SP3616
Village off B4022, 2 miles (3km) S of Charlbury
The 17th-century manor house still graces this expanding village, beautifully situated above the River Evenlode on the fringe of the Wychwood Forest.

FINTRY Central NS6186
Village on B818, 5 miles (8km) E of Balfron
Attractive village in Campsie Fells at the head of Strathendrick. Near by are the 14th-century Culreuch Castle, the waterfall at Loup of Fintry and Carron Valley reservoir.

FIRBECK South Yorkshire SK5688
Village off A634, 3 miles (5km) SE of Maltby
Park Hill was home to the St Leger family and the first 'Leger' race was run here in a field called 'The Racecourse'.

FISHBOURNE West Sussex SU8304
Village on A259, 2 miles (3km) W of Chichester
Unremarkable village beside the remarkable Romano-British palace (English Heritage), excavated from 1960. This is the largest Roman residence north of the Alps. Impressive remains include the garden, as well as celebrated mosaics such as the 'Boy on a Dolphin'. The palace was probably built in the mid-1st century AD for King Cogidubnus, who collaborated with the Roman conquerors, and destroyed by fire in the late 3rd century. Saxon buildings were later built on top of the palace remains.

FISHERTON DE LA MERE Wiltshire SU0038
Hamlet on A36, 1 mile (2km) NW of Wylye
Stone and thatch cottages cluster right down in the Wylye Valley. The village name means 'fishermen's farm belonging to the de la Mere family'.

FISHGUARD (ABERGWAUN) Dyfed SM9537
Small town on A40, 13 miles (21km) N of Haverfordwest
Fishguard (*Abergwaun* in Welsh, the 'mouth of the River Gwaun') comes in three parts. The most picturesque is Lower Fishguard, the old stone quayside lined with fishermen's cottages at the bottom of a steep hill. This harbour was used to depict Dylan Thomas's fictitious seatown of Llareggub when *Under Milk Wood*, starring Elizabeth Taylor and Richard Burton, was filmed in the early 1970s. The 'new' harbour, built 1894–1906, is across the bay at Goodwick. Ferries sail from here across the Irish Sea to Rosslare Dock.

On high ground in between the two harbours stands the main town of Upper Fishguard. The Royal Oak inn contains memorabilia from the 'last invasion of Britain', a farcical episode in 1797 when a poorly-equipped French force led by an Irish-American general landed at nearby Carreg Wastad Point but was soon seen off by the locals. Opposite the inn is the market hall, whose maritime displays include a record of lives saved by the local lifeboat. St Mary's Church contains the headstone of the formidable Jemima Nicholas, who reputedly personally captured 14 French invaders armed only with a pitchfork. Each summer, the town holds a popular and respected music festival.

FISHLAKE South Yorkshire SE6513
Village off A18, 3 miles (5km) N of Hatfield
The village lies between Thorne and Stainforth.It is surrounded by rivers and canals and can only be reached by crossing a bridge.

FISHTOFT Lincolnshire TF3642
Village off A16, 2 miles (3km) SE of Boston
Medieval fenland church between Boston and the Wash, beside Hobhole Drain running into tidal River Witham. Good vegetable-growing country.

FISKERTON Lincolnshire TF0472
Village off A158, 5 miles (8km) E of Lincoln
Quietly situated on north side of River Witham. Norman and later church has puzzling architectural features, thought to incorporate material from nearby abbeys.

FITTLEWORTH West Sussex TQ0119
Village on B2138, 3 miles (5km) SE of Petworth
Attractive village above the River Rother, with stone and timber cottages in Upper Street. Lower Street runs down to an ancient pub and 16th-century bridge.

FIVE SISTERS OF KINTAIL Highland
Mountain peaks N of A87, E of Loch Duich
Impressive chain of five mountain peaks rising above Glen Shiel and part of the Kintail estate (National Trust for Scotland).

FLACKWELL HEATH Buckinghamshire SU8989
Small town off A40, 3 miles (5km) W of Beaconsfield
Sprawl of post-war housing estates, sometimes said to be the largest village in England. Formerly known for cherry orchards.

FLADBURY Hereford and Worcester SO9946
Village off A4538, 3 miles (5km) NW of Evesham
Old houses sit comfortably around the green of this Avonside village, where the 18th-century watermill makes an attractive residence. Good church brasses.

FLAGG Derbyshire SK1368
Village off A515, 5 miles (8km) W of Bakewell
Scattered Peak District farms and cottages on exposed moorland, where the annual point-to-point races on Easter Tuesday attract thousands of visitors.

FLAMBOROUGH Humberside TA2270
Village on B1255, 4 miles (6km) NE of Bridlington
Mentioned in Domesday Book and retaining a small fishing fleet. There are steep cliffs at Flamborough Head. The first lighthouse was built here in the 17th century and the present one dates from 1806. Local schoolchildren still dance the traditional Flamborough 'sword dance', using wooden swords.

FLAMSTEAD Hertfordshire TL0714
Village off A5, 5 miles (8km) N of Hemel Hempstead
Lively commuter village with a rural air. Church has important medieval wall-paintings, and monuments.

FLANDERS MOSS Central NS6398
Scenic area off B822, SW of Thornhill
Flat area, once under the sea and now some of Scotland's richest agricultural land. Some original peat moor remains and other parts have been afforested.

FLASH Staffordshire SK0267
Village off A53, 4 miles (6km) SW of Buxton
Claimed as the highest village in England and close to the source of the River Dove, Flash stands on exposed moorland landscape enjoyed by walkers.

FLAT HOLM South Glamorgan ST2264
Island in Bristol Channel, off Lavernock Point
Small island whose Norse name reflects its role as Viking anchorage. Marconi transmitted from here in early days of radio.

FLAUNDEN Hertfordshire TL0100
Village off B4505, 4 miles (6km) E of Chesham
Sir George Gilbert Scott built the first of his many churches here in 1838, describing it in his memoirs as a 'poor barn', designed for his uncle. Little remains of the medieval church it replaced. The Bricklayers Arms with its old-fashioned garden and the Green Dragon with an aviary are both highly regarded.

FLAX BOURTON Avon ST5069
Village on A370, 5 miles (8km) W of Bristol
Rural village with a pretty Norman doorway and chancel arch in the church and, to the east, a huge workhouse of 1837.

FLEET Dorset SY6360
Hamlet off B3157, 3 miles (5km) W of Weymouth
Just inshore from the lagoon called the Fleet, this tiny village is famous because of J Meade Falkner's novel *Moonfleet*. Only the chancel of the church featured in the story survived the great storm of 1824.

FLEET Hampshire SU8154
Town on A323, 4 miles (6km) W of Farnborough
A 19th-century town which developed because of the railway. Fleet Pond is really a lake. Quirky 1857 church of polychrome brick.

FLEET Lincolnshire TF3823
Hamlet off A17, 2 miles (3km) SE of Holbeach
Fenland village with scattered farmsteads and gathered buildings at Fleet Hargate. Tall-spired church, and a Georgian manor house.

FLEETWOOD Lancashire SD3348
Town on A587, 8 miles (13km) N of Blackpool
Situated at the top of the Fylde coast, and planned in the early 19th century by Sir Peter Hesketh-Fleetwood, who envisaged the creation of a new holiday town. There are two land-based lighthouses which formed part of the plan for the navigation of the Wyre channel. Small inshore fishing fleet.

FLETCHING East Sussex TQ4223
Village off A272, 3 miles (5km) NW of Uckfield
Pleasing L-shaped village street with a green and a variety of architecture, including timber-framed cottages, two old inns, some Georgian houses and modern half-timbered ones. The lovely church dates from about 1230. It appears in Domesday Book as 'Flescinge', possibly named from the fletchers who supplied arrow feathers for Fletching's medieval arrow industry.

FLETTON, NEW AND OLD Cambridgeshire TL1997
Suburb of Peterborough off A15
Old and New Fletton are now modern suburbs of Peterborough, but boast remarkable 9th-century carvings in St Margaret's Church.

FLIMWELL East Sussex TQ7131
Village on A271, 4 miles (6km) SE of Lamberhurst
Crossroads village on the Kentish border on the edge of Bedgebury Forest. Church of 1839 by Decimus Burton. Striking group of Victorian farmworkers' cottages.

FLINT Clwyd SJ2472
Town on A548, 11 miles (17km) NW of Chester
Unassuming town on Dee estuary with significant historic site tucked away behind main street. Flint Castle (Cadw) was first of chain of strongholds built in North Wales by Edward I in his campaign against the Welsh. Castle dates from 1277. Great tower, its most notable remnant, overlooks the estuary.

FLITTON Bedfordshire TL0535
Village off A507, 2 miles (3km) SE of Ampthill
Aristocratic monuments of the 16th to 19th centuries in the De Grey Mausoleum (English Heritage) attached to the church.

FLITWICK Bedfordshire TL0334
Village on A5120, 2 miles (3km) S of Ampthill
Commuter village swollen by post-war housing. Once known for healthy Flitwick Water. Flitwick Moor Nature Reserve has open days.

FLIXTON Suffolk TM3186
Village off B1062, 3 miles (5km) SW of Bungay
Village with Victorian church in woodland, possibly named after the Saxon bishop St Flik. Home of 'Bungay Buckeroos' in World War II.

FLODDEN FIELD Northumberland
see Branxton Battlefield

FLORE Northamptonshire SP6460
Village on A45, 5 miles (8km) E of Daventry
Popular residential village in the triangle formed by the River Nene, Watling Street (A5) and the M1. The 13th-century church and 17th-century old manor lie on the edge of the village. Flore House is Jacobean. According to tradition, the ancestors of John Adams, the second US President, lived in the village, at a thatched property known as Adams' Cottage.

FLOTTA Orkney ND3593
Island between Hoy and South Ronaldsay
Small island in Scapa Flow, housing a major North Sea oil terminal, built in the 1970s.

FLUSHING Cornwall SW8033
Village off A39, 3 miles (5km) E of Penryn
Opposite Falmouth. The village was founded in the 18th century; it has a pleasant row of waterside houses, and a passenger ferry to Falmouth. Good views.

FOBBING Essex TQ7183
Village off B1420, 4 miles (6km) S of Basildon
Among Thames estuary marshes, with a long smuggling history. Fobbing Marsh Nature Reserve. Controversial 1990 monument celebrates 1381 Peasants' Revolt.

Plaque on the cross at Flodden Field.

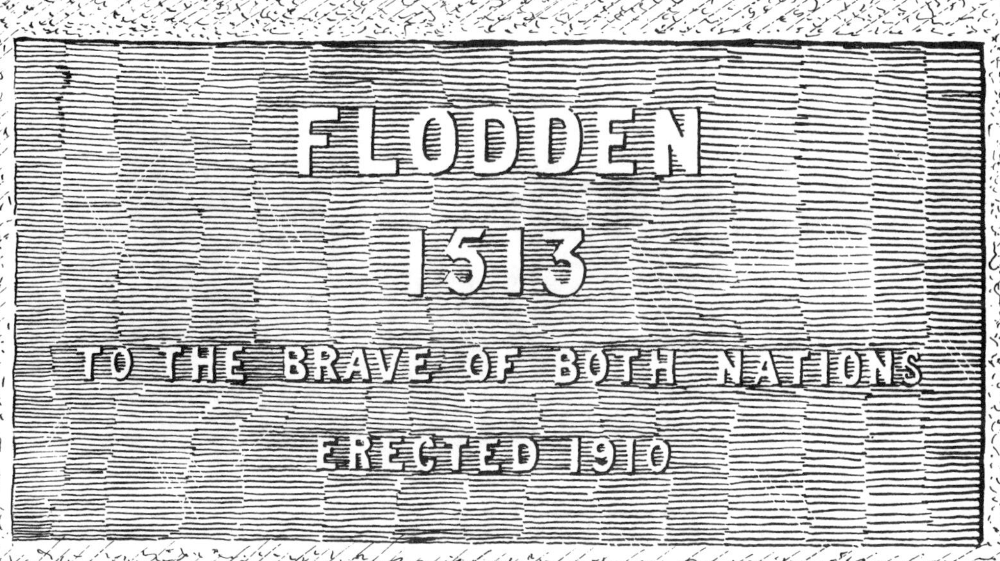

FOCHABERS Grampian NJ3458

Village on A96, 8 miles (13km) E of Elgin

Charming 18th-century village replacing an earlier one, nearer the largely demolished Gordon Castle. George Baxter was a gardener here in the 1860s and opened a grocery in Fochabers which has grown to today's world-renowned food firm. The Folk Museum relates local history. North is Tugnet Ice House, built in 1830 to store ice for packing salmon netted on the River Spey; today it tells the industry's story.

FOLKESTONE Kent TR2235

Town off M20, 14 miles (23km) E of Ashford

The landfall point of the Channel Tunnel and the great mass of overhead power cables for the trains have transformed the coastal scenery at Folkestone, a channel port since Saxon times from which the French coast is visible on clear days.

Two World Wars have battered both the Old Town, with steep narrow streets leading down to the fishing harbour and ferry terminal, and the expansive Victorian resort, developed after the railway arrived in 1842. Yet the old town preserves the Georgian streets (the cobbled High Street is pedestrianised), and the sedate Victorian developments of the 1860s and 70s retain their charm, including the glorious clifftop Promenade called The Leas, backed by stuccoed houses. A lift of 1885, powered by water pressure, takes visitors down to the Maritime Gardens and Undercliff Road. The old fish market, The Stade, at the bottom of High Street, was rebuilt in the 1930s, and leads to East Cliff Sands. The beach is much frequented by windsurfers.

Near by is Folkestone Warren, formed by a coastal landslide in 1915, and dubbed 'Little Switzerland'. It is known for its rare wildflowers.

FOLKINGHAM Lincolnshire TF0733

Village on A15, 8 miles (13km) S of Sleaford

Delightful spacious sloping square surrounded by stone and brick 17th- and 18th-century houses and Greyhound coaching inn. House of Correction gatehouse (1825).

FOLKINGTON East Sussex TQ5503

Hamlet off A27, 5 miles (8km) NW of Eastbourne

On a no-through road beneath the South Downs, with the 13th- to 15th-century church on the edge of a downland hanger.

FOLLY FARM WATERFOWL Gloucestershire

see Bourton-on-the-Water

FONTHILL BISHOP Wiltshire ST9332

Village on B3089, 2 miles (3km) E of Hindon

Interesting stone buildings group by the church. The monumental 17th-century classical gateway to Fonthill survives to the west (see Fonthill Gifford).

FONTHILL GIFFORD Wiltshire ST9231

Village off B3089, 1 mile (2km) SE of Hindon

The eccentric William Beckford built Fonthill Abbey here from 1796, a huge Gothic house with a 275ft (84m) tower and spire. This has gone, but the superbly laid out hilly landscape survives.

The old town hall and ducking stool crane at Fordwich.

FONTWELL West Sussex SU9407
Village on A29, 5 miles (8km) W of Arundel
Village famed for its racecourse, Fontwell Park. Well known for steeplechasing, and for Denmans Gardens, planted with colourful flowers in a framework of evergreens.

FORCETT North Yorkshire NZ1712
Hamlet on B6274, 5 miles (8km) SE of Winston
Small village with a few shops centred around a village green.

FORD Gloucestershire SP0829
Hamlet on B4077, 4 miles (6km) E of Winchcombe
The picturesque 17th-century Plough inn, popular with motorists, stands with one or two cottages in a valley close to the source of the River Windrush.

FORD Northumberland NT9437
Village on B6353, 7 miles (11km) NW of Wooler
Village rebuilt in 1859 by leading Victorian artist Louisa, Marchioness of Waterford, in memory of her husband who was killed in a horse-riding accident. She also decorated the interior walls of Lady Waterford Hall, built as a village school. Ford Castle and the village church both built in the 13th century.

FORD Shropshire SJ4113
Village off A458, 6 miles (8km) W of Shrewsbury
Village overlooking River Severn has a pleasant mix of old houses and a hilltop church with an interesting reredos.

FORD West Sussex SU9903
Village off A259, 3 miles (5km) S of Arundel
Little place at an old ford over the River Arun, opposite Littlehampton, dwarfed by the prison and on the site of an old RAF station. A pretty little church stands alone down by the river.

FORDHAM Cambridgeshire TL6370
Village off A142, 5 miles (8km) N of Newmarket
An attractive village on the River Snail that was once navigable from Soham Lode. The church has an unusual Lady Chapel.

FORDINGBRIDGE Hampshire SU1414
Town on A338, 6 miles (10km) N of Ringwood
Small town on the River Avon with a compact old centre. In the park there is a powerful statue of the painter Augustus John, who lived at Fryern Court (not open) to the north.

FORDWICH Kent TR1859
Village off A28, 2 miles (3km) NE of Canterbury
Pleasant village by a bridge on the River Stour, with a splendid group around the church and smallest town hall in England.

FORDYCE Grampian NJ5563
Village off A98, 3 miles (5km) SW of Portsoy
Fordyce Castle, a four-storey 16th-century L-plan tower house, stands in the centre of this unspoilt village. Parts of St Tarquin's Church date from the 13th century.

FOREMARK Derbyshire SK3326
Hamlet off B5008, 2 miles (3km) E of Repton
Palladian Foremark Hall is a preparatory school for nearby Repton. Fine Robert Bakewell wrought-iron gates. The 1662 church has box pews and three-decker pulpit. Reservoir.

FOREST HILL Greater London TQ3672
District in borough of Lewisham
The delightful Horniman Museum, in its art nouveau building and park, includes shrunken heads, musical instruments and a 1990s aquarium.

FOREST ROW East Sussex TQ4235
Village on A22, 3 miles (5km) SE of East Grinstead
Neat, attractive village in Ashdown Forest, pleasantly situated on hillside above the River Medway. Originally the site of royal hunting lodges. The shopping centre has old buildings.

FORFAR Tayside NO4550
Town off A90 (A94), 12 miles (19km) N of Dundee
This busy market town and royal burgh, formerly the county town of Angus, lies in rich farming country in the Howe of Angus, and was once an important jute and linen-milling centre. In prehistoric times it was a major Pictish site and the present town was founded by David I, who built a castle here, his father, Malcolm Canmore, having held a Parliament on the site in 1057. An octagonal turret marks the spot. In the 17th century Forfar prosecuted many people for witchcraft; the Forfar witch's bridle is displayed in the local museum, an iron head-gag with spikes that fitted inside the victim's mouth.

Today, the town services a large agricultural area and has some solid sandstone buildings, including the 18th-century town hall and the county buildings. It is particularly noted for the 'Forfar Bridie', a crisp pastry turnover with a meat and onion filling.

Two miles (3km) north is the ruined Restenneth Priory, originally a Pictish foundation. The tower dates from the 11th century and is topped by a fine 15th-century octagonal spire.

FORGANDENNY Tayside NO0818
Village on B935, 4 miles (6km) S of Perth
Small village in farming country in Strathearn, noted for the boys' public school, Strathallan, near by.

FORMBY Merseyside SD3306
Town off A565, 11 miles (18km) N of Liverpool
A small coastal town, whose origins go back to Viking times, with a National Trust nature reserve of pine forest. Formby Hall is built on a site that has been occupied since the 12th century. The present building is dated 1523. With the advent of the Liverpool–Southport railway, Formby became a desirable residence for Liverpool businessmen.

FORNCETT, ST MARY AND ST PETER Norfolk TM1693
Villages off B1113, 6 miles (10km) SE of Wymondham
Two pleasant villages set in fertile south Norfolk farmland. It is said that monk John of Forncett wrote the folk song 'Sumer is i-cumin in'.

FORNHAMS, THE Suffolk TL8367

Villages on A1101, 2 miles (3km) NW of Bury St Edmunds

The three Fornhams (All Saints, Genevieve and St Martin) occupy the site of a fierce 13th-century battle.

FORRES Grampian NJ0358

Town on A96, 12 miles (19km) W of Elgin

Ancient royal burgh and agricultural town retaining its medieval layout and well provided with parks and flowers. A Witches' Stone marks the spot where witches were once burnt; there are connections with Shakespeare's *Macbeth*. The 20ft (6m) Sueno Stone possibly commemorates a battle in 1008 and is one of the most important Pictish stones in Scotland.

FORT AUGUSTUS Highland NH3709

Village on A82, 6 miles (10km) NE of Invergarry

A holiday village on the Caledonian Canal at the southwest end of Loch Ness, built on the site of barracks erected after the Jacobite Rising of 1745. Named after George II's son, later to become the infamous Duke of Cumberland, commander of the government troops at Battle of Culloden. A Benedictine abbey now stands on the site of the original fort.

The grave of John Anderson in Fort Augustus.

FORT GEORGE Highland NH7656

Site off B9092, 8 miles (13km) W of Nairn

Classic 18th-century fortress built between 1747 and 1769 to ensure pacification of the Highlands. Architecturally, it is considered to be one of Europe's finest fortifications.

FORT WILLIAM Highland NN1074

Town on A82, 9 miles (14km) SW of Spean Bridge

This Highland town lies in the shadow of brooding Ben Nevis and straggles southwest down Loch Linnhe, while affording beautiful views west across the loch and down Loch Eil. The original fort, built in 1655 to subdue the local clans, was named after William III; it was again strengthened in the 18th century and remained garrisoned until 1855. Shortly afterwards the railway reached the town and the fort was demolished; the town was much expanded and took its present-day form. The West Highland Museum is a splendidly old-fashioned collection dealing with many aspects of local history and Highland culture; it includes the 'secret portrait' of Prince Charles Edward, a blur of paint which resolves into a portrait when reflected against a brass cylinder.

Fort William is one of the Highland's major tourist centres with good public transport links in all directions, ample services, many tourist facilities and a plethora of every type of accommodation. It makes an excellent touring base, and there is easy access to magnificent countryside offering opportunities for many varieties of outdoor activity.

FORTH BRIDGES Lothian NT1278

Bridges carrying A90, and rail bridge

Two bridges across the Firth of Forth, 9 miles (14km) west of Edinburgh. The Forth road bridge was opened in 1964, a graceful suspension bridge carrying the A90 2,000yds (1,828m) over the Firth, one of the world's largest suspension bridges. The Forth railway bridge was completed in 1890; a double rail-line runs through the stone approach viaducts to the cantilevered steel bridge with three towers.

FORTH, RIVER Central

River

Flows east from beneath Ben Lomond through attractive highland scenery to Aberfoyle and Carse of Stirling to open out into an estuary at Firth of Forth.

FORTHAMPTON Gloucestershire SO8532

Village off A438, 2 miles (3km) W of Tewkesbury

Stocks and a whipping-post survive among an array of well-preserved timber-framed houses standing close to a fascinating church.

FORTINGALL Tayside NN7347

Village off B846, 7 miles (11km) W of Aberfeldy

Thatched village at the entrance to Glenlyon, the reputed birthplace of Pontius Pilate. Prehistoric stone circles, and a yew tree in churchyard thought to be the oldest living vegetation in Europe.

FORTROSE Highland NH7256

Small town on A832, 8 miles (13km) NE of Tore

Ancient royal burgh and resort on Black Isle, on the shores of Moray Firth, with fine examples of attractively colour-washed vernacular houses. Remains of the 14th- to 15th-century Fortrose Cathedral include a sacristy and chapter house. Stone from here was used by Cromwell to construct his fort at Inverness. Many Pictish and prehistoric remains in the vicinity.

FORTY GREEN Buckinghamshire SU9291
Village off B474, immediately NW of Beaconsfield
Tiny hamlet in the 19th century, now a commuter and retirement village. Royal Standard of England pub on site of Royalist headquarters.

FOSSE WAY Somerset to Lincolnshire
Roman road
One of the most famous Roman roads, running from Hinton St George in Somerset to Lincoln, on a line still used by modern roads.

FOSTON North Yorkshire SE6965
Hamlet off A64, 7 miles (11km) SW of Malton
A village of stone cottages with pantiled roofs. All Saints Church dates from 1086.

FOTHERINGHAY Northamptonshire TL0593
Village off A605, 4 miles (6km) NE of Oundle
Picturesque grassy mound beside the River Nene marks the site of Fotheringhay Castle, where Mary Stuart was beheaded in 1587. Richard III was born here in 1452. Some of the castle stone was re-used in the attractive village cottages, and some taken to Oundle. The magnificent 15th-century church, with octagonal lantern tower and airy nave of grand proportions, was originally part of a larger collegiate church.

FOULA Shetland HT9639
Island SW of Mainland
The loneliest inhabited island in Britain has a population of about 40, dependant on crofting and fishing. Dramatic cliff scenery and abundant birdlife.

FOULNESS ISLAND Essex TR0092
Island off B1017, 8 miles (13km) NE of Southend-on-Sea
Remote area on edge of Maplin Sands, used for military purposes by Ministry of Defence. Artillery ranges. Access restricted.

FOUNTAINS ABBEY North Yorkshire SE2768
Site off B6265, 3 miles (5km) SW of Ripon
This ruined Cistercian abbey was founded in 1132, one of the richest houses in Western Europe, and now one of the most visited of the National Trust's properties.

FOUR MARKS Hampshire SU6735
Village on A31, 4 miles (6km) SW of Alton
A modern village, named after the stone which marked the junction of four parishes. It has a station on the steam Watercress Line.

FOVANT Wiltshire SU0028
Village on A30, 6 miles (10km) SW of Wilton
Stone cottages, a stream and a handsome church tower of 1492 make up this village. Cut into a chalk hillside to the south are the Fovant Badges, nine different military badges, the first created in 1916. The area has been used by the military for training since before World War I.

FOWEY Cornwall SX1251
Town on A3082, 10 miles (16km) S of Lostwithiel
Set on the pretty Fowey (pronounced 'Foy') estuary, this was a town and port from medieval times, burnt by the French in 1457, and with a reputation for piracy. The narrow main street runs parallel with the estuary, densely packed with small houses dating from 16th century onwards. The handsome 14th-century church has a prominent tower, rising behind the extraordinary early 19th-century towers and battlements of the big house (not open). The little square by the Town Quay has attractive buildings and wonderful river views.

Yachts are everywhere, and just to the north of the town are modern jetties for the big ships which carry china clay. A little car ferry operates over the narrow, fast river to Bodinnic (see) and a passenger ferry runs to Polruan (see).

To the south of the town, on a rocky headland, are the ruins of the small 16th-century St Catherine's Castle.

FOWLIS EASTER Tayside NO3233
Village off A923, 6 miles (10km) NW of Dundee
Small village noted for pre-Reformation church which has a fine sacrament house, a carved font and a series of fine painted panels.

FOWLIS WESTER Tayside NN9224
Village off A85, 4 miles (7km) E of Crieff
A small village many miles from Fowlis Easter, whose restored 15th-century church has two Pictish cross-slabs with exceptional carvings. Standing stones near by.

FOWLMERE Cambridgeshire TL4245
Village on B1368, 5 miles (8km) NE of Royston
Fowlmere (RSPB) has been home to wildfowl for perhaps thousands of years. Its reed beds and ponds are home to kingfishers and water rails.

FOWNHOPE Hereford and Worcester SO5834
Village on B4224, 6 miles (9km) SE of Hereford
Restoration of Charles II is still celebrated annually in this village below wooded Wye Valley. Superb Norman carving in church.

FOXTON Leicestershire SP6989
Village off A6, 3 miles (5km) NW of Market Harborough
Flight of ten locks, completed in 1812, on the Grand Union Canal, with a museum and the remains of an early 1900s boat lift. Church is 13th century.

FOY Hereford and Worcester SO5928
Village off A40, 3 miles (5km) N of Ross-on-Wye
Almost an island within a meander of the River Wye, the village preserves its Victorian suspension bridge and fine chancel screen in its church.

FOYERS Highland NH4921
Village on B852, 11 miles (18km) NE of Fort Augustus
Attractive village nestling at the foot of steep hills running down to the southern shore of Loch Ness in lovely countryside.

FRAMINGHAM, EARL AND PIGOT Norfolk TG2702
Villages off A146, 5 miles (8km) SE of Norwich
The Framinghams lie in peaceful farmland dotted with woodland. Each village has its own church with well-kept churchyards, and they share three pubs.

FRAMLINGHAM Suffolk TM2863
Small town on B1119, 9 miles (14km) N of Woodbridge
With its fine castle, meres, church, and almshouses, Framlingham is steeped in history. The castle (English Heritage) was built by Roger Bigod, Earl of Norfolk. It has been a fortress, a school, and even a fire station in its 800-year history. The town has almshouses (built 1654) and a 16th-century mansion house.

FRAMPTON Lincolnshire TF3239
Village off A16, 3 miles (5km) S of Boston
Pleasant fenland village with imposing church, grand 18th-century hall, brick cottages and larger 18th-century houses.

FRAMPTON COTTERELL Avon ST6681
Village off B4058, 4 miles (6km) W of Chipping Sodbury
The church is set on the River Frome. It is mostly Victorian and surrounded by suburban development.

FRAMPTON ON SEVERN Gloucestershire SO7407
Village off A38, 7 miles (11km) W of Stroud
Old houses and cottages in a variety of styles are strung out beside a huge green next to the Gloucester–Sharpness Canal. The Palladian Frampton Court (open by appointment) is attributed to Vanbrugh and has notable gardens featuring an elegant 18th-century orangery. The medieval church at the southern end of village has a rare lead font.

FRANT East Sussex TQ5935
Village on A267, 3 miles (5km) S of Tunbridge Wells
Attractive hilltop village set around a large, irregularly-shaped green. Fine views over Eridge Park.

FRASERBURGH Grampian NJ9966
Town on A92, 15 miles (24km) NW of Peterhead
Important fishing port founded in 1550s by Sir Alexander Fraser and granted a royal charter in 1592. It boomed as a herring port from the 1870s to the 1890s, and today is a busy whitefish port and commercial harbour complex. The 16th-century castle on Kinnaird Head houses Scotland's oldest lighthouse, built in 1787. The notable 17th-century mercat cross uniquely shows the coats of arms of the old kingdom of Scotland and the new United Kingdom.

FREEFOLK Hampshire SU4848
Hamlet off B3400, 2 miles (3km) E of Whitchurch
Tiny village on the River Test, adjacent to Laverstoke (see). Small church with rustic fittings of 1703.

FREISTON Lincolnshire TF3743
Village off A52, 3 miles (5km) E of Boston
Fenland village between Hobhole Drain and the Wash. Church nave of Norman priory, 15th-century tower and clerestory, north aisle of 15th-century brick.

FRENCHAY Avon ST6477
District in NE Bristol
On the edge of the Frome Valley, now engulfed by Bristol but still with its own character. Georgian houses, a Quaker Meeting House of 1808 and green spaces.

FRENSHAM Surrey SU8441
Village off A287, 4 miles (6km) S of Farnham
Scattered village in the Wey Valley and on the sandy heaths south of Farnham. Arranged in three main clusters, by the church, on a main road at Millbridge and north of the river at Spreakley. The area still grows hops, formerly very important. Famed for its ponds, dug in the Middle Ages and the largest in Surrey. Now in Frensham Country Park; safe sandy beaches; sailing on Great Pond; wide variety of wildlife.

FRESHFORD Avon ST7860
Village off A36, 4 miles (6km) SE of Bath
A pretty stone village on steeply wooded little hills, set in a bend made by the rivers Frome and Avon.

FRESHWATER Isle of Wight SZ3487
Village on A3055, 1 mile (2km) SE of Totland
More like a town than a village, Freshwater comprises several hamlets with an Edwardian centre. The area became popular after Tennyson bought Farringford House, now a hotel 1 mile (2km) south, in 1853. The house of one of his contemporaries is open: Julia Margaret Cameron, the pioneer photographer's, at Freshwater Bay, a tiny chalk inlet with chalk stacks. Also at Freshwater Bay is a little thatched church of 1908, deliberately picturesque. Golden Hill Fort, 1860s, has military displays.

FRESSINGFIELD Suffolk TM2677
Village on B1116, 4 miles (6km) S of Harleston
A large village with a renowned restaurant (the Fox and Goose inn). Church Farm Stable is 14th century. The Baptist church is coffin-shaped.

The village sign at Fressingfield.

FRIDAY STREET Surrey TQ1245

Hamlet off A25, 4 miles (6km) SW of Dorking

Cluster of cottages and pub at end of a lane by the pond on steep pine-clad greensand ridge of Leith Hill; formerly an important iron-working settlement.

FRIDAYTHORPE Humberside SE8759

Village on A166, 9 miles (14km) W of Great Driffield

This is the highest of the Wolds villages. St Mary's Church has an unusual wooden clock copied from an 18th-century French clock.

FRIERN BARNET Greater London TQ2892

District in borough of Barnet

Forested originally, almost all cleared by the 1850s, when the railway arrived and suburban development took wing. Town hall of the 1940s.

FRIMLEY Surrey SU8858

Town on A32, immediately S of Camberley

Ancient village now almost swallowed up by modern Camberley. High Street has some attractive older buildings. Frimley Lodge Park created from 69 acres (28ha) of meadows and woodlands.

FRINTON-ON-SEA Essex TM2320

Town on B1033, 1 mile (2km) SW of Walton on the Naze

A fishing village until the 1880s, when it developed as a restrained, middle-class seaside resort. Attractive beach, smart shops, Victorian and Edwardian houses.

FRISBY ON THE WREAKE Leicestershire SK6917

Village off A6006, 4 miles (6km) W of Melton Mowbray

Between the meandering River Wreake and the Leicester–Melton road. Several 18th-century cottages with date-stones. Village cross. Church mainly 14th century, with an ironstone tower.

FRISKNEY Lincolnshire TF4655

Village off A52, 3 miles (5km) SW of Wainfleet

Late 18th-century vicarage, remains of 19th-century tower mill, farms, 19th-century cottages, and spacious 15th-century fenland church.

FRISTON East Sussex TV5598

Village on A259, 4 miles (6km) W of Eastbourne

A Norman church and a pretty duck pond stand by the main road, in an exposed position 350ft (106m) up on the downs above the sea. Nearby Friston Forest covers 2,000 acres (809 ha).

FRITHELSTOCK Devon SS4619

Village off A386, 2 miles (3km) W of Great Torrington

Hilly and wooded village, with a medieval church and the ruins of a medieval priory.

FRITTON Norfolk TG4600

Village on A143, 6 miles (10km) SW of Great Yarmouth

Fritton Lake is a tree-fringed mere (but duck decoying is no longer practised here). Oak trees line Fritton Common, famous for its cuckoos.

FRITWELL Oxfordshire SP5229

Village off B4100, 3 miles (5km) S of Aynho

Less tranquil following arrival of M40, Fritwell is still worth visiting for the good surviving Norman work in St Olave's Church.

FROCESTER Gloucestershire SO7803

Village off B4066, 4 miles (6km) NE of Dursley

This village beneath the Cotswold Edge has a huge tithe barn, built in about 1300 and standing close to the timber-framed gatehouse of Frocester Court.

FRODSHAM Cheshire SJ5177

Town on A56, 3 miles (5km) S of Runcorn

Close to the Mersey estuary overlooked by Overton Hill. The hill, formed over a million years ago of red, brown and yellow sandstone, rises 365ft (111m) high. In medieval times Frodsham was a thriving port, from where Cheshire's salt and cheese were sent by river to Liverpool.

FROGMORE HOUSE Berkshire SU9777

Mansion off A308, in Windsor Great Park

Eighteenth-century house in Windsor Great Park with fine decorations, especially one room painted with garlands of flowers. Good gardens.

FROME Somerset ST7747

Town off A362, 11 miles (18km) S of Bath

Large town with handsome Georgian stone houses and cottages densely packed in steep streets. Cloth-making made the town rich from medieval times to 1800, with a decline thereafter. The big 1707 classical Congregational chapel and the Blue House of 1726, with figures, are the best buildings. The railway station (1850) is all wood – a rare survivor. Local museum.

FRONCYSYLLTE Clwyd SJ2741

Village on A5, 3 miles (5km) NW of Chirk

At gateway to Vale of Llangollen where English plains meet Welsh mountains. Valley spanned by Telford's Pontcysyllte Aqueduct.

FROSTERLEY Durham NZ0236

Village on A689, 2 miles (3km) SE of Stanhope

An old village in Upper Weardale, where Frosterley black marble is quarried. The marble, actually a limestone speckled with fossils, was in great demand in Victorian times.

Ruined 13th-century priory at Frithelstock.

FROXFIELD Wiltshire SU2968
Village on A4, 3 miles (5km) W of Hungerford
Wide street with some thatched buildings. On the outskirts is the massive Somerset Hospital, actually almshouses, half built in 1694, half in 1775.

FRYERNING Essex TL6300
Village off A12, 5 miles (8km) NE of Brentwood
Attractive village on a hill; the Tudor church tower is a landmark. Green, ponds, simple old Viper pub at Mill Green.

FULBECK Lincolnshire SK9450
Village on A607, 9 miles (14km) N of Grantham
On steep hillside, topped by church with 15th-century pinnacled tower and clerestory, and 18th-century Fulbeck Hall and formal gardens (limited opening).

FULBOURN Cambridgeshire TL5156
Village off A11, 5 miles (8km) SE of Cambridge
Thatched cottages and modern houses rub shoulders in this ancient village. There is a mill, a psychiatric hospital, and an educational nature reserve.

FULHAM Greater London TQ2476
District in borough of Hammersmith and Fulham
This is a fundamentally Victorian residential area west of Chelsea (see), with classy antiques shops and restaurants. Bishop of London's former Fulham Palace, museum, botanic gardens, riverside park; the bishops lived here until 1973. Melancholy tombs and monuments in Brompton Cemetery. Stamford Bridge and Craven Cottage football grounds of Chelsea and Fulham clubs respectively. Hurlingham Club for croquet and other smart sport.

FULKING West Sussex TQ2411
Village off A283, 7 miles (11km) NE of Shoreham
Pretty flint-built cottages huddle beneath the steep downland slopes near the famous Shepherd and Dog inn. Clear spring water flows from the hill.

FULMER Buckinghamshire SU9985
Village off A40, 4 miles (6km) NE of Slough
Neatly kept and attractive, by the River Alderbourne, with a small green. Rare 17th-century church.

FULNECK West Yorkshire SE2232
Village off A6110, 1 mile (2km) S of Pudsey
A large residential district of Pudsey. Home to the Moravian Brethren since 1742 and a museum houses a unique collection from the world-wide Moravian Church.

FULWOOD Lancashire SD5431
Suburb on A6, N area of Preston
Residential suburb of Preston, with office and print works for the *Lancashire Evening Post* and a British Aerospace site.

FUNTLEY Hampshire SU5608
Village off A27, 2 miles (3km) NW of Fareham
Scattered rural hamlet situated on the lower part of the River Meon, with some old timber-framed farmhouses.

FURNACE Strathclyde NN0300
Village on A83, 7 miles (11km) SW of Inveraray
The village was renamed Furnace when iron-smelting began here in the 18th century and continued until 1842. Auchindrain Museum, near by, is an old West Highland township showing Highland life before the Clearances.

FURNESS Cumbria SD2890
Historic region in NW England
This peninsula in the South Lakes owes much of its economic development to the methodical exploitation of all natural resources by the monks of Furness Abbey (see Barrow in Furness).

FURNEUX PELHAM Hertfordshire TL4327
Village off B1038, 5 miles (8km) NW of Bishop's Stortford
On the River Ash. The church has beautiful Burne-Jones stained-glass windows and clock that says 'Time Flies – Mind Your Business'.

FYFIELD Oxfordshire SU4298
Village on A420, 5 miles (8km) W of Abingdon
The unspoilt medieval manor is not open, but there is an interesting church and inn with a built-in medieval chapel.

FYLDE, THE Lancashire
Historic regionin NW England
Fertile plain of flat, treeless lowland with Blackpool, Lytham St Annes and Fleetwood along the sandy coastline (see) and inland Poulton-le-Fylde and Thornton (see).

FYLINGDALES MOOR North Yorkshire SE9299
Scenic area off A171, S of Whitby
A stretch of fine moorland adjoining the North Sea coast. The famous early-warning radar spheres have been dismantled.

FYVIE Grampian NJ7637
Village on B9005, 8 miles (13km) S of Turriff
Village near huge Fyvie Castle (National Trust for Scotland), a grand example of Scottish baronial architecture in a park on the River Ythan. The castle dates from the 13th to 19th centuries and has an extremely important portrait collection.

G

GADDESBY Leicestershire SK6813
Village on B674, 6 miles (10km) SW of Melton Mowbray
One of Leicestershire's finest village churches, 13th and 14th century, with a soaring spire. Almost lifesize equestrian monument of a colonel who fought at Waterloo.

GAILEY Staffordshire SJ9110
Hamlet on A5/A449, 2 miles (3km) S of Penkridge
Nondescript crossroads village on Watling Street. Wharf on Staffordshire and Worcestershire Canal busy in summer. Sailing on reservoirs near by.

GAINFORD Durham NZ1716
Village on A67, 8 miles (13km) W of Darlington
The village once had a spa and the mineral water basin can still be seen on the riverbank a short distance upstream from Gainford. St Mary's Church partly built from stones taken from the Roman fort at Piercebridge. Gainford Hall, hidden behind high gates, is Jacobean.

GAINSBOROUGH Lincolnshire SK8189
Town on A156, 15 miles (24km) NW of Lincoln
Gainsborough's little-known treasure is the Old Hall (English Heritage and Lincolnshire County Council), an outstanding timber-framed medieval manor house with a 15th-century brick tower, a medieval kitchen and a great hall. Concerts, historic re-enactments and other events held here. Near by is the grand Georgian parish church, with medieval tower. The town, an inland port on the River Trent, is mainly 19th-century red brick.

GAIRLOCH Highland NG8076
Village on A832, 5 miles (8km) SW of Poolewe
Scattered crofting township and holiday centre in idyllic coastal scenery on Loch Gairloch. Good local museum, watersports, walking and lovely sandy beach.

GALASHIELS Borders NT4936
Town on A7, 12 miles (19km) N of Hawick
Industrial Border town on Gala Water, famed from the 18th century for woollen textiles. Mills and College of Textiles are open to the public, and the heritage centre tells the town's history.

GALGATE Lancashire SD4855
Village on A6, 4 miles (6km) S of Lancaster
Pleasant village on the River Conder with a number of original mills, many now converted to other uses. Canalside craft centre in farm buildings next to Lancaster Canal.

GALLOWAY Dumfries and Galloway
Scenic area of Scotland
Remote, beautiful area with agriculture and fishing as main industries. Many ruined churches and abbeys. Wild, undiscovered country in Galloway Highlands, and extensive and varied coast.

GALSTON Strathclyde NS5036
Town on A71, 5 miles (8km) E of Kilmarnock
Town in mining area with unusual Byzantine-style, central-domed Roman Catholic church. Loudon Castle, to the north, was fire-damaged in 1941, but the impressive façade remains.

GAMLINGAY Cambridgeshire TL2352
Village on B1040, 2 miles (3km) NE of Potton
This once-prosperous village has about 60 listed buildings, despite the fire in 1600 that destroyed 76 houses. Near by is Gamlingay Cinques Nature Reserve.

GANLLWYD Gwynedd SH7224
Hamlet on A470, 4 miles (6km) N of Dolgellau
Magnificently set amongst steep-sided wooded slopes. National Trust's Dolmelynllyn estate offers walks and the spectacular Rhaeadr Ddu waterfalls.

GANTON North Yorkshire SE9977
Village on A64, 8 miles (13km) W of Filey
A pretty village in the heart of the Yorkshire Wolds, with a 12th-century church.

GARBOLDISHAM Norfolk TM0081
Village on A1066, 7 miles (11km) W of Diss
Lying to the east of Devil's Dyke, Garboldisham is an attractive large village with some cottages built of 'clay lump' (unfired bricks). Pronounced 'Garblesham'.

GARDENSTOWN Grampian NJ8064
Village off B9031, 6 miles (10km) E of Macduff
A fishing port from the 1720s, still partly operational and uniquely situated on a series of narrow terraces on the cliff face above Gamrie Bay.

GARELOCHEAD Strathclyde NS2391
Village on A814, 7 miles (11km) NW of Helensburgh
Pretty village at the head of a sea-loch, a fashionable residential area in the 19th century and popular with sea-anglers and yachtsmen. Faslane nuclear submarine base is near by.

GARGRAVE North Yorkshire SD9354
Village on A65, 4 miles (6km) NW of Skipton
A picturesque village in upper Airedale. There is the site of a Roman villa, excavated in the 1970s, near by.

GARLIESTON Dumfries and Galloway NX4746
Village on B7004, 6 miles (10km) SE of Wigtown
This 1760s planned village, once a ship-building and fishing centre, is today a sea-angling and sailing base. Galloway House has spacious gardens runnng down to the sea.

GARSINGTON Oxfordshire SP5802
Village off B480, 5 miles (8km) SE of Oxford
Mellow houses and an outstanding medieval church stand close to the Tudor manor house famous in 1920s for literary parties of Lady Ottoline Morrell.

GARSTANG Lancashire SD4945
Small town on A6, 10 miles (16km) N of Preston
This old market town appears to have originated in Saxon times. It was one of the last Royalist strongholds north of the River Trent.

GARSTON Merseyside SJ4084
District in SE Liverpool
A sea port on the banks of the River Mersey whose docks were modernised after World War II.

GARTON-ON-THE-WOLDS Humberside SE9859
Village on A166, 3 miles (5km) NW of Great Driffield
Small farming village. St Michael's Church, of Norman origin, restored in 1850s and with highly decorated walls and ceiling.

GARVALD Lothian NT5870
Village off B6370, 8 miles (13km) SW of Dunbar
Village in Lammermuirs, with a partly 12th-century church. Near by is Nunraw Abbey, abandoned after the Reformation and revived by Cistercians in 1946.

GARWAY Hereford and Worcester SO4522
Village off B4521, 5 miles (8km) SE of Pontrilas
The Knights Hospitallers owned the fortress-like Norman church and nearby dovecote of this hillside village on the Welsh border.

GATCOMBE Isle of Wight SZ4985
Village off A3020, 3 miles (5km) S of Newport
Pretty village tucked into a green valley, rather remote. The church has a very fine window of stained glass by William Morris.

GATEHOUSE Northumberland NY7889
Hamlet off B6320, 5 miles (8km) NW of Bellingham
Surrounded by good walking country, this hamlet lies in the heart of the Northumberland National Park. Black Middens Bastle House (English Heritage).

GATEHOUSE OF FLEET Dumfries and Galloway NX5956
Small town off A75, 6 miles (10km) NW of Kirkcudbright
Centre of the cotton industry in the late 18th century, with fine Georgian houses in High Street. Developed by benevolent capitalist James Murray, who founded factories and foundries and built up a ship-building industry, the town declined steadily during the 19th century. To the south lies the ruined tower house of 15th-century Cardoness Castle, overlooking Loch Fleet from a craggy outcrop.

GATESHEAD Tyne and Wear NZ2563
Town on A167, across the river from Newcastle upon Tyne
Administrative centre for the group of industrial towns south of the River Tyne, Gateshead is dominated by concrete tower blocks and the MetroCentre, Europe's largest indoor shopping centre. Built on reclaimed industrial land near the A69 and with 2 million square feet (185,800 sq m) of retail space, said to be the most profitable in the country, the complex has more than 360 shops and restaurants in themed areas, as well as a cinema complex, theme park and bowling centre. The remarkable success of the MetroCentre has turned Gateshead into a major visitor destination for overseas visitors as well as day-trippers.

The town developed around coal deposits discovered in the 14th century, and subsequently around the heavy industries along the riverside during the Victorian era when it was a thriving port.

Gateshead is linked to Newcastle by a number of road and rail bridges which cross the Tyne, the largest of which is the Tyne Bridge. In the shadow of this bridge is St Mary's Church, around which the oldest part of the town is built.

Gateshead International Stadium is a major venue for athletics events.

GATLEY Greater Manchester SJ8488
Town off M56, 3 miles (5km) W of Stockport
A pleasant residential area with Victorian, 1930s and modern houses. Traditional village green.

GATTON Surrey TQ2752
Hamlet off A23, 2 miles (3km) N of Redhill
Once a famous 'rotten borough' of scattered houses, farms and a church containing rare 16th-century woodwork in the park of Gatton Hall, now a school.

GATWICK West Sussex TQ2841
Airport off M23, 3 miles (5km) N of Crawley
One of the world's leading international airports, handling some 20 million passengers each year with direct services to Europe, America and the Far East.

GAWSWORTH Cheshire SJ8969
Hamlet off A536, 3 miles (5km) SW of Macclesfield
Much of the village has been restored by the Roper-Richards family, owners of 15th-century Gawsworth Hall. Also a venue for open-air theatre in the summer. Sandstone church, built in the 15th century, has an eight-spire tower and winged dragon gargoyles.

GAYHURST Buckinghamshire SP8446
Village on B526, 3 miles (5km) NW of Newport Pagnell
Classical-style 1720s church in grounds of Gayhurst House (not open). The former entrance lodge is now a pub, the Sir Francis Drake.

GAYTON Norfolk TF7219
Village on B1145, 7 miles (11km) E of King's Lynn
The mill is still the focal place of this village but is now idle, as are the lime kilns to the north.

GEDDING Suffolk TL9557
Village off A14 (A45), 7 miles (11km) SE of Bury St Edmunds
Boasts traditional Suffolk Red Poll dairy herd, and home of Rolling Stones' Bill Wyman. Gedding Hall (not open) was built in 1273, and rebuilt in the 1600s.

GEDDINGTON Northamptonshire SP8983
Village on A43, 3 miles (5km) NE of Kettering
Near the 13th-century bridge stands the best preserved remaining Eleanor Cross, a monument to the memory of Edward I's queen, marking one of the places her funeral cortège rested on its way to London after her death in 1290. Boughton House, modelled on Versailles, is the treasure-filled home of the Duke of Buccleuch, set in magnificent parkland.

GEDLING Nottinghamshire SK6142
Village off A612, on E outskirts of Nottingham
The elegant, slim early 14th-century spire of All Hallows Church soars above the churchyard where Shrewsbury and Shaw, two Victorian cricketers, lie buried.

GEDNEY Lincolnshire TF4024
Village off A17, 3 miles (5km) E of Holbeach
An outstanding church among many fine fenland churches, with 13th- and 15th-century tower and spectacular clerestory windows.

GELDESTON Norfolk TM3971
Village off A143, 3 miles (5km) NW of Beccles
Sited near River Waveney, Geldeston is a pretty village with a lock. Beer for the local inn once had to be brought in by boat.

GELLIGAER Mid Glamorgan ST1396
Village on B4254, 6 miles (10km) N of Caerphilly
Village at site of Roman camp on the Roman road from Brecon to Cardiff. 'Living history' house of Llancaiach Fawr authentically re-creates Civil War period.

GEORGEHAM Devon SS4639
Village off A3611, 6 miles (10km) SW of Ilfracombe
Set a little way inland from Morte Bay, with many thatched cottages, densely packed in a little valley.

GERMOE Cornwall SW5829
Village off A394, 5 miles (8km) W of Helston
Small and rural granite village with a pretty church. Built into the churchyard wall is St Germoe's Chair, a little covered seat.

GERRARDS CROSS Buckinghamshire TQ0088
Town on A40, 4 miles (6km) NW of Uxbridge
Smart and expensive with comfortable houses in every 20th-century suburban style. Earthworks of extensive Iron Age fort in Bulstrode Park.

GESTINGTHORPE Essex TL8138
Village off B1058, 4 miles (6km) SW of Sudbury
Norman church with massive brick tower added in 1490s; splendid double hammerbeam roof is an Essex rarity.

GIBRALTAR POINT Lincolnshire TF5557
Headland off A52, 4 miles (6km) S of Skegness
Roughly 1,500 acres (607ha) of sand dunes, saltmarsh, sandy and muddy shores, and freshwater habitats which became the first statutory local authority nature reserve in the country, with Lincolnshire Trust for Nature Conservation. Interpretive visitor centre. Residential courses.

GIBSIDE Tyne and Wear NZ1758
Estate off A694, 6 miles (10km) SW of Gateshead
National Trust estate with woodland. The Palladian-style chapel was the Bowes family mausoleum. Park designed by Capability Brown. Gibside Hall, now ruined, is on private property.

GIDLEIGH Devon SX6788
Hamlet off A382, 5 miles (8km) NW of Moretonhampstead
Hamlet on the eastern edge of Dartmoor. Impressive scenery, with wooded lower parts and bare moor above.

GIFFNOCK Strathclyde NS5659
Town on A77, 5 miles (8km) S of Glasgow
Residential area on the southwestern fringes of Glasgow. Many 19th-century merchants' villas, including Greenbank Garden with 13 acres (5ha) of gardens.

GIFFORD Lothian NT5368
Village on B6369, 4 miles (6km) S of Haddington
An 18th-century estate village with a contemporary church and a wide main street. Yester House is an Adam mansion; Yester Castle contains 'Goblin Ha', a 13th-century underground hall.

GIGGLESWICK North Yorkshire SD8063
Village off A65, immediately W of Settle
This village, which faces Settle across the River Ribble, retains an old and gentle charm. Many of the buildings are 17th century. Rising above the village is Giggleswick Scar, a limestone formation which forms part of the Craven Fault. Just outside the village is the famous Ebbing and Flowing Well.

GIGHA Strathclyde NR6449
Island off W Kintyre coast
Fertile island with many prehistoric sites. Ardminish is the only village. Achamore House Gardens (National Trust for Scotland) are renowned for azaleas and rhododendrons.

GILFACH GOCH Mid Glamorgan SS9889
Town on B4564, 2 miles (3km) NW of Tonyrefail
Former mining town tucked away in a cul-de-sac, setting for famous Richard Llewellyn novel about industrial South Wales, *How Green Was My Valley*. Mining site now landscaped.

GILLAMOOR North Yorkshire SE6889
Village off A170, 2 miles (3km) N of Kirkbymoorside
A tiny moorland village with some fine old houses and cottages, lovely views over the River Dove.

GILLING EAST North Yorkshire SE6176
Village on B1363, 2 miles (3km) S of Oswaldkirk
On the edge of the Howardian Hills, the castle, a fortified manor house built in 1349, is now a boys' preparatory school for Ampleforth College (see).

GILLINGHAM Dorset ST8026
Town on B3081, 4 miles (6km) NW of Shaftesbury
This small town on the edge of the Blackmoor Vale (see) was tiny until the railway arrived in 1859. Many buildings in the local Victorian hot-red bricks. Local museum.

GILLINGHAM Kent TQ7767
Town on A2, immediately E of Chatham
Lively town on the Thames estuary, adjoining Chatham, with a variety of sporting facilities, and a country park overlooking the internationally important waterfowl reserves on North Kent Marshes.

GILLINGHAM Norfolk TM4191
Village on A146, 1 mile (2km) NW of Beccles
Village with three churches, one ruinous. A former rector enjoyed riding, and had his saddle fixed into the pulpit so he could 'ride' while preaching.

GILSLAND Northumberland NY6366
Village off B6318, 5 miles (8km) W of Haltwhistle
Hadrian's Wall passes through the village and the Roman fort of Camboglanna is 1 mile (2km) to the west. A bridge abutment stands, rather incongruously, in a field because the River Irthing has changed its course. Sir Walter Scott featured the village in his novel *Guy Mannering*.

GILSTON Hertfordshire TL4413
Hamlet off A414, 3 miles (5km) W of Sawbridgeworth
The church, near the mock-Tudor Gilston Park (not open), has an important 13th-century rood screen and Gore family monuments.

GIMINGHAM Norfolk TG2836
Village off B1145, 4 miles (6km) N of North Walsham
The attractive tower of All Saints' Church dates from about 1500. The watching window allows visitors to look into the church from outside.

GIRVAN Strathclyde NX1897
Town on A77, 17 miles (27km) SW of Ayr
Once a fishing village and handloom weaving centre, this town on the Ayrshire coast boomed after the arrival of the railway in 1860 to become a tourist centre and resort with good beaches and services. It was a boat-building centre in the 1940s. The nearby 16th-century Killochan Castle is a fortified house with a collection of Stuart and Napoleonic relics.

GISBURN Lancashire SD8248
Village on A59, 7 miles (11km) NE of Clitheroe
Delightful village characterised by old stone cottages and cobbled pavements. Parish church has Norman windows with 14th-century stained glass.

GITTISHAM Devon SY1398
Village off A375, 2 miles (3km) SW of Honiton
Pretty thatched village of flint and cob, with a village green. The church still has a Georgian interior with gallery, box pews and memorials.

GLAISDALE North Yorkshire NZ7705
Village off A171, 2 miles (3km) W of Egton
Beggars Bridge was built in the 17th century by Thomas Ferris to prove his love for a wealthy farmer's daughter.

GLAMIS Tayside NO3846
Village on A94, 10 miles (16km) N of Dundee
Angus village with picturesque 17th-century cottages, some housing the Angus Folk Museum, devoted to domestic and agricultural life. Glamis Castle stands near by, a five-storey L-shaped tower block, mainly dating from the 17th century, although parts date from the 14th century. Home of the Lyon family, forebears of the Queen Mother, since 1372. Formal gardens and extensive park.

GLANDFORD Norfolk TG0441
Village on B1156, 3 miles (5km) NW of Holt
An internationally known shell museum is one of the attractions of this pleasant cluster of flint and red-brick houses.

GLAPWELL Derbyshire SK4766
Village on A617, 3 miles (5km) S of Bolsover
Residential village on the main Mansfield to Chesterfield road, close to beautiful Hardwick Hall (see). Well-dressing in July.

GLASBURY Powys SO1739
Village off A438, 4 miles (6km) SW of Hay-on-Wye
Peacefully set in wide valley beside the River Wye. Long history of settlement embracing Roman, early Christian and Norman periods.

GLASGOW Strathclyde NS5865
City off M8, 41 miles (65km) W of Edinburgh
Glasgow is the largest city in Scotland, historically and temperamentally different from Edinburgh in every way. The last two centuries have seen the stupendous growth which made it one of the world's great industrial centres, the economic decline which followed, and the regeneration of the past 20 years which has restored civic pride and made it the European City of Culture in 1990. This has been achieved without losing the strong socialist traditions which are an integral element of city life. Today, this fine Victorian city has strong performing arts, seen at their best during the Mayfest, and excellent museums.

Glasgow was probably founded in the 6th century by St Mungo and received its charter in 1152; it expanded to city status over the next three centuries. The university was founded in 1451 and Glasgow became a busy port, trading linen and manufactured goods with tobacco, then cotton, across the Atlantic. The proximity of coal-fields to the river encouraged iron and steel production and fuelled the city's massive growth during the Industrial Revolution. By the late 19th century Glasgow was known as the Second City of the Empire, hosting international exhibitions in 1888 and 1901. Ship-building and related industries became the basis of the city's wealth; these declined terminally in the mid-20th century, leaving Glasgow an industrial wasteland, with accompanying social problems, by the 1970s. The impressive promotional campaign of the 1980s to restore the city's image has accompanied rebuilding and restoration, which has done much to alleviate past problems. Today, Glasgow faces the future with confidence.

The sprawling city is centred on a grid system around imposing 19th-century George Square, and the adjacent redeveloped Merchant City. To the east lies the cathedral, built from the 12th to the 15th centuries, and the oldest part of the city, including the East End. The western boundary to the city centre is Kelvingrove Park, at the far end of famous Sauchiehall Street. The park contains the Art Gallery and Museum and the imposing neo-Gothic buildings of the main part of the university. The huge Scottish Exhibition and Conference Centre lies to the south, by the river. Other parks ring the city's core, notably Glasgow Green, one of Britain's oldest parks, which contains the People's Palace Museum, devoted to the social history of the city. Glasgow has numerous other museums, galleries and fine buildings; of particular note are the Burrell Museum, housed in a striking modern building south of the river, and the examples of the work of Charles Rennie Mackintosh, particularly the Glasgow School of Art.

Throughout the year Glasgow offers a full range of theatre, music, ballet and opera; the choice of shops, centred on Argyle Street, Buchanan Street and Sauchiehall Street, is the best in Scotland, and there are excellent hotels and restaurants. Football is the major sport, with nine local teams; the passion it evokes is best illustrated by the intense rivalry between Celtic and Rangers.

GLASSON Lancashire SD4456
Village off A588, 4 miles (6km) SW of Lancaster
A recent settlement in the Lune Valley that grew up around Glasson Dock, which first opened in 1787. The Dalton family, who lived at Thurnham Hall, now a country club, played an important part in the development of the town. Many members of the family are buried in the chapter house of Cockersand Abbey, which lies in a remote location southeast of Glasson.

GLASTONBURY Somerset ST5038
Town on A39, 5 miles (8km) S of Wells
A place of ancient legends and mystery, with tales of the Holy Grail and the earliest Christian church in England, King Arthur, and the miraculous Glastonbury thorn which flowers at Christmas.

Glastonbury is a good-looking small market town, full of handsome stone buildings. Many were part of the abbey, including the Tribunal (English Heritage), the 15th-century abbey courthouse (now with a museum on the Iron Age lake villages, see Westhay) and the George and Pilgrims hotel, the 16th-century abbey guest house. The handsome, 15th-century Church of St John is the main town church. There is a pretty market cross of 1846 in the centre, and several 'New Age' shops.

The abbey ruins spread over a large area and are mostly 12th century, with the famous octagonal abbot's kitchen (14th century) and the Holy Thorn Museum. The 14th-century tithe barn is now the Somerset Rural Life Museum, with displays on life in the county. The Chalice Well was the centre of a 18th-century spa, with tales of the Holy Grail grafted on to it.

Glastonbury Tor, 521ft (158m) high, is prominent from miles around, and is topped by the tower of a ruined church. The Somerset Levels (see) extend to the north.

GLATTON Cambridgeshire TL1856
Village on B660, 2 miles (3km) S of Stilton
The splendid 15th-century St Nicholas's Church has a striking tower topped with carvings of the King's Beasts, possibly commemorating the Battle of Agincourt (1415).

GLEMSFORD Suffolk TL8348
Village on B1065, 3 miles (5km) NW of Long Melford
An ancient weaving town once belonging to the bishop who commissioned the Bayeux Tapestry. Cardinal Wolsey's biographer is buried here.

GLEN AFFRIC Highland NH1922
Scenic area off A831, SW of Cannich
Said to be Scotland's loveliest glen, with the tumbling River Glass descending from island-studded Loch Affric through rocky gorges, pine and birch woods.

GLEN ALMOND Tayside NN9128
Scenic area off A822, S of Amulree
Pastoral and agricultural glen reaching from the lower stretches of Sma' Glen almost to Perth. Glenalmond College, a noted boys' public school, is situated here.

GLEN COE Highland NN1557
Scenic and historic area on A82, E of Ballachulish
Glencoe village lies at the west end of the narrow, mountainous and sternly beautiful Glen Coe, a sparsely inhabited glen which today offers outstanding hill-walking and mountaineering. Many famous mountaineers have gained rock and winter mountaineering experience on its demanding peaks. The most noted are the Three Sisters of Glen Coe, with Buachaille Etive Mor being particularly challenging. There is a ski area at the glen's east end.

View of Glen Affric from Loch Benevan.

Glen Coe is mainly renowned for the massacre of 1692, when Alastair MacDonald, chief of a clan notorious for cattle-stealing and unruliness, was late taking an obligatory oath of obedience to William III. This gave the authorities the excuse they wanted to deal with the troublemakers once and for all. Government troops were billeted on the MacDonalds, who entertained them with traditional Highland hospitality for ten days. On the tenth night, in blizzard conditions, the troops turned on their hosts, slaying about 38 and causing more than 300 people to flee into the cold. This act, contrary to all Highland principles of behaviour, was remembered with bitterness for several centuries.

GLEN LYON Tayside
Scenic area off B846, W of Aberfeldy
Scotland's longest glen, with immensely varied mountainous scenery of great beauty. Many prehistoric sites and 16th-century Meggernie Castle situated here. Hydro-electric scheme dam at the western end.

GLEN TANAR Grampian NO4795
Scenic area off B976, SW of Aboyne
Scenically lovely, long, wooded valley in Deeside with exhibitions, ranger services, walks and nature trails at Braeloine Interpretive Centre.

GLENBARR Strathclyde NR6636
Village off A83, 10 miles (16km) N of Machrihanish
Village on the western shores of Kintyre peninsula, with restored Glenbarr Abbey, an 18th-century laird's house with a collection of memorabilia of the once-powerful Clan MacAlister.

GLENBERVIE Grampian NO7680
Village off A90 (A94), 7 miles (11km) SW of Stonehaven
The village, once a weaving centre, is noted as the birthplace of Robert Burns' ancestors, whose tombs lie in the churchyard. There is an annual ploughing competition.

GLENCAPLE Dumfries and Galloway NX9968
Village on B725, 5 miles (8km) S of Dumfries
Sir Walter Scott and Robert Burns are connected with this small sailing resort on the estuary of the River Nith, also known as The Auld Quay.

GLENEAGLES Tayside NN9208
Scenic area on A823, SE of Muirton
Scenic glen in Ochils; 17th-century Gleneagles House was built with an older castle's stones. To the west lies the luxury Gleneagles hotel, with golf courses and many amenities.

GLENELG Highland NG8119
Village off A87, 8 miles (13km) W of Shiel Bridge
Village on an isolated peninsula on the Sound of Sleat, south of Mallaig in magnificent surroundings. The ruins of Bernera Barracks, built after the Jacobite Rising of 1745, are here. Dr Johnson stayed here on his Hebridean journey. Fine Pictish brochs in nearby Glean Beag. Gavin Maxwell wrote *Ring of Bright Water* about neighbouring Sandaig. Ferry to Skye.

GLENFINNAN Highland NM9080
Village on A830, 13 miles (21km) NW of Fort William
Tiny settlement at the northeast end of Loch Shiel, surrounded by mountains and with superb views down the loch. The Glenfinnan Monument commemorates the clansmen from the area who followed Prince Charles Edward during the 1745 Jacobite Rising. It was erected in 1815 on the site where the Prince's standard was raised.

GLENKINDIE Grampian NJ4313
Village on A97, 6 miles (10km) SW of Lumsden
Village in Upper Don Valley. Near by is Glenbuchat Castle, a Z-plan tower house dating from the 1590s, now partly ruinous.

GLENLUCE Dumfries and Galloway NX2057
Village on A75, 9 miles (14km) E of Stranraer
Village with the remains of 12th-century Glenluce Abbey, whose stone was used in the 1590s to build the castellated Castle of Park, on the site of an older tower house.

GLENRIDDING Cumbria NY3817
Village on A592, 1 mile (2km) NW of Patterdale
Village at foot of the Kirkstone Pass as the road descends into the valley towards Ullswater. Start of the Helvellyn Ridge Walk.

GLENROTHES Fife NO2700
New Town on A92, 6 miles (10km) N of Kirkcaldy
Scotland's second New Town was established in 1949 to accomodate the expected increase in the mining community due to the opening of a new coal seam which, in fact, never materialised. The population is mainly employed in light industry. Most of the town dates from the 1960s; mainly low-rise buildings in spacious surroundings with good civic amenities.

GLENTWORTH Lincolnshire SK9488
Village off B1398, 11 miles (18km) N of Lincoln
Below Lincolnshire Cliff. Monument of Sir Christopher Wray, Elizabethan judge and Speaker of House of Commons, lies in church. Hall replaced in 1750s.

GLINTON Cambridgeshire TF1505
Village off A15, 5 miles (8km) NW of Peterborough
Stands in fenland country,with a 17th-century manor house (not open) and some pleasing 17th-century cottages.

GLOMACH, FALLS OF Highland NH0125
Waterfall off A87, 5 miles (8km) NE of Kintail
Scotland's most dramatic falls cascade 370ft (112m) in two streams over a projecting rock into a profound and gloomy chasm. Access on foot only from Morvich Countryside Centre on Kintail.

GLOSSOP Derbyshire SK0393
Town on A57, 13 miles (21km) E of Manchester
Northern Peak District town at the foot of Snake Pass, surrounded by the spectacular moorland scenery of Bleaklow and Kinder Scout. Remains of Melandra Roman fort. Narrow streets and lovely houses in Old

Glossop, mainly 17th century. The Duke of Norfolk built the current town centre in the 1820s and 30s. In the 19th century cotton mills brought the town's growth. Heritage centre. Numerous special events, lively Victorian weekend.

GLOUCESTER Gloucestershire SO8318
City off M5, 32 miles (52km) NE of Bristol
Gloucester is the successor of Roman and Saxon towns, and the church of its Norman abbey was the basis for the cathedral, which retains massive Norman nave piers. They contrast strikingly with the intricate vaulting of the 14th-century choir, which is dominated by England's largest stained-glass window, created in 1349. The north ambulatory houses the tomb of Edward II, interred here after his murder in Berkeley Castle. The south transept is significant as possibly the earliest English essay in the Perpendicular style. There is much more to admire here, including the splendid cloisters and chapter house.

Northgate Street, Eastgate Street, Westgate Street and Southgate Street radiate from the cross, which is still the hub of the city. Prominent in Northgate Street is the New inn, with its galleried courtyard, and it is worth walking on to see the Sainsbury's mural illustrating Gloucester's history. A great attraction in Southgate Street are the animated carved figures over the clockmaker's shop. Almost next door is the Jacobean inn that was the Berkeleys' town residence, and further down is the lovely 15th-century Church of St Mary de Crypt. Southgate Street leads to the docks, once commercially important, being linked to the sea by the Gloucester–Sharpness Canal, and now an attractive business and leisure complex incorporating the old warehouses around the basins, the National Waterways Museum and the entertaining Museum of Advertising and Packaging. The City Museum and Art Gallery, displaying Gloucester's history, can be found in Brunswick Road.

The city's other main attractions are in Westgate Street, notably Bishop Hooper's Lodging, now a Folk Museum, and the Beatrix Potter Centre, in the little house the author chose as the dwelling of her 'Tailor of Gloucester'.

GLYN CEIRIOG Clwyd SJ2037
Village on B4500, 3 miles (5km) S of Llangollen
Former slate-mining village in secluded Vale of Ceiriog. Chwarel Wynne Slate Mine and Museum is a reminder of the past.

GLYNDE East Sussex TQ4509
Village off A27, 3 miles (5km) E of Lewes
Peaceful village beside the River Glynde, under the flank of 491ft (149m) Mount Caburn, a round-topped hill crowned by an Iron Age hillfort with superb views. The extraordinary church of 1763, built in flint in a Grecian style, stands beside the impressive cupola-crowned stables of Elizabethan Glynde Place. John Ellman of Glynde bred the famous Southdown sheep.

GLYNDEBOURNE East Sussex TQ4510
Opera house off B2192, 3 miles (5km) E of Lewes
World-famous opera house set in gardens of Victorian Tudor mansion between Ringmer and Glynde. Opened in 1934. New auditorium built 1992–4, to seat 1,150.

GLYNDYFRDWY Clwyd SJ1542
Village on A5, 4 miles (6km) W of Llangollen
Straddles A5 along shoulder of Vale of Llangollen. The name derives from Owain Glyndwr – his 'mound' (probably his former home) is near by.

GNOSALL Staffordshire SJ8220
Village on A518, 6 miles (10km) W of Stafford
Former industrial village noted for its handbell ringers. Ancient Duke's Head inn, 18th-century lock-up and good medieval church.

GOADBY MARWOOD Leicestershire SK7826
Village off A607, 5 miles (8km) NE of Melton Mowbray
Leicestershire Wolds village, on the route of the Jubilee Way footpath. George Villiers, Duke of Buckingham, spent some of his early years here.

GOATHLAND North Yorkshire NZ8301
Village off A169, 7 miles (11km) SW of Whitby
This picturesque village, high up in the North Yorkshire Moors, has superb examples of stone-built houses. Nearby Mallyan Spout is one of the many waterfalls in the area and just above the village is Moss Swang, a deep and streamless canyon. The North Yorkshire Moors Steam Railway passes through the village.

GOBOWEN Shropshire SJ3033
Village on B5009, 3 miles (5km) N of Oswestry
Victorian railway village with attractive Italianate station. Famous in the medical world as the home of renowned Robert Hunt and Agnes Jones orthopaedic hospital.

GODALMING Surrey SU9643
Town on A3100, 4 miles (6km) SW of Guildford
Still an old-fashioned market town confined in the wooded Wey Valley, with modern development up in the hills. Formerly a very important centre of the Surrey wool industry. The centre has narrow, twisting medieval streets and the High Street features lovely 16th- and 17th-century fronts. Museum in old market hall, 1814. Near by are Busbridge Lakes, with a variety of ornamental wildfowl. Home of Charterhouse School, moved here from London in 1872.

GODMANCHESTER Cambridgeshire TL2470
Small town off A14 (A604), across the Ouse from Huntingdon
A lacey-white Chinese bridge spans the River Great Ouse at Godmanchester, leading to a pleasant lock and the ancient 300 acre (121ha) meadow of Portholme. Godmanchester was important in Roman times, since it was at the junction of three major roads. There are many interesting buildings dotted along old streets, including Island Hall (limited opening), an 18th-century family house.

GODMANSTONE Dorset SY6697
Village on A352, 4 miles (6km) N of Dorchester
The village runs along the River Cerne, with many flint buildings including the thatched Smith's Arms, once a smithy and now supposedly the smallest pub in England.

GODMERSHAM Kent TR0650
Village off A28, 6 miles (10km) NE of Ashford
Tiny place on the River Stour, crossed by a bridge dated 1698. The church, among large old yew trees, was originally Norman, with a unique Norman tower-nave. The big house, Palladian style Godmersham Park (1732) in , was once home to Jane Austen's brother, and the novelist did some of her writing there. Nearby King's Wood covers 1,400 acres (567ha) with waymarked paths.

GODSHILL Isle of Wight SZ5281
Village on A3020, 4 miles (6km) W of Shanklin
The famous picture-postcard view of thatched cottages and church is even better in reality. Many thatched cottages on a surprisingly steep hill. Godshill Model Village. Nostalgia Toy Museum.

GODSTONE Surrey TQ3451
Village on A25, 5 miles (8km) E of Redhill
Attractive crossroads village on greensand ridge with a green, a pond, pretty houses in Church Lane and traditional shops in High Street.

GODSTOW Oxfordshire SP4810
District on NW outskirts of Oxford
Oxonians flock to the popular Trout inn beside the river, and visitors inspect the ruined 15th-century chapel of Godstow Nunnery.

GOG MAGOG HILLS Cambridgeshire TL4953
Hill range off A1307, 4 miles (6km) SE of Cambridge
A chalk grassland site (110 acres/45ha) that includes Wandlebury Iron Age hillfort. The hills rise 300ft (91m) above the flat Cambridgeshire countryside.

GOLANT Cornwall SX1254
Village off B3269, 2 miles (3km) N of Fowey
An interesting church, completed in 1509, and still entirely of that date. Attractive timber roofs. Holy well by the porch.

GOLBORNE Greater Manchester SJ6097
Town off A580, 6 miles (10km) N of Warrington
Older suburb with terraced housing. Golborne Park now a golf course. Culcheth Hall (not open), Georgian home of Culcheth family and then de Traffords.

GOLCAR West Yorkshire SE0915
Village off A62, 3 miles (5km) W of Huddersfield
One of the original weavers' cottages here houses the Colne Valley Museum, which has displays of handweaving and spinning.

GOLDEN VALLEY Hereford and Worcester SO3536
Scenic area along B4347 and B4348, NW of Ewyas Harold
English hills and Welsh mountains flank the River Dore as it links a succession of remote settlements in this beautiful 10 mile (16km) valley.

Old cottages in the village of Godshill.

GOLDERS GREEN Greater London TQ2487
District in borough of Barnet
London's best-known Jewish enclave. Pavlova Museum (limited opening), Ivy House. The ballerina was cremated at Golders Green crematorium, as were Kipling and Freud.

GOLDINGTON Bedfordshire TL0750
District on A428, in E Bedford
Recent housing and high-rises, but some atmosphere survives with the village green and cricket field. Fifteenth-century church enlarged in the 1950s.

GOLDSBOROUGH North Yorkshire SE3856
Village off A59, 2 miles (3km) E of Knaresborough
This was an estate village from the Norman Conquest until 1952, when the land was sold by the present Earl of Harewood.

GOLSPIE Highland NH8399
Village on A9, 7 miles (11km) NE of Dornoch
Administrative centre for Sutherland and a quiet holiday resort with excellent beaches on the North Sea. Baronial Dunrobin Castle, seat of the Dukes of Sutherland, is north of the village, with ornate interior and furnishings. Huge monument to 1st Duke on Beinn a' Bhragaidh behind town, with sweeping views up and down the coast.

GOMERSAL West Yorkshire SE2026
Village on A651, 1 mile (2km) NE of Cleckheaton
Mentioned in Domesday Book when it was owned by Ilbert de Laci. The Methodist church, built in 1827, was known locally as the 'Pork Pie' chapel because of its semi-circular frontage. Charlotte Brontë and John Wesley visited the village, both staying with the Taylor family at Red House.

GOMSHALL Surrey TQ0847
Village on A25, 6 miles (10km) E of Guildford
Houses and shops around a large village green by the River Tillingbourne with a former watermill (wheel in place), now a tea room and craft shop.

GONALSTON Nottinghamshire SK6747
Village off A612, 1 mile (2km) NE of Lowdham
Trent Valley village with a 19th-century hall and estate cottages. Robert Blincoe's apprentice treatment at a 1790s cotton mill led to legislation for improved conditions.

GOOD EASTER Essex TL6212
Village off A1060, 2 miles (3km) E of Leaden Roding
Farming, commuter and retirement village which, in 1985, made the world-record daisy chain, 6,980ft 7in (2,122m) long. For the name, see High Easter.

GOODERSTONE Norfolk TF7602
Village off A134, 4 miles (6km) E of Stoke Ferry
Village noted for its beautiful water gardens, complete with meandering grassy paths, nature walks and aviary.

GOODMANHAM Humberside SE8843
Village off A1079, 1 mile (2km) NE of Market Weighton
The ancient name of the village was Godmundingaham which is derived from the Celtic 'godo', an uncovered sanctuary or temple and 'mynyddis', a hilly place. The ancient Britons had a Druidic temple here and the present village may have been the site of the Roman station Delgovitia. All Hallows' Church dates from the beginning of the 11th century.

GOODNESTONE Kent TR2554
Village off B26046, 2 miles (3km) S of Wingham
The village lies in the great park of Goodnestone House, with gardens, including a walled garden, woodland garden and arboretum, open to the public.

GOODRICH Hereford and Worcester SO5719
Village on B4228, 4 miles (6km) SW of Ross-on-Wye
The extensive remains of a formidable medieval castle (English Heritage) rise from solid rock on a sandstone bluff commanding the Wye Valley.

GOODRINGTON Devon SX8958
Village on B319, 1 mile (2km) S of Paignton
Really part of Paignton, this is mostly a 20th-century seaside development, with the low rocky cliffs interspersed with sandy bays.

GOODSHAW Lancashire SD8125
Village on A682, 2 miles (3km) N of Rawtenstall
Recently restored Baptist chapel was originally built in 1760. Visits to the building can be arranged by local tourist information centre.

GOODWIN SANDS Kent
Sandbanks off E coast of Kent, around Deal
Extensive and dangerous shoal 5 miles (8km) off the east coast of Kent opposite Deal and Sandwich, said to be the drowned remnants of the lost land of Loomea.

GOODWOOD West Sussex SU8808
Mansion off A286, 3 miles (5km) NE of Chichester
This grand 18th-century house, high on the South Downs, is surrounded by a 12,000 acre (4,860ha) estate containing a country park and racecourse. The racecourse, founded in 1801, 500ft (152m) up, hosts 18 flat-racing days a year. The fashionable Glorious Goodwood meeting is held in July. Near by is The Trundle, an Iron Age fort enclosing an older neolithic causeway camp, formerly the site of a medieval chapel and windmill.

GOOLE Humberside SE7423
Town on A161, 23 miles (37km) W of Hull
Goole owes its growth to the Aire and Calder Navigation Company who cut the canal in 1826 linking the West Riding with the River Ouse. They built the system of docks, locks and canal basins. The port is still active and the docks are dominated by the 'Salt and Pepper Pot' water-towers.

GOONHAVERN Cornwall SW7853
Village on A3075, 2 miles (3km) E of Perranporth
Attractions include the World in Miniature model village, and Wild West town and gardens.

GOONHILLY DOWNS Cornwall SW7319
Scenic area off B3293, 5 miles (8km) SE of Helston
Open moorland of sedge and heather on the Lizard peninsula, with the four huge satellite dishes of Goonhilly Satellite Earth Station and a wind farm (see Gunwalloe).

GOOSEY Oxfordshire SU3591
Village off A417, 4 miles (6km) NW of Wantage
Pleasant houses line the wide green of this small settlement in the Vale of White Horse, where the medieval church retains its stone slates.

GOOSNARGH Lancashire SD5536
Village off B5269, 3 miles (5km) W of Longridge
Prosperous village with church dated 1333 and adjacent Georgian almshouse. Chingle Hall, a medieval manor house, is said to be one of the most haunted houses in Britain.

GORDON Borders NT6443
Village on A6089, 8 miles (13km) NW of Kelso
Small village north of Mellerstain House, a fine Adam mansion with superb interior and terraced gardens. The 16th-century L-plan Greenknow Tower lies to the north.

GOREBRIDGE Lothian NT3461
Town off A7, 4 miles (6km) S of Dalkeith
Small town near which stands Arniston House, the Dundas family seat, a fine William Adam mansion commissioned in 1725.

GOREY Channel Islands (Jersey) SY2110
Village on A3, NE of St Helier
Quaint and quiet, with a row of shops and pubs ringing the harbour. Above, Mont Orgueil Castle has a magnificent 13th-century keep (limited opening).

GORING Oxfordshire SU6081
Town on A329, 9 miles (14km) NW of Reading
At the wooded Goring Gap the River Thames passes between the Chiltern Hills and the Berkshire Downs. This idyllic spot began to attract new residents in the Victorian era. Their legacy is a line of palatial riverside houses. Many more houses have appeared since, but the old town centre with fine medieval church and almshouses preserves its appeal.

GORING-BY-SEA West Sussex TQ1102
Town on A259, immediately W of Worthing
Now a suburb of Worthing, with a few older buildings stranded amid the 20th-century developments. The church was rebuilt in 1837 by Decimus Burton.

GORLESTON ON SEA Norfolk TG5203
Town on B1370, immediately S of Great Yarmouth
Standing near the mouth of the River Yare, Gorleston on Sea is a town richly imbued with the atmosphere of an old Norfolk seaport. Small streets wind away from the quayside, which houses a lifeboat station with more than its share of heroic rescues. The Gorleston Psalter is a 14th-century book now on display in the British Museum.

GORRAN HAVEN Cornwall SX0141
Village off B3273, 2 miles (3km) SW of Mevagissey
A small and unspoiled fishing village in a rocky bay with Dodman Point, a prominent headland with wide views, to the south.

GOSBERTON Lincolnshire TF2331
Village on A16, 6 miles (10km) N of Spalding
At busy meeting of Grantham, Boston and Spalding roads. Large airy 14th- and 15th-century church with central tower and crocketed spire.

GOSFIELD Essex TL7829
Village on A1017, 4 miles (6km) NE of Braintree
There's water-skiing, speed-boat riding, fishing and camping at Gosfield Lake Leisure Resort on the county's largest freshwater lake. This is in the grounds of Gosfield Hall (limited opening), a Tudor house remodelled in the 19th century by Samuel Courtauld, the textile magnate of Bocking (see). Courtauld also built attractive mock Tudor houses in the village.

GOSFORTH Cumbria NY0603
Village off A595, 5 miles (8km) NW of Ravenglass
Gosforth Cross, the tallest sandstone monolith in Britain, is carved with both Norse and Christian symbols. There is also a Viking 'fishing stone' and Viking carved stones built into a toolshed, now a Listed Building. The oldest building dates back to 1628, and now houses the library and Supper Room.

GOSFORTH Tyne and Wear NZ2468
Town on A191, immediately N of Newcastle
Mainly residential suburb in rural setting. High Gosforth Park includes a racecourse and a nature reserve.

GOSPORT Hampshire SZ6199
Town on A32, 5 miles (8km) SE of Fareham
On the opposite side of the tight harbour mouth from Portsmouth, the town centre is mostly modern. Passenger ferries run to Portsmouth. Holy Trinity Church has an elaborate organ once used by Handel. The navy's victualling department moved here in 1828, to Weevil Lane. Royal Naval Submarine Museum at Haslar. Gosport Museum. Haslar Hospital (not open) built for the royal navy in 1754, then the largest hospital and the largest brick building in Europe. Fort Brockhurst (English Heritage) is one of a chain built to defend Gosport in 1850s.

GOTHAM Nottinghamshire SK5330
Village off A453, 6 miles (10km) N of Loughborough
Small village below ridge of Gotham Hill. The Wise Men of Gotham tried to rake the moon from a pond and other feigned stupidities to deter the king from taking over their property.

GOUDHURST Kent TQ7237
Village on A262, 4 miles (6km) NW of Cranbrook
A popular and picturesque hilltop village in the High Weald, set among the orchards and hopfields. High Street has attractive tile-hung, weatherboarded and timbered houses and a village pond replete with ducks of several

kinds, including muscovies. Smuggling was rife here in the 18th century and the Star and Eagle pub is said to have a secret passage connecting it to the church. Nearby Finchcocks has a museum of keyboard instruments.

GOUROCK Strathclyde NS2477
Town on A770, 2 miles (3km) W of Greenock
A resort, port and yachting centre, the base for Caledonian MacBrayne, the largest ferry operator in Scotland. Walter Gibson pioneered the curing of red herring-kippers here.

GOVAN Strathclyde NS5565
District in W Glasgow, on River Clyde
Ancient handloom weaving village which became a major Clydeside industrial centre with productive collieries, shipyards and steelworks, now all in decline.

GOWER West Glamorgan SS4889
Scenic area W of Swansea
The stubby Gower peninsula, jutting 14 miles (23km) into Carmarthen Bay from Swansea, was in 1956 the first official Area of Outstanding Natural Beauty. The peninsula's unspoilt coastline has two distinct sides to its personality. In the south and southwest towering limestone cliffs are broken by a succession of sheltered sandy bays. North Gower, in contrast, has a low-lying coastline fringed with saltings and marshland.

The most spectacular part of the peninsula lies in the far west around Rhossili, where the land ends in the narrow promontory of Worms Head. To the north are the dunes of Whiteford Burrows, the transition zone between spectacular and sedate Gower.

Most visitors head for south Gower. The main beaches here can become busy on summer weekends, although those prepared to walk – no hardship, for the coast paths along the cliffs are a joy in themselves – will find a quieter spot. Unexplored north Gower should not be ignored. There are atmospheric views across the peaceful saltings from ruined Weobley Castle, while further east the sands at Penclawdd are still scoured by the village's hardy cockle-pickers.

GOYT, RIVER Derbyshire
River rises in Peak District, tributary of the Mersey
From Axe Edge, the River Goyt flows through Errwood and Fernilee reservoirs in the wooded Goyt Valley, Whaley Bridge and New Mills, before joining the River Tame at Stockport to form the River Mersey.

GRAFHAM WATER Cambridgeshire TL1669
Reservoir off B661, 5 miles (8km) SW of Huntingdon
A man-made reservoir providing a nature reserve, walks, bird-watching hides, fishing and watersports.

GRAFTON REGIS Northamptonshire SP7546
Village on A508, 5 miles (8km) NW of Stony Stratford
'Regis' marks the secret royal marriage of Edward IV to Elizabeth Woodville, whose manor house site is near the Grand Union Canal and the River Tove.

GRAFTON UNDERWOOD Northamptonshire SP9280
Village off A14, 4 miles (6km) E of Kettering
Peaceful village with a stream running through it. American Air Force World War II base, commemorated in roadside memorial and church window.

GRAIG Gwynedd SH8071
Hamlet off A470, 5 miles (8km) SW of Colwyn Bay
Hamlet next to Bodnant Garden (National Trust), Wales's finest formal garden. Terraces, woodlands, lawns, flower beds situated above the Conwy Valley.

GRAIN, ISLE OF Kent TQ8775
Island on A228, off N coast of Kent
Northern tip of the flat and windswept Hoo peninsula at the confluence of the Thames and Medway estuaries. The seaside village of Grain is noted for its oil refinery.

GRAINTHORPE Lincolnshire TF3897
Village on A1031, 7 miles (11km) NE of Louth
Straggling Lincolnshire marsh village, with Georgian brick hall. Wide church with tall tower, brick flooring and wall panelling from box pews.

GRAMPIAN MOUNTAINS Grampian
Mountain range in Scotland
High grass- and heather-covered mountain range stretching across the Highlands from Aberdeen in the northeast to Perthshire and Argyll in the west.

GRANDBOROUGH Warwickshire SP4966
Village off A45, 5 miles (8km) S of Rugby
The village, with its medieval church, stands in watery countryside. To the southeast, beside the Grand Union Canal, is the deserted village of Wolfhamcote.

GRANGE (GRANGE-IN-BORROWDALE) Cumbria NY2517
Hamlet on B5289, 5 miles (8km) S of Keswick
Just outside Borrowdale at the head of Derwentwater. A great double-arched bridge stretches more than 100yds (91m) over the River Derwent. Castle Crag (National Trust) is a famous viewpoint at the Jaws of Borrowdale. Grange Fell includes the hill King's How, 1,363ft (415m), and the Bowder Stone, a huge Ice Age granite mass.

GRANGE-OVER-SANDS Cumbria SD4077
Small town on B5277, 2 miles (3km) SE of Cartmel
Grange-over-Sands is Cumbria's riviera and came into being with the coming of the railway. It has a long Promenade, ornamental gardens and a well-preserved station. The sands here are treacherous and there is an official guide to help those who want to cross them. Climate said to be the mildest in the north of England.

GRANGEMOUTH Central NS9281
Town on A904, 3 miles (5km) E of Falkirk
Major industrial centre and important port since the 1770s. Mainly noted today for chemicals, pipelines and oil refineries.

GRANSDEN, GREAT AND LITTLE Cambridgeshire TL2755
Villages on B1046, 5 miles (8km) NE of Potton
Twin villages near Ermine Street. Great Gransden has a 1674 post mill, and a tract of ancient woodland cared for by the Cambridgeshire Wildlife Trust.

GRANTCHESTER Cambridgeshire TL4355
Village off A603, 2 miles (3km) SW of Cambridge
Immortalised by World War I poet Rupert Brooke, this sleepy little village sits on the meadows by the River Cam, or Granta as it is known locally. Black and white timbered buildings, an abundance of thatched roofs and a photogenic church standing amid time-worn tombs complete the picture in this most English of English villages.

GRANTHAM Lincolnshire SK9135
Town off A1, 21 miles (34km) NW of Stamford
Scientist Sir Isaac Newton and first woman Prime Minister Margaret Thatcher (née Roberts) both have strong connections with this market and industrial town, and feature in displays in the museum. The Roberts' grocer's shop on North Parade became a restaurant, then a chiropractor's. Sir Isaac Newton, born at nearby Woolsthorpe Manor near Colsterworth (see), was educated at the King's School, and his name has been given, perhaps incongruously, to the 1980s shopping centre.

The magnificent St Wulfram's Church neighbouring the school has changed little since Newton's day, with a late 16th-century chained library above the south porch. The splendid spire, rising to a height of 282ft (86m), greets visitors to the town, formerly an important staging post on the Great North road. The medieval Angel and Royal hotel, where King John held court in 1213, and Richard III signed Buckingham's death warrant, was Knights Templar property and continues to offer hospitality today. Another coaching inn, the George, patronised by Dickens, has been converted to pleasant shopping facilities. Grantham House (National Trust, by appointment), 1380 and later, has walled gardens down to the River Witham.

GRANTOWN-ON-SPEY Highland NJ0328
Town on A939, 19 miles (31km) S of Forres
Attractive granite-built Georgian town with a spacious central square in pretty countryside, founded in 1776 by local landowner Sir James Grant. Nowadays this is a major Speyside tourist centre. Old Spey Bridge (1754) crosses the notable salmon river. The railway arrived in 1863 and the town developed as a Victorian health/holiday resort; today it has been somewhat superseded by Aviemore's development.

GRAPPENHALL Cheshire SJ6486
Village on A56, 3 miles (5km) SE of Warrington
The Bridgewater Canal is cut in a loop around the village, and the old part of the village is reached by two hump-backed bridges.

GRASMERE Cumbria NY3307
Village off A591, 3 miles (5km) NW of Ambleside
Famous as the home of William Wordsworth. His house, Dove Cottage, is now a museum dedicated to his life and work and open to the public. Grasmere Lake, on the edge of the village, has an island. The village itself dates from Saxon times and the church is dedicated to the Northumbrian king, St Oswald.

GRASSHOLM Dyfed SM5909
Island 8 miles (12km) W of Skomer
Smallest and most remote of the three Norse-named islands off southwest Pembrokeshire. Famous for its gannet colony, reputedly one of the world's largest.

GRASSINGTON North Yorkshire SE0063
Village on B6265, 8 miles (13km) N of Skipton
One of the best-loved villages of the Yorkshire Dales, parts of which are a conservation area. The village grew in the late 18th century as a result of the lead-mining in the area. The Feast Sports, on a Saturday in October, include many traditional events, especially the 'tea cake eating race'.

GRAVENHURST, UPPER AND LOWER Bedfordshire TL1136
Villages off A600, 3 miles (5km) SW of Shefford
Twin settlements on hills. Redundant little 14th-century church in Lower Gravenhurst has Civil War bullet marks on door.

GRAVESEND Kent TQ6474
Town on A226, 7 miles (11km) NW of Rochester
Busy, noisy, bustling town by the River Thames, where it narrows to become 'London River', and coastal pilots hand over control of their ships to river pilots. It has a long seafaring history and fleets were assembled here in Elizabethan times. Today, sailing clubs keep up the tradition; museum, leisure centre and old-fashioned daily market.

GRAYS (OR GRAYS THURROCK) Essex TQ6177
Town off A13, 2 miles (3km) NW of Tilbury
Busy commercial centre and headquarters of Thurrock borough. Many 1930s and post-war housing estates and high-rise blocks. Thurrock Museum features local history.

GREASBY Merseyside SJ2587
Town on B5139, 4 miles (6km) W of Birkenhead
A small agricultural community that has grown since the 1940s as new housing estates have been built.

GREASLEY Nottinghamshire SK4947
Hamlet on B600, 2 miles (3km) E of Eastwood
In DH Lawrence country. Scanty 14th-century castle remains incorporated into farmhouse. John Robinson, Pilgrim Fathers' pastor, married a local girl here.

GREAT ALNE Warwickshire SP1159
Village on B4089, 2 miles (3km) NE of Alcester
Mother Huff Cap inn welcomes visitors to this pleasant village. Restored watermill on River Alne (not open). Fine views from Alne Hills near by.

GREAT AMWELL Hertfordshire TL3712
Village off A1170, 1 mile (2km) S of Ware
A delightful sylvan and watery spot at one of the sources of the New River (see), with urns on the islands gracefully honouring its presiding genius, Sir Hugh Myddelton, placed here in 1800 by architect Robert Mylne. The striking Mylne family tomb is in the nearby churchyard of St John the Baptist, the Norman church. The village is expensive commuter territory.

GREAT AYTON North Yorkshire NZ5610
Village on A173, 5 miles (8km) SW of Guisborough
This is the most northerly village in the county. It lies on the Captain Cook Heritage Trail .

GREAT BADMINTON Avon ST8082
see Badminton

GREAT BARDFIELD Essex TL6730
Village on B1057, 2 miles (3km) SW of Finchingfield
On the River Pant, this exceptionally attractive village has handsome houses in half-timbering and Georgian brick, a Quaker meeting house of 1804, an 1850s town hall and a 19th-century village lock-up (limited opening). Corn dollies are shown in the 16th-century almshouse, now the Cottage Museum of domestic and farming bygones. An artists' colony here in the 1950s was led by Edward Bawden.

GREAT BARFORD Bedfordshire TL1351
Village on A428, 3 miles (5km) NW of Sandy
Dormitory village on the River Great Ouse, with 17-arched bridge going back to the 15th century and an imposing church. Riverside walks.

GREAT BARR West Midlands SP0495
District on A34, in West Bromwich
Old village engulfed by West Bromwich. Bishop Asbury Cottage (limited opening), Newton Road, was the boyhood home of the first American Methodist bishop.

GREAT BARRINGTON Gloucestershire SP2012
see Barrington

GREAT BEDWYN Wiltshire SU2764
Village off A4, 5 miles (8km) SW of Hungerford
A village now, Great Bedwyn was a town in medieval times and has a large 12th- to 13th-century church. Mason's Yard is decorated all over with old stone carvings and houses the Bedwyn Stone Museum.

GREAT BENTLEY Essex TM1021
Village off A133, 6 miles (10km) NW of Clacton
England's largest village green, over 40 acres (16ha) of it, with cottages distantly in view. Fine peal of bells in Norman church.

GREAT BIRCHAM Norfolk TF7632
Village on B1153, 3 miles (5km) S of Docking
Near the Sandringham estate, Great Bircham boasts an art gallery, sculpture garden, and a fine old corn mill. Houghton Hall is 3 miles (5km) away.

GREAT BOOKHAM Surrey TQ1354
Village on A246, 2 miles (3km) SW of Leatherhead
Pleasant village with old cottages and houses including Fairfield House, High Street, where Fanny Burney wrote *Camilla*. Interesting church, begun in the late 11th century, enlarged over the years and noted for fine monuments. Near by is Polesden Lacey (National Trust), a fine Regency house of 1824, once owned by playwright Sheridan, containing paintings, porcelain, and furniture. Bookham Common (National Trust) covers 450 acres (182ha).

GREAT BRICETT Suffolk TM0350
Village on B1078, 5 miles (8km) N of Hadleigh
Long Norman Church of St Mary and St Lawrence is joined to a farmhouse thought to date from 1250. There was an Augustinian priory here.

GREAT BRINGTON Northamptonshire SP6665
Village off A428, 6 miles (10km) NW of Northampton
Attractive village to the west of Althorp, family home of the Spencers. The house, set in secluded parkland, was built in 1508 by Sir John Spencer, altered by Henry Holland 1790, and has a wealth of paintings, porcelain and other treasures. Splendid range of monuments from the 16th to the 20th centuries commemorating this influential family in the Spencer chapel of the village church.

GREAT BROMLEY Essex TM0826
Village on B1029, 6 miles (10km) E of Colchester
Scattered village with one of Essex's finest churches. Splendid tower, double hammerbeam nave roof and notable brass of priest in vestments.

GREAT BUDWORTH Cheshire SJ6677
Village off A559, 2 miles (3km) N of Northwich
One of Cheshire's prettiest villages with little-changed cottages and a 14th-century church. Arley Hall is an early Victorian mansion house with 12 acres (5ha) of gardens. Still a private residence but open to the public. Budworth Mere, part of Marbury Country Park, is popular with bird-watchers.

GREAT BURDON Durham NZ3116
Hamlet off A66, 2 miles (3km) NE of Darlington
Mill Batts Farm in the village dates back to the 12th century. Until the 1920s a mill race diverted the River Skerne to work the mill.

GREAT BURSTEAD Essex TQ6892
Suburb off A176, 1 mile (2km) S of Billericay
Above the River Crouch. Originally a more important place than Billericay, but now its satellite. Norman church with elegant 18th-century reredos.

GREAT CANFIELD Essex TL5918
Hamlet off B184, 3 miles (5km) SW of Great Dunmow
On the River Roding. Norman church has moving medieval wall-painting of the Virgin and Child. Mound of former castle close by.

GREAT CASTERTON Leicestershire TF0008
Village off A1, 2 miles (3km) NW of Stamford
This was a Stone Age and important Roman settlement where Ermine Street entered Rutland, crossing the River Gwash. Finds from the Roman farmstead, military fort, pottery kiln and cemetery are on display in the Rutland County Museum in Oakham (see). The 'peasant poet', John Clare, married and wrote about local farmer's daughter 'sweet Patty of the Vale'.

GREAT CHALFIELD Wiltshire ST8663
see Chalfield

GREAT CHESTERFORD Essex TL5042
see Chesterford

GREAT COMBERTON Hereford and Worcester SO9542
see Comberton

GREAT COXWELL Oxfordshire SU2693
Village off A420, 2 miles (3km) SW of Faringdon
'Noble as a cathedral' said William Morris of Great Coxwell's huge early 13th-century tithe barn (National Trust).

GREAT CRESSINGHAM Norfolk TF8700
see Cressingham

GREAT DRIFFIELD Humberside TA0257
Town off A166, 11 miles (18km) SW of Bridlington
This agricultural town is known as the 'capital of the Wolds'. The oldest part of the town is Moot Hill which was the meeting place of the Saxon 'Town Moot'. An annual agricultural show has been held here since 1854 and there is a cattle market on Thursdays. The Driffield Canal was opened in 1772.

GREAT DUNMOW Essex TL6222
Town on A120, 9 miles (14km) E of Bishop's Stortford
Known for the Dunmow Flitch of bacon, awarded in leap years to idyllically married couples. The custom died out in the 18th century but was revived in 1855 (see also Little Dunmow). This pleasant old town's New Street was new in the 14th century. Medieval church and Tudor market square. The first self-righting lifeboat was tested out on Doctor's Pond.

GREAT DURNFORD Wiltshire SU1338
Village off A345, 5 miles (8km) N of Salisbury
Flint, stone and brick village with lots of thatched cottages and an 18th-century brick manor house (not open) up by the Norman church.

GREAT ECCLESTON Lancashire SD4240
Village on A586, 5 miles (8km) E of Poulton-le-Fylde
An agricultural community on the River Wyre, the village was known as 'Little London' because it was a social centre for the area.

GREAT GLEMHAM Suffolk TM3461
Village off B1119, 3 miles (5km) W of Saxmundham
A compact village with some handsome buildings, next to the Earl of Cranbrook's estate. The airfield control tower is a war memorial.

GREAT GRANSDEN Cambridgeshire TL2755
see Gransden

GREAT HAMPDEN Buckinghamshire SP8401
Village off A413, 3 miles (5km) E of Princes Risborough
Cottages, village green, and the Hampden Arms. Church in Hampden House grounds, with monuments including one to John Hampden, noted 17th-century Parliamentarian.

GREAT HARWOOD Lancashire SD7332
Town off A680, 4 miles (6m) NE of Blackburn
The town was famous for its textile industry, both wool and cotton, and as the place where John Mercer invented the mercerisation process (technique to give greater strength and shine to material).

GREAT HASELEY Oxfordshire SP6401
Village off A329, 5 miles (8km) SW of Thame
An appealing place where a manor house, an exceptional medieval church and a tithe barn stand around a green, close to attractive stone and timber-framed cottages.

GREAT HAYWOOD Staffordshire SJ9922
Village on A51, 4 miles (6km) NW of Rugeley
The longest packhorse bridge in England spans the River Trent close to this village re-sited by the Ansons of Shugborough. Junction of two popular canals.

GREAT HOCKHAM Norfolk TL9592
Village on A1075, 6 miles (10km) W of Attleborough
A compact Breckland village centred around a triangular green. The church is a short distance away in the grounds of Hockham Hall (not open).

GREAT HORWOOD Buckinghamshire SP7731
Village on B4033, 2 miles (3km) N of Winslow
Attractive thatched and brick cottages, many built after a bad 1781 fire. Housing estate on part of wartime RAF airfield.

GREAT HUCKLOW Derbyshire SK1777
Village off B6049, 2 miles (3km) NE of Tideswell
This Peak District village was the improbable setting for live theatre (1920s–70s), in a former lead-smelting mill. Gliders fly from Hucklow Edge.

GREAT KIMBLE Buckinghamshire SP8205
Village on A4010, 2 miles (3km) NE of Princes Risborough
At foot of Chilterns. Views from prehistoric hillfort up on Pulpit Hill, part of a nature reserve with Grangelands chalk downs.

GREAT LEIGHS Essex TL7217
Village on A131, 4 miles (6km) SW of Braintree
On a stretch of Roman road, later the pilgrim route to Canterbury. Norman church with round tower. Essex County Show held here.

GREAT LINFORD Buckinghamshire SP8542
Village off A422, 2 miles (3km) E of Wolverton (part of Milton Keynes)
Nestled between the A422 road and the Grand Union Canal, the village has been skilfully integrated into Milton Keynes (see) and retains a distinct identity with its green and plenty of trees and paths. Canal towpath walks and ancient church. Landscaped grounds of 17th-century Linford Manor now a public park; 17th-century almshouses have been converted into an arts centre.

GREAT LONGSTONE Derbyshire SK2071
Village off B6465, 2 miles (3km) NW of Bakewell
A stone-built Peak District village with a small green, below Longstone Edge. Attractive hall of brick, used unusually early for this area (1747).

GREAT LUMLEY Durham NZ2949
Small Town off B1284, 2 miles (3km) SE of Chester-le-Street
Once a busy mining village, most of the old village has disappeared and been replaced by modern housing.

GREAT MALVERN Hereford and Worcester SO7845
Town on A449, 7 miles (12km) SW of Worcester
Malvern progressed from village to popular 19th-century spa by heavily promoting its exceptionally pure water and the invigorating fresh air of its hills. The result was an influx not only of tourists but of residents, and this accounts for the pleasingly Victorian character of the town centre, visible in leafy avenues of florid villas, the former Imperial hotel and the ornate railway station, now restored. Earlier architecture, and some original spa buildings can be seen in Belle Vue Terrace above the priory, and the spa character is reinforced by pleasant green spaces such as Priory Gardens and the Winter Gardens.

The Festival Theatre was noted in the 1930s for first performances of several George Bernard Shaw plays. The noble 15th-century tower of the priory, now the parish church, dominates the town centre. Within is a fine Norman nave and 15th-century chancel housing many treasures, including entertaining misericords, splendid medieval glass and a vast array of medieval tiles. Malvern's history is explained at a museum in Abbey Gateway.

Of the other settlements around the hills, Malvern Link, West Malvern and Malvern Wells all have good Victorian churches.

GREAT MASSINGHAM Norfolk TF7922
Village off B1145, 9 miles (14km) N of Swaffham
This picturesque village centres around two ponds and the vast village green. Flint-built houses radiate away from the green.

GREAT MILTON Oxfordshire SP6202
Village off A329, 8 miles (13km) SE of Oxford
Handsome houses, the thatched Bull inn and a church of outstanding interest form the heart of this picturesque village overlooking Thame Valley.

GREAT MISSENDEN Buckinghamshire SP8901
Village on A4128, 4 miles (6km) W of Chesham
Former coaching stop alive with inns which developed into commuter settlement after railway's arrival in 1892. High Street of shops and old houses from 16th century on, many with 18th-century fronts. Half-timbered 16th-century extension tucked away in courtyard of George inn. Isolated church across the A413. Village merges into housing estates of Prestwood.

GREAT MITTON Lancashire SD7138
Village on B6246, 3 miles (5km) SW of Clitheroe
An unspoilt village on the River Ribble. Great Mitton Hall is a fine example of a Tudor, or early Stuart, building.

GREAT OFFLEY (OR OFFLEY) Hertfordshire TL1427
Village off A505, 3 miles (5km) SW of Hitchin
Old houses and a church partly rebuilt in 18th century by Sir Thomas Salusbury with a grandiloquent monument.

GREAT OUSE, RIVER Bedfordshire
River
Rising near Towcester, the river follows a winding course through Buckingham, Bedford, Huntingdon, St Ives and Ely to King's Lynn and the Wash.

GREAT PACKINGTON Warwickshire SP2283
see Packington

GREAT PAXTON Cambridgeshire TL2063
Village on B1043, 3 miles (5km) N of St Neots
The outstanding feature of this village on the River Great Ouse is its cruciform Saxon church, one of the first to be built in England.

GREAT ROLLRIGHT Oxfordshire SP3231
Village off A3400, 3 miles (5km) N of Chipping Campden
This attractive hill village on the Cotswold fringe preserves a church with superb Norman and medieval carving. (See Little Rollright for Rollright Stones.)

GREAT SALKELD Cumbria NY5536
see Salkeld

GREAT SANKEY Cheshire SJ5688
District in W Warrington
A large urban parish on the western edge of Warrington. Sankey Valley Park runs through the parish.

GREAT SAXHAM Suffolk TL8063
see Saxham

GREAT SHEFFORD Berkshire SU3875
Village on A338, 5 miles (8km) NE of Hungerford
In the Lambourn Valley, with a small church which has the only round tower in the county.

GREAT SNORING Norfolk TF9532
see Snoring

GREAT STAMBRIDGE Essex TQ8991
Village off B1013, 2 miles (3km) E of Rochford
On the River Roach. John Winthrop, the first Governor of Massachusetts, lived here before sailing to America. Memorial window in church.

GREAT STRETTON Leicestershire SK6500
Deserted village off A6, 2 miles (3km) N of Great Glen
Great in name only. Earthworks of deserted village remain around the church, rebuilt in 1838. Stretton Hall (18th century) became a hospital. Private flying at Leicester Airport.

GREAT TEW Oxfordshire SP3929
Village on B4022, 5 miles (8km) E of Chipping Norton
Idyllic 'model' estate village for Tew Park offers an absorbing church, picturesque restored cottages, a 17th-century pub and a glimpse of the fine manor house.

GREAT TEY Essex TL8925
Village off A120, 7 miles (11km) W of Colchester
Tremendous Norman tower, using many Roman bricks, distinguishes the Church of St Barnabas in this otherwise unremarkable Essex village.

GREAT THURLOW Suffolk TL6751
see Thurlow

GREAT TORRINGTON Devon SS4919
Town on A386, 5 miles (8km) SE of Bideford
Dramatically sited market town with a steep cliff down to the River Torridge. Classical town hall and pannier market in the dense centre, where there is also a small museum. In the lower part is Dartington Crystal, with displays of glass-making. Rosemoor Garden, 1 mile (2km) southeast, is being expanded by the Royal Horticultural Society to include rose, bog and many other gardens. Great Torrington Steam Railway.

GREAT WAKERING Essex TQ9487
Village on B1017, 2 miles (3km) N of Shoeburyness
Claimed to be the United Kingdom's driest place, with under 20in (51cm) of average annual rainfall.

GREAT WALSINGHAM Norfolk TF9336
see Little Walsingham

GREAT WALTHAM Essex TL6913
Village off A130, 4 miles (6km) N of Chelmsford
Commuter village swollen after the war, but still has attractive old houses. Sizeable church with Norman tower, and an Elizabethan guildhall.

GREAT WARLEY Essex TQ5890
Village on B186, 2 miles (3km) SW of Brentwood
Edwardian church by Harrison Townsend with remarkable art nouveau interior and glass by Heywood Sumner. Old houses in the village.

GREAT WELDON Northamptonshire SP9289
see Weldon

GREAT WENHAM Suffolk TM0839
see Wenham

GREAT WISHFORD Wiltshire SU0735
Village off A36, 3 miles (5km) N of Wilton
A pretty village of cob and thatched cottages, Georgian brick houses and a school of 1722. Stone almshouses date from 1628. There are great celebrations on Oak Apple Day (29 May), asserting local rights to firewood from Groveley Wood.

GREAT WITCHINGHAM Norfolk TG1020
Hamlet off A1067, 2 miles (3km) S of Reepham
Lying to the north of the River Wensum, this pleasant village has a disused mill, some excellent fishing, and Elizabethan Great Witchingham Hall. Norfolk Wildlife Park has British and European animals.

GREAT WITCOMBE Gloucestershire SO9114
Village off A417, 6 miles (10km) SE of Gloucester
Accessible ruins of a Roman villa lie close to Witcombe Park's charming estate village with its Norman and medieval church.

GREAT WITLEY Hereford and Worcester SO7566
Village on A443, 5 miles (8km) SW of Stourport-on-Severn
Two astonishing buildings here. Under successive owners Witley Court became one of biggest houses in Europe but was left to deteriorate after fire in 1937. The ruins have now been made safe and opened by English Heritage. Huge garden fountains should not be missed. Near by is St Michael's, an extravagantly baroque family chapel, with magnificent plasterwork and a painted ceiling.

GREAT WYMONDLEY Hertfordshire TL2128
Village off A602, 2 miles (3km) E of Hitchin
A small place with the earthworks of a vanished Norman castle. The Norman church survives.

GREAT WYRLEY Staffordshire SJ9907
Town on A34, 2 miles (3km) S of Cannock
Neat modern housing estates have replaced the haphazard buildings of this old industrial settlement on the northern edge of a Black Country conurbation.

GREAT YARMOUTH Norfolk TG5207
Town on A47, 18 miles (29km) E of Norwich
Great Yarmouth remained a flourishing port for more than 1,000 years, providing a safe natural harbour behind a spit of land which juts out into the heaving waters of the North Sea. Then, in the 19th century, it was discovered by the Victorians who quickly developed this peaceful little seaside town into a popular holiday resort.

The old part of Great Yarmouth has one of the most attractive waterfronts in England, with an intriguing array of architectural styles jostling for space. Medieval timber-framed merchants' houses rub shoulders with great 19th-century warehouses, while colourful pleasure crafts bob up and down in the water in front of them.

Behind the quay are neatly organised alleys and courtyards known as The Rows, a grid arrangement that dates from medieval times. Although The Rows were badly damaged during World War II, several remain and have been carefully restored. The Old Merchant's House (English Heritage) in Row 117 has displays of 17th- and 18th-century carvings, while the 13th-century tollhouse is said to be the one of the oldest civic buildings in England.

Other interesting buildings include the Tudor house where Anna Sewell, the author of *Black Beauty*, was born, and 4 South Quay, now leased from the National Trust as a museum.

As well as buildings, Great Yarmouth has Nelson's Monument, built in 1819 with 217 steps to the top; the Kingdom of the Sea with its impressive and informative displays of British and tropical fish; a butterfly farm; the Norfolk Rare Breeds Centre; the nearby 15th-century Caister Castle; and 5 miles (8km) of safe, sandy beaches.

GREATFORD Lincolnshire TF0811
Village off A15, 5 miles (8km) NE of Stamford
Stone mushrooms, elephants, crowns and obelisks,

carved in the 1930s, decorate the village. Church monument to Francis Willis, who cured George III's first bout of insanity.

GREATHAM Cleveland NZ4927
Village off A689, 3 miles (5km) S of Hartlepool
The village is perched above Greatham Creek and Cowpen Marsh. The main cobbled street, Westgate, has been the site for the market for the last 600 years and markets are held on Thursday and Saturday. The Hospital of God was founded in 1272, rebuilt in the early 19th century. Greatham Creek is popular with ornithologists.

GREATHAM Hampshire SU7730
Village on A325, 4 miles (6km) W of Liphook
Some old brick and stone cottages, but divided by the main road. Greatham Mill gardens are very good.

GREATSTONE-ON-SEA Kent TR0823
Village off B2071, 1 mile (2km) SE of New Romney
A place of seaside bungalows, developed between the wars on the eastern shore of Dungeness, with a wide sandy beach, Romney Sands, which stretches out for ½ mile (1km) at low tide.

GREEN HAMMERTON North Yorkshire SE4556
Village on A59, 7 miles (11km) SE of Boroughbridge
Small village with mixed old and new housing. Now bypassed by the A59 which has relieved traffic and restored quiet rural atmosphere.

GREENFIELD Clwyd SJ1977
Village on A548, 1 mile (2km) NE of Holywell
On coastal strip of Dee estuary. Wooded vale from Holywell is occupied by the Greenfield Valley Heritage Park, which reflects the area's industrial and rural past – old copper and cotton works, farm buildings, disused railway. Also ruins of Basingwerk Abbey (Cadw), a 12th-century religious site, mainly Cistercian.

GREENFIELD Greater Manchester SE0004
Village off A635, 5 miles (8km) E of Oldham
Pretty, stone-built Saddleworth village in the valley of the River Chew at the edge of the Peak District National Park. Excellent starting point for moorland walks.

GREENHAM Berkshire SU4865
Suburb off A34, on SE edge of Newbury
With a large common, once an American Airforce base – well known for the 'Greenham Common women', protestors against nuclear weaponry.

GREENHEAD Northumberland NY6565
Village on B6318, 3 miles (5km) W of Haltwhistle
Stanegate Roman road crossed the Tipalt Burn here, to serve Hadrian's Wall. The Roman Army Museum stands next to the site of Carvoran fort.

GREENHITHE Kent TQ5875
Small town on A226, 3 miles (5km) E of Dartford
In the Thameside industrial belt with Old Greenhithe facing the river; a narrow street of 18th- and 19th-century buildings ending at little green on the waterfront.

GREENLAW Borders NT7146
Village on A6105, 7 miles (11km) SW of Duns
Once the county town of Berwickshire. Lying on the upper reaches of Blackadder Water. Its 18th-century church tower was built for use as a prison. Near by is an Adam mansion, Marchmont House.

GREENOCK Strathclyde NS2776
Town on A8, 2 miles (3km) W of Port Glasgow
Until the 17th century Greenock was a small fishing village, which benefited from the herring boom of the 1670s. In 1711 the Clyde's first dock was built here; this heralded phenomenal growth during the 18th and early 19th centuries, which made it Scotland's foremost port by 1840. Other industries included ship-building, sugar-refining and the manufacture of pottery and straw hats. The docks were badly damaged during World War II, and since then the town's economic story has been similar to other Clydeside centres: steady decline, despite injections of funding and investment by IBM.

The town contains many fine examples of grandiose Victorian architecture among its public buildings. Two museums concentrate on local history: the Custom House by the docks and the McLean Museum and Art Gallery. The latter records the achievements of James Watt (1736–1819), the pioneer of steam power, born in Greenock. The town is also the supposed birthplace of Captain William Kidd (1645–1701), the notorious pirate. The first post-Reformation church was built in Greenock and the cross on Lyle Hill commemorates the Free French sailors of World War II.

GREENODD Cumbria SD3182
Village off A590, 3 miles (5km) NE of Ulverston
At the mouth of the River Leven; the only means of identifying the old quays is by the Ship inn.

GREENSTED Essex TL5403
Hamlet off A113, 1 mile (2km) SW of Chipping Ongar
Sheltering among trees here is an extraordinary survival, the world's oldest wooden church. It is Saxon, over 1,100 years old, and made of split oak logs held together with dowells. Subsequent generations enlarged the church, adding the chancel, the simple weatherboarded tower and the tiled roof and, in the 19th century, it was restored and stained-glass windows were put in .

GREENWICH Greater London TQ3877
Town and borough off A2, 4 miles (6km) W of Woolwich
You can straddle the Greenwich Meridian, marked on the ground in the Old Royal Observatory, with one foot in the western hemisphere and one in the eastern. The observatory is in Greenwich Park, which stretches south to Blackheath (see) and commands fine prospects of the River Thames, London Docklands and the Queen's House, designed by Inigo Jones and restored in 1990. The majestic baroque buildings of the Royal Naval College, on the site of a favourite riverside palace of the Tudors, are mainly by Wren and Hawksmoor, and include the spectacular Painted Hall. The National Maritime Museum houses the premier collection of material on British naval history.

Close to the Thames waterfront are two icons of the British maritime past: the *Cutty Sark*, the last of the great China tea clippers, and the tiny little *Gipsy Moth IV*, in which Sir Francis Chichester sailed round the world singlehanded in 1966. Other Greenwich attractions include the 18th-century Church of St Alfege, Greenwich Theatre, a fan museum, historic pubs and weekend art and craft markets. River boats travel to Central London and a pedestrian tunnel leads to the Isle of Dogs (see).

GREETHAM Leicestershire SK9214
Village on B668, 6 miles (10km) NE of Oakham
Rutland village off the Great North road, which follows Roman Ermine Street. Saxon and Norman stone fragments built into medieval church walls.

GRENDON Northamptonshire SP8760
Village off A509, 5 miles (8km) S of Wellingborough
Church surrounded by stone houses, some thatched. Grendon Hall (17th and early 18th century), on the edge of the village, is the county's residential youth centre.

GRENDON UNDERWOOD Buckinghamshire SP6820
Village off A41, 6 miles (10km) E of Bicester
Shakespeare often stayed here, allegedly, and based some of his characters on the locals. Now known for Grendon and Springhill prisons.

GRESFORD Clwyd SJ3454
Town on B5445, 3 miles (5km) NE of Wrexham
'Gresford Bells' are one of the traditional Seven Wonders of Wales. Former coal-mining town with memorial to 1934 mining disaster.

GRESHAM Norfolk TG1638
Village off A148, 3 miles (5km) S of Sheringham
Home of founder of Gresham's School (see Holt) founded in 1555. Remains of a medieval fortified manor house can be seen in a meadow.

GRESSENHALL Norfolk TF9615
Village off B1146, 2 miles (3km) NW of East Dereham
The main attraction of this village is the Norfolk Rural Life Museum, a former workhouse now cataloguing 150 years of rural history and development.

GRESSINGHAM Lancashire SD5769
Village off B6254, 5 miles (8km) E of Carnforth
Cluster of stone cottages in the Lune Valley on a steeply sloping site above Gressingham Beck. The church retains a well-preserved Norman doorway.

GRETA BRIDGE Durham NZ0813
Hamlet off A66, 3 miles (5km) SE of Barnard Castle
The hamlet is named after the single-arched bridge over the River Greta which was designed by Sir Thomas Robinson, built by John Morritt in 1774. The ruins of 12th-century Eggleston Abbey stand near by above a dramatic gorge of the River Tees. Murals in Morrit Arms hotel depict scenes from Dickens' novels.

GRETNA Dumfries and Galloway NY3167
Village off A74(M), 9 miles (14km) NW of Carlisle
Border village on the main route north and famous as an elopement destination from the 18th century. Differences in Scots and English law meant that English minors could marry in Scotland without parental consent. Weddings traditionally took place in the old Blacksmith's Shop on Gretna Green. The area was a base for whisky-smuggling throughout the 18th and early 19th centuries.

GRETTON Northamptonshire SP8994
Village off B672, 4 miles (6km) N of Corby
There are several late Tudor houses in this picturesque stone-built village in ancient Rockingham Forest, with views from the hillside over the valley of the River Welland. The Church of St James has substantial Norman features. The stocks and whipping post on the green recall 18th-century punishments.

GREY MARE'S TAIL Dumfries and Galloway NT1815
Waterfall off A708, 9 miles (14km) NE of Moffat
This impressive waterfall with a three-part drop is the highest in the Borders at 200ft (61m). Situated in wild moorland below White Coomb.

GREYSTOKE Cumbria NY4430
Village on B5288, 5 miles (8km) W of Penrith
This pleasant village is home to the racing stable of Gordon Richards who has trained two Grand National winners, Lucius and Hello Dandy. Greystoke Castle is home to the Howard family.

GRIME'S GRAVES Norfolk TL8189
Prehistoric site off A134, 5 miles (8km) NW of Thetford
This series of circular hollows is the remains of a 4,000-year-old neolithic flint mine. More than 300 pits have been discovered (English Heritage).

GRIMSARGH Lancashire SD5834
Village on B6243, 4 miles (6km) NE of Preston
In the Ribble Valley, with one of the largest village greens in the county at 12 acres (5ha).

GRIMSBY Humberside TA2710
Town on the A180
The fishing industry around which Grimsby has grown dominates the town and continues to supply the entire north of England. The waterfront is industrial and rather unattractive although there are some pleasant riverside walks. The newly redeveloped Alexandra Dock area houses the popular National Fishing Heritage Centre.

GRINDLEFORD Derbyshire SK2477
Village on B6001, 3 miles (5km) S of Hathersage
Small Peak District village. Bridge crossing River Derwent, station on Hope Valley line. Annual pilgrimage to Padley Chapel commemorates Catholic martyrs of 1588.

GRINDON Staffordshire SK0854
Village off A523, 8 miles (13km) NW of Ashbourne
Memorial in church to RAF crew who crashed while delivering supplies when this exposed moorland village was snowbound in 1947.

GRINGLEY ON THE HILL Nottinghamshire SK7390
Village off A631, 6 miles (10km) E of Bawtry
Fine views from Beacon Hill across the Idle and Trent rivers into Yorkshire and across to Lincoln. Georgian brick houses cluster round the church.

GRINSHILL Shropshire SJ5223
Village off A49, 7 miles (11km) N of Shrewsbury
Attractive little hilltop village close to overgrown quarries that once produced some of England's most highly-prized building stone.

GRINTON North Yorkshire SE0498
Village on B6270, 1mile (2km) SE of Reeth
This small village, on the banks of the River Swale is dominated by its Norman Church of St Andrew.

GRISEDALE Cumbria
Scenic area SW of Patterdale
Deep-set between the impressive surroundings of Helvellyn range and St Sunday Crag, the valley of Grisedale Beck runs down to Patterdale village amid breathtaking scenery.

GRISTON Norfolk TL9499
Village off B1077, 2 miles (3km) SE of Watton
Griston Hall (not open) is reputed to be the home of the wicked uncle in the 16th-century 'Babes in the Wood' folk tale.

GRIZEDALE Cumbria SD3394
Hamlet off B5285, 3 miles (4km) S of Hawkshead
Grizedale Forest is owned by the Forestry Commission; Grizedale has a sculpture trail, a cycle way, and a visitors' centre in the stables of the now-demolished Grizedale Hall.

GROBY Leicestershire SK5207
Village off A50, 5 miles (8km) NW of Leicester
Charnwood Forest village; picnics at Groby Pool. Manor home of Sir John Grey and Elizabeth Woodville, later Edward IV's wife. Probable birthplace of tragic queen Lady Jane Grey.

GROOMBRIDGE Kent TQ5337
Village on B2110, 4 miles (6km) SW of Tunbridge Wells
Village on the Kent/Sussex border associated with a big house, Groombridge Place. The Kent (northern) part of the village consists of attractively tile-hung cottages of the Groombridge estate grouped around a triangular green with a brick church (1625), originally a private chapel. Groombridge Place gardens feature walled gardens laid out in the 17th century against the backdrop of moated Groombridge Place. Enchanted Forest, with pools and waterfalls, overlooks the Weald.

GROSMONT Gwent SO4024
Village on B4347, 2 miles (3km) S of Pontrilas
Placid Grosmont is the 'gros mont' (French for 'big hill') on which its medieval castle was built. Village church is also interesting.

GROTON Suffolk TL9541
Village off A1071, 4 miles (6km) W of Hadleigh
Famous son is Puritan John Winthrop, who founded Boston, Massachusetts, USA. Church huddles behind a farmhouse on a hill.

GRUINARD Highland NG9489
Hamlet on A832, 20 miles (32km) N of Gairloch
Minute crofting settlement on Gruinard Bay, overlooking Gruinard Island. The island was renowned as the testing ground for anthrax in World War II and closed for many years.

GRUNDISBURGH Suffolk TM2250
Village off B1079, 3 miles (5km) W of Woodbridge
An old Victorian school and St Mary's Church on the green provide the focal point. The River Lark flows through the village.

GUERNSEY Channel Islands
Island in the English Channel
Guernsey, or 'Green Island', is about 25 square miles (65 sq km) in size, with a coastline of attractive bays, wide beaches of sand and shingle, high cliffs (some with caves) and, inland, small farms, mellow farmhouses and red granite churches.

St Saviour's Church, Guernsey's largest country church, has an imposing tower of dressed stone. At Les Vauxbelets, a short distance west of St Andrew's Church, is the Little Chapel, a miniature church built in 1923 by a monk and decorated with thousands of fragments of china, pottery and shells. Sausmarez Manor is a well-preserved 18th-century building (limited opening). L'Ancresse Common, in the extreme north of Guernsey, is rich in prehistoric remains, particularly neolithic tombs.

The German Occupation Museum, near Forest Church, houses an exhaustive collection of Nazi memorabilia. Its detailed documents convey the atmosphere of day-to-day life during the German occupation. The German Underground Hospital in La Vassalerie Road, St Andrews, has been little altered since World War II. Fort Grey, also known as 'cup and saucer', is Guernsey's Maritime Museum.

GUILDEN MORDEN Cambridgeshire TL2744
Village off B1042, 5 miles (8km) NW of Royston
Twenty-three villagers drowned in 1845, and the church bell was said to toll of its own accord. Gabled Morden Hall (not open) and two mills are picturesque.

GUILDFORD Surrey SU9949
Town off A3, 27 miles (43km) SW of London
Surrey's ancient capital is beautifully sited at the old fording point where the River Wey cuts its gap through the North Downs. It was first mentioned in Alfred the Great's will of AD899, but rose to prominence in the 12th century, when Henry II built – or rebuilt – the now ruined castle. It was granted a charter by Henry III and was first represented in parliament in 1295. Guildford was a centre of weaving by Tudor times and an important trading centre following the opening of the canalised Wey in 1653.

Guildford became the centre of a bishopric in 1927

with a cathedral designed by Sir Eward Maufe. It was completed in 1961 and stands near the University of Surrey (1962) on the western side of the river. The old town crowds around High Street, which runs uphill eastwards from the river. It displays a medley of interesting architectural styles and ages, including Abbot's Hospital (1619), Guildford House (1660) and the Royal Grammar School, with its famous chained library, but is dominated by the 1683 façade of the guildhall, with its clock projecting on a beam over the pavement.

GUILSBOROUGH Northamptonshire SP6772
Village off A50, 9 miles (14km) NW of Northampton
Large village, notable Georgian brick and stone houses. Early 17th-century church has windows by Morris and Burne-Jones, commemorating Adelaide Countess Spencer.

GUILSFIELD Powys SJ2111
Village on B4392, 3 miles (5km) N of Welshpool
Noted for its church, a large 15th-century building with unorthodox upper chamber over south porch, magnificent panelled roof and 19th-century vaulting.

GUISBOROUGH Cleveland NZ6116
Town on A171, 6 miles (10km) S of Redcar
Ancient capital of Cleveland. The ruined Gisborough priory (English Heritage), with the remains of its magnificent east window stands, is over 900 years old and the nave and chancel are still recognisable. Guisborough Hall was the home of the Chaloner family. Near by, Tockett's Mill is a working watermill in a wooded dell, open to the public.

GUISELEY West Yorkshire SE1941
Town on A65, 10 miles (16km) NW of Leeds
A stone-built town centred around an old village green with market cross and stocks. Old stone terraces with cobbled streets remain and there is also more modern housing. Patrick and Maria Brontë were married in St Oswald's Church in 1812. Harry Ramsden's, the most famous fish and chip shop in the world, opened its first restaurant here in 1928.

GUITING POWER Gloucestershire SP0924
Village off B4068, 6 miles (10km) W of Stow-on-the-Wold
The great attraction here is the rare breeds centre at Cotswold Farm Park, but the cottages around the village green are also delightful and the church has fine Norman work.

GULLANE Lothian NT4882
Village on A198, 4 miles (6km) SW of North Berwick
Pretty coastal village on the Firth of Forth with dunes, beaches, and fine views. Parts of the old church are Norman. Muirfield championship golf course is near by.

GULVAL Cornwall SW4831
Hamlet off B3311, 1 mile (2km) NE of Penzance
Still a village, despite the proximity of Penzance. The church is set in an odd oval graveyard, right in the middle of the village with roads all around it.

GUMFRESTON Dyfed SN1001
Hamlet on B4318, 2 miles (3km) W of Tenby
Noted for its tiny, primitive church with unusual recess (possibly baptistery) in nave. Manor House Wildlife and Leisure Park, popular with Tenby holiday-makers, near by (see St Florence).

GUNBY Lincolnshire TF4666
Hamlet off A158, 7 miles (11km) NW of Skegness
Red-brick Gunby Hall, built 1700, extended 1870s, reputedly Tennyson's 'haunt of ancient peace'. Ground floor and gardens (National Trust, limited opening).

GUNNISLAKE Cornwall SX4371
Village on A390, 10 miles (16km) NE of Callington
Until the Tamar bridge was built, this was the lowest bridging point on the River Tamar, with a superb granite seven-arched bridge of 1520. Set in a wooded valley.

GUNWALLOE Cornwall SW6522
Hamlet off A3083, 3 miles (5km) S of Helston
Small fishing village on the Lizard peninsula. Marconi made the first wireless transmission across the Atlantic from Poldu Point in 1901.

GURNARD Isle of Wight SZ4795
Village off B3325, immediately W of Cowes
Mostly Victorian seaside development in the centre with a promenade walk along the sea to Cowes. Good views of the New Forest.

GUSSAGE, ALL SAINTS AND ST MICHAEL Dorset SU0010
Villages off A354, 4 miles (6km) SW of Cranborne
Both named after the Gussage River, All Saints' has older cottages and a 14th-century church and St Michael is more 19th century.

GUSSAGE ST ANDREW Dorset ST9714
Hamlet off A354, 2 miles (3km) SW of Sixpenny Handley
Just an old farmhouse and the church, which has 13th-century wall-paintings, set on the Gussage River.

GUTHRIE Tayside NO5650
Village off A932, 7 miles (11km) E of Forfar
Small Angus village in rolling countryside. Turreted Guthrie Castle was the seat of the chiefs of the Clan Guthrie.

GUYHIRN Cambridgeshire TF3903
Village on A47, 6 miles (10km) SW of Wisbech
Straddling the deep and silent River Nene, Guyhirn has a bridge, and a Puritan chapel-of-ease, now redundant.

GWBERT-ON-SEA Dyfed SN1649
Hamlet on B4548, 3 miles (5km) N of Cardigan
Perched above mouth of River Teifi. Small resort, beautiful cliff walks, views across to Cardigan Island, a sanctuary for seals and sea-birds.

GWEEK Cornwall SW7026
Village off B3293, 3 miles (5km) E of Helston
Popular and pretty village at the head of the woody Helford estuary, a port until the river silted. The Cornish Seal Sanctuary, a rescue centre for seals, is based here.

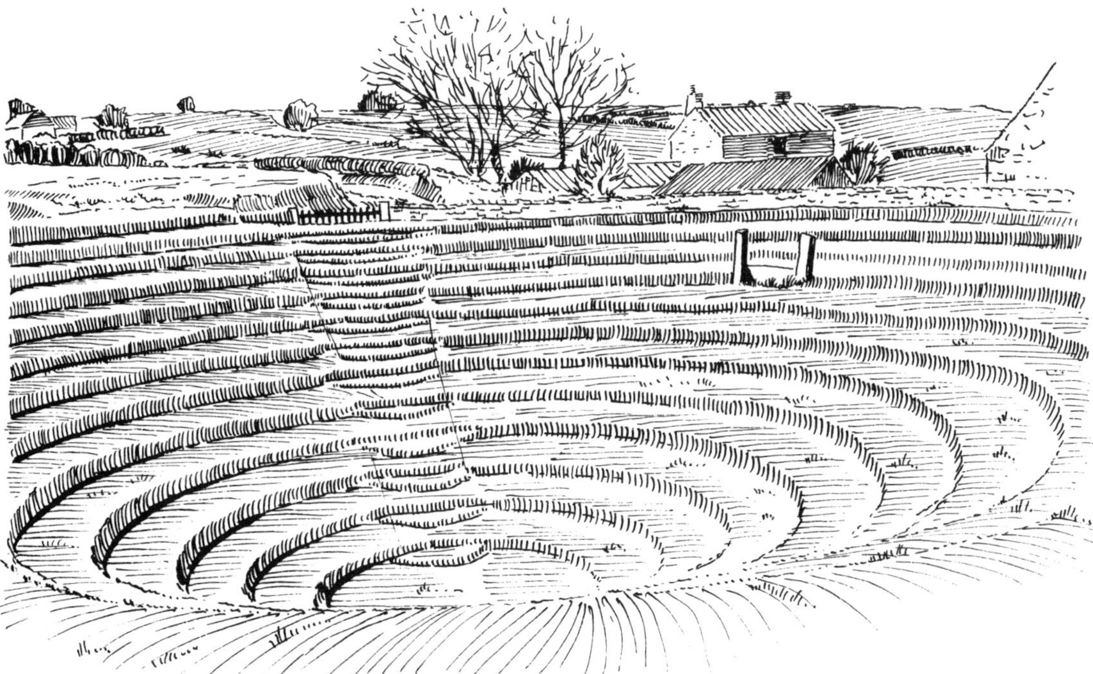

The amphitheatre at Gwennap, where John Wesley preached.

GWENNAP Cornwall SW7340
Village off A393, 3 miles (5km) SE of Redruth
This little village features Gwennap Pit, adapted from mine workings to form an amphitheatre, once preached in by John Wesley.

GWITHIAN Cornwall SW5841
Village on B3301, 4 miles (6km) W of Camborne
Small thatched village, surrounded by sand dunes. Offshore from Godrey Point to the north is a lighthouse.

GYFFIN Gwynedd SH7776
Village on B5106, immediately S of Conwy
Almost a suburb of Conwy on hilly ground to the south. Church has a 15th-century painted chancel roof and 13th-century door.

H

HABBERLEY Shropshire SJ3903
Hamlet off A488, 8 miles (13km) SW of Shrewsbury
A lonely cluster of ancient church, inn, timber-framed manor house and cottages tucked away in the hills above the Rea Valley.

HACCOMBE Devon SX8970
Village off A380, 3 miles (5km) E of Newton Abbot
The village consists virtually only of the big house (not open) and a little church with fine medieval and later memorials, and decorated medieval floor tiles.

HACKNESS North Yorkshire SE9790
Village off A171, 5 miles (8km) W of Scarborough
This attractive village is situated in a delightful wooded valley where the Lowdale Beck meets the River Derwent. Built of mellow, local stone, the estate cottages and houses cluster around the 11th-century Church of St Peter. The old manor house remains in the village (not open).

HACKNEY Greater London TQ3484
Town and borough off A11, in NE London
One of London's poorest districts. The Hackney Empire, an Edwardian music hall, stands ornately ebullient among dingy streets. Sutton House (National Trust), built in 1535, is Hackney's oldest house. Farm trail at Hackney City Farm, sports pitches on Hackney Marshes, drained in the 18th century, greyhound racing at Hackney Stadium. Acres of post-war housing.

HACKTHORPE Cumbria NY5423
Village on A6, 5 miles (8km) S of Penrith
Lowther Leisure Park is in 150 acres (61ha) of parkland with circus, rides and other attractions. Deer park and picnic areas.

HADDENHAM Buckinghamshire SP7308
Village off A418, 3 miles (5km) NE of Thame
Large village of exceptional charm at the older, southern end, with green, duck pond, handsome church and old houses, all beautifully kept. Many buildings and walls of witchert (earth and straw). Walls of Bone House, High Street, are covered with designs made of sheep's knucklebones. Haddenham once specialised in rearing ducks.

HADDENHAM Cambridgeshire TL4674
Village on A1123, 6 miles (10km) SW of Ely
About 120ft (37m) above pancake-flat farmland, Haddenham is the highest village in the Fens. To the south is the site of an ancient causeway associated with 11th-century rebel Hereward the Wake. The excellent Farm Museum is in the High Street, and there is a steam fair each September.

HADDINGTON Lothian NT5173
Town on A1, 16 miles (26km) E of Edinburgh
Once an important inland trading town, the lovely royal burgh of Haddington was besieged and burnt three times by the English during the Middle Ages. It has over 130 buildings listed as being of important historical or architectural interest. The unusually shaped market square is divided by the town house, designed in 1748 by William Adam, and Sidegate contains Haddington House (1680). The late medieval Parish Church of St Mary the Virgin dates from 1462; it was damaged during an English siege in 1548 and finally fully restored in the 1970s. The Lauderdale Aisle includes some Elizabethan alabaster monuments and the plain tomb of Jane Welsh Carlyle, wife of the historian, who was born in Haddington. Haddington was also the birthplace of Alexander II and possibly of John Knox.

South of the town lies Lennoxlove House, seat of the Dukes of Hamilton. Mainly dating from the 17th century, it has Mary Stuart connections and a fine interior. Stevenson House, also outside town, is a 13th-century house with later additions and a lovely garden.

On the hills to the north stands the Hopetoun Monument, commemorating the 4th Earl of Hopetoun.

HADDISCOE Norfolk TM4496
Village on A143, 4 miles (6km) N of Beccles
The Victorian artificial canal joining the rivers Yare and Waveney was intended to provide a better seaport for Norwich at Lowestoft. Near by are Haddiscoe Marshes.

HADLEIGH Essex TQ8187
Town on A13, 4 miles (6km) W of Southend-on-Sea
Hadleigh Castle (English Heritage), a ruined medieval stronghold in an extensive country park, commands views across the marshes and Thames estuary to Kent.

HADLEIGH Suffolk TM0242
Town on B1070, 8 miles (13km) W of Ipswich
Hadleigh's long High Street offers the visitor an enormous variety of architectural styles, ranging from timber-framed to elegant Georgian. Many of them display the carved plasterwork known as pargetting. Especially impressive is Overall House, named after the bishop who helped to translate the Bible for James I, and the magnificent 15th-century guildhall with its overhanging upper storeys.

HADLEY Shropshire SJ6712
Town off M54, immediately E of Wellington
Redeveloped with housing estates and light industry as part of Telford. Short length of Shrewsbury Canal with original lock in Hadley Park.

HADLOW Kent TQ6349
Village on A26, 4 miles (6km) NE of Tonbridge
Village among the orchards with a tower called May's Folly, 170ft (51m) high, built 1838–40 and a landmark for miles around.

HADNALL Shropshire SJ5220
Village on A49, 5 miles (8km) NE of Shrewsbury
A popular residential village in attractive pastoral countrysidewith a church well worth visiting.

HADRIAN'S WALL Northumberland
Roman site
Built by order of the Emperor Hadrian in AD120 to protect the northern frontier of Rome's mighty Empire, the Roman Wall stretched from the Solway Firth to Newcastle upon Tyne. Today, large sections of the wall and a number of forts remain; it is designated a World Heritage Site.

HADSPEN Somerset ST6532
Hamlet off A371, 1 mile (2km) E of Castle Cary
Edwardian gardens around an 18th-century mansion (house not open).

HADSTOCK Essex TL5644
Village on B1052, 4 miles (6km) N of Saffron Walden
The church claims to have England's oldest door in constant use. It may have been the original burial place of St Botolph in the 7th century.

HAGLEY Hereford and Worcester SO9180
Suburb off A491, 2 miles (3km) S of Stourbridge
Hagley Hall, in rural Black Country, is a great Palladian house with virtuoso plasterwork, a painted ceiling, fine furniture and outstanding grounds.

HAGWORTHINGHAM Lincolnshire TF3469
Village on A158, 5 miles (8km) E of Horncastle
Brick-built village with 18th-century and earlier mud-and-stud cottages. Greenstone Norman church with Victorian restoration. Seventeenth-century Stockwith watermill referred to by Tennyson.

HAIGH Greater Manchester SD6009
Village on B5239, 3 miles (5km) NE of Wigan
Dominated by Haigh Hall, now owned by the local authority. The grounds offer woodland walks, a golf course, nature trails and a model village.

HAILES Gloucestershire SP0430
Site off B4632, 2 miles (3km) NE of Winchcombe
Impressive ruins of the famous 13th-century abbey (National Trust/English Heritage) compete for attention with the medieval riches of the parish church.

HAILSHAM East Sussex TQ5809
Town on A295, 7 miles (11km) N of Eastbourne
Busy town, high above Pevensey Levels, with a Friday market, modern shopping arcades and a leisure complex. First mentioned in Domesday Book.

HAINAULT Greater London TQ4591
District in borough of Redbridge
Known for the hornbeams of Hainault Forest Country Park, in 900 acres (364ha) of walking, riding, kite-flying, picnicking territory. Guided walks.

HAINTON Lincolnshire TF1884
Village off A157, 6 miles (10km) SE of Market Rasen
On edge of Lincolnshire Wolds. Seventeenth-century and later hall (closed), 19th-century estate cottages. Heneage family monuments, 16th century onwards, in church.

HALAM Nottinghamshire SK6754
Village off A612, 1 mile (2km) W of Southwell
Red-brick and pantiled village. The church has fine 14th-century and Morris stained glass. Norwood Park (open by appointment), built in the 18th century, has extensive apple and pear orchards.

HALBERTON Devon ST0013
Village off B3391, 3 miles (5km) E of Tiverton
Large village on the Grand Western Canal (1796) with several elegant bridges. Exceptionally fine 15th-century stone pulpit in church.

HALE Cheshire SJ4782
Village off A562, 4 miles (6km) SW of Widnes
Overlooks the River Mersey. Hale Lighthouse, now closed, was first built in 1836 to help ships navigate around Hale Head.

HALE Hampshire SU1918
Village off B3080, 4 miles (6km) NE of Fordingbridge
In the Avon Valley, with an unusual church rebuilt by the architect Thomas Archer in 1717, a little Roman-style building.

HALE (HALE BARNS) Greater Manchester SJ7786
Town on A538, immediately S of Altrincham
Affluent residential area with large Victorian and Edwardian dwellings. Pleasant town centre has exclusive shops and many restaurants.

HALES Norfolk TM3897
Village on A146, 1 mile (2km) SE of Loddon
Old moated manor now a farm. Norman village church with round tower and thatched roof. Council cottages by architects Taylor and Green.

HALES Staffordshire SJ7133
Village off A53, 3 miles (5km) E of Market Drayton
Audley's Cross marks the site of a Wars of the Roses battle in 1459. Church by Sir George Gilbert Scott, and interesting village hall.

HALESOWEN West Midlands SO9683
Town on A458, 7 miles (11km) W of Birmingham
Situated within sight of the Clent Hills, the old nail-making town retains much of its heritage, especially the impressive medieval parish church, timber-framed houses in town centre and The Leasowes, a country park around Mucklow Hill, which offers fine views. The park originated from grounds created by poet William Shenstone. Novelist Francis Brett Young was born here.

HALESWORTH Suffolk TM3877
Town on A144, 24 miles (39km) NE of Ipswich
A little market town with some elegant buildings. The market place has an Elizabethan timber-framed house; the Halesworth and District Museum is housed in a row of converted 17th-century almshouses. Halesworth's most famous residents were William Jackson Hooker and his son Joseph, who lived in the charming Maltings. The Hookers were botanists and directors of Kew Gardens.

HALFORD Warwickshire SP2645
Village on A429, 3 miles (5km) N of Shipston on Stour
Medieval bridge, eccentric Georgian house and church with good Norman carving are the features of this Fosse Way village beside the River Stour.

HALIFAX West Yorkshire SE0925
Town on A58, 7 miles (11km) SW of Bradford
Halifax is the main town of Calderdale rising to prominence during the textile boom of the 18th and 19th centuries. The focal point of the town is Piece Hall, built in 1779 as a market place for the surrounding cottage wool industry.

The subsequent advent of steam power and the Industrial Revolution brought the greatest prosperity to Halifax, which became known as the 'town of 100 trades' because of the many industries that sprang up around the textile industry.

Calderdale Industrial Museum, adjacent to Piece Hall, houses working looms and mill machinery. A 15th-century timber-framed house, just outside the centre, is Shibden Hall which also houses the Folk Museum of West Yorkshire. The interior gives an intimate picture of life in the 17th and 18th centuries and the folk museum depicts life in a 19th-century village.

The town hall was designed by Sir Charles Barry, who also designed the Houses of Parliament in London. Halifax has a large parish church dating from the 12th and 13th centuries, although most of the present building is from the 15th century.

HALKIRK Highland ND1359
Village on B874, 6 miles (10km) S of Thurso
Planned grid-pattern village laid out by agricultural improver Sir John Sinclair in 1803. Massive remains of 14th-century Brawl Castle stand across the River Thurso.

HALKYN Clwyd SJ2171
Village off A55, 3 miles (5km) SE of Holywell
Village between A55 and the Halkyn Mountain, a range of hills – rising to 964ft (294m) – scarred by remnants of ancient lead mines.

HALLAMSHIRE South Yorkshire
Historic region in N England
A district known in the Middle Ages, covering modern-day Sheffield and the area to the north. Formed to facilitate the collection of taxes and administration of justice, a practice common in the north of England.

HALLAND East Sussex TQ5016
Hamlet off A22, 4 miles (6km) SE of Uckfield
Wealden settlement now associated with Bentley Wildfowl: over 155 species of birds in 23 acres (9ha) of parkland. Also Bentley Motor Museum with a collection of rare vehicles.

HALLATON Leicestershire SP7896
Village off A47, 7 miles (11km) NE of Market Harborough
Picturesque village green and conical butter cross, with thatched cottages of local ironstone and limestone. Each Easter Monday, the boisterous Bottle Kicking and Hare Pie Scramble takes place. Hare pie is thrown to the crowds, then Hallaton's team competes with neighbouring Medbourne to get each of three 'bottles' or wooden casks of beer over a boundary.

HALLBANKGATE Cumbria NY5859
Hamlet on A689, 4 miles (6km) E of Brampton
A former lead-mining village at the foot of the Pennine Hills, on the road to Alston.

HALLOW Hereford and Worcester SO8258
Village on A443, 3 miles (5km) NW of Worcester
Pleasant old houses around a green defy modern commuter estates. Rich Victorian craftwork and furnishings in imposing church.

HALLSANDS Devon SX8138
Village off A379, 6 miles (10km) SE of Chillington
Almost deserted after being destroyed by a storm in 1917. To the south is Start Point, a prominent little headland marking a corner of Devon.

HALNAKER West Sussex SU9008
Village on A285, 4 miles (6km) NE of Chichester
Pleasant red-brick main-road village, on the line of Roman Stane Street, with a restored windmill of 1750 crowning a round-topped hill with superb views.

HALSALL Lancashire SD3710
Village on A5147, 3 miles (5km) NW of Ormskirk
A farming village on the Leeds–Liverpool canal with a church, St Cuthbert's, dating from the mid-13th century.

HALSE Somerset ST1427
Village off B3227, 5 miles (8km) NW of Taunton
Thatched cottages and a medieval church with a 15th-century screen and a carving of a pagan Green Man – a face emerging from foliage.

HALSTEAD Essex TL8130
Town on A131, 6 miles (10km) NE of Braintree
Market town on the River Colne, with fine 18th-century weatherboarded watermill converted into an antiques centre. Parish church has Bourchier monuments.

HALTON Buckinghamshire SP8710
Village off A4011, 2 miles (3km) N of Wendover
Fomer Rothschild village, on obsolete arm of Grand Union Canal. RAF camp's officers' mess is in ex-Rothschild stately residence.

HALTON Cheshire SJ5482
District in E Runcorn
An old part of Runcorn. Norton Priory was medieval, converted into a Tudor manor house, then a Georgian mansion. Priory and gardens open.

HALTON Lancashire SD5064
Village off A683, 3 miles (5km) NE of Lancaster
An ancient settlement, with Castle Hill, which was the site of a Roman camp and later a Saxon castle.

HALTON GILL North Yorkshire SD8776
Hamlet off B6160, 4 miles (6km) NW of Arncliffe
An ancient hill-farming community with 17th-century buildings, a resting place for packhorses as they crossed the moors.

HALTON HOLEGATE Lincolnshire TF4165
Village on B1195, 1 mile (2km) SE of Spilsby
Attractive village on southern edge of Lincolnshire Wolds, looking towards Fens. Large greenstone church almost entirely 15th century, with fine clerestory.

HALTWHISTLE Northumberland NY7064
Town on A69, 14 miles (23km) W of Hexham
Market town in a farming area, which suffered badly at the hands of border raiders. Bellister Castle has been burned down and rebuilt twice since the 13th century. Now a National Trust property providing bed and breakfast. The Church of the Holy Cross dates back to 1178.

HAM Greater London TQ1772
District in borough of Richmond
Select area between the Thames and Richmond Park, with imposing houses in Petersham Road, Ham Common and Ham Street, where Sir George Gilbert Scott lived and Cardinal Newman, as a boy. Ham House (National Trust) is a grand 17th-century mansion with fine formal gardens, splendidly set by the river. Polo ground near by.

HAM Wiltshire SU3363
Village off A338, 4 miles (6km) S of Hungerford
Thatched and timber-framed buildings and a green. Unusual wooden roof in the church, much altered in the 18th century and with many fittings of that date.

HAM, HIGH AND LOW Somerset ST4231
Villages off A372, 3 miles (5km) N of Langport
Contrasting sites, with good views from High Ham. Both have fine churches, Low's being 17th century but Gothic. Nearny Stembridge windmill, High Ham (National Trust) dates from 1820.

HAMBLE Hampshire SU4806
Village on B3397, 8 miles (13km) SE of Southampton
A famous yachting centre at the mouth of the Hamble River. The picturesque village runs up the hill with several Georgian brick cottages. The river is full of yachts. Passenger ferry to Warsash (see). Mostly Norman church, quite large.

HAMBLEDEN Buckinghamshire SU7886
Village off A4155, 3 miles (5km) NE of Henley-on-Thames
Picturesquely set on stream deep in wooded valley. Centre with giant chestnut tree, cross, village pump and old cottages. Links with Lord Cardigan, who led the Charge of the Light Brigade, and WH Smith's family. Cardinal Wolsey's heraldic bedhead is in church. Close to the River Thames, with weir and photogenic Hambleden Mill.

HAMBLEDON Hampshire SU6414
Village on B2150, 4 miles (6km) SE of Meonstoke
This attractive village was a market town which declined in the 18th century, leaving a settlement of plain, handsome, mostly Georgian houses. There is a pretty view up to the church. Broadhalfpenny Down, 2 miles (3km) northeast, was the home of the Hambledon Cricket Club in the 18th century, the forerunner of the Marylebone Cricket Club.

HAMBLEDON Surrey SU9638
Village off A283, 3 miles (5km) SE of Milford
Scatter of cottages and houses spread over wooded hills with church rebuilt in 1846. Tiny Oakhurst Cottage (National Trust) and Vann garden.

HAMBLETON HILLS North Yorkshire
Hill range E of A19 in North York Moors National Park
This picturesque hill range forms the western edge of the North York Moors and includes many geological features, including the Hanging Stone.

HAMDON HILL (OR HAM HILL) Somerset ST4716
Hill off A303, 5 miles (8km) W of Yeovil
This prominent hill was a quarry from Roman times for the golden Hamstone, used both locally and further afield. The big Iron Age hillfort has been virtually destroyed by the quarries, and what looks archaeologically interesting is usually the result of quarrying. Now a country park, but with one quarry still working.

HAMILTON Leicestershire SK6407
Deserted village off B667, on NE outskirts of Leicester
Substantial earthworks of village streets, manor and probably chapel deserted in the 15th century.

HAMILTON Strathclyde NS7255
Town off M74, 11 miles (18km) SE of Glasgow
A commercial and administrative centre in the midst of what was once Scotland's largest coal-mining area, Hamilton today sells itself as a leisure area with good shops and recreational facilities, a local museum and racecourse.

Originally Cadzow, its present name was adopted in 1445 in honour of the local ducal family. In the 18th century this wealthy family embarked on a substantial building and landscaping programme around the town. The park around the now-demolished Hamilton Palace was redesigned with a hunting lodge as its centrepiece. James, the 5th Duke, commissioned William Adam to design the building, erected between 1732 and 1744, and known as Chatelherault. It stands today as the centrepiece of the Chatelherault Country Park, which includes the wooded Avon Gorge.

Near by, in the grounds of Strathclyde Country Park, with its lake and watersports facilities, stands the Hamilton Mausoleum, built from 1842 by the 10th Duke, who died before its completion. The massive and idiosyncratic vaulted building contains a chapel as the main feature. The chapel cannot be used as the acoustics make intelligible speech impossible: it has a 15-second echo, the longest of any Scottish building.

HAMMERSMITH Greater London TQ2278
District in borough of Hammersmith and Fulham
On the north bank of the Thames. Ornate Hammersmith Bridge was designed in the 1880s by Sir Joseph Bazalgette. The Dove is one of several riverside pubs of character, and an enjoyable walk leads along the Thames bank to Chiswick (see). Lyric Theatre, Hammersmith Palais for dancing and concerts, former Odeon cinema for pop concerts. Striking 1991 office building, The Ark, by the flyover.

HAMMERWOOD East Sussex TQ4339
Hamlet off A264, 3 miles (5km) E of East Grinstead
No village at all, but a church on the highway and some stately houses, including Hammerwood Park (1792), down a potholed lane.

HAMMOON Dorset ST8114
Village off A357, 2 miles (3km) E of Sturminster Newton
Low-lying village with a pretty manor house (not open) featuring a 16th-century porch and bay window.

HAMPSTEAD Greater London TQ2685
District in borough of Camden
Famously high-minded, egg-headed North London suburb with hilly streets, charming lanes and pleasant pubs. Kenwood House, with rooms by Robert Adam and notable pictures, is on the edge of Hampstead Heath, more than 800 acres (324ha) of open space, boasting views, woods, ponds, riding and boating, summer concerts. Keats House, Freud Museum and the Fenton House musical instrument museum.

HAMPSTEAD NORREYS (OR NORRIS) Berkshire SU5276
Village on B4009, 6 miles (10km) NE of Newbury
On the young River Pang, with attractive old brick houses and barns and an interesting church. Wyld Court Rainforest is small but interesting.

HAMPTON Greater London TQ1369
District in borough of Richmond
On the River Thames, this former market-gardening area is a satellite of the sumptuous red-brick palace of Hampton Court, begun by Cardinal Wolsey, enlarged by Henry VIII and further beautified by Wren for William III. Stately grounds, real tennis court, famous maze. Attractive 18th-century houses near by, 1930s Thames bridge by Lutyens. Hampton parish church rebuilt in the 19th century.

HAMPTON BISHOP Hereford and Worcester SO5538
Village off B4224, 3 miles (5km) SE of Hereford
Protected against floods, this village in a meander of the River Wye has picturesque timber-framed cottages and a Norman church with rare medieval reredos.

HAMPTON IN ARDEN West Midlands SP2080
Village on B4102, 3 miles (5km) E of Solihull
Very large village retaining its independence despite the encroachment of the Birmingham conurbation. Church has notable Norman work, medieval tiles and monuments. Among several buildings of 15th to 17th centuries is the Elizabethan Moat Farm, timber-framed with a medieval core. Hampton Manor (1870s) is by eminent Victorian architect Eden Nesfield.

HAMPTON LUCY Warwickshire SP2557
Village off B4086, 4 miles (6km) NE of Stratford upon Avon
This estate village for Charlecote (see) offers a variety of interesting buildings and outstanding Victorian Arts and Crafts work in its church.

HAMSEY East Sussex TQ4112
Hamlet off A275, 2 miles (3km) N of Lewes
Isolated along a no-through road in the Ouse meadows, leading to a remarkable Norman church on a knoll looped round by the meandering River Ouse.

HAMSTALL RIDWARE Staffordshire SK1019
Village off B5014, 4 miles (6km) E of Rugeley
Attractive Trent Valley village has a good medieval church and interesting buildings in a conservation area, including the turreted gatehouse of its old hall.

HAMSTEAD (OR HAMPSTEAD) MARSHALL Berkshire SU4165
Village off A4, 4 miles (6km) W of Newbury
A small village in the Kennet Valley with the church set apart. Only fine gatepiers survive around the park of the demolished big house.

HAMSTERLEY Durham NZ1131
Village off A68, 2 miles (3km) W of Witton le Wear
Strung along a ridge between the valleys of the River Wear and the River Tees. Hamsterley Forest is a dense coniferous plantation managed by the Forestry Commission. Bedburn Mill, built in the 19th century, is being restored. Evidence that Romans mined for lead here.

HAMSTREET Kent TR0033
Village on A2070, 6 miles (10km) S of Ashford
Village above the old cliff-line behind Romney Marsh. There are a few old houses at the centre, and it is backed by pleasant Ham Street Woods, threaded with paths.

HANBURY Hereford and Worcester SO9664
Village on B4090, 4 miles (6km) S of Bromsgrove
Hanbury Hall (National Trust) was built in 1701 for the Vernon family and displays furniture, pictures and extravagant painted ceilings by James Thornhill. Many Vernon memorials in the parish church, including examples by Roubiliac and Chantrey, masters of monumental sculpture. Also worth a visit is the Jinney Ring craft centre, housed in converted barns.

HANBURY Staffordshire SK1727
Village off A515, 5 miles (8km) NW of Burton-upon-Trent
The huge crater near the village is a grim reminder of the wartime explosion of an ammunition store. Good church monuments. Fine views over Dove Valley from Hanbury Common.

HANDA Highland NC1348
Island off W coast of Sutherland
Island bird reserve run by the Royal Society for the Protection of Birds. Breeding colonies of seabirds including razorbills, kittiwakes, puffins and guillemots. Access from Scourie.

HANDCROSS West Sussex TQ2629
Village off A23, 5 miles (8km) S of Crawley
The friendly Victorian High Street in this little village was once on the London to Brighton road. Nymans Gardens (National Trust), one of the great gardens of Sussex, and High Beeches, are near by.

HANDFORTH Cheshire SJ8583
Village on A34, 1 mile (2km) NE of Wilmslow
Residential area, developed after 1842 when the railway was built from Manchester. Handforth Hall, a 16th-century half-timbered manor house.

HANDSWORTH West Midlands SP0490
District in NW Birmingham
Historically famous for Matthew Boulton's pioneer factory, Soho Manufactory (1760s). His house still stands, and his memorial is in St Mary's Church, together with those of engineers William Murdock and James Watt. Victorian and Edwardian building, fascinating for enthusiasts, is mixed with much modern housing. The extensive Handsworth Park, with woodland and lake, is a pleasant green breathing space.

HANLEY Staffordshire SJ8847
Town on the edge of Stoke-on-Trent
Stanley Matthews, Arnold Bennett and John Smith (captain of the *Titanic*) were born in this old pottery town, now the main shopping, administrative and commercial area of Stoke-on-Trent. Hanley Forest Park is an imaginative green space among a mixture of Victorian and modern buildings. Stoke's City Museum in Bethesda Street has Britain's finest collection of pottery and porcelain.

HANLEY CASTLE Hereford and Worcester SO8442
Village on B4209, 1 mile (2km) NW of Upton-upon-Severn
Attractive Severnside village, the ancient domain of the Lechmere family, with a picturesque pub, timber-framed cottages, almshouses and an interesting church.

HANMER Clwyd SJ4539
Village on A539, 5 miles (8km) W of Whitchurch
Border village with pleasant brick architecture in low-lying landscape beside lake known as Hanmer Mere. Grand church.

HANNINGTON Hampshire SU5355
Village off A339, 3 miles (5km) SE of Kingsclere
High on the chalk, on the summit of a hill. Saxon corner to the church. Classic village green.

HANSLOPE Buckinghamshire SP8046
Village off B526, 5 miles (8km) NW of Newport Pagnell
Former lace-making village has become attractive commuter dormitory for Milton Keynes (see). Good stone houses of 17th and 18th centuries and a church with

beautiful 186ft (57m) spire with whippet weathervane, rebuilt after lightning struck in 1804, and interesting graves and monuments, including one to squire shot by gamekeeper in 1912. Numerous 'ends', originally separate hamlets, in parish.

HANWELL Oxfordshire SP4343
Village on B4100, 2 miles (3km) NW of Banbury
Isolated in hilly countryside, the village is noted for a church with grotesque carving and other fine examples of medieval craftsmanship. Hanwell Castle (not open but accessible) comprises the massive corner tower and part of south wing of a brick 16th-century house erected by William Cope and demolished in 1780s.

HANWORTH Norfolk TG1935
Village off A140, 4 miles (6km) S of Cromer
Lying 4 miles (6km) inland, Hanworth boasts Gunton Park, with its beautiful timber-framed weatherboarded sawmill.

HAPPISBURGH Norfolk TG3731
Village on B1159, 6 miles (10km) E of North Walsham
Pronounced 'Haisbro', with long yellow beaches dominated by the red and white striped lighthouse that warns of the treacherous shifting sandbanks ½ mile (1km) to the south. The fine 14th-century tower of St Mary's Church is also a local landmark, and shrapnel from World War II bombers can still be seen embedded in its walls.

HAPTON Lancashire SD7931
Village off M65, 1 mile (2km) S of Padiham
Village close to the Leeds–Liverpool Canal. The Bridge inn is said to be haunted by the ghost of a young girl who threw herself into the canal.

HARBERTON Devon SX7758
Village off A381, 2 miles (3km) SW of Totnes
In a steep little valley. The prominent church has a fine and unusual 15th-century pulpit.

HARBLEDOWN Kent TR1358
Suburb off A2, immediately W of Canterbury
Old village, traditionally the last halt of pilgrims on their way to Canterbury; the classic view to the cathedral vanished in the expansion of the city that has engulfed Harbledown.

HARBORNE West Midlands SP0284
District in SW Birmingham
This former Staffordshire village became a prosperous Victorian suburb. Many fine houses, including the Harborne Tenants' estate, a 'garden suburb' scheme of 1907.

HARBOTTLE Northumberland NT9304
Village off B6341, 1 mile (2km) SE of Alwinton
On the edge of Ministry of Defence land and therefore with limited access on to Harbottle Moors. Ruins of a stone castle built by Henry II in 1159, some of the stones from which were used to build another castle to the east in 1839. Village surrounded by heather-topped hills known as Harbottle Crags.

HARBY Leicestershire SK7431
Village off A606, 8 miles (13km) N of Melton Mowbray
Large dairy producing Stilton, 'king of cheeses', using milk from the surrounding Vale of Belvoir. Church of the 14th century, windmill stump near disused Grantham Canal.

HARBY Nottinghamshire SK8770
Village off B1190, 6 miles (10km) W of Lincoln
Statue in the church to Edward I's beloved queen, who died here in 1290. Eleanor Crosses were erected later at the body's resting places on the journey to London.

HARDCASTLE CRAGS West Yorkshire SD9630
Beauty spot off A646, 3 miles (5km) NW of Heptonstall
This beauty spot, owned by the National Trust, comprises steep wooded valley and rock outcrops. There is a fine variety of flora and fauna.

HARDENHUISH Wiltshire ST9074
Village on A350, on N edge of Chippenham
Pronounced 'Harnish', this is really a suburb of Chippenham, with an unusual classical church of 1779.

HARDHAM West Sussex TQ0317
Hamlet on A29, 1 mile (2km) SW of Pulborough
A hamlet by the River Arun with picturesque stone and half-timbered cottages, and a neat little 11th-century church with superb medieval wall-paintings. Associated with the vanished priory, and traces of a Roman posting station.

HARDINGSTONE Northamptonshire SP7657
Village off A508, on S outskirts of Northampton
An Eleanor Cross marks the resting place of the body of Edward I's queen during the journey to London after her death in Nottinghamshire in 1290.

HARDKNOTT PASS Cumbria NY2301
Mountain pass between Eskdale Green and Skelwith Bridge
This is a steep pass on the road up Eskdale, single track in places, with hairpin bends and a gradient of 1-in-4. The Roman fort of Hardknott is in an isolated and inaccessible position and is an impressive site. Built in about AD130 by the Emperor Hadrian, it was called *Mediobogdum*.

HARDRAW (OR HARDROW) North Yorkshire SD8691
Hamlet off A684, 1 mile (2km) N of Hawes
A tiny village famous for Hardraw Force, a spectacular waterfall, reached by a path leading from the Green Dragon pub.

HARDWICK Buckinghamshire SP8019
Village on A413, 4 miles (6km) N of Aylesbury
Set round a green. Church partly Saxon, with common grave holding 247 Civil War soldiers from both sides.

HARDWICK HALL Derbyshire SK4663
Mansion off B6014, 5 miles (8km) NW of Mansfield
'More glass than wall', the magnificent result of Bess of Hardwick's building mania dates from 1590 to 1597 (National Trust). Hardwick Old Hall ruins are from the 1580s (English Heritage).

HARDWICKE Gloucestershire SO7912
Village off A38, 5 miles (8km) SW of Gloucester
The ancient church contains a memorial to Olive Lloyd-Baker, pioneer conservationist. She owned Hardwicke Court, a fine house with a 17th-century garden.

HARDY COUNTRY Dorset
Historic and scenic region in S England
Thomas Hardy ranged further afield than Dorset for inspiration for his novels and poetry, but this is the heartland. Hardy was born here (see Bockhampton) and lived in the county most of his life. His novels give wide pictures of life in the county in the 19th century, and include wonderful descriptions of the landscape.

HAREFIELD Greater London TQ0590
Village in borough of Hillingdon
Medieval church with notable monuments, churchyard memorial to Australian soldiers. Timber-framed cottages, old houses. Bayhurst Wood Country Park. Celebrated heart transplant hospital.

HARESFIELD Gloucestershire SO8110
Village off B4008, 4 miles (6km) NW of Stroud
After visiting the medieval church, ascend to Haresfield Beacon (National Trust) on the Cotswold Edge for spectacular views across the Severn Vale.

HARESHAW LINN Northumberland NY8485
Waterfall off B6320, N of Bellingham
Waterfall on Hareshaw Burn, a tributary of the River North Tyne, 30ft (9m) high. Surrounding woods of great botanical and wildlife interest.

HAREWOOD West Yorkshire SE3245
Village on A61, 7 miles (11km) N of Leeds
A fine example of an estate village, on the River Wharfe. Harewood House, home to Lord Harewood, designed by John Carr and built in 1760s, became the first stately home in Britain to be granted museum status in 1994. Extensive parklands with lakes, woods and a pretty 15th-century church.

HARLAXTON Lincolnshire SK8832
Village off A607, 3 miles (5km) SW of Grantham
Close to Grantham, A1, and Leicestershire border. Harlaxton Manor, amazing fusion of baroque and Elizabethan styles built 1837-55 by Salvin for Gregory Gregory, in golden Ancaster stone. Manor used as college by University of Evansville, open for antiques and crafts fairs, events. Fine gardens being restored (open).

HARLECH Gwynedd SH5831
Small town off A496, 10 miles (16km) N of Barmouth
Small town huddled around huge crag surmounted by late 13th-century Harlech Castle (Cadw), one of Wales's most spectacularly sited medieval fortresses. Well-preserved gatehouse and walls, with magnificent views. 'Way from the sea' stairway in rock: sea once lapped castle rock, now a vast area of dune leading to huge beach. Famous golf course.

HARLESTON Norfolk TM2483
Small town off A143, 8 miles (13km) E of Diss
With the new bypass, this lovely Georgian market town has resumed its restful, genteel atmosphere. Attractive courts and streets with names such as Keeling's Yard and Shipp's Close house a wealth of architectural treasures, not least its dressed-flint Victorian church, and the minaret over the Midland Bank building. Artist Alfred Munnings was born 2 miles (3km) away in Mendham.

HARLESTONE Northamptonshire SP7064
Village off A428, 4 miles (6km) NW of Northampton
Attractive village with 19th-century estate houses built by the Spencers of Althorp. Fox and Hounds Georgian inn and a 1320s church with a 17th-century wooden gallery.

HARLINGTON Bedfordshire TL0330
Village off A5120, 7 miles (11km) NW of Luton
John Bunyan often preached here; the church has *Pilgrim's Progress* windows and churchyard views. Sapling planted in 1988 to replace Bunyan's Oak.

HARLOW Essex TL4410
New Town off M11, 5 miles (8km) N of Epping
New Town begun in the 1940s, planned by Sir Frederick Gibberd and embracing several villages and hamlets surrounding the centre, with high-rises, pedestrian precincts and modern sculptures. A visitor centre tells the New Town story, the Harlow Museum covers local history, and the Mark Hall Museum houses a remarkable bicycle collection. Playhouse Theatre and Art Gallery. Parndon Wood Nature Reserve.

HARLTON Cambridgeshire TL3852
Village off A603, 6 miles (10km) SW of Cambridge
Harlton is best known for the ornate 17th-century interior of the Church of the Assumption, restored in memory of Gwen Raverat (author of *Period Piece*).

HARLYN BAY Cornwall SW8775
Hamlet off B3276, 3 miles (5km) W of Padstow
A sandy bay, rocky coast and a little stone village.

HARPENDEN Hertfordshire TL1314
Town on A1081, 5 miles (8km) N of St Albans
Smart Lee Valley commuter town with stylish shops, a broad High Street with plenty of trees, central greens and extensive common attended by substantial expensive houses. The grounds of Rothamsted Manor (not open) are now a public park. It is used by the Experimental Station for agricultural research. Local history centre in Harpenden Hall (limited opening). Disused railway track walks.

HARPHAM Humberside TA0861
Village off A166, 5 miles (8km) NE of Great Driffield
An ancient village with two wells, the Drummerboy's and St John's, the former said to be haunted by a drummerboy who fell in to his death.

HARPSDEN Oxfordshire SU7680
Hamlet off A4155, 1 mile (2km) S of Henley-on-Thames
Enthusiasts for medieval brasses will enjoy the church in this hamlet pleasantly situated in wooded countryside.

HARRIETSHAM Kent TQ8652
Village on A20, 7 miles (11km) SE of Maidstone
Pleasant village, severed by the A20; church on a hill to the north. East Street, with attractive tiled and weatherboarded houses, is beside a lake to the south.

HARRINGTON Lincolnshire TF3671
Village off A158, 4 miles (6km) NW of Spilsby
Hall rebuilt in 1673 and, after a fire, in 1992–4 (closed). Gardens (limited opening) are probably those into which Tennyson's 'Maud' was invited to come.

HARRINGWORTH Northamptonshire SP9197
Village off A43, 6 miles (10km) N of Corby
Attractive stone village with 14th-century cross. The 82-arched blue-brick railway viaduct, built in the 1870s, strides ¾ mile (1km) across Welland Valley.

HARRIS Western Isles
Island in Outer Hebrides, S part of Lewis
Harris is formed by the southern third of the largest Western Isles island, with Loch Seaforth and Loch Resort forming a boundary with Lewis. North Harris is mountainous and rugged; the east is bare and rocky. The west has fertile machair and superb beaches. Many prehistoric sites. Economy based on crofting, fishing, tourism and tweed production. Tarbert is the largest town and ferry port.

HARROGATE North Yorkshire SE3055
Town on A61, 13 miles (21km) N of Leeds
Following the discovery of the first mineral water in 1571, Harrogate evolved as a spa, ranking among the finest in the world, and as such it quickly became a popular venue among the rich Victorians. A handsome town with dignified Victorian buildings, tree-lined boulevards, gardens and wide open spaces, it has never lost its charm and elegance, typified by Montpellier Parade and Gardens in the centre of the town.

Since the building of the town's International Conference Centre, Harrogate has become well established as a major business centre.

Harrogate is also popular with day visitors and with tourists. The Royal Pump Room, now a museum of Harrogate's history, was built in 1842 to enclose the old sulphur well which is still there to this day, and the splendid Turkish baths are still in use at the Royal Baths Assembly Rooms, built in 1897 to house a myriad of water-based treatments. The streets are decorated with ornate cast-iron canopies and floral baskets and lined with old-fashioned shops, tea rooms and restaurants. Harrogate is home to the prestigious Harlow Carr Botanical Gardens, headquarters of the Northern Horticultural Society.

HARROLD Bedfordshire SP9457
Village off A6, 8 miles (13km) NW of Bedford
Attractive former market town on the Great Ouse. Old bridge, photogenic green with 18th-century market house, lock-up, and church whose pinnacled spire is supported by flying buttresses. Harrold-Odell Country Park among Ouse river meadows and worked-out gravel pits has large lake, marsh, masses of wildfowl, walking trails and a visitor centre.

HARROW Greater London TQ1587
Borough in NW London
The hilltop town of Harrow on the Hill is dominated by St Mary's Church and its slender spire. The churchyard with its sweeping view was Lord Byron's favourite spot when he was a boy at Harrow School, whose past pupils also include Sir Winston Churchill and Pandit Nehru. The school buildings are the principal features of the town. Museum and Heritage Centre, Headstone Lane.

HART Cleveland NZ4634
Village off A179, 3 miles (5km) NW of Hartlepool
Peaceful residential district in a rural environment. The church, mainly 17th and 19th century, but dating back to Saxon times, was once mother church of Hartlepool. Hart was once owned by the Bruce family and is reputed to be the birthplace of Robert the Bruce.

HARTBURN Northumberland NZ0885
Village on B6343, 7 miles (11km) W of Morpeth
Picturesque rural village. Parish church is mainly 13th century. Meldon Park, home of the Cookson family since 1832, is open to the public occasionally.

HARTFIELD East Sussex TQ4735
Village on B2026, 6 miles (10km) SE of East Grinstead
Delightful village on the northern edge of Ashdown Forest, the village street lined with weatherboarded, half-timbered and tile-hung cottages and houses. The 13th-century church, with its tall spire, is approached by a curious lych-gate, half cottage and half yew tree. AA Milne wrote *Winnie the Pooh* at nearby Cotchford Farm.

HARTFORD Cheshire SJ6472
Village on A559, 1 mile (2km) SW of Northwich
Administrative centre for the Vale Royal district and site of Mid-Cheshire College of Further Education.

HARTHILL South Yorkshire SK4980
Village off A618, 6 miles (10km) W of Worksop
This is the most southerly parish in Yorkshire and, since 1987, the villagers have revived the tradition of well-dressing.

HARTINGS, THE West Sussex SU7819
Villages on B2146, 3 miles (5km) S of Petersfield
There are three Hartings: East, West and South, tucked below the wooded South Downs near the Hampshire border. South Harting is the main village, with its lovely 18th-century houses and big cruciform church with a copper-clad spire 130ft (39m) high. The others are little clumps of cottages. Uppark (National Trust), a 17th-century house gutted by fire in 1989 and subsequently restored, lies to the south.

HARTINGTON Derbyshire SK1260
Village on B5054, 9 miles (14km) N of Ashbourne
Stone cottages and an 1836 market hall surround the former market place and pond of this charming Peak District village beside the River Dove, forming the Staffordshire border. Higher up are a large medieval

church and Hartington Hall (1611), now a youth hostel. Uniquely in Derbyshire, the cheese factory specialises in Stilton, producing this 'king of cheeses' far from the Vale of Belvoir dairies.

HARTLAND Devon SS2624
Small town on B3248, 4 miles (6km) W of Clovelly
A town in medieval times, but never very successful because it was so remote, Hartland is now more like a village. The church is 2 miles (3km) away towards the sea, and is one of the finest in Devon, with a 130ft (40m) tower. The large and beautiful interior has fine wooden screens and roofs. Hartland Abbey (limited opening) is the big house, converted from monastic buildings. Good gardens.

HARTLAND POINT Devon SS2227
Headland 3 miles (5km) NW of Hartland
The northernmost point of Devon has 350ft (105m) rocky cliffs, bleak and wild, and a big lighthouse to warn shipping. There is nothing between here and America. Hartland Quay is an area a little south of the Point, with particularly contorted geology and a museum. Many coastal waterfalls here. Much of the coast is owned by the National Trust.

HARTLEBURY Hereford and Worcester SO8470
Village off A449, 2 miles (3km) E of Stourport-on-Severn
Modest residence of Bishops of Worcester occupies part of Hartlebury Castle, where 18th-century state rooms can be visited. In another wing is Hereford and Worcester County Museum, featuring the county's archaeology, industry, domestic life and crafts (including Bromsgrove Guild). Hartlebury Common, on outskirts, is a nature reserve for plants, moths and butterflies.

HARTLEPOOL Cleveland NZ5032
Town on A689, 8 miles (13km) N of Middlesbrough
Developed in the 18th century as a port, when railways linked it to the Durham coalfields. Traffic is now more related to oil exploration. Still a thriving fishing industry and parts of the old docks have now been redeveloped to create an attractive marina and the Historic Hartlepool Quay attraction. Maritime Museum in Northgate.

HARTLEY WESPALL Hampshire SU6958
Village off A33, 3 miles (5km) NW of Hook
Famous for the west wall of the church, which has huge arched and decorated timbers from the early 14th century.

HARTLEY WINTNEY Hampshire SU7656
Village on A30, 3 miles (5km) NE of Hook
A former coaching centre, with many inns. Large central green planted with rows of oaks in 1820.

HARTSHEAD West Yorkshire SE1822
Village off A62, 3 miles (5km) W of Batley
Reverend Patrick Brontë was vicar of Hartshead 1811–15. The village, on the edge of Hartshead Moor, has grown in two parts with houses straggling between.

HARTSHILL Warwickshire SP3293
Suburb on B4114, NW of Nuneaton
Queen Boudicca is reputed to have been defeated by Romans at Hartshill Hayes, now an enjoyable wooded country park on a hillside overlooking Anker Valley.

HARTY, ISLE OF Kent TR0267
Island off B2231, part of the Isle of Sheppey
Remote, windswept southeastern tip of Isle of Sheppey, overlooking the estuarine mud of the Swale. Inhabited by flocks of waders and visited by many migrants.

HARVINGTON Hereford and Worcester SO8774
Village on A450, 3 miles (5km) E of Kidderminster
Main attraction in this pleasant old village is Harvington Hall, moated house of a defiant Catholic family, with wall-paintings and priests' hiding places.

HARWELL Oxfordshire SU4989
Village off A417, 2 miles (3km) W of Didcot
The name of the village is synonymous with nuclear research, and the famous Atomic Energy Research Establishment, established in 1946, forms a modern 500 acre (200ha) village of its own. It lies to the south of the old village, which has many attractions, including a good Norman church, almshouses and timber-framed cottages.

HARWICH Essex TM2531
Town on A120, 16 miles (26km) E of Colchester
A busy ferry and container port for Holland, Germany and Scandinavia. Its maritime heritage trail follows the old-fashioned town's long history as a port and dockyard. Low lighthouse with museum, unique 17th-century treadwheel crane, 1808 redoubt fort against French attack and an interesting 19th-century church with cast-iron pillars. Electric Palace cinema of 1911 is Britain's oldest. Harbour and river cruises.

HASCOMBE Surrey SU9939
Village on B2130, 3 miles (5km) SE of Godalming
Friendly village with a green and duck pond tucked into the fold of steep-sided hills. Excellent views from wooded Hascombe Hill, crowned by an Iron Age hillfort.

HASELBURY PLUCKNETT Somerset ST4710
Village on A3066, 2 miles (3km) NE of Crewkerne
The church in this stone village was the home of a famous hermit, St Wulfric, in the 12th century and became a place of miracles and pilgrimages after his death.

HASLEMERE Surrey SU9033
Town on A286, 8 miles (13km) SW of Godalming
Small market town in lovely position in wooded valley, 500ft (152m) up near the heathy uplands of Blackdown and Hindhead. High Street is particularly broad, almost a square, with attractive brick and timber houses. Historical musical instruments are made in workshops founded by Arnold Dolmetsch in the 1920s. A music festival founded by Dolmetsch in 1925 takes place every July.

HASLINGDEN Lancashire SD7823
Town on A680, 4 miles (6km) SE of Accrington
Historic market town in the Rossendale Valley. Haslingden market dates back to 1676 when King Charles II granted the right to charge tolls and stallage. Market days are Tuesday and Friday. Haslingden Grane is an area of moorland with reservoirs. Grane Valley Recreational Centre has pleasant woodland and moorland walks around old Grane Village

HASLINGFIELD Cambridgeshire TL4052
Village off A10, 5 miles (8km) SW of Cambridge
Friendly village strewn down long main street. Seventeenth-century pigeon house is now a private home. Haslingfield Hall (not open) was built by Henry VIII's physician.

HASSOCKS West Sussex TQ3015
Small town on B2116, 2 miles (3km) S of Burgess Hill
Modern housing and a row of shops cluster round the railway station. A large Roman cemetery was discovered just northwest of the crossroads of the A273 and B2116.

HASTINGS East Sussex TQ8109
Town on A259, 4 miles (6km) E of Bexhill
Hastings is an exciting seaside resort with a long history. It was already a thriving port when William the Conqueror landed at Pevensey in 1066, with the harbour between West Hill and White Rock. The harbour silted up and Old Town, with its medieval street pattern and half-timbered buildings, developed to the east. Hastings was one of the original Cinque Ports, but by the 14th century it was reduced to a fishing village with boats drawn up on the shingle, as they are today. The tall weatherboarded fishermen's net stores are a unique feature of Hastings.

Hastings developed as a resort from 1775 onwards, spreading westwards across the site of the original harbour, and until the 1950s it retained an air of Victorian gentility. Unfortunately, this atmosphere has been eroded, although the two cliff railways are lovingly preserved. The pier went up in 1872 and the seafront sports the usual seaside paraphernalia.

The town capitalises on its history. The '1066 Story' is based at the ruins of the Norman castle on West Hill and the Fishermen's Museum, Shipwreck Heritage Centre and Smuggler's Adventure are based in the caves under West Hill.

HASWELL Durham NZ3743
Village on B1280, 3 miles (5km) W of Easington
Part of the old winding house stands as a memorial of the first steel rope winding house in the country. The mine closed in 1895.

HATCH BEAUCHAMP Somerset ST3020
Village off A358, 5 miles (8km) SE of Taunton
Winding village with a 15th-century church and Hatch Court, an elegant mid-18th-century house with gardens and deer park.

HATCLIFFE Humberside TA2100
Hamlet off B1203, 7 miles (11km) SW of Grimsby
An ancient settlement with a well dedicated to St Helen, said to have magical powers.

HATFIELD Hertfordshire TL2308
Town off A1(M), 18 miles (29km) N of London
Old Hatfield is dominated by Hatfield House, the Jacobean Cecil family palace, bulging with treasures. St Etheldreda's Church has monuments; the Eight Bells pub has Dickensian associations. The New Town, developed since 1948, has De Havilland aircraft connections, the Comet hotel and the big Galleria shopping centre. To the north are Mill Green Museum and a working mill.

HATFIELD South Yorkshire SE6609
Town on A18, 7 miles (11km) NE of Doncaster
The village lies in a huge area of drained marsh land. Geoffrey Chaucer once stayed here.

HATFIELD BROAD OAK Essex TL5416
Village on B183, 5 miles (8km) SE of Bishop's Stortford
Desirable commuter village close to Hatfield Forest (see) named after famed Doodle Oak, which has not survived. Priory church.

HATFIELD FOREST Essex TL5320
Scenic area S of A120, 3 miles (5km) E of Bishop's Stortford
Over 1,000 acres (405ha) of woodland (National Trust) – hornbeams, forest glades and rides, plus boating lake with 18th-century Shell House.

HATFIELD HEATH Essex TL5215
Village on A1060, 5 miles (8km) SE of Bishop's Stortford
Ample green and cricket ground in village criss-crossed by a remarkable number of roads. Every type of suburban-style housing.

HATFIELD PEVEREL Essex TL7911
Village on A12, 3 miles (5km) SW of Witham
Commuter village with an old reputation for witchcraft and allegedly stalked by a glaring-eyed spectral dog.

HATFIELD WOODHOUSE South Yorkshire SE6708
Village on A614, 1 mile (2km) SE of Hatfield
A small part of Hatfield Chase, which, 300 years ago, was a royal forest consisting of lakes, woods and marshes.

HATFORD Oxfordshire SU3394
Village on B4508, 3 miles (5km) E of Faringdon
Small cluster of houses in Vale of the White Horse with good Norman church and terrace of cottages attributed to eminent architect GE Street.

HATHERLEIGH Devon SS5404
Village on A386, 7 miles (11km) NW of Okehampton
A tiny market town, still with its weekly market. Hilly, with pleasant buildings. A moorland stream appears in the middle of the town and there is an obelisk of 1860 high above.

HATHERSAGE Derbyshire SK2381
Village on A625, 8 miles (13km) N of Bakewell
This large, lively Peak District village is surrounded by moorland and gritstone edges, popular with walkers arriving by road from 'Surprise View' or by Hope Valley train. The grave of Little John, Robin Hood's lieutenant and perhaps a Hathersage nail-maker, is in the churchyard. Eyre family monuments supplied the heroine's name, and the area became Morton in *Jane Eyre*, after Charlotte Brontë visited in 1845.

HATTON Derbyshire SK2130
Village off A50, 5 miles (8km) N of Burton upon Trent
A mainly 19th-century village, across the River Dove from Tutbury and its castle on the Staffordshire side.

HAUGHLEY Suffolk TM0262
Village off A14 (A45), 3 miles (5km) NW of Stowmarket
Haughley still has a huge 13th-century castle mound and thatched cottages among apple trees. Haughley Park is a 17th-century red-brick mansion.

HAUGHMOND ABBEY Shropshire SJ5313
see Uffington

HAUGHTON Nottinghamshire SK6872
Hamlet on B6387, 4 miles (6km) NE of Ollerton
In the Sherwood Forest area, The World of Robin Hood provides a sound and vision journey through Crusader times to seek Robin Hood.

HAUGHTON LE SKERNE Durham NZ3116
Village on A66, in NE outskirts of Darlington
Originally an independent village, now within the City of Darlington. Although much of its history is now gone, there is still a village green and many of the surrounding houses are Listed Buildings. Bewick House was the home of William Bewick, portrait artist.

HAUXTON Cambridgeshire TL4352
Village off A10, 4 miles (6km) S of Cambridge
Site of a prehistoric crossing of the River Granta. The church has a painting of Thomas Becket of about 1250, and an interesting medieval pulpit.

HAVANT Hampshire SU7106
Town on A27 in N area of Portsmouth
A little town until the 1950s, this is now a large settlement with a small old centre of Georgian brick and some timber-framing. The museum is in the Victorian town hall. Leigh Park has been developed as housing by Portsmouth Corporation, who preserved the well-wooded grounds of the big house as the Sir George Staunton Country Park, with a farm and conservatory.

HAVENSTREET Isle of Wight SZ5690
Village on A3054, 3 miles (5km) SW of Ryde
Small brick village, with Havenstreet Station to the south, the home of the Isle of Wight Steam Railway, museum and trains running for 5 miles (8km).

HAVERFORDWEST (HWLFFORDD) Dyfed SM9515
Town on A40, 20 miles (32km) W of St Clears
Handsome, hilly old county town for Pembrokeshire, centrally located for good access to the coast. The River Cleddau once navigable, giving town a sea-trading past (Old Quay recalls those times). Modern waterside development, ruined medieval priory, elegant Georgian architecture. Panoramic overall view from ruined castle and old gaol (now museum) is on hilltop above the town.

HAVERGATE ISLAND Suffolk TM4147
Island SW of Orford
A long spit of land jutting into the sea is now an RSPB reserve. Flocks of avocets can often be seen flying around it.

HAVERHILL Suffolk TL6745
Town on A604, 16 miles (26km) SE of Cambridge
A large late Victorian and modern town with an abundance of council estates and factories. A parson from Haverhill founded Haverhill, Massachusetts, USA.

HAVERIGG Cumbria SD1578
Village off A5093, 1 mile (2km) SW of Millom
Tiny village at the end of a lane leading to fine sand dunes. An extensive RSPB reserve is located on an old iron-mining site.

HAVERING-ATTE-BOWER Greater London TQ5193
Village in borough of Havering, N of Romford
The Bower was a small royal palace. Today there are enjoyable woods in Havering Country Park, and red deer in Bedfords Park.

HAVERTHWAITE Cumbria SD3483
Village on A590, 2 miles (3km) SW of Newby Bridge
The village lies on the River Leven. The Low Wood Gunpowder Works date from 1849; the gunpowder was removed, for safety reasons, by boat.

HAWARDEN Clwyd SJ3165
Town off A55, 6 miles (10km) W of Chester
Small border town with strong links with William Gladstone. Stands at strategic entry point into Wales from Cheshire Plain. Park contains 'old' and 'new' castles – former is medieval, latter is castellated Broadlane Hall (not open), which was Gladstone's home. The church has a Gladstone memorial chapel and adjacent is St Deiniol's residential library, founded by the politician in the late 19th century.

HAWES North Yorkshire SD8789
Small town on A684, 14 miles (22km) SE of Kirkby Stephen
Situated in Upper Wensleydale on the River Ure, Hawes is the main centre for the northern part of the Yorkshire Dales National Park. This is a farming area and the Gimmer lamb sales in September and the Swaledale tup sales in October are the highlights of the year. The famous Wensleydale cheese is made locally.

HAWESWATER Cumbria NY5015
Reservoir off A590, W of Shap
The lake is used as a reservoir and its banks support many birds, including dippers, grey wagtails and common sandpipers.

HAWFORD Hereford and Worcester SO8460
Village off A443, 4 miles (6km) N of Worcester
On outskirts of Worcester, the National Trust maintains the 16th-century timber-framed Hawford Dovecote.

HAWICK Borders NT5014
Town on A7, 11 miles (18km) S of Selkirk
Pronounced 'Hoyk', this is a centre of the knitwear industry and largest of the Border towns, largely rebuilt after a fire of 1570. An attractive town with good tourist facilities, noted for its Common Riding, held each June. The Horse Monument commemorates the defeat of marauding English troops in 1514 by local teenagers. Local museum in Wilton Lodge, surrounded by a spacious park.

HAWKEDON Suffolk TL7953
Village off A143, 6 miles (10km) NW of Long Melford
The River Glem trickles through meadows below the hall. St Mary's Church is only accessible across the green by mown paths.

HAWKESTONE HALL Shropshire SJ5830
see Weston-under-Redcastle

HAWKHURST Kent TQ7630
Village on A268/A229, 4 miles (6km) S of Cranbrook
Large, straggling Wealden village, with the old centre of church and weatherboarded cottages round a big tree-lined green and a newer centre at the crossroads with an elegant Regency shopping arcade.

HAWKINGE Kent TR2139
Village off A260, 3 miles (5km) N of Folkestone
Village high on the chalk above Folkestone with Battle of Britain Museum and humble little flint church declared redundant in 1980.

HAWKSHAW Greater Manchester SD7615
Village on A676, 2 miles (3km) SW of Ramsbottom
At one time a coal-mining village, now a desirable residential area with much open countryside, surrounding dairy farming.

HAWKSHEAD Cumbria SD3598
Village on B5285, 4 miles (6km) S of Ambleside
It was not until the 19th century that there were roads to the village and the village centre is still not accessible by car. Wordsworth went to the grammar school here that was founded in 1585. The school is now a museum with an important antiquarian library. The National Trust owns, and runs, the Beatrix Potter Gallery and Hawkshead Courthouse.

HAWKSWORTH Nottinghamshire SK7543
Village off A52, 4 miles (6km) NE of Bingham
Quiet village whose long street is lined with houses. Church with 17th-century brick tower on 13th-century stone base, elaborate Norman tympanum.

HAWNBY North Yorkshire SE5487
Village off B1257, 6 miles (10km) NW of Helmsley
A remote village on the River Rye where coal and iron have been worked. Evidence of early settlers in the church.

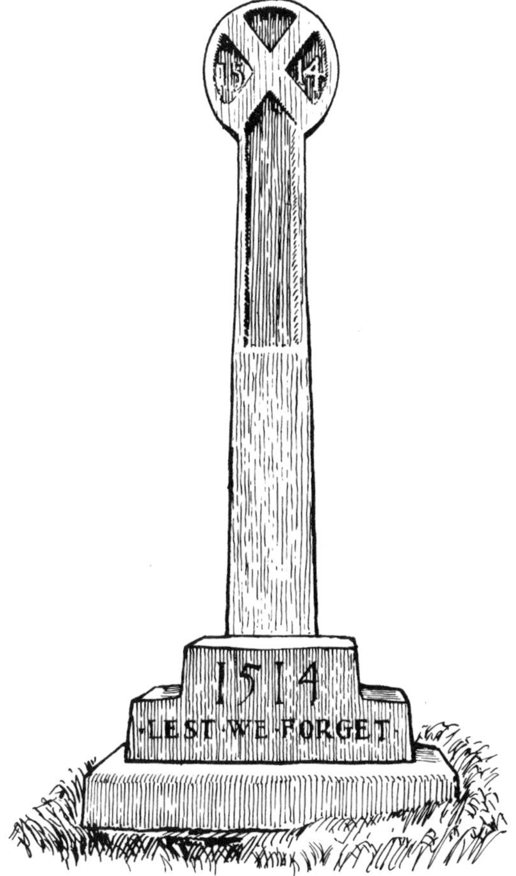

Pillar commemorating the victory of the Hawick youths.

HAWORTH West Yorkshire SE0237
Town off A629, 2 miles (3km) SW of Keighley
This bustling town is on the edge of the Pennine Moors and the steep Main Street is still paved with stone setts, and lined with shops, galleries and cafés. Many of the stone-built handloom weavers' cottages survive, but it is the buildings associated with the Brontë family, including the Parsonage and St Michael's Church, which dominate.

HAWSTEAD Suffolk TL8559
Village off A134, 3 miles (5km) S of Bury St Edmunds
Hawstead has a very fine Norman church with a magnificent hammerbeam roof. The large number of monuments include some to the Bacon family.

HAWTON Nottinghamshire SK7851
Hamlet off A46, 2 miles (3km) S of Newark-on-Trent
Quietly situated beside the River Devon, the church has remarkable 14th-century stone carvings, probably by Southwell Minster craftsmen, and an outstanding stone Easter Sepulchre.

HAXBY North Yorkshire SE6054
Village off B1363, 4 miles (6km) N of York
An agricultural community on the fertile Vale of York, here since before the Norman Conquest.

HAXEY Humberside SK7699
Village on A161, 3 miles (5km) S of Epworth
The parish church is one of the most impressive in the area, dating back to the 12th century. Traditionally the Haxey Hood Game is played every 6 January, when rival teams from Haxey and Westwoodside compete to carry the 'hood' through a scrum to their own village pub.

HAY-ON-WYE Powys SO2242
Small town on B4350, 15 miles (24km) NE of Brecon
Small border town rejuvenated as the 'town of books' or 'second-hand book capital of the world'. Since the 1960s well over 20 bookshops have opened here, followed by antiques and craft shops. All kinds of books are sold, from new novels to antiquarian. Charming covered market place in shadow of Hay Castle (private), a mansion of Norman origin. In early summer the town hosts the prestigious Hay Literature Festival, attracting top names.

HAYDOCK Merseyside SJ5696
Town off M6, 4 miles (6km) E of St Helens
A small industrial town of chiefly Victorian and Edwardian terraced housing. The local coal mines have closed, but the town is near the important crossroads of the Liverpool–East Lancashire and Warrington–Wigan roads. Haydock Park racecourse, the premier course in the northwest of England, lies in the grounds of Haydock Lodge.

HAYDON BRIDGE Northumberland NY8464
Small town on A69, 6 miles (10km) W of Hexham
On the banks of the River South Tyne, the town developed around the river crossing. The old six-arch bridge was gated as protection against Scottish invaders. It is now used only by pedestrians and a modern bridge carries traffic on the busy A69 across the river.

HAYES Greater London TQ0980
District in borough of Hillingdon
Industrial district close to the railway and Grand Union Canal. Towpath walk to Uxbridge (see). Beck Theatre arts centre.

HAYFIELD Derbyshire SK0386
Small town on A624, 4 miles (6km) S of Glossop
Huddled below the exposed moorland of Kinder Scout, the town grew up around wool-weaving and calico-printing works. A popular centre for hillwalkers, with the Sett Valley Trail for gentler walking and riding alongside the river, which rushes down from the plateau to join the River Goyt at New Mills. Flooding was a frequent problem, causing the church to be rebuilt in 1818.

HAYLE Cornwall SW5537
Town off A30, 3 miles (5km) SE of St Ives
Hayle has a huge artificial pond, deliberately impounded to provide water, and deserted wharves. This was an industrial village, established in the 18th century to smelt copper and make mine engines. The estuary is a nature reserve.

HAYLING ISLAND Hampshire SU7200
Island on A3023, S of Havant
A large, flat island, bordered by muddy harbours. The south shore of the island is sandy and started as a resort in the 1820s. The first bridge from the mainland was built in 1824. North Hayling remains rural; the south is more built up, with 1930s and later seaside buildings. Two interesting medieval churches.

HAYTON Cumbria NY5157
Village off A595, 3 miles (5km) S of Brampton
A small rural village overlooked by an 11th-century castle. St James' Church contains an 800-year-old font which stood in the castle chapel.

HAYTOR VALE Devon SX7777
Village off B3387, 5 miles (8km) N of Ashburton
This small village on the eastern side of Dartmoor has Haytor Rocks to the west. This is one of the finest of the granite outcrops on the heights of the moor, 1490ft (453m) up, with wide views. There have been granite quarries here from about 1800, and the remains of the tramway built in 1820 have granite rails for horse-drawn wagons.

HAYWARDS HEATH West Sussex TQ3323
Town on A272, 12 miles (19km) N of Brighton
A modern town on high heathland with housing estates, offices and light industry which has grown around the station. Until the 1980s, the former market was the largest in Sussex. Long, hilly High Street and modern precinct. Old settlement around Muster Green, site of a Civil War battle, where pre-19th-century houses survive among Victorian villas. Borde Hill garden near by.

HAZEL GROVE Greater Manchester SJ9286
Town on A6, 3 miles (5km) SE of Stockport
Busy outskirts of Stockport, and popular residential area. Developed as a coaching stop on the main A6 road to Buxton and Macclesfield.

HAZELWOOD Derbyshire SK3245
Village off B5023, 2 miles (3km) SW of Belper
Village set on a low ridge behind The Chevin, 'the last of the Pennines', above the River Ecclesbourne, with a Victorian church.

HEACHAM Norfolk TF6737
Village off A149, 2 miles (3km) S of Hunstanton
The scent of lavender fills the air for miles around the pretty Wash village of Heacham, wafting from the lavender farm at Caley Mill. The American Indian princess Pocahontas is commemorated in a tablet in St Mary's Church. She married John Rolfe, squire of Heacham Hall, in 1614, and died three years later of smallpox.

HEADBOURNE WORTHY Hampshire SU4832
Village on A33, 2 miles (3km) N of Winchester
Small and rural village, with a rare complete Saxon church, its graveyard surrounded by a stream.

HEADCORN Kent TQ8344
Village on A274, 9 miles (14km) SE of Maidstone
Large, attractive village beside the River Beult, now in commuter land, but with excellent half-timbered houses from its days as a prosperous cloth-making town.

HEADINGLEY West Yorkshire SE2835
District in NW Leeds
Conservation area and prosperous district of Leeds famous as home of Yorkshire County cricket ground.

HEADINGTON Oxfordshire SP5407
District on E edge of Oxford
Stone workers' cottages, affluent Victorian villas and modern estates contribute to enormous architectural variety of this part of Oxford. Shotover Country Park near by.

HEADLAM Durham NZ1818
Village off A67, 3 miles (5km) NW of Piercebridge
Charming rural village. Headlam Hall, a fine Jacobean manor house, surrounded by high walls, is on the outskirts. Converted into a hotel in 1979.

HEAGE Derbyshire SK3750
Village on B6013, 2 miles (3km) W of Ripley
Derbyshire's only tower windmill (open by appointment), built in the 19th century for corn-grinding. Nearby remains of two iron blast furnaces, monument to county's cast-iron industries.

HEALAUGH North Yorkshire SE0399
Village on B6270, 1 mile (2km) W of Reeth
The village lies in the valley of the River Swale. The original 17th- and 18th-century housing has been much altered over the years.

HEANOR Derbyshire SK4346
Town on A608, 3 miles (5km) NW of Ilkeston
Hilltop market town whose Victorian church retains its 15th-century tower, and a monument to Samuel Watson (died 1715), the chief woodcarver at Chatsworth.

HEANTON PUNCHARDON Devon SS5035
Village off A361, 4 miles (6km) W of Barnstaple
Village on the ridge above the Taw estuary, with an impressive late medieval church. Airfield on the flat land by the estuary.

HEATH West Yorkshire SE3510
Village off A655, 2 miles (3km) E of Wakefield
The village is made up of 17th- and 18th-century houses and cottages, built up around Heath Common and now a conservation area.

HEATH AND REACH Bedfordshire SP9228
Village off A5, immediately N of Leighton Buzzard
Really two hamlets combined, in sandy country. Dear little Victorian well-house with clock tower. Stockgrove Country Park has woods, parkland and a lake.

HEATH CHAPEL Shropshire SO5585
Site off B4368, 3 miles (5km) E of Diddlebury
Unspoilt and atmospheric little Norman chapel with 17th-century furnishings, a solitary reminder of long-vanished settlement. Key available.

HEATHFIELD East Sussex TQ5821
Small town on A265, 11 miles (18km) S of Tunbridge Wells
Large, modern settlement, formerly known as Tower Street, which grew up around the railway station, since closed. It now merges with charming Old Heathfield, near by, with its weatherboarded and brick cottages round All Saints' Church. At nearby Horam is the Sussex Farm Museum, with an interpretive centre, country walks and farm trails.

HEATHROW AIRPORT Greater London TQ0775
Airport off M4, 14 miles (23km) W of Charing Cross
London's principal airport since 1946, succeeding Croydon (see), and the world's busiest. Viewing area on Queens Building Roof Gardens. The airport is surrounded by double-glazed suburban housing and numerous attendant hotels, which are generally tawdry or depressing to look at. An exception is the impressive Hilton hotel of 1990 at Terminal Four.

HEBBURN Tyne and Wear NZ3164
Town on A185, 4 miles (6km) NE of Gateshead
Built up around ship-building and heavy engineering. Swan Hunter shipyards were based here until closure.

HEBDEN BRIDGE West Yorkshire SD9927
Town on A646, 7 miles (11km) W of Halifax
An ancient mill town, the 'capital of the Pennines', which has, since 1970, been much restored. Many of the old mill buildings have been converted into museums and other places of interest and the typical 'double-decker' houses can still be seen. The Rochdale Canal has also been cleaned and offers many leisure facilities.

HECKFIELD Hampshire SU7260
Village on A33, 4 miles (6km) N of Hook
A backwater, off the main roads. Odd tower to the church, partly built of sarsen.

HECKINGHAM Norfolk TM3898
Village off A146, 2 miles (3km) E of Loddon
Heckingham has an 18th-century House of Industry and thatched church with a round tower overlooking the pretty River Chet.

HECKINGTON Lincolnshire TF1444
Village off A17, 5 miles (8km) E of Sleaford
Eight-sailed working windmill, Pearoom craft workshops and exhibition centre. One of England's finest 14th-century churches, rich in gargoyles and flowing tracery.

HECKMONDWIKE West Yorkshire SE1824
Town on A638, 2 miles (3km) W of Batley
A textile town with a busy centre which features attractively laid out municipal gardens. There is a clock tower in the market square.

HEDDON'S MOUTH Devon SS6549
Beauty spot off A39, 4 miles (6km) W of Lynton
The seaward end of a spectacularly steep valley, reached by footpath from the little woody hamlet of Hunter's Inn.

HEDDON-ON-THE-WALL Northumberland NZ1366
Village on B6318, 7 miles (11km) W of Newcastle upon Tyne
A residential suburb of Newcastle upon Tyne which was originally a small agricultural village. This is the site of Twelve Mile Castle along Hadrian's Wall. Nothing remains of it, but the most easterly section of the wall and a section of the rampart cut from the rock is still visible to the east of the village.

HEDGE END Hampshire SU4912
District off A334, 1 mile (2km) SE of West End
So named because it was open common until 1863, beyond the hedges. A few Victorian villas in a sea of 1960s onwards housing.

HEDGERLEY Buckinghamshire SU9687
Village off A355, 3 miles (5km) SE of Beaconsfield
In wooded country. Church Wood Royal Society for the Protection of Birds reserve shelters sparrowhawks, woodpeckers, nuthatches and many more, plus plants and butterflies. Victorian church of interest.

HEDNESFORD Staffordshire SK0012
Town off A460, 2 miles (3km) NE of Cannock
The old Cross Keys inn and attractive Anglesey hotel survive in the centre of a former mining town. Valley heritage centre explains the area's history.

HEDON Humberside TA1928
Town off A1033, 6 miles (10km) E of Hull
The Church of St Augustine dominates the town and is known as the 'King of Holderness' because of its cathedral-like proportions. The Kilnsea Cross is a stone relic said to have originally been erected on the site where Henry, Duke of Lancaster, landed prior to his overthrowing Richard II. The town has the oldest civic mace in the country.

HEDSOR Buckinghamshire SU9086
Hamlet off A4094, 3 miles (5km) SW of Beaconsfield
Lord Boston's Folly on Harvest Hill is included in a 1990s house. Cliveden, the former Astor stately home, is now a hotel; the grounds are open.

HEIGHINGTON Durham NZ2422
Village off A6072, 2 miles (3km) SW of Newton Aycliffe
Stephenson's Locomotion Number One was first put on the rails here. Heighington Hall, 18th century, has interesting stonework.

HELENSBURGH Strathclyde NS2982
Town on A814, 8 miles (13km) NW of Dumbarton
Attractive Georgian seaside town with spacious streets, fine buildings and Promenade. Henry Bell (1767–1830), designer of the first practical passenger steamship, moved here; the *Comet*'s flywheel is in Hermitage Park. Charles Rennie Mackintosh's finest work, Hill House, with complementary furnishings and decoration, sits above the town. Birthplace of John Logie Baird (1888–1946), inventor of television.

HELFORD Cornwall SW7526
Village off B3293, 6 miles (10km) E of Helston
Idyllic, tiny village on the Helford estuary. The pretty cottages were described in Daphne du Maurier's novel *Frenchman's Creek.*

HELIONS BUMPSTEAD Essex TL6541
Village off B1054, 3 miles (5km) SW of Haverhill
Junior relation of Steeple Bumpstead (see). Thatched and colour-washed cottages. Church's brick tower is a local landmark.

HELLINGLY East Sussex TQ5812
Village off A271, 2 miles (3km) N of Hailsham
On the edge of Hailsham. The centre is a group of charming old tile-hung cottages around an ancient raised churchyard.

HELMDON Northamptonshire SP5843
Village off A43, 4 miles (6km) N of Brackley
Helmdon stone was used to build Easton Neston, Stowe and Woburn. Medieval glass in church, at the end of the long main street. Former Great Central Railway viaduct.

HELMINGHAM Suffolk TM1857
Village off B1079, 4 miles (6km) S of Debenham
Highland cattle, Soay sheep and red deer can be seen in Tudor Helmingham Hall's 400 acre (160ha) park. Interesting walled kitchen and wildflower gardens.

HELMSDALE Highland ND0315
Village on A9, 15 miles (24km) NE of Golspie
Fishing and holiday town built to house evicted tenants from Strath Kildonan. The Timespan heritage centre tells the local history. Gold was discovered near by in the 19th century.

HELMSHORE Lancashire SD7821
Village on B6214, 1 mile (2km) S of Haslingden
The village is home to the Museum of the Lancashire Textile Industry, housed in an old cotton-spinning mill.

HELMSLEY North Yorkshire SE6183
Small town on A170, 12 miles (19km) E of Thirsk
This is one of the most popular of Yorkshire's market towns, where attractive old inns, houses and shops surround the market square. The town is overlooked by its ruined medieval castle and by All Saints' Church. Duncombe Park is open to the public; the grounds provide an important habitat for wildlife.

HELPSTON Cambridgeshire TF1205
Village on B1443, 6 miles (10km) NW of Peterborough
The poet John Clare was born in a thatched cottage near the village centre in 1793. He is buried in the churchyard and a memorial to him stands opposite the 14th-century village cross. Helpston lies between ancient woodland to the south and west, and the beautiful Welland Valley to the north.

HELSBY Cheshire SJ4975
Village on A56, 8 miles (13km) NE of Chester
Village sits at the foot of Helsby Tor, often used as a practice hill by climbers.

HELSTON Cornwall SW6527
Town on A394, 15 miles (24km) SW of Truro
Helston was a stannary town, where tin was brought to be weighed and taxed, and until the 13th century, when a bar of shingle formed across the mouth of the estuary, it was also a port (see Loe Pool).

Today it is a surprisingly large market town, full of small-scale Victorian and Georgian houses and cottages. The pretty view down the wide main street shows green hills framed by a decorative 1834 archway. An open stream runs by the church and down the main street. The monumental market house was built in 1838. There is a Folklore Museum, and some folk celebrations survive: the Furry Dance on 8 May welcomes spring, and is preceded by a mummers' play the day before.

Helston's unusual Georgian church is built of granite but is austerely classical.

HELVELLYN Cumbria NY3415
Mountain off A591, 4 miles (6km) W of Patterdale
Overlooking Ullswater, the view from the top of the mountain is extensive. There are three memorials on the summit.

HEMEL HEMPSTEAD Hertfordshire TL0507
Town off A41, 7 miles (11km) NW of Watford
On the River Gade and close to the Grand Union Canal. The old market town has a pleasing High Street, handsome Georgian houses, a notable Norman church and an attractive riverside park. Acres of post-war housing mark the New Town, developed since the 1940s. This is prime commuter territory, handy for the M1 and M25.

HEMINGBROUGH North Yorkshire SE6730
Village on A63, 4 miles (6km) E of Selby
The village is situated on the River Ouse and is dominated by St Mary's Church, parts of which date back to the 12th century.

HEMINGFORD, ABBOTS AND GREY Cambridgeshire TL2870
Villages off A14 (A604), 3 miles (5km) SE of Huntingdon
Standing sedately beside the River Ouse and lush water-meadows, these two villages comprise clusters of photogenic cottages around their churches. Hemingford Abbots's church has a fine spire, while that of Hemingford Grey's was lost in a hurricane in 1741. Hemingford Grey has a splendid Norman manor house, said to be the oldest continuously occupied house in England.

HEMPSTEAD Essex TL6338
Village on B1054, 5 miles (8km) N of Thaxted
Dick Turpin, highwayman, was born at the Bell inn, now the Bluebell. Buried here is William Harvey, discoverer of the circulation of the blood.

HEMSBY Norfolk TG4917
Village on B1159, 1 mile (2km) S of Winterton-on-Sea
A Broadland village which was founded and named by Danish invaders. Now it is well known as a popular holiday resort.

HEMSWELL Lincolnshire SK9390
Village off B1398, 5 miles (8km) S of Kirton in Lindsey
Antiques centre of 270 shops at former RAF Hemswell. Craft centre. Village at foot of Lincolnshire Cliff has traditional permanent maypole.

HEMYOCK Devon ST1313
Village off B3391, 5 miles (8km) S of Wellington
Large village with elaborate cast-iron pump of 1902, and Hemyock Castle (limited opening), really a fortified manor house, moated and altered through the ages.

HENBURY Avon ST5678
see Blaise Hamlet

HENDON Greater London TQ2389
District in borough of Barnet
Well-to-do North London suburb with a 1930s air. Medieval Church of St Mary, local museum in 17th-century Church Farm House. The former aerodrome, important in aviation development from 1910, is now home to the Royal Air Force Museum with its Battle of Britain Hall and Bomber Command Hall.

Ruined castle at Helmsley.

Thatched cottage in Henfield.

HENFIELD West Sussex TQ2116
Town on A281, 7 miles (11km) N of Shoreham
Friendly village with a range of traditional shops on bustling High Street. Plenty of architectural detail among the brick, stone and tile-hung houses. The church was first mentioned in AD770. Good local museum. Modern housing to the north and west, trading estate and Woods Mill Countryside Centre to the south. To the east is Henfield's glory: its wide rough common and famous cricket ground with views to the South Downs.

HENGRAVE Suffolk TL8268
Village on A1101, 3 miles (5km) NW of Bury St Edmunds
Charming old-world thatched and flint cottages range through this quaint Suffolk village. Archaeological excavations show that there was a settlement here in neolithic and Bronze Age times. Hengrave's best-known feature is Hengrave Hall, built 1525–38 by wool merchant Thomas Kytson, and now owned by the Convent of Assumption.

HENLEY-IN-ARDEN Warwickshire SP1565
Village on A3400, 7 miles (11km) NW of Stratford upon Avon
The main attractions of this ancient borough, with its long, picturesque main street, are its venerable buildings. They include the 15th-century guildhall, Elizabethan White Swan hotel, and medieval Blue Bell inn. Many other timber-framed and stone buildings rub shoulders with good Georgian houses. Fine Norman Church of St Nicholas at nearby Beaudesert has earthworks of Norman castle behind it.

HENLEY-ON-THAMES Oxfordshire SU7682
Town on A4155, 6 miles (10km) NE of Reading
Home of the world's best-known rowing regatta, Henley lies on a beautiful stretch of the River Thames and boasts a rich variety of well-preserved old buildings dating from the 15th to the 18th centuries. New Street, Hart Street and Bell Street deserve a leisurely walk, and St Mary's Church should not be missed.

HENLLAN Dyfed SN3540
Hamlet off A484, 3 miles (5km) E of Newcastle Emlyn
Picturesque spot by wooded banks of River Teifi. Old stone bridge, site of an ancient fort and the narrow-gauge Teifi Valley Railway.

HENLOW Bedfordshire TL1738
Village off A507, 2 miles (3km) E of Shefford
Close to the River Hiz. Church with imposing tower. Royal Air Force camp has been here since 1918. Good cricket ground.

HEPPLE Northumberland NT9800
Village on B6341, 5 miles (8km) W of Rothbury
A small village in the Coquet valley. Raw Farm has a near complete castle which was the site of the murder of Margaret Crozier by William Winter. Witchy Neuk is a well-preserved Iron Age fort.

HEPTONSTALL West Yorkshire SD9828
Village off A646, 1 mile (2km) NW of Hebden Bridge
The village overlooks Hebden Bridge and the Hardcastle Crags and has become one of the main tourist centres of Calderdale. It is one of only three places in Britain where there are two churches in one churchyard. Every year on Good Friday the 'Paceggers Play' takes place in Weavers Square, telling the story of St George and his heroic deeds.

HEPWORTH West Yorkshire SE1606
Village off A616, 2 miles (3km) SE of Holmfirth
This is an agricultural village that had a large handloom weaving industry which is reflected in the local architecture.

HEREFORD Hereford and Worcester SO5139
City on A49/A438, 30 miles (48km) NW of Gloucester
The ancient capital of West Mercia, and the home town of David Garrick and Nell Gwynne, preserves a quiet centre bounded by the River Wye and a ring road, encouraging a rewarding stroll through the old streets. Individual buildings such as the Green Dragon coaching inn make an immediate impact, but the general impression is of harmonious architecture of many ages set in a comfortable market town.

The cathedral dominates both the riverside and the city centre, the massive strength of its Norman nave contrasting with the intricate architectural detail of the transepts and choir. The extensive chained library and the famous *Mappa Mundi* are its principal treasures, and there is another chained library at the beautiful All Saints' Church in the High Street.

Hereford's long-established attractions are supplemented by a wealth of museums appealing to many tastes – local and natural history at the City Museum, 17th-century domestic exhibits at the timber-framed Old House, steam pumping engines at the Waterworks Museum, furniture and costume at the Churchill Gardens Museum, relics of the Order of St John at Coningsby Hospital and the favourite local tipple at the Cider Museum.

HEREFORDSHIRE BEACON Hereford and Worcester SO7745
see Malvern Hills

HERGEST CROFT GARDENS Hereford and Worcester SO2857
see Kington

HERIOT Borders NT3953
Village on B709, 7 miles (11km) NW of Stow
Upland village in Moorfoot Hills on Heriot Water, tributary of the Tweed, surrounded by rolling grassy heathland.

HERM Channel Islands
Island E of Guernsey
Cliffs, valleys and sandy beaches on an island 2 miles (3km) long, ½ mile (1km) wide. No cars or roads, but an ancient trackway runs along its spine.

HERMITAGE CASTLE Borders NY4996
Site off B6399, 5 miles (8km) N of Newcastleton
Fine example of a massive four-towered medieval border castle on an imposing site in remote Liddesdale. Originally a Douglas stronghold, it passed to the Bothwells in 1492. Restored in the 19th century.

HERNE BAY Kent TR1768
Town on A299, 7 miles (11km) N of Canterbury
Popular resort on the north Kent Coast with a 7 mile (11km) beach, and a seafront dominated by an 80ft (243m) clock tower of 1837. Sailing clubs, golf course, country park and leisure centre on the front, where the former pier (burned down in 1970) stood. Local museum, windmill of 1789 and church inland at the old centre of Herne.

HERNHILL Kent TR0660
Village off A299, 3 miles (5km) E of Faversham
High on wooded hills above Faversham with splendid views over Graveney Marshes and Mount Ephraim Gardens. Church beside a pretty green with an oak tree and characterful buildings.

HERRIARD Hampshire SU6645
Hamlet on A339, 4 miles (6km) SE of Basingstoke
Parkland hamlet, with simple classical brick cottages of the 1820s, built by the owner of the now-demolished big house.

HERRINGFLEET Suffolk TM4797
Hamlet on B1074, 6 miles (10km) NW of Lowestoft
Famous for its splendid windmill and handsome Tudor thatched barn. The Saxon round tower of the church stands over the River Waveney.

HERSTMONCEUX East Sussex TQ6312
Village on A271, 4 miles (6km) NE of Hailsham
Attractive village, centre of the trug-making industry for over 160 years, with all sizes of Sussex trug basket made in the traditional way. Queen Victoria was a customer of the present firm, which exhibited at the Great Exhibition of 1851. The beautiful moated red-brick castle, begun in 1440, and until the 1980s the home of the Royal Observatory, is now an international study centre.

HERTFORD Hertfordshire TL3212
Town on A414, 3 miles (5km) W of Ware
Hertfordshire's historic and charming county town. Four rivers join here as the Mimran, Rib and Beane surrender themselves to the Lee. There are waterside and meadow walks, and riverside gardens in the castle grounds, plus the world's oldest purpose-built Friends Meeting House of 1670s. Enjoyable central streets with pargetting (decorative plasterwork), Georgian fronts, antiques shops and old pubs.

HERTINGFORDBURY Hertfordshire TL3012
Village off A414, 1 mile (2km) W of Hertford
A picturesque, exclusive and expensive place on the River Mimram. Possibly the original of the Bennet family's village in *Pride and Prejudice*. Curious bench-ends and fine monuments to the Cowpers and Grenfells of Panshanger Park in the Victorianised church. There are paths across the park, although the great house was demolished. Cole Green Way is a disused railway walk.

HESKETH BANK Lancashire SD4423
Village off A565, 2 miles (3km) N of Tarleton
On the banks of the Ribble estuary. West Lancashire Light Railway has historic 2ft (61cm) gauge Hunslet steam locomotive *Irish Mail*, built in 1903.

HESLINGTON North Yorkshire SE6250
Village off A19, 2 miles (3km) SE of York
In the 1960s the village of Heslington was chosen as the site of the University of York, and since then the place has developed.

HESSETT Suffolk TL9361
Village off A14 (A45), 5 miles (8km) SE of Bury St Edmunds
Hessett's church is named after St Ethelbert, a king of East Anglia. It is sometimes called the 'museum church', because of its many fine features.

HESSLE Humberside TA0326
Town off A63, 5 miles (8km) W of Hull
Once a major crossing point of River Humber. The 19th-century Hessle Cliff Mill in Humber Bridge Country Park once powered a whiting works. Windmill tower and machinery are preserved.

HESWALL Merseyside SJ2682
Town off A540, 5 miles (8km) SE of West Kirby
A commuter town for Liverpool and beyond, with many large Victorian buildings mingling with modern developments.

HETTON-LE-HOLE Tyne and Wear NZ3547
Town on A182, 6 miles (10km) NE of Durham
A sprawling residential area with no distinguishing features. Faries' Cradle is thought to be a cairn.

HEVENINGHAM Suffolk TM3372
Village on B1177, 5 miles (8km) SW of Halesworth
In tranquil countryside, Heveningham Hall (not open) is one of the grandest Georgian mansions in Suffolk. Its grounds were designed by Capability Brown.

HEVER Kent TQ4744
Village off B2026, 2 miles (3km) SE of Edenbridge
Popular tourist trap with a moated castle where Henry VIII wooed Anne Boleyn. Restored after 1903 by Lord Astor, who created a Tudor-style village and the formal Castle Gardens, with a maze of clipped yew, rose garden and Italian garden with antique sculpture. The castle contains a priceless collection of furniture, paintings and china. The church at the gates has Bullen (Boleyn) tombs.

HEVERSHAM Cumbria SD4983
Village on A6, 2 miles (3km) S of Levens
St Peter's Church, the oldest in Westmoreland, dates from the 8th century. Ephraim Chambers, publisher of the first Chamber's Dictionary, went to school here.

HEWELSFIELD Gloucestershire SO5602
Village on B4228, 4 miles (6km) W of Lydney
A distinctive church with good Norman work is at the centre of a village that commands fine views across the Forest of Dean.

HEXHAM Northumberland NY9364
Town off A69, 20 miles (32km) W of Newcastle
The historic market town of Hexham is now the administrative centre for Tynedale, built on a terrace overlooking the River Tyne.

The focal point of the town is Hexham Abbey. St Wilfrid built it in 674 but the present building dates mainly from 1113, when it was restored following centuries of raids by Danes and Scots. The oldest remains of the original abbey can be found in the Saxon crypt. St Wilfrid's chair, once used as a sanctuary stool, is at least 1,300 years old and reputed to have been the coronation seat of the kings of Northumbria.

The abbey stands at a corner of the market place, where colourful market stalls are set out every Tuesday in the Shambles, a long shelter with a flagged roof. The market place is surrounded by narrow Georgian streets and across the square from the abbey is the moot hall, built in the 14th century, now a gallery for changing exhibitions, and around the corner is the manor office, also 14th century and made from Roman stones, which now houses the Middle March Centre, a small museum devoted to border history.

HEXTABLE Kent TQ5170
Village on B528, 1 mile (2km) N of Swanley
In open countryside between the towns of Swanley and Dartford, Hextable is still a true village, nestled among its market gardens and orchards.

HEXTON Hertfordshire TL1030
Village on B655, 5 miles (8km) W of Hitchin
Next to Barton-le-Clay (see). Ravensburgh Castle is a large Iron Age hillfort among woods in Barton Hills to the southwest.

HEXWORTHY Devon SX6572
Hamlet off B3357, 7 miles (11km) NW of Ashburton
Tiny Dartmoor hamlet on the West Dart River, with extensive remains of 19th-century tin-mining, including an aqueduct and waterwheel pit.

HEYBRIDGE Essex TL8508
Suburb on B1022, immediately N of Maldon
Once a Roman port. Norman church, riverside and canalside walks. Boat moorings at Heybridge Basin, and a seawall path along the Blackwater estuary.

HEYDON Norfolk TG1127
Village off B1149, 3 miles (5km) N of Reepham
Such is the beauty of this little farming village clustered

about its green, that at least 30 film and TV productions have been based here.

HEYDOUR Lincolnshire TF0039
Hamlet off A153, 5 miles (8km) S of Ancaster
Grand medieval church with 14th- and 19th-century stained glass, fine Newton family monuments – including baby being dropped from roof of Culverthorpe Hall by pet monkey.

HEYSHAM Lancashire SD4160
Town on A589, 3 miles (5km) SW of Morecambe
Recorded in Domesday Book as 'Hessam', but there is evidence of a much earlier Saxon settlement here. St Peter's Church was founded in AD967 and is one of the oldest in continuous use in Europe. There is also an 8th-century ruined chapel to St Patrick. A regular ferry service operates to the Isle of Man.

HEYSHOTT West Sussex SU8918
Village off A286, 2 miles (3km) S of Midhurst
A long winding green lies to the north of the village street, which contains half-timbered brick and flint cottages interspersed by fields under the lee of wooded Heyshott Down.

HEYTESBURY Wiltshire ST9242
Village on A36, 4 miles (6km) SE of Warminster
Almost a small town, Heytesbury has almshouses, a little octagonal lock-up and many old malt houses. The writer Siegfried Sassoon lived here for 40 years until his death in 1967.

HEYTHROP Oxfordshire SP3527
Village off A361, 2 miles (3km) E of Chipping Norton
The Victorian church and cottages of this agreeable small estate village stand at the gates of Heythrop Park, now a conference centre.

HEYWOOD Greater Manchester SD8510
Town on A58, 3 miles (5km) E of Bury
A busy cotton town in the 19th century. Unusually constructed Queen's Park Bridge over the River Roch.

HICKLETON South Yorkshire SE4805
Village on A635, 6 miles (10km) W of Doncaster
Commuter village on the old Roman road to Pontefract.

HICKLING Norfolk TG4214
Village off A149, 3 miles (5km) E of Stalham
Hickling Broad forms part of a 1,400 acre (565ha) nature reserve run by the Norfolk Naturalists' Trust, and was formed by medieval peat diggings. Besides migrating birds, it is home to the rare swallowtail butterfly. The charming village of Hickling can be reached by road or boat; despite its remoteness, it was bombed in both world wars.

HICKSTEAD West Sussex TQ2620
Hamlet on A23, 4 miles (6km) SW of Cuckfield
A little place on the old A23 with the All England Showjumping Ground hosting the European Championships every July and other show jumping events throughout spring, summer and autumn.

HIDCOTE BARTRIM Gloucestershire SP1742
Hamlet off B4632, 3 miles (5km) NE of Chipping Campden
This area is a mecca for garden enthusiasts. The renowned Hidcote Manor Garden (National Trust) offers rare trees and shrubs, old rose species and a succession of delightful small gardens created from 11 acres (4ha) of hill landscape. The nearby Kiftsgate Court Gardens feature plants, shrubs, trees and a rose collection on steep hillside terraces overlooking the Vale of Evesham.

HIGH BICKINGTON Devon SS6020
Village on B3217, 7 miles (11km) E of Torrington
The church here has one of the largest collections of 16th-century wooden bench-ends, carved with figures and all sorts of devices.

HIGH CROSS Hertfordshire TL3618
Village on A10, 3 miles (5km) N of Ware
On Ermine Street. Monuments mark the first British hot-air balloon flight in 1784 and the spot where Thomas Clarkson resolved to abolish slave trade in 1785.

HIGH EASTER Essex TL6214
Village off A1060, 2 miles (3km) NE of Leaden Roding
'Easter' may be from the Old English for 'sheepfolds', 'High' because it is higher than Good Easter (see), whose 'Good' comes from a Saxon lady named Godiva.

HIGH ERCALL Shropshire SJ5917
Village on B5062, 8 miles (13km) NE of Shrewsbury
Last major event here was a Civil War siege of the manor house. Adjacent Norman church also suffered, but both survive at the heart of the leafy village.

HIGH FORCE Durham NY8828
Waterfall off B6277, 5 miles (8km) NW of Middleton
On one of the most attractive sections of the Pennine Way, the 70ft (21m) waterfall on the River Tees plunges over Whin Sill rock into a deep pool.

HIGH HALDEN Kent TQ8937
Village on A28, 3 miles (5km) NE of Tenterden
Weatherboarded Wealden village grouped around its central green. The church has a timber tower of about 1300, unique in Kent but similar to those in Essex.

HIGH HALSTOW Kent TQ7875
Village off A228, 5 miles (8km) NE of Strood
On a hill in the middle of the Hoo peninsula with the Northward Hill Royal Society for the Protection of Birds reserve, an important breeding ground for waterbirds, and the largest heronry in Britain.

HIGH HAM Somerset ST4231
see Ham

HIGH LEGH Cheshire SJ7085
Village on A54, 2 miles (3km) SE of Lymm
Popular residential village with two churches, originally the chapels of the Legh and Leigh families, who both owned the manor during Henry II's reign.

HIGH LORTON Cumbria NY1525
see Lorton

HIGH MELTON South Yorkshire SE5001
Village off A6023, 4 miles (6km) W of Doncaster
High Melton Hall, dating from before the 18th century, was purchased in 1948 by the Ministry of Education and is now a teachers' training centre.

HIGH ONGAR Essex TL5603
Village off A414, 1 mile (2km) NE of Chipping Ongar
In Roding Valley, a suburban outlier of Chipping Ongar (see). Norman church with elaborately carved doorway, and a Victorian brick tower.

HIGH RODING Essex TL6017
Village on B184, 3 miles (5km) SW of Great Dunmow
Marginally higher above the River Roding than the other Rodings, along a stretch of Roman road. Thatched cottages and weatherboarding.

HIGH WYCOMBE Buckinghamshire SU8693
Town off M40, 28 miles (45km) NW of London
Old Chilterns Gap market town swollen into a shopping, services, education and administration centre. Office blocks, supermarkets, roundabouts galore, houses crowding steep-sided River Wye valley on old London–Oxford road. Older survivals include 18th-century guildhall, little market house and High Street houses. Chair Museum illuminates historic Chilterns furniture industry and Windsor chairs. Aircraft museum and flying trips at Wycombe Air Park.

HIGHAM Kent TQ7171
Village off A226, 3 miles (5km) NW of Rochester
Scattered place on the edge of the Thames–Medway conurbation, with an ancient marshland church; has submerged three separate hamlets, the most southerly being Gads Hill, where Dickens lived 1857–70.

HIGHAM FERRERS Northamptonshire SP9668
Town on A6, 4 miles (6km) E of Wellingborough
One of the finest Northamptonshire churches, with double nave, woodwork and brasses. It dates mainly from the 13th and 14th centuries, with a splendid spire rebuilt in the 1630s. Archbishop Chichele, born here in 1362, founded the school, Bedehouse and College (English Heritage), in the 1420s. Triangular market place with attractive stone buildings, 14th-century cross, Georgian houses and 1809 town hall.

HIGHBRIDGE Somerset ST3247
Town on A38, 2 miles (3km) SE of Burnham-on-Sea
Now part of Burnham-on-Sea, this was a separate little town in medieval times.

HIGHCLERE Hampshire SU4360
Village on A343, 6 miles (10km) SW of Newbury
A wooded village, with Highclere Castle, a huge mansion of 1840 featuring elaborate Victorian interiors and a fine park.

HIGHCLIFFE Dorset SZ2192
Village on A337, 4 miles (6km) E of Christchurch
Big village centre and built-up area along the coast. Highcliffe Castle (in a public park) is now a ruin, originally an extraordinary 1830s building with medieval French features.

HIGHER ASHTON Devon SX8484
see Ashton

HIGHER WALTON Lancashire SD5727
Village on A675, 4 miles (6km) SE of Preston
A memorial garden has been opened in the village centre in memory of Kathleen Ferrier, who was born here. Large mill now converted into industrial units.

HIGHGATE Greater London TQ2887
District in borough of Haringey
Victorian hilltop suburb with post-war blocks of flats. Lauderdale House, 17th century, is in Waterlow Park. The Whittington Stone with cat, at the foot of Highgate Hill, is where Dick Whittington turned back to become Mayor of London. Highgate Cemetery is being restored and conserved by its Friends: the eastern section is open, guided tours of western section. There are graves of Karl Mar and George Eliot, among many others. Old Highgate is very pretty and villagey.

HIGHNAM Gloucestershire SO7819
Village off B4215, 3 miles (5km) W of Gloucester
Victorian artist Thomas Parry designed the church and filled it with remarkable art work. Nightingales are protected in the ancient Highnam Woods (RSPB) near by.

HIGHWORTH Wiltshire SU2092
Town on A361, 5 miles (8km) NE of Swindon
An old hilltop town, with a wide view. The centre has much Cotswold-type stone building, and 18th-century brick and stone. Jesmond House hotel is a particularly good, early 18th-century building. The large church, of the 15th century and later, has a Norman carving and was used as a strong point by Royalists in the Civil War. A cannon ball is still preserved.

HILBOROUGH Norfolk TF8200
Village off A1065, 6 miles (10km) S of Swaffham
Home of Admiral Nelson's ancestors, Hilborough is a small village with lovely All Saints' Church and a hall dating from 1779.

HILBRE ISLANDS Merseyside SJ1887
Islands off Hilbre Point at head of Wirral Peninsula
The Hilbre Island Nature Reserve provides an important high-tide roost for wading birds. Access is on foot but is restricted by the tides.

HILFIELD Dorset ST6305
Hamlet off A352, 7 miles (11km) S of Sherborne
Secluded hamlet on the lower chalk slopes, with a wide view over the Blackmoor Vale (see).

HILGAY Norfolk TL6298
Village off A10, 3 miles (5km) S of Downham Market
Lime trees line the path to All Saints' Church where Captain Manby, rocket engineer, is buried. The village centre is the delightful market square.

HILL OF FEARN Highland NH8377
Village on B9165, 4 miles (6km) SE of Tain
Attractive inland village on a peninsula between Dornoch and Cromarty Firths. Most noted for three Pictish cross-slabs of major importance found in the area.

HILLEND Lothian NT2566
Village on A702, 5 miles (8km) S of Edinburgh
Outlying suburb on the south side of Edinburgh at the foot of the Pentland Hills, where there is an extensive artificial ski-slope.

HILLESDEN Buckinghamshire SP6828
Hamlet off A421, 3 miles (5km) S of Buckingham
Little place with a wonderful 15th-century church that inspired the young Sir George Gilbert Scott, who later restored it.

HILLINGDON Greater London TQ0782
District in borough of Hillingdon
Notable brasses in the Parish Church of St John, rebuilt by Sir George Gilbert Scott in the 1840s. Parks, playing fields and ski centre.

HILLMORTON Warwickshire SP5374
Village on A428, on SE outskirts of Rugby
This suburb of Rugby preserves its character, with old houses at its centre and a church containing good 18th-century furnishings and interesting monuments.

HILLSBOROUGH South Yorkshire SK3289
District in NW Sheffield
Known as the home ground of Sheffield Wednesday Football Club. A nearby garden serves as a memorial to those who died in the Hillsborough Disaster of 1989.

HILLSIDE Tayside NO7061
Village off A935, 2 miles (3km) N of Montrose
Nearest village to House of Dun, a superb Georgian mansion designed in 1730 by William Adam. Noted for its exceptional interior plasterwork. Walled garden.

HILTON Cambridgeshire TL2866
Village on B1040, 4 miles (6km) SW of St Ives
This pretty village has a famous turf maze, dating from 1660, on its eastern edge next to the green.

HILTON Derbyshire SK2430
Village off A516, 8 miles (13km) SW of Derby
Village set on a long street. Distinctive half-timbered Wakelyn Old Hall manor house became the Bull's Head inn, now a private house.

HILTON Dorset ST7803
Village off A354, 6 miles (10km) NE of Puddletown
Classic English landscape: a green valley with wooded hills, and a prominent 15th-century church.

HIMBLETON Hereford and Worcester SO9458
Village off B4090, 4 miles (6km) SE of Droitwich
Scattered village on Bow Brook in pastoral countryside. Interesting medieval church. Packhorse bridge by timber-framed buildings at Shell, near by.

HIMLEY Staffordshire SO8891
Village on A449, 5 miles (8km) S of Woverhampton
The drunken Glynne Arms vies for attention with a fine classical church. Himley Hall Park caters for outdoor activities and also features fascinating model landscapes.

HINCASTER Cumbria SD5084
Hamlet off A590, 5 miles (8km) S of Kendal
A small hamlet, which had a gunpowder mill until the 1920s. The powder was transported by boat on the Preston to Tewitfield Canal.

HINCKLEY Leicestershire SP4293
Town on A47, 12 miles (19km) SW of Leicester
West Leicestershire town, near Watling Street (A5), which grew through the hosiery industry. Timber-framed 17th-century framework knitters' cottages opposite red-brick late 19th-century hosiery factory. The Great Meeting Unitarian Chapel, 1722, is tucked behind the factory. The castle mound is now a memorial garden. The medieval church was extended and altered in the 19th century. Shakespeare refers to Hinckley market. Joseph Hansom built the prototype Hansom cab in town.

HINDHEAD Surrey SU8835
Small town on A287, 2 miles (3km) NW of Haslemere
Highest town in Surrey, 800ft (243m) up on the plateau top of the greensand ridge. It was developed from the 1880s, when Professor John Tyndall popularised it by claiming that the air was as pure as in Switzerland. Sir Arthur Conan Doyle and George Bernard Shaw both lived here. Hindhead Common (National Trust) is a wild place of gorse, pines and heather.

HINDLEY Greater Manchester SD6104
Town on A577, 2 miles (3km) SE of Wigan
Much residential development has taken place here and at Hindley Green. The library and local park were built by wealthy mill owner Nathaniel Eckersley.

HINDON Wiltshire ST9132
Village on B3089, 7 miles (11km) NE of Shaftesbury
Dense and pretty, with a slightly urban feel. Stone houses built after a bad fire of 1754 trail up the hill.

HINDRINGHAM Norfolk TF9836
Village off A148, 6 miles (10km) NE of Fakenham
Dating back to the Bronze Age, this ancient settlement has some handsome buildings. The sea can be glimpsed 4 miles (6km) distant.

HINGHAM Norfolk TG0202
Town on B1108, 6 miles (10km) W of Wymondham
In the early 17th century rector Robert Peck left Hingham to seek religious freedom. He and his

parishioners founded Hingham, Massachusetts, USA. One of these settlers was Samuel Lincoln, an ancestor of future president Abraham Lincoln. The large market square is fringed by some very elegant Georgian and Queen Anne-style houses.

HINKLEY POINT Somerset ST2146
Headland off A39, 2 miles (3km) N of Stogursey
A low but prominent headland with a huge nuclear power station where there is a visitor centre and guided tours are given.

HINTLESHAM Suffolk TM0843
Village on A1071, 4 miles (6km) E of Hadleigh
Sprawling village set among woods and fields with some handsome houses, an ancient church, and a hall with 14th-century cellars.

HINTON ADMIRAL Hampshire SZ2195
Village off A35, 2 miles (3km) W of New Milton
Little brick village, in a park-like setting. The brick church has an 18th-century tower.

HINTON AMPNER Hampshire SU5927
Hamlet off A272, 3 miles (5km) S of Alresford
A little hamlet and its big neo-Georgian house (National Trust) of the 1930s, with superlative fittings and furniture. Good park and gardens.

HINTON BLEWETT Avon ST5956
Village off B3114, 2 miles (3km) E of West Harptree
Prominent triangular green, with cottages framing the view from the 15th-century church.

HINTON CHARTERHOUSE Avon ST7758
Village on B3110, 4 miles (6km) S of Bath
Stone village with an interesting, partly Norman church and the remains of Hinton Priory, founded in 1232 (limited opening).

HINTON PARVA Wiltshire SU2383
Village off A419, 5 miles (8km) E of Swindon
Also known as Little Hinton, the village has thatched cottages and a small Norman and medieval church, with a Norman font carved with birds and beasts.

HINTON ST GEORGE Somerset ST4212
Village off A356, 2 miles (3km) NW of Crewkerne
One of the prettiest and most unspoiled villages in the country, all golden Hamstone with lots of thatch. Its handsome church, mostly of 1500, has many fine monuments from the 15th century on, many of them to the local Poylett family.

HINTON ST MARY Dorset ST7816
Village on B3092, 1 mile (2km) N of Sturminster Newton
A village of many stone cottages and some thatched. In 1963 a Roman mosaic showing the head of Christ in the centre was discovered here (now in the British Museum).

HINTON-IN-THE-HEDGES Northamptonshire SP5536
Village off A43, 2 miles (3km) W of Brackley
As its name implies, this is a rural place, off the beaten track, with thatched cottages. Medieval church with monuments and a Norman tower.

HINWICK Bedfordshire SP9361
Hamlet off A509, 5 miles (8km) SE of Wellingborough
Reached along a lane in open, unspoiled countryside. Tiny village square. Hinwick House (open occasionally) is 18th century. Hinwick Hall garden centre.

HINXWORTH Hertfordshire TL2340
Village off A1, 4 miles (6km) N of Baldock
Hertfordshire's northernmost village, with an endearing little church. Rumour has it that processions of spectral monks glide through the walls at Hinxworth Place (not open).

HIPSWELL North Yorkshire SE1898
Village on A6136, 2 miles (3km) S of Richmond
Dominated by Catterick Garrison and associated ranges, although some of the original character of the village remains.

HIRWAUN Mid Glamorgan SN9505
Village on A4059, 4 miles (6km) NW of Aberdare
Former industrial village at head of Cynon Valley, beneath great escarpment leading to Rhondda. Workers' Red Flag reputedly originates from 1831 riots here.

HISTON Cambridgeshire TL4363
Village on B1049, 3 miles (5km) N of Cambridge
Home of Chivers jam factory and Unwin's seeds. Despite industry and new housing, Histon has a nice village green with ducks, and a Norman church.

HITCHAM Suffolk TL9851
Village on B1115, 6 miles (10km) NW of Hadleigh
This pretty village has thatched cottages. Hitcham's Horses is a shop selling hand-carved rocking-horses. John Henslow, mentor to Charles Darwin, is buried here.

HITCHIN Hertfordshire TL1829
Town on A505, 8 miles (13km) NE of Luton
Buildings of every period since Tudor times rub along together in this amiable old market town on the River Hiz, famed for Harkness roses. The impressive late medieval parish church demonstrates the town's wealth from the wool trade at that time. There is a substantial costume collection in Hitchin Museum, and a small physic garden of medicinal plants.

HOAR CROSS Staffordshire SK1323
Hamlet off B5234, 4 miles (6km) E of Abbots Bromley
Isolated Needwood Forest hamlet has a magnificent Catholic church by GF Bodley, commissioned by the widow of Hugo Ingram in his memory.

HOARWITHY Hereford and Worcester SO5429
Village off A49, 5 miles (8km) NW of Ross-on-Wye
Hoarwithy maintains the custom of distributing Pax Cakes to the church congregation on Palm Sunday to encourage peace and neighbourliness. The church itself, completed in 1885, is a remarkable building,

reminiscent of an Italian abbey with a tall campanile, mosaic-floored cloister, dome-canopied sanctuary and pulpit inlaid with semi-precious stones.

HOBY Leicestershire SK6617
Village off A607, 5 miles (8km) W of Melton Mowbray
Opposite Brooksby (see), across the valley of the meandering River Wreake, shared with Leicestershire Round footpath. Medieval ironstone church, cruck-built Roof Tree Cottage.

HOCKERTON Nottinghamshire SK7156
Village on A617, 2 miles (3km) NE of Southwell
On the Newark–Mansfield road, across the river from the town of Southwell (see). Norman chancel arch and window in church. Diapered brickwork on manor.

HOCKLEY Essex TQ8392
Suburb on B1013, 5 miles (8km) NW of Southend-on-Sea
Short-lived spa in 1840s, but mainly developed for commuters since the railway's arrival in 1889. Pleasant walks in Hockley Woods.

HOCKLEY HEATH West Midlands SP1572
Village on A3400, 10 miles (16km) NW of Warwick
Convenient roads into Birmingham have turned this small settlement beside the Stratford-upon-Avon Canal into a large dormitory village.

HOCKWOLD CUM WILTON Norfolk TL7388
Village on B1112, 4 miles (6km) W of Brandon
Two settlements, linked as a single village, nestle beside the Little Ouse River. Breckland forests lie to the west and the Fens to the east.

HODDESDON Hertfordshire TL3708
Town on A1170, 3 miles (5km) S of Ware
Medieval market town, today part of a conurbation stretching down the River Lee to London. An 1835 clock tower stands at the centre. The local history comes to life in Lowewood Museum, a Georgian house with budgerigar aviaries in the garden. Wilder birds can be seen in Rye House Marsh RSPB reserve on the east bank of the river. Rye House Gatehouse (limited opening) is 15th century.

HODNET Shropshire SJ6128
Village on A53, 5 miles (8km) SW of Market Drayton
The famous Heber-Percy gardens at Hodnet Hall are reached by a gateway beside the spacious church with its unusual 13th-century octagonal tower and memorial to former incumbent Bishop Reginald Heber, celebrated hymn-writer. In the charming village, quaint timber-framed cottages mix with homely buildings of the 18th and 19th centuries.

HODSOCK Nottinghamshire SK6185
Hamlet off B6045, 1 mile (2km) SW of Blyth
Hodsock Priory Gardens (limited opening), historic garden and woodlands with ponds and streams, belong to the moated Tudor gatehouse of diapered brick.

HOG'S BACK Surrey SU9348
Ridge on A31, W of Guildford
Narrow ridge of chalk, steep on both sides, an extension of the North Downs west of the River Wey; the A31 runs along its crest.

HOGHTON Lancashire SD6125
Village on A675, 5 miles (8km) W of Blackburn
The village is a collection of hamlets of handloom weavers' cottages. Hoghton Tower dates from 1565 and is the only baronial residence in Lancashire. This is where James I knighted the 'Sir Loin of Beef' in 1617. The parish also has a history of 'unlawful' Catholicism during the 17th century.

HOGNASTON Derbyshire SK2350
Village off B5035, 4 miles (6km) NE of Ashbourne
Hillside village of warm-toned stone and brick, close to Carsington Water (reservoir). Astonishing Norman carving on the church doorway, 13th-century tower.

Carving over the church doorway at Hognaston.

HOLBEACH Lincolnshire TF3524
Small town off A151, 7 miles (11km) E of Spalding
Fenland market town between Spalding and the Wash, in rich agricultural land noted for fine flower bulbs and vegetables. Market held since 1252. Church is large, with tower, spire and flowing tracery dating from 14th century when Bishop of Lincoln promised to rebuild chancel. William Stukeley, one of founders of Society of Antiquaries, born here in 1687.

HOLBETON Devon SX6150
Village off A379, 3 miles (5km) SE of Yealmpton
Set back from the wooded shores of the Erme estuary, with thatched cottages and a rich Victorian church interior.

HOLBORN Greater London TQ3181
District in borough of Camden
Lawyers' quarters in Lincoln's Inn and Gray's Inn. Sir John Soane's Museum is a treat in Lincoln's Inn Fields. Holborn Viaduct built in the 1860s.

HOLBROOK Suffolk TM1736
Village on B1080, 5 miles (8km) S of Ipswich
Home of the famous Royal Hospital School, founded in 1712. There is also a mill and a brook that trickles merrily into the mill pond.

HOLCOMBE Somerset ST6749
Village off A367, 4 miles (6km) S of Radstock
Once a coal-mining village. The old church to the north of the village has a charming, unrestored interior with box pews.

HOLCOMBE ROGUS Devon ST0518
Village off A38, 5 miles (8km) W of Wellington
Pretty village leading up the hill to the huge Elizabethan big house (not open) and the church, which has fine woodwork, including a rare Jacobean private pew.

HOLDENBY Northamptonshire SP6967
Village off A428, 6 miles (10km) NW of Northampton
Holdenby House was once the largest house in England, built by Elizabeth I's Chancellor Sir Christopher Hatton. Remains of the Elizabethan garden, with arches, terraces and walks familiar to Charles I, held prisoner here in 1647. Gardens open regularly, with falconry centre, small pets, rare breeds of farm animals. House rebuilt in Victorian times (tours for booked groups).

HOLDERNESS Humberside
Historic region in NE England
Bounded to the east for 30 miles (48km) by the North Sea, the Humber estuary to the south and the floodplain of the River Hull to the west. North Sea Gas comes ashore near Easington, and Holderness is crossed by miles of gas pipeline. Inland, the region is mainly rural with many Saxon villages.

HOLDGATE Shropshire SO5689
Hamlet off B4368, 8 miles (13km) SW of Much Wenlock
Isolated Corvedale hamlet has farmhouse built into ruins of Norman castle and a church with magnificent Norman door and finest Norman font in Shropshire.

HOLE OF HORCUM North Yorkshire SE8493
Scenic feature off A169, 3 miles (5km) N of Lockton
This beauty spot lies on the Levisham Moor – a hollow forming a vast natural amphitheatre.

HOLE-IN-THE-WALL Hereford and Worcester SO6128
Hamlet off A40, 3 miles (5km) N of Ross-on-Wye
This isolated hamlet beneath wooded hills beside River Wye is rarely visited except by walkers and canoeists.

HOLFORD Somerset ST1541
Village on A39, 3 miles (5km) NW of Nether Stowey
A village on the edge of the Quantocks. The poet William Wordsworth lived at Alfoxton Park (now a hotel) for a year in the 1790s.

HOLKHAM Norfolk TF8943
Hamlet on A149, 2 miles (3km) W of Wells-next-the-Sea
Anna, King of the Angles, lived in Holkham, and had four daughters, all of whom were canonised. In the 1730s, Thomas William Coke (pronounced 'Cook') built the splendid Palladian Holkham Hall looking out across the lovely expanse of Holkham beach. In the 19th century, the sand dunes were planted with Corsican pines, now part of Holkham Nature Reserve.

HOLLAND Lincolnshire
Historic region N of The Wash
Fenland area of southeast Lincolnshire, around The Wash, noted for magnificent churches and rich soil producing vegetables and flower bulbs.

HOLLAND-ON-SEA Essex TM1916
District on B1032, immediately NE of Clacton-on-Sea
Former remote village called Little Holland, now a quiet resort and retirement settlement. Country park near shore. Sandy beach and coast walk to Frinton (see).

HOLLESLEY Suffolk TM3544
Village off B1083, 6 miles (10km) SE of Woodbridge
A training ground for pioneer colonists in the 19th century, Hollesley has a prison, a church, and a common on which wildlife thrives.

HOLLINGBOURNE Kent TQ8455
Village on B2163, 5 miles (8km) E of Maidstone
Village with pond, old inn and timbered buildings, lying below a church and manor house under the wooded North Downs. Across the railway is Eyhorne Street, a separate hamlet.

HOLLINGWORTH LAKE Greater Manchester SD9314
Lake off A58, 1 mile (2km) S of Littleborough
The lake covers 118 acres (48ha) in the centre of a large country park with picnic sites, campsite and visitor centre.

HOLLINSCLOUGH Staffordshire SK0666
Hamlet off B5053, 2 miles (3km) NW of Longnor
Tiny stone-built hamlet beside the River Dove amid splendid moorland scenery. Curious church of 1840 with attached house under same roof.

HOLLYM Humberside TA3425
Village on A1033, 2 miles (3km) S of Withernsea
This agricultural village has a pound in the main street, built with large sea boulders to keep stray cattle.

HOLMBURY ST MARY Surrey TQ1144
Village on B2126, 5 miles (8km) SW of Dorking
Village on Hurtwood Common grouped round a wide dell on a wooded hillside with pretty Victorian cottages. The church (1879) is ingeniously designed to cope with the steep slope.

HOLME Cambridgeshire TL1987
Village on B660, 7 miles (11km) S of Peterborough
Village noted for 638 acres (258ha) of birch woodland (Holme Fen) to the southwest of drained Whittlesey Mere. Holme Fen posts indicate peat shrinkage.

HOLME Cumbria SD5278
Village off A6070, 5 miles (8km) N of Carnforth
The village had a prisoner-of-war camp in 1941; it is now a school. The wharf lies on the Preston to Kendal Canal.

HOLME Nottinghamshire SK8059
Village off A1133, 3 miles (5km) N of Newark-on-Trent
Village on the banks of the River Trent. The church is almost entirely early Tudor, rebuilt by the wealth of a Lancashire wool merchant whose fine tomb is here.

HOLME West Yorkshire SE1206
Village on A6024, 3 miles (5km) SW of Holmfirth
A picturesque village with relics of its textile past. Holme Moss is an area of scientific interest, noted for the TV transmitter mast upon it.

HOLME HALE Norfolk TF8807
Village off A47, 5 miles (8km) E of Swaffham
Pink-washed council houses and the Georgian Holme Hale Hall (not open) contrast nicely with the largely 15th-century Church of St Andrew.

HOLME LACY Hereford and Worcester SO5535
Village on B4399, 4 miles (6km) SE of Hereford
John Scudamore, restorer of church at Abbey Dore (see) is buried in St Cuthbert's Church, where misericords and other Scudamore monuments are of great interest.

HOLME NEXT THE SEA Norfolk TF7043
Village off A149, 3 miles (5km) NE of Hunstanton
Standing on a wide expanse of windswept beach, the village of Holme also marks the end of the ancient footpath, the Peddar's Way.

HOLME PIERREPONT Nottinghamshire SK6239
Village off A52, 4 miles (6km) E of Nottingham
Holme Pierrepont Hall (limited opening) is an outstanding brick early Tudor manor, with medieval lodgings, family pictures, furniture and a 19th-century courtyard garden. There are fine Nottinghamshire alabaster monuments in the church. The National Watersports Centre provides a venue for major rowing, canoeing and other watersports training and events on Regatta Lake beside the River Trent. Camping, caravanning, walks and picnics in adjoining country park.

HOLME ST CUTHBERT Cumbria NY1047
Hamlet off B5300, 4 miles (6km) NE of Allonby
Hearse House in the village used to contain a hearse for use, free of charge, by the parishioners. The vehicle is no longer there.

HOLME UPON SPALDING MOOR Humberside SE8138
Village on A163, 5 miles (8km) SW of Market Weighton
Largest village in the former East Riding, at the foot of the Yorkshire Wolds, with industrial estate on site of old aerodrome.

HOLMER Hereford and Worcester SO5042
Village on A49, immediately N of Hereford
Easily overlooked, this little Hereford suburb is worth visiting for the sturdy Norman and medieval church with fine timber roofs.

HOLMES CHAPEL Cheshire SJ7667
Village on A54, 4 miles (6km) E of Middlewich
Village centred around the Church of St Luke, originally half-timbered, later having bricks added. Now a popular residential area close to M6 motorway.

HOLMESFIELD Derbyshire SK3277
Village on B6054, 2 miles (3km) W of Dronfield
On the Pennine ridge, with views over Derbyshire. Cartledge Hall (17th century) was the home of Derbyshire novelist RM Gilchrist, who died in 1917 and is buried in the churchyard.

HOLMFIRTH West Yorkshire SE1408
Town on A635, 5 miles (8km) S of Huddersfield
A small mill town where picturesque groupings of sturdy sandstone cottages, ginnels, and courtyards mix with magnificent textile mills set proudly upon the landscape. Holmfirth is now synonymous with the TV series *Last of the Summer Wine*, which is filmed here. There is a permanent photographic exhibition of the series and also a Postcard Museum.

HOLMPTON Humberside TA3623
Village off A1033, 3 miles (5km) SE of Withernsea
Most of this coastal village is a conservation area and the village has its own coastguard, founded in 1841.

HOLMROOK Cumbria SD0799
Village on A595, 3 miles (5km) SE of Seascale
A small village with St Paul's Church which contains a 9th-century cross of the Irish style and memorials to the Lutwidges, the family of Lewis Carroll.

HOLMWOOD COMMON Surrey TQ1745
Scenic area on A24, 2 miles (3km) S of Dorking
Mixed woodland and grassland, covering 650 acres (263m), owned by the National Trust with the 19th-century villages of North and South Holmwood on the western side of the common.

HOLNE Devon SX7069
Village off B3380, 3 miles (5km) W of Ashburton
Unspoiled stone village on the edge of Dartmoor, the birthplace of Charles Kingsley, author of *The Water Babies*. Lots of archaeological features on the moor.

HOLSWORTHY Devon SS3403
Town on A3072, 9 miles (14km) E of Bude
An agricultural centre, not exciting architecturally. Two big late 19th-century viaducts just outside the town. Lively weekly markets, and an annual agricultural show in May.

HOLT Clwyd SJ4154
Village off A534, 5 miles (8km) E of Wrexham
Village beside River Dee on the Wales/England border. An important crossing point, with a 15th-century bridge. Remnants of a medieval castle.

HOLT Hereford and Worcester SO8262
Hamlet off A433, 5 miles (8km) N of Worcester
Tiny riverside settlement has splendid Norman and Victorian work in its church. Nearby flooded gravel pits are a haven for wildfowl.

HOLT Norfolk TG0738
Small town on A148, 9 miles (14km) W of Cromer
In 1708 a fire destroyed much of the market town of Holt, but the upside of this is that there are many superb Georgian and Victorian buildings, built to replace the medieval ones. The main street is clean and colourful, and particular attractions include Gresham's School (founded 1555), the North Norfolk Steam Railway, and Holt Lowes Country Park.

Rare example of milestone pillar in Holt, Norfolk.

HOLT Wiltshire ST8561
Village on B3107, 2 miles (3km) N of Trowbridge
This was a spa in the 18th century, based around a natural spring. Ham Green is pretty, with Georgian and earlier houses set around the green. The Courts (National Trust) has gardens open to visitors.

HOLT HEATH Hereford and Worcester SO8163
Village on A443, 5 miles (8km) NW of Worcester
Commuter village less interesting than the haphazard fishing and boating resort on opposite bank of River Severn.

HOLTON Suffolk TM4077
Village on B1124, 1 mile (2km) E of Halesworth
A charming village with a 1,000-year-old church tower and splendid post mill. Holton was a US air force base during World War II.

HOLTON CUM BECKERING Lincolnshire TF1181
Village on B1202, 3 miles (5km) NW of Wragby
Church partly medieval, restored by Sir George Gilbert Scott and Sir Giles Gilbert Scott, with Victorian stained glass. Eighteenth-century hall.

HOLTON LE MOOR Lincolnshire TF0897
Village on B1434, 4 miles (6km) SW of Caistor
Wooded village west of Lincolnshire Wolds. Eighteenth-century brick hall. Church rebuilt in 1850s, enlarged in 1926.

HOLTYE East Sussex TQ4539
Village on A264, 4 miles (6km) E of East Grinstead
Tiny main-road village with a golf course on a breezy common. Near by is a stretch of Roman road, surfaced with rusted iron cinders.

HOLY ISLAND Gwynedd (Anglesey)
Island off W coast of Anglesey
An island off an island. Holy Island and the port of Holyhead (see) are linked to the rest of Anglesey by road and rail embankment. Holyhead Mountain is scattered with prehistoric sites, including an Iron Age hillfort at the summit. Mountain meets sea at spectacular South Stack with its lighthouse and bird observatory. Penrhos Coastal Park is at other end of island.

HOLY ISLAND Northumberland NU1242
see Lindisfarne

HOLY ISLAND Strathclyde (Arran) NS0632
Island off E coast of Arran
Lying off Arran, named for the 6th-century resident saint, the island has the remains of a 14th-century monastery and was sold in 1992 to Buddhist monks as a place of retreat.

HOLYHEAD (CAERGYBI) Gwynedd (Anglesey) SH2482
Town on A5, 23 miles (37km) NW of Bangor
Irish sea ferry port for Dun Laoghaire and Dublin. Holyhead has Roman roots – fort (possibly a Roman naval base) stands next to ancient St Cybi's Church, founded in 6th century. Town's long-standing links with the sea recalled at maritime museum. Town

stands at end of A5 from London – 19th-century arch at docks resembles a miniature version of London's Marble Arch.

HOLYMOORSIDE Derbyshire SK3369
Village off A619, 3 miles (5km) W of Chesterfield
Scattered farms and cottages in the valley of the River Hipper, surrounded by beautiful moorland, now grown into a popular residential area for Chesterfield.

HOLYPORT Berkshire SU8977
Hamlet off A308, 2 miles (3km) S of Maidenhead
An old hamlet set around a green, with many attractive houses, some timber-framed.

HOLYSTONE Northumberland NT9502
Hamlet off B6341, 3 miles (5km) SE of Alwinton
Lady's Well, a Roman watering place fed by spring water, is owned by the National Trust. St Paulinus baptised 3,000 people here in the 7th century.

HOLYWELL Clwyd SJ1875
Town off A55, 14 miles (23km) NW of Chester
Town on Dee estuary coastal belt. Named after the holy well and curative springs of St Winefride, one of the traditional Seven Wonders of Wales. The well (Cadw) has been a place of pilgrimage for centuries. The vaulted well chamber is below, with a richly decorated little chapel above. Also notable church.

HOLYWELL Cornwall SW7658
Hamlet off A3075, 3 miles (5km) N of Perranporth
Set between two sets of sand dunes and behind a rocky headland.

HONEYBOURNE, COW AND CHURCH Hereford and Worcester SP1144
Villages off B4035, 5 miles (8km) E of Evesham
Pleasant villages of Cow Honeybourne and Church Honeybourne stand on each side of a Roman road, once the county border. Fine medieval church.

HONEYCHURCH Devon SS6202
Village off A3072, 1 mile (2km) N of Sampford Courtenay
Hamlet on the northern fringe of Dartmoor, with a little partly Norman church with the simple rustic furniture which has rarely survived Victorian improvements.

HONEYSTREET (OR HONEY STREET) Wiltshire SU11061
Hamlet off A342, 6 miles (10km) E of Devizes
A hamlet on the Kennet and Avon Canal, with wharves. Some of the canal buildings survive, and there is still industry here.

HONINGHAM Norfolk TG1011
Village on A47, 8 miles (13km) W of Norwich
Honingham's single street hugs the banks of the River Tud. The church, ½ mile (1km) away, has an upside-down sundial.

HONINGTON Lincolnshire SK9443
Village on A607, 5 miles (8km) N of Grantham
Attractive stone cottages. Earthworks of Roman camp above Grantham–Sleaford road. Norman church with 13th- and 15th-century work and 19th-century restoration.

HONINGTON Suffolk TL9174
Village on A1088, 3 miles (5km) NW of Ixworth
Birthplace of poet Robert Bloomfield. This interesting village is sited in beautiful Breckland country. To the northeast is Knettishall Heath Country Park.

HONINGTON Warwickshire SP2642
Village off A3400, 1 mile (2km) N of Shipston on Stour
The elegant 1680s Honington Hall (limited opening) has a splendid baroque interior. Mellow cottages stand around the village green and the church has appealing monuments.

HONISTER PASS Cumbria NY2213
Mountain pass on B5289, W of Seatoller
A steep stretch of road lying between Buttermere and Seatoller, with an old quarry workings at the summit.

HONITON Devon ST1600
Town off A30, 16 miles (26km) NE of Exeter
Sometimes called the capital of East Devon, Honiton is famous for its lace and memorable wide High Street lined with simple Georgian buildings. A prominent tower belongs to the odd neo-Norman 1830s church. Honiton lace was famous from Elizabethan times, and can be seen in the museum. Tollgates and the tollhouse survive on the Axminster road.

HOO Kent TQ7872
Village off A228, 4 miles (6km) NE of Strood
Pleasant, historic marshland village overlooking the Medway with a big 13th-century church, its spire a sailors' landmark, now overshadowed by Kingsnorth power station.

HOOK Hampshire SU7254
Village on A30, 6 miles (10km) E of Basingstoke
Large modern village, mostly post-war.

HOOK Humberside SE7625
Village off A161, 1 mile (2km) NE of Goole
Lies on a narrow peninsula formed by a loop in the River Ouse, and has a 13th-century church.

HOOK NORTON Oxfordshire SP3533
Village off A361, 5 miles (8km) NE of Chipping Norton
Real-ale enthusiasts acclaim the local brew, and the picturesque village can also be proud of its fine medieval church and well-preserved cottages.

HOOTON Cheshire SJ3678
Village off A41, 3 miles (5km) NW of Ellesmere Port
The parkland of Hooton Hall was used as an aerodrome before the building of Speke Airport. The village is dominated by a Vauxhall car factory.

HOOTON PAGNELL South Yorkshire SE4807
Village on B6422, 7 miles (11km) NW of Doncaster
An estate village, one of the prettiest in the area, with a Norman church, a village cross dating back to 1253 and a medieval manor house.

HOOTON ROBERTS South Yorkshire SK4897
Village on A630, 4 miles (6km) NE of Rotherham
Hillside village above the River Don, with a Norman church and 13th-century stained-glass window. Ralph Vaughan Williams visited the rector's family here.

HOPE Derbyshire SK1783
Village on A625, 4 miles (6km) NW of Hathersage
The River Noe meets Peakshole Water in the Peak District's Hope Valley. Well-dressing takes place in June or July, sheepdog trials and show in August. The college serves a wide rural community.

HOPE Devon SX6740
Village off A381, 5 miles (8km) W of Salcombe
A tiny fishing settlement tucked just inland from the rocky south coast, with just two squares of old cottages and a little sandy cove.

HOPE BAGOT Shropshire SO5873
Hamlet off A4117, 4 miles (6km) N of Tenbury Wells
Beneath the brow of Clee Hill. This tiny settlement has an unspoilt Norman church with a medieval holy well still gushing near by.

HOPE BOWDLER Shropshire SO4792
Village on B4371, 2 miles (3km) SE of Church Stretton
Situated in fine walking country on the slopes of the Church Stretton Hills, the village looks across Apedale to Wenlock Edge.

HOPE UNDER DINMORE Hereford and Worcester SO5052
Village on A49, 4 miles (6km) S of Leominster
Beneath Dinmore Hill, site of Queenswood Country Park. Magnificent medieval font in church. Dinmore Manor, with superb gardens, should not be missed.

HOPEMAN Grampian NJ1469
Village on B9040, 6 miles (10km) W of Lossiemouth
Small fishing port on the Moray Firth, founded in the first half of the 19th century. Egyptian-style ice house, used for storing ice to preserve fish.

HOPESAY Shropshire SO3983
Village off B4368, 3 miles (5km) W of Craven Arms
The village, with its sturdy 13th-century church, stands high on the fringe of Clun Forest next to a fine expanse of National Trust hillside.

HOPTON Suffolk TL9979
Village on B1111, 7 miles (11m) NE of Ixworth
Hopton stands on the Little Ouse River in fenland. It has a 14th-century church, a Methodist chapel, and a High Street chapel.

HOPTON CASTLE Shropshire SO3678
Hamlet off B4385, 5 miles (8km) SW of Craven Arms
The forlorn keep of the 14th-century castle, destroyed during the Civil War, stands in a field close to this small Clun Forest settlement.

HOPTON WAFERS Shropshire SO6376
Village on A4117, 2 miles (3km) W of Cleobury Mortimer
Two impressive Georgian mansions, visible but not open, dominate this pleasant estate village to the east of the Clee Hills.

HOPWAS Staffordshire SK1704
Village on A51, 2 miles (3km) W of Tamworth
Eccentric but charming Victorian church and 18th-century bridge over the River Thame distinguish this commuter village beneath the wooded Hopwas Hays Hills.

HORBLING Lincolnshire TF1135
Village on B1177, 6 miles (10km) W of Donington
Georgian village at edge of Fens, with Tudor-style 19th-century hall. Cruciform church with Norman tower and chancel.

HORBURY West Yorkshire SE2918
Town on A642, 3 miles (5km) SW of Wakefield
Birthplace of architect John Carr (1723–1807). He is buried in Horbury's beautiful, classical church which he designed in 1791.

HORDEN Durham NZ4441
Village on A1086, immediately E of Peterlee
A former mining town. The wheel of the winding gear is now set in a plaque opposite the site of the pit head baths.

HORLEY Oxfordshire SP4243
Village off A41, 3 miles (5km) NW of Banbury
A magnificent church stands at the centre of this attractive village. Old ironstone workings near by are now a nature reserve.

HORLEY Surrey TQ2843
Town on A23, 4 miles (6km) N of Crawley
Medieval village drowned amid Victorian villas and modern housing estates, with a restored 14th-century church and 15th-century half-timbered inn.

HORNBY Lancashire SD5868
Village on A683, 8 miles (13km) NE of Lancaster
The village, on the River Wenning, straddles an ancient north–south trackway that was used for centuries by salters and packhorses. Castle Stede, a fine example of a moated motte and bailey castle, overlooks the River Lune. The present Hornby Castle stands above the river and is mainly 19th century, built around a 13th-century pele tower.

HORNCASTLE Lincolnshire TF2669
Town on A158, 18 miles (29km) E of Lincoln
Roman settlement and market town between Wolds and Fens. Numerous inns indicate importance as trading centre, with famous annual Horse Fair (until 1948). Canal opening 1802, coming of railway 1855 encouraged further building, many bow windows. Cromwell's defeated adversary at 1643 Battle of Winceby, Sir Ingram Hopton, was buried in church – a medieval building with Victorian restoration.

HORNCHURCH Greater London TQ5387
Town on A124, 2 miles (3km) SE of Romford
The town has long been famous for leather. Its badge is a bull's horned head, found, uniquely, at the east end of St Andrew's Church instead of a cross.

HORNCLIFFE Northumberland NT9249
Village off A698, 5 miles (8km) SW of Berwick-upon-Tweed
The chain bridge crossing the River Tweed was a prototype for the Menai Bridge (see), built by Sir Samuel Browne in 1820.

HORNDEAN Hampshire SU7013
Town on A3, 4 miles (6km) N of Havant
An old hamlet on an important road junction, dominated by a huge 1860s brewery.

HORNDON ON THE HILL Essex TQ6683
Village off B1007, 5 miles (8km) SW of Basildon
Attractive hilltop village with 16th-century market hall and numerous ghosts. The Bell inn has a peculiar collection of old hot-cross buns.

HORNING Norfolk TG3417
Village off A1062, 3 miles (5 km) E of Hoveton
Smooth green lawns sweep down to the waters of the River Bure from thatched boathouses at Horning. Near by are peaceful Woodbastwick Fens.

HORNINGHOLD Leicestershire SP8097
Village off B664, 4 miles (6km) SW of Uppingham
East Leicestershire model village acquired in the 1880s by a Lancashire cotton merchant, whose family built new and rebuilt old houses around the 13th-century church.

HORNINGSHAM Wiltshire ST8141
Village off A362, 5 miles (8km) SW of Warminster
Horningsham is a village of thatched cottages and two greens with fine trees. Its plain thatched Meeting House dates from 1700. Longleat House is a vast Elizabethan mansion, with 19th-century interiors and many tourist attractions, including lions and sealions, a railway, maze, exhibitions and a huge and beautiful park.

The bull's head on the church at Hornchurch.

HORNINGTOPS Cornwall SX2760
Hamlet on B3252, 3 miles (5km) SE of Liskeard
Rural hamlet with Great Trethew Pleasure Park, including woodland walks and a rough terrain track.

HORNSEA Humberside TA1947
Small town on B1243, 14 miles (22km) NE of Hull
This is an attractive seaside town with a fine sandy beach and a long history of smuggling. Hornsea Mere is the largest freshwater lake in Humberside and has an RSPB nature reserve. Hornsea Pottery, as well as selling pottery bargains, also has a leisure park with Butterfly World, birds of prey and a plant centre.

HORNTON Oxfordshire SP3945
Village off A422, 5 miles (8km) NW of Banbury
This old quarrying village sent its stone far and wide. Today the manor house, cottages and exceptional medieval church stand peacefully round the green.

HORRABRIDGE Devon SX5169
Village off A386, 4 miles (6km) SE of Tavistock
Some old slate-hung cottages off the main road, and a medieval bridge with arched recesses for pedestrians, but mostly modern.

HORRINGER Suffolk TL8261
Village on A143, 3 miles (5km) SW of Bury St Edmunds
Village dominated by a flint church and a magnificent 18th-century palace, Ickworth Park (National Trust). The front of the palace has an impressive domed rotunda.

HORSEHAY Shropshire SJ6707
Village off A5223, part of Telford New Town
Old industrial village, now part of Telford, with interesting Victorian buildings and a small steam railway museum (limited opening) at the Old Loco Shed.

HORSEHEATH Cambridgeshire TL6147
Village off A604, 4 miles (6km) NW of Haverhill
Wide open country near a Roman road. George V observed some army practice manoeuvres here in 1912. The church has a 14th-century brass.

HORSELL Surrey SU9959
Village in the NW district of Woking
Pleasant curving High Street with varied architecture in a village older than Woking but engulfed by it. Horsell Common was the setting for the landing of the Martians in HG Wells's *War of the Worlds*.

HORSESHOE PASS Clwyd SH1847
Mountain pass on A542, 4 miles (6km) NW of Llangollen
Well-engineered road with sweeping curves climbing north from Llangollen. Links Vale of Llangollen with Vale of Clwyd.

HORSEY Norfolk TG4622

Village on B1159, 9 miles (14km) NE of Acle

Horsey Windpump (National Trust) was built in 1912 to drain the marshy land surrounding Horsey, and can be seen from miles around. Horsey Mere is especially beautiful, edged by reed beds which still yield reeds for the local inhabitants. Horsey stands on a long, unspoiled beach in what was known as 'devil's country' because of its open wildness.

HORSFORTH West Yorkshire SE2338

Village on A6120, on NW outskirts of Leeds

This used to be the biggest village in England but it is now a suburb of Leeds.

HORSHAM West Sussex TQ1730

Town off A24, 12 miles (19km) S of Dorking

Ancient market town with a lively, bustling modern centre, redesigned in 1992 to make it more focused and to get rid of all but essential local traffic. Carfax is a genuine town square with a Victorian bandstand in the middle. The Causeway, Horsham's loveliest street, calm and tree-lined, leads to an impressive Norman church with a tall spire. Excellent museum, big park and nearby the famous Christ's Hospital School.

HORSHAM ST FAITH Norfolk TG2115

Village off A140, 4 miles (6km) N of Norwich

A small stream called the Hor ripples through this pretty village which has the ruins of a 12th-century priory and a 15th-century church.

HORSLEY Derbyshire SK3744

Village off A38, 4 miles (6km) S of Ripley

Fine church on a hill, with clerestory, tower and spire dating from its rededication in 1450. Remains of a 12th-century castle.

HORSMONDEN Kent TQ7040

Village on B2162, 3 miles (5km) NE of Lamberhurst

Big and busy village in the heart of the Kentish hopfields and orchards. Centred on its pleasant green, with agreeable weatherboarded and half-timbered buildings.

HORSPATH Oxfordshire SP5704

Village off B480, 4 miles (6km) E of Oxford

Proximity to Oxford attracts commuters, but the old heart of the village survives near the church, which has unusual carved figures on the tower arch.

HORSTEAD Norfolk TG2619

Village on B1150, 1 mile (2km) W of Coltishall

Horstead Mill was burned down in 1963, but visitors can watch the water gushing through its ruins. Many lovely country footpaths.

HORSTED KEYNES West Sussex TQ3828

Village off B2028, 4 miles (6km) NE of Haywards Heath

This lovely village on a green has a cruciform Norman church with a tall shingled spire down a lane to the north. It contains the diminutive effigy of a 13th-century knight in armour, possibly a heart casket of a member of the de Cahanges family (altered down the years to the pronunciation 'Kanes'), who gave the village its name. Beyond the church is a lake, a former hammerpond of the Wealden iron industry. To the south is a station on the Bluebell Line (see Sheffield Green).

HORTON Avon ST7584

Village off A46, 3 miles (5km) NE of Chipping Sodbury

Long, thin village on the edge of the Cotswolds. Horton Court (National Trust) has a Norman hall and 15th-century parts (Victorian restorations).

HORTON Dorset SU0307

Village off B3078, 5 miles (8km) N of Wimborne Minster

Scattered, low-lying village with an unusual, mostly 18th-century church. Horton Tower (not open) is a big triangular brick folly, six storeys high and built in the mid-18th century.

HORTON IN RIBBLESDALE North Yorkshire SD8071

Village on B6479, 5 miles (8km) N of Settle

An upland village, at the source of the rivers Ribble and Wharge, lying between the three peaks of Whernside, Ingleborough and Pen-y-ghent.

HORTON-CUM-STUDLEY Oxfordshire SP5912

Village off B4027, 6 miles (10km) NE of Oxford

Straggling village on hills overlooking Ot Moor (see), with colourful Victorian church, thatched almshouses and intriguing Studley Priory, now a hotel.

HORWICH Greater Manchester SD6311

Town on A673, 5 miles (8km) W of Bolton

A mill town which has since diversified into other industries and has also become a pleasant residential area.

HOTHAM Humberside SE8934

Village off A1034, 5 miles (8km) S of Market Weighton

Residential village which has an unusual signpost giving the distance to Ypres in France.

HOTHFIELD Kent TQ9644

Village off A20, 3 miles (5km) NW of Ashford

Small village on the edge of parkland near Godinton Park, a rambling red-brick house of 1628 with a garden laid out in formal style in the 18th century and topiary hedges of the 20th century. Nearby Hothfield Common Nature Reserve covers 140 acres (57ha). It is mostly gorse and bracken with bog asphodel in waterlogged places, and rare plants and animals.

HOUGH-ON-THE-HILL Lincolnshire SK9246

Village off A607, 7 miles (11km) N of Grantham

Lincolnshire Cliff village with stone houses and 19th-century brick cottages around small square. Fine church has Saxon tower with rare semi-circular external stair turret.

HOUGHTON Cambridgeshire TL2872

Village off A1123, 3 miles (5km) E of Huntingdon

One of the oldest watermills (National Trust) on the River Great Ouse is at Houghton, a charming, secluded village with a square and a waterpump.

Watermill on the River Great Ouse at Houghton.

HOUGHTON CONQUEST Bedfordshire TL0441
Village off B530, 2 miles (3km) N of Ampthill
Bedfordshire's biggest parish church, with Conquest family brasses and wall-paintings. King's Wood Nature Reserve of woodland and meadows. (For Houghton House, see Ampthill.)

HOUGHTON LE SPRING Tyne and Wear NZ3450
Town on A690, 6 miles (10km) SW of Sunderland
Groups of old stone houses surround the Church of St Michael and All Angels. Some colliery dereliction still to be seen here. Houghton Hall, the manor house of the original village, is now a social club. Bernard Gilpin inaugurated the annual Houghton Feast and Ox Roast which is held on the first Friday in October.

HOUGHTON ON THE HILL Leicestershire SK6703
Village on A47, 6 miles (10km) E of Leicester
Just off the main Leicester–Uppingham road, this is a popular residential village. Traditional red-brick and ironstone cottages, some thatched. Ironstone church with spire, overlooking rolling countryside.

HOUGHTON REGIS Bedfordshire TL0123
Suburb on A5120, on N outskirts of Dunstable
Much 1930s and post-war housing in this Dunstable satellite. Handsome church. Houghton Hall, haunted, has been converted to offices. Railway cutting nature reserve (Sewell Cutting).

HOUGHTON ST GILES Norfolk TF9235
Village on B1105, 1 mile (2km) S of Little Walsingham
The Slipper Chapel was where pilgrims left their shoes to walk barefoot to the shrine at Little Walsingham (see). It is now part of a larger building.

HOUND Hampshire SU4708
Village on A3025, 1 mile (2km) E of Netley
Rural until the 1930s. Little 13th-century church with stunning stained glass of 1959.

HOUND TOR Devon SX7478
Hill off B3387, NE of Widecombe in the Moor
Tiny medieval village on the side of the Tor, with the footings of the little buildings still visible. It was deserted in the 14th century.

HOUNSLOW Greater London TQ1375

Borough off A30, in W London

On an old Roman road to the west and later on a busy stage-coach route, Hounslow grew with the 19th-century arrival of railways. Many Pakistani and Indian immigrants settled here after World War II. The new parish church dates from 1963. Hounslow Heath or Common, once infested by higwaymen, and subsequently briefly an airfield, is now a nature reserve with the River Crane running through it.

HOUSESTEADS Northumberland NY7968

Site off B6318, 3 miles (5km) N of Bardon Mill

Most popular visiting point of Hadrian's Wall, with a museum, the 5 acre (2ha) fort of *Vercovicium*, and the best-preserved section of the wall (National Trust and English Heritage).

HOVE East Sussex TQ2804

Town on A259, immediately W of Brighton

A genteel neighbour of noisy Brighton, this was a fishing village until it developed as a resort in the 19th century. Most of the buildings went up after 1850. A place of elegant Regency squares, lawns, tree-lined avenues, rows of Victorian villas of varied sizes and of 20th-century houses and flats. It has a superb art gallery and the Sussex county cricket ground.

HOVETON Norfolk TG3018

Village on A1151, immediately NE of Wroxham

Adjoining Wroxham over the River Bure, Hoveton is in the very centre of the Broadlands. Boatyards hum with activity in the summer months.

Hoveton village sign.

HOVINGHAM North Yorkshire SE6675

Village on B1257, 8 miles (13km) W of Malton

An unspoilt village in the Vale of Pickering, surrounded by the forest of Galtres. One remaining tree, the King Oak, is over 900 years old.

HOW CAPLE Hereford and Worcester SO6030

Village off B4224, 4 miles (6km) N of Ross-on-Wye

Romantically situated on wooded hills overlooking River Wye. How Caple Court Gardens (limited opening) feature terraced gardens with woodland walks.

HOWARDIAN HILLS North Yorkshire

Hill range lying between B1363 and A64

A limestone hill range covering 77 square miles (199 sq km) separating the vales of York and Pickering. Abundent wildlife and archaeological interest.

HOWDEN Humberside SE7428

Small town on A63, 3 miles (5km) N of Goole

This old market town lies along the River Ouse and is dominated by its minster dedicated to St Peter and St Paul. Howden is from the medieval 'Hovedene' and it was the centre of a vast ecclesiastical establishment. The town has been home to the novelist Nevil Shute and Barnes Wallis, designer of the 'Bouncing Bomb'.

HOWDEN-LE-WEAR Durham NZ1633

Village on A689, 1 mile (2km) S of Crook

The village grew with the opening of collieries in the 1860s. Howden's railway bridge has been moved to stand over the line at Beamish Museum.

HOWICK Northumberland NU2517

Hamlet off B1339, 5 miles (8km) NE of Alnwick

Howick Hall, built in 1782, was home to the 2nd Earl Grey, after whom the tea was named. Gardens open in summer.

HOWSHAM North Yorkshire SE7362

Village off A64, 7 miles (11km) SW of Malton

Pretty, small village with old red-brick cottages, a manor park and a mill from the 14th century. Elizabethan Howsham Hall, built using stone from Kirkham Priory, is now a boys' school.

HOWTOWN Cumbria NY4419

Hamlet off B5320, 4 miles (6km) SW of Pateley Bridge

On the western edge of Ullswater, a popular starting point for walks. Can be reached by steamer which crosses Ullswater from Glenridding.

HOXNE Suffolk TM1877

Village on B1118, 3 miles (5km) NE of Eye

Pronounced 'Hoxen', this ancient village stands along the banks of the River Waveney in rolling countryside of meadows and trees. King Edmund was betrayed here and put to death by Danes in 870. The tree where he died fell suddenly and unexpectedly in 1848; it is marked by a monument in the field where it stood.

HOY Orkney

Island lying W of Scapa Flow

The second largest Orkney island, with vertical cliffs and the Old Man of Hoy, a pinnacle rock-stack 450ft (137m) high, favoured by climbers.

HOYLAKE Merseyside SJ2189

Town on A540, 7 miles (11km) W of Birkenhead

Hoylake is a much sought-after residential area although day-trippers still come here to enjoy the fine beach. The town grew with the coming of the railway in the 1800s and many of the buildings are from that era. There is no amusement park, but there are good sands, wide sea views and a long Promenade.

HOYLAND SWAINE South Yorkshire SE2604

Village on A628, 1 mile (2km) NE of Penistone

A small village with panoramic views of the surrounding countryside. Mainly a farming community.

HUBBERHOLME North Yorkshire SD9278

Village off B6160, 1 mile (2km) NW of Buckden

A small village in a beautiful wooded valley. The church contains fine pews carved by Robert Thompson of Kilburn (see) and JB Priestley is buried here.

HUCKNALL Nottinghamshire SK5349

Town off A611, 6 miles (10km) N of Nottingham

The poet Lord Byron and his daughter, mathematician Ada Lovelace, are buried in the church. Textile industries, furniture-making and Rolls-Royce aero-engine testing.

HUDDERSFIELD West Yorkshire SE1416

Town off M62, 11 miles (18km) S of Bradford

A traditional Yorkshire textile town, Huddersfield has all the hallmarks of Victorian wealth that characterise so many towns in this region. A great Cloth Hall was built in 1766 by the Ramsden family who also brought the Ramsden Canal and the railway to Huddersfield. The Victorian railway station was designed by JP Pritchett in the classical manner with long colonnades. It was completed in 1850 and is considered to be one of the finest railway buildings in England. The town hall was built in 1878 and markets and arcades were built at around the same time.

In 1920 Huddersfield Corporation purchased the Ramsden estate, including almost all of the town centre, from Sir JF Ramsden, the 6th Baronet, and the place is often referred to as 'the town that bought itself'.

Since 1974 Huddersfield has been the administrative headquarters of Kirklees Metropolitan Council. The town centre has been improved considerably by pedestrianisation schemes and stone-cleaning of the Victorian buildings. The cast-iron work, glazed walls and elaborate details of Brook Street outdoor market, built in 1887 as a wholesale market, have been restored and it now serves as a general market.

HUDDINGTON Hereford and Worcester SO9457

Village off A422, 4 miles (6km) E of Worcester

Small village on Bow Brook with rewarding medieval church and view from churchyard of Huddington Court, a perfect example of a moated Tudor manor.

HUGHENDEN VALLEY Buckinghamshire SU8697

Village off A4128, 2 miles (3km) N of High Wycombe

Hughenden Manor and its beautiful grounds (National Trust) were remodelled for Benjamin Disraeli. His monument is in the church.

HUGHLEY Shropshire SO5697

Hamlet off B4371, 4 miles (6km) SW of Much Wenlock

Below Wenlock Edge. The church, with a fine wooden chancel screen, and the timber-framed manor house have little more than a farm for company.

HUISH CHAMPFLOWER Somerset ST0429

Village off B3188, 2 miles (3km) NW of Wiveliscombe

The name means 'Homestead of the Champflower Family'. Consists of cottages and scattered farms on the Brendon Hills.

HUISH EPISCOPI Somerset ST4226

Village on A372, 1 mile (2km) E of Langport

The church at this village, whose name means 'belonging to a bishop', has one of the best of famous Somerset church towers, 99ft (30m) high with elaborate windows, dating from the 15th century.

HULCOTE (OR HOLCOT) Bedfordshire SP9438

Hamlet off A421, 5 miles (8km) NE of Bletchley

Close to M1. Rare Elizabethan gem of a church – its builder's monument shows two generations of a family with 24 children.

HULL (KINGSTON UPON HULL) Humberside TA0928

City on A63, 50 miles (80km) E of Leeds

Hull, officially known as Kingston upon Hull, lies on the southern margin of the plain of Holderness, its port and harbour washed by the tidal flow of the River Humber. Today it is a busy port with much freight and passenger traffic to and from Europe. The Town Docks Museum defines the city's maritime history with galleries on whaling, fishing and shipping.

William Wilberforce, the famous slavery abolitionist, was born in Hull in 1759, and his fine Jacobean house is now a museum commemorating his life and works. The old grammar school, where Wilberforce was a pupil, is now a Museum of Social History called 'The Story of Hull'.

Many of the oldest parts of Hull were bombed out of existence in World War II, but subsequent building in the town centre has been sensitive. The old town, much of which dates back 800 years, is full of narrow cobbled streets and quays with old taverns. Whitefriargate takes its name from the monastery of the Carmelites or White Friars which once stood on the site. Today it is the main shopping street of the old town. The harbour area is now attractively developed as a marina, and the warehouse buildings have been converted into hotels and apartments. In an imaginative scheme to create a city trail, Hull can be explored by following a series of specially commissioned fish reliefs set into the pavements throughout the centre.

The city is pleasantly free from high-rise blocks, offering clear views of the Humber estuary and the famous Humber Bridge (see).

HULLAVINGTON Wiltshire ST8982

Village off A429, 4 miles (6km) SW of Malmesbury

This stone village is reminiscent of the Cotswolds, but is not as pretty as many of the villages in that area.

HULLBRIDGE Essex TQ8095

Village off B1013, 3 miles (5km) N of Rayleigh

On the River Crouch with enjoyable riverside walks. Rare breeds farm.

HULNE PRIORY Northumberland NU1615

Site off B6346, 2 miles (3km) NW of Alnwick

The remains of a monastic house founded in 1240 by the Carmelite order of White Friars.

HUMBER BRIDGE Humberside

Bridge carrying A15 across Humber between Hessle and Barton-upon-Humber

The longest single-span suspension bridge in the world at 4,626ft (1,410m). Building began in 1972 and it was opened in 1981 as a tollbridge. Towers above the supporting piers are 510ft (271m) high and a total of 44,000 miles (71,000km) of wire was used to make the cables.

HUMBER, RIVER Humberside (x)

River flowing past Hull and Grimsby to the North Sea

The River Humber is still a major commercial waterway. Its tributaries drain about 20 per cent of England

HUMBERSTON Humberside TA3105

Village on A1031, 4 miles (6km) SE of Grimsby

Large suburban area with mixed housing. Surrounded by green countryside with a golf course. Excavations revealed site of 12th-century Benedictine abbey.

HUMBIE Lothian NT4562

Village on B6368, 8 miles (13km) SW of Haddington

A village at the foot of the Lammermuir Hills, noted for the Children's Village, a charitable institution founded in 1886 for disabled children in Edinburgh.

HUME Borders NT7041

Village off B6364, 3 miles (5km) S of Greenlaw

Hume Castle, seat of the Homes from 1214 to 1611 and demolished by Cromwell's troops in 1650, stands near the village. There are magnificent views all around.

HUNGARTON Leicestershire SK6907

Village off A47, 7 miles (11km) E of Leicester

Rebuilt between 1766 and 1775, many of the village's red and yellow brick chequer buildings have datestones. Fine early 17th-century brick Quenby Hall (not open) near by.

HUNGERFORD Berkshire SU3368

Town off A4, 9 miles (14km) W of Newbury

A proper market town on the River Kennet and the Kennet and Avon Canal (with several locks near by). Handsome High Street with many pretty brick and stucco houses. The Manor Court, long abolished elsewhere, survives here with great festivities once a year. 'Tutti men' with flowered poles collect pennies and kisses all over the town.

HUNSDON Hertfordshire TL4114

Village on B180, 4 miles (6km) E of Ware

Weatherboarded and half-timbered houses. The church, with brasses and monuments, is close to Hunsdon House (not open,) where Henry VIII's children grew up.

HUNSLET West Yorkshire SE3031

District in S Leeds

A industrial and residential area of Leeds. The Middleton Railway was built in 1758 and lays claim to being the world's oldest railway.

HUNSONBY Cumbria NY5835

Hamlet off A686, 1 mile (2km) E of Salkeld

A small village, lying in the Eden Valley, which has changed very little. The white bridge across the beck was built in 1740.

Humbie, famous for its Children's Village.

HUNSTANTON Norfolk TF6740
Town on A149, 14 miles (23km) N of King's Lynn
The only East Anglian seaside resort to face west, Hunstanton has an essentially Victorian atmosphere, with handsome hotels and lovely Esplanade gardens sloping towards the sea. Hunstanton (pronounced 'Hunston' by some locals) has some remarkable striped cliffs formed by layers of different-coloured rocks. The Kingdom of the Sea is an exhibition of British marine wildlife.

HUNTER'S QUAY Strathclyde NS1879
Village on A815, 2 miles (3km) N of Dunoon
Clyde yachting base at the mouth of Holy Loch, until 1992 a deep-water anchorage and service depot for a United States nuclear submarine base.

HUNTINGDON Cambridgeshire TL2371
Town on A14, 15 miles (24km) NW of Cambridge
The most famous son of Huntingdon is probably Oliver Cromwell, who was born in a small house just off Ermine Street in 1599. The school to which he was sent in about 1610 was later attended by Samuel Pepys, and was originally part of the 12th-century Hospital of St John. In 1962 it was converted from a school to the Cromwell Museum, which contains imaginatively displayed exhibitions on the life and times of the great Parliamentarian.

Huntingdon developed at the spot where Ermine Street crossed the Ouse and became very prosperous in the 10th century as a market town and a mint. By the 12th century it had 16 churches, of which only two survive. During the Civil War, both Cromwell and King Charles used the town as a headquarters at different times, but it was decimated by plague in the 17th century. It regained some prosperity in the 1700s as a major staging post on the Great North road.

Impressive buildings include the two Norman churches, the 1745 town hall, and the George inn, once owned by Cromwell's grandfather.

HUNTINGTON Hereford and Worcester SO2453
Village off A44, 4 miles (6km) SW of Kington
Old Welsh border settlement on hills above River Arrow with simple, sturdy church and remains of a castle.

HUNTLY Grampian NJ5339
Town on A96, 10 miles (16km) SE of Keith
Market town dating from the 18th century and once the seat of the Gordons; ruined Huntly Castle was built on the site of the earlier Palace of Strathbogie. Huntly Museum explains the town and local history. Interesting falconry centre near by with other birds of prey and demonstrations. Leith Hall is a turreted 17th-century mansion house with beautiful park and woodlands.

HURLEY Berkshire SU8283
Village off A423, 4 miles (6km) NW of Maidenhead
On the River Thames, with the remains of a medieval priory, including a big barn and dovecote. The parish church was part of the priory church.

HURSLEY Hampshire SU4225
Village on A3090, 4 miles (6km) SW of Winchester
A large and pretty brick village, with tile-hanging as well. The church was rebuilt in the 1840s for the vicar John Keble, the famous leader of church reform, in the 'correct' medieval style. Complete set of 1840s stained glass.

HURST Berkshire SU7973
Village off B3030, 5 miles (8km) E of Reading
A scattered village, pretty in the centre around the church.

HURST GREEN Lancashire SD6838
Village on B6243, 3 miles (5km) NW of Whalley
A pretty village with almshouses dating from 1706, and Stonyhurst College, which has been a leading Roman Catholic school for 200 years.

HURSTBOURNE PRIORS Hampshire SU4346
Village on B3400, 2 miles (3km) SW of Whitchurch
Set in the Bourne Valley, a famous area for fishing. Brick and flint houses and cottages, and entertaining neo-Norman church tower of 1870, to match some genuine Norman sections.

HURSTBOURNE TARRANT Hampshire SU3853
Village on A343, 5 miles (8km) N of Andover
Unspoiled village with thatched cottages and brick Georgian houses, all looking much as it did when Jane Austen visited. She stayed at Ibthorpe, just to the north, which has changed even less.

HURSTPIERPOINT West Sussex TQ2716
Town on B2116, 3 miles (5km) SW of Burgess Hill
The narrow High Street is most attractive, mainly Georgian with brick pavements. The large church has a landmark spire. Well-known school and a Tudor manor house, Danny, under lee of the Downs.

HURSTWOOD Lancashire SD8831
Hamlet off A671, 3 miles (5km) E of Burnley
An Elizabethan hamlet where the poet Edmund Spenser lived for a while after 1576 and found inspiration for his work *The Shepherd's Calendar*.

HURWORTH-ON-TEES Durham NZ3010
Village off A167, 3 miles (5km) SE of Darlington
The village was once the home of a small community of linen-weavers and agriculturalists. There has been much redevelopment in recent years, but it remains a pretty riverside village.

HUSBANDS BOSWORTH Leicestershire SP6484
Village on A50, 6 miles (10km) W of Market Harborough
At the crossroads of the Leicester–Northampton and Lutterworth–Market Harborough roads. Late 18th-century and early 19th-century red-brick houses, several timber-framed buildings, church with spire.

HUSBORNE CRAWLEY Bedfordshire SP9635
Village on A4012, 2 miles (3km) N of Woburn
Set prettily among sandy hills and woods on the northern edge of Woburn (see) estate. Church has an unusual green sandstone tower.

HUSTHWAITE North Yorkshire SE5175
Village off A19, 4 miles (6km) N of Easingwold
The village, famous for its fruit trees, is a blend of old stone dwellings, mellow Victorian brick houses and more modern properties.

HUTTOFT Lincolnshire TF5176
Village on A52, 4 miles (6km) S of Sutton on Sea
Just inland from Lincolnshire holiday coast, in the salt marshes. Medieval church with 18th-century brick chancel.

HUTTON Essex TQ6395
District on NE outskirts of Brentwood
Once a tiny settlement in a forest clearing, now swallowed by Brentwood suburbs, but the older nucleus survives round All Saints' Church.

HUTTON ROOF Cumbria SD5677
Village off A65, 3 miles (5km) W of Kirkby Lonsdale
The crag at Hutton Roof is an area of Special Scientific Interest because of the limestone pavements and the flora which thrives here.

HUTTON RUDBY North Yorkshire NZ4606
Vilage off A19, 4 miles (6km) W of Stokesley
Small village on the banks of the River Leven with an old watermill and some delightful white-walled cottages.

HUTTON-LE-HOLE North Yorkshire SE7090
Village off A170, 2 miles (3km) N of Kirkbymoorside
A beautiful village lying in the small valley of Hutton Beck. The traditional stone cottages, with pantiled roofs, are built around a large green. The main attraction, however, is the Ryedale Folk Museum which includes a reconstructed medieval thatched cruck house as well as an ancient glassworks, a blacksmith's shop and displays of local crafts.

HUXLEY Cheshire SJ5061
Village off A51, 3 miles (5km) W of Tarporley
Predominantly a farming community although many residents now commute to Chester. Higher Huxley Hall is privately owned.

HUYTON Merseyside SJ4490
Town off M62, 6 miles (10km) E of Liverpool
A residential area for Liverpool's merchants who built many large villa estates. Still has a village green with a cross.

HYDE Greater Manchester SJ9494
Town on A560, 5 miles (8km) NE of Stockport
Busy mill town still dominated by 19th-century mill and warehouse buildings. Newton Hall, a 14th-century cruck-framed hall, open by arrangement.

HYLTON CASTLE Tyne and Wear NZ3558
Castle NW of Sunderland
Hylton Castle (English Heritage) was built in 1400; shaped like an enormous gatehouse or rectangular tower with displays of heraldry.

HYTHE Hampshire SU4207
Village off A326, 2 miles (3km) NE of Dibden Purlieu
On Southampton Water, with a passenger ferry to Southampton. Some industry and ship-building.

HYTHE Kent TR1634
Town on A259, 4 miles (6km) W of Folkestone
Seaside place near Romney Marsh, formerly an important member of the Confederation of Cinque Ports. Today it is the terminus of the Romney, Hythe and Dymchurch Railway. The Royal Military Canal, built against the Napoleonic threat, divides the seaside resort from the Old Town, where narrow alleyways and little streets climb up to the big old church. The church has a crypt lined with skulls and thighbones.

I

IBBERTON Dorset ST7807
Village off A357, 4 miles (6km) S of Sturminster Newton
A winding, well-wooded village, with a church set high above. Leaning chancel and some Elizabethan stained glass.

IBSTOCK Leicestershire SK4009
Village on A447, 3 miles (5km) S of Coalville
Large village which grew through coal-mining and brickworks. William Laud, later the Archbishop of Canterbury, was rector of the mainly 13th-century church, 1617–26.

ICKFORD Buckinghamshire SP6407
Village off A418, 4 miles (6km) W of Thame
Annual tug of war over the River Thame, which is the Oxfordshire border. Hump-backed bridge, old cottages, striking church, pubs.

ICKHAM Kent TR2258
Village off A257, 5 miles (8km) E of Canterbury
Straggling place on the River Little Stour with a big, plain 14th-century church and the Old Rectory, a manor house of 1280 with a hall on the first floor.

ICKLESHAM East Sussex TQ8716
Village on A259, 2 miles (3km) W of Winchelsea
Peaceful village on a ridge above the River Brede, with an exceptional church, its Norman tower rising in three stages.

ICKLETON Cambridgeshire TL4943
Village off A1301, 1 mile (2km) NW of Great Chesterford
Village possesses impressive medieval history. Traces of a fulling mill remain, along with 16th-century Frogge Hall (not open), named for the frogs which lived in the damp streets.

ICKLINGHAM Suffolk TL7772
Village on A1101, 7 miles (11km) NW of Bury St Edmunds
Near the Icknield Way, this attractive village has two churches and a 'high bridge' about 5ft (1.5m) above sea level.

ICKNIELD WAY Hertfordshire
Prehistoric track
Ancient route from the Chilterns to the Wash, now a long-distance trail from Ivinghoe Beacon to near Thetford in Norfolk.

ICKWELL GREEN Bedfordshire TL1545
Village off B658, 3 miles (5km) W of Biggleswade
Noted for May Day ceremonies. Picturesque green and striped maypole. One cottage is the former home of Thomas Tompion, a great 17th-century clock-maker.

IDBURY Oxfordshire SP2319
Village off A424, 5 miles (8km) SE of Stow-on-the-Wold
Benjamin Baker, designer of the Forth Bridge, is buried beside the fine old church in this small village overlooking the Evenlode Valley.

IDDESLEIGH Devon SS5708
Village on B3217, 3 miles (5km) NE of Hatherleigh
Cob and thatch village, with views extending to Dartmoor.

Church spire with external bell at Ickleton.

IDE HILL Kent TQ4851
Village off B2042, 4 miles (6km) SW of Sevenoaks
Cluster of cottages with a pub round the green in a wonderful position on greensand hills. The National Trust owns about 400 acres (162ha) of woodland and heath with fine viewpoints.

IDRIDGEHAY Derbyshire SK2849
Village on B5023, 3 miles (5km) S of Wirksworth
Pleasant village in the valley of the River Ecclesbourne. Half-timbered South Sitch dates from 1621 and earlier. Sir George Gilbert Scott built Elizabethan-style Alton Manor in 1846.

IDSWORTH Hampshire SU7414
Site off B2146, 5 miles (8km) NE of Havant
A deserted village, with only a small, Norman church, set in fields. It has simple 17th- and 18th-century fittings and medieval wall-paintings.

IFFLEY Oxfordshire SP5203
District on S outskirts of Oxford
Generations of undergraduates have strolled beside the River Isis to this ancient waterside village, which has one of England's most important Norman churches.

IGHTHAM Kent TQ5956
Village off A25, 4 miles (6km) E of Sevenoaks
Attractive old village with pretty, half-timbered cottages and houses. Famed for its ancient moated manor house, Ightham Mote (National Trust), which contains a 15th-century great hall, old chapel and crypt, Tudor chapel, fireplace and frieze from the 17th century, and Chinese wallpaper from the 18th century. Near by is Oldbury Hill, with palaeolithic rock shelters and an Iron Age fort.

IKEN Suffolk TM4155
Village off B1069, 4 miles (6km) N of Orford
A most Suffolk of Suffolk villages near where the River Alde widens to look almost like a lake among soft green meadows and woodland.

ILAM Staffordshire SK1350
Village off A515, 4 miles (6km) NW of Ashbourne
The village, with its attractive estate cottages and rewarding church, is the starting point for walks through a beautiful stretch of the Manifold Valley. In summer the River Manifold disappears underground north of Ilam and reappears below Ilam Hall (a youth hostel). The river runs through wooded Ilam Park.

ILCHESTER Somerset ST5222
Village off A303, 5 miles (6km) NW of Yeovil
A Roman and medieval town, now really a large village, with some Georgian stone houses. Town hall of 1810s and a strange 18th-century cross on the green. Local museum.

ILFORD Greater London TQ4486
Town in borough of Redbridge, N of Barking
Acres upon acres of 20th-century housing estates here. Valentine's Park is in the grounds of 17th-century mansion.

ILFRACOMBE Devon SS5247

Town on A361, 9 miles (14km) N of Barnstaple

Until the 19th century this was a little fishing settlement with a sheltered harbour. The dramatic coastline, with its rocky headlands and sheltered bays, attracted visitors from the 1830s, and after the railway arrived in 1874 growth was fast. Now it is a mostly Victorian town, beautifully set out over the small hills and very unspoiled.

The fishing harbour (with boats to Lundy, see) is tucked behind a rocky headland which is crowned with a little medieval chapel (limited opening) that was used as a lighthouse from the 14th century. There are old houses and cottages along the harbour streets, but the High Street inland and most of the rest of the town is later Victorian, with plain, tall boarding-houses of brick. Many public gardens are laid out along the shore, some at amazing angles because of the little hills. The Tunnels have a Greek-style baths building of 1836 in front of the curious tunnels pierced through the rock to give access to little private beaches, linked by further tunnels.

Ilfracome Museum is set in fine gardens, and has displays on Victorian residents and local history. Rolling Falls is a model of Clovelly, and Chambercombe Manor, just to the south, is a late medieval house, altered and restored.

Hele is a pretty hamlet 1 mile (2km) east, with a big 18th-century working watermill.

ILKESTON Derbyshire SK4641

Town on A6096, 8 miles (13km) NE of Derby

On the Derbyshire/Nottinghamshire border, overlooking Erewash Valley, this hilltop market town developed coal, iron and textile industries in the mid-19th century, and has many period buildings. There are elegant 18th-century houses in East Street and art nouveau details in Wharncliffe Road. Erewash Museum, in a Georgian town house, has pleasant gardens. Fine iron Benerley Viaduct. Markets are held twice-weekly and a popular October fair has taken place since 1252. The American Adventure theme park is on the edge of town.

ILKLEY West Yorkshire SE1147

Town on A65, 10 miles (16km) N of Bradford

Ilkley, a well-known spa town on the River Wharfe surrounded by fine moorland scenery, became a fashionable commuter town with the coming of the railway line between Leeds and Bradford in the 1860s and with the Yorkshire woollen industry .

Originally an Iron Age settlement, it was subsequently occupied by the Romans who built a camp here to protect their crossing of the river. They named the town that sprang up *Olicana*, which, with the familiar 'ley' (Anglo-Saxon for pasture) added, gave rise to its existing name. All Saints' Church has three Anglo-Saxon crosses in the churchyard and behind is a grassy mound where a little fort was built. In the town's museum are altars carved in gritstone, dedicated to the Roman gods.

The most famous local attraction is Ilkley Moor, which has been immortalised in the well-known song. The spring at White Wells on Ilkley Moor brought visitors to the town in the 18th century and a small bathhouse was built where elderly patients were encouraged to take a dip in the healing waters of the 'heather spa', as it was known.

ILMINGTON Warwickshire SP2143

Village off A429, 4 miles (6km) NW of Shipston on Stour

Morris dancing flourishes in this picturesque stone village on the Cotswold fringe. Many thatched cottages, a manor house of about 1500 and a church with good brasses.

ILMINSTER Somerset ST3614

Town off A303, 10 miles (16km) SE of Taunton

A handsome 15th-century church with a splendid central tower graces this stone market town. The classical open market house is basically 17th century, and there is an impressive 16th-century grammar school. Ilminster's prosperity was based on cloth-making.

ILSINGTON Devon SX7876

Village off A38, 4 miles (6km) NE of Ashburton

A village high in the valley on the woody western edge of Dartmoor (see Haytor).

IMBER Wiltshire ST9648

Deserted village on Salisbury Plain, 6 miles (10km) NE of Warminster

One of the few villages actually on Salisbury Plain, but ruined and deserted since being taken over in 1943 by the army as part of their training area.

IMMINGHAM Humberside TA1714

Town off A180, 7 miles (11km) NW of Grimsby

The old part of the town is centred around the docks. This was an important port which developed because of its permanent deep-water channel.

IMPINGTON Cambridgeshire TL4463

Village off B1049, 3 miles (5km) N of Cambridge

Impington Village College, built in 1938, was designed by two leading European architects, Walter Gropius and Maxwell Fry. Samuel Pepys was born here in 1633.

INCE Cheshire SJ4576

Village off A5117, 3 miles (5km) E of Ellesmere Port

Small village surrounded by industry, including a power station, which developed when the Manchester Ship Canal gave access to the River Mersey.

INCE BLUNDELL Merseyside SD3203

Village off A565, 3 miles (5km) SE of Formby

A small village that takes part of its name from the Blundell family, who exerted their influence on the area.

INCE-IN-MAKERFIELD Greater Manchester SD5903

Town off A577, 1 mile (2km) SE of Wigan

Coal-mining led to rapid and unsightly expansion during the 19th century, but regeneration has improved the town. Wildlife sanctuaries at the surrounding mosses and flashes.

INCH KENNETH Strathclyde NM4335
Island off W coast of Mull
Island named after a follower of St Colomba, with Celtic crosses and slabs in the churchyard. Unity Mitford, friend of Hitler, lived here after her suicide attempt.

INCHBARE Tayside NO6065
Village on B966, 2 miles (3km) S of Edzell
Strathcathro church was the site of the humiliation of John Balliol in 1296, when Edward I divested him of the title of king.

INCHCAILLOCH Central NS4090
Island in Loch Lomond, off Balmaha
One of a group of attractive wooded islands in Loch Lomond off the holiday centre of Balmaha on the eastern shore of the loch.

INCHCOLM Fife NT1882
Island in Firth of Forth
Island in Firth of Forth, east of Dalgety Bay, mainly noted for the substantial remains of a 13th-century Augustinian abbey, which include a fine octagonal chapter house.

INCHINNAN Strathclyde NS4769
Village on A8, 3 miles (5km) N of Paisley
The present church stands on the site of a Knights Templar church; tombs of Templars, Celtic crosses and mortsafes in churchyard.

INCHKEITH Fife NT2982
Island in Firth of Forth, SE of Kinghorn
Island in Firth of Forth occupied by the French between 1549 and 1567. It has a noted lighthouse.

INCHMURRIN Strathclyde NS3887
Island in Loch Lomond, N of Balloch
The largest island in Loch Lomond, with ruins of Lennox Castle, where the Duchess of Albany sheltered after the murder of her entire family by James I.

INCHNADAMPH Highland NC2521
Village on A837, 36 miles (58km) NW of Bonar Bridge
Remote settlement in a desolate part of wild and mountainous Assynt. Ruined Ardvreck Castle lies on Loch Assynt to the north.

INCHTURE Tayside NO2728
Village on A90 (A85), 8 miles (13km) W of Dundee
Village between Perth and Dundee. Restored 12th- to 15th-century Kinnaird Castle is near by; Rossie Priory (1807) stands on the site of a vanished abbey.

INDIAN QUEENS Cornwall SW9159
Village on A30, 3 miles (5km) S of St Columb Major
A mostly Victorian village on the edge of the china-clay quarrying area.

INGARSBY Leicestershire SK6805
Deserted village off A47, 1 mile (2km) N of Houghton on the Hill
Earthworks of outstanding medieval village site (streets and house sites visible), deserted in 1469 following enclosures for stock-rearing. Old Hall of the 15th and 17th centuries.

INGATESTONE Essex TQ6499
Town off A12, 5 miles (8km) NE of Brentwood
Old houses in High Street. Ingatestone Hall is the historic mansion of the Petre family. The church has a fine tower and Petre monuments.

INGESTRE Staffordshire SJ9824
Village off A51, 4 miles (6km) E of Stafford
Small estate village overlooking the Vale of Trent with remarkably sophisticated 17th-century church attributed to Sir Christopher Wren.

INGLEBY GREENHOW North Yorkshire NZ5706
Village off B1257, 4 miles (6km) E of Stokesley
An isolated village in a valley below the Cleveland Hills. The manor house, built in 1650, now contains luxury flats.

INGLESHAM Wiltshire SU2098
Hamlet off A361, 1 mile (2km) SW of Lechlade
William Morris succeeded in preventing the Victorianisation of the church here in the 1880s and preserved all its old fittings. Very atmospheric.

INGLETON North Yorkshire SD6971
Village on B6255, 6 miles (10km) SE of Kirkby Lonsdale
The village is the gateway to the Three Peaks of Ingleborough, Whernside and Pen-y-ghent. The famous waterfalls were discovered by Joseph Carr in 1865 but it was not until 1885 that they were made accessible to the general public. The village's prime source of income is tourism. The name means 'beacon town'.

INGLEWHITE Lancashire SD5439
Hamlet off A6, 7 miles (11km) N of Preston
Picturesque village with a market cross dating from 1675 and St Anne's Well, said to have great healing properties.

INGLISTON Lothian NT1472
Showground off M8, 7 miles (11km) W of Edinburgh
Permanent showground and home of the Royal Highland Show since 1960, in the grounds of Ingliston House (1846). Large Sunday market and motor-racing near by.

INGOLDMELLS Lincolnshire TF5668
Village on A52, 4 miles (6km) N of Skegness
Family resort on Lincolnshire's holiday coast. Britain's first holiday camp, established in 1936, became Butlin's Funcoast World. Fantasy Island is a huge indoor theme park.

INGRAM Northumberland NU0115
Village off A697, 4 miles (6km) NW of Whittingham
The village is at the foot of Ewe Hill, part of the Cheviot chain. National park information centre just outside the village. Greaves Ash, at the head of Breamish Valley, is the largest hut circle site in Northumberland. Linhope Spout and Davidson's Linn are fine waterfalls near by.

INKBERROW Hereford and Worcester SP0157

Village on A422, 5 miles (8km) W of Alcester

The village claiming to be 'Ambridge' has a picturesque centre where the timber-framed Old Bull proclaims its connections with *The Archers*.

INKPEN Berkshire SU3664

Village off A338, 4 miles (6km) SE of Hungerford

Scattered woody village below the high steep chalk scarp. Inkpen Common has a nature reserve on the acid gravels. Up on top of the scarp is Inkpen Beacon, a neolithic long barrow (see Combe). Immense views.

INNELLAN Strathclyde NS1470

Village on A815, 4 miles (6km) S of Dunoon

A Clyde resort on the southern end of Cowal peninsula, which looks across to Wemyss Bay. Near by lies ruined Castle Toward.

INNER HEBRIDES Highland

Islands off W coast of Scotland

A group of islands off the west coast of Scotland, stretching from Skye in the north to Islay, not far from the Northern Irish coast. Skye is the largest of the group, which also includes Rhum, Eigg, Muck and Canna (known as the Small Isles), Coll and Tiree, Mull, Jura and Colonsay, Oronsay, Iona and Staffa. They offer a wide range of splendid mountain and coastal scenery, including the spectacular Cuillins on Skye and many idyllic white-sand beaches backed by grass and wildflowers.

The islands are rich in prehistoric and historic sites and were first mentioned by Pliny the Elder in AD77. Christianity was introduced through Iona to Scotland from about AD300, and the area became a Gaelic kingdom, despite years of Norwegian sovereignty. It was ceded to the Scottish Crown in 1266, which heralded an attempt to stamp out the native language and import outside landlords. This culminated in the forced emigration of many islanders during the Clearances.

Today, the main industries are crofting and fishing, although tourism is increasingly important as more people escape from stress to these remote and unspoilt surroundings.

INNERLEITHEN Borders NT3336

Small town on A72, 6 miles (10km) SE of Peebles

Famous tweed and knitwear centre on the River Tweed, noted for cashmere and lambswool. It became a spa town in the 19th century and its mineral springs are still open. Sir Walter Scott used the town as inspiration for 'St Ronan's Well' in his eponymous novel. Smail's Printworks (National Trust for Scotland) is a working printing museum and the town's history is explained in the local interpretive centre.

INNERPEFFRAY Tayside NN9018

Site off B8062, 4 miles (6km) SE of Crieff

Ruined Innerpeffray Castle was built in 1610 by James Drummond, 1st Lord Madderty. Fifty years later his grandson established the library, to be used 'for the education of the people'. The present building was erected in 1751, and the last borrowings were in 1968. Books are now available for on-the-spot reference only. The library contains more than 3,000 pre-1800 books, the earliest dating from 1502.

The church at Insh.

INNSWORTH Gloucestershire SO8621
District in NE Gloucester
Northern residential suburb of Gloucester dominated by the big RAF station, responsible for the service's personnel administration.

INSCH Grampian NJ6228
Village on B992, 10 miles (16km) NW of Inverurie
Large village near notable prehistoric remains, including Pictish Picardy Stone and Dunideer Castle,ann early stone castle on a conical hill, once the site of a prehistoric hillfort.

INSH Highland NH8101
Village on B970, 4 miles (6km) E of Kingussie
Secluded village in upper Spey Valley with easy access to Loch Insh, which offers good watersports facilities.

INSTOW Devon SS4730
Village on B3233, 3 miles (5km) N of Bideford
On the Torridge estuary, the old village lies a little inland, with early 19th-century villas towards the shore. Tapely Park Gardens feature the British Jousting Centre. A big Georgian house, altered around 1900, has limited opening.

INVER Tayside NO0142
Village on A9, 1 mile (2km) W of Dunkeld
This small village on the River Braan is associated with the famous Scots fiddler, Neil Gow. Upstream lies The Hermitage, a charming folly built in 1758 on a wooded gorge.

INVERALLOCHY Grampian NK0365
Village on B9107, 3 miles (5km) E of Fraserburgh
Coastal village with good sands east of Fraserburgh. Inverallochy Castle, a Comyns stronghold, 2 miles (3km) south.

INVERARAY Strathclyde NN0908
Small town on A83, 16 miles (26km) NE of Lochgilphead
One of Scotland's loveliest small towns, Inveraray is a planned Georgian settlement founded in 1745 by the 3rd Duke of Argyll, Chief of the Clan Campbell, as a commercial centre for the area, and built on the site of a ruined fishing village beside Loch Fyne. The Duke was rebuilding Inverary Castle and wished to distance himself from the town; its old site now forms the grounds of the castle.

Inveraray Jail Museum is housed in an attractive Georgian courthouse and details the social history of Scottish prisons. The church bell-tower offers splendid views over the town and surroundings; it was built by the 10th Duke and the bell-peal commemorates the Campbells killed in World War I.

Imposing Inveraray Castle is the seat of the Argylls and was built to designs by Roger Morris and others on the site of an earlier fortress. The interior was damaged by a bad fire in 1975, but has been restored and contains fine furniture, pictures, tapestries and porcelain. The landscaped grounds overlook the loch.

Near by is the Argyll Wildlife Park with Scottish indigenous animals and wildfowl.

INVERBERVIE Grampian NO8272
Small town on A92, 9 miles (14km) S of Stonehaven
Flax-spinning and seafood-processing are the main industries of this small town on a rugged coastline. Birthplace of Hercules Linton, designer of the tea clipper, *Cutty Sark*.

INVERESK Lothian NT3472
Suburb immediately S of Musselburgh
Attractive residential village, now a suburb of Musselburgh, developed for Edinburgh merchants in the early 18th century. Inveresk Lodge is owned by the National Trust for Scotland.

INVERGARRY Highland NH3001
Village on A82, 6 miles (10km) SW of Fort Augustus
Village on the north side of Great Glen, overlooking Loch Oich in splendid mountainous countryside. Invergarry Castle was destroyed by the Duke of Cumberland after the Battle of Culloden.

INVERGORDON Highland NH7068
Town on B817, 11 miles (18km) NE of Dingwall
Town on Cromarty Firth, once a naval base, now owing its prosperity to North Sea oil, for which it provides rig construction and maintenance facilities.

INVERKEITHING Fife NT1383
Town off M90, 4 miles (6km) SE of Dunfermline
Ancient royal burgh on the Firth of Forth, chartered in 1165 and still retaining an attractive old centre and sheltered harbour. Its 15th-century buildings include Greyfriars Hospice and parts of the parish church; the mercat cross is 16th century and the old town house, with characteristic outside staircase, dates from 1770.

INVERKIP Strathclyde NS2072
Village on A78, 5 miles (8km) SW of Greenock
Village inland from Firth of Clyde; near by is 15th-century Inverkip Castle and extensive reservoirs lie to the east. Scotland's largest yacht marina here.

INVERLOCHY Highland NN1275
Village on NE edge of Fort William
Village and site of Battle of Inverlochy (1645), won by the Marquis of Montrose over the Covenanters. Two castles: one ruined, dating from the 13th century, the other an expensive hotel.

INVERMORISTON Highland NH4216
Village on A82, 6 miles (10km) NE of Fort Augustus
Pretty village on Loch Ness with attractive walks past waterfalls on the River Moriston. Connections with Dr Johnson on his journey to the Hebrides.

INVERNESS Highland NH6645
Town on A82, 32 miles (52km) NE of Fort Augustus
The 'capital of the Highlands', Inverness is the administrative, service and commercial centre of the region, with good road and rail links all over the Highlands. Situated at the junction of the Beauly and Moray Firths, the town serves a vast hinterland, offering a range of services unobtainable further north.

Inverness developed as a trading port from the 6th

The cathedral on Iona.

century, growing up around the castle, which still dominates the town today. Near by, the Inverness Museum and Art Gallery gives a good overview of the development of the Highlands and some streets in the old centre still contain fine vernacular buildings, such as Abertarff House. St Andrew's Episcopal Cathedral, built in 1866, lies on the west bank of the river, with the Eden Court Theatre complex next door, a bastion of the performing arts in the north. Inverness is endowed with well-kept parks and gardens, and there are attractive riverside walks, while the Caledonian Canal, designed by Thomas Telford in the early 19th century to link the east and west coasts, offers boating opportunities. There are good tourist facilities and accommodation, making it a popular holiday centre.

INVERURIE Grampian NJ7721

Town on A96, 14 miles (23km) NW of Aberdeen

Granite-built service town in rich agricultural country with a paper-making industry. The area is rich in standing and symbol stones and stone circles; the best are at Easter Aquhorthies. Several battles took place in the area; Kinkell church contains the Harlaw monument, a grave slab of armoured knight killed in the Battle of Harlaw (1411).

IONA Strathclyde NM2723

Island off W coast of Mull

The early history of this fertile island, owned mainly by the National Trust for Scotland, is inextricably linked with the story of Scottish Christianity. St Colomba arrived here from Ireland in 563AD with 12 companions to begin the conversion of the mainland, establishing an autonomous Celtic Christian church stretching into northern England. Iona became an influential centre of scholarship and artistry, with a huge library and tradition of building excellence. It was the burial place of numerous Scottish kings.

The Celtic tradition waned under pressure from the established church and Viking raiders, and by the 12th century the island was a conventional Benedictine establishment which flourished until the Reformation. Centuries of disuse followed until the abbey was restored in 1910; in 1938 the Iona Community was set up by the Presbyterian Church to restore the buildings and offer spiritual retreat.

Today the community offers lay and ecumenical retreats and has restored the abbey complex, the 11th-century St Oran's Chapel, and established a museum. The population is now about 90, and most of the income comes from crofting and visitors, who arrive in vast numbers during the summer.

IPING West Sussex SU8522

Village off A272, 2 miles (3km) W of Midhurst

Attractive village with old cottages, a mill, a five-arched bridge over the River Rother and a big rough common to the south, scattered with tumuli.

IPPLEPEN Devon SX8366

Village off A381, 3 miles (5km) SW of Newton Abbot

The village name means 'upland enclosure'. Fine woodwork in the church includes a late medieval screen and a pulpit.

IPSTONES Staffordshire SK0249

Village on B5053, 4 miles (6km) N of Cheadle

Churnet Valley village with venerable stone buildings, outstanding craft work in church and nature reserve popular with bird-watchers.

IPSWICH Suffolk TM1644

Town off A12, 18 miles (29km) NE of Colchester

Ipswich is a flourishing inland port on the River Orwell, and its origins are ancient, although successive generations of townsfolk appear to have striven to maintain a modern appearance. However, Ipswich boasts 12 medieval churches and some fine 16th-century buildings. One of these is the splendid Christchurch mansion, a Tudor country house set in a park. It is open to the public, and attractions include the fine art collection and a museum of children's toys. Other museums include the Ipswich Museum and Art Gallery, which has replicas of the Sutton Hoo archaeological finds, and a charming exhibition of Victorian natural history. The Tolly Cobbold Brewery was built in 1896 and there are displays of brewing equipment dating from 1723.

Famous people connected to Ipswich include Cardinal Wolsey, born about 1475, who became Henry VIII's Lord Chancellor; Gainsborough, who lived here; and Charles Dickens, who reputedly conceived *Pickwick Papers* while staying in the Great White Horse inn.

The Ancient House in Buttermarket is a 15th-century building with some outstanding pargetting symbolising the four continents. Wolsey's Tudor brick gate still stands on Fore Street.

IRCHESTER Northamptonshire SP9265

Village off A45, 3 miles (5km) SE of Wellingborough

Site of a substantial Roman town. Medieval church and 18th-century houses. Former ironstone workings converted to country park with narrow-gauge railway.

IRESHOPEBURN Durham NY8638

Hamlet on A689, 1 mile (2km) SE of Wear Head

The Weardale Museum, adjacent to the Methodist chapel, contains a late 19th-century lead-miner's living room and displays on local minerals.

Façade of the Ancient House in Ipswich.

IRLAM Greater Manchester SJ7193
Town on A57, 8 miles (13km) SW of Manchester
Industrial and residential area developed in the 19th century on low land next to the Manchester Ship Canal.

IRNHAM Lincolnshire TF0226
Village off A151, 6 miles (10km) NW of Bourne
Secluded village. Early 16th-century hall (not open) with some 12th-century work, partly rebuilt after 1887 fire. Georgian landscaped park and Norman and later church.

IRON ACTON Avon ST6783
Village off B4059, 3 miles (5km) NW of Chipping Sodbury
Iron was mined here in early medieval times. Fine 15th-century church and churchyard cross.

IRONBRIDGE Shropshire SJ6703
Town off A4169, 3 miles (5km) S of Dawley
World's first cast-iron bridge dominates straggling old industrial area in Severn Gorge now famous for its outstanding museums, notably outdoor site at Blists Hill. At Coalbrookdale is Museum of Iron and relics of Abraham Darby's pioneering ironworks. Many other attractions, including famous china at Coalport Museum, colourful Victorian tiles displayed at Jackfield and fascinating little town of Ironbridge.

IRTHLINGBOROUGH Northamptonshire SP9470
Town off A6, 4 miles (6km) NE of Wellingborough
St Peter's Church, with its remarkable detached tower of the 13th and 14th centuries, is a landmark between the town and the River Nene. The bridge dates from the 14th century. Medieval cross.

IRVINE Strathclyde NS3239
Town off A78, 7 miles (11km) W of Kilmarnock
An ancient burgh that was the chief seaport for trade between Scotland and Ireland until the development of Port Glasgow. Its 20th-century decline was offset by its establishment as a New Town in the 1970s. Several museums and historic buildings, including Scottish Maritime Museum, Glasgow Vennel Museum and Seagate Castle. Statue of Robert Burns, who learned flax-dressing here.

ISFIELD East Sussex TQ4417
Village off A26, 3 miles (5km) SW of Uckfield
Small place on the Iron River, with a pub, The Laughing Fish, well known for folk singing. Isfield Station is the headquarters of the Lavender Line, part of the old Lewes–Uckfield line.

ISLAY Strathclyde
Island off SW coast of Jura
Pronounced 'Eye-la'. Renowned for its rugged coastline, moorlands and mild climate, Islay was the political centre of the Hebrides in medieval times. Most townships here are planned 18th-century settlements built by the Campbells. Famous for single malt whiskies, it has eight distilleries still in operation. Huge wintering

The 13th-century chapel on the Isle of Whithorne.

ground for white-fronted and barnacle geese. Economy based on crofting, fishing, tourism and whisky.

ISLE ABBOTTS Somerset ST3520
Village off B3168, 4 miles (6km) N of Ilminster
Probably the best of all the lovely Somerset churches.Its tower is a perfect example, dating from the 15th century, as does the fan-vaulting in the porch. Serene interior.

ISLE OF WHITHORN Dumfries and Galloway NX4736
Village on B7004, 3 miles (5km) SE of Whithorn
Village linked to the mainland by a causeway and port of entry for pilgrims to Whithorn in medieval times; now a holiday and sailing resort.

ISLE ORNSAY Highland (Skye) NG7012
Village on A851, 7 miles (11km) SE of Broadford
Attractive old coastal village opposite Oronsay Island on the Sound of Sleat, once Skye's main fishing port. The island has a lighthouse and remains of a convent.

ISLEHAM Cambridgeshire TL6474
Village on B1104, 4 miles (6km) W of Mildenhall
A businesslike village on the edge of the Bedford Levels. There is a lovely 12th-century priory (English Heritage) and a 14th-century parish church.

ISLEWORTH Greater London TQ1675
District in borough of Hounslow
Set on the Thames, with the London Apprentice pub and Syon Park, a stately mansion with superb Robert Adam rooms in lovely grounds with a nursery garden and butterfly house.

ISLINGTON Greater London TQ3184
Borough NE of centre
Once a dairy farming, plague escape and Londoner's day out area, Islington was built over in the 19th century and settled by a strong Irish community. A poor district after the war, it was steadily gentrified, gaining a reputation for its trendy left-wing atmosphere. Canal and New River walks, Chapel Street market, Crafts Council gallery, Business Design Centre exhibitions.

ISLIP Northamptonshire SP9878
Village off A6116, immediately W of Thrapston
The medieval bridge was formerly a major crossing point of the River Nene. The church has monuments to the ancestors of George Washington, the first American President.

ISLIP Oxfordshire SP5214
Village on B4027, 5 miles (8km) N of Oxford
Reputed birthplace of Edward the Confessor straddles the River Ray on the edge of Ot Moor (see), its old buildings grouped near the medieval church.

ITCHEN ABBAS Hampshire SU5332
Village on B3047, 4 miles (6km) NE of Winchester
The neo-Norman church of the 1860s is set right down on the River Itchen, with the grave of the last person in England hanged for horse-stealing (1825).

ITCHEN STOKE Hampshire SU5532
Village on B3047, 1 mile (2km) E of Itchen Abbas
A small village with lots of thatch and a strange church rebuilt in 1866 in French 13th-century style and with a lavish interior.

IVER Buckinghamshire TQ0381
Village on B470, 4 miles (6km) E of Slough
Village atmosphere in lee of M25 with a green, and a church with monuments. Architect GF Bodley and painter Paul Nash lived here.

IVER HEATH Buckinghamshire TQ0283
Suburb on A412, 1 mile (2km) N of Iver
Suburban outgrowth of Iver (see), best known for Pinewood Studios and James Bond films. Walking and riding in Black Park and Langley Park.

IVINGHOE Buckinghamshire SP9416
Village on B489, 3 miles (5km) NE of Tring
Formerly a bigger place, with a massive church suitable to its old role as market town, noted for carvings. King's Head hotel goes back to the 17th century. Ford End watermill, restored, is demonstrated in summer. To the east is Ivinghoe Beacon (National Trust), a tremendous viewpoint from a prehistoric stronghold 750ft (210m) up, the end of the Ridgeway long-distance trail.

IVYBRIDGE Devon SX6356
Town off A38, 10 miles (16km) E of Plymouth
Ivybridge grew as a town in the 19th century because of the paper industry. Medieval bridge and a big 1893 railway viaduct. The Erme Valley, above, is beautiful.

IVYCHURCH Kent TR0227
Village off A259, 3 miles (5km) NW of New Romney
Isolated in a wide expanse of Romney Marsh with one of the finest Marsh churches: big, bare and 14th century. The tower is nearly 100ft (30m) high.

IWERNE COURTNEY Dorset ST8512
Village off A350, 4 miles (6km) N of Blandford Forum
The village, also known as Shroton, is beautifully set in a wide valley with many trees, thatched cottages and an interesting church of 1610.

IWERNE MINSTER Dorset ST8614
Village on A350, 5 miles (8km) N of Blandford Forum
Large village, with old cottages mixed with later ones built by the estate. Half-timbered and complex village hall, 1920s, also built by the local landowner who dressed the village girls in red-hooded cloaks.

IXWORTH Suffolk TL9370
Village on A143, 6 miles (10km) NE of Bury St Edmunds
Pargetted houses range along the long main street. Romans and Saxons lived here, while Ixworth Abbey has 12th- and 15th-century buildings.

IXWORTH THORPE Suffolk TL9173
Village on A1088, 2 miles (3km) NW of Ixworth
Most noted for its lovely little thatched church, complete with Tudor brickwork and some exquisite carved bench-ends.

J

JARLSHOF Shetland HU3909

Site off A970, 27 miles (43km) S of Lerwick

This highly important archaeological site includes remains of seven distinct civilisations, spread over 3,000 year. It was discovered after a winter storm blew off the covering sand. The site occupies a grassy promontory by the sea and reveals a cross-section of Shetland's history from the neolithic to the Viking eras. There are remains of Bronze and Iron Age settlements, 8th-century circular wheelhouses, Viking longhouses and a medieval farmhouse. A museum recalls this fascinating history.

JARROW Tyne and Wear NZ3265

Town on A19, 5 miles (8km) NE of Gateshead

Jarrow is probably best known for the 1930s Hunger Marchers who, led by their MP Ellen Wilkinson, walked to London to draw attention to the region's unemployment brought about by the redundant shipyards. The event is remembered in a bas-relief at the Metro Station.

Thirteen hundred years ago Jarrow was a great Saxon monastery, home of the Venerable Bede. Today, extensive remains of this and a Norman monastery survive. Adjoining it, the Church of St Paul contains the world's only Saxon window with Saxon stained glass. The oldest part of the church was built with Roman stones in about AD681. Bede's Chair, on the south wall, is at least 600 years old, the tower dates from 1075 and the original dedication stone of the church, above the tower arch, is dated St George's Day, 23 April 681.

At the nearby Jarrow Hall's Bede Monastery Museum the story of monastic life in Saxon Northumbria is told through displays. Bede Gallery in nearby Springwell Park holds regular exhibitions of contemporary art, and has a museum of the social history of Jarrow.

JAYWICK Essex TM1513

Suburb off B1027, 2 miles (3km) SW of Clacton-on-Sea

Minor resort and western satellite of Clacton (see), developed since the 1930s. Bungalows by the hundreds, caravan parks, sandy beach, sailing.

JEDBURGH Borders NT6420

Town on B6358, 10 miles (16km) NE of Hawick

Once a quintessential Border fortress town, with a fortified castle and abbey, Jedburgh stands on the Jed Water near the Cheviot Hills. The castle was destroyed in 1409 and the town is now noted for the remains of Jedburgh Abbey, founded by David I in 1138. The abbey and monastic buildings formed a large complex, but from the late 13th century this was continuously damaged, and the monastery was closed in 1560 during the Reformation. The abbey church then became the parish kirk and is well preserved, with a lovely Norman west door, a lofty nave with transitional

Bronze Age excavations at Jarlshof.

Norman-Gothic architectural details and a 12th-century arched and pillared choir.

The town has a charming little market place and two museums: the Jedburgh Castle Jail Museum, featuring 19th-century prison life, andthe crow-stepped, gabled Mary Queen of Scots House, where Mary Stuart once stayed. There is a Riding in July into the attractive surrounding countryside.

Jeddart Handba' was a local ball game, said to originate when local men returned from Border raids and played ball with the heads of their English victims.

JEMIMAVILLE Highland NH7265
Village on B9163, 4 miles (6km) W of Cromarty
Small village overlooking the sands of Cromarty Bay on Black Isle. Good bird-watching opportunities are available at nearby Balblair Nature Reserve.

JERSEY Channel Islands
Island in the English Channel
Jersey, a dependency of the Crown, is the largest, warmest and wealthiest of the Channel Islands, 9 miles (14km) long, 5 miles (8km) wide. Divided into 12 parishes, it has sandy beaches, rugged cliffs, country lanes and busy streets. The finest scenery is along the Route du Nord and Queen's Valley, a National Trust area, is an unspoilt valley with one minor road.

A well-known attraction is the Jersey Wildlife Preservation Trust established by Gerald Durrell at Les Augres off the B31. The Jersey Flower Centre is the largest carnation nursery in the UK.

In St Aubin unusual merchants' houses rise to four or five storeys instead of two. In St Peter the Jersey Motor Museum houses military vehicles, veteran and vintage cars and motorcycles.

Lillie Langtry is buried in the graveyard of St Saviour's Church, and St Matthew's Church (The Glass Church) is renowned for its Lalique glass, particularly the giant glass angel over the altar.

The headquarters of the German Occupation Commander during World War II, St Peter's Bunker Museum on the A12 and the German Underground Hospital at Meadow Bank have been preserved.

Along the B28, at La Hougue Bie, a great burial mound covers a neolithic tomb dating from 3000BC.

JERVAULX ABBEY North Yorkshire SE1785
Site on A6108, 3 miles (5km) SE of Middleham
A Cistercian abbey founded in 1156, now ruined, whose monks were famous for producing Wensleydale cheese and for horse-rearing.

JESMOND Tyne and Wear NZ2566
District in NE Newcastle
Remained as a village until the mid-19th century when it became a residential suburb for Newcastle's wealthiest residents. It is still a fashionable place to live, popular with students.

JEVINGTON East Sussex TQ5601
Village off A259, 4 miles (6km) NW of Eastbourne
Pleasant downland village tucked in a hollow, with the church raised up on the hill, infamous in the 18th century as a haunt of smugglers.

JODRELL BANK Cheshire SJ7970
Site on A535, 3 miles (5km) NE of Holmes Chapel
The Lovell Radio Telescope is the second biggest in the world. Jodrell Bank Science Centre and Arboretum. The site belongs to University of Manchester and includes a 35 acre (14ha) arboretum with trails and picnic areas and an Environmental Discovery Centre.

JOHN O' GROATS Highland ND3872
Hamlet on A9, 542 miles (873km) NE of Land's End
Loosely accepted as the northeastern extremity of the British mainland and a popular destination for the mass tourist market. Named after a Dutchman, Jan de Groot, who was given rights to establish a ferry link from here to the newly acquired Orkney Islands in 1496. The site of his original octagonal house is now marked by a mound with a flagstaff.

JOHNSTONE Strathclyde NS4263
Town on A737, 4 miles (6km) W of Paisley
Town built by local laird George Houston to house workers in spinning, mining and engineering industries. Population grew from ten in 1781 to 7,000 in 1841.

JURA Strathclyde
Island between Islay and the mainland, S of Mull
This sparsely populated, long, wild and rugged island is dominated by the peaks of Paps of Jura, one of Britain's last wildernesses, and has many prehistoric remains and a huge population of red deer. Craighouse, with its distillery, is the only settlement. Notorious Corryvreckan whirlpool lies off the north coast. George Orwell lived here from 1946 to 1948 while writing *1984*.

K

KEARSLEY Greater Manchester SD7504
Town off M61, 4 miles (6km) SE of Bolton
District of Bolton with council housing and a small centre with shops, library and a church.

KEDINGTON Suffolk TL7046
Village off B1061, 2 miles (3km) E of Haverhill
The beautiful Church of St Peter and St Paul has been called the 'cathedral of West Suffolk'; it stands among mature trees.

KEDLESTON Derbyshire SK3041
Hamlet off A52, 4 miles (6km) NW of Derby
The finest Robert Adam house in England (National Trust) is set in classical gardens and parkland with an Adam bridge. It was built in 1759–65 for Nathaniel Curzon, the first Baron Scarsdale, whose family has lived at Kedleston for 700 years. Family portraits, old masters, furniture and other contents in elegant Adam interiors. Numerous Curzon monuments in the late 13th-century church.

KEELBY Lincolnshire TA1609
Village off A18, 7 miles (11km) W of Grimsby
Large village between River Humber and Lincolnshire Wolds. Church has some 13th-century work and a 15th-century tower; heavily restored 1909–10.

KEELE Staffordshire SJ8045
Village on A525, 3 miles (5km) W of Newcastle-under-Lyme
University College of North Staffordshire, established in 1949 in Nissen huts in the grounds of 19th-century Keele Hall, was Britain's first academic campus. It became Keele University in 1962 and now occupies a complex of modern buildings. Despite academic encroachment, Keele retains its estate village character, and the church has monuments to the distinguished Sneyd family, owners of the hall.

KEEVIL Wiltshire ST9258
Village off A350, 4 miles (6km) E of Trowbridge
A pleasant village with brick and timber-framed cottages, some thatched, plus bigger 16th-century houses, some built of stone.

KEGWORTH Leicestershire SK4826
Village on A6, 5 miles (8km) NW of Loughborough
This large village lies close to the Derbyshire and Nottinghamshire borders, near the M1 and East Midlands International Airport. A medieval market town and an important textile centre, it still has a framework knitters' workshop behind Britannia inn. The long windows on all four sides and both floors date from the period between the domestic workshop and powered factory. Of several fine houses, some have cruck trusses and timber-framing; 13th- and 14th-century church.

KEIGHLEY West Yorkshire SE0641
Town on A629, 9 miles (14km) NW of Bradford
A busy market and textile town with fine examples of Victorian and Edwardian architecture along with modern buildings. Many of the cobbled side-streets remain. The Keighley and Worth Valley Railway runs regular services, with steam trains in the summer months, and has been used in films such as *The Railway Children* and *Yanks*.

Inscription on the Smithy at Keir Mill.

KEINTON MANDEVILLE Somerset ST5430
Village on B3153, 6 miles (10km) SE of Glastonbury
A mostly 19th-century and later village, whose name means 'King's Settlement' and whose church stands apart.

KEIR MILL Dumfries and Galloway NX8593
Village off A702, 2 miles (3km) SW of Thornhill
Village at the foot of the Keir Hills. Kirkpatrick MacMillan, inventor of the bicycle in 1839, was born at nearby Courthill Smithy.

KEISS Highland ND3461
Village on A9, 6 miles (10km) N of Wick
Coastal fishing village above Sinclair's Bay to the north of Wick. Remains of an old castle overlook the sea.

KEITH Grampian NJ4250
Town on A96, 15 miles (24km) SE of Elgin
Town at the centre of rich farming country, founded in the 8th century but planned and rebuilt from the 1750s. The local industries are distilling and wool-manufacture. Milton Tower dates from 1480 and the Auld Brig from 1609. Birthplace of St John Ogilvie (1579–1615), a Jesuit priest who was Scotland's first post-Reformation saint.

KELD North Yorkshire NY8900
Village on B6270, 2 miles (3km) NW of Muker
A small, picturesque village on the River Swale. Popular walking country and scenic surroundings including Kisdon Force waterfall.

KELHAM Nottinghamshire SK7755
Village on A617, 2 miles (3km) NW of Newark-on-Trent
Beside the River Trent, red-brick Kelham Hall, now local authority offices, was the major secular work of Sir George Gilbert Scott, 1858–61, after an earlier house burnt down, leaving Salvin's 1840s Jacobean-style service wing. It was bought in 1919 by the Society of Sacred Mission, who added the Arts and Crafts-style quadrangle in 1924–5, and the Byzantine-style domed chapel, now used for concerts, in 1927–8. Other events in grounds.

KELLIE CASTLE Fife NO5105
Mansion off B9171, 3 miles (5km) NW of Pittenweem
Good example of domestic Scottish architecture dating from the 14th to 17th centuries. Fine plasterwork and panelling, and late Victorian walled garden (National Trust for Scotland).

KELMARSH Northamptonshire SP7379
Village on A508, 5 miles (8km) S of Market Harborough
Mellow, red-brick Kelmarsh Hall (limited opening) designed by James Gibbs in 1728. The 15th-century church has a High Victorian interior of 1874.

KELMSCOT Oxfordshire SU2599
Village off A417, 3 miles (5km) E of Lechlade
Craftsman and social philosopher William Morris spent the last years of his life in Kelmscot and is buried in the churchyard. His home, Kelmscot Manor (limited opening), is a living museum of his work. The village, well

worth visiting for its own sake, contains buildings by his disciples Philip Webb and Ernest Gimson.

KELSALE Suffolk TM3865
Village off A12, 1 mile (2km) N of Saxmundham
Once a thriving market town, sleepy Kelsale has a splendid timber guildhall, and an interesting lych-gate in the church.

KELSHALL Hertfordshire TL3336
Village off A505, 3 miles (5km) SW of Royston
A neat and well-kept village among low hills, with broad views. Remains of medieval crosses, and a Victorianised church with an interesting screen and recess.

KELSO Borders NT7234
Town on A698, 8 miles (13km) SW of Coldstream
Set on the confluence of the rivers Teviot and Tweed, Kelso is the site of the remains of a 12th-century abbey, once Scotland's most powerful, destroyed in 1545. The 18th-century Turret House includes Kelso Museum and tells the town's history. Floors Castle, a huge crenellated mansion, dates from 1718 with 1840s additions. It lies in an impressive park west of town.

KELVEDON Essex TL8619
Village off A12, 4 miles (6km) NE of Witham
On the Blackwater. Pleasing High Street, with antiques shops galore and a Thursday market. The museum (limited opening) covers Kelvedon and Feering (see) local history.

KELVEDON HATCH Essex TQ5698
Village on A128, 3 miles (5km) S of Chipping Ongar
Quiet place which did not get gas and electricity until after 1955. Forebears of the Wright Brothers, American aviation pioneers, lived here.

KEMERTON Hereford and Worcester SO9437
Village off A435, 4 miles (6km) NE of Tewkesbury
Bredon Hill village with outstanding Victorian church and array of interesting houses. Home of John Moore, author of *The Brensham Trilogy*.

KEMNAY Grampian NJ7316
Village on B993, 4 miles (6km) SW of Inverurie
Nearby Paradise Hill provided granite for several of London's Thames bridges. Three miles (5km) south is Castle Fraser (National Trust for Scotland), with an outstanding great hall, set in rolling parkland.

KEMPLEY Gloucestershire SO6729
Village off B4215, 4 miles (6km) NW of Newent
The village boasts two richly rewarding churches: St Mary's, with magnificent Norman wall-paintings and St Edward's, a fine example of Arts and Crafts work.

KEMPSEY Hereford and Worcester SO8549
Village on A38, 4 miles (6km) S of Worcester
Popular Severnside commuter village retains good medieval church and many timber-framed and Georgian houses among its modern estates.

KEMPSFORD Gloucestershire SU1696
Village off A417, 3 miles (5km) S of Fairford
Pretty Thames-side village with an impressive church with interesting monuments, picturesque cottages and traces of a once-busy canal wharf.

KEMPSTON Bedfordshire TL0347
Town on A5134, 2 miles (3km) SW of Bedford
Old hamlets scattered like currants within a 20th-century development. Great Ouse riverside church. Veteran inn, the King William IV.

KEMSING Kent TQ5558
Village off A225, 3 miles (5km) NE of Sevenoaks
Pretty little village beneath the North Downs, increasingly hemmed in by overspill from Sevenoaks. There are tile-hung houses around the green and St Edith's Well, whose water is said to cure eye troubles.

KENCHESTER Hereford and Worcester SO4343
Hamlet off A438, 5 miles (8km) W of Hereford
Norman church in a village that has shrunk to a small hamlet. Near by is site of Roman town of *Magnis*.

KENCOT Oxfordshire SP2504
Village off A361, 4 miles (6km) NE of Lechlade
Brize Norton air base is a disturbing presence, but this attractive village has a small church with outstanding Norman carving.

KENDAL Cumbria SD5192
Town on A6, 19 miles (31km) N of Lancaster
Kendal was once an important woollen textile centre, the industry having been founded by John Kemp, a Flemish weaver, in 1331. The town was also famous for its Kendal Bowmen, skilled archers clad in Kendal Green cloth, who fought against the Scots at the Battle of Flodden Field in 1513.

Catherine Parr, the last of Henry VIII's six wives, lived at Kendal Castle in the 16th century before she became Queen of England. Today the castle is a ruin, but Catherine Parr's Book of Devotions is housed in the town hall on Stricklandgate. A distinctive feature of the town's historic centre is the series of named or numbered yards, tucked away down alleyways and through arches, once the focus of local small industry.

Abbot Hall Museum of Lakeland Life and Industry displays traditional rural trades of the region, with blacksmiths' and wheelwrights' workshops, and Abbot Hall Art Gallery includes work by John Ruskin and the Kendal painter George Romney. Adjacent to Abbot Hall is the 13th-century Parish Church of Kendal, one of the largest in England, with five aisles and a peal of 10 bells.

KENFIG Mid Glamorgan SS8081
Village off A4229, 3 miles (5km) N of Porthcawl
Medieval borough of Kenfig lies buried beneath dunes of Kenfig Burrows. Burrows and Kenfig Pool are now a National Nature Reserve, adjacent to surviving village.

KENILWORTH Warwickshire SP2872
Town off A46, 5 miles (8km) SW of Coventry
Extensive remains of a huge castle immortalised by Sir Walter Scott range from the 12th-century keep to

Elizabethan refinements built by the Earl of Leicester. Scott's bedroom is preserved in the 18th-century King's Arms hotel. The church is not outstanding but has a very fine Norman door. The attractive Castle Hill and Castle Green compensate for the nondescript streets of the modern town.

KENMORE Tayside NN7745
Village on A827, 6 miles (10km) SW of Aberfeldy
Estate village at the east end of Loch Tay, near the 19th-century pile of Taymouth Castle on an earlier site. Scotland's oldest inn (1572) is here.

KENNET, RIVER Berkshire
River running through Hungerford and Newbury to Reading
The Kennet River rises in the chalk of the Marlborough Downs and passes through Hungerford, where it is joined by the Kennet and Avon Canal (completed in 1810, re-opened after restoration in 1990). The river and canal run together across Berkshire through Newbury to Reading, where they join the Thames.

KENNINGTON Greater London TQ3177
District in borough of Lambeth
Charlie Chaplin's birthplace. The Oval, the Surrey county cricket headquarters, is used for Test matches. Kennington Park was once Surrey's execution ground.

KENSAL GREEN Greater London TQ2382
District in borough of Brent
Famed for its cemetery (guided tours) beside the Grand Union Canal. There are catacombs, obelisks and romantic mausoleums. Thackeray, Trollope and Brunel are all buried here.

KENSINGTON Greater London TQ2579
District in royal borough of Kensington and Chelsea
A country village until William III settled in Kensington Palace, rebuilt by Wren. The grounds are now Kensington Gardens, next to Hyde Park and containing the Round Pond for toy boats. Holland Park was originally the grounds of a bombed Tudor mansion. Near by, Lord Leighton's house is a museum, as is Linley Sambourne House. The Commonwealth Institute has displays. (See also South Kensington.)

KENSWORTH Bedfordshire TL0319
Village off A5, 2 miles (3km) S of Dunstable
Commuter village with a Norman church and farms on a steep, wooded hill. Old houses to the southeast at Kensworth Lynch.

KENTCHURCH Hereford and Worcester SO4125
Hamlet on B4347, 2 miles (3km) SE of Pontrilas
Worth making an appointment to view Scudamore family's Kentchurch Court, incorporating original castle features, remarkable family portraits and fine Grinling Gibbons carving.

KENTFORD Suffolk TL7066
Village off A14 (A45), 5 miles (8km) NE of Newmarket
A young shepherd committed suicide and was buried outside Kentford. His grave is still tended and furnished with fresh flowers.

KENTISBEARE Devon ST0608
Village off A373, 3 miles (5km) E of Cullompton
In an area of small hills, with a handsome 15th-century church containing a long screen. Late medieval cob and thatch priest's house (not open) close by.

KENTISH TOWN Greater London TQ2884
District in borough of Camden
Originally a forest hamlet which developed from the 1840s, now a mixture of middle-class and council housing. There is a city farm. Karl Marx and George Orwell were past residents.

KENTMERE Cumbria NY4504
Village off A591, 4 miles (6km) N of Staveley
The village is at the source of the River Kent, which provided power for the industry along its banks.

KENTON Devon SX9583
Village on A379, 4 miles (6km) N of Dawlish
Set just back from the Exe estuary, Kenton has a fine 15th-century church with a 120ft (36m) tower. Powderham Castle is close to the estuary, a medieval fortified manor house with fine interiors. It was much altered and extended in the 18th and 19th centuries, and has a deer park.

KERESLEY West Midlands SP3282
Village on B4098, on NW outskirts of Coventry
Unremarkable village, with church by noted Victorian architect Benjamin Ferrey. Site of the big Coventry Colliery.

KERRY Powys SO1490
Village on A489, 3 miles (5km) SE of Newtown
Sleepy border village that gives its name to a famous breed of black-faced sheep. To the north are remnants of Dolforwyn Castle (Cadw), stronghold of Llywelyn the Last.

KERSEY Suffolk TM0044
Village off A1141, 2 miles (3km) NW of Hadleigh
Kersey is reached through vast fields and winding hedgerows. A watersplash grants access to the village which stands on a hill. Its ancient houses are a jumble of gables, timber, and washes of white, pink and ochre. Magnificent St Mary's Church was built from the proceeds of Kersey cloth. The Street is a straggling row of ancient weavers' cottages.

KESSINGLAND Suffolk TM5286
Village off A12, 4 miles (6km) SW of Lowestoft
Once the richest village in England, Kessingland shows signs of former wealth in its houses. It has a long wide beach of sand and shingle.

KESTEVEN Lincolnshire
Historic region in W Lincolnshire
One of three parts into which Lincolnshire was historically divided for administrative purposes, recalled in names of North and South Kesteven District Councils.

KESWICK Cumbria NY2623
Town off A66, 16 miles (26km) W of Penrith
Keswick is the largest town within the Lake District

Old houses in the village of Kersey.

National Park and the main tourist centre of northern Lakeland, situated on the shores of Derwent Water and separating the two distinctive areas of Skiddaw and Borrowdale. It developed as a focus for the mining industry in Elizabethan times and German miners were brought in to help exploit the lead and copper deposits in the hills. Graphite was also mined in Borrowdale resulting in the establishment of a pencil factory which has since operated with imported material. Cumberland Pencil Museum has a realistic reconstruction of a section of a mine and uses exhibits, including the world's largest pencil, 7ft (2m) long, and a video to present the story of the industry.

The local vicar here at one time was Canon Rawnsley, one of the founders of the National Trust.

The Keswick Museum and Art Gallery in Fitz Park houses the original manuscript of *Goldilocks and The Three Bears.*

Nearby Castlerigg Stone Circle, believed to have been erected 3,500 years ago, contains 38 boulders and measures 107ft (33m) across at its widest point.

KETTERING Northamptonshire SP8678

Town on A43, 13 miles (21km) NE of Northampton

This thriving market town's traditional boot and shoe manufacture has broadened to other industries. The parish church has an elegant spire. A fascinating museum is housed in the manor house, and the art gallery collection includes work by local artist Alfred East. Wicksteed Park, on the edge of town, provides hours of amusement for children. The Leisure Village has major facilities for sports, swimming and recreation.

KETTERINGHAM Norfolk TG1602

Village off A11, 6 miles (10km) SW of Norwich

A growing village standing amid rich agricultural land. The Tudor hall is now a racing-car headquarters, and there is a church with marvellous brasses.

KETTLEWELL North Yorkshire SD9672

Village on B6160, 6 miles (10km) N of Grassington

This Upper Wharfedale village, surrounded by drystone walls and the Pennine Hills, is a conservation area.

KETTON Leicestershire SK9704

Village on A6121, 4 miles (6km) SW of Stamford

Beside the River Welland on the Northamptonshire border. Fine Ketton limestone made the Tower of London, York Minster and the village itself. Numerous 17th-century and later houses.

KEW Greater London TQ1876

District in borough of Richmond

Kew's charming green and cricket ground are overlooked by 18th-century houses and the handsome red-brick church, in whose graveyard the painters Gainsborough and Zoffany are buried. Kew Palace, where George III and his family retreated from London, is in the Royal Botanic Gardens, first developed from 1759 by his mother, Princess Augusta of Wales, in her widowhood. The gardens were given to the nation by Queen Victoria in 1841 and now cover 300 acres (122ha) beside the Thames.

Both a pleasure ground and a research centre, Kew Gardens are home to tens of thousands of trees, shrubs and plants, native and foreign. Pleasures include the rhododendron dell and azalea garden, the spectacular glass-and-iron Palm House and Temperate House designed by Decimus Burton, the Water Lily House and the Princess of Wales Conservatory, opened in 1987. The pagoda and the orangery were built for Princess Augusta by Sir William Chambers and the Queen's Cottage was a summerhouse for George III's children. There is a museum of useful plants and flower paintings by Marianne North are shown in a special gallery.

The pagoda at Kew Gardens.

KEWSTOKE Avon ST3363

Village off A370, 2 miles (3km) NE of Weston-super-Mare

Medieval church with pretty Norman doorway. There is a big bay to the north and Weston Woods to the south.

KEYHAVEN Hampshire SZ3091

Village off B3058, 1 mile (2km) W of Milford on Sea

This little hamlet sits on the shore, with huge marshes created by the Hurst Spit protruding into the Solent, halfway to the Isle of Wight. At the end of the spit is Hurst Castle (English Heritage), best approached by boat from Keyhaven. The 1530s fort is dwarfed by 1860s additions. Wonderful views.

KEYMER West Sussex TQ3115

Town on B2116, 1 mile (2km) W of Ditchling

Old village, but the buildings are mostly 20th century, merging westwards with Hassocks. Famous works still produce hand-made bricks and tiles.

KEYNSHAM Avon ST6568

Town off A4, SE of Bristol

A small medieval town, which developed after the railway went through in 1840. Great expansion since World War II as Bristol overspill. Handsome 1634 church tower – the earlier one was destroyed in a thunderstorm of 1632. Town named after St Keyna, who turned all the local serpents into stone – witness the many fossil ammonites in the local building stone. Avon Valley Railway (steam) at Bitton, 1 mile (2km) north. Avon Valley Country Park.

KEYSOE Bedfordshire TL0662

Village on B660, 8 miles (13km) N of Bedford

'Wot's the matter, Lord have mercy upon me', cried William Dickins falling off the steeple, 1718. A tower inscription tells the dramatic tale.

KEYSTON Cambridgeshire TL0475

Village on B663, 4 miles (6km) SE of Thrapston

A quiet village with the charming Pheasant inn, a thatched 17th-century pub decorated with old farming implements.

KEYWORTH Nottinghamshire SK6130

Village off A606, 7 miles (11km) SE of Nottingham

The church's beacon tower signalled to Nottingham and Belvoir Castle in times of danger. Mid-17th-century timber-framed barn. Headquarters of British Geological Survey.

KIBWORTH, BEAUCHAMP AND HARCOURT
Leicestershire SP6893

Villages on A6, 5 miles (8km) NW of Market Harborough

Attractive twin villages on the A6 between Leicester and Market Harborough. The 14th-century ironstone church at Kibworth Beauchamp has an imposing limestone tower rebuilt in the 1830s. Other buildings include the 1725 old grammar school and the 16th-century old manor house. Kibworth Harcourt mostly owned by Merton College, Oxford, since the 13th century. Fine houses include the symmetrical brick Old House of 1678. Post windmill dated 1711 on site of earlier mills.

KIDDERMINSTER Hereford and Worcester SO8376

Town on A456, 16 miles (26km) W of Birmingham

Famous for carpets since the 18th century, the town has lost many older buildings through modern development and road schemes, but some mills survive beside the canal. Local history museum tells story of town, and Brinton's carpet factory is open for tours. Fine monuments in St Mary's Church and statue of Sir Rowland Hill, creator of Penny Post, born here in 1795.

KIDLINGTON Oxfordshire SP4914
Small town on A4260, 5 miles (8km) N of Oxford
Kidlington's extensive modern housing does not detract from the appeal of a richly-furnished medieval church and attractive old town centre.

KIDSGROVE Staffordshire SJ8354
Town on A50, 6 miles (10km) NW of Stoke-on-Trent
Former mining town, now a residential area notable for the long Harecastle Canal tunnels: Brindley's pioneer effort is abandoned, Telford's replacement still in use.

KIDWELLY Dyfed SN4006
Small town off A484, 7 miles (11km) NW of Llanelli
Unhurried little town with surprisingly impressive monuments to medieval and industrial past. Kidwelly Castle (Cadw) is one of Wales's best-preserved fortresses. Massive twin-towered gatehouse guards entrance to remarkably intact castle. On outskirts of town stands an industrial museum based at former tinplate works. Just west are the saltings of the Gwendraeth estuary.

KIELDER Northumberland NY6293
Village off B6357, 5 miles (8km) SE of Myredykes
A popular recreational area comprising Kielder Water, the largest man-made reservoir in Europe, and Kielder Forest, belonging to the Forestry Commission. Watersports, forest trails, fishing and other leisure facilities are now available here and Kielder Castle, once the Duke of Northumberland's shooting lodge, is now a visitor centre.

KIFTSGATE MANOR Gloucestershire SP1742
see Hidcote Bartrim

KILBARCHAN Strathclyde NS4063
Small town off A761, 2 miles (3km) W of Johnstone
This was a handloom weaving centre in the 19th century. The history of the industry is told in the restored 1723 Weavers' Cottage (National Trust for Scotland).

KILBIRNIE Strathclyde NS3154
Town on A760, 4 miles (6km) SW of Lochwinnoch
Noted for Barony Parish Church, possibly dating from 1275, with 16th- and 17th-century aisles and an ornate carved loft. Supposed secret tunnel to Kilbirnie House.

KILBURN North Yorkshire SE5179
Village off A170, 6 miles (10km) E of Thirsk
The village overlooks large parts of the vales of York and Mowbray. The Kilburn white horse, carved in 1857, was the brainchild of Thomas Taylor. It is maintained by a committee of local people. Kilburn was also the home of Robert Thompson whose 'mouse' furniture has sold worldwide.

KILCHOAN Highland NM4863
Village on B8007, 12 miles (19km) W of Salen
Main crofting township in the remote far west of Ardnamurchan peninsula. Ferry link to Mull. Near by is Ardnamurchan Point, the most westerly point of the British mainland.

KILCONQUHAR Fife NO4802
Village on B941, 1 mile (2km) N of Elie
Pretty village on the shores of Kilconquhar Loch. Kilconquhar House, with its 16th-century tower, is now the centre of a time-share holiday development.

KILDWICK North Yorkshire SE0046
Village off A629, 4 miles (6km) NW of Keighley
A picturesque village in the Aire Valley that had many wool- and silk-spinning and weaving mills near by. They are now closed.

KILGETTY Dyfed SN1207
Village off A477, 4 miles (6km) N of Tenby
Stands at key crossroads and gateway point familiar to motorists driving to Tenby and Pembroke. Nearby Folly Farm, based at authentic dairy farm, is a popular attraction.

KILKHAMPTON Cornwall SS2511
Small town on A39, 4 miles (6km) NE of Bude
This small hilltop town is dominated by its large 15th-century church, which has a fine Norman doorway and many 16th-century bench-ends.

KILLEARN Central NS5286
Village on A875, 5 miles (8km) N of Strathblane
Mainly late 18th-century village set around a green at the edge of Campsie Fells. Pots of Gartness, near by, is a popular River Endrick salmon-leap viewpoint.

KILLIECRANKIE Tayside NN9162
Village off A9, 3 miles (5km) SE of Blair Atholl
Village near a gorge which saw the overwhelming defeat of Government forces by Jacobite Highlanders under the command of Graham of Claverhouse, 'Bonnie Dundee', at the Battle of Killiecrankie in 1689. Owned by the National Trust for Scotland, with a visitor centre and trails leading to Soldier's Leap. Near by is a RSPB reserve.

KILLIN Central NN5733
Village on A827, 12 miles (19km) SW of Fearnan
Picturesque village surrounded by hills at the west end of Loch Tay, mainly known for the tumbling and rocky Falls of Dochart, flowing through the village and under 18th-century Dochart bridge. Near by is the burial place of Clan MacNab; ruined 16th-century L-plan Finlarig Castle stands at the end of the loch.

KILLINGWORTH Tyne and Wear NZ2870
Suburb off A189, 4 miles (6km) N of Newcastle
Industrial new town with old centre. Former mining village where George Stephenson lived and worked.

KILMACOLM Strathclyde NS3569
Town on A761, 6 miles (10km) SE of Greenock
Pleasant 19th-century residential town and former weaving centre. Several houses designed by Charles Rennie Mackintosh. Nearby Quarrier's Homes for Orphans founded in 1871.

KILMARNOCK Strathclyde NS4237
Town on A71, 8 miles (13km) NW of Mauchline
A manufacturing town with a long history, Kilmarnock has suffered in the second half of this century from the loss or decline of many of its major industries, and today is economically depressed.

Standing on the route from Ayr to Glasgow, it was a flourishing trading centre by the 15th century, manufacturing carpets and shoes. The town's fortunes wavered during the Jacobite Risings but recovered by the end of the 18th century to boom in the 19th. One of Scotland's first railways served the coal-mines which helped to develop local industry; locomotive-building, engineering, carpet-manufacturing and distilling all flourished until the 1970s. Since then, despite the introduction of new light industries, the town has declined, although Johnnie Walker remains one of the world's biggest whisky-blending and bottling plants.

The town contains some fine Victorian buildings, including the Dick Institute Museum and Art Gallery. Dean Castle dates from the 14th century; now restored, it also houses a museum. There are several pleasant parks: Kay Park contains the Burns Monument, which commemorates the first printing of the poet's work in Kilmarnock in 1786.

KILMARTIN Strathclyde NR8398
Village on A816, 5 miles (8km) N of Lochgilphead
A village in a valley rich in prehistoric remains, including cup-marks, cairns and circles. Overlooked by ruined 16th-century Carnasserie Castle, a fine fortified house.

KILMAURS Strathclyde NS4141
Village on A735, 2 miles (3km) NW of Kilmarnock
Small village, once a weaving centre and Burgh of Barony since 1527; there is an original tollbooth. Also once noted for its cutlery.

KILMELFORD Strathclyde NM8512
Village on A816, 16 miles (26km) N of Lochgilphead
Pretty village attractively situated at the head of Loch Melfort, sheltered by numerous islands – a popular sailing centre. Near by are Arduaine House Gardens (National Trust for Scotland).

KILMERSDON Somerset ST6952
Village on B3139, 2 miles (3km) S of Radstock
A coal-mining area from medieval times to 1973. This pretty stone village has a handsome 15th-century church tower.

KILMORY Strathclyde NR7074
see Knapdale

KILMUIR Highland (Skye) NG3770
Hamlet off A855, 5 miles (8km) N of Uig
Mainly noted as the burial place of Flora MacDonald, who helped Prince Charles Edward evade capture after Culloden. Museum of Island Life tells the crofting story.

The ancient carved cross at Kilmartin.

The Celtic cross at Kilmuir,

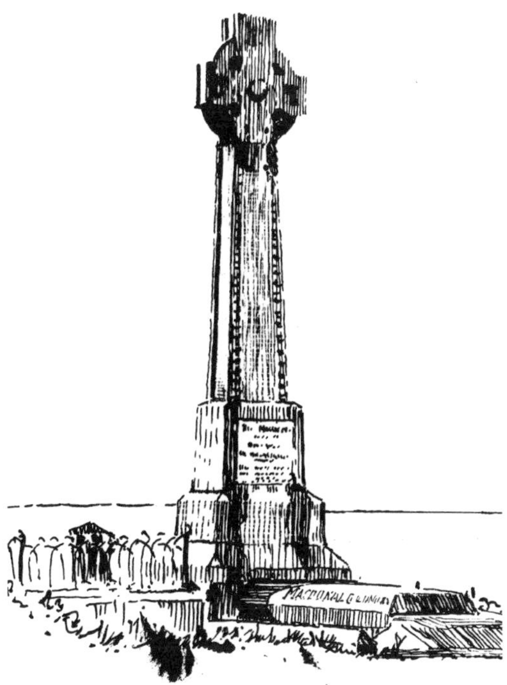

KILMUN Strathclyde NS1781
Village on A880, 5 miles (8km) N of Dunoon
Village on Holy Loch, with extant tower of Collegiate church (1442). Arboretum founded in the 1930s. Nearby Puck's Glen is a stunning walk, following the burn through a gorge.

KILNDOWN Kent TQ7035
Village off A262, 2 miles (3km) SW of Goudhurst
Tiny place with colourful Gothic Revival church built 1839–40, dramatic with stained glass made in Munich, some destroyed during World War II.

KILNSEA Humberside TA4015
Hamlet off B1445, 3 miles (5km) S of Easington
The only habitation of this small hamlet is centred around the lighthouse. Spurn Head is a classified National Nature Reserve.

KILNSEY North Yorkshire SD9767
Hamlet on B6160, 3 miles (5km) NW of Grassington
This ancient fell village is overlooked by the huge limestone Kilnsey Crag, which dominates the landscape for miles around.

KILPECK Hereford and Worcester SO4430
Village off A465, 4 miles (6km) NE of Pontrilas
Kilpeck church is best surviving example of Norman church exuberantly decorated by Hereford School of masons. Corbel table on exterior has wealth of grotesque carving illustrating sins. Magnificent south doorway has shafts and tympanum embellished with dragons, huntsmen and interlaced patterns, while chancel arch is carved with saints and other symbols of holiness. Earthworks of Norman castle near by.

KILSBY Northamptonshire SP5671
Village off A361, 5 miles (8km) SE of Rugby
Focus of communications, near Roman Watling Street, A5, M1, M45, and Robert Stephenson's 2,400yd (2,195m) tunnel for the London–Birmingham Railway, 1838.

KILSYTH Strathclyde NS7178
Town on A803, 3 miles (5km) NW of Cumbernauld
Town at the foot of the Kilsyth Hills in mining country. Site of defeat of the Covenanters by the Marquis of Montrose in 1645.

KILVE Somerset ST1442
Village on A39, 4 miles (6km) NW of Nether Stowey
Set just inland, at the foot of the Quantocks, Kilve has a little medieval church and impressive landscape. Towards the sea are the ruins of late medieval buildings, once a chantry.

KILWINNING Strathclyde NS3043
Town off A78, 5 miles (8km) E of Ardrossan
Noted as the birthplace of Scottish Masonry. Ruins of 12th-century abbey. Water-driven Dalgaven Mill dates from 1620.

KIMBOLTON Cambridgeshire TL0967
Village on A45, 7 miles (11km) NW of St Neots
The sad, discarded wife of Henry VIII, Catherine of Aragon, was confined here 1534–6. Completely rebuilt, Kimbolton Castle (limited opening) is now a school. The River Kym trickles gently through the northeast of the village. Wide main street flanked by large, elegant Georgian houses with tiled roofs. St Andrew's Church dates from 1219.

KIMMERIDGE Dorset SY9179
Village off A351, 5 miles (8km) S of Wareham
Snug, thatched cottages 1 mile (2km) back from Kimmeridge Bay and its short dark cliffs (toll road). Clavell's Tower is a little clifftop folly of the 1820s. Smedmore House (to the east, limited opening) is a smooth stone house of 1761 and earlier, with good gardens.

KIMPTON Hertfordshire TL1718
Village on B652, 4 miles (6km) NE of Harpenden
Commuter village in farming country with walks in local woods. Known for its May Festival. Medieval church.

KINCARDINE Fife NS9387
Small town on A977, 4 miles (6km) SE of Alloa
Once an important port and ship-building centre with a 17th-century mercat cross and the ruins of 15th-century Tulliallan Castle. The bridge opened in 1936; until 1964 the most easterly between Lothian and Fife.

KINCARDINE O'NEIL Grampian NO5999
Village on A93, 7 miles (11km) W of Banchory
One of oldest villages in Deeside which was once an important crossing point on the River Dee. Ruined Auld Kirk built in 1233 as a hospice.

KINCRAIG Highland NH8305
Village off A9, 6 miles (10km) NE of Kingussie
Village in Spey Valley with an 18th-century church. Site of Highland Wildlife Park, a drive-through reserve with a full range of animals indigenous to Scotland.

KINDER SCOUT Derbyshire SK0888
Peak District summit, NW of Edale
This exposed peat plateau is the highest point of the Peak District, 2,088ft (636m), near the starting point of the Pennine Way National Trail. Spectacular Kinder Downfall, wind-sculptured tors. A Mass Trespass here from Hayfield on 24 April 1932 expressed the discontent of walkers at restrictions on moorland access, hastening legislation which created Britain's national parks, of which the Peak District was the first, 1951.

KINETON Warwickshire SP3351
Village on B4086, 10 miles (16km) NW of Banbury
Amid modern development, old stone houses survive in the village beside the River Dene, together with the motte and bailey of 'King John's Castle'.

KING HARRY PASSAGE Cornwall SW8439
River crossing on B3289, 5 miles (8km) S of Truro
A car ferry operates across the Fal estuary, with Trelissick Gardens (National Trust) on the west shore. Very fine gardens and parkland with wonderful river views.

KING'S BROMLEY Staffordshire SK1216
Village on A515, 5 miles (8km) N of Lichfield
A conservation area protects this commuter village's older buildings, including a showpiece cottage called Old Thatch. Interesting medieval church.

KING'S CAPLE Hereford and Worcester SO5628
Village off A49, 4 miles (6km) NW of Ross-on-Wye
On a sharp bend of the River Wye, the village has a rewarding church with fine furnishings of 17th and 18th centuries and a memorial by celebrated artist John Flaxman.

KING'S CLIFFE Northamptonshire TL0097
Village off A47, 5 miles (8km) W of Wansford
A pretty conservation area village in ancient Rockingham Forest, in the valley of the Willow Brook, with limestone houses roofed with Collyweston slate. The schools, almshouses and library were established by 18th-century religious writer William Law, a great influence on John Wesley, founder of Methodism, and tutor to the father of Gibbon the historian. Fine 13th- and 15th-century church with Norman tower.

KING'S HEATH West Midlands SP0781
District in S Birmingham
Sarehole Mill, used until 1919 for grinding corn, is open for working demonstrations. King's Heath Park contains a garden often used in television filming.

KING'S LYNN Norfolk TF6119
Town off A47, 39 miles (63km) W of Norwich
Medieval lanes and alleyways meander back from the quays at King's Lynn's handsome waterfront. The town boasts many fine buildings, some of them ancient — 15th-century St George's guildhall is thought to be the oldest surviving guildhall in England and is owned by the National Trust. Several early medieval and Tudor warehouses have also survived, while at the southern end of the town stands the splendid 17th-century Hampton Court built by a successful master-baker.

The focal point of life in King's Lynn is Saturday Market Place with its 13th-century church. The church has two of the largest brasses in England. North along the River Ouse is the town's second market square, Tuesday Market, which has a 15th-century chapel-of-ease.

King's Lynn is a romantic town, and visitors wandering through its ancient streets will be able to imagine it in former times as a wealthy and active trading community.

Originally called Bishop's Lynn and in the care of the monasteries, the town's name was changed to King's Lynn by Henry VIII during the Dissolution in the 1530s.

KING'S NEWTON Derbyshire SK3926
Village off B587, 1 mile (2km) N of Melbourne
Charming Trent-side village in market gardening country, almost joined to Melbourne (see). Timber-framed cottages and several 18th-century houses. Home of the Newton Wonder apple.

KING'S NORTON West Midlands SP0478
District in S Birmingham
Amid suburban development vestiges of this former Worcestershire village remain, notably the very impressive Church of St Nicholas, the 17th-century timber-framed Saracen's Head and the old grammar school, a brick and timber-frame building with medieval traces. The Patrick Collection, 180 Lifford Lane (limited opening) displays over 80 classic vehicles in a converted papermill.

KING'S NYMPTON Devon SS6819
Village off B3226, 3 miles (5km) N of Chulmleigh
Large village with a handsome, mostly 15th-century church. Superb woodwork inside includes a late medieval screen and roof with intricate bosses. Many 18th-century features.

KING'S PYON Hereford and Worcester SO4350
Village off A4110, 8 miles (13km) NW of Hereford
In deeply rural countryside. The small village with its timber-framed houses clusters round an ancient church.

KING'S SOMBORNE Hampshire SU3631
Village on A3057, 3 miles (5km) S of Stockbridge
Large village in Test Valley, partly consisting of thatched cottages.

KING'S SUTTON Northamptonshire SP4936
Village off B4100, 4 miles (6km) SE of Banbury
Beside the River Cherwell, which forms the Oxfordshire boundary, a beautiful 14th-century spire rises above the Norman, 13th-century and later church. The village also features a Jacobean manor house, half-timbered Tudor Court House, stone-built thatched cottages around the green and village stocks. A

chalybeate spring, in the adjoining hamlet of Astrop, was a fashionable 17th-century spa, and some good ironstone houses of that time remain.

KING'S WALDEN Hertfordshire TL1623
Village off A505, 4 miles (6km) SW of Hitchin
Scattered village with a remote air in rolling, wooded countryside. Beautiful Pre-Raphaelite window in church.

KINGERBY Lincolnshire TF0592
Hamlet off A1103, 4 miles (6km) NW of Market Rasen
Remote, unspoilt redundant church with medieval stained glass, monuments to 14th-century knights and Jacobean timbered roof opposite moated hall. Almshouses.

KINGHAM Oxfordshire SP2624
Village off A436, 4 miles (6km) SW of Chipping Norton
A fine Old Rectory, unusual church details and ancient manor cottages in West Street justify a visit to this Evenlode valley village.

KINGHORN Fife NT2686
Small town on A91, 2 miles (3km) E of Burntisland
Ancient settlement on the Firth of Forth, the scene of the death of Alexander III, the last Celtic King of Scotland. Now a popular holiday resort.

KINGS LANGLEY Hertfordshire TL0702
Village off A41, 3 miles (5km) S of Hemel Hempstead
On the River Gade and the Grand Union Canal, dominated by giant papermills. An impressive viaduct carries the M25 across the valley.

KINGS WORTHY Hampshire SU4932
Village off A33, 2 miles (3km) N of Winchester
Handsome Georgian houses and some older cottages. Abbots Worthy, to the east, is picturesque and full of thatch.

KINGSAND AND CAWSAND Cornwall SX4350
Villages off B3247, 1 mile (2km) SE of Millbrook
The two settlements are always referred to together because they abut. Narrow streets crammed with buildings. Unspoilt rocky and sandy shore. Good views to Devon.

KINGSBRIDGE Devon SX7344
Town on A381, 11 miles (18km) SW of Totnes
This rather remote, old-fashioned small town sits at the head of the Kingsbridge estuary. There is lots of slate-hanging on the steep main street, with stocky granite pillars of 1585 holding up the Shambles. The grammar school of 1670 is now the Cookworthy Museum of Rural Life in South Devon. The town's name reflects the fact that there has been a bridge here from the 10th century.

KINGSBURY Warwickshire SP2196
Village on A4097, 6 miles (10km) S of Tamworth
Tameside village best known today for its Water Park, offering 600 acres (240ha) of lakes, watersports facilities, footpaths and a nature reserve.

KINGSBURY EPISCOPI Somerset ST4321
Village off B3165, 3 miles (5km) NW of Martock
A village on the Levels, with a central green, a little octagonal lock-up and stone cottages. The 15th-century church tower is one of the finest in Somerset. Cider brandy made only here.

KINGSCLERE Hampshire SU5258
Village off A339, 8 miles (13km) NW of Basingstoke
This was once a borough and features much Georgian brick, often grey with red detailing.

KINGSGATE Kent TR3870
Village on B2052, 2 miles (3km) E of Margate
Little Kentish resort near North Foreland, brooded over by battlemented Kingsgate Castle, 1860. Sheltered, sandy Kingsgate Bay at the foot of the cliff; beaches at Joss Bay and Botany Bay.

KINGSKERSWELL Devon SX8868
Small town on A380, 2 miles (3km) NW of Torquay
Cut through by the main road, but the old village survives around the late medieval church.

KINGSLAND Hereford and Worcester SO4461
Village on B4360, 4 miles (6km) NW of Leominster
Picturesque village in Lugg Valley, worth visiting for its timber-framed cottages, good Georgian houses and immensely interesting medieval church.

KINGSLEY Staffordshire SK0246
Village on A524, 8 miles (13km) E of Stoke-on-Trent
Hilltop village with a variety of interesting buildings and good views. Restored Froghall Canal wharf in the Churnet Valley below.

KINGSTEIGNTON Devon SX8773
Small town off A380, 2 miles (3km) N of Newton Abbot
Almost part of Newton Abbot (see), but retaining its old village church.

KINGSTON Cambridgeshire TL3455
Village off B1046, 7 miles (11km) W of Cambridge
The charming Old Rectory (not open) dates from about 1300 and lies to the east of the handsome 15th-century Church of All Saints' and St Andrew.

KINGSTON Dorset SY9579
Village on B3069, 1 mile (2km) S of Corfe Castle
Picturesque stone village in the middle of Purbeck, with a very impressive new church of 1873, built of local stone for the landowner.

KINGSTON BAGPUIZE Oxfordshire SU4098
Village on A415, 6 miles (10km) W of Abingdon
The 17th-century Kingston House, with its fine interior and pleasant grounds, is the main attraction of this village above the Thames Valley.

KINGSTON BLOUNT Oxfordshire SU7599
Village on B4009, 3 miles (5km) NW of Stokenchurch
Against the wooded backdrop of the Chiltern Hills, Kingston Blount's modern houses mix with dwellings of the 16th and 17th centuries.

KINGSTON LISLE Oxfordshire SU3287
Village off B4507, 5 miles (8km) W of Wantage
The village lies below a steep climb to the Ridgeway on Lambourn Downs. The Norman and medieval church displays the crafts of several centuries, and the same can be said of Kingston Lisle Park (limited opening), with its remarkable flying staircase and collections of glass, needlework and furniture of the 17th century.

KINGSTON NEAR LEWES East Sussex TQ3908
Village off A27, 2 miles (3km) SW of Lewes
Modern housing surrounds the green with its row of flint cottages at the Down's foot, where Brighton fishwives used to walk via Kingston carrying fish to Lewes market.

KINGSTON ON SOAR Nottinghamshire SK5027
Village off A453, 6 miles (10km) N of Loughborough
Lord Belper, Edward Strutt, the grandson of Derbyshire industrialist Jedediah Strutt, built Victorian brick estate cottages around the triangular green and the 1840s neo-Elizabethan stone hall, now flats. The church was largely rebuilt in 1900. Babington Chantry (1540) is decorated with babes and tuns, a pun on the family name. Mary Stuart's page, Anthony, was implicated in the Babington Plot to put her on the English throne.

KINGSTON ST MARY Somerset ST2229
Village off A358, 3 miles (5km) N of Taunton
At the southern end of the Quantocks, this pretty stone village has a handsome 15th-century church tower. Many good fittings and memorials.

KINGSTON UPON THAMES Greater London TQ1869
Town/borough on A307, 4 miles (6km) S of Richmond
A leading Surrey market town and shopping centre, which grew up at a ford across the Thames, and later had the first bridge over the river above London Bridge. Saxon kings were crowned on the Coronation Stone, outside the guildhall. The market place has an 1840 town hall. Engaging artwork of leaning phone boxes in London Road. Local museum.

KINGSWEAR Devon SX8851
Town on B3205, 4 miles (6km) SW of Brixham
Opposite Dartmouth (see) on the Dart estuary's woody shore, houses rising steeply from the water. Passenger and car ferries run to Dartmouth and Torbay and the Dartmouth Steam Railway to Paignton (see). Coleton Fishacre Gardens (National Trust) feature shrubs and woodland.

KINGSWINFORD West Midlands SO8888
Town in W area of Dudley
Good Norman and medieval church and interesting old houses survive in the centre of this dormitory suburb. Glass Museum at Broadfield House.

KINGSWOOD Avon ST6473
Town on A420 in E Bristol
Once a coal-mining area, now a suburb of Bristol, with mostly Victorian buildings and a new church of 1820.

KINGTON Hereford and Worcester SO2956
Town on A44, 6 miles (10km) SE of New Radnor
Small and unpretentious Welsh border town beneath high hills. Oxford Arms and old town hall stand out in streets lined with close-set shops and houses of 18th and 19th centuries. To west of town the celebrated Hergest Croft Gardens attract many visitors, while walkers enjoy the fine views from Bradnor Hill (National Trust) and Hergest Ridge.

KINGTON ST MICHAEL Wiltshire ST9077
Village off A350, 3 miles (5km) N of Chippenham
This stone village was the birthplace of John Aubrey, the 17th-century antiquarian and writer. Memorial window in the church.

KINGUSSIE Highland NH7500
Small town on A86, 10 miles (16km) NE of Laggan
Spey Valley resort lying below the Cairngorms, founded in the late 18th century and pronounced 'Kin-youssie'. The Highland Folk Museum, housed in a collection of historic buildings, comprehensively covers every aspect of Highland life. Near by are the impressive Ruthven (pronounced 'Rivven') Barracks, built after the 1745 Jacobite Rising to subdue the area. Insh Marshes RSPB reserve lies to the north.

KINLET Shropshire SO7180
Hamlet on B4363, 4 miles (6km) NE of Cleobury Mortimer
Tiny estate village for Kinlet Hall (now a school) has church with fine medieval work and many interesting monuments.

KINLOCH RANNOCH Tayside NN6658
Village on B846, 7 miles (11km) W of Tummel Bridge
Small village on the Road to the Isles at the east end of Loch Rannoch in wild and impressive landscape. Popular small holiday centre.

KINLOCHBERVIE Highland NC2256
Village on B801, 7 miles (11km) N of Laxford Bridge
Important white-fish port in inhospitable landscape in remotest northwest Sutherland. Access on foot to beautiful Sandwood Bay, the northernmost sandy beach on the west coast.

KINLOCHLEVEN Highland NN1861
Small town on B863, 7 miles (11km) NE of Ballachulish
Formerly a busy aluminium smelting town at the head of Loch Leven which used hydro-electric power from Blackwater Reservoir for 80 years; the process is now explained in the visitor centre.

KINMEL BAY Clwyd SH9880
Village on A548, immediately SW of Rhyl
Resort on a smaller scale than big-brother Rhyl at opposite side of River Clwyd. Long, popular sandy beach with family amenities. Harbour at Foryd.

KINNERSLEY Hereford and Worcester SO3449
Village on A4112, 2 miles (3km) NE of Willersley
Church, 'castle' and cottages form attractive cluster. Castle (limited opening) is actually a fine Elizabethan house. Church is full of interest.

KINNESSWOOD Tayside NO1702
Village on A911, 4 miles (6km) SE of Milnathort
Village at the foot of the Lomond Hills, overlooking Loch Leven. Major gliding centre. Birthplace of Alexander Buchan (1827–1907), whose work inspired modern weather-forecasting.

KINOULTON Nottinghamshire SK6730
Village off A46, 9 miles (14km) NW of Melton Mowbray
Village off the Fosse Way with red-brick 1790s church, near disused Grantham Canal. Poplars commemorate the Battle of the Somme along a farm drive off the Owthorpe road.

KINROSS Tayside NO1102
Town off M90, 9 miles (14km) N of Dunfermline
Market town and important milling centre for cashmere. The tollbooth was restored in 1771 by Robert Adam. Kinross House, in fine gardens, is an outstanding example of late 17th-century architecture.

KINTBURY Berkshire SU3866
Village off A4, 3 miles (5km) E of Hungerford
On the Kennet and Avon Canal and the River Kennet, the village was well known for the production of whiting for paint from the local soft chalk. At Halfway, to the north (on the A4), is a castellated late 18th-century tollhouse.

KINTORE Grampian NJ7916
Village on A96, 4 miles (6km) S of Inverurie
Tiny royal burgh in an area noted for prehistoric remains. The tollbooth (1740) has an outside staircase and the church has a rare sacrament house.

KINTYRE Strathclyde
Peninsula on W coast between Islay and Arran
Long, narrow peninsula, the southern end 12 miles (19km) from Ireland. Campbeltown is the main town, and the industries are farming and forestry. The area is rich in prehistoric sites.

KINVER Staffordshire SO8483
Small town off A449, 4 miles (6km) W of Stourbridge
The town is best viewed from Kinver Edge (National Trust), a high sandstone ridge with intriguing former cave homes. Pleasant streets contain interesting buildings, especially the White Harte inn, 16th-century grammar school (now a house), several good timber-framed and Georgian houses and 19th-century artisans' cottages. St Peter's has many pleasures for church enthusiasts.

KINWARTON DOVECOTE Warwickshire SP1057
see Alcester

KIPPAX West Yorkshire SE4130
Village on B6137, 2 miles (3km) SE of Garforth
A large village of Victorian terraced housing surrounded by modern housing developments and arable land. St Mary's Church is Norman, and features much herring-bone masonry.

KIPPEN Central NS6594
Village off A811, 9 miles (14km) W of Stirling
Traditional village built on the shoulder of Campsie Fells with views of Fintry Hills. Very fine church built in 1825.

The tollbooth at Kintore.

KIRBY BELLARS Leicestershire SK7117
Village on A607, 3 miles (5km) W of Melton Mowbray
Outline of Augustinian priory near a lavish medieval church. Earthworks and surviving stable block of a former manor house, site of a 1645 Civil War skirmish.

KIRBY HILL North Yorkshire NZ1406
Hamlet off A66, 4 miles (6km) NW of Richmond
The village is halfway between London and Edinburgh and the local pub cellar has tethering rings for prisoners that were housed there overnight.

KIRBY LE SOKEN Essex TM2121
Village on B1034, 2 miles (3km) W of Walton on the Naze
In the 19th century this was a bigger place than Walton on the Naze (see), with a busy port and a lively black economy by way of smuggling. There is no commercial traffic now, but boating and watersports on the backwaters and sea wall walks. In winter the Hamford Water Nature Reserve mudflats teem with geese and waterfowl.

KIRBY MISPERTON North Yorkshire SE7779
Village off A169, 3 miles (5km) S of Pickering
Home to the Flamingo Land Funpark and Zoo, set in the grounds of the old Hall. The village is dominated by unattractive 19th-century estate housing.

KIRBY MUXLOE Leicestershire SK5204
Village off A47 on W outskirts of Leicester
Fine medieval moated brick castle (English Heritage), left uncompleted after William Lord Hastings' execution in 1483. Residential village within easy reach of Leicester.

KIRBY UNDERDALE Humberside SE8058
Village off A166, 4 miles (6km) W of Fridaythorpe
A pretty, agricultural village. The Church of All Saints' dates from the 12th century.

KIRBY WISKE North Yorkshire SE3784
Village off A167, 4 miles (6km) NW of Thirsk
Sion Hill Hall, built in 1913, was probably the last country house built in England. It is now open to the public.

KIRDFORD West Sussex TQ0126
Village off A272, 4 miles (6km) NE of Petworth
Attractive village that feels like a tiny town, with a little square green surrounded by tile-hung and stone cottages, church and pub. Once a centre of the Wealden glass industry.

KIRK HAMMERTON North Yorkshire SE4655
Village off A59, 9 miles (14km) W of York
Halfway between Harrogate and York, the village was the last resting-place for many of the slain of the battle of Marston Moor.

KIRK LANGLEY Derbyshire SK2838
Village on A52, 4 miles (6km) NW of Derby
On the Derby–Ashbourne road, with the Meynell Arms and several other good brick houses. The 14th-century and later church has a screen of about 1300.

KIRK MICHAEL Isle of Man SC3190
Village on A3, 6 miles (10km) NE of Peel
Location of 'Douglas Corner' on the TT course. Kirk Michael Church contains some of the finest Viking crosses ever found on the island.

KIRK YETHOLM Borders NT8228
Village on B6352, 7 miles (11km) SE of Kelso
The village is twinned with Town Yetholm, across Bowmount Water, near the English border. It was the headquarters of Scottish gypsies until 1880s, when the last 'Queen' was buried here.

KIRKBEAN Dumfries and Galloway NX9759
Village on A710, 11 miles (18km) S of Dumfries
A village inland from the Solway Firth and birthplace of John Paul Jones (1747–92), founder of the United States navy, whose father was a gardener at Arbigland.

KIRKBRIDE Cumbria NY2256
Village on B5307, 5 miles (8km) N of Wigton
The Church of St Bride dates from before 1189 and was built using stones from Roman buildings. Turf-cutting is still carried out on the marshes.

KIRKBURN Humberside SE9855
Village off A163, 3 miles (5km) SW of Great Driffield
Spread along a busy road and consisting of mainly 19th-century terraced housing. The Church of St Mary contains an impressive font carved with fruit, animals and scenes from the life of Christ.

KIRKBURTON West Yorkshire SE1912
Town off A629, 4 miles (6km) SE of Huddersfield
An attractive historic town, dating mainly from 19th century although church has 13th-century origins.

KIRKBY Merseyside SJ4099
Town off M57, 6 miles (10km) NE of Liverpool
A new town has developed around the old village centre. The name, Scandinavian in origin, means 'church, a fixed residence'.

KIRKBY FLEETHAM North Yorkshire SE2894
Village off A1, 4 miles (6km) SE of Catterick
The village is built around a traditional village green and has maintained its essential character despite new housing developments.

KIRKBY IN ASHFIELD Nottinghamshire SK4956
Town off A38, 4 miles (6km) SW of Mansfield
Originally a clearing in Sherwood Forest, this industrial township grew in the 19th century. The Georgian rectory is now a private house. Church rebuilt after 1907 fire.

KIRKBY LONSDALE Cumbria SD6178
Small town on A683, 14 miles (23km) NE of Lancaster
The name is of Danish origin and marauding seafarers were thought to have settled here. This market town was granted its charter in 1227. The market is held on Thursdays. Devil's Bridge, over the River Lune, dates from the 12th century and the Church of St Mary was built at the time of the Norman Conquest.

KIRKBY MALHAM North Yorkshire SD8960
Village off A65, 5 miles (8km) E of Settle
The name means 'the church place in Malhamdale'. The village has changed little over the years and several of its houses have 17th-century datestones.

KIRKBY MALLORY Leicestershire SK4500
Village off A447, 5 miles (8km) N of Hinckley
Churchyard monument to Byron's daughter, Ada Lovelace, buried in Hucknall (see). Mallory Park motor-racing circuit lies within the grounds of demolished Kirkby Hall.

KIRKBY STEPHEN Cumbria NY7708
Small town on A685, 9 miles (14km) SE of Appleby-in-Westmorland
The town is popular with those travelling between the Lake District and the northeast of England. The church of St Stephen was founded in the 8th century and contains a monument, 'the bound devil', which shows the Norse god Loki as a Gosforth cross. Stenketh Park has spectacular scenery where the River Eden cascades into a ravine.

KIRKBY THORE Cumbria NY6325
Village on A66, 4 miles (6km) NW of Appleby-in-Westmorland
Magnificent view across the Eden Valley and the site of the Roman camp *Braboniacum*.

KIRKBY-IN-FURNESS Cumbria SD2282
Village off A595, 5 miles (8km) NW of Ulverston
Situated on the estuary of the River Duddon. St Cuthbert's Church dates from the 12th century.

KIRKBYMOORSIDE North Yorkshire SE6986
Small town off A170, 7 miles (11km) W of Pickering
A farming town near the North Yorkshire Moors. Buckingham House is named after the Duke of Buckingham who died here in 1687.

KIRKCALDY Fife NT2892
Town on A91, 5 miles (8km) NE of Burntisland
Pronounced 'Kurcawdy', this manufacturing town, a royal burgh from 1450, stretches for miles along the Firth of Forth, and is familiarly known as 'The Lang Toun'. The 4 mile (6km) Esplanade, built in 1922–3 to provide employment, is the scene each April of the Links Market, held since 1305 and nowadays a huge funfair. Weaving, textiles and pottery were the original industries, followed by great prosperity after the invention of linoleum. Coal-mining included mines running underneath the sea, which closed fairly recently after fire damage. Today, floor-coverings still form part of the town's mixed industry, along with rapidly developing electronics.

The Museum and Art Gallery outlines local history and includes fine examples of the collectable Wemyss Ware, manufactured in the town. Ruined 15th-century Ravenscraig Castle is reached by steps from the beach; these were said to be the inspiration for John Buchan's book *The Thirty-Nine Steps*. The architect brothers, Robert and William Adam, were born in Kirkcaldy, and 18th-century economist Adam Smith, author of *Inquiry into the Nature and Causes of the Wealth of Nations*, lived in the town.

KIRKCUDBRIGHT Dumfries and Galloway NX6850
Small town on A711, 10 miles (16km) SW of Castle Douglas
Pronounced 'Kurcoobrie', this royal burgh on the River Dee estuary has a good mix of architectural styles in the streets surrounding the pleasant harbour. MacLellan's Castle was built in the 1580s, the tollbooth dates from 1627 and the mercat cross from 1610. The Stewartry Museum deals with local history and Broughton House was home to Edward Hornel, an important 19th-century Scottish artist.

KIRKDALE North Yorkshire SE6785
Site off A170, 1 mile (2km) W of Kirkbymoorside
The cave here was discovered in 1821, containing the bones of various species no longer found living wild in Britain.

KIRKGUNZEON Dumfries and Galloway NX8666
Village off A711, 4 miles (6km) NE of Dalbeattie
Chiefly noted for nearby Drumcoltran Tower, a 16th-century fortified L-plan tower house. The churchyard has several tall monuments.

KIRKHAM Lancashire SD4232
Town off A583, 8 miles (13km) W of Preston
A market centre for the surrounding area, the town was built on the site of a Roman fort which guarded the road to Ribchester.

KIRKHAM North Yorkshire SE7365
Hamlet off A64, 5 miles (8km) SW of Malton
A quiet village on the River Derwent, dominated by the ruins of the Augustinian monastery of Kirkham Priory (English Heritage).

KIRKHARLE Northumberland NZ0182
Hamlet off A696, 2 miles (3km) SE of Kirkwhelpington
A small compact village, pleasantly situated, noted as the birthplace of Lancelot 'Capability' Brown in 1715.

KIRKINTILLOCH Strathclyde NS6573
Town on A77, 7 miles (11km) NE of Glasgow
Ancient burgh on the Forth–Clyde Canal with Roman traces near by, once a weaving centre; involved in coal-mining from the mid-19th century.

KIRKLEATHAM Cleveland NZ5921
Village on B1269, 2 miles (3km) S of Redcar
Historic village once surrounded by a deerpark, now a conservation area. The Manor House was built by the Turner family as a school in 1710. Now only the stable block and Old Hall Museum remain. Almshouses, dating from 1742, were founded by Sir William Turner. The present church dates from 1763 and contains interesting brasses.

KIRKLINGTON Nottinghamshire SK6757
Village on A617, 3 miles (5km) NW of Southwell
A 19th-century mill sits beside the River Greet at the southern end of the village. Kirklington Hall, mostly 1904, used as Rodney School to the north.

KIRKNEWTON Northumberland NT9130
Village on B6351, 10 miles (16km) SW of Edinburgh
A compact border village at the foot of Yeavering Bell, one of the most northern of the Cheviot Hills. At its summit are the remains of an Iron Age hillfort. The Norman church contains an unusual wall carving of the Adoration of the Magi, depicting the three wise men wearing kilts.

KIRKOSWALD Cumbria NY5541
Village on B6413, 7 miles (11km) N of Penrith
A market town in the Eden Valley with a ruined 11th-century castle devastated by border raiders.

KIRKOSWALD Strathclyde NS2407
Village on A77, 4 miles (6km) W of Maybole
Village noted for its association with Robert Burns, who lived here in 1775. Souter Johnnie's Cottage has Burns memorabilia. The original Tam O' Shanter, farmer Douglas Graham, is buried in the churchyard.

The tombstone of 'Tam O'Shanter' at Kirkoswald.

KIRKPATRICK-FLEMING Dumfries and Galloway NY2770
Village off A74, 6 miles (10km) SE of Ecclefechan
Village on the main routes north, site of Robert Bruce's famous cave where he was allegedly inspired by a spider to persevere in his struggle against the English.

KIRKSTALL West Yorkshire SE2635
District in NW Leeds
The Cistercian monks of the now ruined Kirkstall Abbey had an important influence upon this district of Leeds.

KIRKSTEAD Lincolnshire TF1762
Village on B1191, 2 miles (3km) SW of Woodhall Spa
Remains of 12th-century Cistercian abbey, with outstanding 13th-century St Leonard's Chapel outside gates; roof vaulting, early wooden screen, and monument of knight about 1250.

KIRKSTONE PASS Cumbria NY4008
Mountain pass on A592, 5 miles (8km) S of Patterdale
A steep mountain pass named after the rock at the summit which looks like a church steeple.

KIRKTON OF TEALING Tayside NO4037
Village off A929, 5 miles (8km) N of Dundee
Village north of Dundee with 1st- to 2nd-century souterrain, or earth-house, possibly used for storage, and an unusual dovecote dated 1595.

KIRKWALL Orkney HY4411
Town on A961, 24 miles (39km) N of Duncansby Head across the Pentland Firth
Founded by the Norse earls in about 1035, the city and royal burgh of Kirkwall is the capital and administrative centre of Orkney. It is a busy and prosperous market town with a bustling harbour and a main street which has changed little over the centuries.

The old town is one of the finest examples of an ancient Norse town, dominated by the massive red sandstone cruciform building of St Magnus Cathedral, founded in 1136, and the adjoining ruins of the bishop's palace, dating from the same century. The ruined earl's palace, an excellent example of Renaissance architecture, was built in 1600. Tankerness House is a restored 16th-century merchant's town house with an attractive garden; it houses the Orkney Museum, which tells the 4,000-year history of the islands. Orkney library, founded 1683, is the oldest public library in Scotland. There are two distilleries: Highland Park, operating since 1798, is the world's most northerly whisky distillery.

Kirkwall is the venue at Christmas and on New Year's Day of the world's biggest football game, when two enormous teams play ba' through the town's streets.

KIRKWHELPINTON Northumberland NY9984
Village off A696, 9 miles (14km) SE of Otterburn
Former mining village which now has a more rural character. Norman church with two medieval bells.

KIRRIEMUIR Tayside NO3853
Small town on A926, 5 miles (8km) NW of Forfar
Attractive 18th- to 19th-century town of sandstone

The cathedral at Kirkwall.

houses, retaining its contemporary layout, when it was an important linen-weaving centre. The 1604 Tolbooth dominates the square. Birthplace of James Barrie (1860–1937), author and playwright; his house contains memorabilia. Barrie Pavilion, a gift from the writer to the town, has a camera obscura, giving views across Strathmore. Renowned for the ballad 'Ball of Kirriemuir'.

KIRTLING Cambridgeshire TL6857
Hamlet off B1063, 5 miles (8km) SE of Newmarket
Elizabeth I visited Kirtling Towers (not open) in 1578, although now only the moat and gatehouse remain. All Saints' Church is mainly Norman.

KIRTLINGTON Oxfordshire SP4919
Village on A4095, 6 miles (10km) SW of Bicester
Roman Akeman Street skirts the splendid Kirtlington Park (not open), and other fine houses grace this straggling village close to the River Cherwell.

KIRTON Nottinghamshire SK6969
Village on A6075, 3 miles (5km) E of Ollerton
The 13th-century church sits above a sharp bend in the Tuxford–Ollerton road. L-shaped Hall Farm is 17th century. Kirton Wood Nature Reserve, part of ancient Sherwood Forest, was replanted in the 1930s.

KIRTON IN LINDSEY Humberside SK9398
Small town on B1206, 8 miles (13km) S of Scunthorpe
Small town spread across the side of a hill with criss-crossing streets. Well-preserved 19th-century windmill now houses a transport museum.

KIRTON (OR KIRTON IN HOLLAND) Lincolnshire TF3038
Village on A16, 4 miles (6km) SW of Boston
Former market town, with town-sized medieval church rebuilt in 1800s. Market cross, some Georgian houses, 16th- and 17th-century former inn.

KISLINGBURY Northamptonshire SP6959
Village off A45, 4 miles (6km) W of Northampton
Attractive village, with ironstone and sandstone buildings, 14th-century church close to the River Nene, and charming early 18th-century rectory.

KIT'S COTY HOUSE Kent TQ7460
Prehistoric site off A229, 2 miles (3km) N of Maidstone
Three upright stones, 7 to 8ft (2m) high, and a 13ft (8m) long capstone are all that remains of a neolithic burial chamber once covered by an earthern mound (barrow). There are other ancient stones near by.

KNAPDALE Strathclyde NR8176
Scenic region in Argyll, between the Sound of Jura and Loch Fyne
District of low-lying hills, settled on the coast since early times and noted for cattle-rearing. There are sculptured stones at Kilberry, and the ruined chapel at Keills has a carved Celtic cross. Kilmory Knap Chapel is also known for its carvings, which date from the 8th to the 16th centuries. Castle Sween is a 13th-century stronghold, largely destroyed in 1645.

KNAPTON Norfolk TG3034
Village on B1145, 3 miles (5km) NE of North Walsham
Knapton church has the finest double hammerbeam roof in Norfolk, dating from 1503. It has more than 160 carved angels and other figures.

KNARESBOROUGH North Yorkshire SE3557
Town on A59, 3 miles (5km) NE of Harrogate
A picturesque market town, perched precariously high over the River Nidd, with Georgian houses, narrow streets, a maze of alleys, boating and pleasant riverside walks. Curious attractions include the ruins of a 12th-century castle, England's oldest chemist's shop and the legendary Mother Shipton's Cave with its Petrifying Well.

KNEBWORTH Hertfordshire TL2520
Town off A1(M), 3 miles (5km) S of Stevenage
In the 1840s the best-selling novelist Edward Bulwer-Lytton transformed his ancestral Tudor mansion, Knebworth House, into a wildly romantic fairytale creation. It has a fascinating Indian collection, Dickens associations, Lutyens and Jekyll gardens, a stately park and a church with magnificent family monuments. Lutyens also designed St Martin's Church in the town, and the golf clubhouse.

KNEESALL Nottinghamshire SK7064
Village on A616, 4 miles (6km) SE of Ollerton
Within ancient Sherwood Forest. Old Hall Farm, originally a hunting lodge, is one of the earliest brick houses in the county, about 1515–40.

KNIGHTON ON TEME Hereford and Worcester SO6370
Hamlet off A456, 3 miles (5km) NE of Tenbury Wells
A gated road leads to this remote settlement on hills high above the River Teme – worth the journey for its sturdy Norman church.

KNIGHTON (TREF-Y-CLAWDD) Powys SO2872
Town off A488, 17 miles (27km) NE of Llandrindod Wells
Knighton's Welsh name, Tref-y-Clawdd ('town of the dyke') is a reference to Offa's Dyke. The 8th-century earthwork is well preserved in these parts. Offa's Dyke Heritage Centre has information on the long-distance footpath that follows the dyke. Historic fabric of town reflects long, sometimes turbulent history – remnants of two Norman mottes. The border is marked by the River Teme.

KNOCKAN Highland NC2110
Site on A835, immediately S of Elphin
Crofting settlement in wild countryside to the south of Assynt; Inverpolly National Nature Reserve's visitor centre is here, with information on walking and climbing in the area.

KNOCKHOLT Kent TQ4658
Village off A233, 3 miles (5km) NE of Westerham
The highest village in Kent at 725ft (220m), ranged around its green with a few old houses. Nearby Knockholt Beeches are a landmark from miles around.

KNOCKIN Shropshire SJ3322
Village on B4396, 5 miles (8km) SE of Oswestry
Incongruous radio telescope stands beside attractive village with Norman castle motte, 12th-century church and pleasant main street of timber-framed and brick houses.

KNODISHALL Suffolk TM4261
Village off B1119, 1 mile (2km) W of Leiston
A large area of heathland dominates Knodishall. Ducks bob on the pond, while pylons lead away to nearby Sizewell B power station.

KNOOK Wiltshire ST9341
Village off A36, 6 miles (10km) SW of Warminster
Pretty stone manor house (not open) and a Norman church close together.

KNOTT END-ON-SEA Lancashire SD3548
Village on B5270, 1 mile (2km) NW of Preesall
A small coastal resort which has developed as a place suitable for retirement. The name 'knott' is Danish, and indicates rocky ground.

KNOTTING Bedfordshire TL0063
Village off A6, 4 miles (6km) SE of Rushden
Remote little place with a Norman church dedicated to St Margaret of Antioch; comparatively unspoiled, with 16th- and 17th-century furnishings.

KNOTTINGLEY West Yorkshire SE5023
Town on A645, 11 miles (18km) E of Wakefield
An old coal-mining town of red-brick terraced houses on the River Aire. The red-brick town hall is used as a community centre.

KNOWLE West Midlands SP1876
Village on A4141, 3 miles (5km) SE of Solihull
Housing estates spread northwards from the old centre, worth visiting for its splendid church, 15th-century guildhouse and Elizabethan library with a knot garden.

KNOWLTON Dorset SU0210
Site on B3078, 3 miles (5km) SW of Cranborne
This strange place has a ruined church set inside a neolithic bank and ditch, with a large tree-covered barrow close by.

KNOWLTON Kent TR2853
Hamlet off A256, 5 miles (8km) SW of Sandwich
A tiny place: church, house of 1585 and red-brick farm buildings with dower house and dovecote.

KNOWSLEY Merseyside SJ4395
Village off A580, 7 miles (11km) NE of Liverpool
Knowsley Hall has been the home of the Derby family since the 14th century. Knowsley Safari Park is set in the grounds of the hall.

KNOYDART Highland NG8301
Scenic area on W coast of Scottish mainland
Remote, wild and beautiful peninsula on Sound of Sleat, opposite Skye. Access by boat only; excellent walking and climbing.

KNUCKLAS Powys SO2574
Hamlet on B4355, 3 miles (5km) NW of Knighton
Hamlet in restful, rolling border valley of the River Teme. Remnants of the castle, an early British camp, on hill to northwest.

KNUTSFORD Cheshire SJ7578
Town on A50, 6 miles (10km) W of Wilmslow
Tabley House, built in the 18th century by Carr of York, has a famous collection of paintings. The Gaskell Tower on King Street, Knutsford's picturesque shopping street, is a splendid art nouveau building, now the Belle Epoque restaurant. Cobbled alleys lead off King Street to pretty courtyards.

KNYPERSLEY Staffordshire SJ8856
Village on A527, immediately S of Biddulph
Suburb of Biddulph lying beneath Mow Cop. Church, vicarage and school by Victorian architect RC Hussey remain at centre of modern housing.

KYLE OF LOCHALSH Highland NG7627
Village on A87, 12 miles (19km) NW of Shiel Bridge
Railway terminus on Lochalsh peninsula and the main ferry departure point for Skye until the opening of the Skye road bridge.

KYLEAKIN Highland (Skye) NG7526
Village on A850, opposite Kyle of Lochalsh
A settlement on flat land beside the straits separating Skye from the mainland, until the opening of the Skye bridge the main arrival point for ferries.

KYLES OF BUTE Strathclyde NS0175
Sea lochs at N end of island of Bute
The curved strait which separates the Isle of Bute from the mainland. The beautiful area formed by this, the Firth of Clyde and the sea lochs of Loch Riddon and Loch Striven, penetrating north into the hills, is noted for excellent sailing waters. There is a ferry connection from Bute to Colintraive.

KYMIN, THE Gwent SO5212
Hill off A4136, 1 mile (2km) E of Monmouth
Hill rising to 840ft (256m) above Monmouth with two interesting adornments – 18th-century Round House and Naval Temple of 1801 (National Trust).

KYNANCE COVE Cornwall SW6813
Beauty spot off A3083, 1 mile (2km) NW of Lizard Point
Tiny, rocky cove with many caves and islets on the Lizard peninsula.

KYNNERSLEY Shropshire SJ6716
Village off A442, 3 miles (5km) SE of Crudgington
The village, with its medieval church, stands in the Weald Moors – large fields reclaimed from marshland formed at the end of the Ice Age.

L

LACEY GREEN Buckinghamshire SP8200
Village off A4010, 3 miles (5km) SE of Princes Risborough
Buckinghamshire's and possibly England's oldest smock mill (limited opening), restored, weather-boarded and white-sailed, with massive 17th-century machinery.

LACOCK Wiltshire ST9168
Village off A350, 3 miles (5km) S of Chippenham
One of the prettiest villages in the country, Lacock is mostly stone, with some timber-framing. Lacock Abbey (National Trust) is an odd house, partly medieval, with 1550s alterations and a mock-medieval hall of 1754. Henry Fox Talbot, the pioneer photographer, lived here and the Fox Talbot Museum of Photography is based here. Lackham Gardens and the Museum of Vintage Farm Buildings are to the north.

LADOCK Cornwall SW8950
Village on A39, 6 miles (10km) NE of Truro
A stone village on the Tresillian River. Fine William Morris stained glass in the church.

LADYBANK Fife NO3009
Small town on B9128, 5 miles (8km) SW of Cupar
A small town which grew up around the rail junction of the line leading from Perth with the main Edinburgh–Aberdeen line.

LADYBOWER RESERVOIR Derbyshire SK1986
Reservoir on A57, 10 miles (16km) W of Sheffield
Constructed in the Derwent and Woodlands (Ashop) valleys between 1935 and 1943, below the earlier Derwent Dam where the wartime 'Dambusters' bombers practised. Fairholmes visitor centre, picnics, cycle hire.

LADYKIRK Borders NT8847
Village on B6470, 6 miles (10km) NE of Coldstream
Named after a stone church dedicated to the Virgin, built by James IV in 1499 after his escape from drowning while crossing a River Tweed ford. The present bridge was built in 1839.

LAINDON Essex TQ6889
see Basildon

LAIRG Highland NC5806
Village on A839, 9 miles (14km) N of Bonar Bridge
Important road junction for the north and west in desolate country at the southern end of Loch Shin. Many prehistoric sites near by. Huge annual lamb sale.

LAKE DISTRICT Cumbria
National park covering 885 square miles (2,292 sq km)
The Lake District National Park is Britain's largest, its 885 square miles (2,292 sq km) consisting mostly of moorland and fell. Formed from glacial meltwater, the 16 lakes, of which Windermere (see) is the largest, are arranged like spokes of a wheel in the mountain valleys. Around Skiddaw and in the south of the park are angular and rounded hills; the central area, including Scafell Pike (see), is wild and rugged country.

Crowded in summer, Windermere and Ambleside (see) are boating and touring centres. Grasmere and Rydal (see), noted for their Wordsworth associations, and Coniston for John Ruskin, are finely situated. Environmentally sensitive electric boats can be hired at the National Park Boating Centre. Keswick, on Derwent Water, is a focal point for the northern lakes.

Neolithic stone circles such as Castlerigg (see Keswick), and Roman forts such as Hardknott, reflect Lakeland's long history. Townend at Troutbeck (see) is an example of a local yeoman farmer's house. Former iron workings and more modern slate-quarrying have also left their mark.

The 1,800 miles (2,896km) of public paths provide unrivalled walking and climbing, from gentle lakeside strolls to testing mountain ascents.

LAKE OF MENTEITH Central NN5700
Lake off A811, 5 miles (8km) SW of Callender
Scotland's only 'lake', popular with fishermen and the traditional venue in cold winters for the famous 'bonspiel', a giant outdoor curling contest. The tiny Port of Menteith is the main village and holiday centre. Inchmahome island has the ruins of an Augustinian monastery and was a refuge for Mary Stuart as a child. There is a ruined castle on Inchtulla Island.

The tower on the reservoir, Lake Vyrnwy.

LAKE VYRNWY Powys SJ0119

Lake/reservoir on B4393, 15 miles (24km) NW of Welshpool

Remote, dramatically located reservoir locked away in mountains south of Bala, built in the late 19th century to supply Liverpool. Neo-Gothic water tower adds a spooky touch. Church built to replace flooded place of worship, a visitor centre in converted chapel tells the story of surroundings and lost community. Wooded shores are an important wildlife refuge with RSPB hides. Memorable mountain roads to north and west.

LAKENHEATH Suffolk TL7182

Village on B1112, 5 miles (8km) SW of Brandon

Charles Wesley preached in Lakenheath in 1754, and Lord Kitchener's ancestors lie in the peaceful churchyard of St Mary's Church. Houses are made of flint, chalk, and stone, and straggle out across the border between Breckland and fenland countryside. Near by is a large American airbase, which has had a trans-Atlantic impact on the community.

LALEHAM Surrey TQ0568

Village on B376, 2 miles (3km) SE of Staines

Parkland village beside the River Thames, with attractive 18th- and 19th-century houses in village centre and pretty cottages in lanes leading down to the river. Dr Thomas Arnold ran a school here from 1819 to 1828 before taking up headship of Rugby. Birthplace and burial place of his son, Matthew Arnold, the poet. Laleham House, now converted into flats, was the ancestral home of the Earls of Lucan.

LAMBERHURST Kent TQ6736

Village on A21, 6 miles (10km) SE of Tunbridge Wells

Attractive village in a deep valley on the Kent/Sussex border, where the vineyard started in 1972, is associated with the revival of English wine. Important in the days of the Wealden iron industry, it made railings for St Paul's Cathedral and a sample is displayed in High Street. The National Trust owns and runs the lovely gardensof ruinous Scotney Castle, a 14th-century manor surrounded by a moat.

LAMBETH Greater London TQ3078

District on S bank of Thames

Facing Westminster across the Thames, this is not a glamorous area. Lambeth Palace (not open) is the Archbishop of Canterbury's residence. Museum of Garden History close by in St Mary's Church, and Florence Nightingale Museum in St Thomas's Hospital. The Imperial War Museum, besides its martial exhibits and dramatic Trench and Blitz Experiences, has a notable art collection.

LAMBLEY Nottinghamshire SK6345

Village off A612, 5 miles (8km) NE of Nottingham

Birthplace of Ralph, Lord Cromwell, High Treasurer of England in 1433, whose badge is carved on the mainly 15th-century church. Stockingers' cottages date from the 19th century.

LAMBOURN Berkshire SU3278
Small town on B4001, 12 miles (19km) NW of Newbury
At the head of the Lambourn Valley, a tiny market town with some good small Georgian houses, picturesque almshouses of 1852 and a large medieval church. The chalk downs to the north are largely used for racehorse training. The Seven Barrows on the downs actually number 24.

LAMERTON Devon SX4576
Village off B3362, 3 miles (5km) NW of Tavistock
Just off Dartmoor, in farming land. The large 19th-century vicarage contrasts with the humble late medieval priest's house (not open) close to it.

LAMINGTON Strathclyde NS9731
Village on A702, 6 miles (10km) SW of Biggar
Small Clydesdale village surrounded by rolling hills. Ruins of Lamington Castle, 1598, to the north. The church has a Norman doorway and jougs (stocks) outside.

LAMLASH Strathclyde (Arran) NS0231
Village on A841, 3 miles (5km) S of Brodick
Largest village in southern Arran, with Edwardian houses set around a sheltered, muddy bay. Popular with holiday-makers and sailors.

LAMMERMUIR HILLS Lothian
Hill range S of Haddington in Lothian and Border regions
Rolling, rather bleak and treeless hills which form the eastern end of the Southern Uplands. Lammer Law is one of highest points, at 1,733ft (582m).

LAMORNA Cornwall SW4424
Hamlet off B3315, 4 miles (6km) S of Penzance
Picturesque little wooded valley leading down to the granite cove, with a little jetty and a few old cottages on the shore.

LAMPETER (LLANBEDR PONT STEFFAN) Dyfed SN5748
Small town on A485, 20 miles (32km) NE of Carmarthen
A pleasant university and market town in the upper Vale of Teifi that grew up at fording point on river. The university was founded in 1820s, the oldest in Wales. The town has appealing mix of styles – from traditional coaching inns to student cafés. Motte in university grounds provides evidence of ancient settlement.

LAMPHEY Dyfed SN0100
Village on A4139, 2 miles (3km) E of Pembroke
Lamphey Bishop's Palace (Cadw) was an elegant country retreat of bishops of St David's. Extensive site, with its ornate parapets, gardens and great hall, still has echoes of original comfort.

LAMPLUGH Cumbria NY0820
Hamlet off A5086, 7 miles (11km) S of Cockermouth
Linked to the Lamplugh family, the village has nearby iron-ore mines; one was the third deepest in England when it opened in 1869.

LAMPORT Northamptonshire SP7574
Village on B576, 9 miles (14km) N of Northampton
Elegant Lamport Hall was built in the 1650s for the Isham family, by John Webb, with 18th-century additions by Smiths of Warwick, and some later work. The notable gardens include the first English alpine garden by Sir Charles Isham, 1847, who also introduced the first garden gnome, kept in the library. Fine pictures and furniture now provide the setting for exhibitions, concerts and other regular events.

LANARK Strathclyde NS8843
Town on A73, 11 miles (18km) SE of Motherwell
Town on a plateau above the upper reaches of the River Clyde, in the centre of the fruit- and salad-growing district, today mainly under glass. The broad main street has an 18th-century parish church with a statue of William Wallace, said to have lived in the town, and an old bell, first cast in 1130. Strong Covenanting centre in the 17th century.

LANCASTER Lancashire SD4761
City on A6, 20 miles (32km) N of Preston
Lancaster Castle, a medieval fortress founded by Normans, dominates this historic city from its elevated position. Its huge square keep dates back to 1200 and John of Gaunt, Duke of Lancaster, strengthened the castle in the 15th century. Much of the castle still serves as a prison, but certain sections are open to the public, including the cells where the Witches of Pendle were imprisoned.

Next to the castle is the 15th-century Priory Church of St Mary, originally established as a Benedictine priory in 1094, and near by is the Roman Bath House.

Lancaster grew up at the mouth of the River Lune and it became a busy port in the late 17th and early 18th centuries, receiving shiploads of mahogany, tobacco, rum and sugar from the West Indies. The maritime heritage is celebrated at St George's Quay, and the customs house is now an award-winning museum.

The shopping centre of the city is largely pedestrianised and there are many historic buildings to visit, including the Judges Lodging, built in the 1620s, now housing a furniture and a toy museum, and the City Museum, in the old town hall.

LANCHESTER Durham NZ1647
Small town on A691, 7 miles (11km) NW of Durham
The town gets its name from the nearby Roman fort. It is dominated by All Saints' Church, built by the Normans using stone from the fort, and a Roman altar unearthed locally stands in the south porch. The Derwent Valley Walk runs along the path of the disused branch railway.

LANCING West Sussex TQ1804
Small town on A259, 3 miles (5km) NE of Worthing
Old Lancing, north of the wide A27, has an attractive curved High Street with flint-built cottages. Two thatched cottages opposite the Norman church have birds made of thatch on the roof. The surrounding sprawl fills the plain to the sea. The magnificent Gothic school chapel of Lancing College, 94ft (28m) high, is superbly sited above the River Adur.

LAND OF NOD Hampshire SU8437
Hamlet off B3002, 3 miles (5km) NW of Hindhead
Oddly named, tiny hamlet in the north Hampshire heathlands, with Cain's Farm.

LANDCROSS Devon SS4623
Hamlet on A386, 2 miles (3km) S of Bideford
The smallest parish in the county, enclosed by a loop in the River Torridge. The village is also bordered by the River Yeo.

LANDEWEDNACK Cornwall SW7112
Village off A3083, immediately E of Lizard village
Sheltered old cottages, some thatch, and a church tucked into a hollow set back from the harsh Lizard coast. Lush gardens.

LANDFORD Wiltshire SU2519
Village on B3079, 6 miles (10km) SW of Romsey
Scattered village on the Hampshire border. Brick and stone-banded church of 1858. Hamptworth Lodge, 2 miles (3km) west, is a 1910 reproduction Jacobean manor house.

LANDKEY Devon SS5931
Village off A361, 4 miles (6km) SE of Barnstaple
Big village divided into three parts: Landkey, Landkey Newland and Swimbridge Newland. The church has a very fine knight and lady effigy of 1300.

LANDS END Cornwall SW3425
Headland on A30, 8 miles (13km) SW of Penzance
Rocky headland famous as the most westerly part of England, now with a large theme park featuring displays on Man and the Sea. The land ends with rocky cliffs, then a rocky island and finally lighthouses. The Scillies are sometimes visible.

LANDULPH Cornwall SX4361
Village off A388, 5 miles (8km) N of Saltash
On the banks of the River Tamar, with wonderful marshy river scenery. The church has much good 15th- to 17th-century woodwork.

LANDWADE Cambridgeshire TL6228
Site off A142, 3 miles (5km) NW of Newmarket
Near the lovely Wicken Fen (National Trust), Landwade is an ancient village with a fine parish church standing in lush parkland.

LANEAST Cornwall SX2284
Village off A395, 7 miles (11km) W of Launceston
Set on a steep slope, the church still contains an almost complete set of 16th-century benches and its rood screen.

LANGAR Nottinghamshire SK7234
Village off A52, 4 miles (6km) S of Bingham
Village in the Vale of Belvoir. Langar Rectory was the birthplace of Samuel Butler, the 19th-century author of *Erewhon*. Parachuting and parascending centre at airfield.

LANGBANK Strathclyde NS3873
Village on A8, 5 miles (8km) E of Port Glasgow
Village on the River Clyde, which expanded with the opening of the Glasgow–Greenock railway in 1841. Many Victorian villas, including Finlaystone House, were built on the site of the castle.

LANGCLIFFE North Yorkshire SD8264
Village on B6479, 1 mile (2km) N of Settle
A charming village in the shadow of the 'long cliff', on the edge of the Craven fault. Houses and cottages are clustered around a large green.

LANGDALE PIKES Cumbria NY2807
Hill range in the Lake District, NW of B5343
Spectacular range of high peaks. Great Langdale Valley is a sweeping glaciated valley with steep sides and a wide, flat bottom. National Trust campsite in Great Langdale and car park beneath Stickle Ghyll. Stickle Ghyll Force drops 128ft (38m) on to boulders. Old Dungeon Ghyll hotel was given to the National Trust by historian GM Trevelyan.

LANGFORD Essex TL8309
Village on B1019, 1 mile (2km) NW of Maldon
Originally the 'long ford' over the River Blackwater. Victorianised church with unique west-end apse. Delightful waterside walks.

LANGFORD Oxfordshire SP2402
Village off A361, 3 miles (5km) NE of Lechlade
This village in flat Thames Valley farmland boasts an ancient church with rare Saxon carvings and elegant work of the Middle Ages.

LANGHAM Essex TM0333
Hamlet off A12, 6 miles (10km) NE of Colchester
Above the River Stour. Constable painted here. The Fens cottage garden and nursery. The Discovery apple was first grown in Langham, as Dummer's Pride.

LANGHAM Leicestershire SK8411
Village on A606, 2 miles (3km) N of Oakham
The imposing airy church of this attractive Rutland village has a slender spire and richly decorated south side of the mid-14th century, and two stained-glass windows by Comper. Old hall (closed) dates from 1665, with a 1920s–30s stable wing, entrance front and other alterations, and gardens laid out in the 1920s. The village is the home of Ruddles Brewery, with buildings of 1858 and later.

LANGHAM Norfolk TG0041
Village on B1388, 2 miles (3km) SW of Blakeney
A lovely village, the pub of which has a fascinating collection of antique shoes. The author of *Mr Midshipman Easy*, Frederick Marryat, farmed here.

LANGHO Lancashire SD7034
Village on A666, 4 miles (6km) N of Blackburn
Flourishing community close to rivers Ribble and Calder. The parish traces its history back to Saxon times when a battle was fought at Billangohoh.

LANGHOLM Dumfries and Galloway NY3684
Town on A7, 18 miles (29km) N of Carlisle
An 18th-century mill town with solid stone buildings, whose fortune was founded on textiles. Birthplace of Hugh MacDiarmaid (1892–1978), poet and one of the founders of the Scottish National Party. Craigleuch is a Scottish baronial mansion housing the Scottish Explorers Museum, a huge and diverse collection of artefacts collected by Scottish explorers from all over the world.

LANGLEY Northumberland NY8261
Village on A686, 2 miles (3km) SW of Haydon Bridge
Farming village. Langley Castle is a Victorian reconstruction of a 14th-century castle, now a hotel. Plankey Mill, a local beauty spot, belongs to the National Trust.

LANGLEY CHAPEL Shropshire SJ5300
Site off A49, 2 miles (3km) SE of Acton Burnell
The Langley Chapel (English Heritage), with its original simple furnishings, is an intriguing survival of a small Jacobean Puritan church.

LANGLEY GREEN Norfolk TG3503
Village off A146, 3 miles (5km) N of Loddon
Ruins of the 12th-century Premonstratensian monastery, old farms and pretty cottages stand on the edge of the marshes of the River Yare.

LANGLEY MARSH Berkshire TQ0179
District in E Slough
A modern part of Slough, but with a medieval parish church and a few village buildings. The church was much altered in the early 17th century and has a unique parish library of that date, filled with book cupboards.

LANGOLD Nottinghamshire SK5887
Village on A60, 5 miles (8km) N of Worksop
Country park with a lake created as the feature of the grounds of a house never built. Ancient woodland with West Riding boundary ditch and bank.

LANGPORT Somerset ST4226
Town on A372, 5 miles (8km) SW of Somerton
Despite being small, this has been a town from Saxon times. Dense and hilly, slightly seedy but attractive, it is laid out with narrow streets at the bottom of the hill, while the 15th-century church with its fine tower, sits at the summit. The Hanging Chapel (not open), a little 15th-century chapel, is set on top of a gateway. Wide views of the Somerset Levels.

LANGSTONE Hampshire SU7104
Village on A3023, immediately S of Havant
Hamlet on the shore of Langstone Harbour, a nature reserve for waders, tern and geese. Attractive Georgian cottages, and the black tower of an old windmill. Wonderful views out to sea and over Hayling and Portsmouth (see).

LANGSTROTHDALE North Yorkshire SD9078
Scenic area; part of Wharfedale, NW of Hubberholme
The upper valley of the River Wharfe, mainly of limestone. North of Yockenthwaite the valley becomes narrower and more rugged. Settled in Norse times.

LANGTOFT Humberside TA0066
Village on B1249, 6 miles (10km) N of Great Driffield
The 13th-century poet Peter de Langtoft was born here and is commemorated by the Langtoft Cross on the green.

LANGTON Lincolnshire TF3970
Village off A158, 3 miles (5km) N of Spilsby
Quiet Wolds village with 18th-century brick church; well-preserved interior with box pews and three-decker pulpit. Doctor Johnson visited friend Bennet Langton here.

LANGTON MATRAVERS Dorset SY9978
Village on B3069, 2 miles (3km) W of Swanage
Long, thin, Purbeck stone village, in the middle of the stone-quarrying area. Local museum.

LANGWATHBY Cumbria NY5733
Village on A686, 4 miles (6km) NE of Penrith
Before a bridge was erected over the River Eden, there was a ford (a wath), the longest across the river, hence the village name.

LANIVET Cornwall SX0364
Village on A389, 3 miles (5km) SW of Bodmin
In an old quarrying area, with a number of 5th- to 9th-century inscribed stones and a big cross in the graveyard.

LANLIVERY Cornwall SX0859
Village off A390, 2 miles (3km) W of Lostwithiel
Set high, with wide views over the Fowey Valley. The 15th-century granite church has a landmark tower.

LANNER Cornwall SW7139
Village on A393, 2 miles (3km) SE of Redruth
Scattered moorland village.

LANREATH Cornwall SX1856
Village off B3359, 5 miles (8km) NW of Looe
Pretty cob cottages in the centre, and an interesting well-fitted church. Lanreath Folk and Farm Museum.

LANSALLOS Cornwall SX1751
Village off A387, 3 miles (5km) W of Polperro
A scattered village with a pretty church just inland from the rocky cliffs.

LANSDOWN Avon ST7266
District N of Bath
Ranges from the edge of Bath (see) up on to high downs with Bath Racecourse. Halfway up is Beckford's Tower, 154ft (45m) high, built by the eccentric William Beckford of Fonthill (see) in 1825.

LANTEGLOS Cornwall SX0882
Hamlet off A39, 1 mile (2km) SW of Camelford
The mother parish to the much larger Camelford (see), with the ancient church for the area. There is a 10th-century stone in the graveyard, with an inscription.

LANTEGLOS HIGHWAY Cornwall SX1453
Hamlet off B3269, 3 miles (5km)NE of Fowey
Deep lanes and woods, close to the creek of the Fowey estuary.

LANYON QUOIT Cornwall SW4333
Prehistoric site off A3071, 3 miles (5km) NW of Penzance
Three large upright stones supporting an 18ft (6m) lintel, the remains of a neolithic long barrow. Also Men-an-Tol, two upright stones and a big circular pierced stone, perhaps of the same origin.

LAPFORD Devon SS7308
Village off A377, 5 miles (8km) SE of Chulmleigh
Large village in the Yeo Valley, grown larger since World War II. Very fine 16th-century wooden screen in the church.

LAPWORTH Warwickshire SP1671
Village off B4439, 1 mile (2km) SE of Hockley Heath
This canalside village on the southeastern fringe of Birmingham boasts a rich medieval church of exceptional interest (*Virgin and Child* by Eric Gill). Packwood House (National Trust) is Tudor, timber-framed, with a great hall of 1925 and long gallery of 1932. Outstanding collections of tapestries, needlework and furniture. Grounds include 17th-century formal garden and a unique yew garden.

LARBERT Central NS8582
Town off A9, 2 miles (3km) NW of Falkirk
Town which was known for Carron Ironworks, founded in 1759 and Europe's biggest by 1814. Declined throughout the 20th century and closed in 1982.

LARGO, LOWER AND UPPER Fife NO4102/3
Villages on A915, 2 miles (3km) NE of Leven
Two united villages, once an important fishing centre and now a residential holiday resort with sandy beaches and an attractive harbour, used for small fishing boats. Lower Largo was the birthplace of Alexander Selkirk (1676–1721), the original for Daniel Defoe's *Robinson Crusoe*; his statue stands near the harbour.

LARGS Strathclyde NS2059
Town on A78, 6 miles (10km) S of Wemyss Bay
This popular Clyde holiday resort was once an important weaving centre and fishing port. The Pencil Monument commemorates a 1263 victory by the Scots over the Norwegians which brought Hebrides under Scottish control. Local history is related at Largs Historical Society Museum. Skelmorlie Aisle, once part of a church, is now a baroque-style mausoleum for Sir Robert Montgomerie (1636). Marina facilities at Yacht Haven. Kelburn Castle and Country Centre near by.

LARKHALL Strathclyde NS7651
Town on B7078, 4 miles (6km) SE of Hamilton
Populous town in the Clyde Valley to the southeast of Glasgow, once an important coal-mining centre.

LARKHILL Wiltshire SU1244
Village off A345, 3 miles (5km) NW of Amesbury
Large army settlement on Salisbury Plain, started in 1920, with its own 1937 church.

LASHAM Hampshire SU6742
Village off A339, 3 miles (5km) NW of Alton
Many thatched cottages, and a village pond. The Second World War Aircraft Preservation Society (limited opening) is based at Lasham airfield, to the north, which is also a big gliding centre.

LASTINGHAM North Yorkshire SE7290
Village off A170, 6 miles (10km) NW of Pickering
In AD654 St Cedd built his monastery here in a place described by Bede as 'more like a place for lurking robbers and wild beasts than habitations for man'. The present Church of St Mary was built in 1078 on this site. There are three holy wells in the village, dedicated to St Chad, St Ovin and St Cedd.

LATHBURY Buckinghamshire SP8744
Village on B526, 1 mile (2km) N of Newport Pagnell
Trapped inside a Great Ouse loop. The church has Norman carvings and15th-century wall-paintings.

LATHERON Highland ND2033
Village on A9, 15 miles (24km) SW of Wick
Crofting village south of Wick, best known for outstanding prehistoric standing stones, brochs and cairns in vicinity; particularly at Camster.

LATHKILL DALE Derbyshire SK2066
Beauty spot; valley of River Lathkill E of Monyash
One of several rivers in the White Peak limestone area of the Peak District which disappears underground for parts of its course, the River Lathkill rises in winter in a cave near Monyash. In dry periods, it emerges lower down near Over Haddon. Downstream, the lovely road-free ash and elm wooded dale was designated a National Nature Reserve in 1972.

LATIMER Buckinghamshire TQ0099
Village off A404, 3 miles (5km) SE of Chesham
Pretty Victorian estate village on the River Chess. The grave of a French warhorse lies next to Boer War monument on the green.

LAUDER Borders NT5347
Small town on A68, 9 miles (14km) N of Melrose
Royal burgh and market town in Lauderdale with some fine buildings, including an impressive 18th-century town hall and cruciform church dating from the 1670s. Thirlestane Castle, with castellated sandstone towers, dates from the late 17th century and is based on a 14th-century fortress; it stands in extensive grounds and houses the Border Country Museum.

LAUGHARNE Dyfed SN3010
Village on A4066, 4 miles (6km) S of St Clears
Sleepy seatown now indelibly linked with Dylan Thomas; he lived in the Boathouse on the shores of evocative Taf estuary and is buried in churchyard (died 1953). The place provided inspiration for his play *Under Milk Wood* and the Boathouse is now a museum dedicated to his life and work. Laugharne Castle (Cadw) is medieval with Tudor additions.

LAUGHTON East Sussex TQ5013
Village on B2124, 6 miles (10km) NE of Lewes
Small village, isolated on Glynde Levels. Brickworks, potteries and marble mines flourished here and Laughton Place (1534), was one of the first brick buildings in Sussex.

LAUGHTON Lincolnshire SK8497
Village off A159, 5 miles (8km) NE of Gainsborough
In wooded northeast corner of Lincolnshire near River Trent. Medieval church remodelled by Bodley and Garner in 1894, with colourful roofs, screen and reredos.

LAUGHTON-EN-LE-MORTHEN South Yorkshire SK5188
Village off B6463, 2 miles (3km) E of Thurcroft
A residential village with some attractive buildings. There is a well-preserved motte and bailey castle.

LAUNCELLS Cornwall SS2405
Hamlet off A3072, 2 miles (3km) E of Bude
Set in a wooded valley with an unusual, un-restored church, still with 16th-century benches.

LAUNCESTON Cornwall SX3384
Town off A30, 20 miles (32km) NW of Plymouth
Pronounced 'Lawnston', this is the gateway to Cornwall and was its county town until 1835. The high mound of the medieval castle (English Heritage), its shell keep on top, dominates the town. One castle gatehouse survives, and another from the town walls. Of the steep streets, Castle Street has the best buildings: big 18th-century houses, some of brick. The outer walls of the 15th-century church have decorative carving all over them, an amazing feat in the super-hard granite. Local museum. Narrow-gauge steam railway in the valley.

LAUNDE Leicestershire SK7904
Site off A47, 6 miles (10km) NW of Uppingham
Set in High Leicestershire, Launde's 12th-century Augustinian priory chancel was used as the chapel of the 17th-century house called Launde Abbey. Altered in the 19th century, it is now a Diocesan conference centre.

LAURENCEKIRK Grampian NO7171
Small town off A90 (A94), 10 miles (16km) NE of Brechin
Main town in the fertile farmland of Howe o' Mearns, and site of a large cattle auction mart. Re-modelled in the 18th century and noted for linen-weaving.

LAURISTON CASTLE Lothian NT2076
Mansion in NW Edinburgh
A 16th-century tower house with Jacobean revival additions overlooking the Firth of Forth; the interior is a good example of a fully furnished Scottish country house of the Edwardian era.

LAVANTS, THE West Sussex SU8508
Villages on A286, 2 miles (3km) N of Chichester
Mid Lavant straggles along a main road, with pretty East Lavant on the other side of the river. West Lavant is a huddle of farms without a church.

LAVENDON Buckinghamshire SP9153
Village on A428, 2 miles (3km) NE of Olney
Earthworks of Norman castle, now with farmhouse inside. Minton tiles in the partly Saxon church, with Saxon tower.

LAVENHAM Suffolk TL9149
Small town on A1141, 6 miles (10km) NE of Sudbury
Considerable trouble has been taken to ensure that the medieval character of this lovely little wool-trading town has remained unspoiled by modern development. Charming pastel-hued buildings with sagging roofs abound, and the timber-framed guildhall (National Trust) is one of the finest Tudor buildings in the country. The wool trade financed the magnificent Church of St Peter and St Paul.

LAVERSTOKE Hampshire SU4948
Village on B3400, 2 miles (3km) E of Whitchurch
Set in the Test Valley, this is where water-marked paper for bank notes has been made since 1724. Parts of the Georgian mill survive (not open).

LAWFORD Essex TM0831
Village on A137, 7 miles (11km) NE of Colchester
Close to the Stour estuary. Church noted for exuberant medieval carvings of owls, squirrels, angels and little men dancing, wrestling and playing instruments.

LAWRENNY Dyfed SN0106
Village off A4075, 8 miles (13km) SW of Narberth
On wooded creeks of the Daugleddau and Cresswell and Carew rivers in upper Milford Haven Waterway. Quay (south of village) popular with sailors. Tall church tower looms over village.

LAWSHALL Suffolk TL8654
Village off A134, 5 miles (8km) N of Long Melford
Scattered village so large it has four centres. A member of the Rockwood family, residents of nearby Coldham Hall, was involved in the Gunpowder Plot.

LAXEY Isle of Man SC4384
Small town on A2, 6 miles (10km) NE of Douglas
Set in a deep wooded glen. The Laxey Wheel is the focus of this historic mining valley and the largest working waterwheel in the world, built in 1854 to pump water from the mines of the Great Laxey mining company. The Laxey Woollen Mills were founded by Ruskin in the late 19th century.

LAXFIELD Suffolk TM2972
Village on B1117, 6 miles (10km) N of Framlingham
Laxfield was home to martyr John Noyes, burned for his faith, and the church smasher, Puritan William Dowsing. There is a superb Tudor guildhall.

LAXTON Nottinghamshire SK7267
Village off A6075, 4 miles (6km) E of Ollerton
The last open-field village in England retains a medieval pre-enclosure farming system. Each farmer has strips of land in the village's three large fields, sharing fertile and less good land. The Court Leet meets annually and appoints a jury to administer the system. A visitor

centre provides information. Red-brick farm buildings, yards opening on to the street, mound of well-preserved motte and bailey castle.

LAYCOCK West Yorkshire SE0341
Village off B6143, 2 miles (3km) W of Keighley
An attractive village containing unusual configuration of terraced houses built into steep hillside for mill workers.

LAYER BRETON Essex TL9417
Village off B1026, 6 miles (10km) SW of Colchester
One of three Layer villages with Shalom Hall (limited opening). Attractive church damaged in the great Essex earthquake of 1884 and rebuilt in 1923.

LAYER MARNEY Essex TL9217
Hamlet off B1022, 6 miles (10km) SW of Colchester
Colossal gatehouse of never-to-be-completed stately mansion which might have rivalled Hampton Court. Four tall brick towers, eight storeys high, built by Lord Marney in the 1520s. Tremendous views over the countryside from the roof, attractive gardens, rare breed farm animals, deer. Brick church of same period, with Marney monuments of the 15th and 16th centuries.

LAYER-DE-LA-HAYE Essex TL9620
Village on B1026, 4 miles (6km) SW of Colchester
Sought-after commuter and retirement village close to Abberton Reservoir and Nature Reserve (see Abberton). Waterworks pumping station.

LAZONBY Cumbria NY5439
Village on B6413, 6 miles (10km) N of Penrith
Liverpool's Anglican cathedral has steps made from red sandstone quarried from Lazonby Fell. Burial mounds and a Bronze Age fort have been found here.

LEA Derbyshire SK3257
Village off A615, 3 miles (5km) SE of Matlock
Beautiful rhododendrons at Lea Gardens. Activity centre at Lea Green, the former home of John Smedley, whose famous knitwear factory is near by.

LEA Hereford and Worcester SO6621
Village on A40, 4 miles (6km) SE of Ross-on-Wye
Edwardian benefactor gave outwardly unremarkable church an exotic font made up of Italian sculpture of 11th and 12th centuries.

LEA Lincolnshire SK8286
Village on A156, 2 miles (3km) S of Gainsborough
Village with green, on busy Gainsborough road, beside a meander of the River Trent. Fifteenth-century church tower; 13th-century chancel renewed 1847–9 and nave restored.

LEA MARSTON Warwickshire SP2093
Village off A4097, 3 miles (5km) N of Coleshill
The medieval church remains, but the village's manor house was dismantled after World War I and rebuilt near Cirencester (see), leaving room for a giant power station.

LEADEN RODING Essex TL5913
Village on B184, 6 miles (10km) SW of Great Dunmow
Largest of the Rodings, thought to have got its name because its church was the first with a lead roof.

LEADENHAM Lincolnshire SK9552
Village on A17, 8 miles (13km) NW of Sleaford
Attractive village where Lincoln–Grantham and Newark–Sleaford roads meet and climb the steep slope of the Lincoln Cliff. Fine 17th-century Old Hall, 18th-century Leadenham House, and several other 17th- and 18th-century buildings. The chancel ceiling of the medieval church was painted by Pugin in 1841 when he was here on a visit.

LEADHILLS Strathclyde NS8815
Town on B797, 6 miles (10km) SW of Abington
A village high in the Lowther Hills where lead, first found by the Romans, was mined from the 1510s to 1928. Silver and gold also found in the area.

LEAFIELD Oxfordshire SP3115
Village off B4022, 4 miles (6km) NW of Witney
Well off the beaten track, the village spreads along a minor road beside the Wychwood Forest and looking down on the Evenlode Valley.

LEALHOLM North Yorkshire NZ7607
Village off A171, 3 miles (5km) W of Egton
The village lies on the River Esk and the wall of the Methodist chapel records the levels the river has reached.

LEAMINGTON SPA Warwickshire SP3165
Town on A452, 8 miles (13km) S of Coventry
An insignificant village until its medicinal waters were discovered in the 1780s, Leamington became fashionable after a visit by Queen Victoria in 1838, and the broad, open streets at its centre have the grid pattern and elegant buildings of the Regency period.

Its focal point is the Pump Room, flanked by the attractive Jephson Gardens and Pump Room Gardens, which form an inviting green belt beside the River Leam. The imposing Victorian parish church stands near by, and to the north the long and impressive Parade stretches away, its wealth of shops supplemented by the recently built Royal Priors shopping centre. Prominent in the Parade are the Regent hotel, the largest in England when opened in 1819, and the incongruously styled town hall of 1884, while on each side, streets lead away to sedate residential areas boasting fine Regency and early Victorian architecture (notably the intimate Lansdowne Circus). Some of the best buildings, including the splendid Clarendon Square, lie at the northern end of the Parade.

Leamington's history can be studied at the Art Gallery and Museum in Avenue Road, which also displays outstanding paintings, porcelain and glassware.

LEASOWE Merseyside SJ2791
District in W Wallasey
An old coastal town, now part of Wallasey, with an 18th-century lighthouse and a large hotel set on the shore.

LEATHERHEAD Surrey TQ1656

Town off M25, 8 miles (13km) S of Kingston

Old market town on the River Mole with fine buildings. The old town, centred on a crossroads, is a pleasing area, particularly since the pedestrianisation of the High Street and part of Bridge Street. The church of about 1200 has a massive west tower (1480) at an angle to the nave, on the line of an ancient processional right of way. The town also features the Thorndike Theatre, a museum and the Fire and Iron Gallery of ornamental metalwork.

LEATHLEY North Yorkshire SE2347

Village on B6161, 2 miles (3km) NE of Otley

Farming village situated at the confluence of the rivers Washburn and Wharfe. St Oswald's Church contains rare ironwork. Restored waterpump and stocks, though not in use.

LECHLADE Gloucestershire SU2199

Village on A361 and A417, 10 miles (16km) NE of Swindon

Lechlade is the limit of navigation for larger craft on the Thames, which is joined here by the rivers Coln and Leach. Attractions at the riverside (lively in summer) include Ha'penny Bridge and St John's lock, with Monti's famous statue of Neptune. The magnificent 15th-century church and streets of harmonious buildings make for a rewarding walk in the town centre.

LECHT ROAD Grampian NJ2515

Mountain pass on A939 between Corgarff and Tomintoul

The second highest road in Britain at 2,100ft (640m), the Lecht Road connects Deeside and Speyside, and is regularly blocked in winter. It follows the line of a 1754 military road. Skiing area near summit.

LECKFORD Hampshire SU3737

Village off A3057, 2 miles (3km) NE of Stockbridge

Dense village with a mixture of Victorian and older cottages.

LECKHAMPTON HILL Gloucestershire SO9418

Hill off B4070, 3 miles (5km) S of Cheltenham

Devil's Chimney, a precarious rock pinnacle left by quarrymen, is the famous feature of this vantage point on the Cotswold Edge. Exhilarating walks and splendid views.

LECONFIELD Humberside TA0143

Village on A164, 3 miles (5km) N of Beverley

The name means 'the flat stone in the gloomy shade'. The east coast RAF Search and Rescue Squadron is based here.

LEDBURY Hereford and Worcester SO7137

Town on A438, 12 miles (19km) E of Hereford

Ledbury has been a market town for centuries, and its carefully conserved buildings form an enjoyable series of harmonious frontages, many concealing timber frames. The Barrett Browning Institute of 1892 (commemorating the poet who lived at Hope End to the north of Ledbury) jars somewhat, but the neighbouring almshouses of the St Katharine's Hospital are attractive and retain their 14th-century chapel.

The 17th-century market hall still stands on its wooden pillars in the broad market place, and other reminders of Ledbury's bustling past are the big black and white Feathers inn and the Talbot inn in New Street. Ledbury Park dates from about 1600 and was the Royalist headquarters during a Civil War skirmish here.

Church Lane, containing a heritage centre at the old Grammar School, is an architectural gem leading to the unexpected grandeur of St Michael's Church, where a detached bell tower carries a slender spire. The Norman west door opens on to a fine medieval nave and a chancel with surviving Norman features, but the most distinguished work is found in the beautiful 13th-century north chapel, which houses some interesting monuments.

LEDSHAM West Yorkshire SE4529

Village off A1, 4 miles (6km) NW of Ferrybridge

An old farming village centred around All Saints' Church. A desirable residential area.

LEDSTON West Yorkshire SE4328

Village off A656, 2 miles (3km) N of Castleford

A picturesque old farming village with many stone farmhouses and cottages. Now a very attractive residential area with the new housing built to complement the old style.

LEE Devon SS4846

Village off A361, 2 miles (3km) W of Ilfracombe

Picturesque stone hamlet with a rocky bay and wooded combe behind. It has been a tourist attraction from Victorian times as a 'smugglers' village'.

LEE (OR LEA), RIVER Hertfordshire

River

Rising in Bedfordshire, the river flows east by Luton, Hatfield and Hertford to Ware, where it turns south to flow past Hoddesdon, Cheshunt and Waltham Abbey and down to the Thames at Blackwall. Since 1966 the Lee Valley Regional Park south of Ware has been developed as an extensive recreational area for walking, angling and watersports of all kinds.

LEE, THE Buckinghamshire SP9004

Village off A413, 2 miles (3km) N of Great Missenden

Home of the Liberty department store dynasty, who installed a huge oak figurehead of Admiral Lord Howe unnervingly in a roadside hedge.

LEE-ON-THE-SOLENT Hampshire SU5600

Town on B3333, 4 miles (6km) W of Gosport

Wonderful views from this town include the Isle of Wight. It developed as a resort from 1880, and still has many Victorian and Edwardian villas. The very unusual 1930s church has an impressive interior.

LEEBOTWOOD Shropshire SO4798

Village on A49, 4 miles (6km) NE of Church Stretton

The Pound inn, thatched and timber-framed, is the convivial centre of this straggling village beneath the Church Stretton Hills.

LEEDS Kent TQ8253

Village on B2163, 4 miles (6km) SE of Maidstone

Small village overshadowed by a large and romantic castle on a lake where black swans swim. Built in the 11th century on two small islands on the site of an earlier Saxon castle. Norman castle strengthened in the 13th century remained a royal palace for the next 300 years. Left to the nation in 1974, it has medieval tapestries, armour, statuary, Impressionist paintings and a dog-collar museum. Parkland covers 500 acres (202ha), and includes a maze and aviary. Full programme of events.

LEEDS West Yorkshire SE2933

City off M1, 170 miles (274km) NW of London

The city of Leeds is the largest urban development in Yorkshire and is certainly the economic capital of the county. It has become an important financial centre nationally and its continuing growth is sustained by continuing relocation to Leeds of many national firms. In the 19th century Leeds owed its rapid development as an inland port to the Leeds–Liverpool and Aire and Calder canals, forming a link between Liverpool and Hull from where goods could be exported world-wide. Leeds became an important centre of the woollen industry and for ready-made clothing. The canal basin grew to provide extensive wharves, warehouses, boat-building yards and wet and dry docks until the railways and then roads took over as the main transport routes. However, like other cities with a similar Victorian heritage, interest has been rekindled in the long-neglected waterways and warehouses and Leeds Waterfront is now a stylish district with offices, shops, bars and restaurants. A visitor centre is housed in the former canal office.

The main shopping areas of the city centre have been transformed by pedestrianisation, modernist landscaping and attractive lighting, and old Victorian shopping arcades and halls such as Kirkgate Market, the Corn Exchange and Victorian Quarter have been restored to their former opulence. Kirkgate Market, a busy, traditional market, is particularly impressive with its extravagant domes and a mezzanine balcony supported by the 'Kirkgate Market Dragons'.

The investment in the city centre has clearly paid off, since Leeds is now one of the most desirable retail locations in the country.

The Leeds Industrial Museum in Armley Mill, once the largest textile mill in the world, houses a museum of the textile, clothing and engineering industries.

The city's other industries also included clocks, chemicals, and furniture-making. Thomas Chippendale began his furniture business here. Michael Marks, of Marks and Spencer, began his career at Leeds Penny Bazaar in Leeds Market, and in 1822 Joshua Tetley & Son was founded. The story of the brewery is told at Tetley's Brewery Wharf, a visitor attraction which also relates the history of the English pub.

The £42.5 million Royal Armouries Museum is the first purpose-built national museum to be built tin the 20th century, relocating most of the national collection of weapons and armour that has been stored at the Tower of London.

Founded in 1988, Leeds City Art Gallery houses an excellent collection of works by Renoir, Lowry, Sickert and Leeds artist Atkinson Grimshaw.

Leeds has also developed as a major arts centre, home to Opera North, based at the city's Grand Theatre, the Northern School of Contemporary Dance, Phoenix Dance and the West Yorkshire Playhouse, which opened in 1990. The Henry Moore Institute, which opened in 1993, is the largest gallery in Europe devoted solely to sculpture.

Leeds has three important sporting venues: Elland Road, Leeds United Football Club; Headingley, Yorkshire County Cricket Club; and, next door to it, Leeds Rugby League Club.

LEEDSTOWN Cornwall SW6034

Village on B3280, 3 miles (5km) SE of Hayle

Founded in the early 19th century, when mining started here. Connection with the Dukes of Leeds.

LEEK Staffordshire SJ9856

Town on A53, 10 miles (16km) NE of Stoke-on-Trent

The 'capital' of the Staffordshire moorlands, once famous for silk-weaving. A stroll around its busy streets reveals the Roebuck inn (1627), Ash almshouses (1676), weavers' cottages, Nicholson Institute (art gallery) and former silk mills. Restored Brindley Mill houses displays relating to James Brindley. St Edward's and All Saints' churches feature outstanding work by Victorian architects GE Street and Norman Shaw.

LEEK WOOTTON Warwickshire SP2868

Village off A46, 2 miles (3km) N of Warwick

Piers Gaveston, unsavoury favourite of King Edward II, was executed near by. Determined walkers can reach Gaveston's Cross, which marks the spot.

LEICESTER Leicestershire SK5804

City off M1, 89 miles (143km) NW of London

A major shopping, commercial, industrial and historic city, Leicester is also considered the birthplace of modern tourism, as travel pioneer Thomas Cook organised his first excursion from here in 1841. His statue stands outside the railway station.

Centuries before, the Romans built here on the Lincoln–Cirencester Fosse Way. Mosaic pavements, fine wall-paintings and other finds are displayed in Jewry Wall Museum, overlooking the Roman baths site and impressive Roman masonry. Also within the historic heart (also known as Castle Park) are the half-timbered medieval guildhall, Roger Wygston's 15th-century house providing a setting for the Costume Museum, the Newarke Houses Museum of social history collections, and the 11th-century castle mound. The statue of Richard III stands in pleasant Castle Gardens, near the ancient churches of St Mary de Castro, St Nicholas, and St Martin's (Leicester Cathedral).

The Museum of Technology and the elegant 18th-century Belgrave Hall merit a visit to the city's outskirts, near the Great Central steam railway's southern terminal. New Walk, a tree-lined Regency promenade, leads to the Museum and Art Gallery and De Montfort Hall for shows and concerts. The Haymarket Theatre enjoys a fine reputation, and Leicester's rich cultural diversity is reflected in restaurants, shops, and religious buildings, including Europe's only Jain Temple, beautifully ornamented. Shopping in Leicester's large traditional open market is complemented by specialist arcades and major stores in the Shires and Haymarket centres.

LEICESTERSHIRE WOLDS Leicestershire
Hill range NE of Melton Mowbray
Superb views, honey-coloured ironstone buildings, hedges and woodland planted as fox coverts, in north-east Leicestershire, between the Vale of Belvoir and the Lincolnshire boundary.

LEIGH Greater Manchester SD6500
Town on A572, 12 miles (19km) W of Manchester
Developed during the Industrial Revolution from an agricultural market town. Pennington Flash Country Park is a popular recreational area.

LEIGH Hereford and Worcester SO7853
Village off A4103, 4 miles (6km) W of Worcester
Pride of this Temeside village is Leigh Court Barn (English Heritage), claimed to be Britain's largest cruck-framed building.

LEIGH Kent TQ5446
Village on B2027, 3 miles (5km) W of Tonbridge
Pleasant village built round a green with a large Victorian Tudor-style house and restored 13th-century church. Pronounced 'Lie'.

LEIGH Surrey TQ2246
Village off A217, 3 miles (5km) SW of Reigate
Delightful, secluded village in the heart of the Weald above a tributary of the River Mole. Pleasant old houses surround the village green, with a Victorianised church and manor house near by.

LEIGH DELAMERE Wiltshire ST8879
Village off A350, 4 miles (6km) NW of Chippenham
Estate village, largely rebuilt in the 1840s with a new church, almshouses and cottages.

LEIGH UPON MENDIP Somerset ST6947
Village off A361, 5 miles (8km) W of Frome
A single-street quarrying village, pronounced 'Lie', with one of the famous Somerset church towers. The whole church is basically 15th century, with an elaborately decorated wooden roof.

LEIGH-ON-SEA Essex TQ8486
District off A13 on W edge of Southend-on-Sea
A desirable commuter township in the Southend conurbation. The core is the old Thames estuary fishing village, with boats still landing fish, shrimps and cockles. The church's 80ft (24m) tower is an estuary landmark. There are oak and hornbeam woods in Belfairs Park. Two Tree Island Nature Reserve covers saltmarsh and mudflats with land reclaimed by tipping; interesting plants and teeming birdlife.

LEIGHTON Shropshire SJ6105
Village on B4380, 5 miles (8km) W of Ironbridge
Novelist Mary Webb was born close to the 18th-century hall and church of this village high above the River Severn.

LEIGHTON BROMSWOLD Cambridgeshire TL1175
Village off A14 (A604), 8 miles (13km) NW of Huntingdon
In 1616, a gatehouse into Leighton Bromswold Castle (not open) was erected, intended to be the first stage of the rebuilding of an old manor house. The plans came to nothing, but Leighton Bromswold has a truly splendid medieval church, some of it rebuilt under the watchful eye of poet George Herbert in the 1620s.

LEIGHTON BUZZARD Bedfordshire SP9225
Town on A4146, 11 miles (18km) NW of Luton
Historic market town on River Ouzel, with Linslade on the opposite bank. Beautiful church with 190ft (58m) spire, sumptuously restored after severe damage by 1985 fire. Broad High Street, restored medieval market cross, 1850s former fire station and massive granite war memorial. The town once improbably exported sand to the Sahara Desert; sand-hauling narrow-gauge railway now a tourist attraction.

LEINTWARDINE Hereford and Worcester SO4074
Village on A4113, 7 miles (11km) W of Ludlow
The ancient Roman camp of *Bravonium* lies at the confluence of the rivers Teme and Clun. Chancel of large village church (good medieval stalls with misericords) stands high on the foundations of Roman walls, while the stone houses and cottages still follow early medieval grid plan, with two parallel streets running north from the bridge.

LEIRE Leicestershire SP5290
Village off B577, 4 miles (6km) N of Lutterworth
Small village between the Fosse Way and the Leicester–Lutterworth road. The 17th-century timber-framed manor house has brick infill and thatch. Elegant 1793 brick Glebe House.

LEISTON Suffolk TM4462
Town on B1119, 4 miles (6km) E of Saxmundham
The small town near the Suffolk coast was home to the famous Garrett family. One built Snape Maltings (see), another founded a huge machinery factory in 1728, while yet another became England's first woman doctor. Close to the town in an open field are the remains of Leiston Abbey (English Heritage) with the splendid Lady Chapel and fine great barn. Summerhill School is near by.

LEITH Lothian NT2676
District in N Edinburgh
Scotland's principal port from the mid-12th century until the mid-19th century, trading with France, the Low Countries, the Baltic and America. Attacked several times by the English, it was a ship-building centre from the 17th century and still has well-equipped and important docks and a harbour today. Some fine 16th- to 18th-century buildings; gentrification now in process. Became part of Edinburgh in 1920.

LEITH HILL Surrey TQ1343
Hill off A29, 4 miles (6km) SW of Dorking
At 965ft (293m) this is the highest point in southeast England, and the greatest eminence of the greensand ridge, standing aside from the lower hills. It is covered with

trees and rhododendron plantations and crowned with a folly. Leith Hill tower (National Trust) was built in 1766 to raise the top of Leith Hill to over 1,000ft (304m). Magnificent views from the hilltop, reached by good paths.

LELANT Cornwall SW5437
Village on A3074, 2 miles (3km) SE of St Ives
Once a tiny fishing port. Set on a tidal estuary just around the corner from the sandy shore. Merlin's Magicland Amusement Park.

LEMSFORD Hertfordshire TL2212
Village on B653, 1 mile (2km) W of Welwyn Garden City
Unusual pub names: Long Arm and Short Arm, and Crooked Chimney. Paths in the park allow views of stately Brocket Hall (not open).

LENHAM Kent TQ8952
Small town off A20, 4 miles (6km) NW of Charing
Former market town, still tightly clustered about pleasant market square with the church on one side and half-timbered and 18th-century houses on the other three.

LENTON Nottinghamshire SK5539
District in SW Nottingham
Parts of the Cluniac Lenton Priory, founded in the 1100s and Nottinghamshire's most powerful monastic house, are incorporated in Priory Church. Magnificent font in Holy Trinity Church.

LENWADE Norfolk TG0918
Hamlet on A1067, 2 miles (3km) NW of Attlebridge
This hamlet adjoins the village of Great Witchingham. It is a peaceful settlement and had a railway station on the Melton Constable to Norwich line.

LEOMINSTER Hereford and Worcester SO4959
Town on A49, 12 miles (19km) N of Hereford
Leominster (pronounced 'Lemster') makes no claims to be a tourist showplace. It is a workaday market centre, providing services for a wide area of countryside once famous for the Ryeland sheep that resulted in wool-trading prosperity lasting well into the 18th century. A visit to the Folk Museum is a good introduction to the town. The museum is in Etnam Street, one of Leominster's best thoroughfares, where timber-framing rubs shoulders with pleasant homely Georgian.

More 18th-century architecture is on view in Church Street, but elsewhere in the town there is an attractive jumble of building styles characteristic of an unpretentious country town. Two buildings, however, should not be missed. The priory was originally a 12th-century monastic church, and the finely-carved west doorway and the nave of 1130 still survive. This nave is now the north aisle. Next to it is a second nave added for parish use in about 1240 and rebuilt after a fire in 1699. The south aisle of 1320 is virtually a third nave and is beautifully embellished. The town's other outstanding building is the timber-framed Grange, which once stood in the High Street as the market hall. It is Herefordshire's most elaborately carved building, a rare surviving example of the work of John Abel, the famous local craftsman, builder and king's carpenter (see also Abbey Dore).

LEONARD STANLEY Gloucestershire SO8003
Village off A419, 3 miles (5km) W of Stroud
Only traces remain of the village's medieval priory, but its fine church still stands, offering a wealth of outstanding Norman work.

LEPE Hampshire SZ4598
Hamlet off A326, 5 miles (8km) S of Fawley
A hamlet of slated cottages on the shore, with Lepe Foreshore Country Park. Shipping passes close by.

LERRYN Cornwall SX1457
Village off A390, 3 miles (5km) SE of Lostwithiel
At the head of a small, picturesque wooded estuary, with two small 16th-century bridges and old cottages.

LERWICK Shetland HU4741
Town on A970, 26 miles (42km) N of Sumburgh Airport
Lerwick, founded in the 16th century and Britain's most northerly town, is Shetland's administrative and commercial capital and a thriving port for the fishing and oil industries. Fort Charlotte, built in the 1660s, burnt by the Dutch in 1672 and repaired in 1781, is the oldest building, but the town centre is dominated by solid stone Victorian architecture. The town hall and the Anderson high school are good examples of this style. The Shetland library and museum tells the islands' story with particular reference to the fishing industry. The famous fire festival of Up Helly Aa is held on the last Tuesday in January, when a replica of a Viking longship is burnt.

Lerwick has long been dependant on fishing, supplying the herring fleets in the 16th and 17th centuries and becoming a 19th-century fishing, whaling, and smuggling centre. Today it is Britain's main herring and mackerel port. The oil boom of the 1970s brought prosperity to Lerwick as a supply base for the rigs, and industrial facilities have been improved.

Clickimin Broch, a farmstead from 700BC, later enclosed by defensive walls, stands on Clickimin Loch.

LESLIE Fife NO2501
Town on A911, 2 miles (3km) NW of Glenrothes
This old town is today virtually an extension of Glenrothes. The Bull Stone on the green was used to tether bulls during bull-baiting.

LESMAHAGOW Strathclyde NS8139
Small town off M74, 5 miles (8km) SW of Lanark
Clydesdale town with ruins of a 12th-century priory. This was a Covenanting centre in the 17th century and a coal-mining town in the 19th and 20th centuries. Prehistoric remains on nearby Black Hill.

LETCHWORTH Hertfordshire TL2232
Town off A1(M), 5 miles (8km) N of Stevenage
The first of the 20th century's garden cities, founded in 1903. The Heritage Museum in the original planners' office tells the story, while the results of this pioneering social experimentare all around. Letchworth Museum deals with the area's history and natural history. Working farm and animals at Standalone Farm. Norton Common open space.

LETCOMBE, BASSETT AND REGIS Oxfordshire SU3785
Villages off B4001, 2 miles (3km) SW of Wantage
The two villages stand beneath a steep ascent to the Ridgeway on the edge of the Lambourn Downs. Letcombe Regis is the larger, with much modern housing. Both have old churches, but St Michael's at Bassett has exceptionally good Norman work. Segsbury Camp, a 26 acre (10ha) Iron Age hillfort with sarsen blocks in its ramparts, overlooks the villages.

LETHERINGSETT Norfolk TG0638
Village on A148, 1 mile (2km) W of Holt
Known to many locals as 'Lansett', this beautiful village nestles comfortably in the lovely Glaven Valley, hemmed in by fine old trees and emerald meadows. Many houses are decorated with flint or local pebbles, and the Church of St Andrew has a remarkable 18th-century barrel organ. Letheringsett Hall (not open) is the 18th-century seat of the Cozens Hardy family.

LETWELL South Yorkshire SK5687
Village off A634, 4 miles (6km) SE of Maltby
A pretty village with many Listed Buildings and a restored dovecote. Until 1935 many of the wells were the only source of water for the village.

LEUCHARS Fife NO4521
Village on A919, 5 miles (8km) S of Tayport
Noted for its parish church, an outstanding example of Norman architecture. Near by is 16th-century Earlshall Castle, with beautiful gardens. Important RAF base near by.

LEVEN Fife NO3800
Town on A955, 2 miles (3km) NE of Buckhaven
An important coal-mining centre in the 19th century. Now a holiday resort with good facilities, golf course and beaches.

LEVEN Humberside TA1045
Village off A165, 6 miles (10km) NE of Beverley
The site of the village has changed several times and the name means 'smooth' or 'level'. In 1735, it was known as 'Rosedale in Leven'.

LEVENS Cumbria SD4886
Village off A590, 5 miles (8km) S of Kendal
On the southern tip of Scout Scar, overlooking the Lyth Valley. Levens Hall is a magnificent Elizabethan house built on to a 13th-century pele tower. Open to the public, with fine collection of paintings and furniture, and most noted for its topiary garden, laid out in 1692.

LEVENSHULME Greater Manchester SJ8694
District of SE Manchester
Victorian suburb. The town spreads along the A6 and is known for its antiques shops . Antiques Village in the town hall.

LEVERBURGH Western Isles NG0186
see Rodel

LEVERINGTON Cambridgeshire TF4411
Village off B1169, 2 miles (3km) NW of Wisbech
Leverington Hall is a fine Tudor house. Other old buildings include Beechwood, Lancewood and Park House, all 17th or 18th century (none open).

LEVERTON Lincolnshire TF4047
Village on A52, 5 miles (8km) NE of Boston
Between Boston and The Wash. Church has richly carved chancel and brick clerestory of 1728 altered by James Fowler in 1882–3 restoration.

LEVISHAM North Yorkshire SE8390
Village off A169, 5 miles (8km) NE of Pickering
A tiny remote village overlooking the steep valley of Levisham Beck. The watermill can still be seen.

LEWES East Sussex TQ4110
Town off A27, 8 miles (13km) NE of Brighton
Lewes reached the height of its prosperity in Georgian times, and the agreeable High Street, descending steeply to the River Ouse, is lined by tiled and stuccoed Georgian façades, many of them disguising timber-framed buildings of the medieval town that was an important river port.

Lewes was one of King Alfred's burghs and had two mints by the 10th century. It was granted to William de Warenne after the Norman Conquest. He built the magnificent priory, demolished at the Reformation, and the strong castle whose keep still broods over the town. At the Battle of Lewes (1264) Simon de Montfort defeated Henry III and began the drive towards parliamentary government. Staunchly Protestant in the 16th century, with 17 martyrs burned in the High Street, Lewes still celebrates 5 November in elaborate fashion.

Today Lewes is the bustling county town of East Sussex with a busy High Street and a newer shopping area by the river opposite Harvey's Brewery. There are offices and museums, hotels and specialist shops, delightful twittens (alleyways) lined with pretty cottages and unexpected hidden courtyards.

LEWIS Western Isles
Island in the Outer Hebrides
Lewis comprises the northern two-thirds of the largest island of the Western Isles group. The landscape is mainly flat, made up of peat-bog and lochans and virtually treeless. Some remarkable prehistoric sites. The island is noted for its strong Gaelic language and cultural tradition. The main town, Stornoway, is the administrative and shopping centre for the Western Isles. Economy depends on crofting, fishing, tourism and tweed-production.

LEWISHAM Greater London TQ3774
District in SE London
Former middle-class suburb with a famously long High Street. The area's change of style is summed up by the contrast between the 1897 Jubilee clock tower and the mammoth 1970s shopping centre. The Baring banking dynasty's Manor House in Lee is now a public library. Nearby Catford has the Lewisham Concert Hall and Theatre, and a greyhound-racing stadium.

LEWKNOR Oxfordshire SU7197
Village on B4009, 3 miles (5km) NE of Watlington
A famous pub, the Olde Leathern Bottel, stands with other picturesque buildings at the heart of Lewknor. The church is very interesting.

LEWTRENCHARD Devon SX4586
Village off A30, 8 miles (13km) E of Launceston
Set in a pretty wooded valley, the manor (now a hotel) and church were much altered and enriched by Sabine Baring Gould, composer of 'Onward Christian Soldiers', in the later 19th century.

LEYBOURNE Kent TQ6858
Village on A20, 5 miles (8km) W of Maidstone
West of Maidstone, within earshot of the M20. A blend of old and new, with part of a 14th-century castle incorporated into a modern house.

LEYBURN North Yorkshire SE1190
Small town on A6108, 8 miles (13km) SW of Richmond
This is a busy but spacious town, the administration centre for the area and with a flourishing market. Thornborough Hall, now offices, was once the home of a Catholic family and it has a priest's hiding place. On the western edge of the town is Leyburn Shawl, a limestone terrace, commanding fine views.

LEYLAND Lancashire SD5422
Town off M6, 5 miles (8km) S of Preston
The old village centre, round which the town grew, is marked by a cross. St Andrew's Church was first built in 1050; the oldest parts of the present church date from the 12th century. Leyland is best known for its manufacturing of cars and lorries and it is home to the British Commercial Vehicle Museum.

LEYSDOWN-ON-SEA Kent TR0370
Village on B2231, 3 miles (5km) E of Eastchurch
Seaside resort with a holiday camp and caravan sites on the eastern tip of the Isle of Sheppey, looking down the wide Thames estuary.

LEYTON Greater London TQ3786
Town off A11, NE of Hackney
Forest and marshland originally, residential and industrial today. Sports facilities include Lee Valley Ice Centre for skating and ice-hockey.

LEZANT Cornwall SX3379
Village off B3254, 4 miles (6km) S of Launceston
Very rural, with hamlets scattered all over the parish.

LIBANUS Powys SN9925
Hamlet on A470, 4 miles (6km) SW of Brecon
At the northern approach to Brecon Beacons. Wonderful views – and much information – from the Brecon Beacons Mountain Centre (National Park) on Mynydd Illtyd to the west.

LICHFIELD Staffordshire SK1109
City off A51, 15 miles (24km) N of Birmingham
The centre of Lichfield has a pattern of medieval streets overlaid with 18th-century development. Mellow thoroughfares such as Quoinian's Lane and Bore Street and a variety of specialist shops and welcoming old pubs make strolling and browsing a pleasure in themselves, quite apart from special visitor attractions. Chief among these is the cathedral, built in the 13th and 14th centuries and separated from the city by the attractive Stowe and Minster Pools, which were created from an expanse of marshland.

Lichfield had a cathedral as early as 669, but no visible traces remain of this or of its Norman successor. The cathedral's three tall spires are a unique landmark, and the intricate west front, incorporating well over a hundred statues, gives access to a building full of interest. The superb 16th-century glass in the Lady Chapel, the 8th-century Lichfield Gospels and Francis Chantrey's 'Sleeping Children' memorial should not be missed. The medieval Vicars' Close and other fine houses like the 17th-century bishop's palace form a tranquil setting.

The history of the town is explained at the Lichfield Heritage Exhibition in St Mary's Centre, a redundant church. It reveals the remarkable number of famous people born in Lichfield or associated with it, including the actor David Garrick, the essayist Joseph Addison and the doctor and naturalist Erasmus Darwin. The town's most famous son, however, was Dr Samuel Johnson, poet, novelist and lexicographer. His birthplace in Breadmarket Street is now a Johnsonian museum, and his statue stands near by in the square.

In addition to its ecclesiastical and cultural history, Lichfield has military associations and a visit to the Regimental Museum of the Staffordshire Regiment at Whittington Barracks is highly recommended.

LICKEY Hereford and Worcester SO9975
Village off A38, 4 miles (6km) NE of Bromsgrove
Splendid views and network of walks in woodland, heath and meadowland make Lickey Hills Country Park a favourite day out from Birmingham.

LIDDESDALE Borders
Scenic area, including valley of the Liddel Water
Border Reiver country, stretching north from the border along the Liddel Water Valley with dense forests in the Cheviot foothills and desolate moors.

LIDDINGTON Wiltshire SU2081
Village on B4192, 4 miles (6km) SE of Swindon
Thatched cottages and a 13th-century church make up the old centre. One mile (2km) south is the prominently sited Iron Age hillfort of Liddington Castle, right on the edge of the chalk.

LIDGATE Suffolk TL7257
Village on B1063, 6 miles (10km) SE of Newmarket
Picturesque village with fine 14th-century timber and brick buildings. John Lydgate, a poet who lived just after Chaucer, came from here.

LIFTON Devon SX3885
Village off A30, 4 miles (6km) E of Launceston
Prominent 15th-century church. Many bridges on the rivers Trushel and Lydd and a big milk-based factory.

LIGHTWATER Surrey SU9262
Small town on A322, 1 mile (2km) SE of Bagshot
Modern town with a remaining stretch of once expansive Bagshot Heath, now the 143acre (58ha) Lightwater Country Park. Trails cross varied environments of heathland, woodland and lakes.

LILBOURNE Northamptonshire SP5676
Village off A5, 4 miles (6km) E of Rugby
Once a Roman site, with the remains of a motte and bailey castle, bounded by the infant River Avon, forming the Leicestershire border, and Roman Watling Street.

LILFORD PARK Northamptonshire TL0284
Mansion off A605, 3 miles (5km) S of Oundle
A row of 13 chimneys was added in 1711 to Lilford Hall, built between 1635 and 1656. Park closed in the early 1990s after use as aviaries and events venue.

LILLESHALL Shropshire SJ7513
Village off A518, 3 miles (5km) SW of Newport.
The village stands on a hill crowned by an obelisk in memory of the Duke of Sutherland, a 19th-century magnate whose mansion now serves as the National Sports Centre. The Norman church is well worth visiting, but the compelling attraction is the Lilleshall Abbey (English Heritage), the lonely and evocative ruin of a splendid church.

LILLINGSTONE, DAYRELL AND LOVELL
Buckinghamshire SP7039
Villages off A413, 4 miles (6km) N of Buckingham
Twin villages in the far north of the county. The larger, Lillingstone Lovell, is still a comparatively unspoiled farming village. Brasses and monuments in the attractive church, with its saddleback tower roof and the Georgian former rectory close by. Brasses and monuments of the Dayrell family in the church at Lillingstone Dayrell.

LILLINGTON Warwickshire SP3267
Village on NE outskirts of Leamington Spa
The church is Victorian, but extensive modern housing estates almost entirely monopolise this Leamington Spa suburb.

LILLIPUT Dorset SZ0489
Village on B3369 in SW Bournemouth
This is a mostly 20th-century village, standing on the shores of Poole Harbour. It is named after Jonathan Swift's *Gulliver's Travels* (1726), perhaps because of a local smuggler called Gulliver.

LIMEHOUSE Greater London TQ3681
District in borough of Tower Hamlets, London docks
Former docks and ship-building area, notorious for Chinese opium dens, now extensively redeveloped. St Anne's Church by Hawksmoor is 18th century.

LIMPLEY STOKE Wiltshire ST7860
Village off A36, 3 miles (5km) SE of Bath
Handsome stone buildings on a steep wooded hill, with an unrestored and atmospheric little church.

LIMPSFIELD Surrey TQ4053
Village on A25, 3 miles (5km) W of Westerham
A delightful village on the northern side of the greensand ridge looking to the North Downs. Main Street has attractive houses of different ages. The composer Delius, who always wanted to lie in an English churchyard, is buried here beside the church with its stout 12th-century tower. Limpsfield Chart, on the ridge to the south, is a breezy open space with much gorse.

LINBY Nottinghamshire SK5351
Village on B6011, 1 mile (2km) N of Hucknall
Pretty village with a stream alongside the main street's stone cottages. The 17th- and 19th-century crosses may have marked the Sherwood Forest boundary. An 18th-century cottonmill now houses flats.

LINCLUDEN Dumfries and Galloway NX9677
District in NW Dumfries
Now part of northwest Dumfries and the site of Lincluden Collegiate Church, a superb example of 15th-century architecture of great elegance.

LINCOLN Lincolnshire SK9771
City off A46, 120 miles (193km) N of London
This historic city's magnificent triple-towered hilltop cathedral dominates the skyline from all approaches, a particularly splendid sight when floodlit at night. The impressive Norman west front, 13th-century decagonal chapter house, intricately carved angel choir, two medieval rose windows, and Wren library are among the cathedral's treasures. The Norman castle's wall walks and 19th-century observatory tower provide panoramic views of the cathedral opposite and the town below, with Lincoln's fine Magna Carta displayed adjoining the 18th-century gaol. In the unique Victorian prisoners' chapel, tall cubicles ensured each convict saw only the preacher.

Traffic still passes under Newport Arch, the north gate of the Roman town, settled where the Fosse Way and Ermine Street met. In the Museum of Lincolnshire Life, social and agricultural history is fascinatingly illustrated, while the Incredibly Fantastic Old Toy Show satisfies nostalgia for childhood. The Lawn, in pleasant grounds, is a conference centre, concert hall, and home to the National Cycle Museum.

Linking uphill Bailgate's village atmosphere with the lower town shopping centre is aptly-named Steep Hill, a shock to those who think the county is flat. Twelfth-century Jew's House, adjoining Jew's Court, and numerous other historic buildings such as St Mary's Guildhall merit attention. The Usher Gallery's displays include De Wint paintings and Tennyson memorabilia. Sixteenth-century shops stand on the River Witham bridge near Brayford Pool, an attractive spot for swans and pleasure boats.

LINCOLNSHIRE WOLDS Lincolnshire
Hill range running NW to SE for some 40 miles (64km)
Belying popular belief that Lincolnshire is flat, the Wolds form part of England's chalk uplands from Dorset to Yorkshire. Only about 550ft (168m) at the highest point, yet contrasting sharply with the coastal plain. Prehistoric ridge-top routes such as Bluestone Heath

road give long views over attractive villages with fine churches. It is a designated Area of Outstanding Natural Beauty.

LINDALE Cumbria SD4180
Village off A590, 2 miles (3km) N of Grange-over-Sands
A 40ft (12m) cast-iron obelisk near the crossroads commemorates John Wilkinson, who developed the region's iron industry in the 18th century.

LINDFIELD West Sussex TQ3425
Village on B2028, immediately N of Haywards Heath
Picturesque village with a pond, a large common where cricket is played, and a very attractive long main street where brick alternates with timber-framed, tile-hung and colour-washed houses. Imposing houses stand by the tall-spired church on a hilltop. Fairs and markets used to be held on the common. The sheep fair was large and famous.

LINDISFARNE (HOLY ISLAND) Northumberland NU1242
Island off the coast E of Beal
Small island accessible by causeway from Beal only when tides permit. English Heritage owns the priory, established in AD635, and Lindisfarne Castle, built in 1550 on Beblowe Crag, belongs to the National Trust. St Cuthbert lived and died on the island, now a place of pilgrimage. It has a bird sanctuary and small village.

LINDLEY Leicestershire SP3695
Site on A5, 2 miles (3km) NW of Hinckley
The Motor Industry Research Association's testing track and buildings, on the site of a former airfield and railway line, is used to develop motor vehicles.

LINDLEY West Yorkshire SE1217
District in NW Huddersfield
The art nouveau clock tower, built in 1902 by the Sykes Brothers Wire Company, was a favourite landmark of Sir John Betjeman.

LINDOW MOSS Cheshire SJ8281
Site off A538, NW of Wilmslow
Famous for the discovery in 1984 of Lindow Man, the body of a Celtic Iron Age man preserved in the peat bog since 300BC.

LINDSEY Lincolnshire
Historic region in N area of Lincolnshire
One of the three administrative parts into which Lincolnshire was historically divided, recalled in names of East and West Lindsey District Councils.

LINDSEY Suffolk TL9745
Hamlet off A1141, 4 miles (6km) NW of Hadleigh
Villagers once washed their wool in the tributary of the River Brett that bubbles through this settlement. St James's Chapel is 13th century.

LINGFIELD Surrey TQ3843
Small town on B2028, 4 miles (6km) N of East Grinstead
This pleasant Wealden village has a pretty centre and Victorian and 20th-century buildings near the station. Lingfield Park racecourse was established in 1890. There are attractive weatherboarded tile-hung buildings along the road to the church, and a restored 15th-century cross. The old lock-up (1763) is beside the village pond. The library in Plaistow Street is a former guest house of the College of Priests, 1431. The church, rebuilt in 1431, contains fascinating monuments. Greathed Manor is near by.

LINKINHORNE Cornwall SX3173
Village off B3257, 4 miles (6km) NW of Callington
Prominent 130ft (40m) 15th-century tower of the Church of St Melor, with a holy well dedicated to the saint, too.

LINLITHGOW Lothian NS9977
Town on A803, 16 miles (26km) W of Edinburgh
The ancient royal burgh of Linlithgow, now a residential centre, was once one of Scotland's four main towns and an important industrial centre with a reputation that the place was 'smelt before it was seen'. Local industries included mining, textiles, milling, brewing and the manufacture of candles, soap and glue.

Linlithgow Palace is the chief attraction, a well-preserved 15th-century ruin on the side of Linlithgow Loch and the birthplace of Mary Stuart in 1542. Various rooms remain, including the great hall, with a huge ornate fireplace. There is an octagonal Gothic/Renaissance fountain in the inner courtyard. Next door is St Michael's Church, a 13th-century foundation rebuilt after a fire in 1424 and one of Scotland's largest pre-Reformation churches, topped with an aluminium tower added in the 1960s.

The town retains its medieval layout and many fine buildings; these include early 17th-century houses such as Hamilton House, and a laird's house of 1628. The 17th-century mercat cross is the only complete cross of its type in the country. Linlithgow's history is told at the Linlithgow Story Museum, housed in 18th-century Annet House.

LINN OF DEE Grampian NO0689
Beauty spot off A93, 6 miles (10km) W of Braemar
A famous beauty spot at the head of the Dee Valley where the river tumbles through a rocky cleft in wild countryside. Crossed by a road bridge, opened by Queen Victoria.

LINN OF TUMMEL Tayside NN9060
Beauty spot off A9, 2 miles (3km) S of Killiecrankie
Loch Faskally's creation for hydro-electricity in 1950 has made plunging falls a mere pool. Early fish-pass for salmon. A plaque commemorates Queen Victoria's visit in 1844.

LINTON Cambridgeshire TL5646
Small town on A604, 7 miles (11km) W of Haverhill
The long, narrow High Street is bisected by the Linton branch of the River Cam. The High Street boasts some splendid buildings, including the handsome pargetted Chaundlers, and the early 16th-century black and white Trinity guildhall. The Congregational church was built in 1818, while Linton Zoo is popular with children and adults alike.

The bridge at Linn of Dee.

LINTON Kent TQ7550

Village on A229, 4 miles (6km) S of Maidstone

Pleasant and unpretentious village on a steep hill overlooking the Weald, with pairs of ragstone cottages, a Victorian church and a big house of the 1730s set in parkland.

LINTON IN CRAVEN North Yorkshire SD9962

Village on B6265, 1 mile (2km) S of Grassington

Village built around a wide green which slopes down to Linton Beck. The name is probably derived from the flax grown in the surrounding fields.

LIPHOOK Hampshire SU8331

Small town off A3, 4 miles (6km) SW of Haslemere

This was only a village at the crossroads, with a big coaching inn, until the 20th century. Flora Thompson, author of *Lark Rise to Candleford*, lived here 1916–28, and there is a memorial bust in the main street. Bohunt Manor Gardens are interesting and include a lake. Hollycombe Steam Collection, with woodland walks, is 1½ miles (2km) southeast.

LISKEARD Cornwall SX2564

Town on A38, 11 miles (18km) E of Bodmin

One of Cornwall's medieval stannary towns, where tin was taken to be weighed and taxed. Small today, and rather old-fashioned. Narrow streets, mostly spread over two small hills. Many Victorian buildings, some neo-Gothic. The Pipe Well in the middle is an ancient water supply. Local museum.

LISMORE Strathclyde NM8440
Island in Loch Linnhe
A flat and fertile island at the south end of Loch Linnhe, with lush sheep pastures and notable plants, flowers and birds. Fine broch at Tirefouris on the northeast coast. The seat of the Bishop of Aryll from 1236, it has the remains of his 13th-century Achadun Castle. Traces of the Cathedral of St Moluag were incorporated in the parish church in 1749.

LISS Hampshire SU7727
Village on B3006, 3 miles (5km) NE of Petersfield
A group of scattered villages which have grown because of the railway. West Liss was the original settlement.

LITHERLAND Merseyside SJ3397
Town immediately N of Bootle
Lies at the northern terminus of the former Liverpool overhead railway, constructed in 1893.

LITTLE BADDOW Essex TL7707
Village off A414, 5 miles (8km) E of Chelmsford
Smart village, where a lane runs down to the River Chelmer. Blakes Wood (National Trust) is renowned for bluebells. The church has rare medieval wooden effigies.

LITTLE BARRINGTON Gloucestershire SP2012
see Barrington

LITTLE BAYHAM Kent TQ6336
Hamlet off B2169, 3 miles (5km) W of Lamberhurst
On the Kent/Sussex boundary beside the River Teise. Bayham Abbey ruins, among the most picturesque monastic remains of southern Britain, are on the Sussex side of the river.

LITTLE BERKHAMSTED Hertfordshire TL2907
Village off B158, 4 miles (6km) SW of Hertford
Smart and attractive village that has been home to Bertram Mills and Adam Ant in its time, and was Brian Johnston's birthplace. Notable 18th-century folly tower.

LITTLE BILLING Northamptonshire SP8061
Village off A45, 4 miles (6km) E of Northampton
On the edge of Northampton, beside the River Nene, are Billing Aquadrome's amusements: boating, fishing, outdoor swimming, caravan site.

LITTLE BLAKENHAM Suffolk TM1048
Village off B1113, 5 miles (8km) NW of Ipswich
Central Suffolk village especially noted for its Woodland Garden — 5 acres (2ha) of woodland thick with roses, rhododendrons, azaleas and hydrangeas.

LITTLE BUDWORTH Cheshire SJ5965
Hamlet off A49, 3 miles (5km) NE of Tarporley
Small village near ancient heathland. Little Budworth Country Park represents the last traces of the area's once-large forests. Oulton Park racing circuit holds regular races through the summer.

LITTLE BURSTEAD Essex TQ6692
Village off A176, 2 miles (3km) SW of Billericay
Conservation village in the Green Belt with an attractive church and several Elizabethan houses. Laindon Common woodland.

LITTLE BYTHAM Lincolnshire TF0118
Village on B1176, 7 miles (11km) N of Stamford
East Coast Main Line railway viaduct dominates stone-built village. Church, unusually dedicated to St Medard, has a Norman tower and 14th-century spire.

LITTLE CASTERTON Leicestershire TF0109
Hamlet off A1, 2 miles (3km) N of Stamford
A popular summer season of Shakespeare plays is held in the idyllic open-air theatre, with a covered auditorium, in the grounds of medieval Tolethorpe Hall. Wall-paintings in 13th-century church.

LITTLE CHALFIELD Wiltshire ST8663
see Chalfield

LITTLE CHESTERFORD Essex TL5042
see Chesterford

LITTLE COMBERTON Hereford and Worcester SO9542
see Comberton

LITTLE COWARNE Hereford and Worcester SO6051
Village off A465, 4 miles (6km) SW of Bromyard
Remote settlement with pub and small Victorian church attractively situated in hills above River Lodon.

LITTLE CRESSINGHAM Norfolk TF8700
see Cressingham

LITTLE CROSTHWAITE Cumbria NY2327
Hamlet on A591, 4 miles (6km) NW of Keswick
Mirehouse is a 17th-century manor house with portraits and manuscripts of many literary friends of the Spedding family. Pleasant walk to Bassenthwaite Lake and Norman Church of St Bega.

LITTLE DALBY Leicestershire SK7714
Hamlet off A606, 3 miles (5km) S of Melton Mowbray
The ironstone church on a wooded hill was rebuilt in the 1850s. Mrs Orton of Little Dalby was reputed to be the first person to make Stilton cheese.

LITTLE DUNHAM Norfolk TF8612
Village off A47, 4 miles (6km) NE of Swaffham
In this attractive Georgian village is Dunham Museum, with imaginative displays of working tools and machinery. In the church, the bases of the pillars form seats.

LITTLE DUNMOW Essex TL6521
Village off A120, 2 miles (3km) E of Great Dunmow
Original home of the Dunmow Flitch custom (see Great Dunmow). Church with a chair dubiously identified as the original Flitch chair. Vineyard open to visitors.

LITTLE EASTON Essex TL6023
Village off B184, 2 miles (3km) NW of Great Dunmow
Home of Daisy, Countess of Warwick, mistress of Edward VII. HG Wells lived here, and Ellen Terry frequently visited. Maynard monuments in church.

LITTLE GADDESDEN Hertfordshire SP9913
Village off A4146, 4 miles (6km) N of Berkhamsted
The Ashridge estate (National Trust) covers more than 4,000 acres (1,620ha) of Chilterns woods, downs and commons on the Hertfordshire/Buckinghamshire border. Good walking and bird-watching, with roaming fallow and muntjac deer; the edible dormouse lives here, too. Views from the Bridgewater Monument. Gardens (limited opening) of enormous Ashridge House. Bridgewater family monuments in church.

LITTLE GIDDING Cambridgeshire TL1281
Hamlet off B660, 5 miles (8km) SW of Stilton
TS Eliot wrote *Little Gidding*, the last of his *Four Quartets*, here and for the second time in its history plunged this tiny hamlet into public view. The first time was in 1626, when wealthy merchant Nicholas Ferrar came to found a religious community here. Called the Arminian Nunnery, the community was visited three times by Charles I.

LITTLE GLEMHAM Suffolk TM3458
Village on A12, 2 miles (3km) SW of Friday Street
The founder of Yale University lived in Elizabethan Little Glemham Hall (not open). The charming Lion inn, dating from the 17th century, was a coaching station.

LITTLE GRANSDEN Cambridgeshire TL2755
see Gransden

LITTLE GRIMSBY Lincolnshire TF3291
Hamlet off A16, 3 miles (5km) N of Louth
Tiny church built in 1500 and mellow red-brick hall of about 1720 stand side-by-side, surrounded by trees.

LITTLE HADHAM Hertfordshire TL4322
Village on A120, 3 miles (5km) W of Bishop's Stortford
Attractive village at a crossing of the River Ash. Three-decker pulpit and box pews in St Cecilia's Church.

LITTLE HAMPDEN Buckinghamshire SP8503
Hamlet off A413, 3 miles (5km) S of Wendover
Eric Gill tombstones and remarkable medieval wall-paintings in the tiny church of this hamlet deep in the Chilterns.

LITTLE HEREFORD Hereford and Worcester SO5568
Hamlet off A456, 3 miles (5km) W of Tenbury Wells
Isolated in orchard country close to River Teme, the small village has an 18th-century bridge and unexpectedly splendid medieval church.

LITTLE HORMEAD Hertfordshire TL4028
Hamlet off B1368, 3 miles (5km) E of Buntingford
Close to the River Quin. Noted for an isolated Norman church with 12th-century decorative ironwork on the north door.

LITTLE HORWOOD Buckinghamshire SP7930
Village off A421, 2 miles (3km) NE of Winslow
Pride and the deadly sins depicted in the church. Grand 20th-century mansions, venerably half-timbered Shoulder of Mutton pub.

LITTLE KIMBLE Buckinghamshire SP8207
Village on A4010, 5 miles (8km) S of Aylesbury
Below Chilterns edge. Church's notable medieval wall-paintings include St Francis preaching to the birds. Also medieval Arthurian tiles.

LITTLE LANGDALE Cumbria NY3103
Hamlet off A593, 2 miles (3km) W of Skelwith Bridge
A tiny hamlet. The Three Shires inn gets its name from the fact that the counties Cumberland, Westmorland and Lancashire joined near by.

LITTLE LANGFORD Wiltshire SU0436
Hamlet off A36, 5 miles (8km) NW of Wilton
In the Wylye Valley. The tiny hamlet has a Victorian church with an elaborate Norman doorway.

LITTLE LEVER Greater Manchester SD7507
Town on A6053, 3 miles (5km) SE of Bolton
Close to the confluence of the rivers Croal and Irwell, the town thrived on textile and coal industries.

LITTLE MALVERN Hereford and Worcester SO7740
Village on A4104, 4 miles (6km) S of Great Malvern
In a tranquil situation below Herefordshire Beacon, the tower and choir of the 15th-century priory church retains its carved screen, misericords and medieval tiles. Some monastic buildings survive at neighbouring Little Malvern Court (limited opening), which also houses collection of vestments and embroidery. Sir Edward Elgar's grave can be found at St Wulfstan's Church.

LITTLE MAPLESTEAD Essex TL8234
Village off A131, 2 miles (3km) N of Halstead
One of England's rare round churches is here, built for the Knights Hospitallers in the 14th century but heavily restored in 1850.

The church at Little Maplestead.

LITTLE MARLOW Buckinghamshire SU8787
Village off A4155, 2 miles (3km) NE of Marlow
Attractive backwater near Thames and giant sewage works. Green, church, manor house. Best-selling author Edgar Wallace is buried in the cemetery.

LITTLE MILTON Oxfordshire SP6100
Village on A329, 6 miles (10km) SW of Thame
Village overlooking Thame Valley with the thatched Lamb inn as centrepiece of some appealing old houses. Charming lodges guard the drive to the Tudor manor house.

LITTLE MISSENDEN Buckinghamshire SU9299
Village off A413, 3 miles (5km) NW of Amersham
Set quietly among the Chilterns woods on the River Misbourne. Ancient church with medieval wall-paintings, including St Christopher carrying Christ child and martyrdom of St Catherine. Connections with composers Sir Michael Tippett and Edmund Rubbra. Village began staging annual arts festival in 1960. Crown pub has been kept by same family for 80 years.

LITTLE NESS Shropshire SJ4019
Village off A5, 3 miles (5km) NW of Montford Bridge
A good Norman church here, and architecture buffs should ring Adcote School for permission to view one of Norman Shaw's best country houses.

LITTLE PACKINGTON Warwickshire SP2283
see Packington

LITTLE PETHERICK Cornwall SW9172
Village on A389, 4 miles (6km) W of Wadebridge
At the head of a branch of the Camel estuary. The church has a rich early 20th-century interior.

LITTLE ROLLRIGHT Warwickshire SP2930
Hamlet off A3400, 1 mile (2km) S of Long Compton
Hillside village near the famous Rollright Stones, a circle of 77 stones (King's Men) and a tall single stone (King Stone), probably of the Bronze Age.

LITTLE SALKELD Cumbria NY5536
see Salkeld

LITTLE SAXHAM Suffolk TL8063
see Saxham

LITTLE SNORING Norfolk TF9532
see Snoring

LITTLE SODBURY Avon ST7583
Village off A432, 2 miles (3km) E of Chipping Sodbury
Small stone village, with a partly 15th-century manor house (not open) and a big Iron Age hillfort.

LITTLE SOMBORNE Hampshire SU3832
Hamlet off A272, 3 miles (5km) SE of Stockbridge
In a park-like setting, with only a few cottages and the little Saxon and Norman church.

LITTLE STONHAM Suffolk TM1160
Village off A140, 4 miles (6km) E of Stowmarket
Pretty village with some handsome Georgian buildings. The clock house dates from the 14th century, and has early Tudor chimneys.

LITTLE STRETTON Shropshire SO4491
Village on B4370, 1 mile (2km) S of Church Stretton
At the foot of the Long Mynd (see), with several black and white houses and the distinctive church of 1903, timber-framed and thatched.

LITTLE THURLOW Suffolk TL6751
see Thurlow

LITTLE WALDINGFIELD Suffolk TL9245
Village on B1115, 4 miles (6km) NE of Sudbury
Little Waldingfield has some attractive buildings, such as the 14th-century priory. St Lawrence's Church has some splendid 16th-century brasses.

LITTLE WALSINGHAM Norfolk TF9337
Small town on B1105, 4 miles (6km) S of Wells-next-the-Sea
The shrine of Our Lady of Walsingham has been a pilgrimage site since the 11th century. The spring was said to effect miraculous cures. Walsingham High Street opens out into a pleasant square in the centre of which is a 16th-century pump house and beacon brazier. Great Walsingham is due north and has beautiful 'poppyhead' pews in the church.

LITTLE WARLEY Essex TQ6088
Hamlet off A128, 2 miles (3km) S of Brentwood
Church with 18th-century tower and Strutt family monuments. Ford's office block is on the site of the old East India Company barracks.

LITTLE WELDON Northamptonshire SP9289
see Weldon

LITTLE WENHAM Suffolk TM0839
see Wenham

LITTLE WOLFORD Warwickshire SP2635
Hamlet off A3400, 3 miles (5km) south of Shipston on Stour
On the northern Cotswold fringe. Little Wolford Manor (not open) is a fine example of a 16th-century stone and timber-framed house.

LITTLE WYMONDLEY Hertfordshire TL2127
Village off A602, 3 miles (5km) SE of Hitchin
Bigger than Great Wymondley (see). Attractive village with good pubs, the Plume of Feathers and the Bucks Head.

LITTLE WYRLEY Staffordshire SK0105
Hamlet off A5, 3 miles (5km) SE of Cannock
Little Wyreley Hall (not open), of the 16th and 17th centuries, stands in a former mining area. Canal spur and Wyreley Common to east.

LITTLEBECK North Yorkshire NZ8804
Hamlet off B1416, 4 miles (6km) S of Whitby
An entrancing hamlet of delightful houses surrounding a quiet pool set in the deep wooded valley of the River Esk.

LITTLEBOROUGH Greater Manchester SD9316
Town on A58, 3 miles (5km) NE of Rochdale
The town stands at the junction of two ancient highways on the Yorkshire border. Three original tollhouses still exist.

LITTLEBOROUGH Nottinghamshire SK8282
Hamlet off A156, 4 miles (6km) S of Gainsborough
At the end of a cul-de-sac to the River Trent, once an important ford for the Roman Lincoln–Doncaster road. Tiny Norman church, Roman tiles in herringbone masonry.

LITTLEBREDY AND LONG BREDY Dorset SY5889
Villages off A35, 6 miles (10km) W of Dorchester
Two pretty villages in the scenic Bride Valley, with high chalk downs above them. Littlebredy is the head of the valley, with decorative thatched cottages built in the 19th century in imitation of old ones. Lots of trees and woods, with bare downs above. Long Bredy has old cottages and a little stream. The Kingston Russell stone circle is high on the downs.

LITTLEBURY Essex TL5139
Village on B1383, 2 miles (3km) NW of Saffron Walden
Expensive commuter village right on the River Cam. Victorianised church with brasses and a fine font cover. Iron Age fort on Ring Hill to south.

LITTLECOTE Wiltshire SU3070
Mansion off B4192, 2 miles (3km) W of Hungerford
Pretty 16th-century brick manor house, with many tourist attractions, including a Roman mosaic, jousting and a rare breeds farm.

LITTLEDEAN Gloucestershire SO6713
Village on A4151, 1 mile (2km) E of Cinderford
This former Dean mining village has a fine church and 18th-century 'model' prison. Littledean Hall claims to be England's oldest house.

LITTLEHAM Devon SY0281
Village off B3178, immediately E of Exmouth
On the edge of Exmouth. The church sits high above the village with memorial to Nelson's widow, who died at Exmouth in 1831.

LITTLEHAMPTON West Sussex TQ0202
Town on B2140, 8 miles (13km) W of Worthing
Pleasant coastal resort and working port at the mouth of the River Arun. High Street, inland from the coast and parallel to it, runs eastwards from the harbour. The flint cottages are on an endearingly small scale. The seafront has unpretentious buildings from 1800 onwards, separated from East Beach by The Green (amusement park, putting green). West Beach, across the river, is protected for wildlife. Modern industries include the Body Shop headquarters.

LITTLEHEMPSTON Devon SX8162
Village off A381, 1 mile (2km) N of Totnes
Small, rural and woody, but with the railway running straight through the village.

LITTLEMORE Oxfordshire SP5302
District off A4142 on SE outskirts of Oxford
Residential suburb of Oxford where John (later Cardinal) Newman planned a religious community (some cottages remain). Church contains good Victorian work.

LITTLEOVER Derbyshire SK3334
District of SW Derby
Residential district of Derby, formerly a separate village, with a 16th-century timber-framed thatched cottage.

LITTLEPORT Cambridgeshire TL5686
Small town off A10, 5 miles (8km) NE of Ely
Scene of food riots in 1816 after which five men were hanged. Stands on black Fen soil among vast hedgeless fields.

Inn sign at Littleport.

LITTLESTONE-ON-SEA Kent TR0824
Village on B2071, 1 mile (2km) E of New Romney
Seaside place on east side of Dungeness, with a parade and hotels facing the sea and beach, first laid out in 1886 as a coastal resort planned 'so as in time to form a marine town'.

LITTLETON Surrey TQ0768
Village off B376, 2 miles (3km) NE of Chertsey
Attractive little place (church has exceptional Tudor brickwork in tower) squeezed between massive Queen Mary Reservoir, an important bird sanctuary, and Shepperton Film Studios.

LITTLEWICK GREEN Berkshire SU8479
Village off A4, 3 miles (5km) W of Maidenhead
Still with a green, and a 17th-century well covered by a little roof. Robin Hood's Arbour is an Iron Age embankment to the east. Courage Shire Horse Centre also to the east.

LITTON North Yorkshire SD9074
Village off B6160, 2 miles (3km) NW of Arncliffe
A very picturesque village grouped around a green and with a stream running through it. There is a footbridge over the River Skirfare and footpaths along the river banks. Littondale is a valley of great beauty and is largely unspoilt, one of the few valleys unscarred by lead- mining. The valley has also been used as the setting for ITV's *Emmerdale*.

LITTON Somerset ST5954
Village on B3114, 6 miles (10km) N of Wells
A rural, unspoiled village with a little reservoir to the north created in 1853. Sherborne Gardens have a splendid collection of hollies, themed gardens and other features (limited opening).

LIVERPOOL Merseyside SJ3490
City off M62, 178 miles (287km) NW of London
Liverpool first grew to prominence during the 18th century as a result of its sugar, spice and tobacco trade with the Americas, even dominating the slave trade for a time, until its abolition in 1807. In the 19th century, the port of Liverpool became the gateway to a new world for thousands of British and European emigrants who arrived at the port to travel across the Atlantic to start new lives in America. A statue of Christopher Columbus bears the inscription 'The discoverer of America was the maker of Liverpool'. Today the historic waterfront is a major tourist attraction, centred around the Albert Dock, where monumental 150-year-old former dockside warehouses are the biggest group of Grade 1 Listed Buildings in the country. These have now been converted into a complex of shops, restaurants, bars, television studios and attractions, including the Tate Gallery in the North, with one of the most impressive collections of contemporary art outside London, the Merseyside Maritime Museum which relates much of Liverpool's history as a port, and the Beatles Story, which commemorates the Beatles from their childhood days in Liverpool through to their break-up and pursuit of individual careers.

Passenger ferries across the Mersey still operate from the docks and provide the best view of Liverpool. Overlooking the docks from the city is the Liver Building, whose two 295ft (90m) towers are topped by the famous 'Liver' birds, mythical birds from which the city is said to have taken its name.

Although Liverpool has sadly lost its former prosperity, it has not lost its pride. Many wonderful buildings from that period remain. Great merchant warehouses, banks and trading houses of this once-mighty port survive along broad streets to give Liverpool a sense of grandeur which lives on. The Cunard building along the waterfront and St George's Hall in the city centre, completed in 1854, are equally impressive buildings. Liverpool's two modern cathedrals, both on high ground overlooking the city, are examples of two distinct kinds of ecclesiastical architecture. The Anglican cathedral, begun in 1904 by Sir Giles Gilbert Scott, is built of red sandstone in Gothic style. The Roman Catholic metropolitan cathedral was designed by Sir Frederick Gibberd and consecrated in 1967. The glass was designed by John Piper and Patrick Reyntiens.

Liverpool's museums and art galleries are a great credit to the city. The Walker Art Gallery on William Brown Street has a splendid collection of paintings and sculpture from 1300 to the present day and is especially rich in European Old Masters, Victorian and Pre-Raphaelite paintings and modern British works. Nearby Liverpool Museum contains over one million exhibits from around the world in various galleries.

The Bluecoat Chambers is the oldest building in the city centre, a superb example of Queen Anne architecture and built originally as the Bluecoat School. Today it is a lively arts centre which hosts many exhibitions.

LIVERSEDGE West Yorkshire SE2024
Town off A62, 3 miles (5km) NW of Dewsbury
An old industrial town with many large stone mill buildings evident. The Shears inn is believed to have been a meeting place for the Luddites, where they plotted their activities.

LIVINGSTON Lothian NT0568
New Town off M8, 13 miles (21km) W of Edinburgh
A successful New Town, noted for manufacturing and high-technology industries, established in 1962 in a previous coal-mining and shale oil-extracting area. Adjacent Mid Calder was formerly a coaching stop on the main route from Glasgow to Edinburgh; 16th-century church and connections with John Knox at Calder House. Near by is Almondell and Calderwood Country Park, with a visitor centre.

LIZARD Cornwall SW7012
Village on A3083, N of Lizard Point
The most southerly village in Britain, bleak, and with shops selling objects made from the local serpentine stone. Lighthouse and a very rocky shore.

LIZARD, THE Cornwall
Peninsula SE of Helston
Treeless, flat and bleak, the Lizard is the most southerly part of Britain, with a rocky headland protruding into the Channel. Lots of shipping passes here. The local rock, serpentine, comes in many colours, and is used for buildings as well as ornaments. See also Goonhilly, Kyance and Landewednack.

LLANABER Gwynedd SH6017
Village on A496, 2 miles (3km) N of Barmouth
Mountain-backed village on open, sandy coastline north of Barmouth. Interesting, unexpectedly elaborate church dating from medieval times.

LLANAELHAEARN Gwynedd SH3844
Village on A499, 6 miles (10km) N of Pwllheli
Stands below rocky Yr Eifl mountains which rise to 1,850ft (564m). Path leads to ancient Tre'r Ceiri hill-fort, which has well-preserved remains of huts and ramparts.

LLANANNO Powys SO0974
see Llanbister

LLANARMON DYFFRYN CEIRIOG Clwyd SJ1532
Village on B4500, 8 miles (12km) SW of Llangollen
Peaceful village deep in Vale of Ceiriog on the eastern flanks of the remote Berwyn Mountains. Birthplace of the famous Welsh bard, Ceiriog (John Hughes).

LLANARMON-YN-IAL Clwyd SJ1956
Village on B5431, 4 miles (6km) E of Ruthin
Attractively situated in the valley of the River Alun at the southern end of the Clwydian Range. Interesting church with two naves.

LLANBADARN FAWR Dyfed SN6080
Area in SE Aberystwyth
Once a village in its own right, now a suburb of Aberystwyth. Ancient religious settlement, home of one of Wales's largest churches (13th century).

LLANBEDR Gwynedd SH5826
Village on A496, 3 miles (5km) S of Harlech
Attractive village just inland from Mochras (otherwise known as Shell Island). Inland is lovely Llyn Cwm Bychan and 'Roman Steps' into the Rhinogs. RAF camp.

LLANBEDROG Gwynedd SH3231
Village on A499, 4 miles (6km) SW of Pwllheli
Village and small resort on Lleyn peninsula's south coast with sheltered beach backed by trees. Outcrop above crowned by statue of Tin Man, put there in 1980 to replace an earlier figurehead from a sailing ship. Plas Glyn-y-Weddw is a neo-Gothic mansion which houses a gallery displaying Welsh art and temporary exhibitions.

LLANBERIS Gwynedd SH5760
Town on A4086, 6 miles (10km) SE of Caernarfon
Situated at the foot of the Llanberis Pass, gateway to Snowdon, Llanberis is a popular tourist town. Evidence of a slate-mining past is carved into its steep hillsides, which are disfigured by the scars of quarrying. The Welsh Slate Museum is based at the workshops of the Dinorwig Quarry, once the largest in Wales. Everything has been preserved as it was when the quarry closed in the late 1960s.

The museum is on the shores of Llyn Padarn (see). Llanberis' other lake, Llyn Peris, is guarded by the shell of Dolbadarn Castle (Cadw), a medieval stronghold of the Welsh leader Llywelyn the Great. The mountainside above the lake is riddled with huge tunnels and chambers, created as part of the Dinorwig hydro-electric pumped storage scheme. Tours of this awesome underground world are available from the Power of Wales/Museum of the North, a purpose-built complex which takes a look at Welsh history and natural science in an imaginative way.

A number of footpaths lead upwards from Llanberis to Mount Snowdon (see). Many prefer to take the train, the narrow-gauge rack-and-pinion Snowdon Mountain Railway which climbs almost to the summit. See also Llyn Padarn/Snowdon.

LLANBISTER Powys SO1073
Village on A483, 8 miles (13km) N of Llandrindod Wells
Church has an unusual chimney in place of tower. One mile (2km) northwest at Llananno is a little gem of a church with fabulous carved rood screen.

LLANDAFF South Glamorgan ST1578
District in NW Cardiff
Suburb of encroaching Cardiff beside River Taff, which still preserves its 'village' atmosphere. Small street lined with shops and pubs leads to green above dingle, site of Llandaff Cathedral. Cathedral occupies early Christian place of worship. Present building, medieval, severely damaged by World War II bombing. Interior dominated by modernistic post-war 'Christ in Majesty' sculpture. Riverside walk to city centre.

LLANDAWKE Dyfed SN2811
Hamlet off A4066, 2 miles (3km) W of Laugharne
Sleepy hamlet in unexplored farming country fringeing Carmarthen Bay. Primitive but atmospheric 13th-century church houses ancient inscribed stone.

LLANDDEWI BREFI Dyfed SN6655
Village on B4343, 3 miles (5km) SW of Tregaron
Traditional country village in broad Vale of Teifi between Tregaron and Lampeter. Legendary associations with St David, Wales's patron saint, who held a meeting here.

LLANDDULAS Clwyd SH9078
Village off A55, 2 miles (3km) W of Abergele
Village between Colwyn Bay and Rhyl with pebble and sand beach. One of the quieter stretches of the popular North Wales coast.

LLANDEGAI Gwynedd SH5970
Village off A55, 1 mile (2km) SE of Bangor
Based around model village built by Lord Penrhyn for his estate workers in 19th century. Penrhyn Castle now National Trust.

LLANDEILO Dyfed SN6322
Town on A40, 14 miles (23km) E of Carmarthen
Handsome old country town above pastoral Vale of Towy. Exceptionally long single-spanned bridge across river. Dinefwr Park (National Trust) on outskirts has sweeping landscaped grounds and 'old' and 'new' castles – former was the medieval home of influential South Walean leader, Lord Rhys. Gelli Aur Country Park across the valley, and in hills is Carreg Cennen Castle, spectacularly perched on a lofty crag.

LLANDINABO Hereford and Worcester SO5128
Hamlet on A49, 6 miles (10km) NW of Ross-on-Wye
Hillside hamlet above River Wye has church with fine 16th-century carved rood screen and brass of Thomas Tomkins, aged three.

LLANDINAM Powys SO0288

Village on A470, 2 miles (3km) S of Caersws

Pretty, well-kept village with half-timbered border-style houses. Statue commemorates famous son David Davies, a leading 19th-century Welsh entrepreneur.

LLANDOGO Gwent SO5204

Village on A466, 6 miles (10km) N of Chepstow

Village set in loveliest stretch of Wye Valley near Tintern. To the north is elegant Bigsweir Bridge, which takes the road into England.

LLANDOVERY (LLANYMDDYFRI) Dyfed SN7634

Small town on A40, 17 miles (27km) W of Brecon

Traveller/writer George Borrow called this 'the pleasantest little town in which I have halted'. Llandovery's attractive cobbled market square, clock tower and ruined castle lend it a period charm, enhanced by many old inns. Still a busy farming centre with livestock market. Home of a Welsh-speaking public school. Roman fort near by.

LLANDRILLO Clwyd SJ0337

Village on B4401, 5 miles (8km) SW of Corwen

Llandrillo's pretty cottages sit in the tranquil Vale of Edeyrnion. Good starting point for walks into the Berwyn Mountains.

LLANDRINDOD WELLS Powys SO0561

Town on A483, 7 miles (11km) N of Builth Wells

This spa town is a prized example of undiluted Victorian architecture. Planned as an inland resort to exploit the coming of the railways, Llandrindod Wells has all the expected hallmarks – contrasting brickwork, tall, gabled buildings, decorative ironwork, canopied shopping streets, orderly planning and ornamental parklands. Visitors came here for the 'pure mountain air' and the saline, sulphur, magnesian and chalybeate waters. The lush, wooded Rock Park Gardens close to the centre of town preserve memories of bygone times in the pump house tea rooms, while the town's museum has memorabilia from the heydays of the late 19th and early 20th centuries.

Today, the town – which retains a good choice of hotels and guesthouses – is a popular touring centre for the border country and central Wales. Llandrindod has also kept its excellent range of sporting amenities, including tennis, golf, bowls, fishing and boating, the latter on an attractive lake. Each summer, the town holds a large Victorian Festival.

Remnants of Castell Collen, a Roman camp, stand in fields beside the River Ithon to the north.

LLANDUDNO Gwynedd SH7882

Town on A546, 5 miles (8km) NW of Colwyn Bay

Llandudno is the unrivalled 'Queen of the Welsh resorts'. Not only does it have more hotels and guesthouses than other places, but it has also remained true to its Victorian character. Framed between two headlands – the Great and Little Ormes – are north-facing sands and a long, gently curving promenade, culminating beneath Great Orme in an ornate pier. In the town itself, glass-canopied shops and decorative cast iron make their contribution to the resort's period charm.

The Great Orme headland can be reached by tramway or cabin lift. Attractions on the Orme include gardens, copper mines dating from prehistoric times, a country park and dry ski slope. In the town itself, entertainments and places to visit include theatres, a museum, art gallery and the Alice in Wonderland Visitor Centre, its location explained by Llandudno's links with Charles Dodgson, alias author Lewis Carroll.

A spectacular cliff road runs around the Great Orme to Llandudno's second, west-facing beach, where a statue of the White Rabbit is another reminder of the Alice connection. On the same coastline to the south is Deganwy, whose ruined medieval castle overlooks the Conwy estuary.

LLANDWROG Gwynedd SH4556

Village on A499, 5 miles (8km) SW of Caernarfon

Estate village built in 19th century for neighbouring Parc Glynllifon. The park, with its craft workshops, walks and gardens, is open to visitors.

LLANDYSUL Dyfed SN4140

Small town on A486, 12 miles (19km) N of Carmarthen

Teifiside town in heart of area which once produced Welsh woollens. Spectacular river course a favourite with canoeists as well as fishermen.

LLANEGRYN Gwynedd SH6005

Village on A493, 3 miles (5km) N of Tywyn

Church on hill near village has one of the finest rood screens in Wales, displaying amazingly complex medieval carvings.

LLANELLI Dyfed SN5000

Town on A484, 10 miles (16km) NW of Swansea

Tinplate and steel gave this town its industrial presence. The former steelworks site has now been attractively landscaped. There are more pleasant open spaces in People's Park and Parc Howard. Llanelli is home to the Scarlets, one of Wales's most famous rugby teams. Museum at Parc Howard. Cwm Lleidi Country Park to the north, Wildfowl and Wetlands Centre to the south.

LLANELLTYD Gwynedd SH7119

Village on A470, 1 mile (2km) NW of Dolgellau

Remnants of Cymer Abbey (Cadw), founded in 1199 by Cistercians, evocatively sited in farmland beside the River Mawddach.

LLANERFYL Powys SJ0309

Village on A458, 5 miles (8km) NW of Llanfair Caereinion

Village beside River Banwy. Churchyard is noted for its early Christian tombstone of the 5th or 6th century.

LLANFAIR Gwynedd SH5729

Village on A496, 1 mile (2km) S of Harlech

Former slate-mining village whose 19th-century caverns are now open to the public on two levels.

LLANFAIR CAEREINION Powys SJ1006

Small town off A458, 8 miles (13km) W of Welshpool

Quiet town, once a flannel-making centre. Main terminus for narrow-gauge Welshpool and Llanfair Light Railway which runs to Welshpool.

LLANFAIR PG Gwynedd (Anglesey) SH5271
Village off A5, 2 miles (3km) W of Menai Bridge
Village with the famous tongue-twisting placename, the world's longest – Llanfairpwllgwyngyllgogerychwyrndrobwllllantysilio-gogogoch – meaning 'St Mary's (Church) by the white aspen over the whirlpool, and St Tysilio's (Church) by the red cave'. Also well known for its excellent craft shop complex. Near by is splendid Plas Newydd (National Trust); also prehistoric Bryn Celli Ddu burial chamber (Cadw).

LLANFAIRFECHAN Gwynedd SH6874
Small town on A55, 8 miles (13km) W of Conwy
Huddled beneath steep-sided mountain overlooking Conwy Bay. Retains the character of a small Victorian seaside resort.

LLANFYLLIN Powys SJ1419
Small town on A490, 9 miles (14km) NW of Welshpool
Historic town in lovely upper Cain Valley at the approch to the Berwyn Mountains. St Myllin established religious centre here in early Christian times. Restored holy well. Charter granted in late 13th century. Attractive old buildings in town include Manor House and Hall. Hymn writer Ann Griffiths was converted in 1796 at the Congregational chapel. Llanfyllin Bird and Butterfly World near by.

LLANGADOG Dyfed SN7028
Village on A4069, 5 miles (8km) SW of Llandovery
Substantial village in Vale of Towy. Remains of a Norman motte and bailey castle beside road which climbs across the Black Mountain. Garn Goch hillfort near by.

LLANGAMMARCH WELLS Powys SN9347
Village off A483, 4 miles (6km) E of Llanwrtyd Wells
Quiet village beneath military ranges of Mynydd Eppynt. Few reminders of Llangammarch's days as a spa. Disused pump house in grounds of Lake Hotel.

LLANGARRON Hereford and Worcester SO5221
Village off A466, 5 miles (8km) N of Monmouth
Remotely situated in hills west of Ross-on-Wye, Llangarron is at the centre of widely-scattered farms and isolated country-house estates.

LLANGATHEN Dyfed SN5822
Village off A40, 3 miles (5km) W of Llandeilo
Sits in broad Vale of Towy. Worth visiting for its church with a grand tomb to Bishop Rudd of St David's (died 1615).

LLANGATTOCK Powys SO2117
Village off A4077, 1/2 mile (1km) SW of Crickhowell
Usk Valley village with quaint narrow street leading to Norman church. Monmouthshire and Brecon Canal, caves in limestone cliffs leading to moorlands above.

LLANGATTOCK-VIBON-AVEL Gwent SO4515
Hamlet off B4233, 4 miles (6km) NW of Monmouth
Obscure hamlet in peaceful border country. Charles Rolls (of Rolls-Royce fame) is buried at Llangattock Manor, his former home.

LLANGEFNI Gwynedd (Anglesey) SH4575
Town on A5114, 7 miles (11km) NW of Menai Bridge
Centrally located town which is busy market place and administrative centre for Anglesey. Thursday is the liveliest day, when the town square hosts a large open-air market. Close by is the Cefni Reservoir, popular with fishermen. Oriel Ynys Môn is an attractive art gallery with a historical section covering Anglesey's rich heritage.

LLANGELYNIN Gwynedd SH5707
Hamlet on A493, 4 miles (6km) N of Tywyn
Delightful old rough-and-ready church, dating from medieval times, idyllically situated on hillside above sea. 'New' church at nearby Llwyngwril (see).

LLANGOLLEN Clwyd SJ2141
Town on A5, 11 miles (18km) E of Corwen
Llangollen sits in a steep-sided valley carved by the River Dee. This small town attracts performers and visitors from all over the world every July when it holds its celebrated International Musical Eisteddfod, first staged in 1947 to help heal the wounds of war. Because of its international links, the town is now home to the European Centre for Traditional and Regional Studies, based in a converted chapel. Exhibitions are regularly held here.

High above the town is the gnarled shell of Castell Dinas Brân, the remnants of a 12th-century Welsh native fortress. In the town itself stands Plas Newydd, a striking black and white Tudor-style house which was the home from 1780 of the eccentric 'ladies of Llangollen', whose guests included Wordsworth, Shelley and Sir Walter Scott. Times gone by are again featured in a little museum in an old woollen mill which re-creates a Victorian schoolroom.

The Llangollen Railway, a standard-gauge steam line, runs along the valley from the old station across the 14th-century bridge. Close by is the Canal Museum on the banks of the Llangollen branch of the Shropshire Union Canal. Car enthusiasts are catered for in the town's Motor Museum.

LLANGORSE Powys SO1327
Village on B4560, 4 miles (6km) S of Talgarth
Village close to largest natural lake in South Wales. Church occupies ancient religious site. Small artificial island on lake provides more evidence of ancient settlement.

LLANGRANOG Dyfed SN3154
Village on B4334, 6 miles (10km) SW of New Quay
Beautifully located in sheltered, sandy spot surrounded by cliffs of Cardigan Bay. Exhilarating headland walk from beach up steps to Ynys Lochtyn promontory beneath Iron Age hillfort. Once a thriving ship-building centre, now a holiday village. Home to a centre run by the Welsh youth movement, Urdd Gobaith Cymru. The centre's dry-ski slope is open to the public.

LLANGROVE Hereford and Worcester SO5219
Village off A40, 4 miles (6km) N of Monmouth
Surprisingly large village in empty hill country north of Monmouth boasts early church by eminent Victorian architect GF Bodley.

St Cybi's Well at Llangybi.

LLANGURIG Powys SN9079
Village off A470, 4 miles (6km) SW of Llanidloes
Small village with characterful inns on high, open ground in upper Wye Valley. Church dedicated to St Curig has ancient foundations, medieval remnants.

LLANGYBI Gwynedd SH4241
Hamlet off B4354, 5 miles (8km) NE of Pwllheli
Named after St Cybi, 6th-century Celtic missionary whose holy well was renowned for its healing waters. Located in dingle across field from road.

LLANIDLOES Powys SN9584
Small town offA470, 11 miles (18km) SW of Newtown
Unusual 16th-century black and white market hall on pillars – now the town museum – dominates the centre of Llanidloes. Museum tells of this country town's unlikely past as an industrial centre based on flannel-making and lead-mining industries. Attractive mix of architectural styles, church of ancient origin with wooden belfry. Rollercoaster mountain road to the northwest skirts Clywedog Reservoir and crosses remote farming and forestry country.

LLANRHAEADR-YM-MOCHNANT Clwyd SJ1226
Village on B4580, 4 miles (6km) N of Llanfyllin
Remote village in foothills of Berwyn Mountains. Of great cultural significance as the place where the Bible was first translated into Welsh.

LLANRHAEADR-YNG-NGHINMERCH Clwyd SJ0863
Village off A525, 3 miles (5km) SE of Denbigh
In pastoral Vale of Clwyd. Interesting church with superb Jesse window and a holy well behind.

LLANRHIDIAN West Glamorgan SS4992
Village off B4271, 10 miles (16km) W of Swansea
North Gower village close to Weobley Castle (Cadw), a medieval manor house-cum-stronghold overlooking expanse of Llanrhidian Marsh.

LLANRHYSTUD Dyfed SN5369
Village on A487, 7 miles (11km) NE of Aberaeron
Village close to Cardigan Bay coast where Wyre and Carrog rivers meet. Appealing pebble and sand beach, plus coastal walks.

LLANRUG Gwynedd SH5363
Village on A4086, 4 miles (6km) E of Caernarfon
Village on main road between Llanberis and Caernarfon, noted for its 19th-century castellated house, Bryn Brés Castle, set in attractive gardens.

LLANRWST Gwynedd SH8061
Small town on A470, 11 miles (18km) S of Colwyn Bay
Market town prettily set in Vale of Conwy. Handsome old stone bridge over river, with small 15th-century house (now a tea room) of Tu Hwnt i'r Bont (National Trust) at one end. Interesting Gwydir Chapel in town's parish

church, and Gwydir Uchaf Chapel (Cadw) on forested slopes above. Gwydir Castle on outskirts of town.

LLANSANTFFRAED Powys SO1223
Hamlet on A40, 6 miles (10km) SE of Brecon
Usk Valley hamlet with spired sandstone church. Churchyard contains grave of poet Henry Vaughan (died 1695) who lived at nearby Tretower Court (see Tretower).

LLANSANTFFRAID-YM-MECHAIN Powys SJ2120
Village on A495, 5 miles (8km) E of Llanfyllin
Large border village of red-brick buildings in valley of River Vyrnwy. Church has Jacobean window of 1619 and some good 19th-century stained glass.

LLANSTEFFAN Dyfed SN3510
Village on B4312, 7 miles (11km) SW of Carmarthen
Superb setting on sandy mouth of Towy estuary. Village strung out along shore beneath magnificent headland castle (Cadw).

LLANTHONY Gwent SO2827
Hamlet on B4423, 9 miles (14km) N of Abergavenny
Remote spot in hidden border valley. Llanthony Priory (Cadw) founded in 12th century on earlier religious site (6th century) dedicated to St David. Ruined priory has beautiful Early English archways and – unusually – an inn built into its historic fabric. Stands beneath border ridge of Black Mountains traversed by Offa's Dyke Path.

LLANTILIO CROSSENNY Gwent SO3914
Hamlet on B4233, 6 miles (10km) E of Abergavenny
Border hamlet has ancient origins – the medieval church (restored) was built on a 6th-century religious site. Near by is White Castle (Cadw), one of the Three Castles of Gwent.

LLANTRISANT Mid Glamorgan ST0483
Small town on B4595, 4 miles (6km) S of Pontypridd
Old Llantrisant is on steep hill overlooking new housing and shopping development. Named after three saints, Illtyd, Gwyno and Dyfod – church, Norman in origin, dedicated to them. Statue marks town's associations with 19th-century visionary and eccentric Doctor William Price. Fragments of 13th-century castle, noted craft and design visitor centre. The Royal Mint is located here.

LLANTWIT MAJOR South Glamorgan SS9668
Town on B4265, 4 miles (6km) SW of Cowbridge
Historic town with a maze of old streets. Influential seat of early Christian church in Wales. Cathedral-like Norman church has exceptional collection of Celtic crosses and inscribed stones. Stands on fringes of Vale of Glamorgan only 1 mile (2km) from cliffs and Col-huw beach. Nearby St Donat's is the home of a restored medieval castle, base for Atlantic College, the world's first international sixth-form school.

LLANUWCHLLYN Gwynedd SH8730
Hamlet off A494, 5 miles (8km) SW of Bala
Hamlet well known for its cultural associations with the Welsh language movement. Main terminus of narrow-gauge Bala Lake Railway.

LLANVIHANGEL CRUCORNEY Gwent SO3220
Village on A465, 4 miles (6km) N of Abergavenny
Village in shadow of craggy Skirrid-fawr mountain with ancient Skirrid inn, claimed to be the oldest in Wales. Llanfihangel Court dates from 16th century.

LLANWARNE Hereford and Worcester SO5028
Village off B4348, 6 miles (10km) NW of Ross-on-Wye
Small village in hills above Wye Valley, worth seeking out for the elegant font and old stained glass in its church.

LLANWONNO Mid Glamorgan
Hamlet on minor road, 5 miles (8km) NW of Pontypridd
Attractively set on high ground above industrial valleys among pines of St Gwynno Forest. Associated with the legend of 18th-century Welsh runner Guto Nyth Bran.

LLANWRTYD WELLS Powys SN8746
Small town on A483, 10 miles (16km) NE of Llandovery
Small spa town which preserves its period character well. Large gabled dwellings once served as busy guest-houses. Remains of old sulphur wells in field by River Irfon. At gateway to wildernesses crossed by Abergwesyn Pass. Popular pony-trekking and mountain-biking centre. Cambrian Woollen Mill. Claims to be Britain's smallest town.

LLANYBLODWEL Shropshire SJ2422
Village on B4396, 5 miles (8km) SW of Oswestry
The rambling 16th-century Horseshoe inn beside the River Tanat is a powerful attraction at this idyllic Welsh border village. Another is the eccentric church, of medieval origin but transformed by its vicar John Parker in the 1840s, with a bullet-shaped tower and extravagantly embellished interior. Do not miss Parker's fanciful Gothic vicarage and school.

LLANYBYDDER Dyfed SN5244
Village on B4337, 4 miles (6km) SW of Lampeter
Farming village which comes alive on the last Thursday of each month when its celebrated horse sale (reputedly the largest in Britain) attracts buyers from far and wide.

LLANYMYNECH Powys SJ2621
Village on A483, 6 miles (10km) S of Oswestry
Village on border, partly in England (border runs down main street). By a loop in the River Vyrnwy – picturesque stone bridge and canal aqueduct over river.

LLANYSTUMDWY Gwynedd SH4738
Village off A497, 2 miles (3km) W of Criccieth
Lleyn peninsula village in which statesman David Lloyd George grew up. He lived in cottage known as Highgate, which is open to the public and furnished in 19th-century style. Spent his last years at Ty Newydd. Village also contains memorial museum. A simple grave, designed by Sir Clough Williams-Ellis (of nearby Portmeirion fame), marks Lloyd George's resting place beside River Dwyfor.

LLAWHADEN Dyfed SN0617

Village off A40, 3 miles (5km) NW of Narberth

Village in Pembrokeshire lanes dominated by its castle (Cadw), the fortified palace home of the Bishops of St David's.

LLECHRYD Dyfed SN2143

Village on A484, 3 miles (5km) SE of Cardigan

Set in beautiful Vale of Teifi with old five-arched bridge over river. Popular spot with salmon and trout fishermen.

LLEYN PENINSULA Gwynedd

Peninsula between Caernarfon and Cardigan bays

The Lleyn peninsula – or to give it its correct Welsh spelling, Llyn – is a crooked finger of land about 25 miles (40km) long pointing southwest into the Irish Sea from Snowdonia. Parts of the peninsula remain bastions of the Welsh language, culture and traditions, while resorts such as Abersoch and Criccieth reflect the influences of tourism.

Although popular with visitors, Lleyn's coastline is essentially wild and unspoiled. The peninsula's sheltered coves and sandy beaches are, for the most part, hemmed in by windswept cliffs and rock-bound shores. This is especially true of the far west (the 'Land's End of North Wales') around Aberdaron, the mariners' graveyard of Porth Neigwl or Hell's Mouth, and the dramatic, remote and inaccessible shoreline near Trevor where mountains plunge into the sea. Inland, the peninsula – dotted with small villages and farmsteads – has a quiet rural character.

Many of Lleyn's most beautiful clifflands and beaches (such as Porth Dinllaen and Porth-oer, the latter better known as Whistling Sands) are protected through their ownership by the National Trust, while the coast between Llanbedrog in the south and Clynnog Fawr in the north is a designated Area of Outstanding Natural Beauty.

LLITHFAEN Gwynedd SH3543

Village on B4417, 4 miles (6km) NE of Nefyn

Village which allows access to Nant Gwrtheyrn, a 'ghost village' hidden away at the base of steep cliffs which has been revived as a Welsh language centre.

LLOWES Powys SO1941

Village on A438, 2 miles (3km) W of Hay-on-Wye

Church has two-faced Celtic Cross of St Meilig dating from 7th century. On a hillside to the southwest is Welsh chapel of Maesyronnen, possibly Wales's earliest.

LLWYNGWRIL Gwynedd SH5909

Village on A493, 6 miles (10km) N of Tywyn

Village on mountainous Cardigan Bay coast where Cader Idris meets the sea. 'New' church a replacement for ancient place of worship at nearby Llangelynin (see).

LLYN BRENIG Clwyd SH9756

Reservoir off B4501, 4 miles (6km) S of Bylchau

Moody waters of man-made Llyn Brenig cover the heather moorlands of windswept Mynydd Hiraethog. Reservoir opened in 1976 to help regulate flow of River Dee. Well-developed range of amenities – visitor centre, walks, picnic sites, sailing, fishing, bird-watching, archaeological trail. Smaller Alwen Reservoir close by, together with the conifers of the huge Clocaenog Forest.

LLYN BRIANNE Dyfed SN7948

Reservoir off A483, 11 miles (18km) NW of Llandovery

Giant reservoir created in wild, previously inaccessible hill country in the 1970s to supply Swansea with water. Lake, at the source of the River Towy, held back by huge rock-filled dam. 'New' road runs along eastern shores to link up with the Abergwesyn Pass to Tregaron. Area is the haunt of the rare red kite.

LLYN CELYN Gwynedd SH8740

Reservoir on A4212, 4 miles (6km) NW of Bala

Well-landscaped man-made lake created in 1960s to supply northeast Wales and northwest England. Lakeside memorial commemorates submerged chapel.

LLYN PADARN Gwynedd SH5761

Lake on A4086, immediately NE of Llanberis

Larger of Llanberis's two lakes. Well-developed range of leisure facilities at lakeside Padarn Country Park. Narrow-gauge Llanberis Lake Railway.

LLYWEL Powys SN8730

Hamlet on A40, 1 mile (2km) NW of Trecastle

On southern approach to military ranges of Mynydd Eppynt. Church contains cast of famous ancient stone with carvings from three periods (original now in the British Museum).

LOANHEAD Lothian NT2865

Town on A768, 6 miles (10km) S of Edinburgh

Town in economically troubled previous coal-mining area to the south of Edinburgh with the Pentland Hills to west.

Celtic cross in the church at Llowes.

The upper reaches of Loch Fyne.

LOCH CORUISK Highland (Skye) NG4820
Loch below the Cuillin Hills in SW Skye
Sinister and dramatic loch in the shadows of the Red Cuillins, accessible on foot from Glen Sligachan.

LOCH DOON Strathclyde NX4998
Loch/reservoir off A713, 4 miles (6km) S of Dalmellington
The level of the loch was raised 40ft (12m) for hydro-electricity in the 1930s and the remains of Doon Castle were dismantled from an island and rebuilt on the lochside.

LOCH EIL Highland NN0277
Loch in Lochaber district, NW of Fort William
Sea loch stretching west of Fort William through Lochaber, with fine views east to Ben Nevis. The traditional Road to the Isles ran this way.

LOCH FYNE Strathclyde NR9591
Sea loch in Argyll
Long sea loch with splendid scenery stretching from the Sound of Bute beyond Inveraray. Renowned for its herrings and kippers.

LOCH GARTEN Highland NJ9718
see Boat of Garten

LOCH KATRINE Central NN4409
Loch in the Trossachs, 6 miles (10m) NW of Aberfoyle
Beautiful loch and reservoir in mountainous country in the heart of the Trossachs. Vintage pleasure steamer conveys passengers from Trossachs pier down loch as there is no road access.

LOCH LEVEN Tayside NO1401
Loch E of Kinross
Loch noted for trout-fishing with several islands, including St Serf's, with the remains of an ancient priory, and Castle Island, with the ruins of 15th-century Loch Leven Castle, from which Mary Stuart escaped in 1568 after a year's imprisonment. The loch is a National Nature Reserve, internationally important for breeding and wintering wildfowl; includes Vane Farm RSPB reserve.

LOCH LINNHE Highland NM9354
Sea loch from Fort William to Mull
Long sea loch, stretching northeast from Oban to Fort William. Dramatic mountain scenery and views across the loch to Ardnamurchan.

LOCH LOMOND Strathclyde NS3598
Loch on border of Strathclyde and Central regions
Arguably Scotland's best-known loch, Loch Lomond is the largest expanse of freshwater in Britain and Scotland's third longest and third deepest loch, with a surface area of 27 square miles (70 sq km). Lying within easy reach of Glasgow and the heavily populated central belt, it is easily accessible to the huge numbers of visitors who flock here, attracted by the natural beauty of the loch, with its many wooded islands and splendid mountains to the north.

Fed by numerous small rivers and drained by the River Leven into the River Clyde, the loch supplies much of central Scotland's water supply. It holds many varieties of fish and is popular with anglers and water-sports enthusiasts who come to boat, sail and wind-surf. There is a National Nature Reserve, the wintering ground for geese and other wildfowl, and abundant wildlife along the shore, including red and roe deer, wild goats and a successful colony of escaped wallabies.

One of Scotland's best-known songs, 'The Bonnie Banks of Loch Lomond', was written by a homesick Jacobite in Carlisle gaol.

LOCH LONG Strathclyde NS2192
Sea loch running to Firth of Clyde
Narrow fjord-like sea loch, named after Viking long-ships which raided here, cutting deep from the Clyde estuary into the mountainous country around Arrochar.

LOCH MAREE Highland NG9570
Loch in Wester Ross, NW of Kinlochlewe
Beautiful inland loch with pine-covered islands surrounded by splendid peaks in the midst of renowned deer-stalking country.

LOCH MOIDART Highland NM6472
see Moidart

LOCH NESS Highland NH5023
Loch SW of Inverness
Possibly Scotland's most famous loch, running for 23 miles (37km) along Great Glen with steep hills on either side. Historically important route to west and part of Caledonian Canal system since the early 19th century. Most famous for the monster Nessie, first mentioned in the 7th-century *Life of St Colomba* and sighted at various times in the 20th century since 1932.

LOCH OF STRATHBEG Grampian NK0758
see Rattray Head

LOCH OF THE LOWES Borders NT2319
see St Mary's Loch

LOCH RANNOCH Tayside NN5557
Loch/reservoir W of Kinloch Rannoch
Highland loch and reservoir stretching west from Kinloch Rannoch with excellent stands of Caledonian Forest, composed of Scots pine, which originally covered much of Scotland.

LOCH SHIEL Highland NM8072
Loch SW of Glenfinnan
Long inland loch in wild and mountainous country with many Jacobite connections. Access by road limited.

LOCH TAY Tayside NN6838
see Tay, River

A gravestone at Lochaline.

LOCH TORRIDON Highland NG7560
Sea loch N of Shieldaig
Sea loch in awe-inspiring and sparsely inhabited landscape to the north of Shieldaig and the Applecross peninsula.

LOCH TUMMEL Tayside NN8259
Loch/reservoir on B8019, E of Tummel Bridge
Highland loch, widened by hydro-electric activity, stretching east from Tummel Bridge. Scenically renowned viewpoint at Queen's View, visited by Queen Victoria in 1866.

LOCHABER Highland
Historic region NW of Fort William
Ancient lordship centred on Fort William, extending from Loch Leven to Glen Garry. Includes Ben Nevis. Dominated by the Camerons of Lochiel, fervent Jacobite supporters.

LOCHALINE Highland NM6744
Village on A884, 19 miles (31km) SW of Strontian
Remote and isolated fishing settlement in beautiful surroundings on the Sound of Mull. Ruined Ardtornish Castle is near by. Ferry link to Mull.

LOCHAWE Strathclyde NN1227
Village on A85, 3 miles (5km) W of Dalmally
The River Awe drains this long and narrow loch through the dramatic Pass of Brander. Ruined Kilchurn Castle was built in 1440 and unroofed after the Jacobite Risings.

LOCHCARRON Highland NG8939
Village on A896, 22 miles (35km) SW of Achnasheen
Small holiday and touring centre in lovely position on Loch Carron, with good walking and tourist facilities.

LOCHEARNHEAD Central NN5823
Village on A85, 6 miles (10km) S of Killin
Scattered village in fine mountain scenery at the west end of Loch Earn, renowned as a boating and water-skiing holiday resort.

LOCHGELLY Fife NT1893
Town off A909, 7 miles (11km) SW of Glenrothes
Former mining town on the Fife coalfield, now in economic decline, although Lochgelly Centre provides theatre and sporting facilities.

LOCHGILPHEAD Strathclyde NR8688
Town on A83, 2 miles (3km) N of Ardrishaig
Originally a small fishing village which grew after the opening of the Crinan Canal in 1801. The 18th-century Kilmory Castle, set in pleasant gardens, now houses local government offices.

LOCHINDORB Highland NJ9736
Loch off A939, 8 miles (13km) N of Carrbridge
Loch north of Grantown-on-Spey, chiefly known for islanded ruins of Lochindorb Castle, the lair of the Wolf of Badenoch, third son of Robert II.

The Sugar Loaf double peak of Suilven.

LOCHINVAR Dumfries and Galloway NX6585
Loch off A702, 3 miles (5km) NE of Dalry
Mainly remarkable for its literary connections: the remains of Young Lochinvar's castle (of ballad fame) stands on an island in the loch.

LOCHINVER Highland NC0922
Village on A837, 12 miles (19km) W of Inchnadamph
Important white-fish port and holiday centre in sheltered natural harbour; main community in Assynt. It lies in rugged country dominated by the peaks of Suilven, Canisp and Quinag.

LOCHMABEN Dumfries and Galloway NY0882
Small town on A709, 8 miles (13km) NE of Dumfries
This royal burgh in rolling Annandale is thought to be the birthplace of Robert Bruce. Ruined 13th-century Lochmaben Castle stands on a promontory on Castle Loch; its masonry was used in building many of the town's houses. The loch is home to the rare freshwater vendace. Birthplace of William Jardine (1784–1843), founder of Jardine Matheson.

LOCHORE Fife NT1796
Town on B920, 3 miles (5km) N of Cowdenbeath
Former mining town where extensive land reclamation has created the Lochore Meadows Country Park, with sailing and watersports and other recreational amenities.

LOCHRANZA Strathclyde (Arran) NR9350
Village on A841, 11 miles (18km) NW of Brodick
Village on a sheltered, fertile bay in the north of Arran. The 16th-century ruins of Lochranza Castle stand on a promontory jutting into the loch. Summer ferry to Kintyre.

LOCHWINNOCH Strathclyde NS3559
Small town off A760, 12 miles (19km) SW of Paisley
A small residential town, once a bleaching and weaving centre, surrounded by country parks and leisure facilities, including the RSPB reserve in vast Clyde Muirshiel Regional Park. The park also includes Castle Semple Country Park, with its boating and fishing loch. Substantial remains of square 16th-century Barr Castle.

LOCKERBIE Dumfries and Galloway NY1381
Town off A74 (M), 15 miles (24km) NW of Gretna
A market town of redstone buildings serving an agricultural hinterland, founded in the 17th century and noted for its annual lamb sales. Roman fortifications near by on Birrenswark Hill. Lockerbie came to worldwide attention in December 1988 when wreckage from a sabotaged Boeing 747 fell in and around the town.

LOCKERIDGE Wiltshire SU1467
Village off A4, 3 miles (5km) W of Marlborough
A village with the occasional thatched cottage built from the local sarsens, very hard stones still found scattered over the nature reserve of Fyfield Down, at Piggle Dean by the A4, and at Lockeridge Dean.

LOCKINGTON Leicestershire SK4627
Village of A6, 1 mile (2km) E of Castle Donington
Secluded village near the Derbyshire and Nottinghamshire borders. The 14th-century church has notable monuments. Late 17th-century hall, altered in the 19th century, now offices.

LOCKS HEATH Hampshire SU5107
District off A27, 3 miles (5km) NW of Fareham
The heath was enclosed in 1866, and strawberries were grown on a large scale until the 1970s when the area started to fill with housing and industrial estates. Shopping centre built in 1980s.

LODDISWELL Devon SX7248
Village off B3194, 3 miles (5km) NW of Kingsbridge
This stone village's name is perhaps a corruption of Our Lady's Well – a holy well survives down in the valley. To the north is Blackdown Rings, an Iron Age hillfort with medieval motte and bailey castle added. Vineyard at Lilwell.

LODDON Norfolk TM3698
Small town off A146, 6 miles (10km) NW of Beccles
Once a thriving port on the Broads, Loddon now enjoys a rather more relaxed role as a boating centre. A charming marina has pleasure craft bobbing up and down on the River Chet, and the town, although expanding, has avoided being spoiled by uniform council houses. Hardley Flood is an area of flooded marsh providing an important waterfowl site.

LODE Cambridgeshire TL5362
Village off B1102, 6 miles (10km) NE of Cambridge
A willow-draped canal (lode) arrows through this village of thatch and white brick. Anglesey Abbey (National Trust) is a 12th-century priory with 18th-century gardens.

LODORE FALLS Cumbria NY2618
Waterfall near S end of Derwentwater
A popular beauty spot. Small cascades splash through rocks in the woods to the 40ft (12m) waterfall. Especially impressive after heavy rain.

LOE POOL (OR LOOE POOL OR THE LOE) Cornwall SW6424
Lake off B3304, SE of Porthleven
Lake created in the 13th century when a gravel bar formed across the mouth of the Cober estuary, cutting it off from the sea.

LOFTHOUSE North Yorkshire SE1073
Village off B6265, 6 miles (10km) NW of Pateley Bridge
The village, situated in the Nidd Valley, was a stronghold of early Methodism and has had a Methodist church for 200 years.

LOFTUS Cleveland NZ7218
Town on A174, 4 miles (6km) SE of Saltburn-by-the-Sea
A busy town lying near the coast. Once an important centre for alum manufacture, now more agricultural. A well-marked path leads to the dam and Loftus Mill.

LOGIERAIT Tayside NN9752
Village on A827, 4 miles (6km) SE of Pitlochry
Village near the junction of the rivers Tay and Tummel, with prehistoric stones and circles in the vicinity. A royal castle once stood here. Good examples of mortsafes in churchyard.

LONDESBOROUGH Humberside SE8645
Village off A163, 2 miles (3km) N of Market Weighton
This farming village was mentioned in Domesday Book and various regiments were stationed here in World War II.

LONDON Greater London TQ3079
City
No brief treatment of London can remotely do justice to the character and attractions of Britain's capital, one of the world's largest cities, with a history going back for close on 2,000 years. This entry is inevitably limited largely to the best-known sights, which means that much of genuine fascination is left out.

This entry covers Central London. Many areas of interest further out from the centre have their own individual entries. Central London fundamentally means two areas: the City of London and the City of Westminster, the two nuclei from which today's London has developed. Originally separate settlements along the north bank of the River Thames with open country between them, they expanded over the centuries and eventually joined up, but they are still separate administrative districts today. To them has to be linked a third area, on the opposite side of the river: the cultural enclave of the South Bank.

The Tower and St Paul's
The City of London, or simply 'the City', is Britain's financial capital and the place where the history of London began in Roman times (no evidence has yet been found of a pre-Roman settlement). Leadenhall Market leads a lively existence today at the heart of what was originally the Roman town.

The City's two most important visitor attractions are the Tower of London and St Paul's Cathedral. The Tower, with its long history of torture, misery and death, was begun by William the Conqueror after 1066 and the central keep is still much as the Normans left it. Around it are the massive battlements of subsequent centuries. Inside are the Crown Jewels in their imperial panoply, a superlative arms and armour collection, the headsman's sinister block and axe, and the almost equally sinister Tower ravens, without whom, legend has it, the Tower would fall. Close by is the 19th-century bulk of Tower Bridge and beyond it, the attractively redeveloped St Katharine's Dock with shops and a marina.

St Paul's, under its colossal dome, is the baroque masterpiece of Sir Christopher Wren, completed in 1710. Dizzyingly high up inside is the famous Whispering Gallery. Wren himself and Lord Nelson are buried in the crypt and there is an immense monument to the great Duke of Wellington. Not far away is the Museum of London, whose intriguing displays belie its drearily hideous exterior, with a good view of part of the city's old Roman wall. The Barbican Centre is a 1970s creation with a concert hall, theatres and art gallery.

Westminster and Trafalgar Square
At the heart of Westminster, begun by Edward the Confessor in the 11th century, is Westminster Abbey, Britain's most important church, where almost every monarch of England since William the Conqueror has been crowned. The ancient coronation chair with the Stone of Scone can be seen here, as well as the tombs and monuments of kings and queens and famous figures in British life: from Queen Elizabeth I and Mary, Queen of Scots, bitter enemies in life, to Sir Isaac Newton and David Livingstone, the two Pitts and Ernest Bevin. Great literary figures are commemorated in

Poets' Corner and near the west door is the grave of the Unknown Warrior.

Outside in Parliament Square are statues of distinguished statesmen, including Sir Winston Churchill, and across the road rises the vast 19th-century Gothic edifice of the Houses of Parliament (opening arrangements subject to change). At one end, 320ft (97m) high, is a London landmark, Big Ben, with its giant bell and enormous clock faces; each minute hand is 14ft (4.2m) long.

Whitehall leads away north past the palaces of the bureaucracy and the Cabinet War Rooms, where Churchill and his colleagues directed Britain's World War II effort, to the 17th-century Banqueting House, from which Charles I stepped out to his execution. At the Horse Guards opposite, cavalrymen and their horses stand sentry, to the clicking of tourist cameras.

Next comes Trafalgar Square, with Nelson's Column soaring up to its 17ft (5m) statue of the great naval hero. Below are the Landseer lions and an insatiable army of feedable pigeons. The National Gallery, with the notable Sainsbury Wing of 1991 by Robert Venturi, contains the country's premier old master art collection. The nearby National Portrait Gallery is well worth a visit.

Royal London

From Trafalgar Square, Admiralty Arch opens on to the Mall. Both are part of the Edwardian period development masterminded by Sir Aston Webb which turned this part of the city into an arena of pomp and circumstance. State processions leave Buckingham Palace along this route.

At the far end of the Mall, beyond the noble Queen Victoria Memorial, is the palace itself, the principal royal residence in London, essentially an imposing early 19th-century building by John Nash. The state rooms are open to the public (August to September) and the ceremonial changing of the guard is a major tourist draw.

The magnificent gold state coach and other stately equipages can be admired in the Royal Mews, with the royal horses and their trappings, while the Queen's Gallery is used for exhibitions of items from the royal art collection. South of the Mall there is satisfying strolling in St James's Park, with exotic birds on the lake and views of the surrounding buildings.

It is not a long walk from here to Westminster Cathedral, London's principal Roman Catholic church and another Edwardian creation, a Byzantine-style masterpiece in red brick by JF Bentley, completed in 1903. Further south, by the river, the Tate Gallery holds the nation's collections of British art and 20th-century art. The Turners are in the 1987 extension by Sir James Stirling.

Piccadilly to Harrods

North from the Mall, Piccadilly Circus is probably the best-known single location in the whole of London. Huge advertising signs blink and flash as the traffic grinds its way past Alfred Gilbert's magical statue of Eros, placed here in 1893 on its art nouveau pedestal. This is a crowded spot most of the time. The Criterion Brasserie's lavishly ornate 1870s décor has been handsomely restored and further along is an enjoyable fountain with rearing bronze horses by Rudy Weller. Inside the Edwardian shell of the Trocadero, the Guinness World of Records explores mind-boggling examples of the superlative, while singing wax figures from Madame Tussauds perform in Rock Circus in the frenetic London Pavilion complex.

Heading north from Piccadilly Circus, theatre-lined Shaftesbury Avenue penetrates the fleshpots of Soho (see), while Regent Street curves its way up to Liberty department store, one of London's most stylish emporiums, and on to the shops and crowds of Oxford Street. Westwards from Piccadilly Circus, Piccadilly itself takes a long straight course to Hyde Park Corner. On the way are the Royal Academy of Arts, home of prestigious art exhibitions, and the smart little shops of the Burlington Arcade, where running or whistling are frowned on by uniformed beadles. On the other side of the road, Fortnum and Mason is the capital's fashionable grocer and there are also grandly venerable boot-makers, hatters and wine merchants in St James's Street, beyond which is the Edwardian luxury of the Ritz hotel. Near by, the 18th-century luxury of Spencer House, restored at fabulous expense, is well worth seeing.

To the north lies fashionable Mayfair (see). Apsley House at Hyde Park Corner was the Duke of Wellington's London residence. Hyde Park itself covers over 350 acres (142ha). Further on to the west is the vast terracotta pile of Harrods, where 35,000 customers a day press through the portals of the most famous shop in the world. Further west still are the museums in South Kensington (see).

Covent Garden and the British Museum

To the east of Piccadilly Circus, the Coliseum is one of London's two major opera and ballet houses. The other, the majestic Royal Opera House itself, is further east still, in Covent Garden. The old Covent Garden market area has been transformed into an enjoyable piazza with shops, cafés and street entertainers.

North from here is Holborn (see) and beyond it is another leading visitor attraction, the British Museum, a collection of treasures and antiquities from all over the world. About four million people a year come to see some of the four million objects on display. Guided tours offer a manageable introduction. To the north lies Bloomsbury (see) and to the west is Marylebone (see) and the waxworks of Madame Tussauds.

The South Bank

Psychologically if not geographically part of Central London is the cultural complex on the south bank of the Thames near Waterloo Station. A legacy of the 1951 Festival of Britain, it is dominated by the Royal Festival Hall, the capital's principal modern concert hall. Close by are the Hayward Gallery, persuasively claimed to be the ugliest building in London, and the Museum of the Moving Image, with hi-tech treatment of films and television. On the other side of Waterloo Bridge, the Royal National Theatre has three auditoriums. The National Film Theatre and the much older Old Vic Theatre are not far away.

(For other areas close to the centre of London, see Bayswater; Belgravia; Chelsea; Kensington; Paddington; Pimlico; St John's Wood.)

LONDON APPRENTICE Cornwall SX0050
Village on B3273, 2 miles (3km) S of St Austell
In a wide wooded valley. The village was apparently named after its pub.

LONDON COLNEY Hertfordshire TL1803
Suburb off M25, 3 miles (5km) SE of St Albans
Modest commuter town on the River Colne with Bowmans Open Farm and De Havilland planes in the Mosquito Aircraft Museum (limited opening).

LONDONTHORPE Lincolnshire SK9537
Hamlet off B6403, 3 miles (5km) NE of Grantham
Clustered farms and 1849 estate cottages. Arch with Brownlow arms; 13th-century church with 1852 north aisle and Victorian chancel.

LONG ASHTON Avon ST5470
Village off B3128, 3 miles (5km) SW of Bristol
Big village just outside Bristol, with huge park formed from the grounds of Ashton Court (house not open).

LONG BENNINGTON Lincolnshire SK8344
Village off A1, 7 miles (11km) NW of Grantham
Large village bypassed by A1, with one long straggling street of Georgian houses on old Great North road; church at south end.

LONG BREDY Dorset SY5690
see Littlebredy

LONG BUCKBY Northamptonshire SP6267
Village on B5385, 5 miles (8km) NE of Daventry
Earthworks of 12th-century castle, 13th-century and later ironstone church, older houses near market place. Railway station, canal wharf, M1 motorway links.

LONG COMPTON Warwickshire SP2832
Village on A3400, 4 miles (6km) NW of Chipping Norton
Once notorious for witchcraft, the village occupies a secluded valley in the northern Cotswolds, with old stone and thatched cottages and a unique two-storey lych-gate.

Unusual lych-gate at Long Compton.

LONG CRENDON Buckinghamshire SP6908
Village on B4011, 2 miles (3km) NW of Thame
Delightful half-timbered and thatched showpiece, where needle-making was once the cottage industry. Now a sought-after Oxford commuter village. Many medieval cruck houses. Courthouse (National Trust, limited opening) goes back to the 14th century, when it was perhaps a wool store. Stately church. Medieval mystery plays held every year at Easter.

Courthouse at Long Crendon.

LONG EATON Derbyshire SK4933
Town off M1, 9 miles (14km) E of Derby
A Trent Valley market town which boomed in the mid-19th century with the arrival of railways and machine-lace factories escaping restrictive working practices in Nottingham.

LONG HANBOROUGH Oxfordshire SP4114
Village off A4095, 5 miles (8km) NE of Witney
On the fringe of the Blenheim Palace estate, the village's railway station is the unlikely location for the Oxford Bus Museum.

LONG ITCHINGTON Warwickshire SP4165
Village on A423, 2 miles (3km) N of Southam
The birthplace of St Wulfstan, beside the River Itchen, preserves its venerable houses and rewarding medieval church. The Grand Union Canal passes near by.

LONG LAWFORD Warwickshire SP4776
Village off A428, 2 miles (3km) W of Rugby
Western suburb of Rugby notable for rare example of church of 1839 with its original furnishings intact.

LONG MARSTON North Yorkshire SE5051
Village on B1224, 7 miles (11km) W of York
This is the site of the battle of Marston Moor on 4th July

1644. Cromwell stayed at Long Marston Hall on the eve of battle.

LONG MARSTON Warwickshire SP1548
Village off A46, 5 miles (8km) SW of Stratford-upon-Avon
The story goes that Charles II, disguised as a servant to assist his escape after the Battle of Worcester, was scolded for incompetence in the kitchen of King's Lodge.

LONG MELFORD Suffolk TL8646
Small town off A134, 3 miles (5km) N of Sudbury
Running 3 miles (5km) along an old Roman road, Long Melford High Street starts at the 1792 bridge, and continues past the green to the stately turreted gatehouse of Tudor Melford Hall (National Trust). Kentwell Hall lies at the northern end of the village. There is also a haunted inn, an Elizabethan hospital, and an especially beautiful church.

LONG MYND, THE Shropshire SO4194
Hill off A49, W of Church Stretton
This long massif of high and lonely moorland, mainly National Trust land, rises to 1,700ft (510m). Bleak and dangerous in winter, it is splendid walking country in good weather. The prehistoric Portway runs along its western side, and a feature of the eastern edge is a series of dramatic ravines, including the popular Cardingmill Valley (see Church Stretton).

LONG SLEDDALE Cumbria SD5299
Scenic area off A6, NW of Garnett Bridge
A beautiful valley, Kilnstones was inhabited by monks and the first St Mary's Church was built in the 13th century.

LONG STRATTON Norfolk TM1992
Village on A140, 10 miles (16km) S of Norwich
The village church is one of only two in England to have a Sexton's wheel (a device for working out holy days).

LONG SUTTON Lincolnshire TF4322
Small town off A17, 9 miles (14km) N of Wisbech
Grand Norman and medieval church with highest, oldest and best-preserved lead spire in England. Georgian houses in market town. Butterfly and Falconry Centre.

LONG SUTTON Somerset ST4625
Village on B3165, 2 miles (3km) SW of Somerton
Stone village with a central green and a handsome church of about 1490; its tower, wooden screen and pulpit are all of that date. Contrasting simple 1717 Quaker Meeting House.

LONG WHATTON Leicestershire SK4823
Village on B5401, 4 miles (6km) NW of Loughborough
One long street, with several timber-framed buildings and 18th-century brick. Mainly Victorian Whatton House (not open) has gardens with limited opening in summer.

LONG WITTENHAM Oxfordshire SU5493
Village off B4016, 3 miles (5km) NE of Didcot
Delightful cottages and a fine church are attractions of this village below the Sinodun Hills. Another is the Pendon Museum's collection of intriguing models.

LONGBENTON Tyne and Wear NZ2668
Town on A1058, 3 miles (4km) N of Newcastle
Mostly 1930s housing estates, although the original village is still discernible. The 18th-century manor house has been converted into flats.

LONGBOROUGH Gloucestershire SP1729
Village off A424, 3 miles (5km) N of Stow-on-the-Wold
There is much fine medieval work in the church of this Evenlode Valley village, which abounds in unpretentious Cotswold cottages.

LONGBRIDGE West Midlands SP0077
Town off A38, on SW outskirts of Birmingham
Suburban housing surrounds huge car factory started by Herbert Austin in 1905. Methodist church of 1967 is example of pioneering modern church design.

LONGBRIDGE DEVERILL Wiltshire ST8640
Village on A350, 3 miles (5km) S of Warminster
Stone almshouses of 1655 and a big memorial to the builder of Longleat, 1580, are features of this village on the River Wylye.

Almshouses at Longbridge Deverill.

LONGBURTON Dorset ST6412
Village on A352, 3 miles (5km) S of Sherborne
The 17th-century stone cottages and later developments are rather dominated by the main road. Large 17th-century monuments in the church.

LONGCOMBE Devon SX8359
Hamlet off A385, 2 miles (3km) E of Totnes
Tiny hamlet scattered down the combe to the River Dart, with its mill right down on the creek.

LONGDENDALE Greater Manchester
Valley of the River Etherow, tributary of the Goyt
This valley once marked the northern boundary of the Royal Forest of the Peak. Five reservoirs supply water to Manchester.

LONGDON Hereford and Worcester SO8336
Village on B4211, 4 miles (6km) NW of Tewkesbury
On rising ground at the edge of the empty Longdon Marsh. The village has a very elegant 18th-century church.

LONGDON UPON TERN Shropshire SJ6215
Village on B5063, 3 miles (5km) NW of Wellington
The scattered village on the edge of the Weald Moors has a notable monument to the canal age – the aqueduct that carried the now-vanished Shrewsbury Canal. It is preserved as Thomas Telford's first attempt to replace bulky masonry with a light cast-iron trough, the technology he later used for the spectacular Pontcysyllte Aqueduct near Llangollen.

LONGFIELD Kent TQ6069
Town on B260, 4 miles (6km) SW of Gravesend
Modern development running north from the railway station surrounds older centre with 13th-century church restored in Victorian times

LONGFORD Derbyshire SK2137
Village off A52, 9 miles (14km) W of Derby
Pretty rural village and Tudor hall (not open), rebuilt in 1720 and 1942, in parkland on the line of a Roman road linking Derby to Rocester.

LONGFORGAN Tayside NO2929
Village on A90, 6 miles (10km) W of Dundee
Village between Sidlaw Hills and Firth of Tay. Near by is Huntly Castle, on a rocky outcrop, a 15th-century L-plan tower house with considerable later additions.

LONGFORMACUS Borders NT6957
Village off A6105, 6 miles (10km) W of Duns
Remote village on the southern edge of the Lammermuir Hills. Excellent moorland walking near by and access to the Southern Upland Way.

LONGFRAMLINGTON Northumberland NU1300
Village on A697, 5 miles (8km) E of Rothbury
Home of Museum of Northumbrian Music, devoted to the Northumbrian smallpipe. Nearby Brinkburn Priory (English Heritage) houses modern sculpture.

LONGHORSLEY Northumberland NZ1494
Village on A697, 6 miles (10km) NW of Morpeth
Dormitory village with a 16th-century pele tower. Linden Hall, an early 19th-century manor house, is now a hotel.

LONGNEWTON Cleveland NZ3816
Village on A66, 4 miles (6km) W of Stockton-on-Tees
Modern housing mixed with older, more established properties. Area linked with the Vane family, who developed Seaham Harbour and mine.

LONGNIDDRY Lothian NT4476
Village on A198, 3 miles (5km) SW of Aberlady
Village inland from Firth of Forth, near which stands Gosford House, an 18th-century mansion designed partly by Robert Adam and the seat of the Earls of Wemyss.

LONGNOR Shropshire SJ4800
Village off A49, 8 miles (13km) S of Shrewsbury
Timber-framed Moat House is among interesting houses adjoining the elegant Longnor Hall (1670). Appealing 13th-century church has good 18th-century fittings.

LONGNOR Staffordshire SK0864
Small town on B5053, 6 miles (10km) SE of Buxton
The small grey town between the rivers Manifold and Dove is surrounded by moorland. St Bartholomew's is a classical church of 1780 with a Venetian east window, but it preserves a carved Norman font from its predecessor. The town's old character survives in the cobbled Chapel Street, and a craft centre now occupies the market hall of 1873.

LONGPARISH Hampshire SU4344
Village on B3048, 3 miles (5km) SW of Whitchurch
Runs along the River Test, rural and low-lying with many thatched cottages.

LONGRIDGE Lancashire SD6037
Town on B6243, 7 miles (11km) NE of Preston
Situated at the foot of Longridge Fell from where there are some superb views over the valleys of the Loud and Ribble. Stone-quarrying was important, and several civic buildings in Preston and the Liverpool Docks are built using Longridge stone. Most of the houses date from the time when Longridge was developing as a cotton-spinning town.

LONGSDON Staffordshire SJ9654
Village on A53, 2 miles (3km) SW of Leek
Village on the fringe of the Staffordshire moorlands with a notable Edwardian church. Near by, in the Churnet Valley, is Deep Hayes Country Park.

LONGSHAW ESTATE Derbyshire SK2679
Scenic area off A625, 7 miles (11km) SW of Sheffield
Longshaw Country Park and visitor centre (National Trust) in Peak District, with dramatic views, moorland walks and three-day sheepdog trials in early September.

LONGSTOWE Cambridgeshire TL3054
Village on B1046, 9 miles (14km) NW of Royston
The High Street (1 mile/2km long) leads to Longstowe Hall, an Elizabethan house (extended 1880, not open). A string of lakes run through nearby woods.

LONGTHORPE Cambridgeshire TL1698
Village off A47, in W Peterborough
Longthorpe Tower (English Heritage) is a 14th-century fortified manor house with superb wall-paintings. The upper storey is an art gallery. Near by was a large Roman fortress.

LONGTON Staffordshire SJ9043
Town of Stoke-on-Trent
Small potteries still abound in utilitarian streets, together with the interesting Gladstone Pottery Museum and major firms offering factory tours.

LONGTOWN Cumbria NY3768
Small town on A7, 8 miles (13km) N of Carlisle
The village has long claimed a connection with King Arthur. In the churchyard is the gravestone of Archie Armstrong, jester to Charles I.

LONGTOWN Hereford and Worcester SO3228
Village off A465, 5 miles (8km) W of Pontrilas
Beside the River Monnow in the remote Olchon Valley stone cottages straggle away from ruins of a medieval castle (English Heritage).

LONGVILLE IN THE DALE Shropshire SO5493
Hamlet on B4371, 6 miles (10km) E of Church Stretton
On Wenlock Edge above Longville is Wilderhope Manor (National Trust), an isolated Elizabethan manor house with fine ceiling plasterwork, now a youth hostel.

LONGWORTH Oxfordshire SU3999
Village off A415, 7 miles (11km) W of Abingdon
This village overlooking the upper Thames Valley has a fine medieval church adorned with some distinguished Victorian and Edwardian craft work.

LOOE, EAST AND WEST Cornwall SX2553
Town on A387, 7 miles (11km) S of Liskeard
On both sides of the mouth of the river, joined by a big bridge. East Looe is the famous part, with little stone houses so densely packed that there are no gardens. The streets are much too narrow for cars. Tumbling picturesque green cliffs, and a little sandy bay. West Looe is mostly residential and Victorian.

LOOSE Kent TQ7552
Village on A229, 1 mile (2km) S of Maidstone
Charming place of half-timbered and tile-hung cottages clustered on to steep hillsides above the River Loose. Wool House (15th century) is owned by the National Trust.

LOPHAM, NORTH AND SOUTH Norfolk TM0382
Villages on B1113, 5 miles (8km) NW of Diss
These neighbouring villages have a Fen with the rare great raft spider, and the 'Lopham wonders' — a stile-shaped tree, and an ox's hoofprint in a stone.

LOPPINGTON Shropshire SJ4729
Village on B4397, 3 miles (5km) W of Wem
Mellow old village with cottages in timber-frame and brick and a church with fine 17th-century roofs installed after Civil War damage.

LORNE Strathclyde
Historic region in Argyll
An ancient and beautiful district on the west coast between Loch Leven and Loch Melfort, bounded by Glen Etive to the east, with Oban being the major town. Lynn of Lorne lies between the island of Lismore and the mainland, with wide views south down Firth of Lorne. This was once all Campbell country; the eldest son of the Dukes of Argyll carries the title Marquis Lorne.

LORTON, LOW AND HIGH Cumbria NY1525
Villages on B5292, 4 miles (6km) SE of Cockermouth
The villages have retained their traditional character and most of the houses are 150 to 300 years old. Both George Fox, the founder of the Quaker movement, and John Wesley, the Methodist, have preached here. There is a 1,000-year-old yew tree which was immortalised in Wordsworth's poem *Yew Trees*.

LOSELEY HOUSE Surrey SU9847
Mansion off B3000, 2 miles (3km) N of Godalming
Magnificent Tudor manor house built in 1562 with mellow old stones quarried from Waverley Abbey. Centre of a farming estate famed for luxury dairy products.

LOSSIEMOUTH Grampian NJ2370
Small town on A941, 5 miles (8km) N of Elgin
Fishing port and trim town which doubles as seaside resort. Long sandy beaches, good for dolphin-spotting. The Lossiemouth Fishing and Community Museum tells the local history, including a section on Ramsay MacDonald (1866–1937), Britain's first Labour Prime Minister, who was born in the town. Near by is an important RAF base, established here because of excellent light and low rainfall.

LOSTWITHIEL Cornwall SX1059
Town on A390, 5 miles (8km) SE of Bodmin
Now a very small town. Pretty 14th-century spire on the church. Local museum. Restormel Castle (English Heritage), in ruins but with fine 12th- to 13th-century shell keep, is to the north.

LOUGHBOROUGH Leicestershire SK5319
Town on A6, 10 miles (16km) N of Leicester
An important educational and industrial centre, Loughborough is surrounded by Charnwood Forest's pleasant woodlands and craggy granite outcrops. The large 14th-century church, heavily restored in the 1860s, is next door to the Old Rectory, with its local history collection (limited opening). The copper-capped carillon tower in Queen's Park symbolises the town's link with bells. John Taylor's is the largest working bell foundry complex in the world, with a fascinating museum.

Near by, the Great Central steam railway provides scenic rides to Leicester's outskirts. In 1841, travel pioneer Thomas Cook brought his first excursion from Leicester to a temperance meeting.

Each November, Loughborough's three-day street fair, held since 1221, takes over the market place. Tree-lined walks surround the boys' grammar school, founded 1530 and revived in 1848. In 1850, the girls' grammar school opened, the first in the country. Loughborough's pioneering college of advanced technology became a university in 1966, incorporating the former college of education, its courses complemented by the adjoining College of Art and Design and Loughborough College.

Brush Electrical Engineering, Fisons Pharmaceuticals, 3M Health Care, and Ladybird Books are among the town's major firms.

LOUGHOR West Glamorgan SS5798
Town on A484, 6 miles (10km) NW of Swansea
Industrial town whose ruined castle (Cadw) guards the mouth of River Loughor. At site of fording point originally fortified by Romans.

LOUGHTON Buckinghamshire SP8337
Village in SW part of Milton Keynes
Smart 1980s housing in Milton Keynes suburb. Old village church and green. Loughton Valley Park with Bradwell Abbey remains and Roman villa garden.

LOUGHTON Essex TQ4296
Town on A121, 2 miles (3km) NW of Chigwell
Between the River Roding and Epping Forest (see). Forest information centre organises guided walks. Loughton Camp is a rewarding viewpoint. Victorian churches.

LOUND Suffolk TM5099
Village off A12, 5 miles (8km) NW of Lowestoft
A pleasant village centred around a duck pond. St John the Baptist's Church is mainly 13th century.

LOUTH Lincolnshire TF3287
Town off A16, 14 miles (23km) S of Grimsby
Approaching this unspoilt Georgian market town from the Lincolnshire Wolds, a designated Area of Outstanding National Beauty, travellers glimpse the crocketed spire of St James' Church peeping up from the final folds of the Wolds as they flatten towards the coast.

The splendid spire, said to be the tallest parish church spire in England, was added 1501–15 to the church completed in 1441, reaching a height of 295ft (90m). Wool wealth paid for the church, and Louth still serves a wide rural area with a weekly cattle market and popular general markets. The imposing 1850s town hall is close by. Perhaps the finest red-brick Georgian buildings are on Westgate, where the earlier Wheatsheaf is one of several ancient inns serving the town. Sketches by 19th-century local artist Bennett Hubbard are on show in the local museum.

In 1920, the River Lud caused devastation with a flash flood, the height of which is noted on the 1750s former mill beside the bridge. The river's normally peaceful course through the attractive Hubbards Hills valley at the edge of town makes this a popular spot for paddling and picnics.

LOVE CLOUGH Lancashire SD8127
Village on A682, immediately SW of Dunnockshaw
Small village built around the main road from Burnley to Rawtenstall, surrounded by hills, in popular walking country.

LOVERSALL South Yorkshire SK5798
Village on A60, 3 miles (5km) S of Doncaster
The small, rural village has an attractive 12th-century church with two pairs of misericords in the chancel which came from Roche Abbey.

LOW CATTON Humberside SE7053
Village off A166, 1 mile (2km) S of Stamford Bridge
A tranquil village on the banks of the River Derwent. The cast-iron lampstands in the lane outside the church commemorate the Diamond Jubilee of Queen Victoria.

LOW HAM Somerset ST4321
see Ham

LOW LORTON Cumbria NY1525
see Lorton

LOW NEWTON-BY-THE-SEA Northumberland NU2424
Hamlet off B1340, NE of Embleton
On a sheltered bay with a long stretch of sandy beach and dunes. The little village is mostly owned by the National Trust.

LOWDHAM Nottinghamshire SK6646
Village on A6097, 7 miles (11km) NE of Nottingham
At the busy crossroads of the Nottingham–Newark and Fosse Way–Doncaster roads. The spacious church stands apart from the village, across the beck.

LOWER ARLEY Hereford and Worcester SO7680
see Arley

LOWER ASHTON Devon SX8484
see Ashton

LOWER BASILDON Berkshire SU6078
see Basildon

LOWER BEEDING West Sussex TQ2227
Village on A279, 4 miles (6km) SE of Horsham
Village scattered loosely about crossroads on the edge of St Leonard's forest. Leonardslee Gardens with outstanding collection of rhododendrons, azaleas and camellias is near by.

LOWER BENEFIELD Northamptonshire SP9988
see Benefield

LOWER BRAILES Warwickshire SP3039
Village on B4035, 3 miles (5km) SE of Shipston on Stour
On the edge of the Cotswolds, Lower Brailes has interesting old houses and an unexpectedly imposing church, known as 'the cathedral of the Feldon'.

LOWER BROADHEATH Hereford and Worcester SO8157
Village on B4204, 3 miles (5km) NW of Worcester
The Firs, the small cottage where Sir Edward Elgar was born in 1857, houses scores, letters and other memorabilia; it is open to public.

LOWER BROCKHAMPTON Hereford and Worcester SO6856
see Brockhampton

LOWER CANADA Avon ST3558
see Canada

LOWER DICKER East Sussex TQ5510
see Dicker

LOWER EYTHORNE Kent TR2849
see Eythorne

LOWER GRAVENHURST Bedfordshire TL1035
see Gravenhurst

LOWER HALSTOW Kent TQ8567
Village off A2, 4 miles (6km) NW of Sittingbourne
Little place amid orchards facing a creek on the Medway, with an ancient church separated from the estuary by a dyke.

LOWER HARDRES Kent TR1552
Village off B2068, 3 miles (5km) S of Canterbury
Pleasant, small village on the downs south of Canterbury, with a humble village church of the 1830s.

LOWER HARTWELL Buckinghamshire SP7912
Hamlet off A418, 2 miles (3km) W of Aylesbury
Hartwell House, now a luxurious hotel with 18th-century landscaped grounds, sheltered the exiled Louis XVIII during the French Revolution. Church restored in the 1980s.

LOWER HEYFORD Oxfordshire SP4824
Village on B4030, 6 miles (10km) W of Bicester
Ancient bridge over River Cherwell leads to small village with interesting old church. Nearby Rousham House (limited opening) has superb interior and impressive grounds.

LOWER KINGSWOOD Surrey TQ2453
Village on A217, 2 miles (3km) N of Reigate
Village strung along a main road with an unusual Byzantine-style church with a separate bell-tower built in 1892. Interior of coloured marble, gold mosaic ceiling in apse.

LOWER NITON Isle of Wight SZ5076
see Niton

LOWER PEOVER Cheshire SJ7474
Village on B5081, 6 miles (10km) E of Northwich
The Warren de Tabley Arms, now known as the Bells of Peover, built in 1569, is said to be haunted by George Bell, landlord and brewer in 1871. The church was founded in 1269 and is of Cheshire 'magpie' construction with a Norman sandstone tower. A picturesque village.

LOWER PICKWICK Wiltshire ST8670
Village on A4, immediately NW of Corsham
A pretty stone village with many cottages and a handsome 17th-century stone manor house (not open). Underground Quarry Centre (see Corsham)

LOWER QUINTON Warwickshire SP1847
Village off B4632, 5 miles (8km) SW of Stratford-upon-Avon
Imposing church with rich medieval interior, historic College Arms pub and pleasant old houses lie beneath the prominent Meon Hill.

LOWER SLAUGHTER Gloucestershire SP1622
see Slaughter

LOWER SWELL Gloucestershire SP1725
Village on B4068, 1 mile (2km) W of Stow-on-the-Wold
The village's bid to become a watering-place was unsuccessful, but it can boast superb Norman carvings in its church.

LOWER UPNOR Kent TQ7570
see Upnor

LOWER WEARE Somerset ST4053
Village on A38, 3 miles (5km) W of Cheddar
A failed medieval new town, now very small. Ambleside Bird Gardens have tropical birds.

LOWER WINCHENDON Buckinghamshire SP7312
Village off A418, 4 miles (6km) NE of Thame
Picturesque village on the River Thame. Curious church clock. Nether Winchendon House (limited opening), altered about 1800, is an early example of Gothic Revival.

LOWESTOFT Suffolk TM5493
Town on A12, 38 miles (61km) NE of Ipswich
Like many towns and villages on the East Anglian coast, Lowestoft owes its early wealth to the fishing industry. This has declined in recent years, although indications of former activity are still very much in evidence along the dockside and buildings. The *Lydia Eva* steam drifter in Lowestoft Harbour is one of 3,000 similar vessels that came to Lowestoft for herrings. The quayside has a dry dock and a small shipyard. The outer harbour is used by the Yacht Club and the RNLI lifeboat.

Lowestoft is an excellent place for a holiday. Near by is the lovely Oulton Broad which offers a range of watersports, Pleasurewood Hills American Theme Park, and a variety of piers and pavilions for entertainment. Lowestoft Ness is the most easterly point of the British Isles and is a wild and windswept place frequented by birds.

The town is in two halves, divided by Lake Lothing, which was dug for peat. The old town, to the north, consists of a jumble of Georgian houses crammed along the sides of the steep cobbled streets called The Scores. These were much damaged in World War II.

LOWESWATER Cumbria NY1221
Lake on B5289, 6 miles (10km) S of Cockermouth
The lake, 160 acres (65ha) in size, lies in the Buttermere Valley and is National Trust owned. Rich plant life creates good habitat for waterbirds. The scattered hamlet of Loweswater looks over Crummock to Buttermere; it is said to be one of the region's loveliest views.

LOWICK Northamptonshire SP9780
Village on A6116, 2 miles (3km) NW of Thrapston
Lord Mordaunt, 17th-century owner of Drayton House (limited opening), secluded in the nearby park, was suspected in the Gunpowder Plot. Medieval church with monuments.

LOWICK Northumberland NU0139
Village on B6353, 7 miles (11km) N of Wooler
A cottage on the main street is built on the site of the secret meeting place of Scottish Presbyterians. Local farmers held 'hirings' on the common every year for labourers.

LOWTHER Cumbria NY5323
Hamlet off A6, 4 miles (6km) S of Penrith
Home of the Lowther family from 1283. They lived originally at Lowther Hall, much of which was burnt down in 1720, until Lowther Castle was built in the early 19th century. Lowther village was designed in 1780s by the Adam brothers. 'Hughie' Lowther, 5th Earl of Lonsdale, instituted the Lonsdale Belt, was first president of the Automobile Association and clearly had a passion for yellow!

LOWTHORPE Humberside TA0860
Village off A166, 4 miles (6km) NE of Great Driffield
Elongated village on Holderness plain. The chancel of St Martin's Church, dating from the 13th century, is open to the sky.

LOXWOOD West Sussex TQ0331
Village on B2133, 5 miles (8km) NW of Billingshurst
Pleasant little village off the beaten track with a pond, shops and pub next to the church at a road junction. Associated with John Sirgood, a preacher who founded the religious sect of the Christian Dependents here in the 1850s; they were nicknamed 'Cokelers' as they were assumed to drink cocoa at their meetings. Their chapel and burial ground can be seen in Spy Lane.

LUBENHAM Leicestershire SP7087
Village on A427, 2 miles (3km) W of Market Harborough
Lying beside the River Welland which forms the Northamptonshire border, Lubenham has an 18th-century manor house, the Coach and Horses inn of 1700 and a medieval church, with complete 1812 box pews and pulpit.

LUCCOMBE Somerset SS9144
Village off A39, 2 miles (3km) SE of Porlock
A little Exmoor village with thatched cottages and a surprisingly large medieval church. Horner, a hamlet to the northwest, has idyllic cottages and a little packhorse bridge.

LUCCOMBE VILLAGE Isle of Wight SZ5879
Village off A3055, 1 mile (2km) S of Shanklin
Not really a village, only a few large houses in the Undercliff. Just to the south is Luccombe Chine, narrows with more than 200 steps down to the sea.

LUCKINGTON Wiltshire ST8383
Village off B4040, 7 miles (11km) SW of Malmesbury
Stone village with several small Georgian houses, and Luckington Court, early 18th century, whose formal gardens are open.

LUCTON Hereford and Worcester SO4364
Village on B4362, 5 miles (8km) NW of Leominster
Small village below wooded hills of the Croft Castle estate, notable for Lucton School (1708), a superb Queen Anne house.

LUDDENDEN West Yorkshire SE0426
Village off A646, 2 miles (3km) E of Mytholmroyd
Unspoilt village of old millstone grit cottages at the bottom of steep-sided valley of the River Ludd. The valley had a thriving textile industry throughout the 19th century, from households to mills. At the end of the valley is Luddenden Foot, where the River Ludd joins the River Calder.

LUDDESDOWN Kent TQ6766
Hamlet off A227, 5 miles (8km) S of Gravesend
Hamlet in wooded hilly country with an ancient manor house of about 1200. Holly Hill viewpoint near by and, to the south, a church and the deserted village of Dode.

LUDDINGTON Warwickshire SP1652
Village off B439, 3 miles (5km) SW of Stratford-upon-Avon
There is a strong tradition that William Shakespeare and Anne Hathaway were married in the original church here. Unfortunately, neither church nor registers survive.

LUDGERSHALL Wiltshire SU2650
Village on A342, 7 miles (11km) NW of Andover
Village with the earthworks of a 12th-century castle (English Heritage) and a big medieval cross. Large medieval church with 17th-century tower.

LUDGVAN Cornwall SW5033
Village on B3309, 2 miles (3km) NE of Penzance
Old stone cottages around a square and a fine granite church tower. At Dinas, an Iron Age hillfort to the northwest, is Roger's Tower, an 18th-century folly.

LUDHAM Norfolk TG3818
Village on A1062, 5 miles (8km) E of Hoveton
Picturesque rows of thatched cottages stand next to 18th-century houses around the market place and medieval St Catherine's Church. A reminder that Ludham is on the Broads can be seen at How Hill in Boardman's Mill Windpump. Three miles (5km) away are the romantic ruins of St Benet's Abbey by the River Bure, while restful Womack Water lies near by.

LUDLOW Shropshire SO5174
Town off A49, 24 miles (39km) S of Shrewsbury
Ludlow is one of England's best-preserved medieval and Georgian towns. Its Norman castle, extensively enlarged during the Middle Ages, stands in a strong position on a hill bounded by rivers. The keep and the unique round nave of the chapel survive from the Norman period, together with a range of later state apartments. St Laurence's near by, a monument to wool-trading prosperity, is a magnificent 15th-century church, its tower rising above the town. The poet AE Housman is buried in the churchyard.

Timber-framed buildings abound in the narrow streets of the old centre, their elaborate decoration culminating in the famous Feathers hotel in Corve Street. By contrast, Broad Street and Mill Street are gracious 18th-century thoroughfares, demonstrating a wide variety of Georgian architectural styles.

It is worth walking to the bottom of Broad Street to reach the 15th-century bridge over the River Teme and the fascinating mix of buildings in the suburb of Ludford beyond. The story of Ludlow and its buildings is set out in the museum in the 18th-century Buttercross at the top of Broad Street.

LUGAR Strathclyde NS5921
Village on A70, 2 miles (3km) NE of Cumnock
Birthplace of William Murdoch (1754–1839), founder of the gas-light industry, who conducted experiments in a cave near Lugar Water.

LUGWARDINE Hereford and Worcester SO5541
Village on A438, 3 miles (5km) E of Hereford
Looks across to Hereford from its attractive position on hills above confluence of rivers Frome and Lugg. Medieval bridge over River Lugg.

LULLINGSTONE Kent TQ5264
Site off A225, 1 mile (2km) SW of Eynsford
Church, 18th-century castle and Roman villa in a 600 acre (243ha) park by the River Darent, where it passes through the North Downs. The small flint-built church displays some very grand monuments while the Roman villa, occupied from the 1st to the 5th centuries, incorporates a Christian chapel, unique in Britain. There are waymarked walks in the park and information and displays at the visitor centre.

LULLINGTON East Sussex TQ5302
Hamlet off A27, 4 miles (6km) NE of Sleaford
Tiny place above Cuckmere Valley, with a minute church on the hillside at the end of a brick path, the surviving chancel of a larger building.

LULLINGTON Somerset ST7851
Village off B3090, 3 miles (5km) N of Frome
Picture-postcard village, largely rebuilt in the later 19th century in deliberately picturesque fashion. Norman church with elaborate doorway and font.

LULSGATE BOTTOM Avon ST5165
Hamlet on A38, 7 miles (11km) SW of Bristol
Home of Bristol Airport, a World War II airfield converted for civil use in the 1950s, now a regional airport.

LULWORTH COVE Dorset
see West Lulworth

LUMBUTTS West Yorkshire SD9523
Hamlet off A646, 1 mile (2km) SE of Todmorden
The village was a product of the Industrial Revolution and two of the spinning mills, now ruins, can be seen.

LUMPHANAN Grampian NJ5804
Village on A980, 9 miles (14km) NW of Banchory
Small village in Deeside hills, near which Macbeth was allegedly slain in 1057. Peel Ring is a nearby 12th-century motte.

LUMSDEN Grampian NJ4722
Village on A97, 4 miles (6km) S of Rhynie
High village at the northern edge of the Grampians, noted for nearby St Mary's Kirk, built in the 13th century and remodelled in the 16th century with excellent craftsmanship; now ruined.

LUND Humberside SE9748
Village on B1248, 7 miles (11km) NW of Beverley
Lines of brick houses are grouped around a central green and smaller greens in other parts of village. Market cross is pre-14th century.

LUNDIN LINKS Fife NO4002
Village on A915, immediately W of Lower Largo
Holiday resort on Largo Bay with a golf course and sandy beach. Standing stones to the west date from 2000BC and may have formed part of a Druid temple.

LUNDY ISLAND Devon SS1345
Island off North Devon coast at entrance to Bristol Channel
A long rocky island in the Bristol Channel, 3 miles (5km) long and ½ mile (1km) wide. Steep cliffs rise on all sides; a nature reserve here is well known for seabirds. Three lighthouses and the remains of a medieval castle, plus other cottages, are all available as holiday homes. Ships leave from Bideford or Ilfracombe (depending on the tide); day trips are possible. No cars are allowed on the island. Spectacular views everywhere.

LUNE, RIVER Lancashire
River flowing through Lancaster to Irish Sea at Sunderland Point
River meanders slowly across a wide flood plain. The Lune Valley is a popular recreational area with walks, cycleways, fishing and much wildlife.

LUPPITT Devon ST1606
Village off A30, 4 miles (6km) N of Honiton
Scattered village, running down the hill. Late medieval church with contemporary roofs. At Dumpdon Hill (National Trust), south, there is an Iron Age hillfort.

LURGASHALL West Sussex SU9327
Village off A283, 4 miles (6km) NW of Petworth
The wooded slopes of Black Down, where Tennyson lived in Aldworth House, make a dramatic backdrop for this delightfully rural village. Stone and tile-hung cottages cluster about the green.

LUSS Strathclyde NS3692
Village off A82, 8 miles (13km) S of Tarbet
A lovely conservation village with Glen Luss above on the shores of Loch Lomond. Location for the popular Scottish soap opera *Take the High Road.*

LUSTLEIGH Devon SX7881
Village off A382, 4 miles (6km) SE of Moretonhampstead
Much-visited and well-preserved granite village on the edge of Dartmoor. Wonderful woodland and rock scenery.

LUSTON Hereford and Worcester SO4863
Hamlet on B4367, 3 miles (5km) N of Leominster
Raised above the marshy ground to the east, Luston consists of cottages and cider orchards strung out along the road.

LUTON Bedfordshire TL0921
Town off M1, 28 miles (45km) NW of London
Bedfordshire's largest town, Luton is mainly a graceless 20th-century industrial centre, known particularly for Vauxhall cars, the Luton Town football team and Luton Airport, which opened in 1938. In the past it was a famous hatting town. St Mary's, Bedfordshire's largest church, bears witness to earlier prosperity and there are 1930s churches by Sir Giles Gilbert Scott and Sir Albert Richardson.

Luton Museum has outstanding hat, lace and bobbin collections, as well as material on natural history, costume, toys and dolls, and the Bedfordshire and Hertfordshire Regiment. The Stockwood Craft Museum in Stockwood Country Park, which concentrates on pre-industrial Bedfordshire, covers rural crafts, with contemporary craft workshops, set in attractive gardens. Also here is the Mossman Collection of horse-drawn vehicles, ranging from farm carts to smart carriages and a replica Roman racing chariot from *Ben Hur*.

Other Luton attractions include a waymarked walk along the River Lee and a path following the prehistoric Icknield Way. On the town's southern outskirts is the Woodside Farm wildfowl park, while Luton Hoo (limited opening) is a grand house in a stately park, with a Fabergé collection.

LUTTERWORTH Leicestershire SP5484
Town on A426, 6 miles (10km) NE of Rugby
Granted its market charter in 1214, this was an important staging post and retains its Georgian coaching inns, the Denbigh Arms and the Greyhound. Joseph Hansom, designer of the cab, built the town hall beside the market place. John Wycliffe, translator of the Bible into English, was rector of the large medieval church for ten years until his death in 1384. Local history museum. Birthplace of Whittle's jet engine, commemorated by bust in gardens.

LUTTON Lincolnshire TF4325
Village off A17, 2 miles (3km) N of Long Sutton
Marshland village and former market town. Richard Busby, born here in 1606, was headmaster of Westminster School for nearly 60 years.

LUXULYAN Cornwall SX0558
Village off B3374, 4 miles (6km) NE of St Austell
Village of old granite cottages and a granite church, with moorland above the village and below the picturesque Luxulyan Valley. Deeply wooded, with boulders lying about, and the spectacular Treffry Viaduct, built in 1839 for the railway from Par to Newquay, 660ft (200m) long and up to 100ft (30m) high.

LYBSTER Highland ND2435
Village off A9, 12 miles (19km) SW of Wick
This spacious 19th-century village with a compact harbour was built to house evicted inland tenants during Clearances, and prospered during the herring boom.

LYDBURY NORTH Shropshire SO3585
Village on B4385, 3 miles (5km) SE of Bishop's Castle
Unpretentious Clun Forest village with medieval church of great interest. Nearby Walcot Hall (limited opening) was built for Clive of India in the 1760s.

LYDD Kent TR0240
Town on B2075, 3 miles (5km) SW of New Romney
Large village on Romney Marsh, once an important port but stranded some 3 miles (5km) inland by coastal silting and the great storm of 1287. It has a grand 13th-century church, known as the 'cathedral of Romney Marsh'; High Street curves gently to it, an attractive mixture of stucco and brick. A shingle beach adjoins Camber Sands, largely given over to an army firing range, and there are watersports clubs.

LYDDINGTON Leicestershire SP8797
Village off A6003, 2 miles (3km) S of Uppingham
This picturesque Rutland village has mellow ironstone houses and cottages, many of the 17th century. The bishops of Lincoln had a medieval palace here during King John's reign, a 15th-century range of which was converted to a Bede House in 1602 (English Heritage). Fine panelled wooden ceilings. Grand 14th- and 15th-century church, with acoustic jars in chancel, an early form of amplification.

LYDFORD Devon SX5184
Village off A386, 8 miles (13km) N of Tavistock
A town from the 9th century, with defences, but now only a small village. The square castle (English Heritage) is early medieval, used as a prison. Lydford Gorge (National Trust) is a deep gorge cut by the river, rocky and woody, with narrow parts where the rock walls almost touch, waterfalls and deep pools. This is the best scenery in Devon. Lydford was the largest parish in England, covering most of Dartmoor.

LYDIARD TREGOZE Wiltshire SU1084
Hamlet off A3102, 3 miles (5km) W of Swindon
Now on the edge of Swindon, this is the setting for Lydiard Park, a 1740s mansion, now a museum, with a country park in the grounds. The church has the finest collection of 17th-century monuments anywhere, including the Golden Cavalier of 1645, with pages holding open curtains to reveal him.

LYDIATE Lancashire SD3604
Village on N outskirts of Maghull
A pleasant rural settlement which borders the flat open farmland created on what were the West Lancashire mosses.

LYDNEY Gloucestershire SO6303
Small town on A48, 8 miles (13km) NE of Chepstow
This unglamorous town and former port on the Severn estuary is now the headquarters of Dean Forest Railway, with static displays and steam train rides in summer. Lydney Park contains traces of a Celtic temple and Roman bathhouse, while Lydney Park Museum shows artefacts discovered during Sir Mortimer Wheeler's excavation of the Roman site, plus an interesting Maori exhibition.

LYDSTEP Dyfed SS0898
Hamlet on A4139, 3 miles (5km) SW of Tenby
Pretty South Pembrokeshire coastal spot. Lydstep Haven is a sheltered east-facing beach. Lydstep Point has dramatic cliffs and low-tide caves.

LYME REGIS Dorset SY3492
Town on A3052, 9 miles (14km) W of Bridport
This pretty seaside resort occupies a dramatic setting, with cliffs and landslips on either side of the town (see Axmouth). The Cobb, an artificial harbour, is a handsome 18th-century stone structure which features in John Fowles's *French Lieutenant's Woman* (set in the town in the mid-19th century). Built in medieval times as an island, it was joined to the land only in 1756. The Cobb is away from the main town, and has its own little settlement. The stone steps (Granny's Teeth), where one of Jane Austen's characters in *Persuasion* supposedly fell, are later than her time, but the novel gives a good picture of the town in the early 19th century, after the failing port had become a seaside resort. Along Marine Parade there is attractive seaside architecture.

Landslips on either side have confined the town to the river valley and virtually every street is on a hill, with many pretty houses and cottages, mostly 19th century in the middle because of fires. The narrow Sherborne Lane is picturesque, packed with 18th- and 19th-century cottages.

The area is famous for fossils, revealed by the falling cliffs, and many are displayed in Dinosaurland and in the local museum, which also has displays on the history of the town. There are also fossil shops.

LYMINGE Kent TR1640
Village off A20, 4 miles (6km) N of Hythe
Big, built-up village with interesting 10th-century church on site of Saxon abbey church of St Ethelburga.

LYMINGTON Hampshire SZ3295
Town on A337, 15 miles (24km) E of Bournemouth
This market town has a handsome, mostly Georgian High Street, wide enough to take the market. There is a prominent 17th- and 18th-century church and a pretty quayside. Over the river are car and passenger ferries to the Isle of Wight: ferries were started here in 1200 because this is the shortest crossing.

LYMINSTER West Sussex TQ0204
Village on A284, 2 miles (3km) N of Littlehampton
Large houses hide behind flint walls on flat land near the River Arun. On the site of a 10th-century convent. Views to Arundel.

LYMM Cheshire SJ6887
Town on A56, 5 miles (8km) E of Warrington
Originally a small village, Lymm grew with the expansion of nearby transport networks in the 18th and 19th centuries. The Bridgewater Canal extension boosted local industry. Now a popular and well-to-do residential area serving Warrington and Manchester and close to motorways.

LYMPNE Kent TR1134
Village on B2067, 3 miles (5km) W of Hythe
Village with modern housing and Port Lympne Zoo set on old cliff-line above Romney Marsh. Royal Military Canal at base of cliff. On the cliff is tumble-down Stutfall Castle, the Roman Saxon shore fort *Portus Lemanis*, built in AD270. Lympne Castle is a fortified house; Shepway Cross is a 1923 replacement of a medieval cross, marking the site of the Court of Shepway, which met to administer the affairs of the Cinque Ports.

LYMPSHAM Somerset ST3354
Village off A370, 4 miles (6km) NE of Burnham-on-Sea
Village and church, very Victorianised by two rectors (father and son) who were here for most of the 19th century. Incredibly fanciful Gothic manor house (not open) by the father, 1820; cottages and church inside mostly the work of the son.

LYMPSTONE Devon SX9984
Village off A376, 2 miles (3km) N of Exmouth
Pleasant backwater on the Exe estuary, with many Georgian and early Victorian cottages and small villas. Peter's Tower is a little clock tower of 1885, facing the sea.

LYNDHURST Hampshire SU2908
Small town on A337, 9 miles (14km) N of Lymington
The only town in the New Forest still with the local Verder's Court dealing with forest rights. The Queen's House, of handsome 17th-century brick, was the centre for forest administration. There are many Edwardian houses and shops, and an extravagant Victorian Gothic brick church of 1858, as well as the New Forest Museum. Open grazing areas called Lawns surround the town, and Swan Green is a picturesque hamlet to the west. Holidays Hill Reptiliary, 2 miles (3km) west, has examples of all the local reptiles.

LYNEHAM Wiltshire SU0278
Village on A3102, 5 miles (8km) N of Calne
Tiny old part, swamped by a huge RAF base and airfield. Now a large settlement.

LYNEMOUTH Northumberland NZ2991
Village off A1068, 1 mile (2km) E of Ellington
A compact industrial town which developed in the 1920s around Lynemouth Colliery and an aluminium smelting plant.

LYNG, EAST AND WEST Somerset ST3329
Villages on A361, 6 miles (10km) NW of Langport
Two villages, East and West, both on a low ridge. The 15th-century church at East Lyng has a fine set of 16th- and 17th-century wooden bench-ends, one with a woodcutter.

LYNMOUTH Devon SS7249
Small town on A39, 10 miles (16km) W of Porlock
Quaint fishing village at the mouth of the Lyn River, admired for its picturesqueness from the early 19th century. In August 1952 a disastrous flood killed 34 people and destroyed many houses. The harbour has an odd little Rhenish tower, built in 1885 to supply saltwater for baths to one of the big houses. Wonderful wooded cliffs rise behind the village, where the National Park (Exmoor) Visitor Centre is based (see Lynton).

LYNSTED Kent TQ9460
Village off A2, 3 miles (5km) SE of Sittingbourne
Attractive downland village among Kentish orchards retaining many half-timbered and brick houses and a fine row of cottages south of the churchyard.

LYNTON Devon SS7149
Small town off A39, above Lynmouth
Paired with Lynmouth, Lynton is 500ft (150m) above it, joined by a zig-zag path and a cliff railway of 1890. Lynton was just a hamlet which became a Victorian resort, and features many Victorian and Edwardian buildings and a very fanciful town hall of 1900. The Lynton and Exmouth Museum is here, and the Valley of the Rocks, to the west, has very romantic scenery.

LYONSHALL Hereford and Worcester SO3355
Village off A44, 3 miles (5km) E of Kington
Well-preserved stretch of Offa's Dyke runs west of this Welsh border village with its isolated church and 13th-century castle.

LYTE'S CARY Somerset ST5326
Mansion off B3151, 3 miles (5km) SE of Somerton
The late medieval manor house (National Trust) is very atmospheric and retains its original hall and chapel.

LYTHAM ST ANNE'S Lancashire SD3427
Town on A584, 12 miles (19km) W of Preston
Lytham St Anne's, on the Fylde coast, is in fact two towns which now share the same name but have quite distinctive characteristics, Lytham being the original, older town and St Annes a relatively modern residential town. The town is a popular seaside resort whose pace is more gentle than that of its neighbour, Blackpool. It is also well known for its championship golf courses, especially Royal Lytham St Anne's.

For centuries Lytham was a small fishing village situated at the end of an unbroken range of sandhills that ran northwards to Blackpool. With the coming of the railway in 1846, Lytham became easily accessible from Preston and the industrial towns of Lancashire and it soon became a holiday resort.

Lytham Hall, once the home of the Clifton family, is situated in extensive grounds. It is a fine Georgian buildings with four Ionic columns.

The Green, originally an area of sand dunes, lies in the centre of the town, and was given by the Clifton family to the people of Lytham in 1923. Situated on it is a windmill dating back to about 1805.

LYTHE North Yorkshire NZ8413
Village on A174, 4 miles (6km) NW of Whitby
The village has extensive views of the North Sea and was the home of Rudyard Kipling's grandfather.

LYVEDEN Northamptonshire SP9885
Site off A427, 4 miles (6km) SW of Oundle
Thomas Tresham of Rushton (see) built cross-shaped New Bield (National Trust), incorporating much Catholic symbolism and unfinished at his death in 1605.

M

MABE BURNTHOUSE Cornwall SW7634
Village off A39, 1 mile (2km) W of Penryn
On the edge of Penryn, but still a village. Military vehicle collection here. There are big reservoirs to the south.

MABLETHORPE Lincolnshire TF5085
Small town on A1104, 11 miles (18km) E of Louth
Popular family resort on Lincolnshire holiday coast, developed in late 19th century. Miles of sandy beach, animal and bird garden with seal sanctuary, paddling pool, miniature railway, fairground, crazy golf, numerous sports facilities. Resort developed from two villages. Mablethorpe St Peter's Church was drowned in Henry VIII's reign. St Mary's survives, however; it was founded in 1300, and substantially rebuilt in 1970s.

MACCLESFIELD Cheshire SJ9173
Town on A52 (A523), 10 miles (16km) S of Stockport
Although its origins lie in medieval times, Macclesfield really grew up around the textile industry and retains the look of an early mill town, with terraced weavers' cottages, mills, Georgian town houses and Nonconformist churches, in the foothills of the Pennine Peak District. It became established as the country's silk-weaving centre and the silk history of the town now attracts many visitors. Paradise Mill was the last handloom weaving business to operate in the town, finally closing for production in 1981. It reopened in 1984 as part of the Macclesfield Silk Museum, interpreting the activities of the silk-weaving firm Cartwright and Sheldon and with demonstrations of hand-weaving. The main part of the Silk Museum is at the heritage centre, a former Sunday School building dating from 1813, documenting the history of the silk industry in Macclesfield from its origins to the present day.

The medieval core of the town, embracing the church, the town hall and the market place, is still very much the focal point, at the junction of Chestergate and Mill Street, both of which are busy, pleasant shopping streets.

MACCLESFIELD FOREST Cheshire SJ9772
Hamlet off A537, 4 miles (6km) E of Macclesfield
An isolated hamlet at 1,300ft (396m), surrounded by pine forest and moorland. A popular walking area on the edge of the Peak District National Park.

MACDUFF Grampian NJ7064
Small town on A98, 1 mile (2km) E of Banff
Thriving fishing port and resort on Moray Firth with a large harbour, fish market and seanet-manufacturing industry. Important herring port in the 19th century and also noted as a spa town after the Well of Tarlair, to the east, was found to have healing properties. Known as Doune till 1783, its name was changed in honour of James Duff, Earl of Fife, who had the town cross erected.

MACHEN Mid Glamorgan ST2189
Small town on A468, 4 miles (6km) E of Caerphilly
In forested valley between Caerphilly and Newport. Ruperra Castle (not open) to the south dates from early 17th century in romantic style.

MACHRIHANISH Strathclyde NR6320
Village on B843, 5 miles (8km) W of Campbeltown
Atlantic-facing resort on Kintyre with good beaches and extensive sand dunes, popular with golfers. Caves with stalactites to southwest.

MACHYNLLETH Powys SH7400
Small town on A487, 16 miles (26km) NE of Aberystwyth
Handsome, wide main street dominated by ornate clock tower, erected in 1873 by the Marquess of Londonderry. In the parkland behind is the former home of the marquess which now houses Celtica, a visitor centre that tells the story of Celtic myth and legend. Owain Glyndwr Centre recalls Wales's great medieval hero, Y Tabernacl; the chapel is converted into an arts centre. The fascinating Centre for Alternative Technology is in the forests to the north.

MACKWORTH Derbyshire SK3137
Village on A52, 3 miles (5km) NW of Derby
A 14th-century and later church stands alone in a field. Late 15th-century gatehouse to a vanished castle. Nearby Markeaton Park provides recreation for Derby, overlooked by the university.

MADELEY Shropshire SJ6904
District of Telford New Town
Encroaching Telford New Town has not spoilt Madeley's appeal. Church by Thomas Telford and fascinating array of buildings of 18th and 19th centuries.

MADELEY Staffordshire SJ7744
Village on A525, 5 miles (8km) W of Newcastle-under-Lyme
The road through the village skirts a large pool that served the corn mill, still standing at one end. The timber-framed old hall faces the pool, while near the church are the school (1875) and 17th-century almshouses. The big sandstone church has good Norman, medieval and Victorian work, including a Pre-Raphaelite window.

MADINGLEY Cambridgeshire TL3960
Village off A428 (A45), 4 miles (6km) NW of Cambridge
While a student at Cambridge University, the future Edward VII lodged at Elizabethan Madingley Hall. Madingley also has a mill.

MADLEY Hereford and Worcester SO4138
Village on B4352, 6 miles (10km) W of Hereford
St Dyfrig, who crowned King Arthur, is said to have been born in this village between the River Wye and the Golden Valley. The medieval church is one of the finest village churches in England, with an impressive tower, a spacious nave and chancel and splendid tracery in its windows, one of which contains original glass.

MADRESFIELD Hereford and Worcester SO8047
Village off A449, 2 miles (3km) NE of Great Malvern
With Malvern Hills as a backdrop, the village stands outside the park of Madresfield Court (not open), which became 'Brideshead' in Evelyn Waugh's *Brideshead Revisited.*

MADRON Cornwall SW4531
Village off A3071, 2 miles (3km) NW of Penzance
The mother parish to Penzance, with old cottages and a church, and St Madron's Well, where rags tied to bushes are supposed to cure diseases. Trengwainton Gardens (National Trust) are large woodland gardens.

Cromlech known as Lanyon Quoit, 2 miles (3km) off an unclassified road near Madron.

MAENTWROG Gwynedd SH6640
Village on A496, 3 miles (5km) W of Ffestiniog
Village of handsome stone houses attractively set in wooded Vale of Ffestiniog at key road junction. Plas Tan-y-Bwlch residential study centre for Snowdonia National Park.

MAER Staffordshire SJ7938
Village off A51, 6 miles (10km) SW of Newcastle-under-Lyme
Josiah Wedgwood II lived at the Jacobean Maer Hall and in 1839 Charles Darwin married Emma Wedgwood in the 17th-century church.

MAES HOWE Orkney HY3112
Site off A965, 3 miles (5km) W of Finstown
This is the finest neolithic chambered tomb in Europe, built before 2700BC, with burial cells leading off the main chamber, where sunlight penetrates only at the winter solstice. Runic graffiti was left by Viking invaders. The Ring of Brodgar stone circle, near by, dating from about 1560BC, was perhaps a lunar observatory; 36 out of 60 stones remain. Near the ring are four out of the 12 original Stones of Stenness, dating from around 3000BC.

MAESBURY MARSH Shropshire SJ3125
Village off A483, 3 miles (5km) SE of Oswestry
Navigation inn and restored wharf are reminders of the colourful past of this 19th-century purpose-built canal settlement.

MAESGWM Gwynedd SH7126
Site off A470, 6 miles (10km) N of Dolgellau
Focal point for the surrounding Coed y Brenin Forest. Visitor centre has details of walks, nature displays and local gold-mining exhibits.

MAESTEG Mid Glamorgan SS8591
Town on A4063, 6 miles (10km) E of Port Talbot
Industrial town in Llynfi Valley, flanked by forested hills. The old engine house has been imaginatively converted into a sports centre.

MAGDALEN LAVER Essex TL5108
Hamlet off A414, 4 miles (6km) E of Harlow
One of three Laver villages outside Harlow. Old moated farms and picturesque church where William Webb Ellis, Rugby football inventor, was rector.

MAGHULL Merseyside SD3703
Town on A59, 8 miles (13km) N of Liverpool
A large residential area serving Liverpool. The medieval chapel in the grounds of St Andrew's Church is the oldest ecclesiastical building magnate.

MAGOR Gwent ST4287
Village on B4245, 8 miles (13km) SW of Chepstow
Village on peaceful coastal plain of Severn estuary. Church has interesting history, displaying work by medieval Italian monks.

MAIDEN BRADLEY Wiltshire ST8038
Village on B3092, 4 miles (6km) N of Mere
Set high, with a wooded green. The medieval church contains a superb memorial with a figure of 1730.

MAIDEN CASTLE Dorset SY6688
Prehistoric site off A35, 2 miles (3km) SW of Dorchester
The most massively defended Iron Age hillfort in Britain has three ramparts and two complex entrances. The earliest phases are neolithic, a causewayed enclosure, replaced by a very long bank barrow. The hillfort grew larger through the Iron Age, and was taken by the Romans in AD43 or 44. A cemetery of the Iron Age defenders has been excavated, and finds can be seen in the Dorset County Museum in Dorchester.

MAIDEN NEWTON Dorset SY5997
Village on A356, 8 miles (13km) NW of Dorchester
Almost a tiny town, with the remains of a medieval stone cross in the centre and pleasant buildings.

MAIDENHEAD Berkshire SU8881
Town on A4, 5 miles (8km) W of Slough
Large town close to the River Thames, mostly modern, with remnants of the earlier town including almshouses and a few Georgian houses. At Boyne Hill, to the west, a remarkable group of brick church, parsonage, school and schoolhouse of the 1850s by GE Street. Handsome 1770s bridge across the Thames, and a huge railway bridge built by Brunel in 1837.

MAIDENS Strathclyde NS2107
Village on A719, 5 miles (8km) W of Maybole
A small resort village on the Ayrshire coast, overlooking sandy Maidenhead Bay, within easy reach of several tourist attractions.

MAIDS MORETON Buckinghamshire SP7035
Village on A413, 1 mile (2km) NE of Buckingham
The two 'maids', spinsters of the Peover family, built the 15th-century fan-vaulted church. Developed post-war into a Buckingham suburb.

MAIDSTONE Kent TQ7655
Town off M20, 39 miles (63km) SE of London
Kent's county town, which stands in a countryside of orchards and hop fields on the River Medway, still has a county town atmosphere, with the High Street leading up from the river, originally a wide market place, but later filled in to create parallel Bank Street. Both streets lead to the town centre with the town hall of 1763 and 1960s multi-storey blocks. Maidstone's oldest buildings are the 14th-century Archbishop's Palace, fronting the river, the great church of 1395 and the 15th-century Archbishop's stables.

Maidstone's position on the River Medway, historically an industrial highway, helped it to prosper. Fruit was sent to London; ragstone, Wealden iron, sand and timber were also transported. The Romans and Saxons were here; the Normans gave it its market in 1261; it developed a cloth-manufacturing industry, based on local flocks and fuller's earth, and boosted by refugee Flemish weavers from the 1560s onwards. When the cloth industry died out, paper manufacture took over, and Maidstone remains an industrial centre.

The river is now a pleasure ground with boats and riverside walks. Maidstone hosts fairs including a carnival and river festival.

MALDON Essex TL8506

Town on A414, 9 miles (14km) E of Chelmsford

Beautiful old sailing barges congregate at this historic town, which grew prosperous on barge traffic to London; it stages barge races and a Christmas mud race. There is a characterful waterfront at the old port of Hythe Quay, a park by the River Blackwater and a sea-wall walk to a 10th-century battlefield. The triangular tower of All Saints' Church is unique.

MALHAM North Yorkshire SD9063

Village off A65, 5 miles (8km) E of Settle

The village, although popular with tourists, manages to retain its ancient, picturesque charm, with many of the farmhouses and cottages dating from the 17th century. Just outside the village is spectacular 'Great Scar' limestone scenery with the famous natural features of Malham Cove, the great cliff of Gordale Scar, the dry bed of a waterfall and Malham Tarn. The remains of an Iron Age settlement are close by.

MALLAIG Highland NM6796

Town on A830, 7 miles (11km) N of Arisaig

Busy fishing port, service town for a large area, and road, rail and ferry terminus on the tip of North Morar peninsula, overlooking the Sound of Sleat. Boat connections to Skye, the Small Isles and Knoydart. Popular holiday destination. Mallaig Marine World has an aquarium and exhibits. Impresario Cameron Makintosh holidayed here as child and has done much for the community.

MALLWYD Gwynedd SH8612

Hamlet on A470, 10 miles (16km) NE of Machynlleth

Set among forested mountains in upper Dovey Valley. Brigands' inn named after band of red-haired bandits. Intriguing church.

MALMESBURY Wiltshire ST9387

Town on B4640, 10 miles (16km) N of Chippenham

An ancient settlement that grew up around the abbey, which was founded in the 7th century and became famous under St Aldhelm, who died in 709. His shrine attracted many pilgrims and the church was rebuilt on a huge scale in the 12th century. The huge ruins and church which survive display some of the finest Norman architecture and sculpture in the country, but they are not the complete building: a huge spire fell down in about 1500, and a tower also collapsed.

The town has one of the finest market crosses in the country, elaborate and dating from about 1500. Its 17th-century cottages and some almshouses recall the time when Malmesbury was a weaving centre, and there are handsome Georgian houses and cottages and a big 18th-century silk mill on the river. The Athelstan Museum in the town hall relates the local history.

Charlton Park House, 2 miles (3km) northeast, is of 1607 and the 1770s, and has only a few rooms open.

MALPAS Cheshire SJ4847

Town on B5069, 8 miles (15km) E of Wrexham

A small township in a mainly agricultural area. Cholmondley Castle, home of the Marquis and Marchioness of Cholmondley, was built in the 18th century, and has fine gardens which are open in the summer. The Red Lion inn was visited by King James I in 1624 and his chair is still used.

MALPAS Cornwall SW8442

Village off A39, 2 miles (3km) SE of Truro

Between the Truro and Tresillian estuaries, a little yachting place with superb views.

MALTBY LE MARSH Lincolnshire TF4681

Village on A1104, 4 miles (6km) SW of Mablethorpe

Long village, not far from sea. Remains of brick tower mill built in 1841. Monument to chain-mailed knight (about 1300) in church.

MALTON North Yorkshire SE7871

Town off A64, 17 miles (27km) NE of York

Malton has been the historic centre of Ryedale since Roman times. North of the Roman fort site is the original town of Old Malton, with ancient stone houses and quaint dwellings, in the centre of which stands St Mary's, the only remaining Gilbertine priory in England. Alongside farming, brewing is a traditional Malton industry.

MALVERN HILLS Hereford and Worcester SO7641

Hill range off A449, SW of Worcester

Six miles (10km) long and rising steeply from flat countryside, this narrow hill range presents a dramatic silhouette. The very hard pre-Cambrian rock underlying the hills is responsible for the extreme purity of the famous local water, but Malvern's popularity as a spa was based equally on the accessibility of the hills for vigorous exercise, much appreciated by the young Edward Elgar. This Victorian popularity proved so threatening that in 1884 the Malvern Hills Conservators were established to minimise damage from recreation and quarrying.

Today the range has a network of paths (details from Great Malvern information centre), including an exhilarating end-to-end track which takes in the highest point – the Worcestershire Beacon at 1,394ft (424m). The easiest access (with car park) is at Wynd's Point, the start of an easy climb to the Herefordshire Beacon (1,100ft/334m), where the extensive Iron Age hillfort provides magnificent views. Those seeking more isolation will probably prefer the third major summit at Midsummer Hill (950ft/286m), a National Trust area near the southern end of the range.

Away from the summits there are many opportunities for gentle strolling in unspoilt surroundings.

MAMBLE Hereford and Worcester SO6872

Village off A456, 8 miles (13km) SW of Kidderminster

Solitary village in hilly, wooded countryside. Beautiful 14th-century glass in the church and sadly dilapidated Blount family chapel.

MAN, ISLE OF Isle of Man
Island in Irish Sea, 30 miles (48km) W of English coast
The Isle of Man, famous for kippers, its cat, the annual TT Races and as a tax haven, consists of 227 square miles (588 sq km) of land – 100 miles (161km) of coastline in the Irish Sea. It was annexed by England in the 13th century and is ruled by a Lieutenant Governor. It has its own parliament, the Tynwald, its own laws and taxes and its own Gaelic language, currency and stamps.

It became an island around 10,000 years ago when the meltwater of the Ice Age raised the sea level. Among the first arrivals after this time were the Vikings and much evidence of their inhabitance remains, including Viking burial mounds and treasures that are now displayed at the Manx Museum in Douglas.

The three-legged symbol that now appears on the Manx flag seems to have been adopted in the 13th century by the native kings of the Isle of Man, whose dominion also included the Hebrides. The motto now incorporated with the Three Legs of Man on the official coat of arms is *Quocunque Jeceris Stabit*, meaning 'whichever way you throw I shall stand'.

MANACCAN Cornwall SW7625
Village off B3293, 7 miles (11km) E of Helston
Stone village with steep, wooded roads. The church has a famous 200-year-old fig tree growing out of a wall.

MANACLE POINT Cornwall SW8121
Headland; E point of Lizard peninsula
The easternmost part of the Lizard peninsula. A steep rocky headland with the treacherous Manacles rocks just offshore. Many ships have come to grief here (see St Keverne).

MANATON Devon SX7581
Village off B3387, 4 miles (6km) NW of Bovey Tracey
Attractive granite village on the woody edge of Dartmoor, with steep little valleys and granite outcrops. Becca Falls, in a deep wooded valley to the south, has a 70ft (21m) waterfall, and Grimspound, on the moor 3 miles (5km) away, is a Bronze Age enclosure with hut circles inside it.

MANCETTER Warwickshire SP3296
Village on B4111, immediately SE of Atherstone
The ancient Plough inn dispenses hospitality at the heart of this attractive Anker Valley village .Medieval glass in the church's east window.

MANCHESTER Greater Manchester SJ8398
City off M62/M63, 204 miles (328km) NW of London
The city of Manchester is a major centre of business, commerce and industry. Its heritage is predominantly Victorian when it developed with the cotton industry, but its history dates back to Roman times when a fort was set up here – *Mancunium*. In the 18th century this area, later called Castlefield, developed as the junction of canals which converged on Manchester from surrounding industrial towns and textile mills.

The canal basin of Castlefield now forms the centre of Manchester's tourism district, and has been redeveloped as an urban heritage park. The Roman fort has been reconstructed on its original site and the canals and their towpaths have been renovated and landscaped. The basin now has an outdoor events arena, pubs and cafés, and moorings for narrowboats, and is the centre for a colourful annual boating festival.

The surrounding Victorian warehouse buildings have also been converted into hotels, apartments and offices, as well as tourist attractions such as the Museum of Science and Industry, a modern museum in old buildings, including the old Liverpool Road Railway Station, the world's first passenger rail terminus. The museum relates many aspects of Manchester's industrial history. Granada Studios Tour, home of *Coronation Street* and other famous TV sets, is just around the corner.

Trade was given a considerable boost in 1894 with the opening of the Manchester Ship Canal, linking the city to the sea and turning it into a major inland port. This period of great prosperity has left Manchester with many splendid buildings. In Albert Square is the magnificent Gothic town hall, designed by Alfred Waterhouse and built between 1871 and 1877. The richly decorated interior includes wall-paintings by Ford Madox Brown, illustrating aspects of the city's history. The central library, a spectacular circular building of white Portland stone, was designed by Frank Lloyd Wright and opened in 1934. The John Rylands University Library on Deansgate is an imposing Victorian Gothic building of red sandstone, named after Manchester's first millionaire, a cotton merchant who died in 1888. The cotton exchange building now houses the famous Royal Exchange Theatre and the City Art Galleries contain impressive collections of Pre-Raphaelite and other paintings that were fashionable at this time, bequeathed to the city by its many wealthy merchants and benefactors. The city's 15th-century cathedral is situated on Victoria Street and has the widest nave in England.

Manchester has a strong music tradition, with the Royal Northern College of Music, regarded as one of the country's finest performing music colleges, the Hallé Orchestra and Chetham's School of Music.

With the introduction of Manchester's tram system the city is taking on an increasingly cosmopolitan atmosphere, enhanced by a large student population and a lively Chinatown. It is widely regarded as a centre for youth culture with many clubs and outlets for young fashion designers. The shopping centre is based around the pedestrianised areas of Market Street, King Street and St Ann's Square, with several attractive arcades.

MANGOTSFIELD Avon ST6576
Town on N outskirts of Bristol
Huge suburban area of Bristol, mostly modern.

MANIFOLD, RIVER Staffordshire
River, tributary of the River Dove
The river rises on the northern edge of Staffordshire and runs south through moorlands to join the River Dove near Thorpe. At Ecton, it starts to flow beneath dramatic hills, and there are caves in steep valley sides near Wetton, notably the huge Thor's Cave. Prehistoric sites abound on both sides of the river. The most popular riverside destination for visitors is Ilam (see).

MANKINHOLES West Yorkshire SD9523
Hamlet off A646, 1 mile (2km) SE of Todmorden
Tiny village linked to Lumbutts (see) by flagged paths, or 'causeys' that cross the hills. Housed Belgian refugees from World War I. Youth hostel.

MANNINGFORD BRUCE Wiltshire SU1358
Village off A345, 3 miles (5km) N of Upavon
A village in the Vale of Pewsey, with a Norman church of herringbone flint.

MANNINGTREE Essex TM1031
Town on B1352, 8 miles (13km) NE of Colchester
This was a busy port at the head of the Stour estuary, until the railway came. Matthew Hopkins, 17th-century 'Witchfinder General', is buried here. Surviving from an 18th-century attempt to make neighbouring Mistley a spa are the towers (English Heritage) of a church designed by Robert Adam. Rescued animals are kept in Mistley Place Park, and there are craft workshops at Mistley Quay.

MANORBIER Dyfed SS0697
Village off A1439, 4 miles (6km) SW of Tenby
Well-preserved medieval castle stands above sandy beach in this charming little south Pembrokeshire village. Lovely coastal walks.

MANORDEIFI Dyfed SN2243
Site off A484, 1 mile (2km) SE of Llechryd
Ancient riverside Coracle church (services still held here in summer), very bare and simple with box pews. Contrasts with late 19th-century replacement.

MANSELL LACY Hereford and Worcester SO4245
Village off A480, 6 miles (10km) NW of Hereford
Pretty village beneath woodland first laid out in 18th century by amateur landscape artist Uvedale Price. Village shop has a built-in dovecote.

MANSFIELD Nottinghamshire SK5361
Town on A60, 14 miles (23km) N of Nottingham
This commercial, industrial and market town sits at the traditional centre of Sherwood Forest. One of the largest open markets in the country is complemented by a modern shopping complex and pedestrianised streets. Quarrying, coal-mining and textile industries contributed to the town's growth. Mansfield Museum and Art Gallery reflects local history and arts. Civic Theatre, Water Meadows swimming centre leisure and competition pools.

MANSTON Kent TR3466
Village off B2190, 3 miles (5km) SW of Margate
Village on the Isle of Thanet with camping sites and caravan parks and an associated airfield, Manston Aerodrome, which was an important fighter station in World War II.

MANTHORPE Lincolnshire SK9237
Village on A607, 1 mile (2km) N of Grantham
Mid-19th-century estate village with red-brick and stone Tudor-style cottages. Early 19th-century watermill.

MANTON Leicestershire SK8804
Village on A6003, 3 miles (5km) S of Oakham
Village at the southwest tip of Rutland Water. Homely ironstone church, 13th-century west front, 15th-century transepts, 1796 chancel. The old hall dates from the 17th and 18th centuries.

MANTON Wiltshire SU1768
Village off A4, 1 mile (2km) W of Marlborough
Manton sits on the edge of Marlborough, with a White Horse cut into the chalk hillside by local schoolboys in 1804.

MANUDEN Essex TL4926
Village off A120, 3 miles (5km) N of Bishop's Stortford
Pretty commuter village on the River Stort with half-timbered and thatched cottages. The church, rebuilt in the 1860s, has a notable 15th-century screen.

MAPLEDURHAM Oxfordshire SU6776
Village off A4074, 4 miles (6km) NW of Reading
This unspoilt Thames-side village has a delightful centre with almshouses of 1629 and a wealth of attractive cottages. There are impressive Blount family monuments in St Margaret's Church. Mapledurham House of 1588 (limited opening) has a splendid interior and an 18th-century chapel. Mapledurham Watermill (limited opening) is of Tudor origin and still uses traditional machinery.

MAPPERTON Dorset SY5099
Hamlet off B3163, 2 miles (3km) SE of Beaminster
Set among little green valleys and hills, Mapperton House (stone, 16th to 18th century, not open) has lovely gardens laid out down one of the valleys.

MARAZION Cornwall SW5130
Small town off A394, 3 miles (5km) E of Penzance
An old town, now very small. Pretty along the shore and in the little centre. Ferries to St Michael's Mount (see).

MARBURY Cheshire SJ5645
Village off A49, 3 miles (5km) NE of Whitchurch
The village has a green, two meres and a beautiful 13th-century church with a 1,000-year-old yew tree in the churchyard.

MARCH Cambridgeshire TL4196
Town on B1101, 9 miles (14km) SW of Wisbech
The coming of the railway marked an important stage in the development of this busy market town. Its roots, however, are far more ancient, and there was a Saxon settlement here. St Wendreda's Church has a magnificent roof with carvings of angels and the devil. The High Street Museum has exhibits of local history and a reconstructed forge.

MARCHAM Oxfordshire SU4596
Village on A415, 3 miles (5km) W of Abingdon
Popular commuter village well known to Women's Institute members, whose educational courses take place at Denman College. Tudor brasses in the church.

MARCHINGTON Staffordshire SK1330
Village off B5017, 3 miles (5km) SE of Uttoxeter
Large village overlooking the Dove Valley with a church of 1742 and an interesting variety of buildings from a 17th-century mansion to timber-framed cottages.

MARDEN Hereford and Worcester SO5147
Village off A49, 4 miles (6km) N of Hereford
Sutton Walls, an Iron Age hillfort, rises to the south of this Lugg Valley village, with its 17th-century bridge, medieval well and churchyard conservation area.

MARDEN Kent TQ7444
Village on B2079, 7 miles (11km) S of Maidstone
Village among orchards and hopfields with an attractive High Street of tile-hung and weatherboarded houses, and a medieval church (the belfry topped with a pyramidal roof). The new village centre is by the station.

MARDEN Wiltshire SU0857
Village off A342, 5 miles (8km) SW of Pewsey
A Vale of Pewsey village with thatched cottages and an elaborate Norman doorway to the church, which also has strong 1958 stained glass.

MARDENS, THE West Sussex SU8016
Hamlets on B2141, 6 miles (10 km) SE of Petersfield
Of these remote hamlets, West Marden is the largest but has no church; East Marden has a little centre. North Marden and Up Marden are both little more than a farm and a church, although they do show signs of former streets and houses.

MARFORD Clwyd SJ3556
Village on B5445, 4 miles (6km) N of Wrexham
Estate village of pretty cottages built in the early 19th century. In border country between Wrexham and Chester.

MARGAM West Glamorgan SS7887
District off M4, in SE area of Port Talbot
The wide, open spaces of Margam Park are at the approach to industrial Port Talbot. The park has many attractions, including walking, boating, children's activities, a maze, a deer herd, a sculpture park and beautiful 18th-century orangery. Margam Abbey Church, a Cistercian foundation, is near by. Alongside is a museum containing an important collection of inscribed stones (Cadw).

MARGARET RODING Essex TL5912
Village on A1060, 1 mile (2km) S of Leaden Roding
The smallest Roding, named after a church dedication to St Margaret; with its Norman door, the church is considered to be the best among the Rodings.

MARGARETTING Essex TL6701
Village off A12, 4 miles (6km) SW of Chelmsford
Church belfry and spire held up by a massive wooden construction five centuries old; beautiful 15th-century Jesse window.

MARGATE Kent TR3570
Town on A28, 15 miles (24km) NE of Canterbury
Margate, on the Isle of Thanet, is a bustling seaside resort with 9 miles (14km) of sandy beach, safe swimming, arcades and funfairs, the Winter Gardens with a concert hall that seats 2,000, the Theatre Royal and the Tom Thumb Theatre with the world's smallest stage. The curious Grotto, chambers hollowed from the chalk embedded with shells, possibly prehistoric, is probably an 18th-century folly.

Margate was one of England's earliest coastal resorts, developed after 1753 when Benjamin Beale, a Margate Quaker, invented the bathing machine. The upper classes came to Margate to partake of the new and fashionable craze for sea bathing, making use of Beale's invention – a kind of covered waggon in which the bather was towed into the sea.

The first development, around Cecil Square (1769), was inland from the sea, behind the old fishing village, but soon London trippers were heading to Margate in their droves, first down the Thames and by sea and later by train, and building moved seawards as the 19th century progressed. Today the pier of 1810–15, the parade and the little harbour separate the boisterous seaside sands and fun from the eastern cliffs and 19th-century terraces.

MARHAM Norfolk TF7009
Village off A1122, 7 miles (11km) W of Swaffham
The ruins of a 13th-century Cistercian convent can still be seen on a farm opposite Marham's 15th-century parish church.

MARHAMCHURCH Cornwall SS2203
Village off A39, 2 miles (3km) SE of Bude
Hilltop village, once with an inclined plane to take the barges on the Bude Canal up the hill. The canal survives from just below the village to Bude (see).

MARHOLM Cambridgeshire TF1402
Village off A15, 4 miles (6km) NW of Peterborough
In the heart of Cambridgeshire countryside, and guarded by mighty cedars. St Mary's Church is Norman, but rebuilt in the 13th and 16th centuries.

MARKBY Lincolnshire TF4878
Village on A1111, 3 miles (5km) NE of Alford
Lincolnshire's only thatched church, set back from the road in a farmyard, was completely rebuilt in about 1611 using masonry from Augustinian priory, of which earthworks remain.

MARKET BOSWORTH Leicestershire SK4003
Small town on B585, 6 miles (10km) N of Hinckley
This picturesque small town has numerous 18th-century buildings. The market place is mainly 19th century, with a 16th-century inn and Dixie Grammar School where Samuel Johnson taught. The 14th- and 15th-century church with spire has memorials to the Dixie family, who influenced the town for 300 years. Their former home, 17th-century Bosworth Hall, altered in early Victorian times, is now a hotel and the park is a pleasant country park. For Bosworth Battlefield, see Sutton Cheney.

MARKET DEEPING Lincolnshire TF1310
Small town on A16, 7 miles (11km) E of Stamford
Attractive small former market town at southern boundary of Lincolnshire, at crossing of River Welland. Busy meeting point of Lincoln–Peterborough and Stamford–Spalding roads. Early 14th-century Old Rectory, traditionally thought to be refectory or dormitory of a priory, with medieval timber roof. Medieval church restored in 1870s, when almshouses built. Several fine late 18th-century houses on wide street.

MARKET DRAYTON Shropshire SJ6734
Town off A53, 18 miles (29km) NE of Shrewsbury
Busy market town, crowned by interesting church where future Clive of India startled inhabitants by climbing on to a gargoyle. In the streets below, venerable timber-framed pubs rub shoulders with homely Georgian houses, and a rare country house by Sir John Soane stands on the outskirts. Town's canal wharf and marina bustles with activity in the summer.

MARKET HARBOROUGH Leicestershire SP7387
Town on A427, 14 miles (23km) SE of Leicester
On the A6, Market Harborough flourished as an 18th-century staging post for travellers from London and Northampton to Leicester and beyond. The Angel and the attractively signed Three Swans continue their coaching inn tradition of welcoming visitors.

As befits its name, the town was a planned trading centre, at a crossing of the River Welland, its weekly market starting in 1202–3 and still popular today. In 1614, the timber-framed grammar school was built, its open ground floor sheltering traders as a butter market. From its agricultural base, the town expanded to textiles. Symington's corset factory, busy from the 1860s to 1957, now houses the Harborough Museum, which includes the well-known 'liberty bodice' in its displays.

Near by, St Dionysius Church has a particularly fine 14th-century steeple, and in 1645 was used to house prisoners taken at the Battle of Naseby. High Street has several Georgian buildings, with interesting variations in detailing, and there are substantial 18th-century properties on Leicester Road. Behind the Six Packs inn, the canal basin on the Harborough arm of the Grand Union provides a base for boating holidays.

MARKET LAVINGTON Wiltshire SU0154
Village on B3098, 5 miles (8km) S of Devizes
Once a town, Market Lavington is now only a village, with densely packed houses and cottages, and some old timber-framing.

MARKET OVERTON Leicestershire SK8816
Village off B668, 5 miles (8km) N of Oakham
Attractive 17th- and 18th-century cottages and the early Georgian Market Overton Hall are features of this village. The site of a Roman settlement and two Anglo-Saxon cemeteries are finds made during ironstone quarrying. An Anglo-Saxon tower arch, unique in the county, can be seen in the largely 14th-century church. The sundial on the tower is reputed to have been given by Sir Isaac Newton, whose mother came from here. Stocks and whipping post on green.

MARKET RASEN Lincolnshire TF1089
Town off A46, 14 miles (23km) NE of Lincoln
Market and agricultural town on River Rase, with Lincolnshire Wolds to east. Surrounded by woodland good for pleasant walks and picnics. National Hunt racecourse draws crowds to meetings. Golf course and camp site. Pleasant 18th- and 19th-century residential and commercial buildings, Victorian shop fronts. Church mainly rebuilt 1862. Wesleyan chapel with imposing portico of 1863.

MARKET WEIGHTON Humberside SE8741
Small town off A1079, 10 miles (16km) W of Beverley
Quiet town with 18th-century houses clustered around the church. Village green has a duck pond. Market Weighton Canal leads to Humber estuary.

MARKHAM MOOR Nottinghamshire SK7173
Hamlet on A57, 2 miles (3km) N of Tuxford
Overlooking modern services at a roundabout where the A57 Lincoln–Sheffield road joins the A1 is a Greek Doric mausoleum built by Smirke for the 4th Duke of Newcastle.

MARKINCH Fife NO3001
Small town, immediately E of Glenrothes
Near by is Balgonie Castle, an interesting 15th-century tower with later courtyard, restored in the 1970s. St Drosten's Church has a 12th-century tower.

MARKS HALL COUNTRY ESTATE Essex TL8425
Garden off B1024, 2 miles (3km) NW of Coggeshall
Landscaped grounds and park of a demolished mansion with lakes, cascades, a walled garden, a newly created 1990s arboretum, a barn visitor centre and a picnic area.

MARKS TEY Essex TL9023
Village off A12, 5 miles (8km) W of Colchester
In the past this was mainly a stopping place on the Colchester road; it is now a commuter village. The church has a wooden tower and font.

Stocks and whipping post on the green at Market Overton.

MARKYATE Hertfordshire TL0616
Village off A5, 4 miles (6km) SW of Luton
Former coaching village on Watling Street. The 'wicked lady', 17th-century highwaywoman Katherine Ferrers, lived at Markyate Cell (not open).

MARLBOROUGH Wiltshire SU1869
Town on A4, 10 miles (16km) S of Swindon
Marlborough is famous for its handsome wide High Street, lined with attractive buildings and colonnades – one of the finest market town streets in the country, with Marlborough College (public school founded 1843) and a medieval church at one end, and the classical town hall of 1900 and another church at the other. The Merchant's House of 1656 is being made into a museum. To the north are the rolling Marlborough Downs, with many racehorses.

MARLDON Devon SX8663
Village off A380, 2 miles (3km) NW of Paignton
Stone village on the edge of Paignton. See Compton.

MARLOES Dyfed SM7908
Village off B4327, 7 miles (11km) W of Milford Haven
Village gives its name to nearby Marloes Sands, one of Pembrokeshire's finest beaches. Iron Age promontory fort at beach. Boat trips to Skomer Island.

MARLOW Buckinghamshire SU8486
Town off A4155, 4 miles (6km) NW of Maidenhead
This charming commuter town on the Thames comes complete with imposing riverside residences and expensive post-war estates. The engaging High Street of 18th-century buildings, civilised shops and pubs, leads down to the striking 1830s suspension bridge over the river. All Saints' Church, near by, with its churchyard beside the river, is another 19th-century creation, with monuments from the earlier church which include a dramatic one to Sir Miles Hobart, illustrating his death in a road accident in 1632. The Roman Catholic church is by AWN Pugin, with a 1970 addition.

Marlow seems an odd place to have produced *Frankenstein*, but the elegant houses in West Street include Albion House, where Mary Shelley and her husband, the poet, were living in 1818 when she wrote the book. In Station Road, Marlow Place (National Trust, not open), dating from 1720, is considered the finest house in the town. Hostelries include the Two Brewers, where Jerome K Jerome wrote some of *Three Men in a Boat*, the Ship, with a collection of warship photographs and nautical gear, and the Compleat Angler by the river. Towpath walks and boating.

MARNHULL Dorset ST7818
Village off B3092, 3 miles (5km) N of Sturminster Newton
Many creamy limestone farmhouses and cottages are scattered about this dispersed, very rural village.

MARPLE Greater Manchester SJ9588
Town on A626, 4 miles (6km) E of Stockport
An attractive dormitory town, the meeting point of the Macclesfield and Peak Forest canals. The spectacular Marple Aqueduct, completed in 1800 and 100ft (30m) high, carries the Peak Forest Canal over the River Goyt. Adjacent railway viaduct, completed in 1862, is 124ft (38m) high. Moorings and a flight of locks.

MARSDEN Tyne and Wear NZ3964
District of SE South Shields
Marsden Cliff, several 'stacks', or isolated rocks, dominated by Marsden Rock, is a nesting place for many birds and a Site of Special Scientific Interest. On Lizard Point is Souter Lighthouse, opened in 1871 (National Trust). Popular beach at Marsden Bay.

MARSDEN West Yorkshire SE0411
Town on A62, 7 miles (11km) SW of Huddersfield
The centre of this textile town is a conservation area. On Marsden Moor (National Trust) there is evidence of historic transport routes.

MARSHCHAPEL Lincolnshire TF3599
Village on A1031, 7 miles (11km) SE of Cleethorpes
Substantial village on line of medieval seashore, now 3 miles (5km) inland. Large early 15th-century church, built on salt-trade wealth.

MARSHFIELD Avon ST7873
Small town off A420, 6 miles (10km) N of Bath
Handsome small town, set high and with many 17th- and 18th-century stone buildings. Pretty Norman and 15th-century church. To the south is a 19th-century heap of stones marking the old junction of Gloucestershire, Somerset and Wiltshire.

MARSHWOOD Dorset SY3899
Village on B3165, 5 miles (8km) SW of Broadwindsor
A small village on the rim of the Marshwood Vale, a wide green valley in West Dorset. Lambert's Castle is an Iron Age hillfort; Pilsdon Pen is another, on the highest point in Dorset, at 908ft (277m).

MARSKE (MARSKE-IN-SWALEDALE) North Yorkshire NZ1000
Village off A6108, 4 miles (6km) W of Richmond
The village is the midpoint of the Coast to Coast walk and also the centre for the Swaledale Fell Rescue Group.

MARSKE-BY-THE-SEA Cleveland NZ6322
Town on A1085, 2 miles (3km) SE of Redcar
Modern developments have overshadowed older stone cottages near the High Street. Winkey's Castle, a 16th-century cruck cottage, displays fishing and mining exhibits. Only the tower remains of St Germain's Church which was demolished in 1960. Captain Cook's father is buried here. Like many towns along this coast, it has no harbour and boats are launched from a slipway.

MARSTON MAGNA Somerset ST5922
Village on A359, 5 miles (8km) NE of Yeovil
This stone village has a picturesque stream flowing through the middle and a medieval church.

MARSTON MONTGOMERY Derbyshire SK1337
Village off A515, 4 miles (6km) NW of Sudbury
Quiet south Derbyshire village near the Staffordshire border. The 17th-century half-timbered manor house

has a massive stone chimney. Church has a Norman chancel arch and Victorian bellcote.

MARSTON MORETAINE Bedfordshire SP9941
Village off A421, 7 miles (11km) SW of Bedford
Workaday village close to Stewartby (see) brickworks. Handsome 15th-century church with massive detached bell tower, a rarity.

MARTHAM Norfolk TG4518
Village on B1152, 3 miles (5km) W of Winterton-on-Sea
In summertime, dragonflies and butterflies flutter over peaceful Martham Broad. Martham village is near by, an attractive cluster of Georgian houses around a green.

MARTIN Hampshire SU0619
Village off A354, 8 miles (13km) SW of Salisbury
Pretty chalkland village, with thatched cottages and a little stream which runs only in the winter. Martin Down Nature Reserve has a vast area of downland and much archaeology.

MARTINDALE Cumbria NY4319
Village off B5320, 1 mile (2km) SW of Howtown
The village has the only remaining deer forest in England. Wood from the yew tree at the church was used to make archers' bows.

MARTINHOE Devon SS6648
Village off A39, 3 miles (5km) W of Lynton
Fine coastal scenery, woody and rocky. Wooded bay on the shore; the little village lies inland.

MARTLESHAM Suffolk TM2547
Village off A12, 2 miles (3km) SW of Woodbridge
Martlesham originated around the church on a promontory above the River Deben. It has a thriving nursery and the old Red Lion inn.

Sign of the Red Lion at Martlesham.

MARTLEY Hereford and Worcester SO7559
Village on B4204, 7 miles (11km) NW of Worcester
On the hills above the Teme Valley. The venerable Old Rectory stands close to a fine church with much Norman work and notable wall-paintings.

MARTOCK Somerset ST4619
Village on B3165, 6 miles (10km) NW of Yeovil
Almost a tiny town, Martock has a classical market house of 1753 and a classical market cross. The Treasurer's House (National Trust, open only by appointment) is a very rare medieval small house. The church has plain 17th-century gateways and an impressive 15th-century tower. Intricate wooden roof with topless angels dated 1513.

MARTON Cheshire SJ8568
Village on A34, 3 miles (5km) N of Congleton
The 14th-century church is apparently the oldest black and white church in use in Europe. Village oak tree reputedly the largest in England.

MARTON Cleveland NZ5115
Village off A174, 3 miles (5km) SE of Middlesbrough
Suburb of Middlesbrough, the birthplace of Captain Cook in 1728. The Captain Cook Birthplace Museum in Stewart Park depicts the story of his life, exploits and discoveries. Just outside the museum a granite vase marks the site of the cottage where he was born and the start of Cleveland's Captain Cook Trail.

MARTON Lincolnshire SK8381
Village on A156, 5 miles (8km) S of Gainsborough
Where Lincoln–Gainsborough road crosses Roman Tillbridge Lane linking Ermine Street to River Trent. Anglo-Saxon and Norman church, with herringbone masonry.

MARTON Warwickshire SP4068
Village on A423, 5 miles (8km) N of Southam
The River Leam runs by this pleasant village with its interesting museum of agricultural machinery and domestic bygones.

MARTYR WORTHY Hampshire SU5132
Hamlet on B3047, 3 miles (5km) NE of Winchester
Tiny village on the River Itchen, which here is wide and pretty.

MARWOOD Devon SS5437
Village off A361, 3 miles (5km) N of Barnstaple
Set in attractive scenery, the medieval church has a particularly fine 16th-century wooden screen. Marwood Gardens grow camellias, daffodils and other flowers.

MARY TAVY Devon SX5079
see Tavy

MARYCULTER Grampian NO8599
Village off B9077, 1 mile (2km) SE of Peterculter
Mainly known for the family theme park Storybook Glen, which contains over 100 nursery-rhyme characters set in landscaped gardens.

MARYLEBONE Greater London TQ2881
District in City of Westminster, S of Regent's Park
Named after the Church of St Mary-by-the-bourne. Madame Tussauds is a star attraction with its wax figures of the famous and infamous. and the Planetarium next door. Regent's Park and its spectacular terraces date from the 1820s. Paintings, furniture, arms and armour in the Wallace Collection, instruments of agony in the British Dental Association Museum.

MARYPORT Cumbria NY0336
Town on A596, 6 miles (10km) NE of Workington
The harbour at the mouth of the River Ellen was a considerable ship-building centre up to the end of the 19th century. The Maryport Maritime Museum has many displays from the town's maritime past. There is a pre-Norman Conquest castle hill and a Roman fort. Earthworks are all that is now visible.

MARYSTOW Devon SX4382
Hamlet off B3362, 6 miles (10km) NW of Tavistock
Tiny village high above the River Lyd, with a partly Norman church.

MASHAM North Yorkshire SE2280
Small town on A6108, 8 miles (13km) NW of Ripon
This market town, on the River Ure, was granted its market charter by Richard II in 1393. The annual sheep fair was revived a few years ago. The town is home to Theakston's Brewery, famed for its Old Peculier brew. There is a visitors' centre at the brewery.

MATCHING Essex TL5212
Hamlet off A1060, 2 miles (3km) S of Hatfield Heath
Notable for its 15th-century Marriage Feast Room for wedding breakfasts, in an idyllic setting with church. Augustus John lived here.

MATFEN Northumberland NZ0371
Village off B6318, 5 miles (8km) NE of Corbridge
Unspoilt Victorian village built by the Blackett family who owned Matfen Hall. Village green is surrounded by stone houses with high, pointed windows.

MATFIELD Kent TQ6541
Village on B2160, 2 miles (3km) S of Paddock Wood
Attractive village with lovely row of Georgian houses on the north side of the green with a cricket pitch and duck pond.

MATHERN Gwent ST5291
Village off A48, 2 miles (3km) SW of Chepstow
Stands between Chepstow and the sea. Noted for its house, Mathern Palace, once a residence of the bishops of Llandaff. St Pierre Golf and Country Club near by.

MATHON Hereford and Worcester SO7345
Village off A4103, 3 miles (5km) W of Great Malvern
Attractively situated below the western slopes of the Malvern Hills (see), Mathon has outstanding Norman work in its church.

MATLOCK Derbyshire SK2960
Town on A6, 9 miles (14km) SW of Chesterfield
Matlock is a popular Derbyshire Dales town and tourist centre, bordering the Peak National Park. Peak Rail steam trains provide an enjoyable ride to Northwood from Matlock Riverside. The local authority offices occupy Smedley's grand 1852 hydropathic hotel, which once attracted crowds to rest, recuperate and enjoy views of Riber Castle, now a fauna reserve and wildlife park, perched on the opposite hilltop.

Marriage Feast Room at Matching.

From Hall Leys Park's attractive gardens and recreation facilities, the River Derwent flows on through a deep limestone gorge, shared by both railway and A6, to Matlock Bath's wooded walks and autumn illuminations. A cable car spanning the gorge gives easy access to the Heights of Abraham pleasure grounds, where show caverns dramatically demonstrate the earth's history and local lead-mining activity. Gulliver's Kingdom entertains the family, while High Tor precipice, on the opposite hillside, offers a challenge to rock-climbers, or gentler footpaths to the summit.

An aquarium, a countryside exhibition and the fascinating Lead Mining Museum in the Pavilion, where visits to Temple Mine can be arranged, are among the other attractions in this popular Regency resort, with a full range of accommodation. Nearby Lumsdale Valley industrial trail.

MATTERDALE END Cumbria NY3923
Hamlet on A5091, 1 mile (2km) N of Dockray
Tiny hamlet lying at one end of Matterdale, famous for Wordsworth's daffodils. The huntsman Joe Bowman was born here in 1850.

MATTERSEY Nottinghamshire SK6889
Village on B6045, 3 miles (5km) SE of Bawtry
Beside the River Idle are the remains of a small Gilbertine priory (English Heritage), the only English monastic order, founded in 1185 .

MATTINGLEY Hampshire SU7358
Village off B3349, 3 miles (5km) N of Hook
Rural and wooded village with many timber-framed cottages and, much more unusually, a timber-framed church, mostly 15th century.

MAUCHLINE Strathclyde NS4927
Small town on A76, 8 miles (13km) SE of Kilmarnock
Town with Robert Burns connections; the poet was a tenant at Mossgiel Farm, to the north, for nine years and wrote many famous works there. Burns Memorial Tower (1897) is near by. Mauchline Castle (15th century) has a fine vaulted hall. Souvenir sycamore woodware, known as Mauchline Ware, common in the 19th century and collectable today, originated here.

MAULDEN Bedfordshire TL0538
Village off A507, 1 mile (2km) E of Ampthill
Church with curious 17th-century mausoleum (not open). Ghosts abundant. Trails in Maulden Wood; mixed woodland, conifers, meadows and muntjac deer.

MAULDS MEABURN Cumbria NY6216
Village off B6260, 1 mile (2km) N of Crosby Ravensworth
In an Area of Outstanding Natural Beauty. Monument at Black Dub shows where Charles II stopped with his forces in 1632.

MAVESYN RIDWARE Staffordshire SK0816
Hamlet off B5014, 3 miles (5km) E of Rugeley
Small, attractive hamlet. Good monuments in 18th-century church. Notable buildings are the tithe barn in the main street and the timber-framed gatehouse of the former manor.

MAVIS ENDERBY Lincolnshire TF3666
Village on B1195, 2 miles (3km) W of Spilsby
Small Wolds village. Church chancel and upper part of tower rebuilt; nave and aisles restored in Victorian times.

MAWDESLEY Lancashire SD4914
Village off B5246, 2 miles (3km) E of Rufford
Well-kept village with notable buildings including the church, built in 1840, the village school, founded in 1690, and Mawdesley Hall, built in 1625.

MAWDLAM Mid Glamorgan SS8081
Village off A4229, 3 miles (5km) N of Porthcawl
Takes its name from St Mary Magdalen's Church, built here in the 13th century when neighbouring Kenfig's church was threatened by sands (see Kenfig).

MAWGAN Cornwall SW7025
Village off B3293, 3 miles (5km) SE of Helston
Small old village above a little creek. Deep and wooded roads. Trelowarren House is medieval to 18th century. Trelowarren Woodland Walk leads to a fogou, an Iron Age underground passage, or chamber, lined with stone.

MAWGAN PORTH Cornwall SW8567
Village on B3276, 4 miles (6km) NE of Newquay
Seaside village with sandy bay and rocky headlands.

MAWNAN SMITH Cornwall SW7728
Village off A39, 4 miles (6km) S of Falmouth
Set high, overlooking the Helford River. Two fine woodland and sub-tropical gardens on the steep slopes down to the river – Glendurgan Gardens (National Trust) and Trebah Gardens.

MAXEY Cambridgeshire TF1208
Village off A15, 7 miles (11km) NW of Peterborough
On the Cambridgeshire–Lincolnshire border, beside the River Welland. There is a splendid watermill dating from 1779.

MAXSTOKE Warwickshire SP2386
Village off B4098, 3 miles (5km) SE of Coleshill
Small village full of history. Its priory ruins and medieval castle, adapted over centuries, are not open, but the church has fine 18th-century furnishings.

MAY, ISLE OF Fife NT6599
Island in Firth of Forth SE of Anstruther
This 1 mile (2km) long island with dramatic 150ft (46m) cliffs is now a National Nature Reserve and important seabird nesting site. Puffins nest here, and there is a seal colony on the rocks, as well as the ruins of a 12th-century monastery and a 17th-century lighthouse. The existing lighthouse was designed by Robert Stevenson in 1816.

MAYBOLE Strathclyde NS2909
Town on A77, 8 miles (13km) S of Ayr
Once the capital of Carrick, it developed as a market town with weaving and shoe-making industries, and was once renowned for the longevity of its

inhabitants. Maybole Castle is a four-storey L-plan tower and the ruins of the Collegiate church date from 1371. Crossraguel Abbey, a Cluniac foundation, was built in 1244; extensive remains of high architectural quality.

MAYFAIR Greater London TQ2880
District in City of Westminster, E of Park Lane
The smartest area in London's smart West End. Expensive hotels, restaurants, nightclubs and shops. Bond Street boasts some of the capital's most stylish shops and art dealers. The US Embassy and a statue of President Franklin D Roosevelt dignify Grosvenor Square, while tall plane trees soften Berkeley Square. St George's Church in Hanover Square has seen fashionable weddings galore.

MAYFIELD East Sussex TQ5826
Village on A267, 8 miles (13km) S of Tunbridge Wells
Attractive village where legend says St Dunstan once worked as a smith. The High Street has raised red-brick pavements and fine architecture from Mayfield's days as an important iron town. Catholic convent school incorporates remains of the palace of the Archbishops of Canterbury.

MAYFIELD Lothian NT3565
Town off A7, 1 mile (2km) S of Dalkeith
Town on edge of Edinburgh conurbation with easy access to the coast and Moorfoot Hills.

MAYFIELD Staffordshire SK1546
Village off A52, 2 miles (3km) W of Ashbourne
Riverside mills and terraces of Victorian workers' cottages are features of this straggling village beside the River Dove. Church is rewarding.

MEARE Somerset ST4541
Village on B3151, 4 miles (6km) NW of Glastonbury
Once an island on the Somerset Levels, Meare has a little medieval Fish House (English Heritage), used to process fish caught in the surrounding lakes. Extraordinarily elaborate late medieval iron hinges on the church door.

MEAVY Devon SX5467
Village off A386, 6 miles (10km) SE of Tavistock
Tucked in a bend of the River Meavy, a wooded valley just off Dartmoor. Partly Norman church, and the remains of an oak tree supposedly as old.

MEDBOURNE Leicestershire SP8093
Village on B664, 6 miles (10km) NE of Market Harborough
This attractive village sits on the Uppingham–Market Harborough road, not far from the River Welland, which forms the Northamptonshire boundary. In Roman times, this was a large market settlement. A medieval bridge still crosses the stream. The 17th-century Medbourne Manor incorporates a rare survival of a late 13th- or early 14th-century T-shaped manor house. On Easter Monday the village competes with neighbouring Hallaton (see) in traditional Bottle Kicking.

MEDMENHAM Buckinghamshire SU8084
Village on A4155, 3 miles (5km) W of Marlow
Among sedate Victorian houses on the street leading down to the site of an old ferry over the Thames is Medmenham Abbey (not open), once the scene of Hell-Fire Club orgies organised by Sir Francis Dashwood (see West Wycombe). The Dog and Badger pub on the main road claims Nell Gwynne used it.

MEDWAY, RIVER Kent
River in SE England
Rising in the forest country of Sussex, near West Hoathly, the Medway flows into Kent past Tonbridge and Maidstone to its estuary at Rochester and on to Sheerness, where it joins the Thames estuary. Locks were built on the river as far upstream as Tonbridge. The Medway Court of Admiralty controls fishing in the lower reaches.

MEESDEN Hertfordshire TL4332
Village off B1038, 5 miles (8km) NE of Buntingford
Tiny village with old houses. The church, concealed in a wood, has a Tudor brick porch and medieval mosaic tiles.

MEIFOD Powys SJ1513
Village on A495, 4 miles (6km) S of Llanfyllin
Peaceful village in pastoral vale. Interesting church retains some early medieval features. Once an important religious centre – very large churchyard once contained three separate churches.

MEIGLE Tayside NO2844
Village on B954, 4 miles (6km) SE of Alyth
Important Pictish ecclesiastical centre with many symbol stones in Meigle Sculptured Stone Museum. Sir Henry Campbell-Bannerman (1836–1908), the Liberal Prime Minister, is buried here.

MEIKLEOUR Tayside NO1539
Village on A9484, 4 miles (6km) S of Blairgowrie
Village, pronounced 'M'clour', noted for a beech hedge planted in 1746 and now nearly 90ft (27m) high and 580yds (530m) long.

MELBOURN Cambridgeshire TL3844
Village on A10, 3 miles (5km) NE of Royston
Home to the oldest Baptist chapel in Cambridgeshire (1716), a high-tech science park, a 13th-century church and two outstanding restaurants.

MELBOURNE Derbyshire SK3825
Town on B587, 7 miles (11km) S of Derby
Outstanding Norman church, a gem of English ecclesiastical architecture. Charming 17th- and 18th-century Melbourne Hall, set in attractive gardens with a fine wrought-iron summerhouse by Robert Bakewell, was home to tempestuous Lady Caroline Lamb and Queen Victoria's Prime Minister, Lord Melbourne. Travel pioneer Thomas Cook left a Baptist chapel and almshouses to his native town.

MELBURY ABBAS Dorset ST8820
Village off B3081, 2 miles (3km) SE of Shaftesbury
Small scattered village, with stone cottages. Melbury Abbas Mill still in operation.

MELBURY BUBB Dorset ST5906
Village off A37, 7 miles (11km) SE of Yeovil
The tiny village is tucked under a woody hill in a lovely area. Bubb was the name of the local family.

MELBURY OSMOND Dorset ST5707
Village off A37, 5 miles (8km) S of Yeovil
Picturesque and unspoilt, with stone cottages. Unusual church of 1745: Thomas Hardy's parents were married here.

MELCHBOURNE Bedfordshire TL0265
Village off A6, 5 miles (8km) E of Rushden
Small and pretty place with thatched cottages, farms and an 18th-century church. Owned by Knights Hospitallers in Middle Ages.

MELCOMBE BINGHAM Dorset ST7602
Village off A354, 5 miles (8km) N of Puddletown
The big house (not open) with its 16th-century gatehouse, and the medieval church, are set away from the rest of the village.

MELDRETH Cambridgeshire TL3746
Village off A10, 4 miles (6km) NE of Royston
Ancient Meldreth village green has stocks and the base of a cross. Fruit fields and orchards surround the Norman church.

MELKSHAM Wiltshire ST9063
Town off A350, 6 miles (10km) S of Chippenham
Small town on the River Avon, with a surprising amount of industry and a sizeable 15th-century church. Mostly modern in the centre, it has older buildings around the church and some Regency houses from a small spa which started in 1815. Local museum.

MELLING Lancashire SD5970
Village on A683, 5 miles (8km) S of Kirkby Lonsdale
Charming village in the Lune Valley with a long cluster of mellow stone houses, with mullioned windows, lining the narrow road.

MELLOR Greater Manchester SJ9888
Village off A626, 2 miles (3km) E of Marple
A pretty village surrounded by hills with older terraced cottages alongside the river. Once a base for farming and cottage industries, now popular with commuters.

MELLS Somerset ST7249
Village off A362, 3 miles (5km) W of Frome
Distinguished village, all of honey-coloured stone and wooded. Superb cottages, many thatched, and a big manor house (not open), as well as a handsome early 16th-century church with 104ft (31m) tower. It was planned to rebuild Mells in 1470 on a new plan: New Street was the only part built.

MELMERBY Cumbria NY6137
Village on A686, 8 miles (12km) NE of Penrith
Picturesque village of low, red sandstone buildings – typical of this area – at the foot of the Pennines with almost every house overlooking the large village green.

MELROSE Borders NT5434
Town on A6091, 4 miles (6km) E of Galashiels
Beautifully situated between the River Tweed and the Eildon Hills, Melrose was an important Roman centre, whose story is told at the Trimontium Exhibition in town. Today, its chief attraction is the stone remains of Melrose Abbey, founded by David I in 1136 to replace the 7th-century monastery of St Aidan, to the east. Its fortunes, founded on wool, fluctuated until the Reformation as it was repeatedly razed by the English , mainly in the 1380s and the 1540s. Most of what remains is in Gothic style and dates from the intervening period. The abbey church has well-preserved Perpendicular windows and much finely carved detail on the stonework. There is a museum, housed in the Commendator's House, and Melrose has other museums and lovely gardens, which include Priorwood Gardens (National Trust for Scotland). There is easy access up the Eildon Hills from the town.

Abbotsford, the final home of Sir Walter Scott, lies near by on the River Tweed and clearly shows the hand of the writer in its architecture. It was completed in 1824 and the author died there in 1832. It houses a collection of personal memorabilia and Scottish historical relics.

MELTHAM West Yorkshire SE1110
Town on B6107, 5 miles (8km) SW of Huddersfield
Once a thriving industrial town with several woollen and textile mills, brickworks, a silk mill and thread mill. Now only two woollen mills remain. Bus museum.

MELTON Suffolk TM2850
Village on B1438, immediately NE of Woodbridge
On the outskirts of the charming estuary town of Woodbridge, Melton's new church has an ancient and particularly interesting sacrament font.

MELTON CONSTABLE Norfolk TG0433
Village on B1354, 4 miles (6km) SW of Holt
The Astley family lived in Melton Constable Hall (not open) from 1236 to 1956. They built a tower in 1588 to watch for the Spanish Armada.

MELTON MOWBRAY Leicestershire SK7519
Town on A607, 14 miles (23km) NE of Leicester
Tasty pork pies and Stilton cheese, a popular market, a superb parish church, and a hunt meeting point: these are some of Melton Mowbray's features. The Tuesday street and cattle market, established before 1077, still draws crowds, with market place stalls on Wednesdays and Saturdays, too.

Milk from the rich Vale of Belvoir pastures produces the 'king of cheeses', Stilton, in town and village dairies. At Dickinson and Morris, traditional hand-raised pork pies and rich Melton Hunt cake are made.

Cathedral-sized St Mary's Church, mainly of the 13th and 14th centuries, owes its splendour to wealth from the medieval wool trade. It has a fine central tower and an amazing range of 48 windows in the 15th-century clerestory. Neighbouring 14th-century Anne of Cleves' House is one of Melton's oldest buildings.

Numerous hunting boxes were built or converted in the 19th century, a base for the gentry's social activities. In 1837, the boisterous Marquis of Waterford and his friends added a new saying to the language by literally 'painting the town red'. The Carnegie Museum tells the story, and leisure pools, country park, theatre and sports centre offer further enjoyment.

MELVERLEY Shropshire SJ3316
Hamlet off B4393, 10 miles (16km) W of Shrewsbury
At the confluence of rivers Vyrnwy and Severn, this old boatmen's settlement preserves a rare example of a timber-framed 15th-century church.

MELVICH Highland NC8764
Village on A836, 15 miles (24km) W of Thurso
Lies at the sea end of Strath Halladale, with dramatic cliff scenery near by and views north to the Orkneys.

MENAI BRIDGE Gwynedd (Anglesey) SH5571
Town off A5, 2 miles (3km) W of Bangor
Small town on the north side of Menai Strait named after handsome suspension bridge over the strait designed by Thomas Telford as part of A5 London to Holyhead route. Beautiful views of bridge and strait from waterside Belgian Promenade, which leads to Church Island with its ancient religious site. Neat streets contain Tegfryn Art Gallery. Butterfly farm is a popular tourist attraction.

MENDIP HILLS Somerset
Hill range running SE from above Weston-Super-Mare
This range of limestone hills runs for 30 miles (50km) from the sea at Weston-Super-Mare, right across Somerset to Frome. The summits only reach just over 1,000ft (300m) but give wide views because the surrounding areas are flat. There are many Bronze Age barrows and Iron Age hillforts on the hilltops, and lead was mined here from Roman times until 1800. The limestone has been eroded underground in places, producing caves like those at Cheddar and Wookey (see). There are several picturesque gorges and many smaller combes. The upland fields are divided by characteristic drystone walls and there are many pretty stone villages, also built from limestone quarried locally. Huge modern quarries at the eastern end used for roadstone.

MENDLESHAM Suffolk TM1065
Village off A140, 6 miles (10km) NE of Stowmarket
The 1,000ft (305m) TV mast dominates Mendlesham. St Mary's Church, curiously, houses a collection of armour stored since 1593.

MENHENIOT Cornwall SX2862
Village off A38, 3 miles (5km) SE of Liskeard
Stone village whose prominent church has a spire, rare in Cornwall. Stone quarries here in medieval times.

MENSTRIE Central NS8597
Small town on A91, 4 miles (6km) NE of Stirling
Originally a weaving town with an attractive village green, tucked under the Ochil Hills. Restored 16th-century Menstrie Castle was the birthplace in 1567 of William Alexander, founder of Nova Scotia.

MENTMORE Buckinghamshire SP9019
Village off B488, 4 miles (6km) S of Leighton Buzzard
Mentmore Towers (limited opening), grandiose Rothschild palace designed in mock Elizabethan style by Sir Joseph Paxton, later home of Earls of Rosebery, now belongs to the Transcendental Meditation Movement as its British Seat of the World Government of the Age of Enlightenment. Magnificent grounds, fine views, village green and 19th-century estate cottages, Victorianised church.

MEOLE BRACE Shropshire SJ4810
District on SW outskirts of Shrewsbury
Old village centre, now engulfed by Shrewsbury, boasts Victorian church with celebrated windows by William Morris and Burne-Jones.

MEONSTOKE Hampshire SU6120
Village off A32, 4 miles (6km) E of Bishop's Waltham
The village has a superb High Street of Georgian brick, and a church low in the watermeadows. Set on the River Meon.

MEOPHAM Kent TQ6466
Village on A227, 5 miles (8km) S of Gravesend
Attractive village strung along a main road with its centre at Meopham Green, where the cricketing tradition goes back to the 18th century. Restored windmill of 1807 overlooks the green.

MEPAL Cambridgeshire TL4480
Village off A142, 6 miles (10km) W of Ely
Idyllic setting on the Ouse Washes, overlooking the fenland wilderness and frequented by migrating swans. There is an outdoor centre.

MEPPERSHALL Bedfordshire TL1336
Village off A507, 2 miles (3km) S of Shefford
Earthworks of Norman castle survive, known as The Hills. The Bedfordshire–Hertfordshire border used to run through the rectory dining room.

MERE Wiltshire ST8132
Small town on B3095, 7 miles (11km) NE of Wincanton
Charming small town, with a large medieval church, a famous 18th-century wrought-iron sign on the Ship inn, and many pleasant buildings. Local museum.

MERE BROW Lancashire SD4218
Village off A565, 5 miles (8km) E of Southport
Former site of one of England's biggest lakes until it was drained at the end of the 18th century. Part of the area has reverted back to wetland and in 1972 the Wildfowl Trust acquired 363 acres (147ha) of marshlands and created Martin Mere, now an internationally renowned wildfowl centre. Leisure Lakes is popular parkland.

MEREVALE ABBEY Warwickshire SP2997
see Atherstone

MEREWORTH Kent TQ6653
Village off B2016, 6 miles (10km) W of Maidstone
Model village of the 1740s, built on a new site by the Earl of Westmoreland after he had demolished the old village to build Mereworth Castle, a Palladian villa on a grand scale. The church is the best 18th-century church in Kent, with a spire copied from St Martin-in-the-Fields in London. Near by are Mereworth Woods, a large surviving area of ancient forest.

MERIDEN West Midlands SP2482
Village on B4102, 6 miles (10km) W of Coventry
Sprawling village claiming to be the centre of England. On Meriden Green the medieval village cross marks the spot, and a cyclists' national war memorial is near by. Forest Hall (1788) is headquarters of the Woodmen of Arden, an archery club which holds an annual competition (Grand Wardmote) here in August. The medieval church was reputedly founded by Lady Godiva.

MERLEY Dorset SZ0298
Suburb off A349, 1 mile (2km) S of Wimborne Minster
Modern suburb of Wimborne. Merley House (1750s) has splendid plasterwork inside and displays of model toys. Merley Bird Gardens.

MERRIVALE Devon SX5475
Village on B3357, 4 miles (6km) E of Tavistock
The only granite quarry still working, and the easiest place to see Bronze Age hut circles and enclosures. Discarded 19th-century millstones on the hillside.

MERSEA ISLAND Essex TM0414
Island on B1025, S of Colchester
An island of creeks and marshes. The main settlement is West Mersea (see). Cudmore Grove Country Park, with views and picnic area, on southern shore.

MERSEY, RIVER Merseyside
River, reaching the Irish Sea at Liverpool
The river begins in Stockport and formed the old boundary between Lancashire and Cheshire. A major maritime commercial route, the river reaches the Irish Sea at Liverpool where there are several miles of docks lining its banks. The Kingsway and Queensway tunnels, under the River Mersey, run from the centre of Liverpool to Wallasey and Birkenhead respectively.

MERSHAM Kent TR0539
Village off A20, 3 miles (5km) SE of Ashford
There is modern and older housing in this village between the railway and the M20, where the church has a spectacular 15th-century west window.

MERSTHAM Surrey TQ2953
Village off A23, 2 miles (3km) N of Redhill
Pretty village on London–Redhill road with an old coaching inn and picturesque no-through road. Quality Street (named after a play by J M Barrie) is near by, the site of the Surrey Iron Railway, the first public railway (1805).

MERTHYR MAWR Mid Glamorgan SS8877
Village off A48, 2 miles (3km) SW of Bridgend
Picturesque small village of thatched cottages around green and church – quintessential England transplanted into South Wales. Extensive sand dunes at Merthyr Mawr Warren.

MERTHYR TYDFIL Mid Glamorgan SO0406
Town on A470, 21 miles (34km) NW of Cardiff
Merthyr Tydfil, beside the River Taff, is the former 'iron and steel capital of the world'. In the early 19th century, Merthyr was the largest town in Wales. In districts like Dowlais (see), Penydarren and Cyfarthfa, the ironmasters reigned supreme. Cyfarthfa Castle, former home of the Crawshay family, is a surviving example of their wealth. The 1825 mansion, built in mock-military style in parkland overlooking the Crawshays' ironworks, now houses the town museum.

Other reminders of Merthyr's past pre-eminence are the Ynysfach Engine House, which contains industrial displays, and the memorial to the Merthyr to Abercynon railway, on which in 1804 Cornishman Richard Trevithic ran the world's first steam locomotive.

The cultural life which was a feature of the industrial valleys is represented by a humble terraced cottage, birthplace (1841) of composer Joseph Parry. Politically, Merthyr was a hotbed of dissent. In 1900,the town returned Britain's first Socialist Member of Parliament, James Keir Hardy, founder of the Independent Labour Party.

Although industry dominates Merthyr's story, the town's history stretches back to Roman times (there was a camp at Penydarren). Morlais Castle, north of the town, is a ruined Norman stronghold.

MERTON Greater London TQ2570
Town/borough off A24, in SW London
On the River Wandle, a forerunner of the garden suburb idea. Connections with Lord Nelson, whose pew can be seen in the parish church, and Liberty department store, which produced printed fabrics here. Liberty Board Mill on the Wandle has museum and craft centre. John Innes Park is in the grounds of the famous horticulturalist's mansion.

METFIELD Suffolk TM2980
Village on B1123, 4 miles (6km) SE of Harleston
Most of the large World War II USAAF airbase has been reclaimed for farming. The Church of St John the Baptist has a superb clock.

METHERINGHAM Lincolnshire TF0661
Village off B1188, 9 miles (14km) SE of Lincoln
Large village between Lincoln and Sleaford. Medieval church arches discoloured by 1599 fire, pillars then replaced by Tuscan columns, tower restored.

METHIL Fife NT3799
Town on B931, immediately NE of Buckhaven
This harbour has been here since 1662 and was Scotland's busiest coal port in the early 20th century. Today the dock facilities are used for oil rigs.

METHLEY West Yorkshire SE3926
Village on A639, 5 miles (8km) NE of Wakefield
A residential area. The large village green is surrounded by the old village of stone cottages. There are newer developments of 20th-century houses.

METHLICK Grampian NJ8537
Village on B9170, 6 miles (10km) S of New Deer
Village on the River Ythan near Haddo House, designed by Willam Adam in 1731, but with a Victorian interior. It stands in landscaped parkland.

METHVEN Tayside NO0225
Village on A85, 6 miles (10km) W of Perth
Site of a defeat of Robert Bruce by the English in 1306. Methven Castle (17th century) was one of the last tower houses to be built.

METHWOLD Norfolk TL7394
Village on B1112, 6 miles (10km) NW of Brandon
A large village including several farmsteads and nearby river port of Methwold Hythe. Set in flat fenland, the church, unusually for Norfolk, has a steeple.

MEVAGISSEY Cornwall SX0144
Small town on B3273, 5 miles (8km) S of St Austell
This picturesque little fishing town is rather more urban than most, with larger and higher buildings cramming the narrow streets. The wide inner harbour is 18th-century, using natural rocks for some walls; also an outer harbour. There are more yachts than fishing boats now. Rocky shore; local museum; model railway museum; Mevagissey Harbour Aquarium.

MEYSEY HAMPTON Gloucestershire SP1100
Village on A417, 2 miles (3km) W of Fairford
Pleasant village with a Georgian manor house and fine examples of medieval art in a rewarding church connected with the Knights Templar.

MICHAELCHURCH ESCLEY Hereford and Worcester SO3134
Hamlet off B4347, 7 miles (11km) NW of Pontrilas
This lonely settlement on the eastern edge of the Black Mountains has a church with a rare wall-painting of Christ surrounded by workmen's tools.

MICHELDEVER Hampshire SU5139
Village off A33, 6 miles (10km) N of Winchester
Large and pretty village with lots of timber-framing and thatch. Curious octagon of 1808 at the centre of the church.

MICKLEHAM Surrey TQ1753
Village off A24, 2 miles (3km) S of Leatherhead
Village on the steep side of the wooded Mole Valley near Box Hill, with a pub, The Running Horses, named after a dead-heat in the Derby of 1828. The church in the village centre has a chapel with panelling reputedly saved from the Great Fire of London, 1666. Juniper Hall, now a field studies centre, was a home to French refugees during the Revolution.

MICKLETHWAITE West Yorkshire SE1041
Site off A650, 2 miles (3km) N of Bingley
A picturesque hamlet on the south side of Rombalds Moor.

MICKLETON Gloucestershire SP1643
Village on B4632, 3 miles (5km) N of Chipping Campden
Beneath the northern edge of the Cotswolds, the village has an array of good stone and timber-framed buildings and a treasured 12th-century sculpture in its church.

MICKLEY SQUARE Northumberland NZ0762
Village on A695, 1 mile (2km) W of Prudhoe
Birthplace of Thomas Bewick, naturalist and wood engraver. Cherryburn, owned by the National Trust, was the home of the Bewick family and is now a museum.

MID CALDER Lothian NT0767
see Livingston

MIDDLE CLAYDON Buckinghamshire SP7225
Village off A413, 4 miles (6km) SW of Winslow
Claydon House (National Trust), historic and haunted home of the Verney family, dates from the 17th century to the 19th, but is specially known for its amazing 18th-century rococo interiors and close link with Florence Nightingale, who often stayed here; there is a museum to her. Verney monuments in the church in the grounds.

MIDDLE LITTLETON Hereford and Worcester SP0746
Village off B4085, 3 miles (5km) NE of Evesham
Village in Evesham orchard country has big cruck-framed tithe barn (National Trust) close to the church and a 17th-century manor house.

MIDDLE RASEN Lincolnshire TF0889
Village on A631, 1 mile (2km) W of Market Rasen
Ironstone church with impressive Norman south doorway and chancel arch. Early 14th-century effigy of priest, with flowing vestments, holding chalice.

MIDDLE TYSOE Warwickshire SP3444
Village off A442, 6 miles (10km) NE of Shipston on Stour
Magnificent font and other fine medieval craftsmanship in distinguished church. The 17th-century Upton House (National Trust) displays many treasures.

MIDDLE WALLOP Hampshire SU2937
Village on A343, 7 miles (11km) SW of Andover
Sparse village with some thatched cottages. The large Museum of Army Flying is based here.

MIDDLE WOODFORD Wiltshire SU1136
Village off A360, 4 miles (6km) N of Salisbury
In the Avon Valley, Middle Woodford is bracketed by Upper and Lower Woodford. Heale Gardens grow shrubs, roses and other plants.

MIDDLEHAM North Yorkshire SE1287
Village on A6108, 2 miles (3km) SE of Leyburn
The monks of Jervaulx founded Middleham's main industry when they began training their horses on the Low Moor just above the village. By the late 18th

century there were race meetings held on the moor and the first racing stables had been established. The village has two market crosses, one in each square.

MIDDLETON Cumbria SD6286
Village on A683, 5 miles (8km) N of Kirkby Lonsdale
Scattered village between the Lune Valley and Middleton Fell. A Roman milestone stands on a hill near the church. Middleton Hall is now a farm.

MIDDLETON Derbyshire SK2755
Village on B5023, 1 mile (2km) N of Wirksworth
Limestone-quarrying village. Middleton Top beam-engine, steamed regularly in summer, used to haul wagons up Middleton Incline. Visitor centre and cycle hire along High Peak Trail.

MIDDLETON Greater Manchester SD8606
Town on A664, 6 miles (10km) N of Manchester
An industrial suburb of Manchester which grew as a result of the cotton industry. Spinning, weaving, bleaching and printing of cotton were all carried out here, and earlier in the 18th century, silk weaving was the main industry. Prior to this, the town had been well known for clock-making.

MIDDLETON Warwickshire SP1798
Village off A4091, 4 miles (6km) SW of Tamworth
Middleton Hall offers architecture of many centuries and nature trails in the large grounds. Imaginative children's farm at Ash End House.

MIDDLETON CHENEY Northamptonshire SP4941
Village on A422, 3 miles (5km) E of Banbury
Large village, site of Civil War battle. Church restored by Sir George Gilbert Scott in 1865; outstanding Morris and Burne-Jones stained glass. Farthinghoe Nature Reserve near by.

MIDDLETON, ST GEORGE AND ONE ROW Durham NZ3413/4
Villages off A67, 4 miles (6km) E of Darlington
Middleton One Row is aptly named, originally consisting of one row of Georgian cottages. Its growth was due to the discovery of a sulphurous spring during excavations for coal. In 1860 blast furnaces were set up in Middleton, industry developed and rows of housing were built for the workers. Teesside Airport is near by.

MIDDLETON-IN-TEESDALE Durham NY9425
Small town on B6277, 8 miles (13km) NW of Barnard Castle
Before the 19th century this was an agricultural village and there is still a livestock market. The Quaker-owned London Lead Company arrived in 1815 to mine, establishing offices at Middleton Hall, now a hunting lodge. They were responsible for virtually every 19th-century feature of Middleton.

MIDDLETON-ON-SEA West Sussex SU9700
Town off A259, 3 miles (5km) E of Bognor Regis
Pleasant resort of bungalows, with a shingle bank and sandy beach. The church of 1849 replaced an earlier one lost to sea. Sea defences have arrested massive coastal erosion here.

MIDDLEWICH Cheshire SJ7066
Town on A533, 6 miles (10km) SE of Northwich
A great salt town, supplier of salt to the Romans. Now an important canal centre on the Trent and Mersey Navigation.

MIDDLEZOY Somerset ST3732
Village off A372, 6 miles (10km) SE of Bridgwater
A village in the Somerset Levels, with a handsome 15th-century church tower.

MIDHURST West Sussex SU8821
Town on A286, 11 miles (18km) N of Chichester
Bustling market town with wide, spacious North Street containing many attractive buildings, including an old coaching inn, the Spread Eagle, and the Angel, said to have been patronised by the Pilgrim Fathers. Timber-framed buildings, including the library, cluster along Knockhundred Row. Church Hill and Sheep Lane wear an aspect of Midhurst's prosperous Georgian times. Lovely Cowdray Park is an important polo venue. Tudor Cowdray House, now ruined, burned down in 1793.

MIDSOMER NORTON Avon ST6654
Town on A362, 1 mile (2km) W of Radstock
Not as pretty as its name. In the middle of the old coal-mining area, with tips and remains of collieries all around. A tidied-up stream runs along the High Street. Unusual 17th-century church tower with statue of Charles II, and Roman Catholic church in a converted medieval barn.

MILBORNE PORT Somerset ST6718
Village on A30, 3 miles (5km) NE of Sherborne
Pleasant stone village, with a baby Georgian 'town hall' and a big medieval church with Saxon-Norman features.

MILBURN Cumbria NY6529
Village off A66, 6 miles (10km) N of Appleby
Classic example of a medieval fortified village. Howgill Castle was a former manor house, built in the 14th century. St Cuthbert's Church dates from the Norman Conquest.

MILDENHALL Suffolk TL7174
Village on A1101, 8 miles (13km) NE of Newmarket
In 1946 a ploughman unearthed an astonishing collection of Roman silver plates, spoons, and goblets that became known as the 'Mildenhall treasure'. A great watermill still works on the River Lark, while the hammerbeam ceiling of St Mary and St Andrew's Church is unusually decorated with carved dragons. Near by is the vast American airbase.

MILDENHALL Wiltshire SU2169
Village off A346, 1 mile (2km) E of Marlborough
Pronounced 'Milnal', the village boasts a street lined with thatched brick cottages, an old school of 1824 and a church fitted out in 1815.

MILFORD Derbyshire SK3545
Village on A6, 1 mile (2km) S of Belper
Milford grew from the establishment of Jedediah Strutt's cotton-mill (1780), now mostly demolished. Weirs, stone bridge and 1790s industrial housing using local stone.

MILFORD Staffordshire SJ9721
Village on A513, 4 miles (6km) SE of Stafford
A pleasant village overshadowed by Shugborough, a distinguished 18th-century house (National Trust), the adjacent Staffordshire County Museum and a farm museum in the grounds.

MILFORD Surrey SU9442
Small town on A286, 2 miles (3km) SW of Godalming
Small town on the London–Portsmouth road at the foot of greensand hills in the Wey Valley. Brick and tile-hung cottages scattered among Victorian and later developments.

MILFORD HAVEN (MILFFWRD) Dyfed SM8504
Town on A4076, 5 miles (8km) W of Pembroke
Once an important port on the Milford Haven waterway. The town is spread out in an orderly fashion on hill above the sea. Previously a leading fishing port, the area is now taken over by oil terminals. Has connections with Nantucket whalers. Harbour has been given a new lease of life through a modern marina development. Museum tells of seafaring past.

MILFORD ON SEA Hampshire SZ2891
Town on B3058, 3 miles (5km) SW of Lymington
The village developed as a seaside resort from late Victorian times. Surprisingly complete 13th-century church.

MILL HILL Greater London TQ2292
District in borough of Barnet
Mill Hill Broadway is the shopping centre. Numerous Roman Catholic institutions here include St Joseph's College, 1860s, strikingly topped by the saint's statue 100ft (30m) up. Well-known Mill Hill School, originally Nonconformist, has a classical-style 1820s building on The Ridgeway. The National Institute for Medical Research is housed in a 1930s building.

MILLBROOK Bedfordshire TL0138
Village off A507, 2 miles (3km) NW of Ampthill
Victorianised church with interesting monuments. Link with Valley of Shadow of Death in *Pilgrim's Progress*. Vauxhall Motors testing track.

MILLBROOK Cornwall SX4252
Village on B3247, 3 miles (5km) S of Torpoint
Small village with a big pond on the Tamar estuary, with views of Plymouth.

MILLER'S DALE Derbyshire SK1473
Village on B6049, 5 miles (8km) E of Buxton
The River Wye meanders through this lovely Peak District limestone dale. Walks and picnic sites on Monsal Trail, the line of former railway. Two massive viaducts, 1870s lime kilns.

MILLOM Cumbria SD1780
Town on A5098, 5 miles (8km) SW of Broughton in Furness
Small industrial town on the coast with splendid surrounding beaches. In 1868 a rich seam of haematite was discovered at the tip of the peninsula at Hodbarrow, and Millom was built to work the mine. Working of the seam stopped 100 years later. Folk Museum has an exhibition dedicated to Lakeland poet Norman Nicholson.

MILNATHORT Tayside NO1204
Town on A911, 2 miles (3km) N of Kinross
Small town best known for the ruins of Burleigh Castle, with remains of a 15th-century keep, a curtain wall and moat and a later tower house (1582).

MILNGAVIE Strathclyde NS5574
Town on A81, 6 miles (10km) N of Glasgow
Pleasant residential town lying below Campsie Fells and Kilpatrick Hills to the north of Glasgow, pronounced 'Mull-guy'. Mugdock Country Park lies to the north and contains Mugdock Loch, with the remains of Mugdock Castle on the promontory. The castle was originally a 15th-century fortified tower. A baronial mansion was added in the 19th century; both are now derelict.

MILNROW Greater Manchester SD9212
Town off M62, 2 miles (3km) E of Rochdale
A small industrial town in the foothills of the Pennines with examples of 18th-century weavers' cottages. Several reservoirs near by on the local moors.

MILNTHORPE Cumbria SD4981
Village on A6, 7 miles (11km) S of Kendal
Originally a port, but the River Bela has now silted up. The 'mil' of Milnthorpe referred to the watermills along the river.

MILSTED Kent TQ9058
Village off B2163, 3 miles (5km) S of Sittingbourne
Attractive village with brick and timber cottages, houses and farms, a half-timbered manor house hidden behind a high wall and a flint and stone church.

MILTON Cambridgeshire TL4762
Village off A10, 3 miles (5km) NE of Cambridge
Now a suburb of Cambridge, Milton has some superb houses. Milton Hall has grounds designed by Humphry Repton; Queen Anne House is pargetted (neither is open).

MILTON Oxfordshire SU4892
Village off A34, 3 miles (5km) NW of Didcot
The huge Didcot power station looms large, but Milton is worth visiting for its fine manor house (limited opening), once owned by George III's lace-maker.

MILTON ABBAS Dorset ST8001
Village off A354, 6 miles (10km) SW of Blandford Forum
Famous 'model' village, built on a new site in the 1780s because the landowner wanted it further away from his house. Simple thatched cottages in a beautiful setting. The big house is an elegant stone mansion of 1774, incorporating the abbey hall (limited opening). Huge church, part of the abbey church.

MILTON ABBOT Devon SX4079

Village on B3362, 6 miles (10km) NW of Tavistock

Pretty and wooded landscape above the Tamar estuary, with Endsleigh House (a hotel), an extraordinary, fanciful building of 1810. Equally fanciful gardens (limited opening).

MILTON BRYAN Bedfordshire SP9730

Village off A4012, 2 miles (3km) SE of Woburn

Church window to Sir Joseph Paxton of Crystal Palace fame. Thatched cottages and haunted Mag's Lane.

MILTON ERNEST Bedfordshire TL0156

Village on A6, 5 miles (8km) NW of Bedford

Attractive village close to Great Ouse. Memories of Glenn Miller in Queen's Head pub; he was stationed at Milton Hall.

Bread rack at Milton Ernest.

MILTON KEYNES Buckinghamshire SP8537

New Town off M1, 3 miles (5km) SW of Newport Pagnell

Central Milton Keynes is at the heart of a fascinating new 'urban countryside' development, commenced in the 1960s and still continuing, covering 22,000 acres (8900ha) and several existing towns and villages. Planned with the motor car much in mind, a new road network links local centres in a rural landscape of farms, rivers, lakes, trees and windmills. Parks have been created along the Grand Union Canal and in the Ouse, Ouzel and Loughton Brook valleys. Milton Keynes has more species of wildlife now than before development started.

Housing is being built at the rate of 2,500 new homes a year. In the central grid of streets a huge shopping area with restaurants, bars, offices, railway station, entertainment centre and Buckinghamshire's biggest library has ample parking. The £3 million ecumenical Church of Christ the Cornerstone, with its impressive dome and lantern 101ft (30m) high, was dedicated in 1992. Quirky artworks include concrete cows and there are statues by Elisabeth Frink and other leading contemporary artists. Museums cover the area's archaeology and history, industry and rural life. (For outlying areas, see Bletchley; Fenny Stratford; Great Linford; Loughton; New Bradwell; Newport Pagnell; Stony Stratford; Wolverton.)

MILTON MALSOR Northamptonshire SP7355

Village off A43, 4 miles (6km) S of Northampton

Rural dormitory village for Northampton with Milton House (1777), an early 18th-century manor house, and attractive earlier houses, one of chequered brick.

MILTON REGIS Kent TQ8964

District of Sittingbourne

An ancient royal borough, now a village with paper mills and a well-defined centre, which has spread to Sittingbourne.

MILTON-UNDER-WYCHWOOD Oxfordshire SP2618

Village off A361, 4 miles (6km) N of Burford

This Evenlode Valley village, much expanded by modern housing, has an interesting group of church, lychgate, school and school house designed by GE Street.

MILVERTON Somerset ST1225

Small town on B3187, 7 miles (11km) W of Taunton

A little stone town, mostly small-scale Georgian. Medieval church with many 16th-century bench-ends, some with figures.

MINCHINHAMPTON Gloucestershire SO8700

Small town off A419, 3 miles (5km) S of Stroud

The 17th-century market house on piers is just one of a charming mix of buildings in the streets of this mellow small town above the Frome Valley, and the old textile mills in the valley provide further architectural variety. Minchinhampton Common (National Trust) is a lofty plateau with splendid views over the Frome and Nailsworth valleys.

MINEHEAD Somerset SS9746

Town on A39, 2 miles (3km) NW of Dunster

Minehead is a large town and resort, mostly Victorian. A medieval church stands at the top of the wooded hill with thatched cottages, and the long Church Steps lead down to the Victorian town centre. The sandy bay has older houses and cottages along the front to the harbour. Somerwest World (Butlins holiday camp) is based here, and the steam West Somerset Railway runs 20 miles (32km) to Bishop's Lydeard, near Taunton (see).

MINIONS Cornwall SX2671
Village off B3254, 4 miles (6km) N of Liskeard
A small village at the centre of an area of great archaeological interest on the edge of Bodmin Moor. The most spectacular monuments are Bronze Age: The Hurlers, three stone circles in a row, and Stowe's Pound, two enclosures with stone ramparts, one showing the hut circles inside. The Cheesewring is a natural large heap of stone looking like sculpture. The area was also important for copper- and tin-mining in the 19th century, with remains on Caradon Hill, near Cheesewring and elsewhere.

MINSMERE Suffolk TM4766
Nature reserve off B1122, 3 miles (5km) N of Leiston
On a windswept part of the swampy Suffolk coast is Minsmere Nature Reserve, a refuge for migrating and resident birds, run by the RSPB.

MINSTEAD Hampshire SU2811
Village off A337, 2 miles (3km) NW of Lyndhurst
Scattered, large New Forest village. The inside of the church is crammed with three levels of galleries, like a theatre. Conan Doyle, the creator of Sherlock Holmes, is buried here.

MINSTER LOVELL Oxfordshire SP3111
Village off A40, 3 miles (5km) NW of Witney
The long, cottage-lined street beside the River Windrush leads to a 15th-century bridge. Along the river bank are the ruins of Minster Lovell Hall (English Heritage), a medieval fortified manor house. The nearby church has a wealth of medieval glass. To the south a few cottages survive from an idealistic 19th-century smallholding scheme.

MINSTER (MINSTER IN SHEPPEY) Kent TQ9573
Town on B2008, 2 miles (3km) SE of Sheerness
Grey little town on the highest point of the Isle of Sheppey, looking out over the Thames and Medway estuaries. Double church; nunnery church of 1130 and later parish church.

MINSTER (MINSTER IN THANET) Kent TR3064
Village off A253, 5 miles (8km) W of Ramsgate
Village on the southern slopes of the Isle of Thanet overlooking Minster Marshes, with a fine Norman church and a modern nunnery in the Norman buildings of the abbey grange on a Saxon site.

MINSTERLEY Shropshire SJ3705
Village off A488, 9 miles (14km) SW of Shrewsbury
Beneath the Stiperstones the pleasant village is grouped around its hall and oddly-designed church of 1689, where Maidens' Garlands still hang.

MINTERNE MAGNA Dorset ST6504
Village on A352, 2 miles (3km) N of Cerne Abbas
Lush, wooded parish, with many parkland trees on the small hills. Minterne Gardens are fine woodland with rhododendrons.

MINTLAW Grampian NJ9948
Village on A92, 9 miles (14km) E of Peterhead
The largest Buchan village which has grown in recent years. Near by is Aden Country Park and heritage centre, with woodland, lake and exhibits on farming in the northeast .

MINTO Borders NT5620
Village off A698, 5 miles (8km) NE of Hawick
Small village northeast of Hawick with imposing and rugged Minto Crags near by. On their summit are the wonderfully named ruins of Fatlips Castle.

MINTON Shropshire SO4390
Hamlet off A49, 2 miles (3km) SW of Church Stretton
Ancient settlement at foot of Long Mynd (see), with manor house and cluster of old cottages around a green.

MIRFIELD West Yorkshire SE2019
Town on A644, 3 miles (5km) SW of Dewsbury
Small town on the Calder and Hebble Navigation with a canal basin. Medieval church tower in grounds of modern church.

MISERDEN Gloucestershire SO9309
Village off A417, 7 miles (11km) NW of Cirencester
High above the wooded Frome Valley, Miserden Park Gardens attract many visitors, and the village church of Saxon origin is of interest.

MISTERTON Nottinghamshire SK7694
Village on A161, 5 miles (8km) NW of Gainsborough
Set on low-lying land between the River Idle and the Chesterfield Canal, near the Lincolnshire boundary. The 13th-century and later church spire was rebuilt in the 1840s after a lightning strike.

MISTLEY Essex TM1231
see Manningtree

MITCHAM Greater London TQ2768
District in borough of Merton
Cricket has been played on Mitcham Green since the 18th century. Extensive common with golf course. City farm. The Canons, 17th century, is now a leisure centre.

MITCHELDEAN Gloucestershire SO6618
Small town on A4136, 3 miles (5km) N of Cinderford
Despite modern industry and housing this old Forest of Dean town, set in wooded hills, is worth a visit. The church is particularly impressive.

MITCHELL'S FOLD STONE CIRCLE Shropshire SO3098
see Chirbury

MITFORD Northumberland NZ1786
Village on B6343, 2 miles (3km) W of Morpeth
Unspoilt village at confluence of rivers Wansbeck and Font. Newminster Abbey, formerly a Cistercian house established in 1138, is now in ruins.

MOBBERLEY Cheshire SJ7879
Village on B5085, 2 miles (3km) E of Knutsford
A sprawling village in dairy-farming country, with a mixture of old and new influences. The oldest house in

the village has been inhabited for over 600 years, and the present church was begun in 1245. Large Ilford works are now on the site of a 19th-century crêpe mill.

MOCCAS Hereford and Worcester SO3542
Hamlet off B4352, 10 miles (16km) W of Hereford
Moccas Court (limited opening), house of 1770s by Robert Adam, has elegant interior. Interesting Norman church in riverside grounds by Capability Brown.

MOCHRUM Dumfries and Galloway NX3446
Village off A747, 2 miles (3km) N of Port William
Tiny inland village to the east of Luce Bay. Old Place of Mochrum, to the north, comprises two towers of the 16th and 18th centuries, restored and connected in the 20th century.

MODBURY Devon SX6551
Small town on A379, 7 miles (11km) NW of Kingsbridge
Pretty little market town, with lots of slate-hanging. White Hart hotel and Assembly Rooms, both of 1827, and many other Georgian and early 19th-century buildings. Prominent church with rare medieval spire.

MODDERSHALL Staffordshire SJ9236
Hamlet off A520, 2 miles (3km) NE of Stone
Nine watermills (one restored and open) stand beside Scotch Brook below this unspoilt rural community among hills in the upper Trent Valley.

MOELFRE Gwynedd (Anglesey) SH5186
Village off A5025, 6 miles (10km) SE of Amlwch
Charming coastal village with pebble beach, cottages, and attractive sandy beaches to south and north. Connections with Dickens. Inland are two important historic sites (Cadw). Lligwy burial chamber is a huge prehistoric tomb, one of Britain's largest. Din Lligwy has remains of ancient village dating from Roman times, with nearby ruined medieval chapel of Capel Lligwy.

MOFFAT Dumfries and Galloway NT0805
Small town on A701, 19 miles (31km) NE of Dumfries
Market town at the centre of a sheep-farming district with a wide and spacious High Street lined with Georgian houses and trim cottages. The Colvin fountain is surmounted by a fine brass ram. This was a fashionable spa town in the 18th century: the sulphurous well was patronised by Robert Burns. Moffat Museum tells the town's history. The local speciality is Moffat toffee.

MOIDART Highland
Scenic region W of Loch Shiel
Historic and scenic area between Ardnamurchan and Arisaig, on the route of the Road to the Isles. The evocative Castle Tioram ruins stand on Loch Moidart. Strong Jacobite area.

MOIRA Leicestershire SK3115
Village on B5003, 2 miles (3km) W of Ashby-de-la-Zouch
Industrial settlement developed after 1800. The former Ashby Canal carried coal and bricks. Early 19th-century blast furnace (limited opening) on industrial heritage trail.

MOLD Clwyd SJ2364
Town on A541, 11 miles (18km) NW of Wrexham
The small county town of Clwyd. Home of Theatre Clwyd, leading North Wales cultural and entertainments venue. Busy market place, especially the Wednesday and Saturday open-air markets. Welsh novelist Daniel Owen (the 'Welsh Dickens') born and lived here – Daniel Owen Museum in library. Notable church. To the west is the Loggerheads Country Park with its woods, crags and industrial remains.

MOLE, RIVER Surrey
River
Tributary of River Thames, 30 miles (48 km) long, rises in Sussex, flows into Surrey past Dorking and Leatherhead to join River Thames at Molesey.

MOLLAND Devon SS8028
Village off B3227, 6 miles (10km) E of South Molton
Just to the south of Exmoor, with many little wooded valleys and an atmospheric church, still with all its Georgian fittings. Picturesque thatched cottages.

MOLLINGTON Oxfordshire SP4447
Village off A423, 4 miles (6km) N of Banbury
A village much favoured by commuters, but an early medieval church and old farmhouses are reminders of the origins of this former agricultural settlement.

MONIAIVE Dumfries and Galloway NX7890
Village on A702, 7 miles (11km) SW of Thornhill
Attractive village of colour-washed houses near the 14th-century Maxwelton House, birthplace of Annie Laurie, subject of the famous song.

MONIFIETH Tayside NO4932
Suburb on A930, 2 miles (3km) NE of Broughty Ferry
Residential suburb and resort town with sandy beaches east of Dundee. Prehistoric antiquities in the vicinity.

MONIKIE Tayside NO4938
Village off B961, 5 miles (8km) NW of Carnoustie
Village dominated by Panmure Monument, 105ft (32m) high on a hillside to the south. Affleck Castle, built in the late 15th century, has a notable solar and chapel.

MONK FRYSTON North Yorkshire SE5029
Village on A63, 7 miles (11km) W of Selby
Originally inhabited by Benedictine monks, then a farming community, now a commuter village. Fryston, meaning 'free stone', indicates the number of quarries once worked here.

MONK SHERBORNE Hampshire SU6056
Village off A340, 4 miles (6km) NW of Basingstoke
Rural and wooded, with a big Norman chancel arch in the church.

MONK SOHAM Suffolk TM2165
Village off A1120, 3 miles (5km) NE of Debenham
Approached across meadows and cornfields, Monk Soham's church is most pleasing. The village shared a reedy mere with neighbouring Earl Soham (see).

MONKEN HADLEY Greater London TQ2597
District in borough of Barnet
The highest point on the old Great North road (A1000). Extensive common, large houses and an obelisk on Barnet battle site (1471).

MONKLEIGH Devon SS4520
Village off A386, 4 miles (6km) S of Bideford
Set high above the Torridge Valley, the village has a 15th-century church with the fine Annery chapel, 1432, featuring a monument and superb wooden screen.

MONKOKEHAMPTON Devon SS5805
Village on B3217, 3 miles (5km) E of Hatherleigh
In the Okemont Valley, the village church was mostly rebuilt in 1855. Stained glass in the east window was displayed at the Great Exhibition of 1851.

MONKS ELEIGH Suffolk TL9647
Village on A1141, 5 miles (8km) NW of Hadleigh
A traditional English village with pastel-hued thatched cottages clustered around a 14th-century church.

MONKS HEATH Cheshire SJ8474
Hamlet on A537, 5 miles (8km) W of Macclesfield
Hamlet grew around a busy crossroads. Capesthorne Hall, seat of the Bromley Davenport family, is a striking building in large grounds.

MONKS RISBOROUGH Buckinghamshire SP8104
Village on A4010, immediately N of Princes Risborough
Now continuous with Princes Risborough (see). Picturesque cottages, 16th-century stone dovecote and church with medieval stained glass.

MONKSILVER Somerset ST0737
Village on B3188, 4 miles (6km) S of Watchet
On the edge of Exmoor, with a medieval church. Combe Sydenham lies to the south. The Elizabethan and earlier manor house has a mill, deer park, gardens and nature trails. National Museum of Baking.

MONKTON COMBE Avon ST7762
Village off A36, 2 miles (3km) SE of Bath
Stone village with the famous Dundas Aqueduct to the east, opened in 1805 to carry the Kennet and Avon Canal over the River Avon 60ft (18m) below.

MONKTON FARLEIGH Wiltshire ST8065
Village off A363, 3 miles (5km) E of Bath
A steep street of stone cottages. Monkton Farleigh Mine was used as an underground ammunition store in World War II.

MONKWEARMOUTH Tyne and Wear NZ3958
District in N Sunderland
Now part of Sunderland, originally monastic land. St Peter's Church is Sunderland's oldest building. The station is now the Museum of Land Transport.

MONMOUTH (TREFFYNWY) Gwent SO5012
Town off A40, 20 miles (32km) NE of Newport
This handsome country and market town at the gateway to Wales is as much English as Welsh in its atmosphere. Urbane Georgian town houses stand in the streets leading from Agincourt Square at the town's heart, while a rural flavour is imparted by Monmouth's livestock market.

The town's history is bound up in its border location. Ruined Monmouth Castle (Cadw), one of a chain of border forts built in the 12th century, was later the birthplace of Henry V. A monument to the king, victor at Agincourt, stands in Agincourt Square, which also contains a statue to Monmouth's other famous son, Charles Rolls of Rolls-Royce fame.

Rolls's mother, Lady Llangattock, gave her collection of Nelson memorabilia – which includes his fighting sword and battle plan of Trafalgar – to the museum in Monmouth. The town's most celebrated museum-piece, the Monnow Bridge, is still in use. Reputedly the only one of its kind in Britain, this narrow, fortified bridge built in the late 13th century to guard the western approach to the town continues to hinder access, acting as a traffic bottleneck.

MONNINGTON ON WYE Hereford and Worcester SO3743
Village off A438, 9 miles (14km) W of Hereford
Cider orchard village with outstanding 17th-century church, close to dramatic riverside cliffs. Owain Glyndwr reputed to have died at Monnington Court.

MONSAL DALE Derbyshire SK1771
Beauty spot off A6, E of Taddington
A beautiful Peak District dale, through which the River Wye flows. Views from Monsal Head. Dramatic 1860s viaduct, now part of Monsal Trail.

MONTACUTE Somerset ST4916
Village off A3088, 4 miles (6km) W of Yeovil
Everything here is of golden Hamstone. A superb 15th-century church tower overlooks the perfect village of 17th- and 18th-century cottages. Montacute House (National Trust) is one of the best Elizabethan houses, charming inside and out with a huge long gallery and formal gardens. Montacute Television and Radio Museum.

MONTGOMERY Powys SO2296
Village on B4385, 7 miles (11km) S of Welshpool
Characterful little town crowned by ruined castle, once a key border fortress overlooking Severn Valley. No more than a village really, but given a town charter in 13th century. Almost perfect red-bricked Georgian town square, medieval church with preserved screen and loft, local history museum. Town flanked by Iron Age hillfort and Offa's Dyke.

MONTROSE Tayside NO7157
Town on A92, 12 miles (19km) NE of Arbroath
Spacious and ancient royal burgh and holiday town with fine gabled buildings, virtually surrounded by water; the tidal basin to the west is an important wildfowl wintering area. Castle destroyed in 1297. The town thrived in the 18th century, due to its good harbour and foreign trade; smuggling was also lucrative. Nowadays the economy is based on distilling and oil-related industries. Museum and art gallery date from 1842.

MONYASH Derbyshire SK1566
Village on B5055, 4 miles (6km) W of Bakewell
The base of the cross on the village green marks the village's former status as a market town, once a Peak District lead-mining centre. Gateway to Lathkill Dale (see).

MONYMUSK Grampian NJ6815
Village on B993, 7 miles (11km) SW of Inverurie
A mainly 19th-century village on the River Don, where 12th-century St Mary's Church has Pictish symbol stones. Monymusk House dates from the 16th to 18th centuries.

MORCHARD BISHOP Devon SS7707
Village off A377, 7 miles (11km) NW of Crediton
Large village with several cob and thatched cottages. Prominent church tower.

MORCOTT Leicestershire SK9200
Village off A47, 4 miles (6km) E of Uppingham
Four-storey, four-sailed tower mill, reconstructed in 1986 as a house. Also the most complete Norman church in the county and the 17th-century Sundial House and manor house.

MORDEN Greater London TQ2568
District in borough of Merton
A village until the 1920s. The River Wandle runs through Morden Hall Park (National Trust), with preserved snuff-mills, crafts workshops and a city farm.

MORDIFORD Hereford and Worcester SO5737
Village on B4224, 4 miles (6km) SE of Hereford
Forest trails in Haugh Wood (National Trust) and the Palladian Sufton Court (limited opening) justify a visit to this hillside village on River Wye.

MOREBATTLE Borders NT7724
Village on B6401, 6 miles (10km) SE of Kelso
Near this small village in the northern foothills of the Cheviots is Linton church, with a fine Norman font. Massive remnants of ruined Cessford Castle to the southwest.

MORECAMBE Lancashire SD4364
Town on A589, 3 miles (5km) NW of Lancaster
Situated on the wide, sandy stretch of Morecambe Bay, the holiday resort of Morecambe is of relatively recent origin, having been officially named as such since the last quarter of the 19th century. Before that, it was known as Poulton-le-Sands and consisted of three villages – Bare, Poulton and Torrisholme. With the coming of the railway in 1847, the area developed into a holiday resort and became popular with the textile workers from Yorkshire. Morecambe soon became known as 'Bradford-by-the-Sea'.

The original Winter Gardens, one of the many attractions in Morecambe, was opened in 1878 as a 'People's Palace of Varieties and Aquarium'. Today the Pleasure Park and the Illuminations are still popular with tourists.

Fishing is one of Morecambe's important industries, especially the gathering of mussels and shellfish. Morecambe shrimps are well known and are caught from special trawlers known as 'nobbies'.

It is very popular, although sometimes hazardous, to walk across Morecambe Bay at low tide from Hest Bank to Grange-over-Sands. There are three tidal rivers to ford and walkers are permitted to cross only if accompanied by an official guide.

MORETON Dorset SY8089
Village off B3390, 4 miles (6km) SE of Puddletown
Unspoiled rural village. All the windows in the church are filled with clear glass engraved to magical effect (by Laurence Whistler, 1950s on). TE Lawrence (of Arabia) is buried in the detached graveyard.

MORETON Merseyside SJ2689
District of SW Wallasey
The town, now a district of Wallasey, was built in the 1920s after those made homeless in World War I established a makeshift town here.

MORETON CORBET Shropshire SJ5523
Village on B5063, 8 miles (13km) NE of Shrewsbury
Fascinating church stands beside remains of Norman castle and impressive ruin of fine Renaissance house of 1580s, all open to the public.

MORETON ON LUGG Hereford and Worcester SO5045
Village off A49, 4 miles (6km) N of Hereford
Victorian church contains 15th-century chancel screen and mosaic reredos by noted artist Salviati. Bridge over River Lugg is of 16th-century origin.

MORETON PINKNEY Northamptonshire SP5749
Village off B4525, 9 miles (14km) NE of Banbury
Attractive winding village with 13th-century church, ironstone and limestone cottages, two greens, impressive entrance arch and turreted lodge to 19th-century manor.

MORETON SAY Shropshire SJ6234
Village off A41, 3 miles (5km) W of Market Drayton
Small and isolated village where Clive of India was born and buried anonymously after disgrace and suicide.

MORETON-IN-MARSH Gloucestershire SP2032
Small town on A44 and A429, 4 miles (6km) N of Stow-on-the-Wold
A High Street lined with attractive houses and shops, plus the 16th-century curfew tower, reveals the town's history as a market centre, and its old coaching inns are a reminder that it lies at the crossing of two important roads. Today it bustles with tourists and shoppers. Wellington Aviation Museum in Broadway Road.

MORETONHAMPSTEAD Devon SX7856
Small town on A382, 6 miles (10km) NW of Bovey Tracey
Little crossroads town on the edge of Dartmoor. Most distinctive building is the Almshouse, with granite pillars, dated 1637 (not open). The Miniature Pony Centre is 3 miles (5km) west.

MORFA NEFYN Gwynedd SH2840
Village on B4417, 1 mile (2km) W of Nefyn
Almost an extension of the resort of Nefyn, slightly inland from sweeping crescent-shaped bay of Porth Dinllaen (see entry). Popular golf links.

MORLAND Cumbria NY6022
Village off A66, 6 miles (10km) NW of Appleby-in-Westmorland
Pretty village in the Eden Valley. Morland Beck and mill race once powered small mills along the banks.

MORLEY Derbyshire SK3940
Village on A608, 4 miles (6km) NE of Derby
Fascinating church with Norman nave, medieval stained glass from Dale Abbey and fine monuments. Tithe barn, and a Georgian rectory, now a Diocesan retreat house.

MORLEY West Yorkshire SE2627
Town off M62, 4 miles (6km) SW of Leeds
The earliest mention of Morley is in Domesday Book, as Moreleia, meaning 'field of the moor'. The town was built around seven hills and grew with the cotton industry. Prime Minister Asquith was born here.

MORPETH Northumberland NZ1986
Town off A1, 14 miles (23km) N of Newcastle upon Tyne
The county town of Northumberland and an important border town historically. The 15th-century gatehouse of Morpeth Castle, overlooking the town, has been restored by the Landmark Trust. Telford built the town's bridge over the River Wansbeck in 1831. The ruins of Newminster Abbey can be reached by a riverside footpath.

MORTEHOE Devon SS4545
Village off A361, 4 miles (6km) W of Ilfracombe
Snug slate village, high above the narrow headland of Morte Point. Slate church with 48 16th-century wooden bench-ends. Morte Point, with its jagged reefs and stacks of slate, was a great danger to shipping until the Bull Point Lighthouse was built in 1879. National Trust coastline, with good views of Lundy (see).

MORTIMER'S CROSS Hereford and Worcester SO4263
Hamlet off A4110, 5 miles (8km) NW of Leominster
Restored 18th-century watermill with original machinery (English Heritage) stands on battlefield where Yorkist Edward Mortimer defeated Lancastrian Owen Tudor in 1461.

MORTLAKE Greater London TQ2075
District in borough of Richmond
Oxford and Cambridge Boat Race terminus, and once famed for tapestries. Sir Richard Burton's Arab-tent tomb is at St Mary Magdalene, North Worple Way.

MORVAH Cornwall SW4035
Village on B3306, 3 miles (5km) NE of St Just
Small village in moorland near Land's End, with an impressive double-walled Iron Age hillfort (Chun Castle) to the south, and Chun Quoit, like a box of stone, which is the remains of a neolithic tomb.

MORVAL Cornwall SX2656
Hamlet off A387, 2 miles (3km) N of Looe
A small church and a big house together in a lovely landscape.

MORVILLE Shropshire SO6694
Village on A458, 3 miles (5km) W of Bridgnorth
Above the estate village the impressive frontage of Morville Hall (National Trust) overlooks park containing Norman Church of St Gregory.

MORWELLHAM Devon SX4469
Village off B3257, 4 miles (6km) SW of Tavistock
Village on the Tamar, a large port for copper by the mid-19th century. Preserved and reconstructed, with rides into the copper mine, quays and ships.

MORWENSTOW Cornwall SS2015
Village off A39, 6 miles (10km) N of Bude
This village sits on the harshest part of the hard north Cornwall coast, with its dramatic cliffs and windswept land. The church and rectory huddle in a little valley; Reverend RS Hawker, the rector here, 1834–75, adapted the rectory so that its chimneys looked like the churches with which he had been associated (and the kitchen chimney is based on his mother's tomb). He introduced the Harvest Festival Service.

MOSELEY West Midlands SP0783
District in S Birmingham
The big houses of this affluent Victorian suburb have been joined by modern estates. Moseley Hall Dovecote (limited opening) in Alcester Road.

MOSELEY West Midlands SJ9304
District in N Wolverhampton
Charles II sheltered in Moseley Old Hall (National Trust) after Battle of Worcester. Visitors see his bedroom, plus other 17th-century rooms and a re-created garden.

MOSS SIDE Greater Manchester SJ8495
District of S Manchester
Run-down Victorian inner suburb of Manchester, with terraced houses and council estates. NIA Centre promotes African and Caribbean culture through performing arts.

MOSSAT Grampian NJ4719
Hamlet on A97, 2 miles (3km) S of Lumsden
Village north of Kildrummy Castle, a ruined 13th-century castle dismantled after the Jacobite Rising of 1715. Its layout is still intact.

MOSSLEY Greater Manchester SD9702
Town on A635, 4 miles (6km) SE of Oldham
The town has three parish churches as it is shared by three counties. Whitehall, an Italianate mansion built in 1863, is now the town hall.

MOSTYN Clwyd SJ1580
Village on A548, 3 miles (5km) NW of Holywell
Mostyn Quay grew up as a coal-exporting dock. Near by is estate of Mostyn Hall (not open), partly medieval but added to in Elizabethan style in the 9th century.

MOTHERWELL Strathclyde NS7457
Town on A721, 12 miles (20km) SE of Glasgow
In 1914 the largest steel producer in Scotland, thereafter Motherwell suffered steady decline and the ill-fated Ravenscraig project in the 1950s. Strathclyde Country Park and Dalzell Country Park near by.

MOTTISFONT Hampshire SU3226
Village off B3084, 4 miles (6km) NW of Romsey
Picturesque village famous for Mottisfont Abbey (National Trust), with its wonderful rose gardens. The house (only a few rooms open) has a drawing room painted by Rex Whistler in 1938.

MOTTISTONE Isle of Wight SZ4083
Village on B3399, 3 miles (5km) W of Shorwell
A perfect, small-scale village, with a late medieval church, Elizabethan manor house (gardens limited opening) and a little green.

MOTTRAM IN LONGENDALE Greater Manchester SJ9995
Village off M67, 3 miles (5km) E of Hyde
Although on a busy road, a pleasant district which really marks the outskirts of Manchester and the beginning of the Pennine region.

MOTTRAM ST ANDREW Cheshire SJ8778
Village off A538, 2 miles (3km) SE of Wilmslow
Picturesque, exclusive residential village. Mottram Hall, originally 13th-century residence of the Mottrum family, was rebuilt in 1753. Now a hotel.

MOULDSWORTH Cheshire SJ5071
Village on B5393, 3 miles (5km) SE of Helsby
A small community, notable only for its small motor museum. Surprisingly, there is a station on the Chester–Manchester line.

MOULIN Tayside NN9459
Village on A924, immediately N of Pitlochry
Pretty village in the hills north of Pitlochry, with lovely views from Craigour Hill. Near by is tiny Edradour Distillery, Scotland's smallest.

MOULSFORD Oxfordshire SU5983
Village on A4130, 5 miles (8km) NW of Henley-on-Thames
Pretty Thames-side village with old manor house and small Victorian church, but popular attraction is the Beetle and Wedge, a celebrated riverside inn.

MOULSOE Buckinghamshire SP9141
Village off A509, 3 miles (5km) SE of Newport Pagnell
Carrington estate village. Family monuments in the church, with 1860s chancel and east window by William Burges. Carrington Arms pub.

MOULTON Lincolnshire TF3024
Village on B1357, 4 miles (6km) E of Spalding
Substantial fenland village with a green, fine 15th-century church tower with spire and tall brick tower mill. Several good 18th-century houses.

MOULTON North Yorkshire NZ2303
Village off A1, 4 miles (6km) NE of Richmond
Small, scattered village with old cottages. Moulton Manor, built in 16th century, now offers bed and breakfast accommodation.

MOULTON Suffolk TL6964
Village on B1085, 3 miles (5km) E of Newmarket
Two 15th-century packhorse bridges span the shallow River Kennet. Peaceful Moulton was once on the main thoroughfare between Cambridge and Bury St Edmunds.

MOUNT BURES Essex TL9032
Hamlet off B1508, 1 mile (2km) S of Bures
On a hill above the River Stour. Norman castle mound is the legendary resting place of Boadicea's warriors. Norman church with Roman bricks.

MOUNT EDGCUMBE Cornwall SX4552
Mansion off B3247, just S of Cremyll
A woody peninsula overlooking the Tamar estuary and the sea, now a huge country park. Mount Edgcombe house was rebuilt after bombing in 1941. Wonderful gardens and walks.

MOUNT TABOR West Yorkshire SE0527
Village off A629, 3 miles (5km) NW of Halifax
A scattered village of old stone houses and farms with modern dwellings with no real centre. Jerusalem Farm Estate is a country park with camping and nature trails.

MOUNTAIN ASH Mid Glamorgan ST0499
Town off A4059, 4 miles (6km) SE of Aberdare
Old coal-mining town in Cynon Valley. Typical valleys architecture of terraced houses. Scenic road over forested mountain links with Rhondda valleys.

MOUNTNESSING Essex TQ6297
Village off A12, 3 miles (5km) NE of Brentwood
The main landmark is a handsomely restored early 1800s windmill (limited opening). Church with massive-beamed belfry, isolated near Mountnessing Hall (not open).

MOUNTSORREL Leicestershire SK5814
Village on A6, 4 miles (6km) SE of Loughborough
Former market town with 1793 market cross rotunda. Quarries have provided paving stones for thousands of streets. Stonehurst Family Farm and Museum.

MOUSA Shetland HU4624
Island E of mainland
Uninhabited island noted for Mousa Broch, a large and well-preserved broch with walls 43ft (13m) high. Stormy petrels nest in the broch.

MOUSEHOLE Cornwall SW4626
Village off B3315, 2 miles (3km) S of Penzance
Pronounced 'Mouzall'and set on the rocky coast of Land's End peninsula with a woody backdrop. Its steep, constantly twisting streets and alleyways are packed with stone cottages. The semi-circular 19th-century harbour has huge walls. This is perhaps Cornwall's prettiest fishing village.

MOW COP Staffordshire SJ8557
Hill off A34, 2 miles (3km) NE of Kidsgrove, on border
Eccentric folly marks summit of this rocky hill, 1,100ft (335m) high, owned by the National Trust and worth climbing for magnificent views.

MUCH DEWCHURCH Hereford and Worcester SO4831
Village on B4348, 6 miles (10km) S of Hereford
Village has much new housing, but is worth visiting for fine Norman church with big Tudor monument to local magnate Walter Pye.

MUCH HADHAM Hertfordshire TL4219
Village on B1004, 4 miles (6km) W of Bishop's Stortford
Extremely smart village with the Bishops of London's palace converted into flats. Henry V's French widow, Queen Katharine, lived here. The High Street, as packed with fine Tudor and Georgian houses as a tin with sardines, repays walking its full length. Handsome medieval church with busts by Henry Moore at west door. The old blacksmith's forge is now a museum (limited opening).

MUCH HOOLE Lancashire SD4623
Village on A59, 6 miles (10km) SW of Preston
St Michael's Church dates from 1628. The western tower and pinnacles were added in 1719. Jeremiah Horrocks was curate here when he observed the Transit of Venus in 1639.

MUCH MARCLE Hereford and Worcester SO6532
Village off A449, 7 miles (11km) NE of Ross-on-Wye
Attractions here are Hellens (limited opening), a venerable manor house with fascinating contents, good monuments in the church and a cider distillery open for tours.

MUCH WENLOCK Shropshire SO6299
Small town on A458, 8 miles (13km) NW of Bridgnorth
King Merewalh of Mercia installed his daughter Milburga as head of a priory here in the 7th century, but the present priory ruins (English Heritage) date from the 12th century and are Much Wenlock's major attraction. They reveal a church of cathedral size, its south transept still rising to a height of 70ft (21m). The finest work is the decoration of the chapter house entrance and the vivid carving on a well-head in the lavatorium. The 15th-century Prior's Lodge in the grounds is now a private house.

The town's other prized possession is its 16th-century guildhall, ornately timber-framed and consisting of a fine upper chamber over an open market area. Holy Trinity near by is a spacious Norman and medieval parish church of great interest. The town's narrow streets reveal a rich variety of homely architecture, including the timber-framed Raynald's Mansion in the High Street and some attractive early 19th-century buildings in Sheinton Street. The museum in the High Street illustrates the story of Much Wenlock, including the contribution of Dr William Brookes to the revival of the Olympic Games.

MUCHALLS Grampian NO9092
Village on A90 (A92), 4 miles (6km) N of Stonehaven
Village on a wild and rocky stretch of coastline. Nearby 17th-century Muchalls Castle has a secret passage leading down to a smugglers' cove.

MUCHELNEY Somerset ST4224
Village off A372, 1 mile (2km) S of Langport
A stone village with a fine 15th-century church and 14th-century Priest's House (National Trust, limited opening), a very rare survival. Only the early 16th-century Abbot's Lodging (English Heritage) survives from the big abbey.

Seventeenth-century Muchalls Castle.

MUCK Highland NM4179
Island in Inner Hebrides, SW of Eigg
This fertile island is the smallest and most southerly of the Small Isles. There was much emigration to Canada in the 1900s, and it is now run as a model island unit by the owner and tiny population.

MUDEFORD Dorset SZ1892
District in S Christchurch
On the edge of Christchurch Harbour, with a quay, good views and passenger ferries to Christchurch and Hengistbury Head.

MUGGINTON Derbyshire SK2842
Village off A52, 6 miles (10km) NW of Derby
Hilltop parish church. Halter Devil Chapel built in 1723 by a farmer who, determined to halter his horse in a thunderstorm, found it had horns.

MUIR OF ORD Highland NH5250
Village on A862, 3 miles (5km) N of Beauly
Large and straggling village, noted in the 19th century for the largest cattle fair in northern Scotland. Today, distilling and light engineering are the main industries.

MUIRKIRK Strathclyde NS6927
Town on A70, 9 miles (14km) NE of Cumnock
Town in an industrial area with prehistoric sites near by. To the southwest is Airds Moss, the site of a battle between Royalists and Covenanters in 1680.

MUKER North Yorkshire SD9097
Village on B6270, 8 miles (13km) W of Reeth
The village lies at the foot of Kisdon Hill in Upper Swaledale. The Church of St Mary is the focal point of the village and the grey stone houses huddle around it in a group. Today, the village enjoys prosperity from wool, and in particular Swaledale Woollens, where garments are handknitted by the villagers from wool of the local Swaledale sheep.

MULBARTON Norfolk TG1901
Village on B1113, 5 miles (8km) SW of Norwich
The village common is one of the largest in Norfolk, and the villagers fiercely resist occasional plans to enclose it or build on it.

MULL Strathclyde
Island off Inner Hebrides, N of Colonsay
The second largest island in the Inner Hebrides, with a mountainous landscape, numerous lochs and rivers and a deeply indented coastline giving wonderful views to the mainland and other islands. The main industries are farming, crofting, forestry, fishing and tourism. Scattered population of about 2,500 and the main settlement at Tobermory. Ben More, 3,169ft (966m), is the highest point.

MULLION Cornwall SW6719
Village on B3296, 6 miles (10km) S of Helston
The village is sensibly positioned inland from the rocky shore. It has stone cottages and an interesting church with the best 16th-century bench-ends in Cornwall: wooden and carved with figures. Mullion Cove has a tiny, unspoilt stone harbour built in the 1890s (National Trust).

MUMBLES (THE) West Glamorgan SS6188
Town off A4067, 6 miles (10km) W of Swansea
Small town, sailing centre and little resort on western end of Swansea Bay. Unusual name thought to derive from French *mamelles* (breasts), a reference to pair of rocky islets at Mumbles Head. The pier is a popular fishing spot with panoramic views across to Swansea and Port Talbot. Well-preserved Oystermouth Castle (Cadw) guards the entrance to the Gower peninsula.

MUMBY Lincolnshire TF5174
Village on A52, 4 miles (6km) E of Alford
Inland from seabank between resorts of Chapel St Leonards and Sutton on Sea. Thirteenth-century church with 15th-century tower and Victorian chancel.

MUNDESLEY Norfolk TG3136
Small town on B1145, 4 miles (6km) NE of North Walsham
After the crumbling cliffs and ragged-edged fields which are being ravaged by the encroaching sea, the long, flat beach at Mundesley is a welcome respite. Bathing is safe, and groynes are set at regular intervals to prevent the sand from being washed away. Pronounced 'Munsley', this pleasing seaside town is unspoilt, but still offers golf, bowling and other facilities.

MUNDFORD Norfolk TL8093
Village on A1065, 5 miles (8km) N of Brandon
Large Breckland village on the River Wissey, with flint-built cottages clustered around the green. A Saxon mass grave has been discovered to the west.

MUNDON Essex TL8602
Village on B1018, 3 miles (5km) SE of Maldon
In flat, open country, windswept under huge skies. Tolstoy is thought to have written part of *War and Peace* here.

MUNGRISDALE Cumbria NY3630
Hamlet off A66, 8 miles (13km) NE of Keswick
Pretty setting in the Northern Fells, with a stream, pub, hotel and old church.

MUNSLOW Shropshire SO5287
Village on B4368, 6 miles (10km) NE of Craven Arms
On eastern slopes of Wenlock Edge. This small village, with a fine medieval church and houses in local limestone, overlooks Corvedale.

MUNSTEAD HEATH Surrey SU9842
Hamlet on B2130 1 mile (2km) S of Godalming
Wooded hillsides dotted with late 19th-century country houses, mostly by Sir Edwin Lutyens, and associated with the great gardener, Gertrude Jekyll.

MURRAYFIELD Lothian NT2273
District in W Edinburgh
West Edinburgh suburb, renowned for its Scottish Rugby Union stadium, opened in 1925 and recently extensively modernised. Beechwood House (1790) is now a private hospital.

MURSLEY Buckinghamshire SP8128
Village off B4032, 3 miles (5km) E of Winslow
Market town once, now dormitory for Milton Keynes (see). Old houses and post-war housing estates. Handsome Fortescue family monuments in church.

MURTON North Yorkshire SE6452
Village off A64, 3 miles (5km) E of York
The village remains small and has an important, modern livestock centre. Yowlass Dale is a popular beauty spot. Yorkshire Museum of Farming.

MUSBURY Devon SY2794
Village off A358, 3 miles (5km) SW of Axminster
Named after the Iron Age hillfort on the hill above. The church has a huge monument of 1611 to three generations of one family.

MUSSELBURGH Lothian NT3472
Town off A1, 6 miles (10km) E of Edinburgh
Spacious and attractive old town on the Firth of Forth, known as The Honest Toun. This was a fishing and trading port until the early 19th century, when the harbour silted up. The tollbooth dates from 1591, Pinkie House (now part of a boys' public school) from the 16th century. The golf course was founded in 1774, one of Scotland's oldest. The racecourse first opened in 1816.

MUSWELL HILL Greater London TQ2889
District in borough of Haringey
Mainly Edwardian suburb. Alexandra Palace in park, repaired after 1980 fire, has fine views, an entertainment and exhibition centre, children's activities and funfairs.

The tollbooth at Musselburgh.

MUTHILL Tayside NN8717
Village on A823, 3 miles (5km) S of Crieff
Pronounced 'Mewthle', the village was rebuilt after its destruction in 1715. The church has a ruined nave and choir and an intact 12th-century tower. Drummond Castle and gardens near by.

MWNT Dyfed SN1952
Beauty spot off B4548, 4 miles (6km) NW of Cardigan
Delightful sheltered cove (the so-called 'jewel' of Cardigan Bay) beneath green headland. Ancient whitewashed church adds to the appeal.

MYDDFAI Dyfed SN7730
Hamlet off A4069, 3 miles (5km) S of Llandovery
Peaceful little settlement of stone-built dwellings tucked away in country lanes. Links with the medieval Physicians of Myddfai.

MYDDLE Shropshire SJ4623
Village off A528, 7 miles (11km) N of Shrewsbury
Straggling village with remains of castle, famous as subject of Richard Gough's 18th-century *History of Myddle*, a pioneering classic of local history.

MYLOR, CHURCHTOWN AND BRIDGE Cornwall SW8235
Village off A39, 2 miles (3km) E of Penryn
Mylor Churchtown is on Carrick Roads, a beautiful setting, with lots of yachts and a pretty church with Norman doorways. Mylor Bridge is larger, at the head of a little creek.

MYTHOLMROYD West Yorkshire SE0126
Town on A646, 2 miles (3km) SE of Hebden Bridge
Residential area with much 20th-century housing. Birthplace of Poet Laureate Ted Hughes. Notorious 18th-century counterfeiters, Cragg Vale Coiners, met at Dusty Mill pub.

NACTON Suffolk TM2240
Village of A14 (A45), 5 miles (8km) SE of Ipswich
Famous son was Admiral 'Old Grog' Vernon, after whom the navy drink was named. He lived in Orwell Park, currently a school.

NAFFERTON Humberside TA0559
Village off A166, 2 miles (3km) NE of Great Driffield
Due to the varied types of building, most of the village is a conservation area. Church dates back to the 13th century. Mere attracts many birds.

NAILSEA Avon ST4770
Small town on B3130, 7 miles (11km) W of Bristol
The coal mined here was used in the 19th century for the large glass industry, since gone. Now mostly suburban housing.

NAILSTONE Leicestershire SK4107
Village on A447, 5 miles (8km) S of Coalville
Former mining village. All Saints' Church has a 13th-century chancel, 14th-century tower and broach spire and a wide north aisle making a spacious interior.

NAILSWORTH Gloucestershire ST8599
Town on A46, 4 miles (6km) S of Stroud
The old textile town sprawls along a valley floor beneath Minchinhampton Common (see), with terraces of former millworkers' cottages on the hillsides and in the valley bottom some surviving mills converted to other uses. Other picturesque buildings in Market Street. Many Nonconformist chapels upstage the Victorian church, which is worth visiting for Oliver Heywood's modern mural depicting local life.

NAIRN Highland NH8856
Town on A96, 15 miles (24km) NE of Inverness
Holiday resort, residential town and royal burgh on Moray Firth with excellent sandy beaches, golf course and other facilities. Once a fishing port with a harbour built in 1820 by Thomas Telford; Nairn Fishertown Museum tells the local story. The town has a fine Victorian railway station. Near by is the RSPB Clubin Sands Reserve.

NANPANTAN Leicestershire SK5017
Hamlet off A512, 3 miles (5km) SW of Loughborough
On Charnwood Forest hillside. Mixed woodland and rocky outcrops at Jubilee Wood. Scenic views, with nature trail at Outwoods and Bluebell Woods.

NANT FFRANCON PASS Gwynedd SH6462
Mountain pass on A5, SE of Bethesda
Some of Snowdonia's highest peaks line this dramatic route through the mountains, exploited when engineer Thomas Telford built the A5 linking London with Holyhead.

NANT PERIS Gwynedd SH6058
Village on A4086, 2 miles (3km) SE of Llanberis
Village (otherwise known as Old Llanberis) at foot of Llanberis Pass and southern end of Llyn Peris. Old healing well, simple church with rood screen.

NANT-Y-MOCH RESERVOIR Dyfed SN7586
Reservoir off A44, 4 miles (6km) N of Ponterwyd
Brooding black waters of Nant-y-moch spread themselves across moors of Plynlimon mountain range. Accessible by scenic mountain road linking Ponterwyd with Talybont.

NANTGARW Mid Glamorgan ST1185
Hamlet on A468, 2 miles (4km) SW of Caerphilly
Nantgarw porcelain, produced in early 19th century, is much prized. The site has a small museum. Nearby is the Treforest Industrial Estate (1936), the first of its kind in Wales.

NANTLLE Gwynedd SH5153
Hamlet on B4418, 6 miles (10km) NW of Beddgelert
Old slate-quarrying community, set in ruggedly beautiful countryside beside lake. Mountain road links with A4085 to Beddgelert.

NANTMAWR Shropshire SJ2524
Hamlet off A495, 1 mile (2km) NE of Llanyblodwel
In rugged hill country on the Welsh border. A scattering of cottages close to a vast quarry are reminders of Nantmawr's tough industrial past.

NANTWICH Cheshire SJ6552
Town on A534, 4 miles (6km) SW of Crewe
A small market town in the rich dairy farmlands of South Cheshire. Nantwich Museum includes a Cheshire cheese room. Black and white Tudor Churche's Mansion, the town's oldest building, was saved from being exported to America in 1930 and is now an excellent restaurant. Market every Saturday.

NAPTON ON THE HILL Warwickshire SP4661
Village on A425, 3 miles (5km) E of Southam
Set on a prominent hill, where a windmill commands wide views, the village has a Norman church and an array of mellow houses. Busy canal junction near by.

NARBERTH Dyfed SN1014
Small town on A478, 9 miles (14km) N of Tenby
Town grew up around castle (now ruined) on 'Landsker', medieval dividing line between South and North Pembrokeshire. Lively little place with pleasing Georgian architecture, shops. Local history museum. Close by is Oakwood Park, one of Wales's largest and most successful tourist attractions; also Heron's Brook Country Park and Wildfowl Centre.

NARBOROUGH Norfolk TF7413
Village off A47, 5 miles (8km) NW of Swaffham
Spanning the River Nar, Narborough was one of the biggest aerodromes in England in World War I. Many old buildings were destroyed in the 1950s.

NASEBY Northamptonshire SP6878
Village on B4036, 6 miles (10km) SW of Market Harborough
Site of Civil War Battle in 1645, commemorated by two monuments. Battle and Farm Museum (limited opening). Source of the River Avon.

NASH Gwent ST3483
Village off A455, 4 miles (6km) SE of Newport
At southern approach to Newport on flat esturial lands where the River Usk meets the sea. Noteworthy church.

NASH POINT South Glamorgan SS9168
Headland off B4265, 3 miles (5km) W of Llantwit Major
Headland with strange, stepped limestone cliffs. Site of two lighthouses, a testament to the danger posed to shipping.

NASSINGTON Northamptonshire TL0696
Village off A1, 2 miles (3km) S of Wansford
Beside the River Nene, forming the border with Cambridgeshire. Prebendal Manor House, 1230 (open by appointment), with a museum in the tithe barn, dovecote and gardens.

NASTY Hertfordshire TL3524
Village off A10, 2 miles (3km) W of Puckeridge
A pleasant place with nothing at all nasty about it. The name is said to be derived from 'at the east enclosure'.

NATELY SCURES Hampshire SU7053
Hamlet off A30, 2 miles (3km) SW of Hook
Just a tiny church and a farm. The little church is all Norman, with a tiny apse and nave.

NAUNTON Gloucestershire SP1123
Village off B4068, 5 miles (8km) SW of Stow-on-the-Wold
Once famous for its stone roof tiles, the village lies in the upper Windrush Valley. Its buildings, mainly of local stone, include the Tudor Cromwell House, the 17th-century Old Rectory and some good 19th-century cottages. The church treasures a Saxon cross built into its wall and a fine stone pulpit carved in about 1400.

NAVENBY Lincolnshire SK9857
Village on A607, 9 miles (14km) S of Lincoln
Village on Lincolnshire Cliff with a broad street, a former market site, stone houses and red pantiled roofs. Church has numerous stone carvings and a fine Easter sepulchre.

NAYLAND Suffolk TL9734
Small town off A134, 6 miles (10km) N of Colchester
Alston Court (not open), an elegant 15th-century house with mullioned windows, stands in the heart of Nayland village, surrounded by narrow twisting streets which are overhung by medieval houses washed in different colours. The 15th-century Church of St James has Constable's religious painting *Christ's Blessing of the Bread and Wine*, which he painted in 1809.

NAZE, THE Essex TM2623
Headland off B1034, 1 mile (2km) NW of Walton on the Naze
The 'nose' of Essex, protruding into the North Sea, is a grassy headland above 70ft (21m) cliffs. Nature reserve, nature trail, birds, views.

NAZEING Essex TL4106
Village off B181, 3 miles (5km) SW of Harlow
Above the Lee Valley. Legend has Boadicea and her warriors annihilated here. Flourishing glasshouse industry has declined. Attractive cricket ground.

NEAR SAWREY AND FAR SAWREY Cumbria SD3795
Villages off A592, 3 miles (5km) SW of Bowness-on-Windermere
Both villages are near Lake Windermere. Near Sawrey is furthest from the ferry. Hill Top, a small Lakeland farmhouse, was the home of Beatrix Potter. It is now owned by the National Trust and open to the public. The gardens of Graythwaite Hall are also open and have some fine topiary work.

NEASDEN Greater London TQ2185
District in borough of Brent
Suburbanised between the wars after the North Circular road was built through it in 1921. Unkindly mocked by *Private Eye* satirical magazine.

Naunton, a Cotswold village in the Windrush Valley.

NEASHAM Durham NZ3210
Village off A67, 4 miles (6km) SE of Darlington
Sir Thomas Wrightson of Neasham Hall built estate houses in 1902. Neasham Hill House, built 1757, has gardens open to the public.

NEATH West Glamorgan SS7997
Town on A474, 8 miles (13km) NE of Swansea
Neath was *Nidum* to the Romans. Their fort mostly vanished, though finds are on display at the town museum. Similarly, little left of 13th-century Neath Castle (not open), but Neath Abbey (Cadw) survived the indignity of use as iron foundry during Industrial Revoultion. The town's industrial aspects are balanced by the pretty Gnoll Country Park. Nearby Penscynor Wildlife Park is a top tourist attraction.

NEATISHEAD Norfolk TG3421
Village off A1151, 4 miles (6km) NE of Wroxham
The main street boasts fine late Georgian houses. The village school was founded in 1946 by the Preston family of Beeston Hall.

NEEDHAM MARKET Suffolk TM0855
Town on B1113, 3 miles (5km) SE of Stowmarket
The River Gipping flows to the east of this town, and there is a large picnic site on a pleasant lake which is good for wildlife. Needham Market's crowning glory is the magnificent carvings on the church ceiling. Chain Bridge and Chain House Farm are named for the chains beyond which villagers could not pass during the plague.

NEEDLES, THE Isle of Wight SZ2984
Headland W of Alum Bay, at W end of island
These famous chalk stacks form the western point of the Isle of Wight, with the Victorian Needles Battery (National Trust) perched on the high cliff above. A red and white striped lighthouse of 1859 stands on the outermost stack. Park at Alum Bay (see), as cars are not allowed on the headland road (buses are).

NEEDWOOD FOREST Staffordshire SK1624
Scenic area on B5234, 5 miles (8km) W of Burton upon Trent
A medieval royal hunting forest covered an area (still noticeably wooded) bounded by the rivers Trent, Dove and Blythe and survived until the 17th century.

NEEN SAVAGE Shropshire SO6777
Village off B4363, 1 mile (2km) N of Cleobury Mortimer
Below the high Clee Hills, this small riverside village has a 12th-century church well worth a visit.

NEFYN Gwynedd SH3040
Village on A497, 6 miles (10km) NW of Pwlheli
Small seaside resort linked to Morfa Nefyn and picturesque Porth Dinllaen to form popular north Lleyn holiday area with good sandy beach. Maritime museum.

NELSON Lancashire SD8638
Town on A56, 4 miles (6km) N of Burnley
Victorian cotton town, with many fine mills and a traditional grid-iron pattern of terraced streets. The centre now has pedestrianised streets and the modern Arndale Centre which houses shops and a market hall. Nelson grew from two small villages, and took its name from the railway station, which was named after the local hotel, the Lord Nelson.

NEMPNETT THRUBWELL Avon ST5360
Village off B3114, 2 miles (3km) SW of Chew Stoke
Rural and scattered village just below the Mendip scarp, with a nice little medieval church.

NENE, RIVER Cambridgeshire
River
The River Nene rises near Daventry and meanders through Peterborough to the Wash. The course of the river was altered in the 1490s, but the greatest changes occurred in the 18th century with Smith's Leam between Peterborough and Guyhirn, and Kindersley's Cut near the Wash. Lovely Nene Valley has some beautiful walks, and there are Roman remains in Nene Park.

NENTHEAD Cumbria NY7743
Village on A689, 4 miles (6km) SE of Alston
The village was built by the Quaker owners of the London Lead Company who established here the first free library and the first compulsory schooling in the country. Killhope Lead Mining Centre is the best-preserved site in the country, still dominated by the huge Killhope Wheel that once drove the machinery.

NESSCLIFFE Shropshire SJ3819
Village on A5, 8 miles (13km) NW of Shrewsbury
The ancient Old Three Pigeons is good starting point for woodland walks (including highwayman's cave) on the dramatic sandstone outcrop that shelters the village.

NESTON Cheshire SJ2977
Town on B5133, 7 miles (11km) W of Ellesmere Port
A small market town with medieval origins. The centre has an 18th-century fountain, and there is a four storey, brick-built windmill. Ness Gardens are the botanic gardens of Liverpool University with a large collection of new and rare plants, well displayed and always open to the public.

NETHER ALDERLEY Cheshire SJ8476
Village on A34, 2 miles (3km) S of Alderley Edge
Small village with a 15th-century watermill (National Trust) used for grinding flour, now restored.

NETHER HEYFORD Northamptonshire SP6658
Village off A5, 6 miles (10km) W of Northampton
Between the River Nene and the Grand Union Canal, with a waterway-holidays base. Large village green. Early 18th-century manor house. Church has a fine Tudor monument.

NETHER KELLET Lancashire SD5068
Village off A6, 2 miles (3km) S of Carnforth
A farming community with a traditional village green with old wells and waterpumps. Local industry included quarrying and lime-burning.

NETHER STOWEY Somerset ST1939
Village off A39, 7 miles (11km) W of Bridgwater
Once a town, this attractive stone village has many 17th- and 18th-century houses and cottages, one of which was occupied for three years in the 1790s by the poet Coleridge (National Trust). The pub was renamed the Ancient Mariner in his honour. Castle earthworks survive near by.

NETHER WALLOP Hampshire SU3036
Village off B3084, 4 miles (6km) NW of Stockbridge
Large village with wandering lanes dense with thatched cottages. The church is partly Norman, and has an 11th-century wall-painting. Danebury Ring, to the east, is an Iron Age hillfort.

NETHER WHITACRE Warwickshire SP2392
Village on B4098, 3 miles (5km) NE of Coleshill
On Birmingham's rural fringe, the village conserves its old centre with 17th-century timber-framed houses. The church has 14th-century glass.

NETHERAVON Wiltshire SU1448
Village on A345, 5 miles (8km) N of Amesbury
The army is all around this riverside village with its prominent 18th-century big house (not open). Little brick dovecote in the middle of a field.

NETHERBURY Dorset SY4799
Village off A3066, 1 mile (2km) S of Beaminster
A large village with many buildings in the local orange-coloured stone.

NETHERTHONG West Yorkshire SE1309
Village off A635, 1 mile (2km) N of Holmfirth
The village contains much evidence of its cotton heritage in the 18th-century buildings.

NETHERTON West Yorkshire SE2816
Village on B6117, 2 miles (3km) SW of Horbury
Mining is known to have taken place here since 1401 but the last pit closed in early 1990s. Netherton Hall is supposedly haunted.

NETHY BRIDGE Highland NJ0020
Village off B970, 5 miles (8km) SW of Grantown-on-Spey
Village on the River Nethy, on the edge of Abernethy Forest, in the midst of fine country for outdoor pursuits. Near by stand Castle Roy and the restored Muckerach Castle.

NETLEY Hampshire SU4708
Village off A3025, 2 miles (3km) NW of Hamble
Village on Southampton Water, with the romantically wooded and extensive ruins of Netley Abbey (English Heritage). On the shore is Royal Victoria Country Park, on the site of Netley Hospital, built in 1856 for the army. It was 1,424 ft (433m) long, but only the chapel survives, with a museum.

NETTLEBED Oxfordshire SU7086
Village on A4130, 5 miles (8km) NW of Henley-on-Thames
One brick kiln remains in this affluent village, but the old coaching inn and Georgian houses are the principal relics of its brick-making history.

NETTLECOMBE Somerset ST0537
Hamlet off B3190, 4 miles (6km) S of Watchet
On the edge of Exmoor, Nettlecombe is just an Elizabethan big house (not open) and a rather plain church with a 15th-century tower.

NETTLEHAM Lincolnshire TF0075
Village off A46, 3 miles (5km) NE of Lincoln
Earthworks of Bishop's manor, where Edward I declared his son to be the first Prince of Wales. Ducks on beck, 17th- and 18th-century pantiled cottages around green.

NETTLESTEAD Kent TQ6852
Village on B2015, 5 miles (8km) N of Paddock Wood
A little place in the rural Medway Valley, with a church (rebuilt in 1420) and a modern vineyard near the site of Roman ones.

NETTLETON Wiltshire ST8178
Village off B4039, 7 miles (11km) NW of Chippenham
A scattered village, spread about its little lanes with no focal point.

NEVERN Dyfed SN0839
Village off B4582, 2 miles (3km) NE of Newport
Village noted for its church dedicated to St Brynach, a 5th-century Irish saint. Exceptional ancient carved stones with Latin and Ogham inscriptions. Best of all is the 10th-century Great Cross, one of the finest inscribed Celtic crosses in Wales. Site of overgrown motte and bailey castle with some stone remnants. Also near by is Castell Henllys Iron Age fort, a developed site which re-creates the past.

NEVILL HOLT Leicestershire SP8193
Village off B664, 5 miles (8km) SW of Uppingham
Mainly 13th-century church, hall with 14th-century core (now a school), 17th-century stables and estate cottages. Views across Welland Valley to Rockingham Castle.

NEVILLE'S CROSS Durham NZ2641
Site on A167, on W edge of Durham
Cross erected by Ralph Neville in the 14th century to commemorate the Battle of Neville's Cross in 1346. The stump remains, opposite church.

NEW ABBEY Dumfries and Galloway NX9666
Village on A710, 6 miles (10km) S of Dumfries
Famous for the superb remains of late 13th-century Cistercian Sweetheart Abbey. Unspoilt village with working water-powered mill and Victorian museum.

NEW ADDINGTON Greater London TQ3763
District in borough of Croydon
In effect a minor New Town (unofficially). A 1930s housing estate south of Addington (see) was enlarged by Croydon borough in the 1950s and 60s.

NEW ALRESFORD Hampshire SU5833
see Alresford

NEW ASH GREEN Kent TQ6065
Village off A227, 1 mile (2km) W of Meopham
Self-sufficient New Town begun in 1965, with a pedestrian shopping centre, school, playing fields and church set among neighbourhoods of modern houses.

NEW BRADWELL Buckinghamshire SP8341
Town in Milton Keynes complex, next to Wolverton
Developed from the 1850s for railway company workforce. Grafton Street Aqueduct (1991) carries Grand Union Canal over road. Windmill.

NEW BRIGHTON Merseyside SJ3193
District in E Wallasey
This town, with its long Promenade, panoramic views across the River Mersey and summer open-air concerts, is very popular with day-trippers.

NEW BUCKENHAM Norfolk TM0890
Village on B1113, 4 miles (6km) SE of Attleborough
The castle at New Buckenham was founded in 1145, a few years after the one at nearby Old Buckenham (see). The ramparts and the foundations of a round keep can still be seen. The medieval street pattern still survives, although most buildings are 1800 or later. The fine market house with its nine wooden pillars is 17th century.

NEW CUMNOCK Strathclyde NS6213
Small town on A76, 5 miles (8km) SE of Cumnock
Town near the River Nith which separated from Cumnock in 1650. Formerly an important coal-mining area; mining memorial (1985) dedicated to the 'Past, Present and Future of Mining'.

NEW DEER Grampian NJ8847
Village on A948, 14 miles (23km) SW of Fraserburgh
Founded as an extension to Old Deer in 1805, with a main street leading to a fine viewpoint. Noted for the New Deer annual farming show.

NEW FLETTON Cambridgeshire TL1997
see Fletton

NEW FOREST Hampshire
Scenic area SW of Southampton and E of Ringwood
The New Forest was created by William the Conqueror as a huge area subject to Forest Law, where game was preserved for hunting. There were many forests, but this is the largest to survive. As in medieval times it is a mixture of open grazing, woodland and heath, then preserved for deer, boar and hare. There has always been farming here, with conflicts between the needs of the wild animals and the ponies, cattle and pigs of the foresters. This grew worse from the 15th century, as the Forest was used more as a timber supply for the navy than a hunting forest. The animals (wild or domestic) prevented the trees from regenerating by eating them. The many enclosures in the Forest were made to keep animals out.

The Forest today is a popular area, but large enough to absorb quantities of people. Low, rolling landscape varies from ancient woodlands through boggy heaths to modern plantations. The Ornamental Drive at Bolderwood is one of the best places to see the ancient woodland, with deer observation platforms from which they are often seen. Rhinefield Ornamental Drive has old conifers and rhododendrons.

NEW GALLOWAY Dumfries and Galloway NX6377
Small town on A762, 17 miles (27km) N of Kirkcudbright
The smallest royal burgh in Scotland since its charter in 1633, this long, narrow town of stone-built houses sits at the head of Loch Ken. The 16th-century ruined Kenmure Castle stands on the site of an earlier Gordon stronghold on a hill above the town, and nearby Kells churchyard has charming tombstones and epitaphs. Ken Dee Marshes are the setting for a RSPB nature reserve.

NEW HOLLAND Humberside TA0823
Village on B1206, 2 miles (3km) NE of Barrow-upon-Humber
One of the original crossing points of the Humber estuary. Developed as a railway town and now enjoying a revival as a port.

NEW HOUGHTON Norfolk TR7927
Hamlet off A148, 1 mile (2km) W of West Rudham
On 4 July 1729, Sir Robert Walpole had Houghton village demolished and rebuilt elsewhere as 'New Houghton' to improve the view from his magnificent Palladian mansion. The late medieval church was spared, and still stands in the deer park. Sir Robert and his sons (including writer Horace) are buried here. Breathtaking Houghton Hall and park are open to the public.

NEW INVENTION Shropshire SO2976
Hamlet on A488, 3 miles (5km) N of Knighton
A chapel and a few houses beautifully situated on a stream running through remote hills. Caer Caradoc, Iron Age hillfort, near by.

NEW INVENTION West Midlands SJ9701
District in NW Walsall
Area of residential estates on semi-rural northern fringe of the Black Country. Short Heath Country Park is on its southeastern edge.

NEW LANARK Strathclyde NS8842
Village off A73, immediately S of Lanark
Early industrial cotton-milling village and World Heritage Site surrounded by woodlands on the River Clyde. The village, once Scotland's biggest industrial enterprise, has been superbly restored as living community, working museum and monument to its 18th-century founder Robert Owen, mill-owner and social pioneer. The nearby Falls of Clyde are now part of a Scottish Wildlife Trust reserve.

NEW MILLS Derbyshire SK0085
Town off A6, 8 miles (13km) NW of Buxton
New Mills takes its name from Tudor cornmills, but grew largely through the development of 18th- and 19th-century cottonmills. The textile industry was later joined by engineering industries and the confectionery trade. The Sett Valley Trail provides an attractive walk or cycle ride from Hayfield alongside a tributary of the River Goyt. Torrs Riverside Park; waterfalls in sandstone gorge. Heritage centre.

NEW MILTON Hampshire SZ2495
Town off A337, 5 miles (8km) W of Lymington
Some Edwardian in the middle, but mostly modern. Amazing water tower of 1900 disguised as a castle. Sammy Miller Museum (motorcycles).

NEW PITSLIGO Grampian NJ8855
Village on A950, 10 miles (16km) SW of Fraserburgh
Known in the 19th century for lace-making, which is still practised on a smaller scale today. Commercial peat-cutting near by also brings employment.

NEW QUAY Dyfed SN3859
Village on A486, 5 miles (8km) SW of Aberaeron
Picturesque stone quay still has landing tolls from seafaring days of old. Harbour and beach sheltered by protective headland.

NEW RADNOR Powys SO2161
Village off A44, 6 miles (10km) NW of Kington
Village at meeting of hills and lowlands with long history. Originally a Norman settlement. Substantial motte and bailey castle built in the 11th century, destroyed by Owain Glyndwr in early 15th. Remnants of town walls. Striking 19th-century memorial to famous son, politician George Cornewall Lewis. Former borough and county town of Radnorshire. On doorstep of Radnor Forest, a large conifer plantation.

NEW RIVER Greater London
River, runs from near Ware to Stoke Newington
This remarkable man-made river was constructed to bring water into London from the Hertfordshire springs near Great Amwell (see) by Sir Hugh Myddelton, 1609–13. It ran to a reservoir in Clerkenwell (see), then through wooden pipes to the City. Today it is about 24 miles (39km) long, with its southern end in reservoirs in Stoke Newington and a stretch further south in Islington (see).

NEW ROMNEY Kent TR0264
Town on A259, 9 miles (14km) SW of Hythe
The most important of the Cinque Ports till 1287, when a storm destroyed its harbour. Now 1 mile (2km) from the sea, but Cinque Port documents are still kept in the guildhall. The grandeur of the big Norman church reflects the former greatness of the town in days when ships would anchor at quay just below it. High Street is pleasant, with many attractive Georgian houses. Local steam railway, built to one-third scale.

NEW YORK Lincolnshire TF2455
Hamlet on B1192, 3 miles (5km) SE of Coningsby
Tiny contrast to its American namesake. Settlement in fenland drained in 18th century. Late 19th-century Italianate Wesleyan chapel.

NEWARK-ON-TRENT Nottinghamshire SK7953
Town off A1, 14 miles (23km) N of Grantham
Where the Great North road and the Roman Fosse Way cross, beside the River Trent, this historic market town and commercial centre has at its heart an elegant market square, surrounded by ancient coaching inns, John Carr's splendid town hall and the soaring spire of the grand, mainly 15th-century parish church.

The Bishop of Lincoln's 12th-century castle was one of the most important in the north, where King John died in 1216. The castle gatehouse and the magnificent curtain wall remain, the latter fronting the river, popular for boat trips and waterside walks to the Millgate Museum of social and folk life, in a riverside warehouse. The Gilstrap Centre in pleasant Castle Gardens has displays illustrating the castle story and the town's growth, including its important role in the Civil War, which is further explained in the Newark Museum on Appletongate, not far from the popular Palace Theatre.

On the edge of town, crowds are drawn to Newark Air Museum, and to the show ground, site of the popular county agricultural show in May and the regular antiques fairs for which Newark is internationally renowned.

NEWBALD, NORTH AND SOUTH Humberside SE9136
Villages off A1034, 4 miles (6km) SE of Market Weighton
The villages lie in a hollow, sheltered by the Wolds. The Church of St Nicholas dates from 1125 and is one of the finest Norman churches in Humberside. There are the remains of a Roman villa near by and three quarries have been worked here since that time. The oolitic limestone has been used locally, most notably in Beverley minster.

NEWBIGGIN (NEWBIGGIN-IN-BISHOPDALE) North Yorkshire SE0086
Village on B6160, 2 miles (3km) S of Aysgarth
The village is strung along the base of Wasset Fell; the name means new buildings.

NEWBIGGIN (NEWBIGGIN-IN-TEESDALE) Durham NY9127
Village on B6277, 2 miles (3km) NW of Middleton in Teesdale
Village developed with the lead-mining industry, now reverted to farming. Bowlees visitor centre explains natural history of Upper Teesdale.

NEWBIGGIN-BY-THE-SEA Northumberland NZ3087
Town on A197, 2 miles (3km) E of Ashington
Formerly a fishing and mining village, now catering for holiday-makers. St Bartholomew's Church a shipping landmark on Newbiggin Point, a rocky headland.

NEWBIGGIN-ON-LUNE Cumbria NY7005
Hamlet on A685, 5 miles (8km) SW of Kirkby Stephen
Limestone village in the shadow of Howgill Fells. St Helen's Well is fed by a spring, said to be the start of the River Lune.

NEWBOLD ON AVON Warwickshire SP4877
Village on B4112, on N outskirts of Rugby
In the Rugby suburbs, vestiges of the old village include houses of the 17th and 18th centuries and church memorials to lords of the manor.

NEWBOLD ON STOUR Warwickshire SP2446
Village on A3400, 4 miles (6km) N of Shipston on Stour
Small riverside village on the edge of Ettington Park (see Ettington), where the northern Cotswolds begin to rise.

NEWBOROUGH Gwynedd (Anglesey) SH4265

Village on A4080, 9 miles (14km) SW of Menai Bridge

The 'new borough' established by English invaders in early 14th century. Stands at edge of Newborough Forest, a conifer plantation which leads to dunes of Newborough Warren and vast, empty sands broken by little peninsula of Llanddwyn Island. National Nature Reserve is rich in wildlife. Anglesey Bird World and Bryntirion Open Farm near by.

NEWBOROUGH Staffordshire SK1325

Village on B5234, 4 miles (6km) E of Abbots Bromley

Well-dressing ceremony and maypole dancing take place on spring bank holiday in this planned medieval town that remained a village.

NEWBRIDGE Oxfordshire SP4001

Hamlet on A415, 5 miles (8km) S of Eynsham

Oxfordshire stone was once shipped to London from here, and the mid-15th-century bridge is claimed to be oldest on the Thames.

Inn sign at Newbridge.

NEWBRIDGE ON WYE Powys SO0158

Village on A470, 5 miles (8km) N of Builth Wells

Large village strung out along the A470 north–south trunk road. Set in lovely upper valley of the River Wye.

NEWBURGH Fife NO2318

Town on A913, 9 miles (14km) W of Cupar

Royal burgh on the Firth of Tay, once an important linoleum-manufacturing town but in decline by the beginning of the 20th century. Laing Museum houses local exhibits. Nearby Lindores Abbey was a Benedictine foundation from 1178, sacked in 1543 and afterwards 'reformed' by John Knox. There are few remains, as it was used as a quarry during the construction of Newburgh.

NEWBURGH Lancashire SD4810

Village on A5209, 5 miles (8km) NE of Ormskirk

Picturesque village with 17th-century coaching inn and pleasant green. Woodcock Hall dates from the 14th century: known as Newburgh Hall prior to 1800.

NEWBURN Tyne and Wear NZ1665

Suburb on A6085 on W outskirts of Newcastle

Industrial suburb of Newcastle with Lemington power station. *Puffing Billy*, the first steam locomotive, was built here in 1813.

NEWBURY Berkshire SU4767

Town off A4, 16 miles (25km) W of Reading

A crossroads town, important in late medieval times for cloth production. The fine early 15th-century church was built by a clothier, and one row of humble weavers' cottages survives. Mostly Victorian market place, but Georgian houses elsewhere. The Kennet and Avon Canal has its first lock here. Newbury and District Museum in the 1620s cloth hall. Newbury Racecourse to the east of the town.

NEWBY BRIDGE Cumbria SD3686

Village off A590, 8 miles (13km) NE of Ulverston

A village on the River Kent which got its name from the five-arched stone bridge built in 1651 to replace the existing timber structure.

NEWCASTLE EMLYN Dyfed SN3040

Small town on A484, 11 miles (18km) SE of Cardigan

Market town and meeting place for rural communities of the Teifi Valley with good range of inns and shops. In beautiful wooded river valley setting. Ruined castle on loop in the river is the 'new' castle of 1240. Bethel chapel is an impressive reminder of the flourishing Nonconformism of the 19th century.

NEWCASTLE UPON TYNE Tyne and Wear NZ2464

City off A1(M), 80 miles (129km) N of Leeds

Newcastle, a major commercial centre and capital of the northeast of England, is a city which appears to have survived remarkably well the drastic decline of its surrounding industries, namely ship-building and coal-mining.

The city took its name from the 'new castle' built by William the Conqueror's son in 1080. The castle was rebuilt by Henry II in 1172 and today its Norman keep is one of the finest in England, providing splendid views from its battlements.

The oldest part, and once the heart of the city, is Quayside with historic buildings such as Bessie Surtees' House, a beautiful half-timbered house which is the regional headquarters of English Heritage and open to the public. Quayside has been restored to become a fashionable waterside quarter of the city with restaurants, pubs, antiques and book shops and a Sunday market.

With the decline of river-based trade in the 19th century the city shifted northwards. The Victorian planners John Clayton, Richard Grainger and John Dobson are credited with designing the new commercial city, transforming Newcastle into the elegant Victorian city that it is today, with its wide streets and squares and fine architecture. Grey Street is one of the most handsome streets, curving majestically and lined with beautiful buildings.

The shopping centre of the city is based around Newcastle Street, Pilgrim Street, Granger Street, Market Street, the shopping arcades of Eldon Square and Monument Mall, and the Edwardian Central Arcade. The city has a number of excellent art galleries and five theatres and is well known for its lively nightlife. Newcastle Discovery in Blandon Square is a living museum of Newcastle life as told by the people who live there.

NEWCASTLE-UNDER-LYME Staffordshire SJ8445
Town off M6, immediately W of Stoke-on-Trent
This ancient borough preserves its individuality from neighbouring Stoke-on-Trent. Among extensive modern developments older buildings survive, notably the guildhall of 1713, an unusual Roman Catholic church, good Georgian houses in King Street and the earliest of the town's silk mills in Marsh Parade. Excellent museum in Brampton Park, 'theatre-in-the-round' at New Victoria Theatre.

NEWCASTLETON Borders NY4887
Village on B6357, 17 miles (27km) S of Hawick
Planned symmetrical village founded in 1793 by the Duke of Buccleuch as a handloom weaving centre. Good base for exploring Liddesdale and surrounding country.

NEWCHAPEL Staffordshire SJ8554
Village in NE Kidsgrove
James Brindley, engineer and canal pioneer, is buried in the churchyard of this former mining village on the northern edge of Stoke-on-Trent.

NEWCHAPEL Surrey TQ3642
Hamlet on A22, 1 mile (2km) SW of Lingfield
This complex built around the Mormon temple of 1958 dominates the crossroads on the London–Eastbourne road. First Mormon church in Europe.

NEWCHURCH Isle of Wight SZ5685
Village off A3056, 2 miles (3km) NW of Sandown
Wooded village, with a prominent 18th-century weather-boarded tower to the medieval church. Island Amazon Adventure rainforest with birds and animals.

NEWCHURCH Kent TR0531
Village off A259, 4 miles (6km) N of New Romney
Romney Marsh village, small centre of wide scatter of isolated Marsh farms. Church with spacious 15th-century tower and nearby deserted medieval villages.

NEWCHURCH (NEWCHURCH IN PENDLE) Lancashire SD8239
Hamlet off A6068, 3 miles (5km) NW of Nelson
A typical Pennine hill village which developed a handloom weaving industry in the 18th century. It was associated with witchcraft in the 17th century.

NEWDIGATE Surrey TQ1942
Village off A24, 5 miles (8km) SE of Dorking
Pleasant, scattered Wealden village with timber-framed and tile-hung cottages. Church noted for magnificent 14th-century west tower, constructed entirely in timber.

NEWENDEN Kent TQ8327
Village on A28, 5 miles (8km) SW of Tenterden
Village on the River Rother, the boundary with Sussex, with an early 18th-century bridge and a church raised on a mound with a strange little tower and spire of 1859.

NEWENT Gloucestershire SO7225
Small town on B4215, 8 miles (13km) NW of Gloucester
The timber-framed market house, 17th-century George hotel, a good medieval church and many attractive brick and timber-framed buildings make the 'capital' of the Vale of Leadon an appealing town. Additional attractions include the Shambles Museum of Victorian Life, National Birds of Prey Centre, Butterfly and Natural World Centre, Cowdy Glass Workshop and Three Choirs Vineyard.

NEWGALE Dyfed SM8422
Hamlet on A487, 6 miles (10km) E of St Davids
Newgale's huge, west-facing beach along St Bride's Bay is popular with surfers. Small-scale holiday developments along coast.

NEWHAVEN East Sussex TQ4401
Town on A259, 9 miles (14km) E of Brighton
Cross-Channel ferry and fishing port at the mouth of the River Ouse, also handling some Baltic trade. Known as Meeching until the 1560s, when the River Ouse shifted its mouth from Seaford and the 'new haven' was created. Fort and maze of tunnels built in the 1860s against possible French threat are now restored and open to the public.

NEWICK East Sussex TQ4121
Village on A272, 4 miles (6km) W of Uckfield
Large village with Victorian and Edwardian houses around a big green with the partly Norman church away up the hill.

NEWLAND Gloucestershire SO5509
Village off A4136, 4 miles (6km) SE of Monmouth
The 'cathedral of the Forest' dominates this village on a steep valley side in the Forest of Dean. This spacious church is famous for monuments that include the 15th-century miner's brass, incised with a vivid picture of a medieval miner with pick and candle. The 17th-century old grammar school and almshouses, grouped around the church, complete an attractive picture.

NEWLANDS CORNER Surrey TQ0449
Beauty spot off A25, 3 miles (5km) W of Guildford
Excellent viewpoint at 567ft (172m) on Merrow Down, site of a former racecourse. Noted for fine, springy turf and knarled, ancient yew trees.

NEWLYN Cornwall SW4628

Town on B3315, immediately S of Penzance

Some old winding streets with stone cottages here, but much of the town is modern. Newlyn is a major fishing port, and the harbour is often crammed with fishing boats. It is also famous for the Newlyn School of Artists, started here in the 1880s, a group of painters who produced realistic pictures of local scenes and people (many can be seen in the Penzance Museum).

NEWMARKET Suffolk TL6463

Town on A1303, 13 miles (20km) E of Cambridge

With one of the foremost racecourses in the country, Newmarket has a genteel town centre built largely on the wealth accrued through the horse-racing industry. The Jockey Club stands in the High Street. It was founded in 1752 (the building dates from 1882), and is the governing body of horse-racing, controlling the licensing of jockeys, trainers and racecourses. Next door is the handsome National Horse Racing Museum. Horse-selling has taken place at Newmarket since the 1880s, while the gentle countryside all around is dominated by smooth green paddocks, all enclosed by neat white fences. Outside Newmarket is the National Stud, which possesses some of the best stallions in the world.

When Charles II visited Newmarket in 1683, a fire broke out that destroyed much of the town. Nell Gwynne's home in Palace Street survived, however. The Rutland Arms hotel and White Hart hotel are both former coaching inns. At the end of the long, wide main street is the Jubilee clock tower. The Langtry hotel in Gazeley Road was the home of the queen of the Victorian stage, Lillie Langtry, later the mistress of Edward VII.

NEWMILLERDAM West Yorkshire SE3215

Village on A61, 3 miles (5km) S of Wakefield

An old estate village with new housing in a pleasant setting alongside the lake created by the dam.

NEWMILNS Strathclyde NS5337

Town on A71, 7 miles (11km) E of Kilmarnock

Once a famous muslin-weaving and lace-making town, with an 18th-century town house and crow-stepped tollbooth. Connections with the Covenanters; memorials in churchyard.

NEWNHAM Gloucestershire SO6911

Village on A48, 7 miles (11km) NE of Lydney

The former port on the horseshoe bend in the River Severn retains good Georgian houses in its High Street and interesting converted warehouses of the 18th and 19th centuries, some incorporating blocks of waste from an old glass factory. The Victorian church, a splendid viewpoint on the hill overlooking town, houses an exceptional Norman font from an earlier church.

NEWNHAM Kent TQ9557

Village off A2, 5 miles (8km) SW of Faversham

A long street of cottages amid orchards and parkland. Tudor Calico House recalls that the village was formerly a centre of calico production.

NEWPORT Dyfed SN0539

Small town on A487, 9 miles (14km) SW of Cardigan

In summer, a popular little North Pembrokeshire holiday centre. Good beach. Town has a long history; castle in private ownership. Iron Age hillfort above.

NEWPORT Essex TL5234

Village on B1383, 3 miles (5km) SW of Saffron Walden

This Saxon royal manor and market town stretches narrowly along the River Cam, now a smart, attractive commuter village with much post-war housing. A rewarding history trail includes a medieval church with unique travelling chest, bridge tollhouse, fine old houses, farms and converted former maltings, a former prison, grammar school and the venerable Coach and Horses pub.

NEWPORT Gwent ST3088

Town off M4, 10 miles (16km) NE of Cardiff

Newport is a large, mainly industrial town of over 100,000 people which has grown up around the mouth of the River Usk. Remnants of its medieval castle, hemmed in by road and rail track, stand on the banks of the river. On Stow Hill above the shopping streets is St Woolos Cathedral. This grand building, which blends Anglo-Saxon with Norman influences, occupies the site of a religious settlement dating back as far as the 6th century.

One of a number of Covenanters' monuments in the churchyard at Newmilns.

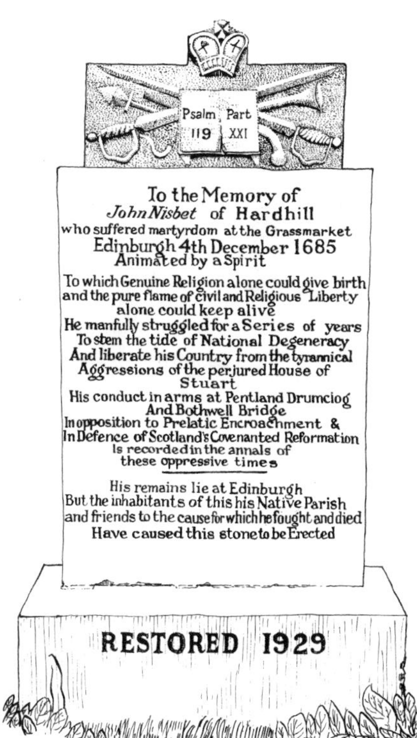

The views from the hill look out to Newport's docklands – responsible for the town's 19th-century growth – and the tall Transporter Bridge across the Usk, a major landmark. Newport's industrial past is just one of the many themes at the wide-ranging museum in the modern town centre.

The splendid 17th-century Tredegar House stands in its 90 acre (36ha) country park on the western approach to Newport. The house, once owned by a wealthy coal magnate, counterpoints glittering 'upstairs' rooms with the 'downstairs' servants' quarters. Also on the outskirts is the Fourteen Locks Canal Centre with its series of giant locks carved into the hillside.

NEWPORT Isle of Wight SZ4989

Town on A3020, 4 miles (6km) S of Cowes

The capital of the Isle of Wight is its largest town and its biggest shopping centre. A handsome central square is the setting of the main church. Two classical buildings were designed in the 1810s by John Nash: the town hall and guildhall. Quay Street, with its Georgian houses, leads to the picturesque river harbour. On the outskirts is a well-displayed Roman villa.

NEWPORT Shropshire SJ7419

Town on A41, 11 miles (18km) SE of Market Drayton

Handsome market town where spacious church is islanded in long High Street. Adams Grammar School, Italianate town hall and Royal Victoria hotel stand out, but street abounds in other mellow Georgian and Victorian buildings built on Norman burgage plots. To the northeast is Aqualate Mere, a vast natural lake accessible by public footpath.

NEWPORT PAGNELL Buckinghamshire SP8743

Town off M1, 6 miles (10km) N of Bletchley

Pleasant dormitory town where River Ouzel joins the Great Ouse, now part of Milton Keynes (see). Plenty of 18th-century red brick; 17th-century Swan Revived inn. Big church with pinnacled tower looks over Ouzel, while cast-iron Tickford Bridge over the river has been in use since 1810. Aston Martin Lagonda make sports cars here.

NEWPORT-ON-TAY Fife NO4228

Town off A92, 5 miles (8km) N of Leuchars

Residential village opposite Dundee, connected to it by rail and road bridges (1887 and 1966). Scene of Tay Bridge Disaster in 1879, when original rail bridge collapsed during a storm, precipitating a crossing train with its passengers into the estuary.

NEWQUAY Cornwall SW8161

Town on A3058, 11 miles (18km) N of Truro

This huge holiday resort has grown from a tiny fishing village. It offers a superb coastline with rocky headlands and sandy bays, and, to the north, 3 miles (5km) of sands. All that survives of the old village is the little harbour tucked in under a rocky cliff and the huers' house, a unique survival of the little huts used by the huers, who watched for shoals of fish.

Crown House in Newport, Essex.

A few Regency buildings survive from the earliest days of tourism here, but most of the town is Victorian or later, having been built after the railway brought hordes of visitors to this splendid coast. The Atlantic rollers make this the home of surf-boarding and the sandy beaches are overlooked by steep cliffs. Huge hotels date from the Victorian era.

Trenance Gardens has good displays of flowers, a boating lake and the Newquay Animal World conservation centre. The Fun Factory is an adventure playground, and Tunnels through Time has displays on Cornwall. The Newquay Sealife Centre is on the seafront.

NEWSHAM North Yorkshire NZ1010
Village off A66, 7 miles (11km) NW of Richmond
An ancient river crossing retaining an attractive 18th-century bridge. Newsham Mill, now used as a pottery, dates from the 16th century and is a rare survival of a small early corn watermill.

NEWSTEAD Nottinghamshire SK5152
Village off A611, 3 miles (5km) SE of Kirkby in Ashfield
Newstead Abbey priory was converted to a 16th-century mansion and underwent a 19th-century neo-Gothic restoration. Fine parkland, lakes, gardens. This was the poet Byron's boyhood home, and has memorabilia and manuscripts.

NEWTIMBER West Sussex TQ2613
Village off A23, 1 mile (2km) NW of Pyecombe
This tiny place is tucked under a steep wooded slope of Newtimber Hill (National Trust). Moated Newtimber Place, an ancient site, has an impressive late 17th-century front.

NEWTON Lancashire SD4430
Village off A583, 2 miles (3km) SE of Kirkham
Situated on the western side of Dunnow Rock, a limestone hill rising from banks of River Hodder. Waddington Fell gives excellent views of Hodder Vale.

NEWTON Norfolk TF8315
Hamlet on A1065, 4 miles (6km) N of Swaffham
Newton's pretty little All Saints' Church was one of very few Norfolk Saxon buildings to escape rebuilding in the 15th century.

NEWTON Northumberland NZ0364
Village off A69, 3 miles (5km) E of Corbridge
Small, peaceful village in a conservation area. Much of the land belongs to the estate of Viscount Allendale.

NEWTON West Midlands SP0393
District NE of West Bromwich
Area of residential estates beside River Tame and adjoining Sandwell Valley Country Park (see West Bromwich).

NEWTON ABBOT Devon SX8671
Town off A380, 6 miles (10km) NW of Torquay
This little medieval settlement at the head of the Teign estuary grew enormously after it became a railway centre in 1856. Older buildings in the centre, but there are rows and rows of Victorian railway workers' housing. Bradley Manor (National Trust) is a 15th-century manor house. Victorian Tucker's Maltings is still working. Stover Country Park to the northwest.

NEWTON ARLOSH Cumbria NY2055
Village on B5307, 2 miles (3km) SW of Kirkbride
Long, straggling village surrounded by peat land and tidal salt marshes. The 14th-century church has a tiny doorway only 2ft 7ins (79cm) wide.

NEWTON AYCLIFFE Durham NZ2724
New Town off A167, 6 miles (10km) N of Darlington
The first of Durham's new towns, started in 1948. Large shopping centre and sports complex provide the focal point, the roads are wide and many trees have been planted in the town. St Andrew's Church, however, dates from the 12th century and has Saxon foundations.

NEWTON FERRERS Devon SX5448
Town on B3186, 3 miles (5km) SW of Yealmpton
On the Yealm estuary, wooded down to the shore. Rather remote.

NEWTON FLOTMAN Norfolk TM2198
Village on A140, 7 miles (11km) S of Norwich
A medieval bridge over the River Tas, the lovely Elizabethan Rainthorpe Hall, and a monument erected in 1571 are just three of Newton Flotman's treasures.

NEWTON HARCOURT Leicestershire SP6396
Village off A6, 6 miles (10km) SE of Leicester
On the far side of the Grand Union Canal and railway from the village, a mainly 17th-century manor house, and 1834 brick church with 13th-century stone tower.

NEWTON KYME North Yorkshire SE4644
Village off A659, 2 miles (3km) NW of Tadcaster
An ancient village by the River Wharfe with a 12th-century church, reached by a footpath through fields past Newton Kyne Hall.

NEWTON LONGVILLE Buckinghamshire SP8431
Village off A421, 2 miles (3km) SW of Bletchley
Picturesque cottages long dominated by brickworks chimneys, but works closed in 1990. Church has unusual dedication to St Faith; it is known for its carvings.

NEWTON MEARNS Strathclyde NS5355
Town on A77, 6 miles (10km) SW of Glasgow
Residential town southwest of Glasgow lying on edge of moorland. Fifteenth-century Blackhouse Castle and monument to local poet Robert Pollock, born 1799.

NEWTON (NEWTON IN THE WILLOWS) Northamptonshire SP8883
Deserted village off A43, 1 mile (2km) W of Geddington
One of the largest Elizabethan dovecotes in the country, bearing the trefoil of the Tresham family (see Rushton), whose home was here. Field Studies Centre in redundant church.

NEWTON POPPLEFORD Devon SY0889
Village on A3052, 3 miles (5km) NW of Sidmouth
A medieval new town, founded in 1226, but a village now, with cob and thatch cottages. Oldest tollhouse in the county (1758), thatched, on the junction of A3052 and A376. Aylesbeare Common Nature Reserve.

NEWTON SOLNEY Derbyshire SK2825
Village on B5008, 3 miles (5km) NE of Burton upon Trent
Beside the River Trent and the Staffordshire border. Red-brick Bladon Castle was designed by Wyatville as a folly and extended to a house. Late 18th-century Newton Park now a hotel.

NEWTON ST CYRES Devon SX8898
Village on A377, 3 miles (5km) SE of Crediton
Cob and thatch village. The medieval church has a large and odd memorial of 1632, showing a figure with high boots.

NEWTON ST LOE Avon ST7064
Village off A39, 3 miles (5km) W of Bath
Stone village with a handsome church and unusually early school (1698).

NEWTON STEWART Dumfries and Galloway NX4065
Small town on A714, 7 miles (11km) N of Wigtown
This market town and holiday centre above Wigtown Bay on the River Cree is a good base for exploring the huge Galloway Forest Park, which encloses the Galloway Hills; the town is also popular with fishermen. There is a local museum and a working mohair mill. The Galloway Monument was erected in 1875 to commemorate the 9th Earl of Galloway.

NEWTON UNDER ROSEBERRY Cleveland NZ5713
Hamlet on A173, 3 miles (5km) SW of Guisborough
Village sits beneath Roseberry Topping, with Norman church on the green. Roseberry Topping, 1,051ft (320m) high, is a prominent feature of the landscape and is part owned by the National Trust, who also own Roseberry Common, an area of heather moorland and rich woodland.

NEWTON-LE-WILLOWS Merseyside SJ5996
Town off A49, 5 miles (8km) E of St Helens
Originally an ancient farming community, the town grew rapidly with the coming of the railways.

NEWTON-LE-WILLOWS North Yorkshire SE2189
Village off A684, 3 miles (5km) NW of Bedale
For centuries under the jurisdiction of Jervaulx Abbey, the village has a history of textile-spinning and weaving.

NEWTONGRANGE Lothian NT3364
Town on A7, 2 miles (3km) S of Dalkeith
Town in economically depressed former coal-mining area. Scottish Mining Museum at Lady Victoria, one of Europe's finest 19th-century collieries.

NEWTONMORE Highland NN7098
Village on A86, 3 miles (5km) W of Kingussie
Stone-built town in the upper Spey Valley, popular as a holiday centre. Clan MacPherson Museum and an indoor water and music spectacular known as Waltzing Waters.

NEWTOWN Isle of Wight SZ4290
Village off A3054, 5 miles (8km) W of Newport
As the name suggests,this was a medieval New Town, founded in 1256, but raided by the French in 1377 and in decline ever since. The classical Georgian town hall (National Trust, limited opening) stands by a rural lane; there are few other houses. The shore, once a port, is quiet and good for birds. Clamerkin Farm Park is to the east.

NEWTOWN (DRENEWYDD) Powys SO1091
Town on A483, 12 miles (19km) SW of Welshpool
Busy town and commercial centre which has attracted significant new investment into rural Wales. Memories of former textile industry in cavernous, red-bricked warehouses, birthplace of 'Father of Socialism' Robert Owen, spacious main street leading to bridge over River Severn, promenade beside river. Museums dedicated to Owen and textile industry. Wide range of performances at Theatr Hafren.

NEWTOWN LINFORD Leicestershire SK5209
Village on B5327, 6 miles (10km) NW of Leicester
Picturesque and popular Charnwood Forest village, at the main entrance to Bradgate Park (see Charnwood Forest). Several timber-framed houses with crucks, and thatched cottages.

NEYLAND Dyfed SM9605
Small town on B4325, 4 miles (6km) E of Milford Haven
Seatown on Milford Haven waterway, once embarkation point for Ireland. Its workmanlike appearance has been improved by the addition of a new marina.

NIDD, RIVER North Yorkshire
River runs through Pateley Bridge and Knaresborough to the Ouse
The River Nidd is sourced high on Great Whernside and Little Whernside. The upper reaches of Nidderdale are thickly wooded and often described as 'Little Switzerland'. The three reservoirs in the valley supply water to Bradford.

NITH, RIVER Dumfries and Galloway
River, runs through Dumfries to Solway Firth
The river rises in Strathclyde and flows through lovely hilly country in Nithsdale to Dumfries, before widening to reach the mudflats of the Solway estuary.

NITON, UPPER AND LOWER Isle of Wight SZ5076
Village on A3055, 4 miles (6km) W of Ventnor
Upper Niton is a large inland village, Lower Niton is part of the deeply wooded steep Undercliff which developed, like Bonchurch (see), in the early 19th century.

NOKE Oxfordshire SP5413
Village off B4027, 5 miles (8km) NE of Oxford
Straggling village on western edge of Ot Moor (see), with appealing rustic church containing interesting 13th-century features and fine brass of 1598.

NOMANSLAND Wiltshire SU2517
Village off B3079, 4 miles (6km) NW of Cadnam
Straggling brick village on the edge of the New Forest, so-called because it was not included in any of the Forest Keepers' areas.

NORBURY Derbyshire SK1242
Village on B5033, 4 miles (6km) SW of Ashbourne
Set by the River Dove which forms the Staffordshire border, Norbury is where George Eliot set scenes of *Adam Bede*. Some of her relations are buried in the churchyard. The church has a 14th-century chancel and stained glass, and 15th-century alabaster tombs of the Fitzherberts. The red-brick late 17th-century manor house (closed) adjoins the church on a hillside above the river. The 13th- to 15th-century Old Manor (National Trust, by appointment) is stone, with a king post roof.

NORE, THE Kent TQ9580
Sandbank, off shore at Sheerness
This sandbank in the Thames estuary, 3 miles (5km) southeast of Sheerness, is marked by a Nore lightship. Traditionally, the name Nore refers to the western Thames estuary, a famous anchorage. Nore gave its name to the Nore Mutiny, a sailors' revolt of 1797.

NORHAM Northumberland NT9047
Village on B6470, 7 miles (11km) SW of Berwick-upon-Tweed
A historic border village built high above the River Tweed. Norham Castle (English Heritage), built in 1157, was repeatedly attacked for centuries afterwards. Sir Walter Scott called it the most dangerous place in Britain in his poem, *Marmion*. St Cuthbert's Church, partly Norman, contains a 17th-century pulpit from Durham Cathedral.

NORMANDY Surrey SU9251
Village on A323, 4 miles (6km) E of Aldershot
Scattered village among commons where William Cobbett, author of *Rural Rides*, once farmed. The cricket ground, surrounded by trees, is claimed to be the most beautiful in Surrey.

NORMANTON Leicestershire SK9305
Site off A606, 1 mile (2km) NE of Edith Weston
Rescued upper part and tower of 19th-century classical church, a landmark on Rutland Water south shore causeway, now used as a museum.

NORMANTON Nottinghamshire SK7054
Hamlet off A612, 1 mile (2km) NE of Southwell
Known as Normanton-on-Trent, although well away from the river. Reg Taylor's Swan Sanctuary shelters injured swans and wildfowl on four lakes.

NORMANTON West Yorkshire SE3822
Town on A655, 4 miles (6km) E of Wakefield
A large and drab former colliery town consisting mainly of red-brick Victorian terraces. There are now many housing estates and an industrial estate. A window in All Saints' Church commemorates the voyages of Sir Martin Frobisher, a locally born 16th-century seaman.

NORTH ANSTON South Yorkshire
see Anston

NORTH BADDESLEY Hampshire SU3920
Village off A27, 3 miles (5km) E of Romsey
Partly modern development, partly rural, with a small and charming church.

NORTH BENFLEET Essex TQ7588
Village off A127, 3 miles (5km) E of Basildon
Junior partner of South Benfleet (see), sandwiched between Basildon and the Southend complex. Colonised by Londoners from the early 20th century.

NORTH BERWICK Lothian NT5585
Town on A198, 19 miles (31km) E of Edinburgh
A seaside town, once a fishing and trading port and now a popular holiday resort, founded earlier than the 12th century. Remains of a 12th-century Cistercian nunnery and a 12th-century parish church. North Berwick Museum tells the local story. North Berwick Law, to the south, is a volcanic rock 613ft (184m) high, surmounted by an archway made from a whale's jawbones.

Archway made from the jawbones of a whale at North Berwick.

NORTH BOVEY Devon SX7483
Village off B3212, 2 miles (3km) SW of Moretonhampstead
Dartmoor village of granite and thatch with a large green dotted with old oak trees.

NORTH BRADLEY Wiltshire ST8555
Village off A350, 2 miles (3km) S of Trowbridge
Large village with modern housing mixed with the old. Classical almshouses of 1810 by the church.

NORTH BURLINGHAM Norfolk TG3610
Village on A47, 2 miles (3km) W of Acle
On main Great Yarmouth to Norwich road, North Burlingham has two churches. Some furnishings were taken from ruinous St Peter's to 15th-century St Andrew's.

NORTH CADBURY Somerset ST6327
Village off A303, 5 miles (8km) W of Wincanton
The large and impressive 15th-century church retains its original wooden roof. The bench-ends (dated 1538) have figures and even a church carved on them. The village itself has many pretty stone cottages.

NORTH CAVE Humberside SE8932
Village on B1230, 6 miles (10km) S of Market Weighton
North Cave Beck runs through this extensive village in the foothills of the Wolds. The Church of All Saints, dated 1318, is the oldest building in the village.

NORTH CERNEY Gloucestershire SP0107
Village on A435, 4 miles (6km) N of Cirencester
Set in the meadows of the upper Churn Valley, the village has a church of exceptional interest, with Norman carving and medieval glass.

NORTH CLIFTON Nottinghamshire SK8272
Village off A1133, 9 miles (14km) W of Lincoln
Trentside village. Pureland Japanese Garden in the grounds of the Relaxation and Meditation Centre, a tranquil place for students and visitors.

NORTH CRAWLEY Buckinghamshire SP9244
Village off A422, 3 miles (5km) E of Newport Pagnell
Church has very rare dedication to St Firmin, a notable 15th-century rood screen with painted figures and an 18th-century pulpit.

NORTH CRAY Greater London TQ4872
District in borough of Bexley
Developed mainly since 1960s, still comparatively countrified. Extensive meadows along the River Cray with an 18th-century bridge. Victorian church.

NORTH CREAKE Norfolk TF8538
see Creake

NORTH CURRY Somerset ST3125
Village off A378, 6 miles (10km) E of Taunton
A pretty village with an elegant church known as the 'cathedral of the Moors', with an unusual octagonal tower and a very attractive 15th-century porch. There is a RSPB reserve at West Sedgemoor. See Somerset Levels and Sedgemoor.

NORTH DALTON Humberside SE9351
Village on B1246, 6 miles (10km) SW of Great Driffield
An agricultural village centred around All Saints' Church and the mere, which is surrounded by elm and sycamore trees.

NORTH DOWNS Surrey
Hill range
Chalk hills running eastwards from Hampshire through Surrey and Kent to plunge into the sea as cliffs at South Foreland. The range is broken by major rivers, particularly the Wey, Mole and Darent. Its steep scarp slope faces south, cut by combes, partly wooded, partly short, springy turf, noted for wildflowers. The North Downs Way follows the hills for 140 miles (224km).

NORTH ELMHAM Norfolk TF9820
Village on B1110, 5 miles (8km) N of East Dereham
This sprawling village with its long main street and walled gardens has the intriguing remains of an enormous early Saxon cathedral, possibly the one in which St Edmund was crowned king in the 9th century. There are also the ruins of a 14th-century bishops' hunting lodge, and a vineyard that produces Elmham Park wines.

NORTH FERRIBY Humberside SE9825
Village off A63, 7 miles (11km) W of Hull
Pleasant residential area on the north bank of the River Humber, developed when rich merchants from Hull's prosperous port built large homes here.

NORTH FORELAND Kent TR4069
Headland off B2052, 1 mile (2km) N of Broadstairs
Prominent white cliffs, the most easterly point in Kent and the southwestern gate to the Thames estuary. Crowned by a lighthouse since 1636.

NORTH GRIMSTON North Yorkshire SE8467
Village on B1248, 4 miles (6km) SE of Malton
Pretty village characterised by white stone cottages with red pantile roofs.

NORTH HILL Cornwall SX2776
Village off B3254, 6 miles (10km) SW of Launceston
Just above the woody valley of the River Lynher, the village has slate cottages and an interesting medieval church.

NORTH HINKSEY Oxfordshire SP4905
Suburb off A34, on W outskirts of Oxford
The old Oxford suburb with Norman church retains village atmosphere. Conduit House (English Heritage) survives from 17th-century water supply project.

NORTH KELSEY Lincolnshire TA0401
Village off B1434, 5 miles (8km) W of Caistor
Black and white painted Tudor-style Church Farm, genuinely Tudor inside. Church mainly 1869, with 13th-century tower. Small Victorian red-brick church on moor, now a house.

NORTH KESSOCK Highland NH6548
Village on A9, across the water from Inverness
Village across the Moray Firth from Inverness, nowadays crouching in the shadow of the A9 road bridge.

NORTH LEIGH Oxfordshire SP3813
Village off A4095, 3 miles (5km) NE of Witney
Saxon church full of medieval riches vies for attention with mosaics, baths and other remains of an extensive Roman villa.

NORTH LEVERTON WITH HABBLESTHORPE
Nottinghamshire SK7882
Village off A620, 5 miles (8km) E of Retford
Working windmill with four sails, built in 1812–15, heightened in 1884. Houses of good 17th- and 18th-century brickwork, with interesting gables.

NORTH LOPHAM Norfolk TM0382
see Lopham

NORTH LUFFENHAM Leicestershire SK9303
Village off A6121, 6 miles (10km) SE of Oakham
Limestone village with 16th-century and later hall. Large medieval church with fine sedilia and inscription to Archdeacon Johnson, founder of Oakham and Uppingham Schools.

NORTH MARSTON Buckinghamshire SP7722
Village off A413, 3 miles (5km) S of Winslow
Pilgrims flocked to the shrine and healing well of miracle-working medieval priest John Schorne, said to have trapped the Devil in a boot. The well, covered now, is in Schorne Lane, near the magnificent church which was restored in 1850s at Queen Victoria's expense in memory of bachelor miser John Camden Nield, who left her his fortune.

NORTH MOLTON Devon SS7329
Village off A361, 3 miles (5km) NE of South Molton
One steep straggling street on the edge of Exmoor. Fine 100ft (30m) church tower.

NORTH MORETON Oxfordshire SU5689
Village off A4130, 2 miles (3km) E of Didcot
Cobbs Cottage and other good timber-framed houses retain traditional character of this popular village. Superb medieval glass in All Saints' Church.

NORTH NEWBALD Humberside SE9136
see Newbald

NORTH NEWTON Somerset ST3031
Village off A38, 1 mile (2km) S of North Petherton
Scattered old farmhouses are set away from the modern village. The church has an elaborate wooden door and screen of the 1630s. The Alfred Jewel (now in the Ashmolean Museum, Oxford) was found here in 1693.

NORTH NIBLEY Gloucestershire ST7495
Village on B4060, 2 miles (3km) NW of Wotton-under-Edge
On Nibley Knoll a tower (key available in village) commemorates William Tyndale, translator of the Bible. The fine church is also well worth a visit.

NORTH NORFOLK COAST Norfolk
Scenic region
The North Norfolk Coast, a designated Area of Outstanding Natural Beauty, is a wild and rugged stretch of coastline that extends from Hunstanton in the north to Great Yarmouth in the east in a great curve. It is an area of England that is constantly changing under the assault of the sea. Some villages have been losing fields, homes, churches, and even graves to the onslaught of the waves, while off the coast, ever-shifting bars of sand and silt provide excellent resting spots for seals and birds. Elsewhere, such as the beaches around Hunstanton, the sea has created huge salt marshes which provide a haven for many species of migrating and resident bird.

The North Norfolk Coast is also renowned for its great expanses of empty beach, golden tracts of sand that stretch away to meet a thin blue ribbon of sea far off in the distance.

Visitors may enjoy the attractions of a busy seaside resort, such as Cromer or Sheringham (see); head for one of the many nature reserves for bird-watching or long walks along deserted paths and trails; or view proud Castle Rising (English Heritage) or exquisite Holkham Hall.

NORTH PERROTT Somerset ST4709
Village on A3066, 2 miles (3km) E of Crewkerne
Plain but attractive stone village, mostly in golden Hamstone.

NORTH PETHERTON Somerset ST2933
Small town on A38, 3 miles (5km) S of Bridgwater
Large village with one of the best of the famous Somerset church towers, 109ft (33m) high and elaborately built in the 15th century.

NORTH PETHERWIN Cornwall SX2889
Village off B3254, 5 miles (8km) NW of Launceston
Small village just above the River Ottery. To the east are Tamar Otter Park and Wildwood, with breeding otters, deer and a wildfowl lake.

NORTH QUEENSFERRY Fife NT1380
Village off A90, at N end of the Forth Road Bridge
Crouching under the Forth Rail Bridge and originally the terminal for ferries across the Firth of Forth, until the road bridge was built in 1964. Deep Sea World is a huge aquarium with the world's largest underwater viewing tunnel.

NORTH RONALDSAY Orkney HY7553
Island, at N end of Orkney group
The most northerly Orkney island is famed for its distinctively flavoured mutton; these seaweed-eating sheep are kept on the beach and off the grass by a stone wall which encircles the island.

NORTH RUNCTON Norfolk TF6415
Village off A47, 3 miles (5km) SE of King's Lynn
The outstanding feature of this small village is its gorgeous 18th-century church, built around 1703–13 by Henry Bell with a lantern tower.

A wooden 'dolly' near the Quay in North Shields.

NORTH SHIELDS
Tyne and Wear NZ3568
Town on A1058, 7 miles (11km) E of Newcastle
Fishing and industrial centre near the mouth of the River Tyne, and terminus for ferries to Norway and Denmark. Birthplace of the steam trawler which revolutionised deep-sea fishing. Museum of fishing at the Fishing Experience Centre, and an early morning fish market at Fish Quay.

NORTH SOMERCOTES
Lincolnshire TF4296
Village on A1031, 3 miles (5km) NW of Saltfleet
Large medieval marshland church, rebuilt in 17th century, restored 1908. Sixteenth-century Locksley Hall, much restored, with stained glass and carving.

NORTH STAINLEY
North Yorkshire SE2876
Village on A6108, 4 miles (6km) N of Ripon
On the banks of the River Ure, the village is home to the Lightwater Valley leisure park, with its roller-coaster rides.

NORTH STOKE
Oxfordshire SU6186
Village on B4009, 2 miles (3km) S of Crowmarsh Gifford.
This small Thames-side settlement has a beautiful and remarkably unspoilt medieval church. Carmel College, a well-known Jewish public school, near by.

NORTH STONEHAM Hampshire SU4417
Village, immediately N of Southampton
In the green gap between Eastleigh and Southampton, with an interesting church of 1600, but dominated by the M27.

NORTH TAWTON Devon SS6601
Village off A3072, 2 miles (3km) E of Sampford Courtenay
Once a market town, now only a village. Low key and mostly 19th century, with an 1887 clock tower. Market house of 1849.

NORTH THORESBY Lincolnshire TF2998
Village on B1201, 7 miles (11km) N of Louth
Large village with 17th-century thatched cottage and an early Victorian villa. Church mostly 13th century, restored 1848 and 1903-5.

NORTH UIST Western Isles
Island in the Outer Hebrides
Island between Harris and Benbecula, with rolling moorland and numerous trout-fishing lochs inland, a rocky east coast, and machair and white-sand beaches in the north and west. Many prehistoric and Norse sites. Lochmaddy is the main settlement and ferry terminal. Small population reliant on crofting, fishing and tourism. Balranald Nature Reserve is a wetland site, protecting breeding grounds of red-necked phalathrope.

NORTH WALSHAM Norfolk TG2830
Town on A149, 14 miles (23km) N of Norwich
Becoming prosperous from the woollen cloth trade in medieval times, North Walsham's wealth was further increased by the digging of the North Walsham and Dilham Canal, which connected it to the Broads. There are many handsome Georgian buildings set along attractive winding streets. The grammar school was founded by John Paston in 1606.

NORTH WARNBOROUGH Hampshire SU7351
Village on B3349, 6 miles (10km) E of Basingstoke
Georgian brick and earlier timber-framed cottages, on the Basingstoke Canal.

NORTH WEALD BASSETT Essex TL4904
Village on B181, 3 miles (5km) NE of Epping
Swollen with post-war housing. Famous wartime fighter airfield here, with a memorial to Norwegian pilots and annual air show. Former radio station.

NORTH WHEATLEY Nottinghamshire SK7685
Village off A620, 4 miles (6km) NE of Retford
Bypassed by the road from Retford to the River Trent and Gainsborough, the village has attractive houses of late 17th and early 18th-century brick.

NORTH WINGFIELD Derbyshire SK4165
Village on A6175, 2 miles (3km) NE of Clay Cross
Between industrial northeast Derbyshire and the Peak District. The church has a 14th-century chancel and a big 15th-century tower. Georgian former rectory.

NORTH WOOTTON Somerset ST5641
Village off A371, 3 miles (5km) SE of Wells
On the edge of the Mendips, with a small 15th-century church.

NORTH WRAXALL Wiltshire ST8175
Village off A420, 6 miles (10km) W of Chippenham
Tiny settlement with an interesting church, mostly 13th century, containing a chapel of 1793. Upper Wraxall is a pretty hamlet near by.

NORTH YORK MOORS NATIONAL PARK North Yorkshire
Scenic region, N of the A170 road
The North York Moors became a National Park in 1952 covering 553 square miles (890 sq km). It is the largest expanse of moorland in England, with open heather moorland, secluded farming dales and a rugged coastline, providing a wonderful habitat for wildlife, flora and fauna.

The national park includes the stretch of coastline that runs alongside the Moors for 35 miles (56km) from Saltburn-by-the Sea to Scalby Ness, Scarborough.

The coastal town of Whitby (see) and the villages of Staithes and Robin Hood's Bay (see) are steeped in history and between them much of the coastline is nature reserve, preserved by the National Trust. Whitby Abbey, perched on a cliff high above Whitby, dates back to AD657.

The North York Moors is essentially a sheep-farming area, the Swaledale breed being the most popular. Throughout the moors and dales there are 1,300 farms rearing sheep and cattle and many attractive villages of stone cottages which have remained unspoilt. In the 19th century a railway line was built to improve trade and much of this is restored to run steam train journeys through the villages and countryside of the national park.

NORTHALLERTON North Yorkshire SE3694
Town on A167, 14 miles (23km) S of Darlington
This is the county town of North Yorkshire, its market serves the surrounding rich farmland of the Vale of Mowbray. The Northallerton Town Trail guides visitors down wide streets and through narrow alleys, past many of the 18th- and 19th-century buildings and the 15th-century almshouse.

NORTHAM Devon SS4429
Town on A386, 2 miles (3km) N of Bideford
Small town at the mouth of the Taw/Torridge estuary. Extensive sand dunes and saltmarsh (Northam Burrows Country Park). There is a bar of pebbles behind the sandy beach.

NORTHAMPTON Northamptonshire SP7560
Town off M1, 60 miles (97km) NW of London
One of England's largest traditional open market squares lies at the heart of the town, surrounded by indoor shopping precincts. A fire in 1675 destroyed most of the town's centre, but two Norman churches, St Peter's and the rare round Holy Sepulchre, survived. The 17th-century Sessions House, county hall, 1817 Judges' Lodgings, Wren-style All Saints' Church, and Doddridge Chapel, an important centre of Nonconformist worship, date from after the fire.

The ornate Victorian Gothic guildhall carries statues and scenes from local history, including Thomas Becket's trial, and Edward I ordering the erection of the Eleanor Cross still standing at Hardingstone (see) on the town outskirts. The traditional boot and shoe industry is illustrated in the Central Museum's astonishing footwear collection.

From the 1960s, Northampton expanded rapidly as a designated New Town. Major companies include Carlsberg Brewery, Avon Cosmetics, Barclaycard and Express Lifts, whose testing tower is affectionately known as the 'Northampton Lighthouse'. The Royal Theatre, a Victorian gem, is joined by the modern Derngate for concerts and other entertainment, while Turner's Musical Merry-Go-Round offers all the fun of the fair.

NORTHBOROUGH Cambridgeshire TF1507
Village off A15, 7 miles (11km) NW of Peterborough
The tragic poet John Clare's wife is buried here. The 14th-century manor house was the last home of Oliver Cromwell's widow.

NORTHBOURNE Kent TR3352
Village off A256, 3 miles (5km) W of Deal
Little country village on chalk hills behind Deal, with a church built by the monks of St Augustine's Abbey, Canterbury.

NORTHCHURCH Hertfordshire SP9708
District on A41, immediately NW of Berkhamsted
There is an attractive walk along the Grand Union Canal here, and the church is partly Saxon. Peter, the 18th-century 'wild boy', is buried here.

NORTHFIELD West Midlands SP0279
District in SW Birmingham
Among sprawling housing estates, few signs remain of former Worcestershire village, but splendid medieval work in St Laurence's Church deserves attention.

NORTHFLEET Kent TQ6274

Town on A226, immediately W of Gravesend

Town on the Thames estuary once famous for shipbuilding, and where Portland cement was first developed. The Norman church contains a 14th-century oak screen, probably the oldest in Kent.

NORTHIAM East Sussex TQ8224

Village on A28, 7 miles (11km) NW of Rye

Lovely village with magnificent weatherboarded 18th-century houses in the High Street, strung along the road down to the River Rother. The church, beside a pretty green, is topped by a gracious stone spire (1505), rare in Sussex. Queen Elizabeth's Oak, alive but virtually branchless, is the tree beneath which Queen Elizabeth I reputedly feasted in 1573. Half-timbered Brickwall House (1633) is now a boarding school; Great Dixter house (1460), with famous gardens, is open to the public.

NORTHILL Bedfordshire TL1446

Village off B658, 2 miles (3km) SW of Sandy

In wooded countryside: village green and pond, veteran Crown inn, Worshipful Company of Grocers' church with 17th-century painted glass.

NORTHINGTON Hampshire SU5637

Hamlet off B3046, 4 miles (6km)NW of Alresford

Neat estate cottages in the village. The Grange (English Heritage) is a pioneering Greek-style house of 1804 which was fire-damaged in 1972 and is now being restored.

NORTHLEACH Gloucestershire SP1114

Small town off A429 and A40, 10 miles (16km) NW of Burford

A magnificent church reflects the town's 15th-century prosperity from the wool trade, with superb medieval craft work and elaborate monuments. An abundance of stone and timber-framed buildings in the town includes an 18th-century House of Correction, now housing the Cotswold Countryside Collection of farming tools, implements and wagons. An unusual attraction is Keith Harding's World of Mechanical Music, featuring music boxes and automata.

NORTHLEW Devon SX5099

Village off A3079, 4 miles (6km) NW of Okehampton

Large rural village with two little squares. Angels and elaborate bosses on the church roof.

NORTHMOOR Oxfordshire SP4202

Village off B4449, 4 miles (6km) S of Eynsham

The straggling village lies marooned between flooded gravel pits and the River Thames. Fine 14th-century church makes a visit rewarding.

NORTHOLT Greater London TQ1384

District in borough of Ealing

Mainly developed since the 1930s. Northolt Aerodrome, a Royal Air Force base, was opened in 1915. War memorial to Polish World War II pilots.

NORTHREPPS Norfolk TG2439

Village off B1159, 3 miles (5km) SE of Cromer

A peaceful village made famous by Verity Anderson's book *The Northrepps Grandchildren*. Northrepps Hall (not open) was the home of Thomas Foxwell-Buxton, an anti-slavery lobbyist.

NORTHUMBERLAND NATIONAL PARK Northumberland

Scenic region in NE of county

Northumberland's uplands achieved national park status in 1956 and the boundary encompasses 640 square miles (1,030 sq km) of hills, moorland and forest. One fifth of the park belongs to the Ministry of Defence, one fifth to the Forestry Commission and the rest belongs to individual farmers and landowners. Only a few sites are in the possession of the National Park Authority, notably Hareshaw Dene near Bellingham and Greenlee Lough to the north of Hadrian's Wall.

Hadrian's Wall spans the park's southern boundary; further north is Wark Forest, the edge of the Border Forest Park. Plantations now cover all but the highest cross-border moors, the watershed for burns and rivers feeding Kielder Water and the Rivers Rede and North Tyne.

Between the Grasslees Valley, Redesdale and Coquetdale, the land is owned by the Ministry of Defence and used as a live firing range, so access is restricted. North of the River Coquet the ground rises steeply and white grassland replaces the dark heather moors. The Cheviot massif is the remains of an extinct volcano and the high hills around the granite core are lava flows, now weathered and turned into grassland.

NORTHWICH Cheshire SJ6673

Town off A556, 20 miles (32km) SW of Manchester

Salt town at the confluence of the rivers Weaver and Dane. The Lion Salt Works is the only traditional 'open pan' salt works still in operation. Britain's only Salt Museum tells the history of the industry. Chemical industry has also developed. Buildings in the town were designed to withstand subsidence common in salt-mining areas.

NORTHWOLD Norfolk TL7597

Village off A134, 4 miles (6km) SE of Stoke Ferry

Distinctive cottages built of chalk, flint, and brick, some washed in pastel colours, characterise this lovely village. The church has an exquisite Easter Sepulchre.

NORTHWOOD Greater London TQ0991

District in borough of Hillingdon

On the Hertfordshire border, this hilly area with fine views was developed after the 1880s. Art nouveau chapel in Mount Vernon Hospital grounds.

NORTON Hereford and Worcester SP0448

Hamlet on A435, 3 miles (5km) N of Evesham

In market garden village. St Egwin's Church has priceless Norman stone lectern from Evesham Abbey and churchyard memorials by Eric Gill.

NORTON North Yorkshire SE7971

Town on B1248 immediately SE of Malton

A small town opposite Malton, across the River Derwent, famous for race-horse stables.

The George inn at Norton St Philip.

NORTON South Yorkshire SE5415
Village off A19, 6 miles (10km) SE of Knottingley
The ancient Parish Church of St Mary Magdalene is reputed to have the finest 14th-century west tower in the area.

NORTON Suffolk TL9565
Village on A1088, 3 miles (5km) SE of Ixworth
Norton stands at a major crossroads and boasts Little Haugh Hall (not open) with its parklands, which was the home of George II's chaplain.

NORTON CANES Staffordshire SK0107
Village off A5, 1 mile (2km) SE of Cannock
Large industrial and residential extension of Cannock, with a Victorian church housing monuments to the Fowke and Hussey families of Little Wyreley.

NORTON DISNEY Lincolnshire SK8859
Village off A46, 7 miles (11km) NE of Newark-on-Trent
Small Witham Valley village with early Victorian Old Rectory. Medieval church, restored by Victorians, has early monuments to Disney family.

NORTON FITZWARREN Somerset ST1925
Village on B3227, 1 mile (2km) W of Taunton
On the edge of Taunton, this is the home of the huge Taunton Cider Company. A wonderful wooden screen in the church is dated 1509.

NORTON IN HALES Shropshire SJ7038
Village off A53, 3 miles (5km) NE of Market Drayton
Popular residential village beside River Tern. Church has a fine 17th-century monument, and to the south are curious prehistoric stones called the Devil's Ring and Finger.

NORTON LINDSEY Warwickshire SP2263
Village off A4189, 4 miles (6km) W of Warwick
A windmill of 1808 stands at the centre of this scattered village on a ridge to the west of Warwick.

NORTON (NORTON JUXTA KEMPSEY) Hereford and Worcester SO8751
Village off A44, 3 miles (5km) SE of Worcester
Rather featureless village next to M5, but bold red-brick army barracks of 1876 are a surprise.

NORTON ST PHILIP Somerset ST7755
Village on A366, 5 miles (8km) N of Frome
Formerly a small town, Norton St Philip's George inn is timber-framed, 15th century and perhaps the best surviving medieval inn in the country.

NORTON SUB HAMDON Somerset ST4715
Village off A356, 5 miles (8km) W of Yeovil
Just below Hamdon Hill (see), the village is built of unspoiled Hamstone and thatch. The handsome 15th-century church has a splendid tower. Dovecote in churchyard.

NORTON SUBCOURSE Norfolk TM4098
Village off B1136, 3 miles (5km) E of Loddon
A ferry village with two drainage mills, a former inn notorious for smuggling, and a tower used by pre-Conquest priests as a fortress.

NORTON-JUXTA-TWYCROSS Leicestershire SK3207
Village off A444, 6 miles (10km) S of Ashby-de-la-Zouch
Near the Warwickshire border, Twycross Zoo has gorillas, chimps, orang-utans, elephants, lions and giraffes. Gopsall Park, 18th-century home of Handel's librettist Jennens, was demolished in 1951.

NORWELL Nottinghamshire SK7761

Village off A1, 5 miles (8km) N of Newark-on-Trent

Moated sites of five manor houses, prebends of Southwell Minster. Timber-framed cottages of the 17th and early 18th centuries. Circular brick pound. Sail-less windmill.

NORWICH Norfolk TG2208

City on A11, 98 miles (158km) NE of London

A sturdy Norman castle frowning down from its vantage point on a hill; a delicate cathedral with a slender spire; crooked cobbled streets and several lively shopping centres are just a few of the many attractions of Norfolk's largest city. Whether the visitor is interested in history, architecture, shopping, art, museums, or leisure activities, Norwich has something to offer.

The castle was built about 1160, and was refaced in the 1830s. For a while it had a grim reputation as the county gaol, but now enjoys a more refined existence as the Castle Museum. Yet even the presence of British ceramic teapots and some splendid paintings does not detract from the sheer power and dominance that exudes from this formidable medieval fortress.

Norwich also boasts 33 medieval churches, although not all are now used. Among the best are St John Maddermarket, with its excellent collection of monumental brasses; spacious St Andrew's, dating from 1478; St Michael-at-Plea, which takes its name from the archdeacon's courts; the 18th-century octagon chapel, which John Wesley called the most elegant meeting house in Europe; and St Peter Mancroft, which dominates the market place. The Friends Meeting House (1826) was where the family of the famous Quaker prison reformer Elizabeth Fry attended.

Outshining all these is the magnificent cathedral, combining sturdy Norman arcades with the soaring splendour of some of the best Gothic architecture in Britain. Norwich's spire is the second highest in Britain after that of Salisbury Cathedral.

Other fine buildings include the Great Hospital, which was founded by Walter de Suffield in 1249 and is centred around the charming Church of St Helen. The old guildhall still stands proudly overlooking the market place, often covered with the brightly coloured awnings of the traders' stalls. Many other fine buildings can be found unexpectedly down little alleys and in secluded courtyards, away from the bustle of the busy modern city. Norwich has an abundance of cobbled streets, meandering away from the old city centre, and it is easy for the visitor to wander at will, enjoying the ancient feel of the city.

Norwich also has several fine parks, and even the roundabouts are carefully tended by the army of council gardeners, and in spring greet the visitor with brilliant displays of flowers and bulbs.

There are several museums in Norwich, including the nationally acclaimed Sainsbury Centre for Visual Arts at the University of East Anglia. There are permanent exhibitions of paintings and sculptures by Picasso, Moore, Bacon and Giacometti, as well as art from Africa, the Pacific and the Americas. The Royal Norfolk Regimental Museum and the Strangers' Hall Museum of Domestic Life offer more specific displays. Norwich also has several new shopping malls, and the Mustard Shop is run by Colman's mustard company. The University of East Anglia occupies a pleasant campus in the suburbs.

NOSELEY Leicestershire SP7398

Site off B6047, 7 miles (11km) N of Market Harborough

The church here was largely completed in around 1305 as a chapel to the medieval manor which, like the village (depopulated in 16th century) does not survive. The present hall is of the 18th century.

NOSS MAYO Devon SX5447

Village off B3186, 3 miles (5km) SW of Yealmpton

Small, rather remote fishing village on the Yealm estuary, with several 1880s estate cottages and an elaborate church of the same date.

NOTGROVE Gloucestershire SP1020

Village off A436, 4 miles (6km) N of Northleach

Descendants of Dick Whittington are commemorated in the Norman church which has a splendid tapestry made by parishioners. Notable neolithic tomb beyond pleasant estate cottages.

NOTTINGHAM Nottinghamshire SK5739

City off M1, 131 miles (211km) NW of London

This historic and commercial city, a major shopping, arts, sports and entertainment centre, is known worldwide because of Robin Hood. An exciting ride at The Tales of Robin Hood tells the outlaw's story, and his statue stands near the castle entrance. Nottingham's present 17th-century castle became a museum in 1878, with fine arts and local historical collections. Below Castle Rock, the Trip to Jerusalem inn was reputedly founded during the Crusades. The neighbouring Brewhouse Yard Museum's collections incorporate period shops.

Modern shopping facilities include the Victoria and Broad Marsh centres, under which regular guided tours show the city's extensive cave system. The Lace Centre, the Costume Museum and the Lace Hall, in a converted church with Burne-Jones and Morris stained glass, illustrate Nottingham's important textile industry. In nearby Shire Hall the history of justice comes to life, and opposite is the mainly 15th-century St Mary's Church, often used for concerts. The Canal Museum, Green's Mill and Science Centre, and further museums at Wollaton (see) make fascinating visits. The 1920s Council House dominates the old market square, where the Goose Fair was traditionally held: moved to the Forest area, it still provides three amusement-packed days each October.

Football, Test cricket, horse-racing, ice-skating and watersports at Holme Pierrepont (see), productions at the Nottingham Playhouse and shows, opera, and concerts at the Royal Theatre and Concert Hall draw crowds to Nottingham from far and wide.

NOTTON West Yorkshire SE3413

Village off A61, 5 miles (8km) S of Wakefield

The village has five Listed Buildings including a railway bridge built by George Stephenson. The remains of Iron Age workings were found in Notton Park.

NUFFIELD Oxfordshire SU6687
Village off A4130, 2 miles (3km) W of Nettlebed
Pleasant village, home of Lord Nuffield for 30 years. Nuffield Place (limited opening), still furnished in 1930s style, gives insight into his life.

NUN MONKTON North Yorkshire SE5057
Village off A59, 9 miles (14km) SE of Boroughbridge
Quaint village of small cottages where there was once a Benedictine nunnery, founded in the 12th century.

NUNBURNHOLME Humberside SE8447
Village off B1246, 3 miles (5km) E of Pocklington
An attractive Wolds village through which the Wolds Way long-distance footpath passes.

NUNEATON Warwickshire SP3691
Town on A444, 8 miles (13km) N of Coventry
Mining and textiles brought prosperity to this busy market town. Its story is told at the museum in Riversley Park, which also celebrates novelist George Eliot, born near by at Astley. Further George Eliot memorabilia can be found at the library. The churches of St Mary (incorporating remains of a 12th-century nunnery) and St Nicholas are both of interest.

NUNEHAM COURTENAY Oxfordshire SU5599
Village on A4074, 5 miles (8km) SE of Oxford
Village overlooking River Thames south of Oxford consists almost entirely of semi-detached cottages built as planned estate village in 1760s by the first Earl Harcourt. Original cottages spoilt view from Nuneham Park, his new house. The Arboretum, now owned by Oxford University, contains 55 acres (22ha) of mixed woodland (limited opening).

NUNNEY Somerset ST7345
Village off A361, 3 miles (5km) SW of Frome
Village with a little story-book 14th-century castle (English Heritage) in the middle. Moated, but on a flat site, with circular towers at the corners. Now a ruin.

NUNNINGTON North Yorkshire SE6679
Village off B1257, 2 miles (3km) N of Hovingham
A delightful little village surrounded by farmland. Nunnington Hall (National Trust) is a manor house on the banks of the River Rye; it has a famous haunted room.

NUNTHORPE Cleveland NZ5314
Village off A172, 4 miles (6km) SE of Middlesbrough
Residential suburb of Middlesbrough takes its name from a 12th-century nunnery once sited on the present site of Nunthorpe Hall, now an old people's home.

NURSLING Hampshire SU3616
Village off A3057, 3 miles (5km) S of Romsey
Tiny old village, dominated by the M27. Pretty 14th-century church with spire.

NUTFIELD Surrey TQ3050
Village on A25, 2 miles (3km) S of Redhill
Victorian village on sandstone ridge overlooking the Weald with a hamlet round the common to the north and a modern village to the south. Known for Fuller's earth quarries.

NUTLEY East Sussex TQ4427
Village on A22, 5 miles (8km) NW of Uckfield
Little community in the heart of Ashdown Forest, overlooked by a post-mill, with a shop, scattered houses, Nutley Hall Rudolf Steiner Home, a church and a pub.

NYMPSFIELD Gloucestershire SO8000
Village off B4066, 3 miles (5km) W of Nailsworth
Attractive village with mellow buildings that include the 17th-century Bell Court and the Rose and Crown, an old coaching inn. On the Cotswold Edge, above the village, Coaley Peak, site of a neolithic tomb, provides panoramic views across the Severn estuary and Forest of Dean. Nearby Woodchester Park, an abandoned Victorian mansion, is preserved as a museum of 19th-century building techniques.

NYNEHEAD Somerset ST1322
Hamlet off B3187, 1 mile (2km) N of Wellington
This little settlement with a Saxon name has a 15th-century church with wooden rood screen.

OADBY Leicestershire SK6200
Town on A6, on SE outskirts of Leicester
Town on southern edge of Leicester, almost part of its suburbs. Many Edwardian houses used as university halls of residence.

OAKAMOOR Staffordshire SK0544
Village on B5417, 3 miles (5km) E of Cheadle
Former industrial village in Churnet Valley, where copper wire for first transatlantic underwater cable was made. Hawksmoor Nature Reserve (National Trust) near by.

OAKDALE Gwent ST1898
Village off A4048, 4 miles (6km) S of Abertillery
Hilly suburb of Blackwood on rise between Ebbw and Sirhowy valleys. Pen-y-Fan Pond Country Park near by.

OAKENGATES Shropshire SJ7010
Town on A5, part of Telford
The old, straggling and charmless Victorian industrial town has now been engulfed by the housing estates and light industry of Telford.

OAKHAM Leicestershire SK8608
Small town on A606, 9 miles (14km) SE of Melton Mowbray
The largest centre of population in little Rutland, and its historic county town, Oakham has much to offer in a small space, as suggested by Rutland's motto *Multum in parvo*. Built of honey-coloured stone, its castle, church and public school buildings form a harmonious group. The late 12th-century castle hall, an important Norman building with fine stone carving by craftsmen

from Canterbury Cathedral, has a huge collection of decorative horseshoes on its walls, given as a toll by visiting peers of the realm. In the market place, the polygonal butter cross has a fine Collyweston slate roof.

Oakham School, founded in 1584 by Archdeacon Johnson, like nearby Uppingham (see), has expanded greatly from its original school room, now converted to a Shakespearean theatre. Above it soars the 14th-century spire of the medieval Church of All Saints.

The Noel family mansion, Catmos, is now council offices, with Rutland Farm Park in the parkland behind. Opposite, the former riding school of the Rutland Fencibles has been attractively converted to form part of the Rutland County Museum, illustrating the agricultural, domestic and social life of this fascinating county.

OAKLEY Bedfordshire TL0153

Village off A6, 4 miles (6km) NW of Bedford

On the Great Ouse. The bridge has a stone showing the height of the great flood of 1823. Church with medieval tower.

OAKLEY Buckinghamshire SP6412

Village on B4011, 6 miles (10km) NW of Thame

Below Brill (see) hill, close to M40. The Great Train Robbery gang's 1963 hideout was here, at secluded Leatherslade Farm.

OAKLEY Fife NT0289

Village on A907, 4 miles (6km) W of Dunfermline

Town in a mining area to the south of the Cleish Hills, west of Dunfermline and north of the Firth of Forth.

OAKLEY (OR CHURCH OAKLEY) Hampshire SU5650

Village off B3400, 5 miles (8km) W of Basingstoke

A village which has grown to be a small town in the last 20 years. The old village part has a big pond and some thatch.

OAKRIDGE (OR OAKRIDGE LYNCH)

Gloucestershire SO9103

Village off A419, 4 miles (6km) E of Stroud

This small village on the steep slopes of Golden Valley near Stroud has an enterprising Village Museum (limited opening) at the Methodist church.

OAKSEY Wiltshire ST9993

Village off A429, 5 miles (8km) NE of Malmesbury

Cotswold stone village, with some old cottages. Medieval church with a wall-painting of St Christopher, a simple screen, and stained glass, all 15th century.

OAKWOODHILL Surrey TQ1337

Hamlet off A29, 5 miles (8km) NW of Horsham

Scatter of hamlets and farms, including 16th- and 17th-century cottages and houses, with a lonely church amid dense woodland to the northwest.

OAKWORTH West Yorkshire SE0338

Village on B6143, on SW edge of Keighley

Old textile village. Oakworth Station, on the Keighley and Worth Valley Railway, was used in the filming of *The Railway Children*. Holden Park opened in 1925, full of grottoes and tree sculptures and with a folly.

OARE Kent TR0063

Village off A2, 1 mile (2km) NW of Faversham

Above Faversham Creek and the marshes that fringe the Swale, this is the site of a nature reserve occupying 170 acres (69ha) of open marsh, with rare plants and varied bird life.

OARE Somerset SS8047

Hamlet off A39, 6 miles (10km) E of Lynton

Remote hamlet in a woody valley on the edge of Exmoor. The little church has many 18th-century fitting; it was the setting for the wedding in RD Blackmore's *Lorna Doone*. Wonderful walking area, with rolling moors to the south and wooded valleys.

OARE Wiltshire SU1563

Village on A345, 2 miles (3km) N of Pewsey

Many old thatched cottages, some Georgian brick with two-colour patterns, and an odd brick church of 1857.

OBAN Strathclyde NM8629

Town on A816, 26 miles (42km) N of Lochgilphead

Oban is the main town in Argyll, servicing a wide catchment area, and the ferry departure point for the Inner Hebrides. The town is well situated on hills around a crescent-shaped bay, with views past the island of Kerrera to the hills of Mull beyond.

Largely a Victorian creation, Oban grew from the small fishing village of the early 19th century to a bustling town after the arrival of the railway and the development of steamships made it the centre of a comprehensive communications network. Travellers could reach Glasgow, the northwest coast, Inverness and the Inner and Outer Hebrides by ship, with rail connections to Glasgow and the south.

Ruined 12th-century Dunollie Castle on a promontory near the harbour is the oldest building, but fine Edwardian edifices line the curving main street around the bay. Above the harbour rises McCaig's Folly, an unfinished replica of the Colosseum in Rome, started in 1897 as a job-creation scheme but never completed. St Colomba's Roman Catholic Cathedral of Argyll and the Isles overlooks the sea, serving an area which was largely untouched by the Reformation.

OCCOLD Suffolk TM1570

Village on B1077, 2 miles (3km) SE of Eye

Occold Hall and Benningham Hall stand in this small village. 'Occold' comes from the Old English 'ac' (oak tree) and 'holt' (wood).

OCHIL HILLS Tayside

Hill range between Bridge of Allan and Newburgh

Hill range running from the River Forth near Stirling to the River Tay near Perth, with its main pass formed by Gleneagles and Glen Devon.

OCHILTREE Strathclyde NS5021

Village on A70, 4 miles (6km) W of Cumnock

Village in a dairy-farming area, possibly where John Knox was married in 1564. Birthplace of Scots author George Douglas Brown (1869–1902).

OCKBROOK Derbyshire SK4235
Village off A52, 4 miles (6km) E of Derby
The church has a 12th-century tower and three monuments by Westmacott. A Moravian settlement was founded here in 1750, with neat brick chapel, houses and school buildings.

OCKHAM Surrey TQ0756
Village on B2039, 1 mile (2km) NW of East Horsley
Village includes many red-brick cottages of the 1860s, set around a triangle of roads to the east of the church and manor house.

OCKLEY Surrey TQ1439
Village on A29, 6 miles (10km) NW of Horsham
The main part of this pleasant village lies along a Roman road, Stane Street, built on a conspicuous embankment and carrying the fast A29. All along it runs a huge, rough green, surrounded by a variety of pleasing houses. Away to the east is a lovely, traditional cluster of church, big house and farm. The railway station stands alone, still further east.

OCLE PYCHARD Hereford and Worcester SO5946
Village off A417, 7 miles (11km) NE of Hereford
Copper-covered spire of St James's Church guides visitors to this small and tranquil rural settlement in the hills.

ODDINGTON Oxfordshire SP5514
Village off B4027, 1 mile (2km) E of Islip
Small village, but traditionally one of the 'seven towns of Otmoor' on the road that skirts the north of the moor.

ODELL Bedfordshire SP9657
Village off A6, 8 miles (13km) NW of Bedford
Attractive limestone village on the Great Ouse. Fine 15th-century church with imposing tower and beautiful interior. Walks among primroses and bluebells in Odell Great Wood, also nearby Harrold-Odell Country Park (see Harrold). Link with Concord, Massachusetts, founded by 17th-century Puritan rector of Odell.

ODIHAM Hampshire SU7451
Small town off A287, 7 miles (11km) E of Basingstoke
Handsome small town. The long High Street is filled with small-scale buildings from the 16th century to Victorian, with much Georgian. Interesting church, with 1649 brick tower. Odiham Castle (to the west) consists of shapeless lumps of flint masonry beside the Basingstoke Canal. At Colt Hill, a wharf on the canal often has barges.

ODSAL West Yorkshire SE1529
District on A6036, in S Bradford
Chiefly residential district with many stone cottages and some more modern housing in keeping with the older buildings.

ODSTOCK Wiltshire SU1426
Village off A338, 3 miles (5km) S of Salisbury
Compact and pretty village with wonderful mixture of building materials – cob, stone, flint and brick. Prettily chequered stone and flint church tower.

OFFA'S DYKE Powys
Earthwork on border of England and Wales
Named after Offa, 8th-century King of Mercia, who built this earthwork as the first official border between England and Wales. Ran from near Chepstow in south to Prestatyn in north, although never continuously, taking advantage of natural barriers such as forests. The dyke, built up to 20ft (6m) high, is still well preserved in parts. The long-distance Offa's Dyke Path (168 miles/270km) follows the line of the dyke wherever practicable.

OFFCHURCH Warwickshire SP3565
Village off A425, 3 miles (5km) E of Leamington
Pleasant traditional village on edge of extensive park of Offchurch Bury, with Grand Union Canal running close by.

OFFENHAM Hereford and Worcester SP0546
Village off B4510, 2 miles (3km) NE of Evesham
A market-garden village with popular riverside pub, a magnet for fishermen and Avon boaters.

OFFHAM East Sussex TQ4012
Village on A275, 2 miles (3km) NW of Lewes
Friendly, pretty village of flint cottages and a church of 1859 on the valleyside above the River Ouse, with a massive old quarry behind the pub. The Battle of Lewes, 1264, in which Simon de Montfort defeated Henry III, was fought on Offham Hill.

OFFHAM Kent TQ6557
Village off A20, 2 miles (3km) SW of West Malling
Attractive old village of local stone and timber cottages and 18th-century brick houses grouped around a green, on which stands a quintain, or tilting post.

OGBOURNE, ST ANDREW AND ST GEORGE
Wiltshire SU2074
Villages off A346, 3 miles (5km) N of Marlborough
Below the chalk downs, in the valley of the River Og. Pretty villages– as is the smaller Ogbourne Maizey, with thatched cottages, some built from the local sarsen stone – and little medieval churches.

OGLE Northumberland NZ1378
Hamlet off A696, 2 miles (3km) E of Belsay
A small attractive village with some stone-built cottages typical of this area. Near by is Kirkley Hall, housing the Northumberland College of Agriculture.

OGMORE VALE Mid Glamorgan SS9390
Village on A4061, 7 miles (11km) N of Bridgend
Former mining village which takes its name from its narrow valley. The road northwards climbs in spectacular loops across forested mountains to Rhondda and Afan valleys.

OGMORE-BY-SEA Mid Glamorgan SS8674
Village on B4524, 4 miles (6km) SW of Bridgend
Village perched on headland above mouth of River Ogmore with views across Bristol Channel. Ogmore Castle was once a key Norman fort.

OKEFORD FITZPAINE Dorset ST8010
Village off A357, 3 miles (5km) SE of Sturminster Newton
A pretty village with many old brick cottages, some still thatched.

OKEHAMPTON Devon SX5895
Town off A30, 23 miles (37km) W of Exeter
Small market town with a large castle on the edge of Dartmoor. Little medieval church prominent in the centre. Handsome granite town hall of 1685; most of the rest Victorian or Edwardian. Shopping arcade of 1900, surprising in such a small town. Museum of Dartmoor Life. The large medieval castle ½ mile (1km) southwest (English Heritage) has a really romantic setting in a wooded valley.

OKEOVER Staffordshire SK1647
Hamlet off A515, 2 miles (3km) NW of Ashbourne
Domain of Okeover family since Norman times. Hall and church stand on banks of River Dove. Family monuments in restored medieval church.

OLD ALRESFORD Hampshire SU5833
see Alresford

OLD BEWICK Northumberland NU0621
Hamlet off B6346, 6 miles (10km) SE of Wooler
Nearby Bewick Hill has remains of two hillforts. Cairns mark a Bronze Age burial ground where graves and artefacts were found.

OLD BOLINGBROKE Lincolnshire TF3465
Village off A155, 3 miles (5km) W of Spilsby
Attractive Wolds village, formerly an important medieval market town. John of Gaunt acquired the 13th-century hexagonal castle through marriage, and the future Henry IV was born here in 1367. Chaucer visited it. Parliamentarians captured the castle and little more than mounds remain (English Heritage). The south aisle of John of Gaunt's church has become the nave and chancel, and there is a Victorian north aisle. Eighteenth-century mud-and-stud cottages.

OLD BRAMPTON Derbyshire SK3371
Village off A61, 3 miles (5km) W of Chesterfield
Above a wooded valley. Medieval church with Norman south door. Hall of 16th/17th centuries. Large cruck barn at Frith Hall Farmhouse.

OLD BUCKENHAM Norfolk TM0691
Village on B1077, 3 miles (5km) SE of Attleborough
One of the largest village greens in England surrounded by scattered hamlets that make up Old Buckenham. The bier in All Saints' Church is one of the oldest in England. Octagonal tower and thatched nave.

OLD DAILLY Strathclyde
see Dailly

OLD DAILLY Strathclyde NX2299
Village on B734, 3 miles (5km) E of Girvan
Lies in the valley of the Water of Girvan. Old and new Dalquharran castles stand near by, Kennedy strongholds, both ruined.

OLD DEER Grampian NJ9747
Village on B9029, 10 miles (16km) W of Peterhead
Cistercian abbey remains on the site of a Celtic monastery, where the illuminated manuscript of the Book of Deer was transcribed in around 800; it is now at Cambridge University.

OLD DILTON Wiltshire ST8649
Hamlet off A3098, on SW edge of Westbury Leigh
Small, with a fascinating unrestored church, still with complete 18th-century fittings – box pews, pulpit, gallery.

OLD FLETTON Cambridgeshire TL1997
see Fletton

OLD KILPATRICK Strathclyde NS4672
Town off A82, 4 miles (6km) SE of Dumbarton
Village near Erskine Bridge at the western end of the Forth–Clyde Canal and reputed birthplace of St Patrick.

OLD LEAKE Lincolnshire TF4050
Village on B1184, 6 miles (10km) NE of Boston
Straggling fenland village. Large Norman and medieval church; tower begun in 1490 took nearly 60 years to finish. Almsbox made from a hollowed oak trunk.

OLD MALTON North Yorkshire SE7972
see Malton

OLD (OR WOLD) Northamptonshire SP7873
Village off A43, 6 miles (10km) SW of Kettering
Village with 18th-century houses, near Pitsford Water reservoir. Medieval church has 15th-century tower, and nave roof with stone angel corbels.

OLD RADNOR Powys SO2559
Hamlet off A44, 3 miles (5km) E of New Radnor
Looks out over the Radnor Forest. Noted church with wealth of features, including huge stone font and medieval choir stall and organ case, reputedly the oldest in Britain.

OLD ROMNEY Kent TR0325
Village on A259, 2 miles (3km) W of New Romney
A tiny Romney Marsh village that was once an important port. Stands beside ancient Rhee Wall, and embankment and channel built by the Romans. The church is remote from village.

OLD SARUM Wiltshire SU1332
Prehistoric site off A345, 2 miles (3km) N of Salisbury
A strong defensive site (English Heritage), with big bank and ditch enclosing 56 acres (22ha). First it was an Iron Age hillfort, then a Roman settlement. Re-occupied from the 10th century, it had a royal castle and cathedral from 1075. Disputes between clergy and castle led to the founding of New Sarum or Salisbury (see) down in the valley in the 13th century. Only footings of the medieval buildings and the defences survive.

OLD SODBURY Avon ST7581
Village on A432, 2 miles (3km) E of Chipping Sodbury
Prominent late Norman church on a knoll. Another tower close by is for the railway tunnel which passes under the village.

OLD TRAFFORD Greater Manchester SJ8196
District of Salford
Famous as the home of Manchester United Football Club and Lancashire's county cricket team. Trafford Park is a large industrial estate, originally an important centre of engineering and manufacturing, now used largely for transportation, distribution and storage.

OLD WARDEN Bedfordshire TL1343
Village off A1, 4 miles (6km) W of Biggleswade
Best known for the Shuttleworth Collection's veteran aircraft, apparently held together with faith and glue, tottering about the sky on flying days at Old Warden Aerodrome. Close by is romantic Swiss Garden with Swiss Cottage summerhouse, fernery, grotto and lake. The picturesque village has thatched cottages, striking 19th-century chimneypots and a church with monuments of Ongley and Shuttleworth squires.

OLD WINDSOR Berkshire SU9874
Village on A308, 2 miles (3km) SE of Windsor
The Saxon royal hunting lodge, the predecessor of Norman Windsor Castle, was here, but the present village is modern. The 13th-century church is down by the River Thames.

OLD WIVES LEES Kent TR0754
Village off A28, 5 miles (8km) W of Canterbury
Village with many converted oasthouses among orchards above the River Stour, on the North Downs Way.

OLD WOKING Surrey TQ0156
see Woking

OLDBURY West Midlands SO9989
District off M5, S of Warley
Industrialised district in heart of Black Country suffers from main roads and elevated M5 motorway but still has good older buildings at its centre.

OLDBURY-ON-SEVERN Avon ST6192
Village off B4061, 2 miles (3km) NW of Thornbury
Scattered village with fine views over Severn Bridge and nuclear power station. Church worth visiting for art nouveau glass in east window.

OLDHAM Greater Manchester SD9305
Town on A62, 7 miles (11km) NE of Manchester
Situated on the edge of Pennine moorland, Oldham was an important cotton-spinning town during the 19th and early 20th centuries and mill buildings still dominate the town, which is largely Victorian. Winston Churchill was first elected as an MP in this constituency, in 1900.

Tommyfield, Oldham's market, claims to be the largest outdoor permanent market in England and, as its name suggests, was once a meadow where fairs and circuses were held, as well as being a rallying point for mass political meetings. Alexandra Park, opened in the middle of the town in 1865, was constructed with a government grant to boost the town at a time when the supply of cotton from America was drying up, leaving many people in Oldham out of work.

Oldham Art Gallery has a fine historic collection, including works by Constable, Turner, Lowry and Pre-Raphaelite painters. Oldham Coliseum, built in 1887, is an important regional repertory theatre which has a reputation for ambitious contemporary productions.

Today the town has a relatively high population of minority communities, and their cultural influences include a number of arts groups and excellent Asian restaurants.

OLDHAMSTOCKS Lothian NT7470
Village off A1, 6 miles (10km) SE of Dunbar
Upland village set about a spacious green. Its name comes from the Saxon for 'old settlement'. A tower in the churchyard was built to watch over graves and prevent body-snatching.

OLDMELDRUM Grampian NJ8127
Small town on A947, 16 miles (26km) NW of Aberdeen
Small town with 17th-century church. Near by are the neolithic–Bronze Age Loanhead Stone Circle and 17th-century Barra Castle.

OLLERTON Nottinghamshire SK6567
Town on A614, 12 miles (19km) NW of Newark-on-Trent
Sherwood Forest village with early 18th-century watermill (limited opening) and 18th-century Hop Pole hotel beside River Maun. Fine undercroft of Cistercian Rufford Abbey (English Heritage) and shell of 17th-century home of Saviles, surrounded by Rufford Country Park with lake, gardens with sculpture collection, craft centre, gallery in former stables and exhibitions in former 18th-century cornmill.

OLNEY Buckinghamshire SP8951
Small town on A509, 5 miles (8km) N of Newport Pagnell
Thriving market and lace town on the Great Ouse, celebrated for its Shrove Tuesday pancake race. The museum cherishes memories of poet William Cowper and his friend John Newton, who wrote *Amazing Grace*; a good lace collection, too. The church has a soaring 180ft (55m) spire and there are handsome Georgian buildings in the town centre. Plentiful antiques shops.

OLTON West Midlands SP1282
District of NW Solihull
Grand Union Canal and large reservoir relieve the monotony of this suburban area where Solihull merges with Birmingham.

OMBERSLEY Hereford and Worcester SO8463
Village on A449, 3 miles (5km) W of Droitwich
Noble church stands at centre of delightful village of well-restored timber-framed houses and 19th-century estate cottages.

ONCE BREWED Northumberland NY7566
Site on B6318, 3 miles (5km) NE of Haltwhistle
National Park Information Centre. Easy access to Housesteads and surrounding moorland and footpaths from the car park on nearby Whinshields Crag.

ONECOTE Staffordshire SK0455
Village on B5053, 4 miles (6km) E of Leek
Jervis Arms beside River Hamps is a welcome feature of this scattered village in high moorland country. Eighteenth-century church with unusual east window.

ONEHOUSE Suffolk TM0158
Village off B1115, 2 miles (3km) W of Stowmarket
United with neighbouring Harleston. Stow Lodge was a 1731 workhouse. Elizabeth I visited Onehouse Hall, when a still-standing grove of lime trees was planted.

ONIBURY Shropshire SO4579
Village off A49, 3 miles (5km) SE of Craven Arms
Iron bridge by Thomas Telford spans River Onny at edge of village. Wernlas Collection in Green Lane displays rare breeds of domestic fowl.

ONICH Highland NN0261
Village on A82, 3 miles (5km) NW of Ballachulish
Village on Loch Linnhe with a prehistoric perforated monolith. Nearby Corran ferry crosses the loch at its narrowest point, providing a short-cut into Ardnamurchan.

ORFORD Suffolk TM4250
Village on B1084, 9 miles (15km) E of Woodbridge
Protected from the rough North Sea by the 6 mile (10km) shingle bank of Orford Ness, Orford village stands on the sheltered banks of the River Alde. It is dominated by the massive 12th-century castle (English Heritage), one of the best in England, built of creamy stone and rising 90ft (27m). Pretty Quay Street has an excellent inn.

ORKNEY ISLANDS Orkney
Island group separated from the N coast of Scotland by the Pentland Firth
The Orkney island group comprises nearly 70 islands, with roughly half inhabited. The largest, Mainland, contains the two most important towns, Kirkwall and Stromness.

First inhabited from 3500BC, the islands have Northern Europe's greatest concentration of prehistoric monuments, which include circles, burial cairns, chambered tombs, Bronze Age brochs and several early Christian Pictish settlements. The islands were settled as Norse earldoms from the 9th until the mid-13th century, when they passed to incoming Scottish earls and became part of Scotland in 1468.

Orcadians have been involved in whaling and fishing and were recruited by the Canadian Hudson's Bay Company. Scapa Flow naval base brought prosperity during the two World Wars, and the oil industry provides employment today. The islands also benefit economically from European Community funding and tourism revenue.

The landscape is flat, treeless and relatively fertile; in summer it is brilliantly green with abundant wildflowers under the clear northern light. The coastal scenery is magnificent, with beautiful white-sand beaches, wonderful seascapes and towering cliffs which support huge bird populations during the breeding season.

ORLETON Hereford and Worcester SO4967
Village off A49, 5 miles (8km) N of Leominster
Modern commuter housing has not spoilt the charm of the old village centre with its black and white cottages.

ORLINGBURY Northamptonshire SP8572
Village off A509, 4 miles (6km) NW of Wellingborough
Early 18th-century hall and old rectory on the green, 19th-century estate houses. Church rebuilt 1843, with tall crossing tower and rose window.

ORMESBY, ST MARGARET AND ST MICHAEL
Norfolk TG4914
Villages on A149, 5 miles (8km) N of Great Yarmouth
These two villages stand on the edge of the Broadlands, near the beautiful reed-bordered Ormesby and Rollesby Broads. Ormesby St Margaret is named for the church that stands on high ground overlooking the village, while Ormesby St Michael has the Norfolk Rare Breeds

Prehistoric standing stones on the Orkney Islands.

Centre, a farm dedicated to breeding unusual farm animals, including pigs, fowl and cattle.

ORMISTON Lothian NT4169
Village on B6371, 2 miles (3km) S of Tranent
Planned village (1735) on Tyne Water, with a wide green and an attractive layout. Simple and important 15th-century mercat cross.

ORMSKIRK Lancashire SD4108
Town on A570, 7 miles (11km) SE of Southport
An important market town on the West Lancashire plain. The late 18th century saw the town's prosperity grow after the partial drainage of Martin Mere (see Mere Brow) to give rich agricultural land near by. A distinctive feature of Ormskirk is the Church of St Peter and St Paul, which has both a tower and a steeple.

ORONSAY Strathclyde NR3588
see Colonsay

ORPINGTON Greater London TQ4666
Town in borough of Bromley
Orpington fowls were bred here in the 1890s when this was still primarily a country area. Between the wars it turned into middle-class commuter territory. The small medieval parish church was hugely enlarged in the 1950s. Nearby Orpington Priory, a medieval clergy house, much altered, now houses the Bromley Museum of local history.

ORRELL Greater Manchester SD5203
Town off M6, 4 miles (6km) W of Wigan
After the construction of the Leeds–Liverpool Canal there was an influx of Liverpool merchants, who bought land to exploit the coalfields. John Clarke, owner of Orrell Colliery, built the mansion known as Orrell Mount. Today Orrell is mainly a suburb of Wigan. Former reservoirs, now called Orrell Lakes, are a popular leisure facility.

ORSETT Essex TQ6482
Village on B188, 4 miles (6km) N of Tilbury
Pleasant backwater with attractive old houses, village green, diminutive pound and lock-up. Impressive church with monuments. Annual show in September.

ORSTON Nottinghamshire SK7641
Village off A52, 4 miles (6km) E of Bingham
Beside River Smite. Medieval St Mary's Church, with 18th-century tower, displays drum from Battle of Waterloo. Slate headstones in churchyard.

ORTON Cumbria NY6208
Village on B6260, 3 miles (5km) N of Tebay
Lovely village at the foot of Orton Scar overlooked by 13th-century All Saints' Church. Orton Hall, built in 1662, is now converted into holiday flats.

ORWELL Cambridgeshire TL3650
Village off A603, 6 miles (10km) N of Royston
Orchards surround the 40 Listed Buildings in Orwell, dating from the 16th to the 19th centuries.

OSBALDESTON Lancashire SD6431
Village on A59, 3 miles (5km) NW of Blackburn
Quiet village on River Ribble. Osbaldeston Hall (private), built in Tudor style, is probably its oldest building, using stone from Roman ruins of Ribchester.

OSBALDWICK North Yorkshire SE6251
District in E York
Once a village, now a suburb of York, Osbaldwick is protected by a conservation order and is home to the Yorkshire Museum of Farming.

OSBOURNBY Lincolnshire TF0638
Village off A15, 5 miles (8km) S of Sleaford
Pleasant brick houses around a triangular square, some Aswarby (see) estate cottages and a Victorian school.

OSMASTON Derbyshire SK1943
Village off A52, 2 miles (3km) SE of Ashbourne
Picturesque thatched brick estate cottages belonging to Osmaston Manor, which was demolished in 1966 leaving a tower of the 1840s. Church of the same date.

OSMINGTON Dorset SY7282
Village on A353, 5 miles (8km) SE of Dorchester
A narrow street of thatched cottages. To the north is a figure of George III on horseback, cut into the chalk. Osmington Mills is a seaside hamlet.

OSMOTHERLEY North Yorkshire SE4596
Village off A19, 6 miles (10km) NE of Northallerton
This beautifully preserved village in the North Yorkshire Moors National Park makes a good centre for exploring the surrounding heather moorland. The village is dominated by the Mount Grace Priory (English Heritage), founded in 1398, and Britain's finest example of a Carthusian monastery.

OSNEY Oxfordshire SP4906
District in W Oxford
Only a small 15th-century room remains of the vast Osney Abbey with a church reckoned to have been 332ft (101m) long.

OSPRINGE Kent TR0060
Hamlet on A2, immediately SW of Faversham
A street of attractive houses running along Roman Watling Street, with a church away to the southwest. Maison Dieu (English Heritage), now housing a museum, was founded as a hospital in 1234.

OSSETT West Yorkshire SE2720
Town off M1, 3 miles (5km) W of Wakefield
Impressive Edwardian town hall with its own restored theatre organ. The town centre is pedestrianised with a large open market.

OSSINGTON Nottinghamshire SK7564
Village off A1, 7 miles (11km) N of Newark-on-Trent
Classical church by Carr of York, 1782–3, separate from village near site of demolished 18th-century hall. Monuments including two by Nollekens.

OSTERLEY Greater London TQ1477
District in borough of Hounslow
Developed as a suburb in the 1930s, along the southern edge of Osterley Park (National Trust), an imposing 18th-century mansion with sumptuous interiors by Robert Adam, set in 140 acres (57ha) of landscaped park with lakes and ancient cedar trees and an Elizabethan stable block. Church of St Francis (1930s), Great West Road.

OSWALDKIRK North Yorkshire SE6278
Village on B1363, 3 miles (5km) S of Helmsley
The village lies at the base of a hanging wood known as The Hag, at the east end of the Hambleton Hills.

OSWALDTWISTLE Lancashire SD7327
Town off A680, immediately SW of Accrington
A typical small Lancashire town that prospered due to the local textile industry. James Hargreaves, inventor of the 'Spinning Jenny' in 1764, lived here.

OSWESTRY Shropshire SJ2929
Town off A5, 16 miles (26km) NW of Shrewsbury
Crowds throng Wednesday market in this Welsh border town, birthplace of Wilfrid Owen, novelist Barbara Pym and composer Walford Davies. Few early buildings, but wealth of 19th-century architecture, result of prosperity when town became headquarters of Cambrian Railways in 1860s (Transport Museum at old station). Old Oswestry, magnificent Iron Age hillfort, stands to north of town.

OTFORD Kent TQ5259
Village off A225, 3 miles (5km) N of Sevenoaks
Historic village in Darent Gap, where the river finds its way through the North Downs, with a village pond included among the county's Listed Buildings, and a 12th-century church by the wide green. Castle of Otford, a ruinous tower and gatehouse of the Archbishop's Palace, was rebuilt splendidly in 1581. Becket's Well – said to have been created miraculously by the Archbishop – supplied water to the palace.

OTHAM Kent TQ7953
Village off A20, 3 miles (5km) SE of Maidstone
Virtually a Maidstone suburb, famous for its timber-framed houses, including Stoneacre (National Trust), a 15th-century manor house and garden.

OTHERY Somerset ST3831
Village on A361, 6 miles (10km) SE of Bridgwater
In the Somerset Levels (see), the land around drained from early medieval times by Glastonbury Abbey. Fifteenth-century church.

OTLEY Suffolk TM2055
Village on B1079, 6 miles (10km) NW of Woodbridge
Tudor timber and brick Otley Hall was the home of the Gosnolds, founders of Jamestown, Virginia, USA, and discoverers of Cape Cod in the 16th century.

OTLEY West Yorkshire SE2045
Town on A660, 10 miles (16km) NW of Leeds
The parish church, dedicated to All Saints, has a fine Norman doorway and fragments of Anglo-Saxon crosses. The market, held on Fridays and Saturdays, dates from Saxon times although the charter was granted in 1222. The Wharfedale Agricultural Show has been held here since 1799. Thomas Chippendale, the cabinet maker, was born here in 1718.

OT MOOR Oxfordshire SP5614
Scenic area off B4027, NE of Oxford
These 4,000 acres (1,620ha) of marshland form valuable wetlands haven for wildlife, one area near Horton-cum-Studley being designated as a Site of Special Scientific Interest. Main waterway is River Ray, fed by numerous natural streams and man-made ditches. Otmoor is crossed north to south by sections of a Roman road running from Alchester, near Bicester, to Dorchester.

OTTERBOURNE Hampshire SU4623
Village off A33, 3 miles (5km) N of Eastleigh
Small and still rural, on the River Itchen. Many 19th-century and earlier buildings in the main street, and a very odd church of 1838. Charlotte M Yonge, the prolific Victorian novelist (160 books), lived here for almost 50 years.

OTTERBURN Northumberland SD8893
Village on A696, 15 miles (24km) SE of Carter Bar
In the valley of the River Rede, and famous for the Battle of Otterburn in 1388 where the Scottish Earl of Douglas was killed and Harry 'Hotspur' of Northumberland's Percy family was taken prisoner. Otterburn Tower, once a fortress to defend against marauding Scots before the battle, is now a hotel.

OTTERTON Devon SX0885
Village off B3178, 2 miles (3km) NE of Budleigh Salterton
Cob and thatch cottages down the wide main street, with a stream. Otterton Mill still works, with bakery and gallery.

OTTERY ST MARY Devon SY0995
Town on B3174, 11 miles (18km) E of Exeter
Pretty little town with narrow twisting streets, and one of the finest churches in the county, large and mid-14th century. Very elaborate plan with a lady chapel. Flaming tar-barrel rolling is still practised annually on 5 November. Cadhay (limited opening) is a charming 16th- and 17th-century manor house with the prettiest courtyard, walled in chequered flint and stone.

OTTRINGHAM Humberside TA2624
Village on A1033, 3 miles (5km) NW of Patrington
During World War II Ottringham was the site of a BBC station from which European broadcasts were relayed.

OUGHTERSHAW North Yorkshire SD8780
Hamlet off B6160, 5 miles (8km) NW of Buckden
An isolated hamlet set in woodland amid a much more barren landscape. The Oughtershaw Beck is the source of the River Wharfe.

OULTON Staffordshire SJ9135
Village off A520, 1 mile (2km) NE of Stone
Attractive village with several large houses built by pottery owners. Four former watermills in valley of Scotch Brook (see Moddershall).

OULTON Suffolk TM5294
District in NW Lowestoft
Oulton Broad is excellent for sailing, but occasionally suffers from noisy speedboats. Oulton Hall, home of eccentric George Borrow, no longer survives.

OULTON West Yorkshire SE3628
Village on A639, 5 miles (9km) SE of Leeds
Picturesque village of stone cottages on a busy main road. Oulton Hall was built in 1851 and is now a hotel.

OUNDLE Northamptonshire TL0388
Small town off A605, 12 miles (19km) SW of Peterborough
Outstanding stone-built town, fine 17th- and 18th-century buildings, many used by Oundle School, founded 1556. Attractive Georgian shopfronts around the market place. Norman and later church, with 208ft (63m) spire. School chapel (1922–3) has stained glass by John Piper. Talbot inn dates from 1626, with staircase from nearby Fotheringhay Castle, reputedly still walked by Mary Stuart's ghost.

OUSE, RIVER East Sussex
River running from St Leonard's Forest to Newhaven
Rising in St Leonard's Forest near Horsham, the Ouse flows east and then south past Lewes to enter the sea at Newhaven. It was an important 'iron river', feeding many hammerponds.

OUSE, RIVER North Yorkshire
River, tributary of the Trent and Humber
Unusually, there is only one accepted source of the River Ouse, marked by an obelisk in the grounds of a seed warehouse at Great Ouseburn. The river is tidal to Naburn Lock, and commercial traffic still reaches York. Although remote from the main cruising network, the reaches above York are much used by local pleasure craft.

OUTER HEBRIDES Western Isles
Island group from Butt of Lewis S to Barra Head
The Outer Hebrides, properly known as the Western Isles, is a chain of Atlantic islands lying at the western edge of Europe. The islands are noted for their natural beauty, the inland landscape being mainly flat, with many small lochans, while the coast is distinguished by the expanses of fertile machair, a type of grassy, sandy, coastal land used for grazing, and sweeping beaches. There are four National Nature Reserves and abundant birdlife and flora. Stornoway is the adminstrative and commercial centre and main ferry port.

Prehistoric cairns, forts, standing stones and brochs date from early in the islands' 6,000-year history. The islands were under Norse control from the 11th century until the Norse defeat at Largs and the Treaty of Perth in 1263. There has been substantial depopulation over the last 200 years through emigration due to Clearances and eviction, though this trend is decreasing. Revenue from crofting, fishing, tourism and tweed is economically important and technological media advances in the shape of the 'Super Highway' are already putting world-wide contacts within reach of people working from home on these remote and beautiful islands.

OUTWELL Norfolk TF5103
Village on A1101, 5 miles (8km) SE of Wisbech
Ranging along small fenland waterways, Outwell and Upwell villages appear almost Dutch. An Outwell farmer amassed a huge collection of Dresden china.

OUTWOOD Surrey TQ3245
Village off A23, 3 miles (5km) NE of Horley
Small Wealden village with a little centre by the green and an open, unspoilt common (National Trust) dominated by an old post mill, 1665, the oldest working windmill in England.

OVER Cambridgeshire TL3770
Village off A14, 9 miles (14km) NW of Cambridge
Splendid Victorian tower mill that has been carefully restored to its former glory. It is open daily to sell the flour it grinds. Blessed Virgin Mary's Church has an impressive array of gargoyles poking from every angle of this 14th-century building, like those on Notre Dame in Paris. Some of the woodwork came from Ramsey Abbey (see Ramsey).

OVER Gloucestershire SO8119
Hamlet on A40, 1 mile (2km) NW of Gloucester
The A40 now passes alongside the fine bridge over the River Severn by Thomas Telford, built 1829 with 150ft (46m) stone span.

OVER ALDERLEY Cheshire SJ8575
Hamlet off A587, 1 mile (2km) NE of Monks Heath
Rural parish with no village centre. Hare Hill Garden (National Trust) is a particularly fine walled garden.

OVER COMPTON Dorset ST5916
Village off A30, 2 miles (3km) E of Yeovil
A small stone village, with Compton House (19th century) used by Worldlife and Lullingstone Silk Farm, with conservation displays and butterflies.

OVER HADDON Derbyshire SK2066
Village off B5055, 2 miles (3km) SW of Bakewell
Peak District village in limestone country overlooking Lathkilldale. Former lead-mining area, and target for 1850s 'gold rush', when iron pyrites (fool's gold) was found. Lathkilldale Trail.

OVER KELLET Lancashire SD5169
Village on B6254, 1 mile (2km) E of Carnforth
Centres on an attractive green with the Church of St Cuthbert, which has links with Cockersand Abbey (see Glasson) lying on higher ground to the south.

OVER NORTON Oxfordshire SP3128
Village on B4206, 1 mile (2km) N of Chipping Norton
Sharing a hill with Chipping Norton, this is the modest estate village for Over Norton House (not open), a rambling mansion of 1875.

OVER PEOVER (HIGHER PEOVER OR PEOVER SUPERIOR) Cheshire SJ7773
Hamlet off A50, 4 miles (6km) S of Knutsford
Peover Hal is a Tudor manor house of 1585.The village church is in the grounds of the hall.

OVER WALLOP Hampshire SU2838
Village on B3084, 7 miles (11km) SW of Andover
Set in watermeadows, with some old thatch and cob.

OVER WHITACRE Warwickshire SP2491
Hamlet on B4114, 4 miles (6km) E of Coleshill
This tiny settlement, standing in a coal-mining landscape, has an unexpected 18th-century church on a hill commanding panoramic views.

OVERBURY Hereford and Worcester SO9537
Village off B4080, 5 miles (8km) NE of Tewkesbury
Estate village below Bredon Hill, prettified by rustic buildings designed by Norman Shaw. Overbury Court built in 1730s for owner of Martin's Bank.

OVERSTRAND Norfolk TG2440
Village on B1159, 2 miles (3km) E of Cromer
Close to Cromer, Overstrand was a much-favoured resort for wealthy Victorians, and boasts some splendid buildings. Overstrand Hall was designed by Lutyens.

OVERTON Clwyd SJ3741
Village on A539, 6 miles (10km) SE of Wrexham
Substantial border village with pleasing architecture and churchyard yew trees, one of the traditional Seven Wonders of Wales.

OVERTON Hampshire SU5149
Village on B3400, 4 miles (6km) E of Whitchurch
A New Town founded in 1217, but only a village now. Pleasant Georgian brick and some thatch. Big ponds for papermills at Quidhampton.

OVERTON Lancashire SD4358
Village off A589, 2 miles (5km) SE of Heysham
On the estuary of the River Lune, consisting of one narrow main street with terraces of white 18th-century cottages, and an ancient church.

OVERTON West Yorkshire SE2516
Village off A642, 2 miles (3km) SW of Horbury
Residential area of red-brick miners' cottages with some modern buildings. Yorkshire Mining Museum is situated at Caphouse Colliery, where guided tours are given by ex-miners.

OVERY Oxfordshire SU5893
Hamlet off A4074, 1 mile (2km) N of Shillingford
Tiny cluster of buildings on the edge of Dorchester, including a manor house of 1712 and a timber-framed mill, built to harness the River Thame.

OVINGDEAN East Sussex TQ3503
Village off B2123, immediately NW of Rottingdean
Pleasant village on the downs above the sea, with some development but surprisingly untouched by the proximity of Brighton.

OVINGHAM Northumberland NZ0863
Village off A695, across the River Tyne from Prudhoe
A quiet village dating back to Norman times. St Mary's Church was founded by Augustinian canons. Its tower is part-Saxon and the tallest in Northumberland at 105ft (32m). George Stephenson's mother is buried in the churchyard. A Goose Fair is held every June. Caravan site on edge of Horsley Wood.

OWER Hampshire SU3216
Village off M27, 3 miles (5km) NE of Cadnam
Forest-edge hamlet, with Paulton's Park, a big leisure park featuring good gardens, wildfowl, Romany and Village Life museums, plus other attractions for children.

OWERMOIGNE Dorset SY7685
Village off A352, 6 miles (10km) SE of Dorchester
A heathland village with many nurseries. The Mill House Cider and Clock Museum has good displays and makes cider.

OWLPEN Gloucestershire ST7998
Hamlet off B4066, 3 miles (5km) E of Dursley
Idyllic estate hamlet, with eight fine brasses in its church, stands near Owlpen Manor (limited opening), restored by famous craftsman Norman Jewson.

OWSTON Leicestershire SK7707
Village off A606, 5 miles (8km) W of Oakham
Remote hillside village, the site of a 12th-century Augustinian abbey, parts incorporated into medieval St Andrew's Church. Early 18th-century manor house, 17th-century The Priory.

OWSTON South Yorkshire SE5511
Village off A19, 5 miles (8km) N of Doncaster
Picturesque, mainly 18th-century village, part of which is a conservation area with a double-arched cart shelter of 1790.

OWSTON FERRY Humberside SE8000
Village off A161, 3 miles (5km) SE of Epworth
A village on the west bank of the River Trent which developed around a Roman river crossing. The earthworks of a medieval castle are a feature.

OWTHORPE Nottinghamshire SK6733
Village off A46, 8 miles (13km) SE of Nottingham
Colonel Hutchinson, Governor of Nottingham during the Civil War, signatory of Charles I's death warrant, lived at the hall (demolished) and is buried in church.

OXBOROUGH Norfolk TF7401
Village off A134, 3 miles (5km) NE of Stoke Ferry
Village dominated by Oxburgh Hall (National Trust), built by Bedingfields in 15th century, restored by Pugin. Church with 16th-century terracotta monuments, and the fine Bedingfield Arms inn.

OXCOMBE Lincolnshire TF3177
Hamlet off A153, 6 miles (10km) NE of Horncastle
Isolated Wolds hamlet off ancient Bluestone Heath road. Tudor-style Oxcombe House, 1845. Tiny brick church (redundant) with octagonal tower, also 1840s.

OXENHOPE West Yorkshire SE0334
Village on B6141, 1 mile (2km) S of Haworth
The village lies in a remote valley and was used as the location for the film *The Railway Children* in 1970.

OXFORD Oxfordshire SP5106
City off M40, 52 miles (84km) NW of London
Modern Oxford is an important industrial, residential and commercial city, but its history and its city centre are both dominated by the university. From the 12th century onwards distinguished scholars attracted students here, forming small residential communities that were later to develop into formal colleges. They were religious in character, and it was not until 1871 that non-Anglicans were admitted. Some knowledge of Oxford's history (often turbulent) is essential for any serious visitor, and one good introduction is the audio-visual experience called The Oxford Story in Broad Street.

Today the colleges are very large institutions indeed, and new ones are still being established. Balliol, Merton and University dispute the claim to be the oldest, but because of periodic rebuilding they do not necessarily look it. In fact New College has some of the oldest buildings, including a gatehouse and hall of 1386. Between them the colleges exhibit virtually every architectural style from early Gothic to modern experimental. Most are open for a few hours each day during term-time and for longer in the vacations. In many cases the attractions include lovely grounds and larger open spaces such as Magdalen's deer park, the Botanic Garden and the Christ Church Meadow. Christ Church ought to be on everyone's list because its chapel doubles as England's smallest cathedral.

The colleges do not have a monopoly of the city centre. It is also possible to visit famous university buildings like the Bodleian Library, the beautiful Divinity School and Wren's Sheldonian Theatre, the scene of the university's great public occasions. There are fine churches too. The 'university church' is St Mary's in the High Street, but St Mary Magdalen's and St Michael's are equally rewarding. The university's long history of academic research has naturally resulted in a number of museums. Among the most accessible are the Ashmolean (art and archaeology), the Pitt Rivers (anthropology), the University Museum (geology and natural history), the Museum of the History of Science, the Bate Collection of Historical Instruments (music), the Museum of Oxford (city and university) and the Museum of Modern Art.

It goes without saying that central Oxford is abundantly provided with services. In addition to the first-class hotels, stores and restaurants expected of a city there are characterful pubs, wine bars and an exceptionally wide range of fine speciality shops, from bookshops such as the famous Blackwell's to tailors, galleries and boutiques. The lively covered market is one of Britain's oldest, having been going since 1773. This bustling commercial life, plus the daily throng of undergraduates on foot or on thousands of bicycles, gives the centre of Oxford its vitality and supplies the abiding impression that most visitors take away with them.

OXHILL Durham NZ1852
Village off B6168, N of Annfield Plain
Mining village. Old waggonway carrying coal to Beamish can still be traced. In 1909 Burns Pit caught fire, killing 168 men and boys.

OXNEY, ISLE OF Kent TQ9127
District in the Rother Levels, 5 miles (8km) N of Rye
Low, hump-backed ridge, a former marshland island surrounded by watercourses, looking over the Rother Levels and Romney Marsh to the sea. Wittersham is its 'capital'.

OXSHOTT Surrey TQ1460
Village on A244, 3 miles (5km) NW of Leatherhead
This 'stockbroker suburb' surrounds an ancient centre with a mineral spring at Jessop's Well. The common to the north is famed for its pines.

OXTED Surrey TQ3852
Town on A25, 4 miles (6km) SW of Westerham
Under the slopes of the North Downs but now very close to the M25. Really two villages: quaint Old Oxted, with its attractive street of pleasant houses and pubs, and the bustling new village, now the main centre, which has grown to the north around the restored Norman church and the railway station.

OXTON Nottinghamshire SK6351
Village off A6097, 4 miles (6km) NW of Lowdham
Attractive village on boundary of Sherwood Forest. Large Iron Age hillfort in sheltered valley to north. Norman chancel arch and rare pillar piscina in 14th-century church with 15th-century tower. Manor house with carriage arch. Stables survive of Sherbrooke family's hall, demolished 1957. Tomb of Robert Sherbrooke, died 1710, surrounded by iron railings near lane.

OXWICH West Glamorgan SS4986
Village off A4118, 11 miles (17km) W of Swansea
Popular, dune-backed beach with wildlife visitor centre. Oxwich Castle (Cadw) is a fortified Tudor house. Penrice Castle in private estate near by.

OYNE Grampian NJ6725
Village on B9002, 7 miles (11km) NW of Inverurie
Village in rolling countryside with three notable castles: 16th-century Westhall, a tower house; ruined Harthill (1638); and Place of Tillyfour, built in 1508 and restored in 1884.

OZLEWORTH Gloucestershire ST7993
Hamlet off B4058, 2 miles (3km) E of Wotton-under-Edge
Standing above this lonely hamlet, Newark Park is a Tudor lodge remodelled by James Wyatt. Church has rare hexagonal Norman tower.

P

PACKINGTON, LITTLE AND GREAT Warwickshire SP2184
Villages on A452, 3 miles (5km) SE of Coleshill
Little Packington has a church with good medieval features but is overshadowed by the hall and park at Great Packington. Packington Hall (not open), the family home of the Earl of Aylesford, stands in a park by Capability Brown that also contains an earlier family house and a notable church of 1790 by Joseph Bonomi.

PADANARAM Tayside NO4251
Village on A926, 2 miles (3km) W of Forfar
Small village between Forfar and Kirriemuir. Near by is the richly carved early Christian St Orland's Stone.

PADBURY Buckinghamshire SP7230
Village on A413, 3 miles (5km) SE of Buckingham
Attractive commuter and weekending village, brick, half-timbering and thatch. Village green. Faded 14th-century wall-paintings in church.

PADDINGTON Greater London TQ2681
District in City of Westminster
Housing here runs from smart to slum. The original village nucleus, Paddington Green with St Mary's Church, is overshadowed by the Westway flyover. The Little Venice canal area, full of houseboats and charm, has canal cruises and water buses. Expensive blocks of flats in Maida Vale. Paddington Station, designed by Isambard Kingdom Brunel, was built in the 1850s.

PADDOCK WOOD Kent TQ6645
Small town on B2160, 5 miles (8km) E of Tonbridge
Sprawling modern industrial town with a grain-drying plant and freight terminal. A hop festival is staged each September.

PADIHAM Lancashire SD7933
Town on A671, 3 miles (5km) W of Burnley
The hilly core of the town, now a conservation area, retains characteristics of the early Industrial Revolution with narrow winding lanes and cobbled alleyways. The terraced streets are later, built as the cotton industry developed. Gawthorpe Hall (National Trust), a beautiful Jacobean mansion built in the 1600s, has been the home of the Shuttleworth family for 400 years.

PADSTOW Cornwall SW9175
Town on A389, 5 miles (8km) NW of Wadebridge
Fishing town on the sheltered Camel estuary, its square harbour surrounded by stone houses from the 16th century onwards. The May Day celebrations here are famous, with the 'Obby 'Oss cavorting round the town. Prideaux Place (limited opening) is late 16th century with fine interiors.

PADWORTH Berkshire SU6166
Village off A4, 8 miles (13km) SW of Reading
Very rural, with a simple Norman church and a handsome Georgian big house (not open). Kennet and Avon Canal, with exhibition and walks.

PAGHAM West Sussex SZ8897
Village off B2166, 4 miles (6km) W of Bognor Regis
An ancient church, a few old cottages and a famous nature reserve sit cheek by jowl with modern estates, bungalows and caravans. Pagham Harbour, formerly Selsey Haven, was an important port shut by storms in the 14th century and reopened at Sidlesham Quay. Partly reclaimed in 1875, it was flooded in 1910. Now the lagoon and fields are an internationally important nature reserve, with migrating waders, and a breeding place of the little tern. Rare flora.

The 'spectacle' stocks next to the churchyard in Painswick.

The abbey church at Paisley.

PAGLESHAM Essex TQ9293
Village off B1013, 4 miles (6km) E of Rochford
Once known for smuggling and oysters in remote country of creek and marsh close to the River Roach.

PAIGNTON Devon SX8960
Town on B3022, 3 miles (5km) SW of Torquay
Just a large village until the middle of the 19th century, then developed as a huge seaside resort because of the sandy beaches. Kirkham House (English Heritage), a late medieval stone house, and Oldway (now council offices), are the best buildings. Oldway is an imitation Versailles, very rich, built late 19th century. Other attractions include Paignton Zoo, Torbay Aircraft Museum and Paignton and Dartmouth Railway.

PAINSCASTLE Powys SO1646
Village on B4594, 5 miles (8km) NW of Hay-on-Wye
Remote spot near border with scant remnants of strategic medieval stronghold which gave the village its name.

PAINSWICK Gloucestershire SO8609
Town on A46, 3 miles (5km) NE of Stroud
The ancient Clipping Ceremony, when children link hands round the church, still takes place each September in this old hillside wool town where former weaving mills stand in the valley bottom and picturesque cottages abound in the steep lanes. Mellow buildings grace the town's streets, and a great attraction near by is the 18th-century Rococo Garden at Painswick House.

PAINTER'S FORSTAL Kent TQ9958
Hamlet off A251, 2 miles (3km) SW of Faversham
Hamlet among the north Kent orchards. To the south is Belmont, an 18th-century mansion with a superb clock collection, mementoes of India, a walled garden, a pinetum and a folly.

PAISLEY Strathclyde NS4864
Town off M8, 7 miles (11km) W of Glasgow
Although appearing to be a continuation of Glasgow, which lies near by to the east, Paisley is very much a distinct town with its own character and history.

It was founded as a monastic settlement with the building of a Cluniac abbey church in 1163; this was rebuilt after its destruction by the English in 1307 but lay ruined from the 16th century until its restoration in the 19th century. Economic expansion began in the 19th century with linen-manufacturing: after the building of the first steam-powered thread mill in 1826 the town became synonomous with cotton and silk production, dominated by the Coats and Clark dynasties. The Kashmiri-influenced tear-drop designs, copied on to colourful shawls, were in huge demand for most of the 19th century and the pattern has borne the town's name ever since. These manufacturing families erected immensely grand civic buildings, including the vast Thomas Coats memorial church.

Today, the industry has declined but others have been developed at the Hillington industrial estate, while the proximity and growth of Glasgow Airport has also created jobs.

PAKEFIELD Suffolk TM5390
District on A12, in S Lowestoft
The 'Roaring Boys' of Pakefield were once notorious smugglers. Pakefield stands on the edge of Lowestoft looking out over the heaving North Sea.

PAKENHAM Suffolk TL9267
Village off A143, 2 miles (3km) S of Ixworth
Pakenham has two superb mills (one water, one wind), a reedy fen, Jacobean Newe House, and 17th-century Nether Hall.

PALGRAVE Suffolk TM1178
Village on A143, 1 mile (2km) S of Diss
A pleasant village with a jumble of plaster and thatched cottages, and two churches – one medieval and the other 19th century.

Gravestone of a waggone in Palgrave churchyard.

PALNACKIE Dumfries and Galloway NX8157
Village on A711, 3 miles (5km) S of Dalbeattie
Village on an inlet of Solway Firth. Near by is 15th-century Orchardton Tower, the only cylindrical Scottish tower house, gutted by Covenanters in the mid-17th century.

PAMBER END Hampshire SU6158
Hamlet on A340, 4 miles (6km) N of Basingstoke
Tiny, with just a few farms and the chancel of the very elegant church of Pamber Priory (1150).

PAMBER HEATH Hampshire SU6162
Village off A340, 7 miles (11km) N of Basingstoke
Big modern settlement on the boundary with Berkshire.

PAMPHILL Dorset ST9800
Village off B3082, 1 mile (2km) NW of Wimborne
Unspoiled, very rural village with three greens and many old brick and timber-framed cottages. Kingston Lacy House (National Trust) is Dorset's grandest house; 1660s and 1835.

PAMPISFORD Cambridgeshire TL4948
Village off A505, 2 miles (3km) SE of Sawston
A quiet, secluded village set among whispering trees and the parkland of Pampisford Hall. St John's Church has superb Norman carvings.

PANGBOURNE Berkshire SU6376
Town on A329, 6 miles (10km) NW of Reading
On the River Thames, with a tollbridge over the river. Many late Victorian and Edwardian villas, including a group of particularly ornate examples known as the Seven Deadly Sins. Kenneth Grahame, author of *The Wind in the Willows*, lived in the cottage by the church.

PANT Shropshire SJ2722
Village off A483, 5 miles (8km) S of Oswestry
Modern housing swamps former quarrying community lying beneath dramatic limestone hill where deep quarries and tramway inclines remain alongside nature reserve.

PANTASAPH Clwyd SJ1575
Village off A55, 2 miles (3km) W of Holywell
Village in countryside west of Holywell with religious community based around mid-19th-century church.

PAPA STOUR Shetland HU1760
Island off W coast of mainland
Rocky island with a wild coastline and fertile west side, which has recovered from the population crisis of the 1970s, when the number of inhabitants fell to 16.

PAPA WESTRAY Orkney HY4952
Island NE of Westray
The island lies across Papa Sound from Westray, to which it is connected by the world's shortest scheduled flight, lasting 100 seconds. The earliest standing building in Europe is at Knap of Howar (3500BC). Ruined St Boniface Church dates from the 12th century, when the island was a medieval pilgrimage centre. The RSPB reserve has a large arctic tern colony.

PAPCASTLE Cumbria NY1031
Village off A594, 1 mile (2km) NW of Cockermouth
Built on and around Roman fort of *Derventio*, a garrison of considerable size built at a major junction. Retains many 18th-century buildings.

PAPPLEWICK Nottinghamshire SK5451
Village on B683, 1 mile (2km) NE of Hucknall
Stone-built Sherwood Forest village with 18th-century cottages. Hall, 1780s (open by appointment), overlooks River Leen. Church in hall grounds, 1795, separated from village; fireplace in squire's pew in gallery, 15th-century stained glass, monuments to Sherwood Forest officials. Papplewick Pumping Station, 1 mile (2km) east, with 1884 James Watt beam engines (limited opening), elaborately decorated cast-iron inside, in beautiful grounds.

PAPWORTH, EVERARD AND ST AGNES
Cambridgeshire TL2862
Villages off A1198, 6 miles (10km) SE of Huntingdon
Nineteenth-century Papworth Everard Hall is famous for the pioneering work in heart transplants carried out here. Papworth Village Settlement was founded in 1916 for disabled people. Papworth St Agnes is a 19th-century estate village, although Manor Farm dates from 1585. This pleasant house has medieval windows, and an elegant frontage rebuilt in 1660.

PAR Cornwall SX0753
Village on A3082, 4 miles (6km) E of St Austell
China-clay port, with a harbour built in 1840, and 1960s terminals for handling the clay.

PARADISE Gloucestershire SO8711
Hamlet off A46, 1 mile (2km) NE of Painswick
Hamlet lies beneath wooded slopes of Painswick Hill, where Painswick Beacon, 250 acres (100 ha) of open countryside, affords magnificent views.

PARBOLD Lancashire SD4911
Village on A5209, 7 miles (11km) NW of Wigan
A pretty village with many grand houses built by wealthy cotton merchants. Parbold Hill is the highest point in the area and offers magnificent views.

PARHAM Suffolk TM3060
Village on B1116, 2 miles (3km) SE of Framlingham
Village with old moated manor house, now a farm, and fascinating Air Museum which tells the story of East Anglian aviation in World War II.

PARKEND Gloucestershire SO6108
Village on B4234, 4 miles (6km) N of Lydney
Scattered village, islanded in a clearing of the Forest of Dean and a good centre for woodland walks. A popular destination is the Nagshead Nature Reserve near by, where 760 acres (310ha) of oak and beech woodland are managed by the Royal Society for the Protection of Birds. In summer, a visitor centre provides information about nature trails.

PARKGATE Cheshire SJ2878
Village on B5135, immediately NW of Neston
Once a main port for travel to Ireland. Extensive salt marshes now lie between village and nearest stretch of water, forming Gayton Sands RSPB Reserve.

PARKHURST Isle of Wight SZ4991
Village on A3020, 1 mile (2km) N of Newport
Famous for its prison, established in 1838, with Albany Prison added in the 1960s. Car parks and waymarked walks in Parkhurst Forest.

PARKMILL West Glamorgan SS5489
Village on A4118, 5 miles (8km) W of Mumbles
Sheltered village allows access to beautiful Three Cliffs Bay, one of Gower's finest. Penmaen Burrows to the southwest have remains of a prehistoric burial chamber, ancient chapel and Norman earthworks. To the north is the impressive Parc le Breos Burial Chamber (Cadw), dating from neolithic times, and Cathole Cave, which contained prehistoric finds. Y Felin Ddwr craft and countryside centre is in the village.

PARKSTONE Dorset SZ0391
District on A35, in E Poole
A suburb of Poole, Victorian and later, with two interesting churches: brick St Osmund, 1920s and stone St Peter, 1880s.

PARRACOMBE Devon SS6644
Village off A39, 4 miles (6km) SW of Lynton
Stone village tightly packed in steep Exmoor Valley, the old church wonderfully preserved up the hill with all its simple 18th-century fittings.

PARRETT, RIVER Somerset
River running to Bristol Channel
Runs right across Somerset from the Dorset border, passing through Langport and Bridgwater. The big estuary, supplemented by the drains, opens into mud flats at Burnham-on-Sea. Steart Point is the low headland, and a nature reserve for seabirds and waders.

PARSON DROVE Cambridgeshire TF3708
Village on B1166, 6 miles (10km) W of Wisbech
Aerial photography reveals that Romans farmed near Parson Drove. It was a woad-producing centre until the invention of synthetic indigo in the 1890s. Samuel Pepys' uncle's horse was stolen here in 1663, leading the diarist to refer to it as a 'heathen place'. There is a long main street, and the whole is surrounded by dykes and fields.

PARTICK Strathclyde NS5467
District in W Glasgow
A ship-building town which became part of Glasgow in 1912, now in economic decline. Noted for the Partick Thistle football club.

PARTINGTON Greater Manchester SJ7191
Town on A6144, 4 miles (6km) NW of Hale
Modern appearance of Partington brought about by its choice as an overspill development site in 1951.

PARTNEY Lincolnshire TF4168
Village on A16, 2 miles (3km) N of Spilsby
Meeting point of Lincoln–Skegness and Alford–Spilsby roads, and of two River Lymn tributaries. Several Georgian houses, and a 14th- and 15th-century church with 1820s chancel.

PARTRISHOW Powys SO2722
Hamlet off A465, 5 miles (8km) N of Abergavenny
Scattered hamlet hidden on southern approach to Black Mountains. Delightful little church much visited for its rood screen, one of Wales's finest.

PARWICH Derbyshire SK1854
Village off A515, 5 miles (8km) N of Ashbourne
Peak District village with stone houses and an 1870s church around a green. Brick Parwich Hall on hillside, completed in 1747. Bronze Age circles on the moor. Royston Grange Trail near by.

Old barn at Paston.

PASSENHAM Northamptonshire SP7839
Village off A422, immediately SW of Stony Stratford
In curve of River Great Ouse. Church with 13th-century nave, 17th-century chancel and furnishings. Two barns, early Tudor and 1626.

PASTON Norfolk TG3234
Hamlet on B1159, 4 miles (6km) NE of North Walsham
Famous for the 'Paston letters' written during the Wars of the Roses. A straggling village with a noble church and an impressive thatched barn.

PATCHAM East Sussex TQ3009
Village off A23, on N outskirts of Brighton
Still has a village atmosphere, although close to Brighton and the A23. Old flint cottages line the lane to the pub and a Norman church crowns the hilltop beside the tithe barn.

PATCHWAY Avon ST6082
Suburb of Bristol on A38, 6 miles (10km) N of Bristol
Like nearby Filton (see), this is part of the local aeroplane industry, producing engines. Housing is mostly modern and suburban.

PATELEY BRIDGE North Yorkshire SE1565
Small town on B6165, 11 miles (18km) NW of Harrogate
A thriving Dales town on the banks of the River Nidd with a steep High Street. Upper Nidderdale Museum is in an original Victorian workhouse and portrays the life of the early Dalesfolk. The town gets its name from the river crossing first used by the monks of Fountains Abbey. The present stone bridge is 18th century.

PATHHEAD Lothian NT3964
Village on A68, 4 miles (6km) SE of Dalkeith
Long, narrow village at the foothills of the Lammermuirs near Tyne Water. Near by is Oxenfoord Castle and grounds, now a girls' school.

PATNA Strathclyde NS4110
Village off A713, 5 miles (8km) NW of Dalmellington
Scattered village by the River Doon in a former mining and iron-producing area.

PATRICK BROMPTON North Yorkshire SE2190
Village on A684, 3 miles (5km) NW of Bedale
Until the Industrial Revolution the village was under the jurisdiction of the estates at Hornby Castle.

PATRINGTON Humberside TA3122
Village on A1033, 4 miles (6km) SW of Withernsea
This large village was recorded in Domesday Book and has the earliest recorded evidence of any settlement in Holderness. St Patrick's Church, built in about 1410, is known locally as the 'queen of Holderness'. A flax-processing mill was built in the 19th century and workers were brought over from Ireland. It was closed in 1881.

PATRIXBOURNE Kent TR1855
Village off A2, 3 miles (5km) SE of Canterbury
Village on Roman Watling Street in the valley of intermittent Nailbourne stream, famous for its late Norman church among the trees in the village centre. Built in 1160, it has a porch with a finely carved doorway and typanum, probably the work of Rochester cathedral masons. Pretty Tudor-style houses with overhanging gables and carved timbers, built in the 1860s for tenants of Bifrons, the demolished manor house.

PATTERDALE Cumbria NY3915
Village on A592, S of Ullswater
At the southern tip of Ullswater, in the shadow of Helvellyn. Holds famous sheepdog trials called the Patterdale Dog Day.

PAUL Cornwall SW4627
Village off B3315, 1 mile (2km) S of Newlyn
Granite village, high on the hill above Mousehole. Almshouses of 1709, and an obelisk to the last speaker of the Cornish language, who died in 1777.

PAULERSPURY Northamptonshire SP7145
Village off A5, 3 miles (5km) SE of Towcester
Long main street off Watling Street. Pury End cairn marks birthplace of Baptist missionary William Carey. Rolls-Royce Enthusiasts Club own Regency-style Stable House.

PAULL Humberside TA1626
Village off A1033, 2 miles (3km) SW of Hedon
In the village there is a lighthouse, with adjoining coastguard cottages, which was built in 1836 along the River Humber.

PAULTON Avon ST6556
Village on B3355, 2 miles (3km) NW of Midsomer Norton
Mostly Victorian village; once a coal-mining area.

PAUNTLEY Gloucestershire SO7429
Hamlet off A417, 3 miles (5km) NE of Newent
Dick Whittington was born here, and his family arms survive in 14th-century glass in the church, which also has a splendid Norman chancel arch.

PAVENHAM Bedfordshire SP9955
Village off A6, 5 miles (8km) NW of Bedford
On high ground above a big loop of the Great Ouse. Thatched and tiled stone cottages. Annual church rush-strewing custom.

PAYHEMBURY Devon ST0801
Village off A373, 5 miles (8km) W of Honiton
Neat thatched cottages around a green. Medieval church with rich Victorian interior.

PEACEHAVEN East Sussex TQ4100
Small town on A259, 2 miles (3km) W of Newhaven
Bungalows and suburban shops on the exposed cliff, the sad failure to realise a 'garden city by the sea', planned to honour World War I Australian and New Zealand troops.

PEAK DISTRICT NATIONAL PARK Derbyshire
Scenic area lying W and SW of Sheffield
The Peak District, at the southern end of the Pennines, was designated Britain's first national park in 1951. It covers 555 square miles (1,438 sq km) of Derbyshire and extends into five neighbouring counties. The Dark Peak peat moorlands fringed by gritstone 'edges' contrast with the deep limestone dales of the White Peak countryside. Surrounded by Manchester, Sheffield, and other heavily populated areas, the Peak District has for many years provided an important and accessible area of countryside for town-dwellers. In the 1930s, this access was increasingly threatened by use of the moors for grouse shooting, and several demonstrations culminated in a Mass Trespass on to Kinder Scout on 24 April 1932, showing the strength of popular feeling, and helping to hasten the establishment of the national parks. The Peak National Park Authority has a responsibility to protect and enhance the landscape and to provide recreational opportunities. It has pioneered planning and traffic management schemes, and the provision of courses at its own Study Centre, Losehill Hall, balancing the needs of visitors with those of the 38,000 people for whom the Peak District is home and workplace.

PEAK FOREST Derbyshire SK1179
Hamlet on A623, 4 miles (6km) SE of Chapel-en-le-Frith
Despite its name this is an almost treeless area, but it came under royal forest law, giving it scope as a venue for clandestine marriages until 1804.

PEAKIRK Cambridgeshire TF1606
Village on B1443, 5 miles (8km) N of Peterborough
Seventeen acres (7ha) of land form the Peakirk Waterfowl Gardens, founded by Peter Scott, on the site of old gravel workings. Through the middle runs the Roman canal Car Dyke, splitting it into different sections for birds that need special protection. The village church is the only one in England dedicated to 8th-century St Pega.

PEASE POTTAGE West Sussex TQ2533
Hamlet off M23, 2 miles (3km) S of Crawley
Hamlet at the southern end of the M23. Its name is said to be from the diet given to prisoners who halted there on the way to Horsham Gaol.

PEASENHALL Suffolk TM3569
Village on A1120, 3 miles (5km) W of Yoxford
Peasenhall with Sibton (see) are separate parishes that function as a single village. Peasenhall has a spacious street that is a conservation area, one house of which is the timbered Woolhall, once an inn. Stuart House was the site of the unsolved murder of a woman. Peasenhall's past is dominated by the agricultural drill factory of James Smyth and Sons.

PEASLAKE Surrey TQ0844
Village off B2127, 4 miles (6km) N of Cranleigh
Pretty tile-hung village along a single-track lane on steep slopes under Hurtwood Common, one of the largest and most untamed areas near London.

PEASMARSH East Sussex TQ8822
Village on A268, 3 miles (5km) NW of Rye
Pretty ridge-top village on the main road, with incongruous supermarket. Ancient centre has a Norman church and a Georgian manor is tucked away down a lane to the south.

PEATLING MAGNA Leicestershire SP5992
Village off A50, 6 miles (10km) NW of Husbands Bosworth
Despite its name, a small village. All Saints' Church is mostly late 13th century: tower with spire, 15th-century nave roof, 17th-century furnishings.

PEBWORTH Hereford and Worcester SP1346
Village off A46, 6 miles (10km) N of Broadway
On edge of Vale of Evesham. The 15th-century church overlooks attractive village with thatched and timber-framed houses.

PECKFORTON Cheshire SJ5356
Hamlet off A49, 4 miles (6km) S of Tarporley
Estate village of Peckforton Castle, built on a sandstone ridge in 1851.

PECKHAM Greater London TQ3476
District in borough of Southwark
Huge post-war council housing estates have replaced much of the Victorian development. Peckham Rye Common and Park are open spaces. North Peckham civic centre is on the Old Kent Road of the music hall song, on the line of Watling Street, the main road to Dover. The Livesey Museum, founded in 1890, has local history exhibitions.

The detached church belfry at Pembridge.

PEDDAR'S WAY Norfolk
Ancient track
This ancient footpath starts in Knettishall and runs through heath and Breckland woods to the rugged North Norfolk coast at Holme.

PEDMORE West Midlands SO9182
Village off A491, on SE edge of Stourbridge
Housing estates have largely eradicated old village beneath Wychbury Hill, but Norman church and 18th-century Pedmore Hall survive.

PEEBLES Borders NT2540
Town on A703, 20 miles (32km) S of Edinburgh
Attractive old royal burgh on River Tweed, popular holiday town and woollen-manufacturing centre. Tweed-dale Museum in Chambers Institute has a collection of casts of famous statues. Beltane Festival in June includes Common Riding of the Marches. To the west lies 14th-century Neidpath Castle, a tower house with pit prison. To the east are Kailzie Gardens, with flower gardens and greenhouses.

PEEL Isle of Man SC2484
Town on A1, 10 miles (16km) NW of Douglas
Home of the Manx kipper and the island's herring trade. Peel Castle is an imposing fortress located on a headland known as St Patrick's Isle. The castle walls enclose the 11th-century church and round tower, and St Germain's Cathedral, built between 1879 and 1884, replacing the 13th-century St Peter's Church.

PEGWELL BAY Kent TR3664
Beach off A256, SW of Ramsgate
Bay and beach at the southernmost point of Isle of Thanet, with cliffs to the north, and marsh to the south. Traditional landing place of Danes (AD499) and St Augustine (AD597).

PELDON Essex TL9816
Village off B1025, 5 miles (8km) S of Colchester
Close to Blackwater estuary creeks and saltings. Famous old low-beamed smugglers' pub, the Rose, partly of 14th century.

PELSALL West Midlands SK0103
Village on A4124, 3 miles (5km) N of Walsall
Former mining and nail-making village is now semi-rural outpost of Walsall with extensive housing developments.

PELTON (PELTON LANE ENDS) Durham NZ2553
Village on A693, 2 miles (3km) NW of Chester-le-Street
A legacy of the mining era, one of numerous self-sufficient communities linked by a network of mines and railways.

PELYNT Cornwall SX2055
Village on B3359, 3 miles (5km) NW of Looe
Large, rather bleak village in open countryside. The church has an unusual classical aisle of 1680. St Nonna's Well, 2 miles (3km) northeast, still has a little building.

PEMBREY Dyfed SN4201
Village on A484, immediately W of Burry Port
Stands on flat lands bordering Carmarthen Bay. Plain village is gateway to Pembrey County Park, an unusual expanse of forest, dune and beach with Cefn Sidan Sands, 7 miles (11km) long. The park has a host of attractions, including waymarked walks, visitor centre, pony trekking, dry skiing, narrow-gauge railway. The flat coastal strip is also home to the Welsh Motor Sports Centre, Wales's premier motor-racing circuit.

PEMBRIDGE Hereford and Worcester SO3958
Village on A44, 6 miles (10km) E of Kington
Picturesque village beside River Arrow. Elizabethan market house looks across tomassive detached tower of

14th-century church with fine woodwork and memorials. Virtually all the houses are timber-framed, including medieval New inn, 16th-century Greyhound inn, Duppa's almshouses (1660s) and Trafford's almshouses (1686). Some cruck-framed houses, including The Forge and Victoria Place in East Street.

PEMBROKE (PENFRO) Dyfed SM9801
Town on A4075, 29 miles (47km) SW of Carmarthen
Pembroke's history is plain to see. Dominating the streets is the town's massive castle, crowning a rock above the Pembroke River. The castle, an important Norman stronghold in the far west of Wales, was never captured by the Welsh. Within its well-preserved walls, approached through the great gatehouse, its most outstanding feature is the cylindrical great keep, still standing 75ft (23m) high. The castle was not the only medieval defence. Pembroke also has a circuit of 14th-century town walls, also exceptionally well preserved in parts.

Pembroke's town centre is spread out across a long ridge. In the main street opposite the castle there are two intriguing attractions – the Museum of the Home, packed with bric-à-brac, and the Sea Historic Galley, which displays marine life. Half-a-mile (1km) to the west is Monkton priory church, restored in the 19th century from a Benedictine foundation dating from the 11th century.

Pembroke Dock, 1 mile (2km) or so to the northwest, is located squarely on the Milford Haven waterway. This port, once an important naval base, is the embarkation point for the Irish Sea ferry to Rosslare.

PEMBROKESHIRE COAST NATIONAL PARK Dyfed
Scenic area of coastline
This is the only coastal-based national park in Britain and one of Europe's most magnificent stretches of coastal natural beauty. The park covers some 225 square miles (583 sq km), essentially in a long and narrow strip running along the coast for 180 miles (288km) between St Dogmael's in the north and Amroth in the south, with one or two exceptions. Breaks in the boundary along parts of the Milford Haven waterway correspond with the inlet's deep-water oil installations, while in north Pembrokeshire the boundary extends inland for some miles to include the Preseli Hills.

The park can be divided into four parts: the rugged rocky north coast between St Dogmael's and St David's; the huge west-facing bay of St Bride with its cliffs and sandy beaches; the Milford Haven waterway and the unexplored wooded creeks of its upper reaches known as the Daugleddau; and the south coast's spectacular headlands and sands, dominated by the resort of Tenby (see).

The park is a haven for wildflowers and birdlife (the razorbill is its official symbol). Walkers can follow a long-distance footpath that runs right around the coast.

PEMBURY Kent TQ6240
Village on A21, 3 miles (5km) E of Tunbridge Wells
Busy sprawling residential place with triangular green south of village centre. Nearby Pembury Woods are excellent for walks.

PEN-Y-GWRYD Gwynedd SH6655
Hotel on A4086, 4 miles (6km) W of Capel Curig
The isloated Pen-y-Gwryd hotel near the top of the Llanberis Pass is a mecca for all climbers and outdoor enthusiasts. Members of the 1953 Everest expedition stayed here; the hotel contains memorabilia. Paths to Snowdon.

PENALLY Dyfed SS1199
Village on A4139, 2 miles (3km) SW of Tenby
Village close to dunes, sea and golf links. The church is noted for its wheelhead cross of about the 10th century, showing Celtic/Northumbrian influences.

PENARTH South Glamorgan ST1871
Town on A4160, 3 miles (5km) S of Cardiff
Satellite town of Cardiff at southern mouth of Cardiff Bay. Seafront retains the flavour of a small seaside resort, complete with pier. Pretty gardens and parklands. Modern marina development in old dock. Turner House Art Gallery. Cosmeston Lakes Country Park to the south has many amenities and contains a village that re-creates medieval life.

PENCARROW HEAD Cornwall SX1550
Headland off A387, SW of Lansallos
Prominent rocky headland on the south Cornwall coast, with long views.

PENCLAWDD West Glamorgan SS5495
Village on B4295, 3 miles (5km) W of Gowerton
Coastal village famous for its cockle pickers. The tidal sands here are Wales's most prolific cockle beds. Cockles are still picked the traditional way, by hand.

PENCOMBE Hereford and Worcester SO6052
Village off A44, 4 miles (6km) SW of Bromyard
Quiet village with small Victorian church at its heart, enviably situated in deserted hills to west of Bromyard.

PENDEEN Cornwall SW3834
Village on B3306, 2 miles (3km) N of St Just
On the Land's End coast, a centre for tin-mining from prehistoric times, and for copper as well from the 19th century. Geevor Tin Mine was worked from the 1920s to 1991, and is now a large museum showing the whole process and giving mine tours. Levant steam engine (National Trust) is the oldest in Cornwall (1840), still in its original building.

PENDENNIS POINT Cornwall SW8231
Headland SE of Falmouth
High, rocky headland at the seaward end of Carrick Roads (see), with a 1540s castle (English Heritage) built along with St Mawes Castle, opposite, to defend the important estuary. Pendennis Castle has big outer defences of 1598. The inner castle is complete, with a complex gatehouse.

PENDINE Dyfed SN2308
Village off A4066, 5 miles (8km) W of Laugharne
Pendine Sands, 6 miles (10km) long, were the scene of land speed record attempts in the 1920s.

PENDLE HILL Lancashire SD8041
Hill off A59, 4 miles (6km) E of Clitheroe
Stands away from the main Pennine chain, with superb views from its summit at 1,830ft (558m). Excellent walking country. Best known for the infamous Witches of Pendle, who lived in villages along the lower slopes of the hill in the early 17th century, the most notorious being Alice Nutter of Roughlee Hall.

PENDLEBURY Greater Manchester SD7802
Town off M62, 5 miles (8km) NW of Manchester
Victorian residential district of Salford with splendid church designed by Bodley. The artist Lowry lived here for much of his life.

PENDLETON Lancashire SD7539
Village off A59, 2 miles (3km) SE of Clitheroe
A small community of stone-built cottages and working farms which has retained its original charm.

PENDOMER Somerset ST5210
Hamlet off A37, 4 miles (6km) SW of Yeovil
Tiny, isolated hamlet with little 15th-century church. Good views.

PENEGOES Powys SH7700
Village on A489, 2 miles (3km) E of Machynlleth
Flour is produced in the traditional way at Felin Crewi, a restored 17th-century watermill. Village is the birthplace of 18th-century landscape painter Richard Wilson.

PENGE Greater London TQ3570
District in borough of Bromley
A suburb fashionable in the 19th century, but not any longer. Watermen's almshouses and nearby Queen Adelaide's Cottages, both striking in Victorian Tudor.

PENHOW Gwent ST4290
Hamlet off A48, 3 miles (5km) W of Caerwent
Fortified manor house of Penhow Castle, standing on a grassy hill above the road, claims to be Wales's oldest lived-in fortress.

PENHURST East Sussex TQ6916
Village off B2096, 4 miles (6km) W of Battle
Hamlet hidden in a maze of lanes in wooded hilly country; a few cottages with church and manor house grouped agreeably by a pond.

PENICUIK Lothian NT2359
Town on A701, 9 miles (14km) S of Edinburgh
Planned village of 1770, now a sizeable town. Home of Edinburgh Crystal Glass Works. Belfry of the parish church dates from the 12th century.

PENIEL HEUGH Borders NT6526
Hill off B6400, 4 miles (6km) N of Jedburgh
Hill topped by well-known Border landmark, the Waterloo Monument, erected in 1815 by the Marquis of Lothian.

PENISTONE South Yorkshire SE2403
Town on B6462, 7 miles (11km) W of Barnsley
Small historic market town on the River Don dominated by a railway viaduct. Adjoining Cubley Garden Village is a 1920s estate village.

PENKRIDGE Staffordshire SJ9214
Small town on A449, 6 miles (10km) S of Stafford
Small town and important livestock centre on fringe of Cannock Chase. Very grand medieval church with fine 18th-century screen and interesting memorials. Littleton Arms and White Hart are former coaching inns. Other good buildings include Old Deanery of around 1600, school of 1818 and pleasant stone, brick and timber-framed houses in School Square.

PENMACHNO Gwynedd SH7950
Village on B4406, 4 miles (6km) S of Betws-y-Coed
Mountain-locked village in quiet valley. Woollen mill, traditional Ty'n-y-coed farmstead, cultural shrine of Ty Mawr Wybrnant in hills above (latter both National Trust).

PENMAENMAWR Gwynedd SH7176
Town off A55, 4 miles (6km) W of Conwy
Small holiday resort with sand-and-shingle beach looking out across Conwy Bay. Steep, mountain-backed hinterland contains significant prehistoric sites.

PENMAENPOOL Gwynedd SH6918
Hamlet on A493, 2 miles (3km) W of Dolgellau
Charming spot by toll bridge across beautiful Mawddach estuary. Old railway signal box is bird-watching centre. Walks along old railway track.

PENMON Gwynedd (Anglesey) SH6380
Site off A5109, 3 miles (5km) NE of Beaumaris
Far-flung historic site of Penmon Priory (Cadw) in eastern corner of Anglesey. Founded by St Seiriol in early Christian times, but as it now stands dates from medieval times when Augustinian monks settled here. Extensive remains, including dovecoet and holy well. Parish church next door. Puffin Island just offshore also settled by Seiriol.

PENN Buckinghamshire SU9193
Village on B474, 3 miles (5km) NW of Beaconsfield
Engaging church and churchyard, high up with Chilterns views shared with Crown inn. The church has a simple interior with a 15th-century Last Judgement painting, Penn family brasses, Curzon family memorials and a Chantrey monument. In the churchyard is the grave of Alison Uttley, author of children's *Little Grey Rabbit* books. Hammer and sickle on grave of traitor Donald Maclean.

PENNAL Gwynedd SH6900
Village on A493, 3 miles (5km) W of Machynlleth
Small village clustered around bridge, once the site of a Roman fort and one of Owain Glyndwr's Welsh parliaments.

PENNAN Grampian NJ8465
Village on B9031, 2 miles (3km) NW of New Aberdour
Fishing village tucked beneath high cliffs with a pebbly beach, once a smuggling base. Used as the location of the film *Local Hero*.

PENNANT-MELANGELL Powys SJ0226

Village off B4391, 2 miles (3km) W of Llangynog

At end of road in isolated corner of Berwyn Mountains. Norman church has medieval effigies and rood screen. Waterfall at Blaen y Cwm.

PENNARD West Glamorgan SS5688

Village on B4436, 3 miles (5km) W of Mumbles

The shifting dunes of Pennard Burrows buried Pennard's main medieval church (its remains lie beside ruined Pennard Castle). The present church is over 1 mile (2km) away.

PENNINES, THE West Yorkshire

Hill range

Known as 'the backbone of England', the Pennine Hills run down the length of northern England, dividing Yorkshire and Cumbria. The range of hills is 145 miles (233km) in length and varies between 20 miles (32km) and 40 miles (64km) in width, forming the main watershed of northern England. Very little of the range rises above 2,000ft (610m) and most of it is between 100ft (305m) and 1,500ft (457m) in height.

The Southern Pennines end in the Edale Valley with a limestone plateau with ridges of acid moorland down each side often edged with long thin crags of millstone grit. The Central Pennines, from the Edale Valley to the Aire Gap, are a region of high millstone grit hills which create a bleak and boggy landscape of endless moorland. The Northern Pennines continue for another 70 miles (112km) to the Tyne Valley and the landscape becomes more dramatic with cliffs such as Malham Cove and Kilnsey Crag, limestone pavements and the highest point of the Pennines in the Cross Fell and Mickle Fell massif.

The Pennine Way is probably Britain's most famous long-distance walk.

PENNINGTON Hampshire SZ3194

Village off A337, on outskirts of Lymington

Almost part of Lymington, with a few older cottages and many Victorian ones. Saltmarsh to the south.

PENNY BRIDGE Cumbria SD3083

Village on A5092, 3 miles (5km) NE of Ulverston

Named after the Penny family who built a stone bridge over the River Crake. Splendid church overlooks the village, which is now purely residential.

PENRHYNDEUDRAETH Gwynedd SH6138

Small town on A487, 3 miles (5km) E of Porthmadog

Unassuming town near foot of Vale of Ffestiniog. Tollbridge over the River Dwyryd for fast connection south; also tollbridge to Porthmadog.

PENRITH Cumbria NY5130

Town off M6, 18 miles (29km) SE of Carlisle

In the 9th and 10th centuries Penrith was the capital of Cumbria and played an important role in defending the surrounding country from marauding Scots. The castle was built around 1399 and enlarged for the Duke of Gloucester (later Richard III) when he was Lord Warden of the Western Marches and responsible for keeping the peace along the border with Scotland. The castle has been in ruins since 1550 but remains an impressive monument.

Nowadays Penrith is a busy market town with a mixture of narrow streets and wide open spaces, such as Great Dockray, the largest market place. St Andrew's Church dates from Norman times but the most recent part, the nave, was rebuilt between 1719 and 1772. Of particular interest is the three-sided gallery and the brass candelabra suspended from the roof, a gift from the Duke of Cumberland in 1745 – a reward for the town's loyalty during the Jacobite Rising.

The town hall, designed by Robert Adam and built in 1791, was originally two houses, one of which was known as the Wordsworth House as it was the home of the poet's cousin, Captain John Wordsworth.

PENRYN Cornwall SW7834

Town on A39, 2 miles (3km) NW of Falmouth

At the head of a side creek off Carrick Roads (see), this was the main medieval Cornish port, but was superseded by Falmouth from the 17th century. The long main street has a town hall of 1839 prominent in the middle. Old-fashioned boatyards line the shore.

PENSFORD Avon ST6163

Village on A37, 6 miles (10km) S of Bristol

Coal was mined here until 1958. The village is dominated by a huge (now disused) railway viaduct of 1873.

PENSHAW Tyne and Wear NZ3253

Village on A183, 3 miles (4km) N of Houghton le Spring

Miners' cottages and red-brick estates, dominated by Penshaw Monument (National Trust), built in 1844 in memory of the 1st Earl of Durham.

PENSHURST Kent TQ5243

Village on B2176, 5 miles (8km) SW of Tonbridge

Charming village at the confluence of the rivers Eden and Medway, dominated by Penshurst Place, its great house, the finest 14th-century manor house in Kent, birthplace of the great Sir Philip Sidney (1554–86). Its chief glory is the splendid great hall of 1341, the best of its age in England. Gardens and vineyard. Tiny half-timbered Leicester Square leads to the church.

PENTEWAN Cornwall SX0147

Village on B3273, 3 miles (5km) S of St Austell

A tiny harbour and a few Regency buildings. Wide sandy bay lined with caravans and small green hills behind.

PENTLAND HILLS Lothian

Hill range

Range of hills to the southwest of Edinburgh, with reservoirs supplying the city's water. Good outdoor recreational facilites and walking for Edinburgh inhabitants.

PENTLOW Essex TL8146

Hamlet off A1092, 3 miles (5km) W of Long Melford

Across the River Stour from Cavendish (see) in Suffolk. Norman church with round tower. Bull's Tower, of the 19th century, has an eerie reputation.

PENTON, MEWSEY AND GRAFTON Hampshire SU3347
Villages off A342, 3 miles (5km) NW of Andover
Dense but rural, these two adjacent villages are difficult to tell apart.

PENTRE IFAN BURIAL CHAMBER Dyfed SN0937
Site off A487, 3 miles (5km) SE of Newport
The cromlech (Cadw) is one of Wales's finest prehistoric tombs. It stands all alone beneath the Preseli Hills.

PENTREFOELAS Clwyd SH8751
Small village on B5113, 8 miles (13km) SE of Llanrwst
Old grey-stoned village, part of which is now a conservation area and scheme to attract new businesses. Heritage trail and working watermill producing flour.

PENZANCE Cornwall SW4730
Town on A30, 7 miles (11km) SW of St Ives
This combined market town and fishing port has grown through tourism into a large town, the most westerly in Britain. It has always been the port for ferries to the Scilly Isles, and now also houses the helicopter service.

Tourism developed here from the Regency period, visitors being attracted by the very mild climate and beautiful scenery. Several Regency terraces in the west of the town survive, but business really took off after the railway arrived in the 1850s.

The centre of the town is the curving main street. In the middle is the handsome, classical domed market house of 1836, with a statue to Sir Humphry Davy (inventor of many things besides his famous lamp). Chapel Street has the best buildings, a mixture of granite and brick, with the amazing Egyptian House of 1835, chapels, inns and houses. Palms and myrtles are among the plants grown in the lush sub-tropical public gardens. The Promenade to Newlyn (laid out in 1840) has a remarkable open-air pool, the 1930s Jubilee Bathing Pool, recently restored. There is a prominent 1832 church. The Penzance Museum and Art Gallery has many Newlyn School paintings, besides other local displays, and Trinity House National Lighthouse Centre has exhibits about lighthouses.

PEOPLETON Hereford and Worcester SO9350
Village off A4538, 3 miles (5km) N of Pershore
Among much modern housing the timber-framed cottages of the old village survive close to the medieval church.

PEPER HAROW Surrey SU9344
Hamlet off A3, 2 miles (3km) W of Godalming
Compact and totally rural hamlet attached to a private park, with access to the church. Park crossed by many footpaths.

PEPPERBOX HILL Wiltshire SU2124
Hill off A36, 5 miles (8km) SE of Salisbury
Spectacular views over Salisbury (see) from the top, with Eyre's Folly, an octagonal brick tower of 1606 (the 'pepperbox').

PERLETHORPE Nottinghamshire SK6471
Hamlet off A614, 2 miles (3km) N of Ollerton
Nineteenth-century estate village for Salvin's 1865–75 Thoresby Hall (not open), one of 'The Dukeries' houses in Sherwood Forest. Gallery, events in landscaped park.

PERRANARWORTHAL Cornwall SW7738
Village on A39, 3 miles (5km) N of Penryn
The older part is down by the wide Carnon River. Perran Wharf, in the wooded valley, has big handsome industrial buildings from the foundry established here in 1750.

PERRANPORTH Cornwall SW7554
Small town B3285, 7 miles (11km) SW of Newquay
With a dramatic rocky shore to the south and 3 miles (5km) of sandy beach to the north, the small town is mostly a modern resort, having grown after the railways arrived in 1906. Perran Sands has a huge area of sand dunes behind, up to 200ft (60m) high. Folk museum.

PERRY BARR West Midlands SP0791
District of N Birmingham
A vast expanse of housing estates. New shopping precinct and St Matthew's Church were acclaimed in 1960s. St Mary's College has important work by Pugin.

PERRY GREEN Hertfordshire TL4317
Hamlet off B1004, 4 miles (6km) SW of Bishop's Stortford
Just outside Much Hadham (see). The great sculptor Henry Moore moved here after his London studio had been bombed in 1940, and made his base here for the rest of his life until his death in 1986. His studio and numerous examples of his work are cared for by the Henry Moore Foundation (open by appointment only).

PERSHORE Hereford and Worcester SO6052
Town on A44, 7 miles (11km) NW of Evesham
Main road passes famous Horticultural College and crosses River Avon on medieval bridge to enter this delightful old market town. Handsome Bridge Street, packed with interesting period houses, leads to Broad Street, which acts as the market square. Beyond it rises the tower of the abbey, where medieval chancel is now parish church.

PERTH Tayside NO1123
Town off M90, 31 miles (50km) N of Edinburgh
Once known as St John's Town, Perth was of major ecclesiastical, commercial and administrative importance throughout the Middle Ages. Few buildings remain from medieval times; the site of the ancient castle is now occupied by the house of The Fair Maid of Perth. St John's Kirk, where John Knox preached, and much-restored Balhousie Castle, now the Regimental Museum of the Black Watch, both date from the Middle Ages, but Perth's architecture is mainly of the 18th and 19th centuries.

Until the 19th century Perth was a cotton-manufacturing centre; today it is a prosperous city serving a large agricultural hinterland. It stands on the River Tay, spanned by two bridges, with Kinnoull Hill rising above and offering wide views of the city and countryside. Several major whisky distillers have their main offices in Perth, and the world headquarters of the General Accident Insurance Company are here.

The North and South Inches form pleasant parks and there are attractive gardens at Branklyn and Cherrybank. The city has good shopping, a museum and art gallery, and recreational facilities include a theatre, leisure pool and ice-rink.

PERTON Staffordshire SO8598
District off A454, on W outskirts of Wolverhampton
Extensive housing developments on site of former Perton airfield. Hamlet of Old Perton survives to south.

PETER TAVY Devon SX5079
see Tavy

PETERBOROUGH Cambridgeshire TL1998
City on A15, 73 miles (118km) N of London
The magnificent Norman cathedral in the busy city of Peterborough is one of the finest in Britain. It was built between 1118 and 1258 on the site of two previous churches. Its vast nave, flanked with massive round Norman columns, rises in layers of handsome arches, achieving a sense of lightness and space as well as strength and grandeur. The roof of the cathedral dates from the 13th century, and is an explosion of colour and intricate designs.

On display in the cathedral is a portrait of Old Scarlett, a 16th-century gravedigger, and the tomb of Catherine of Aragon, Henry VIII's first wife. Mary Queen of Scots was also buried in Peterborough, but her body was removed to Westminster in 1612.

Outside the cathedral is the Norman great gate, while the guildhall dates from 1671. Peterborough offers excellent shopping facilities as well as a museum and art gallery with exhibitions about the Bronze Age Flag Fen archaeological finds. Peterborough's history goes back way further than the Normans, and excavations have revealed a hut dating from about 3700BC, a large Roman fortress, and a 7th-century monastery.

PETERCHURCH Hereford and Worcester SO3438
Village on B4348, 7 miles (11km) NW of Pontrilas
The 'capital' of the Golden Valley, backed by steep hills, clusters beside River Dore. The church has much Norman work.

PETERCULTER Grampian NJ8300
Village on A93, 7 miles (11km) SW of Aberdeen
Established as a paper-making centre, the town is now chiefly a prosperous residential suburb of Aberdeen. To the west is Drum Castle (National Trust for Scotland), one of Scotland's oldest tower houses, dating from the late 13th century. It stands in 100 acres (40ha) of natural oakwood and has a square tower and a superb Jacobean mansion house attached, with later additions.

PETERHEAD Grampian NK1246
Town on A952, 27 miles (43km) N of Aberdeen
A harbour town since 1593, with whaling and herring fishing in previous centuries, this is now a major European white-fish port and a centre for oil-related services. Local history, including fishing and whaling, is explained in the Arbuthnot Museum. It became a spa town in the late 18th century; the town house, built in 1788, has an impressive spire. High-security Peterhead Gaol lies outside the town to the south.

PETERLEE Durham NZ4240
New Town off A19, 7 miles (11km) NW of Hartlepool
One of the most attractive of the New Towns in the northeast. Dates from 1948 and is named after Peter Lee, chairman of first Labour-controlled Durham County Council. Many houses in the flat-roofed style. Castle Eden Dene is a wooded ravine cut deep into limestone, designated a National Nature Reserve.

PETERSFIELD Hampshire SU7423
Town off A3, 11 miles (18km) NE of Portsmouth
Attractive market town, with lots of Georgian brick along with some flint and timber-framing. Statue of William III as a Roman on horseback in the square, which is still used for markets. Impressive Norman church. Physic Garden laid out as 17th-century garden. Many inns, because it was on the main road from London to Portsmouth.

The William III statue in Petersfield.

PETERSTOW Hereford and Worcester SO5624
Village on A49, 2 miles (3km) W of Ross-on-Wye
Workaday village in orchard country near Ross-on-Wye with Norman and medieval church.

PETTAUGH Suffolk TM1659
Village on A1120, 2 miles (3km) S of Debenham
On a Roman road is Pettaugh Hall, the home of the Fastolf (Falstaff) family 1524–1670. The handsome Bull inn is now a private house.

PETTISTREE Suffolk TM2954
Village on B1438, 1 mile (2km) S of Wickham Market
The Greyhound inn may have been raised before the 15th-century church to house its builders. The church has a brass effigy of Francis Bacon.

PETWORTH West Sussex SU9721
Small town on A283, 13 miles (21km) NE of Chichester
Compact town on a hill clustering at the gates of magnificent 17th-century Petworth House (National Trust), set in a 700 acre (283ha) deer park, landscaped by Capability Brown and painted by Turner. Petworth's intricate triangle of streets, which fan out from the market square, provide intimate and interesting townscapes, evidence of the town's prosperity from the Middle Ages onwards. Lombard Street, one of town's oldest, leads to the church.

PEVENSEY East Sussex TQ6404
Village on A259, 4 miles (6km) NE of Eastbourne
On the edge of the wide coastal Pevensey Levels (a reserve with wildfowl and rare plants), and dominated by Pevensey Castle (English Heritage), this ancient village has been inhabited continuously since Roman times. The castle was the Roman fort of *Anderida*, built in AD340 against marauding Saxons. A Norman castle was built within the Roman walls, but fell into disuse after the defeat of the Armada in 1588. It was recommissioned in World War II as a defensive position, observation and radio direction post.

PEWSEY Wiltshire SU1660
Small town on A345, 6 miles (10km) S of Marlborough
More of a village than a town, with the river in the middle, and a little statue of King Alfred (1911). Some old timber-framed and thatched cottages. Pewsey Wharf on the Kennet and Avon Canal has a small display. The White Horse to the south was cut in 1937. The Vale of Pewsey is a wide valley running up to Devizes (see).

PHILLACK Cornwall SW5638
Village off B3301, immediately N of Hayle
An old village set in sand dunes, with many buildings of blocks of strange black material – not stone but waste from furnaces at Hayle (see).

PICKERING North Yorkshire SE7984
Town on A170, 16 miles (26km) W of Scarborough
Pickering is the largest of Rydale's market towns, set on the narrow, fertile plain of the Vale of Pickering. Once an important coaching stop, there are now numerous medieval inns. Remains of Pickering Castle lie to the north of the town. The old cattle market houses the tourist information centre.

PICKWORTH Lincolnshire TF0433
Village off A15, 2 miles (3km) W of Folkingham
Medieval wall-paintings of Doom, Ascension and Weighing of Souls in 14th-century broach-spired church.

PICTON CASTLE Dyfed SN0013
Mansion off A40, 4 miles (6km) E of Haverfordwest
Country mansion dating from medieval times with a castellated wing added in about 1800. Interior mainly 18th century.It stands in splendid grounds and gardens with woodland. Part of the castle houses the Graham Sutherland Gallery, a major collection of the work of this 20th-century artist, who drew much of his inspiration from Pembrokeshire.

PIDDINGHOE East Sussex TQ4302
Village off A259, 1 mile (2km) NW of Newhaven
Former port on the River Ouse, now a peaceful village. Church has a round tower, possibly used as a beacon from Norman times.

PIDDLETRENTHIDE Dorset ST7000
Village on B3143, 6 miles (10km) N of Dorchester
Named after the River Piddle and '30 hides', its land assessment in Domesday Book, the village straggles along the river valley.

PIEL ISLAND Cumbria SD2363
Island between Walney Island and Furness peninsula
The island is reached by boat from Roa Island. There is a castle built by the monks of Furness Abbey in the 1320s.

PIERCEBRIDGE Durham NZ2115
Village on A67, 5 miles (8km) W of Darlington
Built on the site of a Roman fort guarding an important crossing of the River Tees by Dere Street, the Roman road from York to Hadrian's Wall.

PILGRIMS' WAY Kent/Surrey
Ancient track
This prehistoric ridgeway route, on the southern slopes of the dry North Downs, runs from Salisbury Plain to Kent and was in use by traders from mesolithic times, including neolithic stone-axe traders, Bronze and Iron Age traders and Romans. Some medieval pilgrims to Canterbury probably used it (hence its name). Today much of it is incorporated into the North Downs Way (see).

PILL Avon ST5275
Village off M5, 4 miles (6km) SE of Portishead
The name means 'creek', and the pilots who took ships up the estuary to Bristol had their base here. The buildings are mostly modern, and now there are yachts rather than ships.

PILLETH Powys SO2568
Hamlet off B4356, 3 miles (5km) SW of Knighton
Scene of a famous battle of 1402 in which Owain Glyndwr defeated English forces. Motte and bailey castle beside River Lugg dates from 11th century.

PILLING Lancashire SD4048
Village off A588, 3 miles (5km) NE of Preesall
Agricultural village, popular with visitors. Pilling Embankment, designed to protect village and land from flooding, has limited public access to protect over-wintering birds.

PILTDOWN East Sussex TQ4422
Hamlet off A272, 2 miles (3km) NW of Uckfield
Village notorious for an infamous archaeological hoax,

'Piltdown Man', the supposed 'missing link' between apes and humans that fooled the world from 1911 to 1949. Pub sign shows a winking skull.

PILTON Devon SS5534
Village off A361, on N outskirts of Barnstaple
Now a suburb of Barnstaple, with an interesting medieval church with good fittings, and Georgian and later buildings down the main street to the River Taw estuary.

PILTON Somerset ST5840
Village on A361, 3 miles (5km) SW of Shepton Mallet
Hilly stone village, with a huge stone barn (not open) which was built by Glastonbury Abbey. Beautifully set church, partly Norman, partly later medieval. Original roofs, some with angels; 15th-century stained glass with a figure. Pilton Manor Vineyard.

PIMLICO Greater London TQ2978
District in City of Westminster, S of Victoria Station
Laid out by Thomas Cubitt in the 1830s as a less expensive alternative to Belgravia (see), and still an area of character and charm despite some ill-judged post-war developments and the conversion of many houses into small hotels. Good Victorian churches. Dolphin Square was Europe's largest block of flats when built in 1937.

PIMPERNE Dorset ST9009
Village on A354, 2 miles (3km) NE of Blandford Forum
Many brick and flint cottages in this village, which is more rural further off the main road.

PINCHBECK Lincolnshire TF2425
Village off A16, 2 miles (3km) N of Spalding
Substantial fenland village, formerly a market town, with 18th-century rectory and stables. Grand Norman and medieval church with splendid 15th-century clerestory and carved roofs.

PINHOE Devon SX9694
Village on B3181, on NE outskirts of Exeter
Virtually part of Exeter. The hill above with the medieval church has wide views across the Exe estuary.

PINMILL Suffolk TM2037
Hamlet off B1456, 5 miles (8km) SE of Ipswich
Yachting base on the west bank of the River Orwell. Pinmill's 17th-century pub is associated with author Arthur Ransome. Cliff Plantation is an ancient coppice (National Trust).

PINNER Greater London TQ1289
Village in borough of Harrow
Pleasantly 1930s-style Middlesex suburb which still holds its annual fair around Whitsuntide. Old half-timbered houses and inns.

PIRBRIGHT Surrey SU9455
Village on A324, 5 miles (8km) NW of Guildford
Village scattered around an enormous green, actually a fillet of the surrounding heath, sliced off in the 19th century. Similarly large duck pond has two little islands.

PIRTON Hereford and Worcester SO8847
Village off A38, 5 miles (8km) SE of Worcester
The village, with timber-framed manor house and fine Norman and medieval church, stands in empty countryside near Pershore.

PIRTON Hertfordshire TL1431
Village off B655, 3 miles (5km) NW of Hitchin
Attractive houses and village pond. Church in bailey of Norman castle, whose mound has survived.

PISTYLL RHAEADR Clwyd SJ0729
Waterfall off B4580, 4 miles (6km) NW of Llanrhaeadr-ym-Mochnant
Wales's highest waterfall, dropping 240ft (73m) from Berwyn Mountains. One of the traditional Seven Wonders of Wales.

PITCAIRNGREEN Tayside NO0627
Village off A85, 4 miles (6km) NW of Perth
Pretty village set around an English-style green near the River Almond, founded in the early 19th century as a bleaching centre.

PITCAPLE Grampian NJ7225
Village on A96, 4 miles (6km) NW of Inverurie
An inland village with hills to the south. The Z-plan Pitcaple Castle dates from the 15th century, but the present edifice is mainly 17th-and 19th century.

PITCHFORD Shropshire SJ5303
Village off A458, 6 miles (10km) S of Shrewsbury
Attractive cottages stand close to Pitchford Hall, one of Britain's finest Tudor timber-framed mansions (not open), and interesting church.

PITLESSIE Fife NO3309
Village on A92, 4 miles (6km) SW of Cupar
Village in Eden Valley, where historical painter David Wilkie (1785–1841) was born, in Cults Manse.

PITLOCHRY Tayside NN9458
Town off A9, 11 miles (18km) NW of Dunkeld
Major tourist resort, situated in mountainous landscape on the River Tummel at the geographical heart of Scotland, which developed after Queen Victoria's visit in 1844. A renowned hydro-electric dam has a fish-ladder to facilitate the salmon's progress up the river. The Pitlochry Festival Theatre, founded in 1951, is now in a modern building (1981) beside the river. Blair Atholl Distillery has a well-presented visitors' centre. Pictish stone near by at Dunfallandy.

PITMEDDEN Grampian NJ8827
Village off A920, 5 miles (8km) E of Oldmeldrum
Outside the village is the beautifully restored 17th-century Pitmedden Garden (National Trust for Scotland), with terraces, parterres, pavilions and fountains. Near by are the remains of twin-towered Tolquhon Castle (1584–89).

PITMINSTER Somerset ST2219
Village off B3170, 4 miles (6km) S of Taunton
Large and rural, with a rather restored 13th-century church.

PITSEA Essex TQ7488
District off A13, in SE Basildon
Close to the Thames marshes. Pitsea Hall Country Park with marina, motorboat museum, miniature steam train. Sick horse and pony sanctuary (limited opening).

PITSFORD Northamptonshire SP7568
Village off A508, 5 miles (8km) N of Northampton
Intricately carved Norman doorway of church which was mainly rebuilt in 1867. Fishing, sailing, nature reserve at Pitsford Water reservoir, completed 1956.

PITSTONE Buckinghamshire SP9416
Village on B488, 3 miles (5km) N of Tring
Windmill (National Trust, limited opening) of 1620s or earlier, one of Britain's oldest. Farm Museum (limited opening), local history, bygones, engines.

PITTENWEEM Fife NO5502
Town on A917, 1 mile (2km) SW of Anstruther
Thriving and attractive fishing village and royal burgh with a harbour, characteristic streets and wynds and good examples of East Neuk vernacular architecture.

PITTINGTON Durham NZ3244
Village off A690, 4 miles (6km) E of Durham
The village sits at the foot of Pittington Hill, once a thriving limestone quarry and with superb views from its summit.

PITTON Wiltshire SU2131
Village off A30, 5 miles (8km) E of Salisbury
Compact chalkland village with some thatch and timber-framing. Small medieval church.

PITY ME Durham NZ2645
Village on A167, 2 miles (3km) N of Durham
Now a suburb of Durham, the name is derived from the French *petite mer*, meaning little sea, the low-lying area now called The Carrs, once dug for peat.

PLAISTOW West Sussex TQ0031
Village off B2133, 6 miles (10km) NW of Billingshurst
Village among the woods, with a large green, a small pond and a compact cluster of brick and tile-hung cottages.

PLAXTOL Kent TQ6053
Village off A227, 5 miles (8km) N of Tonbridge
Large hilltop village with a long village street, a lovely group of cottages around the church, a working forge making gates and weathervanes and nearby Old Soar Manor (National Trust).

PLAYFORD Suffolk TM2147
Village off B1079, 4 miles (6km) W of Woodbridge
Nestling in the wooded valley of the River Finn, Playford has a mere of great depth, and a cottage once owned by an Astronomer Royal.

PLEASINGTON Lancashire SD6426
Village off A674, 3 miles (5km) W of Blackburn
Village church is also known as Pleasington Priory. Pleasington Old Hall Wood Nature Reserve has a wooded valley, a walled garden and a butterfly garden.

PLESHEY Essex TL6614
Village off A130, 5 miles (8km) NW of Chelmsford
Select, attractive and historic, the village nests in the outer bailey of the Norman castle, whose buildings have long gone, but whose mound looms up 50ft (15m) high, with the moat crossed by a late 14th-century bridge said to be the oldest brick bridge in Britain. Thatched cottages, Victorian church and renowned blacksmith.

PLOCKTON Highland NG8033
Village off A87, 5 miles (8km) N of Kyle of Lochalsh
This picturesque village round a sheltered bay on Loch Carron is a holiday and sailing centre noted for its quality of light, making it popular with artists.

PLUCKLEY Kent TQ9245
Village off A20, 3 miles (5km) SW of Charing
Village famed for its many ghosts – over a dozen – on the serene slopes of greensand hills overlooking the Weald, with an old centre around the church and modern houses beyond.

PLUMPTON Cumbria NY4937
Village on A6, 4 miles (6km) N of Penrith
A scattered community on the River Petteril, somewhat dominated by the busy A6. Site of the Roman fort of *Voreda* just north of the village.

PLUMPTON East Sussex TQ3613
Village on B2116, 4 miles (6km) NW of Lewes
Scattered village with National Hunt racecourse and agricultural college on a plain beneath the steep north slope of the South Downs.

PLUMTREE Nottinghamshire SK6133
Village off A606, 5 miles (8km) SE of Nottingham
Possibly the oldest church in Nottinghamshire, with a Norman church tower. Saxon work was uncovered when tower was rebuilt in 1906, remainder mainly 13th century.

PLUSCARDEN PRIORY Grampian NJ1457
Site off B9010, 5 miles (8km) SW of Elgin
Benedictine monastery founded in 1230, which dissolved and fell into ruin at the Reformation. Restored to the Benedictines in 1943, this is Britain's only medieval monastery still in use. Restoration continues.

PLYMOUTH Devon SX4754
City off A38, 45 miles (72km) SW of Exeter
This is the largest city in the southwest, standing on a superb site flanked by the estuaries of the Rivers Tamar and Plym. Plympton (see) was the earlier settlement, but from the 14th century Plymouth took over.

The Hoe is the famous park and Promenade overlooking Plymouth Sound, with wonderful views of the sea and wooded headlands. Drake's Island (see) is in the middle, with the 1 mile (2km) long breakwater (completed 1847) beyond. Stonehouse and Devonport (see) are to the west. There are many memorials on the Hoe, including Smeaton's Tower (the Eddystone Lighthouse of 1759) and a statue of Sir Francis Drake, who famously completed his game of bowls here in 1588 before going off to defeat the Spanish Armada. Attractions include the Plymouth Dome with its high-tech displays, the Plymouth Gin distillery which can be viewed and the Plymouth Aquarium. Plymouth had miles of elegant Regency terraces: some survive at the western end of the Hoe.

The huge citadel, with vast walls and an ornate gateway, is a barracks of 1666, still in use. The Barbican is the harbour area and has a rich history ranging from Elizabethan seamen to Francis Chichester's triumphant return. The *Mayflower* left for America from here in 1620 and there is an old fish market on the quay. The streets, some still cobbled, are lined with old houses including the Elizabethan House, which is open. The 16th-century Merchant's House Museum can be found further into the town, as can the museum and art gallery.

Plymouth's centre was destroyed by bombing in World War II, and was replaced by a new grid. The ruins of Charles Church (1640s) remain as a memorial to the bombing. Some Victorian churches survived, and the 1870 guildhall was restored, but most of the centre is recent, with large, widely-spaced buildings. Plymouth today is the regional shopping centre, still closely involved with the Royal Navy, as it has been since the 18th century, but also a thriving commercial centre and resort.

PLYMPTON Devon SX5356
District in E Plymouth
Plympton was larger than Plymouth in early medieval times and still has the earthwork of a medieval castle. It is mostly modern now, with older houses only near the castle. Close to the estuary is Saltram House (National Trust), a superlative Georgian mansion with fine rooms by Robert Adam. Large park. Hemerdon House to the northeast is Regency. Plym Valley Railway (steam).

PLYMSTOCK Devon SX5153
District in SE Plymouth
Once a village, now part of Plymouth, with miles of 20th-century housing. The 15th-century church and a few older buildings survive.

PLYMTREE Devon ST0502
Village off A373, 3 miles (5km) SE of Cullompton
Cider apple country. Medieval church of about 1470, with one of the best wooden screens in the county.

PLYNLIMON Dyfed SN7886
Mountain N of A44, 10 miles (16km) W of Llanidloes
High, boggy moorland with few distinctive features, rising to 2,468ft (752m). Marginal hill-sheep land, partly forested.

POCKLINGTON Humberside SE8048
Town on B1246, 7 miles (11km) NW of Market Weighton
A small market town with church dating from 13th and 15th centuries known as 'Cathedral of the Wolds' which dominates the commercial centre. Burnby Hall Gardens is home to one of the finest collections of waterlilies in Europe, left to the town by Percy Marlborough Stewart.

PODIMORE Somerset ST5425
Village off A303, 2 miles (3km) NE of Ilchester
Small stone village with some thatch. Early 14th-century church with distinctive octagonal tower.

PODINGTON Bedfordshire SP9462
Village off A509, 5 miles (8km) SE of Wellingborough
Church with monuments to Orlebars of Hinwick (see). American Airforce commemorated. Santa Pod drag-racing circuit near by.

POLDEN HILLS Somerset
Hill range SW of Glastonbury
Low ridge running through the Somerset Levels (see), packed with medieval villages.

POLEBROOK Northamptonshire TL0687
Village off A605, 2 miles (3km) SE of Oundle
Limestone and thatch, with Jacobean hall (not open), much altered, and rectory around green. Twelfth-century church with 13th-century tower and spire.

POLEGATE East Sussex TQ5804
Suburb on A27, on N outskirts of Eastbourne
Modern place on the line of a Roman road to Pevensey; also on the Lewes–Hastings and Lewes–Eastbourne railways, with an interesting restored windmill (1817) open to the public.

POLESWORTH Warwickshire SK2602
Village on B5000, 4 miles (6km) NW of Atherstone
Areas of new development surround the old village, but important medieval features, including Pooley Hall and the abbey church and gatehouse, remain.

POLING West Sussex TQ0404
Village off A27, 2 miles (3km) NE of Littlehampton
Flint and brick cottages with thatched roofs at the end of a no-through road. The church has a Saxon nave. Site of an early-warning radar system in World War II.

POLMONT Central NS9378
Town off M9, 3 miles (5km) E of Falkirk
The Antonine Wall ran just to the north, and the 1647 Westquarter dovecote lies to the west.

POLPERRO Cornwall SX2051
Village on A387, 3 miles (5km) SW of Looe
Supremely picturesque stone fishing village with a minute harbour, narrow streets, steps and alleyways crammed with little stone cottages. A rocky shore with trees lies behind. Cars have to be left at nearby Crumplehorn, to the north, but there is transport down to and (more importantly) up from the village.

POLRUAN Cornwall SX1250
Village opposite Fowey on E bank of River Fowey
On a rocky headland at the mouth of the Fowey estuary, with good views up the river. Passenger ferry to Fowey.

POLSTEAD Suffolk TL9938
Village off A1071, 4 miles (6km) SW of Hadleigh
Tucked away in gentle wooded hills, Polstead is surrounded by cherry trees. Thatched cottages huddle around village green. Notorious 'Red Barn' murder committed in 1827.

POLTIMORE Devon SX9696
Village off B3181, 4 miles (6km) NE of Exeter
Mixture of cob and thatch and brick estate cottages. Pretty parkland setting, prominent big house, mostly 18th century (not open).

POLYPHANT Cornwall SX2682
Village off A30, 5 miles (8km) SW of Launceston
Set on the River Inny, the village has steep slopes and a big wooded green.

POLZEATH Cornwall SW9378
Village off B3314, 5 miles (8km) NW of Wadebridge
A mostly modern holiday village, with a big, sandy bay. Rumps Point is a wild, rocky headland to the north.

PONT-NEDD-FECHAN Powys SN9007
Village off A465, 4 miles (6km) NW of Hirwaun
At the approach to the limestone country of Brecon Beacons. Walks to waterfalls and remains of gunpowder works and silica mines. Dinas Rock is a noted geological feature.

PONTARDAWE West Glamorgan SN7204
Town on A474, 5 miles (8km) NW of Neath
Town with an industrial history in Tawe Valley. Stands at crossroads close to countryside, a mix of open mountains and forests.

PONTARDDULAIS West Glamorgan SN5903
Small town on A48, 8 miles (13km) NW of Swansea
Former tinplate-manufacturing centre at western fringes of industrial South Wales. Grew up around confluence of Loughor and Dulais rivers

PONTEFRACT West Yorkshire SE4522
Town on A645, 12 miles (19km) SE of Leeds
Historic market town famous for its liquorice confectionery known as Pontefract cakes. Pontefract Castle, now a ruin and open to the public, featured in Shakespeare's *Richard II*, called Pomfret. Pontefract Museum in Salter Row displays the town's history and its industries, especially glass-blowing and confectionery.

PONTELAND Northumberland NZ1673
Village on A696, 5 miles (8km) NW of Newcastle
The core of a Norman castle is now incorporated into the Blackbird inn. Kirkley Hall Gardens are regularly open to the public.

PONTERWYD Dyfed SN7480
Village on A44, 10 miles (16km) E of Aberystwyth
In high country amongst the moors of Plynlimon. The George Borrow hotel is named after the intrepid 19th-century traveller/writer. Area once riddled with lead mines: Llywernog Silver-Lead Mine to the west is a reminder of those times. A little further is Bwlch Nant yr Arian visitor centre, a focal point for forestry, today's main commercial activity in these hills. Walks, picnic sites, superb views.

PONTESBURY Shropshire SJ3906
Village on A488, 7 miles (11km) SW of Shrewsbury
Modern housing surrounds timber-framed and Georgian houses in Rea Valley village that was once railhead for lead mines at Snailbeach.

PONTRHYDFENDIGAID Dyfed SN7366
Village on B4343, 5 miles (8km) NE of Tregaron
Sleepy village which comes alive once a year during major eisteddfod. Ruined Strata Florida Abbey (Cadw), once the 'Westminster Abbey of Wales', near by.

PONTRHYDYGROES Dyfed SN7372
Village on B4343, 3 miles (5km) S of Devil's Bridge
At western gateway to Cwm Ystwyth mountain road to Rhayader. Steep, thickly wooded valley gives this village an Alpine air.

PONTRILAS Hereford and Worcester SO3927
Village on A465, 11 miles (18km) SW of Hereford
Pontrilas Court (not open), a gabled stone house of about 1630, graces this functional village with its big sawmills at foot of Golden Valley.

PONTSTICILL Mid Glamorgan SO0511
Village off A465, 3 miles (5km) N of Merthyr Tydfil
Rural spot only a few miles from Merthyr Tydfil (see). Grave of ironmaster Robert Crawshay is at Vaynor (see) churchyard. The Brecon Mountain Railway runs to Pontsticill Reservoir.

PONTYPOOL Gwent SO2800
Town on A4043, 8 miles (13km) N of Newport
Old tinplate- and iron-making town in eastern valleys. Memories of industrial past on display at Valley Inheritance Centre in converted late-Georgian stable block in Pontypool Park. Attractive wooded park has long dry-ski slope. Pontymoile Canal Basin on Monmouthshire and Brecon Canal south of town centre has an aqueduct and a tollkeeper's cottage.

PONTYPRIDD Mid Glamorgan ST0790
Town off A470, 11 miles (18km) NW of Cardiff
Town in the Taff Valley midway between Merthyr Tydfil and Cardiff. Its industrial history is recalled at the Historical and Cultural Centre, housed in a converted chapel close to the town's most famous landmark, a single-arched 18th-century stone bridge. Popular shopping centre, especially during Wednesday and Saturday markets. Potter John Hughes's 'groggs' draw visitors from far and wide.

POOL-IN-WHARFDALE West Yorkshire SE2445
Village on A659, 3 miles (5km) E of Otley
Pool, on the River Wharfe, is famous for its mills, the first of which, a woollen mill, was dated 1673.

POOLE Dorset SZ0190
Town on A350, 4 miles (6km) W of Bournemouth
A major medieval port, Poole is set on Britain's largest natural harbour. The old town suffered badly after World War II, with many old houses being demolished. A few remain, particularly around the Church of St James, a new and rather austere building of 1820 with characteristic galleries inside. The guildhall (1761) is handsome, but the quay is the most interesting area of the town, the centre of Poole's prosperity from the Middle Ages. The port has moved just over the channel to Hamworthy, but pleasure craft still use the quay, and larger ships pass by. The custom house of 1813 and the Waterfront Museum (in a 15th-century warehouse) are the best buildings. The Waterfront Museum has fine new displays on maritime history, and Scaplen's Court (a house of about 1500) has domestic displays.

Most of the shores around Poole are muddy, and it never developed into a seaside resort. Inland was heathland, now mostly built up. Poole Harbour is vast, with a tiny entrance to the sea which seems too small for the large ships passing through. The Poole side is heavily built up; the Purbeck side still wild and natural.

POOLEWE Highland NG8580
Village on A832, 4 miles (6km) NE of Gairloch
A crofting village at the mouth of the tumultuous River Ewe, attractively scattered around sheltered Loch Ewe. Across the bay are Inverewe Gardens, world-famous sub-tropical wild gardens with a profusion of rare species, which owes its fertility to the sheltering trees and the warmth of the Gulf Stream. Until 1862 its site was a bare rocky peninsula of Torridonian sandstone.

POOLEY BRIDGE Cumbria NY4724
Village on B5320, at NE end of Ullswater
Pretty village where small boats are moored, at the northern end of Ullswater. An attractive 16th-century bridge across the River Eamont leads to the village square.

POPLAR Greater London TQ3780
District in borough of Tower Hamlets
Impoverished dockland area where London socialism flourished between the wars. Severely damaged by World War II bombing, subsequently redeveloped.

PORLOCK Somerset SS8846
Small town on A39, 6 miles (10km) W of Minehead
Seasidey small town, still with thatched cottages in the middle, but lots of Edwardian development too. Porlock Hill is notoriously long and steep. Toll road closer to shore avoids it, and goes through superb scenery. Porlock Weir, 2 miles (3km) west, is a tiny harbour, picturesque with thatched cottages, pebbles and boulder beach and many wooden groynes.

PORT BANNATYNE Strathclyde (Bute) NS0767
Large village on A844, 2 miles (3km) N of Rothesay
Small resort town on northeast coast of Bute. Overlooking the town is 14th-century Kames Castle; 16th-century tower and 18th-century house, now a holiday centre.

PORT CHARLOTTE Strathclyde (Islay) NR2558
Village on A847, 7 miles (11km) NE of Port Wemyss
Charming village at the narrowest point of Loch Indaal. Wonderful walking and sea views at Rhinns of Isla. Museum of Islay Life near by.

PORT CLARENCE Cleveland NZ4921
Village on A178, across River Tees from Middlesbrough
A 19th-century village of terraced housing dominated by the large amount of chemical industry located here. The transporter bridge crosses from here to Middlesbrough (see).

PORT DINORWIC Gwynedd SH5267
Small town on A487, 4 miles (6km) SW of Bangor
Old port on sheltered Menai Strait, built for shipping slate from Llanberis. Now developing as a modern marina. Watersports centre of Plas Menai is near by.

PORT EINON (OR EYNON) West Glamorgan SS4865
Village on A4118, 13 miles (21km) W of Swansea
One-time haunt of smugglers on beautiful sheltered bay. Culver Hole is a mysterious walled section of cliff. Prehistoric Paviland Cave in remote cliffs to the west.

PORT ELLEN Strathclyde (Islay) NR3645
Small town on A846, 10 miles (16km) SE of Bowmore
The largest town on Islay. Its ferry terminal was laid out on a small rocky bay as a planned village in 1821. There are several distilleries near by, including Laphroaig and Lagavulin. To the east are the ruins of 14th-century Dunyvaig Castle. Southwestern Oa peninsula has sheer cliffs with deep caves, once the haunt of smugglers and illicit whisky distillers.

PORT ERIN Isle of Man SC1969
Small town off A36, 9 miles (14km) S of Peel
Popular holiday centre with soft sand and rock pools at the beach. Railway Museum adjoins the station. Boat trips from Port Erin to the Calf of Man.

PORT GAVERNE Cornwall SX0080
Hamlet off B3267, immediately E of Port Isaac
This little north Cornish fishing harbour was once used for shipping the slate from Delabole (see).

PORT GLASGOW Strathclyde NS3274
Town on A8, 3 miles (5km) E of Greenock
Once an important 1690s port, it declined from the 1740s after river-dredging. Newark Castle (15th century) has a tower block, separate gatehouse and later mansion.

PORT ISAAC Cornwall SW9980
Village on B3267, 5 miles (8km) N of Wadebridge
Unspoilt fishing village on the north coast, with a little harbour, stone cottages and fish cellars (the buildings used for salting pilchards).

PORT LOGAN Dumfries and Galloway NX0940
Village on B7065, 4 miles (6km) NW of Drummore
Sailing resort on a sheltered bay with a rare tidal fish pond. Logan Botanic Garden benefits from the Gulf Stream, enabling the propagation of many rare and exotic plants.

PORT MULGRAVE North Yorkshire NZ7917
Hamlet off A174, 1 mile (2km) SE of Staithes
A village of plain, cliff-top houses built in the 19th century, with a tiny disused harbour.

PORT OF MENTEITH Central NN5801
see Lake of Menteith

PORT QUIN Cornwall SW9780
Hamlet off B3314, 5 miles (8km) NW of Wadebridge
Strangely deserted stone fishing village on the north coast, supposedly empty because all the men of the village were drowned in around 1900.

PORT SETON Lothian
see Cockenzie

PORT ST MARY Isle of Man SC2067
Village off A31, 2 miles (3km) SE of Port Erin
Former fishing village, with picturesque harbour and piers, and home of Isle of Man Yacht Club. Lime kilns can still be seen, the remains of local lime industry.

PORT SUNLIGHT Merseyside SJ3484
Village off A41, 3 miles (5km) SE of Birkenhead
This 19th-century model village, now a conservation area, was built by Lord Leverhulme for the workers at his nearby soap factory. The Port Sunlight Heritage Centre displays the history of the village, the factory and the workers; the Lady Lever Art Gallery has collections of 18th- and 19th-century paintings and sculptures.

PORT TALBOT West Glamorgan SS7690
Town off M4, 13 miles (21km) NW of Bridgend
Major industrial centre whose steelworks and attendant services occupy much of the mountain-backed coastal plain. The town itself, which retains a few attractive Victorian features, is named after the Talbot family, who developed the 19th-century docks. Next door is the strange bedfellow of Aberavon, a day-trip seaside resort with large sandy beach, promenade and popular Afan Lido sports and leisure complex.

PORT WILLIAM Dumfries and Galloway NX3343
Small town on A747, 9 miles (14km) SW of Wigtown
A small 18th-century port and resort with sandy beaches on Luce Bay. The nearby remains of 10th- to 11th-century Chapel Finian stand on a long raised beach.

PORTCHESTER Hampshire SU6105
Town on A27, 7 miles (11km) NW of Portsmouth
One old village street lined with simple Georgian brick houses and cottages, the rest of the big settlement is 1930s onwards. The castle (English Heritage) has Roman outer walls, and is the best-preserved Roman fort in northern Europe. The gateways are medieval, and there is a big medieval castle, with a huge stone keep, in one corner. In the opposite corner is a fine Norman church.

PORTESHAM Dorset SY6085
Village on B3157, 6 miles (10km) NW of Weymouth
Partly built in the local, almost white, stone, the village has a backdrop of hills rising behind it. Monument to Thomas Hardy to the northeast.

PORTH Mid Glamorgan ST0291
Town on A4058, 3 miles (5km) W of Pontypridd
Stands at gateway to the two valleys of the Rhondda – the Fach (little) and Fawr (big). Rhondda Heritage Park at nearby Trehafod tells of coal-mining past.

PORTH-Y-WAEN Shropshire SJ2623
Village on A495, 4 miles (6km) SW of Oswestry
Brass band is pride of this haphazard quarrying village in foothills of Berwyn Mountains. Good walking on Llynclys Common, east of village.

PORTHCAWL Mid Glamorgan SS8176
Town on A4229, 6 miles (10km) W of Bridgend
Traditional seaside resort with two sides to its character. Sandy Bay and Trecco Bay boast big funfair and huge caravan park, while Rest Bay to the west has quiet sands and rock pools backed by grassy Lock's Common. Small harbour by esplanade. Newton and Nottage on outskirts preserve their 'village' character. Famous links golf course. Glamorgan Heritage Coast starts to the east.

PORTHCURNO Cornwall SW3822
Village off B3315, 3 miles (5km) SE of Land's End
Rocky shore and sandy bay, with the Minack Theatre cut out of the cliffs in the 1920s, an amphitheatre used for performances.

PORTHGAIN Dyfed SM8133
Hamlet off A487, 4 miles (6km) W of Mathry
The tiny harbour is a strange combination of natural beauty and industrial remains. Old stone-crushing plant next to sheltered quayside and Sloop inn.

PORTHLEVEN Cornwall SW6225
Small town on B3304, 2 miles (3km) SW of Helston
Fishing settlement with a triple harbour built in the mid-19th century. A few older houses.

PORTHMADOG Gwynedd SH5638
Town on A487, 9 miles (14km) SW of Ffestiniog
Old slate-exporting port with large harbour, now a lively town and holiday centre. Scenic narrow-gauge Ffestiniog Railway built to carry slate over 13 miles (21km) from Blaenau Ffestiniog. Welsh Highland Railway also operates on a short route from Porthmadog. Maritime museum on quayside, motor museum and pottery in town. The Cob toll road (part of A487) runs across embankment.

PORTINSCALE Cumbria NY2523
Village off A66, 1 mile (2km) W of Keswick
Village at the northern end of Derwentwater. Lingholm Gardens has a large collection of rhododendron species and others.

PORTISHEAD Avon ST4676
Town on A369, 8 miles (13km) W of Bristol
A little medieval village on the Bristol Channel which became a tiny seaside resort from early Victorian times,

and then developed, with Avonmouth (see), to replace Bristol's docks. Huge Royal Portbury Dock at the mouth of the River Avon opened in 1977, with the largest dock-gates in Britain at that time.

PORTLAND, ISLE OF Dorset SY6972
Peninsula on A354, 4 miles (6km) S of Weymouth
Almost an island, being attached to mainland Dorset only by a shingle bank (see Chesil). Bleak and almost treeless, Portland is all limestone, a famous building stone which has been quarried since medieval times. Cliffs rise on all sides, and there is a wonderful view from Portland Heights. Portland Castle (English Heritage) is of 1540, built to protect Weymouth Harbour: Portland Harbour was not started until 1849. Large prison and borstal (see Easton).

PORTLOE Cornwall SW9339
Village off A3078, 6 miles (10km) SW of Mevagissey
Steep dark cliffs and a little fishing village of stone cottages.

PORTMAHOMACK Highland NH9184
Village on B9165, 3 miles (5km) SW of Tarbat Ness
This windswept village, sprawling downhill to a bay, is a popular sailing centre. Tarbat old church has an interesting tower and balustraded entrance.

PORTMEIRION Gwynedd SH5837
Site off A487, 2 miles (3km) SW of Penrhyndeudraeth
Amazing village created by iconoclastic architect Sir Clough Williams-Ellis on a beautiful wooded peninsula overlooking Traeth Bach estuary. Pastel shaded houses, rich decoration, architectural 'jokes' and fake façades all help to create an engagingly bizarre place. Has been described as Italianate, but combines many styles, from Tudor to oriental. Famously used as location for 1960s cult television series, *The Prisoner*.

PORTMELLON Cornwall SX0143
Hamlet off B3273, immediately S of Mevagissey
Hamlet of old cottages on the shore, with a pretty bay and a green valley.

PORTOBELLO Lothian NT3073
Suburb of Edinburgh
Reputedly named after the capture of Panama's Puerto Bello, the suburb, with its fine Georgian houses, has been a seaside resort since the 19th century. Birthplace of Sir Harry Lauder (1870–1950), the music-hall entertainer.

PORTPATRICK Dumfries and Galloway NX0054
Small town on A77, 6 miles (10km) SW of Stranraer
A holiday resort and fishing village on the Rhinns of Galloway, until the mid-19th century this was the main arrival point from Ireland, where the Irish came to be married under more liberal Scottish law. The 16th-century Dunskey Castle ruins stand on an impressive cliff dominating the town. The Southern Upland Way long-distance footpath starts here and the town is noted as a sea-angling centre.

PORTREATH Cornwall SW6545
Village on B3300, 4 miles (6km) NW of Redruth
A little fishing port, developed from the 18th century for the export of copper.

PORTREE Highland (Skye) NG4843
Town on A850, 10 miles (16km) N of Sligachan
Skye's administrative and commercial centre, with an attractive harbour and trim town centre. The name derives from the Gaelic for 'king's port', named after James V's visit in 1540, when he tried to win the allegiance of the Lords of the Isles. Near by is a heritage centre tracing Skye's history. Busy tourist resort with bus connections and boat excursions.

PORTSCATHO Cornwall SW8735
Village off A3078, 1 mile (2km) S of Trewithian
Natural, unspoiled fishing village, small-scale old stone buildings (including an octagonal fishermen's shelter on the shore). Two little sandy bays, otherwise rocky coast.

PORTSDOWN Hampshire SU6406
Hill running E/W to N of Portsmouth
Long chalk hill behind Portsmouth, giving wonderful views of the harbour. Tall column to the memory of Nelson suitably overlooks the naval base of Portsmouth. Six big forts were built along the hill in the 1860s to defend Portsmouth. Fort Nelson is the artillery museum of the Royal Armouries.

PORTSLADE-BY-SEA East Sussex TQ2605
Town on A27, 3 miles (5km) W of Brighton
Old downland village now engulfed by suburbia. Flint cottages survive in High Street including Kemps, 1580. To the north is Foredown Tower Countryside Centre with a rare camera obscura for viewing surrounding areas.

PORTSMOUTH Hampshire SU6400
Town off M275, 65 miles (105km) SW of London
The town (small until it developed as a naval and garrison town, in the area now called Old Portsmouth) started at the tip of the large flat island. The naval dockyard developed on the sheltered harbour in the 17th century, and grew enormously in the 18th century. Inside the dockyard are the Royal Navy Museum, Nelson's ship *Victory*, the *Mary Rose* (raised from the seabed in 1982), the Mary Rose Museum, and the restored HMS *Warrior*, the first iron-clad warship, built in 1860. The old town was badly damaged by bombing in World War II but patches of 18th-century townscape survive. The Point, the narrow mouth of the harbour, is decidedly picturesque and a wonderful viewing point for shipping.

Portsmouth Cathedral was created from the parish church from 1927 and has a smooth 1930s nave; the west end was completed in 1991. The lantern on top has guided ships into the harbour since 1702.

Portsea (to the north) was virtually destroyed in the last war and is mostly modern apart from St George's Church, which date from 1754.

Beyond Southsea (see) is Eastney, largely a 20th-century development with Eastney Industrial Museum (pumping station of 1887) and the Royal Marines Museum.

Most of the island of Portsmouth is covered with late Victorian and Edwardian housing, with several distinct shopping centres. Charles Dickens' Birthplace Museum is in Landport and the City Museum and Art Gallery is in Museum Road, Old Portsmouth.

Despite the dockyard closing in 1984 Portsmouth is still deeply involved with the sea and is still a naval base. There are car ferries to France, passenger ferries to the Isle of Wight and historic ships to visit.

PORTSOY Grampian NJ5866
Village on A98, 6 miles (10km) W of Banff
Conservation village with attractive buildings set round a harbour, once a fishing port, now a resort. Noted for its green and pink Portsoy marble, cut from a local vein.

PORTWRINKLE Cornwall SX3553
Village on B3247, 6 miles (10km) SW of Torpoint
Little seaside village with a tiny rocky harbour. The Victorian Gothic Whitsand hotel building was moved here from Torpoint in about 1900.

POSTBRIDGE Devon SX6579
Hamlet on B3212, 8 miles (13km) SW of Moretonhampstead
Dull village with wonderful setting in the middle of Dartmoor. Big clapper bridge over the East Dart River.

POTTER HEIGHAM Norfolk TG4119
Village on A149, 10 miles (16km) NW of Great Yarmouth
The medieval hump-backed bridge at Potter Heigham is infamous for having only 7ft (2m) headroom, and professional pilots are recommended for inexperienced sailors. A newer settlement has grown around the bridge, including the colourful marina, while the village proper lies 1 mile (2km) to the north. Helter-Skelter Cottage has part of a real helter-skelter incorporated.

POTTERNE Wiltshire ST9958
Village on A360, 2 miles (3km) S of Devizes
Impressive 13th-century church, in style like Salisbury Cathedral, and one of the finest late 15th-century timber-framed houses in the country (not open). Pretty stone Church House of 1614. Fire Defence Museum (limited opening).

POTTERS BAR Hertfordshire TL2501
Town off M25, 6 miles (10km) W of Waltham Cross
Only a hamlet in the 1850s, now a commuter town. The Church of King Charles the Martyr was built in the 1940s. Walks in Northaw Great Wood.

POTTO North Yorkshire NZ4703
Village off A172, 5 miles (8km) SW of Stokesley
Potto Hall, built in 1861, is now a hotel surrounded by parkland. The village has just a few houses, built around the turn of the20th century.

POTTON Bedfordshire TL2249
Small town on B1040, 4 miles (6km) NE of Biggleswade
A Georgian market and commuter town, largely rebuilt after a 1783 fire. Riotous 18th-century gravestones in the churchyard. Potton Woods walks.

POUGHILL Cornwall SS2207
Village off A39, 1 mile (2km) NE of Bude
Hilly country, thatched cottages and an interesting, typically Cornish church with bench-ends.

POULSHOT Wiltshire ST9759
Village off A361, 3 miles (5km) SW of Devizes
Proper village green at the centre, with many trees and some old cottages. Timber-framed inn.

POULTON Gloucestershire SP1000
Village on A417, 5 miles (8km) E of Cirencester
Cluster of old stone cottages and farmhouses in flat countryside. Victorian church has good modern glass in nave.

POULTON-LE-FYLDE Lancashire SD3439
Town on A586, 3 miles (5km) NE of Blackpool
This market town was listed in Domesday Book as 'Poltun', meaning 'the town by the pool'. St Chad's Church dates largely from the 18th century but the name suggests that this has been a place of worship for over 1,000 years. In 1732, a fire burned all the thatched cottages surrounding the market place to the ground.

POUNDSTOCK Cornwall SX2099
Village off A39, 4 miles (6km) S of Bude
Medieval church and an unusual 14th-century rural guildhall, sitting together in a wooded hollow.

POWERSTOCK Dorset SY5196
Dorset off A3066, 4 miles (6km) NE of Bridport
Large and attractive stone village straggling in a pretty landscape of steep little hills.

POWFOOT Dumfries and Galloway NY1465
Village off B724, 3 miles (5km) W of Annan
A former fishing village on the shores of Solway Firth, now a pleasant resort with sandy beaches and sailing.

POWICK Hereford and Worcester SO8351
Village on A449, 3 miles (5km) SW of Worcester
Scattered village between Worcester and Malvern where Elgar conducted band at the old mental hospital and Pugin built Stanbrook Abbey, a famous convent.

POYNINGS West Sussex TQ2612
Village off A281, 6 miles (10km) NW of Brighton
Small village, cupped in a hollow below the steep slopes of the South Downs, beneath Devil's Dyke hillfort. Remarkable church of 1370, like Alfriston's, in the form of a Greek cross.

POYNTON (POYNTON-WITH-WORTH) Cheshire SJ9283
Town on A52 (A523), 5 miles (8km) S of Stockport
Until the 1930s Poynton was a coal-mining village, the mines, land and property belonging to Lord Vernon. Now a busy crossroads town.

PRAA SANDS Cornwall SW5828
Village off A394, 6 miles (10km) W of Helston
Mostly modern seaside development on the long sandy bay, but with small, late medieval Pengersick Castle (not open) set back from the shore.

PREES Shropshire SJ5533

Village on A49, 5 miles (8km) S of Whitchurch

Scattered community in pleasant open countryside has church worth visiting and some good houses, notably 18th-century Prees Hall opposite church.

PREESALL Lancashire SD3647

Small town off A588, 1 mile (2km) SE of Knott End-on-Sea

Centre of the salt-mining industry in the late 19th century.The mining has brought considerable subsidence problems.

PRESCOT Merseyside SJ4692

Town off A58, 4 miles (6km) SW of St Helens

The medieval street pattern and plot layout remains virtually intact and is evidence of Prescot's importance as one of the oldest settlements in Merseyside.

PRESELI HILLS Dyfed

Hill range SE of Newport

Bare, uninhabited hills of heather and mountain grass rising to 1,760ft (536m) above north Pembrokeshire coast. Empty landscape scattered with a wealth of prehistoric settlements – stone circles, standing stones, burial chambers, camps. Preseli 'bluestones' used in the construction of Stonehenge, but no one knows how they were transported. Hills are within boundary of Pembrokeshire Coast National Park.

PRESTATYN Clwyd SJ0682

Town on A548, 4 miles (6km) E of Rhyl

Popular seaside resort on sandy North Wales coast. Nova Centre at central beach is a major leisure and entertainments complex open day and night. Host of traditional family attractions at Ffrith beach's entertainment centre and boating lake. Quieter Barkby beach is to the east. Prestatyn stands at northern end of the long-distance Offa's Dyke Path. Interpretive centre tells story of the 8th-century earthwork.

PRESTBURY Cheshire SJ8976

Village on A538, 2 miles (3km) NW of Macclesfield

Picturesque, exclusive village on River Bollin with Tudor village centre surrounded by opulent dwellings. Adlington Hall, 15th century.

PRESTEIGNE Powys SO3164

Small town on B4355, 5 miles (8km) S of Knighton

Small border settlement (bridge over River Lugg marks border) with narrow streets and half-timbered architecture. Radnorshire Arms of 1616 is one of a collection of fine buildings that includes Shire Hall (used as a court until relatively recently) and Radnor Buildings. Church contains 16th-century Flemish tapestry. Norman castle once stood on the site of the public park.

PRESTON Dorset SY7083

Village on A353, 3 miles (5km) NE of Weymouth

Largely modern, but with a small older area. The footings of Jordan Hill Roman temple are exposed on the hill by the sea to the west.

PRESTON East Sussex TQ3006

District in N Brighton

Running out of Brighton on the A23, this old village is attached to Preston Manor (1739), given to Brighton in 1932 with pleasant Preston Park.

The Radnorshire Arms in Presteigne.

PRESTON Humberside TA1830

Village on B1239, 1 mile (2km) N of Hedon

The village was founded during Anglo-Saxon invasions and became a principal pig-producing area for East Yorkshire.

PRESTON Lancashire SD5429

Town off M55, 27 miles (43km) NW of Manchester

Strategically situated at the highest navigable point of the River Ribble, Preston is still an active port, although most marine activity now consists of sailing and windsurfing in the Riversway Marina. Now the administrative capital of Lancashire, this was an important cotton-spinning and engineering town.

The town has some fine public buildings, including the town hall, the Harris Art Gallery, the museum and library, all in neo-classical style, which provide a civic focal point close to the covered markets. The parish church has an elegant 205ft (62m) spire which rises above the town centre. Preston has a number of covered shopping centres and pedestrianised areas, including the guildhall and Charter Theatre complex.

The town is possibly most famous for its Guild, and the celebration that takes place once every 20 years, hence the saying 'once every Preston Guild'. The Preston Guild Merchant was established possibly as early as 1179. Its members benefited from exclusive trading rights and employed the Guild Merchant to ensure the quality control of Preston goods. Guild Merchant powers ensured that cottagers could buy in the market before the larger buyers came in.

PRESTON Leicestershire SK8702

Village on A6003, 2 miles (3km) N of Uppingham

Attractive Rutland village of ironstone cottages with mullioned windows. Norman and medieval church, restored 1856.

PRESTON Suffolk TL9450

Village off A1141, 2 miles (3km) NE of Lavenham

Pretty one-street village in pasture and meadowland on a clay ridge. Suffolk historian Robert Reyce built Preston Hall in 1555.

PRESTON BROCKHURST Shropshire SJ5324

Village on A49, 3 miles (5km) SE of Wem

Attractive cluster of houses, some timber-framed, dominated by Preston Hall, stone mansion of late 17th century (not open).

PRESTON CANDOVER Hampshire SU6041

Village on B3046, 6 miles (10km) N of Alresford

Large village with a Victorian church in the middle and the remains of an older one. Two large late Georgian houses (not open).

PRESTON GUBBALS Shropshire SJ4919

Village on A528, 4 miles (6km) N of Shrewsbury

Set in pastoral countryside, village has Victorian church with surviving medieval features and Elizabethan Lea Hall (not open) to north.

PRESTON ON STOUR Warwickshire SP2049

Village off A3400, 3 miles (5km) S of Stratford-upon-Avon

Pretty estate village for Alscot Park has rewarding church, village green and varied array of charming houses.

PRESTON ON WYE Hereford and Worcester SO3842

Village off A438, 8 miles (13km) W of Hereford

In watermeadows to east of the Golden Valley; the ancient church stands beside the manor house, detached from the modern village.

PRESTON UPON THE WEALD MOORS Shropshire SJ6815

Village off A518, 3 miles (5km) NE of Wellington

Unremarkable village with fine 18th-century church and astonishing Preston Hospital – unexpectedly large and sophisticated almshouses of 1720s.

PRESTONPANS Lothian NT3874

Town on B1348, 3 miles (5km) NE of Musselburgh

Medieval mining and salt-producing town, with a good range of lairds' houses of different dates, including 15th-century Preston Tower and Hamilton House (1628). It has a complete and unaltered 17th-century mercat cross. Prestongrange Mining Museum covers 800 years of mining history. This was the site of the Battle of Prestonpans (1745), which resulted in a Jacobite victory over General Cope; a cairn commemorates the battle.

The cairn commemorating the victory at the Battle of Prestonpans.

PRESTWICH Greater Manchester SD8203
Town off M62, 4 miles (6km) NW of Manchester
Victorian residential area with Heaton Hall, one of Manchester's finest 18th-century houses, in extensive parkland.

PRESTWICK Strathclyde NS3525
Town on A79, immediately N of Ayr
Ancient burgh which grew into a fashionable summer resort after the arrival of the railway in 1841. Renowned for golf, the first Open Golf Championship was held here in 1860. The ruined Church of St Nicholas dates from the 12th century. An international civil airport established here because of the good weather has now been eclipsed by Glasgow Airport.

PRIDDY Somerset ST5251
Village off B3135, 4 miles (6km) NW of Wells
High in the Mendips, with a big green used annually for a sheep fair in late August. Thirteenth-century church tower with several good 15th-century fittings, including the wooden screen, stone pulpit and silk altar frontal. Priddy Circles are four large neolithic stone rings to the northeast. Priddy Nine Barrows are to the east.

PRINCES RISBOROUGH Buckinghamshire SP8003
Town on A4010, 7 miles (11km) S of Aylesbury
Indeterminate Chilterns Gap market town swamped by post-1930s housing. Memorial to heroic young American pilot, killed in 1943.

PRINCETOWN Devon SX5873
Town on B3357, 7 miles (11km) E of Tavistock
Grim town in bleak setting, with the prison usually known as Dartmoor.At 1,300ft (400m), the town was founded in the 1780s, with the prison opening in 1808 to house French prisoners-of-war. All buildings are of locally quarried granite, and the church was built by the prison inmates from the granite in 1813.

PRINKNASH ABBEY Gloucestershire SO8813
Site on A46, 3 miles (5km) NE of Painswick
The modern abbey, producing celebrated pottery, and the neighbouring wildlife in Prinknash Park make this hilly spot a major tourist attraction.

PRIOR'S DEAN Hampshire SU7229
Hamlet off A32, 3 miles (5km) SW of Selborne
Tiny unspoilt rural hamlet with a few cottages, a farm and a little Norman church.

PRIORS, HARDWICK AND MARSTON
Warwickshire SP4756
Villages off A423, 5 miles (8km) SE of Southam
Villages in rural countryside. Marston Hardwick, with 17th-century Falcon inn and handsome stone houses, stands on old drovers' road. Interesting church at Priors Hardwick.

PRITTLEWELL Essex TQ8687
District off A127, in NW Southend-on-Sea
Southend's original village nucleus. Priory ruins in park with museum of medieval religious life, natural history, communications, radio and television.

PRIVETT Hampshire SU6726
Hamlet off A272, 3 miles (5km) NE of West Meon
Small, mostly Victorian village with a huge church of 1877; its 160ft (49m) spire is visible from miles around.

PROBUS Cornwall SW8947
Village on A390, 7miles (11km) NE of Truro
Large village, with the best and highest church tower in Cornwall: 124ft (38m) high, 16th century and lavishly decorated. Probus Gardens are attractive trial and demonstration gardens, and Trewithen House (limited opening) is classical 18th century. The gardens and parkland are very fine.

PRUDHOE Northumberland NZ0963
Town off A695, 7 miles (11km) of Newcastle
Prudhoe stands on the banks of the River Tyne. In Norman times a timber castle was built by the river, which was rebuilt in stone by the end of the 12th century. Now owned by English Heritage. A riverside park extends from Prudhoe to Newburn.

PRUSSIA COVE Cornwall SW5528
Village off A394, 7 miles (11km) W of Helston
A lonely, rocky bay, named after a local smuggler nicknamed 'King of Prussia' because of his admiration for Frederick the Great.

PUCKERIDGE Hertfordshire TL3823
Village off A10, 6 miles (10km) N of Ware
Formerly an important Ermine Street coaching stop, now an outlier of Standon (see), with much post-war development. Old inns.

PUDDLETOWN Dorset SY7594
Village on A35, 5 miles (8km) NE of Dorchester
The old village off the main road has a handsome church with good 17th-century fittings and thatched cottages. It was used by Thomas Hardy in his novel *Far from the Madding Crowd*. Ilsington House is 17th to 19th century.

PUDLESTON Hereford and Worcester SO5659
Village off A44, 4 miles (6km) E of Leominster
In deeply rural countryside. A castellated gatehouse marks entrance to 19th-century manor house. Church of Saxon origin stands near by.

PUDSEY West Yorkshire SE2232
Town off A6110, 4 miles (6km) E of Bradford
This is a dormitory town for people working in Leeds and Bradford. The Parish Church of St Laurence was built in the 1840s and is a landmark from miles around. Both Sir Len Hutton and Herbert Sutcliffe started their cricketing careers here. Local industries used to include woollen cloth manufacture, tanning and shoe-making.

PULBOROUGH West Sussex TQ0418
Town on A29, 9 miles (14km) N of Arundel
Attractive village in the beautiful Arun Valley. Historic centre on Roman road, Stane Street (A29), a conservation area with several medieval houses and the 18th-century Chequers hotel. A little lane leads past the spacious church and over the railway to picturesque

Old Place, beside the pond. Pleasant centre by the river, on the A283. Pulborough Brooks Nature Reserve (RSPB) lies in marshy Avon valley, famed for its wintering ducks and waders.

PULHAM, MARKET AND ST MARY Norfolk TM1986
Villages on B1134, 4 miles (6km) NW of Harleston
These two pleasing villages nestle in the River Waveney Valley. Larger Pulham Market has an abundance of old buildings, while Pulham St Mary has a lovely avenue of limes leading to the 15th-century church. The Pulhams became famous during World War I as a base for airships, known as 'Pulham pigs' because of their shape and colour.

PUMSAINT (OR PUMPSAINT) Dyfed SN6540
Hamlet on A482, 7 miles (11km) SE of Lampeter
Pumsaint means 'five saints' in Welsh – name based on local legend. Site of Dolaucothi Roman Gold Mine (National Trust).

PUNCKNOWLE Dorset SY5388
Village off B3157, 5 miles (8km) SE of Bridport
Pronounced 'Punnle', this handsome stone village has an interesting church and good setting.

PURBECK, ISLE OF Dorset SY9681
Peninsula on A351, S and SE of Wareham
Not really an island, but almost cut off from the rest of Dorset by rivers and a long hill. The coastline is famous for its dramatic cliffs and varied geology, and is mostly accessible only on foot. The seaward parts are largely stone, and have been quarried since Roman times.

PURBROOK Hampshire SU6708
Village on A3, immediately S of Waterlooville
An old village much developed since the 1950s. Van Diemen, the discoverer of Tasmania in 1642, lived here.

PURFLEET Essex TQ5578
Village on A1090, 3 miles (5km) W of Grays
On the Thames, dominated by oil terminals, but with much recent commuter housing. Clock tower of former government gunpowder store.

PURLEIGH Essex TL8402
Village off B1010, 3 miles (5km) S of Maldon
Church and fine old Bell pub enjoy views over flat country between Blackwater and Crouch rivers. New Hall Vineyards open.

PURLEY Berkshire SU6576
Village on A329, on NW edge of Reading
Once a village on the River Thames, but now really part of Reading.

PURLEY Greater London TQ3161
Town on A23, in borough of Croydon
The name is thought to relate to pear trees, but the town, set on the main Brighton road and railway, became densely suburbanised.

PURSE CAUNDLE Dorset ST6917
Village off A30, 4 miles (6km) E of Sherborne
A handsome stone village, rather a backwater. Pleasant church and a fine manor house (limited opening) with a 15th-century hall.

PURSTON JAGLIN West Yorkshire SE4319
Village on A645, 1 mile (2km) SW of Pontefract
A village of red-brick Victorian terraced houses with some modern housing developments strung along the main road.

PURTON Wiltshire SU0887
Village off B4553, 5 miles (8km) NW of Swindon
Large scattered village made of several old hamlets. Prettiest around the medieval church. The little Pump Room of 1859 is a reminder of the tiny spa here. Local museum.

PUSEY Oxfordshire SU3596
Village on B4508, 4 miles (6km) E of Faringdon
Pusey's elegant classical church should not be missed, and the beautiful Pusey House Gardens (limited opening) are a great attraction.

PUTLEY Hereford and Worcester SO6437
Village off A438, 4 miles (6km) W of Ledbury
Small village in cider orchard country west of Ledbury, with black and white cottages and two fine early 18th-century houses.

PUTNEY Greater London TQ2375
District in borough of Wandsworth
A comfortable suburb at a medieval ferry crossing of the Thames. Long a convenient place for London merchants and courtiers to have houses, Putney developed rapidly after the railway arrived in 1846. Swinburne lived at The Pines (not open) on Putney Hill. Putney Bridge was designed by Sir Joseph Bazalgette in the 1880s. Wandsworth Museum is housed in the public library. Fashionable cemetery, Putney Vale.

PUTTENHAM Hertfordshire SP8814
Village off B485, 3 miles (5km) NW of Tring
The most westerly village in the county. Small church in pleasant countryside, traces of deserted medieval settlement.

PUTTENHAM Surrey SU9347
Village off A31, 4 miles (6km) SW of Guildford
Attractive little village strung along Harroway (Pilgrims' Way) in lee of Hog's Back. Puttenham Heath, with superb views southward, is a favoured haunt of artists.

PUXTON Avon ST4063
Village off A370, 2 miles (3km) W of Congresbury
The village has an atmospheric church with a leaning tower and, inside, old fittings including box pews and benches.

PWLLHELI Gwynedd SH3735
Town on A497, 8 miles (13km) W of Criccieth
Main town and modest resort on southern shores of Lleyn peninsula. Long beach with miles of spacious sands, harbour. Shopping is focused around Y Maes (The Square), which holds an open-air market each

Wednesday. To the northeast is Butlin's Starcoast World, a big holiday and entertainment centre with many rides. Also in the same direction is the medieval house of Pennarth Fawr (Cadw).

PYE GREEN Staffordshire SJ9814
Village off A34, on N edge of Hednesford
Post office telecommunications tower - concrete pillar surmounted by antennae resembling abstract sculpture – is conspicuous landmark on Cannock Chase.

PYECOMBE West Sussex TQ2812
Village on A23, 6 miles (10km) N of Brighton
Ancient place on a South Downs hillside, in the fork of two main roads, with a small, flint downland church. Once the centre of crook-making for Sussex shepherds.

PYRFORD Surrey TQ0458
Hamlet on B367, 2 miles (3km) E of Woking
A huge old yew tree by a Norman church on a knoll above the River Wey dominates this little red-brick hamlet. View of Newark Priory ruins by river.

PYTCHLEY Northamptonshire SP8574
Village off A509, 3 miles (5km) S of Kettering
Late 16th-century hall, formerly headquarters of the Pytchley Hunt, was demolished in 1824, but 17th-century manor house and Norman and later church remain.

Village cross at Quainton.

Q

QUADRING Lincolnshire TF2233
Village on A152, 7 miles (11km) N of Spalding
Fenland village, pronounced 'Kwaydring', with grand, mainly 15th-century church standing well apart with impressive clerestory and a tapering tower and spire.

QUAINTON Buckinghamshire SP7420
Village off A41, 6 miles (10km) NW of Aylesbury
This Aylesbury commuting village is high up, with sweeping views. The remains of a village cross stand on the green with old houses and the 90ft (27m) tower of an 1830s brick windmill (limited opening) driven by steam. The church is known for its 17th- and 18th-century monuments. At Quainton Road station, Buckinghamshire Railway Centre has a large steam collection with steam rides and a miniature railway.

QUAKING HOUSES Durham NZ1850
Hamlet off A693, 2 miles (3km) S of Stanley
Formerly called Old South Moor, the village was renamed after nearby Quaking Hill when the coal mines were opened.

QUANTOCK HILLS Somerset
Hill range between A39 and A358, NW of Taunton
Running 12 miles (19km) from near Taunton to the Bristol Channel, with open rolling heather or bracken-covered tops and wooded combes on the slopes. Popular for walking. Lanes are narrow and deep, and there are many archaeological remains on the higher parts including Bronze Age barrows and Iron Age hillfort. Many beech woods. Villages cluster at the foot of the hills, or in little sheltered combes. Wordsworth and Coleridge were among the admirers of this classically English landscape, and lived here for a brief period.

QUARLEY Hampshire SU2743
Village off A303, 6 miles (10km) W of Andover
Scattered and rural, with thatched cottages and brick houses. Simple church, partly 11th century with a sophisticated east window of 1723.

QUARNDON Derbyshire SK3341
Village off A52, 3 miles (5km) N of Derby
Close to the edge of Derby. There were unsuccessful plans to establish the village as a spa; a chalybeate well-house remains.

QUARR HILL Isle of Wight SZ5792
Hamlet off A3054, 1 mile (2km) W of Ryde
A few remains of the medieval abbey, including a big barn, and extraordinary early 20th-century brick buildings of the new Quarr Abbey. The church is especially good.

QUATFORD Shropshire SO7390
Village on A442, 2 miles (3km) SE of Bridgnorth
Ancient crossing-point on River Severn still guarded by castle motte. Church stands on high sandstone bluff, with pub and cottages below.

QUATT Shropshire SO7588
Village on A442, 4 miles (6km) SE of Bridgnorth
Rewarding church dominates village outside gates of Dudmaston Hall (National Trust). Good furniture, 17th-century flower paintings and modern pictures.

QUEBEC Durham NZ1843
Village off B6301, 3 miles (5km) S of Lanchester
Small former colliery village, possibly named to commemorate the taking of Quebec in Canada by General Wolfe in 1759.

QUEEN CAMEL Somerset ST5924
Village on A359, 1 mile (2km) SW of Sparkford
Handsome stone village. The 14th-century church has a luxuriant wooden screen and pulpit, both 15th century. The name means 'bare ridge of hills', not the animal.

QUEEN CHARLTON Avon ST6367
Hamlet off A37, 2 miles (3km) SW of Keynsham
Still tucked away and rural, despite the proximity of Keynsham. Norman church tower.

QUEEN ELIZABETH COUNTRY PARK Hampshire SU7118
Scenic area off A3, S of Petersfield
Beech woods lower down, and the high downland of Butser Hill with wide views. Butser Ancient Farm is a reconstructed Iron Age farm.

QUEEN ELIZABETH FOREST PARK Central
Scenic area between Loch Lomond and Aberfoyle
This large and beautiful 75,000 acre (30,375ha) upland area stretching from east Loch Lomondside to the heart of the Trossachs offers woodland walks, cycle routes, riding, fishing and an informative visitors' centre. The park includes part of the West Highland Way long-distance footpath. Good variety of wildlife habitats, including woods with red and roe deer and wild goats.

QUEENBOROUGH Kent TQ9172
Village off A249, 2 miles (3km) S of Sheerness
Industrial place on the Isle of Sheppey, once an important wool port with a castle (1361–77). High Street ends at the water's edge and the Old Guildhall (1793) recalls past glory.

QUEENHILL Hereford and Worcester SO8636
Hamlet off B4211, 3 miles (5km) NW of Tewkesbury
Overshadowed by the M5, the tiny community with its medieval church stands at the gate of Pull Court (Bredon School).

QUEENSBURY West Yorkshire SE1130
Town on A647, 3 miles (5km) N of Halifax
Developed in the 19th century as a textile community. The Albert Memorial Fountain dominates the centre of the town.

QUEENSFERRY Clwyd SJ3168
Town off A55, 6 miles (10km) W of Chester
Bridges have long since replaced the ferries over the River Dee. Town and surrounds mainly industrial. Deeside leisure centre a major attraction.

QUENDON Essex TL5130
Village on B1383, 6 miles (10km) N of Bishop's Stortford
Pretty, picturesque and pricey, with grand mansions and a small and attractive church. Village well has unusual oak shelter.

QUENIBOROUGH Leicestershire SK6412
Village off A607, 6 miles (10km) NE of Leicester
Cruck cottage, 17th- and 18th-century houses near St Mary's Church with fine crocketed spire. Old hall of 1670s, hall of about 1830 and early 20th century.

QUENINGTON Gloucestershire SP1404
Village off A417, 2 miles (3km) N of Fairford
A pretty village above the River Coln with superb Norman carving in its church and 13th-century gatehouse of Quenington Court.

QUERNMORE Lancashire SD5160
Village off A6, 3 miles (5km) E of Lancaster
An agricultural village. The east window of St Paul's Church was rescued from a wreck lost in fog on a river in France.

QUETHIOCK Cornwall SX3164
Village off A390, 4 miles (6km) E of Liskeard
Remote parish with steep, high-hedged lanes, many streams and stone and slate cottages scattered about.

QUIDENHAM Norfolk TM0287
Hamlet off A11, 5 miles (8km) S of Attleborough
Elizabethan Quidenham Hall, remodelled in the 18th century, is now a children's hospice. St Andrew's Church has a Saxon tower and a 1639 poorbox.

QUINTON Northamptonshire SP7754
Village off A508, 4 miles (6km) S of Northampton
Secluded small village with remains of a moat, probably

for a medieval manor house. Late Norman church with 13th-century tower, remodelled in 1801.

QUINTON West Midlands SO9984
Village on A458, on E outskirts of Halesowen
Open Worcestershire countryside lies to the south, but the M5, thunderous dual carriageways and housing estates combine to eradicate any remaining village atmosphere.

QUINTRELL DOWNS Cornwall SW8460
Hamlet on A392, 3 miles (5km) SE of Newquay
A little hamlet of cob cottages on a crossroads, grown since the 1940s into a sizeable village.

QUIRAING, THE Highland (Skye) NG4571
Scenic feature off A855, SW of Flodigarry
Unusual basalt pinnacles and pillars forming part of the Trotternish ridge above Staffin Bay and surrounded by some of Skye's finest scenery.

QUORNDON (QUORN) Leicestershire SK5616
Village off A6, 3 miles (5km) SE of Loughborough
Large Charnwood Forest village. Quorn Hall was home of Hugo Meynell, 'Father of English fox hunting', from 1753–1800, and he added stables and kennels for the Quorn Hunt. Eighteenth-century Bulls Head hotel, 14th- and 15th-century St Bartholomew's Church, with some Norman features, made of local Mountsorrel granite, shared by Anglicans and Methodists. Baptist chapel.

RAASAY Highland NG5640
Island E of Skye
Rugged island off the coast of Skye, the site of an iron-ore mine in the 1910s. There are two tiny villages, excellent walking and outdoor activities at the Raasay outdoor centre.

RADCLIFFE Greater Manchester SD7807
Town on A6053, 2 miles (3km) SW of Bury
Taking its name from the red cliffs on the River Irwell, the canal has been much restored and now provides pleasant walks.

RADCLIFFE ON TRENT Nottinghamshire SK6439
Town on A52, 5 miles (8km) E of Nottingham
Substantial settlement on River Trent, dating from Roman river crossing and Saxon manor. Grown out of estate village of Holme Pierrepont (see).

RADCOT Oxfordshire SU2899
Village on A4095, 3 miles (5km) N of Faringdon
The three-arched bridge of 14th-century origin is said to be the oldest on the River Thames – a claim disputed by Newbridge (see).

RADFORD SEMELE Warwickshire SP3464
Village on A425, 2 miles (3km) E of Leamington
Some picturesque old cottages survive in this residential outpost of Leamington Spa. Church stands aloof beside River Leam.

RADLETT Hertfordshire TQ1600
Town on A5183, 5 miles (8km) S of St Albans
On Watling Street, which is here a broad main shopping avenue. Cat and Fiddle pub uses cat theme and variations.

RADLEY Oxfordshire SU5199
Village off A4183, 2 miles (3km) NE of Abingdon
The church is full of interest, and its congregation maintain the Easter custom of joining hands to encircle it. Radley College is a noted public school.

RADSTOCK Avon ST6854
Town on A367, 8 miles (13km) SW of Bath
Hilly little coal-mining town, very industrial for the Avon countryside. Radstock, Midsomer Norton and District Museum in converted 18th-century barn.

RADWELL Hertfordshire TL2335
Village off A507, 2 miles (3km) NW of Baldock
On the River Ivel, with a millpond and pleasant walks. Touching church monument to Mary Plomer, who died at 30 bearing her eleventh child.

RADWINTER Essex TL6037
Village on B1054, 4 miles (6km) E of Saffron Walden
On the River Pant, with many dependent hamlets. Much attractive High Victorian architecture by Eden Nesfield includes flint-and-tile church.

A view of the southern end of the island of Raasay.

RAGLAN Gwent SO4107
Village off A40, 7 miles (11km) SW of Monmouth
The dual carriageway of A40 separates Raglan from its famous castle. Pretty village with shops and inns is to the south of the road, the castle (Cadw) to the north. Raglan Castle regarded as the last of a breed, built in more peaceful late medieval times when decorative considerations could be indulged. The great tower is its most impressive feature.

RAINFORD Merseyside SD4700
Town off A570, 4 miles (6km) NW of St Helens
The town was the leading centre for the manufacture of clay tobacco pipes for more than 200 years.

RAINHAM Greater London TQ5282
Town in borough of Havering
Norman parish church. Rainham Hall (National Trust, open by appointment) is an 18th-century house with gardens. The future of Rainham Marshes, an extensive open area, is uncertain.

RAINHILL Merseyside SJ4991
Town on A57, 3 miles (5km) SW of St Helens
A pleasant village of red sandstone buildings, Rainhill was the location for the famous locomotive trials in 1829, where George Stephenson's *Rocket* was declared the winner.

RAINOW Cheshire SJ9475
Village on B5470, 3 miles (5km) NE of Macclesfield
Village in the hills, on the border of the Peak District National Park and close to Kerridge Ridge. Stone is still quarried locally.

RAKE West Sussex SU8027
Village on B2070, 3 miles (5km) SW of Liphook
Pleasant little village on a hillcrest in northwestern corner of Sussex, with its wide common across the border in Hampshire.

RAME Cornwall SX4249
Village off B3247, 2 miles (3km) SE of Millbrook
Tiny village on Rame Head. The Head has a splendid wide view down the Cornish coast to the Lizard (see), 50 miles (80km) away. Eddystone Lighthouse is in the English Channel, 9 miles (14km) south. Little medieval chapel on the Head.

RAMPISHAM Dorset ST5602
Village off A356, 4 miles (6km) NW of Maiden Newton
Small, secluded and rambling village with thatched cottages and woods.

RAMPSIDE Cumbria SD2366
Village off A5087, 3 miles (5km) SE of Barrow-in-Furness
An ancient village on the mainland at one end of the causeway to Roa Island. The island is the home of a collection of cottages and the remains of a villa. Foulney Island (not a true island) is a good place from which to observe seabirds.

RAMPTON Cambridgeshire TL4267
Village off B1050, 6 miles (10km) N of Cambridge
Graceful trees fringe the village green, while to the east is a 12th-century fort. A gabled manor house and medieval church complete the picture.

RAMPTON Nottinghamshire SK7978
Village off A57, 6 miles (10km) E of Retford
Medieval church with Tudor brick gateway (and another 19th-century copy gateway, of demolished manor house. Sundown Kiddies Adventureland, with farm animals. Rampton Mental Hospital, 1920s.

RAMSBOTTOM Greater Manchester SD7916
Town on A676, 4 miles (6km) N of Bury
A pretty, unspoilt town lying at the opening of the Rossendale valley. Popular Sunday market. On the East Lancashire Railway, serviced by steam trains.

RAMSBURY Wiltshire SU2771
Village off B4192, 6 miles (10km) E of Marlborough
Small-scale Georgian brick and earlier timber-framed thatched cottages, a Victorian school and an Edwardian pub make a classic village High Street. Interesting church, mostly 15th century, with two intricately carved fragments of 9th-century crosses. Late medieval and 18th-century monuments.

RAMSDEN BELLHOUSE Essex TQ7194
Village off A129, 2 miles (3km) W of Wickford
Pleasant suburban-style development, mainly since 1910. Attractive church. Name comes from medieval lord of the manor, Richard de Belhus.

RAMSEY Cambridgeshire TL2885
Small town on B1040, 10 miles (16km) SE of Peterborough
Once an important town surrounding its medieval abbey, Ramsey declined after the Dissolution, the plague, and finally a series of fires. The main street, the Great Whyte, is exceptionally wide because a stream once ran down it. Remains of the abbey (National Trust) can still be visited, although much of Ramsey town itself is 19th century. The church has William Morris glass.

RAMSEY Isle of Man SC4594
Town on A18, 12 miles (19km) NE of Douglas
Once famous for its ship-building industry the Ramsey shipyard built many vessels, the best known being the *Star of India*, now an attraction in San Diego, USA. The Manx Electric Railway terminus is in the centre of the town, and uses original tramcars, two of which are the oldest working examples in the world.

RAMSEY ISLAND Dyfed SM7023
Island off St David's Head
Beautiful little island accessible by boat from St Justinian's, near St David's. Prolific wildlife, with seals on the rocks.

RAMSGATE Kent TR3865
Town on A253, 15 miles (24km) NE of Canterbury
A seaside resort, fishing village and cross-Channel terminal, Ramsgate has been a harbour with an eye on the

Continent since Roman times. The little circular harbour, built out from the cliffed eastern coast of Thanet, is surrounded by pleasant Georgian terraces, with Victorian development along the front and the Royal Esplanade with its amusement parks and pavilion. Today commercial vessels, the fishing fleet and pleasure craft patronise the harbour near the 500-berth marina. The cross-Channel ferry terminal (1981) is to the south. Every August Ramsgate holds a harbour Heritage Festival.

Most of Ramsgate's worthwhile architecture went up between 1810 and 1850: crescents, terraces and one or two squares, all in softly coloured brick with plenty of cast-iron balconies – a Ramsgate speciality. The harbour became 'royal' in 1827 when George IV stayed there, the same year St George's, the parish church, was built with its 137ft (52m) high tower. Ramsgate is dominated by St Augustine's Church and Abbey (Roman Catholic), Pugin's masterpiece of 1850, externally bleak, internally magnificent. On the hilltop near by is a model village in Tudor style – a 1953 dream of idyllic England.

RAMSHORN Staffordshire SK0845
Village off B5417, 5 miles (8km) E of Cheadle
Pronounced 'Ramser', the small estate village straddles summit of Weaver Hill. Wootton Lodge (not open) of about 1600 is attributed to Robert Smythson.

RANMORE COMMON Surrey TQ1451
Scenic area off A25, 2 miles (3km) NW of Dorking
The wooded southern slopes of the North Downs (National Trust) are famed for bluebells in spring. An imposing cobblestone church (1859) is set on the common, which is crossed by the North Downs Way.

RANNOCH MOOR Strathclyde
Scenic area off A82, SE of Glencoe
Huge upland area of bog, rock and moorland between Glencoe, Loch Rannoch and the Bridge of Orchy. Considered the largest uninhabited wilderness in Britain.

RANTON Staffordshire SJ8524
Village off B5405, 4 miles (6km) W of Stafford
Pleasant agricultural settlement with splendid timber-framed Vicarage farmhouse and ruins of medieval Ranton Abbey.

RANWORTH Norfolk TG3514
Village off B1140, 4 miles (6km) NW of Acle
Ranworth is a beautiful little village set among the Ranworth Marshes. Ranworth (or Malthouse) Broad is lined with staithes (or quays) to which barley was brought for malting. Visitors climbing the towers of St Helen's Church will be rewarded with views across the marshes and five Broads. The Broadlands Conservation Centre is based here.

RASKELF North Yorkshire SE4971
Village off A19, 3 miles (5km) NW of Easingwold
A linear village with a long straight main street. St Mary's Church has a wooden tower believed to be one of the few remaining in Britain.

RATBY Leicestershire SK5105
Village off A50, 5 miles (8km) W of Leicester
On edge of Charnwood Forest. Once a framework knitting village,where two mid-19th-century workshops survive.

RATCLIFFE ON SOAR Nottinghamshire SK4928
Village on A453, 6 miles (10km) NW of Loughborough
Dominated by eight cooling towers of 1967 power station beside River Soar, on Leicestershire border. Church has fine Tudor and Stuart monuments.

RATCLIFFE ON THE WREAKE Leicestershire SK6314
Village off A46, 7 miles (11km) N of Leicester
Attractive village between River Wreake and Fosse Way. Georgian hall. Church with crocketed spire. Roman Catholic Ratcliffe College (1840s) by Pugin.

RATHO Lothian NT1370
Village off B7030, 8 miles (13km) W of Edinburgh
Village and canal-boating centre on Forth–Clyde Canal. Restored church dates from 12th century.

RATTERY Devon SX7461
Village off A385, 4 miles (6km) W of Totnes
Rolling hills. The Church House inn is a late medieval church house, where parish ales were held.

RATTLESDEN Suffolk TL9758
Village off A14 (A45), 5 miles (8km) W of Stowmarket
A scattered village with four main hamlets in pleasant Ratt Valley, surrounded by acres of huge fields. A pair of whalebones stands near the bridge.

RATTRAY HEAD Grampian NK1057
Headland off A952, 7 miles (11km) N of Peterhead
This is the sandy site of old Rattray, deserted in the 18th century when dunes moved in storms. The Loch of Strathbeg bird reserve lies on a main flight path.

RAUNDS Northamptonshire SP9972
Small town off A45 (A605), 6 miles (10km) NE of Wellingborough
Nene Valley footwear town. Medieval church with 15th-century wall-paintings. Major archaeological site, remains of Roman villa, Saxon church and medieval manor.

RAVENFIELD South Yorkshire SK4895
Village off A630, 4 miles (6km) NE of Rotherham
Attractive village in agricultural land. Ravenfield Park is a remnant of the private deer park of the ancient family of Westby.

RAVENGLASS Cumbria SD0896
Village on A595, 4 miles (6km) SE of Seascale
The village was a Roman naval base, and acentre for pearl-fishing and smuggling until the harbour silted up. The narrow-gauge Ravenglass and Eskdale Railway is run for pleasure by enthusiasts. Muncaster Castle has been home to the Penningtons since the 1200s.

RAVENINGHAM Norfolk TM3996
Village off B1140, 4 miles (6km) NW of Beccles
The peaceful village of Raveningham has an elegant

Georgian hall with a notable collection of paintings by Turner, Constable, Gainsborough and Cotman.

RAVENSCAR North Yorkshire NZ9801
Village off A171, 3 miles (5km) SE of Robin Hood's Bay
The village is situated on the east coast and there are superb views across Robin Hood's Bay. George III was a frequent visitor.

RAVENSTONE Buckinghamshire SP8451
Village off A509, 3 miles (5km) W of Olney
Very attractive, correspondingly expensive village in local stone and thatch. Tremendous 17th-century four-poster Finch tomb in church.

RAVENSTONE Leicestershire SK4013
Village off A447, 2 miles (3km) W of Coalville
Georgian brick hall. Large group of almshouses founded in 1711 for 30 women.

RAVENSTONEDALE Cumbria NY7203
Village off A685, 4 miles (6km) SW of Kirkby Stephen
Surrounded by hills, the houses and cottages are mostly built of local limestone. Ruins of a small monastery were excavated in the churchyard.

RAVENSWORTH North Yorkshire NZ1308
Village off A66, 5 miles (8km) NW of Richmond
The village lies in the forgotten dale of Holmedale and has the remains of a 14th-century castle.

RAWMARSH South Yorkshire SK4396
Town on A683, 2 miles (3km) N of Rotherham
Predominantly a residential area. The original 19th-century centre now lies at the southern end as modern development has moved the centre further north.

RAWTENSTALL Lancashire SD8123
Town on A6826, 6 miles (10km) S of Burnley
The town developed as an important woollen centre with the process being undertaken by handworkers using water power until the 19th century. Then the cotton trade began to take over. Fallbarn House is a good example of a 'loomshop', halfway between the handloom weavers' cottages and the mill. Lower Mill, opened in 1840, is now a ruin.

RAYLEIGH Essex TQ8090
Town on A1015, 6 miles (10km) NW of Southend-on-Sea
The old market town expanded in the 1930s and is now a shopping centre and outlier of the Southend conurbation. The tower and sails of the restored windmill (limited opening) with its bygones collection strike a romantic note near the surviving 50ft (15m) mound of the Norman castle (National Trust). Impressive church, lively High Street.

RAYNE Essex TL7222
Village off A120, 2 miles (3km) W of Braintree
Quiet place to which people once went to pray to miraculous image of Virgin in church. Tudor and later houses.

REACH Cambridgeshire TL5666
Village off B1102, 5 miles (8km) W of Newmarket
Reach grew up where the Saxon earthwork Devil's Dyke met Reach Lode. Reach Fair has been held on May Day since before 1201.

READ Lancashire SD7634
Village on A671, 2 miles (3km) W of Padiham
In April 1643 Read saw the downfall of the Royalist cause in Lancashire. Also home of Robert Nowell, a magistrate involved in the Pendle Witches trials.

READING Berkshire SU7173
Town off M4, 36 miles (58km) W of London
Reading has a long history, being a natural junction of rivers (the Kennet and the Thames) and roads, but little remains from earlier periods. The early medieval abbey was one of the wealthiest in the country, but only the inner gatehouse (drastically restored) and some scenic ruins survive. One older area exists around Castle Street with a fine Grecian church, a chequered medieval one and Georgian houses .

The earliest manufacturing was cloth in medieval times, and in the 19th century Reading became a famous factory town, especially for biscuits produced by Huntley and Palmer, who started in 1826 and by 1900 employed 5,000 people. Gigantic Victorian municipal buildings and miles of terraced houses with several Victorian churches bear witness to the growth of the town, while huge modern office blocks attest to current needs. Reading is the main regional shopping centre.

Blake's Lock Museum, in 19th-century industrial buildings by the river, illustrates 19th-century manufacturing and the local waterways. The Museum of Reading has fine new displays on the abbey and the town, and an 1880s life-size reproduction of the Bayeux Tapestry. There is good river scenery, as well as the Kennet and Avon Canal.

REARSBY Leicestershire SK6514
Village on A607, 7 miles (11km) SW of Melton Mowbray
Wreake Valley village, with medieval packhorse bridge; Rearsby Old Hall (1661); timber-framed The Old House, dated 1610, 1613. Medieval churchwas restored in the 19th century.

REAY Highland NC9664
Village on A836, 10 miles (16km) W of Thurso
A solid, stone-built village on the north coast with a fine 18th-century church and Pictish cross-slab at Crosskirk. Fine local examples of Caithness flagstone hedges.

RECULVER Kent TR2269
Village off A299, 3 miles (5km) E of Herne Bay
The twin 12th-century towers ('The Sisters') of the ruined church are built within a Roman fort (both English Heritage) on the north Kent coast and dominate the headland in Reculver Country Park, 91 acres (37ha) of grassy clifftop, seashore and woodland, renowned for bird-watching. The Roman fort was built about AD270 as defence against the Saxons. Two-thirds of the site has since been eroded by the sea. A church

and monastery were built within the Roman walls in AD670. The twin towers were retained in 1820s as a navigational aid.

REDBOURN Hertfordshire TL1012

Town off A5183, 4 miles (6km) NW of St Albans

A former coaching town on Watling Street. Norman church on the common, where cricket has been played since 1666. Handsome Georgian buildings in the town include the Priory (not open), on the site of a medieval priory, where the relics of Saint Amphibalus (see St Albans) were supposedly found. Riverside walk by the Ver down to St Albans (see).

REDBOURNE Humberside SK9799

Village off A15, 5 miles (8km) SW of Brigg

The main road runs alongside the traditional village green and among the trees of this conservation area. The Church of St Andrew contains an impressive stained-glass window of Sodom and Gomorrah.

REDCAR Cleveland NZ6025

Town on A1085, 8 miles (13km) NE of Middlesbrough

Redcar grew rapidly with the advance of railways. Today massive iron and steel complexes with huge blast furnaces dominate the town. Uniquely, there is a race-course almost in the town centre and horses can often be seen exercising on the sandy beaches. Lifeboat Museum contains the Zetland, the world's oldest surviving lifeboat.

REDDITCH Hereford and Worcester SP0467

Town on A441, 12 miles (19km) S of Birmingham

Former needle-making community now expanded into new town. Needle Museum recalls the past, and Arrow Lake Country Park is an impressive town-centre amenity.

REDE, RIVER Northumberland

River, runs from near Carter Bar to the North Tyne

The river follows the line of the A68 for much of its length. It flows through Catcleugh Reservoir and Redesdale Forest, part of the Border Forest Park.

REDENHALL Norfolk TM2684

Village on A143, 1 mile (2km) NE of Harleston

Overlooking the verdant River Waveney Valley is Redenhall, a village especially noted for its elegant late medieval church tower.

The derelict engine house of a former tin mine near Redruth.

REDGRAVE Suffolk TM0477
Village on B1113, 5 miles (8km) W of Diss
Source of the Little Ouse and Waveney rivers which form the Suffolk/Norfolk border. Redgrave is on the edge of Redgrave and Lopham Fens.

REDHILL Surrey TQ2750
Town on A25, immediately E of Reigate
Victorian and 20th-century housing, shopping precinct, offices and light industry sprawling out from the railway station and important crossroads. Airport and open commons.

REDLYNCH Wiltshire SU2021
Village on B3080, 7 miles (11km) SE of Salisbury
On the edge of the New Forest, with much recent development. Newhouse, to the east, is of 1619, with Georgian wings (limited opening).

REDMARLEY D'ABITOT Gloucestershire SO7531
Village off A417, 5 miles (8km) SE of Ledbury
The 16th-century Church House and timber-framed brick cottage distinguish this village in rolling countryside south of Malvern Hills.

REDMARSHALL Cleveland NZ3821
Village off A177, 4 miles (6km) W of Stockton-on-Tees
Small village now favoured by commuters. Norman church with 13th- and 15th-century additions, and 18th-century Ship inn.

REDMIRE North Yorkshire SE0491
Village off A684, 4 miles (6km) W of Leyburn
Over the years the village is thought to have occupied four different sites. The Church of St Mary was built in 1150.

REDNAL West Midlands SP0076
District of SW Birmingham
Dominated by Longbridge car factory, residents of Rednal's housing estates are fortunate to have Lickey Hills and Country Park within easy reach.

REDRUTH Cornwall SW6941
Town on A393, 8 miles (13km) W of Truro
A market town, now continuous with Camborne (see), whose mining history is reflected in terraces of workers' housing and the 1750s church with memorials to mining engineers. Fine views from the 1836 Basset monument on Carn Brae, to the southwest, with a Stone Age enclosure, the remains of a large Iron Age hillfort and a medieval hunting lodge.

REED Hertfordshire TL3636
Village on A10, 3 miles (5km) S of Royston
Unusual grid pattern of streets, possibly Roman in origin, close to Ermine Street. Church partly Saxon.

REEDHAM Norfolk TG4201
Village off B1140, 6 miles (10km) S of Acle
A chain ferry still operates in Reedham, an attractive village that stretches along the banks of the broad River Yare. Reedham has a taxidermist's workshop.

REEPHAM Norfolk TG1022
Village on B1145, 6 miles (10km) SW of Aylsham
A spacious market square is lined by mellow Georgian buildings. Gently undulating countryside surrounds it, and there are two churches in one churchyard (once there were three).

REETH North Yorkshire SE0399
Village on B6270, 9 miles (14km) W of Richmond
The largest village in Swaledale, Reeth lies near the confluence of the rivers Swale and Arkle, surrounded by the Pennine range. The mining of lead, started by the Romans, formed the staple industry for many years. Following its decline the emphasis fell on agriculture. A Folk Museum depicts life and traditions in Swaledale.

REIGATE Surrey TQ2550
Town on A217, 9 miles (14km) N of Crawley
Attractive old market town on Surrey Hills, developed around a Norman castle, today marked by an 18th-century gatehouse. The oldest houses are at the western end of the High Street, and along Upper West Street and Slipshoe Street. The priory was founded in the 13th century. This was once an important coaching town: the London–Brighton road tunnel was cut in 1824 through Castle Hill. The nearby unspoilt tracts of Reigate Common and Reigate Heath have a unique windmill containing a church.

REIGHTON North Yorkshire TA1375
Village on A165, 4 miles (6km) S of Filey
Tiny village of terraced houses and cottages, with large caravan park at Reighton Sands. Popular sandy beach, at the south end of Filey Bay.

REMENHAM Berkshire SU7784
Village off A423, 1 mile (2km) NE of Henley-on-Thames
Scattered village on the River Thames. To the north is Temple Island, with a pretty little 18th-century building. This is the start of the Henley Regatta races.

RENDCOMB Gloucestershire SP0209
Village off A435, 5 miles (8km) N of Cirencester
Estate village for Rendcomb Court has magnificent 'wool church' with 16th-century Crucifixion sculpture, Tudor chancel screen, medieval glass and exceptional Norman font.

RENDLESHAM Suffolk TM3353
Village on A1152, 3 miles (5km) SE of Wickham Market
The peace of this beautiful Deben Valley village is often shattered by the closeness of the nearby Brentwaters American airbase.

RENFREW Strathclyde NS5067
Town off M8, 5 miles (8km) W of Glasgow
Renfrew became a royal burgh in 1396 and by 1614 was the principal port on the River Clyde. The first shipbuilding yard was established in 1844 and some notable public buildings were erected during the following years of prosperity, including the town hall, with its massive square tower, built in 1871.

RENHOLD Bedfordshire TL0952
Village off A428, 4 miles (6km) NE of Bedford
A trimly kept, strung-out aggregation of 'ends', or hamlets, down to the Great Ouse. Church with small spire, brasses and memorial tablets.

RENISHAW Derbyshire SK4477
see Eckington

RENTON Strathclyde NS3877
Town on A82, 2 miles (3km) N of Dumbarton
Town in the Vale of Leven which developed in the 18th century. Birthplace of writer Tobias Smollett (1721–71); there is a monument in his memory.

REPTON Derbyshire SK3026
Small town on B5008, 5 miles (8km) NE of Burton upon Trent
Close to the River Trent. Important 7th-century monastic site and burial place of three Mercian kings. Chancel, crypt and other parts of the Saxon church are incorporated into the medieval church with a 14th-century tower and spire, 15th-century clerestory and timber roof. Parts of an Augustinian priory, founded in the 1170s, are incorporated into the buildings of Repton public school, founded in 1557.

REST AND BE THANKFUL Strathclyde NN2207
Mountain pass on A83, 7 miles (11km) NW of Arrochar
Pass between Loch Long and Loch Fyne; summit at 860ft (262m). It follows an old military road and is named after an inscription on a stone at the summit.

RETFORD, EAST AND WEST Nottinghamshire SK7081
Town on A620, 27 miles (43km) NE of Nottingham
Market town of East Retford owes prosperity to diversion of Great North road through in 1766, and Chesterfield Canal opening 1777. Several Georgian buildings, 1866 town hall beside market place, cruciform St Swithun's Church, museum in 18th-century Amcott House. Separated by River Idle from village of West Retford, where church has fine crocketed broach spire.

RETTENDON Essex TQ7698
Village off A130, 3 miles (5km) NE of Wickford
Royal Horticultural Society's garden is a star attraction. Church has 15th-century priest's house as vestry, and an 18th-century monument 30ft (9m) high.

REVESBY Lincolnshire TF2961
Village on A155, 6 miles (10km) SE of Horncastle
Revesby Abbey is an early Victorian house near the site of a 12th-century Cistercian abbey. On parkland site of home of 18th-century naturalist Sir Joseph Banks, who brought back numerous species from voyages with Captain Cook to develop Kew Gardens, and helped direct fen drainage. Attractive 1850s estate village around green, with former school, Joseph Banks' almshouses (rebuilt 1862) and church, built in 1891.

REWE Devon SX9499
Village on A396, 5 miles (8km) NE of Exeter
Main-road village, with many late 19th-century estate cottages. Church has fine late medieval screen and pulpit, painted in 1870s.

REYNOLDSTON West Glamorgan SS4889
Village off A4118, 11 miles (18km) W of Swansea
Gower village on foot of Cefn Bryn ridge. Road to the northeast climbs over high ground with wonderful views. Prehistoric megalith, Arthur's Stone, on common.

RHANDIRMWYN Dyfed SN7843
Village off A483, 6 miles (10km) N of Llandovery
Pretty village in lovely setting in broad vale of upper Towy Valley. Former lead-mining community. RSPB reserve at Dinas Hill.

Arthur's Stone at Reynoldstone.

RHAYADER (RHAEADR) Powys SN9768
Small town on A470, 11 miles (18km) N of Builth Wells
The clock tower at narrow crossroads in town centre is a familiar traffic hazard for motorists on A470 north–south trunk route. Venue of one of central Wales's busiest livestock markets (Wednesday) with good choice of old inns. Popular fishing, walking, pony trekking and mountain biking centre at gateway to Elan Valley lakelands. Small museum, Welsh Royal Crystal glass factory, farm trail.

RHINNS OF GALLOWAY Dumfries and Galloway NX0552
Peninsula on SW coast of Scotland
This double-headed peninsula runs north to south with Scotland's most southerly mainland point at Mull of Galloway, where there is a RSPB reserve. The hilly countryside features small villages and pastureland; Stranraer and Portpatrick are the main towns. The rugged and windswept coast has good walking and excellent views south to Cumbria and Ireland.

RHONDDA Mid Glamorgan SS9795
Area on A4058/A4233, NW of Pontypridd
Rhondda is a name synonymous with coal-mining. Takes its name from two valleys, the Rhondda Fawr (big) and the Rhondda Fach (little) which meet at Porth (see). Close-knit terraced housing in places like Treorchy, Treherbert and Tylorstown still define character of area, although the mines have disappeared. Unexpectedly beautiful and unspoilt mountains above. Memories of bygone times at Rhondda Heritage Park near Porth.

RHOSLLANERCHRUGROG Clwyd SJ2946
Town off A483, 5 miles (8km) SW of Wrexham
Small town of typical industrial appearance with terraces of local red brick. Stands at foothills of wild Ruabon Mountain and World's End.

RHOSNEIGR Gwynedd (Anglesey) SH3173
Village on A4080, 4 miles (6km) NW of Aberffraw
Attractive, low-key resort on gently-shelving shoreline with twin beaches separated by headland. Lake of Llyn Maelog just inland.

RHOSSILI West Glamorgan SS4188
Village on B4247, 5 miles (8km) SW of Knelston
Small village, perched spectacularly on clifftop in far west of Gower. Walk to narrow promontory of Worms Head (see) possible at low tide. Three mile (5km) west-facing beach popular with surfers. Memorial in church to villager who perished on Scott's doomed South Pole expedition of 1912. Rhossili Down to the north rises to 633ft (193m), the highest point on Gower.

RHU Strathclyde NS2684
Village on A814, 2 miles (3km) NW of Helensburgh
Residential village, resort and yachting centre with marina on Gareloch. Burial place of marine engineer, Henry Bell (1767–1830); imposing statue.

RHUDDLAN Clwyd SJ0278
Town on A525, 2 miles (3km) S of Rhyl
Small town beside River Clwyd which played large role in Welsh history. Long a place of settlement because of strategic location at lowest fording point on the river. Twthill has the remains of a Norman motte and bailey, replaced in stone in 1280s when Edward I built his mighty stone castle here (Cadw). Old stone bridge over river dates from medieval times

RHUM Highland NM3798
see Rum

RHYL Clwyd SJ0081
Town on A548, 4 miles (6km) W of Prestatyn
Unpretentious 'all the fun of the fair' seaside resort with long sandy beach. Spacious seafront backed by the

Ruined castle Rhuddlan.

expected range of attractions and amenities – funfair, amusements, lake, arcades, guest houses. Rhyl's Sun Centre is an early example of an all-weather leisure complex, now commonplace. Great views from 240ft (73m) Skytower on Promenade. Botanical Gardens.

RHYMNEY Mid Glamorgan SO1107
Town on A469, 4 miles (6km) E of Merthyr Tydfil
Old industrial town at head of iron-making and coal-mining Rhymney Valley near southern moors of Brecon Beacons. Rhymney itself was a major iron-making centre by 1820s. Butetown to the north is a superb example of a 'model' village, built by a philanthropic ironmaster at start of 19th century. Small museum. Parc Cwm Darran to the south is an attractive country park on reclaimed colliery site.

RIBBESFORD Hereford and Worcester SO7874
Hamlet off B4194, 1 mile (2km) S of Bewdley
Rudyard Kipling was married in the fascinating church where a Burne-Jones window commemorates his grandmother. Other features include rare wooden nave arcade.

RIBBLE, RIVER Lancashire
River, flows through Preston to the Irish Sea
The river landscape changes from flat, tidal marshes around the estuary through the spectacular limestone scenery of Ribblesdale to open moorland around Lancashire and Yorkshire border. At Ribblehead, a 24-arch viaduct carries the Settle–Carlisle railway across the valley. The Ribble Way middle-distance footpath runs the full 70 miles (113km) of the river from sea to source.

RIBCHESTER Lancashire SD6535
Village on B6245, 6 miles (8km) N of Blackburn
A permanent Roman fort was established here in AD79. Little of the defensive walls remains but several of the internal buildings have been excavated. The village grew from the 1750s onwards to accommodate more handloom weavers. The flax industry was replaced by cotton and related trades such as bobbin-turning. This declined by the mid-19th century.

RICHARDS CASTLE Shropshire SO4969
Village on B4361, 3 miles (5km) S of Ludlow
Disused medieval church and remains of pre-Norman castle stand together well away from featureless modern village. Replacement church by Norman Shaw to north.

RICHBOROUGH CASTLE Kent SO4969
Site off A256, 2 miles (3km) N of Sandwich
Massive walls of Roman fort (English Heritage) built on the site of an earlier Roman fortress and port, traditional landing place of the Roman army (AD43).

RICHMOND Greater London TQ1774
Town in borough of Richmond upon Thames, SW London
Little remains of the royal palace where Henry VII died in 1509, near the delightful Green, but the court's presence gave Richmond a cachet which it did not lose after the railway's arrival in 1840, when well-to-do business and professional people began to move in. Today the town is known for stylish shopping and its two theatres, the one on the Green designed by the great Edwardian theatre architect Frank Matcham.

The Parish Church of St Mary Magdalene is mainly of the 18th century. Close to the 1770s bridge over the Thames is a notable 1980s development by Quinlan Terry. The museum is in the town hall and there's a splendid view over the river from Richmond Hill with its public gardens.

Richmond Park, covering more than 2,000 acres (810ha) and London's largest royal park, was enclosed as a hunting ground by Charles II and still has its deer, along with ponds, streams, the attractive Isabella Plantation and several lodges (not open), including the 18th-century White Lodge, where Edward VIII was born and the Royal Ballet Junior School has its quarters.

RICHMOND North Yorkshire NZ1701
Town on A6108, 11 miles (18km) SW of Darlington
A pretty market town, the capital of Richmondshire, dominated by its castle and centred around its cobbled market square. Buildings such as the town hall (1756) and The King's Head hotel in the market place reflect the prosperity of the town in this period, which came from its thriving market trade, when the town served an area stretching into Lancashire. The Georgian theatre, built in 1788, is the oldest in England and as well as a programme of performances it also houses a museum with collections of playbills, painted scenery and model theatres. St Mary's Church, in existence since at least 1135, contains much medieval work.

Alan Rufus, 1st Earl of Richmond, built the original Norman castle here in 1071. The site, high up on a rocky promontory, with the River Swale passing below, was well chosen for defending the town. The castle is large in its proportions, the keep rising to 109ft (33m) in height with walls 11ft (3m) thick. The curtain walls, keep and towers are still largely intact. Castle Walk goes around the outside of the castle walls, with lovely views over the river.

RICKINGHALL, SUPERIOR AND INFERIOR Suffolk TM0475
Villages on A143, 6 miles (10km) SW of Diss
Two villages divided by the boundary between East and West Suffolk. There was a Roman settlement here, and there are many timber-framed cottages.

RICKMANSWORTH Hertfordshire TQ0694
Town off A412, 5 miles (8km) SW of Watford
Former market town, now commuter territory near the M25. Also close to the River Colne and the Grand Union Canal, with walks, bird-watching, fishing, sailing and watersports facilities. Boat trips from Batchworth Lock Centre. The immensely grand 18th-century mansion of Moor Park, with interiors by Sir James Thornhill, is open to visitors.

RIDDLESDEN West Yorkshire SE0742
Village off A650, 1 mile (2km) NE of Keighley
East Riddlesden Hall (National Trust) was built in the 1640s. The pond, called the 'Stragnum de Riddlesden', is a haven for wildlife.

RIDGE Hertfordshire TL2100

Village off B5378, 3 miles (5km) W of Potters Bar

Little place close to the M25/A1(M) intersection. Field Marshal Earl Alexander of Tunis is buried in the churchyard.

RIDGEWAY, THE Berkshire

Ancient track

This ancient trackway following the crest of the chalk downs is now a long-distance footpath, marked all the way from near Avebury in Wiltshire to the Thames Valley at Streatley, Berkshire. The route is high, with wide views and many archaeological monuments, including hillforts, barrows and the White Horse figure at Uffington.

RIDGMONT Bedfordshire SP9736

Village on A507, 3 miles (5km) NE of Woburn

Handsome 1850s church and Segenhoe Old Church, which it replaced. Rose and Crown pub with *Rupert Annual* covers.

RIEVAULX North Yorkshire SE5785

Village on B1257, 2 miles (3km) W of Helmsley

Rievaulx Abbey (English Heritage), now a ruin, was founded in 1131 by 12 French Cistercian monks. Rievaulx Terrace park (National Trust) has temples overlooking the Rye Valley.

RILLINGTON North Yorkshire SE8574

Village on A64, 5 miles (8km) E of Malton

A large village extending in four directions. Some modern housing is mixed with the older, stone-built cottages. St Andrew's church is located on higher ground.

RIMINGTON Lancashire SD8045

Village off A682, 3 miles (5km) SW of Gisburn

A rural village with a disused lead mine at the nearby hamlet of Stopper Lane. The composer Francis Duckworth lived here.

RINGMER East Sussex TQ4412

Village on B2192, 3 miles (5km) NE of Lewes

Large village strewn around a spacious green where stoolball is played in summer: a Sussex game said to have been invented by milkmaids who used their stools as bats. Village sign shows Timothy the Tortoise, who belonged to Mrs Rebecca Snooke, aunt of the famous naturalist Gilbert White, with whom Timothy lived his last years.

RINGMORE Devon SX6545

Village off B3392, 4 miles (6km) S of Modbury

Just back from the sea, with thatched cottages and a pretty little 13th-century church with steeple.

RINGSFIELD Suffolk TM4088

Village off B1062, 2 miles (3km) SW of Beccles

Set in 'pick your own' berry fields and wooded valleys, the centre of Ringsfield lies at Ringsfield Corner 1 mile (2km) from the church.

RINGSTEAD Norfolk TF7040

Village off A149, 2 miles (3km) E of Hunstanton

Ringstead Downs isan exceptionally pretty chalk valley. St Andrew's Church is early 14th century, and there are also two ruinous churches.

RINGSTEAD Northamptonshire SP9875

Village on A45 (A605), 2 miles (3km) S of Thrapston

Thirteenth-century church with tower and spire. Major archaeological site between Raunds and Stanwick (see).

RINGWAY Greater Manchester SJ8084

Village off M56, 3 miles (5km) SE of Altrincham

Once a rural village, this is the site of Manchester Airport, opened in 1938 and now one of Europe's fastest-growing airports.

RINGWOOD Hampshire SU1405

Town off A31, 10 miles (16km) NE of Bournemouth

Market town on the edge of the New Forest, rather cut about by recent roads. Much small-scale Georgian brick in the middle, and a plain chapel of 1727 with all its original fittings (now a museum). Proper market place, still with a market on Wednesdays. Picturesque Fish inn on the River Avon.

RINGWOULD Kent TR3648

Village on A258, 3 miles (5km) S of Deal

Pleasant old place with pretty cottages above the Deal to Dover road. Church perched high up looking out to sea, west tower topped with jaunty cupola.

RIPE East Sussex TQ5110

Village off A22, 5 miles (8km) W of Hailsham

Quiet little place on a plain beneath the South Downs, with a long history: it lies at the corner of a road grid laid out by the Romans.

RIPLEY Derbyshire SK3950

Town on A38, 10 miles (16km) N of Derby

Market town which expanded during the Industrial Revolution, using local iron, clay and coal deposits. Midland Railway Centre operates a steam-hauled passenger service.

RIPLEY North Yorkshire SE2860

Village on A61, 3 miles (5km) N of Harrogate

A charming estate village adjoining Ripley Castle rebuilt by Sir William Amcotts Ingilby in the style of a village he had seen during his travels in Alsace-Lorraine. Ripley Castle, which has been home of the Ingilbys for over 600 years, is now open to the public along with its gardens.

RIPLEY Surrey TQ0556

Village off A3, 4 miles (6km) SW of Cobham

Attractive village with a wide street of interesting old houses, including Talbot hotel (17th century) and Anchor inn, a 16th-century brick and timber building that could be mistaken for a row of cottages. The village green, said to be the largest in England, has recreation grounds and rough grass, and is faced by tile-hung cottages. Wey Navigation (National Trust) is on the far side of the green.

RIPON North Yorkshire SE3171

City on A61, 10 miles (16km) N of Harrogate

A cathedral city whose history dates back to AD886 when it was granted a charter by Alfred the Great, Ripon's focal point is now the large market place with its 90ft (27m) obelisk. This is surrounded by Georgian and medieval buildings including the town hall, completed in 1801 and the 14th-century half-timbered Wakeman's House. The Ripon Prison and Police Museum, built as a House of Correction in 1686, is in St Mary Gate. From the obelisk the city's official hornblower sounds the 'Setting of the Watch' every evening at 21.00 to assure everyone that they are in safekeeping for the night – a ritual maintained without fail for over 1,100 years.

Ripon Cathedral dates from 672, contains many architectural styles, in particular Gothic, from the 12th to the 16th centuries, has some of the highest vaults and yet is one of the smallest cathedrals in Britain. It has an Anglo-Saxon crypt and treasury with a large collection of silver and silvergilt ecclesiastical treasures.

Newby Hall is a superb Adam house containing Gobelins tapestries, classical sculpture, porcelain and furniture and surrounded by 40 acres (16ha) of gardens.

RIPPINGALE Lincolnshire TF0927

Village off A15, 5 miles (8km) N of Bourne

Large brick-built village between wooded countryside and Fens. Church with 15th-century tower; monuments include a 13th-century deacon holding an open book.

RIPPLE Hereford and Worcester SO8637

Village off A38, 3 miles (5km) N of Tewkesbury

Beautifully situated above the River Severn, the very attractive old village ignores nearby M50. Entertaining misericords in unexpectedly grand church.

RIPPONDEN West Yorkshire SE0319

Town on A58, 5 miles (8km) SW of Halifax

Attractive town in the Ryburn Valley, centred around its church and the bridge over the River Calder, built in 1533.

RISBY Suffolk TL7966

Village off A14 (A45), 4 miles (6km) NW of Bury St Edmunds

The 15th-century manor house is a Grade II Listed Building. The Risby Barn Antiques Centre is in a medieval tithe barn.

RISCA Gwent ST2391

Town on A467, 5 miles (8km) NW of Newport

Town at southern gateway to Welsh Valleys beneath steep, forested slopes crowned by Twmbarlwm Hill, an ancient fortified site. Spectacular views from summit.

RISE Humberside TA1542

Hamlet off B1243, 5 miles (8km) SW of Hornsea

Rise Hall, rebuilt in 1815–20, forms the centre of the village and has been occupied by nuns since 1946.

Half-timbered Wakeman's House in Ripon.

RISELEY Bedfordshire TL0462
Village off A6, 8 miles (13km) N of Bedford
Varied buildings in local brick. Enjoyable church carvings and gargoyles.

RISELEY Berkshire SU7263
Village off B3349, 6 miles (10km) S of Reading
Wellington Country Park, extending into Hampshire, has a lake, children's animal farm, model steam train and nature trails; there is also a small National Dairy Museum.

RISHANGLES Suffolk TM1668
Village on B1077, 4 miles (6km) N of Debenham
Moated farmsteads and an unusual church characterise Rishangles. The church has Norman windows and a rare 16th-century font.

RISHTON Lancashire SD7230
Town off M65, 3 miles (5km) NE of Blackburn
The village is Saxon in origin and the name means 'the fortified village or dwelling place amid the rushes'.

RISLEY Cheshire SJ6592
Town off M62, 5 miles (8km) NE of Warrington
A modern residential and industrial development with Science Park occupied by hi-tech businesses. Risley Moss is a 200 acre (81ha) nature reserve.

RIVENHALL Essex TL8217
Hamlet off A12, 2 miles (3km) N of Witham
Remarkable Saxon church on Roman villa site, remodelled in the 1830s, with beautiful medieval French stained glass and notable monuments.

RIVINGTON Lancashire SD6214
Village off A673, 2 miles (3km) N of Horwich
An historic village which was developed by William Lever, Lord Leverhulme, after he purchased the manor of Rivington in 1900. Rivington Castle was built between 1912 and 1930 as a replica of the ruined Liverpool Castle. The Anglezarke woodland trail runs through 100-year-old woodland on the edge of High Bullough and Anglezarke Reservoir.

ROBERTSBRIDGE East Sussex TQ7323
Village off A21, 5 miles (8km) N of Battle
Gently winding main street of weatherboarded, tile-hung and half-timbered houses of the 15th to 18th centuries. Cricket bats are made here.

ROBERTTOWN West Yorkshire SE1922
Village off A62, 1 mile (2km) SW of Liversedge
The five-storey cottonmill with its tall chimney is a prominent landmark. Cotton-spinning continued here until World War II.

ROBESTON WATHEN Dyfed SN0815
Village on A40, 2 miles (3km) NW of Narberth
Village on A40 with battlemented church tower near upper reaches of Eastern Cleddau River. Black Pool Mill still driven by water.

ROBIN HOOD'S BAY North Yorkshire NZ9505
Small town on B1447, 5 miles (8km) SE of Whitby
This small town clings to a steep cliff overlooking the North Sea. Cobbled slopes, flights of steps and narrow alleyways weave between the terraces and groups of small stone cottages with pink pantiled roofs. Smuggling was a profitable activity here in the 18th and 19th centuries and The Smuggling Experience, open during the summer season, captures the era well.

ROBY Merseyside SJ4390
Town off M62, 6 miles (10km) E of Liverpool
The centre of the town is medieval and is surrounded by Victorian developments of terraced housing. Further expansion has taken place since World War II.

ROCESTER Staffordshire SK1139
Village on B5030, 4 miles (6km) N of Uttoxeter
Home of legendary JCB excavator, with old mills built by Arkwright and terraces of former millworkers' cottages. Lake in JCB grounds is a nature reserve.

ROCHDALE Greater Manchester SD8913
Town off M62, 10 miles (16km) NE of Manchester
Rochdale lies in a shallow valley formed by the little River Roch on the slopes of the Pennines. Once a prosperous cotton town, it has a handsome Victorian Gothic town hall, designed by WH Crossland of Leeds, and opened in 1876. The Esplanade, a busy road which brings traffic into the centre of the town, is still lined with buildings from the Victorian heyday, including Rochdale Art Gallery. Yorkshire Street, the shopping centre of the town, is now pedestrianised and adjoining it is a covered shopping complex with a market.

Rochdale is regarded as the birthplace of the Co-operative movement. The world's first consumer co-operative store, a little shop in Toad Lane called the Rochdale Pioneers, first opened in 1844. It is now a museum and Toad Lane is a conservation area.

St Chad's Parish Church on Sparrow Hill, which runs along the edge of Broadfield Park in the town centre, dates from the 12th century and was extensively renovated in the 15th and 19th centuries. The west window in the tower was designed by Burne-Jones.

ROCHE Cornwall SW9860
Village on B3274, 5 miles (8km) N of St Austell
Large village on the edge of the china-clay district. The famous Roche Rock is a big granite outcrop with a little three-storey 15th-century chapel apparently growing out of it.

ROCHESTER Kent TQ7468
City off M2, 28 miles (45km) E of London
The Romans founded Rochester where Watling Street, their great road from the Channel ports to London, bridged the tidal River Medway. Historically the road has brought travellers to the city, including medieval Canterbury pilgrims and stagecoach passengers.

The Saxons founded the cathedral, consecrated in AD604, the second oldest in England. The Normans rebuilt it from 1077, including the spectacular west doorway. Additions were made in the 12th and 14th centuries, with rebuilding after Civil War damage. The magnificent nave has a superb oak roof supported by carved angels. The close is informal and intimate, and the nearby monastic ruins are set in gardens. The park, The Vines, was probably the monastic vineyard.

The Normans saw the city's strategic value and built a castle. The present castle (English Heritage), which dominates the hill behind the cathedral, was built in 1130. Within the walls are lawns and shrubberies and the massive 120-ft (36-m) keep with walls 12ft (4m) thick.

Rochester's partly pedestrianised High Street has changed little in the last century; the buildings are mostly Georgian, or have Georgian façades. The shops are small, and the scale is human. The former corn exchange, 1705, bears a great clock on an ornamental bracket protruding from its façade, while the old guildhall, now a museum, is a splendid building of 1687 crowned by a copper weathervane of 1780 in the shape of a full-rigged ship. Near by is Watts Charity in a building of 1771.

The novelist, Charles Dickens, knew Rochester well, and it appears in many of his books, notably *Great Expectations*. There is a Charles Dickens Centre and a Dickens' festival in May/June. Other festivals include the Chimney Sweeps (May) and the Carnival and Regatta (July). Rochester has craft and antiques shops, sports and leisure facilities and attractive riverside gardens.

ROCHESTER Northumberland NY8298
Hamlet on A68, 4 miles (6km) NW of Otterburn
Village dominated by an army camp. Few remains of the Roman fort *Bremenium*, the most northerly Roman fortification, can be seen.

ROCHFORD Essex TQ8790
Town on B1013, 3 miles (5km) N of Southend-on-Sea
Old market town, now in the shadow of Southend-on-Sea (see). Attractive market square, church with fine tower. Peculiar People sect was strong here.

ROCK Cornwall SW9476
Village off B3314, 2 miles (3km) SW of St Minver
Opposite Padstow on the Camel estuary, with a ferry between the two which has been running since 1337. Sand dunes to the north.

ROCKBOURNE Hampshire SU1118
Village off B3078, 3 miles (5km) NW of Fordingbridge
Pretty village street, with old brick and timber-framed houses and cottages. Basically Norman church, with oak-shingled spire of 1630. Rockbourne Roman Villa has a museum and footings of the buildings, with mosaics.

ROCKCLIFFE Cumbria NY3561
Village off A74, 4 miles (6km) NW of Carlisle
Village is surrounded by tracts of windswept marshland. Once an important port and ship-building centre with wharfs and quays along the tidal reaches of the River Eden.

ROCKCLIFFE Dumfries and Galloway NX8454
Village off A710, 5 miles (8km) S of Dalbeattie
Small resort best known for Mote of Mark, a 6th-century settlement on a granite outcrop, and Rough Island bird sanctuary, accessible on foot at low tide.

ROCKFIELD Gwent SO4814
Village on B4347, 2 miles (3km) NW of Monmouth
Village with links with the Honourable Charles Rolls, co-founder of Rolls-Royce (his family owned the local estate). Church has tower with timber belfry.

ROCKINGHAM Northamptonshire SP8691
Village on A6003, 3 miles (5km) N of Corby
Charming village of mellow 17th- and 18th-century ironstone cottages below hilltop Rockingham Castle. Royal castle, home of Watson family since 1530, massive Norman gateway leading to Elizabethan buildings, with fine pictures, Rockingham china, extensive gardens. Charles Dickens modelled Chesney Wold in *Bleak House* on Rockingham. Surrounding Rockingham Forest was a royal hunting forest from Norman times.

RODBOROUGH Gloucestershire SO8404
District on A46, immediately S of Stroud
Hilly suburb of Stroud on opposite bank of River Frome where modern houses now outnumber interesting older buildings in local rubble stone.

RODE Somerset ST8053
Village off A361, 4 miles (6km) NE of Frome
Stone village with two churches, one the original medieval, the other a strange, turreted building of 1824, supposedly built for the Wiltshire part of the parish, then split between the two counties.

RODEL Western Isles NG0483
Village on A859, at S end of Harris
Harbour village in the south of Harris. Fine pre-Reformation cruciform Church of St Clement, dating from the 1520s, with castellated tower and some wall tombs with interesting carvings. To the west lies Leverburgh, which Lord Leverhulme tried to transform from a village into a thriving fishing town; developments stopped after his death in 1925. Ferry port with connection to North Uist.

RODMARTON Gloucestershire ST9498
Village off A433, 5 miles (8km) NE of Tetbury
Pleasant cottages stand around small green of village noted for its manor (not open) built in Arts and Crafts style by Ernest Barnsley.

RODMELL East Sussex TQ4106
Village off A26, 3 miles (5km) S of Lewes
Attractive village lying between the Ouse meadows and the downs. It still has a blacksmith. Virginia Woolf lived at Monks House (National Trust) 1919–41.

RODNEY STOKE Somerset ST4850
Village on A371, 3 miles (5km) SE of Cheddar
At the foot of the Mendips. The church has a chapel crammed with elaborate 15th- to 17th-century monuments to the Rodney family.

ROGATE West Sussex SU8023
Village on A272, 4 miles (6km) E of Petersfield
Large, compact village with the wooded slopes of the common to the north. Sandstone cottages line the main road and the church has a bell tower with massive timber-framing.

ROKEBY PARK Durham NZ0713
Estate off A66, 2 miles (3km) SE of Barnard Castle
A Palladian house built in 1735 by Sir Thomas Robinson MP. Contains many works of art, but the *Rokeby Venus* is now in the National Gallery, London.

ROKER Tyne and Wear NZ4059
District in N Sunderland
Home of Sunderland Football Club. Nautical Museum. Fulwell Mill, a windmill in use until 1949, is now open to public. Memorial to the Venerable Bede (see Jarrow).

ROLLESTON Nottinghamshire SK7452
Village off A617, 4 miles (6km) W of Newark-on-Trent
Childhood home of Victorian illustrator of children's books, Kate Greenaway, and of architect CH Fowler, who restored the Norman and medieval church in the 1890s.

ROLLESTON Staffordshire SK2327
Village off A50, 3 miles (5km) N of Burton upon Trent
Commuter village with old centre. Eighteenth-century almshouses and 1640s school room stand near medieval church with monuments of the famous Moseley family.

Saxon churchyard cross at Rolleston, Staffordshire.

ROLVENDEN Kent TQ8431
Village on A28, 3 miles (5km) SW of Tenterden
Large, prosperous village in orchard and hop country with a pleasant village street of white weatherboarded and tile-hung houses.

ROMALDKIRK Durham NY9922
Village on B6277, 5 miles (8km) NW of Barnard Castle
Name is derived from the 10th-century church dedicated to St Romald and known as the 'cathedral of the Dales'. Has three village greens, and the surrounding stone cottages were built in the Middle Ages. The almshouses, built in 1693, now provide homes for the elderly.

ROMANNO BRIDGE Borders NT1647
Village on A701, 3 miles (5km) S of West Linton
Small village on the Lyne Water; near by are the 'Romanno Terraces', believed to be remnants of medieval cultivation cut out of the hillside.

ROMFORD Greater London TQ5188
Town in borough of Havering
Medieval Essex market town on the Roman road between London and Colchester, now a major shopping centre with a lively market three days a week. Many East Enders moved here after the war. Victorian church with monuments. Giant brewery, ice rink, greyhound racing stadium. The Dolphin Centre's pool is heated by solar energy

ROMILEY Greater Manchester SJ9390
Town on A560, 3 miles (5km) E of Stockport
Residential area of terraced and newer housing. Romiley Forum is a prominent local theatre.

ROMNEY MARSH Kent TR0430
Scenic and historic region, W of Dymchurch
This large tract of rich pastureland was a bay of the sea even in historical times. Protected from the sea by a huge earth embankment, Dymchurch Wall, between Hythe and New Romney, and backed by the old cliff-line and Royal Military Canal, constructed in 1807. Reclamation was begun by the Romans, and continued until the 19th century. There are several small isolated churches. Romney Marsh is a breed of sheep noted for its hardy qualities. Area associated with 'owlers' – wool smugglers – in the 18th century.

ROMSEY Hampshire SU3521
Town on A27, 7 miles (11km) NW of Southampton
The market town of Romsey has expanded in recent times on the outskirts but is still full of 18th- and 19th-century brick buildings in the middle. A statue of Lord Palmerston stands in the market place, where there is a big United Reformed Church and a gateway of 1888 which looks more like a church than a chapel. King John's House is partly of 1230, and houses the local museum. The only surviving part of the Andover and Redbridge Canal (1794) is at Romsey.

The huge abbey church, a strong building with much zig-zag decoration, is one of the finest Norman buildings in the country. It is particularly impressive inside and the many memorials include the gravestone of Earl Mountbatten of Burma (died 1979).

Broadlands is close to the town, a late 18th-century brick mansion which was the home of Lord Palmerston (Prime Minister in the middle 19th century) and Earl Mountbatten. It has an odd domed hall and interesting furnishings, plus displays about its famous owners.

ROMSLEY Hereford and Worcester SO9679
Village on B4511, 3 miles (5km) S of Halesowen
Modern village shelters beneath northern edge of Clent Hills while its Norman church and holy well stand isolated to northwest.

ROOKHOPE Durham NY9342
Village off A689, 4 miles (6km) NW of Stanhope
Quiet village surounded by hills and moorland. The Weardale Way footpath passes through the village. Rookhope Nurseries are the highest in Britain.

ROOKLEY Isle of Wight SZ5084
Village on A3020, 3 miles (5km) S of Newport
Small brick village, once with huge brickworks. Rookley Country Park has lakes, birds and animals.

ROOS Humberside TA2930
Village on B1242, 4 miles (6km) NW of Withernsea
A residential area surrounded by agricultural land. Church dates from 13th century and is built of cobble and rubble.

ROPSLEY Lincolnshire SK9934
Village off A52, 5 miles (8km) E of Grantham
Large village with Saxon, Norman and medieval church. Birthplace of Richard Fox, Tudor bishop, statesman and advisor to Henry VII.

ROSE Cornwall SW7754
Hamlet off B3285, 1 mile (2km) E of Perranporth
Small moorland village. Perran Round is an Iron Age enclosure, re-used in medieval times for performances of religious plays. Still used today for all sorts of occasions.

ROSEDALE ABBEY North Yorkshire SE7296
Village off A170, 6 miles (10km) N of Kirkbymoorside
The largest village in Rosedale that grew up around the Cistercian priory; only the tower and staircase remain.

ROSEHEARTY Grampian NJ9267
Village on B9031, 4 miles (6km) W of Fraserburgh
An old fishing port, now a dormitory town for Fraserburgh. Near by lie ruined Pitsligo Castle (1577) and old Pitsligo Kirk (1633). Both have Jacobite connections.

ROSEMARKIE Highland NH7357
Village on A832, immediately N of Fortrose
This Black Isle village is said to have been evangelised by St Boniface. Groam House Museum has fine Pictish stones, notably the 8th-century Rosemarkie cross slab.

ROSLIN (OR ROSSLYN) Lothian NT2763
Village off A701, 2 miles (3km) S of Loanhead
Mining village on the River North Esk. Roslin Castle, built by the St Clair family in the 15th century, stands on a dramatic site high above Roslin Glen, restored in the 1580s, with 16th- and 17th-century additions. The Collegiate Chapel of St Michael, commenced 1446, was destined to be an enormous cruciform church but was never completed; it is magnificently decorated with carvings and sculptures, including the famous spiral 'Prentice Pillar'.

The church at Rosehearty.

ROSNEATH (OR ROSENEATH) Strathclyde NS2583
Village on B833, 2 miles (3km) NE of Kilcreggan
Small resort with nautical associations, once the centre of the farming and herring fishing community on Rosneath peninsula, between Gareloch and Loch Long.

ROSS-ON-WYE Hereford and Worcester SO5924
Town off A40, 9 miles (14km) NE of Monmouth
The small market town stands on a sandstone bluff above the River Wye and has retained its unspoilt charm, needing no man-made visitor attractions. The narrow central streets converge at the busy market square, with a market hall that still has an open ground floor. On one wall is a bust of Charles II, commemorating the town's 17th-century allegiance.

Among many charming buildings in this area is the impressive Royal hotel of 1837, and the streets are full of good Georgian and timber-framed houses. Opposite the market hall is the 16th-century building occupied by John Kyrle (1637–1724), immortalised in verse by Alexander Pope, and Ross's greatest benefactor. He financed not only the elegant spire of St Mary's Church, added in 1721, but also much of the town's commercial development, together with the fine public gardens called The Prospect, which command splendid views. There is a memorial to Kyrle in the imposing church, where other monuments commemorate the influential Rudhall family (the Rudhall almshouses stand near the churchyard). In 1637, the year of Kyrle's birth, Ross was struck by plague, and the cross in the churchyard marks the common grave of over 300 victims.

ROSSENDALE Lancashire
Valley of the River Irwin, S of Burnley
Much of this river valley was a royal hunting ground, hence the name 'Forest of Rossendale'. Settlements grew up only after 1400.

ROSTHERNE Cheshire SJ7483
Village off A556, 3 miles (5km) N of Knutsford
An estate village built in 1909 for the workers on the Tatton estate. Church dates from the 12th century and has been much restored. The cottages leading up to it are all named after different trees and shrubs. Rostherne Mere, the largest mere in Cheshire, is now a bird sanctuary.

ROSTHWAITE Cumbria NY2514
Hamlet on B5289, 3 miles (5km) S of Derwent Water
Picturesque village in Borrowdale, one of the Lake District's prettiest valleys and owned mainly by the National Trust.

ROSTON Derbyshire SK1340
Village off B5033, 5 miles (8km) SW of Ashbourne
Close to the River Dove on the Staffordshire border, in dairy-farming country. George Eliot's father was born in Roston Common cottage; the area was used as a setting for Eliot's novel *Adam Bede*.

ROSYTH Fife NT1082
Town off M90, immediately NW of Inverkeithing
The site of the old town was acquired by the government in 1903 and developed as a dockyard and major naval base during World Wars I and II. A 'garden city' grew up around the base, incorporated with Dunfermline in 1911. It became one of the most important bases for the Royal Navy fleet, but its future now looks extremely uncertain.

ROTHBURY Northumberland NU0501
Small town on B6341, 11 miles (17km) SW of Alnwick
Market town on the banks of the River Coquet, developing as a holiday town for visitors to the Cheviot Hills. Medieval bridge and church with 9th-century sandstone cross shaft. Lord Armstrong built Cragside house and estate (National Trust) in 1865, the first house in the world to have domestic electric lighting.

ROTHER, RIVER Derbyshire
River, runs through Derbyshire and South Yorkshire,
Rises near Clay Cross, flows through Chesterfield and Staveley, Renishaw Park and Rother Valley Country Park before joining the River Don at Rotherham.

ROTHER, RIVER East Sussex
River
Rises on Forest Ridges at Rotherfield and flows east for 30 miles (48 km), passing across the reclaimed Rother Levels to enter the sea at Rye.

ROTHER, RIVER West Sussex
River runs through Hampshire and West Sussex
This tributary of the River Arun, 24 miles (38km) long, rises in Hampshire and meanders past Petersfield and into Sussex. It flows past Midhurst to the River Arun near Stopham.

ROTHERFIELD East Sussex TQ5529
Village on B2100, 3 miles (5km) E of Crowborough
Pleasantly sited at a staggered crossroads on a hilltop, with a very attractive main street of tiled and weather-boarded cottages running on two sides of the 12th-century church, which replaced an earlier monastic building. The tower was blown down in the 1987 hurricane.

ROTHERFIELD GREYS Oxfordshire SU7282
Village off B481, 2 miles (3km) W of Henley-on-Thames
Magnificent brass and other impressive monuments in church, but the main attraction is 17th-century Greys Court and its fine grounds (National Trust – limited opening).

ROTHERFIELD PEPPARD Oxfordshire SU7181
Village on B481, 3 miles (5km) W of Henley-on-Thames
Peppard Common and the heavily wooded Kingswood Common lie above this pleasant village, which has good Norman features in its church.

ROTHERHAM South Yorkshire SK4292
Town off M1, 6 miles (10km) NE of Sheffield
Rotherham lies where the rivers Rother and Don meet. The Romans worked iron here and built a fort on the south bank of the River Don at Templeborough. The site was first excavated over 100 years ago and finds from this and subsequent excavations can be seen at Clifton Park Museum.

The town grew up around heavy industries, mining and engineering, much of which has now declined, although there has been considerable investment in Rotherham's steel production.

At the centre of the town is the Parish Church of All Saints which dates from the 15th century, although there is evidence of an earlier Saxon church on the site. The Chapel of Our Lady on Rotherham Bridge was also built at around the same time and, now renovated and re-consecrated, it is one of the few remaining bridge chapels in the country.

Clifton Park Museum in Clifton House contains a fine collection of locally made Rockingham Pottery including the Rhinoceros Vase which stands almost 4ft (1m) high. The interior of Clifton House has changed little since it was built in 1783 for Rotherham ironmaster Joshua Walker.

ROTHERHITHE Greater London TQ3579
District in borough of Southwark
Parts of this former Surrey Docks area have been satisfyingly redeveloped. The Thames riverside provides attractive walking, with river views from the Mayflower pub, named in honour of the Pilgrim Fathers' ship. Her captain is buried in St Mary's Church. The Rotherhithe Tunnel to the north bank, 48ft (14.5m) below high water, was completed in 1908.

ROTHERWAS CHAPEL Hereford and Worcester SO5338
Site off B4399, 1 mile (2km) SE of Hereford
Fourteenth-century chapel largely rebuilt in 1580s for Roman Catholic Bodenham family. Refurbished 1868. (English Heritage, limited opening).

ROTHERWICK Hampshire SU7156
Village off B3349, 2 miles (3km) NW of Hook
A long main street with brick cottages, thickly hedged, and a pond. Unusual brick church of the 16th century with 17th-century tower.

ROTHES Grampian NJ2749
Small town on A941, 9 miles (14km) SE of Elgin
Originally a crofting township that developed as distilling centre in the 19th century. Home of Glen Grant Distillery, and an animal-feed factory which uses distilling by-products.

ROTHESAY Strathclyde (Bute) NS0864
Town on A844, 2 miles (3km) S of Port Bannatyne
The only town on Bute and a royal burgh since 1401, Rothesay is set in a sheltered bay and is now a popular holiday resort, with promenade and pier. It became popular in the 19th century, when it epitomised 'doon the watter' destinations from Glasgow. Rothesay Castle, built in 1099, is an impressive fortress with curtain walls and towers enclosing a courtyard. Ruined St Michael's Chapel dates from the 14th century.

ROTHIEMURCHUS Highland NH8809
Estate off B970, 2 miles (3km) S of Aviemore
Highland estate near Aviemore which offers a wide range of semi-educational activities, including guided explanatory walks and tours, a fish farm and various shops.

ROTHLEY Leicestershire SK5812
Village off A6, 5 miles (8km) N of Leicester
Delightful Charnwood Forest village with several cruck buildings around green. One of best-preserved 13th-century Knights Templars' chapels. Templars' Hall converted into house by the Babingtons, owners of estate 1565–1845, now Rothley Court hotel. Historian and writer Thomas Babington Macaulay born here in 1800. Numerous Babington monuments in large 13th-century pink granite church.

ROTHWELL Northamptonshire SP8181
Small town on A6, 4 miles (6km) NW of Kettering
Attractive and historic small market town. Magnificent church, on grand scale, dates mainly from 13th century, with remarkable bone crypt. Cruciform 16th-century market house is decorated with trefoils of Sir Thomas Tresham, for whom it was built (see Rushton), and carries coats of arms of local landowners. Sixteenth-century hospital, 17th-century Nunnery Cottage, elegant 18th-century manor house.

ROTHWELL West Yorkshire SE3428
Town off M1, 5 miles (7km) SE of Leeds
An old town, grown from a village, the older buildings interspersed with modern housing developments. Pretty part-timbered cottages and fragments of the wall of a former castle.

ROTTINGDEAN East Sussex TQ3602
Small town on A259, 4 miles (6km) E of Brighton
Kipling, Burne-Jones and William Morris lived in this old settlement in a hollow of the downs overlooking the English Channel, and there is a museum with a Kipling room. A pretty green, with pond, lies in front of the church at the end of High Street, inland from the cliff coast. Landmark Beacon Hill windmill stands on grassy cliffs to the west; modern coastal housing in Saltdean to the east.

ROUGHAM GREEN Suffolk TL9061
Village off A14, 4 miles (6km) SE of Bury St Edmunds
Rougham Green was a 'plague village' and was burned down and rebuilt in a series of hamlets. It has 26 miles (42km) of roads.

ROUS LENCH Hereford and Worcester SP0153
Village off A435, 6 miles (10km) N of Evesham
Pretty village supplied with neo-Tudor cottages, school and sumptuous postbox by benevolent Victorian owner of Rous Lench Court. Church of exceptional interest.

ROUSAY Orkney
Island off N coast of mainland
Island with the finest extant Orcadian broch, at Midhowe, with an adjacent compartmented stalled cairn. Chambered cairn at Taversoe Tuick.

ROWALLAN CASTLE Strathclyde NS4342
Site off B751, 3 miles (5km) N of Kilmarnock
L-plan castle with a courtyard and fine façade, dating from 1562. Two circular towers flank the first-floor Renaissance doorway.

Rowallan Castle.

ROWARDENNAN Central NS3598
Hamlet off B837, 6 miles (10km) N of Balmaha
Village on attractive bay at the end of the road along the east shore of Loch Lomond; access point for Ben Lomond and West Highland Way.

ROWDE Wiltshire ST9762
Village on A342, 2 miles (3km) NW of Devizes
Grown greatly since World War II. Slender 15th-century church tower.

ROWHEDGE Essex TM0221
Village off B1025, 3 miles (5km) SE of Colchester
Old fishing village with picturesque waterfront on west bank of the River Colne. East Donyland's octagonal brick church was built in 1838.

ROWINGTON Warwickshire SP2069
Village on B4439, 6 miles (10km) NW of Warwick
Small canalside settlement has church with good medieval craft work next to the fine timber-framed Shakespeare Hall (not open).

ROWLAND'S CASTLE Hampshire SU7310
Village off B2149, 3 miles (5km) N of Havant
Right on the Sussex border. The long green is lined with Georgian and Victorian houses. Big railway viaduct.

ROWLAND'S GILL Tyne and Wear NZ1658
Village on B6315, 3 miles (5km) SW of Blaydon
Derwentcote Steel Furnace (English Heritage), built in the 18th century, is the earliest and most complete authentic furnace to have survived.

ROWLEY REGIS West Midlands SO9687
Town off A459, just W of Warley
This hillside town quarries hard roadstone called 'Rowley Rag'. Warren's Hall Park, with entrance to long Netherton Tunnel, is a must for canal enthusiasts.

ROWLSTONE Hereford and Worcester SO3727
Hamlet off A465, 1 mile (2km) W of Pontrilas
Magnificent Norman carving adorns the church of this tiny settlement in the hills near the foot of the Golden Valley.

ROWSLEY Derbyshire SK2565
Village on A6, 3 miles (5km) SE of Bakewell
Rivers Wye and Derwent meet here. Seventeenth- and 18th-century houses of Haddon Hall estate village (see Bakewell). Caudwell's Mill is a working 19th-century water-powered flour mill with roller milling machinery.

ROXTON Bedfordshire TL1554
Village off A428, 4 miles (6km) N of Sandy
Thatched cottages above the Great Ouse. Picturesquely rustic, thatched Nonconformist chapel converted from a barn in 1808 by a Congregationalist squire.

ROYDON Essex TL4010
Village on B181, 2 miles (3km) W of Harlow
Commuter settlement on the River Stort. Village stocks and lock-up, Georgian houses. Watersports lake at Roydon Mill Leisure Park.

ROYSTON Hertfordshire TL3540
Town on A10, 12 miles (19km) SW of Cambridge
Market and light industry town at the crossing of Ermine Street and the Icknield Way, once an important coaching stage. Curious man-made cave (limited opening) with carvings of religious scenes. James I's hunting lodge, church of former medieval priory, local history museum. Therfield Heath, a chalk downs nature reserve, and cemetery of prehistoric barrows.

ROYSTON South Yorkshire SE3611
Town on B6428, 3 miles (5km) N of Barnsley
Residential district of Barnsley, formerly a small village with housing of mixed ages and styles. Church of St John the Baptist contains fine 19th-century east window.

ROYTON Greater Manchester SD9207
Town on A671, 2 miles (3km) N of Oldham
Small cotton town on the River Irk. Royton Old Hall (private) a large 17th-century house rebuilt in 18th century.

RUABON Clwyd SJ3043
Town on A483, 5 miles (8km) SW of Wrexham
Partly industrial town at gateway to Vale of Llangollen. Strong links with historically omnipotent Wynnstay family. Church has interesting contents.

RUARDEAN Gloucestershire SO6117
Village off A4136, 3 miles (5km) NW of Cinderford
High on northern fringe of Forest of Dean and enjoying fine views. Church has outstanding Norman carving.

RUBERY Hereford and Worcester SO9877
District on A38 immediately W of Rednal
Residential area on semi-rural fringe of Birmingham. Church of 1950s . Country park at Wasely Hill to west.

RUDCHESTER Northumberland NZ1167
Village on B6318, 1 mile (2km) NW of Houghton
Small village based around the former Roman fort of *Vindobala*, which has been partially excavated.

RUDDINGTON Nottinghamshire SK5733
Village on A60, 5 miles (8km) S of Nottingham
Centre of framework knitting industry: 19th-century workshops and cottages preserved as working museum. Rushcliffe Country Park with Transport Heritage Centre.

RUDSTON Humberside TA0967
Village on B1253, 5 miles (8km) W of Bridlington
In the churchyard is the famous Rudston monolith or rood-stone from which the village gets its name. The monolith stands at the meeting place of four neolithic ditches which enter the village from different directions. Its origin is similar to Stonehenge. Believed to be the oldest inhabited village in England.

RUDYARD Staffordshire SJ9557
Village off A529, 2 miles (3km) NW of Leek
The Kiplings, once holiday-makers here, named their son after this resort village with its beautiful lake. Fishing, boat hire and visitor centre.

RUFFORD Lancashire SD4615
Village on A59, 6 miles (10km) NE of Ormskirk
The ancestral home of the Hesketh family who lived at Rufford Old Hall, now a National Trust property. Contains an early 15th-century great hall.

RUGBY Warwickshire SP5075
Town on A428, 11 miles (18km) E of Coventry
A mere village in the early 19th century, Rugby expanded dramatically as a result of two key developments – its famous public school and the rise of the railway engineering works after 1840. Its new status is reflected in churches by three outstanding architects, Sir George Gilbert Scott, William Butterfield and AWN Pugin. Enthusiasts will also enjoy much of its secular Victorian architecture, and some earlier buildings survive, notably in the market place.

The Lawrence Sheriff almshouses near by are a reminder of the great 16th-century benefactor who founded Rugby School, whose 19th-century buildings dominate the town centre. Dr Arnold, immortalised in *Tom Brown's Schooldays*, established its national reputation, and he features prominently at the Rugby School Museum, also the starting point for tours of the school. Rugby Football is the subject of a museum at the James Gilbert shop in St Matthew's Street. Today a range of modern industries has supplanted railway engineering, and extensive housing estates have developed around the town. With its modern shopping facilities, Rugby retains its traditional role as an unglamorous but essential commercial centre for a wide area.

RUGELEY Staffordshire SK0418
Town off A51, 8 miles (13km) SE of Stafford
Power stations and modern housing surround old centre of this former industrial town, but pedestrianisation makes for pleasant shopping and there are attractive houses of 17th and 18th centuries in Horsefair and the market place. Imposing church of 1822 is well worth visiting. Wolseley Garden Park has 45 acres (18ha) of theme gardens.

RUISLIP Greater London TQ0987
District in borough of Hillingdon
Ruislip turned into a suburb after the railway arrived in 1904, but much of the old village centre has survived. Manor Farm, with its barns, is now a school and a public library. Brasses and monuments in St Martin's Church, frequently restored. Plenty of open space, with a watersports lido and coppiced hornbeams in Ruislip Woods.

RUM (OR RHUM) Highland NM3798
Island to SW of Skye
The largest of the Small Isles, accessible from Mallaig and in the care of the Nature Conservancy Council, with dramatic volcanic peaks and excellent walking. It was cleared for sheep after 1815 and the islanders shipped to Canada. Kinloch is the only village and nearby Kinloch Castle, now a hotel, is an extraordinary Gothic edifice built by Sir George Bullough in 1901. The interior features an electric organ and a superb Edwardian shower.

RUMBLING BRIDGE Central NT0199
Village on A823, 4 miles (6km) E of Dollar
Village near eponymous beauty spot where two bridges span the River Devon; named for the noise of the river in spate. Downstream, Cauldron Linn is a dramatic double waterfall.

RUMBURGH Suffolk TM3481
Village off A14 (A45), 4 miles (6km) NW of Halesworth
Rumburgh was prosperous in medieval times, evidenced by large surviving farmhouses. 'Rumburgh' means 'village surrounded by a ditch or bank reached by a bridge'.

RUNCORN Cheshire SJ5182
New Town off M56, across the River Mersey from Widnes
New Town created in the 1960s, with Bridgewater Canal running through the centre. Surrounded by chemical and hi-tech industries.

RUNNYMEDE Surrey TQ0072
Historic site on A308, 1 mile (2km) NW of Egham
Tranquil watermeadows beside the River Thames, where Magna Carta was signed in 1215. The National Trust owns 300 acres (121ha), with a tea room and shop. Magna Carta Island in the River Thames is frequently cited as the place where King John signed the document, which is more likely to have been signed on the meadows. The 1957 memorial was given by the American Bar Association and the nearby Kennedy memorial (1965) honours the assassinated US president.

RUNSWICK North Yorkshire NZ8016
Village off A174, 6 miles (10km) NW of Whitby
A small fishing village with white painted cottages on the cliff side, overlooking large sandy beaches.

RUSCOMBE Berkshire SU7976
Village off B3024, just NE of Twyford
Almost part of the small town of Twyford, but with its own church, which has a 1638 brick nave and tower; the rest is Norman flint.

RUSHALL Wiltshire SU1255
Village off A342, 1 mile (2km) NW of Upavon
In the Vale of Pewsey, with some old thatched cottages and a rather isolated church, partly rebuilt in brick in 1812.

RUSHBROOKE Suffolk TL8961
Village off A14 (A45), 3 miles (5km) SE of Bury St Edmunds
In the 1840s, Colonel Rushbrooke pillaged some fine medieval wood from the (now demolished) Rushbrooke Hall, and erected it in St Nicholas's Church.

RUSHBURY Shropshire SO5191
Village off B4371, 4 miles (6km) E of Church Stretton
Under steep slope of Wenlock Edge fine Norman church stands next to attractive school of 1821, with Rushbury Manor, expensively timber-framed, near by.

RUSHDEN Northamptonshire SP9566
Town on A6, 4 miles (6km) E of Wellingborough
Footwear-manufacturing town in Nene Valley with grand, mainly 13th-century, parish church. Jacobean Rushden Hall, part local authority offices. Historical Transport Museum.

RUSHMERE ST ANDREW Suffolk TM1946
Village off A1214, on NE edge of Ipswich
About 170 acres (67ha) of common land forms Rushmere Heath in the village centre. Many trees and two duck ponds complete the picture.

The Kirk Port at Rutherglen.

RUSHTON Northamptonshire SP8482
Village off A6003, 3 miles (5km) NW of Kettering
Triangular Lodge (English Heritage) – built by Sir Thomas Tresham 1594–7 to express Catholic faith to which he converted in 1580 – symbolises the Holy Trinity, with three sides, three storeys, and family symbol of trefoils. Other Tresham buildings at Lyveden and Rothwell (see). Mainly 16th- and 17th-century Rushton Hall (not open), home of Treshams from 1438, now a school.

RUSHTON SPENCER Staffordshire SJ9362
Village on A52, 5 miles (8km) NW of Leek
Village in moorland valley is well known for lonely church – 'Chapel in the Wilderness' – where present walls enclose older monastic church.

RUSKINGTON Lincolnshire TF0851
Village on B1188, 4 miles (6km) N of Sleaford
Large residential village, with 17th-century cottages and 1904 almshouses. Norman tower arch in 13th-century church; tower rebuilt in 1620 after collapse. Saxon cemetery site.

RUSPER West Sussex TQ2037
Village off A23, 4 miles (6km) W of Crawley
Unspoilt place of tile-hung and timbered cottages, now with a business centre in renovated barns. The village grew around the 13th-century priory, of which only the church remains.

RUSTINGTON West Sussex TQ0502
Town off A259, immediately N of Littlehampton
Coastal town where thatched flint cottages survive amid a sea of small 20th-century houses. Good sandy beach.

RUTHERGLEN Strathclyde NS6161
Town on A749, immediately SE of Glasgow
The oldest Scottish royal burgh, chartered in the early 12th century and important commercially and politically in the Middle Ages. Became part of Glasgow in 1975.

RUTHIN (RHUTHUN) Clwyd SJ1258
Town on A494, 7 miles (11km) SE of Denbigh
Vale of Clwyd town noted for its distinguished architecture. Many periods represented – medieval, Tudor half-timbered, Georgian red brick. Without the cars, St Peter's Square is like stepping back in time. Tall-spired church a prominent landmark. Old courthouse now a bank. Ruthin Castle (now a hotel) located at site of medieval fortress; medieval banquets. Attractive crafts centre. Market centre for prosperous farmland of vale.

RUTHWELL Dumfries and Galloway NY0967
Village off B724, 6 miles (10km) W of Annan
Ruthwell (pronounced 'Rivvel') parish church contains the 18ft (6m), 8th-century Ruthwell cross, possibly Scotland's most important stone cross, with carved Runic and Latin inscriptions. The cross was restored in 1823 by Reverend Henry Duncan, who also founded the first savings bank in 1810, a forerunner of the Trustee Savings Bank. A museum tells the history of this world-wide movement.

RUTLAND WATER Leicestershire SK9207
Reservoir off A606, 5 miles (8km) W of Stamford
Constructed in 1970s to supply water to nearby towns, Rutland Water (3,100 acres/1,255ha of water) provides major recreational facilities: trout fishing, sailing, watersports. Cycle hire centre for rides round 27 miles (44km) of perimeter track. *Rutland Belle* pleasure cruiser. Butterfly and Aquatic Centre. Nature reserve. Museum in former Normanton church (see).

RUYTON-XI-TOWNS Shropshire SJ3922
Village on B4397, 9 miles (14km) NW of Shrewsbury
Eleven small townships combined in 1300 to form this medieval borough. Interesting church overlooks village street lined with old brick and sandstone houses.

RYCOTE CHAPEL Oxfordshire SP6604
Site off A329, 3 miles (5km) W of Thame
Founded as chantry chapel and original structure unaltered. Medieval benches, musicians' gallery and painted 17th century ceiling (English Heritage).

RYDAL Cumbria NY3606
Hamlet on A591, 1 mile (2km) NW of Ambleside
Rydal Mount (not open) was home to William Wordsworth and his family from 1813 to his death in 1850. Hartley Coleridge also spent the last 11 years of his life in the village. Rydal Water, the centrepiece for many famous views, is a small lake.

RYDE Isle of Wight SZ5992
Town on A3055, 5 miles (8km) N of Sandown
A little hilltop village and a fishing settlement on the shore joined up from the 1820s to create a big seaside resort. Lots of Regency and Victorian stucco houses and terraces line the hill, with the prominent spire of the 1860s church at the top. The long pier was built from 1813 and the pier railway, installed in the 1930s, uses old stock from the London Underground. Ferries to Portsmouth and wonderful sea views. Sandy shore and, to the east, Appley Park with boating lake.

RYE East Sussex TQ9220
Town on A259, 9 miles (14km) NE of Hastings
The flavour is medieval in this little town perched on a knoll between the rivers Rother and Tillingham and still more or less defined by its vanished town walls. Rye was attached to the Cinque Ports and saw great prosperity after a great storm in 1287 brought it good anchorage along the present Strand. It was a royal borough by 1289 but within a century was burnt down by the French and suffering from the silting up of its harbour.

Today Rye is 2½ miles (4km) inland, a cluster of red roofs on a low hill crowned by the church. There is a maze of streets with lovely timbered, weatherboarded and 18th-century houses, including Lamb House (National Trust) where Henry James lived. Attractive cobbled Mermaid Street is named after the Mermaid inn, the one-time haunt of a notorious smugglers' gang. Landgate is the only one of the 14th-century town gates to survive, a massive fortified structure still retaining its portcullis grooves. The museum is housed in the Ypres Tower, also 14th century and fronting the Gun Garden. The hall of the Augustinian friary (about 1380) now houses a pottery.

RYE HARBOUR East Sussex TQ9319
Village off A259, 1 mile (2km) SE of Rye
Village on the edge of saltings above a flat coast, with a nature reserve, important for wildfowl, encompassing a saltmarsh, riverbanks, beach and reclaimed farmland. Camber Castle (English Heritage) was built in Henry VIII's reign.

RYE, RIVER North Yorkshire
River, rises in Cleveland Hills, tributary of the Derwent
Runs through the heart of rural Yorkshire. Ryedale offers a wealth of wildlife habitats and beautiful scenery.

RYHALL Leicestershire TF0310
Village on A6121, 2 miles (3km) N of Stamford
Pretty Rutland village beside River Gwash. Stone cottages. Green Dragon inn with vaulted 13th-century cellar.

RYHILL West Yorkshire SE3814
Village on B6428, 3 miles (5km) NE of Royston
Once the property of the monks of Nostell Priory, the village expanded in the 19th century to house miners and workers building the railway to transport coal.

RYHOPE Tyne and Wear NZ4052
District on S outskirts of Sunderland
Former colliery village. Ryhope Engines Museum, based on Ryhope Pumping Station, has two beam engines dating from 1868; they operate on summer weekends.

RYLSTONE North Yorkshire SD9658
Village on B6265, 5 miles (8km) N of Skipton
A Pennine village with Rylstone Cross standing high on the Fell overlooking the village; it commemorates 'The Peace of Paris' in 1885.

RYME INTRINSECA Dorset ST5810
Village off A37, 4 miles (6km) SE of Yeovil
Stone cottages and the oddest name in the county, meaning 'the home part of the Ryme manor', as opposed to the outer part, once called *Extrinsica*.

RYTHER North Yorkshire SE5539
Village on B1223, 2 miles (3km) NW of Cawood
Very small, picturesque village well away from the main tourist routes, consisting mainly of old cottages with no new housing.

RYTON Tyne and Wear NZ1564
Town off A695, 6 miles (10km) W of Newcastle
Town dominated by Stella power station. Holy Cross Church dates from the 13th century, with Jacobean woodwork. Ryton Willows is picturesque woodland in a riverside setting.

RYTON-ON-DUNSMORE Warwickshire SP3874
Village on A45, 4 miles (6km) SE of Coventry
Ryton Organic Gardens are a popular attraction in this village on Coventry's fringe. Early Norman church.

S

SACRISTON Durham NZ2447

Village on B6312, 3 miles (5km) NW of Durham

Rows of colliery houses were built when two coal shafts were sunk near by. The summit of Findon Hill provides excellent views of Durham city.

SADDELL Strathclyde NR7832

Village on B842, 8 miles (13km) N of Campbeltown

Village with the remains of a Cistercian abbey, founded in about 1160. The stones were taken to build Saddell Castle, a typical 16th-century tower house with an extraordinary pit prison.

Entrance to Saddel Castle.

SAFFRON WALDEN Essex TL5338

Town on B1052, 12 miles (19km) N of Bishop's Stortford

This lovable old market town, whose buildings of historic and architectural interest number hundreds, was until the 18th century the principal centre for growing the saffron crocus, hence its name. Saffron and wool paid for the beautiful, dominating church at its heart, one of the largest in Essex, St Mary the Virgin, magnificently rebuilt in about 1500, with the slender spire added in 1832 and rising to 193ft (59m). The castle ruins are near by, and the town museum.

The town's youth hostel is a 15th-century house and the old Sun inn dates from the 14th century with marvellous 17th-century pargetting (ornamental plasterwork). There are handsome Georgian buildings and impressive 19th-century creations include a bank (now Barclays) by Eden Nesfield, a grand mock-Tudor entrance to the town hall and a stately drinking fountain by the future architect of Westminster Cathedral.

Further out, on the common, is a rarity, a turf maze perhaps 800 years old or more. To penetrate to the centre is a walk of almost 1 mile (2km). The Bridge End Gardens, meanwhile, contain another specimen, a hedge maze of the 1830s.

ST AGNES Cornwall SW7250

Village on B3217, 6 miles (10km) N of Redruth

Large old mining village with one particularly steep street of miners' cottages. St Agnes Beacon (National Trust) is 629ft (191m) high, overlooking the coast.

ST AGNES Isles of Scilly SV8808

Island of the Scilly group

Most southerly of the Scilly group with deeply indented coastline, sandy coves, granite outcrops and a patchwork of tiny fields inland. Disused, 17th-century lighthouse, second oldest in Britain.

ST ALBANS Hertfordshire TL1407

City on A1081, 19 miles (31km) NW of London

The cathedral dominates the scene for miles around from the hilltop where St Alban, England's first recorded Christian martyr, was buried. Down below by the River Ver, a park conceals the site of the Roman town of *Verulamium*, where Alban lived. Some stretches of wall are still standing, a luxurious bath suite has been restored and the Verulamium Museum, with one of the best Roman collections in the country, attracts schoolchildren in droves.

St Alban, according to tradition, was a Roman soldier who was converted to Christianity by a priest named Amphibalus, and enabled him to escape when soldiers came hunting him. Arrested and tortured, Alban refused to sacrifice to pagan gods and was beheaded. The Benedictine abbey founded here in the 8th century grew into one of the richest in England. Its massive stone gateway still stands to the west of the church, which has been a cathedral only since 1877.

The cathedral today is a combination of medieval and Victorian work, with a massive Norman tower built partly of Roman bricks. Appallingly dilapidated by the 19th century, it was rebuilt at his own expense by Sir Edmund Beckett, later Lord Grimthorpe, whose carved head can be seen in the porch as St Matthew and whose grave is outside. Inside, the shrine of St Alban, smashed at the Reformation, has been restored.

Today's St Albans is a shopping and business centre. There's a town museum of local history with a noted collection of craft and trade tools, while mechanical musical instruments lurk in the Organ Museum (limited opening). Outside the city, the stately mansion of Gorhambury (limited opening) has links with Sir Francis Bacon.

ST ANDREWS Fife NO5116
Town on A91, 9 miles (14km) E of Cupar
Historic and prosperous St Andrews stands on a promontory overlooking the North Sea and today is chiefly known for its university and golf courses. The town dates back to the cathedral's foundation in 1160, some centuries after St Andrew's relics were allegedly brought to Scotland by St Regulus; 11th-century St Rules' Church was built in his honour. The cathedral, constructed between 1161 and 1318, was of great ecclesiastical importance until its destruction during the Reformation, when the important Blackfriars foundation was also dissolved.

The secular town, with encircling walls and ports whose remnants exist today, became a prosperous market centre. Its buildings included the clifftop castle, also destroyed at the Reformation, but replaced shortly afterwards. Today's ruins, near the ancient harbour and pier, date from the late 16th century. Scotland's oldest university, founded in 1412, included by the 16th century the colleges of St Salvator, St Leonard and St Mary. It grew steadily over the centuries, and thrives today. Its buildings, many of them of great architectural merit, are scattered around the town.

The railway's arrival opened up the town as a golfing centre and holiday resort, and the town's well-planned suburbs spread to the northwest. Golf has been played here since the 17th century and the Society of St Andrews Golfers dates from 1754, having changed its name to The Royal and Ancient in 1834 and now considered to be the game's ruling authority. The famous Old Course is one of several links golf courses.

St Andrews is a busy commercial centre for the surrounding agricultural countryside, with several excellent schools, good shops and recreational facilities. These, with its history and fine buildings, help to make it a popular tourist destination.

ST ANTHONY-IN-MENEAGE Cornwall SW7825
Hamlet off B3293, 8 miles (13km) E of Helston
Small and remote on the tidal Gillan Creek, with just a few old cottages and the medieval church.

ST ANTHONY-IN-ROSELAND Cornwall SW8532
Hamlet off A3078, 4 miles (6km) SW of Trewithian
Near the end of the long peninsula making one entrance to Carrick Roads (see), with good sea and river views.

ST ARVANS Gwent ST5196
Village on A466, 2 miles (3km) NW of Chepstow
Stands at southern entrance to lovely Wye Valley. Wynd Cliff to the northeast is a famous viewpoint high above the river.

ST ASAPH Clwyd SJ0374
Small town on A525, 5 miles (8km) S of Rhyl
Small town has city status by virtue of its cathedral (Britain's smallest). Ancient origins, though present building dates from medieval times. William Morgan, translator of the Bible into Welsh, was bishop here in early 17th century. Town stands on the River Elwy (tributary of the River Clwyd), with 18th-century bridge. Venue for North Wales Music Festival each September.

ST AUSTELL Cornwall SX0152
Town on A390, 13 miles (20km) NE of Truro
This was a town based on quarrying and mining tin and copper from early times, and on china clay after its discovery here in 1748 by the Plymouth chemist William Cookworthy. The 'Cornish Alps' (or 'White Alps') to the north of the town are waste tips of gritty quartz, by-products of the quarrying. The china clay is today used for paper, paints, medicines, cosmetics and toothpaste, as well as china. The Alps are now being reclaimed and made green: the older ones, with trees, look like natural hills.

The town is not large, and still has some older parts. The central church has a superb late 15th-century tower and wooden roofs of the same date. Buildings include the very plain granite Quaker meeting house of 1829, and the simple market hall of 1844. The St Austell Brewery, which started in the late 19th century, has a visitor centre and gives guided tours.

ST BEES Cumbria NX9711
Village on B5345, 4 miles (6km) S of Whitehaven
Small seaside town which is the start of Wainwright's Coast to Coast Walk. Parish church has a magnificent Norman doorway. St Bees School is a fine building dating from 1583, and a renowned boarding school. Sandstone cliffs of St Bees Head now a nature reserve with many seabirds including guillemots, puffins and terns.

ST BLAZEY Cornwall SX0654
Town on A390, 4 miles (6km) NE of St Austell
Wooded but rather dominated by roads, St Blazey has some Georgian cottages. Tregrehan Gardens, to the west, have woodland and camellias.

ST BOSWELLS Borders NT5930
Village on A68, 4 miles (6km) SE of Melrose
Village boasting Scotland's largest village green, once the venue for horse and cattle fairs. Nearby Mertoun Gardens have shrubs, trees and a walled garden in a beautiful position.

ST BREOCK Cornwall SW9771
Hamlet off A39, 1 mile (2km) SW of Wadebridge
Romantically sited medieval church in a steep, tight little valley filled with trees and with a stream at the bottom.

ST BREWARD Cornwall SX0976
Village off B3266, 4 miles (6km) S of Camelford
Straggling, rather bleak village on the edge of Bodmin Moor (see). Archaeological sites on the moor include stone circles.

ST BRIAVELS Gloucestershire SO5504
Village on B4228, 5 miles (8km) W of Lydney
This attractive stone village high above the River Wye in the Forest of Dean still keeps up the Whit Sunday custom of distributing bread and cheese to parishioners of St Mary's Church, which has a fine Norman font. A youth hostel now lies behind the moat and drum-towered gatehouse of the castle that once housed King John after hunting expeditions.

ST BRIDE'S MAJOR
Mid Glamorgan SS8974

Village on B4265, 3 miles (6km) S of Bridgend

Attractive village, close to Glamorgan Heritage Coast; the church has interesting features, including medieval chancel and tombs.

ST BURYAN
Cornwall SW4025

Village on B3283, 4 miles (6km) E of Land's End

This granite village has one of the finest churches in Cornwall. Its 14th-century tower is prominent from miles around and is used as a sea-mark. The rest of the church is of around 1500, with a lovely rood screen still bearing traces of colour. The Merry Maidens, 2 miles (3km) southeast, is a Bronze Age circle of 19 stones and, close by, in the road verge, are the neolithic Tregiffian burial chamber stones.

ST CLEARS
Dyfed SN2716

Small town on A40, 9 miles (14km) W of Carmarthen

Rural town bypassed by A40. Remnants of a Norman motte, interesting church with Norman arch. Rebecca Riots took place here in mid-19th century.

ST CLEER
Cornwall SX2468

Village off B3254, 2 miles (3km) N of Liskeard

Stone village with a 15th-century church. A holy well is close by, with its little 15th-century building. To the northeast is Trethevy Quoit, the substantial stones forming the centre of a neolithic tomb. The 9th-century King Doniert's Stone, by the roadside 1 mile (2km) northwest, has an inscription stating that 'Doniert ordered it'; a larger contemporary cross stands next to it. The wooded Golitha Falls are on the River Fowey to the west.

ST COLUMB MAJOR
Cornwall SW9163

Village off A39, 6 miles (10km) E of Newquay

Although it claims to be a town, and does have urban Victorian buildings in the middle, this is really more of a village. It was a town in medieval times, however, and still has a large and prominent medieval church. The ancient Cornish form of football, hurling, survives here with an annual match. The goals are 2 miles (3km) apart.

ST COLUMB MINOR
Cornwall SW8462

Village off A392, 1 mile (2km) E of Newquay

On the edge of Newquay, but still a separate place with a fine granite church, mostly 14th century.

ST CROSS
Hampshire SU4727

Village off A333, 1 mile (2km) S of Winchester

Once a village, now part of Winchester. The Hospital of St Cross is a rare survival of a medieval almshouse, a courtyard of buildings dominated by a Norman church, with a proper gatehouse and hall. A path through the watermeadows leads back to Winchester, and it was this walk which inspired Keats to write the poem starting 'Season of mists and mellow fruitfulness' in 1819. St Catherine's Hill, to the south, now cut by the M3, is crowned by an Iron Age hillfort with an 18th-century maze.

ST DAVID'S
Dyfed SM7525

Small town on A487, 15 miles (24km) SW of Fishguard

St David's Cathedral, almost hidden from view in a grassy hollow beneath the main street, occupies the site of a religious settlement founded by St David, Wales's patron saint, in the 6th century. As it now stands, this mellow cathedral with its wonderful oak roof, dates from the 12th century. It was a place of pilgrimage for centuries, two visits to St David's equalling one to Rome. The ruined Bishop's Palace (Cadw) next door would have provided opulent accommodation for medieval prelates.

In the tiny city itself there are two attractions relating to marine life, while St David's Farm Park on the outskirts has rare breeds and a farm trail. West is St David's Head, an intensely beautiful stretch of coastline – Pembrokeshire in miniature – which includes everything from the big sandy beach at Whitesands to the inlet of Porthclais, the original 'port' for St David's. St Non's Bay, named after St David's mother, is David's legendary birthplace (the spot is marked by a ruined chapel, and there is also a holy well here). St Justinian's, with its lifeboat station, is the embarkation point for boat trips to Ramsey Island (see).

ST DAY
Cornwall SW7342

Village off B3298, 2 miles (3km) E of Redruth

Known in the 19th century as the richest square mile in the world because of the number of tin (and copper) mines. None are now working, but there are many waste tips and buildings.

ST DOGMAEL'S
Dyfed SN1646

Village off A487, 1 mile (2km) W of Cardigan

Village opposite Cardigan on western shores of the Teifi estuary. Ruined abbey (Cadw) founded by the Benedictines in 12th century. Attractive views from the ruins to the rivermouth. Y Felin watermill still produces flour the traditional way. Pretty Poppit Sands to the north is the boundary for the Pembrokeshire Coast National Park.

ST ENDELLION
Cornwall SW9978

Hamlet on B3314, 4 miles (6km) N of Wadebridge

Inland from the north Cornish coast, but still rugged and windswept, with a fine late medieval church dedicated to St Endellienta.

ST FAGANS
South Glamorgan ST1277

Village off A48, 4 miles (6km) W of Cardiff

Picturesque village on western fringes of Cardiff. Home of the Museum of Welsh Life which reflects life in bygone Wales. Centrepiece is large parkland, where buildings from all over Wales – including farmhouses, a school, chapel, workshops and industrial terraced cottages – have been re-erected stone by stone. Demonstrations of craft and rural skills. Extensive site also contains conventional museum block, Elizabethan mansion, gardens.

ST FERGUS
Grampian NK0952

Village on A952, 4 miles (6km) N of Peterhead

Noted for its huge terminal, processing over one-third of all Britain's North Sea gas, with another terminal under construction.

ST FILLANS Tayside NN6924
Village on A85, 5 miles (8km) W of Comrie
Attractive village with good watersports facilities at the east end of Loch Earn, founded in the 18th century. Dundurn Hill was the site of a 7th-century Pictish fort.

ST FLORENCE Dyfed SN0801
Village off B4318, 3 miles (5km) W of Tenby
Little village just inland from Tenby. Distinctive chimneys on some houses display influence of Flemish immigrants.

ST GEORGE Clwyd SH9775
Hamlet off A55, 2 miles (3km) SE of Abergele
Hamlet close to Kinmel Park (not open), whose house was remodelled in second half of 19th century in Queen Anne style. Iron Age fort of Dinorben near by.

ST GERMANS Cornwall SX3657
Village on B3249, 8 miles (13km) SE of Liskeard
This very pretty stone village, once a small town, is set in woodland and has a famous church, the most important in Cornwall before Truro Cathedral was built. Its elaborate Norman doorway has seven layers of arches. Port Eliot, the big house (not open) below the church, is quaintly castellated, and the 17th-century almshouses to the west are picturesque. The quay on the river is now used by yachts. Big railway viaduct.

ST HARMON Powys SN9872
Village on B4518, 3 miles (5km) N of Rhayader
Village on empty, open ground above Rhayader. Francis Kilvert, author of *Kilvert's Diaries*, was vicar here 1876–7.

ST HELEN AUCKLAND Durham NZ1826
Village on A688, 1 mile (2km) SW of Bishop Auckland
The ancient Church of St Helen Auckland dates from 1150. Rare parvis above the porch provided accommodation for visiting priests.

ST HELENS Isle of Wight SZ6289
Village on B3330, 3 miles (5km) SE of Ryde
A huge, high green, with the rest of the village falling down to Bembridge Harbour.

ST HELENS Merseyside SJ5195
Town on A571, 11 miles (18km) E of Liverpool
The name of St Helens is derived from the chapel of Saint Elyn which was situated within the extensive ecclesiastical parish of Prescot. The town's growth came during the Victorian period, the town hall being completed in 1876. A building of particular interest is the Friends' Meeting House in Church Street, a charming stone building with mullioned windows and an old sundial above the doorway.

During the reign of Elizabeth I the district also became known for its ironstone quarries. St Helens is famed for its glass production and is the headquarters of Pilkington PLC, where the company has its own glass museum. The 'Hotties' is the name given to the point in the town where the Pilkington glass factory drew water from the canal and where the used, hot water was returned after use, creating permanent clouds of steam in the vicinity. The Hotties Science and Arts Centre, is planned as a new visitor centre, housed in the renovated Victorian furnace building at this point, describing the Hotties and the history of St Helens as an industrial glass-making town.

ST HELIER Channel Islands (Jersey) JS1508
Town on A1, 6 miles (10km) E of St Aubin
On the south side of Royal Square, originally the market, an attractive, granite-paved pedestrian area, stand the government buildings, the States, the Royal Court and the public library. John Wesley preached here in 1787, and the Battle of Jersey was fought here in 1781. Splendid mid-19th-century terraced houses survive in Rouge Bouillon and Queen's Road, and there is distinguished Regency-style architecture in Almorah Crescent. Fort Regent, now a leisure complex, looms above the harbour.

Elizabeth Castle, in St Helier Bay, named by Sir Walter Raleigh, is reached by a causeway (limited opening) at low tide . The Island Fortress Museum at the Weighbridge houses German militaria and an audio-visual theatre. The Jersey Museum, a magnificent four-storey house in Pier Road, houses a portrait of Lillie Langtry painted by John Everett Millais.

The ormer (*oreille de mer*) – a rare delicacy – and conger eel (conger soup being a local speciality) can be found at the fish market.

Parades and ceremonies take place in the Parade Gardens and Howard Davies Parks; the annual Jersey Battle of the Flowers takes place in Victoria Avenue in August.

ST IPPOLLITTS Hertfordshire TL1927
Village off B656, 2 miles (3km) S of Hitchin
Pretty village, whose saint was originally Hippolytus, a figure of Greek myth linked with horses; there was a medieval horse cult here.

ST IVES Cambridgeshire TL3171
Town on A1123, 5 miles (8km) E of Huntingdon
St Ives has one of only three remaining chapel bridges in England, a pretty building dating from 1426 astride the River Ouse. St Ives is named after a Persian bishop called Ivo, whose bones are said to have been found near by. The town declined during the Black Death, and again after a fire in 1680 which destroyed 122 houses.

ST IVES Cornwall SW5140
Town on A3074, 7 miles (12km) NE of Penzance
Until the 1890s the prosperity of this picturesque town was based on pilchards and tin, but this century it has converted to tourists and art. Beautifully situated, with sandy beaches on either side and a rocky headland in the middle, the town itself is small-scale and well preserved, with little cobbled streets, flowers everywhere, many external staircases and steep alleyways. Fishing boats still use the harbour and the town museum is close by.

Out on the headland is the little Chapel of St Michael, and in the town is St Ia's Church, early 15th century with a Madonna and Child by Barbara Hepworth. She lived here, and her studio and garden have many sculptures on view.

From the late 19th century St Ives attracted artists, but the St Ives colony dates from the 1930s, with Hepworth and Ben Nicholson the earliest members, along with Bernard Leach, who established his pottery at Upper Stennack, high in the town, in the 1920s. The Tate St Ives displays modern art created in Cornwall in its striking new (1993) building on Porthmeor beach, a spot popular with surfers.

ST JOHN'S CHAPEL Durham NY8838
Village on A689, 7 miles (11km) W of Stanhope
Once an important lead centre, quarrying is still important. Although a village, there is a town hall. Regular sheep and cattle markets are held.

ST JOHN'S WOOD Greater London TQ2683
District W of Regent's Park, in City of Westminster
With its substantial houses and elegant terraces, this smart area was once notorious for the number of rich men's mistresses it accommodated. It attracted artists and authors, too, including Landseer and George Eliot. Lord's cricket ground, the game's hallowed headquarters, has a museum of cricket. Contemporary art is on show in the Saatchi Gallery.

ST JUST Cornwall SW3731
Small town on A3071, 4 miles (6km) N of Land's End
An important mining centre, whose impressive central square is lined with low granite buildings and a big 15th-century church. Cape Cornwall is the headland to the west, with fine views. About 1 mile (2km) south is Land's End Airport, offering scenic flights. There are many industrial remains from mining, and archaeological features include Balloball neolithic barrow cairn.

ST JUST-IN-ROSELAND Cornwall SW8435
Village on A3078, 2 miles (3km) N of St Mawes
Famous (uniquely) for its churchyard, steep and wooded, planted since the 19th century with decorative trees and shrubs. Winding paths lead to the tidal creek.

St Just-in-Roseland signpost.

ST KEVERNE Cornwall SW7921
Village on B3293, 9 miles (14km) SE of Helston
High and windy village with a rather urban square and the prominently-spired church at the middle, a beacon for those navigating near the treacherous Manacles (see).

ST KEW Cornwall SX0276
Village off A39, 4 miles (6km) NE of Wadebridge
The large 15th-century church stands with the inn and a huge rectory in a wooded hollow. Stained glass dated 1469 in the church. St Kew Highway is a developing hamlet just off the main road.

ST KEYNE Cornwall SX2461
Village on B3254, 2 miles (3km) S of Liskeard
Famous for the holy well, southeast of the village. The first one of a married couple to drink from it is supposed to have mastery over the other. Magnificent Music Machines features Wurlitzer organs, among other things.

ST KILDA Western Isles NF0999
Island W of Harris
World Heritage Site, owned by the National Trust for Scotland, 110 miles (177km) west of the mainland, uninhabited since 1930, when the last residents asked to be evacuated. Economy was based on fowling fulmar and gannet-breeding colonies on the 1,400ft (427m) cliffs. The island's unique way of life was destroyed by ill-health and discovery by the Victorians.The old village is now restored.

ST LAWRENCE Isle of Wight SZ5376
Village off A3055, 2 miles (3km) W of Ventnor
Romantic Victorian stone and timber-framed houses scattered about in the wooded Undercliff, with a steep cliff behind. Tropical Bird Park and Isle of Wight Rare Breeds and Waterfowl Park.

ST LEONARD'S FOREST West Sussex TQ2131
Scenic area off A264, E of Horsham
Part of the forest ridges of Sussex associated with a legend of a dragon, fought by St Leonard. Sandstone heights, reaching 480ft (146m). Characteristic vegetation: pine, larch and birch woods, open commons.

ST LEONARDS East Sussex TQ8009
Town on A259, immediately W of Hastings
Genteel suburb of Hastings, originally a separate development of the 1820s by James and Decimus Burton; centres on St Leonards gardens, a landscaped ravine surrounded by Regency villas.

ST LEVAN Cornwall SW3822
Hamlet off B3315, 3 miles (5km) SE of Land's End
Close to Land's End, with the church tucked into a sheltered valley. Holy well in the cliff at Porthchapel Bay, on the rocky granite coast.

ST MARGARET'S AT CLIFFE Kent TR3544
Small town off A258, 4 miles (6km) NE of Dover
Little town with weatherboarded houses perched above delightful St Margaret's Bay, a secluded resort and beach on the Channel shore down a steep cliff road near South Foreland. The Pines gardens take advantage of the warm micro-climate at the cliff foot with specimen trees, shrubs and lakes. Traditional starting point for cross-Channel swimmers, as it is the nearest point to France.

ST MARGARET'S HOPE Orkney ND4493
Village on South Ronaldsay
Picturesque village on a sheltered bay, with two small museums. Margaret, Maid of Norway, died here on her way to marry Edward II in 1290.

ST MARTIN'S Isles of Scilly SV9315
Island of the Scilly group
The third biggest island in the Scilly group, 2 miles (3km) long. Magnificent views from Chapel Down, where a daylight navigational aid, the Day Mark, was built in 1687.

ST MARY BOURNE Hampshire SU4250
Village on B3048, 3 miles (5km) NW of Whitchurch
Many thatched cottages around the medieval church, with flat watermeadows beyond. The church has a fine Norman Tournai marble font.

ST MARY IN THE MARSH Kent TR0627
Village off A259, 2 miles (3km) N of New Romney
Cottages huddle together in this small place, remote and lonely on the flats of Romney Marsh. Unrestored 13th-century church stands by a bridge over a drainage channel.

ST MARY'S Isles of Scilly SV9111
Island in the Scilly group
The largest island in the Scilly group, 3 miles (5km) by 2 miles (3km). Star Castle, an eight-pointed fortress (now a hotel) completed in 1593, formed part of the Garrison built in the 1740s. Harry's Walls, uncompleted 16th-century fortifications, are found at Porth Harry. Bant's Carn (English Heritage), a prehistoric burial chamber, overlooks Romano-British village and Innisidgen Carn.

ST MARY'S LOCH Borders NT2422
Loch on A708, 13 miles (21km) W of Selkirk
Stretch of water which includes Loch of the Lowes. Tibbie Shiels inn on its banks has literary connections: near by is statue of poet James Hogg.

ST MAWES Cornwall SW8433
Town on A3078, 5 miles (8km) SW of Trewithian
Exclusive yachting centre on Carrick Roads, the shore road lined with white houses and villas. Passenger ferries to Falmouth and St Anthony (summer only). St Mawes Castle (English Heritage) was built in the 1540s as a pair to Pendennis (see) opposite.

ST MAWGAN Cornwall SW8765
Village off B3276, 5 miles (8km) NE of Newquay
A pretty village in a lovely wooded valley. The medieval church has a 15th-century rood screen and there has been a nunnery here since 1794.

ST MELLION Cornwall SX3865
Village on A388, 3 miles (5km) SE of Callington
High village with views to Dartmoor. The lower parts, with woody valleys, used to be a fruit-growing area.

ST MERRYN Cornwall SW8874
Village on B3276, 2 miles (3km) W of Padstow
Tiny slate village consisting of a cluster of cottages and the church.

A carved Celtic cross at the Carmelite chapel of Lanherne, 1 mile (2km) north of St Mawgan.

ST MICHAEL PENKEVIL Cornwall SW8542
Village off A3078, 6 miles (10km) SW of Probus
On a wooded peninsula between the Truro and Fal rivers, still with a pump on the village green. Many estate cottages.

ST MICHAEL'S MOUNT Cornwall SW5129
Island in Mount's Bay, off Marazion
The famous romantic view is of the fairy-tale castle (National Trust) perched on top of the rocky island dominating Mount's Bay, joined to the mainland by a causeway at low tide, and by ferries from Marazion (see) at high tide. The village at the bottom, with its harbour, is beautifully preserved. The castle feels like a ship inside, with impressive views, and its interesting interior includes a fanciful 1750s drawing room and priory church.

ST MICHAEL'S ON WYRE Lancashire SD4641
Village on A586, 3 miles (5km) SW of Garstang
The Norman church stands close to the River Wyre on a spot probably first chosen in 6th century by Irish missionaries.

ST MINVER Cornwall SW9677
Village off B3314, 3 miles (5km) NW of Wadebridge
Old cottages dominated by a 19th-century octagonal spire. See Polzeath.

ST MONANS (OR ST MONANCE) Fife NO5201
Small town off A917, 3 miles (5km) W of Anstruther
Fishing town with attractive old houses round harbour. The parish church was built between 1362 and 1370, and restored in the 1820s. Ruined Newark Castle stands on a clifftop near by.

ST NEOT Cornwall SX1867
Village off A38, 5 miles (8km) NW of Liskeard
On the edge of Bodmin Moor, with a fine 15th-century church most unusually still having its original early 16th-century stained glass.

ST NEOTS Cambridgeshire TL1860
Town off A1, 8 miles (13km) SW of Huntingdon
This market town was founded in the 10th century by Benedictine monks. St Neot, who was said to have been adviser to King Alfred, was buried in Cornwall, and it is possible the monks stole his bones for their new priory in Cambridgeshire. Fine buildings include the 17th-century Bridge hotel and the 15th-century Church of St Mary. Attractive riverside park.

ST NEWLYN EAST Cornwall SW8256
Village off A3075, 4 miles (6km) S of Newquay
The church in this high, stone-built village is dedicated to St Newlina, and the fig growing from its wall is supposed to be her staff. In 1846 39 villagers were killed in a mining accident, and the village cockpit (once used for cockfighting) was restored as a memorial. Trerice (National Trust), to the north, is a perfect little Elizabethan manor house. Lappa Valley Steam Railway is to the east.

ST NICHOLAS South Glamorgan ST0974
Village on A48, 6 miles (10km) W of Cardiff
St Nicholas stands close to the beautifully landscaped Dyffryn Gardens, a 70 acre (28ha) expanse ranged around a late 19th-century mansion. Also close by is Tinkinswood Long Cairn, a communal burial chamber dating from around 4000BC whose large tomb is topped by a massive capstone, possibly the biggest in Britain. Its less impressive companion piece, St Lythans Burial Chamber, stands in fields to the south.

ST NICHOLAS AT WADE Kent TR2666
Village off A28, 6 miles (10km) SW of Margate
Delightful Thanet village away from main roads with many brick cottages and houses in the centre.

ST NINIAN'S ISLE Shetland HU3620
Peninsula on W coast of mainland
This beautiful island is linked by a white-sand causeway to Mainland, with the remains of a 12th-century church. Pictish silver hoard found in 1858.

ST OLAVES Norfolk TM4599
Village on A143, 1 mile (2km) SW of Fritton
This remote hamlet, standing on the shores of Fritton Lake, has the remains of an Augustinian priory (English Heritage) and a small trestle mill.

ST OSYTH Essex TM1215
Village on B1027, 3 miles (5km) W of Clacton-on-Sea
Holiday village on a creek off the River Colne, close to the seaside. Pilgrims came to the shrine of St Osyth, martyred by Vikings. The impressive 15th-century gatehouse of St Osyth's Priory is the entrance to a stately home and gardens, with an enjoyable picture collection. Church with interior in 16th-century brick and monuments of D'Arcy family. Woodland and waterside walks.

ST PAUL'S WALDEN Hertfordshire TL1922
Village on B651, 3 miles (5km) W of Stevenage
The Queen Mother spent some of her childhood here at the Bury (gardens open occasionally), the Bowes Lyon family's Victorian mansion, whose formal gardens were originally laid out by an earlier squire in the 18th century. He also provided the Church of All Saints' with its handsome chancel. The romantic ruins of Minsden Chapel lie to the north.

ST PETER PORT Channel Islands (Guernsey) GN5308
Principal town on Guernsey, on E coast
Narrow, cobbled streets, lined with Regency and Victorian buildings, cling to the slopes above the harbour. The 13th-century Castle Cornet (limited opening) dominates the harbour entrance and houses three military museums. The fine, granite, medieval town church stands at the harbour's edge and high above is Hauteville House (limited opening), the home of Victor Hugo between 1856 and 1870.

ST SAMPSON Channel Islands (Guernsey) GN5411
Town on Guernsey, on E coast
A small commercial port with a depot for grading and packing tomatoes. St Sampson's Church is the oldest in Guernsey.

ST STEPHEN IN BRANNEL Cornwall SW9453
Village on A3058, 4 miles (6km) W of St Austell
Granite village on the edge of the china-clay-quarrying area (see St Austell).

ST TUDY Cornwall SX0676
Village off B3266, 5 miles (8km) NE of Wadebridge
Little slate and granite village. The war memorial is shaded by a large chestnut tree grown from a conker brought home from the battlefield of Ypres in World War I.

ST VIGEANS Tayside NO6443
Village off A92, 1 mile (2km) N of Arbroath
Village noted for its church, with parts dating from 1100 and a 15th-century tower. Important collection of inscribed Pictish stones.

ST WEONARDS Hereford and Worcester SO4924
Village on A466, 7 miles (11km) N of Monmouth
In hill country north of Monmouth old stone cottages stand around unspoilt 15th-century church with medieval glass and ancient furnishings.

ST WINNOW Cornwall SX1157
Hamlet off A390, 2 miles (3km) S of Lostwithiel
Tiny hamlet, beautifully situated on the wooded Fowey estuary, with the church right down on the water.

SAINTBURY Gloucestershire SP1139
Village off A44, 2 miles (3km) NE of Broadway
Small village overlooking Vale of Evesham from high Cotswold Edge, with finely restored old houses and cottages in sloping main street.

SALCEY FOREST Northamptonshire SP8052
Scenic area on B526, 7 miles (11km) NW of Newport Pagnell
Substantial wooded areas of ancient hunting forest, with trails, picnic areas and nature reserves. Oaks grown in early 18th century for ship timbers.

SALCOMBE Devon SX7439
Town on A381, 6 miles (10km) S of Kingsbridge
Fishing and yachting centre. The old village slowly developed from the early 19th century as a resort. Still with narrow streets and a wonderful setting. Very mild climate, so lush greenery. At Sharpitor to the south is Overbecks Museum and Garden (National Trust); gardens are semi-tropical, full of strange and beautiful tender plants. Museum has a great variety of exhibits collected by one of the owners of the house.

SALCOMBE REGIS Devon SY1488
Village off A3052, 2 miles (3km) NE of Sidmouth
Tiny village set back from the sea in a beautiful little valley, with red sandstone cliffs on the shore.

SALE Greater Manchester SJ7892
Town on A56, 5 miles (8km) SW of Manchester
A popular residential area which developed with the opening of the Manchester to Altrincham railway. Town centre is largely pedestrianised and provides pleasant shopping. Trafford Watersports Centre is a 45 acre (18ha) park with a lake, conservation area, picnic sites and various watersports activities.

SALEN Highland NM6864
Village on A861, 6 miles (10km) S of Kinlochmoidart
A crofting settlement on the remote Ardnamurchan peninsula at a junction where the main route north joins the tortuous and scenic road to Ardnamurchan Point.

SALFORD Greater Manchester SJ8298
Town off M62, immediately W of Manchester
The city of Salford is Manchester's twin across the River Irwell. Its Art Gallery at Peel Park now contains the Lowry Centre, a tribute to LS Lowry who was born and lived in Salford, which displays much of his work.

Salford grew with industrialisation. Cloth was made, silk-weaving, dyeing and fulling were carried on. Factories were substituted for homeworkers and the population grew from 12,000 in 1812 to almost 220,000 by the end of the 19th century by which time several large mills had been built. This rapid growth was reflected in the vast areas of poor-quality housing that was built throughout the Victorian period when overcrowding led to serious social problems.

The opening of the Manchester Ship Canal in 1894 turned Salford into a major inland port which employed a large proportion of Salford's population for almost a century.

Salford Docks has now been developed into a leisure and residential district. Renamed Salford Quays, the waterfronts now provide a backdrop to apartments, pubs, walkways and a large cinema complex. The area will also be served by a planned extension to Manchester's Metrolink tram system.

SALFORD PRIORS Warwickshire SP0751
Village on B439, 5 miles (8km) NE of Evesham
Village in market garden country overlooking confluence of rivers Arrow and Avon. Fine Norman and medieval church.

SALISBURY Wiltshire SU1429
City on A30, 82 miles (132km) SW of London
Perhaps the best English cathedral city, created from 1220 when the settlement moved from Old Sarum (see) down to New Sarum in the valley. The cathedral was built 1220–60, and is the only English cathedral built all in one style. It is the finest example of Early English style, and one of the greatest medieval buildings in the country. The 404ft (123m) spire was added from 1334, the highest in Great Britain, and visible from miles around. The cathedral is stone vaulted, and especially rich in chantry chapels and memorials. The chapter house has a copy of Magna Carta.

The cathedral close is still cut off from the city by walls and medieval gates, and is the largest in the country. Fine houses of all dates line the roads, with a sea of green lawns around the cathedral. Mompesson House (National Trust) is of 1700, with fine 1740s plasterwork, Malmsbury House is of a similar date, and Salisbury Museum is in the King's House, 15th century onwards. Redcoats in the Wardrobe is the military museum.

The city itself is all on a proper human scale, a huge area of streets full of a happy mixture of medieval to Victorian buildings, with many Georgian, in brick, stone and even timber-framing. There are many inns, and several medieval churches. Buildings of note include the market place, still with stalls, the 1780s guildhall and the elaborate 15th-century market cross. The John Creasy Museum (contemporary art) is in the library.

The River Avon runs very close to the city and walks along the watermeadows give superb views of the cathedral.

Salisbury today is a bustling prosperous city, an important shopping centre and large market town which still preserves the feel of an ancient city, with no modern office blocks or other high buildings to challenge the dominance of the medieval cathedral.

SALISBURY PLAIN Wiltshire
Scenic area N of Salisbury
Huge area of empty chalkland, virtually without villages and ringed by towns. The Plain is 20 miles (30km) by 12 miles (20km), grassy downland from prehistoric times until World War I, when it was ploughed up. The army uses most of it for training, and there are many prehistoric remains, most famously Stonehenge (see).

SALKELD, GREAT AND LITTLE Cumbria NY5536
Villages on B6412, 5 miles (8km) NE of Penrith
The villages are home to Long Meg and Her Daughters, a large stone circle situated on a hill overlooking the River Eden with a large monolith. There is a water-powered flour mill, still producing wholemeal flour, that has been in existence on this site since 1345. St Cuthbert's Church stands on the site of an older, probably Saxon, church.

SALLE Norfolk TG1024
Village off B1145, 1 mile (2km) N of Reepham
Some people insist that Salle (pronounced 'Saul') church is the final resting place of Anne Boleyn. A pleasant little village with a glorious church, grander than many a cathedral.

SALTAIRE West Yorkshire SE1438
Town off A650, just W of Shipley
This model town is named after its founder, Sir Titus Salt, and the River Aire on which it stands. Many of the buildings are well preserved and the town has become a popular tourist attraction. Salts Mill houses a permanent exhibition of the works of David Hockney.

SALTASH Cornwall SX4358
Town on A38, across the Tamar from Plymouth
This little medieval port on the Tamar River is dominated by two huge bridges, the railway bridge of 1857 by Brunel and the elegant suspension road tollbridge of 1961.

SALTBURN-BY-THE-SEA Cleveland NZ6621
Town on A174, 4 miles (6km) SE of Redcar
On a high sandy cliff and a seaside resort in Victorian times, with the northeast's only pier. Tramway, built in 1883 and still working, transports passengers from the seafront up to the town. The Ship inn, a former smugglers' haunt, is now a museum and tourist attraction.

SALTCOATS Strathclyde NS2441
Town on A738, 3 miles (5km) SW of Kilwinning
Seaside town whose prosperity was derived from salt production; local coal was used in the evaporation of seawater. The harbour, with its 19th-century Martello Tower, was reconstructed in 1914. North Ayrshire Museum tells the local story. Nowadays this is a popular resort with neighbouring Ardrossan, built in the 19th century, for families from central industrial Scotland. Offshore lies Horse Island.

SALTDEAN East Sussex TQ3802
District on A259, 1 mile (2km) SE of Rottingdean
An inter-war development, with estates grouped around a combe above coastal cliffs with a 1930s outdoor lido and a holiday camp.

SALTFLEET Lincolnshire TF4593
Village on A1031, 9 miles (14km) NE of Louth
Wide sandy beaches and dunes of coastal strip designated a National Nature Reserve. Part of medieval market town of Saltfleet and its church were washed away by the sea. Norman and later church with leaning 15th-century tower at nearby hamlet of Saltfleetby All Saints (now redundant). Saltfleetby's St Clements Church, converted into craft workshop, and St Peter's Church, Victorian.

SALTFLEETBY ALL SAINTS Lincolnshire TF4591
see Saltfleet

SALTON North Yorkshire SE7179
Village off A170, 4 miles (6km) S of Kirkbymoorside
The village is bounded by the rivers Rye and Dove. Its name comes from the French word *saule*, meaning willow.

SALWARPE Hereford and Worcester SO8761
Village off A38, 2 miles (3km) SW of Droitwich
Sixteenth-century Salwarpe Court and medieval church with Talbot family monuments stand at heart of village sandwiched between River Salwarpe and Droitwich Canal.

SAMLESBURY Lancashire SD5930
Village off A59, 3 miles (5km) E of Preston
Samlesbury Hall, dating from 1325, houses a valuable collection of antiques and paintings. Roach Bridge papermill has been working for two centuries.

SAMPFORD COURTENAY Devon SS6301
Village off A3072, 5 miles (8km) NE of Okehampton
Picturesque thatched village with cob and some stone, and an impressive 15th-century church. Typical of Devon, with rolling red hills.

SANCREED Cornwall SW4229
Village off A30, 3 miles (5km) W of Penzance
In the middle of Land's End peninsula, with Carn Euny 1 mile (2km) west, the impressive remains of an Iron Age village, with a long fogou, or passage chamber.

SANDAY Orkney
Island S of North Ronaldsay
Sandy farming and fishing island of great natural beauty with abundant wildlife. Lovely beaches. Start Point lighthouse stands at the east. Chambered cairn (3000BC) at Quoyness.

SANDBACH Cheshire SJ7560
Town on A534, 5 miles (8km) NE of Crewe
Market town served by the Trent and Mersey Canal. In the market place are two richly carved Anglo-Saxon sandstone crosses of 8th and 9th centuries, said to have been set up when Peada, son of heathen warrior King Penda, married the daughter of King of Northumbria. Market day is Thursday.

Ancient crosses at Sandbach.

SANDBANK Strathclyde NS1680
Village on A815, 2 miles (3km) N of Dunoon
Village with a reputation for yacht-building, on the south shores of Holy Loch with views across to Argyll Forest Park.

SANDEND Grampian NJ5566
Village off A98, 3 miles (5km) E of Cullen
Once a thriving fishing port with a tiny harbour, now a fish-curing centre. Set at the end of a wide, sandy bay, very popular with visitors.

SANDFORD ORCAS Dorset ST6220
Village off B3145, 3 miles (5km) N of Sherborne
This secluded stone village has a fine 1530s manor house, reached through its own little gatehouse.

SANDHEAD Dumfries and Galloway NX0949
Village on A716, 7 miles (11km) S of Stranraer
A village near the Sands of Luce. Kirkmadrine church, 2 miles (3km) northeast, has inscribed 5th-century stones and some of the earliest Scottish Christian monuments.

SANDHURST Berkshire SU8361
Town on A321, 3 miles (5km) W of Camberley
Originally sandy heathland, now wooded, with a Royal Military Academy established in 1907. Large buildings and a lake. Trilakes Country Park has lakes and animals.

SANDHURST Kent TQ7928
Village on A268, 5 miles (8km) SW of Cranbrook
Village of weatherboarded houses straggling along a main road, with a delightful secluded green tucked away from the bustle, and a church away from the village on a hilltop to the south.

SANDIACRE Derbyshire SK4736
Town on A52, 2 miles (3km) N of Long Eaton
Former market town bordering Nottinghamshire, along the Erewash Canal beside the M1. Church on sandstone outcrop, with Norman nave, 13th-century tower and 14th-century chancel. Lace factory of 1888 and village lock-up.

SANDON Staffordshire SJ9429
Village on A51, 4 miles (6km) NE of Stafford
Appealing estate village with timber-framed cottages and pub designed by famous architect Guy Dawber. Church has fine 17th-century interior.

SANDOWN Isle of Wight SZ5984
Town on A3055, 5 miles (8km) S of Ryde
Sandown started to develop later than most of the Isle of Wight resorts, mostly in the later Victorian and Edwardian eras. It has a fine sandy beach and a long Victorian pier with a 1930s theatre, as well as one of the best sunshine records in the country. Isle of Wight Geology Museum.

SANDRIDGE Hertfordshire TL1710
Village on B651, 3 miles (5km) NE of St Albans
Locally pronounced 'Sarndridge'. Now a satellite of St Albans (see), but with Roman bricks and a Norman font in the Victorianised church.

SANDRINGHAM Norfolk TF6928
Village off A149, 7 miles (11km) NE of King's Lynn
Sandringham is not a village, but a number of adjoining parishes and the 7,000 acre (2,830ha) Sandringham estate, country home of the royal family. The present house was built after 1870 designed to look like a Jacobean mansion. The gardens and park are superb, and may be visited by the public when the royal family is away.

SANDSEND North Yorkshire NZ8612
Village on A174, 3 miles (4km) NW of Whitby
A picturesque village at the foot of the steep gradient of Lythe Bank, the two halves spanning separate valleys and joined along the seafront by a promenade with houses and hotels. The valleys, with prominent railway viaducts, have delightful small cottages and the village is a favourite spot for sailing and windsurfing.

SANDTOFT Humberside SE7408
Hamlet off A161, 3 miles (5km) NW of Belton
Sandtoft Transport Centre has a large displayed collection of trolley buses and motor buses. Sandtoft Flying Club airfield base.

SANDWICH Kent TR3358
Town on A257, 11 miles (18km) E of Canterbury
Sandwich was founded by the Saxons on the coast at the mouth of the River Stour. Since then the river has silted up and Sandwich is 2 miles (3km) inland, with fields and golf courses juxtaposed between it and the sea. An original Cinque Port, Sandwich was one of England's most important naval bases, yet by the 15th century it was no longer even a harbour, but a cloth-manufacturing town, its continued prosperity coming from refugee Flemish weavers who settled there. When the cloth industry declined Sandwich became an exclusive golfing resort, with the Royal St George's Golf Club between the town and Sandwich Bay, where there is a nature reserve.

Today it is a quiet little market town with narrow streets and alleys radiating from Cattle Market, the central square with its Elizabethan town hall housing the museum. Strand Street, which runs along the former seafront, now riverside, is full of timber-framed buildings including the magnificent Weaver's Hall and King's Arms. Two of the town gates survive: massive Barbican Gate to the north, leading to the swing bridge over the river, and Fisher Gate, 1384, overlooking the quay.

SANDY Bedfordshire TL1749
Town off A1, 8 miles (13km) E of Bedford
A nondescript town in a market gardening area on the River Ivel, with overspill London council estates. The King's Arms remains from former Great North road coaching days. The Royal Society for the Protection of Birds has its headquarters at The Lodge, an 1870s mansion to the east on the B1042, in extensive grounds with nature trails and hides. The Locomotive pub on the B1042 has railway pictures and memorabilia.

SANDY LANE Wiltshire ST9668
Village on A342, 3 miles (5km) SW of Calne
Lots of thatched cottages, and a sweet little thatch and timber church of 1892.

SANQUHAR Dumfries and Galloway NS7809
Town on A76, 10 miles (16km) NW of Thornhill
A royal burgh (pronounced 'Sanker') on the Southern Upland Way, founded in 1598 on the River Nith and once a coal-mining and cotton-milling centre. Covenanters fixed their Declarations of 1680 to the town cross, a site now marked by an obelisk. The tollbooth was designed by William Adam in 1735 and built with stones from ruined Sanquhar Castle. The world's oldest post office has been in use here since 1738.

SAPPERTON Gloucestershire SO9403
Village off A419, 5 miles (8km) W of Cirencester
Beautifully situated overlooking Frome Valley, Sapperton is interesting for its connections with Ernest Gimson and the Barnsley brothers, craftsmen who lived at Daneway House and designed some of the village cottages. They are buried in the graveyard of the elegant church. Canal enthusiasts will want to visit the famous Sapperton Tunnel, 2 miles (3km) long.

SARK Channel Islands
Island in the English Channel between Guernsey and Jersey
Smallest of the four main Channel Islands islands, 3 miles (5km) long, 2 miles (3km) wide, an erosion plateau with steep cliffs and bays. La Coupée, a narrow, high isthmus, separates Great Sark from Little Sark. The only motor vehicles are farm tractors, otherwise horse-drawn carriages or bicycles. The Sark Derby, with mounted draught horses, is held in September.

SARN HELEN Gwynedd
Roman road
This important strategic link built by the Romans ran from their camp of *Segontium* near Caernarfon, through Snowdonia, and thence on to Chester. Some sections survive.

SARNESFIELD Hereford and Worcester SO3750
Village off A480, 11 miles (18km) NW of Hereford
John Abel, 17th-century master craftsman, whose work survives at Abbey Dore and old Leominster town hall, is buried in churchyard here.

SARRATT Hertfordshire TQ0499
Village off A404, 3 miles (5km) N of Rickmansworth
Village green with pond and picturesque cottages, often used for filming. Church with unusual saddleback tower.

SARRE Kent TR2565
Village on A28, 4 miles (6km) SW of Birchington
Shrunken place with a large windmill on the edge of marshes between the mainland and the Isle of Thanet. An important harbour and ferry when the marshes were an arm of the sea.

SATLEY Durham NZ1143
Village on B6296, 3 miles (5km) N of Tow Law
Attractive village surrounded by farmland. Hall Hill Farm stages demonstrations of farm skills and crafts.

SAUCHEN Grampian NJ7011
Village off A944, 4 miles (6km) SW of Kemnay
A village near Castle Fraser (Natonal Trust for Scotland), a magnificent Z-plan building built between 1575 and 1636. Very fine and simple main hall. Restored walled garden.

SAUNDERSFOOT Dyfed SN1304
Small town off A478, 3 miles (5km) N of Tenby
Tenby's little brother. A small but busy seaside resort with long sandy beach. Boat-filled harbour popular base for sailing and watersports. Unlikely history as a coal-exporting port. In woods above is Stepaside Heritage Project, an intriguing place at which industrial history of area is revealed. Nearby Wiseman's beach was used for D-Day rehearsals.

SAUNTON Devon SS4537
Village on B3231, 7 miles (11km) NW of Barnstaple
Saunton Sands run for 3 miles (5km) with Braunton Burrows (see) sand dunes behind. Little village tucked up under the rocky headland.

SAVERNAKE FOREST Wiltshire SU2266
Scenic area on A4, SE of Marlborough
An enormous area of woodland, formerly a medieval hunting forest, with the Grand Avenue flanked by huge old beech trees. Straight rides cut right across it, one with a column of 1781. Wonderful walking country. Tottenham House (limited opening) is a huge mansion of 1825, with a lavish church of 1861, at St Katherines.

SAWBRIDGEWORTH Hertfordshire TL4814
Town on A1184, 4 miles (6km) NE of Harlow
Nice old town unmarred by high-rises. Boat trips on River Stort. Rare breeds at working Kecksys Farm (limited opening).

SAWLEY Derbyshire SK4731
Village on B6540, immediately SW of Long Eaton
Norman and medieval church beside the River Trent where Derbyshire meets Nottinghamshire and Leicestershire. Monument to John Bothe, Treasurer of Lichfield Cathedral, who died in 1496.

SAWLEY Lancashire SD7746
Village off A59, 4 miles (6km) NE of Clitheroe
The village is home to Salley Abbey, founded in 1174 as a Cistercian establishment and now a ruin.

SAWSTON Cambridgeshire TL4849
Small town off A1301, 6 miles (10km) SE of Cambridge
Two branches of the River Cam drove the papermills here. Sawston Hall is an elegant Elizabethan mansion rebuilt in 1553.

SAXHAM, GREAT AND LITTLE Suffolk TL7862
Villages off A14 (A45), 4 miles (6km) W of Bury St Edmunds
At the edge of the hilly, wooded countryside of

southwest Suffolk, with lovely churches; Saxham Hall has a Moorish temple.

SAXILBY Lincolnshire SK8975
Village off A57, 6 miles (10km) NW of Lincoln
Large dormitory village on Roman Fossdyke Canal, some expansion dating from railway arrival in 1849. Manor house with diaper brickwork.

SAXMUNDHAM Suffolk TM3863
Small town off A12, 18 miles (29km) NE of Ipswich
The coming of the railway in 19th-century England changed the face of many rural towns, and this is especially evident in Saxmundham. Improved communications brought industry and a frenzy of Victorian buildings. Small terraces of cottages and large, grand 19th-century edifices dominate the town, belying its roots as a far more ancient settlement.

SAXTEAD GREEN Suffolk TM2564
Village on B1119, 2 miles (3km) NW of Framlingham
Has an especially fine 18th-century working post windmill (English Heritage). It stands on the marshy green towering over surrounding trees.

SAXTHORPE Norfolk TG1130
Village on B1149, 6 miles (10km) SE of Holt
Saxthorpe has a mill and a history of successful industry, from the medieval wool trade to a 19th-century agricultural foundry. Mannington Hall has spectacular gardens.

SCA FELL AND SCAFELL PIKE Cumbria NY2006
Mountains in the Lake District, W of Langdale
Popular walking and climbing region. Scafell Pike is England's highest mountain at 3,210ft (978m). Most of the range now belongs to the National Trust.

SCALBY North Yorkshire TA0090
Small town on A170, 2 miles (4km) NW of Scarborough
A small coastal town which has been developed since World War II. Its scenic, sheltered position makes it an ideal holiday base.

SCALLOWAY Shetland HU4039
Small town on A970, 5 miles (8km) W of Lerwick
Small town and white-fish port on the west coast of Mainland, once Shetland's capital. Home of the North Atlantic Fisheries College, with courses in fishing and fish-farming. Ruined Scalloway Castle dominates the harbour, built in 1600 by the unpopular Earl Patrick Stewart. An important World War II base for ferrying supplies to the Norwegian resistance, the service known as 'Shetland Bus'; a local museum tells the story.

SCAPA FLOW Orkney
Harbour S of mainland
Huge naval base during World Wars I and II, penetrated by the Germans in 1939, who sank the *Royal Oak*. Churchill Barriers were then constructed to prevent access from the east, and are now part of the road network. This remarkable engineering feat was partly built by Italian prisoners-of-war, who created the lovely Italian chapel from two Nissen huts, since restored and still in use today.

SCARBOROUGH North Yorkshire TA0488
Town on A170, 35 miles (56km) NE of York
The two bays and the town of Scarborough are dominated by Castle Hill, a flat-topped promontory upon which the gaunt remains of Scarborough Castle stand.

Visitors to this traditional seaside resort could not fail to be impressed by the panoramic setting of cliffs and bays here. It was Scarborough's spring water, however, discovered in 1626 by Mrs Tomazyn Farrer, that first

Working windmill at Saxtead Green.

drew the crowds and the coming of the railway from York in 1846 really established Scarborough as a resort. It still retains a very traditional feel, with Regency and Victorian buildings, bandstands and gardens, donkey rides and Punch and Judy tents. The Spa, or 'Spaw House', originally built in 1700 and rebuilt in 1877, is now a huge entertainment and conference complex, housing the grand hall, a ballroom, a theatre and numerous shops and cafés.

Scarborough Castle dates from the 12th century and in its time was twice besieged by Parliamentarian forces, in 1643 and 1648. The Quaker George Fox was imprisoned here in 1665. In the Civil War Scarborough was ultimately the only Royalist port on the east coast and it was not until 1645 that the Castle surrendered to Parliament. Today staged battles in the summer holiday season are a popular attraction for tourists.

There are visible remains of a Roman signal station on Castle Hill, believed to have been built in AD370 as a look-out post.

The port consists of three piers enclosing an outer and inner harbour. Up to 1950 the main industry was fishing but since then the commercial traffic of the port has increased.

Anne Brontë, who died at the age of 28 on 28 May 1849, is buried in the churchyard of the Parish Church of St Mary.

SCARISBRICK Lancashire SD3713
Village on A570, 4 miles (6km) SE of Southport
Pronounced 'Scazebrick', the hall, with its extensive grounds, was sold in 1945 for use as an independent boarding school.

SCARRINGTON Nottinghamshire SK7341
Village off A52, 2 miles (3km) NE of Bingham
Amazing stack of 50,000 discarded horseshoes outside former forge, built up over 20 years from 1945 to a height of 17ft (5m).

SCHIEHALLION Tayside NN7154
Mountain off B846, 4 miles (6km) SE of Kinloch Rannoch
Impressive peak, 3,547ft (1,081m) high, in the Central Highlands used to establish density of earth in the 18th century. Associated with Gaelic folklore.

SCHOLAR GREEN Cheshire SJ8357
Village on A34, 1 mile (2km) N of Kidsgrove
The village is now disturbed by the busy A34 road. Rode Hall is an 18th-century country house, home of Sir Richard Baker Wilbraham and open to the public.

SCILLY, ISLES OF Cornwall
Island group lying W of Land's End
The Scillies consist of well over 100 islands, 28 miles (45km) west of Land's End. Warmed by the Gulf Stream, they have a mild climate with exotic and subtropical plants, and flower-farming as an industry. The population of about 2,000 nearly all live on St Mary's. There is very little traffic, as visitors are not permitted to bring cars or caravans over.

Samson, once inhabited, now has only the ruins of cottages with hedges marking the outlines of ancient fields. Tean was once used for grazing, and people lived there in the summer, burning seaweed for kelp. The ruined hermitage on St Helen's is reputed to be the oldest Christian building on the islands, built between Roman times and the 8th century. Western Rocks are renowned as a graveyard for ships through the centuries and Eastern Isles are home to seabirds and seals. There are remains of a late megalithic settlement on Nornour. Bishop Rock, Britain's tallest lighthouse, is on the southwest tip of the Scillies. The Old Man of Gugh, a standing stone 9ft (3m) high, was erected by Gugh's Bronze Age inhabitants.

The sport of gig-racing can be watched in the summer, and the pilot gig, *Klondyke*, built in 1873, is exhibited in St Mary's Museum.

Hugh Town is the capital of the islands.

SCOLE Norfolk TM1579
Village on A140, 2 miles (3km) E of Diss
Interesting buildings in Scole include the Scole inn, a huge old coaching inn built in 1655 of red brick, and the 16th-century Crossways hotel.

SCOLTON MANOR Dyfed SM9922
Estate off B4329, 5 miles (8km) NE of Haverfordwest
Attractive Scolton Manor Country Park based around 19th-century manor house. Lots of attractions – museum, arboretum, walks, railway exhibits.

SCONE PALACE Tayside NO1126
Mansion off A93, 2 miles (3km) N of Perth
Castellated, mainly Gothic mansion outside New Scone (pronounced 'Scoon'), with remains of the village of Old Scone in its grounds. Scone Abbey was the traditional enthronement place of Scottish monarchs, and Moot Hill was the site of the Stone of Destiny, now in Westminster Abbey. The palace is now the seat of the Earls of Mansfield, with fine collections of furniture, paintings and porcelain.

SCOT'S GAP Northumberland NZ0386
Hamlet on B6343, 1 mile (2km) E of Cambo
Rothley Lake, designed by Capability Brown, is popular with bird-watchers. Two castle follies, Codger Fort (1769) and Rothley Castle (1740s). Prehistoric hillfort on Rothley Crags.

SCOTCH CORNER North Yorkshire NZ2105
Road junction of A1/A66, 9 miles (14km) SW of Darlington
A notable road junction and prominent landmark for motorists. There is a large service station and lorry park serving the needs of travellers.

SCOTLANDWELL Tayside NO1801
Village on A911, 4 miles (6km) W of Leslie
Village to the east of Loch Leven, named from the springs that well up in a stone cistern, built in 1858.

SCOTTER Lincolnshire SE8800
Village on A159, 6 miles (10km) S of Scunthorpe
Large village between Lincolnshire Cliff and the River Trent. Eighteenth-century old manor house, Norman and medieval church beside River Eau.

Stone cistern at Scotlandwell.

SCOURIE Highland NC1544
Village on A894, 8 miles (13km) NW of Kylesku
Tiny crofting village north of Edrachillis Bay, with a fine sandy beach. Noted as the furthest point north where the Atlantic palm grows.

SCRABSTER Highland ND1070
Village on A836, 2 miles (3km) NW of Thurso
Mainland ferry port for Orkney and Faroe Islands at the northwestern end of Thurso Bay.

SCRIVELSBY Lincolnshire TF2665
Site on B1183, 2 miles (3km) S of Horncastle
Hereditary Grand Champion of England lives in medieval gatehouse to demolished Scrivelsby Court. Impressive Lion Gate entrance to deer park.

SCROOBY Nottinghamshire SK6590
Village on A638, 1 mile (2km) S of Bawtry
Home of William Brewster, leader of the *Mayflower* pilgrims. Site of Archbishop's Palace, on Great North road, which received many important visitors.

SCUNTHORPE Humberside SE8910
Town on A18, 21 miles (33km) E of Doncaster
Built on one of the largest ironstone deposits in Europe, Scunthorpe, originally five small agricultural villages, has grown up around its iron and steel industry. By 1875 four ironworks were in operation and by 1890 steel was being produced. Within the span of a century the population rose from 3,000 to 70,000 and railways were built to import coal. By 1960 Scunthorpe's four works were producing one-tenth of the national steel output.

Today only one steelworks remains in Scunthorpe, but modernisation has accelerated its steel output to around one-quarter of the national figure. Much of the former industrial land has been given over to housing and leisure. The town centre has been modernised and has a pedestrian precinct and a large market in High Street.

Scunthorpe Museum and Art Gallery, in the former vicarage of the Church of St Lawrence, incorporates a reconstructed ironworker's cottage and the galleries cover local history, archaeology, natural sciences, and a history of Scunthorpe's steel industry. St Lawrence's Church is the oldest building in Scunthorpe, dating from the 12th century and restored in 1841.

SEA PALLING Norfolk TG4226
Village on B1159, 4 miles (6km) SE of Happisburgh
Safe bathing is available at this small coastal village. The sand dunes have been planted with marram grass to stabilise them.

SEABURN Tyne & Wear NZ4060
District on A183, on N edge of Sunderland
Small, quiet seaside resort with pleasant beaches. Some attractive gardens and the Sunderland greyhound stadium.

SEAFORD East Sussex TV4899
Town on A259, 3 miles (5km) SE of Newhaven
Seaside resort on the open breezy Channel coast, once an important harbour and associate member of the Cinque Ports at the mouth of River Ouse. Its harbour silted up and the river shifted course dramatically during a storm in 1579, leaving the old harbour dry and creating a new one at Newhaven. Shingle beach and superb chalk headland, Seaford Head, with nature reserve.

SEAHAM (OR SEAHAM HARBOUR) Durham NZ4249
Town off A19, 5 miles (8km) S of Sunderland
Lord Londonderry bought Seaham to build a harbour to ship coal. He lived at Seaham Hall, where earlier, in 1815, poet Byron married Isabella Milbanke.

SEAHOUSES Northumberland NU2231
Town on B1340, 3 miles (5km) SE of Bamburgh
Holiday and fishing village. Harbour serves an active fishing fleet and boat trips to Farne Islands. Original kipper smokehouse still functions.

SEALE Surrey SU8947
Village off A31, 4 miles (6km) E of Farnham
A tiny village on Harroway (Pilgrims' Way) under the steep slopes of the Hog's Back. Hog's Back hotel is the site of a 19th-century Admiralty semaphore station.

SEALYHAM Dyfed SM9627
Hamlet off A40, 6 miles (9km) S of Fishguard
Pembrokeshire hamlet famous with dog-lovers for its associations with the Sealyham terrier, a small, white and sometimes cantankerous canine.

SEAMER North Yorkshire TA0183
Village off A64, 4 miles (6km) SW of Scarborough
The earliest trace of a settlement here was in 8000BC when mesolithic men settled on the shore of a lake at Starr Carr.

SEASCALE Cumbria NY0301
Small town on B5343, 12 miles (19km) S of Whitehaven
Once a Victorian seaside resort, now residential area mainly for workers at Sellafield nuclear power station.

SEATHWAITE Cumbria SD2295
Hamlet off A593, 6 miles (10km) N of Broughton in Furness
Claims to be Britain's wettest inhabited spot, with an average annual rainfall of 140in (325cm).

SEATON Cornwall SX3054
Village on B3247, 3 miles (5km) E of Looe
Recent seaside settlement in a wooded valley. Near by, to the west, is the Monkey Sanctuary, with a breeding colony of woolly monkeys.

SEATON Devon SY2490
Small town on B3172, 6 miles (10km) SW of Axminster
A village until the late 19th century, then a coastal resort. Beautiful coastal scenery, especially the chalk stacks of Beer Head to the southwest. Town mostly small-scale and dull. Medieval church a little inland, where the original village was. The Seaton Tramway runs 6 miles (10km) up the Axe Valley.

SEATON CAREW Cleveland NZ5229
Village on A178, at S edge of Hartlepool
Former fishing village with miles of sandy beaches, a popular day out from Middlesbrough.

SEATON DELAVAL Northumberland NZ3075
Town off A190, 4 miles (6km) S of Blyth
A former colliery town. Seaton Delaval Hall was built by Sir John Vanbrugh in Palladian style for Admiral George Delaval. The tiny harbour at Seaton Sluice was built to export coal and an impressive cut through the cliff enables Seaton Burn to sluice the harbour to prevent it from silting up.

SEATON ROSS Humberside SE7840
Village off A163, 6 miles (10km) W of Market Weighton
The village was originally built on the edge of marshland and has the remains of two windmills.

SEAVIEW Isle of Wight SZ6291
Village on B3330, 2 miles (3km) E of Ryde
A rural village developed from late Victorian times as a seaside resort. Toll road along the sea. Flamingo Park has many other birds, too.

SEDBERGH Cumbria SD6591
Small town on A684, 9 miles (14km) E of Kendal
Small stone-built town at the foot of the Howgill Fells has been in Cumbria since 1974 but remains in the Yorkshire Dales National Park. Popular as a holiday base for exploring Yorkshire and Lake District. Narrow main street with 'yards' tucked down alleyways. Sedbergh School, famous 400-year-old boarding school, is in centre of town.

SEDGEFIELD Durham NZ3528
Small town off A689, 8 miles (13km) NW of Stockton-on-Tees
Sedgefield has the only racecourse in County Durham and came to prominence in the equestrian world in 1804 as headquarters of the Lambton Hunt.

SEDGEMOOR Somerset
see North Curry; Somerset Levels; Westonzoyland

SEDLESCOMBE East Sussex TQ7718
Village on B2244, 3 miles (5km) NE of Battle
Large village grouped on either side of a long green with a parish pump under a little stone building of 1900. Former centre of the iron industry, both in Roman times and in the 15th century.

SEEND Wiltshire ST9461
Village on A361, 4 miles (6km) W of Devizes
Full of handsome stone or brick houses, many Georgian. Nice 15th-century church. Iron ore mined here in mid-Victorian times.

SEER GREEN Buckinghamshire SU9692
Village off A355, 2 miles (3km) NE of Beaconsfield
This is pricey commuter territory, and Quaker territory at nearby Jordans, connected with William Penn, founder of Pennsylvania. He, his two wives and ten of his 16 children are buried outside the 1688 Meeting House. Mayflower barn was built of the Pilgrim Fathers' ship's timbers. Jordans village was designed by Fred Rowntree in 1916 as a Quaker garden suburb.

SEFTON Merseyside SD3501
Village on B5422, 3 miles (5km) NE of Crosby
A quaint old agricultural village on the edge of rich arable farmland which retains many of its old stone houses and cottages.

SELATTYN Shropshire SJ2633
Village on B4579, 3 miles (5km) NW of Oswestry
Isolated hill village near Welsh border. Pub and old stone cottages stand beside church with fine medieval wagon roof over chancel.

SELBORNE Hampshire SU7433
Village on B3006, 4 miles (6km) SE of Alton
Beautiful small-scale hills and valleys with lots of beech woods and the popular Selborne Hangar (steep zig-zag steps). Slightly austere village, famous because of *The Natural History of Selborne* (1788), written by Gilbert White who lived here all his life. The Wakes, his home for 60 years, is a museum and includes material on the Oates family too. Lovely walking country. The Mallinson Collection of Rural Relics.

SELBY North Yorkshire SE6132
Town on A19, 13 miles (21km) S of York
The town, dominated by its famous abbey church, is an important local market and shopping centre and a thriving port. Many of the buildings date from the 19th century when the town expanded with the coming of the railway, but its history goes back to the 11th century and the founding of Selby Abbey.

SELHAM West Sussex SU9320
Village off A272, 3 miles (5km) E of Midhurst
No village centre, but stone, tile-hung and brick and timber houses scattered among meadows and heaths near the River Rother. Remarkable old Saxo-Norman church.

SELKIRK Borders NT4728
Town on A7, 9 miles (14km) N of Hawick
Ancient tweed-manufacturing royal burgh above the Ettrick and Yarrow valleys. Halliwells House is a museum telling the story of industrialisation of Tweed Valley. A statue shows explorer Mungo Park (1771–1806), born locally. Flodden Monument was erected in 1913. About 3 miles (5km) west is Bowhill House, a Georgian mansion with superb French antiques and European paintings and woodland walks in the grounds.

The Old Court House at Selkirk.

SELLY OAK West Midlands SP0482
District off A38, in SW Birmingham
Vestiges of the former leafy Victorian suburb linger here, with generous open spaces and pleasant streets, especially in Selly Park.

SELMESTON East Sussex TQ5006
Village off A27, 8 miles (13km) E of Lewes
Attractive village on the plain beneath the South Downs with an old church in a circular Saxon churchyard. Charleston Farmhouse, once home to artists of the Bloomsbury Group, lies to the southwest.

SELSEY West Sussex SZ8593
Town on B2145, 8 miles (13km) S of Chichester
Modern town on Selsey Bill, the most southerly point in Sussex, a low-lying, blunt-nosed headland. Main Street has some flint cottages, bungalows and caravans. Site of first Saxon invasion, AD447, and of St Wilfred's Cathedral, now lost through coastal erosion along with monastic buildings and deer park. A sea wall prevents further erosion. There is a 5 mile (8km) sandy beach at Bracklesham Bay.

SELSLEY Gloucestershire SO8304
Village off B4066, 1 mile (2km) SW of Stroud
Victorian church with array of Pre-Raphaelite windows and walks on Selsley Common draw visitors to this hill village on outskirts of Stroud.

SELWORTHY Somerset SS9146
Village off A39, 2 miles (3km) E of Porlock
Picturesque village on the side of a wooded hill with 1820s thatched cottages built higgeldy piggeldy in large plots around a green. The church is beautifully set, with steep woods behind and dramatic wide views in front. Selworthy Beacon is one of the highest points in the huge area owned by the National Trust here.

SEMPRINGHAM Lincolnshire TF1032
Site off B1177, 8 miles (12km) N of Bourne
Norman church with later tower and chancel, where St Gilbert, who died here in 1189, founded the only English monastic order in 1132. Monastic church, buildings and village have gone.

SENNEN Cornwall SW3525
Village on A30, 1 mile (2km) NE of Land's End
The most westerly village in Britain, just inland from Land's End. Sennen Cove has a small harbour, a famous surfing beach fringed with sand, and a footpath up to Land's End.

SENNYBRIDGE Powys SN9228
Village on A40, 8 miles (13km) W of Brecon
Village largely dating from arrival of railway (line now disused) in 1870s. Army camp serves military training ranges of Mynydd Eppynt to the north.

SETON MAINS Lothian NT4275
Site on A198, 3 miles (5km) E of Prestonpans
Seton Palace was replaced in 1790 by Robert Adam's Seton Castle. Seton collegiate church stands in the grounds, unfinished, but with remarkable vaulted apses.

SETTLE North Yorkshire SD8163
Town off A65, 13 miles (21km) NW of Skipton
Lying at one end of the scenic Settle–Carlisle Railway, this market town has an unusual row of 18th-century

double-decker shops – The Shambles – and a wealth of Georgian buildings. The Museum of North Craven Life illustrates aspects of local history and archaeology.

SEVEN SISTERS East Sussex TV5396

Cliffs E of Cuckmere Haven

This famous landmark is made up of a switchback of vertical chalk cliffs between Cuckmere Haven and Birling Gap, now a clifftop country park with trails, interpretation centre and natural history exhibition at Cuckmere Haven.

SEVEN SISTERS West Glamorgan SN8208

Village off A4109, 8 miles (13km) NE of Neath

Village in former coal-mining area of Dulais Valley. Seven Sisters Museum and Sawmill is a quirky attraction – working sawmill, exhibits plus 'Wild West' Gunsmoke Cowboy Town.

SEVEN SPRINGS Gloucestershire SO9617

Site on A435, 4 miles (6km) SE of Cheltenham

The spring here is source of the River Churn – and firmly believed by locals to be the ultimate source of the River Thames.

SEVENHAMPTON Gloucestershire SP0321

Village off A436, 5 miles (8km) E of Cheltenham

Manor house and stone cottages cluster beside infant River Coln. Fine brass commemorates benefactor who rebuilt impressive church in 15th century.

SEVENOAKS Kent TQ5255

Town off A21, 6 miles (10km) N of Tonbridge

A pleasant country town 500ft (152m) up, overlooking the Weald, Sevenoaks stands at the gates of its great house, Knole (National Trust), set in a superb deer park. Knole was built from 1456 and has been home to the Sackville family since 1603. The High Street is very attractive with many 17th- to 19th-century houses. There is a museum, theatre, a famous school and a wildfowl reserve. Sevenoaks hosts a summer festival.

SEVENOAKS WEALD Kent TQ5250

Village off A21, 3 miles (5km) SW of Sevenoaks

Pretty village with a little green in wooded countryside, with a church of 1820 and Else's Farm, where poet Edward Thomas lived in the early 20th century.

SEVERN BEACH Avon ST5484

Village off A403, 8 miles (13km) NW of Bristol

Tiny village on the Bristol Channel shore, the take-off point for the new Severn road bridge and a massive new road system.

SEVERN BRIDGE Avon

see Aust

SEVERN, RIVER Gloucestershire/Powys

River, rises on Plynlimon

Flowing from mid-Wales to the Bristol Channel, the River Severn was for centuries the main commercial outlet for the Midlands and now provides a popular route for pleasure craft.

The Severn Bore, a small tidal wave occurring above the estuary, attracts many onlookers, and further upstream tourists enjoy views of river from steam trains on the restored Severn Valley Railway between Bridgnorth and Kidderminster.

The River Severn eventually flows into the Severn estuary along the South Wales coast.

SHADFORTH Durham NZ3441

Village off B1283, 5 miles (8km) E of Durham

A quiet village with mainly white and grey houses lining a long, narrow green. In its present form dates from around 1080.

SHAFTESBURY Dorset ST8622

Small town on A30, 18 miles (29km) W of Salisbury

This hilltop town, overlooking the Blackmoor Vale (see), was an important centre in medieval times, but is a quiet backwater today. Many older cottages (some still thatched) are built of the local greensand. The steep cobbled Gold Hill, with cottages down one side and buttressed stone wall down the other, is the most famous view in the town.

The medieval town had 12 churches and chapels, but only three survive. The footings of the abbey church, where the bones of St Edward the Martyr were housed from his death in 978, can be seen, but little else of the huge abbey.

The old suburb of St James is at the foot of one of the steep slopes which border the town. Local museum.

SHAKESPEARE COUNTRY Warwickshire

Historic region

Impossible to define, and largely an invention of the tourist industry, this is a convenient term for Stratford-upon-Avon and nearby villages such as Shottery with Shakespeare family connections. The name has also been applied to the surrounding countryside in Warwickshire and Worcestershire that lingered in Shakespeare's memory and occasionally shows through in the characters and settings of his plays.

SHALDON Devon SX9372

Village on B3199, 5 miles (8km) NE of Torquay

Regency resort on the Teign estuary opposite Teignmouth (see). White stucco villas and cottages, with a foot ferry across the narrow river mouth.

SHALFLEET Isle of Wight SZ4189

Village on A3054, 4 miles (6km) E of Yarmouth

Pretty village with a large, squat Norman church tower, and a quiet creek to the north.

SHALFORD Surrey TQ0047

Village on A281, immediately S of Guildford

Attractive village, centred on a tiny square flanked by old cottages and a church, with a long green to south. Watermeadows along the River Wey separate the village from Guildford. Shalford Fair may have been the original of Bunyan's Vanity Fair.

SHAMLEY GREEN Surrey TQ0343
Village on B2128, 4 miles (6km) SE of Guildford
Enormous irregularly shaped village green, more of a common, with Victorian houses and half-timbered 16th- and 17th-century cottages.

SHANKLIN Isle of Wight SZ5881
Town on A3055, 2 miles (3km) SW of Sandown
This interesting town is separated from its sandy shore and promenade by a vertical cliff (with a lift). The old village has picturesque thatched cottages and Shanklin Chine, a little woody ravine with a stream falling to the sea, is floodlit at dusk. Rylestone Gardens have good displays of plants and, in summer, the Island Countryside Centre, with displays.

SHAP Cumbria NY5615
Small town on A6, 9 miles (14km) S of Penrith
The town is famous for its bad weather, as almost every winter the A6 over Shap summit is blocked by snow. Keld Chapel, preserved by the National Trust, is 15th century and used only once a year, in August. Shap Abbey (English Heritage) was established in 1201 in this remote location.

SHAPINSAY Orkney
Island to E of mainland
Large and comparatively fertile island off Mainland. Water-powered mill at Elwick Hall. Balfour Castle is Victorian baronial, with a walled garden.

SHAPWICK Dorset ST9301
Village off A350, 5 miles (8km) SE of Blandford Forum
Down in the flat valley of the River Stour, Shapwick has many thatched cottages. Badbury Rings is an Iron Age hillfort with a Roman road close by.

SHARDLOW Derbyshire SK4330
Village on A6, 6 miles (10km) SE of Derby
Former inland port on the Trent and Mersey Canal (1777). Cavendish Bridge, opened 17 years earlier, provided easier road route over River Trent than Swarkestone (see). Mix of warehouses and domestic buildings. Late 18th-century Shardlow Lodge, now a restaurant, was a canal carrier's house. Shardlow Hall (now offices) is late 17th century with Palladian wings and late 18th-century pavilions.

SHARESHILL Staffordshire SJ9406
Village off A460, 5 miles (8km) NE of Wolverhampton
Commuter village on rural fringe of Wolverhampton retains a few old houses and boasts elegant 18th-century church.

SHARNBROOK Bedfordshire SP9959
Village off A6, 7 miles (11km) NW of Bedford
Home of Unilever's food research laboratories. An amateur theatre occupies the former mill.

SHARPENHOE Bedfordshire TL0630
Village off A6, 6 miles (10km) N of Luton
At the foot of Sharpenhoe Clappers (National Trust), a tree-crowned Chilterns spur commanding wide views over the Great Ouse.

SHARPNESS Gloucestershire SO6702
Village on B4066, 3 miles (5km) NW of Berkeley
A busy port on the Severn estuary, outlet of Gloucester–Sharpness Canal, completed in 1827 to bring large ships into Gloucester.

SHAW Greater Manchester SD9308
Town on A663, 3 miles (5km) N of Oldham
An undistinguished market town, Shaw is founded on the cotton industry and was the home of some of its most dynamic leaders.

SHAWELL Leicestershire SP5480
Village off A426, 4 miles (6km) NE of Rugby
Close to Watling Street (A5),the Roman settlement of *Tripontium*, and Warwickshire border. Hilltop church of 1860s, with 15th-century tower.

SHEBBEAR Devon SS4309
Village off A3072, 7 miles (11km) NE of Holsworthy
Village set around a large square. The Devil's Stone hotel is named after a stone in the churchyard which has to be turned each year to let the devil out.

SHEEPSTOR Devon SX5667
Village off B3212, 4 miles (6km) SW of Princetown
Granite Dartmoor hamlet, with the rocky tor one side and the huge Burrator Reservoir, created 1891, on the other. Supplies water to Plymouth, and looks like a natural lake.

SHEEPWASH Devon SS4806
Village off A3072, 4 miles (6km) W of Hatherleigh
Partly set around a square, pretty with several thatched cottages.

SHEEPY MAGNA Leicestershire SK3201
Village on B4116, 3 miles (5km) N of Atherstone
On River Sence, close to Warwickshire border. New House Grange, moated site with house of about 1700, early 16th-century timber-framed tithe barn.

SHEERNESS Kent TQ9175
Town on A249, 10 miles (16km) N of Sittingbourne
A dockyard town, deep-water port and seaside resort on the extreme northwest tip of the Isle of Sheppey at the confluence of the rivers Thames and Medway. The Promenade, resplendent with gardens and amusements, overlooks the busy Thames estuary and beach. Deep-water container port near the site of naval dockyards (1665–1961), now a trading estate.

SHEFFIELD South Yorkshire SK3587
City off M1, 144 miles (232km) NW of London
Sheffield is Britain's fifth largest city with a population of 520,000, famous for its manufacture of steel and cutlery. It sits in the southern foothills of the Pennines on the River Don in a surrounding landscape predominantly of valleys and trees, and is very much an industrial city in a country setting.

By the 17th century this small town had already acquired a reputation for its knives and tools, exploiting the fast-flowing rivers which turned grindstones and hammers. In the second half of the 17th century

Sheffield also began to make its own steel. Although of a much later period, the only visible reminder today of Sheffield's first steel-making technology is the cementation furnace preserved at Hoyle Street in the Netherhope district of the city.

During the Industrial Revolution steel, cutlery and tool production expanded enormously. Benjamin Huntsman's invention in 1742 of a way to make a superior form of steel, crucible steel, transformed steel-making processes. By 1850 Sheffield was producing 90 per cent of Britain's steel.

In 1913 Harry Brearley accidentally discovered stainless steel as he sought to prevent the rusting of barrels in Lee Enfield Rifles. He was quick to see the commercial potential of his discovery and it was soon used for cutlery, engineering, and surgical instruments.

Although Sheffield's metal-manufacturing industries contracted in terms of employment during the post-war era, the output of steel, cutting edges and cutlery has never been higher. To maintain employment levels the city has diversified into the service sector which now employs over 70 per cent of the workforce.

Along the central corridor from Castlegate in the north of the city to Moorfoot in the south are the city's main shopping areas. The Moor and Fargate are pedestrianised and Orchard Square, in the heart of the city centre, is now a courtyard-style shopping precinct but was once a clutter of small workshops. Here John Brown, inventor of the railway buffer and pioneer manufacturer of railway lines and armour plate, began his career. His achievements are commemorated by Elsie the buffer girl, who appears each quarter hour on the square's clock tower.

Sheffield has few early buildings of note. Those of the 19th century include the Cutlers' Hall with its Grecian façade, and there are some Georgian houses close by in Paradise Square. At Cutlers' Hall, visitors can see the Norfolk Knife which was two years in the making and a top prize-winner for its unsurpassed craftsmanship at the 1851 Great Exhibition.

Kelham Island Industrial Museum on Alma Street contains a 10 ton bomb and the 400 ton working River Don Engine. Abbeydale Industrial Hamlet is a restored 18th-century working site with forges, furnaces and water-driven hammers.

Sheffield's Crucible Theatre is probably best known as the venue of the annual World Snooker Championship, but it is also a leading repertory theatre.

SHEFFIELD GREEN East Sussex TQ4125
Village on A275, 2 miles (3km) S of Danehill
Crossroads village on the edge of Sheffield Park, a privately owned mansion with National Trust garden of over 100 acres (40ha), landscaped in the 18th century by Capability Brown. Sheffield Park is the headquarters of the Bluebell Railway, which runs 10 miles (16km) to Kingscote (to be extended to East Grinstead). The locomotive sheds house a large collection of vintage steam trains.

SHEFFORD Bedfordshire TL1439
Small town off A600, 9 miles (14km) SE of Bedford
Originally a 'sheep-ford', on the rivers Flitt, Hitt and the19th-century Ivel Navigation. Nearby Chicksands Priory (limited opening) was the home of the Osborne family from 1576 to 1936, now in the Royal Air Force station; mainly of the 18th and early 19th centuries, with stained glass, Coade statues, and numerous ghosts, including that of a walled-up nun. Dorothy Osborne wrote famous letters here.

SHELDON MANOR Wiltshire ST8874
Mansion off A420, 2 miles (3km) W of Chippenham
Superb stone manor house, with an amazingly large porch of about 1282. Little 15th-century chapel. Good gardens.

SHELLOW BOWELLS Essex TL6007
Hamlet off A1060, 4 miles (6km) S of Leaden Roding
Scattered farms and houses. Curious name comes from the de Buella lords of the manor, of Bouelles in France.

SHELSLEY WALSH Hereford and Worcester SO7263
Hamlet off B4204, 7 miles (11km) NE of Bromyard
Peaceful cluster of timber-framed cottages and an Elizabethan manor house beside the River Teme. Superlative woodwork in nearby church.

SHELTON Bedfordshire TL0368
Village off B645 (A45), 5 miles (8km) E of Higham Ferrers
One of Bedfordshire's prettiest villages with cottages, a former manor house, a rectory and a simple, unspoiled medieval church.

SHELTON Norfolk TM2291
Hamlet off A140, 5 miles (8km) N of Harleston
A peaceful hamlet with an abundance of wildlife, Shelton was not so idyllic when it was ruled by the powerful 16th-century Boleyn family.

SHELVE Shropshire SO3399
Hamlet off A488, 7 miles (11km) N of Bishop's Castle
Small, rubble-built church is centre of lonely hamlet in former lead-mining country below the Stiperstones (see Shropshire Hills).

SHENLEY Hertfordshire TL1800
Village on B5378, 5 miles (8km) SE of St Albans
Set among hospitals. 'Be sober, Do well, Fear not, Be vigilant', says old village lock-up. Nicholas Hawksmoor, architect, buried in churchyard.

SHENSTONE Staffordshire SK1104
Village off A5127, 3 miles (5km) S of Lichfield
Popular village in wooded surroundings. Old magistrate's courtroom survives in Bull's Head and pleasant old houses in centre compensate for modern estates.

SHEPPERTON Surrey TQ0867
Town on B375, SW of Sunbury
Attractive village famed for its film studios on a meander of the River Thames, on to which Ferry Square opens. Behind is Church Square, the centre of the old village, with a church, a 400-year-old inn and elegant 18th-century houses. The new part of Shepperton centres on the railway station, joined to the old village by High Street. Reinstated ferry crosses the Thames to Weybridge from Shepperton Lock.

SHEPPEY, ISLE OF Kent TQ9770
Island on A249, off N coast of Kent
Island off the north Kent coast, 9 miles (14km) long, 5 miles (8km) broad, separated from the mainland by the Swale and Medway estuary. The main towns are Sheerness and Queenborough. Accessible by Kingsferry Bridge over the Swale. A ridge runs east–west along the island, dropping north to the Thames estuary as cliffs. To the south are reclaimed marshes broken by creeks, with the internationally important nature reserve of the Swale, rich in birdlife.

SHEPRETH Cambridgeshire TL3947
Village off A10, 5 miles (8km) NE of Royston
Docwra's Manor is an 18th-century house with excellent gardens, while Manor Farm dates from 1500. There is also a fish farm and wildlife sanctuary.

SHEPSHED Leicestershire SK4719
Town off A512, 4 miles (6km) W of Loughborough
Small industrial town whose 19th-century growth was based on footwear and hosiery industries. Some cottages used by framework knitters remain near the medieval church. Galleries were inserted into the church in 1844 to cater for growing population. Fine monuments to Phillipps family of Garendon, from 1696–1830. Nearby Blackbrook windmill has been converted into a house.

SHEPTON MALLET Somerset ST6143
Town off A37, 18 miles (29km) S of Bristol
Small, mostly of stone. In the centre there is an elaborate market cross, and wooden medieval market stalls. The church has a fine Somerset tower, and perhaps the finest wagon roof in the country, with angels, 350 panels and bosses. Brewing has been an important industry, with a big Victorian brewery on the outskirts. Babycham is made here. Local museum.

SHERBORNE Dorset ST6316
Town on A30, 5 miles (8km) E of Yeovil
The prettiest town in Dorset is like a miniature cathedral city. Its huge and beautiful church (the best in the county) was once the abbey church, with famous stone fan-vaulting and many fine monuments ranging from medieval abbots to later local landowners. The famous public school developed from the abbey school, and now has buildings all over the town, as well as on the original site of the abbey buildings.

Most of the town is built of the local orange stone, but the main street has timber-framing as well, a good mixture of small-scale buildings running up the hill from the little market house, a monastic building of the 16th century. Local museum. The Almshouse of St John (limited opening) still has its original 1440s buildings, including the chapel.

Just outside the town are two castles: the Old Castle (English Heritage) has the substantial ruins of a fortified palace built by a bishop of Salisbury in the 12th century, and the New Castle was started by Sir Walter Raleigh in the 1590s, with later wings.

SHERBORNE Gloucestershire SP1714
Village off A40, 5 miles (8km) W of Burford
National Trust owns Sherborne Park and rows of attractive estate cottages of 17th, 18th and 19th centuries.

SHERBORNE ST JOHN Hampshire SU6255
Village off A340, 3 miles (5km) NW of Basingstoke
Unusual 1533 brick porch to the church. The 16th-century Vyne (National Trust) was the first English house to be given a classical portico (1655). Fine 18th-century rooms.

SHERBURN IN ELMET North Yorkshire SE4933
Small town on A162, 6 miles (10km) S of Tadcaster
The village lies in the shadow of All Saints' Church. Steeton Hall was a late medieval castle of which only the gatehouse (English Heritage) remains.

SHERE Surrey TQ0747
Village off A25, 5 miles (8km) E of Guildford
In the wooded Tillingbourne Valley, this lovely compact little village is claimed to be the prettiest in Surrey. A small green known as The Square is surrounded by well-kept half-timbered houses of the 18th and 19th centuries, with older half-timbering in the rest of the village. Exceptional, cruciform 12th-century church on a Saxon foundation with a 'squint' for the 14th-century anchoress who lived in a vanished external cell.

Cottage with Norman doorway in Sherborne, Gloucestershire.

SHERFIELD ON LODDON Hampshire SU6758
Village off A33, 5 miles (8km) NE of Basingstoke
The old village surrounds a large green, which has wooded parts, ponds and bogs. Several older houses are moated.

SHERIFF HUTTON North Yorkshire SE6566
Village off B1363, 4 miles (6km) NE of Strensall
The substantial ruins of the Sheriff's stone castle, which was built in 1382, remain a landmark and are owned by the village.

SHERINGHAM Norfolk TG1543
Town on A149, 4 miles (6km) W of Cromer
This bustling old fishing village slips easily into its more recent role as a popular holiday resort. Elegant Georgian and Edwardian houses surround the small flint-built fishermen's cottages. Rugged cliffs turn into rolling wooded hills rich in wildlife. Sheringham Park (National Trust) is 770 acres (312ha) of parkland, some of which was landscaped by Sir Humphry Repton. Terminus of North Norfolk Railway.

SHERINGTON Buckinghamshire SP8846
Village off A509, 2 miles (3km) NE of Newport Pagnell
Dormitory for Newport Pagnell (see) and Milton Keynes (see). England's only church dedicated to St Laud, an obscure French bishop.

SHERNBORNE Norfolk TF7132
Hamlet off A149, 6 miles (10km) S of Hunstanton
Moated Shernborne Hall (not open) is built on the site of an earlier house. The church was restored in 1898 with money from the Prince of Wales.

SHERSTON Wiltshire ST8586
Village on B4040, 5 miles (8km) W of Malmesbury
Once a small market town on the edge of the Cotswolds. Wide High Street with 16th-century onwards houses. Impressive medieval church with 1730 tower.

SHERWOOD FOREST Nottinghamshire
Historic area NE of Nottingham
Extensive royal hunting forest of woodland and open areas, formerly covering 160 square miles (414 sq km), about 20 per cent of the county, nearly reaching the city. Known worldwide as setting for outlaw Robin Hood and his men. Oaks and silver birches of ancient woodland form Sherwood Forest Country Park near Edwinstowe (see). Footpaths, cycle trails, picnic sites.

SHETLAND ISLANDS Shetland
Island group N of the Orkneys
This far-northerly 100-island group, of which 15 are inhabited, lies as close to Norway as to the southern Highlands of Scotland, a fact reflected in its history and attitudes. Although so far north, the Gulf Stream produces a mild, though windy climate and the islands support many sheep on gently undulating moorlands. The coastal scenery is superb, with dramatic cliffs and huge vistas suffused with light of exceptional clarity.

There are many notable prehistoric and Pictish remains. Peaceful Norse settlement probably began before the Shetlands came under Norwegian sovereignty in 911, where they remained until 1470. Fishing was developed by the Dutch and became economically vital, along with knitting and the Merchant Navy service. During the mid-20th century fishing declined and economic depression followed, the situation being dramatically rescued by the oil boom of the 1970s, which has brought huge prosperity. The oil revenue proceeds have been used to develop new industries and expand existing ones; fishing today employs 20 per cent of the population. Tourism is becoming increasingly important as modern transport makes the islands easier to reach for those seeking tranquillity in unforgettable surroundings.

SHEVIOCK Cornwall SX3755
Village on A374, 4 miles (6km) W of Torpoint
Small village rather dominated by the road. The church has a medieval spire, rare in this county. Lovely estuary scenery to the north and south.

SHIFNAL Shropshire SJ7407
Small town on A464, 2 miles (3km) E of Telford
Railway viaduct crossing centre of this old market town does not detract from array of handsome buildings, including timber-framed Nell Gwyn pub, 17th-century Old Idsall House, Idsall House of 1699, Georgian Old Rectory and elegant Decker Hall (golf clubhouse) of 1810. Very big church has Norman and medieval work of exceptional architectural interest.

SHILBOTTLE Northumberland NU1908
Village off A1, 3 miles (5km) S of Alnwick
Grew to house workers employed in local industries of drift mining, quarrying and limeworks. The colliery closed in 1982.

SHILDON Durham NZ2226
Town on B6282, 2 miles (3km) SE of Bishop Auckland
Victorian railway town, once the centre for wagon-building and repair. The Timothy Hackworth Museum has a working replica of his famous engine *Sans Pareil*.

SHILLINGFORD Oxfordshire SU5992
Village on A4074, 5 miles (8km) N of Wallingford
This small settlement on a pretty stretch of River Thames near Dorchester has some fine old buildings and an attractive balustraded bridge.

SHILLINGTON Bedfordshire TL1234
Village off A507, 3 miles (5km) SW of Shefford
Handsome medieval church set commandingly on a hill. Pleasant atmosphere, with old houses. Deacon Hill viewpoint to south.

SHINCLIFFE Durham NZ2940
Village on A177, 2 miles (3km) SE of Durham
Made up of two distinct parts, the older Shincliffe Village, now a conservation area, and newer High Shincliffe.

SHINFIELD Berkshire SU7268
Village on A327, 4 miles (6km) S of Reading
Still a village, despite being so near Reading. School Green has the original school of 1707 flanked by Victorian additions.

SHIPBOURNE Kent TQ5952
Village on A227, 4 miles (6km) N of Tonbridge
Scattered village with a large green faced by a few houses, a Victorian church and a pub.

SHIPDHAM Norfolk TF9507
Village on A1075, 4 miles (6km) SW of East Dereham
Lively village which had a World War II airbase. The church has a cupola and one of the finest Tudor wooden lecterns in the world.

SHIPLAKE Oxfordshire SU7678
Village on A4155, 3 miles (5km) S of Henley-on-Thames
Poet Alfred Tennyson was married here in church that has fine collection of medieval French glass. Some notable houses reflect Shiplake's Edwardian popularity.

SHIPLEY Derbyshire SK4445
Village on A6007, 2 miles (3km) NW of Ilkeston
Shipley Hall demolished. Country park of lakes and woodland, open spaces, nature trails and a visitor centre. Farming project for groups, by appointment.

SHIPLEY West Sussex TQ1421
Village off A272, 4 miles (6km) W of Cowfold
Quiet little village of scattered houses on the River Adur with a renovated smock mill (associated with Hilaire Belloc) and interesting church built in 1125 by the Knights Templar.

Restored windmill at Shipley, West Sussex.

SHIPLEY West Yorkshire SE1437
Town on A657, 3 miles (5km) NW of Bradford
Several notable houses including one dated 1593, with mullioned windows and gargoyles. The town is the home of the World of Sooty exhibition.

SHIPSTON ON STOUR Warwickshire SP2540
Small town on A3400, 10 miles (16km) SE of Stratford upon Avon
Former wool village is now pleasant small market town with wealth of old pubs and handsome buildings in its main streets.

SHIPTON Shropshire SO5691
Village on B4378, 6 miles (10km) SW of Much Wenlock
Shipton Hall of 1587 (limited opening), built in local limestone, graces this small village overlooking Corvedale. Norman and Tudor church in grounds.

SHIPTON-UNDER-WYCHWOOD Oxfordshire SP2717
Village on A361, 4 miles (6km) NE of Burford
Large village in the Evenlode Valley, once the centre of Wychwood Forest. Its church has interesting Norman and medieval features and the handsome old buildings include Shipton Court (not open), one of England's largest Jacobean houses, the 15th-century Shaven Crown hotel (once the guesthouse of Bruern Abbey) and Prebendal House with its medieval tithe barn.

SHIREBROOK Derbyshire SK5267
Town on B6407, 4 miles (6km) N of Mansfield
On Nottinghamshire border, in area developed for coal-mining (now finished), close to pleasant wooded country. Kissingate leisure centre.

SHIREOAKS Nottinghamshire SK5580
Village off A57, 2 miles (3km) NW of Worksop
Nineteenth-century church and miners' cottages by Duke of Newcastle. Shireoaks Hall, of about 1600 but much altered, and remains of outstanding water garden.

SHIRLEY Derbyshire SK2141
Village off A52, 4 miles (6km) SE of Ashbourne
Shirley Hall is a 16th-century timber-framed house. Shirley House, neo-Tudor, dates from 1939. The old rectory was the birthplace of writer John Cowper Powys in 1872.

SHIRLEY West Midlands SP1178
District off A34, on W edge of Solihull
Suburban housing, offices and light industry mingle pleasantly here, within easy reach of open countryside south of Birmingham.

SHOBDON Hereford and Worcester SO4062
Village on B4362, 6 miles (10km) W of Leominster
Plain church exterior conceals extravagant Gothick furnishings installed by 18th-century owner of Shobdon Court. Three arches from original church on hill above.

SHOEBURYNESS Essex TQ9385
District off A13, on E edge of Southend-on-Sea
Developed after the Royal Artillery's arrival in the mid-19th century to establish coastal firing ranges here. Minor seaside resort, council estates.

SHOREDITCH Greater London TQ3382
District in borough of Hackney
St Leonard's Church, 18th century, has a 1990s peal of bells. Geffrye Museum in former almshouses covers English domestic interiors.

SHOREHAM Kent TQ5161
Village off A225, 4 miles (6km) N of Sevenoaks
Peaceful village in Darent Valley under steep downland slopes, associated with early 19th-century artist and visionary, Samuel Palmer.

SHOREHAM-BY-SEA West Sussex TQ2105
Town on A259, 6 miles (10km) W of Brighton
Commercial port, industrial centre and seaside resort at the mouth of the River Adur. The present harbour is in a natural lagoon parallel to the coast. Earlier harbours were at Old Shoreham, up the valley, and New Shoreham, at the river mouth. Charles II escaped to France from Shoreham in 1651. There were important ship-building yards here from the Middle Ages to the end of the 19th century. Airport. Shingle beach, museum and parish church (1140), in style unique in England, at New Shoreham.

SHORWELL Isle of Wight SZ4582
Village on B3323, 5 miles (8km) SW of Newport
Thatched stone cottages set just below the chalk downs. Little spire on the church and several Elizabethan or Jacobean houses. Yafford Mill and Farm Park.

SHOTESHAM Norfolk TM2499
Village off B1332, 6 miles (10km) S of Norwich
Hidden in rural south Norfolk, Shotesham stands near a tributary of the River Tas, and lines it with thatched cottages and weeping willows.

SHOTLEY Suffolk TM2336
Village on B1456, 7 miles (11km) SE of Ipswich
Situated on hill overlooking the Stour estuary marshes, with Royal Naval School HMS *Ganges*. Hundreds of sailors are buried in the churchyard.

SHOTLEY BRIDGE Durham NZ0952
Village on B6278, on NW outskirts of Consett
Although much has changed, the village is still pleasant. It was largely dependent for many years upon the steelworks at Consett.

SHOTTERY Warwickshire SP1854
see Stratford-upon-Avon

SHOTTESBROOKE Berkshire SU8477
Site off B3024, 3 miles (5km) E of Twyford
Shottesbrooke Park (not open) is an unusual late 18th-century neo-Gothic house, close to the superb church – 14th century with a central spire like a cathedral.

SHOTTON Clywd SJ3068
Town on A548, immediately W of Queensferry
Parts of conurbation along mouth of River Dee stretching from Queensferry to Connah's Quay. Site of British Steel works.

SHOTTON Durham NZ4139
Village off A19 in SW outskirts of Peterlee
Old mining village now incorporated into the outskirts of Peterlee (see). Shotton Colliery opened in 1840 and finally closed down in 1972.

SHOTTS Strathclyde NS8759
Town off A71, 6 miles (10km) NW of Wishaw
An Industrial Revolution show town on the old Edinburgh–Glasgow route, famed for iron- and coal-mining. The pits are now closed but a new prison provides employment.

SHOTWICK Cheshire SJ3371
Village off A550, 5 miles (8km) NW of Chester
Dominated by St Michael's Church, which overlooks the River Dee. Once a port, the churchyard wall still has an iron ring for mooring boats.

SHREWSBURY Shropshire SJ4912
Town off A5, 39 miles (63 km) NW of Birmingham
Shrewsbury became important soon after the Norman invasion when William the Conqueror's trusted colleague Roger de Montgomery established a castle in a remarkable loop of the River Severn, which makes the old town centre almost an island. The castle still stands, greatly changed after its conversion to a house in the 18th century, and so does the fine church of the abbey founded by Roger de Montgomery and made famous by Ellis Peters in the Brother Cadfael novels.

Later medieval and Tudor development gave the town the superb St Mary's Church and the rich array of timber-framed buildings in the town centre streets and across the Welsh Bridge in Frankwell. Outstanding among these are the medieval Bear Steps, the market hall in the square, the huge Ireland's Mansion in High Street, the Abbot's House in Butcher Row and Rowley's House in Barker Street. Equally distinguished are the Tudor and Jacobean stone buildings opposite the castle, originally occupied by Shrewsbury School and now housing the library.

Shrewsbury's popularity among fashionable society in the 18th century produced a wealth of good Georgian building, largely concentrated in the south-eastern area up against the old town walls and overlooking the river. There is much to admire in these quiet and elegant streets, especially the classical church of St Chad with its round nave.

The town's early history is interpreted at Rowley's House Museum, and its later life is illustrated at the Clive House Museum on College Hill. There is also a fascinating military museum at the Castle. But Shrewsbury does not live in the past. It is a bustling county town with excellent shopping facilities, including large stores in Castle Street and modern shopping centres unobtrusively developed in Pride Hill and Mardol.

SHREWTON Wiltshire ST0643
Village on A360, 6 miles (10km) W of Amesbury
Large village on the River Avon but rather dominated by the main road. Little domed 18th-century lock-up in the middle.

SHRIVENHAM Oxfordshire SU2489
Village off A420, 6 miles (10km) NE of Swindon
Extensive buildings of Royal Military College of Science dominate this village below Lambourn Downs. Fine monuments in the rewarding church.

SHROPSHIRE HILLS
Area of Outstanding Natural Beauty
Church Stretton, the 'capital' of the Shropshire Hills, is the best centre for exploring this unspoilt upland area. The town overlooks the Stretton Gap, where road and railway find the only easy route between the Long Mynd to the west and the looming ridge to the east known as the Church Stretton Hills. A ridge-top walk along this range from the south will take in three minor peaks at over 1,000ft (366m) before rising to the stark summit of Caer Caradoc (1,500ft/550m), crowned with an Iron Age hillfort. The gentler whaleback of Lawley Hill completes the walk.

There are no peaks on the Long Mynd (see), which is an exhilarating high plateau crossed by a minor road from Church Stretton. The road travels north-west, eventually arriving beneath the jagged Stiperstones – huge outcrops of quartzite with the 'Devil's Chair' at the centre. They create a sinister atmosphere and have attracted various superstitions, but they make a fine objective for a walk, which can also take in the surviving buildings and spoil heaps of the lead mines that flourished below them at Snailbeach.

SHUDY CAMPS Cambridgeshire TL6244
Village off A604, 3 miles (5km) W of Haverhill
'Shudy' was added in the 13th century, apparently implying 'shanty'. The approach from the east is past parkland with thatched cottages and willows.

SHUTE Devon SY2597
Village on B3161, 3 miles (5km) W of Axminster
Small and rural, with the Elizabethan gatehouse (not open) to Shute Barton (National Trust), a 15th-century house. Many memorials in the church to the Pole family who built the big Georgian house.

SIBLE HEDINGHAM Essex TL7734
Small town off A604, 3 miles (5km) NW of Halstead
On a Roman road. Something of a village flavour surviving round the church, 15th-century White Horse inn and old houses.

SIBSEY Lincolnshire TF3550
Village on A16, 5 miles (7km) NE of Boston
Sibsey Trader windmill (English Heritage) of 1877, with six sails and machinery intact, open and operated occasionally. Norman and medieval church.

SIBTHORPE Nottinghamshire SK7645
Village off A46, 6 miles (10km) SW of Newark-on-Trent
Large round 13th- or 14th-century dovecote with 1,260 nesting boxes. Church has 13th-century tower, 14th-century chancel, 18th-century nave, 16th-century alabaster monument.

SIBTON Suffolk TM3669
Village on A1120, 2 miles (3km) W of Yoxford
Linked to Peasenhall (see), Sibton has a spacious 19th-century atmosphere. An abbey was founded here in 1150.

SIDBURY Devon SY1391
Village on A375, 3 miles (5km) N of Sidmouth
Beautifully set in a green valley with many cob cottages and a proper village church, a mixture of dates from Saxon onwards. Sand (limited opening) is a 16th-century stone manor house.

SIDCUP Greater London TQ4672
District in borough of Bexley
Extensively developed from the 1920s on, now studded with post-war blocks of flats and offices. Scadbury Park Nature Reserve to south.

SIDDINGTON Gloucestershire SU0399
Village off A419, 1 mile (2km) SE of Cirencester
In this former canal village a medieval barn stands next to a church with good Norman carving, an unusual font and medieval craft work.

SIDLAW HILLS Tayside
Hill range between Perth and Glamis
Long, low range of hills running east to west from near Montrose to Perth and forming the southern boundary of Strathmore.

SIDMOUTH Devon SY1287
Town on B3175, 13 miles (21km) E of Exeter
Charming Regency seaside resort set in a narrow valley between high red sandstone cliffs. A little fishing village until the late 18th century, Sidmouth then developed quickly as a select resort. The town still has quantities of Regency buildings, most of them stuccoed. Elegant

Circular dovecote at Sibthorpe.

villas and quirky Gothic-windowed cottages – some large, some thatched – are still surrounded by green spaces. The little Esplanade has terraces too. The infant Princess Victoria was staying here with her parents in 1819 when her father died. Her presence added to the fashionable appeal of the town, and she contributed towards the rebuilding of the church, in 1860. There is a Vintage Toy and Train Museum and a local museum, and an International Folk Festival every August.

A pretty walk up the River Sid leads to Sidford, once a hamlet on the main road, now joined to Sidmouth. Medieval bridge over the river. Donkey Sanctuary to the east.

SILBURY HILL Wiltshire SU0968
Village on A4, 1 mile (2km) S of Avebury
One of the most impressive archaeological monuments in the country – a mound 550ft (167m) across the base and 130ft (39m) high, with a ditch round it. Part of the Avebury (see) complex of sites, and probably neolithic.

SILCHESTER Hampshire SU6262
Village off A340, 7 miles (11km) N of Basingstoke
A Roman town, *Calleva Atrebatum*, which was deserted after the Romans left and is now farmland. The walls and the amphitheatre survive. Parts of the town were excavated in the 19th century. Little museum. The medieval church is tucked up next to part of the Roman wall, and has a very pretty 16th-century screen.

SILK WILLOUGHBY Lincolnshire TF0542
Village on A15, 2 miles (3km) S of Sleaford
Ornate steeple on 14th-century St Denis' Church, which has ancient pews. Village cross on carved base.

SILLOTH Cumbria NY1153
Town on B5302, 10 miles (16km) NW of Wigton
Airy seaside town with wide, cobbled streets, spacious greens, sandy beaches and dunes. Magnificent views across the Solway Firth to the southern lowlands of Scotland.

SILSDEN West Yorkshire SE0446
Town on A6034, 4 miles (6km) N of Keighley
A well-contained stone-built industrial town which spreads uphill from the Leeds and Liverpool Canal. Newer housing on the outskirts.

SILSOE Bedfordshire TL0835
Village off A6, 1 mile (2km) S of Clophill
Gleaming white cottages and a striking mock-medieval 1830s church. Wrest Park (English Heritage, limited opening) was the seat of the de Grey family, Earls of Kent, whose mausoleum is at Flitton (see). Now occupied by quangocrats, the house dates from the 1830s, with sumptuous grounds in every style from around 1700 to 1850.

SILVERDALE Lancashire SD4674
Village off A6, 4 miles (6km) NW of Carnforth
To the east of the village is Leighton Moss, managed as a nature reserve by the RSPB. The large areas of reed bed are the major British breeding grounds for the bittern. By the latter half of the 19th century Silverdale had become a seaside resort with medicinal baths of fresh seawater.

SILVERSTONE Northamptonshire SP6744
Village on A43, 3 miles (5km) SW of Towcester
Major motor-racing circuit draws crowds to ancient limestone village. Remains of fish ponds probably indicates site of medieval royal hunting lodge.

SIMONBURN Northumberland NY8773
Village off B6320, 7 miles (11km) NW of Hexham
The village was moved in the 18th century when owners of nearby Nunwick House decided to landscape the gardens. These gardens are now open to the public.

SIMONSBATH Somerset SS7739
Village on B3223, 7 miles (11km) SE of Lynton
A small village set in a little valley in the middle of Exmoor; developed from the 17th century.

SINGLETON West Sussex SU8713
Village on A286, 5 miles (8km) N of Chichester
Village of flint and brick cottages in the Lavant Valley, famed for the Weald and Downland Open Air Museum. It covers 40 acres (16ha) and is a collection of old vernacular buildings from the southeast that were threatened with destruction. Re-created medieval farmstead, working horses; hands-on gallery explaining building materials and techniques. Shop. Programme of special events.

SISSINGHURST Kent TQ7937
Village on A229, 1 mile (2km) NE of Cranbrook
Village with a pleasant main street of delightful Kentish houses of many eras, adjacent to Tudor Sissinghurst Castle, with its gardens created by Vita Sackville-West (National Trust).

SITTINGBOURNE Kent TQ9063
Town on A2, 8 miles (13km) E of Gillingham
Industrial town with a long history as a market town and staging post. Near Roman Watling Street on a creek off the Swale in the heart of Kentish cherry orchards. In the Middle Ages this was a stopping place for pilgrims to Canterbury and had a thriving market. Today industries include paper-manufacture and fruit-preserving and packing. Steam railway, nature reserve and museums.

SIXPENNY HANDLEY Dorset ST9917
Village on B3081, 5 miles (8km) NW of Cranborne
The older signposts still say '6d Handley'. Large and well wooded; the old village was mostly destroyed by fire in 1892.

SIZERGH CASTLE Cumbria SD4987
Mansion off A591, 3 miles (5km) S of Kendal
Built around a 14th-century pele tower, mansion now belongs to National Trust. Contains relics of early Jacobite Rebellion, excellent early Elizabethan woodwork and extensive gardens.

SIZEWELL Suffolk TM4762
Site off B1122, 2 miles (3km) E of Leiston
Famous for its nuclear power station, Sizewell is an attractive fishing village. The building of the Sizewell B power station was highly controversial.

Prehistoric village of Skara Brae.

SKARA BRAE Orkney HY2218
Prehistoric site off B9056, 4 miles (6km) W of Dounby
Unique remains of a fishing and farming village of 3000–2500BC. Europe's most complete neolithic village, with much domestic detail preserved during long burial under dunes.

SKEGNESS Lincolnshire TF5663
Town on A52, 19 miles (31km) NE of Boston
Medieval Skegness was a victim of the sea. By the early 19th century the farming and fishing village was becoming known as a watering place. Excursion traffic arrived with the railway in 1873, and the town's development was carefully planned by landowner the Earl of Scarborough, with wide tree-lined streets. From the 1920s, when the town council bought the foreshore, further amenities were developed to create a popular major seaside resort. The town's widely known slogan, 'Skegness is so bracing', and the rotund Jolly Fisherman character skipping happily along the sands in boots and sou'wester, have been associated with the resort since their introduction on a railway excursion poster in 1908. The clock tower is almost as well known.
Sandy beaches still form one of the main holiday ingredients, with summer entertainment at the Embassy Centre, and late summer illuminations. Visitors can see the seal hospital at Skegness Natureland, where stranded and injured animals are cared for, while Church Farm Museum demonstrates domestic and agricultural life in an 18th- and 19th-century setting. A model village, funfairs and amusements complete the holiday picture.

SKELMERSDALE Lancashire SD4606
New Town off M58, 4 miles (6km) SE of Ormskirk
Since the 1960s the village has grown into a New Town, having been developed and promoted as a business park.

SKELTON Cleveland NZ6518
Small town on A173, 2 miles (3km) S of Saltburn
An elevated town in the picturesque dale of Skelton Beck, based around ironstone-mining, the last mine closing in the 1960s. Skelton Castle was the Norman home of Robert de Bruce (King Robert I), rebuilt as a castellated mansion in 1794. Grounds are open to the public on certain days.

SKELTON North Yorkshire SE5756
Village off A19, 4 miles (6km) NW of York
The parish church of St Giles was built with stones left over from the building of York Minster in the 13th century.

SKELTON (SKELTON ON URE) North Yorkshire SE3668
Village off A1, 2 miles (3km) NW of Boroughbridge
The village is situated on the River Ure and is home to Newby Hall, a Queen Anne house set in exceptional gardens.

SKELWITH BRIDGE Cumbria NY3403
Hamlet on A593, 2 miles (3km) W of Ambleside
Crossing point of the River Brathay. Further upstream, Skelwith Force, although only 15ft (3m) high, is dramatic after rain. Workshops and slate showroom at Kirkstone Galleries.

SKENFRITH Gwent SO4520

Village on B4521, 6 miles (10km) NW of Monmouth

Village on loop on the River Monnow almost on the Wales/England border. Medieval Skenfrith Castle (Cadw) is one of the Three Castles of Gwent.

SKIDBY Humberside TA0133

Village off A164, 6 miles (10km) NW of Hull

The village is of Danish origin, founded in about AD890. The old windmill buildings house a museum of old implements associated with flour production.

SKIDDAW Cumbria NY2629

Mountain in Lake District, 4 miles (6km) NW of Keswick

The region's third highest peak, it is composed of softer rock, containing graphite, than that found in nearby Borrowdale.

SKILLINGTON Lincolnshire SK8925

Village off A1, 2 miles (3km) NW of Colsterworth

Stone-built village around green, between A1 and Leicestershire border, along which Viking Way footpath runs.

SKINNINGROVE Cleveland NZ7119

Village off A174, 1 mile (2km) NW of Loftus

Industrial village in deep ravine cut by Kilton Beck; Catersty Sands is a fine, quiet beach. Tom Leonard Mining Museum is attached to a former drift mine.

SKIPNESS Strathclyde NR9057

Village on B8001, 2 miles (3km) NE of Claonaig

Remote village overlooking Arran at the north end of Kintyre. Ruined Skipness Castle dates from the 1260s and commands Kilbrannan Sound and the Clyde estuary.

SKIPSEA Humberside TA1655

Village on B1242, 5 miles (8km) NW of Hornsea

Close to the North Sea, with an attractive beach. The 13th-century remains of a castle are owned by English Heritage.

SKIPTON North Yorkshire SD9851

Town off A629, 16 miles (26km) NW of Bradford

Known as the 'gateway to the Dales', Skipton's origins can be traced to the 7th century when Anglian farmers named it 'Sheeptown'. The Normans built the first castle here in the 12th century, and established the markets and fairs which have carried on here ever since, in the wide cobbled market place.

The town is dominated by Skipton Castle, standing behind the 14th-century Church of the Holy Trinity, and 200ft (60m) above Eller Beck. Only one gateway is left of the original Norman castle begun by Robert de Romille. Most of what is visible today was built by the Cliffords in the 14th century, but Lady Anne Clifford remodelled much of it in the 17th century, rebuilding the upper part of the 14th-century doorway visible from the High Street and adorning it with the Clifford family motto, *Desormais* ('henceforth'). The castle has an enormous banqueting hall, a series of kitchens, a beautiful Tudor courtyard with an ancient yew tree and an unusual 19th-century room decorated with exotic seashells brought back by George Clifford, the 3rd Earl of Cumberland, from his sea voyages.

SKOKHOLM AND SKOMER Dyfed SM7305

Islands off SW coast of Wales at S end of St Bride's Bay

The names of these two islands reflect Viking influence in Pembrokeshire in the Dark Ages. The islands are important bird sanctuaries. Skomer, the larger of the two, has one of the finest seabird populations in north-west Europe – fulmars, shags, razorbills, puffins, guillemots, oystercatchers, kittiwakes and Manx shearwaters. Accessible by boat in summer. Skokholm (less accessible) was Britain's first bird observatory, established in 1933.

SKYE, ISLE OF Highland

Island, of the Inner Hebrides

Skye, the furthest north of the Inner Hebrides, offers magnificent mountain scenery and a superb coastline, and attracts over one million visitors annually. The Cuillins, the Neist peninsula and fertile Sleat (pronounced 'Slate') are diverse and beautiful. Skye's history is that of the other Inner Hebridean islands: Viking and Gaelic influences were strong, which can be seen in many of the place names, and by the 15th century a strong Gaelic culture had emerged, the principal clans being the MacDonalds of Sleat and the MacLeods of Dunvegan. Huge emigration occurred between 1840 and 1888; this was stemmed by Gladstone's Crofters' Act of 1886, which gave security of tenure at a fair rent to crofters; the system still operates today.

Fishing and crofting are the traditional economic activities, both of major importance and doing much to preserve the traditional way of life: Gaelic is still widely spoken. There is some light industry, notably electronics, distilling, and the vital revenue from tourism. Portree and Broadford are the main settlements, and there are numerous crofting townships. Skye is served by ferries to and from the mainland and the Outer Hebrides.

SLAD Gloucestershire SO8707

Village on B4070, 2 miles (3km) NE of Stroud

Birthplace of Laurie Lee and immortalised in *Cider with Rosie*. His old home (not open) stands among other unremarkable cottages.

SLAIDBURN Lancashire SD7152

Village on B6478, 7 miles (11km) N of Clitheroe

A pretty village of stone cottages and cobbled pavements in the Forest of Bowland. The focal point is the 13th-century pub Hark to the Bounty.

SLAITHWAITE West Yorkshire SE0713

Town off A62, 4 miles (6km) SW of Huddersfield

Slaithwaite had a busy dock on the Huddersfield Narrow Canal (built in 1795) until a trunk road was built in 1820–2.

SLALEY Northumberland NZ9758

Village off B6306, 5 miles (8km) S of Corbridge

A linear village made up of buildings on both sides of the road, most having been built since World War II and some converted from old farm buildings.

SLAPTON Devon SX8245

Village off A379, 5 miles (8km) SW of Dartmouth

Pretty village just inland, dominated by the 80ft (24m)

ruined tower from a chantry. Slapton Ley is a strange lake (the largest in the county) separated from the sea by a shingle bank. The long sandy beach has an obelisk commemorating the use of the area by the American army in 1944 practising for D-Day; 3,000 people were evacuated for ten months for this.

SLAPTON Northamptonshire SP6446
Village off A43, 4 miles (6km) W of Towcester
Quiet village beside the River Tove. Unspoilt small Norman and 13th-century church, with medieval wall-paintings.

SLAUGHAM West Sussex TQ2528
Village off A23, 5 miles (8km) SE of Horsham
Picture-postcard village of stone and tile-hung houses and cottages round a green, facing a medieval church. Near by are the ruins of Elizabethan Slaugham Place and tranquil Slaugham Pond.

SLAUGHTER, UPPER AND LOWER Gloucestershire SP1622
Villages off A429, 3 miles (5km) SW of Stow-on-the-Wold
These showpiece Cotswold villages are a magnet for tourists who come to admire Lower Slaughter's idyllic cottages and 17th-century manor house (now a hotel) around the green and on manicured river banks. Upper Slaughter has a Tudor manor (also a hotel) and cottages restored by Lutyens. Memorial to Reverend FE Witts, author of *Diary of a Cotswold Parson*, in the church.

SLEAFORD Lincolnshire TF0645
Town on A15, 11 miles (18km) NE of Grantham
Market town between limestone country and the Fens. Earthworks of 12th-century castle, ruined by early 17th century. St Denys' Church, beside the market place, has notable flowing tracery. The sail-less windmill is the home of tourist information centre. Handley memorial commemorates a local MP. Numerous buildings of historic and architectural interest, including 17th-century Cogglesford Mill and massive brick maltings of 1905.

SLEDMERE Humberside SE9364
Village on B1252, 7 miles (11km) NW of Great Driffield
Sledmere House, set in parkland and gardens landscaped by Capability Brown, was built in 1751. The Church of St Mary is in the grounds of the mansion house. The village has two monuments dedicated to victims of World War I.

SLIGACHAN Highland (Skye) NG4829
Hamlet on A850, 8 miles (13km) S of Portree
Known mainly as the access point for walks south down Glen Sligachan between the Red and Black Cuillins; access also to the peaks themselves.

SLIMBRIDGE Gloucestershire SO7403
Village off A38, 4 miles (6km) N of Dursley
Slimbridge Wildfowl and Wetlands Trust, founded by Peter Scott in 1946, is now the world's largest collection of wildfowl, with 150 different species (most spectacular in winter). The village also boasts an outstanding early medieval church with original glass, a rare lead font and a monument to William Tyndale, Bible translator, thought to have been born here.

SLINDON West Sussex SU9608
Village off A29, 4 miles (6km) W of Arundel
The National Trust owns the 3,500 acre (1,417ha) Slindon estate, on southern slopes of the South Downs with magnificent views across the West Sussex coastal plain. The unspoilt little village is 200ft (61m) up; it has a square of lanes with 17th-century brick and flint cottages, an attractive little green and a restored Norman church. Footpaths and a bridleway cross the estate, which includes a 3¾ mile (6km) stretch of Roman road, Stane Street.

SLINFOLD West Sussex TQ1131
Village on A29, 4 miles (6km) W of Horsham
Mellow little village, turning its back on Stane Street and grouped along The Street, a tree-lined road with houses of the 15th to 20th centuries, all set in their own gardens.

SLINGSBY North Yorkshire SE6974
Village on B1257, 6 miles (10km) W of Malton
A limestone-built village of Victorian and modern houses. All Saints' Church contains a monument to William Wycliffe, a 14th-century knight, who supposedly killed a serpent that was terrorising the villagers.

SLOUGH Berkshire SU9779
Town on A4, 21 miles (34km) W of London
'Come friendly bombs, and fall on Slough/It isn't fit for humans now' wrote John Betjeman in 1937. Until 1838, when the railway arrived, Slough was only a few scattered villages. The town then grew and in 1920 the world's first trading estate was established here. From the 1930s, stylish office buildings were used along the roads to screen the factories behind. The town centre dates from the 1960s and 70s. Local museum.

SMA' GLEN Tayside NN9029
Beauty spot on A822, 6 miles (10km) N of Crieff
The River Almond flows through this scenic, rocky and narrow glen on the Highland fault line. General Wade's road (1730) followed the line of the glen.

SMAILHOLM Borders NT6436
Village on B6397, 5 miles (8km) W of Kelso
Smailholm Tower stands on a high outcrop near the village, an excellent and well-restored example of 15th-century Border pele tower.

SMALL HYTHE Kent TQ8930
Hamlet on B2082, 2 miles (3km) S of Tenterden
Charming roadside hamlet to the north of the Isle of Oxney, originally a port for Tenterden. Excellent timber buildings including Smallhythe Place (National Trust), once the home of actress Ellen Terry.

SMALLTHORNE Staffordshire SJ8850
District of Stoke-on-Trent
Pride of this nondescript former village is Ford Green Hall (limited opening), a 16th-century timber-framed yeoman's house with period furniture.

SMARDEN Kent TQ8842
Village off A262, 7 miles (11km) N of Tenterden
Lovely 'black and white' Kent village on the River Beult; an old Wealden market town, centre of the medieval cloth industry. It has never grown, and still consists of one short High Street of very pleasing half-timbered Wealden cottages and houses. Its 14th-century church is sometimes called the 'Barn of Kent' because of its huge roof span.

SMETHWICK West Midlands SP0288
District of Warley, 2 miles (3km) from centre
Victorian terraces and modern estates dominate the area. At Galton Valley canal heritage site three phases of historic canal-building come together.

SMISBY Derbyshire SK3419
Village on B5006, 2 miles (3km) N of Ashby-de-la-Zouch
Beside Tournament Field, the setting for a scene in Walter Scott's *Ivanhoe*. Close to Ashby-de-la-Zouch Castle across Leicestershire boundary. Brick village lock-up.

SNAEFELL Isle of Man SC3988
Mountain off A18, 4 miles (6km) NW of Laxey
The highest point on the island, at 2,036ft (621m). Snaefell Mountain Railway, 100 years old, operates from Laxey to the summit, with original tramcars.

SNAILWELL Cambridgeshire TL6467
Village off A142, 3 miles (5km) N of Newmarket
Huddled along the tiny River Snail, Snailwell stands in gently rolling countryside on the 'Old Fenland shore'. Has an especially fine Norman church.

SNAITH Humberside SE6422
Village on A1041, 1 mile (2km) S of Carlton
The name of this thriving village means 'enclosed by water' and the area is known locally as the Three Rivers area. The old village lock-up, the Penny Cells, has been restored by the local Heritage Society and exhibitions are held there. The Priory Church of St Lawrence has a Saxon foundation.

SNAKE PASS Derbyshire SK0892
Mountain pass on A57, SE of Glossop
Splendid Sheffield–Glossop moorland route, frequently closed by winter snow. Takes its name from the Snake inn, built by the Duke of Devonshire soon after he built the road, and named after his family's emblem.

SNAPE North Yorkshire SE2684
Village off B6268, 2 miles (3km) S of Bedale
The village is dominated by its castle which was once home to Catherine Parr, the last wife of Henry VIII.

SNAPE Suffolk TM3959
Village on A1094, 5 miles (8km) NW of Aldeburgh
Famous as a lively centre for opera, jazz, and classical music. The Maltings Proms occur from April to October, and is the venue of the Aldeburgh festival founded by Benjamin Britten. A 48ft (15m) ship dating to AD625 was unearthed in 1862 near the lovely 12th-century flint and brick church. The name means 'boggy place'.

SNARFORD Lincolnshire TF0582
Hamlet on A46, 6 miles (10km) SW of Market Rasen
Church and 17th-century farm remain alone, village gone. Medieval church has three fine monuments to 16th- and 17th-century St Paul family.

SNETTERTON Norfolk TL9991
Hamlet off A11, 4 miles (6km) SW of Attleborough
Tiny village famous for its motor-racing track, and the Equine Race and Rehabilitation Centre run by the International League for the Protection of Horses.

SNETTISHAM Norfolk TF6834
Village on A149, 4 miles (6km) S of Hunstanton
Snettisham has much to offer the visitor. There is a magnificent 14th-century church, which is an unusual shape because the east chancel is missing. The spire soars 175ft (53m) over the village, and features in JP Hartley's *The Shrimp and the Anenome*. Other attractions include the gabled Old Hall, now a Sue Ryder home, and Park Farm.

SNITTERFIELD Warwickshire SP2159
Village off A46, 3 miles (5km) N of Stratford-upon-Avon
Shakespeare's father, born here, would not recognise the village with its modernised old houses and affluent new ones. Welcombe hotel, a haunt of celebrities, is near by.

SNODLAND Kent TQ7061
Village on A228, 5 miles (8km) NW of Maidstone
Industrial place on the west bank of the River Medway, dominated by cement works and papemills, with steep wooded hillsides climbing up behind the village.

SNORING, GREAT AND LITTLE Norfolk TF9434
Villages off A148, 3 miles (5km) NE of Fakenham
Two neat, charming villages which owe their name to a Saxon family named Snear. Little Snoring grew dramatically during World War II.

SNOWDONIA NATIONAL PARK Gwynedd
Scenic area around Snowdon and principal peaks
The Snowdonia National Park takes its name from Snowdon, at 3,560ft (1,085m) the highest mountain in England and Wales. Yet the park's name is misleading, for it covers 840 square miles (2,176 sq km) in all, extending southwards into central Wales all the way to Machynlleth.

Although essentially mountainous, the park embraces a varied landscape. In the north, the rugged, volcanic peaks and glaciated valleys of the Snowdon massif inevitably attract most of the attention. In addition to Snowdon itself, outdoor enthusiasts make for the Glyders, Tryfan and the Carneddau, each as challenging as its more famous neighbour.

Around Betws-y-Coed there is gentler forest walking country, in contrast to the exhilarating open hillsides of the unexplored Aran and Arennig mountains around Bala. The bleak, damp moors of the Migneint above Ffestiniog attract only hardy hill sheep, while the wild Rhinogs inland from Harlech represent one of southern Britain's last remaining areas of true wilderness.

The park's southern gateway is guarded by the massive bulk of Cader Idris, a mountain which sweeps down to the sea to give the park a spectacular coastline.

SNOWSHILL Gloucestershire SP0933

Village off A44, 3 miles (5km) S of Broadway

High on the Cotswold Edge above Broadway and the Vale of Evesham stands this village of attractive stone cottages. Its handsome old manor house (National Trust – limited opening) shows architectural features from the 15th to the 18th centuries and is famous for the astonishing range of collections built up by its eccentric owner Charles Wade from 1919 to 1950s.

SOBERTON Hampshire SU6116

Village off A32, 2 miles (3km) S of Meonstoke

Straggling village along a hill parallel with the River Meon. Wide views from the church, which has a pretty 16th-century stone and flint chequered tower.

SOCKBURN Durham NZ3407

Hamlet off A66, 6 miles (10km) SE of Darlington

Farmhouse adjacent to Sockburn Hall was home of Mary Hutchinson, who married William Wordsworth. Best known for legendary Sockburn Worm, a dragon which lived in River Tees.

SOHAM Cambridgeshire TL5973

Village off A142, 5 miles (8km) SE of Ely

A 7th-century cathedral was built here on an earlier Saxon cemetery. Soham was once only reachable by water, and the Ely causeway was only built in the 12th century. There is a 17th-century steelyard once used for weighing carts leaving the market, and Downfield Mill dates from 1726. St Andrew's Church has an especially fine roof.

Rare example of a 17th-century steelyard at Soham.

SOHO Greater London TQ2981

District in City of Westminster

London's leading restaurant and sex-entertainment area has had a cosmopolitan atmosphere since Huguenot refugees from France settled here in the 17th century. Soho Square still has its French Protestant church, while Gerrard Street is the centre of London's Chinatown. Theatres in Shaftesbury Avenue, film companies in Wardour Street, raucous Berwick Street market. Restaurants, delicatessens, art galleries, characterful pubs.

SOKE OF PETERBOROUGH Cambridgeshire

Historic region NW of Peterborough

'Soke' was Saxon for an area with special privileges. Much wealth came from trading routes along the Great North road and the River Ouse.

SOLIHULL West Midlands SP1479

Town off M42, 7 miles (11km) SE of Birmingham

Generous open space and rural eastern fringe make Solihull a pleasant place. Very impressive Church of St Alphege dominates town centre, where older buildings like the 15th-century manor house vie with modern shopping and office developments. Interesting buildings away from town centre include Malvern Park Farm, Berry Hall and Ravenshaw, all timber-framed. Land Rovers are produced here.

SOLVA Dyfed SM8024

Village on A487, 3 miles (5km) E of St David's

Picturesque Lower Solva, at end of a long tidal inlet, is one of Pembrokeshire's most sheltered harbours. Seafaring past reflected in its architecture. Good range of craft shops.

SOLWAY COAST Cumbria

Scenic region

The length of coastline known as the Solway Coast stretches from the River Esk near the Scottish border to Maryport on the Irish Sea. The name Solway is generally accepted to be derived from two old Norse words, 'sul' meaning pillar, probably referring to the Lochmaben Stone, a large ice-borne granite boulder which marked the Scottish end of a ford, and 'vath' meaning ford. Together they refer to the crossing at the mouth of the River Esk.

The Solway Coast is rich in flora and fauna, with a mixture of sand dunes, salt marshes, shingle beds and peat mosses – a haven for birds and other wildlife. The Cumbrian Wildlife Trust and RSPB are responsible for the protection and management of much of the coastline. Campfield Marsh, Grune Point, Drumburgh Moss and the dunes at Silloth are all havens for migrating birds and a variety of plant species.

There is much evidence of Roman occupation here. The coast was protected by forts at Kirkbride, Beckfoot and Maryport and milecastles were built between the forts along the entire stretch of coastline.

SOMERLEYTON Suffolk TM4897

Village off B1074, 5 miles (8km) NW of Lowestoft

Neo-Tudor red-brick cottages huddle around the well-tended green. Somerleyton Hall to the east is a splendid high-Victorian palace.

SOMERSAL HERBERT Derbyshire SK1335
Village off A50, 2 miles (3km) NW of Sudbury
Elizabethan half-timbered Somersal Hall, a 1712 brick block with 1850 additions. Seventeenth-century box-framed Old Cottage; 17th-century Montgomery House has timber-framed barn; 1874 church.

SOMERSBY Lincolnshire TF3472
Village off A158, 6 miles (10km) E of Horncastle
Attractive Wolds village where the poet Tennyson was born in 1809 at the rectory, now Somersby House (not open). Area featured in his poetry. Memorabilia in church.

SOMERSET LEVELS Somerset
Scenic region SE of Bridgwater
Very low-lying flat land at the centre of Somerset which was marsh until drained, a process which started in medieval times. The straight drainage ditches are known as 'rhynes', and the characteristic view is pollarded willows with straight roads. Much of the area is peat, which has been dug since medieval times and is still extracted. The Glastonbury Iron Age Lake Village (see Glastonbury) was a settlement when the area was still watery, and timber trackways dating from between 6,000 and 2,700 years ago are being excavated (see Westhay and Stoke St Gregory).

SOMERTON Oxfordshire SP4928
Village off A4260, 3 miles (5km) S of Aynho
Standing above River Cherwell, the village has Norman church with fine Fermor monuments. Somerton Meads is a nature reserve for wildfowl and aquatic plants.

SOMERTON Somerset ST4828
Small town on B3151, 4 miles (6km) NW of Ilchester
A quiet and rather old-fashioned small town, with many interesting buildings. The 16th- and 17th-century houses include the Hext almshouses of 1626, and there are many good Georgian houses and several inns. The market cross was rebuilt in 1673. Town hall of about 1700. Large earlier medieval church with 15th-century wooden roof.

SOMPTING West Sussex TQ1705
Village off A27, 2 miles (3km) NE of Worthing
Brick and flint characterise the village street, engulfed by suburbia, and the splendid Saxon church tower capped by its 'Rhenish helm', of about AD1000, now unique in England, although common in Germany.

SONNING Berkshire SU7575
Village on B478, 4 miles (6km) NE of Reading
Pronounced 'Sunning', this large and pretty, much-visited village on the River Thames has many old brick houses and cottages, including a fine house, The Grove, which was used as a weekend retreat by General (later President) Eisenhower during World War II. An 18th-century bridge spans the Thames, and there is a picturesque lock.

SOPLEY Hampshire SZ1597
Village on B3347, 3 miles (5km) N of Christchurch
On the River Avon, and full of 18th-century brick houses and cottages. Medieval church on a big artificial mound.

SOULBURY Buckinghamshire SP8826
Village on B4032, 3 miles (5km) NW of Leighton Buzzard
The mysterious glacial boulder here is supposedly able to move by itself. Grand Union Canal.

SOUTH ANSTON South Yorkshire
see Anston

Unusual church tower at Sompting.

SOUTH BENFLEET Essex TQ7787
Small town off A13, W area of Southend-on-Sea
Former fishing village on Benfleet Creek, off the Thames estuary. Now a Southend (see) suburb, with an interesting church and old pubs.

SOUTH BRENT Devon SX6960
Village off A38, 5 miles (8km) SW of Buckfastleigh
Large village on the edge of Dartmoor, with a handsome 15th-century church. Big railway viaduct.

SOUTH CADBURY Somerset ST6325
Village off A303, 2 miles (3km) E of Sparkford
Stone village in lovely countryside, best known for Cadbury Castle, a big Iron Age hillfort, woody and with good views. It has been traditionally associated with King Arthur, and excavations in the 1960s showed that the hillfort had been re-occupied in the 5th and 6th centuries, the time of the real King Arthur.

SOUTH CAVE Humberside SE9230
Village on A1034, 8 miles (13km) SE of Market Weighton
The village has a town hall built in 1796 and South Cave Castle, built in the 18th century, is now a hotel.

SOUTH CERNEY Gloucestershire SU0497
Village off A419, 4 miles (6km) SE of Cirencester
Attractions of village with pleasant old houses and superb Norman church carving are now enhanced by lakes of the nearby Cotswold Water Park.

SOUTH CREAKE Norfolk TF8538
see Creake

SOUTH DALTON Humberside SE9645
Village off A1079, 6 miles (10km) NE of Market Weighton
A picturesque Wolds village with small, 18th-century houses. The Kiplingcotes Derby has been run every year since 1519 and was one of the original steeplechases.

SOUTH DOWNS East Sussex
Hill range
A range of chalk hills, designated an Area of Outstanding Natural Beauty, extending 100 miles (160km) from near Petersfield in the Hampshire basin through Sussex to plunge into the sea at Beachy Head. The downs are an escarpment with a steep north-facing slope cut by combes (the most impressive is the Devil's Dyke), rising to an undulating crest before falling to the coast as an irregular south-sloping plateau cut by dry valleys. The downs' highest point is Butser Hill in Hampshire, at 889ft (270m). Three major rivers, the Arun, Adur and Ouse, cut through the hills.

In the west the downs are bare rolling country, ploughed for grain and grazed by sheep and cattle. West of the River Arun the landscape is more wooded. Settlements are few on the dry chalk, but cluster along the springlines north and south. There are many tumuli, several hillforts and plenty of ancient trackways, giving evidence of early activity in the hills. The South Downs Way is an 106 mile (160km) bridleway from Winchester to Eastbourne, which follows the crest of the hills.

The South Downs have given their name to a famous breed of sheep.

SOUTH FORELAND Kent TR3643
Headland off A258, 3 miles (5km) NE of Dover
Chalk headland, the eastern extremity of the White Cliffs of Dover, guarding the strait. Two lighthouses; the older (1843) is now owned by the National Trust, and was used in 1898 for the first radio navigation aid.

SOUTH HAMS Devon
Scenic region of S Devon
The southernmost part of Devon, tucked between Paignton and Plymouth. Very green and fertile, with a beautiful coastline.

SOUTH KENSINGTON Greater London TQ2678
District in borough of Kensington and Chelsea
Famous for culture and museums, including the Victoria and Albert Museum of art and design, with a ravishing collection of treasures, the Natural History Museum in a much-loved building by Alfred Waterhouse, and the Science Museum. To the north are the red-brick Royal Albert Hall, of 1871, and the Albert Memorial, repaired in the 1990s.

SOUTH KYME Lincolnshire TF1749
Village on B1395, 7 miles (11km) NE of Sleaford
On edge of fenland village, with 14th-century tower house, and part of 12th-century Augustinian priory with Saxon carving and 1888 additions.

SOUTH LEIGH Oxfordshire SP3908
Village off A40, 3 miles (5km) SE of Witney
John Wesley preached his first sermon in Norman church of this village looking over the Windrush Valley. Splendid medieval wall-paintings.

SOUTH LOPHAM Norfolk TM0382
see Lopham

SOUTH MIMMS Hertfordshire TL2201
Village off A1000, 2 miles (3km) W of Potters Bar
Close to the M25/A1(M) complex. Remains of Norman motte and bailey castle, church with monuments and 16th-century stained glass.

SOUTH MOLTON Devon SS7125
Town on B3227, 11 miles (17km) E of Barnstaple
Proper market town, the middle with a dense square packed with Georgian and Regency buildings. The guildhall of 1740 arches over the pavement. Classical pannier market of 1863. Local museum. International Animal Rescue at Ash Mill. Quince Honey Farm, Hancock's Devon Cider, Clapworthy Mill.

SOUTH NEWBALD Humberside SE9136
see Newbald

SOUTH NEWINGTON Oxfordshire SP4033
Village on A361, 6 miles (10km) SW of Banbury
Village beside River Swere has handsome houses and a stunning church with a wealth of 14th-century glass and an array of medieval wall-paintings.

SOUTH OCKENDON Essex TQ5983
Suburb on B186, 3 miles (5km) NW of Grays
London overspill estates from 1940s. Church with round tower. Davy Down open space in Mar Dyke Valley, watersports at Grange Waters.

SOUTH PETHERTON Somerset ST4316
Small town off A303, 5 miles (8km) E of Ilminster
Tiny town, mostly 19th century in the centre, with Blake Hall (originally the 18th-century market hall) in the middle of the road.

SOUTH POOL Devon SX7740
Village off A379, 3 miles (5km) SE of Kingsbridge
At the head of one of the creeks on the Kingsbridge estuary, remote and unspoilt. Handsome 15th-century church.

SOUTH QUEENSFERRY Lothian NT1278
Small town off A90, at S end of Forth bridges
A pilgrim ferry port founded by St Margaret of Scotland in the 11th century; trade was important in the 16th and 17th centuries. Queensferry Museum relates the local history. Hawes inn has associations with Sir Walter Scott and Robert Louis Stevenson. Nearby Hopetoun House, designed by William Bruce in 1699–1702, with Adam additions from 1721, epitomises the great country house. Abercorn church has Hopetoun Loft (1708).

SOUTH RONALDSAY Orkney
Island in the Orkneys
Most southerly of the main Orkneys, this well-cultivated island is connected to the mainland by a causeway, with a summer ferry connection to John O' Groats. The Tomb of the Eagles is a chamber tomb from 3000BC.

SOUTH SCARLE Nottinghamshire SK8464
Village off A1133, 7 miles (11km) NE of Newark-on-Trent
Close to Lincolnshire boundary, with views of Lincoln Cathedral. Church has fine Norman and 13th-century interior, 15th-century clerestory and nave roof and 18th-century vamping horn – one of only nine in the country, a sort of trumpet used to 'vamp up' the singing. Several 17th-century buildings, including timber-framed Old Vicarage. Dovecotes in grounds of hall and at Beecher's Farm.

SOUTH SHIELDS Tyne and Wear NZ3666
Town on A185, 7 miles (11km) E of Gateshead
Modern town grew as a Victorian seaside resort and colliery town. Roman fort of *Arbeia*, built at the mouth of the River Tyne as a seaward defence and supply base in the 2nd century, has been extensively excavated. On the site of West Gate is a replica fort and Roman museum.

SOUTH STOKE Avon ST7461
Village off A367, 2 miles (3km) S of Bath
Little stone village just outside Bath, but still separate. Attractive Packhorse inn dates from 1674.

SOUTH TAWTON Devon SX6594
Village off A30, 4 miles (6km) E of Okehampton
Little granite village on the northern edge of Dartmoor. Picturesque centre, with external stairs to the church house, and a 15th-century church.

SOUTH UIST Western Isles
Island in the Outer Hebrides
Second largest of the Western Isles, with a peat and lochan interior and hilly east side, and extensive beaches and machair down the west coast. Prehistoric and early Christian sites and connections with Prince Charles Edward and Flora MacDonald. Depopulation in the 19th century due to Clearances; much employment today from an army missile range, with crofting and tourism also important.

SOUTH WALSHAM Norfolk TG3613
Village on B1140, 3 miles (5km) NW of Acle
Formed by ancient peat-diggings, South Walsham Broad is just one of many tranquil expanses of reedy water in this region. Lovely South Walsham stands on its tree-fringed banks. This ancient village has the Fairhaven Garden Trust, about 60 acres (24ha) of bird sanctuary on a private broad; the Elizabethan South Walsham Hall (hotel); and the 17th-century Ship inn.

SOUTH WARNBOROUGH Hampshire SU7247
Village on B3349, 5 miles (8km) N of Alton
The older parts lie off the main road, with neat brick or timber-framed cottages. Medieval church with interesting fittings and monuments.

SOUTH WINGFIELD Derbyshire SK3755
Village on B5035, 3 miles (5km) W of Alfreton
Substantial ruins of 15th-century manor house built by Ralph Lord Cromwell. Mary Stuart was held here (1569 and 1584) in the care of the Earl of Shrewsbury. Stone-built village with a stylish railway station (disused).

SOUTH WOODHAM FERRERS Essex TQ8097
Small town off B1012, 5 miles (8km) NE of Wickford
A freshly minted post-modernist Essex market town, whose town square was formally opened by the Queen in 1981. No high rises, no concrete, buildings in traditional styles. Superstore with handsome weatherboarded clock tower, low-slung church, shops, restaurants, pubs, friendly atmosphere. Working farm with pigs, sheep and pets' corner at Marsh Farm Country Park.

SOUTH WRAXALL Wiltshire ST8364
Village off B3109, 3 miles (5km) N of Bradford-on-Avon
Seventeenth-century stone cottages around the church, and to the north the manor with a 15th-century gatehouse.

SOUTH ZEAL Devon SX6593
Village off A30, 4 miles (6km) E of Okehampton
A medieval New Town, but a village now, on the northern edge of Dartmoor. Many old cottages, and the Oxenham Arms – picturesque and early 16th century.

SOUTHAM Warwickshire SP4161
Small town off A425, 7 miles (11km) SE of Leamington
Old Mint pub, of medieval origin, attracts far-flung clientele to this small market town. The church has a splendid roof and windows.

SOUTHAMPTON Hampshire SU4112
City off M27, 70 miles (113km) SW of London
Sited on the sheltered inlet of Southampton Water, the city has been a port from Saxon times. Southampton has no seaside (the shores are all muddy) but it is still a big commercial port and the old town has preserved a remarkable number of historic attractions. Despite bombing damage, much of the medieval town remains and more than half the impressive town-wall towers and gates survive. Bargate is one of the finest town gates in the country, with a museum in the guildhall above. God's House Tower houses the archaeological museum, and there are remnants of the castle too.

Inside the walls are many historic buildings including St Michael's Church, with its 165ft (50m) sea-mark spire; the 13th-century medieval Merchant's House (English Heritage), furnished in medieval style; the Tudor House Museum; and the 14th-century Wool House, now a maritime museum.

Land reclamation has altered the shoreline of Southampton dramatically. Town Quay is a viewpoint for the long stretch of docks, once used by cruise liners, and beyond are new container-ship docks. Passenger ferries operate to Hythe and the Isle of Wight.

The docks on the southern side have mostly been converted into housing and shops now, with one dock preserved at Ocean Village where the Victorian steam-powered cargo vessel *Shieldhall* can be seen. Near by is the Southampton Hall of Aviation. An amazingly high tollbridge was built in 1977 over the River Itchen to Woolston.

Modern Southampton extends way beyond the medieval town and the main shopping streets were rebuilt in the 1950s after bombing. The 1930s guildhall with its prominent clock tower survived, as did the fine art gallery. The city is a thriving shopping and business centre, with many big new office blocks and new shopping malls.

There are big parks around the centre of the city, with the huge common to the north. In medieval times it was used for grazing.

SOUTHBOURNE Dorset SZ1391
Village off B3059, on E outskirts of Bournemouth
Virtually part of Bournemouth, Southbourne developed from the 1850s. CS Rolls (of Rolls-Royce) died here in a flying accident in 1911, the first pilot to be killed in Britain.

SOUTHEASE East Sussex TQ4205
Village off A259, 3 miles (5km) NW of Newhaven
Pretty little village in the broad Ouse Valley, grouped around a triangular green with a Norman round-towered church on a Saxon foundation.

SOUTHEND Strathclyde NR6908
Village on B842, 8 miles (13km) S of Campbeltown
Holiday village in southern Kintyre. The flat rock at nearby Keil is the traditional landing place of St Colomba; an imprint of the saint's footsteps can be seen.

SOUTHEND-ON-SEA Essex TQ8786
Town on A13, 35 miles (56km) E of London
A combination of popular seaside resort, shopping metropolis and business centre, Southend began life as the 'south end' of the village of Prittlewell (see). A fashionable resort developed here on the Thames estuary coast in the first years of the 19th century, trading on its brisk sea air and low rainfall within easy reach of London. With the arrival of the railways the town turned into a brash and breezy popular resort and began to spread over the surrounding towns and villages. It is famed especially for its immensely long, frequently endangered iron pier of 1889, which Sir John Betjeman described as 'beautiful and incomparable'.

Southend has 7 miles (11km) of seafront with a sand and shingle beach, the big Sea Life Centre aquarium, watersports of all kinds, high-technology adventure parks for children, gardens and parks, museums, theatres and night clubs, restaurants of every style and hotels for every pocket. At the same time, the town's office blocks indicate that it has ceased to rely only on the seaside for its living. (See also Hadleigh; Leigh-on-Sea; South Benfleet; Shoeburyness; Thorpe Bay; Thundersley; Westcliff-on-Sea.)

SOUTHERNDOWN Mid Glamorgan SS8873
Village on B4524, 4 miles (6km) S of Bridgend
Village on headland above cliff-backed Glamorgan Heritage Coast. Road leads to sheltered beach with Heritage Coast Centre and walks in Dunraven Park.

SOUTHERNESS Dumfries and Galloway NX9754
Village off A710, 3 miles (5km) S of Kirkbean
Small resort village on a headland in Solway Firth with excellent sands near by and wide views south to the hills of the Lake District.

SOUTHFLEET Kent TQ6171
Village off A2, 3 miles (5km) SW of Gravesend
Timbered cottages survive at the crossroads in this residential village, being absorbed into the industrial belt of Gravesend.

SOUTHILL Bedfordshire TL1542
Village off B658, 2 miles (3km) N of Shefford
Whitbread brewing dynasty estate village. Church with Admiral Byng and Dr Johnson connections. Stately Southill House grounds open occasionally.

SOUTHMINSTER Essex TQ9599
Village on B1021, 2 miles (3km) N of Burnham-on-Crouch
Commuter settlement among the Dengie peninsula streams and marshes. In the church are relics of Nelson, whose chaplain was vicar here.

SOUTHPORT Merseyside SD3317
Town on A565, 16 miles (25km) N of Liverpool
Seaside resort and residential area, Southport has retained an air of Victorian elegance while becoming a modern shoppers' paradise. Tree-lined Lord Street, with its wide pavements, is almost 1 mile (2km) long and is decorated with ornamental wrought-iron arcades and hanging flower baskets.

Pleasureland Amusement Park, with its 'white knuckle' rides annually attracts over two million visitors. The town also has the largest marine lake in Britain, the second longest seaside pier in the country and a 7 mile (11km) beach plus a Promenade, ornamental gardens, theatres, cinemas, discos, open-air afternoon concerts and a wide variety of restaurants and pubs.

Royal Birkdale Golf Course regularly hosts the British Open and the three-day Southport Flower Show, held every August for over 150 years, is Britain's biggest summer flower show. The Atkinson Art Gallery, Lord Street, has collections of British art and Chinese porcelain.

Meols Hall, Churchtown, the private house of the Hesketh family, is set in its own parkland opposite the Hesketh Arms public house and the village church. The grounds are opened for spring and summer shows and fairs.

SOUTHREPPS Norfolk TG2536
Village off A149, 4 miles (6km) SE of Cromer
Near the sea, and set in quiet English countryside, Southrepps has a peaceful Quaker cemetery, a new village hall, and a sturdy church.

SOUTHROP Gloucestershire SP2003
Village off A361, 3 miles (5km) N of Lechlade
The picturesque Swan inn stands among attractive cottages in charming village beside River Leach. Church has a wealth of Norman carving.

SOUTHSEA Hampshire SU6498
District of Portsmouth
Southsea developed as a select residential area from Regency times, and became a seaside resort from about 1860, resulting in many Victorian buildings. The big common was preserved along the seafront, and along the shore are the 1540s castle (now a museum), the Sea Life Centre, the D-day Museum with extensive displays and huge tapestry, and Cumberland House Natural History Museum. Spitbank Fort, in the sea, is one of three built in the1860s.

SOUTHWARK Greater London TQ3279
District in borough of Southwark, on S bank of Thames
Lying at the southern end of London Bridge, of which it was the 'south work', Southwark or 'the borough' was the historic gateway to the capital from the south, thronged for centuries with travellers and inns, theatres, brothels and prisons. The tremendous George inn (National Trust), a 17th-century replica of the old galleried hostelry that Shakespeare knew, preserves something of the atmosphere of a vanished age. Dickens knew it well, too, and also the Church of St George the Martyr in Borough High Street.

Shakespeare has a modern monument in Southwark Cathedral, close to London Bridge, one of the city's most impressive churches. The Harvard Chapel commemorates the founder of Harvard University, who was born in Southwark. The Southwark heritage centre is near by and the Clink Museum, on the site of the prison of that name, tells its own story.

Over to the west among the cramped streets of the Bankside area, with its wonderful views of St Paul's, the Globe Theatre, where Shakespeare's plays were put on, is being recreated. It has its own museum of the Elizabethan theatre. Bankside power station is being redeveloped to house the Tate's modern art collection.

SOUTHWELL Nottinghamshire SK7053
Town on A612, 6 miles (10km) W of Newark-on-Trent
The delightful and historic minster town of Southwell is surprisingly little discovered by visitors, being hidden away from major roads on the fringe of Sherwood Forest. The building of the minster began just after 1100, the Norman nave, transepts and three towers having the choir added in the early 13th century, before the beautiful foliage carving of the chapter house, probably Europe's finest, completed the work in about 1295. The church was raised to its present cathedral status only in 1884, but the remains of the 14th-century Palace of the Archbishops of York adjoin the church, incorporating the present Bishop's Manor.

Elegant Georgian houses surround the minster, and opposite is the Saracen's Head, the ancient coaching inn where Charles I surrendered to the Scots Commissioners in 1646. The young Lord Byron lived in the town for some five years, in one of the houses facing the attractive green.

An exhibition at the Merryweather Garden Centre explains the origins of the popular Bramley apple which was first grown in Southwell, an area still important for fruit-growing (see Norwood). Just outside the town are the popular Southwell racecourse, and Brackenhurst Agricultural College.

SOUTHWICK Hampshire SU6208
Village off B2177, 3 miles (5km) NW of Cosham
Pronounced 'Suthick', this superbly preserved large village has many thatched cottages and an unusual church of 1566 with interesting 18th-century fittings.

SOUTHWICK Northamptonshire TL0292
Village off A605, 3 miles (5km) NW of Oundle
Fourteenth-century and Elizabethan Southwick Hall, still a family home (limited opening), has exhibitions of Victorian and Edwardian life. Roubiliac monument in church.

SOUTHWICK West Sussex TQ2405
Town on A27, immediately E of Shoreham-by-Sea
Very suburban coastal town, with a green and some flint and 18th-century buildings. Site of a large 1st- to 4th-century Roman villa.

SOUTHWOLD Suffolk TM5076
Town on A1095, 4 miles (6km) E of Blythburgh
Southwold is an ancient town, and was a Saxon port. It became an important harbour in medieval times, but declined when the approaches to it began to silt up. It was given another breath of life in the last century when it became a popular holiday resort, although in a quiet, restrained way with none of the glitter of Great Yarmouth or Sheringham.

Today, Southwold is an elegant town boasting some handsome buildings, all dominated by the 100ft (30m) white lighthouse that looms over them. The lighthouse was built in 1890, and its light could be seen from as far away as 17 miles (27km) out to sea.

Southwold's town centre comprises pretty houses and cottages of pink and blue with tiled roofs. It has nine greens of various sizes and shapes. The main church is that of St Edmund King and Martyr with its famous mechanical jack that chimes the bell. The jack has a stubbled chin and bloodshot eyes. Real-ale lovers will know Adnams brewery, which is on the site of a brewery founded in the 16th century.

SOUTRA HILL Lothian NT4559
Hill off B6368, 4 miles (6km) N of Oxton
A noted viewpoint on the road between Moorfoot and Lammermuir Hills, southeast of Edinburgh. Soutra Aisle is a remnant of a 15th-century hospice.

SOWERBY North Yorkshire SE4380
Village on A61, immediately W of Thirsk
A charming village of old houses and cottages. Pudding Pie Hill is a Saxon burial mound excavated in 1855.

SOWERBY BRIDGE North Yorkshire SE0523
Town on A58, 2 miles (4km) SW of Halifax
An industrial town lying on the River Calder; despite the number of mill chimneys and factory roofs, dominated by the surrounding countryside. The bridge from which the town takes its name was originally built in the 17th century and is over the River Calder. Each September the Sowerby Rushbearing Festival is held here.

SPALDING Lincolnshire TF2422
Town on A16, 14 miles (23km) SW of Boston
Capital of Lincolnshire's flower bulb industry, this attractive Dutch-influenced town draws thousands of visitors to Springfields show gardens and to its annual flower parade of huge colourfully decorated floats in early May. River Welland runs through town, with Georgian terraces facing 15th-century Ayscoughfee Hall, home to a fascinating museum. Spalding Gentlemen's Society, founded 1710, also has a museum.

SPALDWICK Cambridgeshire TL1272
Village on A14, 7 miles (11km) W of Huntingdon
The pretty spired church is decorated in part with snail shells, meant to represent St James, the patron saint of pilgrims.

SPARKFORD Somerset ST6026
Village on A359, 4 miles (6km) SW of Castle Cary
Main-roadish, now bypassed. Sparkford Motor Museum has more than 200 vehicles.

SPARSHOLT Hampshire SU4331
Village off A272, 3 miles (5km) NW of Winchester
Set high on the chalk at 420ft (128m), well wooded and hedged. Classical church doorway of 1631, still with its original door. Sparsholt Agricultural College.

SPARSHOLT Oxfordshire SU3587
Village off B4507, 3 miles (5km) W of Wantage
A pretty, well-wooded village below the Berkshire Downs, with a Norman and medieval church of exceptional interest.

SPAXTON Somerset ST2237
Village off A39, 5 miles (8km) W of Bridgwater
Scattered hamlets. One of them (Four Forks) was notorious from 1846 as the home of a strange religious sect called Agapenome or 'the abode of love'. Its buildings and chapel still survive.

SPEAN BRIDGE Highland NN2281
Village on A82, 9 miles (14km) NE of Fort William
Village overlooking the southern end of Great Glen, where commandos trained during World War II; a fine bronze statue of three soldiers (1952) commemorates them. Near by is Glen Roy, with the outstanding signs of glacial retreat on its hills, known as the Parallel Roads. Achnacarry, between Loch Lochy and Loch Arkaig has Clan Cameron Museum: this was a strong Jacobite clan.

SPEEN Berkshire SU4568
District off A4, on W edge of Newbury
A few Georgian houses and the church are all that remain of the village, which has been swallowed up by Newbury.

SPEEN Buckinghamshire SU8499
Village off A4128, 2 miles (3km) NW of Hughenden Valley
Home of Rest for Horses, at Speen Farm, cares for horses, ponies, donkeys. Eric Gill's grave is in Speen burial ground.

SPEKE Merseyside SJ4283
District in SE Liverpool
This area is home to Liverpool's airport and Speke Hall (National Trust), a Tudor manor house.

SPELDHURST Kent TQ5541
Village off A264, 2 miles (3km) NW of Tunbridge Wells
Attractive residential village up in the wooded hills, with old pub, and a Victorian church containing ten colourful windows designed by Burne-Jones.

SPELSBURY Oxfordshire SP3521
Village on B4026, 2 miles (3km) N of Charlbury
Picturesque cottages and almshouses grace this village above Evenlode Valley where Earl of Rochester, licentious 17th-century poet, lies in unmarked grave.

SPENNYMOOR Durham NZ2533
Town on A688, 4 miles (6km) NE of Bishop Auckland
A sprawl of modern tower blocks and Victorian houses surrounds traditional red-brick terraces of this former mining village.

SPETCHLEY Hereford and Worcester SO8593
Village on A422, 3 miles (5km) E of Worcester
Fine gardens of Spetchley Park (limited opening) dominate this estate village of the Berkeley family, whose monuments can be found in the small church.

SPEY BAY Grampian NJ3565
Village on B9104, 4 miles (6km) N of Fochabers
This River Spey-mouth village is a salmon-netting industry base, with Scotland's largest ice-house at Tugnet. Massive shingle banks to the west are pushed constantly to shore by the drift.

SPEY, RIVER Grampian
River
The second longest river in Scotland rises in the Monadhliath Mountains and runs through Aviemore and Newtownmore to Strath Spey, where the best of its noted salmon-fishing starts. Through Strath Spey the magnificent Highland scenery makes the valley popular with tourists, while further down it houses many distilleries, before the river swings north through lusher wooded countryside to the Moray Firth.

SPILSBY Lincolnshire TF4066
Small town on A16, 16 miles (26km) NE of Boston
Small market town at southern end of the Wolds. Bronze statue of explorer Sir John Franklin in market place. Born here 1786, he died 1847 while commanding expedition which discovered the North-west Passage, between Greenland and Canada. Church has Willoughby chapel with tombs from 1349–1610, until family moved to Grimsthorpe Castle (see Edenham).

SPOFFORTH North Yorkshire SE3651
Village on A661, 3 miles (5km) NW of Wetherby
An old village, expanded greatly in the 1960s with the demand for private housing. Stockeld Park is a Palladian mansion (open by appointment). Ruins of Spofforth Castle (English Heritage).

SPONDON Derbyshire SK4036
Village on A52, 4 miles (6km) E of Derby
Georgian brick houses near church, including The Homestead, and former coach house. Church completely rebuilt after a fire in 1340; heavily restored in 1826 and 1890s. Nearby Locko Park.

SPOTT Lothian NT6775
Village off A1, 2 miles (3km) S of Dunbar
Village where the last witch to be burnt south of the Forth perished. Prehistoric remains in the vicinity. Churchyard has a watch-house as protection against body-snatchers.

SPRATTON Northamptonshire SP7170
Village off A50, 6 miles (10km) NW of Northampton
Hilltop church has ornately carved late Norman tower, 14th-century spire and tomb of Sir John Swinford, died 1371, with earliest SS (Lancastrian) collar in England.

SPROATLEY Humberside TA1934
Village on B1238, 4 miles (6km) N of Hedon
On a hill above the flat land of Holderness, with an Ice Age glacier stone in the churchyard.

SPROTBROUGH South Yorkshire SE5301
Village off A638, 3 miles (5km) W of Doncaster
The village overlooks the River Don and the 800-year-old church has a 'Frith Stool', one of only three remaining in England.

SPROWSTON Norfolk TG2411
Village on A1151, on NE edge of Norwich
Now a suburb of Norwich, Sprowston has a restored church with some fine monuments. Lazar House, once a hospital, is now a library.

SPROXTON Leicestershire SK8524
Village off B676, 5 miles (8km) W of Colsterworth
Wolds village with ironstone church on higher ground, 13th-century tower, splendid faces on corbels of nave roof. Complete 10th-century Saxon cross in churchyard.

STACKPOLE AND STACKPOLE ELIDÔR (OR CHERITON) Dyfed SR9896
Hamlets off B4584, 3 miles (5km) S of Pembroke
Hamlet of Stackpole is a little way inland from Stackpole Quay, a simple but delightful little stone harbour (reputedly Britain's smallest) once used for shipping limestone. Just north is Stackpole Elidôr (or Cheriton) whose church has interesting effigies. Walk across headland from quay leads to beautiful Barafundle Bay and spectacular Stackpole Head. National Trust has its only residential school in Britain here.

STAFFA Strathclyde NM3235
Island of Inner Hebrides, N of Iona
Uninhabited grassy island of columnar basalt with extraordinary caves – the best known of which, Fingal's Cave, inspired Mendelssohn's *Hebridean Overture*.

STAFFORD Staffordshire SJ9223
Town on A34, 14 miles (23km) S of Stoke-on-Trent
The county town of Staffordshire is of Saxon origin, although little of its early history is visible. Only the extensive earthworks remain of the medieval castle, but beside St Mary's Church are the foundations of a tiny Saxon chapel, a startling contrast to the church itself, which is impressively large. It contains a memorial to Izaak Walton, a reminder that the legendary angler was born here in 1593. (Church enthusiasts will probably prefer the little Norman and medieval St Chad's in Greengate Street.) The big market square, Stafford's natural centre, is dominated by the imposing 18th-century Shirehall, and here too is the Judge's House of about 1800. In spite of some intrusive modern development the lively central streets retain their attractive character. Occasionally buildings leap to the attention – for example the huge and handsome timber-framed High House (open) in Greengate Street – but the main pleasure for the stroller is in more modest buildings such as the Noel almshouses of 1660, the fine 18th-century Chetwynd House, Eastgate House, the Swan hotel and the Friends' Meeting House of 1730. There are also curiosities, such as the Town Mill with its two waterwheels and the former 18th-century windmill.

STAFFORDSHIRE MOORLANDS Staffordshire
Scenic region, N of Leek
Exposed uplands, partly within Peak District National Park, draw visitors to the Roaches rocks and picturesque valleys of rivers Hamps, Manifold and Dove.

STAGSDEN Bedfordshire SP9848
Village off A422, 4 miles (6km) W of Bedford
Thatched cottages, with church nicely renovated in the 1970s. Some 150 species of birds, British and other, on view in Stagsden Bird Gardens.

STAINDROP Durham NZ1220
Village on A688, 5 miles (8km) NE of Barnard Castle
A pretty village, once the market centre of the district and on the estate of Raby Castle. The medieval, battlemented castle, mainly 14th century, is open to the public and stands in 200 acres (81ha) of deer park. The Lords of Raby are buried in splendid tombs at the Parish Church of St Mary.

STAINES Surrey TQ0371
Town off M25, 17 miles (27km) W of London
On the site of a Roman town, *Pontes*, Staines was built where bridges carried the London–Exeter road across the River Thames. The town centres on a modern bridge, still the focal point of the settlement. Church Street is the architectural heart of the town, with many styles, mostly post-17th century. Modern developments including offices and light industry sprawl away from the centre, but The Lammas remains, an open common by the river.

STAINFORTH North Yorkshire SD8267
Village on B6479, 2 miles (3km) N of Settle
The village was destroyed during the Civil War and rebuilt simply using local materials. Packhorse bridge, crossing the River Ribble, belongs to the National Trust.

STAINFORTH South Yorkshire SE6411
Town off A18, 7 miles (11km) NE of Doncaster
Pretty town on River Don giving its name to the Stainforth and Kearby Canal which runs from here to the River Trent.

STAINTON Cleveland NZ4814
Village off A174, 4miles (6km) S of Middlesbrough
A dormitory village in a wooded setting, radiating from the village green at its centre. Now a conservation area. A disused quarry is being converted into a nature reserve.

STAITHES North Yorkshire NZ7818
Village on A174, 9miles (14km) NW of Whitby
This village, a favourite with artists, is set on the cliffs near Whitby. The modern part is set up on the main road while the older village, from which cars are restricted, lies below the cliff. The old fishing community, with the cottages jumbled around the tiny harbour, is where Captain Cook was apprenticed to a grocer.

Replica of the London Stone at Staines.

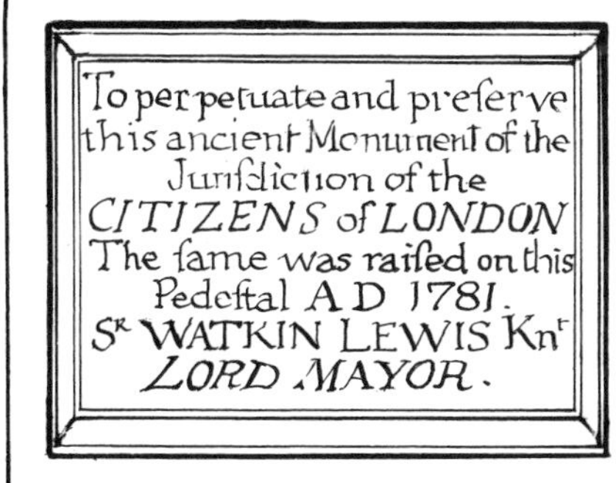
To perpetuate and preserve
this ancient Monument of the
Jurisdiction of the
CITIZENS of LONDON
The same was raised on this
Pedestal A D 1781.
S^R WATKIN LEWIS Kn^t
LORD MAYOR.

STALBRIDGE Dorset ST7317
Village on A357, 7 miles (11km) S of Wincanton
Almost a small town, plain and old-fashioned in the local greying stone, with a late 15th-century market cross.

STALHAM Norfolk TG3725
Village off A149, 7 miles (11km) SE of North Walsham
The ancient market town of Stalham lies at the northern reaches of the Broads on the beautiful River Ant. Boats at South Staithe allow visitors to explore How Hill Water Gardens, the River Ant itself, and nearby Hickling Broad. Composer E J Moeran wrote some evocative music here, based on the haunting waters of the Broads and Stalham Windmill.

STALYBRIDGE Greater Manchester SJ9698
Town off A635, 8 miles (12km) E of Manchester
One of the oldest cotton towns in the country which grew rapidly during the Industrial Revolution. Retains a handsome Victorian appearance.

STAMFORD Lincolnshire TF0307
Town off A1, 12 miles (19km) NW of Peterborough
An outstanding stone-built town on the River Welland, Stamford was designated England's first conservation area in 1967. One of the Five Boroughs of the Danelaw in the 10th century, Stamford later developed a cloth industry, iron-working and pottery. Browne's Hospital, founded 1475–6, is a fine survival of medieval almshouses, partly rebuilt in 1870.

On the edge of the town is magnificent Burghley House, built in 1546–87 by William Cecil, Elizabeth I's chief adviser. His monument and those of numerous other Cecils are in St Martin's Church, one of the town's five surviving medieval churches. Famous horse trials take place in Burghley Park each September.

The present mellow stone townscape dates mainly from the 17th and 18th centuries. Bypassed by the busy A1 in 1961, the town was formerly an important staging post on the Great North road. The George retains its 'gallows' inn sign across the road, and waiting rooms marked for passengers for London and York. The early 18th-century assembly rooms and 1768 theatre are among the beautiful buildings which make up this unique town, with further details available from the museum.

STAMFORD BRIDGE Humberside SE7155
Village on A166, 7 miles (11km) E of York
Attractive village, once an important crossing point of River Derwent. Stone commemorates the Battle of Stamford Bridge in 1066.

STAMFORDHAM Northumberland NZ0771
Village on B6309, 6 miles (10km) N of Prudhoe
An elongated agricultural village with a green and mainly Georgian terraced houses, a Best Kept Village winner and now a conservation area. The church tower is 13th century, but the rest of the church was rebuilt in 1849. There is a preaching cross and a gaol-house.

STANDISH Greater Manchester SD5610
Town on A49, 3 miles (5km) N of Wigan
The town's medieval past is still evidenced by the wooden stocks, market cross, dipping well and St Wilfrid's Church dating mainly from the 16th century.

STANDON Hertfordshire TL3922
Village on A120, 6 miles (10km) W of Bishop's Stortford
Prosperous commuter village on the River Rib. Handsome old houses and a wide main street where markets and fairs were held. Once belonged to the Knights Hospitallers, who had a commandery here. Later the squires were the Sadleirs, whose monuments are in the church, which has a rare detached bell tower. Notable Roman Catholic school, St Edmund's College.

STANE STREET West Sussex
Roman road from London to Chichester
One of Britain's most famous Roman roads. Runs for 56 miles (90km) from London to Chichester via Epsom, Dorking and Pulborough. Partly followed by the A29.

STANFORD DINGLEY Berkshire SU5771
Village off A340, 5 miles (8km) SW of Pangbourne
In the Pang Valley, with timber-framing and brick.

STANFORD IN THE VALE Oxfordshire SU3493
Village off A417, 5 miles (8km) NW of Wantage
Popular and expanding village in Vale of White Horse has two greens, some handsome Georgian houses and church with Norman work and large brass.

STANFORD LE HOPE Essex TQ6882
Town off A13, 5 miles (8km) NE of Tilbury
Developed for Thames-side industrial workers. Striking church with big, pinnacled tower. Joseph Conrad wrote *The Nigger of the Narcissus* here.

STANFORD ON AVON Northamptonshire SP5878
Village off A427, 5 miles (8km) SE of Lutterworth
Stanford Hall (1690s), with motorcycle museum and events, on Leicestershire bank of infant River Avon; separated from 14th-century church which has numerous Cave family monuments.

STANHOPE Durham NY9939
Small town on A689, 5 miles (8km) W of Wolsingham
A crossroads town which also grew around lead-mining. Industry is now mostly quarrying and flourspar-mining. Stanhope Castle, built in 1798 for Cuthbert Rippon, MP for Gateshead, now converted into flats. The Stone House, former rectory and one of Stanhope's oldest houses, is now a hotel.

STANLEY Durham NZ1953
Town on A693, 5 miles (8km) W of Chester-le-Street
Coal-mining town with mainly modern housing estates. Spoil heaps are being grassed over and landscaped.

STANMER East Sussex TQ3309
Village off A27, 4 miles (6km) NE of Brighton
Farming village within the grounds of Stanmer Place, now the nucleus of the University of Sussex. Wooded Stanmer Park covers 537 acres (217ha), with pleasant wide lawns laid out in the 18th century.

STANMORE Greater London TQ1692
District in borough of Harrow
Quite countrified until the 20th century. Old houses and cottages. Stanmore Common and Bentley Priory are open spaces both noted for fungi.

STANNINGFIELD Suffolk TL8756
Hamlet off A134, 5 miles (8km) S of Bury St Edmunds
Coldham Hall, 1 mile (2km) west, was built in 1574 for Robert Rookwood. St Nicholas' Church has some superb Norman stonework.

STANSTEAD ABBOTS Hertfordshire TL3811
Village on B180, 3 miles (5km) SE of Ware
In London commuterland, with a small boat marina at the northern end of the Lee Valley Regional Park.

STANSTED AIRPORT Essex TL5222
Airport off M11, 2 miles (3km) NE of Bishop's Stortford
London's newest airport, whose much praised, hangar-like passenger terminal opened in 1991. Airfield originally constructed by wartime American Airforce.

STANSTED MOUNTFITCHET Essex TL5125
Village on B1383, 3 miles (5km) NE of Bishop's Stortford
Imaginatively reconstructed Norman castle and village on ancient site. Large toy museum includes animated displays. Restored windmill (limited opening).

STANTON Gloucestershire SP0634
Village off A44, 3 miles (5km) SW of Broadway
Idyllic village at foot of Cotswold Edge. Delightful cottages line sloping main street, and church reveals outstanding medieval and Victorian craft work.

STANTON DREW Avon ST5963
Village off B3130, 6 miles (10km) S of Bristol
Famous for three stone circles with two avenues and a burial chamber, all dating from the neolithic period, about 4,000 years ago. Pretty village.

STANTON HARCOURT Oxfordshire SP4105
Village on B4449, 3 miles (5km) SW of Eynsham
A traditional cluster of manor house, church and picturesque cottages form the centre of this village in meadowland near River Thames. The church is full of treasures, including much Norman work, rare chancel screen, medieval shrine and array of brasses. Stanton Harcourt Manor (limited opening) is fascinating remaining portion of medieval home of Harcourt family.

STANTON IN PEAK Derbyshire SK2464
Village off A6, 1 mile (2km) SW of Rowsley
Nine Ladies prehistoric stone circle on Stanton Moor. Stanton Hall, 16th and 17th century, with 1799 addition. Stanton Old Hall dated 1667.

STANTON LACY Shropshire SO4978
Village off B4365, 3 miles (5km) N of Ludlow
This tranquil village beside River Corve has the only Shropshire church with substantial Saxon work. Circular churchyard indicates a Celtic site.

STANTON ON THE WOLDS Nottinghamshire SK6330
Village off A606, 7 miles (11km) SE of Nottingham
Smaller than in former times, this Wolds hamlet has a tiny church with some Norman masonry in the nave.

STANTON ST JOHN Oxfordshire SP5709
Village on B4027, 5 miles (8km) E of Oxford
This attractive estate village, looking across to Oxford from its low hill, was the home of John White, who founded the State of Massachusetts. His home, Rectory Farm (not open), still stands, as do the 17th-century estate cottages. The church contains glass and other exceptionally fine embellishment of the 13th century.

STANWAY Gloucestershire SP0632
Village off B4077, 4 miles (6km) NE of Winchcombe
A picturesque place of stone and thatched cottages at foot of wooded Stanway Hill. Playwright James Barrie designed its cricket pavilion, and Eric Gill carved lettering on its war memorial. Near the church stand a huge medieval tithe barn and the impressive 17th-century gatehouse of Stanway House (limited opening), a repository of fine furniture and paintings.

STANWICK Northamptonshire SP9871
Village off A45 (A605), 2 miles (3km) NE of Higham Ferrers
Overlooking River Nene with 13th-century church with its octagonal tower. Major archaeological site between Raunds and Ringstead; remains of Roman villa, Saxon church, medieval manor.

STANWICK ST JOHN North Yorkshire NZ1811
Site off B6274, 2 miles (2km) SE of Caldwell
Stanwick Camp (English Heritage, open to the public) is an enormous complex of earthworks, largely excavated in the 1950s.

STAPELEY Cheshire SJ6749
Hamlet on A51, 3 miles (5km) SE of Nantwich
Mainly noted for Stapeley Water Gardens which occupies a 64 acre (26ha) site and is a popular visitor attraction.

STAPLE FITZPAINE Somerset ST2618
Village off B3710, 5 miles (8km) SE of Taunton
One of the fine Somerset church towers, ornate 15th century. Castle Neroche to the south has large medieval earthworks.

STAPLEFORD Leicestershire SK8118
Hamlet off B676, 4 miles (6km) E of Melton Mowbray
Medieval village disappeared about 1500. Stapleford Park dates partly from the same period, was Jacobeanised in 1890s, and is now a country-house hotel in parkland. Outstanding 18th-century Gothic church, with Rysbrack monument.

STAPLEFORD Nottinghamshire SK4837
Town off A52, 3 miles (5km) W of Beeston
Between Nottingham and the River Erewash, on the Derbyshire border. Church, with important Saxon cross shaft of about 1050. Framework knitters' cottages.

STAPLEFORD Wiltshire SU0737
Village on B3083, 4 miles (6km) N of Wilton
Off the Wylye Valley, well wooded and with some old cottages. The Norman piers in the church are striped in two different coloured stones.

STAPLEHURST Kent TQ7843
Village on A229, 6 miles (10km) N of Cranbrook
Pleasant old village with a particularly fine main street with raised pavements and lovely Kentish houses, including an 18th-century post office and half-timbered Fuller House.

STARBOTTON North Yorkshire SD9574
Village on B6160, 2miles (3km) N of Kettlewell
A quiet village over Cam Gill, with 17th-century buildings and later cottages built for the lead-miners.

STARCROSS Devon SX9781
Village on A379, 3 miles (5km) N of Dawlish
Riverside hamlet on the Exe estuary, with passenger ferries in summer to Exmouth. The Brunel Pumping Station was one of ten on the short-lived (1846–7) 'atmospheric' railway built by Brunel from Exeter to Plymouth, worked by vacuum in the rails. Big chimney.

START POINT Devon SX8337
Headland off A379, SE of Hallsands
Rocky headland marking the southwestern corner of Devon, with lighthouse of 1836. Wild rocky coast.

STARTFORTH Durham NZ0416
Village off A67, outside Barnard Castle
Sixteenth-century bridge crosses the River Tees, joining the village to Barnard Castle.

STAUNTON Gloucestershire SO5412
Village on A4136, 2 miles (3km) E of Monmouth
Huge and precarious Buck Stone stands near this Forest of Dean village, which also boasts a fine medieval church.

STAUNTON HAROLD Leicestershire SK3720
Site off B587, 3 miles (5km) NE of Ashby-de-la-Zouch
Picturesque group of 17th- and 18th-century hall (Sue Ryder Home) with church (National Trust) built during the Commonwealth, beside lake. Craft workshops in stables.

STAUNTON IN THE VALE Nottinghamshire SK8043
Village off A1, 6 miles (10km) S of Newark
In Vale of Belvoir, where Nottinghamshire meets Lincolnshire and Leicestershire. Hall and medieval church form harmonious group, both restored. Hall, altered 1794, part early 19th century, said to be Willingham of Scott's *Heart of Midlothian*. Church, much rebuilt in 1853, has monuments to the Staunton family, and a figure by Westmacott, 1811. Tall 17th-century brick dovecote at Staunton Grange.

STAVELEY Derbyshire SK4374
Town off A619, 4 miles (6km) NE of Chesterfield
Developed on coal and iron. Staveley Hall , built 1604, was classicised in 1710, remodelled in 1867, now council offices. Medieval The Chantry. School of 1840s.

STAVERTON Devon SX7964
Village off A384, 2 miles (3km) N of Totnes
In the wooded valley of the River Dart, with a stone bridge of 1413 and a 14th-century church with 15th-century wooden screens.

STAVERTON Gloucestershire SO8923
Village on B4063, 4 miles (6km) W of Cheltenham
Memories of the Gloster Aircraft Company, pioneers of jet propulsion, linger at the Gloucester and Cheltenham airport.

STAWELL Somerset ST3638
Village off A39, 5 miles (8km) E of Bridgwater
Has some handsome Georgian brick houses. Church tower unfinished.

STAYLITTLE Powys SN8892
Hamlet on B4518, 6 miles (10km) NW of Llanidloes
Located high in Cambrian Mountains on edge of Hafen Forest and Llyn Clywedog. The name is said to derive from a local speedy blacksmith, where you had to 'stay little' to have horseshoes changed.

STEBBING Essex TL6624
Village off B1057, 3 miles (5km) NE of Great Dunmow
Delightful old cottages and farmhouses, graceful 14th-century church with notable rood screen. Wartime American airfield here.

STECHFORD West Midlands SP1287
District off A4040, area in E Birmingham
Once a Worcestershire village beside the River Cole, Stechford has been progressively engulfed by housing, but area around All Saints' Church preserves leafy Edwardian atmosphere.

STEEP Hampshire SU7425
Village off A3, 1 mile (2km) N of Petersfield
Dominated by the steep wooded scarp of the chalk. Scattered traditional cottages, some built in the 20th century, and many fine modern fittings in the church.

STEEP HOLME Avon ST2260
Island in Bristol Channel
Uninhabited island west of Weston-super-Mare, now a nature reserve, with steep cliffs.

STEEPLE Dorset SY9180
Village off A351, 3 miles (5km) W of Corfe Castle
A tiny village in the middle of Purbeck with stone cottages. Its isolated church contains the 17th-century Lawrence family coat of arms, whose stars and stripes inspired the American flag.

STEEPLE ASHTON Wiltshire ST9056
Village off A350, 3 miles (5km) E of Trowbridge
One of the most photographed villages in Wiltshire, with a very pretty 15th-century church, a wonderful range of houses and cottages around its triangular green, and a little domed lock-up. Market cross of 1679. Stone and timber-framed buildings.

STEEPLE ASTON Oxfordshire SP4726
Village off A4260, 4 miles (6km) S of Deddington
The village straddles a small valley in hills above the River Cherwell. Among its very rewarding buildings are Manor Farm House, Grange Cottage, a school and almshouses, all of the 17th century and an eccentric early 19th century 'castle'. The church has fine medieval work and a remarkable monument of 1730.

STEEPLE BUMPSTEAD Essex TL6841
Village on B1054, 3 miles (5km) S of Haverhill
Sizeable village at a ford, with large Victorianised church going back to the 11th century. Handsome guildhall. Edith Cavell worked here.

STEEPLE CLAYDON Buckinghamshire SP7026
Village off A413, 5 miles (8km) S of Buckingham
Calvert brickworks village. No steeple until 1862. Interesting public library. Plaque on site where Cromwell's army camped in 1644.

STEEPLE LANGFORD Wiltshire SU0337
Village on A36, 5 miles (8km) NW of Wilton
Down by the River Wylye, with several chequered flint and stone cottages alongside brick and thatch.

STELLA Tyne & Wear NZ1763
Village off A695, 1 mile (2km) E of Ryton
A small ancient settlement whose name refers to the two power stations that were built here. Both stations are now closed down.

STENG CROSS Northumberland NY9690
Site off B6341, SE of Elsdon
Winter's Gibbet, where William Winter was hung in 1791, found guilty of murder. At the base are the remains of Steng Cross.

STENHOUSEMUIR Central NS8783
Town off A88, 2 miles (3km) NW of Falkirk
Now virtually part of Falkirk, the town features the 19th-century site of Scotland's largest livestock market, where half a million head are sold at a series of fairs.

STENTON Lothian NT6274
Village on B6370, 5 miles (8km) SW of Dunbar
A pretty village with a medieval wool stone on the green and a 14th-century rood well. The 16th-century Biel terraced gardens lie to the northeast.

STEPNEY Greater London TQ3681
District in borough of Tower Hamlets
One of London's poorest districts, in the heart of the old East End, Stepney was a noisome docklands slum until knocked flat in the Blitz. Afterwards much of the population was decanted and the area was redeveloped. Stepney Green has some 18th-century houses and the Church of St Dunstan, whose graveyard is packed with monuments.

STEVENAGE Hertfordshire TL2325
New Town off A1(M), 28 miles (45km) N of London
Old Stevenage is the original town on the old Great North road, with the New Town added on since the 1940s and 1950s. The story since the Stone Age is told in the Stevenage Museum. Traffic-free shopping area, extensive web of cycle paths, Gordon Craig Theatre. Fishing and boating in Fairlands Valley Park, with wildfowl reserve.

STEVENSTON Strathclyde NS2742
Town on A78, 2 miles (3km) E of Ardrossan
Industrial town with a history of mining; an explosives factory now provides employment. High Kirk (1883) dominates the town.

STEVENTON Hampshire SU5448
Village off B3400, 6 miles (10km) SW of Basingstoke
Small, scattered and rural, the birthplace of Jane Austen (1775), whose family lived at the rectory (demolished) for 25 years.

STEVENTON Oxfordshire SU4691
Village on B4017, 4 miles (6km) W of Didcot
The best houses in this village beneath the Berkshire Downs, including the timber-framed Priory, stand alongside the tree-lined road called The Causeway.

STEVINGTON Bedfordshire SP9853
Village off A6, 4 miles (6km) NW of Bedford
Stone village with a striking 18th-century windmill, the only post mill in Bedfordshire, now preserved by the county council. Medieval pilgrims came to the holy, healing well which can be found tucked away in the churchyard wall. In the church are quaint medieval carvings on pew ends. The medieval village cross was restored in the 19th century.

STEWARTBY Bedfordshire TL0142
Village off A421, 3 miles (5km) N of Ampthill
Neatly marshalled model village of the 1920s and later, built for the workforce of massive brickworks. Village hall with clock tower. Country park.

STEWARTON Strathclyde NS4245
Small town on A735, 5 miles (8km) N of Kilmarnock
Town once renowned for hat-making, including regimental headgear; it later made knitwear and hosiery. Birthplace of David Dale (1739–1806), New Lanark pioneer cotton-miller .

STEWKLEY Buckinghamshire SP8526
Village on B4032, 5 miles (8km) W of Leighton Buzzard
Perhaps England's longest village, its main street running for almost 2 miles (3km). One of the country's best-preserved Norman churches.

STEYNING West Sussex TQ1711
Town off A283, 5 miles (8km) NW of Shoreham-by-Sea
Fine old market town and former port on the River Adur. Associated with St Cuthman, who built the first church here in the 8th century. Royal burgh and site of the Royal Mint. There are two main streets: the curving, architecturally diverse High Street, and Church Street, claimed as the finest village street in Sussex and famed for its lovely old houses.

STICKLEPATH Devon SX6494
Village off A30, 3 miles (5km) E of Okehampton
Small village on the northern edge of Dartmoor with the Museum of Water Power, a preserved edge-tool works powered by a watermill, founded 1815.

STIFFKEY Norfolk TF9743
Village on A149, 4 miles (6km) E of Wells-next-the Sea
Pronounced 'Stiff-key' or 'Stew-key'. It means 'islands of stumps', relating to marshland with fallen trees and reeds. Stiffkey Hall has an attractive garden open to the public. One 1920s rector earned a name for himself by crusading for London's 'fallen women'. Stiffkey Salt Marshes are run by the National Trust.

STILLINGFLEET North Yorkshire SE5940
Village on B1222, 2 miles (4km) NE of Cawood
The village, a conservation area, lies on Stillingfleet Beck. Traces of ancient inhabitation can be seen in the area.

STILLINGTON Cleveland NZ3723
Village off A177, 4 miles (6km) S of Sedgefield
A 20th-century industrial village in a rural setting with predominantly Victorian housing.

STILTON Cambridgeshire TL1689
Village on A1, 6 miles (10km) SW of Peterborough
Although one of England's most famous cheeses is named after this village, it has never been produced here. It was made in Leicestershire and transported to Stilton to be loaded on to the coaches travelling on the Great North road. The Bell, restored to its former coaching splendour, has a chimney stack date of 1642, although the inn is probably older.

STINSFORD Dorset SY7191
Village off A35, 2 miles (3km) E of Dorchester
The little church is visited for its association with Thomas Hardy, who is buried here. The whole area features in his novels. Kingston Maurward Animal Park, Farm and Gardens has good gardens and grounds, with rare breeds.

STIRLING Central NS7993
Town off M9, 21 miles (34km) NE of Glasgow
Stirling, lying on the River Forth and dominated by its crag-top castle, is an ancient royal burgh and was of great strategic importance in medieval times. Several important battles during the Wars of Independence were fought around the town, which spread down the hill during the stable years that followed to become a favourite residence of the Stuart monarchs and a thriving trading centre with notable buildings. Today, Stirling is an important commercial centre, serving a prosperous agricultural hinterland, with some major tourist attractions and a well-known university near by.

Stirling Castle's superb defensive position gives excellent views over the town; its buildings include the great hall, the palace and chapel royal. Other historically and architecturally interesting constructions in the old part of the town are Mar's Wark, the Church of the Holy Rude, the guildhall, tollbooth and Darnley's House. The Lower Town houses the Smith Art Gallery and Museum and the main shopping area, while Stirling Old Bridge lies on the outskirts.

Across the river to the north lie the scant remains of Cambuskenneth Abbey, founded in 1147, which was the site of Robert Bruce's Scottish Parliament in 1326.

STOCK Essex TQ6998

Village on B1007, 3 miles (5km) N of Billericay

Attractive village, green, windmill, three excellent pubs, church with weatherboarded belfry, slender spire. Fishing, nature trail at nearby Hanningfield Reservoir.

STOCKBRIDGE Hampshire SU3535

Small town on A30, 15 miles (24km) NE of Salisbury

Very large village or small town on the River Test, a famous centre for trout-fishing. One long street, with lots of Georgian brick including the town hall of 1810 and several inns. Many shallow bridges over the river. Stockbridge Down to the east is a downland nature reserve. Houghton Lodge, to the south, has gardens and a hydroponicum.

STOCKLINCH, MAGDALEN AND OTTERSEY Somerset ST3817

Villages off B3168, 2 miles (3km) NE of Ilminster

Both villages have medieval churches. Stocklinch Magdalen has many old stone and thatch cottages.

STOCKPORT Greater Manchester SJ8989

Town off M63, 6 miles (10km) SE of Manchester

Stockport is a large market town originally built on a red sandstone cliff overlooking the River Mersey. The 700-year-old market place, adjacent to the Merseyway shopping precinct and built on massive stilts over the River Mersey, is surrounded by buildings of historic interest, including the Parish Church of St Mary. The chancel dates from the 14th century but there is evidence of a church dating from 1150 on this site. The nave and the tower were rebuilt in 1813, following a partial collapse which was blamed on a marathon bell-ringing session to celebrate Nelson's victory at Trafalgar.

Stockport has thrived as a market town for hundreds of years and during the Industrial Revolution was a centre for textile and hat manufacture. Stockport Museum records the town's history of hatmaking.

Other noteworthy buildings include Stockport's 'wedding cake' town hall, so called because of its white façade and high, tiered clock tower. The Tunnel Shelters, a maze of underground tunnels cut for use as air-raid shelters during World War II, are open to the public, and the famous, illuminated Stockport Railway Viaduct with 27 arches, built in 1840, dominates the town.

STOCKSBRIDGE South Yorkshire SK2798

Town off A6102, 8 miles (14km) NW of Sheffield

Self-contained, semi-rural community in the valley of the River Don and on the edge of Howden Moors, which grew around the still-dominant steelworks.

STOCKTON Wiltshire ST9838

Village off A303, 5 miles (8km) SE of Heytesbury

In the Wylye Valley, with thatched cottages close to the medieval church.

STOCKTON ON TEME Hereford and Worcester SO7167

Village on A443, 6 miles (10km) SE of Cleobury Mortimer

The village is beautifully situated in unspoilt hills above River Teme. Carved Norman chancel arch and fine timber roof in church.

STOCKTON-ON-TEES Cleveland NZ4418

Town on A17, across the Tees from Middlesbrough

Stockton was the main port on the River Tees for over 900 years, particularly in the 18th century, until development at Middlesbrough and the construction of larger vessels brought about its decline. It was the railway era that brought prosperity to the town, marked by the arrival of England's first steam passenger train on the Stockton and Darlington Railway on 27 September 1825.

The tiny church of St Edwold at Stockwood.

Modern Stockton is a mixture of old and new. The Town Hall and Market Cross both date from the mid-18th century, but even though they and the Parish Church make an attractive group the town is somewhat dominated by tower blocks and ring roads. The Georgian High Street is impressive, and original façades can still be seen above modern shop fronts. There are still signs of the old warehouses and narrow riverside alleys off the High Street. There was a castle here at one time, belonging to the Bishops of Durham during the Middle Ages, but no trace of it remains. The notorious dockside taverns have gone too, replaced by a new riverside walk and pleasure craft moorings.

STOCKWOOD Dorset ST5806
Hamlet off A37, 2 miles (3km) NE of Evershot
Still well wooded, with the smallest church in the county, smaller even than the Georgian farmhouse next door.

STOGUMBER Somerset ST0937
Village off A358, 4 miles (6km) SE of Watchet
Picturesque, with many thatched cottages down the hill and a fine medieval church. Bee World and Animal Centre to the east.

STOGURSEY Somerset ST2042
Village off A39, 7 miles (11km) NW of Bridgwater
Unspoilt stone village, once a small town, with an impressive, mostly Norman church and the moated remains of a small medieval castle, with a medieval bridge and later gatehouse.

STOKE Devon SS2324
see Hartland

STOKE ABBOT Dorset ST4500
Village off B3162, 2 miles (3km) W of Beaminster
Large and unspoilt, with cottages of great variety. Tiny wooded gorge on the Broadwindsor road.

STOKE BRUERNE Northamptonshire SP7449
Village off A508, 4 miles (6km) E of Towcester
Canal Museum in 19th-century grain warehouse beside Grand Union Canal, with locks and attractive canal bridge. Narrowboat trips and towpath walks to Blisworth Tunnel, the longest navigable tunnel on British Waterways (3,075yds/2,812m long), completed in 1805. Seventeenth-century Pavilions of demolished Stoke Park, attributed to Inigo Jones, the first country house in England modelled on a Palladian villa.

STOKE BY CLARE Suffolk TL7443
Village on A1092, 2 miles (3km) SW of Clare
Has lovely, minute pulpit and story of notorious 18th-century miser who would not clean his boots lest they wore out. Elwes Houses was a priests' college.

STOKE CHARITY Hampshire SU4839
Village off A30, 6 miles (10km) N of Winchester
Small village down in the river meadows. The ordinary-looking Norman church is crammed with medieval and 17th-century memorials.

STOKE D'ABERNON Surrey TQ1259
Village on A244, 3 miles (5km) NW of Leatherhead
An idyllic group of church and manor house (now a boys' school) is set by the peaceful windings of the River Mole, now cheek-by-jowl with the M25. Suburbia lies beyond, around the railway. The church is famed for brasses to Sir John D'Abernon, who died in 1277, the oldest brass in England, and one to his son, another Sir John (died 1327).

STOKE DOYLE Northamptonshire TL0286
Village off A605, 1 mile (2km) SW of Oundle
Small village on stream running to River Nene. Church of 1720s with original furnishings and early Rysbrack monument, unusually dedicated to St Rumbald.

STOKE DRY Leicestershire SP8596
Village off A6003, 2 miles (3km) S of Uppingham
Little village above Eyebrook Reservoir. Fascinating medieval church, with richly carved Norman columns of chancel arch. Everard Digby, Gunpowder Plot conspirator, born here.

STOKE EDITH Hereford and Worcester SO6040
Village off A438, 6 miles (10km) E of Hereford
Stoke Edith Park burned down in 1927, but its former estate village with good 18th-century church still stands overlooking Frome Valley.

STOKE FLEMING Devon SX8648
Village on A379, 2 miles (3km) SW of Dartmouth
Set high above the shore with wide views. The church has a fine 15th-century tower.

STOKE GABRIEL Devon SX8457
Village off A385, 3 miles (5km) SW of Paignton
Pretty village centre. On a side creek from the River Dart, which is dammed to make a lake to supply the tide-mill with power. Salmon-fishing here. Medieval church with ancient yew, possibly older than the church.

STOKE GOLDING Leicestershire SP3997
Village off A447, 3 miles (5km) NW of Hinckley
According to tradition, where Richard III's crown was found in bush after his Bosworth defeat (see Sutton Cheney).

STOKE MANDEVILLE Buckinghamshire SP8310
Village on A4010, 3 miles (5km) SE of Aylesbury
Much 1930s housing. Stoke Mandeville Hospital, on the outskirts of Aylesbury, is world famous for the treatment of spinal injuries.

STOKE ORCHARD Gloucestershire SO9228
Village off A435, 4 miles (6km) NW of Cheltenham
Pleasant village with timber-framed houses and interesting Norman church with series of early wall-paintings.

STOKE POGES Buckinghamshire SU9783
Village off A355, 3 miles (5km) N of Slough
Delightful church indelibly associated with the 18th-century poet Thomas Gray and the *Elegy in a Country*

Churchyard. His tomb is in the churchyard, with a monument (National Trust) by James Wyatt close by. A beautiful landscaped cemetery next to the churchyard is open to the public. The village is still remarkably rural, although so close to Slough (see).

STOKE PRIOR Hereford and Worcester SO9567
Village on B4091, 2 miles (3km) S of Bromsgrove
Cottages survive from the 'model village' created by saltworks entrepreneur John Corbett, together with traces of his factory beside popular Worcester and Birmingham Canal.

STOKE ROW Oxfordshire SU6883
Village off B481, 5 miles (8km) W of Henley-on-Thames
Village famous for its unique well, given by Maharajah of Benares in 1864. Iron pillars support gilded dome over winding gear decorated with elephant.

STOKE ST GREGORY Somerset ST3427
Village off A361, 8 miles (12km) E of Taunton
Long village with distinctive octagonal church tower. Willows and Wetlands Centre has basket-making and displays on natural history of the Somerset Levels.

STOKE SUB HAMDON Somerset ST4717
Village off A303, 5 miles (8km) W of Yeovil
Under Ham Hill, and built from the beautiful local golden stone. Two villages: West Stoke, denser, with more cottages and The Priory (National Trust), a 14th-century hall; East Stoke has a partly Norman church.

STOKE-BY-NAYLAND Suffolk TL9836
Village on B1068, 2 miles (3km) N of Nayland
Stands on raised ground above Dedham Vale meadows and near the River Stour. It is an Area of Outstanding Natural Beauty in the heart of Constable Country.

STOKE-ON-TRENT Staffordshire SJ8745
City off M6, 135 miles (217km) NW of London
Local novelist Arnold Bennett established his reputation with his novels set in the Five Towns – Tunstall, Burslem, Hanley, Longton and Stoke – that made up the Potteries conurbation in his day. Fiercely independent, the towns became progressively more involved together in the improvement of roads, water supplies, sewage and other amenities and were forced towards amalgamation. In 1910 Fenton joined them to form the town of Stoke-on-Trent, now a city sprawling over 36 square miles (93 sq km).

The presence in the area of marl clay, coal, water, iron, copper and lead, the essential raw materials for the manufacture and decoration of ceramics, led to the concentration of pottery manufacture here. Volume production started in the 17th century, but the industry leapt forward in the 18th century, thanks to entrepreneurs like Josiah Wedgwood, Josiah Spode and Thomas Minton, who brought individual potters together into organised workplaces. It should be remembered, however, that these famous names associated with fine decorative china represented only a fraction of the total output of the pottery towns; they were outnumbered by the hundreds of small factories turning out utilitarian household and sanitary chinaware.

Production reached its height towards the end of the 19th century, when the smoke pall produced by countless 'pot banks' and the diseases caused by toxic raw materials made the Potteries the least healthy environment in Britain. Something of the atmosphere of those days (without the smoke) survives in the many terraces of small houses, the gaunt old factories and the waste land that still exist – together with the haphazard streets that can be a nightmare for motorists. They form a marked contrast to the modern shopping centres, big office blocks and green open spaces that have started to replace them.

For anyone interested in industrial archaeology or Victorian architecture Stoke-on-Trent is a paradise, and in recent years the city has done much to celebrate its past with the establishment of museums and the opening up of famous factories to visitors. Individual attractions in Tunstall, Burslem, Hanley, Longton and Fenton are described in separate entries; Stoke itself has the Minton and Spode factories, as well as a very grand town hall, one of Britain's most splendid railway stations and the ground of the venerable Stoke City Football Club, always associated with local boy Stanley Matthews.

STOKEINTEIGNHEAD Devon SX9170
Village off B3199, 4 miles (6km) E of Newton Abbot
Small village. The late medieval church, tucked into a little combe, has an unusually early wooden screen of 1400 and the earliest (1375) brass in the county.

STOKENCHURCH Buckinghamshire SU7696
Village on A40, 7 miles (11km) NW of High Wycombe
Former Chilterns chair-making centre. Large green, much 20th-century housing. Strange-looking dish-festooned concrete communications tower of 1961.

STOKENHAM Devon SX8042
Village on A379, 5 miles (8km) E of Kingsbridge
Large village with old slate and thatch cottages in the middle near the big 15th-century church. Inland from Slapton Sands (see).

STOKESLEY North Yorkshire NZ5208
Small town off A172, 8 miles (13km) S of Middlesbrough
The town lies on the River Leven and there are various bridges over the river in the town. The narrow pack-horse bridge has low walls which allowed animals carrying heavy packs to cross the water. The town was home to Jane Pace, the first white woman to settle in Victoria, Australia, in 1836.

STONDON MASSEY Essex TL5800
Village off A414, 3 miles (5km) SE of Chipping Ongar
Village green, pond and pub. Memorial in the Norman church to Elizabethan composer William Byrd, who lived and died here.

STONE Staffordshire SJ9034
Town off A34, 7 miles (11km) N of Stafford
Admiral Jervis, colleague of Nelson, was born in this market town. Nautical activity is now confined to the busy Trent and Mersey Canal, but the town is worth exploring for buildings such as the early Gothic Revival church, stately neo-Jacobean railway station, thatched Crown

and Anchor pub, Crown hotel of 1778 and pleasant Georgian buildings. Canoeing is popular on the River Trent.

STONE (STONE-CUM-EBONY) Kent TQ9327
Village off B2080, 2 miles (3km) SW of Appledore
Little village perched on the former seacliff of the Isle of Oxney with Roman altar preserved in the church.

STONE STREET Kent
Roman road
This Roman road is one of several radiating from the major route centre, Canterbury, heading south to Lympne, an important Roman port. Largely followed by the B2068.

Rare example in the church at Stone of a Mithraic altar, which at one time served as a mounting block.

STONEGRAVE North Yorkshire SE6577
Village on B1257, 2 miles (3km) NW of Hovingham
An attractive village. Stonegrave House is former home of the late Sir Herbert Read (occasionally open).

STONEHAVEN Grampian NO8786
Town off A90 (A92), 13 miles (21km) S of Aberdeen
Once an important fishing port; composed of the old town south of the River Carron, Cowie at the north end of the bay and the new town of 1795. Some 17th- and 18th-century buildings, including a crow-stepped tollbooth housing a local museum. Noted for New Year celebrations, when young men swing fireballs round their heads to ward off evil.

STONEHENGE Wiltshire SU1242
Site on A360, 2 miles (3km) W of Amesbury
The most famous prehistoric monument (English Heritage) in the country, a ring of huge sarsen stones 13ft (4m) high, some still carrying other stones across their tops. Inside, a ring of smaller stones and at the centre more huge sarsens. This was started 5,000 years ago, and was altered and added to several times. Very impressive despite modern roads close to it. (See Salisbury Museum.)

STONEHOUSE Devon SX4654
District in W Plymouth
A little port taken over by the royal navy in the 18th century, with the big 1750s Royal Naval Hospital, the 1780s Royal Marine Barracks and, largest of all, the Royal William Yard – the navy's Victualling Yard started in 1825 on the waterfront. Huge complex of buildings, with a grand entrance gateway topped by a big statue of William IV. Now part of Plymouth. Passenger ferry to Cremyll (see).

STONELEIGH Warwickshire SP3372
Village off A46, 3 miles (5km) E of Kenilworth
Once a humble estate village, Stoneleigh has become a showpiece, with an important Norman church, a manor house, almshouses and a rich array of picturesque cottages, mostly of brick and timber-frame. The grounds of historic Stoneleigh Abbey (not open) house the National Agricultural Centre and the site of the vast Royal Show, held in July each year.

STONESFIELD Oxfordshire SP3917
Village off B4022, 3 miles (5km) SE of Charlbury
Village once famous for stone roofing slates stands above meandering River Evenlode. Intriguing tiny lock-up near church, which has good Tudor glass.

STONEY MIDDLETON Derbyshire SK2375
Village on A623, 5 miles (8km) N of Bakewell
Peak District limestone village with unusual octagonal church added to 15th-century tower. Middleton Dale much quarried. Well-dressing in July.

STONHAM ASPAL Suffolk TM1359
Village on A1120, 5 miles (8km) E of Stowmarket
Roman bathhouse found in 1962, and huge hoard of 17th-century coins discovered in 1980, possibly highwayman's treasure. Broughton Hall is moated.

STONOR Oxfordshire SU7388
Village on B480, 4 miles (6km) NW of Henley-on-Thames
Wooded Chiltern estate village for Stonor Park (limited opening), a fine old house displaying exceptional treasures. Also gardens, deer park and chapel.

STONY STRATFORD Buckinghamshire SP7940
Small town on A5, in NW Milton Keynes
Old coaching town on Watling Street with many 18th-century buildings and an astonishing number of inns.

Rivalry between the Cock and the Bull pubs in the High Street is supposed to account for the phrase 'cock and bull story'. Wildfowl conservation area among meadows and gravel pits by the Great Ouse.

STOPHAM West Sussex TQ0219
Village off A283, 1 mile (2km) W of Pulborough
A few cottages cluster round the tall, very early Norman church at the end of a no-through road. Near by is a famous bridge over the River Rother, rebuilt in 1424.

STOREY ARMS Powys SN9820
Site on A470, 7 miles (11km) SW of Brecon
Popular spot at high point of Merthyr Tydfil to Brecon road through Brecon Beacons. Walks to Pen-y-fan, Beacons' summit. Storey Arms itself is an outdoor pursuits centre.

STORNOWAY Western Isles NB4232
Town on A859, principal town of Lewis
Stornoway is the largest town and the adminstrative centre for the Western Isles, and the transport hub of Lewis. The harbour was enlarged and modernised in the 19th century, when the town was a major herring port. Today it is used for shelter by many fish factory ships, from Eastern Europe in particular. It is also the ferry terminal from the mainland, while the island's airport lies 4 miles (6km) to the east.

The medieval castle was destroyed by Cromwell's troops in 1654; the present Gothic-style Lews Castle was built by James Matheson, who bought Lewis in 1844 and effected much development until his death in 1878. In 1918 Lewis was purchased by Lord Leverhulme, but his philanthropic economic development plans came to nothing and in 1923 the area of Stornoway parish was gifted to the town council.

The wooded castle grounds are now a public park. There are a number of churches, including St Colomba (1794), and an art gallery in the town hall. There is a certain amount of suburban sprawl and the industrial estate provides facilities for the finishing processes of the famous Harris tweed.

STORR, THE Highland (Skye) NG4954
Mountain ridge off A855, 7 miles (11km) N of Portree
Mountain ridge with massive landslip which formed the Old Man of Storr, a 165ft (50m) column of rock offering challenging climbing.

STORRINGTON West Sussex TQ0814
Small town on A283, 4 miles (6km) SE of Pulborough
An old market town of many different building styles, with a heavily restored Norman church. Nearby Parham Park is the best Elizabethan house in Sussex, with a big deer park.

STOTTESDON Shropshire SO6782
Village off B4363, 4 miles (6km) N of Cleobury Mortimer
Isolated hill village with fine Saxon, Norman and medieval features in its church. Magnificent Norman font and Arts and Crafts screen.

STOULTON Hereford and Worcester SO9049
Village on A44, 5 miles (8km) SE of Worcester
Old cottages mingle with modern housing development in this pleasant village in market garden country. Norman church has fine nave roof.

STOUR, RIVER Kent
River, combining Great Stour and Little Stour
Rising near Hythe, the River Stour flows 40 miles (64km) across Kent past Canterbury to Stourmouth; it then flows across marshlands past Sandwich to Pegwell Bay and the sea.

STOUR, RIVER Suffolk
River, running through Clare and Dedham to Harwich
Running through Constable Country, the Stour passes through typical English countryside of ancient trees, rolling meadows, and quaint villages.

STOUR, RIVER West Midlands
River, tributary of the Severn
Once important for early industry, the River Stour rises in Clent Hills, loops round Halesowen and Stourbridge and passes through Kidderminster to join the River Severn at Stourport.

STOURBRIDGE West Midlands SO9084
Town on A458, 10 miles (16km) W of Birmingham
The Redhouse Glassworks Museum and two crystal factories open to visitors are reminders of the glass-making history of this town on the edge of the Worcestershire countryside. The restored canal warehouse in Canal Street is an additional attraction, and there are pleasant older buildings in the town centre.

STOURPAINE Dorset ST8609
Village on A350, 3 miles (5km) NW of Blandford Forum
Thatched cottages are set off the main road. Hod Hill, to the north, is an Iron Age hillfort with a Roman fort in one corner.

STOURPORT-ON-SEVERN Hereford and Worcester SO8171
Town on A451, 3 miles (5km) SW of Kidderminster
The small canal town, busy with pleasure craft in summer, developed in late 18th century when Brindley constructed junction of Worcestershire and Staffordshire Canal with River Severn. Interesting complex of locks and basins survive. Main dock, with original buildings such as the Tontine hotel, now used as marina. Eighteenth-century houses remain in streets around dock area.

STOURTON Wiltshire ST7734
Village off B3092, 3 miles (5km) NW of Mere
Little estate village with medieval church, part of the wonderful Stourhead landscape (National Trust) created in the 18th century. Three classical temples, a Gothic cottage, grotto and bridge over the lake were constructed and the medieval market cross from Bristol was moved here as an ornament. Severely classical 18th-century big house, with fine collection of pictures and furniture. King Alfred's Tower 2 miles (3km) away was completed in 1772, a landmark from miles around. Stourton House Garden.

STOW Borders NT4544
Village on A7, 5 miles (8km) W of Lauder
Village to the east of Moorfoot Hills on Gala Water, with a packhorse bridge built in 1655.

STOW Lincolnshire SK8881
Village on B1241, 4 miles (6km) N of Saxilby
Just off Roman Tillbridge Lane. Outstanding church with lofty Saxon tower arches, early Norman nave and later Norman chancel. Late 17th-century Manor Farm.

STOW BARDOLPH Norfolk TF6205
Village on A10; 2 miles (3km) NE of Downham Market
Stow Bardolph boasts some handsome houses, a fine park with rolling meadows and proud trees, a lovingly restored hall, and a church with an unusual effigy. Inside a mahogany cupboard is a lifesized fully-dressed wax model of Sarah Hare, a parishioner of Holy Trinity, complete with warts and staring eyes, who died in 1744 from pricking her finger while sewing.

STOW CUM QUY Cambridgeshire TL5260
Village on B1102, 5 miles (8km) E of Cambridge
Quy Fen is fringed with hedgerows and scrub, proving plentiful nesting for birds. Stow means 'holy place', and Quy means 'cow island'.

STOW-ON-THE-WOLD Gloucestershire SP1925
Small town on A429, 4 miles (6km) S of Moreton-in-Marsh
The highest town in the Cotswolds has a fine medieval church into which Royalist prisoners were herded after one of the last Civil War battles. Shopping is a pleasure in the bustling town centre where handsome shops, inns and houses of the 17th and 18th centuries line the market square and neighbouring streets.

STOWE Buckinghamshire SP6737
Parish off A413, 3 miles (5km) NW of Buckingham
Stowe Mansion is occupied by Stowe School (limited opening) in 18th-century grounds (National Trust) of the utmost magnificence by Bridgeman, Kent and Capability Brown.

STOWE-BY-CHARTLEY Staffordshire SK0026
Village off A518, 6 miles (10km) NE of Stafford
Utilitarian village in Trent Valley has the ancient Cock inn, a good Norman church with monuments by Lutyens and the entertaining Amerton Working Farm.

STOWE-IX-CHURCHES Northamptonshire SP6357
Village off A5, 6 miles (10km) SE of Daventry
Evil presence reputedly deflected Saxon builders from eight church sites, before allowing building on a ninth, hence curious name. Saxon church tower, fine monuments. Old Dairy Farm craft centre.

STOWLANGTOFT Suffolk TL9568
Village off A1088, 2 miles (3km) SE of Ixworth
Church is especially fine with nine 15th-century Flemish carved wooden panels and 60 carved figures in the bench-ends.

STOWMARKET Suffolk TM0458
Town off A14 (A45), 11 miles (18km) NW of Ipswich
An ancient market town which stands at a junction of major roads. It is still busy, although its heyday was in the 17th and 18th centuries as a centre for the wool trade. Notable buildings include Abbot's Hall, now the Museum of East Anglian Life. Alton watermill is also on the museum site.

STRADBROKE Suffolk TM2373
Village on B1117, 4 miles (6km) NW of Laxfield
This sleepy village was once larger. It has the 14th-century All Saints' Church, and the timber-framed Town House, built in 1587.

STRAITON Strathclyde NS3804
Village on B741, 6 miles (10km) SE of Maybole
Village on the Water of Girvan. Restored church has a pre-Reformation aisle. Blairquhan House lies to the west.

STRANRAER Dumfries and Galloway NX0560
Town off A75, 9 miles (14km) NW of Glenluce
The main Scottish ferry port to Northern Ireland and Eire, which developed in the 1820s–40s, when piers were built into Loch Ryan. The town has been a royal burgh since 1617. The 16th-century Stranraer Castle is a complete tower house in the centre, which houses a heritage centre devoted to the history of prisons. Northwest, Castle House was the home of John Ross (1777–1856), Arctic explorer.

STRATFIELD MORTIMER Berkshire SU6664
Village off A33, 6 miles (10km) SW of Reading
Flat and well wooded, on the border with Hampshire. The 19th-century church has an unusually early tomb slab of 1017.

STRATFIELD SAYE Hampshire SU6861
Village off A33, 8 miles (12km) SW of Reading
The big house was presented to the 1st Duke of Wellington after he defeated Napoleon at Waterloo (1815). Lots of French furniture and reminders of the duke, with a superb display on his life. Little Victorian village and a plain classical church of 1755 .

STRATFORD Greater London TQ3884
Town in borough of Newham
Grim former industrial area. Theatre Royal, staging controversial productions, Passmore Edwards Museum, relating local history, huge Abbey Mills pumping station (open by appointment).

STRATFORD ST MARY Suffolk TM0434
Village off A12, 6 miles (10km) NE of Colchester
Delightful Tudor village with many fine buildings, such as the Weaver's House and Norman church. Stratford St Mary was a Roman staging point.

STRATFORD SUB CASTLE Wiltshire SU1332
Village off A345, just NW of Salisbury
Tucked under Old Sarum (see), hence the name. Several large stone houses, Elizabethan to Georgian, and a medieval church with a tower and many fittings of 1711.

STRATFORD TONY Wiltshire SU0926
Village off A354, 3 miles (5km) S of Wilton
Pretty chalkland village in the River Ebble Valley, with the little medieval church right by the river.

STRATFORD-UPON-AVON Warwickshire SP2054
Town on A439, 8 miles (13km) SW of Warwick
Even without Shakespeare Stratford-upon-Avon would be an appealing town, with a fine riverside position and streets full of mellow buildings. But the Shakespeare associations have brought some splendid bonuses, such as R S Gower's lively monument near the 15th-century Clopton Bridge and the attractive gardens fronting the Royal Shakespeare Theatre.

The summer tourist activity here is matched by the shopping bustle in the wide Bridge Street that leads towards the town centre. Henley Street, branching to the right, contains the solid middle-class house where Shakespeare was born, while High Street, to the left, is the way to several famous attractions – Harvard House (home of the mother of the university's founder), New Place (the site of Shakespeare's retirement home, now marked by a garden), Nash's House (the home of his grand-daughter and a museum of Stratford history) and the lovely timber-framed group comprising the grammar school, the guildhall and the guild chapel. Beyond these, in the road leading to the church, is Hall's Croft, home of Shakespeare's doctor son-in-law, where a 17th-century dispensary is re-created.

Holy Trinity is the church of a prosperous market town, with a stately nave and chancel of the 14th and 15th centuries and a fine chapel commemorating the influential Clopton family. It would justify a leisurely inspection even without Shakespeare's monument in the chancel.

Apart from these special attractions, Stratford boasts interesting shops and a wealth of other notable buildings, and it is also worth investigating the exhibitions and audio-visual presentations at The World of Shakespeare in Waterside and the informal performance studios set up by the Royal Shakespeare Company.

The picturesque thatched farmhouse where Anne Hathaway, Shakespeare's wife, grew up is at Shottery on the town's western outskirts, while his mother's house is at Wilmcote (see).

STRATHAVEN Strathclyde NS7044
Town on A723, 7 miles (11km) S of Hamilton
Former weaving centre, pronounced 'Straiven', where markets were once held on Common Green. Local history is told at the John Hastie Museum. East Church (1777) is the main landmark.

STRATHMIGLO Fife NO2109
Small town off A91, 2 miles (3km) SW of Auchtermuchty
Small town, founded in the 15th century, with a tollbooth dating from 1734 and noted for the manufacture of footwear.

STRATHPEFFER Highland NH4858
Village on A834, 4 miles (6km) W of Dingwall
Victorian spa town in a hilly wooded valley west of Dingwall (see). Sulphur springs were used from 1770 and the pump room was built in 1820; the spa developed after this and was renowned all over Europe until 1914. Water-sampling pavilion in main square. Abundant Pictish remains in area, including vitrified fort at Knockfarrel and Eagle Stone, engraved with an angel.

STRATHY Highland NC8465
Village on A836, 17 miles (27km) W of Thurso
Scattered crofting settlement near Strathy Point, which has many caves, a lighthouse and a sandy beach near by. Fine bird-watching and a wide variety of flora, including rare Scottish primrose.

STRATTON Cornwall SS2306
Town off A39, just E of Bude
Small town on a steep hill, with a fine medieval church at the top.

STRATTON-ON-THE-FOSSE Somerset ST6550
Village on A367, 3 miles (5km) SW of Radstock
Named after the Roman road (see Fosse Way), and dominated by Downside Abbey, a school and monastery with huge Victorian and later buildings. Vast church.

STREATHAM Greater London TQ3071
District in borough of Lambeth
A typical South London suburb of 19th/20th-century houses and flats, but there was also a spa in Streatham in the 17th century, and London merchants built fine houses here. The Parish Church of St Leonard was sympathetically restored in the 1970s after a fire; monuments to the Thrales, Dr Johnson's friends. Streatham Common. Ice rink.

STREATLEY Berkshire SU5980
Village on A329, 4 miles (6km) NW of Pangbourne
Tucked up by the River Thames and below steep downland, with the High Street leading straight down to the river. Good mixture of buildings, including Georgian houses. The church is on the river, which has weirs here. The ornamental Edwardian barge usually moored here originally belonged to an Oxford college.

STREET Somerset ST4836
Town on A39, 2 miles (3km) SW of Glastonbury
Famous for shoe-making. Street was only a village when the Clark family started making shoes here in 1829. Their original factory is now the Shoe Museum. The Clarks were Quakers, and Street has a stately and classical meeting house of 1850. Also a prominent 1897 clock tower, and a big sculpture by Henry Moore.

STRELLEY Nottinghamshire SK5141
Village on A6002, 4 miles (6km) W of Nottingham
Fine 14th-century church chancel endowed by Samson de Strelley, containing his tomb. Eighteenth-century hall in landscaped park, some medieval walls in stables.

STRENSHAM Hereford and Worcester SO9140
Hamlet off A38, 5 miles (8km) N of Tewkesbury
Hamlet beside M5 north of Tewkesbury has superb riverside church with fine furnishings from 16th to 18th centuries and many brasses and monuments.

STRETFORD Greater Manchester SJ7994
Town off A56, 4 miles (6km) SW of Manchester
Residential area built up around busy A56 Manchester to Chester road. Large shopping centre. Longford Hall was home to prominent Victorian entrepreneur John Rylands.

STRETHALL Essex TL4839
Village off B1383, 4 miles (6km) W of Saffron Walden
Small, quiet, secluded place among chalk hills near Cambridgeshire border, lovely setting for remarkable Saxon and medieval church.

STRETHAM Cambridgeshire TL5174
Village on A10, 4 miles (6km) SW of Ely
Stretham stands on the edge of the Fens where its Old Engine, installed in 1831, pumped 120 tons of water each minute to keep Waterbeach Levels drained. This fascinating engine, first steam then diesel, now silent, is well maintained and open to the public. Stretham also has a 20ft (6m) village cross dating from about 1400.

STRETTON Cheshire SJ4452
Village off A534, 1 mile (2km) NW of Tilston
Mainly agricultural, surrounded by dairy and arable farms in pretty countryside. Restored Stretton Watermill.

STRETTON Cheshire SJ6283
Village on B5386, 2 miles (3km) S of Warrington
Wallspit House, a Georgian Listed Building, is now a pub and restaurant, renamed The Hollow Tree.

STRETTON Leicestershire SK9415
Village off A1, 8 miles (13km) NW of Stamford
On Great North road. Ram Jam inn may take curious name from 18th-century drink popular with travellers. Church mainly 13th century, Norman doorway.

STRETTON SUGWAS Hereford and Worcester SO4642
Village on A480, 4 miles (6km) NW of Hereford
Large village looking over the River Lugg to Hereford has a church worth visiting for carved Norman tympanum and unusual timber-framed tower.

STRETTON-ON-DUNSMORE Warwickshire SP4072
Village off A45, 6 miles (10km) W of Rugby
Large village on Dunsmore Heath, with church by Gothic Revival pioneer Thomas Rickman and attractive brick and timber-framed cottages around its green.

STRID, THE North Yorkshire SE0656
Beauty spot off B6160, 2 miles (3km) NW of Bolton Abbey
At this beauty spot the River Wharfe flows through a ferocious white-water ravine where many have died.

STROMEFERRY Highland NG8634
Village on A980, 8 miles (13km) NE of Kyle of Lochalsh
Village on the south shore of Loch Carron, once linked by ferry to the north side of the loch. Ruined Strome Castle (destroyed in 1602) stands opposite.

STROMNESS Orkney HY2509
Small town on A965, 12 miles (19km) W of Kirkwall
The main seaport for centuries, this sailors' haven, with narrow alleys and closes, boomed in the 19th century with the herring trade and Hudson's Bay Company recruitment. Modern ferry terminal.

STRONTIAN Highland NM8161
Village on A861, 8 miles (13km) W of Inversanda
Loch Sunart village. The Strontian Lead Mines (1722) produced bullets for the Napoleonic wars. The 'Floating Church' anchored here when the Free Church broke away from the Church of Scotland (1843).

STROOD Kent TQ7369
Town on A2, across River Medway from Rochester
Big old town looking over the River Medway to Rochester, joined by a bridge which carries Roman Watling Street. Frequented by Canterbury pilgrims in the Middle Ages; several hospitals were built for them. High Street is narrow and winding and the town is hemmed in by industry. The 14th-century church (founded pre-1193) was rebuilt in 1812 by Sir Robert Smirke, his first work.

STROUD Gloucestershire SO8305
Town on A46, 8 miles (13km) S of Gloucester
At the junction of five valleys with fast-flowing streams, Stroud was a notable weaving town and still produces broadcloth. Never picturesque, its rugged Nonconformist character lingers in interesting buildings such as an early Methodist chapel, 18th-century houses in Rowcroft and the neo-classical Subscription Rooms. The Stroud Museum specialises in local history and an industrial museum recalls local crafts and industries.

STRUAN Tayside NN8065
Village off A9, 4 miles (6km) W of Blair Atholl
Tiny village in the heart of Clan Robertson country; the churchyard is a burial place for clan chiefs. Clan museum near by at Bruar Falls.

STRUBBY Lincolnshire TF4582
Village off A157, 4 miles (6km) N of Alford
Between Wolds and coast. Seventeenth-century Woodthorpe Hall, Georgian Old Rectory, early 18th-century Grange Farm. Church with Victorian exterior and medieval interior.

STRUMBLE HEAD Dyfed SM8941
Headland off A487, 5 miles (8km) NW of Fishguard
Savage coastal headland with far-reaching views. Lighthouse. Close to Carreg Wastad Point, scene of farcical French 'invasion' in 1797.

STRUMPSHAW Norfolk TG3407
Village off A47, 4 miles (6km) SW of Acle
Merging with neighbouring Lingwood, Strumpshaw nevertheless has its own distinct character. It has a hill (a rarity in East Anglia) from which Norwich can be seen, and a little 14th-century church. Strumpshaw Fen is an RSPB sanctuary on the River Yare. Hides allow visitors to watch marsh harriers and many other birds.

STUDHAM Bedfordshire TL0215
Village off A5, 6 miles (10km) SW of Luton
Highest and southernmost Bedfordshire village, among woods near Whipsnade (see). Unusual war memorial in church.

STUDLAND Dorset SZ0382
Village on B3351, 3 miles (5km) N of Swanage
A seaside village, mostly Edwardian in the middle, with an attractive and interesting Norman church. Studland Bay has a long sandy beach backed by wild heathland. Ferry (passenger and car) across the narrow mouth of Poole Harbour.

STUDLEY Warwickshire SP0763
Village on A435, 4 miles (6km) SE of Redditch
The old village centre of this residential outpost of Redditch has a fine Norman and medieval church and some venerable buildings.

STUDLEY ROYAL North Yorkshire SE2770
Hamlet off B6265, 2 miles (4km) W of Ripon
A tiny hamlet in the valley of the River Skell, close to Fountains Abbey, whose buildings (mainly National Trust) have been restored to their original glory. The formal water gardens, laid out by John Aislabie in 1720, encompass many fine monuments. Splendid Church of St Mary (English Heritage).

STUMP CROSS CAVERNS North Yorkshire SE0863
Caves on B6265, 5m (8km) SW of Pateley Bridge
An impressive show cave with beautiful displays of colour-illuminated stalactites, stalagmites and crystal formations.

STUNTNEY Cambridgeshire TL5578
Village on A142, 2 miles (3km) SE of Ely
Stunt means 'steep' in old Cambridgeshire, and referred to the sloping sides of what was once an island in the Fens. Excellent views of Ely.

STURMINSTER MARSHALL Dorset ST9500
Village off A350, 4 miles (6km) W of Wimborne
A large village down in the Stour Valley, one of its two greens having a maypole. White Mill Bridge and mill, to the north, are picturesque.

STURMINSTER NEWTON Dorset ST7814
Small town off A357, 8 miles (13km) NW of Blandford Forum
Traditionally the capital of the Blackmore Vale (see), this is a small market town with a huge market. Pretty, but quiet and sleepy apart from Mondays (market day), it has many Georgian brick buildings and a dense centre. William Barnes, the Dorset poet, went to school here in the early 19th century. Sturminster Newton Mill, 17th and 18th century, still works.

STURRY Kent TR1760
Village on A28, 3 miles (5km) NE of Canterbury
Village on the River Stour, largely rebuilt after bomb damage in World War II, but retaining a Norman church tower and huge old weatherboarded and brick barn.

STYAL Cheshire SJ8383
Village off B5166, 1 mile (2km) N of Wilmslow
Model village built to house workers at nearby Quarry Bank Mill, a large cottonmill. The National Trust owns the mill, village and woodlands.

SUDBOROUGH Northamptonshire SP9682
Village off A6116, 3 miles (5km) NW of Thrapston
In wooded Rockingham Forest countryside, on Harper's Brook tributary of River Nene. Circular tollhouse dated 1660, and 13th-century church.

SUDBOURNE Suffolk TM4153
Village off B1084, 2 miles (3km) N of Orford
Sudbourne Forest was much damaged by the 1987 hurricane, although this was merely the most recent of a history of natural disasters to have befallen lovely Sudbourne. Sudbourne Hall was abandoned during World War II when German bombs came uncomfortably close. It remained empty for six years, doubtless to the disgust of the ghost who is said to haunt it.

SUDBURY Derbyshire SK1632
Village off A50, 5 miles (8km) E of Uttoxeter
Late 17th-century Sudbury Hall (National Trust), with superb plasterwork and woodcarving. Museum of Childhood illustrates Victorian and Edwardian life. Estate village, with inn of 1671.

SUDBURY Suffolk TL8741
Town on A134, 13 miles (21km) NW of Colchester
Still a weaving town, Sudbury was once one of the largest East Anglian woollen centres. Gainsborough was born here in 1727, and the elegant Tudor house with added Georgian façade is now a museum. Market Hill forms the town centre, while below it stands the medieval Salter's Hall and Anchor inn. The 'Sudbury Pall' is a famous 15th-century embroidery.

SUGAR LOAF Gwent SO2718
Mountain off A40, 3 miles (5km) NW of Abergavenny
Mountain 1,955ft (596m) high above Abergavenny and the Usk Valley. A major landmark. Walks to top from car park off the A40.

SUILVEN Highland NC1518
Mountain off A837, 5 miles (8km) SE of Lochinver
Distinctive and spectacular mountain in Assynt with a long ridge of three peaks forming a summit, 2,399ft (731m) high. Formed of Torridonian sandstone on granite.

SULBY Isle of Man SC3894
Village on A3, 4 miles (6km) W of Ramsey
Next to the Sulby River. Sulby Straight is a famous stretch of the TT racecourse. Sulby Reservoir was built in the 1980s.

SULGRAVE Northamptonshire SP5545
Village off B4525, 6 miles (10km) N of Brackley
Attractive limestone village with thatched houses and 17th-century Thatched House hotel, popular with American visitors drawn to Sulgrave Manor, home from 1539 of Washington family, ancestors of first

Sulgrave Manor.

US President: Elizabethan house and gardens open regularly for visits, concerts, special events. In St James's Church, 17th-century Washington pew and family monuments. Stocks on village green.

SULHAMSTEAD Berkshire SU6368
Village off A4, 6 miles (10km) SW of Reading
Scattered wooded village in the Kennet Valley. At Sulhampstead Abbots, to the southeast, there is a little Norman church.

SULLOM VOE Shetland HU3573
Harbour off Yell Sound
This deep-water inlet, which served as a World War II seaplane base, houses Britain's largest oil terminal, stabilising crude piped oil from Brent and Ninian fields and shipping it to refineries.

SUMMER ISLES Highland
Islands at mouth of Loch Broom, reached from Ullapool
Group of islands to north-west of Loch Broom, largely uninhabited; Tanera Mhor is the largest. Isle Martin is owned by the RSPB.

SUMMERBRIDGE North Yorkshire SE2062
Village on B6165, 3 miles (5km) SE of Pateley Bridge
The village is home to the Brimham Rocks, owned by the National Trust, which have been eroded to form fantastic shapes.

SUMMERCOURT Cornwall SW8856
Village on A3058, 6 miles (10km) SE of Newquay
Crossroads town, now bypassed, with a famous fair on 25 September which used to close the main road all day.

SUMMERSEAT Greater Manchester SD7914
Village off A56, 2 miles (3km) N of Bury
A typical, quaint English village with a station on the East Lancashire Railway. Brooksbottoms Mill, a former cottonmill, has been converted into flats.

SUNBURY Surrey TQ1068
Town off M3, 4 miles (6km) SE of Staines
Elegant residential town on the River Thames with an extraordinary 18th-century church. Thames Street is busy thoroughfare parallel to the river, lined with 18th-century buildings, with alleyways leading between them to the river. The newer part of the town is at Sunbury Cross. The grounds of the demolished Sunbury House are now a 12 acre (5ha) park with a walled garden. Nearby Kempton Park Racecourse hosts flat and National Hunt meetings.

SUNDERLAND Lancashire SD4255
Village off A589, 1 mile (2km) SW of Overton
A cotton port in the 18th century, most of whose properties were built by Lancaster merchant Robert Lawson between 1715 and 1720. A Georgian gate-pier is all that remains on the deserted quay at Sunderland Point. At high tides this little peninsula in the Lune estuary virtually becomes an island.

SUNDERLAND Tyne and Wear NZ3956
Town on A184, 11 miles (18km) SE of Newcastle
The town grew around three villages on the banks of the River Wear, Monkwearmouth and Bishopwearmouth, monastic lands from the 10th and 13th centuries, and Sunderland, land 'sundered' from the monastic estates of Monkwearmouth. The Industrial Revolution turned Sunderland into the biggest shipbuilding town in the world for a time; now the riverside is changing and the scars of derelict land are being cleared to create a greener environment. Wearmouth Bridge, opened in 1929 with massive steel arches spanning the river, brings traffic into the modernised town which has built up around a late Victorian and Edwardian commercial centre.

The Empire Theatre on High Street West is a splendid example of Edwardian theatre architecture, opened in 1907 by Vesta Tilley. It is now a civic theatre presenting a wide range of music, comedy, opera and ballet. Grindon Museum on Grindon Lane is a former shipbuilder's house with Edwardian period rooms.

Sunderland stages a series of annual events, including the International Festival of the Air, Roker Regatta, Sunderland Air Show and the Illuminations, from mid-September to the beginning of November, when 6 miles (10km) of the seafront are festooned with lights.

SUNDRIDGE Kent TQ4855
Village off A25, 3 miles (5km) W of Sevenoaks
Characterful village with a square and several delightful houses strung out along the road between Sevenoaks and Westerham.

SUNNINGDALE Berkshire SU9567
Small town off A30, 6 miles (10km) SW of Staines
A wooded Edwardian development with villas, the home of many celebrities. Famous golf course.

SURBITON Greater London TQ1867
District off A3, in borough of Kingston
Archetypal middle-class suburb, originally created by the railway's arrival in the 1840s. Good Victorian churches and waterworks.

SURFLEET Lincolnshire TF2528
Village on A16, 4 miles (6km) N of Spalding
In rich agricultural fenland, with Lincolnshire's Pisa, the alarmingly leaning tower of medieval St Laurence's Church, with early 15th-century chancel and clerestory.

SURLINGHAM Norfolk TG3106
Village off A47, 6 miles (10km) E of Norwich
Surlingham huddles at the edge of Surlingham Broad, now a reserve under the care of Norfolk Naturalists' Trust. Linked with naturalist and writer Ted Ellis.

SUTCOMBE Devon SS3411
Village off A388, 5 miles (8km) N of Holsworthy
Remote and rural with a pleasant late medieval church, almshouses of 1674 and some old cottages.

SUTHERLAND Highland
Historic region in N Scotland
A former county in the northern Highlands, the Vikings' 'Southland'. Scenically stunning, with fine mountains and coastline. Fishing, crofting and tourism are the main industries.

SUTTON Bedfordshire TL2247
Village off B1040, 1 mile (2km) S of Potton
Photogenic packhorse bridge and (normally) shallow ford. Burgoyne memorials and barrel organ in church.

SUTTON Cambridgeshire TL4478
Village on B1381, 6 miles (10km) W of Ely
Crouched on the edge of the Isle of Ely, Sutton offers vast skies and endless fenland to visitors. St Andrew's Church was built in 1400.

SUTTON Greater London TQ2564
Town/borough off A232, 4 miles (6km) W of Croydon
A major shopping, business and administrative centre, with a long High Street and 1960s/1970s high-rise commercial blocks. Sutton was a farming village until the London to Brighton turnpike road came through in 1755, followed by the railway in 1847. Victorian churches plus notable Methodist church of 1907 and Baptist church of 1934; 1930s civic centre.

SUTTON Norfolk TG3823
Village on A149, 1 mile (2km) SE of Stalham
Sutton has the tallest windmill in Britain and the Broadlands Museum. Sutton Broad is a peaceful stretch of water frequented by birds.

SUTTON Suffolk TM3046
Village on B1083, 3 miles (5km) SE of Woodbridge
A track over Sutton Common leads to the 11 barrows of Sutton Hoo, excavated in 1938 by Basil Brown to yield the stunning ship burial.

SUTTON AT HONE Kent TQ5570
Village on A225, 3 miles (5km) S of Dartford
Busy industrial village by the River Darent, on an ancient site with St John's Jerusalem Garden (National Trust) beside a moated house, originally a commandery of the Knights Hospitallers.

SUTTON BONINGTON Nottinghamshire SK5025
Village off A6006, 4 miles (6km) NW of Loughborough
In south of county, near River Soar. Medieval St Michael's Church, with tower and spire. Smaller St Anne's Church. University of Nottingham's School of Agriculture.

SUTTON BRIDGE Lincolnshire TF4721
Town on A17, 9 miles (14km) W of King's Lynn
Settlement grew from building of new bridge in 1832 over the River Nene, part of a massive drainage scheme by Telford and Rennie. Present bridge 1894–7. Peter Scott, ornithologist and artist, lived in one of two disused lighthouses at mouth of river, built 1820s. Victorian church of knapped flint.

SUTTON CHENEY Leicestershire SK4100
Village off A447, 2 miles (3km) S of Market Bosworth
Richard III is reputed to have celebrated mass at St James' Church before Battle of Bosworth Field, fought on 22 August 1485. The Battlefield Centre at Ambion Hill and battlefield trails explain events which resulted in Richard's defeat and death, bringing bitter Wars of the Roses to an end, and starting Tudor dynasty with crowning of Henry VII.

SUTTON COLDFIELD West Midlands SP1296
Town on A453, 7 miles (11km) NE of Birmingham
The imposing Holy Trinity Church stands among offices and busy shops in the town centre, with handsome Georgian houses near by. The cruck-built Old Smithy, moated New Hall and survivors of 50 stone cottages built by Bishop Veysey for 16th-century weavers are reminders of earlier history. Pride of the town, however,

is Sutton Park, 2,400 acres (960 ha) of woodland, heath and lakes.

SUTTON COURTENAY Oxfordshire SU5093
Village on B4016, 3 miles (5km) NW of Didcot.
Splendid houses and appealing old cottages in brick, stone and timber-frame make up the centre of this showpiece village beside the River Thames. George Orwell, Prime Minister Lord Asquith and Martha Pye (aged 117) are buried in the graveyard of All Saints' Church, which has outstanding Norman and medieval work and fine furnishings.

SUTTON IN ASHFIELD Nottinghamshire SK4958
Town on A38, 3 miles (5km) SW of Mansfield
Market town and, from 17th century, a textile-manufacturing centre. Norman and medieval church, restored in Victorian times.

SUTTON MANDEVILLE Wiltshire ST9828
Village off A30, 1 mile (2km) W of Fovant
Pretty setting in a wooded combe. A few stone cottages and a prominent church mostly of 1862.

SUTTON ON TRENT Nottinghamshire SK7965
Village on B1164, 8 miles (12km) N of Newark
Between A1 and River Trent, with some pleasant houses. Medieval church with 13th-century tower rebuilt 1902–3, church sympathetically restored 1932, highlight is splendid early 16th-century Mering Chapel with battlements, pinnacles, tomb-chest with Purbeck marble top. At south of village, early 19th-century brick tower mill. To north, Grassthorpe Manor House, 1697.

SUTTON POYNTZ Dorset SY7083
Village off A353, 4 miles (6km) NE of Weymouth
Set under the chalk hills, with a picturesque central millpond, and is celebrated as a beauty spot. Wessex Water Museum.

SUTTON SCARSDALE Derbyshire SK4469
Village off A617, 4 miles (6km) E of Chesterfield
Hilltop shell of early 18th-century baroque mansion (English Heritage) which had been remodelled from a 17th-century house by Francis Smith of Warwick.

SUTTON (SUTTON CUM LOUND) Nottinghamshire SK6884
Village off A638, 3 miles (5km) N of Retford
Pair of small villages, between Great North road and River Idle. Waterfowl reserve in former gravel pits.

SUTTON VALENCE Kent TQ8149
Village on A274, 4 miles (6km) NW of Headcorn
Charming village among orchards on steep south-facing Quarry Hills with superb views over the Weald from attractive High Street.

SUTTON-ON-SEA Lincolnshire TF5281
Village on A52, just SE of Mablethorpe
Village seaside resort, with sandy beaches, gardens and paddling pool. Major work on sea defences followed disastrous 1953 floods.

SUTTON-ON-THE-FOREST North Yorkshire SE5864
Village on B1363, 8 miles (13km) N of York
A pretty village in the countryside. Sutton Park, an early Georgian stately home with gardens laid out by Capability Brown, is open to the public.

SUTTON-UNDER-WHITESTONECLIFFE North Yorkshire SE4882
Village on A170, 3 miles (5km) E of Thirsk
A small village below Sutton Bank, a ridge on the western edge of the North York Moors and popular with hang-gliders. Osgodby Hall is open to the public.

SWADLINCOTE Derbyshire SK2919
Town off A514, 5 miles (8km) SE of Burton upon Trent
Close to Leicestershire and Staffordshire borders. Growth based on coal and clay industries. Dry-ski slope on landscaped colliery site.

SWAFFHAM Norfolk TF8109
Town off A47, 14 miles (23km) SE of King's Lynn
This charming market town, centred around Butter Cross in the main square, was once known as the 'Montpellier of England'. The market square is flanked with elegant 18th-century buildings. The northern end is dominated by the 1817 Assembly Rooms, while the Corn Exchange and Plowright Place are Victorian. Butter, or Market, Cross was presented to Swaffham by the Earl of Orford in 1783, and the handsome dome supported by pillars is topped by a statue of Ceres, the Roman goddess of agriculture.

Swaffham's heyday was during the Regency period, where it was especially noted for its hare coursing.

The church is built of expensive Barnack stone, and tells of the wealth of medieval Swaffham. The north aisle owes its splendour to a poor peddler in the 15th century. The story goes that John Chapman dreamt that he would meet a man who would make him rich in London. He set off, and met a man who told him that there was a pot of gold buried in his garden. He found two pots, and gave most of his new wealth to the church.

SWAFFHAM, BULBECK AND PRIOR Cambridgeshire TL5562
Villages on B1102, 6 miles (10km) W of Newmarket
Tucked away in pretty countryside, the two fen-edge villages stand about 1½ miles (2km) apart. Swaffham Bulbeck is linear with picturesque thatched cottages and the 18th-century yellow and red Abbey House, on the site of an old nunnery. Swaffham Prior has a collection of elegant Georgian houses and a churchyard with two churches.

SWAINSHILL Hereford and Worcester SO4641
Village on A438, 3 miles (5km) W of Hereford
At western end of village is The Weir (National Trust), woodland garden on banks of River Wye, famous for wealth of springtime bulbs.

SWALCLIFFE Oxfordshire SP3737
Village on B4035, 5 miles (8km) W of Banbury
Village on fringe of Cotswolds with ancient manor house and rewarding church of Saxon origin. Iron Age hillfort on Madmarston Hill near by.

SWALE, RIVER North Yorkshire
River, runs through Reeth and Richmond, tributary of the Ure
Despite its picturesque appearance, the River Swale is one of the most ferocious rivers in England. Swaledale is patterned with drystone walls.

SWALLOWFIELD Berkshire SU7264
Village off B3349, 6 miles (10km) S of Reading
The church has interesting late medieval engineering: sturdy wooden bracing inside to carry the bell-turret. Swallowfield Park is a late 17th-century mansion.

SWANAGE Dorset SZ0278
Town on A351, 9 miles (14km) SE of Wareham
Swanage is a holiday resort which has grown from a little fishing port. It enjoys a beautiful setting, with the hills of Purbeck behind and the wide bay in front. The chalk cliff to the west leads to the detached stack of chalk called Old Harry.

Swanage was deliberately developed as a resort from the 1820s, but until the railway arrived in 1885 growth was slow. The railway line has been rebuilt to Corfe and has steam trains. The town is largely Victorian, and ornamented with odd bits of architecture brought from London: the Wellington Tower on the beach is one, and the centre of the town hall another. Behind the town hall is a little lock-up of 1802.

The millpond is famously picturesque, surrounded by cottages built and roofed in the local stone. Durlston Country Park, to the southwest, includes a large area of wild land on two of the cliffs, a mock castle tea house of the 1880s, caves made by stone-quarrying and a big lighthouse.

SWANBOURNE Buckinghamshire SP8026
Village on B4032, 2 miles (3km) E of Winslow
Attractive Aylesbury Vale village of brick and half-timbered houses, largely built since an 18th-century fire.

SWANLEY Kent TQ5168
Town on B258, 4 miles (6km) SW of Dartford
Industrial town that was a tiny village until the railway came in 1861; it still has a small church beneath a grove of pines overlooking the green.

SWANNINGTON Leicestershire SK4116
Village off A50, 2 miles (3km) NW of Coalville
Incline of Stephenson's Leicester–Swannington railway, 1832, one of earliest railway lines operated by steam locomotives, improving coal transport.

SWANSCOMBE Kent TQ6074
Town off A226, 3 miles (5km) W of Gravesend
Former agricultural village swamped by Thames-side industry, with a partly Saxon church tower. An important palaeolithic skull ('Swanscombe Man' or, more correctly, 'Woman') was found in 1935 in an old gravel pit, now the site of a nature reserve.

SWANSEA (ABERTAWE) West Glamorgan SS6593
City off M4, 35 miles (56km) W of Cardiff
Swansea, Wales's second city, has an enviable location beside the grand sweep of sandy Swansea Bay. Always a maritime town, Swansea grew up in the 18th and 19th centuries as an industrial port serving the local metal-smelting industries. Swansea was severely damaged by bombing during World War II, after which the city centre was rebuilt to a modern plan, although fragments of the medieval castle survive. In the 1970s and 1980s, the developers turned their attentions to the redundant old waterfront, remodelling it into a stylish Maritime Quarter, complete with large marina, which has won praise for its architectural qualities.

Despite this rebuilding, Swansea is still a very Welsh city. Visitors will often hear Welsh spoken in the streets, and Swansea market boasts one of the best selections of traditional fresh foods in Wales, ranging from home-baked Welshcakes to the seaweed-based local delicacy known as laverbread.

This go-ahead city boasts many attractions old and new. Traditionalists will make for Swansea Museum with its noted collection of ceramics, reflecting the city's history of porcelain manufacture. There are also exquisite displays of Swansea porcelain and pottery at the Glynn Vivian Art Gallery, while a converted warehouse in the Maritime Quarter houses the excellent Maritime and Industrial Museum.

Swansea's Guildhall is noted for its Brangwyn Panels, huge murals originally intended for the House of Lords. One of the city's more novel attractions is Plantasia, a giant hothouse with thousands of plants in desert and tropical environments.

A statue of poet Dylan Thomas, Swansea's most famous son, looks out across the boat-filled marina. Fittingly, it is close to Ty Llên, Britain's first purpose-built literature centre. To the west, Swansea Bay is fringed by pleasant parklands and the university campus.

SWANTON MORLEY Norfolk TG0116
Village on B1147, 3 miles (5km) NE of East Dereham
This thriving, lively village has three pubs (one once lived in by Abraham Lincoln's forebears), several shops, and the remains of a windmill. RAF personnel were stationed here during World War II.

SWARDESTON Norfolk TG2002
Village on B1113, 4 miles (6km) S of Norwich
The pretty church at Swardeston has a window dedicated to Edith Cavell, the daughter of the rector. Cavell was executed in World War I by the Germans.

SWARKESTONE Derbyshire SK3728
Village on A514, 5 miles (8km) S of Derby
Medieval causeway and bridge cross the River Trent at the point reached by Prince Charles Edward's army in 1745 before they turned back for Scotland. Bowling pavilion by John Smythson in grounds of 17th-century hall. Trent and Mersey Canal near by.

SWARLAND Northumberland NU1602
Hamlet on B6345, 2 miles (3km) NW of Felton
Developed from smallholdings which were privately funded here in the 1930s for men to pursue a life in agriculture.

SWARTHMOOR Cumbria SD2777
Village on A590, 1 mile (2km) SW of Ulverston
Grew to accommodate workers from Lindal Moor

Mines. George Fox, founder of the Quaker movement, lived at Swarthmoor Hall.

SWAVESEY Cambridgeshire TL3668
Village off A14 (A604), 9 miles (14km) NW of Cambridge
Cedars and larches rustle in Swavesey's atmospheric churchyard in the Great Ouse Valley. An 11th-century Benedictine priory stood here.

SWAY Hampshire SZ2798
Small town on B3055, 3 miles (5km) SW of Brockenhurst
On southern fringes of New Forest, with much modern development. Sway tower at 218ft (66m) is a landmark from miles around, a folly dating from the 1880s.

SWIMBRIDGE Devon SS6230
Village off A361, 5 miles (8km) SE of Barnstaple
For 40 years the home of Reverend John (Jack) Russell who bred the famous terriers. Smallish late medieval church, with one of the finest wooden screens in the county.

SWINBROOK Oxfordshire SP2812
Village off A361, 2 miles (3km) E of Burford
In Hons and Rebels (1960) Jessica Mitford described the girlhood of herself and her sisters at Swinbrook House (not open). Nancy and Unity Mitford lie in the churchyard. The village beside the River Windrush is charming, with its 19th-century neo-Tudor cottages, old farmhouses and the picturesque Swan inn, once a mill. Outstanding memorials in the church.

SWINDON Wiltshire SU1584
Town off M4, 70 miles (113km) W of London
The largest town in Wiltshire and a thriving business centre, part of Silicon Valley, with many recent office blocks. This was a little market town until 1840s, when New Swindon was built down the hill from the old town as a locomotive works, making and repairing engines for the new railways. About 300 cottages were built for the workforce, plus a church and pubs. Most of it still survives, with the Great Western Railway Museum and one of the workers' cottages fitted out as it was in the 19th century.

The old and new towns have expanded and joined, with a big modern shopping centre. There are huge business parks, Windmill Hill with its 18th-century brick windmill, and Greenbridge to the northeast with three statues by Elisabeth Frink. At Shaw Ridge there is a coloured statue of Diana Dors, who was born locally.

The Old Town has its best buildings around the market square, with a Greek-style town hall of 1853 and Georgian houses. Most of the town is Victorian or modern. Swindon has a Museum and Art Gallery and the Swindon and Cricklade Railway (steam).

SWINE Humberside TA1335
Village off A165, 5 miles (8km) NE of Hull
The village is named after the Saxon king, Swaine, and the large mound, called Giant's Hill, is his burial place.

SWINESHEAD Bedfordshire TL0565
Village off B660, 10 miles (16km) N of Bedford
More attractive than its name. Pleasing village street with old houses, dominated by tall tower and spire of church.

SWINESHEAD Lincolnshire TF2340
Village off A17, 6 miles (10km) SW of Boston
After losing his baggage in the Wash in 1216, King John stayed at Swineshead Abbey. House of 1607 superseded abbey. Medieval church and Georgian houses.

SWINGFIELD MINNIS Kent TR2143
Village on A260, 5 miles (8km) N of Folkestone
Scatter of houses along a main road on the windy chalk uplands above Folkestone with a butterfly reserve incorporating free-flying butterflies in a greenhouse garden.

SWINTON Greater Manchester SD7701
Town on A6, 5 miles (8km) NW of Manchester
Descends to Irwell Valley, around Salford's old coal-mining area. Agecroft Hall, Tudor house, was dismantled and rebuilt in USA. Now site of power station.

SWINTON North Yorkshire SE2179
Village off A6108, 1 mile (2km) SW of Masham
An attractive hamlet with a few estate houses and no real centre. Swinton Park is an early 18th-century mansion house.

SWINTON South Yorkshire SK4599
Town on A6022, 4 miles (6km) N of Rotherham
Suburb of Rotherham. Little remains of the famous Rockingham pottery which was once sited here.

SWITHLAND Leicestershire SK5512
Village off B591, 4 miles (6km) S of Loughborough
Charnwood Forest village noted for slates, used widely for roofing and headstones. Mid-19th-century hall. Reservoir causeway carries scenic steam Great Central Railway.

SWYNCOMBE Oxfordshire SU6890
Site off B481, 7 miles (11km) NW of Henley-on-Thames
Swyncombe House (not open) and an ancient church stand alone on Swyncombe Downs, an expanse of Chiltern chalk landscape with panoramic views over Thames Valley.

SWYNNERTON Staffordshire SJ8535
Village off A51, 3 miles (5km) NW of Stone
Handsome traditional village with outstanding medieval church, Jacobean Fitzherbert Arms and many attractive cottages. Mill Meece pumping station is near by.

SWYRE Dorset SY5288
Village on B3157, 5 miles (8km) SE of Bridport
This fishing village, set a little back from the sea, was largely rebuilt from the mid-19th century.

SYDE Gloucestershire SO9410
Village off A417, 8 miles (13km) NW of Cirencester
Overlooking the wooded Upper Frome Valley, Syde has a church featuring work of several centuries and a fine medieval tithe barn.

SYDENHAM Greater London TQ3671
District in borough of Lewisham
Once a popular spa; the springs are now in Sydenham Wells Park. Suburban development after the Crystal Palace (see) was moved here in 1854.

SYDLING ST NICHOLAS Dorset SY6399
Village off A352, 2 miles (3km) SW of Cerne Abbas
Picturesque, full of pretty flint and stone-banded cottages, many of them thatched. A small stream with many little bridges completes the picture.

SYMINGTON Strathclyde NS9935
Village on A72, 3 miles (5km) SW of Biggar
Village below Tinto Hill, the 2,335ft (711m) landmark prominent from miles around.

SYMONDS YAT Hereford and Worcester SO5516
Beauty spot on B4432, 3 miles (5km) N of Coleford
Yat Rock, high above spectacular meander in River Wye, provides panoramic views. Wye Valley heritage centre and woodland walks near by.

SYMONDSBURY Dorset SY4493
Village off A35, 1 mile (2km) W of Bridport
Secluded village with virtually every building in the local golden sandstone.

SYSTON Leicestershire SK6211
Village off A607, 5 miles (8km) NE of Leicester
On edge of Leicester, where Melton Mowbray road leaves Fosse Way. Some cruck-framed and early brick-fronted buildings. Large medieval church.

SYWELL Northamptonshire SP8267
Village off A4500, 5 miles (8km) W of Wellingborough
Elizabethan hall and 12th-century and later church beside village green; village rebuilt 1860s. Business and private flying from aerodrome. Sywell Reservoir Country Park.

T

TACKLEY Oxfordshire SP4719
Village off A4260, 3 miles (5km) NE of Woodstock
In this straggling settlement above River Cherwell only the gateway, barn and dovecote remain of manor house, but hillside church contains notable Victorian work.

TACOLNESTON Norfolk TM1495
Village on B1113, 5 miles (8km) S of Wymondham
A lovely Norfolk village with a medieval church nestling amid pine trees, a 17th-century pub, and a green hemmed by thatched cottages.

TADCASTER North Yorkshire SE4843
Town off A64, 9 miles (14km) SW of York
Standing on the banks of the River Wharfe, Tadcaster is dominated by the brewing industry, located here because of the river. There are still three breweries in the town: John Smiths, Samuel Smiths and Bass Charringtons. Tadcaster also had a thriving quarrying industry and many of the buildings of the town are constructed from the local limestone.

TADDINGTON Derbyshire SK1471
Village off A6, 5 miles (8km) W of Bakewell
Peak District village at top of Taddington Dale. Well-positioned 14th-century church with ancient cross shaft in churchyard. Eighteenth-century hall. Well-dressing in August.

TADLEY Hampshire SU6060
Village on A340, 6 miles (10km) NW of Basingstoke
A few older cottages in the middle and much modern development. St Paul's is an interesting modern church (1965) and St Peter's has a brick tower dated 1685.

TADMARTON Oxfordshire SP3937
Village on B4035, 4 miles (6km) SW of Banbury
On northern Cotswold fringe with some substantial houses and rewarding Norman and medieval church.

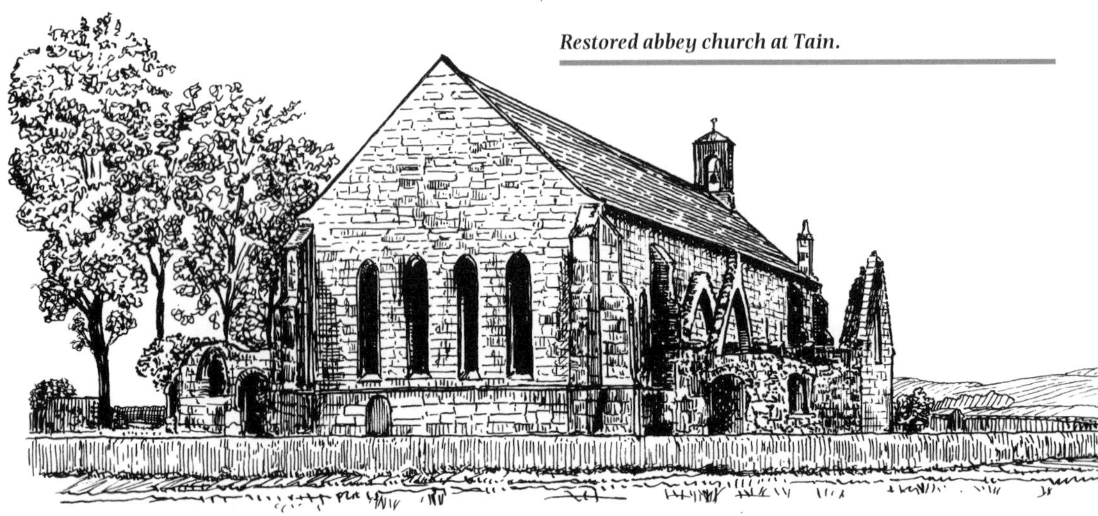

Restored abbey church at Tain.

TADWORTH Surrey TQ2356
Village on B290, 2 miles (3km) S of Epsom
Green and leafy 20th-century village in a downland valley near a railway station, with a handsome 17th-century manor house.

TAF, RIVER Dyfed
River
Flows beside Laugharne (see), resting place of celebrated writer Dylan Thomas, to join waters of Tawe and Gwendraeth rivers entering Carmarthen Bay.

TAFF, RIVER Mid Glamorgan/Powys/South Glamorgan
River, runs to mouth of River Severn
Begins its journey to Cardiff and the sea high in the Brecon Beacons (its headwaters are now captured in a string of scenic reservoirs alongside A470). Historic valley of the Taff rich in industrial heritage – ironworks at Merthyr Tydfil, coal-mining maily between Merthyr and Pontypridd. Canal (disused) and railway built in valley to carry materials between Merthyr and Cardiff.

TAIN Highland NH7782
Small town off A9, 10 miles (16km) NE of Invergordon
Compact and attractive royal burgh on Dornoch Firth, once important pilgrimage centre for devotees of 11th-century St Duthac, born here. Fine Collegiate Church built 1371, 17th-century tollbooth with spire-topped square tower and mercat cross. Tain Museum tells local history. Southeast lies restored Fearn Abbey, moved to present site in 1338.

TAKELEY Essex TL5621
Village off A120, 5 miles (8km) E of Bishop's Stortford
Traffic pours through on the A120. The Norman church, using Roman bricks, stands apart by itself, and has a modern rood screen.

TAL-Y-BONT Gwynedd SH5921
Village on A496, 4 miles (6km) N of Barmouth
Village near coast in Snowdonia National Park, near sandy beach backed by shingle and dune. Museum of Transport and Rural Life has old advertisements, toys, vehicles.

TAL-Y-LLYN Gwynedd SH7109
Village on B4405, 5 miles (8km) S of Dolgellau
Village below Cader Idris at southwestern end of lovely, 1 mile (2km) long Tal-y-llyn Lake, source of River Dysynni.

TALATON Devon SY0699
Village off A30, 3 miles (5km) NW of Ottery St Mary
Pretty cob and thatch village, with some 17th-century brick, rare in Devon, and a 15th-century church with good wooden screen.

TALBOT VILLAGE Dorset SZ0794
Village on A3049, 2 miles (3km) NW of Bournemouth
Early Victorian model village, funded by Miss Georgina Talbot, but swamped from the 1980s onwards and now virtually part of Bournemouth.

TALGARTH Powys SO1533
Small town on A4078, 7 miles (11km) SW of Hay-on-Wye
On northern edge of Black Mountains in Brecon Becons National Park. Associated with Methodist revivalist Hywel Harris, who set up an experimental religious community at nearby Trefecca based on self-sufficient social commune principles. Museum housed in what is now a Presbyterian college. Bronllys Castle (Cadw) is a lone tower on steep mound dating from around 1100.

TALKIN Cumbria NY5457
Hamlet off B6413, 3 miles (5km) SE of Brampton
The River Milbourne flows through the village, now popular with tourists. Talkin Tarn is surrounded by woods and the country park has recreational facilities.

TALLAND Cornwall SX2251
Hamlet off A387, 2 miles (3km) SW of Looe
Scattered up the steep valley sides from a little wild bay, with deep, wooded lanes. The little medieval church has a detached tower.

TALLEY Dyfed SN6332
Village on B4302, 6 miles (10km) N of Llandeilo
Rolling hills form backdrop to tranquil, late 12th-century remains of Talley Abbey (Cadw) beside twin lakes.

TALLINGTON Lincolnshire TF0908
Village on A16, 4 miles (6km) E of Stamford
On southern boundary of county. Georgian brick Manor Farm, old thatched cottage, and early 18th-century watermill. Watersports park in former gravel pits.

TALSARNAU Gwynedd SH6135
Village on A496, 4 miles (6km) NE of Harlech
Small village in Snowdonia National Park above Traeth Bach's estuary and sands with views across to Italianate village of Portmeirion (see).

TALYBONT Dyfed SN6589
Village on A487, 6 miles (10km) NE of Aberystwyth
Village at foot of scenic drive to Nant-y-moch reservoir and Ponterwyd. Bedd Taliesin, traditionally grave of 6th-century bard Taliesin, or mythical Welsh sage, is in hills 1 mile (2km) north-east. The grave is possibly made of the stone of a burial chamber. On A487 north of Talybont is the village named after Taliesin.

TALYBONT-ON-USK Powys SO1122
Village on B4558, 6 miles (10km) SE of Brecon
On Monmouthshire and Brecon Canal, not – despite name – on River Usk, which flows near by. Talybont Reservoir a nature reserve rich in birdlife.

TAMAR, RIVER Cornwall
River, flows S to Plymouth Sound
The river cuts Cornwall off from the rest of the country, rising only 6 miles (10km) from the north Cornwall coast and running south right across the county, with a big estuary around Saltash. Upper and Lower Tamar lakes are reservoirs on the upper part of the river.

TAME, RIVER Staffordshire
River
River passes secretively through Birmingham, leaves city on eastern side and turns north past lakes at Kingsbury to reach Tamworth before joining River Trent.

TAMERTON FOLIOT Devon SX4760
District on B3373, on N edge of Plymouth
Plymouth has grown around it, but the village is still recognisable, with some Georgian houses and a late medieval church.

TAMWORTH Staffordshire SK2004
Town off A453, 14 miles (22km) NE of Birmingham
Once capital of the Saxon kingdom of Mercia, Tamworth is now a market town surrounded by large 'overspill' housing estates. High-rise flats now adjoin its oldest building, the castle, which has a Norman keep but otherwise consists of progressive additions, including a Tudor chapel and hall and Jacobean apartments. It houses the interesting local history museum. Another significant building is the fine town hall of 1701, from the steps of which Robert Peel, local MP and later Prime Minister, issued his famous 'Tamworth Manifesto' in 1834.

The town's old centre has some harmonious Georgian and Victorian frontages, and it is worth seeking out individual buildings such as the attractive almshouses in Gungate, the Spital Chapel in Wiggington Road, the 16th-century Moat House in Lichfield Street and the nearby Georgian manor house which has an older core. In the impressive Church of St Editha interesting tombs stand among architectural features of many centuries and there is some notable pre-Raphaelite glass.

Inevitably, Tamworth has acquired shopping precincts, new offices and a wide range of leisure facilities in keeping with its status as a busy modern town.

TAN HILL North Yorkshire NY8906
Site off B6270, just N of Keld
The site of England's highest inn (1,732ft/528m), at the head of Stonedale. Coal was mined here in shallow, bell-shaped pits.

TANDRIDGE Surrey TQ3750
Village off A25, 2 miles (3km) SE of Godstone
Pleasant village standing alone on a sandy hilltop south of the North Downs, with a massive old churchyard yew, a medieval church and plenty of old Wealden farmhouses in the parish.

TANFIELD Durham NZ1855
Village off A6076, 2 miles (3km) N of Stanley
A pleasant rural village noted for the Tanfield Railway, which now runs steam trains from Sunniside station to Causey Arch.

TANGMERE West Sussex SU9006
Village off A27, 3 miles (5km) E of Chichester
A village associated with the former Battle of Britain base, RAF Tangmere. Old runways have now been turned back to farmland and built on by new housing estates, but the memory of the struggle for control of the skies is maintained by the pub, The Bader Arms, named after flying ace Sir Douglas Bader, and by the Tangmere Military Aviation Museum.

TANKERSLEY South Yorkshire SK3399
Village off A6135, 2 miles (3km) W of Hoyland Nether
Ancient village with a medieval church dedicated to St Peter which houses cannonballs from the Civil War.

TANKERTON Kent TR1267
District in E of Whitstable
Residential extension of Whitstable, suburban in appearance, with a grassy promenade along the clifftop, undercliff and beach huts facing pleasant shingle beach.

TANNINGTON Suffolk TM2467
Village off A1120, 4 miles (6km) NW of Framlingham
The agricultural land around Tannington is wide, flat, and virtually treeless, hedgeless, and ditchless. Tannington village has two halls, and 14th-century St Ethelbert's Church.

TANSOR Northamptonshire TL0590
Village off A605, 2 miles (3km) NE of Oundle
St Mary's Church, on bank of River Nene, has an intriguing architectural history, with a double Norman and 13th-century tower arch.

TANTALLON CASTLE Lothian (E) NT5985
Site off A198, 3 miles (5km) E of North Berwick
Curtain walls of this dramatically sited 14th-century ruin enclose entire headland; magnificent views. Tantallon was impregnable until sacked by Cromwell's artillery in 1651.

TANTOBIE Durham NZ1754
Village off A6076, 2 miles (3km) NW of Stanley
Inhabitants were mostly employed in coal-mining at Tanfield Moor Colliery. Once had a large isolation hospital, subsequently converted to a factory.

TANWORTH IN ARDEN Warwickshire SP1170
Village off B4101, 4 miles (6km) NW of Henley-in-Arden
In attractive hilly countryside near Redditch. Medieval church with interesting monuments to the Archer family, who once occupied the early 18th-century Umberslade Park (not open). The Georgian Aspley House and a pleasant scatter of old brick and timber-framed houses stand near the church, and a farm outside the village caters specially for young visitors.

TAPLOW Buckinghamshire SU9182
Village off A4, 4 miles (6km) W of Slough
Desirable commuter location above the Thames, which is crossed by Sir Robert Taylor's handsome 1770s bridge into Maidenhead (see). Georgian houses, timber and brick cottages and a church rebuilt in 1912, with a copper-covered spire. Taplow Vineyard is open to the public. To the north is Cliveden (see Hedsor).

TARBAT NESS Highland NH9487
Headland off B9165, 3 miles (5km) NE of Portmahomack
Headland at northern tip of promontory stretching into North Sea southeast of Dornoch Firth. Lighthouse, good walking, bird-watching and wide views.

TARBERT Strathclyde NR8668
Small town on A83, 5 miles (8km) NE of Kennacraig
Small fishing and yachting harbour town off Loch Fyne, a boat-building and sail-making centre. Overlooked by 14th-century castle, stronghold of Robert Bruce.

TARBERT Western Isles (Harris) NB1500
Small town on A859, capital of Harris
Main settlement on Harris and ferry terminal for services from Skye. Stands on isthmus in sheltered valley. Noted for local tweed-weaving.

TARBET Strathclyde NN3104
Village on A82, 7 miles (11km) S of Ardlui
Small holiday resort on west Loch Lomondside with lovely views across to Ben Lomond and easy access to Arrochar and Loch Long.

TARBOLTON Strathclyde NS4327
Village on B730, 2 miles (3km) NW of Stair
Mining village where Robert Burns lived for seven years and founded Bachelors' Club in 1781, housed in cottage now restored by National Trust for Scotland.

TARDEBIGGE Hereford and Worcester SO9969
Village off A448, 3 miles (5km) E of Bromsgrove
Old canal settlement, now dominated by prison complex, has church of 1770s with splendid interior containing fine tombs and beautiful craft work by local people. Well-known canal features here are intimidating flight of over 30 locks raising Worcester and Birmingham Canal by 300ft (91m) in 3 miles (5 km) and Tardebigge Tunnel, 580yds (528m) long.

TARLAND Grampian NJ4804
Village on B9119, 9 miles (14km) NE of Ballater
Village noted for MacRobert Trust RAF rest centre at Cromar House; Trust encompasses charitable and farming foundations. Nearby important prehistoric sites at Culsh and Tomnaverrie.

TARLETON Lancashire SD4520
Village off A565, 8 miles (12km) E of Southport
On the banks of the River Douglas. A busy seafaring port in the 18th century. Market gardening an important industry.

TARN HOWS Cumbria NY3300
Lake off A593, 2 miles (3km) NE of Coniston
The lake was bought and sold on to the National Trust by Beatrix Potter. Popular beauty spot with magnificent surrounding mountain views.

TARPORLEY Cheshire SJ5562
Village off A51, 9 miles (14km) NW of Nantwich
An attractive village, now a desirable residential area. The Anglican church dates back to the 13th century and was restored in Victorian times. The Swan hotel is headquarters of the Tarporley Hunt meetings. The Tarporley Fire Brigade, founded in 1869, was the first voluntary fire brigade in the country.

TARR Somerset SS8632
Hamlet off B3223, 1 mile (2km) SW of Liscombe
Just a farm and the famous Tarr Steps, a long, low, clapper bridge over the River Barle.

TARRANT, CRAWFORD AND KEYNSTON Dorset ST9203/4
Villages off A350, 3 miles (5km) SE of Blandford Forum
The two southernmost villages on the little River Tarrant, Keynston the larger, Crawford the more interesting. Crawford was the site of one of the richest nunneries in medieval England, but only a few fragments of barns survive in the little hamlet. Tiny medieval parish church.

TARRANT, GUNVILLE AND HINTON Dorset ST9212
Villages off A354, 5 miles (8km) NE of Blandford Forum
Hinton is cut by the main road, but these are otherwise similar villages with thatched cottages and medieval churches. Gunville was the site of the huge early 18th-century mansion of Eastbury: only the gates and stables survive.

TARRANT, LAUNCESTON AND MONKTON Dorset ST9409
Villages off A354, 4 miles (6km) NE of Blandford Forum
Two pretty villages close together on the little River Tarrant, both with thatched brick or cob cottages. Monkton has the best centre, with a humped bridge and a ford.

TARRANT, RAWSTON AND RUSHTON Dorset ST9306
Villages off A354, 3 miles (5km) E of Blandford Forum
Close together on the River Tarrant, Tarrant Rawston is a hamlet of a big farm and little church, Tarrant Rushton a village with thatched cottages and an unusual church.

TARRING NEVILLE East Sussex TQ4403
Village on A26, 2 miles (3km) N of Newhaven
Shrunken village, now only a cluster of farms cupped in a hollow of the South Downs in a gap cut through the hills by the River Ouse, with pleasant views over the valley.

TARRINGTON Hereford and Worcester SO6140
Village on A438, 7 miles (11km) E of Hereford
Handsome 18th-century Foley Arms is attractive feature of this village on hillside overlooking River Frome. Church worth visiting for its Norman carving.

TARVES Grampian NJ8631
Village on B999, 4 miles (6km) NE of Oldmeldrum
Village church contains elaborate tomb with fine Renaissance carving and statues of William Forbes and his wife who lived at nearby Tolquhon Castle.

TARVIN Cheshire SJ4967
Village off A51, 5 miles (8km) E of Chester
Georgian in appearance, after a fire in 1752 destroyed many old timber-framed cottages. Attractive 14th- and 15th-century village church.

TASBURGH Norfolk TM2095
Village off A140, 8 miles (12km) S of Norwich
River Tas winds its way through this pleasing village, and through the Elizabethan gardens of 16th-century Rainthorpe Hall.

TASTON Oxfordshire SP3621

Hamlet off A44, 2 miles (3km) SW of Enstone

Tiny settlement on hills above River Evenlode. Its name derives from its mysterious Thor Stone, standing over 6ft (2m) high.

TATSFIELD Surrey TQ4157

Village off B2024, 3 miles (5km) NW of Westerham

Leafy 20th-century development high on the North Downs close to the Kent border, with an old church with Norman walls on the Downs' crest.

TATTERSHALL Lincolnshire TF2157

Village on A153, 8 miles (13km) SW of Horncastle

Huge moated brick keep, 100ft (30m) high, of Tattershall Castle (National Trust), built about 1440 by Ralph Cromwell, Lord Treasurer of England. State apartments and fireplaces. Views of Lincoln Cathedral and Boston Stump from top on clear days. Holy Trinity Church, begun 1469, with fine medieval glass in east window, has notable collection of medieval brasses. Dogdyke Pumping Station, 1855 (limited opening).

TATTINGSTONE Suffolk TM1337

Village on A137, 5 miles (8km) S of Ipswich

The Tattingstone Wonder are workers' cottages disguised as a church in 1790. Tattingstone itself stands on the western edge of beautiful Alton Water, a man-made reservoir.

TATTON PARK Cheshire SJ7481

Estate off A50, 3 miles (5km) N of Knutsford

A 2,000 acre (809ha) estate with deer park, medieval hall, mansion built between 1780 and 1813, beautiful gardens and a working estate farm and two meres. The estate belonged to the Egerton family until 1958. A National Trust property managed by Cheshire County Council.

TATWORTH Somerset ST3205

Village off A358, 2 miles (3km) S of Chard

Formed as a village in the 19th century. A meadow here is still let annually by candle auction: the successful bid is the last one before the candle goes out.

TAUNTON Somerset ST2224

Town off M5, 167 miles (269km) SW of London

County town of Somerset from 1935, a regional shopping centre with many modern malls, and much modern industry and big office blocks. The old centre is small. St Mary's has one of the largest and finest of the Somerset church towers – 163ft (49m) high and elaborately pinnacled. The 1770s market house is very classical. Other Georgian and earlier buildings include brick almshouses of 1635.

Taunton was a town from Saxon times, and had a castle from the 12th century. The surviving buildings are 13th century, much adapted in the 18th and 19th centuries. Somerset County Museum and Somerset Light Infantry Military Museum are both housed in the castle. The municipal buildings include the grammar school of 1522.

Taunton takes its name from the River Tone, and was the terminus of the Bridgwater and Taunton Canal, completed in 1827 and now being restored. The Duke of Monmouth was proclaimed King of England here in 1685, and many citizens paid for this treason with their lives.

The opening of the M5 to Taunton has caused the town to grow even more than it did when the railway arrived in 1842.

Almshouses in Taunton.

TAVERHAM Norfolk TG1614
Small town on A1067, 5 miles (8km) NW of Norwich
On the north bank of the River Wensum, Taverham has a huge garden centre, and 10 purpose-built workshops comprise the Craft Centre.

TAVISTOCK Devon SX4874
Town on A386, 13 miles (21km) N of Plymouth
This market town, on the western side of Dartmoor, was in medieval times a stannary town where tin was taken to be taxed. In the 18th and 19th centuries, it was a centre for copper-mining, and the town was much altered in the first half of the 19th century with the copper profits.

The big medieval abbey buildings have mostly gone, but the prominent gatehouse was restored in 1824, and other smaller buildings survive in the middle of the town. A big pannier market is attached to the mock-medieval town hall of 1860, one of several castellated buildings which, along with the lawns, give Tavistock its particular character. The big church is 15th century.

Fitzford forms another centre, with a Victorian statue of Sir Francis Drake (born locally) and a prominent 1860s church. Many miners' cottages of the 1860s are here, and others are on the outskirts of the town. A short canal to Morwellham (see) was built in the early 19th century to carry the copper, and the dominating railway viaduct was built in 1892.

TAVY, MARY AND PETER Devon SX5079
Villages off A386, 4 miles (6km) NE of Tavistock
Two villages on the edge of Dartmoor. Mary Tavy was an important mining centre in the 19th century, while Peter Tavy was more rural. Wheal Betsy, to the north of Mary Tavy, has the impressive remains of an engine house. There are many archaeological remains on the moor above Peter Tavy. Ambulance museum at Peter Tavy.

TAW, RIVER Devon
River
The Taw rises as a little Dartmoor stream, and runs right across Devon to Barnstaple. Below that town it forms a wide estuary.

TAWSTOCK Devon SS5529
Village off B3232, 2 miles (3km) S of Barnstaple
Set in lovely countryside, down in the Taw Valley. The church in the grounds of 18th-century Tawstock Court (not open), with a Tudor gatehouse, is one of the best in Devon, mostly early 14th century, with fine wooden screens and a huge collection of monuments to the owners of the big house.

TAXAL Derbyshire SK0079
Hamlet off A5002, 1 mile (2km) S of Whaley Bridge
In picturesque Goyt Valley. Church monument to Michael Heathcote (died 1768), 'Gentleman of the Pantry and Yeoman of the Mouth' to George III.

TAY, RIVER Tayside
River, flows to North Sea
Scotland's longest river whose headwaters are River Lochay and River Dochart rising west of Killin and flowing into Loch Tay. River Tay emerges at east end of loch, joined along course by rivers Lyon, Tummel, Isla and Almond. Flows through Highland scenery and agricultural land to Perth and estuary at Dundee on Firth of Tay. Noted salmon-fishing river.

TAYNTON Oxfordshire SP2313
Village off A424, 1 mile (2km) NW of Burford
Abandoned quarries are reminder that stone from this Windrush Valley village was once in national demand. Flamboyant 14th-century work in church.

TAYNUILT Strathclyde NN0031
Village on A85, 3 miles (5km) E of Connel
Village near shores of Loch Etive, where former Bonawe Ironworks is Britain's most complete charcoal-fired ironwork remains with displays on industry's 18th- to 19th-century history. To southeast lies Ardanaiseig Garden on Loch Awe, with herbaceous borders, fruit, vegetables and shrubs. In Taynuilt is Barguillean's Angus Garden, a natural garden with bulbs, azaleas and rhododendrons.

TAYPORT Fife NO4528
Town on B945, 4 miles (6km) N of Leuchars
Residential town, ferry departure point before construction of Tay rail and road bridges. Tentsmuir National Nature Reserve to southeast, with bird-watching, woods and beaches.

TEALBY Lincolnshire TF1590
Village on B1203, 3 miles (5km) E of Market Rasen
One of the loveliest villages of the Lincolnshire Wolds, on route of Viking Way footpath. Norman and medieval church at top of village.

TEBAY Cumbria NY6104
Village on A685, 10 miles (16km) NE of Kendal
A long rambling village with the ruins of a Roman fort and a rounded mound called Castlehow.

TEBWORTH Bedfordshire SP9926
Village off A5, 4 miles (6km) NW of Dunstable
An off-the-beaten-track little place with farmhouses and cottages in brick and thatch.

TEDBURN ST MARY Devon SX8194
Village on A30, 7 miles (11km) W of Exeter
The village has grown around the old main road, leaving the medieval church isolated.

TEDDINGTON Greater London TQ1670
District in borough of Richmond
This quiet suburb lies between the River Thames and Bushy Park. The riverside is pleasant at Teddington Lock and Weir, the furthest point from the sea where the river is affected by the tides. Thames Television has studios close by. An avenue of chestnuts 1 mile (2km) long and attractive woodland gardens distinguish the 1,000 acre (405ha) Bushy Park.

TEDSTONE, WAFRE AND DELAMERE Hereford and Worcester SO6759
Hamlets off B4203, 4 miles (6km) NE of Bromyard
Interesting Saxon and medieval church stands to west of these remote hamlets. Footpath access to National Trust land on wooded slopes below.

TEES, RIVER Cleveland
River, flows through Barnard Castle to Stockton-on-Tees and Middlesbrough
An attractive river noted for its waterfalls in the upper reaches. Rising on Cross Fell it gradually widens giving way to meadowland in Teesdale, an area scarred by stone-quarrying. At the river mouth there is a large amount of heavy industry. Upper Teesdale National Nature Reserve is famous for its gentians and other alpine flowers.

TEESPORT Cleveland NZ5423
Town off A1085, 4 miles (6km) NE of Middlesbrough
An intensively industrial area centred around Tees Dock. There is a large amount of heavy industry located here.

TEESSIDE AIRPORT Cleveland NZ3713
Airport off A67, 6 miles (9km) E of Darlington
Located at Middleton St George and opened in 1964 this is a modern regional airport. It is surrounded by warehouses and an industrial estate.

TEFFONT, EVIAS AND MAGNA Wiltshire ST9832
Villages on B3089, 7 miles (11km) W of Wilton
Pretty villages on the little River Teff, both with thatched cottages (and bus shelters). Evias has a particularly beautiful setting, with the 1825 church and its 125ft (38m) steeple on the lawns of the manor house. Magna has a medieval church, stone cottages and Fitz House Gardens (limited opening).

TEGG'S NOSE Cheshire SJ9472
Beauty spot off A537, 2 miles (3km) E of Macclesfield
Originally a large stone quarry in the foothills of the Pennines. Now a country park with waymarked walks and beautiful views over Cheshire and Derbyshire.

TEIFI, RIVER Dyfed
River
River source lies in wild country northeast of Tregaron in cluster of small lakes called Teifi Pools. Continues through towns of Lampeter and Newcastle Emlyn to the sea. Particularly beautiful stretch from Llandysul. Noted for historic woollen industry when scores of mills were located on its banks. Coracles – ancient fishing craft – can still be seen at Cenarth, Cilgerran.

TEIGH Leicestershire SK8616
Village off A606, 5 miles (8km) N of Oakham
Pleasant Rutland village with 1782 church retaining medieval tower, in which pews face inwards in college chapel fashion; pulpit and reading desks on west wall.

TEIGN, RIVER Devon
River, runs from Dartmoor to English Channel
The Teign rises on Dartmoor, with a picturesque steep wooded valley to Chudleigh (see Dunsford), where it widens. It forms a wide but short estuary below Kingsteignton, and enters the sea at Teignmouth (see).

TEIGNGRACE Devon SX8473
Village off A382, 2 miles (3km) NW of Newton Abbot
A small village in the Teign Valley. The church was rebuilt in 1786, and has a fine collection of Georgian monuments.

TEIGNMOUTH Devon SX9473
Town off A381, 3 miles (5km) SW of Dawlish
A port before it became a seaside resort in the 19th century, Teignmouth has sandy beaches, an 1860s pier and much Victorian development. The town extends on to the bar across the mouth of the Teign estuary, with a passenger ferry across to Shaldon (see). Some Regency stucco survives, the best being Den Crescent of 1826, with the Assembly Rooms in the middle. Local museum.

TELFORD Shropshire SJ6807
New Town off M54, 12 miles (19km) E of Shrewsbury
The New Town of Telford originated in an imaginative scheme of the 1960s to make use of the huge area of derelict land left by the abandoned Shropshire coalfield. This wasteland in the shadow of the Wrekin (see) stretched northwards from the Ironbridge Gorge on the River Severn and included some well-established small towns and industrial villages. The aim was to attract new industry and overspill population from the West Midlands.

The name Telford was chosen to honour the famous engineer who had been Shropshire's county surveyor. Things have not gone entirely to plan, but there is no doubt that an ugly landscape has been transformed. Big new housing estates are scattered over newly-greened sites and sophisticated modern industry (including many companies from overseas) have been attracted here. A fine new shopping centre has been established and a huge town park created. At the same time the old towns (see Dawley, Oakengates, Madeley and Wellington) have retained their character and much of their distinctive 19th-century architecture, while the museum complex at Ironbridge (see) has become a world-class visitor attraction. The M54 links the town to the motorway network.

TELSCOMBE East Sussex TQ4003
Village off A26, 3 miles (5km) NW of Newhaven
A few old cottages, a church and a manor house folded among the South Downs at end of a no-through road, now maintained as a rural spot.

TEME, RIVER Hereford and Worcester
River
River flows idyllically through Shropshire, skirts Ludlow Castle, enters Worcestershire at Tenbury and approaches Worcester in a series of tortuous loops before joining the River Severn.

TEMPLE BALSALL West Midlands SP2076
Village on B4101, 4 miles (6km) SE of Solihull
This small village beside the River Blythe was an important medieval headquarters of the Knights Templar,

and remnants of their hall still remain behind a Victorian façade. The unexpectedly grand St Mary's Church was their chapel, although it was heavily restored in Victorian times. The impressive almshouses of 1677 stand near by.

TEMPLE BRUER Lincolnshire TF0053
Site off A607, 3 miles (5km) E of Welbourn
Isolated surviving late 12th-century tower of Knights Templar's church, with pyramid roof added in 19th-century restoration.

TEMPLE EWELL Kent TR2844
Suburb off A256, 3 miles (5km) NW of Dover
In the Dour Valley, once the property of the Knights Templar, but now a suburban extension of Dover, with a church containing panels of 17th-century Swiss glass.

TEMPLE GRAFTON Warwickshire SP1254
Village off A46, 5 miles (8km) W of Stratford-upon-Avon
Ann Whateley, apparently Shakespeare's first choice of bride, lived in this windswept hill village, which has unspoilt cottages in local stone.

TEMPLE GUITING Gloucestershire SP0928
Village off B4077, 6 miles (10km) W of Stow-on-the-Wold
Charming, unspoilt village in wooded Windrush Valley. Church is well worth visiting for its Norman carving and medieval glass.

TEMPLE SOWERBY Cumbria NY6127
Village on A66, 6 miles (10km) NW of Appleby-in-Westmorland
Sloping green surrounded by red sandstone Georgian houses, typical of Eden Valley. Acorn Bank Garden (National Trust), with orchard, gardens, and woodland walk beside Crowdundle Beck.

TEMPLECOMBE Somerset ST7022
Village on A357, 4 miles (6km) S of Wincanton
Large brick and grey stone village on the railway, with a squat but prominent church. Abbas Combe, a suburb, is more picturesque, with old cottages and the stocks still preserved.

TEMPSFORD Bedfordshire TL1653
Village on A1, 3 miles (5km) N of Sandy
Ruthlessly split by the thundering A1 road. Wartime undercover agents took off secretly from here for occupied Europe.

TENBURY WELLS Hereford and Worcester SO5968
Small town on A456, 13 miles (21km) SW of Bewdley
Tenbury Museum in Cross Street tells the story of this small Teme-side market town. Harmonious array of buildings of many ages includes market house (1811), picturesque Royal Oak and Pembroke inns and remains of spa erected in 1862. Burford House Gardens to west of town houses National Clematis Collection and displays unusual species of shrubs, roses and herbaceous plants.

TENBY (DINBYCH Y PYSGOD) Dyfed SN1300
Town on A4139, 9 miles (14km) E of Pembroke
Colour-washed Georgian houses lead down to this characterful resort's harbour from a maze of medieval lanes and ancient town walls. A grassy headland, crowned by the remains of a 12th-century castle and a Victorian memorial to Prince Albert, divides the sands and cliffs of North Beach from the small Castle Beach and dune-backed South Beach, the latter over 1 mile (2km) long. Also on the headland's Castle Hill are the town museum's maritime exhibits and an excellent art gallery displaying the work of local artist Augustus John.

Just offshore are the tidal rocky outcrop of St Catherine's Island with the ruins of a Victorian fort, and Caldy Island's monastic settlement (see), reached by boat from the busy harbour.

The well-preserved medieval town walls stand 20ft (6m) at their highest point. Their surviving gate, known as the Five Arches, still acts as a main entrance into the medieval town. St Mary's Church, largely 15th century, has a landmark spire 152ft (46m) high but the oldest building here is probably the 15th-century Tudor Merchant's House (National Trust) with contemporary wall frescoes and period furnishing.

TENDRING Essex TM1424
Village on B1035, 6 miles (10km) NW of Clacton-on-Sea
A dormitory village between Colchester and Clacton. The medieval church has a timber porch and notable hammerbeam roof.

TENTERDEN Kent TQ8833
Small town on A28, 10 miles (16km) SW of Ashford
Delightful old town above Rother Levels which grew rich on wool and weaving in the Middle Ages. Broad High Street with stylish shops, especially antiques, in fine half-timbered houses from prosperous weaving days and elegant 18th-century buildings from its days as an agricultural market town. The church, founded in 1180, has a magnificent 15th-century tower, 125ft (38m) high.

TERLING Essex TL7715
Village off A12, 3 miles (5km) W of Witham
Known for Lord Rayleigh's Farms dairy products, this is the picturesque estate village of the Strutt family, Earls of Rayleigh, who bred two distinguished scientists in the 20th century at their Georgian mansion, Terling Place (not open). The church has an 18th-century red-brick tower and there are cottages in pink and white and a half-timbered manor house (not open). A photographer's delight.

TERRINGTON ST CLEMENT Norfolk TF5520
Village off A17, 4 miles (6km) W of King's Lynn
A lovely Norfolk village dating from Saxon times. Traces of a windmill and the cathedral-like St Clement's Church remain.

TERRINGTON ST JOHN Norfolk TF5315
Village off A47, 6 miles (10km) NE of Wisbech
Marshland village with a splendid church. It has a little passage connecting the tower to the nave and a fine clerestory.

TEST, RIVER Hampshire
River
Famous trout-fishing river, running across western Hampshire, through Whitchurch, Stockbridge and Romsey. Below Totton it forms a wide estuary, the start of Southampton Water.

TESTON Kent TQ7053
Village on A26, 4 miles (6km) W of Maidstone
A cluster of old houses, a big house and a church rebuilt in 1736 make up this hillside village amid orchards above the River Medway, spanned by a lovely six-arched bridge.

TETBURY Gloucestershire ST8993
Small town on A433, 10 miles (16km) SW of Cirencester
On Spring Bank Holiday locals celebrate Woolsack Day by racing up Tetbury's steep Gumstool Hill carrying heavy sacks of wool. More leisurely strollers will enjoy delightful streets of mellow buildings, especially in the old market place called The Chipping. Additional attractions are the Police Bygones Museum in Long Street and arguably the most elegant 18th-century church in the Cotswolds.

TETFORD Lincolnshire TF3374
Village off A158, 6 miles (10km) NE of Horncastle
Attractive Wolds village at foot of Tetford Hill, below Bluestone Heath ancient trackway. Village street forms a circle. Seventeenth-century watermill with wooden breast-shot wheel. Late 17th-century Mansion House, built for John Dymoke, was altered in 19th century and has a 1973 library wing. St Mary's Church, of greenstone, has 15th-century tower and clerestory.

TETNEY Lincolnshire TA3100
Village on A1031, 5 miles (8km) S of Cleethorpes
Large marshland village. Spacious Church of St Peter and St Paul has impressive high 15th-century tower. Unusually, an inscription dates work on church to 1363. Church was restored and chancel rebuilt in 1860s. At Tetney Lock, a small hamlet grew up alongside the Louth Navigation Canal, opened in 1770. Bird reserve at Tetney Marshes.

TETTENHALL West Midlands SJ8700
District in NW Wolverhampton
Leafy suburb with pleasant Victorian houses and unique 1950s church stands on its ridge, aloof from nearby Wolverhampton.

TEVERSAL Nottinghamshire SK4861
Village on B6407, 3 miles (5km) W of Mansfield
Isolated rural village whose stone buildings have characteristics of neighbouring Derbyshire. St Catherine's Church has exceptionally complete 17th-century furnishings.

TEVERSHAM Cambridgeshire TL4958
Village off A1303, 3 miles (5km) E of Cambridge
On the outskirts of historic Cambridge, Teversham is close to the site of Cambridge Airport. The church on the village green offers splendid views of Cambridge's skyline.

TEVIOT, RIVER Borders
River
River rising in the Teviothead Hills near Dumfries border and flowing northeast through woollen-manufacturing town of Hawick to join River Tweed at Kelso.

TEWIN Hertfordshire TL2714
Village off B1000, 4 miles (6km) NW of Hertford
In attractive and expensive commuter territory, with big, imposing houses and a well-known cricket side. The Plume of Feathers pub goes back to the 17th century. Trees grow eerily out of Lady Anne Grimston's grave in the churchyard, where the Beit diamond magnates and members of the De Havilland family are also buried.

TEWKESBURY Gloucestershire SO8932
Town off M5, 10 miles (16km) N of Gloucester
This splendid medieval town at the meeting of the Rivers Severn and Avon prospered from the early Middle Ages onwards. Its medieval status is proclaimed by the cathedral-like abbey, now the parish church, where the great Norman tower and massive nave arcades contrast with the colour and delicacy of the rich medieval chancel.

The Y-shaped town centre abounds in fascinating buildings. In Old Baptist Chapel Court is one of England's earliest Nonconformist chapels, while near by stands a unique row of tiny 15th-century shops. A stroll along Church Street and High Street will reveal an array of timber-framed and Georgian frontages, including the Hop Pole hotel (Mr Pickwick stayed here), the top-heavy House of the Nodding Gables and venerable pubs such as the Old Fleece, the Swan hotel and the Tudor House hotel. Many of the old houses are now good shops.

Away from the main streets there is much to explore in the side alleys that are a feature of the town – several of them lead to the enjoyable waterfront area. Tewkesbury's long history is explained at the timber-framed town museum in Barton Street.

TEYNHAM Kent TQ9562
Village off A2, 3 miles (5km) E of Sittingbourne
A long street and scattered development in the historic centre of Kentish cherry orchards, where Richard Harris, Henry VIII's fruiterer, planted over 100 acres (40ha) of fruit trees.

THAKEHAM West Sussex TQ1017
Village on B2139, 3 miles (5km) N of Washington
The best part of the village is down a no-through road, with an attractive group about the church on a knoll. Little Thakeham, a Lutyens house, now a hotel, is on a ridge to south.

THAME Oxfordshire SP7005
Town off A418, 9 miles (14km) SW of Aylesbury
Venerable inns, timber-framed houses and fine Georgian residences make a walk through the streets of this old riverside market town a delightful experience. The impressive church is richly endowed with furnishings of several centuries, including a superlative array of brasses and a monument to Lord Williams, whose grammar school (Milton was a pupil) still stands.

THAMES DITTON Surrey TQ1667
Suburb off A307, 1 mile (2km) W of Surbiton
A sea of suburbia laps around this unspoilt Thames-side village, with narrow streets, a church with a 13th-century tower and a slipway beside the 16th-century inn.

THAMES, RIVER Greater London
River
England's premier river runs for some 220 miles (350km) from the Cotswolds eastward and southeastward through Oxford and Reading to London, and then through a wide estuary to the North Sea. Until the coming of modern roads, the Thames was a major artery of commerce and communication, and London owes its existence and history to the river.

THAMESMEAD Greater London TQ4780
New Town on A2041, 3 miles (5km) NE of Woolwich
Created since the 1960s on the River Thames. Modernist and post-modernist architecture, with parks and lakes. St Paul's (1970s) is a multi-denominational worship centre.

THANET, ISLE OF Kent
Area in NE Kent, containing Margate and Ramsgate
The northeast corner of Kent, including the North Foreland, was a true island well into historical times, but the old strait is now Minster and Chislet Marshes.

THARSTON Norfolk TM1894
Village off B1135, 2 miles (3km) E of Forncett St Mary
Tharston's origins pre-date Domesday Book, although the church is mainly 13th century. 'Hollow ways' are sunken lanes between high banks that are common here.

THATCHAM Berkshire SU5167
Suburb on A4, 3 miles (5km) E of Newbury
Once a small village, but now really a huge suburb of Newbury. Thatcham Moor Nature Reserve is the largest surviving area of freshwater reed beds.

THAXTED Essex TL6131
Small town on B184, 6 miles (10km) SE of Saffron Walden
A striking little town, where Gustav Holst wrote part of *The Planets*. Good shops, restaurants and pubs and a great place for Morris dancing. The wonderfully venerable timber-framed guildhall (limited opening) of the Thaxted cutlers now has a museum. A beautiful, soaring 180ft (55m) spire distinguishes the church where Holst was organist. John Webb's windmill (limited opening) of 1804 has been restored.

THEALE Berkshire SU6471
Village off A4, 5 miles (8km) W of Reading
Theale has much Georgian brick and an odd church, built in the 1820s in the style of Salisbury Cathedral. Despite its large size, much of the detailing is too big for the church.

THEBERTON Suffolk TM4365
Village on B1122, 2 miles (3km) N of Leiston
Home of the 19th-century travel writer Charles Montagu Doughty. An exceptionally pretty church displays a scrap of German zeppelin shot down in 1917.

THEDDINGWORTH Leicestershire SP6685
Village on A427, 5 miles (8km) W of Market Harborough
Close to River Welland and Northamptonshire border. Norman and medieval church restored 1858 by Sir George Gilbert Scott. Snetzler organ, 1754. Nineteenth-century estate cottages.

THEDDLETHORPE ALL SAINTS Lincolnshire TF4688
Village off A1031, 3 miles (5km) NW of Mablethorpe
Large All Saints' Church, from which the village takes its name, is known as the 'cathedral of the marsh'. Too big for the village's present scattered population, it is cared for by the Redundant Churches Fund. Built of greenstone, with limestone and brick repairs. Some Norman work, otherwise built about 1380, with 19th-century restorations.

THELWALL Cheshire SJ6587
Town off A50, 3 miles (5km) E of Warrington
Dormitory town of Warrington, familiar to many for its viaduct carrying the M6 motorway over the Manchester Ship Canal.

The old black and white Pickering Arms at Thelwall.

THERFIELD Hertfordshire TL3337
Village off A505, 3 miles (5km) S of Royston
Attractive 'best kept village' winner, with half-timbered and brick houses, earthworks of Norman castle, Victorian church. (For Therfield Heath, see Royston.)

THETFORD Norfolk TL8683
Town on A134, 12 miles (19km) N of Bury St Edmunds
Pretty Thetford is associated with the atmospheric remains of a once-powerful abbey, a towering Norman castle mound set among Iron Age earthworks, and the great forest to the west. The town centre is a conservation area, so that the abundant medieval and Georgian houses in almost every street are protected.

Evidence of Thetford's early importance can be seen in its wealth of archaeological finds. There was a powerful Iron Age fortress here, which the practical Normans used as the base of their own castle in the 12th century. Perhaps even more important was the huge cluniac priory (English Heritage) that was founded in 1103, its picturesque ruins standing on the banks of the Little Ouse River.

In the town centre is the 15th-century Ancient House, now a museum. The fine carved oak ceilings can still be admired while visitors can wander through the exhibitions on local history and archaeology. In the pretty courtyard is a Tudor herb garden.

But perhaps best of Thetford's many treasures is the 50,000 acre (20,235ha) Thetford Forest Park, great tracts of pine trees and heathland criss-crossed by ancient trackways.

THEYDON BOIS Essex TQ4499
Village on B172, 2 miles (3km) S of Epping
This leafy commuter village lies close to Epping Forest (see) and the attractive village green with its pond and oak trees is part of the forest. The Victorian church dates from 1850. Pleasant pubs include the 300-year-old Bull and the Sixteen-String Jack, named after a notorious 18th-century highwayman and the ribbons he sported.

THEYDON, GARNON AND MOUNT Essex TQ4799
Villages off B172, 2 miles (3km) SE of Epping
In pleasant country, audibly close to motorways. Both villages have interesting churches. Hobbs Cross Open Farm is near Theydon Garnon.

THIRKLEBY North Yorkshire SE4778
Village off A19, 4 miles (6km) SE of Thirsk
A small farming community. The village consists of two halves connected by a footbridge over the beck.

THIRLSPOT Cumbria NY3118
Village on A591, 5 miles (8km) SE of Keswick
At the northern end of Thirlmere, one of the largest lakes which was appropriated as a reservoir. The valley was flooded to create a water supply for Manchester.

THIRSK North Yorkshire SE4282
Town off A168, 8 miles (13km) SE of Northallerton
Thirsk was a major stopping point in the days of stage coaches and many of the traditional coaching inns can still be seen around the cobbled market square. The splendid Parish Church of St Mary is known as the 'cathedral of the north'. The town has a racecourse and there are many horses stabled here.

THISTLETON Leicestershire SK9117
Village off B668, 7 miles (11km) NE of Oakham
Rutland village, site of numerous Roman finds, excavated before ironstone-quarrying. Church has tower of 14th century, remainder rebuilt 1879–80.

THIXENDALE North Yorkshire SE8461
Village off A166, 2 miles (4km) NW of Fridaythorpe
Small traditional village built along one main street. On the path of Wolds Way and Centenary Way walks, this is a popular base for walkers.

THOMPSON Norfolk TL9296
Village off A1075, 3 miles (5km) S of Watton
Situated near the 'Battle Area' of the army, Thompson is a quiet village with Thompson Water, a marshy man-made lake, and wild Thompson Common.

THORLEY Hertfordshire TL4718
Village off B1004, on SW edge of Bishop's Stortford
Much development since the 1970s. The famous Dick Whittington was lord of the manor. Interesting church with Norman doorway.

THORNABY-ON-TEES Cleveland NZ4517
Small town off A1045, on SE edge of Stockton-on-Tees
An industrial suburb of Stockton-on-Tees and Middlesbrough. The original village, with an 11th-century church, is now a conservation area.

THORNBOROUGH Buckinghamshire SP7433
Village off A421, 3 miles (5km) E of Buckingham
Lively village with a green and pond, and a Norman church. The six-arched 14th-century bridge over the Claydon Brook is Buckinghamshire's only surviving medieval bridge. Two big mounds close by were opened in 1839 and found to contain objects of the Roman period, and it is known that there was a Romano-Celtic temple here.

THORNBURY Avon ST6390
Town on B4061, 12 miles (19km) N of Bristol
Dense stone buildings in the middle of this old market town, a cloth-making centre in medieval times, range from 16th century to Victorian. The church, with its fine early 16th-century tower, stands away from the town, near the Tudor Castle (not open), a sophisticated building.

THORNBY Northamptonshire SP6775
Village on A50, 8 miles (13km) SW of Market Harborough
Tudor-style hall, with 19th- and 20th-century additions to 17th-century core. Stone House of about 1700, and early 20th-century Thornby Grange.

THORNDON Suffolk TM1469
Village off B1077, 3 miles (5km) S of Eye
Peaceful village standing in rich cornfields. The famous Dowlands Restaurant is a handsome building, parts of which are Elizabethan.

THORNE South Yorkshire SE6813
Town off M18, 9 miles (15km) NE of Doncaster
The area around this small market town used to be marshland until it was drained in 1626 by Dutch engineer Cornelius Vermuyden.

THORNEY Cambridgeshire TF2804
Village on A47, 7 miles (11km) NE of Peterborough
Thorney became important in the 7th century, when a monastery was founded here. Fragments of it remain in grand St Mary and St Botolph's Church. Today, Thorney is predominantly 19th century, with a massive mock-Jacobean water tower at its centre. The Dukes of Bedford lived here, and are responsible for much of the later development.

THORNEY ISLAND West Sussex SU7503
Peninsula in Chichester Harbour
This low-lying peninsula, with a big former RAF airfield, was a true island in Chichester Harbour until drainage work in the 19th century.

THORNGUMBALD Humberside TA2026
Village on A1033, 2 miles (3km) SE of Hedon
On a busy main road. This was a traditional farming and market garden community, now a large sprawling suburban area serving Hull.

THORNHAM Norfolk TF7343
Village on A149, 4 miles (6km) E of Hunstanton
A tiny harbour and peaceful beaches mark this charming village with its attractive flint and chalkstone cottages. Coastal walks and bird-watching are on offer.

THORNHAM, MAGNA AND PARVA Suffolk TM1071
Villages off A140, 3 miles (5km) SW of Eye
Two delightful villages 1 mile (2km) apart. Thornham Parva's main treasure is its exquisite altar painting dating to about 1300 (to see it, ask for the key from the house nearest the church). Thornham Magna has the excellent Three Horseshoes, which has been an inn since 1150. The Thornham estate is a working farm open to visitors.

THORNHAUGH Cambridgeshire TF0600
Village off A1, 5 miles (8km) SE of Stamford
Standing on a tributary of the River Nene, Thornhaugh has Sacrewell Farm and Country Centre, a working farm with a watermill and fine gardens.

THORNHILL Dumfries and Galloway NX8795
Small town on A76, 13 miles (21km) NW of Dumfries
Attractive village on early Christian site on River Nith. Tall column topped by winged horse replaces usual mercat cross, erected in 1714 by Marquess of Queensberry.

THORNHILL Mid Glamorgan ST1584
Village on A469, 1 mile (2km) S of Caerphilly
Northern suburb of Cardiff blessed with two fine parks: Cefn Onn is noted for rhododendrons and azaleas; The Wenallt's has rolling woodland, heathland. Extensive views.

THORNHILL West Yorkshire SE2518
Village off B6117, 2 miles (3km) S of Dewsbury
An ancient textile and coal-mining village. There has been a church here for over 1,000 years.

THORNLEY Durham NZ3639
Village on B1279, 6 miles (10km) E of Durham
Former colliery village. The remains of original medieval village, now only earthworks, are contained within the parkland of 18th-century Thornley Old Hall.

THORNTHWAITE Cumbria NY2225
Hamlet off A66, 3 miles (5km) NW of Keswick
Hamlet at the foot of Seat Howe. The Thornthwaite Gallery is an attractive 18th-century barn which deals in fine arts.

THORNTON Leicestershire SK4607
Village on B585, 5 miles (8km) SE of Coalville
On a ridge of high ground with views over Thornton Reservoir. Church close to reservoir has 15th-century tower, 1864 chancel.

THORNTON West Yorkshire SE1032
Village on B6145, 4 miles (6km) W of Bradford
Old part of the village, where many streets are cobbled, has been well preserved, being by-passed by the main road. The Old Parsonage, birthplace of three of the Brontë sisters, has been restored and is now a restaurant.

THORNTON CURTIS Humberside TA0817
Village on A1077, 6 miles (10km) E of Immingham
A small farming village. The magnificent gatehouse of the ruined Thornton Abbey (English Heritage) is the largest in England.

THORNTON DALE (OR THORNTON-LE-DALE) North Yorkshire SE8383
Village on A170, 3 miles (5km) E of Pickering
This attractive village, at one end of the scenic North Yorkshire Moors Railway, takes its shape from the Middle Ages but its character is from later times. There are many Georgian houses as well as pretty, stone thatched cottages. There is a rustic bridge over Thornton Beck which flows through the village.

THORNTON HOUGH Merseyside SJ3080
Village on B5136, 2 miles (3km) N of Neston
A model estate village, centred around a large village green, built in the late 19th century in the heart of rural Wirral.

THORNTON STEWARD North Yorkshire SE1787
Village off A6108, 5 miles (8km) SE of Leyburn
An old village in Wensleydale with a small castellated square tower built as a store-room and armoury during the French war of 1804–15.

THORNTON (THORNTON CLEVELEYS OR THORNTON-LE-FYLDE) Lancashire SD3442
Town off A585, 2 miles (3km) E of Cleveleys
Marsh Mill-in-Wyre is the last complete windmill in the region; it is now restored and, with surrounding Marsh Village, is a popular attraction.

THORNTON WATLASS North Yorkshire SE2385
Village on B6268, 3 miles (5km) SW of Bedale
An ancient village on the River Ure with a triangular village green used as a cricket pitch.

THORNTON-IN-CRAVEN North Yorkshire SD9048
Village on A56, 6 miles (10km) SW of Skipton
Pretty village which stands on the course of the Pennine Way, with lovely views of surrounding countryside.

THORNTON-LE-BEANS AND THORNTON-LE-MOOR North Yorkshire SE3990
Villages off A168, 3 miles (5km) SE of Northallerton
Two villages in the heart of rural North Yorkshire. Thornton-le-Beans, known as The Beans to distinguish it from the other, is a small, attractive village with several 18th-century houses and more modern housing off the main street. A large well behind Hawnby House supplied the village with water before 1950.

THORNTON-LE-MOORS Cheshire SJ4474
Village on A5117, 3 miles (5km) SE of Ellesmere Port
This small, agricultural village, overshadowed by the vast oil refinery, has remained virtually untouched over the years.

THOROTON Nottinghamshire SK7642
Village off A52, 4 miles (6km) NE of Bingham
In Vale of Belvoir. Medieval church with 14th-century tower and crocketed spire, Victorian restoration. Remains of circular medieval dovecote in farmyard.

THORP ARCH West Yorkshire SE4345
Village off A659, 1 mile (2km) E of Boston Spa
Bound on the east by Rudgate, the Roman road which forded the River Wharfe here, a fine village with stone houses grouped around a village green.

THORPE Derbyshire SK1550
Village off A515, 3 miles (5km) NW of Ashbourne
Where the River Manifold joins the River Dove, which forms the border with Staffordshire. Conical hill of Thorpe Cloud, 942ft (287m) high, guards the entrance to dramatic Dovedale.

THORPE Surrey TQ0268
Village off M25, 2 miles (3km) SW of Staines
A village in the Thames Valley amid gravel pits and motorways. Its houses are hidden behind curving stone walls, with an attractive historic group, in a pleasing mixture of styles, around the parish church which has a 12th-century chancel and brick tower. Nearby 500 acre (202ha) Thorpe Park puts the accent on watery themes, including Loggers' Leap, a famous water flume.

THORPE ABBOTTS Norfolk TM1979
Village off A143, 5 miles (8km) E of Diss
Thorpe Abbotts is up a hill, a pretty group of houses around chestnut trees and a well. The church stands at the hill foot.

THORPE BAY Essex TQ9185
District in E of Southend-on-Sea
The smartest residential area of Southend (see). Particularly expensive houses close to the seafront. Golf course.

THORPE BY WATER Leicestershire SP8996
Hamlet on B672, 3 miles (5km) SE of Uppingham
Beside River Welland, the Northamptonshire border. Attractive ironstone and limestone houses, mainly with Collyweston slate roofs.

THORPE END Norfolk TG2810
District in NE Norwich
Once quite separate from Norwich, Thorpe End is now a suburb. It is a garden village, its houses attractively arranged around neat lawns and verges.

THORPE HESLEY South Yorkshire SK3795
Village off A629, 4 miles (6km) NW of Rotherham
Isolated rural community once nicknamed 'Mutton Town'. Wesley Steps, built in 1979, mark the place from which John and Charles Wesley once preached.

THORPE MANDEVILLE Northamptonshire SP5344
Village on B4525, 6 miles (10km) NE of Banbury
Fine early 18th-century manor house, 1622 sundial on Three Conies pub and 14th-century church. Closer to the Oxfordshire boundary is The Hill, built in the 1890s by Voysey.

THORPE MARKET Norfolk TG2436
Village on A149, 4 miles (6km) S of Cromer
The spacious village green has a 16th-century house at one end. The attractive church was built in 1795, with decorative turrets on the roof.

THORPE SALVIN South Yorkshire SK5281
Village off A57, 4 miles (7km) W of Worksop
Small rural village. St Peter's Church has interesting font which depicts the four seasons. The manor house is now in ruins.

THORPE ST ANDREW Norfolk TG2609
District in E Norwich
The River Yare winds sluggishly through this suburb of Norwich, passing handsome 18th-century houses, grand trees and modern flats.

THORPE THEWLES Cleveland NZ4023
Village on A177, 4 miles (6km) NW of Stockton-on-Tees
Residential area once overshadowed by viaduct, demolished in 1978. The old Catle Eden railway line is now a footpath and cycle track.

THORPE-LE-SOKEN Essex TM1722
Village on B1033, 5 miles (8km) N of Clacton-on-Sea
Pleasant village. Victorian church with Tudor tower. Arnold Bennet lived here and Sir William Gull was ostensibly buried here, but was he Jack the Ripper?

THORPENESS SuffolkTM4759
Small town on B1353, 2 miles (3km) SE of Leiston
An eccentric holiday village conceived by Glencairn Stuart Ogilvie in the early 1900s. The houses and Dolphin inn are mock-Tudor, and stand around the 65 acre (26ha) boating lake known as The Meare. The

House in the Clouds is a five-storey house topped by a 50,000 gallon (227,000 litre) water tank (disguised as a timber-framed house).

THORRINGTON Essex TM0919
Village on B1027, 2 miles (3km) N of Brightlingsea
A sprawling village among creeks and marshes. The church has a fine tower and a lovely churchyard. A disused tide mill on Alresford Creek is being restored.

THORVERTON Devon SS9202
Village off A396, 6 miles (10km) N of Exeter
A large, pretty village with thatched cottages, cobbled pavements, a green and a stream.

THRAPSTON Northamptonshire SP9978
Village off A605, 7 miles (11km) SW of Oundle
Medieval nine-arched bridge over River Nene. Medieval and later church, memorial to Sir John Washington has three stars and stripes, forerunner of American flag. Montague House, his home, now offices. Eighteenth-century cottages and Oakleigh House. Former corn exchange of 1850. Titchmarsh Nature Reserve, bird sanctuary and heronry off A605. Wildflowers, songbirds at Denford Churchyard reserve, between church and river.

THREE BRIDGES West Sussex TQ2837
District off A264, in E Crawley
An important railway junction and a modern settlement merged imperceptibly with Crawley (see); it was named after bridges spanning the River Mole.

THREE HOLES Norfolk TF5000
Hamlet on A1101, 7 miles (11km) SE of Wisbech
Name came from the three arches in the 17th-century bridge over the Old Croft River. Was originally called 'Waldingstow'.

THREE LEGGED CROSS Dorset SU0805
Village on B3072, 4 miles (6km) W of Ringwood
Mostly recent, presumably named after the road junction. The area was once heathland.

THREE MILE CROSS Berkshire SU7167
Village off A33, 4 miles (6km) S of Reading
This small village where Mary Russel Mitford, author of *Our Village*, was born is now dominated by the M4.

THREEKINGHAM Lincolnshire TF0836
Village on A52, 6 miles (10km) S of Sleaford
Supposed to take its name from three Danish kings killed in battle in 870, but tombs in church are 14th century. Whalebone arch .

THRELKELD Cumbria NY3225
Village on A66, 4 miles (6km) E of Keswick
This is a quiet village overlooked by the peak Blencathra. In 1904, one of the first English sanatoria was built for tubercular patients, now Blencathra Holiday Centre. The Blencathra Hunt have their kennels here and there is a monument in the churchyard to former members of the hunt.

THRIGBY Norfolk TG4612
Hamlet off A1064, 4 miles (6km) W of Caister-on-Sea
Set among orchards and pretty hedgerows, Thrigby is a pleasant village boasting Thrigby Hall, built in 1876, with its interesting wildlife gardens.

THRINGSTONE Leicestershire SK4217
Village off A512, 2 miles (3km) N of Coalville
Ruins of Grace Dieu Priory, founded 1235–40 for Augustinian canonesses. Grace Dieu Manor, 1830s, by Railton, was centre of Catholic Revival; it has a Pugin chapel.

THRIPLOW Cambridgeshire TL4346
Village off A505, 6 miles (10km) NE of Royston
Set among pretty meadows famous for marsh orchids. A smithy stands on the village green, and there is evidence of Iron and Bronze Age settlements.

THROCKING Hertfordshire TL3330
Village off A10, 2 miles (3km) NW of Buntingford
Highest church in Hertfordshire, with Elwes family monuments and curious tower, completed in red brick in 1660.

THROCKLEY Tyne and Wear NZ1566
District off A69, 6 miles (10km) W of Newcastle
Dormitory suburb high above the River Tyne. Main street follows line of Hadrian's Wall, with many houses and shops built over the Vallum.

THROWLEIGH Devon SX6690
Village off A382, 6 miles (10km) SE of Okehampton
On the edge of Dartmoor, with a medieval church, 16th-century church house and thatched cottages, all of granite.

THROWLEY AND THROWLEY FORSTAL Kent TQ9955
Hamlets off A251, 4 miles (6km) SW of Faversham
Hidden among Kentish cherry orchards on the North Downs, Throwley is a scatter of farms, but Throwley Forstal is a small cluster grouped about its green.

THRUMPTON Nottinghamshire SK5031
Village off A453, 1 mile (2km) NE of Ratcliffe on Soar
Quiet village, in cul-de-sac to River Trent. Church with 13th-century tower. Mainly Jacobean hall (limited opening), an H-shaped brick house in delightful grounds.

THRUSSINGTON Leicestershire SK6415
Village off A607, 7 miles (11km) W of Melton Mowbray
On River Wreake. Red-brick houses around green. Small ironstone church with 13th-century chancel and 15th-century tower.

THRUXTON Hampshire SU2945
Village off A303, 5 miles (8km) W of Andover
Well known for its motor-racing circuit, on a World War II airfield. Large village, with many thatched cottages. The church has an unusual Elizabethan oak effigy of a woman.

THUNDERSLEY Essex TQ7988
Town off A13, 4 miles (6km) E of Basildon
Part of the Southend (see) built-up complex. Sweeping views from a hill on which stands St Peter's Church, enlarged in the 1960s.

THUNDRIDGE AND WADESMILL Hertfordshire TL3517
Villages on A10, 2 miles (3km) N of Ware
On either side of the River Rib where Ermine Street crosses it. The bridge dates from the 1820s.

THURCASTON Leicestershire SK5610
Village off B5328, 4 miles (6km) N of Leicester
Fifteenth-century cruck-built Latimer's House may be birthplace of Bishop Latimer, certainly born in village. He was burnt as a heretic under Mary I; memorial to him in church.

THURCROFT South Yorkshire SK4988
Village on B6060, 5 miles (8km) SE of Rotherham
Village built to house miners when the local colliery was opened in 1909. Colliery closed in 1960s.

THURGARTON Nottinghamshire SK6949
Village on A612, 3 miles (5km) S of Southwell
Thirteenth-century church incorporating parts of Augustinian priory church, Victorian timber roof and chancel. Manor house on site of priory.

THURLASTON Leicestershire SP5099
Village off A47, 6 miles (10km) SW of Leicester
All Saints' Church has 15th-century tower and monuments of the Turville family, of whose mansion only fragments remain, on a moated site.

THURLEIGH Bedfordshire TL0558
Village off B660, 6 miles (9km) N of Bedford
A village of thatched houses. An American airforce wartime airfield was subsequently used for research and testing. Bury Hill is a Norman castle mound.

THURLESTONE Devon SX6742
Village off A379, 4 miles (6km) W of Kingsbridge
Just inland from the rocky coast, with a big sandy bay, Thurlestone enjoys a mild climate and luxuriant greenery and has picturesque thatched cottages.

THURLOW, LITTLE AND GREAT Suffolk TL6751
Hamlets on B1061, 4 miles (6km) N of Haverhill
Adjoining Great Thurlow, Little Thurlow straggles along the River Stour. Interesting buildings line the main street, including School House, founded in 1614 by a former Lord Mayor of London.

THURLOXTON Somerset ST2730
Village off A38, 2 miles (3km) SW of North Petherton
Small village. The church has an interesting and unusual set of wooden furnishings – screen, pulpit and pews – all dating from the 1630s.

THURLSTONE South Yorkshire SE2303
Village on A628, 1 mile (2km) W of Penistone
Many fine examples of early weavers' cottages built for those working in the woollen industry. Today, agriculture is the main occupation.

THURLTON Norfolk TM4198
Village off B1140, 5 miles (8km) N of Beccles
The old White Hart is now a private house, but there was an inn here since the 1300s. The mill remains are called Great Goliath.

THURNBY AND BUSHBY Leicestershire SK6403
Villages off A47, 4 miles (6km) E of Leicester
Residential area close to city, retaining old village core. Church rebuilt 1870–3, using old materials, with central tower.

THURNE Norfolk TG4015
Village off B1152, 9 miles (14km) NW of Great Yarmouth
This charming village stands on the banks of the River Thurne, from which it takes its name. The Lion inn stands in pleasant gardens.

THURNHAM Lancashire SD4654
Village off A588, 5 miles (8km) S of Lancaster
Thurnham Mill, on the banks of the Lancaster Canal, is now a hotel. Tiny village with only a handful of houses and a pretty church.

THURNSCOE South Yorkshire SE4505
Town off A635, 7 miles (11km) E of Barnsley
Largely a residential area with a mixture of housing, mostly terraces, of a variety of ages.

THURSBY Cumbria NY3250
Village on A595, 6 miles (10km) SW of Carlisle
The village lies on the old Roman road to Carlisle and takes its name from the Saxon god Thor.

THURSFORD Norfolk TF9933
Hamlet off A148, 5 miles (8km) NE of Fakenham
This lovely village is best known for its fascinating 'Thursford Collection', an incredible exhibition of fairground memorabilia, including several steam engines. At the centre is the 'Mighty Wurlitzer', the fourth largest organ for cinemas in Europe. Fairs were significant events in Norfolk life, and the Thursford Collection is an important insight into our past.

THURSLEY Surrey SU9039
Village off A3, 3 miles (5km) N of Hindhead
This village was a centre of the medieval glass and iron industries and has an old hammerpond, now a nature reserve, on the sandy common. There are two parts to the village, the main one on a no-through road, The Street, with tile-hung, stone, brick and timber houses and a remarkable church with windows of 1030. The other is around a triangular green with pleasant old cottages and houses, including the birthplace of architect Sir Edwin Lutyens.

THURSO Highland ND1168
Town on A882, 18 miles (30km) NW of Wick
Thurso is the most northerly town on the British mainland and a major service centre for a large area; its neighbouring port of Scrabster is the departure point for

the Orkney ferries. Historically it was a Norse settlement which developed into a trading and fishing town, and the area of Fishertown beside Thurso Bay, with its narrow streets and traditional architecture, is the oldest part of the town. The remains of Old St Peter's Kirk, dating from the 12th to 16th centuries are here. Sir John Sinclair, the local 'improving' laird, was responsible for the 18th-century expansion of the town; a grid-plan of streets lies around a central square containing a statue of this benefactor. Local history is told in the Thurso Museum, which also contains the fine carved Pictish Ulbster Stone.

Employment from the 1950s was chiefly provided by the nuclear power station at nearby Dounreay; it is still a major employer although the fast reactor has closed and there is some anxiety about its future. The quarrying of Caithness flagstones was a traditional industry, while today many people are involved in tourism.

THURSTASTON Merseyside SJ2484
Village on A540, 3 miles (5km) SE of West Kirby
Thurstaston Hill, part of Thurstaston Common (National Trust), is a popular vantage point to view the Wirral and the Dee and Mersey estuaries. The main visitors' centre of Wirral Country Park is here. The village itself is a cluster of red-stone buildings grouped around a large grassy area.

THURSTON Suffolk TL9265
Village off A14 (A45), 5 miles (8km) E of Bury St Edmunds
An expanding village with three pubs, and a village hall named after William Tyrell Cavendish, who went down with the *Titanic* in 1912.

THURSTONFIELD Cumbria NY3156
Village on B5307, 5 miles (8km) W of Carlisle
A farming village with the Lough, a millpond surrounded by woodland, which is now a private fishing centre.

THURTON Norfolk TG3200
Village on A146, 3 miles (5km) NW of Loddon
A rapidly expanding village centred around the fine old Church of St Ethelbert, with its thatched roof. The George and Dragon inn is 400 years old.

THWAITE ST MARY Norfolk TM3394
Village off B1332, 3 miles (5km) N of Bungay
Tiny village with many interesting buildings, including Queen Anne Thwaite Hall and Tudor Old Messauge. The church is Norman.

THWING Humberside TA0470
Village off B1253, 8 miles (13km) W of Bridlington
A quiet backwater, the site of the Anglo-Saxon 'Dic Ring' excavated in 1984. Obelisk marks spot where huge meteorite fell in 1795, and 12th-century church.

TIBBERTON Hereford and Worcester SO9057
Village off A4538, 4 miles (6km) NE of Worcester
New housing now dominates ancient centre of village, but picturesque Rectory Farm still stands next to Victorian church with its surprising polychrome interior.

TIBTHORPE Humberside SE9655
Village off A163, 4 miles (7km) W of Great Driffield
The approach roads are flanked by avenues of trees and there are beautiful views of the surrounding countryside.

TICEHURST East Sussex TQ6830
Village on B2099, 3 miles (5km) SE of Wadhurst
Attractive village of weatherboarded cottages and houses high on a little ridge. Victorian arcade of shops. Pashley Manor with its lovely gardens is near by.

TICHBORNE Hampshire SU5730
Village off A31, 2 miles (3km) SW of New Alresford
Charming unspoilt village, with brick and timber-framed cottages. Interesting partly 11th-century church with superb Jacobean box pews and good 17th-century memorials. The Tichborne Dole – a gallon of flour for each inhabitant – is still presented at an annual ceremony. The Tichborne trial was a mid-Victorian drama: a long-lost heir (or a pretender) appeared from Australia to claim the estate. He lost the long court case.

TICKENCOTE Leicestershire SK9909
Village off A1, 3 miles (5km) NW of Stamford
Impressive Norman chancel arch of church tucked away from roar of A1 traffic. Much other Norman work, nave rebuilt and tower added 1792.

TICKENHAM Avon ST4571
Village on B3130, 3 miles (5km) E of Clevedon
Tickenham runs along the edge of the northernmost part of the Somerset Levels. Cadbury Camp, an Iron Age hillfort, stands on the woody hill to the north. The unusual, mostly early medieval church, is next door to a late medieval manor house (not open).

TICKHILL South Yorkshire SK5993
Town on A60, 6 miles (10km) S of Doncaster
Small, characterful town in attractive agricultural area. Development over the last 20 years has provided homes for commuters although Tickhill retains some of its medieval grandeur and charm. The castle, now owned by the Duchy of Lancaster, retains its gatehouse, moat and curtain wall. The grounds are opened to the public several times a year for special events.

TICKNALL Derbyshire SK3523
Village on A514, 2 miles (3km) W of Melbourne
Estate village of red-brick houses, including 1772 Harpur almshouses. Pumps line village street. Tramway bridge near entrance to Calke Abbey, 'the house that time forgot'. The early 18th-century house (National Trust) displays the amazing collections squirreled away by the Harpur-Crewe family. Village lock-up. Church of 1842.

TIDCOMBE Wiltshire SU2958
Hamlet off A338, 3 miles (5km) SW of Shalbourne
Small, with many beech trees. Medieval church with Elizabethan tower.

TIDDINGTON Oxfordshire SP6504
Village off A418, 4 miles (6km) W of Thame
Nondescript residential area on rising ground above the River Thame.

TIDESWELL Derbyshire SK1575
Small town on B6049, 6 miles (10km) E of Buxton
Peak District town between limestone dales and uplands, with large cruciform church known as the 'cathedral of the Peak', built over a period of 75 years in the 14th century, finishing with pinnacled tower. Musical events held in church. Well-dressing in June.

TIDMARSH Berkshire SU6374
Village on A340, 1 mile (2km) S of Pangbourne
On the River Pang, with brick cottages. There is a fine Norman doorway to the church; the heavy timber supports inside for the bell-turret were carved to match in Victorian times.

TIDWORTH (NORTH TIDWORTH) Wiltshire SU2349
Town on A3026, 3 miles (5km) SW of Ludgershall
In the military area, with lots of suburban army housing and a medieval church. North Tidworth is in Wiltshire, South is in Hampshire.

TIGHNABRUAICH Strathclyde NR9772
Small town on A8003, 1 mile (2km) N of Kames
Sailing resort on Kyles of Bute; road leads up to National Trust for Scotland viewpoint above Kyles, with walking on Caladh Castle Forest Trail.

TILBROOK Cambridgeshire TL0769
Village on B645, (A45) 7 miles (11km) E of Higham Ferrers
Tiny Tilbrook stands near the meandering River Til. The southern end of the village lines the side of what was the busy A45 between Higham Ferrers and Kimbolton.

TILBURY Essex TQ6476
Town off A1089, 2 miles (3km) SE of Grays
A Thames estuary container port, with a ferry across to Gravesend (see) and fine river views. It developed round the docks, opened in the 1880s as ships grew too big to go further upstream, and was taken over by the Port of London Authority in 1909. Tilbury Fort (English Heritage) is Britain's best piece of 17th-century military architecture. (See also East Tilbury.)

TILEHURST Berkshire SU6673
District in W of Reading
Only the village church and a few older farmhouses and cottages survive from the old village, now engulfed by Reading.

TILFORD Surrey SU8743
Village off A287, 3 miles (5km) SE of Farnham
A delightful village beside the River Wey with two medieval bridges and a huge triangular green dominated by three large oak trees, including the reputed 'oak at Kynghoc', mentioned in 1128.

TILGATE West Sussex TQ2735
District in S Crawley
District in the New Town of Crawley named after an old forest, now Tilgate Forest Park, a former iron-smelting area where the first dinosaur was discovered in 1830.

TILLICOULTRY Central NS9197
Town on A91, 3 miles (5km) NE of Alloa
Hillfoot village with tradition of milling and weaving, using water power in tartan and woollen manufacture. Clock Mill heritage centre tells local industrial story.

TILLINGHAM Essex TL9904
Village on B1021, 5 miles (8km) NE of Burnham-on-Crouch
Owned by St Paul's Cathedral, London, for a record period of some 1,400 years, Tillingham has weather-boarded cottages and a delightful old pub, the Cap and Feathers.

TILLINGTON West Sussex SU9622
Village on A272, 1 mile (2km) W of Petworth
A tidy village on the Petworth estate, standing high on a ridge top commanding superb views to the South Downs, with attractive small houses and an unusual church tower.

The 19th-century church at Tillington.

TILNEY ALL SAINTS Norfolk TF5618
Village off A17, 4 miles (6km) W of King's Lynn
The splendid church at Tilney All Saints is well worth visiting, especially for its double hammerbeam roof. There is also a thatched 16th-century hall.

TILSHEAD Wiltshire SU0347
Village on A360, 9 miles (14km) NW of Amesbury
On Salisbury Plain (see) with some thatched cottages of flint and stone chequer. The church is partly chequered too, and partly Norman.

TILSWORTH Bedfordshire SP9824
Village off A5, 3 miles (5km) NW of Dunstable
The grave of a murdered 'female unknown' has a melancholy inscription in the churchyard, which commands a fine Chilterns view. Manor gatehouse.

TILTON ON THE HILL Leicestershire SK7405
Village on B6047, 9 miles (14km) NW of Uppingham
As name might imply, extensive views over surrounding countryside from this spot. Ironstone church has fine spire, numerous gargoyles.

TIMBERSCOMBE Somerset SS9542
Village on A396, 3 miles (5km) W of Dunster
Dense narrow streets, tucked between Exmoor and the Brendon Hills. Superb walking country.

TINTAGEL Cornwall SX0588
Village on B3263, 4 miles (6km) NW of Camelford
Famous for its castle (English Heritage) spectacularly set on a headland, almost an island off the steep slaty shore. Remnants of a medieval castle and indications of 6th-century buildings can be seen; the castle has been associated with King Arthur since medieval times, and much visited from Victorian times. The village is touristy, with a huge Victorian hotel; the Old Post Office (National Trust) is a 14th-century stone house. Bleak and treeless coastline.

TINTERN PARVA Gwent SO5200
Village on A466, 4 miles (6km) N of Chepstow
In the celebrated Wye Valley, immortalised by William Wordsworth's poem and internationally known for its Cistercian abbey (Cadw) founded in 1131. The great abbey church, rebuilt in the 13th century, is one of Britain's most impressive monastic ruins, with superb east and west windows. Exhibitions and rail memorabilia at former Victorian railway station, crafts complex, Offa's Dyke and Wye Valley walks.

TINTINHULL Somerset ST4919
Village off A303, 4 miles (6km) NW of Yeovil
Golden Ham Hill stone village, with 17th-century Tintinhull House (National Trust, only a tiny part open) with very fine formal gardens filled with unusual plants.

TINTWISTLE Derbyshire SK0297
Village on A628, 2 miles (3km) N of Glossop
Weavers' cottages of 18th- and 19th-century cotton centre; views over Bottoms Reservoir in Longdendale Valley. Close to border with Cheshire, of which it was formerly a part.

TIPTON West Midlands SO9592
District on A4037, in West Bromwich
This old Black Country mining and industrial village is now transformed by residential estates and town centre conservation area.

TIPTREE Essex TL8916
Small town on B1022, 9 miles (14km) SW of Colchester
The jam capital of Essex, among fields full of fruit and, in spring, of blossom. Commuters blossom here, too, amid sprawls of inter-war and post-war housing. Local farmer Arthur C Wilkin founded Wilkin's Tiptree Preserves in 1885. A pot appears on the village sign and the jam factory shop is open to the public.

TIREE Strathclyde
Island in the Inner Hebrides, SW of Coll
Beautiful and windswept crofting island to west of Mull with excellent windsurfing off fine beaches. Highest average hours of sunshine in Britain.

TIRRIL Cumbria NY5026
Village on B5320, 2 miles (3km) S of Penrith
At the foot of Ullswater. The village has a house dated 1699 which belonged to William Wordsworth's grandfather: it is called Wordsworth House.

TISBURY Wiltshire ST9429
Village off A30, 10 miles (16km) W of Wilton
Almost like a small town, with a winding main street. Older buildings in stone, Victorian onwards in brick. Large and complex church. Pythouse, to the west, dates from 1805 and is severely classical (limited opening).

TISSINGTON Derbyshire SK1752
Village off A515, 4 miles (6km) N of Ashbourne
Beautiful Peak District estate village of stone houses, with Jacobean Tissington Hall, church with Norman tower, and triangular green. Pagan custom of well-dressing, a thanksgiving for water, may have originated here, although date uncertain. Custom observed here each May, with blessing on Ascension Day. Tissington Trail near by.

TITCHFIELD Hampshire SU5305
Village off B3334, 3 miles (5km) W of Fareham
Beautifully preserved village, with many Georgian buildings in the central square and older cottages in other streets. The church has a Saxon doorway, and a lovely memorial to the Earls of Southampton of 1594. They converted the medieval abbey (English Heritage) to the north into a house in the 1540s – now mostly ruined apart from the gatehouse.

TITCHMARSH Northamptonshire TL0279
Village off A605, 2 miles (3km) NE of Thrapston
Unspoilt village with 18th-century thatched almshouses and splendid 15th-century church tower. Poet John Dryden spent his childhood in demolished manor; church monuments of his parents and family.

TITHBY Nottinghamshire SK6936
Hamlet off A46, 2 miles (3km) S of Bingham
Hamlet between Fosse Way and Vale of Belvoir. Georgian church furnishings, box pews, squire's pew, pulpit with reader's desk, west gallery.

TITLEY Hereford and Worcester SO3360
Hamlet on B4355, 3 miles (5km) NE of Kington
Hamlet in hills overlooking Arrow Valley consist of little more than Titley Court (17th century inside Victorian exterior) and church of 1868.

TITSEY Surrey TQ4055
Hamlet on B269, 1 mile (2km) N of Limpsfield
The famed viewpoint overlooks the parkland of Titsey Place and a cluster of cottages under a scarp of the North Downs, with the remains of a Roman villa and Romano-Celtic temple.

TITTLESHALL Norfolk TF8921
Village off A1065, 6 miles (10km) S of Fakenham
The fine medieval Church of St Mary contains some especially splendid monuments to the Coke family (Earls of Leicester) dating from the 17th century.

TIVERTON Devon SS9512
Town on A396, 12 miles (19km) N of Exeter
A real market town, its medieval wealth based on cloth-making, with many later 18th-century buildings, and a fine early 18th-century church. Tiverton Castle has a medieval gateway, and there is a richly decorated porch of 1517 on the medieval church close by. The 1864 town hall is very impressive. West Exe, over the river, has much mid-19th-century housing, built for the textile workers. Tiverton museum has rural displays and the Great Western canal basin, uphill from the town, has barges and is now a country park.

TIVETSHALL ST MARGARET Norfolk TM1687
Village off B1134, 6 miles (10km) NW of Harleston
St Margaret's Church is outstanding for its enormous and impressive royal arms of Elizabeth I. Nearby St Mary's Church is a ruin.

TIVINGTON Somerset SS9345
Hamlet off A39, 3 miles (5km) W of Minehead
Hamlet on the edge of Exmoor, with a tiny chapel in part of a thatched cottage. High woods beyond.

TIXALL Staffordshire SJ9722
Hamlet off A513, 4 miles (6km) E of Stafford
Attractive hamlet of old estate cottages faces Shugborough (see Milford) across River Sow. Worth catching a glimpse of imposing Tudor gatehouse of demolished Tixall Hall.

TIXOVER Leicestershire SK9700
Village off A47, 5 miles (8km) SW of Stamford
On River Welland, the Northamptonshire border. Eighteenth-century and earlier hall. Church with Norman tower, across fields by river.

TOADHOLE Derbyshire SK3856
Hamlet on B6013, 1 mile (2km) S of Higham
Two late 18th-century houses – Furnace House and Amber Mill House. Former Friends' Meeting House of 1743, with school room over stable. Higham Mill near by.

TOBERMORY Strathclyde (Mull) NM5055
Town on A848, principal town on Mull
Attractive town, Mull's main resort and administrative centre, with brightly painted houses built around sheltered harbour. Founded on site of earlier settlement as fishing village in 1789, with grid-plan of streets on bluff above harbour. Mull Museum tells local story, including the 1588 sinking in harbour of ship from Spanish Armada, reputed to be carrying treasure.

TODDINGTON Bedfordshire TL0128
Village on A5120, 5 miles (8km) N of Dunstable
An important market town in its day, and still a sizeable place set charmingly round a green and boasting an astonishing array of pubs, among them the Sow and Pigs, Angel, Bedford Arms and Oddfellows Arms, as well as the Church of St George of England. Rare breed farm animals, a vintage tractor collection and beautiful grounds can be seen at Toddington Manor. Conger Hill has a fine viewpoint.

TODDINGTON Gloucestershire SP0333
Village off B4077, 3 miles (5km) N of Winchcombe
The village has a good Victorian church and the Gloucestershire and Warwickshire Steam Railway, a mecca for railway enthusiasts, at its restored station.

TODENHAM Gloucestershire SP2436
Village off A429, 3 miles (5km) NE of Moreton-in-Marsh
An isolated, unspoilt village with an 18th-century pub, attractive cottages and a fine medieval church.

TODMORDEN West Yorkshire SD9324
Town on A6033, 8 miles (12km) NE of Rochdale
Market town which grew after the Rochdale Canal was built and because of this link to Lancashire, cotton rather than wool was the predominant industry. Todmorden Hall dates from 17th century; with new-found wealth from textiles, many older buildings were replaced in the 19th century and public buildings were erected.

TODWICK South Yorkshire SK4984
Village off A57, 6 miles (10km) NW of Worksop
Only the moat remains of the Old Manor House, demolished in 1945, and reputed to be the Torquilstone Castle of Sir Walter Scott's novel *Ivanhoe*.

TOFT HILL Durham NZ1528
Village on A68, 3 miles (5km) W of Bishop Auckland
Once a mining village, the cottages have mainly been converted into modern homes. Panoramic views of Weardale, Teesdale and the hills of Swaledale.

TOFT MONKS Norfolk TM4294
Village on A143, 3 miles (5km) N of Beccles
Standing in a region of wide open treeless fields, with two moated houses and some attractive farm buildings.

TOFTREES Norfolk TF8927
Hamlet on A1065, 2 miles (3km) SW of Fakenham
All Saints' Church was in a sorry state until recently. It has been carefully restored, and boasts a lovely Norman font.

TOLLAND Somerset ST1032
Village off B3188, 3 miles (5km) NE of Wiveliscombe
Stone village. Interesting 17th-century manor house (Gaulden Manor) with fine 17th-century plasterwork and themed gardens (limited opening).

TOLLARD ROYAL Wiltshire ST9417
Village on B3081, 6 miles (10km) SE of Shaftesbury
A wooded village in Cranborne Chase (see). King John's House (not open) is partly 13th century; Rushmore Park is vast.

TOLLER, FRATRUM AND PORCORUM Dorset SY5797
Villages off A356, 2 miles (3km) W of Maiden Newton
Toller Porcorum, in the valley (the name means 'of the pigs') is larger, with several thatched cottages. Fratrum is higher, a little hamlet with 16th-century manor house and stables (not open) and tiny church with an odd Norman font.

TOLLERTON Nottinghamshire SK6134
Village off A52, 4 miles (6km) SE of Nottingham
Seventeenth-century hall Palladianised, then Gothicised in about 1800 by Pendock Barry, now St Hugh's College. Church rebuilt about 1812 with mausoleum to Barry's wife.

TOLLESBURY Essex TL9510
Village on B1023, 7 miles (11km) E of Maldon
Once known for delectable oysters. Tall sailmakers' lofts rise above Woodrolfe Creek and the coastal mudflats. Busy yacht marina.

TOLLESHUNT D'ARCY Essex TL9212
Village off B1026, 6 miles (10km) NE of Maldon
The crime novelist Margery Allingham, creator of Mr Campion, lived here from the 1930s until her death in 1966. The stylish red-brick Queen Anne house in the main street is marked with a plaque and her grave is in the churchyard. The Victorian maypole has a wooden cage round its base.

TOLPUDDLE Dorset SY7994
Village on A35, 4 miles (6km) W of Bere Regis
Large village in watermeadows, famous for the Tolpuddle Martyrs, six farm labourers who formed a tiny trade union in 1834, were prosecuted and transported to Australia. Memorial cottages on the outskirts of the village, with a small museum.

Shelter at Tolpuddle, erected to commemorate the centenary of the Martyrs.

TOMINTOUL Grampian NJ1618
Village on A939, 10 miles (16km) SE of Grantown-on-Spey
One of the highest villages in the Highlands, laid out in 1750s near River Avon. Mainly noted for Glenlivet and Tamnavulin distilleries, set amidst high and desolate country.

TONBRIDGE Kent TQ5946
Town off A21, 6 miles (10km) SE of Sevenoaks
A pleasant old town dominated by the 13th-century gatehouse of a Norman castle demolished in the Civil War, and now surrounded by landscaped gardens. The town has spread along the road away from the River Medway, spanned by a Victorian cast-iron bridge, and the northern part of High Street has many attractive 18th- and 19th-century buildings. The famous school was founded in 1553.

TONG Shropshire SJ7907
Village on A41, 2 miles (3km) NW of Albrighton
Dickens set closing chapters of *The Old Curiosity Shop* in Tong, which has a handsome mix of brick and timber-framed houses and an array of distinguished memorials in its splendid church of 1410. Near by are White Ladies Priory (English Heritage), ruins of a 12th-century nunnery of St Leonard, and Boscobel House (English Heritage), timber-framed hiding place of Charles II.

TONG West Yorkshire SE2230
Village off A650, 4 miles (6km) SE of Bradford
Picturesque small village, now a residential district of Bradford and once described as 'an oasis in the desert of industrialism'.

TONGHAM Surrey SU8848
Village off A324, 2 miles (3km) SE of Aldershot
Twentieth-century building sprawls from Aldershot, swamping a handful of timber-framed houses at a crossroads, the old centre of this former brewing village.

TONGLAND Dumfries and Galloway NX6953
Village on A711, 2 miles (3km) NE of Kirkcudbright
Village mainly noted for 1935 Tongland Hydro Power Station, part of Galloway hydro-electric scheme. Dam and adjacent fish ladder for spawning salmon.

TONGWYNLAIS South Glamorgan ST1382
Village off A470, 5 miles (8km) NW of Cardiff
Dominated by fairytale castle on wooded hill above River Taff's gorge. Castell Coch (Cadw) is a Victorian Gothic fantasy with fabulously imaginative decoration.

TONYPANDY Mid Glamorgan SS9992
Town on A4119, 5 miles (8km) NW of Pontypridd
In famous former mining valley of the Rhondda, scene of miners' riots of 1910 when Home Secretary Winston Churchill sent in the troops.

TOOTING Greater London TQ2771
District in borough of Wandsworth
Heavily built up since the 1890s and best known for the Granada cinema, now a bingo hall, which has a fantastically extravagant 1930s interior designed by Theodore Komisarjevsky. Tooting Bec Common is a sizeable open space and Tooting Bec Lido, which dates from 1907, is one of England's biggest open-air swimming pools.

TOPCLIFFE North Yorkshire SE4076
Village off A168, 4 miles (6km) SW of Thirsk
An old village, mentioned in Domesday Book, with many modern houses. The mill produced flour until the 1960s.

TOPPESFIELD Essex TL7437
Village off B1057, 5 miles (8km) NE of Finchingfield
A few old houses are left in this windy place on a hill. The Church of St Margaret of Antioch has a 1699 tower in red brick.

TOPSHAM Devon SX9688
District off A376, 4 miles (6km) SE of Exeter
Having served as a port for Exeter from medieval times, Topsham is now a picturesque yachting centre. Its narrow streets, luckily with no through traffic, are filled with handsome 17th- and 18th-century brick houses. The prettiest and best-preserved townscape in Devon, it has views of the wide estuary and a local museum.

TORBAY
see Brixham, Paignton, Torquay

TORBRYAN Devon SX8266
Hamlet off A381, 4 miles (6km) SW of Newton Abbot
A sheltered hamlet with a 16th-century church house turned into an inn, a few cottages and a 15th-century church with good fittings including a screen and box pews.

TORCROSS Devon SX8242
Village on A379, 7 miles (11km) SW of Dartmouth
On the southern end of Slapton Ley (see), the largest lake in Devon, right on the shore. Old cottages.

TORKSEY Lincolnshire SK8378
Village on A156, 7 miles (11km) S of Gainsborough
Once significant town, now a popular leisure spot, where Roman Foss Dyke leaves River Trent, linking it to River Witham. Remains of Elizabethan mansion, known as Torksey Castle.

TORPENHOW Cumbria NY2039
Village off A595, 1 mile (2km) NE of Bothel
Superb views of Solway, Lakeland hills and Pennines from elevated position of fine Norman church.

TORPHICHEN Lothian NS9672
Village on B792, 2 miles (3km) N of Bathgate
Pretty hill-backed village founded as only Scottish house of Knights of St John of Jerusalem and important medieval sanctuary. Part of original church incorporated into present 17th-century parish church, fine example of fortified church architecture. Cairnpapple Hill near by is site of underground burial cist on hilltop used for ritual from about 2500BC–100AD.

TORPOINT Cornwall SX4355
Town on A374, across the Hamoaze from Plymouth
Town created by the ferry across from Plymouth, which started a regular service in the 18th century. Bleak, but with good views of Devonport and the Rame peninsula.

TORQUAY Devon SX9164
Town on A3022, 18 miles (30km) S of Exeter
At the heart of 'the English Riviera', this huge seaside resort developed from the late 18th century. It has a very mild climate, encouraging exotic greenery and even palm trees, and a yachting and fishing harbour. The town centre is rather spoilt by big blocks of flats, but the outskirts still have dignified Victorian villas, set in large gardens with winding drives.

Many Victorian churches are scattered about the town, and an exotic pavilion of 1911 sits down by the harbour, with domes and tiles. There are parks and gardens everywhere, and the headland Torquay covers has small, dramatic hills, adding to the romantic effect. Rocky cliffs are all around, with sandy beaches.

Torre Abbey is unusual in being so close to the sea and has a 14th-century gatehouse, the rest of the buildings having been converted into a house in the 18th century. Torbay museum displays local archaeology. In Kent's Caverns limestone caves, early prehistoric remains were found, along with the bones of extinct animals. See Babbacombe and Cockington.

TORRIDGE, RIVER Devon
River, runs by Torrington to Bideford
The river rises near the north Devon coast, but takes a long loop through south Devon before heading north through Great Torrington. Large estuary at Bideford.

TORRIDON Highland NG9055
Village on A896, 6 miles (10km) E of Shieldaig
Wilderness area between Loch Maree and Loch Torridon with outstanding mountain scenery which includes the ancient Torridonian sandstone peaks of Ben Eighe and the ridge of Liathach. Torridon estate owned by National Trust for Scotland who run a countryside centre with displays on wildlife, flora and fauna. Renowned area for climbing and taxing hill-walking, and geologically of great interest.

TORTHORWALD Dumfries and Galloway NY0378
Village on A709, 4 miles (6km) NE of Dumfries
Village above Lochar Water and Nith Valley with near-by ruins of 14th-century Castle of the Carlyles prominent on hilltop.

TORTINGTON West Sussex TQ0005
Hamlet off A27, 2 miles (3km) SW of Arundel
This tiny place overlooking the River Arun clusters around its 12th-century church, famed for rich Norman mouldings and beakhead ornamentation. Remains of priory in farm to north.

TORTWORTH Avon ST7093
Village off B4509, 3 miles (5km) W of Wotton-under-Edge
Tiny village, with an ancient chestnut tree in a field close to the church, supposedly 600 years old. Now decayed but surrounded by many mature offspring.

TORVER Cumbria SD2894
Hamlet on A593, 2 miles (3km) SW of Coniston
The Furness Railway came here in 1859, to carry stone and slate from quarries. The Green Cottages, so called because of the colour of the stone, were built by the railway company.

TORWORTH Nottinghamshire SK6586
Village on A638, 2 miles (3km) E of Blyth
On old Great North road in north Nottinghamshire. Daneshill Lakes Nature Reserve of woodland and water in former gravel pits.

TOSELAND Cambridgeshire TL2462
Village off B1043, 4 miles (6km) NE of St Neots
A tiny fenland village with Toseland Hall, a lovely red-brick Tudor house with three gables, mullioned windows and picturesque chimneys.

TOSSIDE Lancashire SD7656
Hamlet on B6478, 4 miles (6km) W of Long Preston
On the edge of Forest of Bowland, half in Lancashire, half in Yorkshire. A 17th-century church. Village post office was once the smithy.

TOSTOCK Suffolk TL9563
Village off A14 (A45), 6 miles (10km) E of Bury St Edmunds
Standing among watermeadows, Tostock has some handsome white brick Georgian buildings, and a late 13th-century church.

TOTLAND Isle of Wight SZ3287
Village off A3054, 3 miles (5km) SW of Yarmouth
A little seaside resort which developed from a hamlet in the late 19th century. Lots of Edwardian brick houses, some turreted.

TOTLEY South Yorkshire SK3180
District on SW edge of Sheffield
A surprisingly rural area of stone-built houses dominated by meadows and moorland of the Peak District. Sizeable student population.

TOTNES Devon SX8060
Town on A385, 7 miles (11km) W of Torquay
Totnes is one of the best towns in the county, dense but on a human scale. The High Street runs down the hill, closely packed with buildings from the 16th century onwards. Some are picturesquely carried on pillars over the pavement, and the striking Eastgate (remodelled in 1837 and damaged by fire in 1990) stands over the road. The 16th-century buildings include the pillared guildhall and timber-framed houses. Totnes museum is in a fine Elizabethan town house built by a rich merchant. The castle (English Heritage) at the top of the town still has an impressive motte with a 14th-century shell keep on top, and the church has a handsome 15th-century 120ft (36m) tower and an outstanding stone screen of 1459. Totnes is at the lowest bridging point on the River Dart, with a handsome stone bridge of 1826 alongside the new (1982) one.

Other attractions include the Devonshire Collection of Period Costume and a motor museum.

TOTTENHAM Greater London TQ3390
District in borough of Haringey
North London residential suburb with industrial estates, developed from the 1870s onwards and home of Tottenham Hotspur Football Club, whose ground is at White Hart Lane. The area was once owned by Robert the Bruce and Haringey museum at Bruce Castle covers local history, with a specialist postal history section and the museum of the Middlesex Regiment.

TOTTERIDGE Greater London TQ2494
District in borough of Barnet
This was a rural backwater until between the wars. The parish church was rebuilt in the 1790s, with many of the Pepys family buried in the churchyard.

TOTTERNHOE Bedfordshire SP9821
Village off B489, 2 miles (3km) W of Dunstable
Famed for its stone, which was used in the construction of Westminster Abbey and many other important buildings, and for the church here. Thatched and timbered houses in the village include the Cross Keys pub. Tremendous views over the Ouzel Valley from the Norman castle mound up on top of Totternhoe Knolls, a chalk grassland nature reserve.

TOTTINGTON Greater Manchester SD7712
Town on B6213, 2 miles (3km) NW of Bury
Mainly a farming and residential area with some attractive streets. The Dungeon dates from 1835 and is of unknown origin.

TOTTON Hampshire SU3613
Town on A35, 4 miles (6km) W of Southampton
On the lowest bridging point of the River Test, once a small village, now large. It developed from the later 19th century, with much industry. Lower Test nature reserve is marshy. New Forest butterfly farm and Longdown dairy farm to the south.

TOW LAW Durham NZ1238
Village on A68, 8 miles (13km) NW of Bishop Auckland
Not an attractive place. Formerly a centre of coal and iron-ore mining, and headquarters of the Weardale Iron Company.

TOWCESTER Northamptonshire SP6948
Small town on A43, 8 miles (13km) SW of Northampton
Pronounced 'Toaster'. Roman town of *Lactodorum* on Watling Street (A5), where it crosses River Tove. Norman castle motte, near ironstone parish church, with tall tower. Medieval market town and 19th-century coaching centre, where A5 crosses Northampton–Oxford road. Saracen's Head appears in Dickens' *Pickwick Papers*. Numerous Georgian and earlier buildings. Italianate Town Hall. Racecourse is part of Easton Neston park.

TOWEDNACK Cornwall SW4838
Hamlet off B3306, 2 miles (3km) SW of St Ives
Winding lanes through moorland, scattered old farms and a little medieval church. Everything is made of granite.

TOWN YETHOLM Borders NT8228
see Kirk Yetholm

TOWNSHEND Cornwall SW5932
Village on B3280, 3 miles (5km) SE of Hayle
Peaceful, small and pretty village in the River Hayle Valley.

TOWY, RIVER Dyfed
River
Begins its journey above huge reservoir of Llyn Brianne. Flows through Llandovery and Carmarthen to Carmarthen Bay. Coracles (ancient fishing boats) sometimes work river at Carmarthen.

TRANENT Lothian NT4072

Town off A1, 4 miles (6km) E of Musselburgh

Industrial and mining town a little inland from Firth of Forth. Church dates from 1800 with 1587 dovecote near by.

TRAPRAIN LAW Lothian NT5874

Hill off A1, 2 miles (3km) SW of East Linton

Distinctively shaped hill (734ft/220m) and well-known landmark formed by volcanic activity. Site of largest southeast Scottish Iron Age fort, surrounded by turf ramparts, inhabited until the 5th century. Excavations in 1919 uncovered remarkable collection of Roman silver including jugs, bowls, goblets and spoons, dating from about 415AD. Silver now in National Museum of Antiquities, Edinburgh.

TRAQUAIR Borders NT3334

Village on B709, 1 mile (2km) S of Innerleithen

Attractive village with 13th-century Traquair House, Scotland's oldest inhabited house, at its centre. This has strong Jacobite associations, and the Bear Gates to the main avenue have been closed since 1745; they will traditionally re-open when the Stewarts are reinstalled. Eighteenth-century working brewery with extensive gardens which produces renowned Traquair Ale.

TRAWDEN Lancashire SD9138

Village off A6068, 2 miles (3km) SE of Colne

Good starting point for walks up Pendle Hill. Nearby moorland is characterised by 'hushings' – mounds, gorges and piles of stone left from open-cast mining.

TRAWSFYNYDD Gwynedd SH7035

Village off A470, 4 miles (6km) S of Ffestiniog

Made famous by Britain's first inland nuclear power station, opened in 1965 on man-made lake. Now being decommissioned but open for tours.

TRE'R-DDÔL Dyfed SN6592

Village off A487, 2 miles (3km) N of Talybont

Village near Dovey estuary and its National Nature Reserve, a combination of sand dunes and beach at Ynyslas, the raised bog of Cors Fochno, and estuary waters rich in wildfowl and migrant wading birds. Visitor centre, trail. Village's Yr Hen Gapel (The Old Chapel) is a Wesleyan chapel of 1845 housing a folk collection.

TREALES Lancashire SD4432

Village off A585, 1 mile (2km) NE of Kirkham

Rural settlement of farms and thatched cottages, part of a large parish which includes Wharles and Roseacre.

TREBARWITH Cornwall SX0586

Hamlet off B3263, 2 miles (3km) S of Tintagel

Wild remote slate coast near Tintagel (see) with Trebarwith Strand sandy beach. Slate has been quarried from the cliffs.

TREBETHERICK Cornwall SW9378

Village off B3314, 5 miles (8km) NW of Wadebridge

The Norman church, with its little 13th-century spire, was buried in the sand dunes, and dug out in 1863. John Betjeman is buried here. Lovely setting on the Camel estuary.

TRECASTLE Powys SN8829

Village on A40, 8 miles (13km) SE of Llandovery

Small Norman motte and bailey survives in this village on northern boundary of Brecon Beacons National Park.

Traquair House.

TREDEGAR Gwent SO1409

Town on A4048, 21 miles (33km) N of Cardiff

Industrial town, at top of Sirhowy Valley. Town's focal point, a sturdy iron clock, symbolises Tredegar's metal-smelting past. Bedwellty House, now occupied by the local authority, was 19th-century ironmaster's house. On reclaimed land to the north is Bryn Bach Park, whose lake is popular for fishing and watersports.

TREDINGTON Gloucestershire SO9029

Village off A38, 2 miles (3km) S of Tewkesbury

Big, much-worn fossil of the prehistoric ichthyosaurus in porch floor is a unique feature of the sturdy Norman church here.

TREDINNICK Cornwall SW9270

Village off A39, 4 miles (6km) SW of Wadebridge

Small old stone village. Shire Horse Adventure Park to the south.

TREEN Cornwall SW3923

Village on B3315, 3 miles (5km) SE of Land's End

Unspoilt but windswept granite village. The famous Logan Rock used to balance on the cliff, moving at a touch, but after being pushed down the cliff in 1824 and replaced it lost its delicate balance.

The modern sign at the inn in Treen, recalling the overturning in 1824 of the Logan Rock.

TREETON South Yorkshire SK4387

Village on B6067, 3 miles (5km) S of Rotherham

Attractive village built mainly from red and yellow sandstone. Framing was the main industry until a pit was sunk in 1875 (closed in 1990).

TREFRIW Gwynedd SH7863

Village on B5106, 2 miles (3km) NW of Llanrwst

On western flank of beautiful Conwy Valley. Village is best known for two attractions: Trefriw Woollen Mill, in production since about 1830, illustrates the traditional processes of turning wool into cloth; the local chalybeate springs, discovered by the Romans, were developed into a tourist attraction by the Victorians. Original Roman cave and Victorian bathhouse survive, with tastings of mineral water.

TREGARON Dyfed SN6759

Small town on A485, 10 miles (16km) NE of Lampeter

Small market town in remote uplands on tributary of River Teifi at western end of daunting Abergwesyn Pass. The 19th-century cattle drovers gathered in the square for their long and arduous trek to the English markets. Cors Caron Nature Reserve (noted for birdlife) consists of three raised peat bogs either side of the River Teifi.

TREGONY Cornwall SW9245

Village on B3287, 7 miles (11km) SW of St Austell

A port in medieval times, before the river silted. Long steep main street, with stone, cob and thatch. Victorian clock tower.

TREGYNON Powys SO0998

Village off B4389, 5 miles (8km) N of Newtown

In rolling farmland, home of splendid half-timbered Gregynog Hall, bequeathed to University of Wales by wealthy Davies sisters, grand-daughters of philanthropic industrialist David Davies.

TREHARRIS Mid Glamorgan ST0996

Small town on A4054, 5 miles (8km) N of Pontypridd

Industrial community in Taff Valley between Pontypridd and Merthyr Tydfil, next to oddly named Quaker's Yard, a Quaker burial ground.

TREHERBERT Mid Glamorgan SS9498

Village on A4061, 10 miles (16km) NW of Pontypridd

This former industrial village was the scene of the first mining of the world-famous Rhondda steam coal, at the Bute Merthyr Colliery.

TRELLECK Gwent SO5005

Village on B4293, 5 miles (8km) S of Monmouth

Quiet spot, once capital of the area, full of historical interest. Prehistoric standing stones (Harold Stones), ancient church and well.

TREMADOG Gwynedd SH5640

Village on A498, 1 mile (2km) N of Porthmadog

Spacious, well-planned early 19th-century village designed to be part of recognised route to Ireland which never materialised. Birthplace of TE Lawrence, 'Lawrence of Arabia'.

TREMATON Cornwall SX3959

Village off A38, 2 miles (3km) W of Saltash

Market gardening area. The castle (not open), to the southeast, is a substantial ruin with a Georgian house inserted.

TREMEIRCHION Clwyd SJ0873
Village on B5429, 5 miles (8km) NE of Denbigh
On the hillside above the Vale of Clwyd. Old church has memorial tablet to local lady, Hester Piozzi, formerly Mrs Thrale, Doctor Johnson's close friend.

TRENT Dorset ST5918
Village off A359, 3 miles (5km) NE of Yeovil
Lots of golden-orange limestone houses and cottages, some late medieval, and an interesting church with the best wooden screen in the county, 13th century and fan-vaulted.

TRENT, RIVER Nottinghamshire
River
Major Midlands river, rising near Biddulph Moor, Staffordshire, flowing southeast through the Potteries and Stoke-on-Trent, then northeast through brewery town of Burton, and beside test cricket ground and National Water Sports Centre at Nottingham. On through Newark and Gainsborough (tidal bore, or aegir) to join River Ouse and flow through Humber estuary into North Sea.

TRENTHAM Staffordshire SJ8641
Village on A5035, on S outskirts of Stoke-on-Trent
Trentham Gardens, an immensely popular pleasure park, occupies grounds once owned by Duke of Sutherland. Interesting church by Charles Barry.

TRENTISHOE Devon SS6448
Hamlet off A39, 5 miles (8km) W of Lynton
A remote settlement, set back from the rocky cliffs and comprising only a farm and a little church, where the musicians' gallery is so small it needed a hole for the bass viol. See Heddon's Mouth.

TREORCHY Mid Glamorgan SS9596
Town on A4061, 9 miles (14km) NW of Pontypridd
Terraced industrial town, once capital of the Rhondda Fawr Valley, known for the celebrated Treorchy Male Voice Choir.

TREREIFE Cornwall SW4529
Hamlet off A30, 2 miles (3km) W of Penzance
This little inland hamlet has an animal park, a brass-rubbing centre and farm displays.

TRESCO Isles of Scilly SV8915
Island of the Scilly group
The second largest of the Scilly isles, Treso is a private estate with no cars, only farm tractors. The island is wild and barren in the north, while its central section has green fields and cottages. Tresco Abbey Gardens are world-renowned subtropical gardens, housing the Shipwreck Museum at Valhalla, which contains figure-heads and sternplates from wrecks around the islands. Cromwell's Castle was built in 1651, and King Charles's Castle 100 years before.

TRESHNISH ISLANDS Strathclyde
Islands in the Inner Hebrides, SE of Coll
Group of uninhabited rocky islands, the largest being Lunga, noted for seabirds, particularly puffins. Aptly-named Dutchman's Cap forms distinctive landmark.

TRESILLIAN Cornwall SW8646
Village on A39, 3 miles (5km) NE of Truro
At the head of a lovely estuary, this village is rather dominated by the main road. The Wheel inn was used as Parliamentarian headquarters when the Royalist forces surrendered at the bridge here in 1646.

TRETIRE Hereford and Worcester SO5223
Hamlet off B4521, 5 miles (8km) W of Ross-on-Wye
Victorian church and 18th-century old rectory form the heart of this tranquil hamlet in hills west of Ross-on-Wye.

TRETOWER Powys SO1821
Village on A479, 3 miles (5km) NW of Crickhowell
Peaceful village in Brecon Beacons National Park. Tretower Court and Castle (Cadw) a cluster of medieval buildings unmatched in Wales. Medieval-style garden also.

TREVOSE Cornwall SW8675
Hamlet off B3276, 4 miles (6km) W of Padstow
Remote and scenic rocky headland, with a lighthouse of 1847 to warn shipping. Toll road to Trevose Head.

TRIMDON Durham NZ3634
Village on B1278, 3 miles (5km) N of Sedgefield
Norman church built on a mound in the village centre. Fiction writer Mary Stewart lived here as a child when her father was the vicar.

TRIMINGHAM Norfolk TG2838
Village on B1159, 4 miles (6km) SE of Cromer
North Norfolk coastal village with a church dedicated to the Head of John the Baptist. Plenty of exquisite wood-carving by a former rector.

TRIMLEY, ST MARTIN AND ST MARY Suffolk TM2736
Villages off A14, 2 miles (3km) NW of Felixstowe
Twin villages of Trimley St Martin and Trimley St Mary have their churches in one graveyard. Elizabethan adventurer Thomas Cavendish lived here.

TRING Hertfordshire SP9211
Town off A41, 5 miles (8km) NW of Berkhamsted
Nicely set in a gap in the Chilterns. Stuffed and pre-served creatures ranging from giant sloths to fleas, collected by the 2nd Lord Rothschild, are shown in the amazing zoological museum. The Rose and Crown inn of 1905 is another Rothschild creation. Victorianised church. Grand Union Canal walks and wildfowl at Tring Reservoirs, towpath walk to Hemel Hempstead (see).

TROON Cornwall SW6638
Village off B3303, 2 miles (3km) SE of Camborne
Miners' village, with many Victorian terraces and remains of tin mines.

TROON Strathclyde NS3230
Town on A759, 6 miles (10km) N of Ayr
Seaside town which developed as coal-port for Ireland in early 19th century, with boat-building a secondary industry. Today a holiday resort town with excellent

Bridge across the River Rother at Trotton.

sandy beaches and five golf courses; more golf is played here than anywhere else in Scotland. Three miles (5km) offshore lies Lady Isle, a bird sanctuary.

TROSSACHS, THE Central

Scenic area, N of Aberfoyle

The name Trossachs, meaning 'bristly country', was applied originally to the narrow gorge which runs between Loch Katrine and Loch Achray. Today, the term is applied to the whole area between Callander and Loch Lomond, one of the loveliest parts of the Highlands, with a wide variety of landscape and easy access from Scotland's most populous urban districts. Sir Walter Scott did much to popularise the area through his writings, and visits by Queen Victoria and growing admiration for the folk-hero, Rob Roy MacGregor, indubitably helped. Scenically, the mountains stretching east to Ben Ledi from the northern end of Loch Lomond complement the hilly wooded landscape around Lochs Katrine, Achray and Vennachar. This diversity provides a range of habitats for vegetation, animals, birds and flora.

Forestry provides employment and led to the creation of the Queen Elizabeth Forest Park, a huge recreational area run by the Forestry Commission. At Loch Katrine, Trossachs holiday-makers can cruise the loch's length by steamer. All in all, the area's outdoor facilities and scenic beauty have combined to make tourism of increasing importance.

TROSTON Suffolk TL8972

Village off A1088, 3 miles (5km) NW of Ixworth

Beautiful Troston has a handsome 17th-century hall, and a church with some lovely medieval wall-paintings. Famous residents include Edward Lefft, who edited Shakespeare's plays and published them as a 10-volume edition. His nephew, Capel Lefft, worked with Wilberforce to end the slave trade. He was also a patron of the village poet Robert Blomefield.

TROTTERNISH Highland (Skye) NG4552

Peninsula N of Portree

Scenic peninsula in northeast Skye with unusual geological features formed by volcanic upheavals; Trotternish Ridge is Britain's longest landslip. Local employment from crofting and fishing.

TROTTISCLIFFE Kent TQ6460

Village off A20, 1 mile (2km) N of Wrotham Heath

Pronounced 'Trosley', an old village of weatherboarded houses just beneath the North Downs, with a fascinating church including parts of a former palace of the bishops of Rochester. Nearby Trosley Country Park covers 160 acres (65ha) of downland, and includes three waymarked paths, one to Coldrum Stones, a neolithic long barrow excavated in 1910 to reveal 22 skeletons and given to the National Trust in 1926.

TROTTON West Sussex SU8322

Hamlet on A272, 3 miles (5km) W of Midhurst

Pleasant sandstone village with a superb early 15th-century bridge over the River Rother and a church famed for 14th-century wall-paintings.

TROUGH OF BOWLAND Lancashire SD6253

Scenic area NW of Dunsop Bridge

The largest area of unspoiled and remote countryside in Lancashire. Moors rise to 1,804ft (550m) to give breathtaking views.

TROUTBECK Cumbria NY3827

Village off A5091, 3 miles (5km) N of Windermere

An unspoilt village which gets its name from the river, Trout Beck. Beatrix Potter lived in the village, at Troutbeck Farm, and her flock of Herdwick sheep remain. Townend, built in 1626, is a yeoman farmer's house. Now owned by the National Trust, the Browne family collections are open to the public.

TROWBRIDGE Wiltshire ST8557
Town off A363, 8 miles (13km) SE of Bath
The county town of Wiltshire, although not large, has been an important cloth-making town from medieval times and has Victorian mill buildings and many Georgian stone houses, some large and grand. There is a pretty 15th-century church (very restored) and many late 19th-century churches and chapels. Local museum.

TROWELL Nottinghamshire SK4839
Village on A6007, immediately SE of Ilkeston
Beside River Erewash, on Derbyshire border, and close to M1 motorway. Medieval church. Victorian hall. Chosen as Festival of Britain Village in 1951.

TRULL Somerset ST2122
Village off A38, 2 miles (3km) S of Taunton
Scattered old farms and more recent centre. The attractive medieval church has a unique wooden pulpit of about 1500, complete with all its figures of saints.

TRUMPINGTON Cambridgeshire TL4454
District on A1301, on S edge of Cambridge
Straddling the old Cambridge–London road, a village with ancient origins. Sir Roger de Trumpington was a knight, and his brass, the second oldest in England, dates from 1289. It can be seen in the lovely Parish Church of St Mary and St Nicholas. Near by is Byron's Pool, a peaceful backwater of the River Cam.

TRUNCH Norfolk TG2834
Village off B1145, 3 miles (5km) N of North Walsham
In the heart of 'flint country', with many flint-built buildings. Famous for the grave of Nelson's son by his mistress, Lady Hamilton.

TRURO Cornwall SW8244
City off A39, 13 miles (21km) SW of St Austell
The county town of Cornwall was a medieval stannary town where tin was taken to be weighed and taxed, and the principal port for tin. It became a city in 1887, and a huge new cathedral was designed in 1880 by JL Pearson, the first Anglican cathedral to be built in England since St Paul's in London.

Little remains of Truro's medieval past, but there are many later Georgian buildings, most impressively in wide Lemon Street, full of austere classical houses. The centre has more Victorian architecture, and is very varied. Notable buildings include the classical granite city hall of 1846 and there is much Regency and Victorian stucco. The town is dominated by the cathedral, with its three towers, stone-vaulted inside and rather French in style.

The wide river was used for cargoes into the 20th century and now has an attractive walk beside it. The Royal Cornwall museum has extensive displays on the county.

TRUSLEY Derbyshire SK2535
Village off A516, 6 miles (10km) W of Derby
Trusley Hall, part of a Tudor brick house with separate Elizabethan summer house. Small brick church dating from 1713, with original furnishings.

TRUSTHORPE Lincolnshire TF5183
Small town, immediately S of Mablethorpe
Seaside village with pleasant sandy beaches between Mablethorpe and Sutton on Sea. Holiday centres provide entertainment and amenities.

TUCKENHAY Devon SX8156
Hamlet off A381, 3 miles (5km) S of Totnes
Industrial hamlet on a creek at the head of the Dart estuary, founded in 1806. Picturesque, with many warehouses remaining.

TUFNELL PARK Greater London TQ2985
District in borough of Islington
Inconspicuous suburb north of Kentish Town (see), largely Victorian in character. Holloway Prison for women was rebuilt in the 1970s.

TUFTON Hampshire SU4546
Hamlet off A34, 1 mile (2km) SW of Whitchurch
Farming hamlet in the Test Valley, with some thatched cottages and a little medieval church.

TULLIBARDINE Tayside NN9113
Site off A823, 2 miles (3km) W of Auchterarder
Pre-Reformation Collegiate Church at Tullibardine Chapel (1446). Cruciform sandstone church with tower and tracery windows; interior has fine timber roof and carvings.

TULLIBODY Central NS8695
Town on A907, 2 miles (3km) NW of Alloa
Village situated near the junction of the River Devon with the Forth estuary. Ruins of medieval St Serf's Church, destroyed during the Reformation in 1559.

TULLYNESSIE Grampian NJ5519
Village off A944, 3 miles (5km) NW of Alford
Terpersie Castle stands near by, an early Z-plan castle dating from 1561 with two round towers at opposite corners of the main block.

TULSE HILL Greater London TQ3173
District in borough of Lambeth
Originally developed early in the 19th century for a well-to-do clientele. Ornamental lakes and a walled garden in Brockwell Park.

TUMBY Lincolnshire TF2359
Hamlet on A155, 2 miles (3km) NE of Tattershall
Early 19th-century Tumby Lawn, close to disused Horncastle Canal and oak and larch woods.

TUMMEL BRIDGE Tayside NN7659
Site on B846, 6 miles (10km) E of Kinloch Rannoch
Tiny village at west end of Loch Tummel with Wade bridge across River Tummel and hydro-electric power station. Known for low winter temperatures.

TUNBRIDGE WELLS Kent TQ5839
Town on A26, 31 miles (50km) SE of London
This cheerful former spa town grew up amid the Wealden forests after Lord North discovered its chalybeate spring in 1606. Until that time there were only a

few scattered cottages and farms hereabouts, so Tunbridge Wells has no medieval or Tudor buildings. The initial visitors roughed it in cottages, lodged in nearby towns or, like Queen Henrietta Maria, camped out on the common.

Building began in 1638 when a grassy promenade, called The Walk, was laid out beside the medicinal spring and visitors 'took the waters' in the morning and socialised afterwards. Later The Walk was paved with square earthenware tiles, giving rise to its present name, The Pantiles.

Tunbridge Wells grew haphazardly and informally, and is a very attractive town, its charm arising from 18th- and 19th-century elegance including Decimus Burton's Calverley Park and Calverly Park Terrace and the buildings on Mount Sion and Mount Ephrahim. The common is a superb open space, while the most famous area, The Pantiles, is in effect an 18th-century shopping precinct: a raised paved walkway shaded by lime trees, and fronted by shops behind a colonnade, which gives uniformity to otherwise varied architecture.

TUNSTALL Kent TQ8961
Village on B2163, 1 mile (2km) SW of Sittingbourne
Pretty village-cum-suburb of Sittingbourne among the Kentish orchards, with some old houses and a restored 14th-century church.

TUNSTALL Lancashire SD6073
Village on A683, 3 miles (5km) S of Kirkby Lonsdale
Tunstall church now stands alone on the site where the village originally stood. Charlotte Brontë and her sisters came to church here while at a nearby school.

Thirteenth-century ironwork on the south door of the church at Tunstead, Norfolk.

TUNSTALL Staffordshire SJ8651
Town, part of Stoke-on-Trent
Most northerly of towns making up Stoke-on-Trent is no beauty, but enthusiasts for no-nonsense Victorian architecture will enjoy a stroll.

TUNSTALL Suffolk TM3555
Village on B1078, 4 miles (6km) E of Wickham Market
On the edge of a rolling heath, Tunstall has St Michael's Church with its tall, slender, late medieval tower.

TUNSTEAD Derbyshire SK1074
Village off B6049, 2 miles (3km) NW of Miller's Dale
Quarried for limestone since 1929, and therefore kept just outside boundary drawn for Peak National Park in 1951. Birthplace of engineer James Brindley.

TUNSTEAD Norfolk TG3022
Hamlet off A1151, 4 miles (6km) N of Wroxham
A history of prosperity in weaving explains Tunstead's handsome 14th-century church. There are fine painted screens and an unusual windowless clerestory.

TUR LANGTON Leicestershire SP7194
Village off A6, 5 miles (8km) N of Market Harborough
Early 17th-century manor house, part of once-larger building. Thirteenth-century remnant of old church. High Victorian brick St Andrew's Church, 1865–6, by H Goddard and Son.

TURKDEAN Gloucestershire SP1017
Village off A40, 2 miles (3km) N of Northleach
A beech avenue joins the two halves of this pleasant village set on a wooded hillside, with its handsome houses and engrossing church.

TURNBERRY Strathclyde NS2005
Village on A77, 5 miles (8km) N of Girvan
Mainly renowned for seaside golf course, overlooked by the famous Turnberry hotel, which incorporates promontory with lighthouse and ruins of Turnberry Castle.

TURNER'S HILL West Sussex TQ3435
Village on B2110, 4 miles (6km) SW of East Grinstead
Hilltop village, with attractive village street, old inn, a church with interesting reredos reputedly from a demolished Wren church, and a magnificent view over the Weald.

TURRIFF Grampian NJ7249
Town on A947, 9 miles (14km) S of Banff
Historic and busy service and market town with 1557 mercat cross and ruins of 11th-century church. Annual Turriff Show is a major European agricultural event.

TURTON BOTTOMS Lancashire SD7315
Village off B6391, 4 miles (6km) N of Bolton
Turton Tower is a beautiful medieval manor house standing in 8 acres (3ha) of gardens and woodland. The oldest part is a 15th-century pele tower, the rest being a 16th-century half-timbered farmhouse. Jumbles Country Park and Reservoir provides a popular leisure facility.

TURVEY Bedfordshire SP9452
Village on A428, 7 miles (11km) W of Bedford
A handsome village on the Great Ouse, whose flood levels are marked on the Three Fyshes pub wall. Mordaunt monuments can be seen in the notable church.

TURVILLE Buckinghamshire SU7691
Village off B480, 5 miles (8km) N of Henley-on-Thames
A pretty village in a remote and beguiling valley, containing a Victorianised church, a 1950s bungalow by Erno Goldfinger and an excellent pub, and offering fine views from Turville Hill.

TUTBURY Staffordshire SK2128
Small town on A50, 4 miles (6km) NW of Burton upon Trent
Market town beside River Dove, where timber-framed Dog and Partridge pub stands among other harmonious buildings in High Street. Remains of castle where Mary Stuart was imprisoned are a major attraction, and so is the very fine medieval church with its stunning doorway. Tutbury Crystal Glass, Georgian Crystal Company and Roundhouse Gallery (ceramics and glass) welcome visitors.

TUXFORD Nottinghamshire SK7371
Village off A1, 7 miles (11km) S of Retford
Mainly Georgian village, formerly a market town, rebuilt after fire in 1702, at crossing of Great North road with Lincoln–Ollerton road. Church with 14th-century tower and spire, 1495 chancel, 18th-century north chancel chapel widened for monuments of White family. Georgian Newcastle Arms. Seventeenth-century grammar school, now a library. Remains of two tower windmills.

TWEED, RIVER Borders
River
Fourth longest Scottish river, which in places forms the border with England. It rises in the hills above Moffat and flows east through Peebles, Melrose and Kelso to reach the North Sea at Berwick. Deep pools and pebble banks have kept it a beautiful river, free from manufacturing and long famous for its salmon-fishing.

TWEEDMOUTH Northumberland NT9952
Village on A1167, on the estuary of the River Tweed
A small village, once a busy port on the estuary of the River Tweed, now overshadowed by Berwick.

TWEEDSMUIR Borders NT0924
Village on A701, 8 miles (12km) S of Broughton
Village at foot of Talla Reservoir, built in 1905 to provide Edinburgh's water. Writer John Buchan took title Lord Tweedsmuir. Inscribed 1685 Covenanters' Stone in churchyard.

TWICKENHAM Greater London TQ1673
District in borough of Richmond
A suburb with 18th-century memories. Marble Hill House, a grand 1720s villa, has grounds running down to the River Thames and Orleans House, with its handsome Octagon of the same period, is an art gallery. Horace Walpole's 'Gothick' villa at Strawberry Hill (not open) is now a training college. Twickenham rugby football ground is Rugby Union's premier stadium and headquarters of the game.

TWIGWORTH Gloucestershire SO8422
Village on A38, 3 miles (5km) N of Gloucester
Ivor Gurney, poet and composer, lies in the churchyard here. Appealing array of wildlife art displayed at the Nature in Art gallery at Wallsworth Hall.

TWINEHAM West Sussex TQ2519
Hamlet off A23, 1 mile (2km) W of Hickstead
A scattered hamlet deep in the Weald on two streams of the River Adur, with several ancient farmsteads and a rare Tudor church built in brick.

TWIZEL BRIDGE Northumberland NT8843
Bridge over River Till, close to confluence with the Tweed, 3 miles (5km) S of Norham
A single-arched 15th-century bridge over the River Till, which provided the turning point of the Battle of Flodden Field.

Twizel Bridge over the River Till.

TWO BRIDGES Devon SX6075
Hamlet on B3357, 8 miles (13km) E of Tavistock
On the only major road junction on Dartmoor, a lonely valley with a few buildings and two bridges, one of 1780, over the West Dart River. The South Devon railway (steam) runs along the Dart Valley to Buckfastleigh (see).

TWYCROSS Leicestershire SK3304
Village on B4116, 5 miles (8km) NE of Atherstone
Twycross House, red and blue chequered brick front, 1703. Manor Farm, about 1712. Outstanding 13th-century French stained glass in east window of church. For Twycross Zoo, see Norton-juxta-Twycross.

TWYFORD Berkshire SU7876
Town off A4, 5 miles (8km) E of Reading
Set on the River Lodden, Twyford has a double stream and many lakes from gravel-digging. Largely Victorian brick, but some Georgian and even earlier buildings.

TWYFORD Buckinghamshire SP6626
Village off A421, 6 miles (10km) NE of Bicester
A haven of peace close to the Oxfordshire border. The church embraces all periods since Norman.

TWYFORD Hampshire SU4824
Village on B3335, 3 miles (5km) S of Winchester
Large village with much Georgian brick, a striped flint and brick church of 1876, Twyford Waterworks of 1900, and Marwell Zoo, extensive and very good.

TWYFORD Leicestershire SK7210
Village on B674, 6 miles (10km) S of Melton Mowbray
Named from two fords that spanned the brook. In 1826, mourners came from afar to burial of Absalom Smith, king of the gypsies.

TWYFORD Norfolk TG0124
Village on A1067, 7 miles (11km) SE of Fakenham
Twyford Hall has parts dating from medieval times, and stands in a park that adjoins the churchyard. The church porch has a wooden cupola.

TWYWELL Northamptonshire SP9578
Village off A604, 3 miles (5km) W of Thrapston
Unlikely rural England location for editing of Livingstone's African journals, by 19th-century rector Horace Waller, the explorer's friend. Carved African animals decorate the choir stalls.

TYBERTON Hereford and Worcester SO3839
Village on B4352, 8 miles (13km) W of Hereford
Village lies below steep wooded hills, and its 18th-century church is worth visiting for fine interior containing superb woodwork and furnishings.

TYDD ST GILES Cambridgeshire TF4216
Village on B1165, 5 miles (8km) NW of Wisbech
Adrian IV, the only English pope (1154–9) was possibly curate here. Church is 12th to 13th century, but partly demolished during 19th-century restoration.

TYLDESLEY Greater Manchester SD6902
Town on A577, 5 miles (8km) SW of Bolton
A small industrial town with coal-mining country to the north and Chat Moss to the south.

TYNDRUM Central NN3330
Village on A82, 5 miles (8km) NW of Crianlarich
Highland village on main route west with good rail and road connections. Surrounded by fine mountains, where there is recent gold-mining activity.

TYNE, RIVER Lothian
River
Rises in Moorfoot Hills and runs mainly northeast through fertile country, passing Haddington and East Linton en route, to reach North Sea near Dunbar.

TYNE, RIVER Tyne & Wear
River
An attractive river in its upper reaches formed from the Rivers North and South Tyne which join near Hexham to form the River Tyne. The banks of the river, in the city of Newcastle, have been revitalised to create an attractive area for pleasure activities. Nearer the North Sea it becomes more industrialised, dominated by the steel industry and ship-building.

TYNEHAM Dorset SY8880
Deserted village off A351, 5 miles (8km) SW of Wareham
Deserted village at the centre of the huge estate taken over by the army in 1943 for a firing range. Display in the church, accessible when no firing. Lovely coast.

TYNEMOUTH Tyne and Wear NZ3669
Town on A193, 8 miles (13km) E of Newcastle
Coastal town with long maritime history. Ancient kings of Northumbria are buried by ruins of Tynemouth Castle and priory. Above headland rocks known as Black Middens is a 50ft (15m) statue of Lord Collingwood, hero at Battle of Trafalgar. Sandy beaches at Long Sands.

TYNINGHAME Lothian NT6179
Village on B1407, 2 miles (3km) NE of East Linton
Attractive estate village built in the 17th century to serve Tyninghame House, which was transformed in 1820s into a Scottish baronial mansion.

TYNRON Dumfries and Galloway NX8093
Village off A702, 2 miles (3km) NE of Moniaive
Small upland village. Tynron Doon ramparts have signs of occupation from Iron Age to 16th century.

TYNWALD HILL Isle of Man SC2781
Hill at St John's, 3 miles (5km) SE of Peel
A stepped hill which dates back over 1,000 years, the meeting site of the Manx Parliament. The Tynwald ceremony is held here each July.

TYRINGHAM Buckinghamshire SP8547
Hamlet off B526, 2 miles (3km) N of Newport Pagnell
An imposing gateway by Sir John Soane gives access to the massively impressive Tyringham House, now a private medical centre. A humped bridge crosses the Great Ouse.

TYSELEY West Midlands SP1083
District in SE Birmingham
The Birmingham Railway Museum (limited opening) has brought new life to this old residential and industrial quarter of Birmingham.

TYWARDREATH Cornwall SX0854
Village off A390, 5 miles (8km) E of St Austell
A big village, old in the centre, with Menabilly, the house where novelist Daphne du Maurier lived for 21 years. Polkerris is a picturesque fishing hamlet.

TYWYN Gwynedd SH5800
Town on A493, 10 miles (16km) W of Machynlleth
Coastal town-cum-seaside-resort on Cardigan Bay. Long sandy beach, dunes, promenade. Home of Talyllyn Railway, the narrow-gauge Great Little Train with the longest continuous service in Wales (opened 1865). Runs into mountains near Abergynolwyn. Railway museum at station. Church contains famous St Cadfan's Stone, said to bear the earliest example of written Welsh (estimated 7th century).

U

UBLEY Avon ST5258
Village off A368, 2 miles (3km) E of Blagdon
Red sandstone church and cottages, mixed with modern development.

UCKFIELD East Sussex TQ4721
Town off A26, 8 miles (13km) NE of Lewes
In the wooded Weald on the River Uck, this pleasant old town, once a centre for the iron industry, has an attractive High Street which descends a hill towards the railway. Georgian buildings in the upper part and Victorian and neo-Georgian lower down. There are modern suburbs and modern light industries.

UDDINGSTON Strathclyde NS6960
Town off M74, 2 miles (3km) NW of Bothwell
Manufacturing town to southeast of Glasgow on River Clyde with good road and rail links throughout central Scotland.

UDIMORE East Sussex TQ8718
Village on B2089, 4 miles (6km) W of Rye
Strung along a ridge between the rivers Brede and Tillingham, with views southwards to Fairlight and Winchelsea; the church of 1170, rebuilt in the 13th century, is down a lane to the south.

UDNY GREEN Grampian NJ8826
Village off A920, 5 miles (8km) E of Oldmeldrum
Village with Udney Castle, five-storeyed 16th-century tower house. Mort House protected corpses against body-snatchers.

UFFCULME Devon ST0612
Village off B3391, 5 miles (8km) NE of Cullompton
This large village, with a square at the centre, has a handsome church with an impressive early 15th-century fan-vaulted screen. Coldharbour Mill is now a working museum, with a big building of 1799, producing woollen yarn.

UFFINGTON Lincolnshire TF0607
Village on A16, 2 miles (3km) E of Stamford
Stone-built, at southern edge of the county. Uffington House burned down in 1904, leaving the splendid gate-piers. Seventeenth-century cottages, Georgian lodges and 19th-century estate housing.

UFFINGTON Oxfordshire SU3089
Village off B4508, 4 miles (6km) S of Faringdon
Village gives its name to famous White Horse (English Heritage), 3,000-year-old chalk figure carved into hill to south. Near it is Iron Age hillfort called Uffington Castle (National Trust). Uffington itself is notable for its many buildings constructed of chalk, and St Mary's is a 13th-century church so unspoilt that it has its original door hinges.

UFFINGTON Shropshire SJ5213
Village off B5062, 3 miles (5km) E of Shrewsbury
Beneath wooded Haughmond Hill. Church with old Continental glass. To northeast are substantial ruins of Haughmond Abbey (English Heritage).

UFFORD Suffolk TM2952
Village off A1152, 3 miles (5km) NE of Woodbridge
A huddle of charming thatched cottages on the River Deben. Uffa, the Saxon from whom the village takes its name, was the founder of the dynasty connected to the fascinating archaeological discoveries at Sutton Hoo. The 15th-century font cover at St Mary's Church is said to be the finest in the country.

UFTON NERVET Berkshire SU6367
Village off A4, 6 miles (10km) SW of Reading
Rural and woody village, with a many-gabled big house dating from the 1570s.

The old stocks and whipping post outside the church at Ufford.

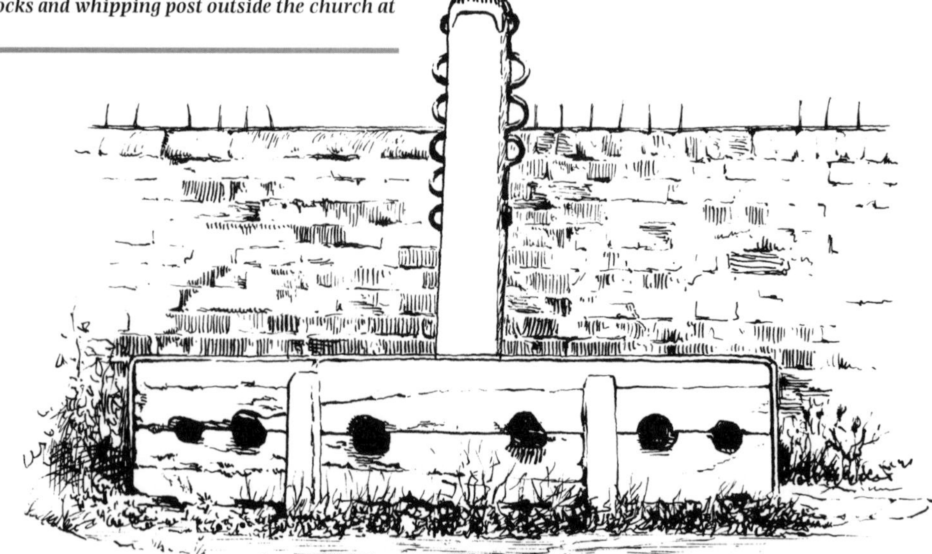

UGBOROUGH Devon SX6755
Village off A38, 3 miles (5km) E of Ivybridge
Just off Dartmoor, on a hill, with its 15th-century granite church set high. Impressive screen with painted figures of about 1525.

UGGLEBARNBY North Yorkshire NZ8707
Village off A169, 3 miles (5km) S of Whitby
An isolated settlement with the remains of two stone circles near by. Some features remain of a Norman church where the 19th-century church now stands.

UGLEY Essex TL5228
Village off B1383, 5 miles (8km) NE of Bishop's Stortford
An attractive place, despite its curious name. Bluebell woods, and a Victorian church on the hill.

UGTHORPE North Yorkshire NZ7911
Village off A171, 6 miles (10km) W of Whitby
A small village in a remote situation on the moors with an old windmill and some sturdy stone houses and farms.

UIG Highland (Skye) NG3963
Village on A856, on W coast of Trotternish peninsula
Village and Western Isles ferry terminal on sheltered bay off Loch Snizort. Landing point after Prince Charles Edward came 'over the sea to Skye'.

UIG Western Isles (Lewis) NB0534
Village off B8011, on W coast of Lewis
Village on sheltered bay where famous 12th-century Norse chessmen were discovered in 1831. Carved from walrus ivory, they are Europe's oldest authentic chess pieces.

ULBSTER Highland ND3240
Village on A9, 7 miles (11km) S of Wick
Cliff-top village in prehistorically rich area. Near by, the 365 Whaligoe Steps descend cliff to old herring station; women used to carry catch up in creels on their backs.

ULCEBY Lincolnshire TF4272
Village on A1028, 3 miles (5km) SW of Alford
In wooded Wolds setting. Brick church of 1826, interior restored 1885. Former rectory of 1850, The Peacocks, with huge columns supporting centre bay.

ULCOMBE Kent TQ8449
Village off A20, 3 miles (5km) SW of Harrietsham
Scattered village on the ragstone hills among orchards and hopfields. The village ascends a hill along the road to the church with panoramic Wealden views and a huge churchyard yew.

ULDALE Cumbria NY2436
Village off B5299, 7 miles (11km) S of Wigton
An isolated village whose name means 'wolf's dale'. Close by, at Aughertree, are the remains of a Roman camp.

ULEY Gloucestershire ST7998
Village on B4066, 2 miles (3km) E of Dursley
Wealth of interest in this old weaving village includes church exemplifying Victorian High Church principles, delightful houses and cottages around the green and two notable prehistoric sites on hills to northwest. Hetty Pegler's Tump is a big chambered long barrow (take a torch) and Uley Bury hillfort is an Iron Age camp with splendid views.

ULLAPOOL Highland NH1294
Small town on A835, 12 miles (18km) SW of Elphin
Planned 1788 fishing port laid out on grid pattern and beautifully situated in lovely Highland scenery near mouth of Loch Broom. Good harbour, much used recently by Eastern European factory fishing ships, known locally as Klondykers. Major tourist centre with good facilities including Ullapool Museum which tells local story. Ferry departure point for Stornoway in Outer Hebrides.

ULLENHALL Warwickshire SP1267
Village off A4189, 2 miles (3km) NW of Henley-in-Arden
A scattered settlement in a hilly landscape. The Victorian church has fine wagon roofs and the chancel of its medieval predecessor still stands.

ULLESTHORPE Leicestershire SP5087
Village on B577, 3 miles (5km) NW of Lutterworth
Moated site of former manor house. The 17th-century manor house now converted to a hotel and golf course. Shell of 1800 brick tower mill.

ULLINGSWICK Hereford and Worcester SO5949
Hamlet off A417, 8 miles (13km) NE of Hereford
At the centre of this small hill settlement a timber-framed farmhouse is neighbour to a church with medieval glass and unusual painted memorial.

ULLSWATER Cumbria NY4220
Lake on A592, N of Patterdale
The second largest lake in the Lake District, 7 miles (11km) long. The northern and western shorelines are National Trust owned. Often considered one of the most beautiful lakes, its setting is spectacular, in a steep glaciated valley. Cruisers serve the length of the lake from Glenridding to Pooley Bridge and Howtown.

ULPHA Cumbria SD1993
Village off A593, 4 miles (6km) N of Broughton-in-Furness
Pleasant village near the River Duddon. The church was restored in the 19th century but the 16th-century east window remains.

ULVA Strathclyde (Mull) NM3640
Island off W coast of Mull, S of Loch Tuacth
Sparsely inhabited island off west coast of Mull, mainly remembered as the scene of the elopement and drowning of 'Lord Ullin's Daughter' in ballad by Thomas Campbell.

ULVERSCROFT Leicestershire SK5012
Site off A50, 1 mile (2km) N of Markfield
Charnwood Forest ruins of Augustinian priory, founded 1174. Prior's lodgings incorporated into farmhouse. Near by, three summer cottages by Ernest Gimson, 1897–1908.

ULVERSTON Cumbria SD2878
Town on A590, 8 miles (13km) NE of Barrow-in-Furness
Market town with old buildings, cobbled streets and alleys, linked to the Leven estuary by England's shortest ship canal. Birthplace of Stan Laurel, the Laurel and Hardy Museum off the market square has photos, mementoes and a small cinema. On Hoad Hill is a monument to Sir John Barrow, founder of the Royal Geographic Society.

UMBERLEIGH Devon SS6023
Village on A377, 7 miles (11km) SE of Barnstaple
A hamlet in the valley of the River Taw, which has grown up around the railway station.

UNDERBARROW Cumbria SD4692
Village off B5284, 3 miles (5km) W of Kendal
A farming village, with a mild climate, in the Morecambe Bay horseshoe. It has won the Best Kept Village award on several occasions.

UNDERWOOD Nottinghamshire SK4750
Village on A608, 2 miles (5km) N of Eastwood
Near Derbyshire border. Victorian church, with a massive tower and an oak-shingled spire, built for Earl Cowper of Beauvale.

UNST Shetland
Island of the main Shetland group
Britain's most northerly island with impressive cliff scenery. Main port Baltasound, once an important herring-fishing base. Historic ruins include 12th-century Kirk of Lund and 1598 Muness Castle. Nature reserves at Hermaness, with cliff-nesting seabirds, and Keen of Hamar, with arctic flora. Employment from RAF base, fishing and crofting. Muckle Flugga Lighthouse stands on rock off Unsts's north coast.

UNTHANK Cumbria NY4436
Village on B5305, 5 miles (8km) NW of Penrith
Hutton-in-the-Forest was converted from an old medieval pele tower into a dwelling in 1605. It is open to the public.

UP CERNE Dorset ST6502
Hamlet on A352, 1 mile (2km) N of Cerne Abbas
Tiny hamlet in a lovely chalk valley.

UP EXE Devon SS9402
Village off A396, 6 miles (10km) N of Exeter
Scattered hamlet in the Exe Valley. Nether Exe to the south is even sparser, but has a tiny late medieval church.

UP HOLLAND Lancashire SD5205
Town on A577, 4 miles (6km) W of Wigan
Retains much original character with narrow, steep cobbled streets, many allowing lovely views of the Pennines, and 14th-century parish church.

UPAVON Wiltshire SU1355
Village on A345, 4 miles (6km) SW of Pewsey
Pretty village, with thatched cottages, flint and stone chequering, brick and timber-framing. RAF housing on outskirts and tank crossings on the roads.

UPCHURCH Kent TQ8467
Village off A2, 4 miles (6km) E of Gillingham
A little place amid orchards on the edge of the muddy creeks of the Medway estuary, with a large early 14th-century church where Sir Francis Drake's father was vicar.

UPHILL Avon ST3158
Suburb off A370, on S outskirts of Weston-super-Mare
Now joined up to Weston-super-Mare, but originally a separate village. Old St Nicholas Church (mostly Norman) is on its own, overlooking the Axe estuary. Summer ferry across to Brean (see).

UPLEADON Gloucestershire SO7526
Village off B4215, 2 miles (3km) E of Newent
Straggling village on the northern fringes of Forest of Dean. Its riverside church, away to the west, should not be missed.

Timbered 16th-century church tower at Upleadon.

UPLEATHAM Cleveland NZ6319
Village on B1268, 2 miles (3km) SW of Saltburn
Rural village in an ironstone region on northern edge of the Cleveland Hills. There are some original stone cottages, although some have become victims of subsidence, caused by the intensive mining. The Church of St Andrew claims to be smallest in England – a misnomer, as it is only the remains of a larger structure.

UPLYME Devon SY3293
Village on B3165, 2 miles (3km) NW of Lyme Regis
Woody and hilly village with some old cottages mixed with modern.

UPMINSTER Greater London TQ5686
Town in borough of Havering
Commuter suburb mainly developed between the wars at the far end of the London Underground District Line, with a Norman parish church, an impressive 1803 windmill (limited opening) and a magnificent late 14th-century tithe barn, which is now a museum (limited opening). Upminster Hall, of the 15th century and later, is now the golf clubhouse.

UPNOR, UPPER AND LOWER Kent TQ7570
Villages off A228, 2 miles (3km) NE of Strood
Medway villages with a church built in 1878, a flourishing yacht club and an Elizabethan gun station, Upnor Castle. The castle was built in 1561 looking across Upnor Reach to the Royal Naval Dockyards, Chatham (see), intended to guard them. At this it was singularly unsuccessful, for in 1667 the Dutch sailed past the castle, destroyed half the English fleet and sailed back unharmed.

UPOTTERY Devon ST2007
Village off A30, 5 miles (8km) NE of Honiton
Small and rural, with several buildings in the pretty early Victorian Tudor revival style.

UPPER ARLEY Hereford and Worcester SO7680
see Arley

UPPER BASILDON Berkshire SU6078
see Basildon

UPPER BEEDING West Sussex TQ1910
Village on A2037, 1 mile (2km) E of Steyning
A little street of cottages on the River Adur opposite Bramber, the site of a Norman priory. All around are bungalows and late 19th- and 20th-century houses.

UPPER BENEFIELD Northamptonshire SP9988
see Benefield

UPPER BROUGHTON Nottinghamshire SK6826
Village on A606, 6 miles (10km) NW of Melton Mowbray
Above Vale of Belvoir, close to Leicestershire border. Several timber-framed cottages. Medieval church with north aisle and chancel rebuilt by Teulon in 1855.

UPPER CANADA Avon ST3558
see Canada, Avon

UPPER CANTERTON Hampshire SU2612
Hamlet off B3078, 1 mile (2km) S of Brook
New Forest hamlet of a few cottages. The Rufus Stone marks the spot where William II, the unpopular son of the Conqueror, was killed while hunting.

UPPER CHEDDON Somerset ST2328
Village off A358, 2 miles (3km) N of Taunton
Victorian Hestercombe House has impressive Edwardian garden, designed by Lutyens and Gertrude Jekyll.

UPPER CLATFORD Hampshire SU3543
Village off A303, 1 mile (2km) S of Andover
Many thatched cottages in the middle, medieval church with very unusual double chancel arch, and a charming cast-iron bridge of 1843, made locally.

UPPER DICKER East Sussex TQ5510
see Dicker

UPPER EYETHORNE Kent TR2849
see Eyethorne

UPPER GRAVENHURST Bedfordshire TL1035
see Gravenhurst

UPPER HAMBLETON Leicestershire SK9007
Village off A606, 3 miles (5km) E of Oakham
On peninsula of Rutland Water, which drowned Nether Hambleton. Early 17th-century Hambleton Old hall. Hambleton Hall, 1881,is now a country house hotel. Estate cottages of 1892.

UPPER MILTON Somerset ST5447
Hamlet off A39, 1 mile (2km) N of Wells
On the slopes of the Mendips, with Milton Lodge Gardens, started in 1919, and an arboretum.

UPPER NITON Isle of Wight SZ5076
see Niton

UPPER NORWOOD Greater London TQ3369
District in boroughs of Lambeth and Croydon
Once wild, dangerous forest, now a blameless suburb. Big houses along Beulah Hill, a smart spa in the 1830s.

UPPER SHERINGHAM Norfolk TG1441
Village on B1157, 1 mile (2km) SW of Sheringham
Lying 1 mile (2km) inland from Sheringham (see), this pretty village among the heather and tree-clad hills has evidence of Roman occupation.

UPPER SLAUGHTER Gloucestershire SP1622
see Slaughter

UPPER SOUDLEY Gloucestershire SO6510
Village on B4227, 2 miles (3km) S of Cinderford
A school and a scatter of cottages make up this old iron-making hamlet in the wooded Soudley Valley. Good walking to north.

UPPER SUNDON Bedfordshire TL0428
Village off B579, 5 miles (8km) NW of Luton
Fine views to the north from Sundon Hills Country Park on the edge of chalk downs. Woodland walks.

UPPER SWELL Gloucestershire SP1726
Village on B4077, 1 mile (2km) NW of Stow-on-the-Wold
Pretty village with some charming buildings, an 18th-century bridge over the River Dikler and a rewarding Norman church.

UPPER TEAN Staffordshire SK0139
Village on A522, 6 miles (10km) NW of Uttoxeter
The huge Tean Mill, built to manufacture linen tape, looms in this village on the edge of moorlands. Rows of weavers' cottages remain.

UPPER TYSOE Warwickshire SP3343
Village of A422, 5 miles (8km) S of Kineton
From the village, with manor house and old stone cottages, there is a good walk to Tysoe Windmill – not open, but commanding splendid views.

UPPER UPNOR Kent TQ7570
see Upnor

UPPERMILL Greater Manchester SD9905
Village on A670, 5 miles (8km) E of Oldham
Largest of Saddleworth's picturesque villages, on the moor. Saddleworth Museum, in a mill next to the Huddersfield Canal, tells history of Saddleworth.

UPPERTHONG West Yorkshire SE1208
Village off A635, 1 mile (2km) W of Holmfirth
The village is a conservation area and many of the buildings reflect the large handloom weaving industry that played an important part in village life.

UPPINGHAM Leicestershire SP8699
Small town on A6003, 7 miles (11km) N of Corby
Delightful mellow stone Rutland market town with numerous fine 17th-century buildings, many with early 18th- or early 19th-century frontages. School, founded 1584, dominates town. It flourished and grew, particularly in 19th century, and some buildings are now open for visitors to tour. Church beside market place has 14th-century tower and tall spire, 17th-century Falcon hotel has an 1870 front.

UPSALL North Yorkshire SE4587
Village off A19, 4 miles (6km) NE of Thirsk
A tiny village in the Hambleton Hills. It has had three castles, the present one now being used as a private house.

UPSHIRE Essex TL4101
Village off A121, 2 miles (3km) E of Waltham Abbey
Battered by the M25's noise, but attractive to commuters. A church and white weatherboarded cottages sit on a windy hilltop, with jumbled post-war housing below.

UPTON Cheshire SJ4069
Village off A41, 2 miles (3km) N of Chester
Small village with a large zoo. Chester Zoo was begun by George Mottershead from a house on the edge of the village in 1930.

UPTON Dorset SY9893
District off A35, 3 miles (5km) NW of Poole
On the shores of Poole Harbour, mostly 1930s onwards and suburban. Upton House is early 19th-century mansion with fine country park and gardens.

UPTON Dyfed SN0104
Site off A477, 3 miles (5km) NE of Pembroke
Upton Castle's gardens lie in a sheltered valley and contain over 250 kinds of trees and shrubs, flower beds, and a small chapel.

UPTON Lincolnshire SK8686
Village off B1241, 4 miles (6km) SE of Gainsborough
Small village near River Till. Church has 11th-century chancel with herringbone masonry and Norman and 13th-century work. The tower was rebuilt in 1776, the chancel renewed in 1867.

UPTON Norfolk TG3912
Village off B1140, 2 miles (3km) N of Acle
A lovely village standing near a marshy stretch of land locally called The Doles near Upton Broad. Palmers Hollow post mill is a drainage pump.

UPTON Nottinghamshire SK7354
Village on A612, 2 miles (3km) E of Southwell
Neo-Georgian Upton Hall (British Horological Institute headquarters, limited opening). Early 18th-century Cross Keys inn, church with dovecote tower, attractive cottages.

UPTON Oxfordshire SU5187
Village on A417, 2 miles (3km) S of Didcot
Upton's proximity to Harwell and Didcot has led to much modern housing, but the small Norman church is worth visiting.

UPTON BISHOP Hereford and Worcester SO6527
Village off B4224, 4 miles (6km) NE of Ross-on-Wye
The Norman church of this small hill settlement has several interesting features, including a Roman tombstone on its wall.

UPTON CRESSETT Shropshire SO6592
Hamlet off A458, 4 miles (6km) W of Bridgnorth
Upton Cresset Hall (limited opening), fine Tudor manor house with impressive brick gatehouse, shares this lonely hamlet with interesting Norman church.

UPTON GREY Hampshire SU6948
Village off B3349, 4 miles (6km) SE of Basingstoke
Many pretty cottages, especially around the big pond. On Oak Apple Day branches of oak are placed on the church and cottages.

UPTON PYNE Devon SX9197
Village off A377, 3 miles (5km) north of Exeter
Laid out down a hill, with old cottages and cobbled paths. The 14th-century church tower has statues, unusual for a village church.

UPTON SNODSBURY Hereford and Worcester SO9454
Village off A422, 6 miles (10km) E of Worcester
Older cottages of this large village in market garden country east of Worcester are now upstaged by modern commuter homes.

UPTON ST LEONARDS Gloucestershire SO8614
Village on B4073, 3 miles (5km) SE of Gloucester
Commuter housing surrounds old village centre with its picturesque timber-framed cottages. Fine Victorian chancel and huge 18th-century memorial in church.

UPTON UPON SEVERN Hereford and Worcester SO8540
Village on A4104, 6 miles (10km) NW of Tewkesbury
Heritage centre in former church tower explains history of this delightful Severnside village with generous choice of pubs and many handsome buildings.

UPWALTHAM West Sussex SU9413
Hamlet on A285, 5 miles (8km) SW of Petworth
A delightful little group of barns, farms and an unsullied 12th-century church tucked in a hollow of the South Downs between Chichester and Petworth.

UPWEY Dorset SY6684
Village on B3159, 4 miles (6km) N of Weymouth
Pretty stone village in a wooded valley. Upwey Wishing Well is a spring, a sizeable stream emerging from the ground.

UPWOOD Cambridgeshire TL2582
Village off B1040, 2 miles (3km) SW of Ramsey
Upwood is a peaceful fenland village. It lies to the south of the former war-time airfield.

URCHFONT Wiltshire SU0457
Village on B3098, 4 miles (6km) SE of Devizes
Pretty village with two greens and a village pond. Many attractive houses, especially around the green near the church.

URE, RIVER North Yorkshire
River
The tiny River Ure rises in Abbotside Common, flows through Wensleydale and into the River Humber.

URMSTON Greater Manchester SJ7694
Town off M63, 5 miles (8km) SW of Manchester
Grew as a pleasant residential area with the development of railway network and Trafford Park Industrial Estate.

URSWICK Cumbria SD2674
Village off A590, 6 miles (10km) NE of Barrow-in-Furness
The village has been formed from the two hamlets of Great and Little Urswick. Traditionally, those born in Urswick are known as 'Ossick Coots'. Urswick Tarn covers a substantial area and is an important habitat for water birds including coots, grebe, wild geese and mallards. There have been swans here since 1767.

USHAW MOOR Durham NZ2242
Village off B6302, 3 miles (5km) W of Durham
Industrial village above the Deerness Valley. Ushaw College, now part of Durham University, was founded by monks fleeing Douai during the French Revolution.

USK Gwent/Powys SO3700
Town off A449, 9 miles (14km) NE of Newport
Small historic country town on River Usk, nowadays known for its floral displays which have won it numerous 'Britain in Bloom' awards. Gwent Rural Life Museum in old malt barn, cottage re-creates period farmhouse interiors with authentic rural craft implements and agricultural machinery. Church has interesting 12th- to 15th-century work. Ruined Norman castle in private hands.

USK, RIVER Gwent
River
Flows from Usk Reservoir in Brecon Beacons National Park through Brecon, widening into shallow vale en route to Usk, Newport and the sea.

UTKINTON Cheshire SJ5465
Hamlet off A49, 2 miles (3km) N of Tarporley
Attractive village in the Forest of Delamere. Nearby High Billinge has spectacular views over the Cheshire Plain towards Wales.

UTTERBY Lincolnshire TF3093
Village on A16, 4 miles (6km) N of Louth
Just east of Lincolnshire Wolds. Fourteenth-century packhorse bridge. Figures carved in porch of 14th- and 15th-century church. Utterby Manor is 17th century, Utterby House is 18th century.

UTTOXETER Staffordshire SK0933
Town on A518, 13 miles (21km) NE of Stafford
History of this busy rural market town in lower Dove Valley is interpreted at the heritage centre occupying old timber-framed cottages in Carter Street. St Mary's Church has typical 'preaching box' of 1828. Few other old buildings remain, but central area, especially the market square, High Street and Church Street is pleasant enough. Well-known racecourse lies to southeast.

UXBRIDGE Greater London TQ0584
Town in borough of Hillingdon
Old market town on the River Colne and the Grand Union Canal, an important London–Oxford coaching stop, hence the pubs along Oxford Road. The Piccadilly Underground line arrived in the 1930s, and the 1970s Hillingdon Civic Centre has been described as 'quintessential Metroland'. The old town centre was destroyed in the 1960s. Brunel University is to the south.

V

VALLE CRUCIS ABBEY Clwyd SJ2044
Site on A542, 1 mile (2km) NW of Llangollen
Cistercian abbey (Cadw) rebuilt late 13th/early 14th century. Fine vaulting and medieval memorial sculptures. Name means 'valley of the cross'.

VATERNISH Highland (Skye) NG2658
Peninsula area in NW Skye
Wild and isolated peninsula in northwest Skye lying between Loch Snizort and Loch Dunvegan. Ruined Trumpan Church was scene of Macleod massacre in 1570s.

VATERSAY Western Isles
Island in Outer Hebrides, to SW of Barra
Tiny island connected by modern causeway to Barra with scattered crofts, idyllic beaches and sparse population. Uninhabited Bishop's Isle and Mingulay to south.

VAUXHALL Greater London TQ3078
District in borough of Lambeth
Londoners enjoyed Vauxhall Pleasure Gardens from the 17th century to the 19th. The story is told in the heritage centre in St Peter's Church, built in the 1860s. Vauxhall Bridge dates from 1906, the Secret Service lurks in Terry Farrell's flamboyant 1993 Vauxhall Cross building and Covent Garden Market moved to Nine Elms Road in 1974.

VAYNOR Mid Glamorgan SO0410
Hamlet off A470, 3 miles (5km) N of Merthyr Tydfil
Hamlet on southern fringes of Brecon Beacons National Park by Taf Fechan's gorge. Merthyr ironmaster's grave in church.

VENTNOR Isle of Wight SZ5677
Town on A3055, 3 miles (5km) SW of Shanklin
This seaside resort sits at the southern tip of the Isle of Wight, the centre of the Undercliff, the strange, steep, wooded landslip area bordering the sea. Ventnor developed from the 1840s as the island, and particularly the Undercliff, became fashionable, and many mid-Victorian buildings still survive, including churches. The site is steep, with smaller hills and hummocks on the way down.

Visitors were attracted by the very mild climate, as well as the romantic scenery. Wooded Boniface Down is prominent from the town and wooded cliffs rise on either side, formalised in the centre as the road to the sea, the Cascades, with gardens and a natural waterfall. The Esplanade was laid out in 1848 and there are sandy beaches.

Ventnor Botanic Garden, to the west, has huge gardens and a Temperate House. Many tender plants grow out of doors here.

VER, RIVER Hertfordshire
River
This Hertfordshire stream rises at Redbourn and runs by St Albans (Roman *Verulamium*) to the River Colne. It has suffered from abstraction and pollution in the 1990s.

VERNHAM DEAN Hampshire SU3456
Village off A343, 3 miles (5km) NW of Hurstbourne Tarrant
Lots of thatched cottages in this very rural village. Elaborate Norman doorway on the little church. Manor House has gardens by Gertrude Jekyll.

VERYAN Cornwall SW9139
Village off A3078, 3 miles (5m) S of Tregony
This pretty village is full of trees and has a water garden at the centre. Many thatched cottages include five round ones, built in the early 19th century; one stands at each end of the village, supposedly to stop the devil entering. Nare Head to the south is a prominent rocky headland, with Veryan Bay, wild and unspoilt.

VICKERSTOWN Cumbria SD1868
Small town on Walney Island, opposite Barrow-in-Furness
Purpose-built town of terraced houses, dating from the turn of the 20th century, built by ship-building firm Vickers for their employees.

VIGO Kent TQ6361
Village off A227, 4 miles (6km) NE of Borough Green
Modern self-contained village built in a wood from 1965–75. It is based on a central footpath with roads around the edge.

VIRGINIA WATER Surrey TQ0067
District off A30, 3 miles (5km) SW of Staines
Exclusive residential suburb at the heart of Wentworth estate on the edge of Windsor Great Park, named after the ornamental lake, 2 miles (3km) long, created in 1746–68 by Thomas and Paul Sandby for the 1st Duke of Cumberland. It has private gated roads, with large neo-Tudor houses behind rhododendron hedges. Valley Gardens, laid out in the 1930s, are public gardens covering some 400 acres (162ha).

Totem pole at Virginia Water.

VOWCHURCH Hereford and Worcester SO3636
Village on B4348, 6 miles (10km) NW of Pontrilas
Church with interesting primitive interior stands near cluster of old cottages in this small riverside village beneath wooded hills.

VULCAN VILLAGE Cheshire SJ5894
Village, immediately S of Newton-le-Willows
A model village founded in 1830s, for workers at the locomotive factory, which retains many features from that era.

W

WADDESDON Buckinghamshire SP7416
Village on A41, 5 miles (8km) NW of Aylesbury
Spick-and-span Rothschild village in respectful attendance on the glories of Waddesdon Manor (National

Trust), built in the 1870s in *château* style for Baron Ferdinand de Rothschild and restored at staggering expense in the 1980s and 90s. Exquisite treasures of art and craft, sumptuously landscaped grounds with fountains, statues and aviary.

WADDINGTON Lancashire SD7243
Village on B6478, 2 miles (3km) NW of Clitheroe
Picturesque village with a brook, almshouses and a 16th-century church. Waddington Old Hall (not open) dates back to 1464.

WADDINGTON Lincolnshire SK9764
Village on A607, 5 miles (8km) S of Lincoln
On Lincolnshire Cliff, overlooking Witham and Trent valleys. Stone cottages. RAF station.

WADEBRIDGE Cornwall SW9972
Town off A389, 6 miles (10km) NW of Bodmin
A market town (and once a port) on the Camel estuary, with one of the finest medieval bridges in the country, built in about 1468 and 320ft (97m) long. The town has some Victorian architecture. The Royal Cornwall Show is held here annually.

WADENHOE Northamptonshire TL0183
Village off A605, 4 miles (6km) SW of Oundle
Seventeenth-century houses facing green. Wadenhoe House of 1657, rebuilt 1858. Church, with saddleback Norman tower, separated from village on knoll above River Nene.

WADESMILL Hertfordshire TL3617
see Thundridge

WADHURST East Sussex TQ6431
Village on B2099, 6 miles (10km) SE of Tunbridge Wells
Pretty ridge-top village with an attractive High Street, a long road of tile-hung and weatherboarded cottages. The church is known for its tall, slender spire, 130ft (40m) high, and for its remarkable collection of 30 iron tomb slabs, dating from 1617 to 1790, a relic of Wadhurst's days as the most important of Wealden iron-smelting villages.

WADWORTH South Yorkshire SK5697
Village on A60, 4 miles (6km) S of Doncaster
Ancient village with some modern housing, dominated by the A1 and M18. Wadworth Hall, designed by Paine, is now used for commercial purposes.

WAINFLEET ALL SAINTS Lincolnshire TF4958
Village on B1195, 5 miles (8km) SW of Skegness
Once a port, but business declined with silting up of haven in 15th century. A few Georgian fronts in High Street. Wainfleet School, founded 1484 by Bishop Waynflete of Winchester, is now the public library. Bateman's Brewery, established 1874, incorporates brick tower mill in 19th-century buildings, with beer-bottle-shaped weathervane.

WAKEFIELD West Yorkshire SE3320
City off M1, 8 miles (13km) S of Leeds
The cathedral city of Wakefield prospered for many years as an inland grain and cloth port. The old town, built on a hill overlooking the River Calder, grew up around the crossroads of the main streets Westgate, Northgate and Kirkgate.

At the very centre of the town is the Cathedral of All Saints, built in the 13th century, whose spire dominates the skyline and at 247ft (75m) high is the tallest in Yorkshire. The cathedral is now surrounded by pedestrianised shopping areas leading to the traditional outdoor market, market halls and the Ridings shopping centre.

The city's museum has a fine collection of exotic birds and animals from South America, and local archaeological finds dating back 300 years. The Art Gallery includes some works by two Yorkshire sculptors, Barbara Hepworth and Henry Moore.

St Mary's Chantry Chapel, built in the 14th century on the old Wakefield Bridge spanning the River Calder, is the sole survivor of four chapels built in Wakefield as resting places for travellers. Wakefield Bridge was built in the early 1340s.

The Theatre Royal and Opera House were designed by the renowned Edwardian architect Frank Matcham.

WAKERLEY Northamptonshire SP9599
Village off A47, 7 miles (11km) SW of Stamford
Medieval bridge across River Welland to Rutland. Norman and later church on hill outside village. Wakerley Woods, part of ancient Rockingham Forest, has trails and picnic areas.

WAKES COLNE Essex TL8928
Village on A604, 5 miles (8km) E of Halstead
Next to Chappel (see) and the impressive railway viaduct. East Anglian Railway museum of steam locomotives and memorabilia, steam rides.

WALBERSWICK Suffolk TM4974
Village on B1387, 3 miles (5km) E of Blythburgh
The neat, tidy village of Walberswick has some large, handsome houses and is a pleasant river port with many little fishing craft bobbing up and down on the water. St Andrew's Church is built partly inside the ruins of its predecessor that was dismantled in the 17th century because of a lack of funds.

WALBURY HILL Berkshire SU3761
Hill off A338, 5 miles (8km) SE of Hungerford
An Iron Age hillfort stands on the highest point in Berkshire, at 974ft (297m). (See Combe.)

WALCOT Lincolnshire TF0635
Village off A15, 7 miles (11km) S of Sleaford
Pleasant village, with medieval church; Norman and 13th-century interior, 14th-century tower with crocketed broach spire, chancel, 15th-century clerestory, 1907 restoration.

WALCOTT Norfolk TG3632
Village off B1150, 2 miles (3km) NW of Happisburgh
Long, safe beaches of golden sand are easily accessible from this attractive, peaceful village. Money for the 19th-century church restoration came from Nelson's godson.

WALES South Yorkshire SK4782
Village on B6060, 7 miles (11km) W of Worksop
Former mining community with many of the characteristics of a small town, dominated by the M1.

WALESBY Lincolnshire TF1392
Village off B1203, 3 miles (5km) NE of Market Rasen
Attractive Wolds village. Hilltop All Saints' Church, maintained by Redundant Churches Fund, is now the Rambler's Church on the Viking Way. It has box pews and a Jacobean pulpit.

WALKDEN Greater Manchester SD7303
Town on A6, 2 miles (3km) NW of Swinton
An industrial town with good recreational facilities and a shopping centre with a covered market.

WALKERBURN Borders NT3637
Village on A72, 2 miles (3km) E of Innerleithen
Village on River Tweed founded in 1854 for textile-manufacturing. Industry's history told in Scottish Museum of Woollen Textiles. Near by is ruined 16th-century Elibank Tower.

WALKERINGHAM Nottinghamshire SK7792
Village off A161, 4 miles (6km) NW of Gainsborough
Straggling village between River Trent and Chesterfield Canal. Manor House of Elizabethan brickwork, 13th- and 15th-century church with 17th-century monument by Edward Marshall.

WALKERN Hertfordshire TL2826
Village on B1037, 4 miles (6km) E of Stevenage
Commuter village with a rural air, near a ford over the River Beane. St Mary's Church goes back to Saxon and Norman times. The 17th-century octagonal brick dovecote is now a house. Jane Wenham of Church Lane, Walkern was in 1712 the last person condemned to death for witchcraft in England, but was reprieved.

WALKHAMPTON Devon SX5369
Village off B3212, 5 miles (8km) SE of Tavistock
Just off Dartmoor, the church on a hill has a big granite tower, and the 16th-century church house is now an inn.

WALL Northumberland NY9168
Village on A6079, 3 miles (5km) N of Hexham
A small cluster of houses close to Hadrian's Wall and the site of the Battle of Heavenfield.

WALL Staffordshire SK1006
Village off A5, 2 miles (3km) SW of Lichfield
Small village on Watling Street, once the Roman settlement of *Letocetum*. Remains of inn and bathhouse survive. Museum of excavated finds (English Heritage).

WALLAND MARSH Kent TQ9823
Scenic region NW of Lydd
To the west of Romney Marsh, the wide stretch of marshland between new Romney, Appledore and Rye was reclaimed in medieval times.

WALLASEY Merseyside SJ3291
Town off M53, at N point of Wirral peninsula
An urban area made up of several townships, whose development really began in 1823 when the steam ferry service came from Liverpool to Seacombe. This rapid growth, which continued well into the 20th century, is largely responsible for the town's appearance today. The centre of the old village, along with the church, stands on a hill overlooking the River Mersey.

WALLINGFORD Oxfordshire SU6089
Town off A329, 12 miles (19km) SE of Oxford
The Wallingford Museum relates this bustling town's long history, revealed in Saxon masonry in St Leonard's Church, and the earthworks of the castle. Other old buildings, like the old town hall (limited opening), Augier's almshouses, George inn, White Hart and Lamb hotel date from 16th to 18th centuries. The important bridge, much rebuilt, is of 13th-century origin.

WALLINGTON Hertfordshire TL2933
Village off A505, 3 miles (5km) E of Baldock
Hertfordshire seems to have influenced George Orwell's *Animal Farm*. He lived here, next to the Plough pub, and ran the village shop.

WALLSEND Tyne and Wear NZ3066
Town on A193, 4 miles (6km) E of Newcastle
Town marks the end of Hadrian's Wall. Model of the fort, *Segedunum*, and artefacts displayed in Wallsend heritage centre. Main employment was mining and ship-building.

WALMER Kent TR3750
District off A258, immediately S of Deal
Plenty of Victorian houses as well as 20th-century ones in this residential seaside place that merges north up the coast with Deal. There are two churches, one Norman, the other Victorian, and ruins of a semi-fortified Norman house beside the old churchyard. On the promenade, Walmer Castle, one of Henry VIII's gun stations, has been the official residence of Lord Warden of the Cinque Ports since the 18th century.

WALMLEY West Midlands SP1393
District in SE Sutton Coldfield
Insulated from Sutton Coldfield by golf courses, the housing estates of Walmeley face the pleasant Warwickshire countryside.

WALNEY ISLAND Cumbria SD1868
Island on A590, across the water from Barrow-in-Furness
The southern part of the island is a bird sanctuary and one of the largest gulleries in Europe. To the north of the island is a nature reserve known for the Natterjack toad. The island also has a golf course and several beaches.

WALPOLE Suffolk TM3674
Village on B1117, 3 miles (5km) SW of Halesworth
A 17th-century house was converted for use as a Congregational Chapel during the Civil War. One of the fine houses has pargetting dating from 1708.

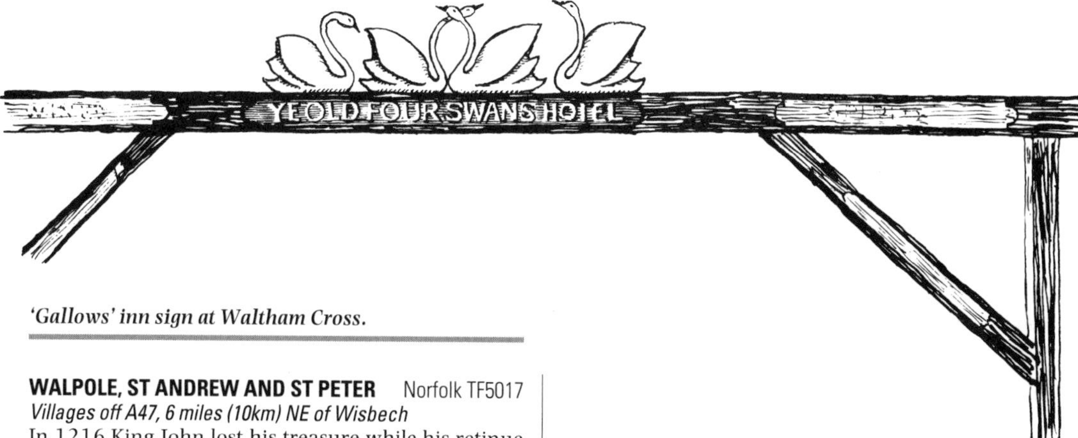

'Gallows' inn sign at Waltham Cross.

WALPOLE, ST ANDREW AND ST PETER Norfolk TF5017
Villages off A47, 6 miles (10km) NE of Wisbech
In 1216 King John lost his treasure while his retinue passed through the parish of Walpole St Andrew. Searches for this fabled wealth continue today. Walpole St Peter boasts one of the finest churches in the Norfolk marshlands, a magnificent building with a sumptuous interior. The family of Hugh Walpole, Britain's first Prime Minister, left Walpole in the 13th century.

WALSALL West Midlands SP0198
Town off M6, 8 miles (13km) NW of Birmingham
Medieval Walsall developed on a steep limestone hill, and the parish church still stands at the top. It overlooks a pedestrianised High Street that becomes an enormous open-air market on Tuesdays and Saturdays, while the more distant view is of modern housing estates and open countryside to the east.

Today's smoke-free Walsall is very different from the 19th-century 'town of a hundred trades', famous for a huge range of leather goods and specialist metalwork. Leather is still a major product and is celebrated at the Walsall Leather Museum in Wisemore, while other aspects of local history feature at the Museum and Art Gallery in Lichfield Street, along with a fine art collection. The square called The Bridge is the centre of Walsall.

Modern shopping precincts have replaced the unhealthy Victorian streets, recalled by the statue of 'Sister Dora', a Victorian nun who became a legendary local nurse. In nearby Bradford Street is the birthplace of the humorist Jerome K Jerome, his house now a commemorative museum. The pride of Walsall, however, is its series of open spaces, including a fine arboretum and a country park.

WALSHAM LE WILLOWS Suffolk TM0071
Village off A143, 5 miles (8km) E of Ixworth
A fringe of willow trees overhangs a tributary of the Black Bourn. Timber-framed cottages and handsome church with medallion commemorating girl who died of a broken heart.

WALSINGHAM, GREAT AND LITTLE Norfolk
see Little Walsingham

WALSOKEN Cambridgeshire TF4710
Village off A47, on NE edge of Wisbech
Stands on the Norfolk–Cambridgeshire border, with a church described by architectural historian Nikolaus Pevsner as the grandest in Norfolk. It is Norman with beautiful carvings.

WALTHAM ABBEY Essex TL3800
Town off M25, 7 miles (11km) SW of Harlow
King Harold, killed at Hastings, was buried in the abbey church, which he had rebuilt. Later rebuilt again, the building has an impressive Norman nave, monuments, fine Victorian work by William Burges and Burne-Jones windows. Thomas Tallis was organist here. Epping Forest District Museum of local history, Welsh Harp inn, countryside centre for the Lee Valley Park.

WALTHAM CROSS Hertfordshire TL3600
District on A1010, immediately S of Cheshunt
A dispiriting post-war shopping centre, named after the beautiful 13th-century Eleanor Cross, one of only three originals left, restored in the 19th century. Four swans sail across a nearby gallows sign, although the Four Swans pub has gone for ever. Cedars Park has a heritage trail and pets' corner. In Theobalds Park is Temple Bar, former City of London gateway.

WALTHAM ON THE WOLDS Leicestershire SK8024
Village on A607, 5 miles (8km) NE of Melton Mowbray
Attractive Wolds village on main road between Grantham and Melton Mowbray. Ironstone houses, some thatched, others with slate or pantiled roofs. There was a market here until 1921, and the Agricultural Hall was built in Tudor style in 1838. Large medieval church with tower and crocketed spire, Norman doorways and angels supporting wooden roof. Television mast near by.

WALTHAM ST LAWRENCE Berkshire SU8276
Village on B3024, 3 miles (5km) E of Twyford
A pretty brick and timber-framed village; the Bell inn has particularly good timbering. Georgian and earlier brick houses.

WALTHAMSTOW Greater London TQ3689
Town in borough of Waltham Forest
A fashionable area before being overtaken by 19th-century working-class housing. It has a thriving street market. Vestry House museum records local history in a

former police station. The William Morris Gallery has an excellent collection in Morris's childhood home, whose grounds are now a park. Walthamstow Marshes Nature Reserve is a wetland area with hay meadows, wildflowers and butterflies.

WALTON Somerset ST4636
Village on A39, 1 mile (2km) W of Street
At the foot of the Polden Hills, with wide views over the Somerset Levels from Walton Hill (with remains of old windmill) and Ivythorn Hill.

WALTON ON THE HILL Surrey TQ2255
Village off B2220, 4 miles (6km) SW of Banstead
On the downs but with Walton Heath to the south, the pleasant Victorian village centre has a pond at one end of the High Street and a green at the other.

WALTON ON THE NAZE Essex TM2521
Town on B1034, 7 miles (11km) NE of Clacton-on Sea
A seaside resort with a sandy beach and one of England's longest piers, developed as a bathing resort from the 1820s on and featuring a Martello tower and a big boating lake. To the north lies the open space of the Naze (see) and a maze of winding channels and inlets off the North Sea which attract small-boat sailors, walkers and bird-watchers.

WALTON-IN-GORDANO Avon ST4273
Village on B3124, 2 miles (3km) NE of Clevedon
Very small village on the outskirts of Clevedon. On the hill above is Walton Castle (not open), fanciful and tall, built in 1625.

WALTON-LE-DALE Lancashire SD5528
Village on A6, on SE outskirts of Preston
Historic village in an attractive wooded area in the Ribble Valley. Church, dating back to 1190, contains memorials to the de Hoghton family.

WALTON-ON-THAMES Surrey TQ1066
Town on A3050 immediately NE of Weybridge
Cheerful, friendly town with modern shopping facilities and a sports centre. The old town centre is set back from the River Thames, around Manor Road, with attractive houses including Long Cottage, Thames Cottage and timber-framed Old Manor House where lived John Bradshaw, president of the judges who tried Charles I. The church has a monument to New Zealanders who died in Walton hospitals during World War I.

WALTON-ON-TRENT Derbyshire SK2118
Village off A38, 4 miles (6km) SW of Burton-upon-Trent
Beside the River Trent, on the Staffordshire border. Eighteenth-century brick hall. Church with late Norman interior, 13th-century chancel, 15th-century tower and early 20th-century woodwork.

WALWORTH Greater London TQ3278
District in borough of Southwark
Off the Old Kent Road, Walworth has a market in East Street. The history of Southwark (see) since Roman times is covered in the Cuming Museum.

WAMBROOK Somerset ST2907
Village off A30, 2 miles (3km) SW of Chard
Scattered village of several hamlets, very rural. Part of Dorset until 1896.

WANBOROUGH Surrey SU9348
Hamlet off A31, 4 miles (6km) W of Guildford
Compact bundle of a manor house, once Asquith's home, a 13th-century chapel and a big tithe barn, grouped round a farmyard on the north slope of the Hog's Back.

WANBOROUGH, HIGHER AND LOWER Wiltshire SU2082
Village off A419, 4 miles (6km) E of Swindon
Divided into Higher and Lower Wanborough. Higher with the medieval church (distinctive hexagonal tower), and Lower with more houses and inns.

WANDSWORTH Greater London TQ2574
District in borough of SW London
On the River Wandle, which joins the Thames at Young's Brewery. The Wandle Trail follows the river back to Croydon (see). All Saints' Church in the High Street is impressively 18th-century and St Anne's Church is in 1820s Greek Revival style. The grim bulk of Wandsworth Prison dates back to the 1850s. (For Wandsworth Museum, see Putney.)

WANGFORD Suffolk TM4679
Village on B1126, 3 miles (5km) NW of Southwold
A large village on the River Wang with a pleasant church and and two old pubs.

WANLIP Leicestershire SK6010
Village off A6, 4 miles (6km) N of Leicester
Small village in watermeadows on west bank of River Soar. Church has first inscription on brass in English, 1393.

WANLOCKHEAD Dumfries and Galloway NS8712
Village on B797, 2 miles (3km) S of Leadhills
Scotland's highest village (1,380ft/420m), noted from 17th century until 1950s for lead-mining; Scottish Lead Mining Museum traces industry's history. Rare example of water-powered beam engine, built to drain Straitsteps Mine. Restored miners' cottages, mine and visitor centre are other attractions. Good local walking on Southern Upland Way.

WANNOCK East Sussex TQ5703
Village off A22, immediately S of Polegate
Old village at the foot of the South Downs, with a little lane running up a deep combe to timber-framed Filching Manor. Now a suburb of Polegate.

WANSBECK, RIVER Northumberland
River, runs through Morpeth to North Sea
Source is in hills above Kirkharle, running into a wooded valley with nature reserves. Wansbeck Country Park has a camp site, boat hire, walks and picnic areas.

WANSDYKE Wiltshire
Site in S England
One of the longest earthworks in the country, running

50 miles (80km) across Wiltshire and Avon, mainly on chalk uplands. A single bank and ditch, it was built during the unsettled times of the 5th or 6th centuries, probably as a defence against the Saxon invaders. The best-preserved parts are on the Marlborough Downs.

WANSFORD Cambridgeshire TL0799
Village off A1, 7 miles (11km) W of Peterborough
The 12-arched bridge over the River Nene is truly splendid. The first arches date from 1577, the second were built 1672–4, while the last were added in 1795. The Haycock, a nearby 17th-century inn, once had stabling for 150 horses, and was one of the largest coaching inns ever built. Wansford is headquarters of the Nene Valley Railway.

WANSFORD Humberside TA0656
Village on B1249, 3 miles (5km) E of Great Driffield
Picturesque village on the banks of the Driffield Navigation and River Hull, with many houses dating back to the 1700s.

WANSTEAD Greater London TQ4088
District in borough of Redbridge
Rows of dreary streets, but ornamental lakes, woods, a heronry and the remains of an 18th-century mansion dignify Wanstead Park, which is run as part of Epping Forest (see). There are interesting graves and monuments in the massive City of London cemetery. Wanstead Flats is an appropriately named open space of over 100 acres (40ha).

WANTAGE Oxfordshire SU3988
Town on A338, 13 miles (21km) SW of Oxford
The long history of Wantage, which includes a Roman settlement, the birth of Alfred the Great here in AD849 and the destruction of the town by the Danes in 1001, is interpreted at the Vale and Downland Museum in Church Street. Alfred is remembered with a statue in the market place, but little of that early history is visible today, and this pleasant traditional market town is characterised by harmonious buildings of the 17th century onwards, many set in narrow cobbled passages. (The courtyard of Stile's almshouses is cobbled with the knuckle bones of sheep.)

A feature of the townscape is the distinctive use of the local red and blue brick in many Georgian buildings. There is evidence of the town's medieval prosperity in the Church of St Peter and St Paul, which has a rich interior with several brasses and a lady chapel built by the Wantage trade guilds. The Anglican Convent of St Mary, with buildings by three distinguished Victorian architects, Street, Butterfield and Pearson, is less accessible, but the work of the nuns has made the name of Wantage widely known.

WAPPING Greater London TQ3480
District in borough of Tower Hamlets
Archetypal old London docks area where pirates once swung at Execution Dock. Wapping High Street runs past the river wharves. St George in the East Church was designed by Hawksmoor in the 1720s. Tobacco Dock was redeveloped by Terry Farrell in the 1980s as a shop and restaurant complex. Pepys and Dickens both knew the famous Prospect of Whitby pub on the river.

WARBLINGTON Hampshire SU7205
Hamlet off A27, 1 mile (2km) W of Emsworth
There is an old village down by Chichester Harbour and a big modern settlement to the north. The Saxon and Norman church has little flint huts of 1800 in the corners of the graveyard, for watchmen who prevented grave-robbing. One tower survives from Warblington Castle (not open).

WARBOROUGH Oxfordshire SU5993
Village on A329, 3 miles (5km) N of Wallingford
Stuart manor house, 13th-century church and timber-framed cottages form pleasant centre of this straggling village close to River Thames.

WARBOYS Cambridgeshire TL3080
Village on B1040, 7 miles (11km) NE of Huntingdon
Famous for its three so-called witches, who were hanged in 1593 for the grisly murder of a woman.

WARBSTOW Cornwall SX2090
Village off A39, 7 miles (11km) E of Boscastle
Old slate cottages and a simple church. On the green is the earthen bank of a pound. Warbstow Bury Iron Age hillfort overlooks the village.

WARBURTON Greater Manchester SJ6989
Village off A6144, 1 mile (2km) SW of Partington
A pretty rural village where the modern houses have been blended with the much older half-timbered cottages and farms.

WARCOP Cumbria NY7415
Village on B6259, 3 miles (5km) W of Brough
A pleasant village with an ancient bridge over the River Eden which is so narrow that it has recesses for pedestrians.

WARDEN Northumberland NY9166
Hamlet off A69, 2 miles (3km) NW of Hexham
At the confluence of the North and South Tyne rivers and sheltered by Warden Hill. Warden's papermill industry dates back to 1763.

WARDINGTON Oxfordshire SP4946
Village on A361, 4 miles (6km) NE of Banbury
Village overlooks the infant River Cherwell. Its manor house has been much remodelled but other venerable buildings remain near the medieval church.

WARDLE Greater Manchester SD9116
Town off A58, 3 miles (5km) NE of Rochdale
Pretty village which has retained its rural character, with 18th- and 19th-century cottages around the square.

WARDOUR Wiltshire ST9227
Hamlet off A350, 5 miles (8km) NE of Shaftesbury
No village, only the Old Castle (English Heritage) and the big, severely classical 1770s mansion which replaced it. The Old Castle, elegant and hexagonal with 1570s alterations, is now a ruin. Georgian summer house and lake.

WARE Hertfordshire TL3514
Town on A1170, 4 miles (6km) N of Hoddesdon
This charming old market town, where Ermine Street crossed the River Lee, has former maltings converted into flats, a delightful riverside walk and a town museum (limited opening). The monster Great Bed of Ware is in London, but Scott's Grotto (limited opening), built by 18th-century poet John Scott and lined with shells, restored in the 1990s, is an aristocrat of its kind.

WAREHAM Dorset SY9287
Town on A351, 6 miles (10km) W of Poole
A port until the 14th century, with ships coming right up the River Frome. The quay on the river is pretty, but only for pleasure boats now.

On three sides are the green banks of the Saxon defences; on top of one is the little Saxon church of St Martin, full of fragments of wall-paintings and a superb effigy of Lawrence of Arabia in Arab dress. The main parish church (St Mary) has very unusual 7th- to 9th-century inscribed stones.

The outskirts have older cottages mixed with modern, but the centre mostly dates from after a bad fire in 1762, with lots of Georgian brick and many inns (one with a huge figure of a bear). There is a town hall of 1870 and a local museum.

WARESLEY Cambridgeshire TL2554
Village on B1040, 4 miles (6km) NE of Potton
Pretty Waresley stands in peaceful countryside between two old Roman roads. Gransden and Waresley Woods lie near by .

WARFIELD Berkshire SU8872
Hamlet off B3034, 2 miles (3km) N of Bracknell
Some old brick and timber-framing. The fine church is mostly 14th century, the north chapel screen still, very unusually, having its rood loft.

WARGRAVE Berkshire SU7878
Village on A321, 2 miles (3km) N of Twyford
Set on the River Thames, Wargrave is crammed with timber-framed cottages and Georgian brick mixed with Edwardian imitations. A brick church tower of 1635 stands; the rest was burnt down by suffragettes in 1914. Pretty green around the church.

WARK Northumberland NY8577
Village on B6320, 4 miles (6km) S of Bellingham
A pleasant village with attractive cottages and a village green. Chipchase Castle is a pele tower to which a Jacobean mansion was added. Wark Forest lies on the edge of the Northumberland National Park. Abel Chapman, the naturalist, once lived here. Wark is pronounced locally as 'ark'.

WARK Northumberland NT8238
Village on B6350, 2 miles (3km) W of Cornhill-on-Tweed
On the south bank of the River Tweed, with ruins of a castle built around 1126 on a rocky outcrop, once an important fortress.

WARKTON Northamptonshire SP8979
Village off A43, 2 miles (3km) NE of Kettering
Estate village planned by Montagus of Boughton House (see Geddington). Church chancel built for magnificent Montagu monuments, two by Roubiliac, one by Adam.

WARKWORTH Northamptonshire SP4840
Hamlet off A422, 2 miles (3km) E of Banbury
Medieval castle, succeeded by Jacobean house, demolished 1805. Fine Lyons tombs and Chetwode brasses remain in church, set apart on hillside.

WARKWORTH Northumberland NU2406
Village on A1068, 1 mile (2km) NW of Amble
In a horseshoe bend of the River Coquet. Warkworth Castle (English Heritage) dominates the village from the top of the main street. A hermitage was created by Bertram, a Northumbrian knight, who accidentally killed his brother and sweetheart. Overcome by remorse, he spent the reminder of his life in solitude.

WARLEGGAN Cornwall SX1569
Village off A30, 6 miles (10km) E of Bodmin
Tiny slate and granite village, very remote, running down from Bodmin Moor to a wooded valley.

WARLEY West Midlands SP0086
District off A456, 4 miles (6km) W of Birmingham
Avery, famous makers of weighing-machines, run a museum of their craft in Foundry Lane, making history of weights and scales unexpectedly fascinating.

WARLINGHAM Surrey TQ3558
Town on B269, 5 miles (8km) SE of Croydon
A green with shops, pub and old cottages now hemmed in by the urban growth of Croydon. The church, now in a housing estate, dates from about 1250 but was rebuilt by the Victorians.

WARMINGTON Northamptonshire TL0791
Village off A605, 3 miles (5km) NE of Oundle
Large church built almost entirely 1180–1280. Jacobean manor house, altered 1677. Interior door at 17th-century Eaglethorpe House said to come from Fotheringhay Castle.

WARMINGTON Warwickshire SP4147
Village on B4100, 5 miles (8km) NW of Banbury
A picture-postcard village beneath western slopes of Edge Hill. The 17th-century manor house and other attractive dwellings grace the sloping village green with its pond, and cottages in local stone abound. The ancient Plough is an inviting pub, standing close to a church with fascinating medieval details and casualties of the Battle of Edgehill buried in its churchyard.

WARMINSTER Wiltshire ST8745
Town off A36, 6 miles (10km) SE of Frome
One main street, a mixture of brick, stone and timber-framed buildings, ranging from the 16th to 19th centuries. Imitation Jacobean town hall of 1832, pretty 15th-century church and grammar school of 1707; downs close by. Local museum.

WARNFORD Hampshire SU6223
Village on A32, 2 miles (3km) NE of Meonstoke
In the Meon Valley, with many watercress beds and flint and brick cottages of many dates and styles. Norman church with an odd tower and very unusual 12th-century dedicatory inscriptions. Ruins of a 13th-century house behind the church. Millions of snowdrops in season.

WARNHAM West Sussex TQ1533
Village off A24, 2 miles (3km) NW of Horsham
Attractive village with a variety of architectural styles from Tudor to 20th century, a restored Tudor church and a millpond dug in 1600 as a hammerpond for the nearby iron furnace.

WARNINGLID West Sussex TQ2526
Village on B2115, 5 miles (8km) SE of Horsham
A little ridge-top village centred on a crossroads, with brick and tile-hung cottages, a church of the 1830s and a quaint little pond with a hump-backed stone bridge.

WARRINGTON Cheshire SJ6088
Town off M62, 16 miles (25km) E of Liverpool
A manufacturing town on the River Mersey, Warrington has rapidly expanded with large industrial and commercial parks and it has been granted New Town status.

Many visitors to Warrington assume that it is a completely modern town until they venture into the centre where many of the buildings are Georgian in style. The town hall is a fine example of Georgian architecture and was once the home of the Patten family. At the front are some magnificent cast-iron gates which were made for exhibition in 1860 at Ironbridge in Shropshire. Originally they were to be erected at Sandringham for Queen Victoria, but were purchased by a local industrialist, Frederick Monks, in 1895 for Warrington.

The Barley Mow inn in the old market place dates from 1561 and has a fine frontage of carved woodwork.

The parish church, a short distance from the centre, is Warrington's oldest building. Founded in the 7th century, the church is dedicated to St Elphin, Warrington's own saint, and the chancel and crypt date from 1354.

Warrington Museum and Art Gallery is a Victorian building where regular exhibitions are held.

WARSASH Hampshire SU4906
Village off A27, 6 miles (10km) W of Fareham
On the River Hamble estuary, mostly Victorian and modern. Lots of yachts on the river.

WARSLOW Staffordshire SK0858
Village on B5053, 7 miles (11km) E of Leek
Stone cottages and 18th-century church with good furnishings stand at heart of this moorland village in Peak District National Park.

WARSOP Nottinghamshire SK5667
Town on A60, 5 miles (8km) NE of Mansfield
Separated by the River Meden (with an 18th-century watermill) from older Church Warsop, where stone houses and farms gather around the Norman and medieval church.

WARTER Humberside SE8650
Village on B1246, 4 miles (6km) E of Pocklington
Picturesque, tiny estate village set in a leafy hollow of the Wolds. The 19th-century church overlooks the village green.

WARTON Lancashire SD4128
Village on A584, 4 miles (6km) E of Lytham St Anne's
Village now with a suburban appearance, on low-lying ground overlooking the Ribble estuary.

WARTON Lancashire SD5072
Village off A6, 1 mile (2km) N of Carnforth
Pretty village at foot of Warton Crag with 14th-century church, once home of the Washington family. On Independence Day the church flies the American flag.

WARWICK Warwickshire SP2865
Town off A46, 9 miles (14km) SW of Coventry
A disastrous fire in 1694 destroyed Warwick's original centre, but something of its medieval atmosphere can be captured at the little enclave of Bridge End and in the profusion of timber-framing in nearby Mill Street. The bridge itself provides a famous view of the castle above the river. Norman in origin, it was greatly enlarged by the powerful Beauchamp family in the 14th century, eventually becoming a stately home. The tour of the state rooms, great hall, the dungeons and much more is enlivened by audio-visual presentations and a waxwork re-creation of a Victorian house party.

Warwick's other renowned attraction is St Mary's Church. Its tower and nave were rebuilt after the fire, but the Norman crypt and 14th-century chancel survived, as did the magnificent chapel erected in the 1440s to house the sumptuous tomb of Richard Beauchamp.

Jury Street and Northgate Street contain some of the best buildings erected after the fire, among them the Court House of 1730 (the public rooms can be visited), the Northgate House of 1698 and the shire hall, with its octagonal courtrooms and grim gaol. At the narrow Westgate ancient houses squeeze along the road, dominated by the 15th-century Lord Leycester Hospital, a home for old soldiers since 1571. The chapel, guildhall and great hall are open to the public. Another fascinating building of the same period is Oken's House in Castle Street, which now houses an intriguing collection of antique dolls and toys.

A reminder of workaday Warwick life is supplied at the 17th-century St John's House, a museum of folk history and the regimental museum of the Royal Warwickshire Regiment, while the wider history of the county can be studied at the Warwickshire Museum in the market place.

WASDALE HEAD Cumbria NY1808
Hamlet on minor road, off A595, N of Wast Water
British rock-climbing began here in the 1880s and it is now a climbing centre for the local high peaks.

WASHFIELD Devon SS9315
Village off A396, 2 miles (3km) NW of Tiverton
Above the Exe valley, isolated and rural, the village has a 15th-century church tower.

WASHFORD Somerset ST0441
Village on A39, 2 miles (3km) SW of Watchet
Stone village on the main road. Tropiquaria, housed in 1933 Radio Station, has fish and animals. Cleeve Abbey (English Heritage) has the gatehouse and more domestic buildings of the little medieval abbey surviving. Washford Station (on the West Somerset Railway) has displays about the Somerset and Dorset Railway.

WASHINGBOROUGH Lincolnshire TF0170
Village off B1188, 3 miles (5km) E of Lincoln
Across River Witham from Lincoln. Stone cottages and 13th-century church, restored in mid-19th century. Late Georgian Washingborough Hall, now a hotel.

WASHINGTON Tyne and Wear NZ2956
New Town on A1231, 6 miles (10km) W of Sunderland
Washington Old Hall was home to the de Wessington family between 1183 and 1288, ancestors of George Washington. Rebuilt in 1613 and saved from demolition in 1936 when it was restored and given to the National Trust. Disused colliery now houses the 'F' Pit Industrial Museum.

WASHINGTON West Sussex TQ1212
Village off A24, 7 miles (11km) N of Worthing
A little place under the South Downs, beneath Chanctonbury (see Wiston), with an interesting church, a famous inn and several pretty cottages.

WASING Berkshire SU5764
Site off A340, 1 mile (2km) SW of Aldermaston
Consists only of the little medieval and 18th-century church and the big house in its park.

WAST WATER Cumbria NY1606
Lake on minor road off A595, 3 miles (5km) NE of Santon Bridge
The deepest lake in England(260ft/79m), surrounded by wild, rugged countryside. An important habitat for crustacea and unusual plants.

WATCHET Somerset ST0743
Town off A39, 15 miles (24km) NW of Bridgwater
Tiny port, with harbour, mostly Victorian or later. Museum in the pretty early Victorian market house. Big and handsome 15th-century church to southwest; fine monuments in Wyndham chapel. St Decaman's Well close by. Local museum. Kentsford House gardens.

WATENDLATH Cumbria NY2716
Hamlet off B5289, 3 miles (5km) NE of Seatoller
Ancient village which now belongs to the National Trust in a picturesque valley south of Derwentwater, on the slopes of High Seat. Watendlath is a popular beauty spot. Sir Hugh Walpole used the village as a setting in his novel *Rogue Herries*.

WATER END Hertfordshire TL0310
Hamlet on A4146, 2 miles (3km) NW of Hemel Hempstead
In the valley of the River Gade, the village green by the river is protected by the National Trust.

WATER NEWTON Cambridgeshire TL1097
Village off A1, 3 miles (5km) SE of Wansford
Located to the west of the significant Roman settlement of *Durobrivae*, close to where Ermine Street crossed the River Nene. Many treasures have been found, including gold and silver plates. Now bypassed by the A1.

Effigy on the church tower at Water Newton.

WATER OF LEITH Lothian
River
Flows from Pentland Hills southwest of Edinburgh, northeast through Balerno and Edinburgh to the Firth of Forth at Leith, dropping over 1,250ft (381m) in 20 miles (32km). Formerly used as power-source for mills, particularly at Dean Village, now a conservation area of Edinburgh with attractive old buildings. Pleasant 13 mile (20km) walkway runs beside the Water into Edinburgh.

WATER ORTON Warwickshire SP1791
Village off A446, 2 miles (3km) NW of Coleshill
With a huge sewage works and equally huge power station near by (now decommissioned), this suburban village is not romantic, but the bizarre Digby inn is worth visiting.

WATERBEACH Cambridgeshire TL4965
Village off A10, 5 miles (8km) NE of Cambridge
Once a dry port on the marshy fens, Waterbeach has Roman Car Dyke to the south, and medieval Denny Abbey (English Heritage) to the north.

WATERFORD Hertfordshire TL3114
Village on A119, 2 miles (3km) NW of Hertford
On the River Beane. The small 1870s church has a splendid Victorian interior and outstanding Pre-Raphaelite stained glass.

WATERINGBURY Kent TQ6853
Village on A26, 5 miles (8km) W of Maidstone
A pleasant brewing village among the hopfields and orchards of the Medway Valley, with attractive houses, both old and new.

WATERLOO Merseyside SJ3197
District in S Crosby
This area of north Liverpool is chiefly residential, having developed in the 1920s.

WATERLOOVILLE Hampshire SU6809
Town on A3, 7 miles (11km) NE of Portsmouth
Mostly 1920s onwards, with a modern shopping centre. Named after an inn called The Heroes of Waterloo.

WATERPERRY Oxfordshire SP6206
Village off A418, 7 miles (11km) E of Oxford
Attractions in this riverside village include a fascinating church, old cottages and Waterperry Gardens (limited opening), part of the horticultural centre founded by Beatrix Havergal as a women's training college.

WATERSMEET Somerset SS7448
Beauty spot off A39, 1 mile (2km) N of Hillsford Bridge
Famous picturesque meeting of the Hoar Oak Water and East Lyn River in a deep woody valley (National Trust).

WATFORD Hertfordshire TQ1196
Town off M1, 16 miles (26km) NW of London
The butt of much unkind humour, and ill served by post-war planning and development, Watford was an old market town which developed into an industrial centre after the arrival of the Grand Union Canal and the railway in the 19th century. It grew into Hertfordshire's biggest town, connected to London by an almost uninterrupted chain of suburbs. Printing and brewing were front runners in this process and the town museum is in an 18th-century mansion which formerly housed the offices of Benskin's Brewery. Besides covering local history and Watford Football Club, it has a good art collection.

The parish church, St Mary's, boasts a notable 16th-century chapel, while the 1880s Roman Catholic Church of the Holy Rood was designed by JF Bentley, architect of London's Westminster Cathedral. Marie Lloyd, Charlie Chaplin and a host of music hall stars played the Watford Palace theatre with its sumptuous Edwardian interior. For open-air pleasures there's attractive walking in Cassiobury Park, with canal cruises from Ironbridge Lock, and nature trails explore Whippendell Woods further west. The more formal Cheslyn Gardens provide colour and interest all year.

WATH North Yorkshire SE3277
Village off A1, 4 miles (6km) N of Ripon
Small village with a cement plant. Norton Conyers is a medieval mansion house with 16th-century extensions. Open to public occasionally.

WATH UPON DEARNE South Yorkshire SE4300
Town on A633, 5 miles (8km) N of Rotherham
Small market town on River Dearne which until recent years had two collieries.

WATLING STREET Greater London)
Roman road
The Roman road from Dover to London, St Albans and Wroxeter. Long stretches of the A2 and A5 roads follow its line today.

WATLINGTON Oxfordshire SU6894
Small town on B480, 7 miles (11km) S of Thame
Elizabethan cottages and a charming range of Georgian houses are preserved in the narrow streets of this ancient town below the Chiltern Hills. The Hare and Hounds is a fine Georgian inn, and the town still has its town hall of 1665. Watlington Hill (National Trust) offers 250 acres (100ha) of beech woodland and chalk grassland on the downs.

WATTON Humberside TA0150
Village on A164, 5 miles (8km) S of Great Driffield
Small village surrounded by outlying farms. Some buildings remain of World War II RAF station.

WATTON Norfolk TF9100
Village on B1077, 8 miles (13km) SE of Swaffham
Connected with local legend 'Babes in the Wood', Watton has a long, pleasing High Street, and near by is ancient Watton Wood.

WATTON-AT-STONE Hertfordshire TL3019
Village off A602, 5 miles (8km) SE of Stevenage
A pretty village on the River Beane, with a curious 19th-century pump and an old hostelry, the George and Dragon.

Pump at Watton-at-Stone.

WAVENEY, RIVER Norfolk
River, tributary of the Yare
The River Waveney rises near Redgrave, and part of its length forms the Suffolk/Norfolk border. Its limit of navigation is Geldeston Lock.

WAVERLEY Surrey SU8645
Site off B3001, 2 miles (3km) SE of Farnham
Beside the peaceful windings of the River Wey, the beautiful ruins of the great Cistercian abbey that inspired Sir Walter Scott.

WAXHAM Norfolk TG4426
Hamlet on B1159, 4 miles (6km) E of Stalham
A tiny coastal village with tree-strewn sand dunes. There is a derelict church and the remains of a Tudor hall.

WEALD, THE East Sussex
Historic region
The Weald is the region of varied landscape between the chalklands of the North and South Downs. In ancient times known as Andredsweald, its name comes from the Old English for woodland. Densely forested in Anglo Saxon times, it still looks wooded from downland viewpoints. It was once an important iron-producing region and is now given over to agriculture, modern industries and residential settlements.

WEAR HEAD Durham NY8539
Village on A689, 9 miles (14km) W of Stanhope
One of the highest villages in England, which can be cut off in winter. Killhope and Burnhope urns converge in the village to form the River Wear.

WEAR, RIVER Durham
River, runs through Bishop Auckland and Durham to Sunderland
Rises high in beautiful North Pennines countryside and flows through lead-mining country of Weardale into more industrial landscape towards Sunderland.

WEARE Somerset ST4152
Village off A38, 2 miles (3km) SW of Axbridge
On the edge of the Somerset Levels, with a 15th-century church. See Lower Weare.

WEARE GIFFARD Devon SS4721
Village off A386, 2 miles (3km) NW of Great Torrington
Along the Torridge Valley, a 15th-century church and 16th-century manor house complete with gatehouse.

WEASENHAM ST PETER Norfolk TF8522
Village on A1065, 6 miles (10km) SW of Fakenham
An attractive village with cottages clustered around the village green. St Peter's Church was restored in the 19th century.

WEAVER, RIVER Cheshire
River, runs through Nantwich and Northwich, tributary of the Mersey
The river flows north through the county of Cheshire and played an important part in the development of the salt industry.

WEAVERHAM Cheshire SJ6174
Village on B5153, on W outskirts of Northwich
Noted for its open spring which was said to have medicinal qualities, the only source of water for many houses into the 20th century.

WEAVERTHORPE North Yorkshire SE9670
Village off B1253, 4 miles (6km) NW of Langtoft
Long and substantial village. The church, which stands alone above the village, has fine early 12th-century Norman features.

WEDMORE Somerset ST4347
Village on B3151, 4 miles (6km) S of Cheddar
Large stone village in the Somerset Levels, with a handsome 15th-century church.

WEDNESBURY West Midlands SO9894
District on A41, in NW West Bromwich
An interesting church and museum and art gallery reward visitors to this town once celebrated for its tubes and gun barrels.

WEDNESFIELD West Midlands SJ9400
District in NE Wolverhampton
Pioneering overspill estates reinvigorated industrial town once noted for making animal traps. It now houses Wolverhampton's main hospital.

WEEDON Buckinghamshire SP8118
Village off A413, 3 miles (5km) N of Aylesbury
A smart place, set among trees on an eminence. Brick houses, thatched or tiled, and some striking Dutch gables. Five Elms pub.

WEEDON BEC Northamptonshire SP6259
Village off A5, 4 miles (6km) SE of Daventry
At busy crossroads of Roman Watling Street (A5) and A45 Northampton–Coventry road. Extensive barracks built from 1803 to protect George III and army, site chosen as farthest from any possible coastal invasion. Some buildings demolished, others turned to commercial and industrial use. Nineteenth-century church with Norman tower, sandwiched between main-line railway viaduct and bank of Grand Union Canal.

WEEDON LOIS Northamptonshire SP606
Village off A43, 6 miles (10km) N of Brackley
Henry Moore monument in churchyard to Edith Sitwell, whose brother, Sacheverell, lived at nearby Weston Hall, where composer William Walton stayed and wrote in the 1930s.

WEEK ST MARY Cornwall SX2397
Village off A39, 6 miles (10km) S of Bude
Now a rather bleak village, Week St Mary was much larger in medieval times. Two greens and earthworks of a medieval castle.

WEEKLEY Northamptonshire SP8880
Village on A43, 2 miles (3km) NE of Kettering
Attractive estate village alongside Boughton Park (see Geddington). Montagu monuments in church. Early 17th-century former Montagu Hospital, and former Free School.

WEELEY Essex TM1422
Village on A133, 5 miles (8km) NW of Clacton-on-Sea
Small, inconspicuous place with a Victorian church. Weeley Hall Wood, one of the biggest woods in Essex, has occasional open days.

WEEM Tayside NN8449
Village on B846, 1 mile (2km) NW of Aberfeldy
Named after St David's Cave on Weem Rock, the village has two churches, one mentioned in 13th-century charters and one dating from the 15th century. Hotel is an old coaching inn, where General Wade lived during construction of Tay Bridge in 1733. To the west is Z-plan 15th-century Castle Menzies, with 19th-century additions, seat of the Clan Menzies.

WEETING Norfolk TL7788
Village on B1106, 2 miles (3km) N of Brandon
Neolithic flint mines Grimes Graves are in Weeting parish. The ruins of a castle (English Heritage) stand romantically in their own parkland near the pretty church.

WEETON Lancashire SD3834
Village on B5260, 3 miles (5km) NW of Kirkham
Attractive village. On one side of the green is a 17th-century thatched house, and on the other the village pub dating from the same period.

WELBECK ABBEY Nottinghamshire SK5674
Estate off A60, 3 miles (5km) SW of Worksop
One of 'The Dukeries', home of Dukes of Portland, now an army college (not open). Harley Gallery exhibition and craft centre. Dukeries Adventure Park and Garden Centre.

WELBOURN Lincolnshire SK9654
Village off A607, 11 miles (18km) S of Lincoln
Attractive village below Lincolnshire Cliff. Substantial 17th-century and 18th-century houses. Church with crocketed spire.

WELBURN North Yorkshire SE7267
Village off A64, 5 miles (8km) SW of Malton
An attractive village with many of the buildings constructed of Ryedale stone. The magnificent Castle Howard estate lies just south of the village.

WELCOMBE Devon SS2218
Village off A39, 8 miles (13km) N of Bude
Remote village named after the holy well close to the tiny medieval church. Set in a valley just back from the harsh rocky coast.

WELDON Northamptonshire SP9289
Village off A43, 2 miles (3km) E of Corby
Lantern tower of Great Weldon church was beacon for travellers through ancient Rockingham Forest. Many fine houses of local Weldon limestone.

WELFORD Berkshire SU4073
Village off B4000, 5 miles (8km) NW of Newbury
Low in the Lambourn Valley, with many racehorses. Prominent church spire and lots of brick.

WELFORD Northamptonshire SP6480
Village on A50, 3 miles (5km) S of Husbands Bosworth
Brick-built village on arm of Grand Union Canal and infant River Avon, forming Leicestershire border. Church with 13th-century south arcade.

WELFORD-ON-AVON Warwickshire SP1452
Village off B439, 4 miles (6km) W of Stratford-upon-Avon
Charming village in a loop of the River Avon, where picturesque cottages in colourful gardens surround the village green and its famous maypole.

The striped village maypole at Welford-on-Avon.

WELL Lincolnshire TF4473
Hamlet off A1104, 1 mile (2km) SW of Alford
Well Hall (Well Vale House) built in 1720s with landscaped park and lakes. Elegant Palladian church built 1733, Tuscan columns, Georgian interior. Walks in Well Vale.

WELL North Yorkshire SE2681
Village off B6267, 8 miles (12km) N of Ripon
An attractive and desirable village. A stream runs down the main street and the houses are reached by small bridges.

WELLAND, RIVER Lincolnshire
River
Rises west of Market Harborough, forming border between Leicestershire and Northamptonshire below Rockingham Castle, then flows into southern Lincolnshire through Stamford, Market Deeping and Spalding to the Wash.

WELLESBOURNE, HASTINGS AND MOUNTFORD Warwickshire SP2855
Villages on A429, 5 miles (8km) E of Stratford-upon-Avon
Wellesbourne Hastings and Wellesbourne Mountford stand on opposite banks of the River Dene. The church has impressive Norman and Victorian work, and both settlements offer an attractive mixture of old cottages and larger houses. There is a restored watermill (limited opening) in Kineton Road, and the Wellesbourne Wartime Museum (limited opening), on former airfield to west of village.

WELLINGBOROUGH Northamptonshire SP8967
Town off A45, 10 miles (16km) NE of Northampton
Nene Valley market town whose industrial base expanded rapidly from 1960s, from traditional footwear to modern high-tech and distribution companies. Ironstone and limestone 15th-century thatched tithe barn, 17th-century Hind hotel, mainly 14th-century All Hallows' Church with 13th-century tower and spire. Church of St Mary the Virgin, 1908–30, by Sir Ninian Comper, with blue and gold interior.

WELLINGHAM Norfolk TF8722
Village off A1065, 6 miles (10km) SW of Fakenham
St Andrew's Church in pretty Wellingham has some very vivid screen-paintings. One shows George fighting the dragon, watched by a kneeling princess.

WELLINGTON Shropshire SJ6511
Town off M54, part of Telford
In the shadow of the Wrekin (see), this utilitarian market town is now incorporated into Telford, but it retains its individuality with narrow shopping streets and homely architecture of early 19th century and later. Standing on its own raised green, All Saints' (1790) is by distinguished architect George Steuart, although his classical interior has been altered.

WELLINGTON Somerset ST1320
Town off A38, 6 miles (10km) SW of Taunton
Small market town, from which the Duke of Wellington (victor at Waterloo) took his title. A 170ft (53m) monument to his memory lies to the south on the Blackdown Hills (see). Old-fashioned, small-scale town, with the market hall of 1833 in the centre, and a few Georgian houses. Local museum.

WELLOW Avon ST7458
Village off A367, 4 miles (6km) S of Bath
Tucked in the valley of the Wellow Brook, the village has a handsome 14th-century church. Stoney Littleton long barrow (to the south) is the best in the area, 107ft (32m) long with stone passage and chambers.

WELLOW Nottinghamshire SK6766
Village on A616, 1 mile (2km) SE of Ollerton
Pretty village with brick and timber-framed houses and cottages, pond and village green with permanent maypole, the centre of annual celebrations. Norman circular earthworks, surrounded by bank and ditch. Medieval church, much restored in Victorian times with east window of 1878 by Kempe. Methodist chapel. Wellow Hall, dated 1700, remodelled in 18th century, with 19th-century wing behind.

WELLS Somerset ST5445
City on A39, 17 miles (24km) S of Bristol
England's smallest city, with one of the finest cathedrals and bishop's palaces. The perfect market square seems to have every type and date of building, with two medieval gatehouses, one leading to the cathedral, the other to the bishop's palace. The palace has the most picturesque setting: walled, moated and with old trees. It includes a 13th-century chapel, ruins of the huge hall, and the Henderson Rooms. The wells or springs which gave the town its name are in the garden.

The most memorable parts of the cathedral are the 13th-century west front, and inside the huge 1330s scissor-braces inserted to stop the tower falling down. There are quantities of fine fittings and monuments, and a famous view up the stone steps to the chapter house.

Vicar's Close is the most complete medieval street in Europe, built in the mid-14th century. The rest of the town is pretty, with a fine 15th-century church (St Cuthbert). Local museum.

WELLS-NEXT-THE-SEA Norfolk TF9143
Small town on A149, 6 miles (10km) E of Burnham Market
A working harbour town with a quayside filled with colourful boats and dock equipment. No longer by the sea, Wells stands on a muddy creek. The Embankment, 1 mile (2km) long, was built to prevent the harbour from silting up altogether, and provides a pleasant walk to the sea. A local delicacy, pickled samphire, can be bought here.

WELNEY Norfolk TL5294
Village on A1101, 5 miles (8km) NW of Littleport
Small village sited on the Ouse Washes. Famous as the home of Welney Washes Nature Reserve, which each winter hosts the spectacle of migrating swans.

WELSH BICKNOR Hereford and Worcester SO5917
Hamlet of B4228, 2 miles (3km) NW of English Bicknor
Welsh border hamlet high above River Wye in Forest of Dean with unexpectedly rich Victorian carving in its church.

WELSH FRANKTON Shropshire SJ3633
Hamlet on A495, 3 miles (5km) SW of Ellesmere
Hamlet of great interest to canal enthusiasts as junction of three of Ellesmere Canal Company's waterways. Llangollen branch, still operational, is very busy in summer.

WELSH NEWTON Hereford and Worcester SO4918
Village on A466, 3 miles (5km) N of Monmouth
Village in hilly countryside, where John Kemble, martyred in 1679 and canonised by Roman Catholic Church in 1970, lies in churchyard.

WELSH ROAD Warwickshire SP4558
Ancient track
Old trackway used by Welsh cattle-drovers on way to London markets survives as minor road passing through Southam and Priors Marston to Byfield in Oxfordshire.

WELSHAMPTON Shropshire SJ4335
Village on A495, 2 miles (3km) E of Ellesmere
Traditional village on Clwyd border has small church by Sir George Gilbert Scott and attractive Victorian school and cottages.

WELSHPOOL (TRALLWNG) Powys SJ2207
Town on A458, 17 miles (27km) W of Shrewsbury
This handsome border town stands in the lush valley of the River Severn beside the Montgomery Canal. Its fine Tudor, Georgian and Victorian buildings include the highly carved 15th/16th-century Buttery and adjacent Prentice Traders. A hexagonal cockpit, the only one in Wales surviving on its original site, stands just off the main street.

Pride of place, however, must go to Powis Castle (National Trust), a border stronghold on the western approach to Welshpool. Dating from around 1200, it evolved into a stately Elizabethan mansion and is now home to a magnificent country house collection and 'Clive of India' memorabilia. Interior features include an elegant long gallery with 16th-century plasterwork and a 17th-century great staircase. The castle's spacious grounds contain a famous terraced garden of the late 17th century and what is claimed to be the tallest tree in Britain, a Douglas Fir.

Welshpool's Powysland Museum (local history and archaeology displays) and the Montgomery Canal Centre are housed at the Canal Wharf. Canal boat trips run from here. The narrow-gauge Welshpool and Llanfair Light Railway connects the town to Llanfair Caereinion (see). The farm-based Moors Collection near by has farm animals, rare breeds and waterfowl.

WELTON Cumbria NY3544
Hamlet on B5299, 4 miles (6km) S of Dalston
The village's name originates from the large number of wells that are in the area.

WELTON Humberside SE9527
Village off A63, 1 mile (2km) SE of Elloughton
Reputedly the prettiest village in Humberside with a mixture of old and new buildings. The Green Dragon inn is famous as the place where Dick Turpin, the highwayman, was nearly captured. Once called the Town of Wells, the village has a well in its centre where water pours continually from an iron pipe, its source being an underground spring.

WELWICK Humberside TA3421
Village on B1445, 2 miles (3km) SE of Patrington
A pleasant village at the east end of Holderness. John and Christopher Wright, born in the village, were involved in the Gunpowder Plot.

WELWYN Hertfordshire TL2316
Town off A1(M), 5 miles (8km) S of Stevenage
On the River Mimram and the old Great North road, which accounts for the coaching inns, including the White Hart and the Wellington, Welwyn has plenty of Georgian houses. A curiosity is a Roman bathhouse (limited opening), discovered in the 1960s when the A1(M) was being built, originally part of a 3rd-century villa and now tucked under the motorway.

WELWYN GARDEN CITY Hertfordshire TL2312
New Town off A1(M), immediately S of Welwyn
This sought-after, if regimented town blends garden and city in attractive accordance with the ideals of Ebenezer Howard, which had been pioneered previously at Letchworth (see). There are broad shopping avenues and tree-lined residential streets with neo-Georgian houses and plenty of greenery.

An enjoyable town trail steers visitors around the garden city. Building began in 1920, with the Frenchman Louis de Soissons as the principal architect, and the early residents, who were often mocked as earnest teetotallers, vegetarians and arty-crafty types, commuted to work in London. Industry, kept in a separate area beyond the railway line, soon began to move in – the Shredded Wheat factory opened in 1925 – and provided jobs. Many residents today, however, are still London commuters.

Open spaces include Sherrardspark Woods, where hornbeams and oaks are clustered in 200 acres (81ha) of woodland near the town centre. Stanborough Park covers 126 acres (51ha), with fishing, sailing and watersports on the lake and bird-watching in a nature reserve among reed marshes. The Campus West complex, meanwhile, functions as cinema, theatre, roller rink and entertainment centre.

WEM Shropshire SJ5128
Small town on B5476, 10 miles (16km) N of Shrewsbury
Essayist William Hazlitt grew up in this pleasant small town, and notorious Judge Jeffreys became Baron Wem. Fire destroyed many early buildings, but the timber-framed old hall remains, together with homely early 19th-century buildings such as Wem Brewery, Castle inn, market hall and Roden House. Aston Hall and Ditches Hall, just outside town, are fine timber-framed manor houses.

WEMBLEY Greater London TQ1885
District in borough of Brent
Largely developed between the wars, Wembley is dominated by Wembley Stadium (guided tours), designed in the 1920s by Sir John Simpson and Maxwell Ayrton, scene of the Cup Final, sports events and pop concerts. Show-jumping and other events at the 1930s Wembley Arena, previously the Empire Pool. Conference centre and exhibition hall. Market on Sundays.

WEMBURY Devon SX5249
District off A379, 5 miles (8km) SE of Plymouth
Old village by the rocky shore, modern inland. The 15th-century church is right by the sea with a good view of the Great Mew Stone just offshore.

WEMYSS BAY Strathclyde NS1969
Village on A78, 7 miles (11km) SW of Greenock
Glasgow's ferry embarkation point for Rothesay on Bute. Outstanding wrought-iron and glass station rebuilt twice since first opening in 1865.

WENDENS AMBO Essex TL5136
Village on B1039, 2 miles (3km) SW of Saffron Walden
One of the smart, expensive villages in the valley of the River Cam, with picture-book thatched cottages and a

charming little church. The tower is Norman and there are medieval wall-paintings inside. The nice old-fashioned Bell pub has a pet goat. *Ambo* is Latin for 'both' and the village combines the earlier Great and Little Wenden, united in 1662.

WENDOVER Buckinghamshire SP8607
Town on A413, 5 miles (8km) SE of Aylesbury
A charming old market town of timber-framed buildings and Georgian red brick in a Chilterns gap, containing antiques shops, tea rooms and a good bookshop. A path runs beside the Misbourne stream from the 19th-century clock tower to the church. Excellent walking country, with nature trails in Wendover Woods and National Trust land including the 852ft (260m) viewpoint of Coombe Hill.

WENDRON Cornwall SW6731
Village on B3297, 2 miles (3km) N of Helston
Bleak hamlet, once a mining area. Granite late medieval church; the lych-gate, unusually, has a room over it.

WENHAM, GREAT AND LITTLE Suffolk TM0738
Villages off B1070, 4 miles (6km) SE of Hadleigh
Two pleasing villages in south Suffolk with the beautiful fortified manor house of Little Wenham Hall, a 13th-century brick building.

WENHASTON Suffolk TM4275
Village off B1123, 3 miles (5km) SE of Halesworth
Sited on flat marshes, Wenhaston appears very Dutch standing on the tidal river. People drowned here during devastating 1953 floods. Church has famous carved panel.

WENLOCK EDGE Shropshire SO5392
Hill ridge
Dramatic wooded ridge with steep eastern escarpment runs for 15 miles (24km) between Much Wenlock and Craven Arms. Immortalised by AE Housman.

WENSLEY North Yorkshire SE0989
Village on A684, 1 mile (2km) W of Leyburn
Once the principal market town of the dale, Wensley is an unspoilt village of neat houses set in beautiful surroundings.

WENSLEYDALE North Yorkshire
Valley of the River Ure above Masham
This beautiful and scenic valley of the River Ure has been immortalised in the novels of James Herriot. The hills along the valley have a characteristic flat-topped appearance, with a jutting cap or lip of hard gritstone and the patterns of ancient drystone walls can still be seen. The area is also noted for its distinctive Wensleydale cheese.

WENTWORTH South Yorkshire SK3898
Village on B6090, 4 miles (7km) NW of Rotherham
Village built along busy road. Wentworth Woodhouse, an 18th-century mansion (not open), has one of the longest frontages in England at 606 feet (185 metres).

WEOBLEY Hereford and Worcester SO4051
Village on B4230, 10 miles (16km) NW of Hereford
The soaring needle spire of the big medieval church guides visitors to this black and white village where picturesque houses and shops line the streets. The timber-framed Unicorn and Red Lion inns and a cruck-framed cottage form a fine group at the centre.

WEOLEY CASTLE West Midlands SP0281
District in SW Birmingham
Within this residential district are the ruins of Weoley Castle (limited opening), a 13th-century fortified manor house. Museum on site.

WERRINGTON Cornwall SX3287
Hamlet off B3254, 2 miles (3km) N of Launceston
Just the church of 1742 and the big Georgian mansion, set in a large, beautiful park.

WESSEX Wiltshire
Historic region in S England
The ancient kingdom of Wessex was the area ruled over by King Alfred the Great in the 9th century. The country of England grew from this kingdom.

WEST ACRE Norfolk TF7715
Village off A1065, 2 miles (3km) W of Castle Acre
The handsome Stag inn and All Saints' Church form the centre of this peaceful village. The remains of an Augustinian priory straddle the River Nar.

WEST ALVINGTON Devon SX7243
Village off A381, 1 mile (2km) W of Kingsbridge
High above the Kingsbridge estuary, with a few stone cottages and a late medieval church.

WEST AUCKLAND Durham NZ1826
Village on A688, immediately SW of Bishop Auckland
One of the ancient green villages of County Durham. Two manor houses face each other across the green, one is now a hotel.

WEST BAY Dorset SY4690
Village on B3157, 2 miles (3km) S of Bridport
Village-sized seaside resort, with a proper harbour still used by fishing boats. Big Victorian block of flats, local museum, fine wild cliffs on either side.

WEST BECKHAM Norfolk TG1439
Village off A148, 2 miles (3km) S of Sheringham
Typical North Norfolk inland coastal village. Its houses are built of blue flint from nearby beaches and are roofed with red pantiles.

WEST BLATCHINGTON East Sussex TQ2807
District in N Hove
Former downland village swallowed up by Hove but with a curious old smock mill of 1820, once sketched by Constable.

WEST BRETTON West Yorkshire SE2813
Village on A637, 5 miles (8km) SW of Wakefield
Rural village. Bretton Park includes Yorkshire Sculpture Park, an open-air gallery exhibiting the work

of celebrated sculptors such as Henry Moore and Barbara Hepworth.

WEST BRIDGFORD Nottinghamshire SK5837
Town off A52, in SE Nottingham
Across Trent Bridge from city of Nottingham. Home of test and county cricket ground, and of Nottingham Forest Football Club.

WEST BROMWICH West Midlands SP0091
Town off M5, 5 miles (8km) NW of Birmingham
The 'capital' of the Metropolitan borough of Sandwell was an agricultural town before industrial development caught up with it in the 18th century, after which it thrived on coal-mining and metal-working, specialising in the making of springs. Today it is primarily a residential, commercial and administrative centre.

The pedestrianised Sandwell Centre, a complex of shops, market hall and car parks, is just one of a number of redevelopment schemes that have transformed the town, but there is evidence of an older history in the restored 16th-century manor house (now a pub and restaurant) in Hall Green Road and in the timber-framed Oak House (open) in Oak Street. The town's Victorian prosperity is reflected in the Gothic town hall in the High Street and the nearby library of 1907.

The great local attraction, however, is Sandwell Valley Country Park, 1,700 acres (680ha) of woodlands, meadows and lakes on the eastern side of the town. Among the many attractive features are nature trails, a restored working farm and the remains of a medieval priory. The park is a welcome amenity for the extensive housing estates that now surround the old town centre.

The windmill at West Blatchington.

WEST BURTON North Yorkshire SE0186
Village on B6160, 1 mile (2km) SE of Aysgarth
The village is built around a large, central green with a distinctive pyramidical market cross dating from 1820 when a large weekly market was held on the green. Mill Force waterfall is best viewed from the little packhorse bridge leading to a footpath to the fells.

WEST BURTON West Sussex SU9913
Village off A29, 4 miles (6km) N of Arundel
Pleasant old houses built around a tight little quadrilateral of lanes beneath the great green downs, just like neighbouring Bignor (see), but with no church.

WEST CHALLOW Oxfordshire SU3688
Village off A417, 2 miles (3km) W of Wantage
Small village below steep edge of Lambourn Downs. The church, roofed with stone slates, has rare 14th-century bellcote and some medieval glass.

WEST CHELBOROUGH Dorset ST5405
Hamlet off A37, 2 miles (3km) W of Evershot
A remote and well-wooded small stone village.

WEST CHILTINGTON West Sussex TQ0918
Village off A283, 3 miles (5km) E of Pulborough
In the complicated sandstone country of the Weald, with deeply cut, twisting lanes, this compact little showpiece of a village is based on crossroads where a small green is surrounded by pretty cottages. The green is dominated by a lovely unrestored 11th- to 12th-century church famed for its medieval wall-paintings. To the southwest is modern housing on an old common, making for a pleasant green suburb.

WEST CLANDON Surrey TQ0452
Village on A247, 4 miles (6km) NE of Guildford
This attractive village is strung along the Guildford–Leatherhead road, with a great house, Clandon Park, rebuilt in the 1730s and set in a park by Capability Brown.

WEST COKER Somerset ST5113
Village on A30, 3 miles (5km) SW of Yeovil
Handsome Ham Hill stone village, with unusual classical almshouses of 1718, and many stone cottages. Some Georgian building, too.

WEST DEAN West Sussex SU8612
Village on A286, 5 miles (8km) N of Chichester
A little place with plenty of flint cottages and a church rebuilt after a fire in 1934, and dominated by West Dean College, with its lovely garden and museum of gardening.

WEST DEAN Wiltshire SU2527
Village off A27, 2 miles (3km) NE of Whiteparish
A large green, thatched cottages and a pub which is half in Wiltshire, half in Hampshire. Part of the old church survives; it is full of monuments.

WEST DERBY Merseyside SJ4092
District in E Liverpool
An attractive area with an interesting centre. Croxteth Hall, historic home of the Earls of Sefton, has nature trails, guided walks and a Home Farm.

WEST DRAYTON Greater London TQ0579
District in borough of Hillingdon
Developed since the 1920s, close to Heathrow Airport (see). Attractive green. Parish church and the remains of a Tudor manor house.

WEST END Hampshire SU4614
Suburb off A27, 4 miles (6km) NE of Southampton
Well wooded with some Victorian houses, but mostly 1950s onwards.

WEST FARLEIGH Kent TQ7153
Village on B2010, 3 miles (5km) SW of Maidstone
Scatter of big houses, an early Norman church and the lovely Kentish cricket ground at Farleigh Green among orchards and hopfields beside the River Medway.

WEST FELTON Shropshire SJ3524
Village off A5, 3 miles (5km) SE of Oswestry
Norman church and castle motte stand together among pleasant houses in leafy village centre, while modern village expands on other side of A5.

WEST FIRLE East Sussex TQ4707
Village off A27, 4 miles (6km) SE of Lewes
A little village tucked under the South Downs at Firle Beacon. This famous viewpoint, 618ft (188m) up, commands sweeping vistas northwards over the Weald to Leith Hill and the North Downs and southwards to the English Channel above Newhaven. Firle Place, one of the loveliest great houses of Sussex with a mellow Georgian façade on a Tudor building, has been the home of the Gage family for 500 years.

WEST GRINSTEAD West Sussex TQ1720
Village off A24, 3 miles (5km) SW of Cowfold
Deep in the Weald, hidden from prying eyes, with a scatter of great houses including Knepp Castle, the ancient parish church, and a Roman Catholic connection.

WEST HADDON Northamptonshire SP6371
Village on A428, 7 miles (11km) NE of Daventry
Thirteenth-century and later church, medieval ironstone and limestone patterning in wall, fine timber roof, carved Norman font, 1850 window by Pugin.

WEST HAM Greater London TQ3983
Town in borough of Newham
A former Essex town, swallowed up by London. The famous football club plays at Upton Park. West Ham Park opened in the 1870s.

WEST HANNEY Oxfordshire SU4092
Village off A338, 3 miles (5km) N of Wantage
Popular village in the Vale of the White Horse. Small church with rich medieval carving and memorial brasses.

WEST HANNINGFIELD Essex TQ7399
Village off A130, 5 miles (8km) S of Chelmsford
Fishing, watersports, nature trails and bird-watching at the huge Hanningfield Reservoir to the south. Interesting church with wooden tower.

WEST HARDWICK West Yorkshire SE4118
Hamlet off B6428, 1 mile (2km) NE of Wragby
Isolated and rural hamlet consisting of a handful of arable farms with no real centre.

WEST HARPTREE Avon ST5656
Village on A368, 7 miles (11km) N of Wells
On the slopes of the Mendips, the older buildings all in the local stone, Dolomitic Conglomerate.

WEST HENDRED Oxfordshire SU4488
Village off A417, 3 miles (5km) E of Wantage
The village, sprawling on the slopes overlooking the Vale of the White Horse, boasts a fine collection of medieval tiles in its 14th-century church.

WEST HOATHLY West Sussex TQ3632
Village off B2028, 4 miles (6km) SW of East Grinstead
A hilltop village with an attractive street lined with historic houses, including the 17th-century manor house and half-timbered Priest House, now a museum. The medieval church, opposite the well-known Cat inn, dominates the village, and has an unusual terraced churchyard – built on a medieval vineyard – with lovely views over the Weald. Nearby Gravetye Manor, now a hotel, is an Elizabethan manor house with an imposing south front; it was the home of the great gardener, William Robinson.

A brass in the side chapel of the church at West Hoathly.

WEST HORSLEY Surrey TQ0752
Village off A246, 6 miles (10km) E of Guildford
A single long street runs north from the main road; the church lies on the main road to the east, with some Saxon remains, remnants of early 13th-century murals and the supposed resting place of the head of Sir Walter Raleigh. West Horsley Place, which Raleigh's son inherited, is a large medieval building, rebuilt in about 1630.

WEST HUNTINGTOWER Tayside NO0725
Village on A85, 3 miles (5km) NW of Perth
Noted for Huntingtower Castle, formerly Ruthven Castle, built in the 15th and 16th centuries as two separate houses and joined in the 17th century.

WEST ITCHENOR West Sussex SU7901
Village off B2179, 5 miles (8km) SW of Chichester
An attractive village on Chichester Harbour with the harbour office, attractive 18th-century cottages, a pub, a prestigious sailing club and plenty of boats.

WEST KENNETT Wiltshire SU1168
Hamlet on A4, 1 mile (2km) SE of Avebury
Just the Georgian big house and a famous neolithic long barrow with stone chambered tomb.

WEST KILBRIDE Strathclyde NS2048
Town on B781, 4 miles (6km) NW of Ardrossan
With contiguous Seamill, a Clyde coast resort with good sandy beaches and views to the Cumbrae Islands. To northwest ruined Portencross Castle stands on Farland Head, off which a Spanish galleon was reputed to have sunk. West Kilbride Museum Society runs local museum with textile displays, costumes, lace, and changing exhibits.

WEST KINGTON Wiltshire ST8077
Village off B4039, 7 miles (11km) W of Chippenham
Pretty stone and thatch cottages close to the old bridge. Well wooded.

WEST KIRBY Merseyside SJ2186
Town on A540, 1 mile (2km) S of Hoylake
A seaside resort, with long promenade, beach and marine lake, along the Dee estuary. Much development took place in the latter part of the 19th century.

WEST LAVINGTON West Sussex SU8920
Village off A286, immediately SE of Midhurst
Small village consisting of a Victorian church and a few big houses folded among trees close to Midhurst.

WEST LAVINGTON Wiltshire SU0053
Village on A360, 5 miles (8km) S of Devizes
Large straggling village, the old buildings a mixture of brick, stone and timber-framing, but much modern housing too.

WEST LINTON Borders NT1551
Village on A702, 7 miles (11km) SW of Penicuik
Picturesque village on edge of Pentland Hills, which was once important toll point on the northwest drove road, and noted for its large sheep fairs. Whipman Society formed in 1803, horsemen's mutual aid society, which still holds annual week of celebration in June. Noted for stone-carving, with fine examples in main street and old churchyard.

WEST LULWORTH Dorset SY8280
Village on B3071, 4 miles (6km) S of Wool
Famous for Lulworth Cove, a circular bay almost encircled by cliffs. Wild countryside, wonderful for walking, extends on both sides, with the natural rock arch of Durdle Door in the sea to the west. The village of thatched stone cottages is set back from the sea. Lulworth Heritage Centre has displays about the area.

WEST LYNN Norfolk TF6120
District across the River Ouse from King's Lynn
West Lynn is a straggle of pretty fishermen's cottages along the banks of the River Ouse facing King's Lynn.

WEST MALLING Kent TQ6857
Village on A20, 5 miles (8km) W of Maidstone
Large village with a wide High Street, where most buildings are scheduled for architectural interest. It includes plenty of fine 18th-century façades and 600-year-old Ford House. St Mary's Abbey incorporates parts of a nunnery founded in 1090; St Leonard's Tower is the remains of a Norman manor house; the Tudor Swan hotel, in Swan Street, was a coaching inn where Dr Johnson stayed.

WEST MALVERN Hereford and Worcester SO7646
see Great Malvern

WEST MEON Hampshire SU6424
Village on A32, 3 miles (5km) NE of Meonstoke
Many brick and timber-framed thatched cottages, and an impressive 1840s church, built of small squared flints.

WEST MERSEA Essex TM0112
Town at W end of Mersea Island
Resort with shingle and sand beach, sailing and fishing, attendant bungalows. Mersea Island museum covers local and natural history.

WEST MONKTON Somerset ST2628
Village off A38, 4 miles (6km) NE of Taunton
Belonged to Glastonbury Abbey, hence the name. Big plain 14th-century church tower, elaborate late medieval wooden roof with angels.

WEST MOORS Dorset SU0703
Small town on B3072, 8 miles (13km) N of Bournemouth
Heathland village grown large since the 1970s. West Moors Country Park and Forest, including very good adventure trails.

WEST NORWOOD Greater London TQ3272
District in borough of Lambeth
Suburbanised in the 19th century, this was originally Lower Norwood; the name changed in 1885. Notable Victorian cemetery, with Greek Orthodox section.

WEST PECKHAM Kent TQ6452
Village off A26, 5 miles (8km) NE of Tonbridge
Cottages, manor farm, inn and church in a tight cluster near the village cricket green among Kentish orchards.

WEST PENNARD Somerset ST5438
Village on A361, 3 miles (5km) E of Glastonbury
On the lower slopes of Pennard Hill. One mile (2km) to the south is 14th-century Court Barn (National Trust).

WEST PUTFORD Devon SS3515
Village off A388, 8 miles (13km) N of Holsworthy
Rural village on the River Torridge. Medieval church with an unusually large number of 16th-century Barnstaple floor tiles.

WEST QUANTOXHEAD Somerset ST1142
Village on A39, 3 miles (5km) E of Watchet
At the seaward end of the Quantocks, a 19th-century village in park-like setting, with church, manor house and school all rebuilt in the mid-19th century.

WEST RASEN Lincolnshire TF0689
Village on A631, 3 miles (5km) W of Market Rasen
Small village, outgrown by Market Rasen. Packhorse bridge crosses River Rase. Ironstone church has Norman arcading and medieval stone seats around pillars.

WEST ROW Suffolk TL6775
Village off A1101, 2 miles (3km) W of Mildenhall
A peaceful little village standing near the River Lark on the Cambridgeshire/Suffolk border. A house was converted into St Peter's Church in 1850.

WEST RUNTON Norfolk TG1842
Village on A149, 2 miles (3km) E of Sheringham
Home of North Norfolk Heavy Horse and Pony Centre. The beach is safe for swimming, and was once a source of amber.

WEST SOMERTON Norfolk TG4520
Village on B1159, 2 miles (3km) W of Winterton-on-Sea
Pleasing little village near Martham Broad and the River Thurne. 'Norfolk giant' Robert Hales born here. He was almost 8ft (2m) tall.

WEST STAFFORD Dorset SY7389
Village off A352, 3 miles (5km) E of Dorchester
Village in the Frome Valley, with many thatched cottages. Little 16th- and 17th-century church with many 1640 fittings.

WEST STOCKWITH Nottinghamshire SK7994
Village off A161, 5 miles (8km) NW of Gainsborough
Brick village beside River Trent, the Lincolnshire boundary. Rectangular brick church, restored 1963, with monument to ship's carpenter.

WEST STOW Suffolk TL8170
Village off A1101, 5 miles (8km) NW of Bury St Edmunds
In 1849 a Saxon cemetery was found in West Stow; in 1940 Roman kilns were discovered; in 1947, remains of a Saxon village were revealed. A group of thatched wooden huts and a hall were reconstructed, and are open daily. The village lies within the 125 acres (51ha) of woodland, marsh and heath that comprise the West Stow Country Park.

WEST TANFIELD North Yorkshire SE2678
Village off A6108, 5 miles (8km) NW of Ripon
Attractive stone-built village along the River Ure. A remarkable Tudor gatehouse, Marmion Tower, overlooks the riverside (open to the public).

WEST TARRING West Sussex TQ1303
District in NW Worthing
Fine old village caught up within modern Worthing, centred on a crossroads with a High Street lined with flint and stucco cottages and one half-timbered house.

WEST THORNEY West Sussex SU7602
Village off A27, 3 miles (5km) SE of Emsworth (on Thorney Island)
Church, cottages and RAF housing lurk behind an old airfield on the eastern shore of low-lying mud-girt Thorney Island in Chichester Harbour.

WEST THURROCK Essex TQ5877
Village off A13, 4 miles (6km) W of Tilbury
The enormous Lakeside shopping centre stands in regenerated industrial wasteland. St Clement's Church has a wildlife sanctuary. Queen Elizabeth II Bridge opened in 1991.

WEST WALTON Norfolk TF4713
Village off A47, 3 miles (5km) N of Wisbech
West Walton has a wonderful 13th-century detached church tower standing tall and aloof from the houses clustered around it.

WEST WEMYSS Fife NT3194
Village off A955, 4 miles (6km) NE of Kirkcaldy
Once a coal port, taking its name from coastal 'weems', or caves. Some near by contain Bronze, Iron Age and Pictish carvings. Castle and 18th-century tollbooth.

WEST WITTERING West Sussex SZ7898
Village on B2179, 6 miles (10km) NW of Selsey
Attractive houses and gardens and a row of restored cottages by the western shore of Selsey peninsula overlooking long, sandy Bracklesham Bay.

WEST WYCOMBE Buckinghamshire SU8294
Village on A40, immediately NW of High Wycombe
Wonderfully picturesque main street owned by the National Trust. West Wycombe Park (National Trust) is the grand 18th-century mansion of Sir Francis Dashwood, notorious leader of the Hell-Fire Club, who remodelled the magnificent hilltop church, built the mausoleum and dug out the caves, where he and his riotous friends are portrayed in tableaux.

WESTBOROUGH Lincolnshire SK8544
Village off A1, 7 miles (11km) NW of Grantham
Attractive 17th- and 18th-century houses. Church beside River Witham has a pleasing mixture of styles from late 12th-century nave to 1752 tower.

WESTBOURNE West Sussex SU7507
Village on B2147, 2 miles (3km) E of Havant
Attractive former market town on the Hampshire border, now dwindled to a quiet village with 18th- and 19th-century houses and a little 'square' beside the big medieval church.

WESTBROOK Kent TR3369
District off A28, W extension of Margate
Residential suburb of Margate with famous sea-bathing hospital founded in 1791 by Dr Lettsom, founder of the British Medical Society.

WESTBURY Shropshire SJ3509
Village on B4386, 9 miles (14km) W of Shrewsbury
Fascinating earthworks of Caus Castle (access with permission) lie to southwest of this pleasant mix of traditional dwellings above Rea Valley.

WESTBURY Wiltshire ST8751
Town on A350, 4 miles (6km) S of Trowbridge
A woollen cloth town from medieval times, with a large market place. Pleasant Georgian houses, everything small-scale. The town hall was built in 1815, and the indoor swimming pool of 1887 is supposedly the oldest still in use in Britain. A museum is housed in a restored woollen cloth mill and a 400ft (122m) chimney to the north was built for a large cement factory. The Woodland Park is to the west. Westbury White Horse (see Bratton).

WESTBURY ON SEVERN Gloucestershire SO7114
Village on A48, 4 miles (6km) E of Cinderford
Scattered village close to the Severn estuary has an unusual church with a massive detached tower (impressive timber-framing inside) and a soaring 14th-century spire. Westbury Court Garden (National Trust, limited opening) is the earliest example in England of a formal Dutch water garden with canals and yew hedges. Laid out by Maynard Colchester in about 1700.

WESTBURY-ON-TRYM Avon ST5777
District on A4018 in N Bristol
Mostly 1930s suburban development, but with the 15th-century gatehouse and church surviving from a college of priests. The church is partly 13th century with a 15th-century tower.

WESTCLIFF-ON-SEA Essex TQ8685
District in SW Southend
This sedate Victorian suburb of Southend (see) features the Beecroft art gallery, cliff gardens overlooking the seafront, the Cliffs Pavilion entertainment centre and an Edwardian church.

WESTCOTT Surrey TQ1448
Village on A25, 1 mile (2km) W of Dorking
Cheerful village centred on a little green with pleasant Victorian houses and an open common to the west. This was the birthplace, in 1766, of the famous economist, Thomas Malthus.

WESTDEAN East Sussex TV5299
Hamlet off A259, 2 miles (3km) S of Alfriston
An enchanting little hamlet on the South Downs Way in Friston Forest, over 1,500 acres (607ha) planted in 1926 with beeches and conifers. Westdean is probably the 'Dene' where Alfred the Great had a palace and met the famous Saxon historian Asser. The ruins of the manor house are on the palace site, and stand opposite the old rectory built in 1220, Westdean's oldest building.

WESTENHANGER Kent TR1237
Village off A20, 3 miles (5km) NW of Hythe
Village beside Folkestone Racecourse. Strewn along Stone Street, the Roman Canterbury–Lympne road, with a nearby ruinous fragment of a 14th-century manor house, similar to Bodiam Castle (see).

WESTER ROSS Highland
Scenic region in NW Highlands
Mountainous and scenic western half of former county of Ross and Cromarty, stretching from Kyle of Lochalsh to Ullapool and Summer Isles, and eastwards to flatter country south of Dornoch Firth. Coastline is deeply indented with numerous sea-lochs. Area of great natural beauty with crofting and tourism providing most local employment.

WESTERGATE West Sussex SU9305
Village on A29, 4 miles (6km) N of Bognor Regis
This residential area of modern houses and flint cottages (without a church) marks the location of the western gate on to a former common lying between it and Eastergate.

WESTERHAM Kent TQ4454
Small town on A25, 5 miles (8km) W of Sevenoaks
A pleasant town set on a rise beneath the Kentish sandstone hills close to the M25. Its High Street, the busy A25, twists over the hill, broadening past the little green to form the old market place, fronted by two former coaching inns. The church, on the northern corner of the green, has an unusual staircase to the tower. The tapering green is surrounded by attractive 17th- and 18th-century houses and dominated by two statues of famous Westerham men. One is a seated likeness of Sir Winston Churchill by Oscar Nemon (1969), the other shows General Wolfe, brandishing his sword.

There are several fine houses, including Quebec House, a gabled building of the early 17th century, childhood home of General James Wolfe, victor at Quebec, 1759, where he was killed. Now National Trust, it houses the Wolfe Museum. To the south is Squerries Court, a William and Mary house, home of the Ward family. Chartwell, Sir Winston Churchill's home for 40 years, is 1 mile (2km) south. This Tudor manor house (National Trust) was rebuilt for Sir Winston in 1923, and houses a museum and exhibition.

WESTFIELD East Sussex TQ8115
Village on A28, 4 miles (6km) N of Hastings
Modern red-brick village and ancient church strung along the main road to Hastings, with the old centre tucked down a by-road with weatherboarded cottages and an inn.

WESTGATE ON SEA Kent TR3270
District off A28, on W outskirts of Margate
Family resort on north Kent coast with clean, sandy beach backed by chalk cliffs with a grassy clifftop.

WESTHALL Suffolk TM4280
Hamlet off B1124, 3 miles (5km) NE of Halesworth
An atmospheric village set in a secluded valley. The Norman church is thatched and stands in a churchyard with trees.

WESTHAM East Sussex TQ6404
Village off A27, immediately W of Pevensey
Old village with some timber buildings and a path from the Norman church to the west gate of Pevensey Castle. The church was probably the first built in England after the Conquest in 1066.

WESTHAMPNETT West Sussex SU8806
Village on A285, 2 miles (3km) NE of Chichester
Attractive village of simple cottages with an interesting church overshadowed by Chichester Cathedral spire. Now bypassed by busy A-roads, it is able to breathe again.

WESTHAY Somerset ST4342
Village on B3151, 5 miles (8km) NW of Glastonbury
Village in the Somerset Levels, with Peat Moors visitor centre which includes replicas of the prehistoric trackways, an Iron Age settlement and the history of peat. Nature reserve.

WESTHORPE Suffolk TM0469
Village off B1113, 7 miles (11km) N of Stowmarket
The pretty Church of St Margaret's is impressive because it has not suffered from heavy-handed restoration. The floor is uneven brick and medieval tiles.

WESTHOUGHTON Greater Manchester SD6505
Town on A58, 5 miles (8km) E of Wigan
A small industrial town in the coal measures between Wigan and Bolton.

WESTLETON Suffolk TM4469
Village on B1125, 3 miles (5km) E of Yoxford
Nature reserves surround pleasant Westleton village with its ancient green, duck pond, and medieval thatched church. North Warren is RSPB heathland.

WESTLEY WATERLESS Cambridgeshire TL6256
Village off B1061, 5 miles (8km) S of Newmarket
The pretty Church of St Mary the Less has especially fine brasses to Sir John and Lady Alyne de Creke dating to 1324.

WESTMESTON East Sussex TQ3313
Village on B2166, 5 miles (8km) NW of Lewes
An attractive little village at the foot of the South Downs with a church, 17th-century cottages and a manor house; haunted by several well-attested ghosts.

WESTMILL Hertfordshire TL3627
Village off A10, 2 miles (3km) S of Buntingford
A delightful village off the beaten track, with a broad main street, old houses, green and pump. The Sword in Hand pub has an interesting sign.

WESTMINSTER, CITY OF Greater London TQ2979
see London (Central)

WESTON Hertfordshire TL2530
Village off A507, 3 miles (5km) SE of Baldock
A pretty place with a green and duck pond. Guardsmen's furry busbies are made here. The Norman church has a legendary giant's grave.

WESTON Lincolnshire TF2924
Village on A151, 3 miles (5km) E of Spalding
Fenland village, with one of the county's purest examples of a 13th-century church, later tower. Wykeham Chapel (1311) built as country house chapel. Georgian farmhouses.

WESTON Staffordshire SJ9727
Village off A518, 4 miles (6km) NE of Stafford
Village beside River Trent with interesting medieval church, appealing houses and cottages (some 17th century) and old Woolpack inn facing village green.

WESTON LONGVILLE Norfolk TG1115
Village off A1067, 9 miles (14km) NW of Norwich
Life-sized prehistoric beasts lurk among the woods and parkland of Weston Longville Dinosaur Natural History Park. The village overlooks the peaceful River Wensum, and there are several handsome 19th-century houses and a 13th-century church. Parson James Woodforde arrived here in 1776 and kept a diary (full of details of rural life, especially his meals) until 1803.

WESTON RHYN Shropshire SJ2835
Village off A5, 4 miles (6km) N of Oswestry
Workaday village with Victorian church and chapels befitting former coal-mining community and now attracting much modern housing.

WESTON SUBEDGE Gloucestershire SP1240
Village off A44, 2 miles (3km) NW of Chipping Campden
Roman Ryknild Street skirts this orchard village with its array of appealing stone and timber-framed cottages. Interesting church interior.

WESTON UNDER PENYARD Hereford and Worcester SO6323
Village on A40, 2 miles (3km) E of Ross-on-Wye
The Romans smelted iron here on fringe of Forest of Dean, but village today is a scatter of stone cottages and handsome larger houses.

WESTON UNDERWOOD Buckinghamshire SP8650
Village off A509, 2 miles (3km) W of Olney
Georgian houses dignify 'one of the prettiest villages in the kingdom', as the poet William Cowper described it. He lived here in the 1780s and 90s. The 'wilderness' gardens where he liked to write are now home to birds of 150 species in the Flamingo Gardens and Zoological Park, one of the best collections of exotic birds in the country.

WESTON (WESTON-UNDER-REDCASTLE) Shropshire SJ5629
Village off A49, 3 miles (5km) E of Wem
Appealing estate village lying beside sandstone cliffs and spectacular 18th-century follies of Hawkstone Park. Georgian Hawkstone Hall (college) is occasionally open.

WESTON-IN-GORDANO Avon ST4474
Village on B3124, 3 miles (5km) NE of Clevedon
Tiny village,with a medieval church tucked under the ridge overlooking the valley which gives the second part of the name.

WESTON-ON-THE-GREEN Oxfordshire SP5318
Village off A34, 4 miles (6km) SW of Bicester
Village on edge of Otmoor (see), where the elegant Weston Manor House (hotel) hides a medieval core. Church is unusual mixture of medieval and classical.

WESTON-SUPER-MARE Avon ST3261
Town on A370, 18 miles (28km) SW of Bristol
Big seaside resort on a sandy bay between two headlands. Developed from the 1840s, it has many Victorian buildings. Weston Woods, on the ridge to the north, have a toll road running through them. The Woodspring Museum has local displays, and the International Helicopter Museum displays many helicopters. New sea-life centre.

WESTON-UNDER-LIZARD Staffordshire SJ8010
Village on A5, 7 miles (11km) E of Telford
Estate village for Weston Park (limited opening), 17th-century mansion of Earl of Bradford with distinguished decoration and furnishings. Grounds by Capability Brown.

WESTONING Bedfordshire TL0332
Village on A5120, 4 miles (6km) S of Ampthill
A village of some timber-framed buildings and a clock tower put up to celebrate Queen Victoria's 1897 Diamond Jubilee.

WESTONZOYLAND Somerset ST3534
Village on A372, 4 miles (6km) E of Bridgwater
In the Somerset Levels, the site of the Battle of Sedgemoor (1685), when the Duke of Monmouth, claimant to the throne and illegitimate son of Charles II, was defeated by King James II. Very fine 15th-century church with 100ft (30m) tower and one of the finest wooden roofs, with angel supports. The 19th-century steam-powered pumping station, which helped to drain the levels, is occasionally open.

WESTOW North Yorkshire SE7565
Village off A64, 5 miles (8km) SW of Malton
Small village of grey stone cottages and several surrounding farms. Church was rebuilt in the 19th century but contains much earlier features.

WESTRAY Orkney
Island lying N of Rousay
Island to northwest of Orkney group, with fertile, gentler slopes to south rising to dramatic cliffs of Noup Head in northwest. Main village is Pierowall with ruins of 17th-century Notland Castle near by and St Mary's Parish Church with interesting inscribed tombstones. Economy is based on fishing, beef-cattle and sheep-rearing. Excellent bird-watching and maritime flora.

WESTWARD HO! Devon SS4329
Village on B3236, 2 miles (3km) NW of Bideford
Charles Kingsley's book, *Westward Ho!* (1855), popularised this remote area of the coast, and the settlement developed from the 1870s. The Victorian buildings are cluttered up with modern alterations, and there is much modern development too, as well as a sandy surfing beach (see Northam).

WESTWELL Kent TQ9947
Village off A251, 3 miles (5km) N of Ashford
Pretty village with a 13th-century church tucked among chestnut trees in the hills close to the Pilgrims' Way.

WESTWELL Oxfordshire SP2209
Village off A361, 2 miles (3km) SW of Burford
Fine Norman church, 17th-century rectory and manor house of Tudor origin form attractive picture by village green. Unusual war memorial.

WESTWOOD Wiltshire ST8159
Village off A363, 1 mile (2km) SW of Bradford-on-Avon
A handsome stone village with a fine medieval church. Westwood Manor (National Trust) is a perfect stone manor house, late medieval and early 17th century, with a topiary garden. Iford Manor is a handsome Georgian stone mansion, with fascinating gardens ornamented with old Italian sculpture. Lovely setting by the River Frome.

The 'Shrapnel' gateway of Midway Manor at Westwood.

WETHERAL Cumbria NY4654
Village on B6263, 4 miles (6km) E of Carlisle
The village has the only church in England dedicated to St Constantine and a viaduct, built in 1830, by Francis Giles.

WETHERBY West Yorkshire SE4048
Small town off A1, 12 miles (23km) SE of Boroughbridge
Ancient market town. Original stone bridge with six arches, parts of it medieval, carries Great North road over River Wharfe.

WETHERDEN Suffolk TM0062
Village off A14 (A45), 4 miles (6km) NW of Stowmarket
An ancient village whose origins lie in sheep-rearing and wool. Delightful old cottages and church stand near much newer buildings.

WETHERINGSETT Suffolk TM1266
Village off B1077, 4 miles (6km) NW of Debenham
A pleasant agricultural village famous for two rectors – the 17th-century geographer Richard Hakluyt, and GW Ellis, who was not a priest at all.

WETHERSFIELD Essex TL7131
Village on B1053, 2 miles (3km) SE of Finchingfield
Attractive, hilly village with a green at the centre and many timber-framed houses.

WETTON Staffordshire SK1055
Village off A515, 7 miles (11km) NW of Ashbourne
Exposed moorland village of old stone cottages with Castern Wood Nature Reserve and dramatic Thor's Cave overlooking the Manifold Valley near by. Splendid views.

WETWANG Humberside SE9359
Village on A166, 6 miles (10km) W of Great Driffield
Located on a busy road, Wetwang has expanded greatly in the latter half of the 20th century. A craftsman here uses the symbol of a rabbit on his work.

WEY, RIVER Surrey
River
The Wey flows 35 miles (56km) from Alton, through Godalming and Guildford to the River Thames at Weybridge. This was England's first 'improved' river, with locks built in 1653, creating the 'Wey and Godalming Navigation'.

WEYBOURNE Norfolk TG1143
Village on A149, 3 miles (5km) W of Sheringham
The steep shingle beach is called Weybourne Hoop (or Hope). It was considered a vulnerable spot during the Armada crisis and in both world wars.

WEYBREAD Suffolk TM2480
Village on B1116, 2 miles (3km) S of Harleston
St Andrew's Church has a lovely Norman tower, although the church itself has been Victorianised inside. One house has 17th-century pargetting.

WEYBRIDGE Surrey TQ0764
Town on A317, 4 miles (6km) W of Esher
Old town on the confluence of the rivers Thames and Wey, after which it is named. The iron bridge which spans the Wey was built in 1865. Near by, close to a modern housing estate, are the remains of Oatlands Palace, built by Henry VIII with masonry from various Surrey monastic institutions. The church of 1848 has a tall spire and highly decorative interior.

WEYHILL Hampshire SU3146
Village on A342, 3 miles (5km) W of Andover
Just a little roadside settlement now, but until 1957 the site of a famous fair, one of the largest in medieval England.

WEYMOUTH Dorset SY6778
Town on A353, 26 miles (42km) W of Bournemouth
A port from medieval times, and one of the earliest seaside resorts, made fashionable from 1789 because George III spent his summers there.

The natural harbour of the River Wey is still used by fishing vessels, big ferries and lots of pleasure craft. The harbour has the Diving and Shipwreck Museum, and Brewer's Quay with Timewalk, modern displays on the history of the area and the Discovery scientific exhibition. Tudor House is one of the few earlier survivors, fitted out with old furniture. The Nothe is the headland sheltering the harbour, crowned by an 1860s fort, now with good displays.

The long sandy bay of the resort is round the corner from the harbour, and lined with fine late Georgian terraces, also found in many other areas of the town. A big statue of George III is colourfully painted, and buildings include the stone guildhall of 1836 and classical church of 1815.

Radipole Lake is a nature reserve, particularly good for birds, and at Lodmoor the sea-life park has many fish and other sea creatures.

Weymouth combines three completely different areas: the harbour, with its ships and boats, bordered by attractive buildings; the town proper with the shopping centre; and the long sandy bay of the resort, lined with Georgian terraces.

WHADDON Buckinghamshire SP8034
Village off A421, 4 miles (6km) W of Bletchley
From its hilltop, Whaddon surveys the former hunting forest of Whaddon Chase. It is now a dormitory village for Milton Keynes (see).

WHALEY BRIDGE Derbyshire SK0181
Town off A6, 6 miles (10km) NW of Buxton
Small industrial town of cotton-spinning and engineering at entrance to wooded Goyt Valley, surrounded by hills. Canal boat hire on Peak Forest Canal with 1832 wharf buildings, canal cottage and stable block for horses who worked here. Nearby Buxworth Basin provided interchange for limestone from horse-drawn trams to canal boats.

WHALLEY Lancashire SD7336
Small town off A59, 6 miles (10km) NE of Blackburn
Attractive historic village on the River Calder, with 13th-century church. The remains of Whalley Abbey, also 13th century, include a well-preserved gateway and part of the chapter house. Large, 48-arch viaduct

carries the Blackburn to Clitheroe railway line across the Calder Valley.

WHALSAY Shetland
Island lying E of mainland
Shetland's most prosperous fishing community with majority of 1,000 population involved in industry. Once herring-based, modern fleet of purse seiners was developed in 1970s and operates from 1980s harbour at Symbister. Pier House recalls early Hanseatic trade. White fishing, net manufacture, fish-processing and fish-farming provide employment. Prehistoric sites at Yoxie and Bennie Hoose.

WHALTON Northumberland NZ1381
Village on B6524, 5 miles (8km) SW of Morpeth
An agricultural village with some houses built around pele towers. Church is mainly 13th century.

WHAPLODE Lincolnshire TF3224
Village on A151, 2 miles (3km) W of Holbeach
Large fenland village, on main road between Spalding and Holbeach. Impressive church with Norman nave and clerestory, almost detached 12th-century tower, 14th-century south porch, grand Stuart tomb. At Whaplode St Catherine is the Museum of Entertainment – working museum of fairground and mechanical music (limited opening).

WHARFE, RIVER North Yorkshire
River, runs through Ilkley and Tadcaster to the Ouse
Wharfedale is the longest and one of the most spectacular of the Yorkshire dales, dominated by Great Scar limestone. The river begins almost as a moorland stream high on Cam Fell, and its peat-coloured water runs broad and shallow, capable of rising at great speed, through mid-Wharfedale.

WHARNCLIFFE SIDE South Yorkshire SK2994
Village on A6102, 6 miles (10km) NW of Sheffield
Small village on the edge of Howden Moors, nestling below Wharncliffe Crags, a millstone grit escarpment, and dominated by Wharncliffe Wood.

WHARRAM PERCY North Yorkshire SE8564
Deserted village off B1248, 1 mile (2km) SW of Wharram-le-Street
This deserted village has been made accessible to visitors and many house and croft walls can be traced.

WHARRAM-LE-STREET North Yorkshire SE8665
Village on B1248, 6 miles (10km) SE of Malton
At the crossing of a Roman road with an even older route, the village is clustered around its 11th-century church.

WHATSTANDWELL Derbyshire SK3354
Hamlet on B5035, 4 miles (6km) N of Belper
Where A6 crosses River Derwent. Florence Nightingale walked home from the station here to Lea to avoid the crowds waiting to greet her return from Scutari. Railway, canal and road follow river valley.

WHATTON Nottinghamshire SK7439
Village off A52, 3 miles (5km) E of Bingham
Between River Smite and Nottingham–Grantham road. Church with Norman and 14th-century work, Victorian restoration. Windmill, about 1820, with five storeys and no cap.

WHEATFIELD Oxfordshire SU6899
Site off A40, 3 miles (5km) N of Watlington
Below Chiltern Hills a farm and church stand alone in park of former Wheatfield House. Church combines medieval features with elegant classical interior.

WHEATHAMPSTEAD Hertfordshire TL1714
Village off B653, 3 miles (5km) E of Harpenden
A pleasant village featuring a Norman church with monuments. A Roman road crossed the River Lee here below the Devil's Dyke (National Trust), the massive rampart of a big Iron Age encampment, possibly the principal settlement and stronghold of Cassivellaunus, the British chieftain who fought Julius Caesar. Nomansland Common is where the 'wicked lady' highwaywoman (see Markyate) used to waylay travellers.

WHEATLEY Oxfordshire SP5905
Village off A40, 5 miles (8km) E of Oxford
This former quarrying village has been transformed, but splendid older buildings remain, among them some venerable pubs, a Tudor manor house and a curious lock-up.

WHEELDALE ROMAN ROAD North Yorkshire SE8197
Roman site on Wheeldale Moor, 3 miles (5km) SW of Goathland
A 1 mile (2km) stretch of Roman road running across isloated moorland, still with hardcore and drainage ditches (English Heritage).

WHERWELL Hampshire SU3840
Village on B3048, 3 miles (5km) SE of Andover
Many handsome thatched cottages on the wide River Test. Lovely watermeadows.

WHESTON Derbyshire SK1376
Village off A623, 1 mile (2km) W of Tideswell
Fifteenth-century village cross, perhaps a boundary marker for the royal forest of the High Peak. Seventeenth-century Vicarage Farm. Mid-Georgian hall.

WHICHAM Cumbria SD1382
Hamlet on A595, 3 miles (5km) NW of Millom
Pleasant hamlet at the foot of the Whicham Valley. Small dales chapel has a plain Norman doorway.

WHICHFORD Warwickshire SP3134
Village off A3400, 5 miles (8km) N of Chipping Norton
Hill village overlooking Stour Valley, with an interesting Norman and medieval church and attractive thatched cottages in local stone.

WHICKHAM Tyne and Wear NZ2061
Town off A1, 3 miles (5km) W of Gateshead
Residential and industrial area on hillside above Derwent Valley. Power station near by at Derwent Haugh.

WHIMPLE Devon SY0497
Village off A30, 4 miles (6km) NW of Ottery St Mary
A village on the railway, grown large in recent years, with many orchards, some for cider apples. The old village is set around a square, with streams.

WHINLATTER PASS Cumbria NY1924
Mountain pass on B5292, W of Portinscale
Steep scenic road with excellent views at eastern end over Bassenthwaite Lake to Skiddaw. Whinlatter visitor centre has exhibitions and forest trails.

WHINNYFOLD Grampian NK0833
Village off A975, 2 miles (3km) S of Cruden Bay
Cliff-top village where fishing boats were beached on shingle due to lack of harbour. Bram Stoker, author of *Dracula*, had holiday home near by.

WHIPPINGHAM Isle of Wight SZ5193
Hamlet off A3021, 1 mile (2km) SE of East Cowes
The royal church for Osborne House (see) was built here in the 1850s and 60s for Queen Victoria. Prince Albert is said to have partly designed the very odd building with its elaborate tower, and there are the royal pew and many rich fittings inside. There is no village – just orange-brick almshouses of 1880 and one house.

WHIPSNADE Bedfordshire TL0117
Village on B4540, 3 miles (5km) S of Dunstable
Whipsnade Wild Animal Park was opened in 1931 to provide spacious enclosures for London Zoo animals, and Berthold Lubetkin designed some modernistic buildings for it in the 1930s. Today more than 3,000 animals live in its 570 acres (231ha), and it has success in breeding rare species. The 'tree cathedral' plantation belongs to the National Trust and there are magnificent views.The Whipsnade Lion is cut into the hillside.

WHISSENDINE Leicestershire SK8314
Village off A606, 4 miles (6km) NW of Oakham
Rutland village, with large medieval church, moated manor site, sail-less windmill, and 19th-century estate cottage moved from Stapleford (see).

WHISTON Merseyside SJ4791
Town off A57, immediately S of Prescot
An old mining town surrounded by parkland. The Stadt Moers Country Park is built on the remains of the coal-mining and brick-working industries.

WHISTON Northamptonshire SP8460
Village off A428, 6 miles (10km) E of Northampton
Church on hill, separate from village, entirely early 16th century with light and dark stone tower and numerous carvings. Two 18th-century monuments by Nollekens.

WHISTON South Yorkshire SK4590
Town on A618, 2 miles (3km) SE of Rotherham
Pretty village built on the site of a Stone Age settlement. Church of St James was founded over 800 years ago and is in a combination of styles.

WHITBURN Lothian NS9465
Town on A706, 3 miles (5km) SW of Bathgate
Town in Scotland's industrial central belt between Edinburgh and Glasgow, once noted for its coal mines and iron foundries.

WHITBURN Tyne and Wear NZ4061
Town on A183, 4 miles (6km) SE of South Shields
Pleasant village with sloping village green surrounded by houses of great character. Mostly residential since the colliery closed down. Sandy beach at Whitburn Bay.

WHITBY North Yorkshire NZ8911
Town on A171, 17 miles (27km) NW of Scarborough
Situated at the mouth of the River Esk, Whitby is a bustling fishing port and seaside resort on the east coast. Captain Cook sailed from Whitby in the *Endeavour* in 1768 and as a young man lived in the town. His house in Grape Street is now the Captain Cook Memorial Museum.

The attractive harbour has two lighthouses at its entrance, dating from 1855 and 1835. The West Lighthouse is open to the public in summer. On the cliffs high above the town are the jagged sandstone ruins of Whitby Abbey and 12th-century St Mary's Church, reached by 199 steps. The first abbey was founded by St Hilda in AD657 on land given by the King of Northumbria. Later the Danes destroyed it and it was rebuilt by the Normans. In the 7th century the abbey was the home of Caedmon, the first English Christian poet and a cross commemorating him stands in St Mary's churchyard. The ruins that stand today are 13th century.

Abraham 'Bram' Stoker set three chapters of his novel *Dracula* around Whitby and a Dracula Trail can be followed around the town.

WHITCHURCH Buckinghamshire SP8020
Village on A413, 5 miles (8km) N of Aylesbury
Rex Whistler lived and painted here, enjoying the views over the Vale of Aylesbury. Veteran timber and brick houses include the Priory hotel, which goes back 500 years, while formidable earthworks survive of medieval Bolebec Castle. In the church the monument to the noted 19th-century agriculturist John Westcar portrays him with his prize bull and some sheep.

WHITCHURCH Hampshire SU4648
Small town on B3400, 6 miles (10km) E of Andover
Handsome small town on the River Test with lots of red brick. Many Georgian buildings, including several inns. Whitchurch Silk Mill is a large plain brick building of 1800, where silk is still woven.

WHITCHURCH Hereford and Worcester SO5517
Village on A40, 4 miles (6km) NE of Monmouth
Part of sprawling settlement below Symonds Yat. Nature trails and good walking on Little Doward and Great Doward, limestone outcrops to southwest.

WHITCHURCH Oxfordshire SU6377
Village on B471, immediately N of Pangbourne
The tollbridge of 1891 still operates at this attractive Thames-side village, where old cottages and a mill cluster by the river.

WHITCHURCH Shropshire SJ5441
Town off A49, 18 miles (29km) N of Shrewsbury
Market town on north Shropshire border and birthplace of composer Edward German. Notable classical church of 1712 and narrow streets revealing buildings of several centuries. Timber-framed pubs, 17th-century almshouses and good Georgian houses in Dodington contrast with modern civic centre and shops. JB Joyce, famous makers of railway and tower clocks based here. Brown Moss Nature Reserve to southeast.

WHITCHURCH Warwickshire SP2248
Site off A3400, 4 miles (6km) S of Stratford-upon-Avon
Only a farm remains of settlement served by this isolated church by River Stour. It has a fine east window and some medieval glass.

WHITCHURCH CANONICORUM Dorset SY3995
Village off A35, 4 miles (6km) NE of Lyme Regis
In the Marshwood Vale, with several thatched cottages and a distinguished early medieval church, still with the shrine to St Candida, a rare survival.

WHITCOMBE Dorset SY7188
Hamlet on A352, 3 miles (5km) SE of Dorchester
Perfect stone hamlet, with a few thatched cottages, the big house and the church where the poet William Barnes was rector.

WHITE HORSE, VALE OF THE Oxfordshire
Scenic region of the Berkshire Downs
Vale extends southwest from Abingdon to Swindon, still remarkably empty and scattered with isolated hamlets and occasional larger villages. Bronze and Iron Age sites abound.

WHITE LADIES ASTON Hereford and Worcester SO9252
Village off A422, 5 miles (8km) E of Worcester
Pleasant village in pastoral countryside east of Worcester. Picturesque name derives from association with medieval Cistercian nunnery.

WHITE NOTLEY Essex TL7818
Village off B1018, 3 miles (5km) NW of Witham
Down the road from Black Notley (see). The small Norman church using Roman bricks has some medieval stained glass.

WHITE RODING Essex TL5613
Village on A1060, 2 miles (3km) W of Leaden Roding
The village is called 'White' because of the pale-coloured walls of the church, whose spire is a local landmark.

WHITE WALTHAM Berkshire SU8577
Village off B3024, 3 miles (5km) SW of Maidenhead
Rambling groups of farm buildings and timber-framed cottages. Stocks and a whipping post are preserved near the church.

WHITECHAPEL Greater London TQ3381
District in borough of Tower Hamlets
Multi-racial East End area, which originally flourished on the main road between London and Essex. Named after a 13th-century chapel, it saw substantial Jewish immigration in the 19th century. The Whitechapel slums were the scene of Jack the Ripper's murders in 1888 and Fascist marches in the 1930s. The lively Whitechapel art gallery is set in an art nouveau building. The East London Mosque was built in 1985 and a market is held in Whitechapel Road.

WHITEFIELD Greater Manchester SD8006
Town on A56, 3 miles (5km) S of Bury
Textile town where the cottage industry began in the 15th century. Fine Gothic Revival parish church designed by Sir Charles Barry, built in 1820s.

WHITEGATE Cheshire SJ6269
Village off A54, 3 miles (5km) NW of Winsford
Picturesque village with thatched cottages. Vale Royal, a country house once owned by the Lords of Delamere, gave the district its name.

WHITEHAVEN Cumbria NX9718
Town off A595, 7 miles (11km) S of Workington
A seaside port situated on the west Cumbrian coast, Whitehaven was the first post-Renaissance planned town in Britain, often referred to as the 'Georgian port' due to its wealth of 18th-century architecture. Although much of the town centre has been rebuilt, the remaining 17th- and 18th-century buildings are now Listed. The town was owned at this time by the Lowther family, who also owned the surrounding mines.

The harbour is now a conservation area and the port is still busy with the fishing fleet and small pleasure boats. West Pier was built by Scottish engineer Sir John Rennie. Along South Harbour are monuments to the mining industry such as the Candlestick Chimney, the mine bogeys and the winding wheel. The last mine closed in 1986.

In the mid-18th century the port of Whitehaven was larger than Liverpool. Its prosperity grew through the export of coal and the import of tobacco and rum from North America. Cumberland rum butter remains a popular local delicacy.

George Washington's grandmother, Mildred Warner Gale, lived in Whitehaven and is buried in St Nicholas Gardens.

WHITEHILLS Grampian NJ6565
Village on B9038, 2 miles (3km) NW of Banff
Small fishing village, unchanged architecturally since the 19th century, with own white-fish fleet and market. Harbour dates from 1900.

WHITEKIRK Lothian NT5981
Village on A198, 4 miles (6km) SE of North Berwick
Village, once renowned for its healing well, with interesting 15th-century cruciform church. Two-storeyed tithe barn near by encloses part of 16th-century castle.

WHITELEAF Buckinghamshire SP8104
Hamlet off A4010, 1 mile (2km) NE of Princes Risborough
Known for the Whiteleaf Cross, cut into the Chilterns hillside, of uncertain antiquity. Aylesbury Vale views from Whiteleaf Fields (National Trust).

WHITELEY VILLAGE Surrey TQ0962

Village on B365, 2 miles (3km) SE of Weybridge

Founded on the bequest of Bayswater store millionaire William Whiteley, a specially built, symmetrically planned garden suburb for the elderly, completed in 1921 and centred on Whiteley Monument.

WHITEPARISH Wiltshire SU2423

Village on A27, 7 miles (11km) W of Romsey

Large village, with distinctive Victorian oak-shingled bell tower on central church and a few brick cottages.

Folly (1606) on Pepperbox Hill, Whiteparish.

WHITESTAUNTON Somerset ST2810

Village off A30, 3 miles (5km) NW of Chard

Wooded stone-built hamlet, with 15th-century church and late medieval manor house, at the eastern end of the Blackdown Hills.

WHITEWELL Lancashire SD6546

Hamlet off B6478, 6 miles (10km) NW of Clitheroe

Locally known as 'Little Switzerland' for the beauty of its wooded valley, with River Hodden at the bottom. The village consists of an inn and a small church.

WHITFIELD Kent TR3045

Suburb on A256, on N edge of Dover

The tiny old centre with church stands alone, pleasingly rural, at Church Whitfield; the modern estates of Whitfield loom a couple of fields away on the outskirts of Dover.

WHITFORD Clwyd SJ1478

Village off A55, 3 miles (5km) NW of Holywell

Dominated by grand 19th-century church, burial place of renowned 18th-century travel writer Thomas Pennant. Exceptionally tall (11ft/3m) Maen Achwyfan Celtic cross near by.

WHITGIFT Humberside SE8223

Hamlet off A166, 4 miles (6km) E of Goole

Small settlement on the south bank of the River Ouse. The Church of St Magdalene has a unusual clock, numbered up to 13.

WHITHORN Dumfries and Galloway NX4440

Small town on A746, 9 miles (14km) S of Wigtown

Site of Scotland's first Christian settlement, dating from St Ninian's arrival in 5th century, with remains of 12th-century priory. Archaeological visitor centre tells local Christian story with guided tours and exhibitions. Museum contains 5th-century Latinus Stone, Scotland's oldest Christian memorial. St Ninian's Cave lies to the south, with 8th-century carvings, once used as retreat .

WHITKIRK West Yorkshire SE3633

District in W Leeds

Residential district centred around busy main road. Temple Newsam House is a Tudor-Jacobean mansion (open).

WHITLAND Dyfed SN1916

Small town off A40, 6 miles (10km) E of Narberth

Small market town of historical significance for 10th-century assembly called by Hywel Dda to establish unified legal system for Wales. Commemorative gardens and visitor centre.

WHITLEY BAY Tyne & Wear NZ3572

Town on A193, 2 miles (3km) N of Tynemouth

Popular family seaside resort with beach, ideal for bathing and popular with holiday-makers and day trippers. Cullercoats, traditional fishing village, has effectively become a part of Whitley Bay. St Mary's Island once used by smugglers and now home to a variety of wildlife. The island can be reached by a short causeway.

WHITMORE Staffordshire SJ8140

Village on A53, 4 miles (6km) SW of Newcastle-under-Lyme

Attractive pub and estate cottages grace old village centre. Good church interior. Seventeenth-century Whitmore Hall (limited opening) has notable family portraits.

WHITNEY-ON-WYE Hereford and Worcester SO2647

Village on A438, 4 miles (6km) NE of Hay-on-Wye

Tollbridge over River Wye still operates here. Church has attractive interior, and Rhydspence inn, an old drovers' hostelry, stands beside road to west.

WHITSTABLE Kent TR1166

Town on A290, 6 miles (10km) NW of Canterbury

Seaside resort on the north Kent coast famed for its oysters, introduced into the area by the Romans. There are late 18th-/early 19th-century houses at Island Wall and Middle Wall by a 7 mile (11km) shingle beach. The little harbour, now devoted to yachting and fishing, was the port for Canterbury and for steamboats to Australia in 1827. It was the first port served by a railway link (1830).

WHITTINGHAM Northumberland NU0611
Village off A697, 6 miles (10km) N of Rothbury
An attractive village divided in two by the River Aln, once the estate village for Eslington Park.

WHITTINGTON Gloucestershire SP0120
Hamlet off A40, 4 miles (6km) E of Cheltenham
Old and unspoilt estate cottages grace this hamlet beneath wooded hills. Church has Norman and medieval interior.

WHITTINGTON Shropshire SJ3231
Village on A495, 3 miles (5km) NE of Oswestry
Ruins of moated castle with impressive gatehouse stand opposite church with outstanding Victorian woodwork. Hymnwriter William Walsham How was vicar here.

WHITTINGTON Staffordshire SK1608
Village off A51, 3 miles (5km) E of Lichfield
Church is well worth visiting, but main attraction here is Regimental Museum of Staffordshire Regiment, housed in the Victorian Whittington Barracks.

WHITTLEBURY Northamptonshire SP6944
Village on A413, 3 miles (5km) S of Towcester
Once in middle of vast medieval royal hunting forest of Whittlewood. Church with 13th-century tower, restored 1878, overlooking Tove Valley.

WHITTLESEY Cambridgeshire TL2797
Town on A605, 5 miles (8km) E of Peterborough
This attractive fenland town has some handsome 17th- and 18th-century houses, but most buildings are later. There is a lovely butter cross in the market place. To the north is the Roman Fen Causeway, while King's Dyke lies to the south. Local hero Harry Smith, one of Wellington's generals, has a statue and a pub named after him.

WHITTLESFORD Cambridgeshire TL4748
Village off A1301, 7 miles (11km) S of Cambridge
This spacious village standing amid mature trees has a timbered guildhall, the blue and white Tickell Arms, a pretty Norman church, and a mill.

WHITTON Shropshire SO5772
Hamlet off B4214, 3 miles (5km) NW of Tenbury Wells
Isolated on lower slopes of Clee Hill at a respectful distance from ancient Whitton Court. Norman church has a Burne-Jones window.

WHITWELL Leicestershire SK9208
Village on A606, 4 miles (6km) E of Oakham
Village beside Rutland Water (see), with 17th-century hall near shore. Medieval church with 13th-century bellcote. Village twinned with rather larger Paris!

WHITWELL-ON-THE-HILL North Yorkshire SE7265
Village off A64, 5 miles (9km) SW of Malton
Village lines approach road of Whitwell Hall, built 1835 in the Tudor Gothic style and surrounded by parkland.

WHITWORTH Lancashire SD8818
Town on A671, 4 miles (6km) N of Rochdale
Pleasant town with stone-built cottages and farmsteads. Near by, the Dell is a gorge with waterfalls, ruins and stone arches crossing the River Spodden.

WHORLTON Durham NZ1014
Village off A67, 4 miles (6km) E of Barnard Castle
On the north bank of the River Tees. Bridge was built in 1831; it is the oldest suspension bridge in England still supported unaided by its original chains.

WICHENFORD Hereford and Worcester SO7860
Village off B4204, 5 miles (8km) NW of Worcester
Pleasant village in orchard country where National Trust maintains handsome timber-framed dovecote (limited opening) in grounds of Wichenford Court.

WICK Avon ST7072
Village on A420, 7 miles (11km) E of Bristol
A stone village on the River Boyd, with large limestone quarries to the north.

WICK Highland ND3650
Town on A9, 15 miles (24km) NE of Latheron
Historic county town of former Caithness and Britain's most northerly east coast town. Extensive harbour dates from the 19th century when Wick was Europe's largest herring port with over 1,000 boats in the fleet. Wick heritage centre is large and there is an excellent local museum. Today, the town is an administrative centre with employment from fishing, tourism, and the Caithness Glass factory.

WICKEN Cambridgeshire TL5670
Village off A1123, 2 miles (3km) SW of Soham
Pretty village with reed-thatched cottages is best known for the National Trust's Wicken Fen. It is really three fens in one – Wicken Sedge Fen, St Edmund's Fen, and Adventurers' Fen. There is a well-maintained drainage mill on Adventurers' Fen, a boardwalk, and a marked nature trail around peaceful lodes, sedge fens and reedy ponds.

WICKEN BONHUNT Essex TL4933
Village on B1038, 4 miles (6km) SW of Saffron Walden
Expensive and exclusive. The evening curfew was rung here up until the 1960s. The Coach and Horses pub has an unusual sign.

WICKFORD Essex TQ7493
Town on A129, 3 miles (5km) NE of Basildon
On the River Crouch, still merely a village in the 1880s, but now a smartish London commuter town with many post-war estates.

WICKHAM Berkshire SU3971
Village on B4000, 6 miles (10km) NW of Newbury
Rural village with a church well known for its Saxon tower, and for the gilded *papier mâché* elephants which hold up the elaborate Victorian roof.

WICKHAM Hampshire SU5711
Village on A32, 3 miles (5km) N of Fareham
One of the finest villages in the south, with very varied cottages and houses of all dates from the 16th century lining a huge square. Vineyard to the north.

WICKHAM MARKET Suffolk TM3055
Small town off A12, 5 miles (8km) NE of Woodbridge
A market no more, Wickham has a picturesque watermill by the River Deben. Two local farms provide nature trails, working farm demonstrations and equestrian arts.

WICKHAMBREAUX Kent TR2258
Village off A257, 5 miles (8km) E of Canterbury
Attractive village with triangular-shaped green overhung by big lime and chestnut trees on the banks of the River Little Stour near a tall, white, weatherboarded watermill. Characterful buildings, including 18th- and 19th-century brick cottages, stand around the green and in Gutter Street. The late 14th-century church, restored in 1878, has a colourful art nouveau window by American Arlid Rosencrantz.

WICKHAMBROOK Suffolk TL7554
Village on A143, 9 miles (14km) SW of Bury St Edmunds
Isolated Wickhambrook is really a series of hamlets, and has 11 village greens. Gifford's Hall's gardens are open under the National Gardens Scheme.

WICKHAMFORD Hereford and Worcester SP0641
Village off A44, 2 miles (3km) SE of Evesham
In *Ancestral Voices* (1975) James Lees-Milne described his boyhood in this attractive old orchard village near Evesham, although modern housing has encroached since. He lived in the rambling, timber-framed 16th-century manor house close to the church, which retains its impressive 18th-century interior and has a monument to Penelope Washington, ancestor of George.

WICKHAMPTON Norfolk TG4205
Village off B1140, 2 miles (3km) N of Reedham
Standing remote in an area of fields and dykes, Wickhampton is near flat marshes dotted with windmills. St Andrew's Church has two interesting stone figures.

WICKWAR Avon ST7288
Village on B4060, 4 miles (6km) N of Chipping Sodbury
A large village with many stone buildings including the surprisingly urban town hall of 1795 and grammar school of 1684.

WIDCOMBE Avon ST7563
District in SE Bath
On the outskirts of Bath, this hilly area has many villas, mostly in classical style, built from the early 19th century onwards. Crowe Hall has romantic gardens (occasionally open).

WIDDINGTON Essex TL5331
Village off B1383, 4 miles (6km) S of Saffron Walden
A quiet and pricey village. Mole Hall Wildlife Park, developed over the last 40 years or so, breeds otters and is home to creatures from chimps and eagle owls to exotic butterflies. Prior's Hall Barn (English Heritage), restored to its medieval grandeur, is a big 14th-century barn with a crown post roof.

WIDDRINGTON Northumberland NZ2595
Village on A1068, 7 miles (11km) NE of Morpeth
A quiet inland village from Druridge Bay with outstanding views of Coquet Island. Two nature reserves near by.

WIDE OPEN Tyne and Wear NZ2472
Hamlet off A1056, 5 miles (8km) N of Newcastle
The centre of a large overspill area, virtually a suburb of Newcastle, with a mixture of housing. On the outskirts there is some light industry.

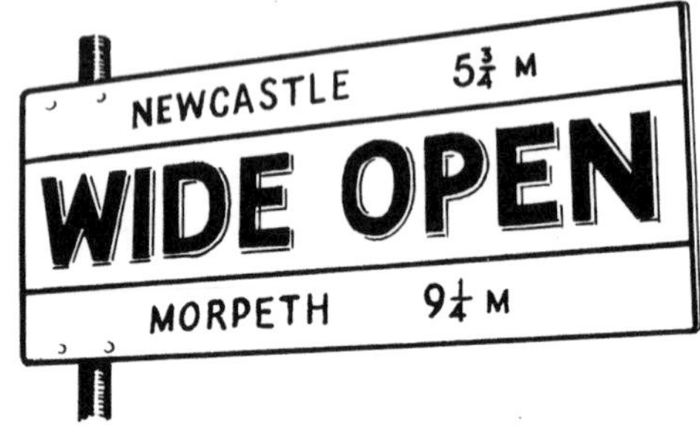

Sign on the former Great North Road.

WIDECOMBE IN THE MOOR Devon SX7176
Village on B3387, 5 miles (8km) NW of Ashburton
The most famous village on Dartmoor, over- popular in summer, set in a valley and dominated by the 15th-century elegant and slender church tower, granite like all the rest of the village. The elaborate 16th-century church house (National Trust) has a pillared loggia.

WIDEMOUTH BAY Cornwall SS2002
Village off A39, 3 miles (5km) S of Bude
Since the 1930s this has been a little seaside resort, set on a sandy bay. Rocky shore on either side of the bay.

WIDFORD Hertfordshire TL4216
Village on B1004, 4 miles (6km) E of Ware
Above the Ash. Authors Charles and Mary Lamb stayed here as children and loved it. Their grandmother is buried here.

WIDFORD Oxfordshire SP2712
Site off A40, 1 mile (2km) E of Burford
Tiny church beside the River Windrush has Norman masonry, wall-paintings and areas of Roman mosaic pavement in chancel.

WIDMERPOOL Nottinghamshire SK6327
Village off A606, 10 miles (16km) NW of Melton Mowbray
Wolds village, off Fosse Way. Church almost rebuilt 1888–95, 14th-century tower. Victorian hall, with Italianate tower, bought in 1950 by the Automobile Association as a patrol school.

WIDNES Cheshire SJ5185
Town off M62, 6 miles (10km) W of Warrington
Widnes is a large industrial town on the River Mersey which developed in the 19th century through large-scale chemical manufacture, once the canals and railways had arrived. Widnes Dock, now known as Spike Island, offered cheap land, good transport and ready access to salt, coal and water and the chemical industry really began when John Hutchinson set up business here as an alkali manufacturer. The industry boomed, bringing with it appalling housing conditions and pollution on a terrifying scale. Towards the end of the 19th century things began to improve, however. Poor housing was demolished, the environment became cleaner and industry diversified, removing the dependence on the heavy chemical industry and with it the grime and pollution.

Catalyst, The Museum of the Chemical Industry, gives an insight into the development of the industry. Housed in one of Hutchinson's Victorian buildings, it overlooks the River Mersey and Spike Island, original heart of the chemical industry and named after the 'spikes', or lodgings, that were thrown up between plants to accommodate factory workers. Spike Island is cleared now and has a more pleasant function as the site of the annual Halton Show.

WIGAN Greater Manchester SD5805
Town off M61, 17 miles (27km) NW of Manchester
Wigan is an industrial town and one of the oldest boroughs in Lancashire. Its industry developed around coal-mining which began as early as 1450 and by the 19th century there were over 1,000 pit shafts in operation, providing coal for the region's booming textile industry.

Wigan Pier, on the Liverpool to Leeds Canal, was the key loading point on the canal for the distribution of coal to the cotton mills of Lancashire. With the decline of these industries and the waterways the town suffered and the pier fell into dereliction, but today the canal and the warehouse buildings around it have been renovated and the area is now a premier heritage centre.

The main attractions are Tencherfield Mill, home of the world's largest working mill steam engine which is still in its original state and the canal-side complex, where four restored warehouse buildings now house a pub and restaurant, souvenir shop, education centre and The Way We Were, an imaginative living history exhibition which describes Wigan at the turn of the century. The pier is also the home of the North's Jazz Centre, where regular concerts are held.

WIGGENHALLS, THE Norfolk TF5914
Villages off A10, 4 miles (6km) SW of King's Lynn
St Germans, St Mary Magdalene, St Mary the Virgin, St Peter: these four villages range along the River Great Ouse on the flat Norfolk marshes. Each village has a church. Two bridges connect the villages across the river. St Germans has three pubs; St Mary the Virgin has a huge pumping station; St Peter's church is a ruin on the river bank; and St Mary Magdalene was famous for its eels.

WIGGLESWORTH North Yorkshire SD8156
Village on B6478, 2 miles (3km) SW of Long Preston
A small settlement of predominantly stone-built houses surrounded by open countryside. Modern houses in keeping with rest of village.

WIGHILL North Yorkshire SE4746
Village off A659, 2 miles (3km) N of Tadcaster
A very rural settlement surrounded by open fields. The few houses are typical of this area; stone-built and dating from the 19th century.

WIGHT, ISLE OF Isle of Wight
Island off Hampshire coast
Known locally simply as The Island, the Isle of Wight has been called 'England in miniature', because of its great variety of scenery. The smallest county in England, it measures 23 miles (37km) by 13 miles (21km), and has been appreciated by visitors since the early 19th century. The mild climate and remote simplicity attracted famous residents such as the poet Tennyson, as well as holiday-makers. Queen Victoria built a retreat for her family at Osborne, and all through the 19th century tourism increased.

The island still has wonderfully unspoilt countryside and a very varied coastline, with chalk stacks at the Needles, sandy beaches and the wooded Undercliff. Old manor houses, picturesque villages and a fine castle at Carisbrook combine with many museums and other attractions for the visitor. Car ferries run from Southampton to East Cowes, Portsmouth to Fishbourne, and Lymington to Yarmouth, with a passenger ferry also from Portsmouth to Ryde. The fastest crossing from the mainland is the hovercraft from Southsea to Ryde.

WIGHTWICK MANOR West Midlands SO8698
Mansion on A454, on W outskirts of Wolverhampton
Theodore Mander's Victorian house (National Trust) houses fine array of Pre-Raphaelite art and furnishings in William Morris tradition.

WIGMORE Hereford and Worcester SO4169
Village on A4110, 8 miles (13km) NW of Leominster
Mortimer Forest, hilly and wooded domain of powerful Mortimer family, stretches from Ludlow to this large village, offering good walks and much geological interest. Another walk leads to Wigmore Castle (not open), on hills behind village. The Norman and medieval church is built on different levels and the picturesque village centre was laid out in Norman times.

WIGSTON (OR WIGSTON MAGNA) Leicestershire SP6099
Town on A50, on SE outskirts of Leicester
All Saints' Church, mainly early 14th century, at heart of old village centre. Master hosier's house and workshop illustrate framework knitting industry.

WIGTOFT Lincolnshire TF2636
Village on A17, 6 miles (10km) SW of Boston
In fenland farming country. Church of 14th and 15th centuries, tower with stone spirelet. Late 18th-century Casterton House with Regency coach house and granary.

WIGTON Cumbria NY2548
Town on A596, 11 miles (17km) SW of Carlisle
Market town on the Solway Plain with medieval layout and Georgian architecture. The cobbled area in front of the church is the old corn market.

WIGTOWN Dumfries and Galloway NX4355
Small town on A714, 6 miles (10km) S of Newtown Stewart
Peaceful small town on hill overlooking Wigtown Bay, with wide main street and square, containing two mercat crosses. Pillar on shoreline commemorates the two Wigtown Covenanter female martyrs of 1685, who drowned in estuary. Near by is Torhouskie Stone Circle, dating from around 2000BC and one of the finest in Britain.

WILBURTON Cambridgeshire TL4874
Village on A1123, 5 miles (8km) SW of Ely
Standing in pancake-flat Fen country, Wilburton has a 1600 red-brick manor house. Fourteenth-century wall-painting of St Blaise in church.

WILBY Norfolk TM0389
Hamlet off A11, 4 miles (6km) SW of Attleborough
In 1633 a fire damaged much of pretty All Saints' Church (now refurbished). Wilby also has thatched cottages and some restored 17th-century almshouses.

WILBY Northamptonshire SP8666
Village on A4500, 2 miles (3km) SW of Wellingborough
Above Nene Valley, 14th-century church with unusual tower, square topped by octagonal lantern and spire, Victorian chancel. Georgian Wilby Hall.

WILBY Suffolk TM2472
Village on B1118, 1 mile (2km) SE of Stradbroke
A tiny village almost hidden among the vast rolling cornfields. Ballroom dancing in the Coronation Hall attracts Saturday-night visitors.

WILDBOARCLOUGH Cheshire SJ9868
Village off A54, 5 miles (8km) SE of Macclesfield
Remote hamlet in the Pennine foothills, surrounded by sheep farms. Panoramic views from the top of Shutlingsloe Hill,

WILFORD Nottinghamshire SK5637
Village on A606, in S Nottingham
On southeast bank of River Trent, linked by 1870 bridge to Nottingham. Medieval church, rectory of about 1700, Wilford Hall 1781, some 18th-century cottages.

WILLASTON Cheshire SJ6852
Village on A534, 2 miles (3km) E of Nantwich
Many buildings of historical interest. Willaston Mill is the tallest of the old Wirral flour mills. Willaston Old Hall gardens (limited opening).

WILLEN Buckinghamshire SP8741
Village off A509, 2 miles (3km) NE of Milton Keynes
Part of Milton Keynes (see), but preserves an earlier atmosphere. Noble 17th-century church by Robert Hooke, Japanese peace pagoda by the lake.

WILLENHALL West Midlands SO9698
Town in W Walsall
The acknowledged centre of the lock-making industry received a boost when American Linus Yale set up his works here. Willenhall Museum (social history) and the Lock Museum in Victorian locksmith's house celebrate this and other aspects of this interesting town. One grim episode is commemorated at Doctor's Piece, gardens on the site of a mass grave of cholera victims.

WILLENHALL West Midlands SP3676
District in SE Coventry
This residential suburb near Coventry Airport boasts a church of 1957 by Sir Basil Spence, architect of Coventry Cathedral.

WILLERSEY Gloucestershire SP1039
Village off A44, 2 miles (3km) N of Broadway
A pleasant village under the northern Cotswold Edge with a sturdy old church and a wide main street lined with handsome stone houses.

WILLESDEN Greater London TQ2284
District in borough of Brent
A creation of the 19th and 20th centuries. St Mary's Church is a survivor of the medieval village. Impressive monuments in the Jewish Cemetery include those of the Rothschilds and the Samuels. Features include the Grange Museum of Community History, Willesden Green sports centre and stadium (1960s) and the well-known Spotted Dog pub in Willesden Green High Road.

WILLEY Shropshire SO6799
Hamlet off B4373, 2 miles (3km) S of Broseley
Willey Hall (not open), built in 1820s by Lewis Wyatt, shares hamlet with a farm and a Norman church with interesting memorials.

WILLEY Warwickshire SP4984
Village off A5, 3 miles (5km) W of Lutterworth
Village stands between two Roman roads – Watling Street (the county boundary here) and Fosse Way. Church has houseling tables (rare form of communion rail).

WILLINGALE, DOE AND SPAIN Essex TL5907
Villages off B184, 4 miles (6km) NE of Chipping Ongar
Two former parish churches, of Willingale Doe and Willingale Spain, share the one churchyard and views of the Roding Valley.

WILLINGDON East Sussex TQ5802
Suburb in N Eastbourne
Old-established village with some pretty cottages and a 13th-century church, nearly lost in Eastbourne's suburbia.

WILLINGHAM Cambridgeshire TL4070
Village on B1050, 8 miles (12km) NW of Cambridge
Standing on the ancient fenland 'shoreline', Willingham is a large village with a splendid church. It has an impressive hammerbeam roof, bristling with angels, and some Saxon and Norman work. To the east of the village is a prehistoric fort named after one of William the Conqueror's generals, Belsar, who built the causeway to Ely.

WILLINGTON Bedfordshire TL1150
Village off A603, 4 miles (6km) E of Bedford
A former Bedford estate village with a harbour on the Great Ouse where the Danes once kept their longships, and much post-war housing. The notable Tudor church contains the tomb of its builder, Sir John Gostwick, who was Master of Horse to Cardinal Wolsey. His manor house is no more, but the capacious dovecote has survived (National Trust, open by appointment only).

WILLINGTON Derbyshire SK2928
Village on A5137, 6 miles (10km) SW of Derby
Between Trent and Mersey Canal and meandering River Trent, dominated by five cooling towers of the power station built in 1962. Church mainly of 1842.

WILLINGTON Durham NZ1935
Town on A690, 4 miles (6km) N of Bishop Auckland
Originally a settlement on Roman Dere Street. A former pit village much transformed by reclamation.

WILLITON Somerset ST0741
Village on A39, 1 mile (2km) S of Watchet
Large village, mostly 19th century in the middle. Orchard Wyndham is a late medieval onwards manor house, with hall. Orchard Mill is early 19th century.

WILLOUGHBRIDGE Staffordshire SJ7440
Hamlet on A51, 2 miles (3km) SE of Woore
Hamlet on western slopes of wooded Maer Hills notable for Dorothy Clive Garden, 8 acres (3ha) of woodland, rock and scree gardens.

WILLOUGHBY Lincolnshire TF4771
Village on B1196, 3 miles (5km) S of Alford
At meeting point of Wolds and marsh. Birthplace of Captain John Smith, founder of Virginia, USA, rescued from death by Princess Pocahontas.

WILLOUGHBY WATERLEYS Leicestershire SP5792
Village off A426, 5 miles (8km) N of Lutterworth
Fine brick-built houses, mainly early 18th century, Manor Farm dated 1693. Old hall is a 16th- or early 17th-century timber house with 1712 brick front.

WILLOUGHBY-ON-THE-WOLDS Nottinghamshire SK6325
Village off A46, 8 miles (13km) NW of Melton Mowbray
Wolds village near Fosse Way and Leicestershire border. Medieval church, tombs of Willoughby family, brass commemorating Stanhope, killed at Willoughby Field in 1648, one of the last Civil War skirmishes.

WILMCOTE Warwickshire SP1658
Village off A3400, 3 miles (5km) NW of Stratford-upon-Avon
Mary Arden's House, home of Shakespeare's mother, and adjacent countryside museum are both open to public. Richly furnished Victorian church is worth visiting.

WILMINGTON East Sussex TQ5404
Village on A27, 2 miles (3km) W of Polegate
Attractive village of well-kept cottages strung along a street beneath the South Downs heading to ruined Wilmington Priory (founded in 1243, suppressed in 1414) with the remains built into a farmhouse, and the enigmatic chalk-cut figure of Long Man. There is no written record of this human figure, 226ft (69m) high, with a staff in each hand, until the 18th century, but he was probably cut by the Saxons.

WILMSLOW Cheshire SJ8481
Town on A34, 11 miles (17km) S of Manchester
Developed in the 19th century as a desirable residential area for Manchester's wealthy merchants when the railway was built out of Manchester.

WILPSHIRE Lancashire SD6832
Village on A666, 3 miles (5km) N of Blackburn
Residential district of Blackburn on the edge of the Ribble Valley, with a popular golf course.

WILSFORD Lincolnshire TF0042
Village off A153, 4 miles (6km) SW of Sleaford
Stone-built village in valley off Grantham–Sleaford road. Graceful spire of Saxon, Norman and medieval church. Heath quarries are source of famous Ancaster limestone.

WILSFORD Wiltshire SU1057
Village off A342, 3 miles (5km) NW of Upavon
In the Vale of Pewsey, with some thatched and timber-framed cottages, and a medieval church.

WILSFORD Wiltshire SU1339
Hamlet off A303, 2 miles (3km) SW of Amesbury
Tiny hamlet in the Avon Valley with a Norman church tower. Lake, a hamlet to the south, is picturesque.

WILTON Cleveland NZ5819
Hamlet off A174, 3 miles (5km) NW of Guisborough
Compact village built around Wilton Castle, once home of the Bulmer family, now the property of ICI Chemicals.

WILTON Hereford and Worcester SO5824
Village on A40, 1 mile (2km) W of Ross-on-Wye
The village confronts Ross-on-Wye across river bridge damaged in Civil War, which also accounted for ruined Wilton Castle (not open).

WILTON Wiltshire SU0931
Small town on A30, 3 miles (5km) W of Salisbury
An ancient borough and the county town of Wiltshire in early medieval times, Wilton was famous for its many monastic houses, of which little remains. It now seems like a very large village rather than a town, with many Georgian houses of various colour bricks, and a town hall of 1738, with a Victorian clock turret. The parish church is very odd, built in Italian Romanesque style in 1841, with a detached bell tower, lots of decoration and many rich fittings inside. The Wilton carpet factory has buildings from Georgian onwards, and was founded here in the 17th century.

The classical Triumph Arch gateway to Wilton House is right in the town, and dates from 1755. The house is partly Elizabethan, partly 1630s, with 1801 mock-medieval rooms and the famous state rooms of the mid-17th century, sumptuous and rich, with much gilding and many fine paintings. The single and double cube rooms are the most elaborate. The grounds have large ancient ornamental trees, and the Palladian bridge of 1737. Displays on model soldiers, a 1907 dolls' house and a scenic model railway.

WILTON Wiltshire SU2661
Village off A338, 3 miles (5km) E of Burbage
Thatched cottages and a duck pond. The little lake of Wilton Water is a reservoir for the Kennet and Avon Canal. Wilton Windmill (1821) is restored and working.

WIMBISH Essex T5936
Village off B1053,4 miles (6km) E of Saffron Walden
A collection of scattered hamlets close to the River Pant. Remarkable 14th-century brass in the church.

WIMBLEDON Greater London TQ2370
District in borough of Merton
Famed for the tennis championships and the All England Club's engaging museum. The broad expanse of Wimbledon Common has a history of duels, highway robberies and murders. The restored windmill (limited opening) dates from 1817. There are formal grounds and pleasant walks in Canizzaro Park, while Southside House (limited opening) has an interesting past. Smart atmosphere in Wimbledon Village. Theatre and stadium.

WIMBORNE MINSTER Dorset SZ0099
Town off A31, 7 miles (11km) NW of Bournemouth
Handsome market town on the River Stour, with a long history. The Minster Church of St Cuthberga is dedicated to a royal princess who was abbess here in the 8th century. Nothing remains from her time, but the church is mostly high-quality Norman work, with two towers, one 15th century, one Norman with a 1608 top. The astronomical clock is 17th century. Outside, a figure of a Napoleonic soldier strikes the hours.

The town centre has curving streets and a square, all with lots of Georgian brick. The cornmarket has a 1738 market house and is superb small-scale townscape. Priest's House museum is in a fine town house, with good displays. The Model Town shows the area in the 1950s, at one-tenth scale. A big market is held on the outskirts, Friday to Sunday.

On the edge of town, Dean's Court gardens are large and informal, with fine trees. To the east, Stapehill Experience has large gardens, a Victorian nunnery and huge agricultural displays.

WIMBORNE ST GILES Dorset SU0312
Village off B3081, 2 miles (3km) SW of Cranborne
In the well-wooded landscape of Cranborne Chase (see), lots of brick cottages in a variety of styles. Brick almshouses of 1624, and an unusual church, partly 1732, partly 1908 rebuilding after a fire. Rich fittings of 1908 and a good series of monuments to the Shaftesbury family.

WINCANTON Somerset ST7128
Small town off A303, 12 miles (19km) NE of Yeovil
Small-scale, rather old-fashioned town with High Street winding up the hill with many small Georgian houses, mostly in the local yellowy-orange stone. Local museum. Wincanton Racecourse to the north, and much industry on the outskirts.

WINCHCOMBE Gloucestershire SP0228
Town on B4632, 6 miles (10km) NE of Cheltenham
Outstanding here are the very grand 'wool church', the 15th-century George inn with galleried courtyard and the array of stone and timber-framed buildings in town centre. Other attractions include Folk and Police Museum and intriguing private railway museum. To southeast of the town is Sudeley Castle (limited opening), rich in historical associations and surrounded by splendid grounds.

WINCHELSEA East Sussex TQ9017
Town on A259, 2 miles (3km) SW of Rye
The shadowy remnants of the 'new' town of 1288, built after the destruction of the old town by the sea in 1287. Laid out on grid-iron pattern, the present town covers only one-third of the area, thanks to 14th-century French raiders. Three town gates, but no walls, survive; the church is a fragment of the original. Houses are mostly late 19th- and 20th-century, widely spaced along garden suburb-like streets with grass verges.

WINCHESTER Hampshire SU4829
City off M3, 12 miles (19km) N of Southampton
Capital of Wessex from the time of Alfred, and capital of all England from the 10th century until the Norman Conquest, this is one of the most historic cities in the country, crammed with medieval and later buildings.

The huge cathedral is the second on the site, Norman and a mixture of later medieval styles, and is the second longest in Europe – a beautiful building, full of superb fittings including the best set of medieval chantry chapels in the country and early 14th-century wooden quire stalls of the highest quality. The Triforuim gallery has a very good display on the buildings. The statue of William Walker the diver records his dangerous work replacing the footings. The small cathedral close has a medieval pilgrim hall and other attractive corners.

The 14th-century Kingsgate has the little Church of St Swithun above. Jane Austen died in College Street, and is buried in the cathedral. Winchester College, the famous public school, still inhabits the original medieval courts, with chapel and hall. The ruins of the medieval bishop's palace, Wolvesey Palace (English Heritage) are extensive.

The town itself is dense, full of Georgian brick houses. One of the best is the Royal Hampshire Regiment Museum, and there are four more military museums in Peninsula Barracks and the City Museum in the pretty little square. Opposite the decorative Victorian guildhall (with exhibition gallery) is a huge statue of King Alfred (1901). The City Mill (National Trust) of 1774 has a pretty little garden.

The 13th-century great hall is the only surviving part of the castle, and one of the finest medieval halls in the country, displaying the so-called King Arthur's table, an early medieval fake, and with a little 'medieval garden' attached. Westgate, part of the medieval city walls, has a museum above. See also St Cross.

WINCHFIELD Hampshire SU7654

Village off A30, 2 miles (3km) E of Hook

Rural and wooded, with a Norman church. Basingstoke Canal near by.

WINCLE Cheshire SJ9566

Hamlet off A54, 5 miles (8km) SE of Macclesfield

Pretty hamlet in the Dane Valley on the edge of the Peak District National Park. Ship inn is a popular country pub.

WINDERMERE Cumbria SD4198

Town on A591, 7 miles (11km) NW of Kendal

The confusion of names between the town and the lake stems from the days when the Kendal and Windermere Railway Company was opened in 1847. Its terminal station was at the village of Birthwaite, hardly a name to bring tourists flocking in, so the railway company changed the name of the station to Windermere, even though it is 1 mile (2km) from the lake. A footpath opposite the railway station and beside the Windermere hotel leads through the woods to the top of Orrest Head, a 784ft (239m) hill north of the town, to one of the finest viewpoints in Lakeland.

The town quickly developed around the station, filled with hotels, boarding houses and shops, and spread down the hill towards the village of Bowness on the lakeside. These days Bowness has taken over as the tourist centre, but Windermere remains a busy town.

Windermere, the lake, is the largest in England, being 10½ miles (17km) long and about 1 mile (2km) wide at its broadest point. It can be crossed by car ferry from Bowness to Far Sawrey, or by passenger boat between Lakeside, Bowness and Ambleside.

WINDLESHAM Surrey SU9364

Village off A30, 1 mile (2km) E of Bagshot

Amid heath and meadowland, Updown Hill, the main street, lined by Victorian houses, has a green at the bottom and the Field of Remembrance at the top.

WINDRUSH Gloucestershire SP1913

Village off A40, 4 miles (6km) W of Burford

Old quarrying village now has idyllic houses and cottages in local stone around its small green and an outstanding Norman and medieval church.

WINDSOR Berkshire SU9676

Town off M4, 2 miles (3km) S of Slough

This handsome market town sits at the foot of the most royal of castles. Still occupied by the Queen, the romantic masses of the castle dominate the town. Picturesque streets and cobbled lanes reveal many Georgian houses and earlier timber-framing, and a classical guildhall of 1687, designed by Sir Christopher Wren. The especially elaborate railway station dates from 1850, and has a royal waiting room. The Royalty and Empire display includes Queen Victoria's arrival in Jubilee year.

Windsor is the largest castle in England and inside is like a little walled town. Building started on this naturally strong site in the 11th century, but most of the buildings are 12th century, greatly altered in the early 19th century. The exception is St George's Chapel, one of the finest chapels anywhere, built 1475–1510, in the latest medieval style. Fan-vaulted inside, it has sumptuous carved wooden stalls for the Knights of the Garter, with banners above, and a richly decorated chapel to the memory of Prince Albert attached, a pinnacle of Victorian piety and taste.

The Round Tower is the most prominent building, built in the 12th century on an artificial mound. Like all the other buildings it was made more impressive and romantic in the early 19th century, when the architect Wyatville 'restored' the castle. The state apartments are largely 19th-century inside, ranging from the Victorian grand staircase to rooms altered for George IV. A fire in St George's Hall in 1992 closed many rooms, and St George's Hall is to be rebuilt in modern medieval style, with a modern 'Gothic' octagonal anteroom. Three rooms in rich later 17th-century style survived all the alterations. Rich furnishings and fine paintings are displayed throughout. Queen Mary's dolls' house was designed by Lutyens and finished in 1923 (see Windsor Great Park). The guard is changed ceremonially most days in the middle of the morning, and the Queen's Presents and royal carriages are displayed in the town.

WINDSOR GREAT PARK Berkshire

Scenic area, S of Windsor

This huge park attached to Windsor Castle is really part of a royal hunting forest. Nearly 5,000 acres (2,000ha) and 14 miles (72km) round, it has a famous view up the tree-lined Long Walk to the castle, with a statue of George III at the other end. Savill Garden, a very fine woodland garden, has been developed since 1932. See also Frogmore and Virginia Water.

The carved Norman church doorway in Windrush.

WINESTEAD Humberside TA2924
Village off A1033, 2 miles (3km) NW of Patrington
The 12th-century church, unusually dedicated to St German, is the only part of the village visible from the main road.

WING Buckinghamshire SP8822
Village on A418, 3 miles (5km) SW of Leighton Buzzard
Ascott (National Trust), remodelled by George Devey for Leopold de Rothschild in the 19th century, is today largely a 1930s black and white creation, with pictures, furniture, porcelain and outstanding gardens. The famous Saxon church in the village boasts impressive monuments of the Dormer family, earlier owners of Ascott. The wartime airfield might have been London's dreaded third airport.

WING Leicestershire SK8903
Village off A6003, 4 miles (6km) SE of Oakham
Intriguing medieval circular turf maze, 40ft (12m) diameter, on roadside verge. It has the same pattern as the one at Chartres Cathedral.

WINGATE Durham NZ4037
Village on B1280, 4 miles (6km) S of Easington
Former mining settlement. Peter Lee, miners' leader and local politician, worked in this pit in the late 19th century.

WINGERWORTH Derbyshire SK3867
Village off A6, 2 miles (3km) S of Chesterfield
Wingerworth Hall completed in 1729, was demolished 200 years later. The new church nave, added 1963–4, incorporates Norman and 13th-century work.

WINGFIELD Suffolk TM2276
Village off B1118, 2 miles (3km) N of Stradbroke
Set in some of the loveliest countryside in Suffolk, Wingfield boasts several treasures. The castle is a timber-framed house enclosed within great stone walls and a moat, while fascinating Wingfield College is a 14th-century priests' college founded by the de la Pole family. Next door is the glorious collegiate church.

WINGHAM Kent TR2457
Village on A257, 6 miles (10km) E of Canterbury
An old village which feels more like a town, on the Canterbury–Sandwich road. The church with its tall, green spire and famous Oxinden family monument stands close to row of half-timbered old buildings, including the Old Canonry at a right-angle bend in the road. The spacious and attractive High Street, with grass verges and pollarded lime trees, is lined with handsome Tudor and Georgian houses. Wingham Bird Park is near by.

WINGRAVE Buckinghamshire SP8619
Village off A418, 5 miles (8km) NE of Aylesbury
On the Mentmore (see) estate, Wingrave has a strong Rothschild influence. Exiled Czech patriot Jan Masaryk occupied the manor house during the war.

WINKBURN Nottinghamshire SK7158
Village off A617, 6 miles (10km) NW of Newark
William and Mary hall (open by appointment) next to church with box pews and monuments, virtually unaltered since early 18th century.

WINKFIELD Berkshire SU9072
Village on A330, 3 miles (5km) NE of Bracknell
A rural village, despite the proximity of Bracknell. The church has a brick tower of 1629 and unusual octagonal wooden columns of 1592 inside.

WINKLEIGH Devon SS6308
Village on B3220, 9 miles (14km) NE of Okehampton
Hilltop village, once a small town, dense with stucco and cob, and with a pyramidal conduit head in the middle, 1832.

WINKWORTH ARBORETUM Surrey SU9941
Beauty spot on B2130, 2 miles (3km) SE of Godalming
The National Trust's magnificent arboretum, a glorious display of colourful shrubs and trees covering over 90 acres (26ha) of the Surrey Hills.

WINLATON Tyne and Wear NZ1762
Town off A694, immediately S of Blaydon
Compact residential community surrounded by open countryside on three sides. In Hood Square, small museum housed in a preserved chain forge.

WINSCOMBE Avon ST4257
Village on A371, 2 miles (3km) N of Axbridge
Set in the attractive Winscombe Vale, the village has a 15th-century church with a handsome 100ft (30m) tower and three windows of original stained glass. Very fine William Morris window, too.

WINSFORD Cheshire SJ6566
Town on A54, 5 miles (8km) S of Northwich
Salt is still mined here and the town is largely modernised. Lake at Winsford Flashes created by subsidence due to salt mining.

WINSFORD Somerset SS9034
Village off A396, 5 miles (8km) N of Dulverton
Pretty thatched village in a woody Exmoor valley, with a packhorse bridge (and several others) and a prominent 15th-century church. Winsford Hill has a stone bearing a 5th century inscription – the Caratacus stone – and several Bronze Age barrows.

WINSHAM Somerset ST3706
Village on B3162, 4 miles (6km) SE of Chard
Largish village, with an interesting medieval church which has a large and rather rustic 16th-century painting of the Crucifixion.

WINSLOW Buckinghamshire SP7727
Small town on A413, 6 miles (10km) SE of Buckingham
Houses of the 17th and 18th centuries in this comfortable old market town include imposing Winslow Hall (limited opening), designed in the early 1700s, probably by Sir Christopher Wren, for a self-made Winslow man, William Lowndes. Good furniture, Chinese art,

satisfying gardens. Much humbler is Keach's Meeting House, a brick shed of 1695, for breakaway Baptists.

WINSTER Cumbria SD4193
Village on A5074, 3 miles (5km) S of Windermere
An unspoilt, scattered village of whitewashed stone cottages. The River Winster, which formed the border between Westmorland and Lancashire, flows through the centre.

WINSTER Derbyshire SK2460
Village off B5057, 4 miles (6km) W of Matlock
Attractive gritstone village, once a lead-mining centre and market town. The 15th- or 16th-century ground floor of its Market House (National Trust) originally had open arches, the later upper storey is brick. Early Georgian Winster Hall, 17th-century Dower House (remodelled in 18th century), and many 18th-century houses. Church dates mainly from 1840s, with 1721 tower. Shrove Tuesday pancake races.

WINSTON Durham NZ1416
Village on A67, 6 miles (10km) E of Barnard Castle
Charming village overlooking the River Tees. Single-arched bridge below the village built in 1764, at that time the longest semi-circular arch in Europe.

WINTERBORNE CAME Dorset SY7088
Hamlet off A352, 2 miles (3km) SE of Dorchester
Classical mansion of 1754 (not open) and a little late medieval church. William Barnes, the Dorset poet, is buried here.

WINTERBORNE, CLENSTON AND WHITCHURCH
Dorset ST8303/8300
Villages off A354, 4 miles (6km) SW of Blandford Forum
Both in the valley of the River Winterborne; Clenston is the smaller and prettier

WINTERBORNE, ZELSTON AND TOMSON Dorset SY8997
Village and hamlet off A31, 4 miles (6km) NE of Bere Regis
Zelston has many thatched cottages and a duck pond; Tomson is only a hamlet, with a farm, a few cottages and a tiny Norman church with unspoilt rustic fittings inside, painstakingly restored in 1930 with money raised by the sale of Thomas Hardy's letters to the Society for the Protection of Ancient Buildings.

WINTERBOURNE Avon ST6480
Suburb off B4058, 6 miles (10km) NE of Bristol
An old village that has recently grown large. The church is a proper medieval mixture, with 14th-century knight and lady effigies and a very early brass of 1370.

WINTERBOURNE ABBAS Dorset SY6190
Village on A35, 4 miles (6km) W of Dorchester
Rather dominated by the main road, but with older cottages. Nine Stones Circle is a little Bronze Age stone circle in woodland to the west.

WINTERBOURNE, DAUNTSEY, EARLS AND GUNNER
Wiltshire SU1734
Villages on A338, 4 miles (6km) NE of Salisbury
These three villages lie close together on the River Bourne. Dauntsey and Earls are very close together and share a Victorian church across their boundary. All have thatched cottages, but Gunner is the quietest, off the main road and with a medieval church. St Thomas Path recalls Thomas à Becket, parish priest here in the 13th century. Figsbury Rings Iron Age hillfort is to the southeast.

WINTERBOURNE STEEPLETON Dorset SY6289
Village on B3159, 4 miles (6km) W of Dorchester
Many thatched stone cottages, lots of trees and a partly Saxon church.

WINTERBOURNE STOKE Wiltshire SU0741
Village on A303, 5 miles (8km) W of Amesbury
Winding lanes, thatch and stone cottages, some chequered with flint, and a stream off the main road. Two Norman doorways to the church.

WINTERSLOW Wiltshire SU2232
Village off A30, 6 miles (10km) E of Salisbury
Large village scattered about several hamlets. Much development from 1930s onwards.

WINTERTON-ON-SEA Norfolk TG4919
Village on B1159, 8 miles (12km) N of Great Yarmouth
A small windswept village with a history of shipwrecks. The church tower acts as a landmark for sailors and has an anchorite's cell.

WINTOUR'S LEAP Gloucestershire ST5496
Viewpoint on B4228, 1 mile (2km) N of Tutshill
Spectacular viewpoint at top of steep limestone cliff overlooking River Wye. Pursued by Parliamentarians, Sir John Wintour jumped off and survived in 1642.

WINWICK Cheshire SJ6092
Village on A49, 3 miles (5km) N of Warrington
Small suburb of Warrington, dominated by village church with a magnificent spire. Bronze Age burial site and Roman road have been discovered in the parish.

WIRKSWORTH Derbyshire SK2854
Town on B5023, 4 miles (6km) S of Matlock
This small market town was once the centre of the lead-mining industry, and the Barmote Court which regulates the industry still meets twice a year in the 19th-century Moot Hall. The area surrounding Wirksworth is still extensively used for quarrying, with the nearby National Stone Centre demonstrating many everyday uses for stone. At the heart of the town is the sloping market place, and the nearby heritage centre illustrates aspects of the town's past in its displays. Substantial 17th- and 18th-century houses contribute to the pleasant townscape, with some earlier buildings including 16th-century Gell's Bedehouses. The impressive cruciform church dates mainly from 1272, its 13th- and 14th-century tower topped by a lead-covered spike. The clerestory was added and the east end altered in the 19th century, while an Anglo-Saxon coffin lid and Norman fragments give clues to an earlier building.

Elizabeth Evans, George Eliot's aunt, is buried in the churchyard, and the novelist used the town as Snowfield in *Adam Bede*. Arkwright's 1770s Haarlem Mill, and Providence Mill of about a century later, bear witness to the town's textile history.

WIRRAL Merseyside
Historic region, peninsula between River Mersey and River Dee
For centuries the Wirral peninsula was a wild and inaccessible spot jutting out into and separating the estuaries of the rivers Mersey and Dee. Modern Wirral dates from the day the Mersey ferries began a regular service to and from Liverpool. The local villages and towns have since been developed to house Liverpool commuters.

WISBECH Cambridgeshire TF4609
Town on A1101, 12 miles (19km) SW of King's Lynn
Wisbech has been a port since medieval times, when the River Nene flowed only another 4 miles (6km) to the sea (it is now 11 miles/18km to the Wash). It is still busy, although perhaps less so than its neighbour King's Lynn. Prosperity in the 18th century is especially evident in The Brinks, two lines of graceful buildings, mainly Georgian, that face each other across the River Nene. Peckover House (National Trust) is one of these, dating from 1722, and with a magnificent rococo wood and plaster interior.

There is a museum to the founder of the National Trust, Octavia Hill, who was born on the South Brink in 1838. Other fine buildings include the old market and the 19th-century Crescent.

There is a monument to Thomas Clarkson, who fought to abolish slavery, while the active Angles Theatre has been entertaining the locals since 1793.

WISBECH ST MARY Cambridgeshire TF4208
Village off B1169, 3 miles (5km) SW of Wisbech
Wisbech St Mary stands near the River Nene in an area of Cambridgeshire where all waterways and roads run in straight lines.

WISBOROUGH GREEN West Sussex TQ0525
Village on A272, 2 miles (3km) W of Billingshurst
Attractive village in the hilly, wooded country of the Weald, looking south to the downs. Magnificent big green with mature trees surrounded by little knots of houses and cottages, some tile-hung, some brick, some half-timber, with a little stucco. The green is overlooked by the tall-spired church, hidden behind cottages on a little rise beside the duck pond.

WISHAW Strathclyde NS7954
Town on A721, 3 miles (5km) SE of Motherwell
Town in the industrial Clyde Valley. Two Victorian mansions by Gillespie Graham lie near by; Wishaw House and Cambusnethen Priory.

WISLEY Surrey TQ0659
Hamlet off A3, 4 miles (6km) E of Woking
A lovely little cluster of church, farm and cottages by the River Wey, with nearby Royal Horticultural Gardens and an open, sandy common.

WISSINGTON Suffolk TL9533
Hamlet off A134, 1 mile (2km) SW of Nayland
Attached to nearby Nayland, Wissington is a pretty farming hamlet with a mill, a Norman church, and pleasant cottages. A revolutionary TB clinic stood near by .

WISTANSTOW Shropshire SO4385
Village off A49, 2 miles (3km) N of Craven Arms
Village comprises a few houses lining a stretch of Watling Street West, a Roman road. At centre is rewarding church of about 1200.

WISTMAN'S WOOD Devon SX6177
Beauty spot on Dartmoor, 1 mile (2km) N of Two Bridges
Possibly the only original woodland in southern England, stunted and twisted short oak trees growing amongst big rocks. Very remote.

WISTON Dyfed SM0217
Village off A40, 5 miles (8km) E of Haverfordwest
In quiet rural spot with slight remains of 12th-century motte and bailey castle and later keep.

WISTON West Sussex TQ1512
Hamlet off A283, 2 miles (3km) E of Washington
A lovely park and Elizabethan house are tucked beneath the steep slope of the South Downs, crowned by Chanctonbury Ring, an early Iron Age hillfort marked by an eye-catching clump of beech trees planted in 1760 by Charles Goring of Wiston, but decimated by the great storm of October 1987. The remains of a Romano-Celtic temple of the 1st and 2nd centuries and a 19th-centrury dewpond lie in the centre of the fort.

WISTOW Leicestershire SP6495
Village off A6, 6 miles (10km) SE of Leicester
Wistow Hall, modernised in late 18th century, in parkland. Norman and medieval church remodelled 1746. Wistan le Dale model village, at garden centre.

WISTOW North Yorkshire SE5935
Village on B1223, 3 miles (5km) NW of Selby
Village centre is dominated by the parish church which dates back to 1213. The village is reputedly haunted. The surrounding area contains some of the best arable land in the north of England.

WITCHAMPTON Dorset ST9806
Village off B3082, 6 miles (10km) E of Blandford Forum
Unusually for Dorset, a largely brick village, with 17th-century onwards brick cottages, some timber-framed.

WITHAM Essex TL8214
Town off A12, 9 miles (14km) NE of Chelmsford
An old market town, much expanded since the 1960s with London overspill estates. A plaque marks where Dorothy L Sayers, creator of Lord Peter Wimsey, lived in Newland Street and there is a perky statue of her with her pet cat opposite. Georgian buildings and coaching inns in the main street. Parkland by the River Brain.

WITHAM FRIARY Somerset ST7441
Village off A359, 6 miles (10km) NE of Bruton
Scattered and rural. The plain early Norman church and dovecote both belonged to the priory.

WITHAM ON THE HILL Lincolnshire TF0516
Village off A6121, 4 miles (6km) SW of Bourne
On rise between East and West Glen rivers. Medieval

church with medievalised 1730s tower. Seventeenth-century Palace Farm may incorporate remains of a medieval building of Bishops of Lincoln. Eighteenth-century Witham Hall has additions of 1903–5, now a school. Massive Bowthorpe Oak on Bowthorpe Park Farm is said to have seated 13 people for tea in its hollow trunk.

WITHERIDGE Devon SS8014
Village on B3137, 9 miles (14km) W of Tiverton
Now a village, but once a market town, with a huge market place lined with cob and thatch cottages and small Georgian houses.

WITHERNSEA Humberside TA3428
Small town on A1033, 15 miles (24km) E of Hull
A lively, traditional seaside resort with several stretches of sandy beach. The old lighthouse, surrounded by houses, is now a museum dedicated to the RNLI.

WITHERSFIELD Suffolk TL6547
Village off A604, 2 miles (3km) NW of Haverhill
Village set in a pleasant valley with some unusual carved benches in the Church of St Mary. A deep ditch still forms the parish boundary.

WITHERSLACK Cumbria SD4384
Hamlet off A590, 3 miles (4km) N of Lindale
A tranquil village where, until the mid-19th century, the Earls of Derby held manor courts at the Derby Arms inn.

WITHINGTON Gloucestershire SP0315
Village off A40, 5 miles (8km) W of Northleach
Straddling the River Coln beneath extensive woodland, Withington has fine Norman and medieval church, a Jacobean manor house and charming houses and cottages.

WITHINGTON Greater Manchester SJ8492
District in S Manchester
Fashionable residential area of large Victorian dwellings, many of which have been converted into flats. Popular with students.

WITHINGTON Hereford and Worcester SO5643
Village off A4103, 4 miles (6km) NE of Hereford
Slender spire proclaims rewarding Norman and medieval church in this large village looking across River Lugg to Hereford. Roman road runs to north.

WITHNELL Lancashire SD6322
Town off A675, 5 miles (8km) SW of Blackburn
Withnell Fold Mill Village, now a conservation area, is a 19th-century estate village built to house workers of nearby papermill.

WITHYBROOK Warwickshire SP4384
Village on B4112, 7 miles (11km) NW of Rugby
Isolated settlement near Fosse Way, where church has notable Easter Sepulchre and some medieval glass. Two deserted villages in countryside to southwest.

WITHYCOMBE Somerset ST0141
Village off A39, 2 miles (3km) SE of Dunster
Red sandstone village with an unusual 13th and early 14th-century church, small and simple.

WITHYHAM East Sussex TQ4935
Village on B2110, 6 miles (10km) SW of Tunbridge Wells
Pleasant hamlet with a little street of tile-hung houses, the earliest, Duckings, is close to a former hammerpond and once belonged to an ironmaster. The hamlet is connected with the Sackville family, who are buried in its church up a steep lane outside the village. The church was rebuilt after a lightning strike in 1663, and houses the famous tomb of Thomas Sackville, who died in 1667 aged 13. Memorial to Vita Sackville-West.

WITHYPOOL Somerset SS8435
Village off B3223, 2 miles (3km) S of Exford
Remote village on Exmoor, set in a little valley with a big stone bridge over the River Barle. Many beech-hedged banks.

Landacre Bridge over the River Barle at Withypool.

WITLEY Surrey SU9434

Village on A283, 2 miles (3km) S of Milford

Pretty commuters' village strung along a main road in wooded, hilly country, with an interesting church containing a window with oak frame over 1,000 years old and an 11th-century south door. The best buildings of this brick, tile-hung and timber village are around the church and include the 15th-century Old Cottage and 16th-century Step Cottage. Nearby Witley Common covers 500 acres (202ha).

WITNEY Oxfordshire SP3510

Town off A40, 10 miles (16km) W of Oxford

Old weaving town straddling the River Windrush. Famous blankets are still made here, and the trade's long history shows in many buildings, including Staple Hall, Blanket Hall, Bridge Street mills and workers' cottages. Medieval prosperity produced the grammar school, almshouses and imposing parish church full of 15th-century artistry. Eighteenth-century town hall and butter cross remain, contrasting with Woolgate Centre shopping precinct.

WITTENHAM CLUMPS Oxfordshire SU5692

Hill off A4074, 3 miles (5km) NW of Wallingford

These copses on Sinodun Hills, with Iron Age hillfort near by, command spectacular views. Surrounding grassland and woodland is nature reserve and popular picnic spot.

WITTERING Cambridgeshire TF0502

Village off A1, 3 miles (5km) SE of Stamford

A coaching stop when on the Great North road. Now, thankfully, the heavy traffic of the A1 rumbles to the east of the village.

WITTERSHAM Kent TQ8927

Village on B2082, 4 miles (6km) S of Tenterden

A big old village, the 'capital' of the Isle of Oxney, 214ft (65m) up, high above Rother Levels, with the nearby Stocks windmill, 1781, the tallest post mill in Kent.

WITTON GILBERT Durham NZ2345

Village on A691, 3 miles (5km) NW of Durham

In Browney Valley. The village grew as a mining community. The original blacksmith's shop still stands and is a Listed Building.

WITTON LE WEAR Durham NZ1431

Village off A68, 3 miles (5km) SW of Crook

An attractive village of great character near the River Wear. Witton Castle was built in the 15th century by the Eures family who prospered from mining. Only the walls remain now and the site is a recreation area. Low Barns Nature Reserve has woods, ponds, meadows and riverside walks and hides.

WIVELISCOMBE Somerset ST0827

Small town on B3227, 9 miles (14km) W of Taunton

Very small town, largely Victorian or later in the middle, set just below the Brendon Hills (see).

WIVELSFIELD East Sussex TQ3420

Village on B2112, 2 miles (3km) S of Haywards Heath

The old-established farming village clusters round a church with modern housing at nearby Wivelsfield Green, with a Victorian pub, and a railway station to the west of the village.

WIVENHOE Essex TM0321

Town on B1028, 4 miles (6km) SE of Colchester

Set on the River Colne,Wivenhoe has a quayside, craft shops and river views from the Black Buoy and Rose and Crown pubs. Notable 16th-century brasses are contained in the Victorianised church, which was damaged by the 1884 earthquake. Wivenhoe Park, on the way to Colchester, was bought in 1962 for the new University of Essex campus with its tower blocks and university art gallery.

WIVETON Norfolk TG0442

Village on B1156, 1 mile (2km) SE of Blakeney

Wiveton is a quiet coastal village that was once a thriving port on the River Glaven. The handsome church tells of the village's former wealth.

WIX Essex TM1628

Village on A120, 6 miles (10km) SW of Harwich

Once owned by Edward the Confessor's queen, more recently known for its timberyard.

WIXFORD Warwickshire SP0854

Village on B4085, 7 miles (11km) W of Stratford-upon-Avon

Small village on River Arrow with 17th-century pub, charming cottages and a superb memorial brass in its very rewarding church.

WOBURN Bedfordshire SP9433

Village on A4012, 5 miles (8km) N of Leighton Buzzard

An exceptionally handsome Georgian village with a splendid 1860s church built for the 8th Duke of Bedford. Woburn Abbey is the Bedford stately home, packed with treasures of art, china and silver, and set in a lavishly beautiful deer park. Antiques Centre with 40 shops. Woburn Wild Animal Kingdom is Europe's biggest drive-through safari park.

WOBURN SANDS Buckinghamshire SP9235

Village on A5130, 4 miles (6km) E of Bletchley

Set right on the Bedfordshire border, which crosses the main street, the village has a curious war memorial and the Swan pub has a 'green lady' ghost.

WOKING Surrey TQ0058

Town on A247, 6 miles (10km) N of Guildford

Woking itself developed on the arrival of the railway in 1838; the centre was redesigned for pedestrians in 1992 and, with its theatres, shops and industry, is also renowned for possessing the first mosque built in Britain (1889). Old Woking, 2 miles (3km) to the south, is a charming old market town mentioned in Domesday Book.

WOKINGHAM Berkshire SU8168

Town off M4, 7 miles (11km) SE of Reading

This old market town still has an old centre, but much

modern development as well. The odd and fanciful 1860 town hall is triangular, and several streets have Georgian brick and earlier timber-framing. On the outskirts to the south is Lucas Hospital, classical almshouses of 1665 (limited opening).

WOLD NEWTON Humberside TA0473
Village off A1039, 7 miles (11km) SW of Filey
The most northerly village in Humberside, set in an attractive setting on the Wolds uplands. The village lies in the Gypsey Race Valley which stays dry for years before suddenly becoming fast-flowing.

WOLDINGHAM Surrey TQ3755
Suburb off B269, 2 miles (3km) S of Warlingham
Commuter village on high downland amid plenty of trees and with two churches: tiny, ancient St Agatha's and St Paul's, built in 1933.

WOLFERTON Norfolk TF6528
Village off A149, 6 miles (10km) NE of King's Lynn
Visitors to the royal estate at Sandringham passed through Wolferton Station until 1966. The station is now a museum of royal memorabilia.

Carved village cross at Wolferton.

WOLLASTON Northamptonshire SP9062
Village on A509, 4 miles (6km) S of Wellingborough
Between River Nene and Bedfordshire border. Eighteenth-century church with 14th-century crossing tower and spire. Village museum. Hall, 18th century, in commercial use.

WOLLATON Nottinghamshire SK5239
District on A609, in W Nottingham
Grand symmetrical Elizabethan Wollaton Hall, 1580–8, by Robert Smythson for Francis Willoughby, in deer park with lake, cast-iron camellia house. Hall used as natural history museum. Industrial Museum in 18th-century stables, with beam engine. Medieval church, 1880s south chapel to accommodate Willoughby monuments from 1471. Eighteenth-century brick cottages around village square. Rectangular brick dovecote of 1585.

WOLSINGHAM Durham NZ0737
Town on A689, 10 miles (16km) NW of Bishop Auckland
Industrial town in central Weardale, a mixture of old stone cottages and modern developments. The church was rebuilt in Victorian times but retains a 12th-century tower. Wolsingham gained prosperity as a market town and its annual agricultural show is the oldest in England.

WOLSTON Warwickshire SP4175
Village off B4455, 5 miles (8km) SE of Coventry
Popular commuter village beside River Avon has worthwhile church and 18th-century houses in old village street. Earthworks of Brandon Castle across river.

WOLVERCOTE Oxfordshire SP4909
District in N Oxford
Popular residential suburb with modern estates and big papermill still has its village church and pleasant older houses, especially around Wolvercote Green.

WOLVERHAMPTON West Midlands SO82977
Town on A41, 12 miles (20km) NW of Birmingham
Best known today for its old-established football club and its sophisticated racecourse, Wolverhampton has a distinguished history. The grand parish church testifies to its success in the medieval wool trade, but in the 18th century the town went over to metal-working and was also noted for enamelled and japanned ware, displayed at Bantock House Museum in Finchfield Road. Later still it was an early centre of the motor industry, boasting such names as Sunbeam, Villiers, AJS Motorcycles and Guy Motors.

The metal trades are still important but they no longer impinge on the town centre, marked today by Queen Square and the vast array of shops in the Mander and Wulfrun Centres. Industrialisation spared few of the town's early buildings, although a timber-framed house survives in Victoria Street and there are good 18th-century houses in King Street and George Street. Victorian architecture predominates, ranging from artisan cottages through affluent villas to major buildings such as the Royal Wolverhampton School, the Grand Theatre and the excellent Museum and Art Gallery in Lichfield Street.

Wolverhampton was always a leader in council housing, and huge areas of residential development are a feature of the town.

WOLVERTON Buckinghamshire SP8141
Town off A5, in NW area of Milton Keynes
Formerly a major railway town, Wolverton has a big railway embankment and the Grand Union Canal aqueduct in Ouse Valley Park. Museum of Industry and Rural Life.

WOLVERTON Hampshire SU5558
Hamlet off A339, 2 miles (3km) E of Kingclere
A well wooded, dispersed village, with big hedges and a very fine 1716 church, still with many original fittings.

WOLVERTON Warwickshire SP2062
Village off A46, 5 miles (8km) N of Stratford-upon-Avon
Visitors seek out this small, lonely village west of Warwick to see the remarkable medieval glass and Pre-Raphaelite window in its church.

WOLVEY Warwickshire SP4287
Village on B4065, 4 miles (6km) S of Hinckley
Medieval market centre is now modern commuter village. Its interesting Norman and medieval church stands aloof beside the infant River Anker.

WOLVISTON Cleveland NZ4525
Village off A689, 4 miles (6km) N of Stockton-on-Tees
A middle-class residential area comprising 19th-century terraced housing and modern detached developments. Frequent winner of the 'Britain in Bloom' award.

WOMBOURNE Staffordshire SO8793
Town off A449, 4 miles (6km) SW of Wolverhampton
Commuter town of limited interest apart from The Bratch, site of James Brindley's picturesque locks and lockkeeper's cottage on Staffordshire and Worcestershire Canal.

WOMBWELL South Yorkshire SE3902
Town on A633, 4 miles (6km) SE of Barnsley
Residential area with some light industry. Pit-head baths of the former Wombwell Colliery are among the best in the county.

WONERSH Surrey TQ0145
Village on B2128, 3 miles (5km) SE of Guildford
Compact village, once a centre of cloth manufacture, with a minute central square, village cross and wide green under the slopes of Chinthurst Hill.

WOOBURN AND WOOBURN GREEN Buckinghamshire SU9087
Village and suburb on A4094, 5 miles (8km) SE of High Wycombe
Twin suburban settlements in the Wye Valley. Rare breeds are kept at Odds Farm Park and the Glass Market has glass craftsmanship in action.

WOOD DALLING Norfolk TG0827
Hamlet off B1145, 3 miles (5km) N of Reepham
A remote Norfolk village with a 14th- and 15th-century church with a 13th-century chancel. Wood Dalling Hall was built in 1582.

WOOD WALTON Cambridgeshire TL2180
Village off B1090, 6 miles (10km) N of Huntingdon
In the flat region near Peterborough, Wood Walton's Fen (Nature Conservancy Council) is an area of natural marsh that is carefully managed to protect plants and insects.

WOODBASTWICK Norfolk TG3315
Village off A1151, 8 miles (12km) NE of Norwich
Bordered by River Yare, Woodbastwick is sited in Broadland Marsh Conservation area. Two thatched almshouses, round thatched pumphouse and church stand near village green.

WOODBOROUGH Nottinghamshire SK6347
Village off A6097, 6 miles (10km) NE of Nottingham
Cottages and knitters' workshops of former framework knitting centre. Fine 14th-century chancel in church, Kempe and Burne-Jones windows.

WOODBRIDGE Suffolk TM2749
Town off A12, 8 miles (12km) NE of Ipswich
There is no wooden bridge at this attractive estuarine town. Its name is ancient, and meant 'Woden's town' in Saxon times. The town grew up at the head of the Deben estuary, its main industries traditionally shipbuilding and sail-making.

There are many fine buildings, but among the most impressive is the handsome tide mill, an 18th-century weatherboarded mill which was working until 1957 when part of the waterwheel broke. It is open to the public, and restored to full working order. Also along the atmospheric quayside is the 17th-century ferry house, and the pretty row of cottages that form numbers 1–5 Quayside that used to be the Ship inn.

One of the town's most generous benefactors was Thomas Seckford, an Elizabethan statesman who was responsible for commissioning the first proper maps of England. He provided money for the Seckford almshouses (although the present buildings are Victorian), and the shire hall. He was buried in 1857 in the fine Parish Church of St Mary the Virgin, a short walk across cobbled paths from Market Hill.

Near by is Sutton Hoo ship burial site.

WOODBURY Devon SY0187
Village on B3179, 4 miles (6km) N of Exmouth
A large village with a mixture of late 19th-century brick estate cottages and older ones. Woodbury Salterton to the north has an interesting collection of buildings from the 1840s: church, school, vicarage and well-house. Woodbury Common is high and heathy, with views of the Exe estuary and much archaeology including Woodbury Castle, an Iron Age hillfort.

WOODCHESTER Gloucestershire SO8402
Village off A46, 2 miles (3km) S of Stroud
Former industrial village has old mills in valley bottom and millworkers' cottages on hillside above. Spectacular Roman mosaic pavement buried beneath churchyard.

WOODCHURCH Kent TQ9434
Village off B2067, 4 miles (6km) E of Tenterden
Big friendly village grouped around a large green with weatherboarded and timber houses, a noble church with a very tall spire and a working white smock mill of 1820.

WOODDITTON Cambridgeshire TL6559
Hamlet off B1061, 3 miles (5km) S of Newmarket
Once standing in forest at the end of Devil's Dyke, Woodditton has a church with a 1393 brass to Henry Englissh and his wife.

WOODEATON Oxfordshire SP5311
Village off B4027, 4 miles (6km) NE of Oxford
Small village overlooking River Cherwell with medieval church and older houses around green with remains of 13th-century cross.

WOODFORD Greater London TQ4191
District in borough of Redbridge
Comfortable suburb developed after the railway came through in the 1850s. Statue on Woodford Green of Sir Winston Churchill, Woodford's MP.

WOODFORD Greater Manchester SJ8882
Village on A5102, 3 miles (5km) E of Wilmslow
Agricultural village in prosperous area. Dominated by aerodrome and British Aerospace works. Annual air show is renowned.

WOODFORD Northamptonshire SP9676
Village off A14, 2 miles (3km) SW of Thrapston
On bank of River Nene. Norman and medieval church has two early 14th-century wooden effigies, and a heart found in 1860 in recess of column.

WOODFORD, UPPER, MIDDLE AND LOWER Wiltshire SU1236/7
Villages off A360, 4 miles (6km) N of Salisbury
Three pretty villages in the Avon Valley with thatched cottages, many close to the wide river, and all set in lush meadows. Middle Woodford has the church, and Heale House (17th century, not open), with fine gardens including a Japanese one. At Upper Woodford one of the farm stables has an ornate wooden turret with a clock of 1935.

WOODGREEN Hampshire SU1717
Village off A338, 3 miles (5km) NE of Fordingbridge
Big New Forest village, famous for the wall-paintings in the village hall (limited opening) of 1931 showing local rural scenes and people.

WOODHALL SPA Lincolnshire TF1963
Town on B1191, 6 miles (10km) SW of Horncastle
Nineteenth-century spa, at height of fame in Edwardian period, and today a popular inland resort. There are tree-lined streets, pine and birch woodlands, elegant hotels and guesthouses. Championship golf course. Open-air swimming pool in Jubilee Park. Tiny barge-boarded Kinema in the Woods (1922), using back projection. Remains of 15th-century brick tower house – Tower on the Moor.

WOODHAM FERRERS Essex TQ7999
Village on B1418, 2 miles (3km) N of South Woodham Ferrers
The old village from which South Woodham Ferrers (see) sprang is set in farming country. Unusual war memorial.

WOODHAM MORTIMER Essex TL8104
Village on A414, 3 miles (5km) SW of Maldon
Victorian church with sad Tudor brass to a three-year-old child.

WOODHAM WALTER Essex TL8007
Village off A414, 3 miles (5km) W of Maldon
Lying south of the River Chelmer, the village has an unusual Tudor church in a brick version of the Perpendicular style. The Bell pub is Elizabethan.

WOODHEAD Derbyshire SK0999
Site on A628, 5 miles (8km) NE of Glossop
Woodhead Reservoir is one of a series in the Longdendale Valley. Woodhead railway tunnel was the longest in the world when opened in 1845; a second was completed in 1852 which was replaced by a third in 1954.

WOODHOUSE EAVES Leicestershire SK5314
Village on B591, 4 miles (6km) S of Loughborough
Charnwood Forest village, cottages from Swithland slate stones. Church and 1840s Beaumanor Hall by Railton, of Nelson's Column fame. Woodhouse Beacon viewpoint.

WOODHURST Cambridgeshire TL3176
Village off B1040, 3 miles (5km) N of St Ives
Sited in wide open country, the little village of Woodhurst has a single main street that is oval and ringed by cottages.

WOODMANCOTE Gloucestershire ST7597
Village off A435, immediately SE of Bishop's Cleeve
Now a popular residential suburb of Dursley, the village retains some good Georgian houses in its old centre.

WOODPLUMPTON Lancashire SD5034
Village on B5411, 4 miles (6km) NW of Preston
Attractive village of old cottages. Parts of church date back to 14th century. There are 17th-century buildings in the village centre.

WOODSTOCK Oxfordshire SP4416
Town on A44, 8 miles (13km) NW of Oxford
The world-famous Blenheim Palace and Park (limited opening) are the big attraction here, but the charming small town at its gates deserves a leisurely tour. Harmonious stone buildings of 17th and 18th centuries rub shoulders with inviting old pubs and hotels, and the Oxfordshire County Museum in Park Street covers most aspects of the county's history.

WOODY BAY Devon SS6749
Hamlet off A39, 3 miles (5km) W of Lynton
Romantic wooded cliffs and a rocky bay, with a few houses on the amazingly steep road.

WOOKEY HOLE Somerset ST5347
Village off A371, 2 miles (3km) NW of Wells
Mendip village, famous for the caves in the limestone from which the River Axe appears. Large caves are accessible, with a famous echo, stalactites and stalagmites. Fairground museum, and traditional paper-making. Paper has been produced here since the 17th century.

WOOL Dorset SY8486
Village off B3071, 5 miles (8km) W of Wareham
Large modern part, but an old centre with cob cottages, and the famous Woolbridge to the north, a fine 16th-century stone bridge with early 17th-century stone manor house (not open) beyond. Part of the setting for Thomas Hardy's *Tess of the D'Urbervilles*.

WOOLACOMBE Devon SS4543
Village on B3343, 5 miles (8km) SW of Ilfracombe
Two miles (3km) of sandy beach, with a rocky headland at each end. Developed from the 1880s as a resort. Views of Lundy (see) and the Once Upon a Time tourist attraction.

WOOLBEDING West Sussex SU8722
Hamlet off A286, 1 mile (2km) NW of Midhurst
Compact little cluster of Saxon church, delightful big house and farms on a meandering loop of the River Rother, spanned by a three-arched medieval bridge.

WOOLER Northumberland NT9928
Small town on A697, 15 miles (24km) NW of Alnwick
A market town and centre for walking in the Cheviot Hills, with salmon- and trout-fishing on the River Till. A rock known as King's Chair hangs over Pin Well. Ancient kings are supposed to have directed battles from the chair, and a pagan custom was to drop a crooked pin into the well.

WOOLFARDISWORTHY (WOOLSERY) Devon SS3321
Village off A39, 3 miles (5km) SE of Clovelly
Usually called Woolsery, which seems a waste, this large village has many thatched cottages. Buck's Mills on the shore to the north is a miniature Clovelly, wooded to the shore.

WOOLHAMPTON Berkshire SU5766
Village on A4, 6 miles (10km) E of Newbury
Partly in the Kennet Valley, and partly on wooded slopes, Woolhampton has Georgian brick and some timber-framing. Douai Abbey, refounded here in 1903, has some 1840s buildings.

WOOLHOPE Hereford and Worcester SO6135
Village off B4224, 7 miles (11km) SE of Hereford
The old Butcher's Arms and Crown inn grace the village, along with many houses in pale sandstone. They stand on 'Woolhope Dome', a heavily wooded outcrop of limestone and sandstone, a complex landscape of ridges and valleys. Interesting coffin lids in medieval church. Trails and forest walks in Haugh Wood (National Trust) to northwest of the village.

WOOLLEY Avon ST7468
Hamlet off A46, 3 miles (5km) N of Bath
Tiny stone hamlet on the slopes of a hill, with a church of 1761 designed by John Wood of nearby Bath.

WOOLLEY West Yorkshire SE3213
Village off A61, 5 miles (8km) S of Wakefield
Retains a rural character despite being surrounded by industrial towns. Woolley Hall is now a college.

WOOLPIT Suffolk TL9762
Village off A14 (A45), 5 miles (8km) NW of Stowmarket
An atmospheric town with mellow honey-coloured buildings around an elegant church. The Swan inn is more than 400 years old, just one of several medieval houses in Woolpit. St Mary's Church was started in the 11th century, but has 15th-century additions. On the village green is a charming roofed pump.

WOOLSINGTON Tyne & Wear NZ1969
Village off A696, 5 miles (8km) NW of Newcastle
Small village separated from Newcastle by fields and inevitably dominated by Newcastle International Airport which is undergoing a continuous programme of expansion.

WOOLSTHORPE (WOOLSTHORPE-BY-BELVOIR)
Lincolnshire SK8333
Village off A52, 5 miles (8km) W of Grantham
Pretty village on River Devon, the Leicestershire boundary, opposite Belvoir Castle. Wharf on Grantham Canal used to unload stone for Belvoir and Harlaxton.

WOOLSTON Shropshire SJ3224
Hamlet off A5, 4 miles (6km) SE of Oswestry
Timber-framed building (holiday cottage) stands over St Winefride's Well, reputedly spot where saint's body rested on way to Shrewsbury Abbey. Access possible.

WOOLTON Merseyside SJ4286
District on B5171, in SE Liverpool
A dignified area which was once an estate village of Georgian and Victorian buildings. Older buildings, such as Woolton Hall, are in local red sandstone.

WOOLWICH Greater London TQ4478
District in borough of Greenwich
A visitor centre commands a spectacular view of the massive gates of the Thames Barrier. Woolwich, birthplace of Arsenal football club, has historic military connections. The Royal Arsenal closed in 1963. The magnificent Royal Artillery Barracks are not open, but there are plans to open the regimental museum in the Arsenal. Meanwhile, the museum in John Nash's 1814 Rotunda has an impressive collection.

WOORE Shropshire SJ7342
Village on A525, 6 miles (10km) NE of Market Drayton
Pleasant village on border with Staffordshire has classical church of 1830. Hospitable Swan hotel, an attractive early 19th-century inn, stands opposite.

WOOTTON Bedfordshire TL0045
Village off A421, 4 miles (6km) SW of Bedford
Former brick-making village, itself naturally built of brick; many Bedfordshire church bells were cast here, too.

WOOTTON Isle of Wight SZ5492
Village off A3054, 3 miles (5km) W of Ryde
On the Blackbridge Brook estuary, a mostly modern settlement with many yachts.

WOOTTON Oxfordshire SP4319
Village off B4027, 2 miles (3km) N of Woodstock
Pleasant village sprawls beside long lane on both sides of the River Glyme. Unspoilt medieval church accepts a Victorian mosaic reredos with good grace.

WOOTTON BASSETT Wiltshire SU0682
Small town on A3102, 6 miles (10km) W of Swindon
A very small market town, the main street full of Georgian houses and cottages, and centring on the extraordinary town hall of 1700 (looking much earlier). Picturesque timber-framed top, stone pillars below. Now a museum (limited opening).

WOOTTON RIVERS Wiltshire SU1962
Village off B3087, 3 miles (5km) NE of Pewsey
Many timber-framed thatched cottages and the Kennet and Avon Canal at one end of the village, with a lock and lock-keeper's house.

WOOTTON ST LAWRENCE Hampshire SU5953
Village off A339, 3 miles (5km) W of Basingstoke
Old cottages mixed with modern infill. Partly Norman church, with two fine modern windows engraved by Laurence Whistler.

WOOTTON WAWEN Warwickshire SP1563
Village on A3400, 2 miles (3km) S of Henley-in-Arden
This scattered village has one of Warwickshire's most fascinating churches. St Peter's incorporates a Saxon tower that forms a small sanctuary at the church's centre, and there is a wealth of fine medieval craft work. The timber-framed Bull's Head stands out among an array of much-restored cottages, and there is a four-storey mill (not open) beside the River Alne.

WORCESTER Hereford and Worcester SO8555
City off M5, 24 miles (38km) SW of Birmingham
The familiar view of the cathedral high above the River Severn is almost the only good view here because Worcester suffered savage development in the 1960s and its gems have to be sought out.

The cathedral is the obvious start, and a visit must include the strikingly vaulted Norman crypt, the surviving part of the church built by the Saxon bishop Wulfstan. The nave houses the tombs of King John and Prince Arthur (eldest son of Henry VIII) and the restored misericords should not be missed.

College Green, outside the cathedral, is a restful close, and by walking through Edgar's Tower it is possible to visit the Royal Worcester factory and Dyson-Perrins Museum of porcelain in Severn Street. Another attraction near the cathedral is the 16th-century Commandery with its Civil War displays. In nearby Friar Street are the timber-framed Old Talbot, Greyfriars and Tudor House, which houses a local social history museum.

Friar Street leads to New Street, with the three-storey timber-framed Nash's House and the picturesque King Charles House from which Charles II made one of his many escapes. St Swithun's Church, close by, has one of England's most perfect classical church interiors. The main street to the north of the cross contains the handsome St Nicholas' Church, the former Hopmarket hotel and the delightful Berkeley Hospital. Keep going beyond the railway bridge to reach the City Museum and Art Gallery.

The walk back to the cathedral past the Cross and through the pedestrianised shopping area passes by Worcester's best building – the baroque guildhall, beautifully embellished. Near by stands a statue of Elgar, forever associated with the city and the Three Choirs Festival, which Worcester hosts in turn with Hereford and Gloucester.

WORFIELD Shropshire SO7595
Village off A454, 3 miles (5km) NE of Bridgnorth
Charming estate village of Davenport House (not open). Impressive medieval church and lanes lined with appealing brick and timber-framed houses.

WORKINGTON Cumbria NX9928
Town on A597, 17 miles (27km) W of Keswick
The town is situated at the mouth of the River Derwent and the harbour has the Vanguard sailing club. Workington Hall, now demolished, was built in 1379 and Mary Stuart stayed here when fleeing to England in 1568. The Helena Thomson Museum has a collection of 19th-century costumes and other artefacts.

WORKSOP Nottinghamshire SK5879
Town on A60, 12 miles (19km) N of Mansfield
Market town surrounded by 'The Dukeries' (see Clumber Park, Ollerton, Welbeck Abbey). Priory church incorporates part of church of Augustinian canons, Norman nave, 13th-century lady chapel and 20th-century transepts, central tower and east end. Unique 1314 priory gatehouse with wayside shrine and chapel. Mid-19th-century town hall beside market place. Some Georgian buildings.

WORLINGTON Suffolk TL6973
Village on B1102, 1 mile (2km) SW of Mildenhall
Small village near the River Lark. Sixteenth-century mansion Wamil Hall is reputed to be haunted by a woman called Lady Rainbow.

WORLINGWORTH Suffolk TM2368
Village off A1120, 5 miles (8km) NW of Framlingham
A long, winding road leads through avenues of trees, past Worlingworth Hall gallops and the 12th-century church to the old Swan pub.

WORMEGAY Norfolk TF6611
Village off A134, 6 miles (10km) SE of King's Lynn
The old motte and bailey castle is now grass-covered. St Michael's Church has a 15th-century tower, but other parts were rebuilt in 1893.

WORMINGFORD Essex TL9332
Village off B1508, 6 miles (10km) NW of Colchester
Fine views over the Stour Valley. The painter John Nash lived and is buried here.

WORMINGHALL Buckinghamshire SP6408
Village off A418, 5 miles (8km) NW of Thame
A village above the River Thame with post-war housing estates, old almshouses and a veteran half-timbered, thatched pub, the Clifden Arms.

WORMIT Fife NO3926
Village off A914, 2 miles (3km) SW of Newport-on-Tay
Village on Firth of Tay opposite Dundee on southern landfall of Tay Rail Bridge, built 1883–8 to replace original bridge of 1871.

WORMLEIGHTON Warwickshire SP4453
Village off A423, 8 miles (13km) N of Banbury
A magnificent gatehouse recalls the splendour of the Spencer family's manor, largely destroyed during Civil War. Outstanding chancel screen in the fine church.

WORMLEY Surrey SU9438
Village on A283, 3 miles (5km) S of Milford
Scattered village in beautiful wooded hill country south of Witley, once favoured by Victorian artists and writers, including Myles Birkett Foster and George Eliot.

WORMS HEAD West Glamorgan SS3887
Headland at SW end of Gower Peninsula
Two connecting rocky islets make up Worms Head, connected to the southern end of vast Rhossili Bay by a causeway accessible for two and a half hours either side of low water. The highest point is at 200ft (61m) with a cave at its foot. The name, reflecting Viking influence, derives from its serpent-like shape ('Worm' is Norse for serpent).

WORPLESDON Surrey SU9753
Village on A322, 3 miles (5km) NW of Guildford
Heathland village with a large green and old houses, but increasingly hemmed in by the expansion of Guildford and Woking.

WORSBROUGH South Yorkshire SE3503
District on A61, immediately S of Barnsley
Worsbrough Country Park has a beautiful reservoir and a fully restored working Saxon watermill (open to visitors).

WORSLEY Greater Manchester SD7400
Town off M63, 6 miles (10km) W of Manchester
Attractive historic and residential area. Bridgewater Canal runs through the picturesque village centre, which has a green and Tudor, Jacobean and Victorian buildings.

WORSTEAD Norfolk TG3026
Village off A149, 3 miles (5km) SE of North Walsham
Famous for its cloth since medieval times, Worstead is now a peaceful village with a cluster of Jacobean houses at its centre.

WORSTHORNE Lancashire SD8732
Village off A671, 3 miles (5km) E of Burnley
Pretty village, relatively unchanged. Long associations with the Thursby family, great local benefactors.

WORTH West Sussex TQ3036
Hamlet off B2036, 2 miles (3km) E of Crawley
A pleasant suburb of Crawley close to the M23, with one of England's best churches, a remarkable Saxon survival, built AD950–1050, cruciform with a wide, tall nave and mighty chancel arch. It was restored in 1871, when the tower and spire were built, and again after a fire in 1986. Worth Forest, which rises to 505ft (154m), was a centre of the medieval iron industry and is now a beautifully wooded region.

WORTH MATRAVERS Dorset SY9777
Village off B3069, 4 miles (6km) W of Swanage
One of the prettiest Purbeck villages, set just back from the sea and full of stone cottages and houses. Famous picture-postcard view across the pond. Mostly Norman church, with lots of zig-zag decoration. Rocky shore, good walking.

WORTHAM Suffolk TM0877
Village off A143, 3 miles (5km) SW of Diss
St Mary's Church in Wortham has the broadest round tower in England. The first-floor entrance suggests that it may have been used for defence.

WORTHEN Shropshire SJ3204
Village on B4386, 6 miles (10km) SE of Welshpool
Well situated in Rea Valley at foot of Long Mountain, this compact village has church with interesting work of several centuries.

The tower of the 14th-century 'wool' church at Worstead.

WORTHENBURY Clwyd SJ4246
Village on B5069, 4 miles (6km) NE of Overton
Border village near River Dee's loops. Church has well-preserved 18th-century interior pews with fireplaces, and 14th-century stained glass from Winchester College chapel.

WORTHING West Sussex TQ1402
Town on A259, 10 miles (16km) W of Brighton
Worthing combines the amenities of a large town and popular seaside resort, as well as possessing a sizeable fishing fleet. The fishing boats are drawn up on to the beach in time-honoured fashion for the catch to be sold on the shore, with customers coming from all over West Sussex.

Modern Worthing developed from a fishing hamlet after a visit by Princess Amelia, sister to the Prince Regent, in 1798. In 1806 The Steine was laid out, surrounded by houses in cream-coloured brick, soon followed by Montagu Place, Liverpool Terrace and the most ambitious of Worthing's early 19th-century developments, Park Crescent, which is entered through a triumphal arch.

Victorian, Edwardian and 20th-century buildings crowd in around Worthing's Regency beginnings and shoppers can enjoy the award-winning Montague shopping centre. Worthing is a famous venue for bowls, and major championships are held here. The 5 mile (8km) seafront is backed by a promenade with colourful flower beds, and there is sea-fishing from the pier. The Pavilion Theatre hosts variety shows, plus a summer talent-spotting contest, while the Connaught Theatre presents drama by leading touring companies and concerts are given at the Assembly Hall.

WORTHINGTON Leicestershire SK4020
Village off A453, 4 miles (6km) NE of Ashby-de-la-Zouch
Northwest Leicestershire village with views to Charnwood Forest. Brick cottage dated 1714, and octagonal brick lock-up. Norman church extended in 13th century.

WORTLEY South Yorkshire SE3099
Village on A629, 5 miles (8km) SE of Penistone
Compact village with a mixture of old and new housing. The Top Forge, 17th-century ironworks, has been restored and hosts frequent open days.

WOTTON Surrey TQ1247
Hamlet on A25, 3 miles (5km) W of Dorking
In beautiful hill country, with a church, where diarist John Evelyn is buried, isolated in a field away from the pub, Wotton House and a few cottages.

WOTTON UNDERWOOD Buckinghamshire SP6815
Village off B4011, 6 miles (10km) N of Thame
Interesting church and estate cottages stand respectfully attendant on the 18th-century hauteur of Wotton House (not open) and its magnificent grounds.

WOTTON-UNDER-EDGE Gloucestershire ST7593
Small town on B4058, 9 miles (14km) SW of Stroud
Isaac Pitman invented his shorthand system in 1837 while he was working in this pleasant market town. His terraced house is one of a splendid variety of buildings on view, including a noble church with superb brasses, 17th-century Tolsey House, Perry and Dawes almshouses and fine collection of houses and cottages once occupied by weaving-mill owners and their workers.

WOULDHAM Kent TQ7164
Village off A2, 3 miles (5km) SW of Rochester
A village with an interesting old church beside the tidal River Medway, surrounded by marshes and overgrown chalk pits and medieval Starkey Castle Farm to the north.

WRABNESS Essex TM1731
Village off B1352, 5 miles (8km) W of Harwich
On the Stour estuary. Wood and estuary mudflats support flourishing birdlife in Stour Wood and Copperas Bay RSPB reserve.

WRAGBY Lincolnshire TF1378
Small town on A158, 7 miles (11km) S of Market Rasen
Small former market town midway between Lincoln and Horncastle. Early 19th-century Turnor Arms. Church of 1839, almshouses of 1840.

WRAGBY West Yorkshire SE4117
Hamlet on A638, 4 miles (6km) SW of Pontefract
Nostell Priory (National Trust), fine Palladian house built in 1733. Contains one of the finest collections of Chippendale furniture. Pleasant grounds include 16th-century church.

WRANGLE Lincolnshire TF4250
Village on A52, 7 miles (12km) NE of Boston
Fenland settlement along Boston–Skegness road with farmhouses dating from period of land drainage. Medieval church with much 14th-century stained glass.

WRAXALL Avon ST4971
Village on B3130, 6 miles (10km) W of Bristol
Hilly, with some older stone buildings and a handsome 15th-century church tower. Birdcombe Court, 1 mile (2km) west, has a medieval tower (not open).

WRAY Lancashire SD6067
Village on B6480, 7 miles (11km) S of Kirkby Lonsdale
A lovely row of stone farmhouses and cottages lines the long main street through the village.

WRAYSBURY Berkshire TQ0074
Village on B376, 3 miles (5km) NW of Staines
Surrounded by reservoirs and gravel-digging lakes. Old farmhouses are scattered about, but the village is mostly modern suburban.

WREAY Cumbria NY4348
Village off A6, 5 miles (8km) SE of Carlisle
On the River Petteril. The Twelve Men, a group once responsible for villagers' welfare, still meet in the Plough inn, although they now have little responsibility.

WREKIN, THE Shropshire SJ6208
Hill off M54, 3 miles (5km) SW of Wellington
Long, domed hill outside Telford, heavily wooded, with steep promontory overlooking Severn Valley. Hillfort on summit once capital of Celtic tribe (see Wroxeter).

WRENBURY Cheshire SJ5947
Village off A530, 5 miles (8km) SW of Nantwich
Small country village with 16th-century church. The estate of Comber Mere Abbey, founded in 12th century, encompasses England's largest privately owned lake.

WRENTHAM Suffolk TM4982
Village on A12, 4 miles (6km) N of Southwold
An ancient village that has changed very little through the years. St Nicholas' Church tower dates from the 15th century.

WRESSLE Humberside SE7031
Village off A63, 3 miles (5km) NW of Howden
Village on the River Derwent with a station on the main line into Hull resulting in there being three level crossings. Wressle Castle is still standing.

WRESTLINGWORTH Bedfordshire TL2547
Village on B1042, 3 miles (5km) SE of Potton
A small place in Brussel sprout country close to the River Cam and the Cambridgeshire border.

WREXHAM Clwyd SJ3350
Town on A483, 11 miles (17km) SW of Chester
This border town was once noted for its industries which included brick and tile manufacture. It has made a special effort to preserve its past, an initiative which focuses on the Clywedog Valley Heritage Park and Trail.

The town's heritage centre concentrates on Wrexham's booming 19th-century industries, while the Clywedog Valley has been rejuvenated to re-create its pioneering role during the Industrial Revolution – and also to show off the natural beauty which has been restored to the area. King's Mill tells the story of an 18th-century miller's life, while Nant Mill and the Plas Power woodlands focus on local nature. The trail also links with other sites in the area, including Bersham (see).

Dominating the centre of Wrexham itself is St Giles's Church with its 16th-century tower, which rises to 136ft (41m). Elihu Yale, whose family came from near by and who founded America's Yale University, is buried here.

The jewel in the district's crown is Erddig Hall (National Trust), a supreme example of an 'upstairs, downstairs' house virtually unchanged since 18th-century alterations were made to the 17th-century building. Of outstanding interest are the perfectly preserved servants' quarters and outbuildings.

WRINGTON Avon ST4762
Village off A38, 2 miles (3km) E of Congresbury
A large village, feeling almost like a small town. Many stone buildings stand along the curving main street, and the very handsome 15th-century church has one of the famous Somerset towers, 114ft (34m) high. Memorial to the 17th-century philosopher John Locke, who was born here.

WRITTLE Essex TL6706
Suburb off A414, 2 miles (3km) W of Chelmsford
Attractive, sought-after place close to the River Wid with a charming green and pond, a pleasing variety of old houses and a church which is particularly rich in brasses. The church tower fell down in 1800 and had to be rebuilt. Marconi broadcast the world's first radio entertainment programme from a hut here in 1922.

WROTHAM Kent TQ6159
Village off M20, 8 miles (13km) N of Tonbridge
An ancient village, pronounced 'Root-em', beneath the steep tree-clad slopes of the North Downs, which keeps its identity despite nearby motorways (the M20 and M26). The lovely little village square has an Elizabethan manor house on one side and a 14th/15th-century church on the other. Remains of an archbishop's palace are close to the church. The attractive High Street runs off westwards. Wrotham Water (National Trust) lies between the village and Trottiscliffe.

WROUGHTON Wiltshire SU1480
Village on A4361, 3 miles (5km) S of Swindon
Grown large since the 1960s because of its proximity to Swindon, but with an older centre on the main road. The Science Museum has the airfield to the south (very limited opening) for vehicles and planes.

WROXALL Isle of Wight SZ5579
Village on B3327, 2 miles (3km) N of Ventnor
A mostly 19th-century onwards village, with Appuldurcombe House (English Heritage) to the west – the shell of an early 18th-century mansion, hit by a landmine in World War II. Isle of Wight donkey sanctuary.

WROXALL Warwickshire SP2271
Hamlet on A4141, 6 miles (10km) NW of Warwick
Within grounds of Wroxall Abbey School is a medieval convent church containing a fine collection of medieval glass. Open by arrangement.

WROXETER Shropshire SJ5608
Village on B4380, 5 miles (8km) SE of Shrewsbury
The site of Roman city of *Viriconium* (open). Started as military fortress in about AD50, developed as civilian town for local Cornovii tribe, whose capital was The Wrekin (see). Visible remains include large bathhouse complex with massive section of wall and bases of forum pillars. Visitor centre on site interprets ruins and displays smaller items. Ancient church near by.

WROXHAM Norfolk TG2917
Village on A1151, 7 miles (11km) NE of Norwich
Linked to Hoveton (see) by an attractive hump-backed bridge, Wroxham is the capital of the Norfolk Broads. The river banks are jammed tightly with boats of all sizes and colours. Roy's supermarket once claimed to be the biggest village store in the world. One house has a garden with a miniature passenger steam engine.

WROXTON Oxfordshire SP4141
Village on A422, 3 miles (5km) W of Banbury
Lord North, 18th-century Prime Minister, lived in Wroxton Abbey, now a college. He provided a new

tower for the medieval church, which, despite a fine monument by Flaxman, is almost upstaged by the thatched Roman Catholic church. The very pretty village has thatched cottages in local ironstone, especially attractive around the green.

WRYNOSE PASS Cumbria NY2702
Mountain pass off A593, on minor road to Eskdale Green
One of the most dramatic roads in the Lake District, the summit of the pass is 1,281ft (391m). The steep road can get very crowded in summer.

WYBOSTON Bedfordshire TL1656
Village off A1, 3 miles (5km) SW of St Neots
Split in two by the A1 road. Angling and watersports are available at Wyboston Lakes.

WYBUNBURY Cheshire SJ6949
Village off A500, 4 miles (6km) S of Crewe
Village has suffered from subsidence caused by running sand, salt and water below ground. Nature reserve at Wybunbury Moss.

WYCHBOLD Hereford and Worcester SO9265
Village on A38, 2 miles (5km) NE of Droitwich
Modern housing has transformed village formerly domain of Corbett family, whose saltworks were at neighbouring Stoke Prior (see). They built isolated church in 1889.

WYCHNOR Staffordshire SK1716
Hamlet off A38, 1 mile (2km) NE of Alrewas
Earthworks of medieval deserted village (accessible) are visible in front of the church and former school here.

WYCLIFFE Durham NZ1114
Hamlet off A66, 4 miles (6km) E of Barnard Castle
Birthplace of John Wycliffe (1324–84), reformer and translator of the Bible. Wycliffe Hall Botanical Gardens contain important collections. Tiny 13th-century church.

WYCOLLER Lancashire SD9339
Hamlet off A6068, 3 miles (5km) E of Colne
Pretty country village contained within a country park. Wycoller Hall is a romantic ruin immortalised as Ferndean Manor by Charlotte Brontë.

Bridge spanning the River Bure at Wroxham.

WYDDIAL Hertfordshire TL3731
Village off A10, 1 mile (2km) NE of Buntingford
Quiet, scattered place with an unusual church built partly in brick in 1532, with 16th-century Flemish stained glass.

WYE Kent TR0546
Town off A28, 4 miles (6km) NE of Ashford
Old market town on the North Downs, famed for its agricultural college. There are pleasant Georgian houses in the old part of town near the 15th-century collegiate church, as well as older half-timbered buildings. Wye College occupies the buildings of a college of priests founded in 1447, while Stour Music Festival is held partly in Olantigh Hall. A nearby nature reserve on Wye Downs covers 250 acres (101ha).

WYE, RIVER Derbyshire
River, tributary of the Derwent
Rises near Buxton, flows through Miller's Dale, dramatic Monsal Dale, Bakewell, past Haddon Hall, drives Caudwell's Mill and joins River Derwent at Rowsley.

WYE, RIVER Hereford and Worcester
River
Rising on Plynlimon, the river flows through Rhayader and Builth Wells, attracting anglers seeking salmon, grayling and trout. After Hereford it begins a series of striking meanders that continue to Ross and Monmouth. Then begins the dramatic stretch through the Wye Valley, with a spectacular loop around Symonds Yat (see) before the steep limestone gorge above Chepstow, where it joins the Severn estuary.

WYE, RIVER Powys/Gwent
River
Has its source in Plynlimon Mountains, flows through Rhayader, Builth Wells to leave Wales at Hay-on-Wye; re-enters near Monmouth to flow down lovely valley to the sea.

WYKE West Yorkshire SE1526
Town on A58, 5 miles (8km) E of Halifax
A large residential area of Bradford centred around the older, Victorian town centre. The Church of St Mary the Virgin stands on a hill overlooking the town.

WYKE CHAMPFLOWER Somerset ST6634
Hamlet off A359, 1 mile (2km) W of Bruton
Tiny hamlet, mostly the manor house (not open) and attached tiny 1624 church, still with original panelling, pulpit and box pews.

WYKEHAM North Yorkshire SE9683
Village on A170, 6 miles 10km) SW of Scarborough
This is an ancient village of mellow stone houses and nearby Wykeham Forest offers some fine views.

WYKEN West Midlands SP3680
District in NE Coventry
A Coventry suburb that still has its old Norman village church. Remains of medieval Caludon Castle and Coombe Abbey Country Park near by.

WYLAM Northumberland NZ1164
Village off B6528, 8 miles (13km) W of Newcastle-upon-Tyne
Points Bridge, built for the railway over the River Tyne in 1876, is now a historic monument. Pretty sandstone village and birthplace of George Stephenson.

WYLYE Wiltshire SU0037
Village off A303, 7 miles (11km) NW of Wilton
Old thatched cottages around the church and, in Teapot Lane, some of chequered flint and stone. Standing in the river by the mill is an 18th-century statue of a man blowing a horn, supposedly a memorial to a post-boy who fell from a stage coach and drowned here.

WYMINGTON Bedfordshire SP9564
Village off A6, 2 miles (3km) S of Rushden
An attractive village of stone and thatch, famed for its striking 14th-century church with a soaring spire and fine brasses.

WYMONDHAM Leicestershire SK8518
Village off B676, 6 miles (10km) E of Melton Mowbray
Wolds village, once a market centre, with 17th-century former grammar school. Six-sailed windmill of 1814, being restored, with adjoining tea room.

WYMONDHAM Norfolk TG1001
Small town on A11, 9 miles (14km) SW of Norwich
The centre of Wymondham (pronounced 'Windham') is its handsome 17th-century market cross. The splendid abbey church of St Mary and St Thomas of Canterbury has two towers built because of a 14th-century dispute between the monks and the townspeople. In 1559, Kett's Rebellion (a revolt by peasants against the loss of common land) began in Wymondham.

WYNFORD EAGLE Dorset SY5895
Hamlet off A356, 2 miles (3km) SW of Maiden Newton
Small and scattered, with a fine 1630s stone manor house (not open) and church with Norman carving and inscription.

WYRE Orkney HY4426
Island off SE coast of Rousay
Low-lying island near Rousay with remains of 12th-century Cubbie Roo's Castle. Norse stronghold, and scant ruins of medieval St Mary's Chapel.

WYRE FOREST Hereford and Worcester SO7476
Forest off B4194, NW of Bewdley
About 6,000acres (2,400ha) of ancient forest landscape, now oak and conifer woodland. Rare plants and roaming deer. Visitor centre near Far Forest (see).

WYRE PIDDLE Hereford and Worcester SO9747
Village on A4538, 2 miles (3km) NE of Pershore
Despite promising name, the village, pleasantly situated beside River Avon, is merely functional with many new houses.

WYRE, RIVER Lancashire
River, runs from Forest of Bowland to Irish Sea at Fleetwood
Flows through rich farmland. Wyre Estuary Country Park comprises whole estuary from the mouth to Shard Bridge, and contains Wyreside Ecology Centre.

WYSALL Nottinghamshire SK6027
Village off A60, 6 miles (10km) NE of Loughborough
Attractive village on edge of Wolds. Manor house with brick barn. Manor farmhouse with diaper-patterned brickwork. Norman and medieval church.

WYTHAM Oxfordshire SP4708
Village off A34, 3 miles (5km) NW of Oxford
Lying beneath prominent and heavily wooded Wytham Hill. Church rebuilt with materials from Cumnor Place, including medieval windows and churchyard gate.

WYTHENSHAWE Greater Manchester SJ8188
District off M56, immediately S of Gatley
Designed in the 1920s as a full-scale garden suburb, and became known as one of Europe's largest council estates. Wythenshawe Hall dates back to the Tudor period.

WYTON Cambridgeshire TL2772
Village on A1123, 3 miles (5km) E of Huntingdon
Pretty Wyton standing near the River Ouse is a pleasant place for picnics. There is a boat slipway to allow water-craft on to Ouse and lakes.

WYVERSTONE Suffolk TM0467
Village off B1113, 6 miles (10km) N of Stowmarket
A small, scattered farming community which dates from Saxon times. It has a church surrounded by mature trees, and wide open, hedgeless fields.

Y

Y GAER Powys SO0029
Roman site off minor road, 3 miles (5km) W of Brecon
Remains of Roman fort established by AD80, rebuilt in middle of 2nd century. West and south gateways, corner turret, northern fort wall.

Y PIGWN Powys SN8231
Roman site off A40, 4 miles (6km) NW of Trecastle
Earthworks possibly of 1st century constructed by Romans alongside ancient road across lonely moorland. Usk Reservoir to the south.

YAFFORD Isle of Wight SZ4481
Hamlet off B3399, 1 mile (2km) SW of Shorwell
Small settlement with old cottages scattered about. Yafford Mill is a restored 18th-century watermill, still working.

YALDING Kent TQ6950
Village on B2010, 5 miles (8km) SW of Maidstone
Unspoilt village on the River Beult in a traditional hop-growing area near the Teise and Medway confluences. The main street curves gently uphill with grass verges,

flanked by attractive cobbled walks fronted by timber and thatched buildings. There is a superb view over the Weald from the top of the 13th-century church tower. Yalding Leas is common meadowland where the three rivers meet near the seven-arched medieval town bridge.

YANWATH Cumbria NY5127
Hamlet on B5320, 2 miles (3km) S of Penrith
Small village on the River Eamont. Yanwath Hall (not open) is a well-preserved 14th-century manor house, now a farm.

YAPTON West Sussex SU9703
Village on B2233, 3 miles (5km) W of Littlehampton
Set amid wide cornfields on the coastal plain, this village has flint cottages, 19th- and 20th-century houses, a rustic 12th-century church and an attractive garden, Berri Court, open to the public.

YARCOMBE Devon ST2408
Village off A30, 5 miles (8km) W of Chard
On the slopes above the River Yarty Valley is the 15th-century church, with the old church house (now an inn) abutting the churchyard.

YARDLEY West Midlands SP1285
District in E Birmingham
This former village, heavily developed between the wars, received an early and much-acclaimed new shopping precinct in 1960s. But it retains older buildings around its fine medieval church, which has interesting monuments. Blakesley Hall (limited opening) is a large 16th-century house with period furnishings, 17th-century pottery and exhibition of timber-framing techniques.

YARDLEY GOBION Northamptonshire SP7644
Village on A508, 3 miles (5km) NW of Stony Stratford
Limestone village between Roman Watling Street (A5) and River Tove forming Buckinghamshire border, alongside Grand Union Canal. Victorian church.

YARDLEY HASTINGS Northamptonshire SP8656
Village on A428, 4 miles (6km) NW of Olney
Norman and later church. Yardley Chase – favourite walks of poet Cowper from his home in nearby Olney.

YARE, RIVER Norfolk
River, flows into North Sea at Great Yarmouth
Flowing through the heart of the lovely Norfolk Broads, the River Yare first curves south around Norwich. Flows into Breydon Water.

YARM Cleveland NZ4112
Town on A67, 4 miles (6km) S of Stockton-on-Tees
Old market town standing within a horseshoe-shaped loop of the River Tees. Elegant Georgian merchants' houses indicate its earlier prosperity. A Dominican friary first stood on the site of the Friarage which was built in 1770. The 43-arched viaduct which crosses the Tees is one of the biggest in England.

YARMOUTH Isle of Wight SZ3589
Town on A3054, 9 miles (14km) W of Newport
An important medieval town which declined to become a village from 1800. It now consists of a couple of streets and a square of old houses in a mixture of brick, stone and timber-framing. The church is 17th century onwards, with a peculiar late 17th-century effigy. Yarmouth Castle (English Heritage), built by Henry VII in the 1540s, is dense and atmospheric inside. Passenger and car ferries run to Lymington. Fort Victoria Country Park includes a planetarium, a marine aquarium and a maritime heritage exhibition.

YARMOUTH Norfolk TG5207
see Great Yarmouth

YARNSCOMBE Devon SS5623
Village off B3227, 5 miles (8km) NE of Great Torrington
Set high, with green hills all around. Norman and 15th-century church.

YARNTON Oxfordshire SP4712
Village off A44, 4 miles (6km) NW of Oxford
Village distinguished by splendid church with rich interior and vast collection of stained glass. Pixey and Yarnton Meads, traditional grassland, is a nature reserve.

YARPOLE Hereford and Worcester SO4764
Village off B4361, 4 miles (6km) NW of Leominster
Pretty village lying below Croft Castle (see), with attractive timber-framed cottages. Church has big detached tower with massive internal supporting timbers.

YARROW WATER Borders
River
River flowing through green hills and connecting St Mary's Loch to Ettrick Water. Yarrow Kirk replaced two earlier structures. Area strong in literary connections.

YARWELL Northamptonshire TL0697
Village off B671, 1 mile (2km) S of Wansford
Attractive village with 17th-century houses. Caravan and camping site at Yarwell Mill beside River Nene.

YATE Avon ST7182
Suburb on A432, on W outskirts of Chipping Sodbury
This small old village with a handsome 15th-century church tower has grown enormously since the 1960s.

YATELEY Hampshire SU8160
Small town on B3272, 3 miles (5km) W of Camberley
The old village is around the green, and the church has a fine wooden porch of 1500. There are vast amounts of 1950s onwards development. Yateley Common is a huge nature reserve of heathland with marsh and ponds. Blackbushe Airport to the south.

YATTENDON Berkshire SU5574
Village off B4009, 5 miles (8km) W of Pangbourne
Mixed Victorian estate buildings and Georgian, all brick. Robert Bridges, poet laureate, lived here for many years.

YATTON Avon ST4365
Village on B3133, 4 miles (6km) S of Clevedon
On the edge of the Somerset Levels, the main street of Yatton is lined with stone houses and cottages. The handsome church has a fine 14th-century tower (the spire was added in the 15th century) and a magnificent late 15th-century elaborate porch. The Newton Chapel has effigies of Sir John and Lady Newton, who paid for the late 15th-century rebuilding of the church.

YATTON KEYNELL Wiltshire ST8676
Village on B4039, 4 miles (6km) NW of Chippenham
Stone village on the edge of the Cotswolds, with a fine manor house of 1659 (not open). Pretty hamlets at West Yatton and Long Dean.

YAVERLAND Isle of Wight SZ6185
Village on B3395, 1 mile (2km) NE of Sandown
Straggling inland, but larger and more modern on the shore, with the Isle of Wight zoological gardens.

YAXHAM Norfolk TG0010
Village on B1135, 2 miles (3km) S of East Dereham
In this compact little village is the simple Church of St Peter with its round Saxon tower. The village has associations with poet William Cowper.

YAXLEY Cambridgeshire TL1892
Village on B1091, 4 miles (6km) S of Peterborough
Yaxley is a large village surrounded by interesting features. To the east are Whittlesey Mere, Farcet Fen and the Nene Washes; to the south is Holme Fen (the lowest point in Britain); to the north lies the historic city of Peterborough; and to the west is Norman Cross, site of a POW camp in the 18th and 19th centuries.

YAXLEY Suffolk TM1274
Village on A140, 2 miles (3km) W of Eye
Yaxley was recorded in 1066. One of its famous inhabitants was Sir Frederick Ashton, the choreographer (died 1988).

YEADON West Yorkshire SE2041
Town off A65, 7 miles (11km) NW of Leeds
The town lies on a hillside and is predominantly residential with stone houses dating from the early 19th century to the present day. Leeds Bradford International Airport is near by.

YEALAND, CONYERS AND REDMAYNE Lancashire SD5074/5076
Villages off A6, 2/3 miles (3/5km) N of Carnforth
Two pretty villages on the lower slopes of Warton Crag. Friends' Meeting House in Yealand Conyers dates from 1692. Leighton Hall is an impressive stately home with 19th-century white limestone façade, in a broad expanse of open parkland. It is open to the public and owned by the Gillow-Reynolds family.

YEALMPTON Devon SX5751
Village on A379, 7 miles (11km) E of Plymouth
A village set on the River Yealm, with an early 19th-century bridge with tollhouse, just above the estuary. Church, school and school house are early works (around 1850) of the architect Butterfield. Old Mother Hubbard's Cottage in the main street is a reminder that the nursery rhyme was written at Kitley in 1804. Kitley Caves and Country Park, National Shire Horse Centre.

YEARBY Cleveland NZ6020
Village on B1269, 3 miles (4km) S of Redcar
An increasingly residential settlement consisting of two rows of houses with long front gardens. It became a conservation area in 1974.

YEARSLEY North Yorkshire SE5874
Hamlet off B1363, 5 miles (8km) NE of Easingwold
An estate village until 1944, its sandstone cottages with slate or pantiled roofs huddling down each side of the main street.

YEDINGHAM North Yorkshire SE8979
Village on B1258, 8 miles (13km) NE of Malton
This quiet old village had its own priory, founded in 1163, the site of which can still be seen.

YELL Shetland
Island, lies between mainland and Unst
Large island to north of mainland with somewhat monotonous landscape redeemed by fine natural harbours, or 'voes'. Mid Yell is the main settlement, with its own fishing fleet. More fishing activity centres around Cullivoe to the north. The oldest building is Haa of Brough to the south, a trading post built in 1672 and now a museum. RSPB reserve at Lumbister.

YELLING Cambridgeshire TL2562
Village off B1040, 6 miles (10km) S of Huntingdon
A linear village sprawled along a peaceful back road, Yelling stands in pleasant countryside near a tributary of the River Great Ouse.

YELVERTON Devon SX5267
Small town on B3212, 5 miles (8km) SE of Tavistock
On the edge of Dartmoor, but rather suburban, being a dormitory to Plymouth. The 1591 Plymouth Leat, made to carry water to Plymouth, runs to the south of the church, and the 1793 Devonport Leat to the north.

YEO, RIVER Devon
River, flows from N Dartmoor
The Yeo rises just north of Dartmoor, runs east to Crediton, and joins the Exe just above Exeter.

YEO, RIVER Dorset
River
The Yeo rises above Sherborne, runs past Yeovil, and then runs westwards to join the River Parrett near Langport.

YEOLMBRIDGE Cornwall SX3187
Village on B3254, 2 miles (3km) N of Launceston
A little village on the River Ottery with a fine stone bridge, the oldest in Cornwall, 14th century.

YEOVIL Somerset ST5515
Town on A30, 5 miles (8km) W of Sherborne
Largish town, much cut about by modern roads, and with many of the older buildings recently demolished. Named after the River Yeo (also called River Ivel), it has been a town since early medieval times. Yeovil has some older buildings in the centre, along with modern shopping developments and the Museum of South Somerset. The large Church of St John is late 14th century, with a rather solid-looking tower. The town produced cloth until the late 18th century; the major industry now is helicopters.

YEOVILTON Somerset ST5422
Village off B3151, 2 miles (3km) E of Ilchester
Medieval church and some old cottages, but best known for the large Fleet Air Arm Museum.

YES TOR Devon SX5890
Hill on Dartmoor, 3 miles (5km) S of Okehampton
Second highest point on Dartmoor – 2,030ft (618m) – with wonderful views. Not always accessible as in a military area. Wild moorland.

YETMINSTER Dorset ST5910
Village off A352, 5 miles (8km) SW of Sherborne
Old-fashioned large village, full of stone farmhouses and cottages, many of them 17th century. Pretty stone church, mostly of about 1450.

YETTS O' MUCKHART Central NO0001
Village on A91, 4 miles (6km) NE of Dollar
Well-kept village on River Devon at foot of Ochil Hills. Stands with neighbouring Pool of Muckhart near Cauldron Linn beauty spot with pretty walks.

YIELDEN (OR YELDEN) Bedfordshire TL0167
Village off A6, 4 miles (6km) E of Rushden
On the River Til, guarded by the substantial earthworks of a vanished castle. Bunyan preached in the handsome church.

YOCKENTHWAITE North Yorkshire SD9079
Hamlet off B6160, 4 miles (6km) NW of Buckden
Once a prosperous place with a school and inn, the hamlet now consists of a few stone farms and a packhorse bridge. Bronze Age stone circle near by.

YOCKLETON Shropshire SJ3910
Vilage on B4386, 6 miles (10km) W of Shrewsbury
Village on Roman road west of Shrewsbury. Fanciful Gothic church in different coloured stone, with tower and spire with dormer windows.

YORK North Yorkshire SE6051
City off A64, 212 miles (341km) N of London
Few cities look as completely medieval as York. It began life as a fortress, built in AD71 by the Roman 9th Legion and grew into an important city known as *Eboracum*.

The Vikings gave York its name, derived from Jorvik, during their brief but flourishing reign. Jorvik Viking Centre is built on the site of Viking remains discovered by archaeologists beneath Coppergate, and provides a vivid description of Viking Age York.

Norman rule lasted longer and the Normans made the city a vital centre of government, commerce and religion for the north, preparing the city well for its important role in the reigns of the Plantaganet kings. In 1485, when this era ended and the Tudor age began, York was already at its zenith.

The pride of York is its magnificent minster which towers over the whole city. It contains England's greatest concentration of medieval stained glass, the two most famous windows being the 'Five Sisters' in the north transept, and the great east window which covers 2,000 square feet (186sq m), thought to be the largest area of medieval coloured glass in the world. The minster took 250 years to build and was completed and consecrated in 1472.

Treasurer's House was the residence for Treasurers of the Minster until 1547. It now belongs to the National Trust and has a fine collection of period furnishings. The medieval centre of the city is reached through the four great Bars in the city walls, Micklegate, Bootham, Monk and Walmgate Bars. A walk around the walls, built during the reign of Henry II (1216–72) is a good introduction to the city.

In the Middle Ages York was an important wool-trading centre and fine cloth was woven here. The prosperity that this trade brought allowed other trades and craftspeople to thrive in the city, such as goldsmiths, silversmiths, saddlers, barbers, butchers and shoe-makers. They lived and worked in Stonegate, Goodramgate and the Shambles, the old butchers' quarter, all still very medieval in appearance. Today these areas have an excellent range of shops, including interesting antique and jewellery specialists.

York's splendid Georgian Mansion House was built between 1725 and 1730, and is the only house in England today which is used solely as the official private residence for a Lord Mayor during his term of office.

The Industrial Revolution for the most part passed York by but the city did become a great railway centre when the first railway line to York opened in 1839. The city has a splendid station and the station hotel, The Royal York, has also been restored to its original grandeur. The National Railway Museum is located in York.

Besides the railways, the other major employer in York has for many years been the confectionery trade. Rowntree's, Terry's and Craven's all began here and the industry continues to thrive on the outskirts of the city centre.

YORK TOWN Surrey SU8660
District in W Camberley
The earliest part of Camberley, a grid of streets built on the heathy uplands after 1809, and named after Frederick, the famous Duke of York.

YORKSHIRE DALES NATIONAL PARK North Yorkshire
The Yorkshire Dales National Park is an area of outstanding scenery covering an area of approximately 691 square miles (1,769sq km). It lies astride the Pennines in the north of England and the area is rich in contrast, with wild rugged moorlands, lush green dales with their distinctive patchwork of drystone walls, limestone caverns and unspoilt rural villages.

There are 20 main dales, each having its own character. To the south of the area lies a highly populated industrial area while to the north thinly settled uplands stretch to the Tees and beyond.

The area has been inhabited for over 10,000 years and early settlers have left their mark on the landscape in the form of ancient settlement sites, disused mineral workings and barns typical of the Dales. Today, some 20,000 people live in the scattered farms, villages and small market towns of the park.

The home knitting industry thrived in some Dales villages, and the area is famous for Wensleydale cheese.

The Dales are often referred to as 'James Herriot country' as this was the setting for the vet books by James Herriot, and the location for the ensuing television series All Creatures Great and Small.

YORKSHIRE WOLDS Humberside
Hill range extending from Flamborough Head to the Humber estuary
A landscape of rolling hills and dales lying mainly between 400ft (122m) and 600ft (183m), with their highest point at Garrowby Top. Arable farmland dominates, and there are some scattered villages and some grand houses. The Wolds Way is a long-distance footpath running from Hessle on the Humber estuary to Scarborough in Yorkshire.

YOULGREAVE Derbyshire SK2164
Village off B5056, 3 miles (5km) S of Bakewell
Straggling Peak District village with Georgian houses, a 17th-century old hall and Old Hall Farm. Co-operative Society shop, now a youth hostel, dates from 1887. Large Norman church with 15th-century tower. Well-dressing in June.

YOXALL Staffordshire SK1418
Village on A515, 6 miles (10km) N of Lichfield
Good Norman and medieval church and some distinguished houses justify conservation area in centre of this village on fringe of Needwood Forest.

YOXFORD Suffolk TM3968
Village on A1120, 4 miles (6km) N of Saxmundham
Standing in the peaceful valley of the River Yox, Yoxford is a former 18th-century coaching town on the London to Yarmouth road.

YSBYTY CYNFYN Dyfed SN7579
Site on A4120, 2 miles (3km) NE of Devil's Bridge
In remote country between Devil's Bridge and Ponterwyd. Church built in what was a megalithic stone circle (no longer complete). Parson's Bridge beauty spot near by.

Thatched cottages in Zeal Monachorum.

YSBYTY IFAN Gwynedd SH8448

Village on B4407, 3 miles (5km) SW of Pentrefoelas

Farming village in remote corner of Snowdonia National Park by infant River Conwy. Llyn Conwy, river's headwaters, on moors to the southwest.

YSTALYFERA West Glamorgan SN7608

Small town on A4067, 4 miles (6km) NE of Pontardawe

Former mining town in the upper part of Tawe Valley, overlooked by forested slopes and Y Darren Widdon, 'Rock of Sighs'.

YSTRAD MEURIG Dyfed SN7067

Hamlet on B4340, 2 miles (3km) W of Pontrhydfendigaid

Hamlet in lonely upland setting of upper Teifi Valley. Only a few mounds remain of 12th-century castle.

YSTRADFELLTE Powys SN9213

Hamlet off A4059, 5 miles (8km) NW of Hirwaun

Hamlet in limestone area of southern Brecon Beacons National Park, famous for spectacular collection of waterfalls, caves, potholes, gorges. Porth yr Ogof is possibly biggest cave entrance in Wales, where River Mellte disappears underground before reappearing to form series of waterfalls: Sgwd Clun-gwyn, Sgwd Isaf Clun-gwyn, Sgwd y Pannwr. Path along valley also links with Sgwd yr Eira (which you can walk behind) on River Hepste.

YSTRADGYNLAIS Powys SN7810

Small town off A4067, 2 miles (3km) NE of Ystalyfera

Former mining community in the upper part of the Tawe Valley on northern edge of coalfield. Close to boundary of Brecon Beacons National Park.

YTHAN, RIVER Grampian

River

River flowing southeast from Strathbogie through Methlick and Ellon to reach North Sea through noted estuary, with nature reserve at Forvie Ness.

Z

ZEAL MONACHORUM Devon SS7204

Village off B3220, 8 miles (13km) NW of Crediton

Dense village with many thatched cottages and a 15th-century church.

ZEALS Wiltshire ST7831

Village off A303, 2 miles (4km) W of Mere

Large and recently bypassed village with mostly modern buildings. Right on the boundary of Somerset and Dorset.

ZELAH Cornwall SW8151

Village on A30, 5 miles (8km) N of Truro

A long, thin village with two Nonconformist chapels, recently bypassed.

ZENNOR Cornwall SW4538

Village on B3306, 4 miles (6km) W of St Ives

Wild and remote, the little village is set between open moors and rocky cliffs. Its Norman and later medieval church has a mermaid portrait on a bench-end – she is said to have lured a local to his doom. DH Lawrence and his German wife were driven away from here in World War I, assumed to be spies. Zennor Head has rocky cliffs and Zennor Quoit is one of the largest neolithic chamber tombs. Zennor Wayside museum.

Mermaid carving in the church at Zennor.

VEHICLE INDEX MARKS

BRITAIN

Since 1983 vehicle registration numbers in Britain (excluding Northern Ireland, see below) have been arranged to show a letter denoting the year of issue; a serial three-figure number; a serial letter and, finally, two letters indicating the office which first registers the vehicle. The following list gives the index marks of Local Vehicle Licensing Offices in England, Scotland and Wales.

AA	Bournemouth
AB	Worcester
AC	Coventry
AD	Gloucester
AE	Bristol
AF	Truro
AG	Hull
AH	Norwich
AJ	Middlesbrough
AK	Sheffield
AL	Nottingham
AM	Swindon
AN	Reading
AO	Carlisle
AP	Brighton
AR	Chelmsford
AS	Inverness
AT	Hull
AU	Nottingham
AV	Peterborough
AW	Shrewsbury
AX	Cardiff
AY	Leicester
BA	Manchester
BB	Newcastle upon Tyne
BC	Leicester
BD	Northampton
BE	Lincoln
BF	Stoke-on-Trent
BG	Liverpool
BH	Luton
BJ	Ipswich
BK	Portsmouth
BL	Reading
BM	Luton
BN	Manchester
BO	Cardiff
BP	Portsmouth
BR	Newcastle upon Tyne
BS	Inverness
BT	Leeds
BU	Manchester
BV	Preston
BW	Oxford
BX	Haverfordwest
BY	London NW
CA	Chester
CB	Manchester
CC	Bangor
CD	Brighton
CE	Peterborough
CF	Reading
CG	Bournemouth
CH	Nottingham
CJ	Gloucester
CK	Preston
CL	Norwich
CM	Liverpool
CN	Newcastle upon Tyne
CO	Exeter
CP	Huddersfield
CR	Portsmouth
CS	Glasgow
CT	Lincoln
CU	Newcastle upon Tyne
CV	Truro
CW	Preston
CX	Huddersfield
CY	Swansea
DA	Birmingham
DB	Manchester
DC	Middlesbrough
DD	Gloucester
DE	Haverfordwest
DF	Gloucester
DG	Gloucester
DH	Dudley
DJ	Liverpool
DK	Manchester
DL	Portsmouth
DM	Chester
DN	Leeds
DO	Lincoln
DP	Reading
DR	Exeter
DS	Glasgow
DT	Sheffield
DU	Coventry
DV	Exeter
DW	Cardiff
DX	Ipswich
DY	Brighton
EA	Dudley
EB	Peterborough
EC	Preston
ED	Liverpool
EE	Lincoln
EF	Middlesbrough
EG	Peterborough
EH	Stoke-on-Trent
EJ	Haverfordwest
EK	Liverpool
EL	Bournemouth
EM	Liverpool
EN	Manchester
EO	Preston
EP	Swansea
ER	Peterborough
ES	Dundee
ET	Sheffield
EU	Bristol
EV	Chelmsford
EW	Peterborough
EX	Norwich
EY	Bangor
FA	Stoke-on-Trent
FB	Bristol
FC	Oxford
FD	Dudley
FE	Lincoln
FF	Bangor
FG	Brighton
FH	Gloucester
FJ	Exeter
FK	Dudley
FL	Peterborough
FM	Chester
FN	Maidstone
FO	Gloucester
FP	Leicester
FR	Preston
FS	Edinburgh
FT	Newcastle upon Tyne
FU	Lincoln
FV	Preston
FW	Lincoln
FX	Bournemouth
FY	Liverpool
GA	Glasgow
GB	Glasgow
GC	London SW
GD	Glasgow
GE	Glasgow
GF	London SW
GG	Glasgow
GH	London SW
GJ	London SW
GK	London SW
GL	Truro
GM	Reading
GN	London SW
GO	London SW
GP	London SW
GR	Newcastle upon Tyne
GS	Luton
GT	London SW
GU	London SE
GV	Ipswich
GW	London SE
GX	London SE
GY	London SE
HA	Dudley
HB	Cardiff
HC	Brighton
HD	Huddersfield
HE	Sheffield
HF	Liverpool
HG	Preston
HH	Carlisle
HJ	Chelmsford
HK	Chelmsford
HL	Sheffield
HM	London (Central)
HN	Middlesbrough
HO	Bournemouth
HP	Coventry
HR	Swindon
HS	Glasgow
HT	Bristol
HU	Bristol
HV	London (Central)
HW	Bristol
HX	London (Central)
HY	Bristol
JA	Manchester
JB	Reading
JC	Bangor
JD	London (Central)
JE	Peterborough
JF	Leicester
JG	Maidstone
JH	Reading
JJ	Maidstone
JK	Brighton
JL	Lincoln
JM	Reading
JN	Chelmsford
JO	Oxford
JP	Liverpool
JR	Newcastle upon Tyne
JS	Inverness
JT	Bournemouth
JU	Leicester
JV	Lincoln
JW	Birmingham
JX	Huddersfield
JY	Exeter
KA	Liverpool
KB	Liverpool
KC	Liverpool
KD	Liverpool
KE	Maidstone
KF	Liverpool
KG	Cardiff
KH	Hull
KJ	Maidstone
KK	Maidstone
KL	Maidstone
KM	Maidstone
KN	Maidstone
KO	Maidstone
KP	Maidstone
KR	Maidstone
KS	Edinburgh
KT	Maidstone
KU	Sheffield
KV	Coventry
KW	Sheffield
KX	Luton
KY	Sheffield
LA	London NW
LB	London NW
LC	London NW
LD	London NW
LE	London NW
LF	London NW
LG	Chester
LH	London NW
LJ	Bournemouth
LK	London NW
LL	London NW
LM	London NW
LN	London NW
LO	London NW
LP	London NW
LR	London NW
LS	Edinburgh
LT	London NW
LU	London NW
LV	Liverpool
LW	London NW
LX	London NW
LY	London NW
MA	Chester
MB	Chester

MC	London NE
MD	London NE
ME	London NE
MF	London NE
MG	London NE
MH	London NE
MJ	Luton
MK	London NE
ML	London NE
MM	London NE
MO	Reading
MP	London NE
MR	Swindon
MS	Edinburgh
MT	London NE
MU	London NE
MV	London SE
MW	Swindon
MX	London SE
MY	London SE
NA	Manchester
NB	Manchester
NC	Manchester
ND	Manchester
NE	Manchester
NF	Manchester
NG	Norwich
NH	Northampton
NJ	Brighton
NK	Luton
NL	Newcastle upon Tyne
NM	Luton
NN	Nottingham
NO	Chelmsford
NP	Worcester
NR	Leicester
NS	Glasgow
NT	Shrewsbury
NU	Nottingham
NV	Northampton
NW	Leeds
NX	Dudley
NY	Cardiff
OA	Birmingham
OB	Birmingham
OC	Birmingham
OD	Exeter
OE	Birmingham
OF	Birmingham
OG	Birmingham
OH	Birmingham
OJ	Birmingham
OK	Birmingham
OL	Birmingham
OM	Birmingham
ON	Birmingham
OO	Chelmsford
OP	Birmingham
OR	Portsmouth
OS	Glasgow
OT	Portsmouth
OU	Bristol
OV	Birmingham
OW	Portsmouth
OX	Birmingham
OY	London NW
PA	Guildford
PB	Guildford
PC	Guildford
PD	Guildford
PE	Guildford
PF	Guildford
PG	Guildford
PH	Guildford
PJ	Guildford
PK	Guildford
PL	Guildford
PM	Guildford
PN	Brighton
PO	Portsmouth
PP	Luton
PR	Bournemouth
PS	Aberdeen
PT	Newcastle upon Tyne
PU	Chelmsford
PV	Ipswich
PW	Norwich
PX	Portsmouth
PY	Middlesbrough
RA	Nottingham
RB	Nottingham
RC	Nottingham
RD	Reading
RE	Stoke-on-Trent
RF	Stoke-on-Trent
RG	Newcastle upon Tyne
RH	Hull
RJ	Manchester
RK	London NW
RL	Truro
RM	Carlisle
RN	Preston
RO	Luton
RP	Northampton
RR	Nottingham
RS	Aberdeen
RT	Ipswich
RU	Bournemouth
RV	Portsmouth
RW	Coventry
RX	Reading
RY	Leicester
SA	Aberdeen
SB	Glasgow
SC	Edinburgh
SCY	Truro (Isles of Scilly)
SD	Glasgow
SE	Aberdeen
SF	Edinburgh
SG	Edinburgh
SH	Edinburgh
SJ	Glasgow
SK	Inverness
SL	Dundee
SM	Glasgow
SN	Dundee
SO	Aberdeen
SP	Dundee
SR	Dundee
SS	Aberdeen
ST	Inverness
SU	Glasgow
SW	Glasgow
SX	Edinburgh
TA	Exeter
TB	Liverpool
TC	Bristol
TD	Manchester
TE	Manchester
TF	Reading
TG	Cardiff
TH	Swansea
TJ	Liverpool
TK	Exeter
TL	Lincoln
TM	Luton
TN	Newcastle upon Tyne
TO	Nottingham
TP	Portsmouth
TR	Portsmouth
TS	Dundee
TT	Exeter
TU	Chester
TV	Nottingham
TW	Chelmsford
TX	Cardiff
TY	Newcastle upon Tyne
UA	Leeds
UB	Leeds
UC	London (Central)
UD	Oxford
UE	Dudley
UF	Brighton
UG	Leeds
UH	Cardiff
UJ	Shrewsbury
UK	Birmingham
UL	London (Central)
UM	Leeds
UN	Exeter
UO	Exeter
UP	Newcastle upon Tyne
UR	Luton
US	Glasgow
UT	Leicester
UU	London (Central)
UV	London (Central)
UW	London (Central)
UX	Shrewsbury
UY	Worcester
VA	Peterborough
VB	Maidstone
VC	Coventry
VE	Peterborough
VF	Norwich
VG	Norwich
VH	Huddersfield
VJ	Gloucester
VK	Newcastle upon Tyne
VL	Lincoln
VM	Manchester
VN	Middlesbrough
VO	Nottingham
VP	Birmingham
VR	Manchester
VS	Luton
VT	Stoke-on-Trent
VU	Manchester
VV	Northampton
VW	Chelmsford
VX	Chelmsford
VY	Leeds
WA	Sheffield
WB	Sheffield
WC	Chelmsford
WD	Dudley
WE	Sheffield
WF	Sheffield
WG	Sheffield
WH	Manchester
WJ	Sheffield
WK	Coventry
WL	Oxford
WM	Liverpool
WN	Swansea
WO	Cardiff
WP	Worcester
WR	Leeds
WS	Bristol
WT	Leeds
WU	Leeds
WV	Brighton
WW	Leeds
WX	Leeds
WY	Leeds
YA	Taunton
YB	Taunton
YC	Taunton
YD	Taunton
YE	London (Central)
YF	London (Central)
YG	Leeds
YH	London (Central)
YJ	Brighton
YK	London (Central)
YL	London (Central)
YM	London (Central)
YN	London (Central)
YO	London (Central)
YP	London (Central)
YR	London (Central)
YS	Glasgow
YT	London (Central)
YU	London (Central)
YV	London (Central)
YW	London (Central)
YX	London (Central)
YY	London (Central)

NORTHERN IRELAND AND EIRE

Vehicle index marks in Northern Ireland have been made up of two or three letters and four figures since 1958. The Republic of Ireland (Eire) has a system similar to that of the UK.

Z	Dublin
ZA	Dublin
ZB	Cork
ZC	Dublin
ZD	Dublin
ZE	Dublin
ZF	Cork
ZG	Dublin
ZH	Dublin
ZI	Dublin
ZJ	Dublin
ZK	Cork
ZL	Dublin
ZM	Galway
ZN	Meath
ZO	Dublin
ZP	Donegal
ZR	Wexford
ZS	Dublin
ZT	Cork
ZU	Dublin
ZV	Dublin
ZW	Kildare
ZX	Kerry
ZY	Louth
AZ	Belfast
BZ	Down

CZ Belfast
DZ Antrim
EZ Belfast
FZ Belfast
GZ Belfast
HZ Tyrone
JZ Down
KZ Antrim
LZ Armagh
MZ Belfast
NZ Londonderry
OZ Belfast
PZ Belfast
RZ Antrim
SZ Down
TZ Belfast
UZ Belfast
VZ Tyrone
WZ Belfast
XZ Armagh
YZ Londonderry
ZZ Dublin *used only for vehicles temporarily imported by visitors, and temporarily registered by a registration body)*
IA Antrim
IB Armagh
IC Carlow
ID Cavan
IE Clare
IF Cork
IH Donegal
IJ Down
IK Dublin
IL Fermanagh
IM Galway
IN Kerry
IO Kildare
IP Kilkenny
IR Offaly
IS Mayo
IT Leitrim
IU Limerick
IV Limerick
IW Londonderry
IX Longford
IY Louth
IZ Mayo
AI Meath
BI Monaghan
CI Laois
DI Roscommon
EI Silgo
FI Tipperary (N Riding)
GI Tipperary (S Riding)
HI Tipperary (S Riding)
JI Tyrone
KI Waterford
LI Westmeath
MI Wexford
NI Wicklow
OI Belfast
PI Cork
RI Dublin
SI Dublin
TI Limerick
UI Londonderry
WI Waterford
XI Belfast
YI Dublin

ISLE OF MAN

From August 1987 index marks consisted of the letters **BMN**, followed by up to three figures and a letter, ending at **BMN 999Y** and continuing with **CMN** and so on.

CHANNEL ISLANDS

States of Alderney: AY followed by up to four figures
States of Guernsey: figures only, 1–56,000
States of Jersey: J followed by up to five figures

INTERNATIONAL DISTINGUISHING SIGNS

Foreign registered vehicles should show an international distinguishing sign indicating the country of registration. Some are unofficial; most are established signs, listed by the United Nations.

A Austria
ADN Yemen People's Democratic Republic
AFG Afghanistan
AL Albania
AND Andorra
AUS Australia
B Belgium
BD Bangladesh
BDS Barbados
BG Bulgaria
BH Belize
BR Brazil
BRN Bahrain
BRU Brunei
BS Bahamas
BUR Burma
C Cuba
CDN Canada
CH Switzerland
CI Ivory Coast
CL Sri Lanka
CO Colombia
CR Costa Rica
CZ Czech Republic
CY Cyprus
D Germany
DK Denmark
DOM Dominican Republic
DY Benin
DZ Algeria
E Spain
EAK Kenya
EAT Tanzania
EAU Uganda
EC Ecuador
ES El Salvador
ET Egypt
ETH Ethiopia
EW Estonia
F France
FJI Fiji
FIN Finland
FL Liechtenstein
FR Faroe Islands
GB Great Britain and Northern Ireland
GBA Alderney (Channel Islands)
GBG Guernsey (Channel Islands)
GBJ Jersey (Channel Islands)
GBM Isle of Man
GBZ Gibraltar
GCA Guatemala
GH Ghana
GR Greece
GUY Guyana
H Hungary
HK Hong Kong
HKJ Jordan
HR Croatia
I Italy
IL Israel
IND India
IR Iran
IRL Ireland
IRQ Iraq
IS Iceland
J Japan
JA Jamaica
K Cambodia
KWT Kuwait
L Luxembourg
LAO Lao People's Democratic Republic
LAR Libya
LB Liberia
LS Lesotho
LT Lithuania
LV Latvia
M Malta
MA Morocco
MAL Malaysia
MC Monaco
MEX Mexico
MS Mauritius
MW Malawi
N Norway
NA Netherlands Antilles
NIC Nicaragua
NL Netherlands
NZ New Zealand
OMAN Oman
P Portugal
PA Panama
PK Pakistan
PE Peru
PL Poland
PNG Papua New Guinea
PY Paraguay
RA Argentina
RB Botswana
RC Taiwan
RCA Central African Republic
RCB Congo
RCH Chile
RH Haiti
RI Indonesia
RIM Mauritania
RL Lebanon
RM Madagascar
RMM Mali
RN Niger
RO Romania
ROK Korea, Republic of
ROU Uruguay
RP Philippines
RSM San Marino
RU Burundi
RUS Russia
RWA Rwanda
S Sweden
SD Swaziland
SGP Singapore
SK Slovakia
SME Suriname
SN Senegal
SWA/ZA Namibia
SY Seychelles
SYR Syria
T Thailand
TG Togo
TN Tunisia
TR Turkey
TT Trinidad and Tobago
USA United States of America
V Vatican City
VN Vietnam, Socialist Republic
WAG Gambia
WAL Sierra Leone
WAN Nigeria
WD Dominica (Windward Islands)
WG Grenada (Windward Islands)
WL St Lucia (Windward Islands)
WS Western Samoa
WV St Vincent (Windward Islands)
YU Yugoslavia
YV Venezuela
Z Zambia
ZA South Africa
ZRE Zaire
ZW Zimbabwe

Picnic sites

The following list gives a selection of inspected picnic sites in England, Wales and Scotland, with national grid references, locations and an indication of the facilities that are available.

England

AVON

Swineford ST691692

Picnic tables on the site of an old iron foundry, approached along a private track off the A431 between the villages of Bitton and Kelston.

Tog Hill ST733728

Spectacular views over the Severn Valley from a 2-acre (1ha) site off the A420, 8 miles (13km) east of Bristol. Car park, toilets and drinking water available.

CAMBRIDGESHIRE

Grafham Water TL141670 and TL162665

Sailing and fishing (by permit only) at two extensive sites overlooking Grafham Water, reached from the B661. Car park, tables, toilets and drinking water available.

CHESHIRE

Teggs Nose SJ950732

Waymarked trails and guided walks are among the attractions at this site off the A537, where there is also an information centre, toposcope, car park, tables, toilets and drinking water.

CUMBRIA

Aira Force NY398205

Views of Ullswater and the Fells, with a waterfall and wooded walks at this National Trust site covering 50 acres (20ha), southwest of Pooley Bridge. Car park, tables and drinking water available.

Bowness SD403985

Set back from Lake Windermere, a mile (2km) from Bowness, this site with tables and toilets is situated in pleasant countryside and has access to the lake.

Crosscanonby Saltpass NY067402

Excavations of saltpans can be seen here along with descriptions and an ancient monument. Car parking and tables are available at the site, which is 3 miles (5km) north of Maryport, on the B5300.

White Moss Common Old Quarry NY348066

An attractively landscaped car park in a former quarry near Grasmere gives access to a common and conservation area. Features include a car park, toilets and drinking water, facilities for the disabled and a tourist map. Fishing can be arranged.

DERBYSHIRE

Alsop en la Dale Station SK156549

Managed by the Peak District National Park, this site with car park and tables is set at a former railway station on the Buxton–Ashourne line, now the Tissington Trail.

Middleton Top SK275551

Access to the High Peak Trail and Middleton Top Engine House from this site with car park, tables, toilets and drinking water, off the B5023 1 mile (2km) northwest of Wirksworth.

DEVON

Stoke Hill SX923952

Panoramic views on the west side of Pennsylvania Road, 2 miles (3km) north of Exeter.

DORSET

Bishops Limekiln SY588859

Fine views towards Chesil Beach and the Isle of Portland, northeast of the B3157 in the centre of Abbotsbury. A lime kiln still exists on the site.

DURHAM

Causey Arch NZ205562

A reconstruction of the Waggonway (an early railway) can be seen near this site with car park, tables and toilets, on the A6076 north of Stanley.

GLOUCESTERSHIRE

Beechenhurst, Forest of Dean SO614119

Open lawns and oak woodland covering 5 acres (2ha) near Coleford on the B4226. Fire hearths, refreshment kiosk, car park, toilets (closed in winter) and drinking water. A forest trail leads from the site.

Coaley Park SO794014

A superb viewpoint near a gliding centre, on the Cotswold Way. Nympsfield long barrow, of about 2800BC, is on the site, which has extensive parking, toilets and a site plan featuring wildlife and archaeology notes and signed woodland walks.

GREATER LONDON

Mad Bess Wood TQ075895

Northwest of Ruislip, on the A4180, this is a pleasant woodland area covering 186 acres (75ha), part of which is a bird sanctuary.

HAMPSHIRE

Abbotstone Down SU585362

Extensive grass clearings in wood and scrub land on the B3046 north of Alresford. Car park, tables and toilets are available; signed footpaths lead to Alresford, Itchen Abbas, Winchester, Micheldever and Preston Candover.

HEREFORD AND WORCESTER

Beacon Hill SO985758

A viewpoint with pedestal-mounted map and telescope on the hilltop reached via Monument Lane, off the B4096 northeast of Bromsgrove. A car park, tables and drinking water are available on the 523-acre (211ha) site.

Goodrich Castle SO576197

A well positioned site in the Wye Valley, overlooking forest and near Goodrich Castle. The site has a car park, tables, toilets, drinking water and signed scenic walks, and is reached from the A40 (signposted from the village centre).

HERTFORDSHIRE

Stanborough Park TL228114

A lakeside setting with car park (fee), tables and toilet off the A6129 east of the junction with the A1 at Welwyn Garden City. For an extra charge visitors can use a heated open-air swimming pool and boating facilities.

HUMBERSIDE

South Skirlaugh TA154375

Set on the Hornsea rail trail, a recreational path along a disused railway, the site has tables and a car park and is reached via the A165, south of South Skirlaugh.

LANCASHIRE

Lane Ends SD457562

Overlooking the estuary and giving access to the coastal path and creek, this site off the A588 west of Conder Green has a car park, tables and toilet, and wildlife information posters.

LEICESTERSHIRE

Rutland Water (Skyes Lane) SK936083

Set near the shore, this site off the A606, 5 miles (8km) east of Empingham, is well equipped, with a tourist information centre, public telephone, playground, refreshments, toilets, tables, drinking water and a car park (fee).

NORFOLK

Lynford Arboretum TL825943

This secluded site sits among varied woodland, 1 mile (2km) east of the A1065, and has tables and forest and wheelchair tracks leading through the arboretum.

NORTHUMBRIA

Housesteads NY790687

Set on Hadrian's Wall, at an ideal starting point for walkers, near the remains of a Roman fort and a museum, 9 miles (14km) east of Greenhead on the B6318. Car parking is available.

NORTH YORKSHIRE

Staxton Brow TA009779

A sloping, tree-planted grassy area with panoramic views, south of Staxton village on the B1249. Car parking, tables and toilet available.

OXFORDSHIRE

Abbey Meadow SU500970

A swimming pool, tennis courts and a pitch and putt course are provided on this 5-acre (2ha) site with toilet off the A415 near Abingdon town centre, alongside the River Thames by the Abbey Gardens.

SHROPSHIRE

Whittington Castle SJ325312

The castle ruins are the main feature of this landscaped area of grass on the banks of the moat. The site covers 20 acres (8ha) at Whittington, and has car parking, table and a playground.

SOMERSET

County Gate Transit SS794486

Views of Exmoor, Doone Valley and the Bristol Channel at a hilltop site in Exmoor National Park. Reached via the A39, 7 miles (11km) west of Porlock, it has car parking (fee Easter–September), tables, toilet and tourist information.

STAFFORDSHIRE

Waterhouses SK086511

Cycle hire is available at this interesting site between the village (off the A523) and the industrial quarries of Cauldon. Cyclists and walkers can cross the main road to the Manifold Valley Track. Car parking, tables, toilet and drinking water available.

SURREY

Virginia Water SU977687

Part of Windsor Great Park, this site with toilet facilities is set on the large lake and surrounded by parkland, on the A30 northeast of Sunningdale.

Wales

CLWYD

Llyn Brenig SH967547

This lakeside area has several sites, with facilities including car parking, tables, toilets, an information centre, shop, café and a viewpoint and archaeological trail. Fly-fishing is permitted. The lake is located 5 miles (8km) north of Cerrigydrudion, off the B4501.

DYFED

The Arch SN765756

A Forestry Commission site near a Georgian folly (hence the name), 2 miles (3km) southeast of Devil's Bridge waterfall. Three forest trails lead from the site, which has a car park, tables and toilet.

Bwlch Nant-yr-Arian SN718813

This award-winning site in a wooded area 10 miles (16km) east of Aberystwyth has a visitor centre, toilet, tables, drinking water, information board and viewpoint overlooking beautiful Cardigan Bay.

Dyfi National Nature Reserve SN609941
Overlooking the Dyfi estuary, this beach site is set among sand dunes at the end of an unclassified road north of the B4353 at Ynyslas. With a conservation shop and tables.

GWENT

Tintern Railway Station ST536005
This seasonal site, on the A466 north of Tintern, is set by a former branch-line railway station in a lovely wooded valley. The station now provides a railway exhibition and information service, on the route of the Wye Valley Walk.

GWYNEDD

Llyn Tegid SH905327
Southwest of Bala at Llangower station, alongside the B4403, this site with car park, tables and toilet gives access to Bala Lake (Llyn Tegid) and is divided by the lakeside narrow-gauge railway.

Oriel Eryri SH580602
Beside Llyn Padarn (Lake Padarn) on the A4086 at Llanberis, in the heart of Snowdonia, this site is next to the National Power for Wales Museum and has a car park, tables and a launching ramp on the lakeside.

MID GLAMORGAN

Garwnant Forest Centre SO003132
A visitor centre, forest walks and a miniature assault course are features of this forestry site on wood high ground, with views of the Llwyn Reservoir. Equipped with a car park, tables and toilet, it sits 5 miles (8km) north of Merthyr Tydfil.

POWYS

Elan Valley SN929644
An attractive level site on the banks of the River Elan near the vast Caban Coch reservoir and dam, a mile (2km) southwest of Elan Village. Facilities include a café, shop, visitor centre, tables and toilet.

Scotland

BORDERS

Mayfield NT730337
A grass and mature tree-studded area alongside the River Tweed near Abbotsford Grove and Kelso Abbey. Facilities include car parking, tables, drinking water and fishing.

Whiteadder Reservoir NT666633
An extensive grassy site amid the rolling Lammermuir Hills beside the River Whiteadder, 10 miles (16km) east of Gifford. Car park.

CENTRAL

Queens View NS508808
A viewpoint on the edge of moorland and walking country, on the A809 southeast of Drymen. Car park, tables.

Carron Valley Forest NS721838
Located next to a forest, this level, grassy site is set by the River Carron. There is a children's play area, tables, toilets and car parking, and there are a number of signed walks. The site is 1.5 miles (3km) from Carron Bridge.

DUMFRIES AND GALLOWAY

Bruces Stone NX555766
An attractive secluded area on the shores of Clatteringshaws Loch, among thick pine woods between the Forestry Commission's Galloway Deer Park and the National Trust Monument, Bruces Stone. Car park, drinking water, museum. The site is 5 miles (8km) west of New Galloway, off the A712.

Mabie NX950709
A half-mile (1km) woodland drive from the A710, 4 miles (7km) south of Dumfries, leads to this attractive site surrounded by hills and thick forest. There are tables and toilets available, and forest walks.

GRAMPIAN

Glen Muick NO309852
A visitor centre, telescope and information boards are available at this red deer reserve 8 miles (13km) southwest of Ballater. Car park, tables, toilet.

Newburgh NK006284
North of Newburgh itself, by the Ythan estuary, this small site offers views of the water and of a bird sanctuary. Car park, tables.

HIGHLANDS

Daviot Wood NH710414
This attractive, well maintained site 3 miles (5km) southeast of Inverness is set in bays cut in to the Scots pine woods and forms part of the Daviot Wood tourist information centre. Facilities include a car park, tables, toilet, drinking water and a viewpoint.

Kilt Road NG509655
A remote, grassy site south of Staffin, with a viewpoint over the cliff edge across the Sound of Raasay and an outlook over Loch Mealt Falls and Kilt Rock. Car park, tables.

STRATHCLYDE

Arran, Isle of North Sannox NS015466
Overlooking the Firth of Clyde, this site on the A841 has extensive views of Bute and Cumbrae and the mainland coastline, and is backed by mature trees and Goat Fell. A footpath leads to the beach. Tables, toilet and drinking water are available.

Glenfinart Beach NS189886
North of Ardentinny, off an unclassified road, this site on a sand and shingle beach offers views down to Loch Long, and there are walks to Carrick Castle. Car park, tables and toilet are available.

National Parks and National Scenic Areas

The 11 National Parks of England and Wales represent a remarkably varied range of landscapes, covering 10 per cent of the countries' land surface. Established in the late 1940s, British National Parks are specially protected areas designated by Parliament for their outstanding beauty. National Park authorities control development in their areas, protect the environment and wildlife and maintain facilities for visitors.

Scotland has no National Parks, and consequently has fewer visitor services and signed footpaths. There are, however, 40 National Scenic Areas, selected by the 1978 Countryside Commission for Scotland as protected regions of 'national scenic significance'.

England

The Broads

Over 124 miles (200km) of navigable inland waterways are the main feature of this area of East Anglian wetlands. The Norfolk and Suffolk Broads, created when sea levels rose and flooded medieval peat cuttings, provide boating and fishing country and a home for water-birds. Windmills, river ports and wide, flat landscapes characterise the area.
Information: The Broads Authority, Thomas Harvey House, 18 Colegate, Norwich.

Dartmoor

In contrast to the lush hills of the surrounding Devon countryside, Dartmoor is a wild, exposed area of moorland dotted with 'tors' or rocky outcrops. Evidence of Bronze and Iron Age occupation can be found in the remains of settlements, stone circles and cairns, and the part-wild Dartmoor ponies roam on the lower land and along the roadsides.
Information: Dartmoor National Park, Parke, Haytor Road, Bovey Tracey, Devon.

Exmoor

The smallest national park lies across the Somerset–Devon border and embraces rolling, heather-covered moors, wooded valleys and dramatic coastal cliffs. Wild red deer live on the moor, and Exmoor ponies graze on open land.
Information: Exmoor National Park, Exmoor House, Dulverton, Somerset.

Lake District

England's highest peak, Scafell Pike, soars to 3,209 feet (978m) above this craggy Cumbrian landscape of ancient mountains and wide lakes. Wordsworth sang the area's praises, triggering a huge influx of sightseers. Lake Windermere, England's largest lake, 11 miles (17km) long, is particularly popular, and walkers have access to many of the Lake District mountains.
Information: Visitor Services, Lake District National Park Authority, Murley Moss, Oxenholme Road, Kendal, Cumbria.

North York Moors

High, open moorland forms the heart of this park, dropping to deep valleys, or dales, and extending in the east to spectacular cliffs facing the North Sea. Fine monastic ruins can be seen at Rievaulx and Mount Grace Priory.
Information: North York Moors National Park, The Old Vicarage, Bondgate, Helmsley, York.

Northumberland

Gentle, flat-topped sandstone hills define this remote park, edging the border between Scotland and England. To its south is the 75 mile (120km) Hadrian's Wall, built by Romans in AD122 to repel the Picts.
Information: Northumberland National Park, Eastburn, South Park, Hexham, Northumberland.

Peak District

The Peak District is geologically split into the northern sandstone and millstone grit 'Dark Peak' of high, wild moors and rugged outcrops; and the southern limestone 'White Peak', with its farmland and fertile valleys. The 250 mile (402km) Pennine Way starts at Edale.
Information: Peak National Park, Aldern House, Baslow Road, Bakewell, Derbyshire.

Yorkshire Dales

Rich farmland, high moorland and plunging valleys give this limestone area its open beauty. Stone villages and archaeological remains are scattered through the area, and the Dales Way and the Pennine Way cut through it.
Information: Yorkshire Dales National Park, Colvend, Hebden Road, Grassington, Via Skipton, North Yorkshire.

Wales

Brecon Beacons

Marking the division between the industrial South Wales valleys and the remote countryside of Mid Wales, this National Park focuses on the Brecon Beacons mountain range, running from the Black Mountain in the west to the gentler Black Mountains in the east.
Information: Brecon Beacons National Park, 7 Glamorgan Street, Brecon, Powys.

Pembrokeshire Coast

This is the only British National Park to consist entirely of coastal land. The Pembrokeshire Coast runs around the southwestern 'foot' of Wales, taking in magnificent cliffs, hidden bays and high moors. St David's, Britain's smallest city, boasts a fine cathedral, and the Pembrokeshire Coast Path runs 181 miles (292km) from Cardigan (Aberteifi) to Amroth.
Information: Pembrokeshire Coast National Park, County Offices, Haverfordwest, Dyfed.

Snowdonia
The highest mountain in England and Wales, Snowdon (Yr Wyddfa), dominates this area of rugged mountain scenery in North Wales. Rising to 3,560 feet (1,085m), Snowdon forms the main peak of the Snowdonia range (Eryri), in the heart of Welsh-speaking Wales. The park also encompasses impressive castles, legacies of English conquest, and attractive, sandy coastline.
Information: Snowdonia National Park, Penrhyndeudraeth, Gwynedd.

Scotland

Splendid coastal scenery, lochs and fjords, islands, moors, mountains and marshes combine to form the most beautiful and dramatic of Scotland's landscapes, protected as National Scenic Areas. The 40 areas and their information offices are listed below.

Assynt–Coigach
Haunting lochs, peat bogs and hills in the northwest of the region.
Tourist Information Centre (open March to October), Main Street, Lochinver, Dumfries and Galloway.

Ben Nevis and Glen Coe
Ben Nevis is the highest mountain in Britain at 4,410 feet (1,344m). Beautiful Glen Coe was the setting for the 1691 Campbell massacre of the MacDonalds.
Tourist Information Centre, Cameron Centre, Cameron Square, Fort William, Highland.

Cairngorm Mountains
High moors, ski slopes and deep forests, where deer roam, make this a popular and attractive area.
Tourist Information Centre, Grampian Road, Aviemore, Highland.

Cuillin Hills, Isle of Skye
Climbing country in the south of Skye.
Tourist Information Centre, Meall House, Portree, Isle of Skye, Highland.

Deeside and Lochnagar
Caledonian pine forest in a wide valley including the Balmoral royal estate.
Tourist Information Centre, The Mews, Mar Road, Braemar, Grampian.

Dornoch Firth
Estuary and mud flats attracting rich bird-life and backed by gentle hills.
Tourist Information Centre, The Square, Dornoch, Highland.

East Stewartry Coast
Sandy bays and rocks along the coastline near Dalbeattie.
Tourist Information Centre, Whitesands, Dumfries, Dumfries and Galloway.

Eildon and Leaderfoot
Melrose Abbey stands in this attractive Border country, where the rivers Tweed and Leader flow beneath the Eildon Hills.
Tourist Information Centre (open April to October), 3 St John's Street, Galashiels, Borders.

Fleet Bay
Farmland, moors and woods surrounding the River Fleet and its estuary.
Tourist Information Centre (open Easter to October), Car Park, Gatehouse of Fleet, Dumfries and Galloway.

Glen Affric
Ancient forests grow in this remote Highland area.
Tourist Information Centre, Castle Wynd, Inverness, Highland.

Glen Strathfarrar
Forested with Caledonian pine trees in wild Highland country.
Tourist Information Centre, Castle Wynd, Inverness, Highland.

Hoy and West Mainland, Orkney Islands
Fertile farmland, hill country and sandstone cliffs.
Tourist Information Centre, Ferry Terminal Building, The Pierhead, Stromness, Orkney.

Jura and Knapdale
The quartzite Paps of Jura loom over the island's moors. Sea cuts into the rocky shore of Knapdale, which also has woods and farmland.
West Highlands and Island of Argyll Tourist Board, MacKinnon House, The Pier, Campbelltown, Highland.

Kintail
The Five Sisters of Kintail form a range of peaks at the head of the lovely Loch Duich.
Tourist Information Centre (open April to October), Car Park, Kyle of Lochalsh, Highland.

Knoydart
Two lochs in mountain country in a wild and remote part of the Highlands.
Tourist Information Centre (open April to October), Mallaig, Highland.

Kyle of Tongue
Highland crofts and lochs on the mountainous north coast of the Highlands.
Tourist Information Centre (open April to October), Car Park, Riverside, Thurso, Highland.

Kyles of Bute
Narrow sea lochs between wooded hills.
Tourist Information Centre, 15 Victoria Street, Rothesay, Isle of Bute, Strathclyde.

Loch Lomond
The largest loch in Britain in mountain country, surrounded by woods and waterfalls.
Loch Lomond, Stirling and Trossachs Tourist Board, 41 Dumbarton Road, Stirling, Central.

Loch na Keal, Isle of Mull
Lochs and inlets on Mull and smaller islands including rocky Staffa, where Fingal's Cave inspired Mendelssohn's overture of the same name.
Tourist Information Centre, 48 Main Street, Tobermory, Isle of Mull, Strathclyde.

Loch Rannoch and Glen Lyon
Wild flowers on the uplands, green valley slopes in Glen Lyon and wooded Loch Rannoch.
Tourist Information Centre, The Square, Aberfeldy, Tayside.

Loch Shiel
Narrow loch cutting between mountains and leading to the memorial to Bonny Prince Charlie's landing in 1745.
Tourist Information Centre, Cameron Centre, Cameron Square, Fort William, Highland.

Loch Tummel
Lochs, woods and moors and the Pass of Killiecrankie.
Tourist Information Centre, 22 Atholl Road, Pitlochry, Tayside.

Lynn of Lorn
A string of islands, including Lismore, and limestone coastline.
Tourist Information Centre, Boswell House, Argyll Square, Oban, Strathclyde.

Morar, Moidart and Ardnamurchan
Heather moors, lochs and woods and fine coastline.
Tourist Information Centre, Mallaig, Highland.

Nith Estuary
Mountains, estuary and pastures rising to Criffell.
Tourist Information Centre, Whitesands, Dumfries, Dumfries and Galloway.

North Arran
Valleys and woods overlooked by Goat Fell peak.
Tourist Information Centre, The Pier, Brodick, Isle of Arran, Strathclyde.

Northwest Sunderland
Mountains and cliffs, moors and bird colonies on Handa.
Tourist Information Centre (open March to October), Main Street, Lochinver, Dumfries and Galloway.

River Earn (Comrie to St Fillans)
Farms and craggy hills between Highlands and Lowlands.
Tourist Information Centre, Town Hall, High Street, Crieff, Tayside.

River Tay (Dunkeld)
Waterfalls, woods and the cathedral of Dunkeld along the Tay Valley.
Tourist Information Centre (open March to October), The Cross, Dunkeld, Tayside.

St Kilda
Uninhabited volcanic islands rich in bird life.
Tourist Information Centre, Boswell House, Argyll Square, Oban, Strathclyde.

Scarba, Lunga and the Garvellachs
A group of islands of pink limestone, including the treacherous waters around Scarba.
Tourist Information Centre, Boswell House, Argyll Square, Oban, Strathclyde.

Shetland Islands
Dramatic cliffs, bird life and prehistoric remains.
Tourist Information Centre, Market Cross, Lerwick, Shetland.

The Small Isles (Rhum, Eigg, Muck and Canna)
Circle of islets in the Inner Hebrides.
Tourist Information Centre (open April to October), Mallaig, Highland.

South Lewis, Harris and North Uist
Beaches, crofts and moors on Outer Hebrides islands.
Tourist Information Centre (open April to October), Pier Road, Tarbert, Isle of Harris, Western Isles.

South Uist Machair
Machair (flower pastures and water-meadows) and beaches in the Outer Hebrides.
Tourist Information Centre (open April to October), Pier Road, Tarbert, Isle of Harris, Western Isles.

Trossachs
Low mountains, woods and lochs form popular walking country.
Loch Lomond, Stirling and Trossachs Tourist Board, 41 Dumbarton Road, Stirling, Central.

Trotternish, Isle of Skye
Rocks and cliffs on the northeastern tip of Skye.
Tourist Information Centre, Meall House, Portree, Isle of Skye, Highland.

Upper Tweeddale
Gentle hills and the deep Tweed Valley scattered with castles, villages and woods.
Tourist Information Centre, High Street, Peebles, Borders.

Wester Ross
Beautiful mountain country with lochs and fjords.
Tourist Information Centre (open April to October), Car Park, Kyle of Lochalsh, Highland.

British Kings and Queens

The English and Scottish monarchies were united in 1603, with the accession of James VI of Scotland to the English throne as James I. The Welsh principalities were brought under English rule after the death of the last native prince, Llywelyn, in 1283 during Edward I's conquest of Wales. Since that time the eldest son of the English monarch has traditionally been known as the Prince of Wales.

The Anglo-Saxons and Normans

ANGLO-SAXON
EARLY SAXON KINGS 978–1042
EDWARD THE CONFESSOR 1042–66
HAROLD II 1066

NORMAN
WILLIAM I (THE CONQUEROR) 1066–87
WILLIAM II 1087–1100
HENRY I 1100–35
STEPHEN 1135–54

William, Duke of Normandy, lay claim to the English throne as a distant cousin of Edward the Confessor. Edward had at one time suggested that he might succeed him, but on his death-bed passed the crown to his brother-in-law Harold. William promptly invaded England and was crowned after Harold's death at the Battle of Hastings. The Norman knights who accompanied him acquired English lands and titles and in 1086 he sent tax inspectors to ascertain the revenue of all major landowners, recorded in the Domesday Book.

The Conqueror was succeeded by his red-haired son, William Rufus, a successful soldier and diplomat whose reign was marred by conflict with the church. He was killed by an arrow while hunting in the New Forest – some say deliberately. One of the prime suspects was his brother, who now became Henry I and made peace with the church by renouncing the crown's right to appoint abbots and bishops. After Henry's death the throne was claimed both by his daughter, the Empress Matilda (widow of the Holy Roman Emperor) and by her cousin Stephen. Civil war raged between the two factions until 1153, when Matilda's son Henry, by her second husband Geoffrey of Anjou, was adopted as Stephen's heir.

The Angevins

HENRY II 1154–89
RICHARD I 1189–99
JOHN 1199–1216

Energetic and charismatic, Henry II came to the throne with wealth, power and a beautiful wife, Eleanor of Aquitaine. His reign saw conflict in France, where he tried to suppress threats to his continental territories, and a re-emergence of the power struggle with the church, culminating in the murder of the king's former friend Thomas Becket, Archbishop of Canterbury. In England, Henry's reign saw the development of an effective and durable bureaucracy.

Henry's eldest son Richard, jealous of his father's favourite John, joined forces with Philip II of France to secure his succession as Richard I. 'The Lionheart' spent most of his reign on crusades in the Holy Land or defending territory in France. He died in 1199 of a battle wound, leaving no heir, and was succeeded by his brother John. The French wars continued. To pay for his attempts to regain lost territories, John taxed his subjects heavily, causing resentment and rebellion, which was only settled in 1215 when the king was forced to sign the Magna Carta, asserting the rights of the nobility.

The Plantagenets

HENRY III 1216–72
EDWARD I 1272–1307
EDWARD II 1307–27
EDWARD III 1327–77
RICHARD II 1377–99

John's son was crowned Henry III at the age of nine, and grew to be a pious man and a poor soldier, who gave up many of his territorial rights abroad. The power struggle with the barons, led by Simon de Montfort, erupted into war in 1264, during which Henry was captured. His son Edward escaped and restored the king, who devoted the rest of his reign to art and architecture and the completion of Westminster Abbey.

Edward I was a warrior and a law-maker, who tightened up royal government, conquered Wales and earned the name 'Hammer of the Scots' from his constant wars across the border. In sharp contrast, Edward II was effete and bored by royal duties. He made enemies of the barons, bestowing favours and power on his favourites, Piers Gaveston and later the Despensers. Rebellion found its focus in the queen, Isabella, and her lover Roger Mortimer who, together with the heir to the throne, Edward, imprisoned the king and forced him to renounce the crown before having him horribly murdered at Berkely Castle.

Edward III made an impressive start to a glorious reign by leading a successful coup against his mother and her lover. He then broadcast his claim to the French throne and led his barons to France for the first battles of the Hundred Years' War. With his eldest son, Edward the Black Prince, he won a string of military successes and control of a quarter of France. But the tide turned: the French won back much land; the Black Prince died; the ageing king's advisers were attacked in the House of Commons and the Black Death decimated the population.

Richard II was proud and brave, but was no soldier. Early in his reign he negotiated with Wat Tyler, leader of the Peasants' Revolt and, after Tyler's murder by the king's men, won the support of the angry rebels. But Richard's arrogance provoked a new revolt by the powerful Lords Appellant, who had several of the king's friends executed. Richard took his revenge, exiling and killing his adversaries including Henry Bolingbroke, who was sent abroad. But Bolingbroke returned, imprisoning the king and claiming the throne for himself. Richard, like Edward II, a dangerous focus for opposition, was also murdered in his prison.

Lancaster

HENRY IV 1399–13
HENRY V 1413–22
HENRY VI 1422–71

During his 13-year reign, Henry IV faced rebellion on several fronts. The Welsh rose under the leadership of Owain Glyndwr; Charles IV of France refused to recognise him as king; and supporters of Richard II attempted a coup. Worn down by a troubled reign, the king died of leprosy, to be succeeded by his son, Henry V. The new king had one obsession: the conquest of France. He was an excellent tactician and led a series of triumphs culminating in recognition of his claim as heir to Charles VI's throne and his marriage to the French king's daughter. Henry died of fever while fighting off new raids on his French territories.

Henry VI, crowned at nine months old, was to become a compassionate and devout man who wore a hair shirt and hated violence. He fell victim to recurring bouts of insanity, used as a pawn in the fierce rivalry between the descendants of Lancastrian John of Gaunt, Richard II's uncle, and those of Gaunt's brothers, led by the Duke of York. Edward, inheritor of the duchy of York, snatched the crown as Edward IV and put Henry in the Tower of London; then alliances shifted and brought Henry back to the throne. But Edward returned, had Henry executed and brought the succession to the House of York.

EDWARD IV 1461–83
RICHARD III 1483–85

York

After spending the first 10 years of his reign engaged in power-games with his ambitious cousin Richard Neville 'the kingmaker', Edward IV concentrated on sorting out the crown's finances and making peace with France. When he died in 1483 his son Edward was 12 and was placed, as the king had demanded, under the protection of his uncle, Richard of Gloucester. Having led an exemplary career as the king's loyal lieutenant in the north, Richard now took on a dangerous role. As Protector he faced the enmity of the late king's wife, Elizabeth Woodville, and was almost certain to be disposed of once Prince Edward was crowned. Richard moved first, declaring the prince and his brother illegitimate, putting them in the tower (where he probably had them murdered) and taking the throne as Richard III. This sparked off the invasion of the Lancastrian claimant, Henry Tudor, grandson of Henry V's widow Catherine and her second husband, Welsh squire Owen Tudor. The Lancastrian party won the day at the Battle of Bosworth, where Richard was killed and Henry Tudor became Henry VII.

HENRY VII 1485–1509
HENRY VIII 1509–47
EDWARD VI 1547–53
MARY I 1553–58
ELIZABETH I 1558–1603

Tudor

Henry's marriage to Elizabeth Woodville's daughter, Elizabeth of York, took the sting out of the York–Lancaster rivalry, and the great Tudor dynasty was established. Henry's solvent and efficient rule brought peace to the country for the first time in 100 years. His eldest son, Arthur, died of consumption at 16 and the second son, Henry, who married his brother's widow, Catherine of Aragon, came to the throne as Henry VIII. He is best known now as the king who had six wives, but this first match lasted 20 years, after which Henry's longing for a male heir and his infatuation with Anne Boleyn led to its annulment in 1533. Previously a staunch defender of the Catholic church, Henry broke with the Papacy when Clement VII refused to grant his divorce, and took the opportunity as Supreme Head of the Church of England to empty and destroy church buildings and lay his hands on their wealth. Anne Boleyn produced another daughter, Elizabeth (Catherine had given birth to Mary in 1516) and the impatient king had her beheaded for adultery. His third wife, Jane Seymour, finally gave Henry his son, Edward, but died in childbirth. Three more wives failed to add to his male progeny and the last, Catherine Parr, outlived the now overweight and gouty king.

Under the influence of his Protector, the Duke of Somerset, nine-year-old Edward embarked on a reign of Protestant activity, including the new English Prayer Book, and met with bitter protests. Edward's fragile health and the prospect of the accession of the passionately Catholic Mary Tudor led to the desperate move of declaring Lady Jane Grey, a great niece of Henry VIII, the rightful heir. When Edward died of consumption in 1553 there was little support for this manufactured succession and the unfortunate Lady Jane was executed.

Mary soon put her Catholic policies into action, earning notoriety as 'Bloody Mary' for her ruthless 'turn or burn' tactics, having recalcitrant Protestants burned at the stake. She married the Catholic King of Spain, Philip II and her pregnancy was announced, but turned out to be the symptoms of dropsy, and Mary died childless in 1558. Her half-sister Elizabeth took the throne and embarked on a 45-year reign.

Elizabeth never married, despite attempts by Parliament to press the issue. Her own right to the throne was disputed by Mary Stuart, Queen of Scots; faced with the threat of rebellion Elizabeth reluctantly had her rival executed. Good Queen Bess reached the pinnacle of her popularity in 1588, when Philip's invading Spanish Armada was driven back by the British fleet. Her death in 1603 was widely mourned, and brought to an end the Tudor dynasty.

JAMES I 1603–25
CHARLES I 1625–49
INTERREGNUM (COMMONWEALTH) 1649–660
CHARLES II 1660–85
JAMES II 1685–88
WILLIAM III (OF ORANGE) 1688–1702 AND MARY II 1688–94
ANNE 1702–14

Stuart

James I, the son of Mary Queen of Scots, had been James VI of Scotland since he was a year old. His reign was marked by continuing religious controversy. In 1605 Roman Catholic conspirators were discovered trying to blow up king and Parliament in the Gunpowder Plot, and James reintroduced severe penalties for anyone not attending Anglican services. His belief in the supremacy of the monarch made for uneasy relations with the increasingly confident House of Commons, and foreshadowed the crisis that overtook his son and heir Charles I.

The clash between Charles, with his elevated ideas of kingship and High Church sympathies, and an assertive and anti-Catholic Parliament came to a head in 1642, when the king entered the Commons to arrest five of his leading critics, only to find that his 'birds had flown'. The two factions, Royalists and Parliamentarians, embarked on civil war, which ended with the execution of Charles I in 1649.

For the following 11 years Britain was governed by a largely unpopular Puritan Parliament, led by the anti-Royalist general, Oliver Cromwell. When Cromwell died and his place as Lord Protector was taken by his son, it seemed that one dynasty had simply been replaced by another.

Charles II, who had escaped to France during the war, was restored to the throne in 1660 and ensured his popularity by proposing religious toleration and compromise. But disputes about the succession continued to rage: Charles's brother, James, Duke of York, was a Catholic convert and his opponents, the Whigs, made repeated attempts to exclude him from the succession, resisted by the king and his Tory supporters.

Charles died in 1685 and James II confirmed his opponents' suspicions by enacting a number of measures in favour of Catholics. The Bishop of London and a party of conspirators invited the king's Dutch nephew, William of Orange, and his wife, Mary, to invade and take the throne. James fled to France and William III and Mary II became joint monarchs of Britain. Their reign saw the partial establishment of a constitutional monarchy, rejecting the use of royal prerogative and confirming the necessity of a regular Parliament.

Mary's sister Anne, who presided over the Union with Scotland in 1707, had several children but the only child to survive infancy, William, died aged 11, bringing the Stuart dynasty to an end.

Hanover

George I 1714–27
George II 1727–60
George III 1760–1820
George IV 1820–30
William IV 1830–37
Victoria 1837–1901

According to the 1701 Act of Settlement, the crown now passed to the eldest child of Sophia, wife of the Elector of Hanover and grand-daughter of James I. Her son, George, took the throne in 1714, disliked for being foreign and for having had his wife's lover hacked to bits. The two disasters of his British reign were the Jacobite rebellion of 1715, supporting the claim of James II's son to the throne, and the bursting of the South Sea Bubble in 1720, when a speculative company crashed. Robert Walpole, the first prime minister, steered the government through several crises and confirmed the limitations of the monarchy.

George's son, George II, became king at the age of 44 and reigned for 33 years. He despised and distrusted his eldest son, Frederick, who gained Tory support in opposition to the king's faction, but outlived him, and survived the threat of a new Pretender, James II's grandson. George's diplomatic machinations paved the way for Britain's involvement in the Seven Years' War with France, but military conquests brought control of the seas and worldwide territories.

George was succeeded by his grandson, George III, who took more interest in politics than his previous namesakes, but was condemned as a fool after the loss of the American colonies. He later supported the young William Pitt, prime minister at 24, who led the country through the turbulent years when revolution threatened to spread from France. In later years the king suffered recurring periods of insanity – possibly the symptoms of porphyria – and the last 10 years of his life were spent in isolation in Windsor Castle.

Because of his father's illness, George IV had exercised power as Prince Regent since 1812. He had developed from a handsome man-about-town to a gross, debt-ridden womaniser. His secret marriage to a Catholic widow, Mrs Fitzherbert, was shortlived; his arranged marriage with Caroline of Brunswick was disastrous. After 24 years of separation she reappeared in 1820 to claim her share of the throne and was locked out of the coronation ceremony. George IV is chiefly remembered as a style-setter, responsible for the creation of the exotic Brighton Pavilion.

After the deaths of George IV's daughter and brother, the succession passed to his second brother, William. William IV was 64 when he became king and had served in the navy for many years. He was bluff, eccentric and popular, and his reign saw the introduction of the 1832 Reform Bill, extending the right to vote. On his death in 1837, his niece Victoria began her 64-year reign.

The happy marriage of Victoria and Prince Albert of Saxe-Coburg set a new moral tone in the 19th century and marked the transition of royalty from a seat of power to a national symbol. This was the zenith of British Imperialism, as well as a period of great social change at home. Under the premierships of Gladstone and Disraeli industry developed rapidly and electoral rights were further extended. After the death of Albert in 1861 the queen became a more remote figure, but her own death 40 years later was the occasion of deep public mourning and the end of a unique era.

Saxe-Coburg-Gotha

Edward VII 1901–10

Edward VII had served a long apprenticeship as Prince of Wales when he came to the throne at 59 and had a reputation for social and gambling scandals. He died at the peak of a constitutional crisis – which was then passed to his second son (the eldest had died), George V – as the government pressed for the creation of more Liberal peers to push through Lloyd George's 'People's Budget'.

Windsor

George V 1910–36
Edward VIII 1936
George VI 1936–52
Elizabeth II 1952–

The new king agreed to the Liberals' demand, though unhappy at being used by party politics. His reign saw the carnage of World War I, uprisings in Ireland and the election of the first Labour government. It also saw, as a result of the war, a change in the name of the royal family. Victoria's children took the name of Prince Albert, Saxe-Coburg-Gotha. But, anti-German feelings ran high during the war, and a British royal family with a German name was uncomfortable to many. To account for public sentiment, George V decreed to change the family name to Windsor. With his death in 1936 the crown passed to Edward VIII, who reigned for only 11 months before abdicating in order to marry an American divorcee, Mrs Wallace Simpson.

His brother, George VI, was an unprepared and unwilling monarch at first, but with the help of his wife, Lady Elizabeth Bowes-Lyon, became one of the most popular of British kings. During World War II the king and queen endeared themselves to the public by visiting bomb sites in East London and refusing to leave the capital, despite bomb damage to Buckingham Palace. Their reign saw the fragmentation of the Empire, as independence or dominion status were achieved by a succession of nations.

Elizabeth, George VI's eldest daughter, was on tour in Kenya with her new husband, Philip, Duke of Edinburgh, when the king died in 1952. The new queen, Elizabeth II, was to encourage a more open relationship between the royal family and the expanding public media. In recent years that relationship has been somewhat soured by the focus of the press on marital and other troubles of younger members of the family.

THE PARISH CHURCH

The parish churches of Britain are a living record of a thousand years of Christianity – their architecture and contents eloquently recording a significant part of our heritage.

The outline ground plans below illustrate a typical evolution of a parish church through the periods. Early extensions were necessary to cope with a rising population; as communties became more prosperous additions and extensions were financed by wealthy members of the parish.

The cutaway drawing to the right identifies some of the more important parts of a typical parish church, keyed to the numbered list below.

1 stair tower
2 flagpole
3 castellations
4 pinnacle
5 louvres (belfry)
6 clocks
7 west door
8 doom painting
9 rood cross
10 rood loft
11 rood screen
12 rood stairs
13 chest
14 war memorial

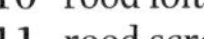

Norman
12th century
A two-cell structure with an apse at the east end containing the altar. Windows are narrow slits.

Early medieval
13th – 14th centuries
Space for more worshippers in north aisle, with enlarged altar space; tower and chantry chapel extensions.

Late medieval
15th – 16th centuries
Extended south aisle, north chapel extension and new rood and screen. New porch.

Post-Reformation
17th – 18th centuries
Galleried seating to accommodate larger congregations, new altar.

Victorian restoration
19th century
Choir stalls built for the village choir; new vestry extension.

15 choir stalls
16 aumbry (sacred store)
17 candlestick
18 Easter sepulchre
19 aumbry lamp
20 reredos
21 altar
22 communion rail
23 piscina
24 secilia
25 north chapel
26 dossal (back) and riddell (side) curtains
27 east window
28 buttress
29 porch
30 parvise (room above porch)
31 niche and statue
32 table tomb
33 gravestone
34 lych gate
35 brass monuments
36 ledger stone
37 pier
38 pews
39 houselling benches
40 nave altar frontal
41 eagle lectern
42 pulpit
43 hymn board
44 organ pipes
45 coat of arms
46 angel
47 galleried seating
48 chantry chapel
49 parclose screen
50 alms box
51 font
52 stairs
53 lancet window
54 bell ringers floor
55 finial
56 nave
57 north aisle
58 south aisle

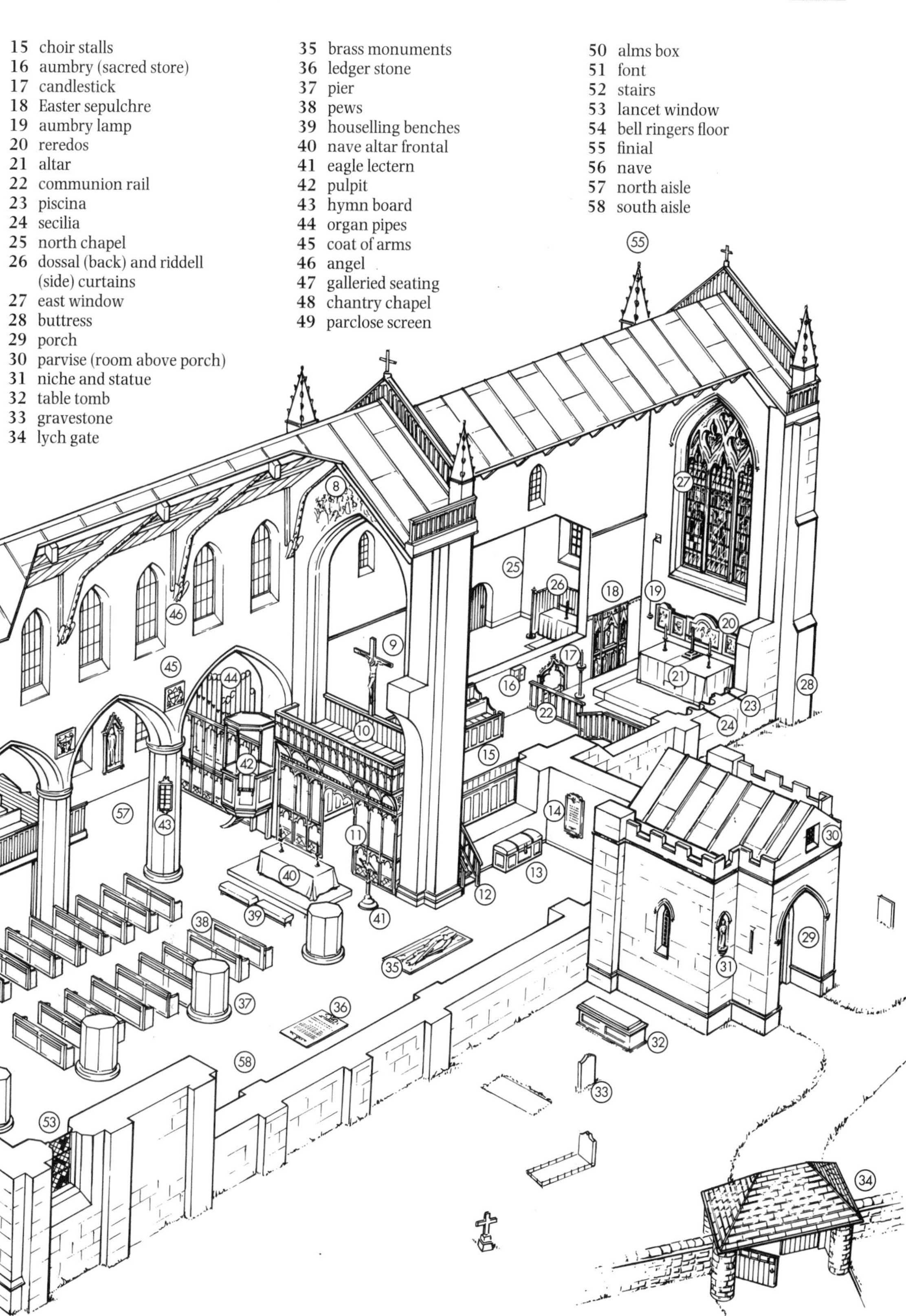

ARCHITECTURAL GLOSSARY

arcade covered walk between a series of arches supporting a roof, or a passageway that has an arched roof
architrave (classical) main beam resting on columns; moulded frame around a doorway or window; moulding around the outside of an arch
bailey court enclosed by a fortified wall
barbican fortified tower over a gateway outside a castle or city
bas-relief moulding or carving standing out from the surface of the material
Brutalism post World War II architectural style using stark designs in concrete, especially for large public buildings
cantilever beam projecting from a wall, fixed at one end
capital carved head of a column or pillar

Decorated capital, Natural History Museum, London

cartouche ornament representing a scroll, possibly with an inscription
caryatid pillar carved in the form of a woman
chancel eastern end of the church, where the altar is set, used by clergy and choir
chevron zig-zagging moulding carved around doors, windows and arches
clerestory row of high windows in a church or hall
cob building material using a mix of clay and straw
collar-beam horizontal timber beam connecting the rafters of a sloping roof
colonnade row of columns
console ornamental bracket supporting a shelf
corbel horizontal support of stone, timber or brick jutting from a wall
Corinthian one of the Greek Orders (see also Doric, Ionic) introduced as measures of proportion in Greek architecture and adapted by the Romans; characterised by ornate decoration and flared capitals
cornice moulded projection at the top of a building or wall
cove concave arch or moulding between the top of a wall and the ceiling
crenellation decorative use of battlements
crocket carved ornament, usually representing foliage, on the side of a spire or canopy

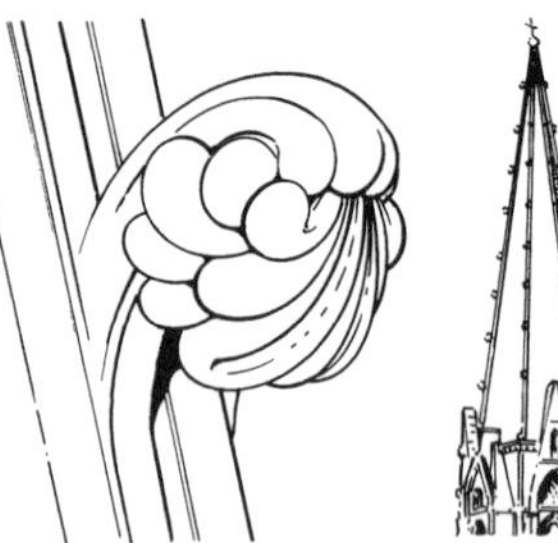

Crocket

crypt underground room, usually a burial place beneath a church
cupola small dome crowning a roof
curtain wall wall connecting castle towers; or a wall which is not used as a support
dado lower part of a wall, painted or decorated to look different from the upper wall
Doric the oldest and simplest of the Classical Orders of architecture (see Corinthian, Ionic)
dormer window upper floor window projecting through a sloping roof
dressed stone smooth-finished stonework used on the exterior corners of brick and stone buildings
entablature the upper part of a classical building above its columns: the architrave, frieze and cornice
façade the front of a building

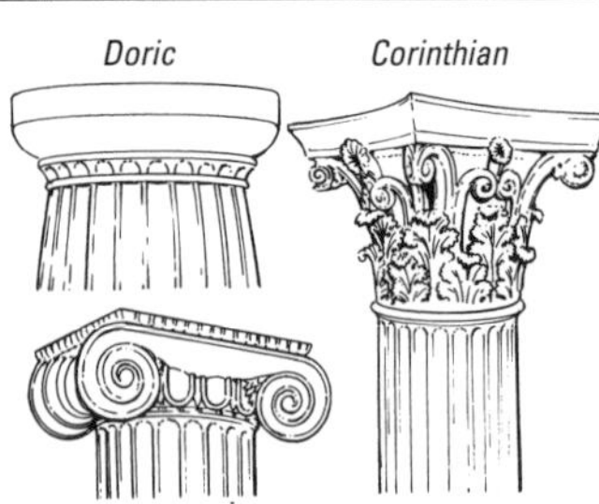

Capitals of the three classical orders

fluting vertical grooves used to decorate columns
folly A tower or 'ruin' built only for decoration
frieze central section of the entablature, between architrave and cornice; or decorated section of wall near the ceiling
gable triangular upper section of wall at the end of a sloping roof
gargoyle grotesque carving of a beast's or a human's head used as a spout to carry water away from a gutter or wall
gate-house building, usually a tower, over the gate to a city or fort, sometimes housing a prison or other rooms
gazebo small building or summer-house, giving a wide view of grounds
half-timbered timber framework surrounding a brick or plaster filling

Half timbered Little Moreton Hall, Cheshire

inglenook seating space built into a large fireplace
Ionic one of the Classical Orders of architecture (see Corinthian, Doric), characterised by a column with scrolls on each side of the capital
keep tower and main stronghold within a castle
keystone central stone at the top of an arch
lancet window tall, pointed window
lintel horizontal stone or timber support above a door or window
mezzanine floor between two others, usually the ground and first floors
motte man-made mound within castle grounds, usually forming the site of the keep
moulding ornamental feature on a cornice or other projection or recess

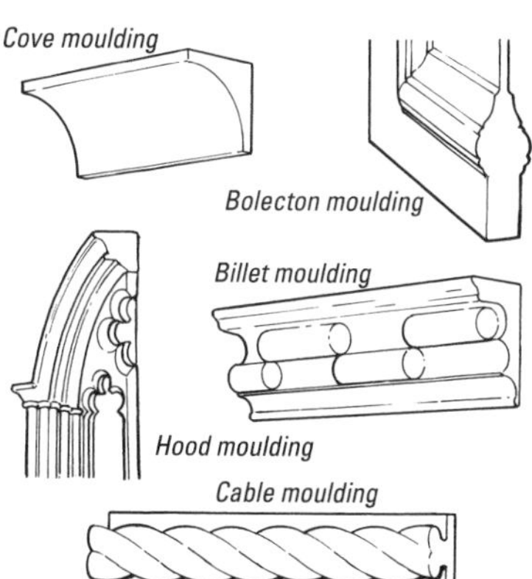

Mouldings

mullion vertical bar dividing the sections of a window
nave central part of a church, excluding side aisles and chancel
oratory small chapel for private worship
oriel window projecting upper-floor window supported by corbels
pantile s-shaped roof tile
parapet low wall or balustrade on the edge of a balcony or roof
pargeting decorated plasterwork
pebble-dash external decoration using small pebbles stuck into cement or plaster
pilaster false pillar used as decoration
pinnacle the top of a buttress or tower, usually pyramid-shaped and ornamented
pointing mortar between bricks or stonework to finish or repair the joints

Oriel window, Port Sunlight, Merseyside

portcullis defensive iron or wooden railing, lowered to bar the way through an entrance to a castle or fortified town
portico covered porch or walkway, usually forming the entrance of a building

Baroque portico, St Anne's Limehouse

quatrefoil carved design, usually in window tracery, depicting four pointed leaves around a circle
retaining wall wall built to hold back earth, rubble or water
rib decorative or structural band projecting from a vault or ceiling
rose window circular Gothic window, using tracery radiating from a central circle to depict a rose-like design

rotunda a circular, usually domed building or room
shaft the body of a supporting column
stucco plaster used to coat external walls; decorative work moulded into the plaster

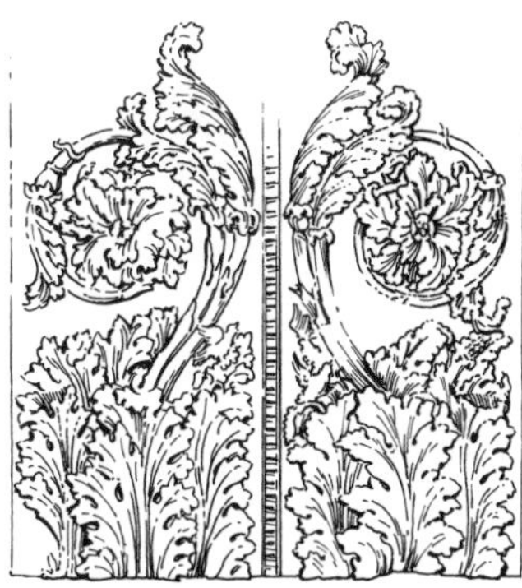

Stucco wall decoration by Robert Adam, Kenwood, London

tracery carved and interlaced mullions used to decorate Gothic windows

Fourteenth-century Gothic tracery, Exeter Cathedral

transept the short bar of a cross-shaped church building, at right angles to the nave
transom in a window, the horizontal bar that separates the panes of glass
tympanum recess, usually decorated, between the top of a door or window and the arch above it
undercroft a vaulted basement, sometimes found in monasteries

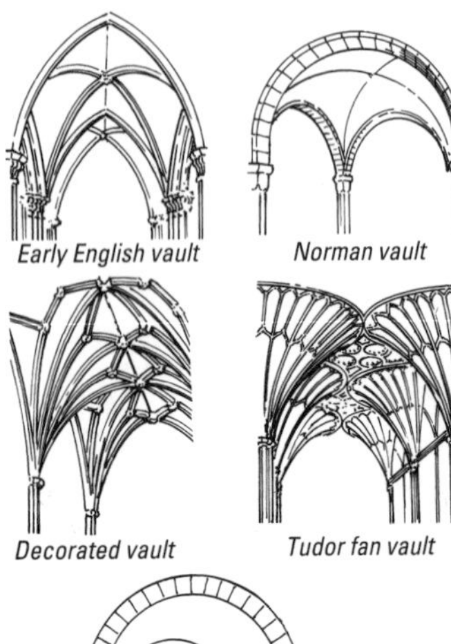

Vaulting

vaulting the use of arches, usually intersected, to support the weight of a roof or ceiling

A brief guide to British architectural periods

Anglo-Saxon
Churches and castles were built of stone and are characterised by their simple arched windows with thick central supports.

Examples: Bradford-on-Avon church, Wiltshire; Sompting church tower, West Sussex; Brixworth church, Northamptonshire

Anglo-Saxon:
Tenth-century window, Worth church, West Sussex

Norman (Romanesque)
In the late 11th and 12th centuries the Norman invaders brought new styles and craftsmen from Normandy. Massive fortified buildings and churches were thrown up in the wake of theNorman Conquest, easily recognisable by their round arches, heavy masonry and highly decorated walls and doorways.

Examples: Rochester Castle, Kent; Durham Cathedral; Oxford Cathedral

Norman:
Canterbury Cathedral crypt

Early English
Architecture of the late 12th and 13th centuries became lighter, using pointed rather than rounded arches, especially in lancet windows. This period marked the move towards the long, vertical lines of the Gothic style and an increasing focus on window space. As windows became bigger, buttresses were added to transfer the outward thrust of the roof to the ground.

Examples: Lincoln Cathedral; Salisbury Cathedral; Wells Cathedral: Five Sisters Window, York Minster

Early English:
Lancet window, Hereford Cathedral

Decorated Gothic
Increasingly elaborate tracery and decoration were employed on arches, doorways and especially on windows during the 13th and 14th centuries.

Examples: Westminster Abbey, London; Exeter Cathedral; Chapter House, York Minster

Perpendicular Gothic
Evolving from the Decorated style, simpler lines and more uniform tracery on windows and walls emerged during the late 14th and 15th centuries, with much use of fan-vaulting and four-centred arches. Designs became lighter, using greater areas of glass.

Examples: King's College Chapel, Cambridge; Henry VII Chapel, Westminster Abbey, London; Bath Abbey; Transept and Choir, Gloucester Cathedral

Perpendicular Gothic:
Decorated Gothic tracery, York Minster

Tudor and Early Stuart
The late 15th and 16th centuries marked a shift from the Gothic to the Renaissance styles, with the emphasis on domestic architecture for the expanding aristocracy and gentry. During the reigns of Elizabeth I (1558–1603) and James I (1603–25) manor houses were built to E-shaped ground plans, set in formal gardens and decorated with ornamental plasterwork. Brick and wood-panelling were popular.

Examples: Hampton Court Palace, Kingston upon Thames, Surrey; Burghley House, Stamford, Leicestershire; Longleat House, Wiltshire

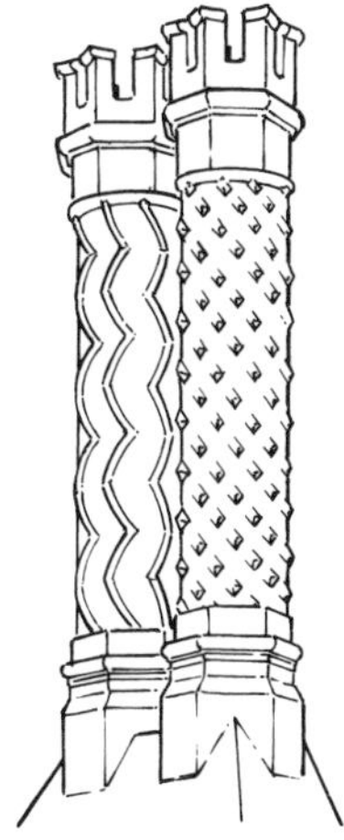

Tudor and Early Stuart: Chimney stacks, Oxburgh Hall, Norfolk

Late Stuart
The Palladian style, recalling the work of 16th-century Italian architect Andrea Palladio, reflected Roman classical influences in porticos and restrained symmetrical façades. Classical styles merged in the 18th century with baroque ornamentation and rich detail.

Examples: The Queen's House, Greenwich; St Paul's Cathedral, London; St Martin-in-the-Fields, London; Castle Howard, North Yorkshire

Late Stuart: Bridge at Blenheim Palace by Vanbrugh

Major architects:
Inigo Jones (1573–1652): designed The Queen's House, Banqueting Hall, Whitehall, London. Brought the Palladian style from Italy, as well as the use of movable scenery and the proscenium arch.
Christopher Wren (1632–1723): designed St Paul's Cathedral, Greenwich Hospital, Pembroke College, Cambridge etc. Became Professor of Astronomy at London (1657) and Oxford (1661) and was a co-founder of the Royal Society, Britain's oldest scientific society.
Nicholas Hawksmoor (1661–1736): apprenticed to Wren; designed north quadrangle of All Souls, Oxford; worked with Vanburgh on several projects; favoured monumental classicism.
Sir John Vanburgh (1664–1726): designed Castle Howard, Blenheim Palace etc. A leading exponent of the baroque style. Also a playwright.
James Gibbs (1682–1754): Scottish architect who designed St Martin-in-the-Fields, Radcliff Camera, Oxford etc.

Georgian and Regency
During the Georgian period architects turned back to the Palladian style, and in the late 18th and early 19th centuries, Greek classical influences came to the fore, prompting an emphasis on simplicity and symmetry, especially in the new terraced town houses. The Regency period saw the introduction of floor-to-roof bow windows and elaborate wrought-ironwork in staircases and balconies. Trade was expanding overseas, bringing in a range of stylistic influences, and the use of oriental motifs and decoration became increasingly popular towards the end of this era.

Examples: Georgian: Holkham Hall, Norfolk; The Royal Crescent, Bath; New Town, Edinburgh. Regency: Brighton Pavilion
Major architects:
William Kent (1685–1748): designed Holkham Hall; worked closely with his patron Lord Burlington, advocating the return to Palladianism.
Robert Adam (1728–92): designed Osterley House and Syon House in London and major parts of the New Town in Edinburgh. Took great care in designing interior decoration and furniture as well as exteriors.
John Nash (1752–1835): designed Brighton Pavilion, Regent Street in London etc. Responsible for many of the country's best known country houses.
Sir John Soane (1753–1837): designed the Bank of England, London, Dulwich Art Gallery, London. Used austere classical designs.

Georgian and Regency: Robert Adam doorway, Adelphi, London

Victorian
Architecture of the period 1837–1901 called on a mish-mash of influences as new public buildings such as railway termini and municipal offices sprang up all over the country. Neo-Gothic designs, florid and romanticised medieval motifs, rich details and extensive use of steel, iron and glass all marked the Victorian urban developments, while, in contrast, mass housing was built for the new industrial towns.

Examples: Keble College, Oxford; Halifax Town Hall; Albert Memorial, Hyde Park, London; The Houses of Parliament, London; Manchester Town Hall; Cardiff Castle
Major architects:
Sir Charles Barry (1795–1860): designed the Houses of Parliament in London after the fire of 1834, as well as the Travellers' Club (1829) and the Reform Club (1837). An exponent of classicism.
Sir Gilbert Scott (1811–78): designed St Pancras railway station, London. Compelled to alter his neo-Gothic design for the Foreign Office in London to a more restrained classical style.
Augustus Welby Northmore Pugin (1812–52): designed several Catholic churches and cathedrals and worked on the Houses of Parliament with Barry. Led the neo-Gothic movement.
William Burges (1827–71): rebuilt the living quarters of Cardiff Castle; designed Castell Coch, near Cardiff. Heavily influenced by French Gothic architecture.

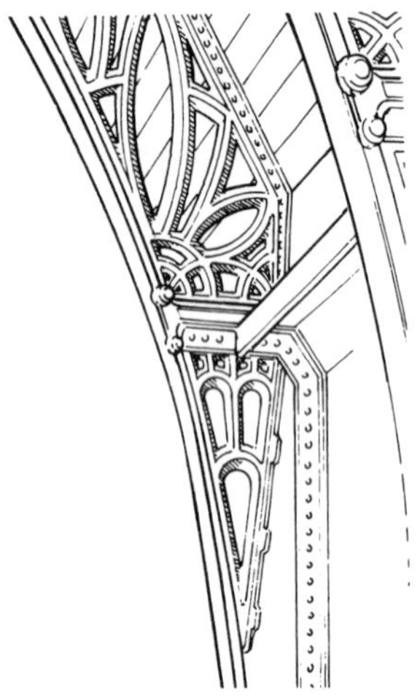

Victorian:
Cast-iron roof of Paddington Station by Brunel and Wyatt

Late Victorian and Edwardian
In the late 19th century the Arts and Crafts movement was promoted by William Morris as a reaction against mass production. Its aim was to make hand-made objects and fine art an integral part of daily life. The Arts and Crafts influence extended to architecture as suburban brick houses, with terracotta panelling, balconies and large gardens, were built at a comfortable distance from city and town centres. The flowing, organic motifs of art nouveau were popular in decoration and architecture until about 1914.

Examples: Letchworth Garden City, Hertfordshire; Cardiff Civic Centre; Glasgow School of Art
Major architects:
Charles Rennie Mackintosh (1868–1928): redesigned Glasgow School of Art (1909) and produced distinctive furniture. Major exponent of Scottish school of art nouveau.
Sir Edwin Landseer Lutyens (1869–1944); designed characterful country houses for the wealthy, including Castle Drogo, Devon, and converted Lindisfarne Castle, Northumbria. Shifted further towards neo-classicism after World War I.

Edwardian:
Art nouveau staircase
1819

Inter-War
Public and domestic buildings made full use of Art Deco's geometric lines, bold colours and exotic motifs (often using Egyptian themes, marking the huge public interest in Howard Carter's discovery of Tutankhamun's tomb). Traditional materials such as coloured tiles and stained glass were combined with modern chromium plating in imaginative designs.

Examples: BBC Broadcasting House, Langham Place, London; Odeon Cinema, Weston-super-Mare; Odeon Cinema, Islington, London; Hoover Building, Perivale, London

Post World War II
After 1945 designs became increasingly stark and massive, using materials such as concrete, especially in the tower blocks of the 1960s and the rough, unfinished designs of Brutalism. In contrast, the High-tech style of the 1970s and 1980s exposed the inner workings of public buildings, with functional features such as pipes, lifts and escalators visible on the outside. Stainless steel and glass were popular materials and bright colours and lights were favoured means of decoration.

Examples: Brutalism: National Theatre, London; High-Tech: Lloyds Building, London
Major architects:
Richard Rodgers (1933–): designed the Lloyds Building (1986) and the Centre Georges Pompidou in Paris (1977).
Sir Norman Foster (1935–): designed the Sainsbury Centre, University of East Anglia and the Hong Kong and Shanghai Bank in Hong Kong, using bold structures and careful detailing.

Post World War II:
Lloyds Building, London

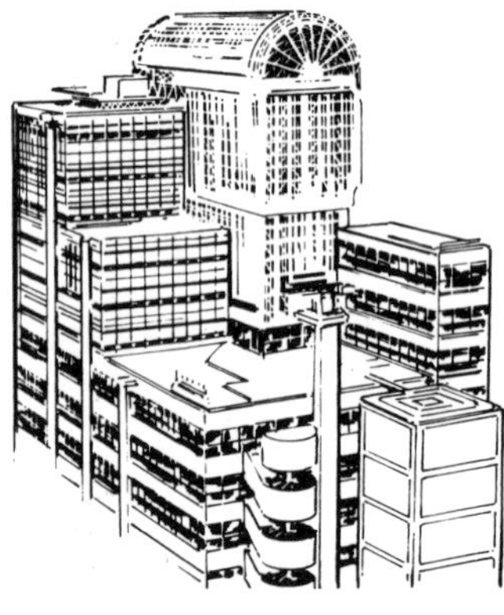

INDEX TO FAMOUS PEOPLE

Where to Find ...

This is an index to well-known places of interest that have not been listed alphabetically in the gazetteer; information for those found in the text of the towns or cities that they are in or near, in the right-hand column below.

D

E

F

G

H